PIMLICO

665

THE DEVIL'S DISCIPLES

Anthony Read is the author or co-author of ten non-fiction books, and has also written more than 200 television scripts, winning awards in both areas. Before devoting himself to full-time writing, he had successful careers in advertising, journalism, publishing and as a BBC television drama producer.

D0291304

THE DEVIL'S DISCIPLES

The Lives and Times of Hitler's Inner Circle

ANTHONY READ

PIMLICO

Published by Pimlico 2004

8 10 9 7

First published in Great Britain by Jonathan Cape 2003

Pimlico edition 2004

Pimlico
Random House, 20 Vauxhall Bridge Road,
London SW1V 2SA

www.randomhouse.co.uk

Addresses for companies within The Random House Group Limited
can be found at:
www.randomhouse.co.uk/offices.htm

The Random House Group Limited Reg. No. 954009

A CIP catalogue record for this book
is available from the British Library

ISBN 9780712664165

The Random House Group Limited supports The Forest Stewardship
Council (FSC®), the leading international forest certification organisation.
Our books carrying the FSC label are printed on FSC® certified paper.
FSC is the only forest certification scheme endorsed by the leading
environmental organisations, including Greenpeace. Our
paper procurement policy can be found at
www.randomhouse.co.uk/environment

Printed and bound in Great Britain by Clays Ltd, St Ives PLC

For Rosemary,
with eternal love and gratitude

CONTENTS

PART FOUR: Expansion:
The Greater German Reich 1937–1939

PART FIVE: War: Germany Triumphant

PART SIX: War: Defeat

PROLOGUE

THEY called it ASHCAN, a sardonic acronym for Allied Supreme Headquarters Centre for Axis Nationals. Into it, in May 1945, the American and British victors of the Second World War dumped what remained of the leadership of Hitler's Third Reich: fifty-two assorted politicians, military commanders and high officials to be interrogated, investigated, and prepared for trial at Nuremberg as war criminals.

ASHCAN was housed in the Palace Hotel in Mondorf-les-Bains, a genteel spa town with quiet, tree-lined streets around a manicured public park, set amid woodland and vineyards in the rolling country-side of the south-east corner of the Duchy of Luxembourg. A small stream on the southern edge of the town marked the border with France; the border with Germany lay about six kilometres to the east, in the gorge of the Mosel river. The Palace was the principal among the town's dozen or so hotels, standing in a raised position in its own extensive gardens and grounds. It was an undistinguished building, eight storeys tall with the top two in a mansard roof, its two wings forming a shallow V, its pale stuccoed walls enlivened with art-deco style panels, a far cry from the tawdry glories of the Reich.

In peacetime, the Palace catered discreetly for well-to-do visitors seeking relief from rheumatism and liver complaints at the town's two thermal springs. But in May 1945, the fine fittings and furnishings – chandeliers, carpets and drapes, soft furniture – were all stripped out. In the bedrooms, folding camp cots with no pillows, straw-filled palliasses and rough army blankets replaced the comfortable beds and interior sprung mattresses. The only other furniture in each room was a hard upright chair and a flimsy table designed to collapse immedi-ately under a man's weight, to foil any suicide attempt. The glass in the windows was replaced, first with wire netting and later with shatter-proof Perspex and metal bars. There were no lights or electricity in the rooms, no mirrors, and no locks on the doors, but an opening was cut into each to allow guards to look in at all times. Outside, a private airstrip was laid in the grounds, which were enclosed by a barbed wire stockade with an electric alarm system and four watchtowers equipped with machine guns and searchlights, more for the protection of the prisoners than to prevent escapes.[1]

The Americans who had requisitioned the hotel were taking no chances over the safety of their guests – but it was made abundantly clear to those guests that their status had changed abruptly, and perma-nently. Only a few days before, they would have demanded every scrap of luxury the hotel could provide. For years they had wallowed in power, position and privilege. Now they were reduced to empty husks, some pitiful, some posturing as they tried to hold on to their illusions, clinging to the last shreds of authority.

From the moment they arrived, prisoners were subjected to humil-iation and obloquy, beginning with an intimate strip search by a prison doctor. Their clothes were taken away and examined minutely for poison capsules or suicide weapons, which were often found sewn into uniforms or concealed in the heels of shoes. Anything sharp was confis-cated, including the pins on medals, insignia and badges of rank; so, too, were shoe laces, belts, braces, suspenders, neckties, steel-shod shoes, spectacles, and all walking sticks, canes and batons, a loss which rankled particularly with the field marshals. In the face of such indig-nities, most of the men – for they were all men, women having been restricted to supporting roles in Nazi ideology – found it difficult to maintain any sort of dignity, let alone the hauteur which had become second nature over the previous twelve years.[2]

The first important Nazi to arrive was Arthur Seyss-Inquart, tall and thin, limping heavily on his left leg as a result of a wound received during the First World War when he had been an officer in the Austrian army. His captors found it difficult to believe that this man, peering vapidly about him through thick spectacles, had for seven years exer-cised the power of life and death over millions. This was the man who, in 1938 as Minister of the Interior in Vienna, had handed Austria to Hitler on a plate by opening the frontier to the German army. He had then unleashed 40,000 police and Death's Head SS men on the country's 300,000 Jews, and provided a former palace of the Rothschilds as headquarters for Adolf Eichmann and his 'Central Office for Jewish

Emigration'. After a year as Governor of Austria, Seyss-Inquart had become Deputy Governor-General of Poland and then, from May 1940, Commissioner in the Netherlands, where over the following five years he was responsible for tens of thousands of deportations to concentration camps, countless summary executions, and in the final weeks of the war the death by starvation of at least 16,000 Dutch citizens.

Seyss-Inquart was followed by Hans Frank, who arrived in a US army ambulance, 'a pitiful wreck of a man' still in a serious condition after slashing his wrists and throat in a suicide attempt.[3] Now forty-five years old, with thinning dark hair, Frank had joined the German Workers Party, forerunner of the National Socialists, as a nineteen-year-old law student in Munich; he became a member of the SA in 1923, marching behind Hitler in the abortive *putsch* on 9 November. He had later become the Party's legal adviser and leading jurist, making his name as defence counsel for members charged with criminal and civil offences before Hitler came to power. He was also Hitler's personal lawyer. After 1933, he had been responsible for transforming the German legal system to serve National Socialism. In spite of his culpability for countless cases of perverted justice, he might still have escaped trial as a major war criminal had he not been appointed Governor-General of Poland in October 1939.

Hitler's orders to Frank when he appointed him as his viceroy were unequivocal: he was 'to assume the administration of the conquered territories with the special order ruthlessly to exploit this region as a war zone and booty country, to reduce it, as it were, to a heap of rubble in its economic, social, cultural and political structure'.[4] Ruling like some oriental despot from the splendour of Cracow Castle, Frank more than fulfilled his brief, turning his fiefdom into the bloodiest of all the occupied territories, with the possible exception of the western Soviet Union under Alfred Rosenberg's tender care. Basically insecure, and with his authority threatened by a constant power struggle with the SS, Frank compensated for his weakness with exaggerated brutality. He supervised the slaughter of the Polish intelligentsia, shipped hundreds of thousands of slave labourers to the Reich, and provided the sites for several of the most notorious death camps, including Auschwitz, Treblinka and Sobibor, proclaiming that his mission was 'to rid Poland of lice and Jews'.

For all the blood on their hands, however, men like Seyss-Inquart and Frank were not in the first rank of the Nazi leadership. They were essentially functionaries, never among the movers and shakers of the

Party at the highest level, which was Hitler's inner circle. This tiny group, never numbering more than half a dozen at any one time, enjoyed Hitler's exclusive confidence; only its members had any influence on him or were able to instigate policy decisions. They alone had the authority to interpret his wishes, which – except in the military sphere during the war – were usually expressed in the vaguest and most generalised terms, and put them into execution as they saw fit. This was the basis of their power. It was also its deepest flaw, for each depended entirely on Hitler's favour, which could be withdrawn at any moment and for which they were continually required to compete. As a consequence, it was inevitable that they should all seek approval by demonstrating themselves to be, as it were, more Catholic than the Pope in both word and deed. Each strove to out-do the others in brutality – which Hitler professed to admire – the virulence of their anti-Semitism, and their total commitment to the cause. Their rivalry was therefore at the root of many of the worst excesses of Nazi policy.

Hitler, of course, was not only aware of this rivalry, but actively encouraged it, constantly fomenting insecurity and mutual mistrust among his lieutenants. The ancient principle of divide and rule was an essential element in his *modus operandi*: a little healthy competition is inevitable among ambitious politicians, but while a democratic leader may seek to create harmony among his immediate subordinates in order to facilitate consensus, a dictator needs dissension, to prevent their combining to overthrow him. While they were always quick to close ranks in the face of any external threat, each member of Hitler's inner circle owed his loyalty to the Führer alone. Each of them in his own way was in love with him, deeply and totally besotted, desperate to please him, and bitterly jealous of any attention he bestowed on other suitors.

Hermann Göring, in other circumstances an outrageously ebullient figure, was reduced to a helpless supplicant in Hitler's presence. In the early days of the Party he confessed to the banker Hjalmar Schacht, 'Every time I stand before the Führer, my heart falls into my trousers.' And when they took power in 1933 he declared: 'No title and no distinction can make me as happy as the designation bestowed on me by the German people: "The most faithful paladin of the Führer."'

Joseph Goebbels was almost literally seduced by Hitler, who turned the full force of his charm upon him to win him away from the troublesome left wing of the Party in 1925. In his diary on 6 November, Goebbels recorded the impact of their first meeting: 'We drive to Hitler. He is having his meal. He jumps to his feet, there he is. Shakes my hand.

Like an old friend. And those big blue eyes. Like stars. He is glad to see me. I am in heaven. That man has got everything to be a king. A born tribune. The coming dictator.'[5] Seventeen days later, on 23 November, the conquest was complete: 'Hitler is there. Great joy. He greets me like an old friend. And looks after me. How I love him! What a fellow! Then he speaks. How small I am! He gives me his photograph. With a greeting to the Rhineland. Heil Hitler! I want Hitler to be my friend. His photograph is on my desk.'[6] By mid February 1926, hero worship had turned to personal adoration: 'Adolf Hitler, I love you'.

Heinrich Himmler also went in for photographs of his Führer. While working tirelessly for the Party in the rural heartland of Upper Bavaria, long before he came to national prominence, he was regularly seen holding murmured conversations with a picture of Hitler on his office wall. In 1929, he told his friend Otto Strasser: 'For him I could do anything. Believe me, if Hitler were to say I should shoot my mother, I would do it and be proud of his confidence.'[7] Strasser, incidentally, was one of those few Party members who were impervious to Hitler's spell, but he was nevertheless fully aware of it: he believed that Hitler had the psychic powers of a medium.[8]

Göring, Goebbels and Himmler had been the three most important members of Hitler's inner circle for most of his time in power. For twelve years they had circled each other warily, each with his eyes fixed hungrily on the ultimate prize – the succession. Now, the contest was finally over: Goebbels had succeeded Hitler as Reich Chancellor for just forty-two hours before following his example and taking his own life in the ruins of the Führer bunker; Himmler, too, had committed suicide after being captured by the British; only Göring remained. He was, at last, the undisputed number one in the Nazi hierarchy.

When Göring arrived at ASHCAN on 20 May, the gulf between him and the lesser Nazis was immediately obvious. While most of them had slunk into captivity looking dejected and apprehensive, the Reich Marshal swept in confidently, resplendent in an immaculate pearl-grey uniform. His fingernails were varnished – as were his toenails, it was discovered when he was stripped for examination. He brought with him sixteen matching, monogrammed blue leather suitcases, a red hatbox, and his valet, Robert Kropp.

One of the suitcases was found to contain about 20,000 white tablets, which proved to be paracodeine, a mild derivative of morphine at 1/6 strength, a more than adequate supply for Göring's needs, since he was in the habit of taking twenty of them each morning and night. It was in fact Germany's, and indeed the world's entire stock, since at that time it was not available anywhere else. There was also a tin of Nescafé, in which searchers found a 9-mm brass cartridge case housing an ampoule containing enough cyanide to kill ten men. A second ampoule was discovered sewn into one of the many uniforms that filled most of the other suitcases.

Göring was anticipating a comfortable confinement, befitting his status as the world's highest-ranking military officer and Hitler's successor as Führer of Germany. He expected to hold talks with General Eisenhower and the other Allied leaders, and had brought with him enough outfits to present himself in what he felt was the appropriate style for such occasions. He had managed to refrain from bringing the jars of loose diamonds that he liked to run through his fingers at times of stress as some men play with 'worry beads', but he had brought a number of personal effects that he clearly regarded as essentials. It came as a profound shock to him when the officious commandant of ASHCAN, Colonel Burton C. Andrus, took them all away and locked them up in the gun room.

Andrus made a careful inventory of the valuable items. It reads like the contents of a jeweller's shop:

1 gold Luftwaffe badge
1 gold Luftwaffe badge with diamonds
1 desk watch
1 travelling clock by Movado
1 large personal toilet case
1 gold cigarette case, inlaid with amethyst and monogrammed by
   Prince Paul of Yugoslavia
1 silver pill-box
1 gold and velvet cigar case
1 square watch by Cartier, set with diamonds
1 gold chain, gold pencil and cutter
3 keys
1 emerald ring
1 diamond ring
1 ruby ring
4 semi-precious buttons
1 small eagle with diamond clips

1 diamond A/C badge
4 cuff links with semi-precious stones
1 gold pin (evergreen twig)
1 pearl stick-pin
1 gold stick-pin with swastika of diamond chips
1 watch fob (platinum, onyx stones, diamond, inlaid A/C insignia)
1 personal seal (in silver)
1 small watch set with artificial diamonds
1 medal *Pour le Mérite*
1 Iron Cross, class I, 1914
1 *Gross Kreuz*
1 gold cigarette lighter
1 wrist watch
2 old Norse collar buckles
1 brass compass
1 fountain pen inscribed 'Hermann Göring'
1 silver cigar cutter
1 brooch
1 silver watch
1 set of lapis lazuli cuff buttons
1 silver box, heart-shaped
1 platinum Iron Cross
1 gilded pencil
1 large Swiss wrist watch
81,268 Reichsmarks[9]

For two days, even though deprived of his precious decorations, Göring basked in his unquestioned leadership of the prisoners in ASHCAN. Then, on 23 May, he suddenly found his position challenged by the arrival of another group which included Grand Admiral Dönitz, who had been named by Hitler as Reich President, and Albert Speer, the forty-year-old former architect and Armaments Minister, who had been one of the inner circle since 1942. Speer had been Hitler's Benjamin, enjoying a particularly close personal relationship with him; although he had entered the race late in the day he had been a definite contender for the succession. He had also, during the second half of the war, taken over many of Göring's areas of responsibility, steadily eroding his power base and reducing his authority. Göring was not pleased to see him.

By the end of the war, Speer had become disillusioned with Hitler and the regime, and had no interest in jockeying for meaningless position: all he was concerned with was saving his neck by proving he had never been a dyed-in-the-wool Nazi or responsible for any atrocities. He only stayed in ASHCAN for about two weeks, before being moved first to Eisenhower's headquarters at Versailles and then to DUSTBIN, the British-run interrogation centre for technicians and scientists, near Frankfurt.

Speer may have posed no threat to Göring's supremacy, but Dönitz was acutely conscious of status: although Göring outranked him militarily, he was determined to exert his authority as the rightfully designated head of state. Colonel Andrus described him as 'imperious' and said he 'looked down on all of us – Americans and fellow prisoners alike'.[10] He certainly looked down on Göring, despising his self-indulgence and unmilitary flamboyance. Göring, for his part, refused to recognise Dönitz's position or his right to it: the admiral had played no part in the political leadership of the Reich, or the Nazi Party's battles for power, whereas he himself had been at the very heart of both, and had for several years been Hitler's nominated successor. He regarded his own disinheritance at the very end as invalid, the result of Machiavellian manipulation of Hitler by his sworn enemy in the inner circle, Martin Bormann, aided by Goebbels, Himmler and Ribbentrop.

Bormann had disappeared – though no one knew it at that time, he was in fact lying dead in the rubble of Berlin's Lehrter railway station, having taken cyanide after being wounded by Soviet troops while trying to escape – so he was no longer a threat to Göring. The only other surviving member of the inner circle was the former Foreign Minister, Joachim von Ribbentrop, who was brought to ASHCAN on 15 June. But Ribbentrop had never been a serious contender. His place in the inner circle had always been dubious, due only to his position and the influence he had been able to exert on Hitler in foreign policy matters. He had always been regarded by the others as an outsider. Now, he was a total wreck, bereft of any dignity, incapable even of the pomposity that had been his trademark, and in a suicidal condition. In marked contrast to Göring's impressive collection, his valuables were listed as simply one Longines watch and 24,410 Reichsmarks.

With no other former leaders left to contend with, Dönitz was therefore Göring's only competitor. True to form, the Reich Marshal found it impossible to resist entering into a bizarre contest for precedence, a challenge that the Grand Admiral haughtily took up. Their American jailers watched their antics with incredulity, until an uneasy truce was declared: it was tacitly agreed that they would avoid arriving anywhere simultaneously, while the dining room was rearranged so each could preside at the head of a separate main table. Even then, the sniping continued. Speer later recalled Göring complaining loudly at lunch one day that he had suffered more than any of the others, because he had had so much more to lose, whereupon Dönitz, sitting with his back to Speer, remarked to his neighbour, 'Yes, and all of it stolen!'[11]

When they reached Nuremberg, however, and the trial began, there was no longer any question who was the number one: Göring's name was first on the list of indictments; Dönitz a mere fourteenth out of twenty-four. No doubt Göring was further gratified to note that although Hess was second and Ribbentrop third, the absent Bormann was down at nineteen and Speer even lower at twenty-two. In the courtroom they were seated strictly in the order of the indictment, which gave Göring pride of place and the chance to show off. Colonel Andrus, who had noted at ASHCAN that Göring 'never failed to grab an opportunity for self-aggrandisement', watched his performance with interest. 'In the first few minutes,' he recalled later, 'Göring began the extroverted, flamboyant play-acting that was to go on throughout the trial. He lounged with one fat arm spread out behind his thin neighbour, Hess, the other elbow hanging over the edge of the dock. Then he would lean forward, elbows on the barrier of the wooden dock in front of him, a grin spreading across his huge face.'[12]

Britain's alternate judge at the tribunal, Sir Norman (later Lord) Birkett, noted: 'Göring is the man who has really dominated the proceedings, and that, remarkably enough without ever uttering a word in public up to the moment he went into the witness box. That in itself is a very remarkable achievement and illuminates much that was obscure in the past few years . . . Nobody seems to have been quite prepared for his immense ability and knowledge . . .' With grudging admiration, Birkett's description of Göring went on: 'Suave, shrewd, adroit, capable, resourceful, he quickly saw the elements of the situation, and as his self-confidence grew, his mastery became more apparent.'[13]

Göring's mastery in the courtroom was not enough to save him from the death sentence. But it did confirm his final victory in the struggle among that gang of the most vicious and amoral men the world has ever seen. While stressing in court that everything he had done had been to build a greater Germany and not for his personal advancement, in the privacy of his cell Göring confessed to an American psychiatrist at Nuremberg, Dr Douglas M. Kelley, that 'his basic motive had been that single, driving ambition – to achieve for Hermann Göring supreme command of the Third Reich'. Describing his decision to tie his fortunes to the fledgling Nazi Party in the first place, he told Kelley: 'You see, I was right. The people flocked to us, the old soldiers swore by us – and I became the head of the nation. Too late, you would say? But perhaps not . . . Anyway, I made it.'14 It was, of course, a hollow victory, a victory by default, but an unrepentant Göring refused to recognise that. 'I am determined to go down in German history as a great man,' he boasted. 'In fifty or sixty years there will be statues of Hermann Göring all over Germany. Little statues, maybe, but one in every German home.'15

The contest for power had lasted more than twenty years. Through all its twists and turns it had had a profound effect not only on the personalities involved and those surrounding them, but also on all aspects of the governance of the Reich, including the formulation of policies and their execution. Just how ruthless the internecine struggles had been was revealed by Göring himself, when describing to Kelley how he had ordered his former friend, Ernst Röhm, to be shot during the purge of the SA brownshirts in 1934, after they had become rivals for Hitler's approval. When Kelley asked how he could bring himself to order the killing of his old friend, 'Göring stopped talking and stared at me, puzzled, as if I were not quite bright. Then he shrugged his great shoulders, turned up his palms and said slowly, in simple, one-syllable words: "But he was in my way . . ."'16

PART ONE

ROOTS
1918–1923

I

'OUR TIME WILL COME AGAIN'

ON 9 November 1918, the German nation was plunged into a state of deep trauma, from which it would not recover for at least a generation. Even to those who saw the end of the war on any terms as a blessed relief, news that the government was suing for peace, that the Kaiser had abdicated and a republic had been declared, came as a profound shock. As recently as 27 September, their newspapers had been proclaiming that the war was won. Now, suddenly, they were being told that all was lost, that all the sacrifices and pain of the previous four years had been wasted. It was hardly surprising that the German people, both soldiers and civilians, felt bewildered and betrayed.

Germany had been in a state of total confusion, fed by rumours and half-truths, throughout the whole of 1918. Civil order was breaking down as the country became ever more polarised between the extremes of left and right. On the right, organisations such as the Fatherland Party, founded in 1917 by Grand Admiral Tirpitz and a Prussian bureaucrat called Wolfgang Kapp, still banged the big drum of nationalism, blindly insisting Germany must fight on. To raise more money for the war, they erected a gigantic wooden statue of Field Marshal Hindenburg, Chief of the General Staff, in Berlin's Königsplatz, in front of the Reichstag, and persuaded patriotic citizens to pay for the privilege of hammering nails into it. Tens of thousands were happy to do so. Dozens of smaller but equally right-wing organisations and parties erupted all over Germany including, in Munich, the Thule Society, successor to the pre-war Germanic League, which preached extreme nationalism with Nordic overtones and took as its emblem the ancient symbol of the *Hakenkreuz,* the 'hooked cross' or swastika. They all refused to recognise the inevitability of defeat, and went on demanding total victory, with the annexation of Luxembourg, parts of Belgium, and vast swathes of territory in the east, imperialist policies that attracted 1.25 million members[1] to the Fatherland Party alone by July 1918.

On the left, in stark contrast, the socialists were calling for the old order to be overthrown and the war ended immediately. What little faith they had in Germany's military leaders had been destroyed by the draconian peace treaty forced on the new Russian regime at Brest-Litovsk on 3 March that year, on terms far more savage than those the Entente powers would impose on Germany at Versailles. Former prisoners of war were coming home from Russian camps infected with the bacillus of Bolshevism: it found a fertile breeding ground among a population worn down by the continual deaths of loved ones and four years of growing deprivation as a result of the Allied blockade and the insatiable demands of the war.

The people's resolution had been sapped still further by near starvation during the 'Turnip Winter' of 1917–18, when the failure of the potato harvest reduced them to eating root crops normally used only for animal feed. Even those were in short supply, and their consumption meant there was nothing to feed the animals on, thus adding a fresh spin to the vicious spiral of shortage. There had been no chance to recover from this before the arrival of the deadly world-wide influenza epidemic added to the general sense of hopelessness. Strikes became commonplace, there was unrest everywhere, and when strikers and protesters were arrested and sent to the front as punishment, they took their discontent with them and spread it through the trenches, further undermining morale among the exhausted troops, who by late summer of 1918 had been driven back to the line of the Western Front of 1914.

Lance-Corporal Adolf Hitler recalled the situation later:

At the height of the summer of 1918 it was stiflingly hot all over the front. There were quarrels going on at home. What about? In the various units of the army there were many rumours. It seemed that the war was now hopeless, and only fools could think we were going to win . . . By the end of September my division arrived, for the third time, at the positions we had stormed as a young volunteer regiment. What a memory. Now, in the autumn of 1918, the men had become different, there was political discussion among the troops. The poison from home was beginning to have its effect here, as everywhere. The young drafts succumbed to it altogether. They had come straight from home.[2]

Earlier in the year, everything had looked very different. 1918 had begun with victory over Russia, after a staggering advance of 150 miles in one week. The peace treaty forced the Russians to cede some 290,000 square miles of territory – an area three times the size of Germany itself, containing a quarter of Russia's population and a third of its agricultural land.[3] Shortly afterwards, the Romanians, too, were knocked out, finally ending the war in the east. General Erich Ludendorff, First Quartermaster General and *de facto* head of the High Command, was able to transfer successful divisions to the Western Front, to take part in a great offensive on the Somme starting on 21 March.

Ludendorff's spring offensive was an all-out gamble designed to smash the Entente, splitting the French and British armies and forcing them to beg for peace on German terms before the inexhaustible supply of fresh troops from America could make a significant impact. It began magnificently, breaking the British line on a front nineteen miles long on the first day. Indeed, so successful was the attack that the Kaiser gave all German schoolchildren a 'victory' holiday on 23 March, and rewarded Hindenburg with the Grand Cross of the Iron Cross 'with Golden Rays', a decoration last given to Field Marshal Blücher for his part in the defeat of Napoleon at Waterloo.[4]

Despite British and French counter-attacks, by 5 April the German armies had pushed forward twenty miles along a front of fifty miles, and were within five miles of the city of Amiens before they were halted. The very speed and distance of the offensive, however, stretched the Germans to breaking point and Ludendorff had neither the reserves nor the supply structures to consolidate his victory. Nevertheless, on 9 April he launched a fresh onslaught further north in Flanders, which so frightened the British Commander-in-Chief, Field Marshal Sir Douglas Haig, that he issued what became known as the 'Backs to the Wall' order, calling on his men to fight to the end, defending every position to the last man, and forbidding any retirement. At this point, it was the British and French, not the Germans, who feared they were about to lose the war.

Once again, however, the German advance was halted before it had achieved its objective. The great gamble had come very close to success, but eventually it had failed. It had been an expensive failure, too, costing 423,450 irreplaceable men. Inevitably, German morale plummeted: by mid April, Sixth Army was reporting that 'The troops will not attack, despite orders. The offensive has come to a halt.'[5] Three more German offensives in the spring and early summer also began in triumph – at one point they advanced to within forty miles of Paris and were able to rain shells down on the city from Krupp's long-range 'Big Bertha' guns – but all were eventually repulsed with heavy losses, bringing their casualty figures for the year to 800,000.

Germany had, quite literally, been bled dry. There were not enough young men left to fill the gaps at the front, even by advancing the call-up of the next draft of eighteen-year-olds. And there was precious little materiel – tanks, guns, ammunition, aircraft, were all in short supply. So, of course, was food – the advances in the spring and early summer offensives had frequently been held up by half-starved troops stopping to gorge themselves on the stocks of food and drink they found behind the Allied front line.

On the other side, the Allied armies had suffered even heavier losses than the Germans, with almost a million casualties. British and French reserves, too, were almost exhausted, but fresh blood was pouring across the Atlantic at the rate of 250,000 men a month. By June, the Americans had twenty-five enormous, 18,000-strong divisions in France, with another fifty-five being formed in the United States. The balance was changing irrevocably. There was now no way Germany could win a war of attrition.

The people back home knew little or nothing of the deteriorating situation at the front. By 1917, Ludendorff had become quasi-military dictator of Germany and, using the indolent and rather dim Hindenburg as a figurehead, controlled all aspects of the war both at home and at the front, without reference to the government except when it suited him. This included information, of course. Letters from the troops were heavily censored. Successes were trumpeted, but reverses were never admitted, not just to the German public but, incredibly, not even to the government or the army. Foreign Minister Admiral Paul von Hintze refused to release news of the defeat on the Marne in July 1918 because it was essential to 'deny defeat' and 'nurse the patriotic feelings of the German people'. Their patriotic feelings were further nursed by not being told of the disaster of 8 August, Germany's 'black day', when a massive force of 530 British and 70 French tanks, supported by Australian and Canadian infantry, crashed through the German lines in front of Amiens and proceeded to retake the entire Somme battle-field in four days. Nor were they told of General Pershing's first all-American offensive of the war on 12 September, which drove the Germans out of positions south of Verdun which they had occupied since 1914, capturing 466 guns and 13,251 prisoners.

The German retreat, however, never turned into a rout. The army withdrew in good order to prepared positions on the Hindenburg Line, and as the troops found themselves approaching their *Heimat* their fighting spirit was rekindled. They were reminded that during four years of war no foreign soldier had set foot on German soil except as a prisoner. Since they, too, had been told nothing about the general situation, many were persuaded that victory was still possible after all. It was a vain belief, born out of desperation, but it took hold in thousands of men eager to clutch at anything that offered to salvage their pride in themselves and their country.

26 September marked the start of the end game, as the British, French, American and Belgian armies, under a unified command for the first time in the war, launched a concerted attack. Although the Germans fought valiantly in defence, it was clear to their commanders that they could do nothing more than delay the inevitable. On 28 September, one day after those wild claims in the Berlin papers that the war was won, Ludendorff's nerve broke. Locking himself in his office at the High Command headquarters in Spa, he ranted and raged all day, blaming the Kaiser, the Reichstag, the navy, the home front – everybody except himself, the true architect of the disaster – for the situation in which his army now found itself. At six o'clock, when he had finally vented his spleen, he descended one floor to Hindenburg's office and told the Field Marshal there was now no alternative to seeking an armistice. Sorrowfully, Hindenburg agreed. On 2 October he informed a meeting of the Crown Council in Berlin, presided over by the Kaiser, that an immediate truce was vital. 'The army,' he told them, somewhat melodramatically, 'cannot wait forty-eight hours.'[6] The Council members, totally unprepared for such a sudden reversal, were thunderstruck.

Ludendorff hoped to persuade the Allies to agree to a negotiated armistice broadly on the terms of the Fourteen Points for peace proposed by American President Woodrow Wilson in January 1918. He also hoped to gain some concessions, including the retention of a German Poland and at least part of Alsace-Lorraine with its valuable iron and coal fields. Perhaps most of all, though, he hoped to end the war with the German army intact and technically undefeated; he was determined at all costs to avoid any suggestion of unconditional surrender.

If there was to be any hope of persuading the Allies to talk, they had to be convinced that a measure of democracy was at last being introduced into the German government. The Chancellor, Count Georg von Hertling, had broken down completely under the strain, and even begged to be given the last rites. He was replaced by Prince Maximilian of Baden – a seemingly odd choice, since he was the Kaiser's brother-in-law, but Prince Max was in fact a liberal, a known exponent of a negotiated peace, and a prominent figure in the German Red Cross. And for the first time ever, the Reichstag, the German national parliament, was given a few genuine powers, not least among them the right to appoint the War Minister and thus to exert at least some control over the military.

During October and into November, as Prince Max and his government tried to prepare the way for peace talks, the chaos and confusion worsened. One by one, Germany's allies – the Bulgarians, Turks, Hungarians and Austrians – collapsed, leaving her standing alone. But at the same time the army rallied and seemed to be holding its own among the water obstacles of Flanders, reviving the mirage of ultimate victory. Haig was not alone in believing the Germans were capable of retiring to their own frontier and holding that line indefinitely.

Desperate to save face, both for himself and the army, Ludendorff now declared that they no longer needed an armistice. Totally undermining Prince Max's peace negotiations, he issued a rallying call to the army rejecting Wilson's Fourteen Points as an unacceptable demand for unconditional surrender, and a challenge to continue resistance 'with all our strength'. Typically, he then panicked and tried to retract his proclamation, which in any case had been suppressed by an officer of the General Staff. But a signal clerk leaked it to the Independent Socialist Party in Berlin, who immediately fed it to the press. Ludendorff was not worried by its publication: he was eager to shift the blame for the surrender on to the supine politicians, presenting it as a betrayal of himself, the High Command and the brave army, who in his version of events all wanted to fight on. He was planting the myth of the 'stab in the back', which would bedevil Germany over the next quarter century.

On 26 October, in the furore that followed publication of his war cry, Ludendorff was forced to resign. He was replaced by General Wilhelm Groener, the son of a sergeant, a specialist in rail transport and logistics who was more than willing to work with Prince Max and the politicians to negotiate peace. Ludendorff fled to Sweden in disguise, complete with false beard, blue sunglasses and a passport in the name of Lindström, an ignominious end to one of the most illustrious careers in German military history.

Even as the army steadied, Prince Max and his government faced a new threat. The need for an armistice was still a race against time, but now it was not the army that was in danger of disintegrating but the home front. Over the last few months, Germany had become a vast tinderbox of revolution waiting for a spark. At the beginning of November, that spark was struck in Kiel, base of the Imperial Navy's High Seas Fleet.

For most of the war, the fleet's dreadnoughts, battleships and cruisers had been bottled up in port or coastal waters by the British Royal Navy. It had dared to emerge in force only three times, to fight what were little more than skirmishes off Heligoland and on the Dogger Bank and then in 1916 the only full-scale engagement between the two main fleets, the Battle of Jutland. This, the last great naval surface battle in history, ended with the High Seas Fleet withdrawing to Kiel and the British Grand Fleet to Scapa Flow, a result which may in all fairness only be described as a draw; the German Navy, typically, labelled it 'the Victory of the Skaggerak'. A German journalist more accurately described it as 'an assault on the jailer followed by a return to jail'.[7]

On 30 October 1918, with the end of the war upon them, the officers of the High Seas Fleet decided to salvage their honour by steaming out into the North Sea for one last battle. It was a quixotic gesture, grand but futile, and hopelessly suicidal: the officers had visions of gaining a place in history by going down in glory with all guns blazing. However, their sailors, who had not of course been consulted, had no intention of allowing themselves to be sacrificed to their officers' hubris. They refused to raise steam, or to prepare their ships to leave port. When the officers tried to discipline them, the revolt escalated into a full-scale mutiny. The men stormed the armouries, seized weapons, and took over the port and city, calling for revolution. Dockyard workers downed tools and joined them enthusiastically. The port admiral, the Kaiser's brother Prince Heinrich, was forced to follow Ludendorff's example and flee in disguise, hiding behind false whiskers.

Within days, the conflagration had spread throughout the Reich. Gangs of sailors roamed the country, spreading the message of revolution. Mutiny and insurrection were everywhere. Modelling themselves on the soviets set up by the Bolsheviks in Russia, soldiers', sailors' and workers' councils seized control in towns and cities and barracks. The old order was finished.

At that moment, Hitler was lying in a hospital bed at Pasewalk, near Stettin in Pomerania, temporarily blinded after a British gas attack at Werwick, just south of Ypres. He recalled his bewilderment and something of his angst in *Mein Kampf*:

Bad rumours kept on coming in from the Navy, which was said to be in a ferment, but this seemed to me to be something born of the excited imagination of a few youths rather than a matter affecting large numbers of men. In hospital everyone talked about the end of the war, which they hoped was swiftly approaching, but no one imagined it was to come immediately. I was unable to read the newspapers.

In November the general tension increased. Then one day the disaster came upon us suddenly and without warning. Sailors arrived in lorries and called on all to revolt, a few Jewish youths being the leaders in the struggle for the 'freedom, beauty and dignity' of our national life. Not one of them had ever been to the front.

The following days brought with them the worst realisation of my life. The rumours grew more and more definite. What I had imagined to be a local affair was apparently a general revolution. In addition to all this, distressing news came back from the front. They wanted to capitulate. Yes – was such a thing possible?

On 10 November the aged pastor came to the hospital for a short address; then we heard everything.

I was present and was profoundly affected. The good old man seemed to be trembling when he told us that the House of Hohenzollern was to wear the Imperial crown no more – that the Fatherland had become a republic.[8]

Hitler's old pastor was right: after 500 years of ruling Berlin, Brandenburg, Prussia, and finally the whole of Germany, the Hohenzollerns had been thrown out of power, along with all the other royal houses. The even older house of Wittelsbach, which had ruled in Bavaria without interruption for more than a thousand years, had been the first domino to fall. On 7 November, the ageing King Ludwig III was stopped on his daily stroll through Munich by a working man, who gently advised him 'Majesty, go home, and stay there, otherwise something unpleasant might happen to you.' Back at the palace, his ministers told him it was all over, and he and his family had better leave while they still could. They did so that evening, the ailing queen carrying a few jewels wrapped in a kerchief, and the king with a box of cigars stuffed under his arm – but first they had to beg a can of petrol from a local garage, as the royal chauffeur had drained the tanks of the royal cars and absconded with the fuel.[9] They had barely left the city before the leader of Munich's Independent Socialists, Kurt Eisner, proclaimed a republic in Bavaria, with himself as Chancellor.

Over the next two days, the rest of Germany's twenty-two lesser kings, princes and dukes were all deposed without resistance. By midday on Saturday 9 November, only Kaiser Wilhelm II, the King of Prussia, remained. He was not in Berlin, having left for military headquarters at Spa on 30 October, in the mistaken belief that 'his' soldiers would always obey their oath and protect him. Prince Max knew better. With hundreds of thousands of armed and rebellious troops and workers rampaging through the streets of the capital, he sought to forestall violent revolution by issuing a press statement announcing that the Kaiser had renounced the throne – though in fact Wilhelm had bluntly refused to do any such thing. Prince Max then bowed out, handing over the government to the moderate leader of the Social Democrats, Friedrich Ebert, a forty-seven-year-old former saddler and trade union leader.

Like many other Social Democrats, Ebert favoured the establishment of a constitutional monarchy on the British pattern, but his hopes were scuppered by his deputy, Philipp Scheidemann, who proclaimed a republic almost accidentally. Scheidemann had rushed to the Reichstag to tell his colleagues of Ebert's appointment. Having done so, he was eating lunch in the restaurant when he was told that Karl Liebknecht, the leader of the extreme left Spartacus Party, was setting up camp in the Royal Palace, from where he intended to announce a soviet-style republic modelled on Lenin's Russia. If the moderate socialists were to prevent a Spartacus *coup*, they had to get in first. 'I saw the Russian madness before me,' Scheidemann wrote later, 'the replacement of the Tsarist terror by the Bolshevist one. No! Not in Germany.'[10] There was no time to lose. Leaving his meal, he strode out on to the small balcony outside the Reichstag library. The vast crowd cheered his appearance, then quietened as he began an off-the-cuff speech. He told them of the new government, and spoke briefly about the horrors of war and the misery of defeat, then, needing a rousing finish, he cried: 'The rotten old monarchy has collapsed. Long live the new! Long live the German Republic!' And so it was done, almost as an afterthought.

Liebknecht made his announcement two hours later, but by then the Social Democrats had already formed their legitimate government, winning over the left-wing Independent Socialists by agreeing that workers' and soldiers' councils should exercise 'all power' until the election of a new national assembly.

At Spa, meanwhile, General Groener had finally managed to persuade the Kaiser that his troops would no longer obey their oath and die for him, that he could not use the army to suppress the revolution, and that he must either abdicate immediately or do the honourable thing and seek death in the trenches. Wilhelm was appalled at either prospect. He declared that suicide in any guise was not compatible with his position as head of the Lutheran Church in Germany, and 'A successor to Frederick the Great does not abdicate.' He then fled in a convoy of twelve cars driven by Prussian officers to seek sanctuary in neutral Holland, suffering the ultimate indignity of being denied entry at the frontier until he had surrendered his sword to a Dutch customs officer. The rest of his personal belongings followed by rail in twenty coaches of the imperial train – not for Wilhelm the small bundle of jewels and a single box of cigars. He did not formally abdicate until 28 November, his indecision adding to the political chaos that engulfed the German nation.

The armistice came into effect at 11 a.m. on Monday 11 November. It was signed not by Hindenburg or Groener or any of the generals who had called for it, but by a brave Catholic politician, Matthias Erzberger, who a full year earlier had persuaded the Reichstag to pass a resolution calling for peace. The armistice terms were swingeing, but they did not call for unconditional surrender. Germany was to hand over, in good condition, 5,000 heavy guns, 30,000 machine guns, 2,000 aircraft, and all her U-boats, plus 5,000 rail locomotives, 150,000 freight wagons and 5,000 lorries. The navy's surface fleet was to be interned in British waters. Allied troops were to occupy the Rhineland, their upkeep paid for by Germany. And the Allied blockade would not yet be lifted. Erzberger balked at these conditions, and referred back to the High Command. Hindenburg told him to sign.

When Hitler heard the news of the armistice, he wept openly:

As everything went black before my eyes again, I groped and tottered my way back to the ward and threw myself on the bed, burying my burning head in the pillow and blankets . . . The days that followed were terrible and the nights were even worse. I knew that all was lost. In those nights hatred grew in me, hatred for those responsible for this dastardly crime. Miserable and degenerate criminals! The more I tried in that hour to get clear ideas about that monstrous event, the more my brow burned with shame and rage. What was all the pain in my eyes compared to this misery?[11]

According to his account in *Mein Kampf*, the effect of 'this misery' on Hitler was that he 'discovered his own fate' and determined to become a politician himself – an odd decision considering that he had just described politicians as degenerate criminals. He was, of course, writing for effect, six years after the event: his move into active politics was not the result of a sudden flash of inspiration, but took place over a period of several months. At the time, his dismay must have been intensified by the prospect of having to return to his previous miserable existence as a failed artist, from which the war had rescued him in 1914. For four years, he had been clothed, fed and given a useful role to play, and the hardships and dangers involved were a small price to pay for the chance to belong somewhere, for the first time since he had left home. His first priority in 1918 would have been to avoid slipping back into his old life. Nevertheless, the shock and distress were real enough, and undoubtedly became the catalyst that precipitated the change in direction not only for Hitler but also for thousands of other angry young men in Germany at that time.

One of the angriest of the young men was twenty-five-year-old Lieutenant Hermann Göring, then a much decorated air ace and commander of the elite Jagdgeschwader Richthofen No 1 (JG1), a super-squadron or wing created by combining four crack fighter squadrons, which had been commanded until his death in action by the legendary Red Baron. Reduced by enemy action to well under half its full strength, JG1 had been forced to pull back on 7 November from its well-equipped base at Guise in Picardy to a muddy field at Tellancourt close to the Luxembourg border (and ironically less than thirty miles from the Palace Hotel at Mondorf, the future ASHCAN). Bad weather prevented flying, forcing the crack pilots and their ground crews to sit around kicking their heels in frustration. With plenty of time to speculate on the alarming situation, their mood was understandably grim. Göring, however, remained belligerent, refusing to heed the prophets of doom. On 9 November, he called together the surviving 53 officers and 473 other ranks of JG1 and told them to ignore 'absurd rumours that our beloved Kaiser is preparing to desert us in our hour of need'. The Kaiser, he insisted, would stand by them, and they must stand by him, ready as always to die for him and the honour of the Fatherland. He called on them to be prepared for a last death or glory battle, and they rose to their feet and cheered him to a man.

The cheers had hardly died away before orders arrived halting all air operations on the Western Front. Göring could hardly believe it. He told his adjutant, Karl Bodenschatz, he would like to climb into his plane, lead his squadron to army headquarters, and 'strafe its

cowardly crew out of existence'.[12] Fortunately, the weather was still
too bad for flying, so the generals – and Hermann Göring – were
spared. Whether or not he would have done it we shall never know;
it would certainly have been in character, but so, too, would a show
of bluster and bravado.

Göring's chance to display his defiance came next day, after the
devastating news that, far from standing by them, the Kaiser had fled
to Holland and an armistice was indeed about to be signed. The chaos
in headquarters was reflected in a flurry of conflicting signals to JG1
and the other squadrons, first ordering them to ground their aircraft,
then to fly them back to Germany, then to hand them over to the
Americans, and then to surrender them to the French. Göring assembled his men again and announced that he did not intend to obey the
orders to surrender. 'I will allow neither my men nor my machines to
fall into the hands of the enemy,' he went on. 'We cannot stay here
and fight on. But we can make sure that when the end comes we will
be in Germany.' Records and valuable equipment would be evacuated
by road, under the command of Bodenschatz; the planes would be
flown out to Darmstadt, some twenty miles south of Frankfurt am
Main.[13]

The planes were already revving up their engines for take-off when
a staff car appeared and slewed to a halt in front of them. An agitated
officer clambered out and presented written orders to Göring to disarm
his planes at once and fly them to French air headquarters at Strasbourg.
A refusal, he said, could jeopardise the entire armistice negotiations,
and provoke a resumed attack by the Allies. Göring talked to his leading
officers, and came up with a compromise solution. Five pilots, chosen
by lot, would fly to Strasbourg, giving the impression that the rest
were to follow. On landing, they would crash and wreck their planes,
so that they would be of no use to the French. The others, meanwhile,
would fly back to Germany. To avoid any interference, the staff officer
would be escorted back to Germany with the ground party's convoy.

Honour, it seemed, was satisfied – but there was to be one more
twist in the tale before it was done. Mist, drizzle and low cloud made
navigation difficult, and some of the pilots landed by mistake at
Mannheim, some thirty miles south of their objective. Mannheim was
under the control of a workers' and soldiers' council, who saw the
pilots' pistols and the planes' machine guns as gifts from heaven for
their revolutionary struggle. They seized them and the planes, but
allowed the pilots to proceed by truck to Darmstadt, where they

reported the incident to Göring. He, of course, was furious, and immediately took off for Mannheim at the head of a flight of nine aircraft, two of them flown by pilots who had been disarmed. While Göring and the others flew low around the field, beating it up threateningly, they landed and delivered an ultimatum from their commander: the revolutionaries had four minutes to return the confiscated weapons, or they would be machine-gunned and bombed. The weapons were promptly handed over. This time, there can be little doubt that Göring would have relished carrying out his threat.

After crash-landing and destroying his plane back at Darmstadt, an example followed by all the other pilots, Göring wrote his final report:

11 November. Armistice. Squadron flight in bad weather to Darmstadt. Mist. Since its establishment the squadron has shot down 644 enemy planes. Death by enemy action came to 56 officers and non-commissioned pilots, six men. Wounded 52 officers and non-commissioned pilots, seven men. (Signed) Hermann Göring, Lieutenant, O.C. Squadron.

Without its aircraft, the squadron was ordered to move to Aschaffenburg, near Frankfurt, where it occupied a paper mill until it was officially disbanded seven days later, on 19 November. Göring, as befitted his status, stayed in the house of the owner, together with his second-in-command, the top ace Ernst Udet. During that final week, with no duties to perform, the officers spent most of their time in the local restaurant and bar, the Stiftskeller, where, Bodenschatz recalled: 'They were often very drunk and always very bitter. It was understandable. The Germany we had known and loved and fought for was going to pieces in front of our eyes, and we were helpless to do anything about it. Officers were being insulted in the streets by the men, the medals they had risked their lives to earn torn from their breasts.' Göring's mood, Bodenschatz said, ranged from the cynical to the savage. 'One moment he talked of emigrating to South America and washing his hands of Germany for ever, but the next he spoke of a great crusade to raise the Fatherland back to the heights from which it had fallen.'[14]

At the actual disbandment, in the courtyard of the paper mill, there was no ceremony and no speeches. Later that evening, however, Göring climbed on to the Stiftskeller's little bandstand to address those officers who had stayed behind for one last drink together, and for the first time found his voice as an orator. As he stood there, a glass in his hand, the shouting and roistering suddenly died, for the men realised that this was a new Hermann Göring. He had, of course, spoken to the squadron many times as its commander, but always in the conventional tone of a Prussian officer, barking out short, sharp sentences, to drive his points home. This time it was different. 'He hardly raised his voice at all,' said Bodenschatz, 'but there was a strange quality to it, an emotional underbeat, that seemed to slip through the chinks in your flesh and reach right into your heart.' Unlike some of the other officers in JG1, Bodenschatz was an admirer of Göring and remained one to the end, carrying his hero worship right through the dark days of the Nazi regime and the Second World War, so his memories may be a little rosy. But even taking this bias into account, it is clear that that evening marked a turning point in Göring's life, not only because it was the end of his chosen career as a regular officer, but also because he discovered a new purpose, a new ability, and a new path, though it would be another two or three years before he set out upon it in earnest.

That evening, he spoke of the proud record of the Richthofen Squadron, and the way its achievements had made it famous throughout the world. Then his tone changed. 'Only in Germany today,' he went on savagely, 'is its name now dragged in the mud, its record forgotten, its officers jeered at.' He denounced the disgraceful behaviour of the revolutionaries who were bringing shame upon the officers and men of the armed forces who had sacrificed themselves for their country. He spoke of his love for Germany and his faith in its future: 'The forces of freedom and right and morality will win through in the end. We will fight against those forces that are seeking to enslave us, and we will win through. Those same qualities that made the Richthofen Squadron great will prevail in peacetime as well as in war.' Surveying his rapt audience, before proposing a final toast and smashing his glass on the floor, he concluded with a solemn prophecy: 'Our time will come again!' No one could doubt that he meant every word.

Hermann Wilhelm Göring was born and bred to be a German nationalist. He later claimed that his pregnant mother travelled back all the way from Haiti simply so that her fourth child and second son could be born in Germany, though the fact that she had had a difficult time with a previous birth in primitive surroundings is a more likely reason. Either way, Hermann was born in the Marienbad Sanatorium just outside the little town of Rosenheim, some forty miles south of Munich, on 12 January 1893. Both his origins and his early years were unconventional, a fact which had a great influence on the development of his highly individual personality.

Hermann's father, Dr Heinrich Ernst Göring, appeared to be the very picture of solid bourgeois respectability. Until the age of forty-five he had followed his own father in a humdrum career as a district judge in Prussia, fathering five children by his wife, Ida, who died in 1879 after ten years of marriage. But then, in about 1885, he met a buxom, blue-eyed young Bavarian woman of Austrian descent, Franziska 'Fanny' Tiefenbrunn, and everything changed. He resigned his position as a judge, applied for an overseas posting with the German Consular Service, and was selected by Bismarck to be the Reich Commissar, or governor, of the newly acquired territory of German South-West Africa, today's Namibia. He left Germany at short notice for England, to study British methods of colonial administration before taking up his post: unlike countries such as Britain, France and Holland, Germany had no culture or experience of overseas colonialism. Fanny accompanied him to London, where they were married in a quiet ceremony with only two witnesses in the German Chapel Royal in St James's.

Reading between the lines, it seems clear that Dr Göring had been forced to abandon his career as a judge and leave the country to avoid a scandal. Fanny was pregnant – she had reached five months by the time of the marriage – and the Prussian Protestant Göring family disapproved of this, and of her. She was, after all, twenty-six, well beyond the age at which a respectable young woman should have been married, she came from humble, probably peasant, stock – the marriage register declared her father to be a merchant, a description that could cover almost anything – and to top it all she was a Catholic and a Bavarian. Such a woman was clearly an unsuitable partner for Dr Göring, and could not be allowed to bring up his four surviving children by his first marriage. From that point the children disappear from the history books, 'taken off his hands' by relatives. It would appear that he never saw them again.

South-West Africa was no plum posting; it was rough, tough and primitive, and Fanny stayed behind in Germany to give birth to her first child, Karl-Ernst, before sailing out to join her husband in Windhoek. Their second child, Olga, was born there, but there were complications, and neither mother nor baby would have survived without the attention of a young half-Jewish Austrian doctor, Hermann Epenstein, who became a close family friend. During five years of discomfort and danger, Dr Göring fashioned a successful colony out of the unpromising material of South-West Africa, dealing shrewdly with the local chiefs and making it safe for German traders. It was a considerable achievement, but sadly, his legacy of trust and fair dealing was destroyed by his successors, who treated the black tribesmen with typically Prussian arrogance and contempt.

Returning to Germany, Dr Göring found it hard to settle. It may be that his family was still hostile, and that the shadow of the scandal still lingered. It may be that he had developed a taste for life in exotic foreign parts, and for the prestige of position. In any case, he looked around for another overseas posting. The only one available was as Consul-General in Haiti, which may have sounded exotic, but was certainly not prestigious. Nevertheless he took the job, once again sailing away and leaving his wife to bear a child, Paula, before following him to the steamy, disease-ridden delights of Port-au-Prince. When she became pregnant again, she returned to Germany for the confinement, in a clinic in Bavaria recommended by Dr Epenstein.

The morning after the baby was born the good doctor, now back home on extended leave, was her first visitor. She named the child Hermann, after him, adding Wilhelm, for the Kaiser. Epenstein, whose father had converted to Christianity in order to marry the daughter of a wealthy Roman Catholic banker, insisted on being his godfather. He called on Fanny virtually every day until, after only a few weeks, she left both her new son and his godfather and returned to her husband and her other three children in Haiti.

Prematurely weaned, baby Hermann was handed over to one of her friends, Frau Graf, in Fürth, on the outskirts of Nuremberg. He did not see his mother again for three years. Far from being abused or ill treated by his foster family, however, he was thoroughly spoilt by Frau Graf and her two daughters, both only a little older than himself. With his golden hair and bright blue eyes he was an angelic-looking child, and they were delighted to pamper and indulge him, setting a pattern of expectation that would remain with him for the rest of his life. As Douglas M. Kelley, the American psychiatrist who studied Göring in Mondorf and Nuremberg, noted: 'The lack of early parental control undoubtedly accounts for the development of some of Göring's aggressiveness and uncontrolled drive. Without a father's or mother's supervision, he did much as he pleased in those first three years, and early established habit traits that are shown later in his inability to conform to authority.'[15]

When his real family returned from Haiti to reclaim him, Hermann attacked his mother, beating her face and chest with his fists as she tried to embrace him. He ignored his father completely. Hermann and his mother were quickly reconciled, and he came to adore her unconditionally. But this only fuelled both his resentment at being separated from her during those crucial early years and his jealousy of his elder brother and sisters, who had not been abandoned. He demanded constant attention, which his mother and sisters were happy to provide, spoiling him even more than Frau Graf and her girls had done. Retired at the age of fifty-six, Dr Göring was more like a grandfather than a father to young Hermann, and they were never really close, but he, too, indulged the boy and treated him as his favourite.

For the next five years, the Görings lived in the Berlin district of Friedenau, a newly-built suburb in the south of Schöneberg, described by the developer as providing 'properties for the superior middle class'.[16] Hermann's dreams of a career as an officer, and his lifelong obsession with uniforms began at that time: Berlin was still very much a military city, where the uniform was everything and the Prussian officer caste was above the law. Dr Göring's circle of acquaintances included army officers as well as civil servants, and young Hermann delighted in persuading Johann, the family servant, to bring their gleaming helmets and swords to his bedroom for him to gaze at and touch while they were dining. His favourite outings with his father were to watch the grand parades at Potsdam, and when Dr Göring bought him a miniature hussar's outfit at the age of five, he was deliriously happy. In that respect, as well as several others, he was never to grow up.

One regular visitor who was neither a civil servant nor a soldier – though he had served for a while as an army physician with a cavalry regiment – was Dr Epenstein, now ennobled by the Austrian Emperor Franz Josef as Ritter (Knight) von Epenstein after generous contributions in the right quarters. His relationship with Fanny Göring had grown steadily closer – indeed, her last child, Albert, looked remarkably like him. If Dr Göring noticed, he said nothing. He sought solace in the bottle, drinking more and more heavily but never becoming objectionable, simply subsiding each evening into an amiable stupor. Life had not been kind to him: he looked and felt older than his years, he had only an inadequate government pension to live on, and his health was failing; soon after Albert was born, he was ill for several months with pneumonia and bronchitis.

It was Epenstein who provided the solution to the Görings' problems. He had always been a seriously wealthy man, and a few years earlier had gratified his passion for romantic medievalism by buying a ruined castle perched in the Austrian mountains at Mautendorf, some fifty miles south-east of Salzburg, restoring it and filling it with antiquities. Now he bought and restored a second castle, Burg Veldenstein, in Franconia, about twenty miles north of Nuremberg, and installed his mistress and her family in it, 'for the sake of Heinrich's health'. His concern for Heinrich's health did not extend to giving him the best bedroom, which was reserved for his own use. While Fanny occupied an adjoining room almost as grand as his, her cuckolded husband was assigned to meaner quarters on the ground floor. When the family went to stay with Epenstein at Mautendorf, as they frequently did since Fanny always acted as his hostess when he entertained, the complaisant Dr Göring was consigned to a lodge in the grounds.

To an impressionable boy like Hermann, the difference between his weak, depressed father and the dashing Epenstein with his smart clothes and glamorous life on the fringes of court circles in Berlin and Vienna was striking. It was only natural that Hermann should come to idolise him and take him, rather than his own father, as a role model. Epenstein was a flamboyant character, who liked to play the feudal lord, dressing both himself and his staff in fanciful period costume to fit the style of the castle, and demanding that the servants bow or curtsey whenever they encountered him. His manner was domineering and arrogant, but this was the normal mark of the aristocrat in Germany at that time, following the example set by the Kaiser. The children had to stand to attention and call him 'sir' whenever they spoke to him – which they were not allowed to do without his permission – but although they found him intimidating, they all admired him, and none more than Hermann, his favourite.

Veldenstein, perched dramatically on a sheer, rocky cliff above the little Pegnitz river, was every boy's dream playground with its turrets and towers and banners and battlements, and it was here that Hermann Göring's character was irrevocably shaped. His fantasies and childhood games were all to do with Teutonic legends, knights and warriors, as he marshalled his friends in sieges and battles, always under his command. He climbed the walls and cliffs effortlessly, and graduated early to scaling crags and peaks that would have daunted older and more experienced mountaineers, always choosing the most difficult routes to the top, and never displaying the slightest hint of fear. He also acquired his lifelong love of nature and hunting; when he was not climbing or dreaming of the age of chivalry, his greatest treat was to be taken out by Epenstein to stalk and shoot chamois and other game.

Hermann soon came to regard Burg Veldenstein as his ancestral home, revelling in the ornate medieval-style furnishings and pictures, the suits of armour and the ancient weapons displayed on walls and chimney breasts. Mautendorf, where the family spent most summers, was even more impressive: a former residence of the powerful bishops of Salzburg, it was now a treasure house of valuable antique furniture, Gobelin tapestries, precious silver, old master paintings and carvings. It was here that Hermann Göring's lavish taste and insatiable appetite for works of art was formed.

School came as a nasty shock to Hermann, bringing the unwelcome discovery that the universe did not revolve around him alone. First at a small private school in Fürth, and from the age of eleven at boarding school in Ansbach, he was constantly in trouble for wild and rebellious behaviour, for fighting and trying to boss his fellow pupils about. He showed little inclination for book learning or any intellectual pursuit. There are many conflicting versions of how he came to leave Ansbach after three tumultuous and miserable years – he always claimed that he had led a strike by fellow pupils against the bad food and harsh discipline before packing his bedding, selling a violin to raise his train fare and heading for home – but whatever the truth, there was obviously no going back.

Hermann's salvation came when his father and Epenstein found him a place at one of Germany's best military colleges, the Cadet School at Karlsruhe. 'Emphasis at Karlsruhe,' a contemporary of Göring's later told journalist Willi Frischauer, 'was on military training. Book learning took second place.'[17] It was exactly what Hermann needed, and wanted. He took to the life immediately, flourishing under a discipline that he could understand and accept, and finished his time with excellent results for discipline, riding, history, English, French and music. 'Göring has been an exemplary pupil,' his final report stated, continuing prophetically, 'and he has developed a quality that should take him far: he is not afraid to take a risk.'[18]

With his successful time at Karlsruhe behind him, Göring was able to win a place at the Prussian Military Academy at Lichterfelde, in the south of Berlin, Germany's Sandhurst or West Point. Again, he sailed happily through the course, becoming a member of the most exclusive student fraternity and enjoying the social life of an officer cadet in Berlin to the full before passing the ensign examination with the highest grade on 13 May 1911. He was later to claim that he achieved a total of 232 marks, 100 more than was needed for a pass, which according to him was the highest in the history of the Academy. His family was delighted with his success, and his hero, Epenstein, rewarded him with a gift of 2,000 marks. He used some of it on a tour of northern Italy with a group of fellow graduates, where he spent hours in galleries and palazzos, going from painting to painting and sculpture, enraptured by the beauty of works by masters like Leonardo, Titian, Rubens, Raphael and Michelangelo.[19]

The newly-commissioned Lieutenant Göring was gazetted to the 112 Baden Regiment, the 'Prince Wilhelm', which was stationed at Mülhausen (now Mulhouse) in Alsace, close to the frontier with France and facing the strategically important Belfort Gap. But his joy was tempered by bad news from home. Epenstein had found a new love, a vivacious young woman called Lilli, who insisted on marriage and, not unnaturally, was unhappy at the thought of his previous mistress living rent-free in one of his castles. Dr Göring, meanwhile, was becoming increasingly fractious and quarrelsome, and had at last rebelled against his wife's infidelity. The result was that the Görings were having to move out of Veldenstein and find other, less grand, quarters in Munich. Göring was dismayed not only because he loved Veldenstein, but also because he had boasted to his fellow officers and friends about the glories of his 'family seat'. For old Heinrich, already seriously ill, it was too much: he died shortly afterwards. Göring, smart in his new lieutenant's uniform, wept at the graveside.

When war broke out in August 1914, Göring's regiment was immediately withdrawn from Mülhausen and repositioned back across the Rhine, ready to repel the expected French attack on the Fatherland. A disappointed Göring managed to find some adventure by leading patrols on reconnaissance missions back into Mülhausen, first in an armoured train and later on bicycles, claiming later to have torn down the tricolour and several French posters and to have almost kidnapped a French general. He did manage to seize four French cavalry horses and took four prisoners. Within the next few weeks, however, he saw real action in the battles of Mülhausen, Saarburg and Baccarat, winning the Iron Cross, Second Class, before being struck down with arthritis in both knees as the first rains of the war began to fall. He was evacuated from the front, first to Metz and then for further treatment at a hospital in Freiburg, in southern Germany.

The move to Freiburg was fortuitous in more ways than one. First, he escaped the slaughterhouse of the Battle of the Marne, and second he met up with a friend from Mülhausen, Lieutenant Bruno Loerzer, who had been posted to the flying school at Freiburg as a trainee pilot. Flying sounded exciting, a challenge that appealed greatly to Göring, and he applied at once for a posting as an airborne observer. Like much in his early years, the story of how he achieved his ambition was embroidered and inflated later, both by himself and by over-eager hagiographers, to boost his image as a dashing hero. He is popularly supposed to have discharged himself from hospital, forged transfer papers, stolen a plane and begun flying as Loerzer's observer without permission, and then to have eluded the military police and survived a military court with the help of a great deal of string-pulling by his godfather and the personal intervention of the Crown Prince, Friedrich Wilhelm. The truth, as usual, is more mundane: with his arthritic knees making it unlikely he would be able to continue as an infantry officer, his application for a transfer was approved at once and he was posted, perfectly normally, to 3 Air Reserve Detachment at Darmstadt for training as an observer. He was, of course, already experienced as observation officer on the ground, and the course seems to have lasted only two weeks, before he was posted to fly with Loerzer from Stenay, near Verdun.

Göring and Loerzer made a good partnership – however exaggerated tales of their exploits became, there can be no doubt that both were brave young men with a zest for adventure. Loerzer was a fine natural pilot, and Göring a fearless observer who made a name for himself as 'the Flying Trapezist', hanging precariously over the side of the plane to get better photographs of enemy positions and installations while under heavy fire from the ground. When not taking pictures or directing artillery fire by morse code over a primitive radio transmitter, he kept busy shooting back at the troops below, at first with his revolver and later with a light machine gun on an improvised mounting – he claimed to have been the first observer to fit such a weapon to his plane.

Göring's pictures of the French fortifications, trench systems and gun emplacements were the best, and despite their junior rank he and Loerzer were regularly called into conferences to brief the top brass of 5th Army, including its commander, the Crown Prince, with further details of their observations. After a particularly hazardous flight they were both rewarded with the Iron Cross, First Class, by the Prince himself. 'The airforce lieutenants Göhring and Lörzer [sic] were among those who displayed conspicuous dash and zeal,' the Crown Prince recalled in his memoirs in 1923.[20] On one famous occasion, when French aircraft raided Stenay, the two young airmen distinguished themselves by taking off and, although their plane was unarmed, forcing one of the raiders down. The Crown Prince was particularly impressed and grateful for their action, since his wife was visiting at the time, and had been in danger. The two young heroes dined frequently in the royal mess, where Göring, naturally, relished every chance of mixing with the highest in the land, developing connections that were to prove most valuable in future years.

When first the French aircraft designer Raymond Saulnier, and then the Dutchman Anthony Fokker, devised systems of synchronising machine guns to allow them to fire through the propeller of an aircraft, the nature of aerial warfare was changed forever. Until the spring of 1915, the priority had been reconnaissance, and the observer had been the man who counted, the pilot often being seen as merely his chauffeur. Now that it was possible to mount forward firing machine guns, the pilot was transformed into a knight, 'riding' his plane to engage in single combat in the sky. It was a prospect Göring could not possibly resist, and at the end of June 1915 he returned to Freiburg to begin training, returning to 5th Army as a pilot in mid September.

Göring's first solo operational flight was on 3 October when, in what sounds like a typical piece of Göring overstatement, he reported that he had 'fought off seven French planes one after the other', but he had to wait until 16 November before he scored his first official kill. Over the next year, his tally climbed slowly: his second came only in March 1916, and it was another four and a half months before he was credited with his third. In between, he had made several claims that were disallowed, while moving constantly around the front. By the autumn of 1916, he was back with his friend Bruno Loerzer in the newly-formed Jasta (short for *Jagdstaffel*, Fighter Squadron) 5, mainly engaged in escort duty for bombers.

On patrol on 2 November, he spotted a giant British Handley-Page bomber lumbering out of the cloud ahead. It looked like a perfect sitting duck and he swooped joyfully in for his fourth kill – forgetting that no bomber would fly alone without an escort. He was brutally reminded of his mistake when the bomber's top cover of Sopwith fighters suddenly swarmed around him, guns blazing. Bullets raked his plane, one of them smashing into his hip. He managed to escape, and to crash land in the cemetery of a country church, which by great good fortune was being used as a field hospital. Without the prompt attention he received, he might well have bled to death. As it was, he spent the next four months in hospital.

Returning to duty in mid February 1917, he was posted to Loerzer's latest command, Jasta 26, based in upper Alsace, and almost immediately began to increase his score of kills, notching up another three before being given command of his own squadron, Jasta 27, flying out of the same airfield as Loerzer's, on 17 May. By the beginning of November, he and Loerzer had each reached a total of fifteen kills, a respectable number but well below the top aces like Manfred von Richthofen, who by then had disposed of sixty-one Allied aircraft.

Göring was a good commander, though his manner often verged on arrogance. His years of military training had prepared him for administration as well as fighting, and he ran a tight and efficient squadron. Although he still enjoyed the high life – one of the great benefits of the air force was that its pilots had unlimited supplies of champagne and good food, and lived in conditions that would have seemed luxurious to men in the trenches – he was a strict disciplinarian while on duty. He was ruthless in demanding total obedience, both on the ground and in the air, where his pilots had to forgo individual brilliance and follow the plans he had prepared. It was initially unpopular, but it worked. The day of the maverick was over; a pilot's chances of success, and survival, were greater as part of a well-drilled team.

In addition to his Iron Cross, First and Second Class, Göring had by this time received three other major decorations: the Zähring Lion with Swords, the Order of Karl Friedrich, and the Hohenzollern Medal with Swords, Third Class. But the supreme award, the *Pour le Mérite*, Germany's equivalent to Britain's Victoria Cross or America's Congressional Medal of Honour, still eluded him: the convention was that pilots automatically qualified for it when they had shot down twenty-five enemy planes, and not before. He was also niggled by the fact that when the four new fighter wings or super squadrons, the *Jagdgeschwaders*, were formed early in 1918, Loerzer was given command of JG2, but he was passed over, remaining as CO of Jasta 27, which was incorporated into Loerzer's unit. And when Richthofen was killed in April, command of JG1 went to one of his own officers, Captain Wilhelm Reinhardt, another blow to Göring's fierce ambition.

Within a few weeks, however, everything was to change. At the end of May, the Kaiser suddenly decided to award Göring his coveted *Pour le Mérite*, 'for continuous courage in action', although he had still only recorded fifteen kills. It may have been in recognition of his earlier exploits or his achievements as a squadron commander – Loerzer received the honour, too, with the same score – or it may simply have been that Germany needed heroes and they fitted the bill. Shortly afterwards Reinhardt was killed while trying to outdo Göring in test flying a new aircraft type; after Göring had given a spectacular display of aerobatics in the new plane, Reinhardt tried to follow suit, but broke a wing strut and plunged into the ground. To the surprise of most of the officers of JG1, Reinhardt's replacement was not one of them, but an outsider, Hermann Göring.

Göring managed Germany's most glamorous military formation well, and earned the grudging respect of most of the pilots under his command. Although there were always a few who disliked his braggadocio and suspected that he had inflated his score with dishonest claims, there were others who liked and admired him, and who became his friends for life. By the end of the war, he had increased his personal total of kills to twenty-two, and had achieved the status of a national hero, one of the select few whose photographs were sold as picture postcards.

After the squadron had been disbanded and its pilots dispersed, Göring stayed briefly with his fellow ace, Ernst Udet, in Berlin, before making his way back to his mother's apartment in Munich. If he had been upset by the unrest and republicanism in the capital, he was furious at the situation in Munich, and the regime of Kurt Eisner. Eisner had been jailed earlier in the year for organising strikes in aircraft and munitions factories – activities that hardly endeared him to Göring, who regarded his government as rabidly Bolshevik. Bands of revolutionary soldiers, sailors and workers still roamed the streets, setting on anyone they regarded as a class enemy. They took particular delight in attacking officers, tearing decorations and insignia of rank from their uniforms. Göring almost lost his epaulettes and his treasured medals to one such gang, but managed to fight them off, his bitterness and anger reinforced by what he saw as ingratitude and a lack of respect for the uniform that would have been quite incomprehensible only a few months earlier.

At some point around this time, according to his later testimony, Göring flew to Vienna, perhaps hoping things would be quieter there, or maybe hoping to reach his godfather at Mautendorf, only to find himself in the middle of another revolution as the Habsburg Empire collapsed.[21] He stayed for two days, then, unsettled and bitter, returned to Berlin, where the situation was little better than in Munich. While Ebert's national government was less extreme than Eisner's, it was still socialist. It also had to keep the workers' and soldiers' councils on its side, to prevent their going over to the Spartacists under Liebknecht and Rosa Luxemburg. Banning the old imperial badges of rank was one simple way of placating the revolutionaries, and a law was passed ordering officers to replace their traditional silver and gold shoulder straps with simple stripes worn on the sleeves. Not unnaturally, many officers objected strongly to this, Göring among them, and when they called a protest meeting in the Philharmonic Hall he turned up in full dress uniform, sporting all his medals. The new War Minister, General Hans-Georg Reinhardt, addressed them, calling on them to support the new government and obey its orders, including the one to abandon the old badges of rank, as he himself had done. He had barely finished when Göring rose to his feet and mounted the platform, to applause from the audience as they recognised him or spotted the *Pour le Mérite* at his throat. Begging the general's pardon, he began to speak, summoning up all his recently-found gift for oratory, his words ringing round the famous old hall:

I had guessed, sir, that as Minister for War you would be here today to address us. But I had hoped to see a black band on your sleeve that would symbolise your deep regret for the outrage you are proposing to inflict on us. Instead of that black band, you are wearing blue stripes on your arm. I think, sir, it would have been more appropriate for you to wear red stripes.

The audience broke into loud applause, but Göring had hardly begun. Holding up his hand for silence, he continued:

For four long years we officers did our duty and risked our lives for the Fatherland. Now we come home and how do they treat us? They spit on us and deprive us of what we gloried in wearing. This I will tell you, the people are not to blame for such conduct. The people were our comrades – the comrades of each of us, regardless of social distinctions, for four long years of war. No, the ones who are to blame are those who have stirred up the people, who stabbed our glorious army in the back and who thought of nothing but attaining power and enriching themselves at the expense of the people. And therefore I ask everyone here tonight to cherish hatred, a deep and abiding hatred, of those swine who have outraged the German people and our traditions. But the day will come when we will drive them out of our Germany. Prepare for that day. Arm yourselves for that day. Work for that day. It will surely come.[22]

The text of Göring's speech was made public in 1935, after the Nazis had come to power, by Dr Erich Gritzbach, head of Goring's secretariat in the Prussian ministry, and its wording must therefore be treated with some suspicion – especially the reference to the 'stab in the back', a phrase that was not in general use until November 1919, when Hindenburg used it to a committee of inquiry of the National Assembly. But contemporary reports confirm that Göring did speak to the meeting, and they back up the general tone and content of what he said. His speech gives us a clear and concise account of his credo, and of the deep feelings that were to lead him into a political career.

For the moment, however, Göring was not yet ready for active politics. He was still adrift, cut off from the only career he had ever wanted, the only life he had ever known as an adult – after speaking to General Reinhardt like that, there would certainly be no place for him in a reduced Reichswehr, the regular army. He did not even join one of the Freikorps, companies of former soldiers, which were being raised by his fellow officers as a right-wing reaction to the workers' and soldiers' councils. Instead, he decided to cash in on the connections he had made when, as a leading air ace and squadron commander, he had regularly visited aircraft and aero engine manufacturers to advise them and to test and assess their new models. Surprisingly, although they had disbanded the German air force, the Allies had not banned German firms from continuing to make planes, but since there was obviously no longer a market in Germany, they had to look elsewhere for sales. Göring contacted Anthony Fokker, whose D VII had been the most successful German fighter of the war, and was engaged to demonstrate his new F-7 model at an air show in Denmark. He persuaded Fokker to allow him to keep the plane, which he would continue to promote at air displays all over Scandinavia. Early in 1919, he flew out of Germany, away from the mayhem that he so despised. He had no plans to return.

II

'IF ONLY THERE COULD BE FIGHTING AGAIN'

HEINRICH Himmler returned to Munich for demobilisation at the end of the war despondent and disappointed. Unlike Göring, who had achieved glory as a swashbuckling aerial killer, the eighteen-year-old Himmler had seen no action, had failed to receive a commission as an officer, and his dreams of a military career were in tatters. Any thought that he would one day become Göring's chief rival for power in Germany would have seemed too ludicrous to contemplate, for there was nothing in his character or background that was in any way extraordinary.

Himmler was born in Munich on 7 October 1900, into a background that could hardly have been more solidly bourgeois or conventional, if one ignores the fact that his paternal grandfather was the illegitimate son of a peasant, who joined the 1st Royal Bavarian Regiment as a private, transferred to the Bavarian police force and reached the rank of sergeant, before finally achieving respectability as a minor local government official in the district of Lindau in the Bavarian Alps. There, he married the daughter of a watchmaker, who bore him one son, Gebhard, a clever boy who attended *Gymnasium* (the equivalent of the British grammar school or French *lycée*) and then Munich University, where he read philosophy and then philology, the study of classical languages and literature.

After graduation in 1894, Gebhard became a classics teacher in a Munich *Gymnasium*, and at the same time managed to get an appointment as tutor to Prince Arnulf of Bavaria's son Heinrich. No doubt this provided him with welcome extra money, but for a staunch monarchist and ambitious social climber the satisfaction of such a connection with

the royal house of Bavaria must have easily outweighed financial considerations. And in any event, within three years he became comfortably
off when he married Anna Heyder, who brought with her a modest
inheritance from her dead father, who had been in trade.

The Himmlers set up home in a second floor apartment at 2
Hildegardstrasse, in the centre of Munich. Their first child, a boy they
called Gebhard after his father, was born in 1898, and their second
two years later. They named him Heinrich, after Professor Himmler's
former royal pupil, Prince Heinrich, who agreed to be his godfather.
A third son, Ernst, was born five years later, by which time the family
was living in slightly grander style in Amalienstrasse, just behind the
university. Their apartment was furnished with antiques, and one room,
according to Himmler's brother Gebhard, 'was set aside and turned
into a shrine devoted to the memory of the family's ancestors'.[1]
Professor Himmler was obsessed with family history, much of it fanciful;
conveniently ignoring his grandfather's humble origins and illegitimacy
he insisted that the Himmler line could be traced back as far as 1297,
the date on a 'Himmler house' in Basle, and that the family had also
been prominent citizens of Mainz and Oberhein.

Professor Himmler was an avid collector of writings on Germanic
history, as well as coins and postage stamps, indexing and cataloguing
every item with meticulous care. Most evenings he read to his sons
from his library, so that by the time young Heinrich was ten years old
he knew the date of every famous German battle by heart. As a teacher,
the professor was a pedant, a strict disciplinarian and a bully, but his
sons, including Heinrich, all seem to have loved and respected him,
allowing him to mould them in his own image without protest or any
sign of rebellion. Like his parents, Heinrich was a devout Catholic,
dutifully attending church every Sunday and holy day and saying his
prayers every night in front of an ivory crucifix. In fact, in matters of
religion and morality he was already something of a prig.

When Heinrich entered the Royal Wilhelm Gymnasium in September
1910, he naturally became a model pupil in almost everything. The
exception was gymnastics, the school's only organised sporting activity:
he tried hard but he was short-sighted, rather plump, and had a congen-
itally weak constitution – or congenital hypochondria – as a result of
which his mother had tended to mollycoddle him. He was always a
swot, always near the top of his class, and never showed any wish to
step out of line. Although he was not the most popular boy in the
school, he was not a loner, and had a reasonable circle of friends. His

greatest ambition at that time was to be an officer in the Imperial Navy, which unlike the army did not demand aristocracy as a qualification for a commission, but his poor eyesight would have made that career impossible for him.

In 1913, Professor Himmler became deputy headmaster of the *Gymnasium* in Landshut, an attractive medieval town complete with an impressive castle, on the River Isar about forty miles north-east of Munich. His sons became pupils at his school, where they seem to have settled in without difficulty, and their lives continued on their unremarkable way. When the war came, it was some time before it affected them directly, though it did of course feed Heinrich's military fantasies and he followed its course avidly. Like all boys of that time, he was intensely nationalistic, rejoicing in the German army's successes and lamenting its setbacks. And like most boys of his age, he became an enthusiastic member of the Jugendwehr, the Youth Defence Force, in preparation for the time when he would be old enough to join the army proper. That time came when he reached the age of seventeen. His elder brother had been called up the year before, his best friend had left school for officer training earlier in the year, and Heinrich was desperate to follow suit, despite his father's wish that he complete his final exams first. He was also desperate to avoid being drafted into the ranks as a common soldier, like his brother. Heinrich wanted to fight for his country, but clearly not at any price.

The old restrictions on entry to the officer corps had been relaxed because of the war, but without influence in the right quarters it was still extremely difficult for middle-class applicants to find a place, particularly in a good regiment. Heinrich, of course, had a royal godfather, which should have opened the doors for him, but Prince Heinrich had been killed in action a year earlier. Professor Himmler contacted the chamberlain in the late prince's household, who duly wrote a letter of recommendation to the commanding officer of the 1st Bavarian Infantry Regiment and sent Heinrich 1,000 marks to buy his way in. Unfortunately, the chamberlain's letter was not enough – the regiment already had too many applications, and no room even on its waiting list, so the Himmlers had to look elsewhere.

Increasingly anxious that his son might be called up into the ranks, Professor Himmler began writing to every regiment in Bavaria, and every friend or acquaintance who might be able to pull the vital strings. As the rejections mounted, Heinrich tried to avoid the draft by leaving school and taking a job with the War Relief Office, but when it was announced that students in their final year at *Gymnasium* were exempt, he went back to school with some relief. In the Christmas holidays, however, the 11th Bavarian Regiment suddenly offered him a place as a *Fahnenjunker*, an officer cadet, and on 1 January 1918, he reported to the regimental depot at Regensburg, to begin his training.

In spite of his keenness, Himmler was no more than an average officer cadet. The inevitable homesickness of a callow youth living away from his close family for the first time soon passed as the cadets were allowed home most weekends. By the middle of October he was drilling new recruits and waiting for the posting to the front that was necessary before receiving a commission. The armistice put a stop to that.

While Munich was seething with left-wing revolutionaries, the smaller towns and villages of Bavaria remained deeply conservative. Regensburg was the birthplace of the Bayerische Volkspartei, the Bavarian People's Party (BVP), a right-wing, heavily Catholic organisation, which fitted Heinrich's own beliefs. Kicking his heels there in the vain hope that somehow or other he might still get his coveted commission, he attended meetings of the new party, and wrote home telling his father he, too, must join the BVP, as it was their only hope. It was his first experience of party politics, but it failed to spark any political ambitions in him: all he wanted, still, was to be an officer – his brother Gebhard had won a battlefield commission as a *Fähnrich*, an ensign, together with the Iron Cross, First Class. When Heinrich and his fellow cadets were discharged in mid December, his disappointment overshadowed everything else. He returned home to Landshut in time for Christmas, and in the new year went back to school to complete his studies and obtain his *Abitur*, so that he could move on to college.

Landshut, like Regensburg, remained relatively calm amid the political storms that were sweeping through Germany. Elsewhere, however, things were far more turbulent. In December 1918, the workers' and soldiers' councils held their first congress in Berlin. Delegates from all parts of the country demanded the socialisation of key industries, the breaking up of the great Junker estates, and a purge of the army starting with the dismissal of Hindenburg, pending its replacement by a people's militia whose officers were to be elected by the men. To the officer corps, this threat to its privileged existence was not just dangerous but positively sacrilegious. General Groener warned that he and the entire High Command would resign immediately if the councils' demands were met. In the face of the generals' ultimatum, Ebert caved in and simply ignored the congress's demands. In doing so, he lost perhaps his only chance to bring the army to heel, to overturn centuries of Prussian practice and make it answerable to the government and not itself in the person of the commander-in-chief. It was to prove a costly mistake for Germany in the future.

In fact, Ebert had capitulated to the military on his very first day in office: in the evening of 9 November Groener had called him on the secret direct line between GHQ and the Chancellery, pledging the army's support in the battle against Bolshevism in return for a promise that the government would not interfere in army affairs. Ebert had given him that promise. When the Spartacists called a general strike on 5 January 1919, took to the streets and occupied key buildings in the capital, Ebert called in Groener's pledge, and the army moved on Berlin. For five days, there was virtual civil war in the capital, but it was an unequal contest from the start – most of the workers rejected the revolutionaries' call to arms and stayed at home. Within the week the revolt had been crushed in the most brutal fashion. Karl Liebknecht and Rosa Luxemburg were arrested and murdered by officers of the Guards Cavalry Division, and their bodies dumped in the Tiergarten. Luxemburg's corpse was dropped through the ice into the Landwehr Canal, where it was not discovered until the thaw many weeks later, along with dozens more in other canals and waterways. The murders were never investigated and the culprits, though known, were never brought to justice: even under the new regime, it seemed that army officers were still above the law.

For those who had visions of creating a genuine democracy out of the wreckage of defeat, the events of January 1919 were a chilling reminder of the power and ruthlessness of the old order. Britain's *Manchester Guardian* newspaper reported on 15 January: 'The formidable military machine, which seemed to be crushed for ever, has risen with astounding rapidity. Prussian officers are stalking the streets of Berlin, soldiers marching, shouting and shooting at their command. Indeed Ebert and Scheidemann very likely got more than they bargained for.'

The army had played its part in putting down the second revolution, but the real victors were the Freikorps – a name that properly translates as 'volunteer corps', and which dates back to the struggle for liberation and a national German identity during the Napoleonic occupation between 1806 and 1813. The Freikorps of 1918 and 1919, however, were not bands of freedom fighters but freebooting private armies formed by embittered former officers to fight the Poles in Silesia, and to combat the revolutionary forces of the extreme left. In contrast to the soldiers' and workers' councils, which like all left-wing organisations were riven by constant internal squabbles, they were tightly disciplined, single-minded and well-equipped by the regular army with machine guns, mortars and even field guns as well as rifles and pistols. Based initially on the so-called storm-troops, elite squads that had led suicidal attacks across no man's land during the war, they were tough, hard, fighting units. With the size of the army strictly controlled by the Allies, the Freikorps were an essential and totally reliable auxiliary force in the fight against Bolshevism. In hindsight, it is clear that the Bolshevik threat was grossly exaggerated, but at the time it seemed terrifyingly real and the officer corps, the civil service and conservatives and liberals of all classes were only too ready to use any weapon to defeat it, no matter how double-edged that weapon might prove to be.

Having brought the situation in Berlin under control, the army and the Freikorps turned their attention to Munich, where trouble was boiling up even as Berlin was cooling down. In the national and local elections held on 19 January, the day after the first formal session of the Peace Conference in Paris, the parties of the radical left were resoundingly defeated everywhere by the moderates. In Bavaria, Kurt Eisner's revolutionary socialists could muster only 2.5 per cent of the votes, entitling them to a mere three seats in the Bavarian Diet compared with sixty-six for the middle-class Bavarian People's Party. Eisner tried to cling on to power by prevaricating and procrastinating, but eventually he was forced to call the new Diet. It was to be the last political act of his life: on his way to the opening ceremony he was shot dead by a young monarchist officer, Count Anton Arco-Valley, scion of one of Bavaria's most prominent dynasties.

The assassination of Eisner led to chaos, starting in the chamber of the Diet itself, where there was more shooting and at least two more deaths, as opposing factions sought vengeance on each other. For several weeks, there was no proper government in Bavaria. The soldiers' and workers' council was nominally in charge, but in reality a state of near anarchy prevailed, with armed bands roaming the streets and occupying public buildings, banks and hotels. Eisner was raised to the status of a martyr, and public sentiment swung to the left again, in a sympathetic reaction to his killing.

The Diet was finally reconvened on 17 March, and a Majority Socialist former schoolteacher, Johannes Hoffmann, was elected Minister-President. Just as it seemed, however, that the Spartacists might be subdued and some semblance of order restored, news arrived from Hungary that galvanised them into fresh action: the communists there had overthrown the government and set up a full-scale soviet republic under Bela Kun. It was the first soviet regime at national level outside Russia, and it proved that it could be done. On 6 April, an assorted group representing most of the left-wing parties and organisations – but not, significantly, the communists – met in the unlikely surroundings of the queen's bedchamber in the royal palace, and proclaimed a Räterepublik, a soviet republic, of Bavaria, under the leadership of a twenty-six-year-old bohemian poet called Ernst Toller.

The legitimate Hoffmann government fled Munich for the safety of Bamberg, just as the German National Assembly had left Berlin for Weimar. Both moves were eminently sensible in the circumstances: there was a new Spartacist uprising in Berlin during March, which was put down with even greater savagery than before by Gustav Noske, Ebert's Minister of Defence, who sent in troops and tanks. Noske, a former butcher, was the closest thing to a strong man in the government; he had accepted his appointment gladly, declaring: 'Someone must be the bloodhound',[2] and he had no hesitation in translating his words into brutal action. Square-jawed and stocky, often wearing a workman's cap to remind everyone of his proletarian credentials, he had risen through the trade union movement to become a Reichstag deputy and the party's expert on military matters. Although he was a Social Democrat, he was also a committed nationalist, and had been sent by Prince Max to put down the mutiny in Kiel at the beginning of November, a task he had accomplished with grim relish. It was Noske who gave official approval to the Freikorps, and saw that they were properly armed and housed.

The Toller Räterepublik in Bavaria lasted just seven days before it was overthrown by army troops loyal to the Hoffmann government, but the troops were defeated in their turn by Spartacist fighters – armed workers, rebel soldiers from the garrison and red sailors. Power was then seized by hard-core communists, who proclaimed a Second Räterepublik under Eugen Leviné, a Russian-born agent sent by the Communist Party in Berlin with Moscow's backing to put some steel into the Bavarian party and foment revolution. Leviné's supporters began a reign of terror in Munich. Toller was released from prison and appointed commanding general of the 'Red Army', which defeated the Hoffmann troops in a pitched battle at Dachau, a quiet little market town about ten miles from the city. In desperation, Hoffmann appealed to Noske for help. Noske's response was prompt and ominous: 'The Munich insane asylum must be put in order.'[3] He sent the Prussian Major-General von Oven with a force of regular army units, which were to be supplemented by Freikorps, to see to it.

The regular troops were assembled on the army training ground at Ohrdurf in Thuringia, the state immediately to the north of Bavaria, where they were joined by thousands of Freikorps men. So many ex-officers flocked to volunteer their services that they were formed into whole companies with no other ranks or enlisted men. Himmler, who was just about to begin the second term of his crash course at school, immediately joined the Landshut Freikorps, and then the reserve company of the larger Freikorps Oberland, which belonged to the Thule Society, becoming aide to the commanding officer. He had high hopes that the Oberland would be incorporated into the regular army, taking him with it and so reviving his military career.

Von Oven's force of 20,000 men moved on Munich towards the end of April, and by the twenty-ninth had the city surrounded. The Red government began to fall apart amid growing anarchy. Toller resigned as commander of the Red Army, and was replaced by a young sailor, Rudolf Egelhöfer, who appealed to the regular troops of the Munich garrison for support.

Adolf Hitler was one of the troops in the city barracks. He had been back in Munich since 21 November, during which time he had done guard duty at a prisoner-of-war camp and at the main rail station, and was now in the demobilisation battalion of the 2nd Infantry Regiment, reluctantly awaiting discharge. Presenting himself as a Social Democrat and a supporter of Hoffmann's government, he was actively involved in the soldiers' councils, and had been elected as his battalion's deputy representative a couple of weeks earlier. It was his first political position. At the meeting called to discuss Egelhöfer's appeal, he is said to have leapt on to a chair and made a speech exhorting his fellow soldiers to refuse: 'We are not revolutionary guards for a lot of carpetbagging Jews!' Interestingly, however, he did not urge them to fight against the Räterepublik, but to stay neutral in the coming battle, which they did.[4]

The battle for Munich was brief but bloody. The Spartacists alienated everybody by murdering ten hostages they had been holding, putting them up against the wall of the Luitpold Gymnasium and shooting them. Among the victims were seven members of the Thule Society, including its secretary, the beautiful Countess Hella von Westarp – a grave mistake, since her murder gave the counter-revolutionaries a wonderful excuse for righteous indignation and vicious retribution. At the same time, the advancing White Army came upon a camp holding some fifty Russian prisoners of war, who were all slaughtered without thought. This was only the beginning. As the army and the Freikorps moved into the city, they killed hundreds of people, many of them innocent, and the Red forces did the same, while Hitler and his comrades sat in their barracks and did nothing.

Himmler and his Freikorps fellows also did nothing. They were a reserve unit, but were not needed, so once again Himmler was denied action, and his hopes of moving back into the army with the Freikorps Oberland were destroyed when the government ordered it to disband. He returned to school, completed his course, then began looking for a new career. In consultation with his father, who was keen to find some way of distancing his son from the very real dangers of politics, he chose agriculture. He had always liked plants, and as a boy had acquired a large collection of herbs, an interest that was later to become an obsession.

The choice of farming was not such a huge departure from Heinrich's military ambitions as it might seem. In his mind he held a romantic vision of himself following in the footsteps of the Teutonic knights of old, warriors who settled on the land they had conquered and became farmers. The concept of *Blut und Boden*, the mystical link between blood and soil, had become popular in the nineteenth century, triggering a nationalist-*völkisch* movement to return to the land and spread the Germanic empire and race far beyond the confines of Germany itself. A diary entry later that year reveals something of Himmler's thinking: 'At the moment, I do not know for whom I work. I work because it is my duty, because I find peace in work, and I work for my ideal of German womanhood with whom, some day, I shall live my life in the east and fight my battles as a German far from beautiful Germany.'[5] It was a vision that he was never to lose.

Professor Himmler was moving up the ladder again, having secured a new appointment as *Rektor*, headmaster, of a *Gymnasium* in

Ingoldstadt, about thirty miles north-west of Landshut and forty-five miles north of Munich. He found Heinrich a position on a farm near the town, with the idea that he would gain a year's practical experience before going on to Munich University's Technical High School to study agronomy.

Heinrich started on 1 August, at the peak of the harvest and all the backbreaking work that that entailed, but after only a month was taken ill and admitted to hospital, diagnosed as suffering from a paratyphoid infection. Whether the disease was real or the symptoms were psychosomatic must remain speculation, but throughout his life he suffered unexplained intestinal cramps and disorders, a problem he shared with Hitler and which was almost certainly stress related. Real or not, it was enough to take him off the farm and away from the heavy physical work involved, and from the foreman, with whom, he recorded in his diary, he had 'an unpleasant last conversation'.

Himmler seems to have spent most of his three weeks in hospital reading, and started recording dates, details and his opinions of the books he read in a series of notebooks, much as his father catalogued and indexed all his collections. It was a habit that he continued for the next fifteen years, and the notes that survive give us a fascinating insight into some of the influences that helped shape his idiosyncratic philosophy. At the beginning, he read mostly German classics – probably brought to the hospital by his father – and novels, particularly those of his favourite author, Jules Verne, something else that he shared with Hitler. His later reading was a mish-mash of polemics and popular philosophy, ranging from Nietzsche and H. Stewart Chamberlain (another of Hitler's favourites) to works on Jews and freemasons and dubious racial theories. Occasionally, banned erotic books appear on his list; he always condemned them as degenerate, giving the impression that he had only read them out of moral duty, but he read them all the same.

After he was discharged from hospital, Himmler still felt unwell. His family doctor diagnosed an enlarged heart caused by overwork, and recommended that he convalesce for a while, taking only light exercise and avoiding nervous stress. Instructed to 'interrupt for a year and study',[6] he enrolled at the Technical High School on 18 October 1919, moved to Munich and rented a room in Amalienstrasse, near the flat where the family had once lived. His elder brother, Gebhard, was already a student at the university, living close by.

At the Technical High School, Himmler was, as ever, a model student, diligent, conscientious and hard working, clever but not brilliant. Although he was always rather gauche, he had a surprisingly active social life, going to parties – on one occasion dressing up as 'Abdul Hamid, the Sultan of Turkey' – taking dancing lessons, learning to play the guitar, and joining a whole host of clubs and societies. The impression we are left with is of an eager, earnest, and rather boring young man, still something of a mother's boy, anxiously seeking the acceptance of his peers while retaining the approval of his parents and teachers.

He was accepted into one of the best student fraternities, the Apollo, though this raised certain problems for him. Fraternities like the Apollo were centred on two activities, drinking huge quantities of beer, and duelling. His delicate stomach made swilling beer difficult, but the fraternity leaders understood and granted him a special dispensation excusing him from drinking. Duelling, however, was a struggle for his conscience: the Catholic church had strictly forbidden it, and he was still a devout Catholic, but he desperately wanted to conform to student mores, and he desperately wanted the duelling scars that were the mark of the German gentleman. The need to conform won. His diary entry for 15 December 1919 reads: 'I believe I have come into conflict with my religion. Come what may, I shall always love God, pray to him and adhere to the Catholic Church and defend it, even if I should be expelled from it.'[7] For all the *Angst*, though, he seems to have been in no great hurry – or it may be that he had difficulty finding a partner – and it was not until June 1922, towards the end of his last term, that he achieved his objective with five cuts needing five stitches.

Like any typical, repressed adolescent with two brothers and no sisters, Heinrich was awkward with girls and suffered the pains of unrequited love. When one girl turned him down, his old ambitions surfaced again, as he recorded in his diary on 28 November 1919: 'If I could only face dangers now, could risk my life, could fight, it would be a relief to me.'[8] Clearly, he still hankered after the military life. Earlier that month, he, his brother Gebhard and his cousin and best friend Ludwig 'Lu' Zahler had applied to join the 14th Alarm Company of the Protection Brigade in Munich, an official army reserve force like Britain's Territorials or the National Guard in America. At the beginning of December, he noted happily: 'Today I have my uniform on again. It is always quite my favourite dress.'[9]

* * *

As the new decade dawned, the political situation in Germany generally and Munich in particular was still as volatile as ever. On 7 January 1920, a 7,000-strong mass meeting in Munich of the Deutschvölkischer Schutz- und Trutz-Bund, the German Nationalist Defence and Defiance Confederation, a pan-German umbrella organisation for right-wing groups, which used the swastika as its symbol, had ended in violent uproar, and the authorities were understandably nervous. On 13 January a demonstration in Berlin against planned legislation to make works councils obligatory turned into a nightmare when the crowd tried to storm the Reichstag and the police opened fire on them with rifles and machine guns, killing and wounding dozens of marchers. Fearful of similar scenes in Munich, the Bavarian government imposed a ban on political meetings in the city.

Adolf Hitler had been one of those who spoke briefly at the Schutz- und Trutz-Bund meeting in Munich: it was the first time he had appeared on such a stage, the first time he had tasted the addictive rush of adrenaline at facing a huge audience. Though still a serving corporal in the army, he was now the star speaker of the Deutsche Arbeiterpartei (DAP), the German Workers' Party, which he had joined in September 1919 on the orders of his commanding officer. The DAP was one of at least fifteen small right-wing parties which had mushroomed in Munich since the war, but it was growing more quickly than most of the others, thanks in part to Hitler's rapidly developing speaking skills. Audiences at its first seven public meetings had grown steadily from a few dozen to some 400, but now that he had experienced the buzz of a real mass meeting, he could hardly wait to take the DAP down the same road. He persuaded the chairman, Anton Drexler, to go along with him, and they booked the Bürgerbräukeller, a large beer hall on Rosenheimer Strasse, about half a mile south-east of the city centre across the River Isar, for later that month, to re-launch the party.

Because of the ban, the meeting had to be rescheduled for Tuesday 24 February, in a new venue, the more central Hofbräuhaus. The delay turned out to be useful, for it not only gave Hitler more time to prepare his speech and to draft, with Drexler, a party manifesto to be announced at the meeting, it also made his subject more timely and more emotive. To fill the cavernous hall, they needed an audience of 2,000. But Hitler and Drexler were both unknowns, so Drexler persuaded Dr Johannes Dingfelder, not a party member but a well-known figure in *völkisch* circles in Munich, to make what he was assured would be the main speech of the evening, '*Was uns not tut*', 'What we need to do'. With blazing red posters and handbills plastered around the city they got their 2,000 people to fill the hall, a large number of them communists responding to Hitler's deliberately provocative red posters and there to cause trouble. Drexler seems to have lost his nerve at this point, and Hitler took the chair, another first and another step forward in his burgeoning career.

Dingfelder's address was worthy and unexceptional, and was received politely. Hitler followed. He presented the twenty-five points in the party's new manifesto, then turned to attacks on the Jews and the Versailles diktat, all of which went down very well. His raw oratory set the place alight, and there was some heckling and barracking but, contrary to his wishful claims in *Mein Kampf,* the meeting ended with little or no violence. There were no riots, no broken heads, and therefore no banner headlines to provide much-needed publicity. Heinrich Himmler and his friends in the Protection Brigades were not called out, and indeed seem to have been totally unaware of Hitler's debut as a speaker on the grand scale. They were, however, very much aware of the main subject of his speech and its effects on the German people.

The Versailles Treaty had come into effect on 10 January, and three weeks later the Allies had demanded the extradition of the Kaiser from Holland and the handing over by the German government of nearly 900 former officers, starting with Hindenburg, for trial as war criminals. The government refused, but the officer corps was barely placated, using the incident to attack President Ebert and his colleagues for signing the Treaty in the first place. Their feelings became more and more heated as rumours, accusations and counter accusations mounted. They finally boiled over when the government succumbed to Allied pressure, accepted the demobilisation of 60,000 troops, including 20,000 officers, and ordered the disbanding of the Freikorps.

The toughest and most ruthless of the Freikorps, the 2nd Marine Brigade, known as the Ehrhardt Brigade after its commander Naval Captain Hermann Ehrhardt, was stationed at Döberitz, some fifteen miles outside Berlin. It had distinguished itself in savage battles against the Poles on the eastern frontier and the Bolsheviks in the Baltic states, as well as fighting the Spartacists in Berlin, and it had been one of the main units in the force that had crushed the Räterepublik in Munich the previous year. The very thought of disbanding was anathema to its officers and men. Through the commander of the Berlin Military District, General Freiherr Walther von Lüttwitz, they sent an ultimatum to the government, demanding a halt to all demobilisation of both army and Freikorps, plus various other measures including fresh elections, the forcible suppression of all strikes, and the restoration of the old imperial colours of red, white and black, which had been replaced under the new Weimar constitution by the black, red and gold of the revolutionaries of 1848.

When Ebert rejected their ultimatum, the Brigade marched on Berlin, led by their assault company and a field artillery battery, singing their brigade song:

> Swastika on our helmets
> Black-white-red our band
> The Brigade of Ehrhardt
> Is known throughout the land.
>
> Worker, worker, what's to become of you
> When the Brigade is ready to fight?
> The Ehrhardt Brigade smashes all to bits
> So woe, woe, woe to you, you worker son-of-a-bitch![10]

As they goose-stepped through the Brandenburg Gate at 7 a.m. on 13 March, they were greeted by General Ludendorff, who happened, 'quite by chance', to be taking his early morning constitutional at that precise time and place, and by Dr Wolfgang Kapp, the co-founder of the wartime Fatherland Party. Kapp and Lüttwitz made their way to the Reich Chancellery on Wilhelmstrasse, and issued a proclamation stating that the Reich government had ceased to exist. 'The full state power has devolved on Commissioner Dr Kapp of Königsberg as Reich Chancellor and Minister-President of Prussia,' it continued. 'We need two things, order and work. Agitators will be exterminated without compunction.'

Ebert and his government had wisely decamped during the night, first to Dresden and then to Stuttgart, having failed to persuade the Chief of the General Staff, Colonel-General Hans von Seekt, to provide military support. Seekt's response had been brief and blunt: 'Troops do not fire on troops . . . When Reichswehr fires on Reichswehr, then all comradeship within the officer corps will have vanished.'

The army – renamed the Reichswehr during the Weimar Republic – may have stood aside, but it offered no active support to the *putsch*. When the one member of the government who had stayed behind, Privy Councillor Arnold Brecht, called for a general strike and the whole city came to an abrupt standstill, the troops stayed in their barracks. Civil servants and bureaucrats at every level also refused to co-operate: the new regime's first difficulty came when they could find no one to type out their manifesto, since they had made the mistake of trying to seize power on a Saturday, and consequently it was too late to make the Sunday newspapers. Then Brecht hid the rubber stamps needed to authenticate all documents – and no one would accept unstamped orders. The next blow came when the Freikorps troopers demanded pay, and Kapp realised his regime had no money to give them. He tried to persuade Ehrhardt to take it from the state bank, but Ehrhardt refused indignantly, saying he was an officer not a bank robber.

The general strike was the most complete stoppage in German history. Everything came to a halt immediately: there was no water, no power, no transport, nothing. In the midst of the increasing chaos there were more mutinies in the army and navy in various parts of the country, the security police and troops declared their allegiance to the Ebert government, and after only four and a half days the *putsch* collapsed. Kapp climbed into a taxicab and headed for Tempelhof Airport, emulating Ludendorff by flying out to Sweden, though he did not feel the need for false whiskers.

The Freikorps troops formed up and marched out of Berlin, watched by a hostile crowd, but the farce into which the attempted *putsch* had descended had a vicious edge. A boy in the crowd jeered at the departing troopers, and two of them broke ranks, clubbed him to the ground with their rifle butts and kicked him to death. When the crowd tried to intervene, other troopers opened fire on them with rifles and machine guns, before continuing on their way, leaving hundreds of dead and dying behind them.

Shortly after Kapp took off from Tempelhof, a small plane flew in from Munich, carrying Corporal Adolf Hitler of the 'Information Department', Abteilung 1b/P, of the Reichswehr's Bavarian Command, and his mentor in the DAP, Dietrich Eckart. They had been sent by Captain Mayr, commander of Abteilung 1b/P, to inform Kapp and Lüttwitz of the political situation in Munich, and to find out exactly what was happening in Berlin. By the time they arrived it was all over, but the journey was not wasted – they made contacts with *völkisch* circles and right-wing groups like the Stahlhelm veterans' association, which would be valuable to Hitler in the future. The well-connected Eckart was able to introduce his protégé to a number of influential people in Berlin, most notably Frau Helene Bechstein, wife of the piano manufacturer and one of Berlin's premier political hostesses, who took a lasting shine to the intense young man with the piercing blue eyes.

For Hitler, the high point of his visit to Berlin came when General Ludendorff received him and Eckart in his suite at the Adlon Hotel, a meeting that was probably the most significant of his life so far: the backing of the former *de facto* military dictator would give him the credibility he needed if he was to fulfil his ambitions. Returning to Munich at the end of March, he resigned from the army in order to devote himself full-time to the life of a political activist. At the same time, he announced a change of name for the DAP: in order to attract a broader spectrum of support, it would in future be known as the NSDAP, the National Socialist German Workers' Party, a title that was soon abbreviated, in the usual German fashion, to the Nazi Party.

The situation in Munich, which Hitler and Eckart had gone to Berlin to report, was very different from that in the Reich capital. While Kapp and Ehrhardt were making a complete botch of trying to unseat the Social Democratic national government, in Munich the army and the leaders of the powerful Einwohnerwehr, the Citizens' Defence Force or Home Guard, had 'persuaded' Hoffmann's Bavarian socialist government to resign. In its place, they had installed their own right-wing government, under Gustav Ritter von Kahr, an old-style monarchist autocrat. Unlike Kapp and Lüttwitz, Kahr had the crucial support of both the army and the police – indeed his government was in many ways little more than a front for the military – so the Munich *putsch* was relatively smooth and trouble-free. But it was still a highly nervous time, and Himmler's 14th Alarm Company was among those called out to preserve order. Himmler, his brother and cousin had a great time wearing their uniforms for real and patrolling the streets in armoured cars, machine guns at the ready.

Soon afterwards, the protection brigades were disbanded on the orders of the Allied Control Commission, which saw them, quite rightly, as devices for getting round the restrictions on the size of the Reichswehr imposed by the Versailles Treaty. Disappointed but undaunted, Himmler immediately joined the Einwohnerwehr, which was not officially connected to the army but had a military structure and still gave him a chance to wear a uniform. He was issued with '1 rifle and 50 rounds,

1 steel helmet, 2 ammunition pouches and 1 haversack', significantly from the stores of the Reichswehr's 21 Rifle Brigade.[11]

Throughout the Reich, the political situation remained volatile, particularly in the industrial regions where the communists had their power bases. In Saxony a soviet republic was proclaimed amid the most violent threats and atrocities on both sides. In the Ruhr, the general strike escalated into a series of pitched battles between workers and the army, which gave the French the excuse to march in and impose a military occupation, raising tensions still further. With so much of Germany in turmoil, the forces of the far right saw Bavaria as a safe haven, and began to migrate there, quickly turning Munich into the centre for all anti-Weimar activity. Anyone in danger of arrest for right-wing subversive activity could be sure of finding a refuge in Bavaria, often with a job as a labourer or a supervisor on one of the great estates.

Ludendorff was presented by an admirer with a villa in the Munich suburb of Ludwigshöhe, which rapidly became a centre of pilgrimage for nationalist opponents of the Weimar Republic. It was guarded round the clock by troopers of the Ehrhardt Brigade, which had left Döberitz and established a new base in Munich, at the express invitation of the city's Police President, Ernst Pöhner, a tall, arrogant former army lieutenant. It was Pöhner who, when asked if he knew that there were political murder gangs operating in the city, was reputed to have replied, 'Yes – but not enough of them!'[12] Most of the gangs were made up of former Freikorps members, who had gone underground when their brigades and corps were banned, forming themselves into so-called sporting and social clubs to stay together and bide their time. Their most popular sporting activities were rifle shooting and marching.

Himmler left Munich in September 1920, for a year's practical experience on a farm at Fridolfing, near the Austrian border. When he returned in August 1921 to begin his final year at college, he resumed his activities with his many organisations and societies – he was clearly still driven by a compulsion to belong – but showed no interest in political parties. As far as we know, he was not even aware of Hitler or the NSDAP. Like many young men facing an uncertain future, he thought seriously about emigrating. 'Today I cut an article out of the newspaper about emigration to Peru,' he wrote in his diary on 23 November 1921. 'Where will I end up: Spain, Turkey, the Baltic countries, Russia, Peru? I often think about it. In two years' time I will no longer be in Germany.' Three years later, he was still toying with the idea, inquiring at the Russian embassy about going to the Ukraine as an estate manager.

His great passion, however, was still the army. 'If only there could be fighting again,' he wrote in his diary, 'war, departing troops!'[13] A few months later he was still on the same tack: 'Perhaps I will join up in one way or another. For basically I am a soldier.'[14] The Einwohnerwehr had gone the way of the protection brigades, but Himmler could draw some consolation from the fact that before they were dissolved he had at last been given a commission, as a *Fähnrich*. For now, however, he had to make do with the officers' association of his old regiment, and a shadowy veterans' organisation calling itself the Freiweg Rifle Club.

The Freiweg had some connection with the much-feared Organisation Consul, which carried out hundreds of political assassinations throughout Germany between 1919 and 1922, claiming the lives of, among others, Matthias Erzberger, the man who had signed the armistice in 1918, and the Foreign Minister, Walther Rathenau. The 'Consul' after whom it was named was none other than Captain Ehrhardt, who had fled to Hungary immediately after the débâcle of the Kapp *putsch* but had returned to Bavaria on false papers under the name of 'Consul H. von Eschwige'. The papers had been provided by Police President Pöhner, who continued to provide protection for Ehrhardt and his officers in Munich. He also provided false papers for Erzberger's assassins, enabling them to escape to Hungary, where the government refused to extradite them until 1946.

Himmler's diary entry after the Rathenau killing shows that he had at least some knowledge of the affair: 'Organisation "C". Dreadful if everything should become known.'[15] The following week he volunteered for 'special missions' with the Freiweg. Nothing seems to have come of it, but it does show that he was now taking a more active interest in politics. In fact, he obtained a place on the political science course at the university for the following year, and was even granted exemption from fees, but his father was unable to go on supporting him. Although Professor Himmler had reached the peak of his profession that year when he was appointed *Rektor* of the Wittlesbach Gymnasium, one of Munich's top schools, inflation was already hitting hard, and he had two other sons to consider. So Heinrich completed his course, fought his duel, gained his diploma and looked for a job

in agriculture. The best he could find in those difficult times, with inflation and unemployment both soaring, was a post as an assistant in a
fertiliser company, Stickstoff-Land Ltd in Schleissheim on the outskirts
of Munich. He began work there at the beginning of September 1922.

No longer a student, and with a secure if not very well-paid job,
Himmler might have been expected to settle down to a steady career
connected with the land, a life of farmers and fertilisers and crop yields.
But in the previous year he had met a man who offered him the chance
to wear a uniform again, even though it was only at weekends and
even though it was only the grey windcheater, ski cap and gaiters of
a nationalist association which called itself the Reichsflagge (Imperial
Flag). The man was a battle-scarred veteran of the trenches, Captain
Ernst Röhm. Himmler, still young and impressionable, still eager for
acceptance, became his devoted follower.

A much-decorated war hero, three times wounded and with the scars
to prove it – the upper part of his nose had been shot away in 1914,
and another bullet had scored a deep channel across his left cheek –
Röhm was a swaggering, bellicose, regular officer who had served on
the Western Front as a company commander in the 10th Bavarian
Infantry. Although he was a practising, but still secret, homosexual
there was nothing effete in his manner, and nothing to arouse the young
Himmler's suspicions in this area – if there had been, he would probably have been deeply shocked and certainly would never have followed
him. The son of a railway employee, Röhm had never wanted to be
anything but a soldier: the army had been his life, his entire *raison
d'être*, encompassing all his dreams and ambitions. He had suffered
the humiliation of the Armistice with particular bitterness, and now
devoted all his considerable energies to finding ways of maintaining
the army's influence and restoring its power, by any and every possible
means. He despised the Republic and all it stood for, especially the
threat it posed to his military career, and he intrigued constantly to
bring about its downfall – when he came to write his memoirs in 1928,
he entitled them *Die Geschichte eines Hochverräters (The Story of a
Traitor)*.

By the end of the war, Röhm, then aged thirty-one, had been invalided
away from the front after being wounded seriously for a third time,
to serve as supply officer on the staff of 12 Bavarian Infantry Division,
based in Himmler's home town of Landshut.[16] He had then become

Armaments and Equipment Officer of 21 Rifle Brigade in Munich, where he had been responsible for arming the various paramilitary outfits, including Himmler's.[17] Finally, he had been appointed to the staff of the Reichswehr VII District Command in Munich, as adjutant to Major-General Ritter von Epp, who had led the Freikorps Oberland in the defeat of the Räterepublik and was now commander of all infantry forces in Bavaria. Working for Epp, Röhm had been responsible for organising, arming and co-ordinating the paramilitaries, especially his particular baby, the Einwohnerwehr. He had also been in charge of removing arms and equipment from army stores and stockpiling them in clandestine dumps, securely hidden from both the Allied Control Commission and the German government, against whom they would be used in the anticipated confrontation between the army and the Republic. When the Bavarian government was finally forced to dissolve the Einwohnerwehr and confiscate the weapons of the other paramilitary organisations, many of those organisations chose to hand them over to Röhm for safe keeping, earning him the nickname 'the machine-gun king'. Controlling such an arsenal gave him considerable power and influence in nationalist right-wing politics.

Although his interests were military-political rather than party-political, Röhm took an active interest in most of the right-wing organisations and parties, an involvement that had increased when he took over Abteilung 1b/P from Captain Mayr in 1920. Before he handed over, Mayr had introduced him to his star prospect, taking Hitler to meet him at sessions of the Iron Fist, a secret club that Röhm had founded for radical right-wing officers. Shortly afterwards, Röhm began attending meetings of the DAP (as it then was), joined the party as member number 623, and began providing much-needed money from his department's slush fund. Having heard Hitler speak, he recognised the potential behind his raw intensity: here, he believed, was a man he could use.

For the moment, Hitler was only one member of the party, and the DAP was only one among the many small parties in Munich that Röhm was interested in. Hitler's own ambitions were still limited to being 'the drummer', the man who could rouse the masses and set them on the march, and this suited Röhm's purposes admirably. He began giving Hitler practical help to become what he, Röhm, needed him to be. Hitler was a man without contacts; Röhm knew everybody. Over the next two years, in addition to subsidising him financially, he promoted his protégé's career by introducing him to patriotic officers and politicians, overcoming their reservations about the difference in rank by insisting that Hitler address him with the familiar 'Du', 'thou', instead of the formal 'Sie'. (The habit stuck: in later years, Röhm was the only one among Hitler's associates who was allowed – or who was bold enough to claim – this privilege.) He also bolstered the DAP's credibility by persuading many other Reichswehr officers to join. When the Thule Society's newspaper, the *Völkischer Beobachter*, was about to go bankrupt in December 1920, Röhm was instrumental, along with Hitler's other mentor, Dietrich Eckart, in persuading Ritter von Epp to provide 60,000 marks from the army's secret funds to help the NSDAP to buy it as a mouthpiece.

Röhm's main interest was still with the paramilitaries rather than parties like the NSDAP, but before long he found a way of combining the two. When the Einwohnerwehr was dissolved, its members dispersed into a rash of new or strengthened 'patriotic associations' which sprang up throughout Bavaria, mostly formed around the remnants of the Freikorps. Many of their names, and those of their leaders, had a familiar ring: they included Epp's Bund Oberland, Ehrhardt's Wiking-Bund, and the Reichsflagge, headed by Röhm. When Hitler staged an internal coup in the NSDAP in July 1921, seizing power as chairman and relaunching the party with bigger ambitions, it was to Röhm that he turned to strengthen the 'hall protection squad' of heavies and bouncers used to control or disrupt meetings, and transform it into the party's own paramilitary group. Röhm brought in Ehrhardt, who reached an agreement with Hitler for the seasoned troopers of his former Brigade to join the party's 'Sports Section' – it was just at the time of the Erzberger assassination, and Ehrhardt no doubt found it useful to have an extra layer of cover for his men.

By the autumn the section, commanded by an Ehrhardt veteran, Lieutenant Klintzsch, had 300 members and a new name: the Sturmabteilung, 'Storm Section', or SA for short. Röhm had no direct involvement with it – he was too busy with his own Reichsflagge, and with keeping an eye on the many other groups in which he had an interest. But he continued to provide financial support and encouragement.

Himmler met Röhm at least as early as January 1922, when his diary records being with him in Munich's Arzberger Keller after a meeting of one of the many organisations he belonged to: 'Captain Röhm and Major Angerer [Himmler's former company commander] were also there; very friendly. Röhm pessimistic as to Bolshevism.'

Himmler was captivated by the force of Röhm's personality, and Röhm was happy to take the young man under his wing and to steer him in the right direction. When he graduated from college and started work for Stickstoff-Land, Röhm persuaded him to join both the Reichsflagge and, a year later, the NSDAP. Himmler joined the party willingly, in August 1923, receiving the membership number 42,404. But he was not yet a Nazi: his banner was the imperial flag of the German monarchy not the swastika, and his leader was not Hitler, but Röhm.

III

FIGHTING THE NOVEMBER CRIMINALS

HERMANN Göring returned to Germany in the summer of 1921, to study history and political science at Munich University, and to look for a new career, a new future. He was also fleeing from scandal in Stockholm, where he had followed the racy traditions of his own family by falling in love with another man's wife, persuading her to leave her husband and young son and set up home with him.

After leaving Germany for Denmark at the end of 1918, Göring had led the life of a barnstorming showman for several months, flying his white-cowled Fokker monoplane around air displays and fairs, often in company with four other former members of JG1. As famous German air aces, they were treated as celebrities wherever they went. Rich young Danes fêted them with champagne, good food, and girls. Women swooned over all of them, but the star was undoubtedly the handsome, dashing, twenty-six-year-old Lieutenant Göring, who took full advantage of all that was offered. According to Karl Bodenschatz, he lived 'like a world boxing champion. He had more money than he needed and any girl he wanted.' In one of his letters to Bodenschatz, he wrote about going home with an attractive Danish woman and spending the night with her 'in a bath of champagne'. Bodenschatz never dared to ask if he meant it literally, but said he would not have been surprised if the answer had been yes.[1]

Göring billed himself as the last commander of the Richthofen Flying Circus, and if the crowds wanted to believe his plane was the one in which he had fought and killed on the Western Front, why should he disabuse them? He was never one for letting the truth get in the way of a good story, particularly stories that promoted his image as a hero. In any case, it was good for business, and his business sense was developing rapidly. In between the parties and the aerobatics, he was advising the Danish government on aircraft and equipment for their embryonic air force, and there can be little doubt that he enjoyed handsome fees from them and equally handsome commissions from the suppliers he recommended.

By the summer of 1919, however, the high life in Denmark was beginning to pall. It may be that his behaviour, both sexually and socially, and his increasingly strident criticism of the Versailles Treaty were wearing out his welcome. Maybe the consultancy fees and sales commissions were starting to dry up as the Danish Air Force became fully equipped. Maybe Göring got bored – like most ex-combatants he was finding it hard to settle into peacetime life. Or maybe he was simply offered a good job in Sweden. In any case, he flew on to Stockholm, where he joined the fledgling Svenska Lufttrafik airline, flying air taxis. He had no plans to return to Germany, seeing no future there as a flier while the country was denied an air force. On 13 February he wrote to the German army's settlement office applying for discharge, and offering to forgo his pension rights in exchange for the rank of captain and the right to continue wearing uniform. The higher rank, he explained, would be 'of particular advantage in my civilian career'.[2] After four months' delay, he got his discharge, and his promotion. He was now Captain Göring (retired).

On 20 February 1920, Göring was hired to fly a young Swedish nobleman, Count Eric von Rosen, to his castle on Lake Baven some forty-five miles south-west of Stockholm. The weather was filthy – according to Göring's version, which sounds like a typical piece of hyperbole, there was a blizzard building up and three other pilots had already turned Rosen down, but the fearless Hermann accepted the challenge. Rosen was something of a daredevil himself – he was well-known as an explorer both in Africa and the Arctic – so there may be at least a grain of truth in the story. In any case, they got there, and Göring made an expert landing on the frozen lake, under the red stone battlements of Rockelstad castle. Whatever the weather had been like at the start, it was now definitely too bad for a return journey, and Rosen invited his 'air-chauffeur' to stay the night.

Göring was enchanted by Rockelstad. This was his natural habitat. A blazing fire welcomed them into the great hall where the walls were hung with old weapons and armour, family portraits, rich tapestries depicting heroic Nordic myths, and countless hunting trophies. A huge stuffed bear stood at the head of the stairs, killed with a spear by the head of the house. In the hearth, two large wrought iron swastikas hung on either side of the fire – at that time the swastika had no political significance for either Rosen or Göring, but was merely an ancient Nordic good luck symbol which Count von Rosen had discovered on rune stones in Gotland and adopted as a personal emblem.

While the two men were warming themselves in front of the fire, brandy glasses in their hands, Rosen's sister-in-law, Carin, Baroness von Kantzow, appeared at the top of the staircase. It could have been a scene from a romantic novelette: as she descended to meet them, tall, elegant, her fine features and deep blue eyes framed by soft brown hair, Göring gazed up at her as though he had seen a vision. For him, it was a complete *coup de foudre*, from which he never recovered. Carin reciprocated his feelings: 'He is the man I have always dreamed about,' she told her sister Fanny, later.[3] Back in Stockholm, they began a passionate affair, which quickly rocketed out of control.

Carin von Kantzow was thirty-one, five years older than Göring, and came from a military background, which must have added to her attraction for him. She was the fourth of five daughters of Baron Karl von Fock, a colonel in the Swedish army, and his Anglo-Irish wife Huldine, a member of the Beamish brewing family, County Cork's answer to Dublin's Guinness dynasty. Her grandfather had served in Britain's Coldstream Guards; her husband, Baron Nils von Kantzow, was also a regular army officer, who had been military attaché in Paris from 1912 to 1914. She had an eight-year-old son, Thomas, whom she loved, but she was bored with her dull life as an army wife, and with her dull husband – when she was with Göring, she told her sister later, it was a delight to be with someone who did not take two days to see the point of a joke.

But for all his dullness, Nils von Kantzow was a decent, honourable man. When his wife left him to set up home with the penniless Göring, he made her an allowance that enabled them to live in at least a little of the comfort to which she had always been accustomed. In return, he retained custody of Thomas. Like the divorce which he eventually gave Carin, it was a very civilised arrangement: he seems to have been remarkably free of bitterness, and imposed no restriction on her access to her son, who liked and admired his new stepfather from the start.

In his seduction of Carin, Göring took no chances, wooing her and winning over her family with his youthful glamour as a brave military hero, mixed with wildly romantic gestures, and outrageous flattery. How much of it was genuinely felt and how much coolly calculated is impossible to say: he had already demonstrated throughout his youth and military career that once he had set his heart on something he was totally ruthless in pursuit of his goal. At the same time, he had the capacity to mask that ruthlessness behind a winning charm. This was perhaps the most important trait in a character that appeared to be simple but was in fact extremely complex. It was to serve him well throughout his future career, and he employed it now with great success.

Carin's maternal grandmother had founded a private religious sisterhood, the Edelweiss Society, based on vaguely pantheistic beliefs, and Göring embraced it enthusiastically. After visiting its tiny chapel in the garden of the Focks' house, he wrote to Carin's mother, the high priestess:

I should like to thank you from my heart for the beautiful moment I was allowed to spend in the Edelweiss chapel. You have no idea how I felt in this wonderful atmosphere. It was so quiet, so lovely, that I forgot all earthly noise, all my worries, and felt as if in another world. I closed my eyes and absorbed the clean, celestial atmosphere which filled the whole room. I was like a swimmer resting on a lonely island to gather new strength before he throws himself once more into the raging steam of life. I thanked God, and sent up warm prayers.[4]

The letter was no doubt written with at least one eye on its effect, but at the same time much of it was certainly genuine, typical of the sentimental streak in Göring's nature. When they left the chapel, Carin gave him a sprig of edelweiss: he put it in his hat, and wore one constantly from then on. When he took her to Munich to meet his mother – who strongly disapproved of his stealing her from her husband and child – he filled her hotel room with roses before carrying her off to a picture-postcard chalet in the mountains. Carin herself lived by her emotions, and stood no chance of resisting such a determined onslaught on them. She left her husband and lived with Göring for several months in a small apartment before the sharp tongues and disapproving eyes of Stockholm society became too much and they fled to Germany.

At the time of his trial after the Second World War, Göring always claimed that he had had no interest in politics until he met Hitler. The facts, however, do not bear this out. Carin's sister recorded that even on that first night in Rockelstad castle, Eric von Rosen had raised his glass of German wine and proposed a toast to the day when 'Germany would find the leader who would once more make her people free', adding 'Perhaps we have heard from him tonight.'[5] Clearly, Göring had been holding forth over dinner with his usual passion. Two years later, the German legation in Stockholm reported that the thirty-year-old former air ace was describing himself in Sweden as 'a candidate for the post of Reich President'.[6]

'In some way I wanted to participate in the fate of my country,' Göring told the Nuremberg court. 'Since I could not and would not do that as an officer . . . I had first of all to build up the necessary foundation, and I attended the University of Munich in order to study history and political science.'[7] While Carin stayed in Sweden to remain close to her son and organise her divorce, he took a hunting lodge at Bayrichszell, in the mountains some thirty-five miles south of Munich, almost on the Austrian frontier, and settled down to his studies. He did not find it easy. He was, after all, twenty-nine years old, in every way a man among boys compared with the other students, and had always seen himself as a man of action rather than ideas. Nevertheless, he persevered, though he found himself learning more on the streets and in the cafés and beer halls, where the best education in political reality was to be found, than in the lecture room.

The political situation in Munich was still fluid, though for a brief period during the first half of 1922, an unfamiliar calm settled over the city. The hard-line monarchist Ritter von Kahr had been forced to step down as Minister-President after the dissolution of the Einwohnerwehr and the other paramilitary organisations, and he had been replaced by a mild conservative, Graf Lerchenfeld, who broadly supported the federal government and so offered some relief from the stresses of separatism. The dangers of anarchy and revolution seemed to have receded. It was, of course, another illusion.

The illusion was shattered on 24 June when the Jewish Foreign Minister Walther Rathenau was assassinated by two members of Ehrhardt's Organisation Consul, hard on the heels of a failed attempt on the life of Philipp Scheidemann, the former Chancellor who had proclaimed the Republic from the balcony of the Reichstag. Rathenau's killing was in Berlin, but everybody knew it had been planned in Munich. His murderers died in a ferocious gun battle with police at a remote castle, their young driver was caught and sentenced to ten years' imprisonment, but the Bavarian authorities, true to form, made no attempt to bring Ehrhardt and his associates to justice.

The federal government reacted by passing a new Law for the Protection of the Republic, cracking down hard on terrorism and all subversive activity, including extremist political parties. One of its first victims was Adolf Hitler. At the beginning of the year he had been sentenced to three months in prison for inciting a beer hall brawl, suspended against future good behaviour – a condition that was easily overlooked by the Bavarian government, who saw him as a valuable tool in their fight against Bolshevism. Under the new law, however, there could be no excuse for ignoring his blatant attacks on the Republic, and they were forced to imprison him, albeit for only one of the three suspended months. He served his time from 24 June to 27 July, in the most comfortable cell in Munich's Stadelheim Prison.

The right-wing organisations in Munich naturally saw the Law for the Protection of the Republic as a direct threat to their own existence, and they forced Lerchenfeld to pass an emergency decree virtually excluding Bavaria from its provisions. The federal government recognised this as a serious challenge to its own authority, and in turn forced Lerchenfeld to withdraw his decree. This provoked a new wave of protest and agitation in Munich, culminating in a huge demonstration on the Königsplatz on 16 August, billed as 'For Germany – Against Berlin'. The newly-released Hitler was the principal speaker, marking his growing stature with a savage attack on 'the approaching Jewish Bolshevism under the protection of the Republic'.[8] The SA marched in the demonstration, its first public outing with drums and banners, though with only 800 members it was still tiny by comparison with the large, well-armed contingents of the Bund Oberland, Reichsflagge and the Bund Bayern und Reich, the biggest of the Bavarian patriotic leagues, which alone had 30,000 men on parade.

The political temperature was rising rapidly again, with a powerful new factor adding to popular discontent. In addition to resentment at what they saw as the Berlin government's spineless acquiescence with the Versailles diktat, all the extremist parties fed on the alarming rise in inflation since the war. The mark had stood at 4.16 to the US dollar in 1914, and 7.45 at the time of the armistice, an uncomfortable but bearable loss in value. Since then its fall had accelerated steadily, and by mid June 1922 it had reached 272 to the dollar. Rathenau's murder added new spin to the vicious spiral: within a week the rate plummeted to 401, and ten days later it was 527 and still falling. As salaries and savings became worthless, the only response of the federal government in Berlin was to print more and more banknotes, increasing the financial chaos and quenching any remaining glimmers of confidence in the economy. It was a situation ripe for revolution, both nationally and locally.

In Munich, Röhm, Pöhner, the former Munich police chief, and Dr Pittinger, head of the Bund Bayern und Reich, planned a *putsch* to overthrow both the Bavarian and Reich governments, counting on the support of the Bavarian District Command of the Reichswehr to back up their own paramilitaries. Hitler agreed to join them. In the event, however, the police found out about the plot and it came to nothing. Lerchenfeld resigned, and a new, right-wing government took over. But it failed to bring any greater stability – the unrest continued to simmer over the next twelve months, threatening to boil over at any moment.

One of the main reasons why the planned *putsch* failed to materialise was that the right in Munich was hopelessly divided, with no single leader capable of uniting the various factions. Some wanted greater autonomy for Bavaria within the Republic; some wanted complete separation under a restored Bavarian monarchy; some favoured joining with Austria in a new south German Catholic state; some wanted to turn back the clock and restore the Kaiser in Berlin; and some, like Hitler, wanted to destroy the hated Republic and replace it with a unified Germany under a dictator. Apart from their fear of socialism and communism, almost the only thing they all had in common was hatred of the Weimar Republic.

Göring, studying the situation from the sidelines, shared that feeling. 'I hated the Republic,' he told Douglas M. Kelley at Nuremberg. 'I knew it could not last. I saw that as soon as the Allies withdrew their support, a new government would take over Germany. I wanted to help destroy the Republic and to be, perhaps, the ruler of the new Reich.'[9] As always, Göring was thinking big. Before he could begin working towards his ambition, however, he needed a political party. For a time, he tried to found his own, but soon realised that there was too much competition and that he would be better off joining one that was already up and running. The only question was, which one? 'There were at that time about fifty organisations – call them parties – of World War veterans in Germany,' he explained.

They didn't like the government. They didn't like the Versailles Treaty. They didn't like the peace – a peace in which there were no jobs, no food, no shoes. I knew that the overthrow of the Republic would be done by these dissatisfied men. So I looked over their parties to see which ones showed promise.

After studying each one, I decided to join the National Socialist Party. It was small – that meant I could soon be a big man in it. It appealed to the unhappy veterans – that meant it would have the manpower for a *putsch*. It attacked Versailles – that gave it character and a target for the emotions of the veteran. Even its anti-Semitism served a purpose – it won over those who needed something more elemental than a political error as a focus for their emotions.[10]

Göring first encountered Hitler on a Sunday evening in November 1922, at another mass demonstration in Königsplatz. Having failed to get the Kaiser extradited from Holland to stand trial as a war criminal, the Allies were now pressing for the arrest and trial of his generals, a demand that raised even greater indignation among Germans. Göring was spitting mad: the military commanders were his heroes, and he went along to the meeting eager to contribute to the protest. What he heard left him deeply depressed. One speaker after another stood up and spouted empty, long-winded platitudes, and no one called for direct action. Finally, with the crowd growing impatient, people began calling for Hitler, who happened to be standing close by, surrounded by a small group of supporters. Göring knew Hitler's reputation as a rousing orator, and looked forward to hearing him speak for the first time. He was disappointed when Hitler refused, but fascinated to overhear the reasons he gave: 'He could not see himself speaking, as he put it, to these tame, bourgeois pirates. He considered it senseless to launch protests with no weight behind them. This made a deep impression on me; I was of the same opinion.'[11]

Intrigued by this intense young man with the pale face and small moustache, wearing his habitual slouch hat and shabby trench coat and carrying a dog whip, Göring asked around and discovered that Hitler held court every Monday evening in the old-world Café Neumaier on the edge of the Viktualenmarkt. Next day he went there, to hear what this unconventional politician had to say. Carin, who had now joined him in Munich after obtaining her divorce, went with him. They found Hitler at his regular table, surrounded by his usual entourage. As his subject for the evening, he had chosen 'The Versailles Peace Treaty and the Extradition of the German Army Commanders'. He spoke about the meeting the previous evening, declaring that there was no sense in the empty protests made there, and that a protest could only succeed if it was backed by power to give it weight. Until Germany had become strong again, this sort of thing was useless: 'You've got to have bayonets to back up any threats!'

This was fighting talk, exactly what Göring wanted to hear. 'This conviction,' he told the court in Nuremberg, 'was spoken word for word as if from my own soul.'[12] At last, he had found a man 'who had a clear and definite aim'. Hitler in turn was impressed by Göring's contribution to the evening, a passionate speech about officers putting honour first in any conflict of interest, and took note of the newcomer.[13] That night, after earnest discussions with Carin, Göring decided Hitler was the man for him. He knew little about the Nazi programme or policies, but that hardly mattered: 'I joined the Party because it was revolutionary,' he explained to Dr Kelley, 'not because of the ideological stuff . . . The thing that attracted me to the Nazi Party was that it was the only one that had the guts to say "to hell with Versailles", while the others were smiling and appeasing. That's what got me.'[14]

Next day, he called on Hitler at party headquarters, and offered his services. Hitler could hardly believe his luck: 'Splendid, a war ace with the *Pour le Mérite* – imagine it! Excellent propaganda!' he crowed later to his well-connected supporter, Kurt Lüdecke. 'Moreover, he has money and doesn't cost me a cent.'[15] Turning on the full force of his charm, he told Göring their meeting was 'an extraordinary turn of fate'. Göring, though flattered, was well aware of his own worth: 'Naturally, Hitler was glad to have me because I had a great reputation among officers of the First World War. I was of value, and in turn I was to become leader of the Reich.'[16]

The astonishing claim that they struck such a deal at their first meeting is typical of Göring's unique mixture of naïve enthusiasm and cool calculation, to say nothing of his egotism. But such a deal is entirely typical of Hitler's intuitive ability to win people over by making them feel special and offering them their heart's desire. From that moment, Göring was hooked. He had sold his soul to Hitler as surely as Dr Faustus sold his to Mephistopheles; his price was not youth but the promise of power. It was a promise that would haunt him for the rest of his days.[17]

It may be that Hitler genuinely saw Göring as the future leader he was seeking for Germany, a role for which Göring certainly had the charisma and personality, however flawed his character might be. At that time Hitler still regarded himself as merely the 'drummer', a John the Baptist figure preparing the way for a heroic Messiah who would somehow emerge as 'a gift from heaven'. 'Our task,' he declared, 'is to create the sword that this person will need when he is there. Our task is to give the dictator, when he comes, a people ready for him.'

It was only during the following year that Hitler finally became convinced that he himself was the Messiah figure, that it was his own destiny to be the supreme leader, the Führer, of the German people. By then, Göring was so enamoured of him, so in thrall to him as a substitute father figure replacing Epenstein, that he was content to be his crown prince, his Simon Peter. Indeed, on Hitler's thirty-fourth birthday in 1923, Göring proclaimed him 'the beloved leader of the German freedom movement' – though he was still referring to himself as a prospective candidate for the presidency.

At their first meeting, Hitler talked, inevitably, about the 'unbearable shackles' of the Treaty of Versailles, insisting that it would only be possible to free Germany from them by rousing the 'broad masses of the people', and not through the existing nationalist parties and organisations. He then gave what Göring described as 'a very wonderful and profound explanation of the concept of National Socialism', combining bourgeois nationalism and Marxist socialism to 'create a new vehicle for these new thoughts'. It was all heady, if empty stuff. Göring, who was extremely clever but essentially shallow, swallowed it whole. When Hitler went on to say that he had made a 'special selection' of those people within the party 'who were convinced followers, and who were ready at any moment to devote themselves completely and unreservedly to the dissemination of our idea',[18] Göring was desperate to be counted as one of them.

He was given the chance immediately, when Hitler offered him command of the SA. The present leaders were too young, Hitler said, and for some time he had been looking out for someone with a distinguished war record, ideally a *Pour le Mérite* airman or submariner, who would have more authority. It seemed especially fortunate, he continued, that Hermann Göring of all people, the last commander of the Richthofen Squadron, should place himself at his disposal. Göring accepted at once, but with the proviso that he should not officially take over for two months, so that it would not appear that he had only joined the party because of the position. Until then, he would remain in the background, but would 'make his influence felt immediately'. Hitler agreed, they shook hands and Göring swore a solemn oath of allegiance: 'I pledge my destiny to you for better or for worse, I dedicate myself to you in good times and in bad, even unto death.'

Göring had a second, more personal reason to delay taking command of the SA. Carin's divorce became absolute in December, and he needed time to put his domestic affairs in order and to make arrangements for their wedding – in fact for two weddings, one in Stockholm on 25 January 1923, the second in Munich on 3 February. He had already moved his bride into a villa they had bought in Obermenzing, a fashionable suburb of Munich just beyond the Nymphenburg Palace, in November. Carin had brought her own elegant furniture and effects from Sweden, including Chinese embroidery, romantic pictures and a white harmonium on which she would accompany her new husband while he sang folk songs, ballads and even operatic arias in a light baritone voice.

Göring filled his own quarters with the heavy gothic pieces he had always liked, especially in one room that was to be the most important in the house. 'On the ground floor,' Carin's sister Fanny recorded, 'was a large, attractive smoking room, with an alcove lit from outside by a bulls-eye window. A few steps down from it was a wine cellar with an open fire, wooden stools and a great sofa.' This room became a meeting place for 'all those who had dedicated themselves to Hitler and his freedom movement'. Hitler himself was a regular visitor, generally arriving late at night, and even learned to relax in this private, congenial setting, so different from his sparsely furnished, shabby room at 41 Thierschstrasse. According to Fanny, his 'sense of humour showed itself in gay stories, observations and witticisms, and Carin's spontaneous and wholehearted reaction to them made her a delightful audience'.[19]

As with all that he did, Göring threw himself wholeheartedly into the Party and the SA to the exclusion of everything else, including his studies. Fortunately, Carin shared his enthusiasm. Uniquely among the Nazi womenfolk, she took an active part in the endless talk of Hitler's inner circle, both in her own home and in the regular drinking sessions in the Bratwurstglöckel tavern, just behind the Frauenkirche church in the heart of old Munich, where a large table, their *Stammtisch*, was permanently reserved for the group. Since Carin's money was in hard Swedish currency, the Görings were able to live in some comfort during the time of rampant inflation, and even to put money into the Party. They were able to afford a splendid new car, a twenty-five horsepower Mercedes-Benz 16, which Hitler used as a saluting base while reviewing an SA march-past at Easter 1923. At the same rally, Göring was reportedly seen giving Hitler pocket money. All this helped to cement the personal relationship between the two men, but although they were close for many years, they always addressed each other with the formal

'*Sie*', never progressing to the more intimate '*Du*'. Göring was never allowed to forget – nor did he wish to – that Hitler was 'The Chief'.

Göring never had any wish to supplant Hitler, but he was determined from the very beginning to be his chosen successor, his deputy, perhaps even his partner. One of his reasons for choosing the Nazi Party was that it was a small organisation where he could swiftly move to the top, and he had only to look at the rest of the men in the inner circle at that time to know that he was right. They were an unimpressive bunch: ineffectual dreamers, drunks, thugs – and mostly unsophisticated provincials to boot. Anton Drexler, co-founder of the original DAP, who had been supplanted by Hitler the previous year, was a locksmith in the Munich railyards; tall, thin and bespectacled, he was a plodder both physically and mentally. In marked contrast, Dietrich Eckart, the man who had accompanied Hitler to Berlin at the time of the Kapp Putsch, was big, bluff, and gregarious, with a rumbustious sense of humour, but he was a drunk and a morphine addict, a bohemian who spent most of his time in cafés and bars.

Eckart, son of a prosperous lawyer in Neumarkt, was a *völkisch* poet and playwright who had made his name with a translation of Ibsen's *Peer Gynt,* which brought him a steady income, some of which he gave to the struggling Party. He edited and published a scurrilous anti-Semitic weekly called *Auf gut deutsch* (*In Plain German*), knew everybody who counted in Munich society, and was able to persuade some of them to give substantial financial help. Twenty years older than Hitler, he regarded him as his protégé: he had coached and tutored and attempted to civilise the young firebrand, polishing his table manners, introducing him to political hostesses and even buying him his first trench coat. Hitler labelled him 'the spiritual father' of the movement – it was Eckart who had coined the party slogan, '*Deutschland erwache!*' ('Germany awake!') – but by the beginning of 1923, he was growing weary of his mentor, and they were drifting apart. In any case, Eckart was drinking himself to death – he would be gone by the end of the year – and so posed no threat to anyone in the hierarchy.

Others in the inner circle included Rudolf Hess, the son of an expatriate merchant, born and raised in Alexandria, Egypt, a fighter pilot during the war, who was still studying politics at Munich University; Alfred Rosenberg, a Baltic-German émigré, who fancied himself as a philosopher and wrote woolly articles for Eckart's magazine; Max Erwin von Scheubner-Richter, another Baltic-German, an engineer by profession with valuable contacts among wealthy Russian refugees; Hitler's former sergeant in the List Regiment, Max Amman, a rough-neck who was a good organiser and so was made the Party's business manager; Hermann Esser, a deeply unsavoury young activist who had been press agent for Captain Mayr, a gifted rabble-rouser whose oratory almost matched Hitler's, whose Jew-baiting articles were a feature of the *Völkischer Beobachter*, and who was not above blackmailing his associates.

The latest recruit, arriving at much the same time as Göring, was Ernst 'Putzi' Hanfstaengl, a fleshy six-foot-four Harvard graduate whose American mother was descended from two Civil War generals. Hanfstaengl's family were noted art dealers, and he was a partner in an art publishing firm. He was cultured, witty and rich, extremely well connected, and had a beautiful wife who, like Carin Göring, doted on the Nazi leader. Putzi endeared himself to Hitler not only through his generous financial contributions, which included an interest-free loan of US$1,000, a vast sum in those inflationary times, to buy new rotary printing presses for the *Völkischer Beobachter*, but also by his ability as a pianist, playing Wagner while Hitler paced to and fro, whistling the tune and 'conducting'. But although he was valuable as a milk cow and as a sort of social secretary, Hanfstaengl had only a superficial intelligence, and no personal political ambition. There was no steel in his character, and he, too, posed no threat to Göring.

There was not an intelligent man of action among the entire inner circle, with one exception: Ernst Röhm. It was immediately apparent that Röhm was Göring's only serious rival, but he was in many ways a semi-detached member of the Party, which was only one of his many interests and involvements. He was also the one man Göring had to work closely with in reshaping the SA.

Röhm was still a serving army officer, and had just been trans-ferred from Major-General Epp's infantry command to the staff of the new GOC in Bavaria, General Otto von Lossow. Lossow, a tall, well-built man with a shaven head, had been sent by Berlin to bring maverick right-wing officers like Röhm to heel, and to enforce the army's loyalty to the federal government. But from the beginning his attitude was ambivalent: as a Bavarian himself, he was sympathetic to the separatists, and like so many senior officers, he was obsessed with the threat of Bolshevism, regarding right-wing organisations, including their paramilitaries, as allies. His main concern was not whether they threatened the Republic, for which, as a right-wing monarchist, he had no affection and even less loyalty, but whether they threatened the authority of the army. As long as they knew their place in this respect, he was happy to tolerate and even encourage them, especially in their battles with the Communist paramilitaries of the Red Front.

The German army had always depended on the existence of a large reserve army, closely integrated with the active army, consisting of men who had completed their period of conscription but who were still subject to military discipline, kept up to scratch by annual training and ready for mobilisation at very short notice. The Versailles Treaty had removed this reservoir, limiting the army in its entirety to 100,000 men. Lossow and his fellow generals saw the paramilitary organisations as the basis of a hidden reserve army, a means of circumventing the Versailles restrictions in preparation for the day when Germany would rise again and take revenge on her enemies. Hitler did not accept this role for the SA: for him it was a weapon in the internal fight against the Republic and the 'November criminals'. It must remain under his control, and not that of the generals; it must never become a mere adjunct of the Reichswehr. But while the generals were providing money, equipment and support, he was quite prepared to go along with them. Göring, despite his military background, agreed with him on both counts. In January 1923, shortly before Göring officially took command, Röhm brokered a meeting between Hitler and Lossow, at which they agreed that the SA would receive clandestine army training.

The SA at that time was little more than an unruly and ill-organised club composed mainly of freebooting remnants of the Freikorps. Officially charged with protection duties at political meetings, they spent most of their time picking fights and breaking heads wherever they could and with whatever they could lay their hands on – beer steins and chair legs were among their favourite weapons, along with brass knuckledusters and rubber truncheons, though they occasionally used pistols and even home-made bombs and grenades. Göring's first task was to instil discipline and structure, and transform it into a reliable formation that would carry out his or Hitler's orders without question. It would not be easy. However, delighted to be commanding men again, he set about whipping them into shape, drawing on his years of military training and experience to create a tough, professional force.

He began by introducing a number of his own friends and acquaintances to raise the general tone and create an upper echelon, and drawing in members of the Party 'who were young and idealistic enough to devote their free time and their entire energies to it'. Then he looked for recruits from the working class to provide extra muscle among the rank and file. Drilling and training them with all the rigour of the Prussian officer he had once been, he soon began to produce results, not only in Munich, but throughout Bavaria, with companies and regiments parading weekly in every town and city. 'I gave him a dishevelled rabble,' Hitler recalled later. 'In a very short time he had organised a division of eleven thousand men.'[20]

Hitler's admiration for Göring's achievement was lasting – 'He is the only one of its heads that ran the SA properly,' he said later – and extended to other areas, too. While Göring came to worship Hitler and accept his own subservience without question, Hitler was always slightly in awe of Göring for his war record, his decorations and the undoubted bravery they represented, his education and training, his easy manner, and the fact that although he may not have actually been an aristocrat he could move confidently in the very highest circles. To Hitler, Göring was always a hero, a fact that coloured their relationship to the very end.

When Göring officially took command of the SA at the beginning of February 1923, it was in the midst of a national crisis that promised great opportunity for Hitler and the Nazi Party. Three weeks earlier, on 11 January, French and Belgian troops had marched into the Ruhr, Germany's industrial heartland, triggering a remarkable train of events which in ten months was to raise Hitler from an insignificant beer hall agitator on the margins of provincial politics to a potential national leader. Everything that ensued, not only during that year but through to 1933 and even 1945, can be traced back to that action.

The French and Belgians were seen by many, including Britain and the United States, as vindictive and arrogant, and so they were. But they had good cause. They were understandably nervous at the unstable situation in Germany, which threatened their own security, and their war wounds were still too sore for any forgiveness or trust of their former enemy, whom they blamed entirely for everything that had happened. Their own industrial regions, where most of the heaviest fighting on the Western Front had taken place, had been totally devastated. Germany's, on the other hand, remained physically unscathed – apart from some early fighting in East Prussia, there had been no battles on German soil. What was more, the French were deeply in debt to Britain and the United States, which had largely financed their war effort, and the Americans were insisting on early repayment. Although they had been given the use of the Saar mines, and had regained Alsace-Lorraine with its iron and steel, they still needed the heavy reparations imposed at Versailles to fund their own reconstruction.

From the beginning, the Germans had dragged their feet and tried to avoid paying. In the autumn of 1922, they asked the Allies to grant a moratorium. Britain and the United States were prepared to agree, but the French refused point blank, insisting that the Germans were perfectly capable of raising the money by taxing the rich. This was something the German government, despite being socialist, was not prepared to do: there were three groups, the army, the rich industrialists and the landowners, that no German government was prepared to offend – the war itself had been financed entirely by bonds and war loans, public donations and, in an ominous portent, by printing more paper money, but not through taxation. Far from raising taxes on the rich, the government actually reduced them in 1921. At the end of 1922, Germany defaulted on payments – specifically on delivery of 135,000 metres of timber telegraph poles and coal to the value of 24 million gold marks – to France. This was not the first time they had deliberately tried to evade their obligations, and what little French patience remained now expired. They marched their troops into the Ruhr, along with the equally aggrieved Belgians, to exact payment in kind.

For Germany this was an economic disaster. Since the loss of the industrial regions of Alsace-Lorraine, the Saar and Upper Silesia, which had been ceded to Poland, the Ruhr accounted for more than eighty per cent of her entire production of coal, iron and steel. Without it, she could not survive, never mind rebuild. The French were well aware of this – indeed, one of the underlying reasons behind their move was to weaken Germany's reviving power – but it did not sap their resolve. If anything, it strengthened it. They even made a point of sending in black colonial troops, knowing their presence would add to the distress and unease of a local population that was inherently racist.

The workers of the Ruhr immediately downed tools in a general strike. The Berlin government called for a campaign of passive resistance that was taken up by everyone except some mine owners, who continued unpatriotically but profitably delivering coal to France. The army did its bit by organising sabotage and guerrilla warfare, clandestinely arming and reactivating former Freikorps groups. The French responded with imprisonments, deportations and executions. The state of undeclared war swiftly spread to the Saar and the Rhineland, which had been under Allied military occupation since 1918.

The Berlin government supported the beleaguered population financially, but the only way it could manage this without increasing taxation was once again by printing more money, and thus exacerbating the rocketing inflation. At the beginning of the year, the mark stood at 7,000 to the US dollar. Within days of the occupation of the Ruhr, it had plunged to 18,000, and it continued to fall exponentially throughout the rest of the year. By 1 July the rate was 160,000. A month later it had reached one million, by November four billion, and then on into uncountable trillions, but still the government refused to call a halt, stop the printing presses and balance the budget.

Apart from the government itself, which was able to frustrate the French and clear all its public debt, only three groups in Germany profited from the collapse of the currency. They were, of course, the rich industrialists, the landlords and the army, who pressured the government to continue with a policy that brought nothing but ruination to the vast majority of the people. The rich capitalists who knew how to manipulate credit became super rich as they bought up factories, mines and other property with worthless currency, while at the same time heavy industry was able to wipe out all its debts in the same way. And the army was delighted to find that all the war debts were cleared, leaving the country financially free to start planning another war. For the rest of the population, there was only misery, despair and bankruptcy as both savings and wages became utterly worthless.

On the face of it, the crisis seemed to present Hitler with a golden opportunity to cash in on the widespread unrest caused by the collapse of the mark, and public anger at the occupation of the Ruhr. But the French action had united the German nation behind the government as it had never been since August 1914, and it would be brave, even foolhardy, to swim against the tide of popular sentiment and attack it. Nevertheless, that is just what Hitler did. He, like Lenin in Russia only five years earlier, was concerned first and foremost with the enemy within, rather than the enemy without. France could wait; the 'November criminals' could not.

'The external rebirth of Germany is only possible,' he screamed to a packed meeting in the Circus Krone on the day the French and

Belgians marched into the Ruhr, 'when the criminals are faced with their responsibility and delivered to their just fate.' He blamed the government and the forces behind it – Marxism, democracy, internationalism, all of which were part of the 'global Jewish conspiracy' – for the weakness that allowed the French to treat Germany like a colony.[21] Deriding the calls for national unity, he announced that any member of the party who took part in active resistance to the occupation would be expelled. Göring, though not yet in his position, stood solidly behind Hitler. When Röhm demanded that the SA join the other paramilitaries and the Reichswehr to march against the French to liberate the Ruhr, he opposed him vigorously.

Surprisingly, Hitler's bold move paid off. As he stepped up his propaganda campaign, support for the Nazi Party grew, and he began planning his first 'Reich Party Rally', to take place between 27 and 29 January with twelve mass meetings and a parade on the Marsfeld, close to the centre of Munich, at which the standards of the principal SA units, based in Munich, Nuremberg and Landshut, were to be dedicated in front of 6,000 storm-troopers. The Bavarian government was decidedly nervous about this – there had been persistent rumours since November that Hitler was plotting a *putsch*. On 26 January they banned the rally and declared a state of emergency. Hitler was furious, and threatened to go ahead anyway, personally marching at the head of his troops, ready to take the first bullets if they were fired on.

It was the arch-fixer Röhm who calmed Hitler down and with the help of Epp persuaded General von Lossow, former Minister-President Kahr, who was then presiding over Upper Bavaria, and the new Munich Police President, Eduard Nortz, who had replaced the sympathetic Pöhner, to weigh in on Hitler's side. Lossow was persuaded to talk to Hitler, and after obtaining a promise 'on his word of honour' that he would not attempt a *putsch*, agreed not to oppose the rally. The others followed suit. Faced with the fact that neither the army nor the city police would move against the Nazis, the government capitulated. The rally took place triumphantly, with Hitler receiving the adulation of the crowds as 'the leader of the German freedom movement', a significant step forward on his progress from drummer to Führer, from prophet to Messiah. Göring, hurrying back from his marriage in Stockholm two days before, took his bride to the parade, to bathe in the reflected glory and to cast a critical eye on the men he was about to command.

*   *   *

The Nazis were on their way, at least in Bavaria – they had been banned in almost every other German state since the previous autumn. Between February and November, some 35,000 new members flocked to join the party, swelling the total membership to about 55,000, and making it a force to be reckoned with. Over the same period, Göring reorganised the SA along military lines, establishing a headquarters staff similar to that of a divisional HQ, with a Chief of Staff and infantry and artillery commanders, and amalgamating local units into companies and regiments.[22] He also created an elite guard squad which he at first called the Stabswache, the Staff Watch, distinguished from the rest of the SA by black ski caps with a death's head badge, and a black border on their swastika armbands. This quickly became the Stosstrupp Hitler, the Hitler Shock Troop, and in due course would form the basis of the SS.

Under Göring's energetic direction, the overall strength of the SA grew to some 15,000. But Hitler still depended on the goodwill of the Bavarian government, the police, and above all the army, which meant Lossow, whose ambivalent attitude dogged him throughout the year. The training of the SA by the army, which Hitler and Lossow had agreed shortly before the Party Day, went ahead through the spring and summer in the woods outside Munich. But there was a price to be paid for Reichswehr support: the SA had to share its training with other radical paramilitary groups, joining them in an umbrella organisation formed by Röhm in February, which he named the Arbeitsgemeinschaft der Vaterländischen Kampfverbände (Working Association of Patriotic Combat Formations). The SA was by no means the biggest or most powerful member of the Working Association, and overall military command was given to retired Lieutenant-Colonel Hermann Kriebel, who had previously been Chief of Staff in the Bavarian Einwohnerwehr.

Though there was never any question of the SA losing its individual identity, Göring must have been disappointed at this subordination of his power, but he never showed it. And in any case there was a much bigger prize for the party: again at Röhm's behest, Hitler moved to the front of the political leadership of the Working Association. This raised his stature immediately, and allowed him to move in the highest circles, bringing him, and his SA commander, into regular contact with leading figures including Ludendorff, the former Quartermaster General and military dictator, who was able to provide a link with the radical right in north Germany.

When General von Seeckt, Chief of the Army High Command, visited

Munich in March, it was only natural that Lossow should arrange a meeting with Hitler. It lasted four hours, but was hardly momentous – Seeckt was not impressed by the Nazi leader, and Hitler was disappointed that the general refused to commit the army to direct action in the Ruhr, or to unseating the Republican government. Nevertheless, it was another step in establishing Hitler's credentials as a serious politician. Lossow was impressed: he shared Hitler's hatred of the Republic and its government, but they disagreed violently on what was to be done. Lossow wanted Bavaria to secede from the Reich and go its own way. Hitler wanted to retain a unified Reich, but under a dictatorship. When it came to a march on Berlin, emulating Mussolini's successful march on Rome at the end of the previous October, Lossow vacillated.

The intensive training of the SA by the army was ostensibly in preparation for a concerted attack on the French, and indeed plans for such an operation were drawn up by the Werhmacht High Command in Berlin under the code name 'Spring Training'. Göring brought his storm troopers to a high state of readiness, both physically and mentally. They still fought battles in the streets and beer halls against the Communists, but they were ready and eager for bigger battles elsewhere. On 15 April, Easter Sunday, Göring showed them off to his leader, standing next to him in his open Mercedes as he took the salute. Carin wrote to her son back in Stockholm, describing the scene:

Today, the Beloved One [as she always described Göring] paraded his army of true young Germans before his Führer, and I saw his face light up as he watched them pass by. The Beloved One has worked so hard with them, has instilled so much of his own bravery and heroism into them, that what was once a rabble – and I must confess sometimes a rough and rather terrifying one – has been transformed into a veritable Army of Light, a band of eager crusaders ready to march as the Führer's orders to render this unhappy country free once more . . .

After it was over, the Führer embraced the Beloved One and told me that if he said what he really thought of his achievement, the Beloved One would get a swollen head.

I said that my own head was already swollen with pride, and he kissed my hand and said, 'No head so pretty as yours could ever be swollen.'[23]

'Spring Training' eventually came to nothing – Berlin had got cold feet. Even when French troops shot down strikers at the Krupp works in Essen on 31 March, killing thirteen and wounding forty-one, Seeckt refused to let his men and their paramilitary auxiliaries off the leash.

Seeckt was simply being realistic, knowing that his relatively small force stood no chance against the powerful French army, but the storm-troopers were spoiling for a fight, and Göring was finding it increasingly difficult to hold them back. He found some release for their energies by turning them loose against the Communists, revelling in the rough and tumble of beer hall battles. 'Boy, how those beer mugs flew,' he enthused twenty years later to American historian George Schuster. 'One nearly laid me out!'[24]

Beer mugs were not the only weapons used; in April, Göring and a heavily armed squad occupied the offices of the *Völkischer Beobachter* to prevent the arrest of the editor, Dietrich Eckart, and on 26 April storm-troopers and Communists exchanged gunfire in the streets. No one was killed, but four men were seriously wounded. This was all part of the build-up to a major confrontation between the two sides, planned by Hitler and Göring for the Socialists' and Communists' traditional May Day celebrations. The police had already given approval for a Socialist parade through the city. But 1 May was also the anniversary of the overthrow of the Bavarian Räterepublik in 1919, which gave the right an excuse for celebrations, too.

Hitler dithered until the last minute, waiting to see if the Bavarian authorities would submit to his demand that they ban the Socialists' demonstration. When it became clear that they were only prepared to ban the parade but not the demonstration, he called a meeting of the Working Association leaders on 30 April, at which they decided to stage a counter-demonstration the next day, and to attack the Socialists. This was what Göring and the other paramilitary leaders had been waiting for. Göring sent out emergency orders to his regiments, in Nuremberg and Landshut as well as Munich, to report to the city's Oberwiesenfeld next morning, armed and ready for action. It was short notice, but they obeyed eagerly.

The local SA leaders had been collecting weapons for some time – the commander of the Lower Bavarian regiment in Landshut, for example, a local pharmacist called Gregor Strasser, had accumulated 140 rifles and a number of light machine guns – and early next morning they handed them out to their men and set off to do their duty. From the start, however, the plans for a bloody confrontation began to go wrong. Strasser's lorry convoy was stopped by police and he was ordered to hand their weapons in at the nearest army barracks. He got the police off his back by giving his word that he would comply, then promptly broke his promise and drove straight to Munich. It was disconcerting that the police were not looking the other way as they usually did. Hitler, meanwhile, was discovering that the army, too, was showing a disturbing lack of support. He had met Lossow and demanded the arms that were being stored for the Munich SA in army barracks, declaring he needed them to combat a *putsch* which he claimed the Communists were plotting. Lossow, no doubt mindful of the gunfight between SA and Communists four days earlier, had refused, and warned him that the army would fire on anyone, from right or left, who tried to create disorder on the streets.

Röhm appeared to have saved the day by taking it upon himself to drive to the barracks with an escort of storm-troopers, drawing the weapons from the armoury on his own authority as a staff officer. Hitler, wearing a steel helmet and his Iron Cross, prepared to lead the march, with Göring, also helmeted and bemedalled, at his side. Excitement was running high, but before they could start, a chastened Röhm arrived, guarded by a detachment of armed troops and police, with orders from Lossow that Hitler must return the weapons immediately, and stand down his men.

The 2,000 paramilitaries vastly outnumbered the soldiers and police, and could easily have overwhelmed them – indeed, Kriebel, their commander, along with Strasser and others, were all for taking them on as an hors-d'oeuvre to their battle against the left. There is no record of Göring's attitude. Hitler, however, still smarting from his interview with Lossow, believed that the general would have no hesitation in calling out the full force of the army and police against them. He backed down. The weapons were returned. The march was cancelled. Hitler tried to save what face he could with a fiery speech to the assembled troopers, followed by another to a mass meeting that evening at the Circus Krone. But there was no disguising the fact that it was a severe humiliation for him, and for Göring and the SA, and a sharp reminder that they still depended on the goodwill, if not the active support, of the army. 'What mattered,' Lossow later explained, 'was this: who was in charge of the country? . . . The first trial of strength ended with Hitler's defeat, and we had nothing more to do with one another.'[25] This was not strictly true, but it got Lossow off the hook in 1924, which seems to have been his main concern.

For Hitler and Göring the May Day débâcle was an embarrassment they would overcome. It was merely a temporary setback, when it

could have been the end – Hitler could have been arrested and imprisoned, or even deported back to Austria, but he was not. Although
proceedings were started against him for breach of the peace, they were
quietly dropped when he took the audacious step of inviting prosecution, announcing that he would welcome his chance to speak openly
in court, implying that he would reveal how the Reichswehr was arming
and training the paramilitaries for action against the French.

Hitler took off soon afterwards for a holiday with Eckart at a small
hotel, the Pension Moritz, on the Obersalzberg, near Berchtesgaden,
whose owners were supporters of the movement. It was his second
visit – Eckart had introduced him to it the previous winter – and he
fell in love with the area's beauty, peace and quiet, where he could
restore his wounded pride and recharge his energy before resuming the
fight against the 'November criminals'. He spent much of the summer
in the mountains, returning to Munich from time to time to make
speeches and beat the drum.

Göring stayed in Munich, immersing himself in work, repairing the
damaged morale of his men and continuing the process of building up
the SA for the great day, which he still believed was imminent. Looking
back the following year, exiled in Italy, he boasted to an Italian correspondent:

Often, I was on the go until 4 a.m. and was back at the office at 7 a.m. the
next day. I didn't have a moment's respite all day . . . Believe me, I have often
– very often – come home dead tired at 11 p.m., spent fifteen minutes grabbing some tea or supper with my wife and then, instead of going to bed,
reviewed the day's activities for two or three hours; the next morning at 7
a.m. the first adjutant would come to report.[26]

Throughout the summer, the SA continued to pick bloody fights with
Communists and Socialists, and was prominent at a series of 'German
Days' with pseudo-military programmes, held at weekends in various
parts of Bavaria. And as its profile rose, so new recruits flocked to
join.

For Röhm, the events of May Day threatened at first to be much
more serious. He was carpeted by a furious General von Lossow,
reminded of his obligations and duties as a serving officer, and informed
that he would be posted forthwith to the backwater of Bayreuth. But
when it came to political infighting, Lossow was no match for Röhm.
With his usual acuity, Röhm promptly resigned his commission – thus
freeing himself to speak openly. He then wrote to the commander of

the Munich garrison, General von Danner, complaining about Lossow's attitude. It was a sharp reminder that Röhm knew far too much to be antagonised, and the hint was taken. He was persuaded to withdraw his resignation, while Lossow took immediate steps to quash his dismissal, which had been telegraphed from Berlin in the meantime. Röhm retained his position on Lossow's staff, but went on sick leave, until the affair had blown over, or the time became right for the full-blown *putsch* for which everyone was waiting.

IV

BEER HALL REVOLUTION

'THINGS fall apart; the centre cannot hold; mere anarchy is loosed upon the world . . .' W.B. Yeats's memorable lines from his 1920 poem, 'The Second Coming', could have been written for Germany in the summer of 1923, as the political scene whirled faster and faster, like a centrifuge flinging people outwards to the extremes of left and right, driving out reason and moderation. Hyper-inflation, resentment of the French and a series of strikes and disturbances fuelled constant rumours of an impending *putsch*. In Bavaria, the main threat was from the right, but in its immediate northern neighbour, Thuringia, and in Saxony and Hamburg, the Communists were flexing their muscles and planning revolutionary uprisings.

By August things were so bad that the centre-right Chancellor, Wilhelm Cuno, who had been responsible for the campaign of passive resistance to the French, was forced to resign: far from uniting the nation, his policies had brought it to the brink of disintegration as well as economic collapse. He was replaced by Gustav Stresemann, leader of the bourgeois German People's Party (DVP), who became the seventh Chancellor in five years. Stresemann, a pragmatic republican, formed a grand coalition that included the Social Democrats and set about trying to stabilise the situation and reunify the nation. He was rewarded by more strikes and Communist-led disturbances, including food riots when trains and trucks were attacked and looted by desperate city dwellers close to starvation. Stresemann knew that the essential first step along the road to recovery was to end passive resistance to the French occupation and resume reparations payments, but the mood of the country made such a move dangerous and he hesitated to take it. Even the suggestion, however, was enough to spark more trouble. It

gave Hitler the opportunity to come storming back into the ring, shamelessly changing tack and accusing the Berlin government of betraying
the national resistance by capitulating to the French, as well as doing
nothing to bring inflation under control.

On 1 and 2 September, the anniversary of the Prussian victory over
France at Sedan in 1870, the biggest 'German Day' yet was held at
Nuremberg. The police estimated that 100,000 nationalists poured into
the city. The ceremonial march past took a full two hours, with Hitler
standing alongside Ludendorff, Prince Ludwig Ferdinand of Bavaria
and Colonel Kriebel on the reviewing stand, while the crowds roared
their approval, waving handkerchiefs and throwing flowers, in a show
of 'such enthusiasm as had not been seen in Nuremberg since 1914',
according to the official police report. 'Many men and women wept,
so overcome were they by emotion.'[1]

For the Nazis this was a great showcase. Göring proudly marched
his SA through the streets behind its band, the smartest outfit on parade
and the most impressive, with its numbers swollen to 15,000 – considerably more than the entire strength of a regular army division. This
transformation from the rag-tag 800 who had turned out for the SA's
first public outing in Munich barely fourteen months earlier was a
remarkable tribute to Göring's energy, organising ability and leadership. His joy, however, was tempered by the fact that neither of the
two women who meant most in the world to him could be there to
share in his triumph. His mother had died suddenly a few days before,
which had upset him deeply. The day of her funeral had been bitterly
cold, the graveyard swept by one of Munich's notorious *Föhn* winds,
and Carin had caught a chill, which had turned to pneumonia. She
was now lying in bed with a high fever. Desperately concerned for her
as he was, Göring had been determined to do his duty – and, no doubt,
to claim his share of the glory at the head of 'his' troops.

There is no record of whether or not Heinrich Himmler took part
in the great rally, but it is hard to believe he would have missed it.
Two weeks before, at Röhm's behest, he had joined the Nazi Party,
even though this meant falling out with his father, who was still an
ardent supporter of the BVP and its separatist policies, and who
regarded Hitler and his followers as lower-class rowdies. He did not,
however, join the SA, but remained true to the Reichsflagge, and would
undoubtedly have marched with them in Nuremberg, just one among
the many thousands. He would certainly have been free to do so, for
he had left his job with Stickstoff-Land at the end of August, possibly

because he had been laid off as a result of the deteriorating economic situation, more probably because he saw a chance of pursuing the military career that was still his ultimate dream. With the threat of red revolution in Thuringia, detachments of the Bavarian army were moved to the state border. Replacement units were being formed from paramilitary groups and Ensign Himmler applied to join one of these, Kompanie Werner of the 1st Battalion, 19th Infantry.[2] He was accepted on 15 September, though he was once again fated not to see action. Whatever the reason for his leaving Stickstoff-Land, from then on he devoted his time entirely to political and paramilitary activities.

Although Ludendorff was the acknowledged figurehead of the nationalist movement, it was Hitler who made the keynote speech in Nuremberg, flaying the federal government and promising his wildly cheering audience: 'In a few weeks the dice will roll . . . What is in the making today will be greater than the World War. It will be fought out on German soil for the whole world.' The rapturous reception he received from the vast crowd wiped out the humiliation of May Day, re-establishing him as a revolutionary leader and revitalising the SA with the promise of action.

On the second day of the rally, the three leading groups in the Working Association, the NSDAP, Bund Oberland and Reichsflagge, agreed to join together in a tighter, more radical group, which they called the Deutscher Kampfbund (German Combat League). Its aims were clearly stated in its manifesto: the overthrow of the Republic and the tearing up of the Treaty of Versailles. Colonel Kriebel was once again given overall command of the paramilitary arms, but Max Erwin von Scheubner-Richter, one of Hitler's inner circle in the Nazi Party, was appointed secretary-general. The action plan he drew up, undoubtedly in consultation with Hitler if not at his dictation, called for the seizure of power in Bavaria as a first step, beginning by putting Kampfbund leaders in charge of the Bavarian Ministry of the Interior and the Bavarian police – the lessons of May Day had been well learned.

On 25 September, as fresh crises threatened to engulf Germany and Bavaria, Hitler was given sole political leadership of the Kampfbund, after a long meeting with Röhm, Kriebel, Captain Heiss, the leader of Reichsflagge, Friedrich Weber, the leader of Bund Oberland, and Göring, who had now secured his position in the front rank of the movement and was involved in every top-level discussion. His strategy of choosing the small Nazi Party to achieve rapid advancement had paid off handsomely: here he was, less than twelve months after joining, one of the acknowledged leaders of the revolutionary movement, poised for the great leap for power. Since 24 August, in fact, he had enjoyed Hitler's *Vollmacht,* complete authority, to act on his behalf. The others – apart from Göring – saw Hitler's new position as a subsidiary role, mainly concerned with propaganda, supporting rather than controlling the military leadership, more in line perhaps with Hitler's old army job as a political instructor. Hitler, of course, had other ideas – but as always, he was adept at allowing people the illusion that they were using him, while he was in fact manipulating them to suit his own purposes.

The very next day, the crisis broke. Stresemann announced the end of passive resistance to the French, and the nation erupted in protest. Hitler ordered Göring to put the SA on alert, and announced he would speak at fourteen mass meetings in Munich alone on 27 September. Röhm finally resigned his Reichswehr commission, to be ready to lead his Reichsflagge troopers in support of Hitler. Alarmed, the Bavarian Minister-President, Eugen von Knilling of the BVP, proclaimed a state of emergency, suspended all civil rights, and appointed Ritter von Kahr General State Commissioner, making him *de facto* dictator. This was bad news for Hitler and his followers, since although Kahr was a right-winger and strongly anti-Berlin, he was a committed Bavarian separatist, and a monarchist to boot. His first action on his appointment was to ban Hitler's fourteen meetings, refusing to budge when Hitler raged at him and threatened bloody revolution.

The appointment of Kahr was equally bad news for the federal government, heightening the danger of Bavarian secession and possible civil war between Berlin and Munich. Stresemann immediately called his government together under the chairmanship of President Ebert, to decide what to do. Their main problem was where did the army stand? Seeckt, ever the Prussian officer, small, neat, and as calm and disdainful of the political civilian as he had been when he stood aside during the Kapp *putsch* in 1920, gave Ebert his inimical answer: 'The army, Mr President, stands behind me.'

Seeckt was confirming what everyone already knew – that no matter what the constitutional position, the army was in fact an independent state within a state, and that it would do whatever its military chief, not its political supreme commander, decided. Seeckt decided that for the sake of the army itself, whose future depended on the unity of the state, he would support the Republic and its government. Ebert there-upon declared a national state of emergency, placing all executive power in the hands of the Defence Minister, Otto Gessler – which meant Seeckt, and through him his local commanders in each of the German states. Any attempt, by anyone, to march on Berlin or to bring down the Republic, would be met with force by the army. Less than a week later, Seeckt proved that he meant what he said when the army moved swiftly to quash an ill-organised right-wing *putsch* by the so-called Black Reichswehr, a 20,000-strong direct descendant of the old Freikorps based on the north-eastern frontier as a defence against the Poles. As October progressed, the threatened Communist take-overs in Hamburg, Saxony and Thuringia were averted by firm action by police and military, leaving only Bavaria as a centre of revolutionary activity.

In Bavaria, Kahr was ruling as leader of a triumvirate with Lossow and Colonel Hans Ritter von Seisser, chief of the state police. While this aristocratic trio of 'vons' shared the Kampfbund's hatred of Berlin and the Republic, they had their own agenda, and were actively planning their own national revolution, in concert with right-wing groups in northern Germany. This would start with a military operation using the army to overthrow the government and install a directorate in Berlin, which might include Kahr but not, of course, Hitler and Ludendorff. The Kampfbund also wanted a directorate, but based in Munich and including Hitler and Ludendorff but definitely not Kahr, with a march by the paramilitaries to take Berlin by force.

Hitler was acutely aware that his window of opportunity was rapidly closing. As well as the threat of his being forestalled and sidelined by Kahr, there was also a growing danger that Stresemann and Seeckt were getting the national situation under control at last, stabilising the country and thus depriving the Nazis and their allies of the oxygen of crisis, which they needed in order to succeed. Hitler managed to provoke a fresh rift in Berlin–Munich relations by publishing virulent personal attacks on Seeckt, Stresemann and Gessler in the *Volkischer Beobachter*. Seeckt ordered Lossow to close down the paper, and also to arrest the three most troublesome former Freikorps leaders, Ehrhardt, Rossbach and Captain Heiss of the Reichsflagge, for whom arrest warrants were still out in the rest of Germany. Lossow refused, claiming it would endanger pubic security and bring the Reichswehr into conflict with the Bavarian government. Seeckt then dismissed Lossow, but Kahr refused to accept his replacement, and confirmed him as commander of Reichswehr troops in Bavaria. When Seeckt reminded Lossow of his and his troops' oath of obedience, Kahr forced the officers and men to take a fresh oath, pledging their allegiance to the Bavarian government, and not the Republic. This was serious stuff, barely one step from secession and civil war, but Seeckt stayed calm and did nothing, biding his time and avoiding setting Reichswehr against Reichswehr, exactly as he had in 1920.

The six weeks following the declaration of a state of emergency were a time of frantic and confused activity for all the conspirators, but for none more so than Göring. Carin, although still very ill, had recovered enough to be moved, and he sent her home to her mother in Sweden. There, the infected lungs improved slightly, but she developed heart problems and entered a clinic for treatment. He worried about her constantly, and wrote begging Countess von Fock to take good care of her, because 'she is everything to me'. 'Over here,' he wrote, 'life is like a seething volcano whose destructive lava may at any moment spew forth across the country . . . We are working feverishly and stand by our aim: the liberation and revival of Germany.' Unable to bear being parted from her Beloved One, Carin returned to the 'seething volcano' in mid October, before she was fully recovered, and had to stay in bed in Obermenzing while he dashed back to see her between engagements. 'He is very busy these days and great events are in the offing,' she wrote to her mother, adding: 'He looks tired and doesn't get enough sleep, and he wears himself out travelling miles just to see me for a few moments.'3

Great events were indeed in the offing, and Göring was at the heart of them, plotting, scheming, and doing his best to keep the lid on the pressure cooker that was the SA as the heat continued to build. 'The day is coming when I can no longer hold back my men,' Lieutenant Wilhelm Brückner, commander of the Munich SA regiment told him and Hitler. 'If nothing happens now, they will run away from us.'4 The same demands for action were creating great strains within the Kampfbund as a whole, which as Hitler himself acknowledged was in danger of falling apart. And what was more, the money was running out fast. If they did not move soon, they would lose everything.

All the signs were that something was about to happen. Freed from the constraints imposed by Berlin, Lossow revived and updated his 'Spring Training' plan as 'Autumn Training', and began openly declaring his intention of marching on Berlin, promising Göring and the other Kampfbund chiefs on 24 October that he would start within fourteen days. He ordered the army in Bavaria to resume training the

SA and the other paramilitary units with greater urgency. Seisser, for his part, told his state police officers that armed police units would join the army in the march on Berlin to overthrow the Reich government and replace it with a nationalist dictatorship.

Göring was in constant touch with Lossow and Seisser, discussing closer co-operation and arranging for the SA's weapons to be cleaned and serviced by military armourers. When he chaired a meeting in Munich of all his SA leaders on 23 October, he announced the planned *putsch*, called for a list of 'personalities who will have to be eliminated and at least one of whom will have to be shot immediately after the proclamation as an example',[5] and told them they would be marching side by side with the Bavarian army and police. Hitler confirmed this in a ten-minute speech, ending by calling on them to be ready for national revolution. The commander of the Lower Bavaria SA regiment, Gregor Strasser, later recorded how delighted he was to hear those words, saying that the meeting 'was for me perhaps the most beautiful since 1918 because from then on I thought things would change'.[6]

The thing that changed first was the attitude of the triumvirate. From the end of October, Lossow suddenly banned all Hitler's public meetings, and the next day Hitler learned that Kahr was sending Seisser to Berlin for talks with Seeckt and the federal government. This looked suspiciously as though Kahr intended to sidestep Hitler and do some sort of deal. Fearing that they were about to be ditched, the Kampfbund leaders decided to strike first: they would seize Kahr, Lossow and Seisser, together with Minister-President Knilling, at the dedication of Munich's new war memorial on German Remembrance Day, 4 November, and force them to support the Kampfbund's revolution. Their hastily devised plan had to be abandoned, however, when the police and army were deployed in force to block off the street in advance of the ceremony.

Kahr had meanwhile suffered a setback of his own. At their meeting in Berlin the day before, Seeckt had told Seisser in no uncertain terms that the army would actively resist any move against the federal government, a statement that he underlined publicly in his Order of the Day on 4 November. Two days later, the triumvirate met the heads of the patriotic associations and, without mentioning their own rebuff from Seeckt, warned them all against precipitate action. Lossow, ambivalent as ever, told them he would support a move against Berlin, but only if it was carefully planned, fully prepared, and had more than a fifty-one per cent chance of success.

In the face of yet more prevarication, Hitler, Göring, and the other Kampfbund leaders became convinced that Lossow was merely playing them along. They decided to go ahead at once with their own *putsch*. Meeting secretly on 7 November, Hitler, Göring, Weber, Kriebel and Scheubner-Richter drew up their plans for arresting members of the government in their beds, simultaneously seizing control of communications, town halls and police stations throughout Bavaria. At first, they set the date for the night of Saturday 10 November – weekends have always been the best time for staging a *coup* – with a march into the centre of Munich with bands playing on the Sunday morning, which happened to be the fifth anniversary of the hated Armistice. But there was a strong chance that the weekend would be too late. Kahr was due to address a public meeting, hurriedly called for the very next day, 8 November, in the huge Bürgerbräukeller, at which all the leading figures in Munich would be present. He was supposed to outline his economic and political programme, but Hitler and his cronies feared he intended to use the occasion to declare Bavarian independence from Berlin. Their suspicions were strengthened when Kahr refused to meet Hitler either before or immediately after the meeting. If they were to avoid being bypassed, they would have to act immediately.

It would be a scramble to assemble their forces in a matter of hours, but Göring's efficient organisation of the SA meant it should be possible. And at least they knew that the triumvirate would all be in one place, on the platform of the Bürgerbräukeller, at a specific time. If they could all be taken, and persuaded to give their backing, in public, before a gathering of Munich's notables, there would be no need for elaborate plans to seize key points and communications. Everything would drop into place without opposition. Kahr would have been outflanked. The *putsch* would be a *fait accompli* before anyone even left the beer hall.

The meeting of the Kampfbund leadership ended at about 1 a.m. on the morning of 8 November. The triumvirate were to be seized at 8.30 p.m. that evening. In those few hours, Göring had to alert his SA troops throughout Bavaria, almost all of them spare-time storm-troopers with full-time jobs elsewhere, mobilise them and bring them into Munich within that time, and without telling any but a few selected senior officers what was going on. Somehow, he managed it. So, too, did Weber with his Bund Oberland fighters, and Heiss with the Reichsflagge, from which Röhm had split his own unit, renaming it Reichskriegsflagge (Reich War Flag). Göring booked three other beer halls, the Artzberger, Hofbräu and Torbräu, as assembly points, while

Röhm chose the Löwenbräukeller for his 400 men, who included Heinrich Himmler and his elder brother Gebhard.

Everything went smoothly throughout the day. Göring found time to look in on Carin, still in her sickbed, to tell her there was to be 'a great meeting' that night and that he might be late home, but she was not to worry. Then he hung his *Pour le Mérite* medal round his neck, picked up his black leather coat and black steel helmet with a big white swastika painted on the front, and drove back into the centre of the city.

Kahr began reading his dry, prepared speech to a packed audience of some 3000 in the Bürgerbräukeller at 8 p.m. that evening. Almost as many people had failed to get into the hall when the doors were closed at 7.15, and were milling around in the garden and square outside. Göring arrived almost on schedule at 8.34, at the head of the elite 100-strong SA Shock Troop, the Stosstrupp Hitler, all carrying weapons and wearing steel helmets. Because of their disciplined appearance, the police on duty assumed they were Reichswehr troops, and made no move to stop them as they leaped from their trucks and ran to take up positions in and around the hall. Hitler was waiting nervously in the foyer, looking like the head waiter in a seedy hotel in an ill-fitting black morning coat with his Iron Cross pinned on his breast. He was attended by his bodyguard, former butcher and wrestler Ulrich Graf, and a small group, including Rudolf Hess, Max Amman, Erwin von Scheubner-Richter and Putzi Hanfstaengl. Göring and his men crashed open the doors into the main room, set up a Maxim machine-gun in the opening, then marched forward towards the platform, forcing a way through the crammed tables for Hitler, who followed holding a Browning pistol and flanked by Graf, Hess and the others.[7]

It took a few minutes for Kahr to realise what was happening, and for his speech to tail off into silence. But there was no silence in the rest of the hall: voices were raised in a hubbub of consternation and confusion as people began to stampede for the exits, only to find them blocked by storm-troopers. Unable to reach the platform, Hitler climbed on to a chair and shouted for quiet. Failing to make himself heard, he raised his pistol and fired a shot into the ceiling. In the sudden hush that ensued, he announced that the national revolution had begun, that the hall was surrounded by 600 heavily armed men, and no one was to leave. The Bavarian government was deposed, he said, and a provisional Reich government was to be formed. The barracks of the Reichswehr and state police had been occupied, and army and police were marching on the city under the swastika banner. Clambering over the remaining tables, he stepped on to the platform. One of Seisser's police aides, Major Hunglinger, moved towards him, his hand in his pocket. Hitler, suspecting that he was holding a gun, immediately pressed his own pistol to the major's temple, ordering him to remove his hand; it was empty. Turning to Kahr, Lossow and Seisser, he 'invited' them to accompany him into an adjoining ante-room, assuring them that he guaranteed their safety. After a moment's hesitation, they agreed – Lossow later claimed that he whispered to the others as they went 'Put on an act'.

Göring was left in charge in the main hall. As the crowd grew restless again, with shouts of 'Theatre!' and 'South America!', he followed Hitler's example by drawing his pistol and firing a shot into the ceiling. Then, opening the neck of his leather jacket to display his *Pour le Mérite* more clearly, he told them that the action was entirely friendly: it was not directed against Kahr, or the army and police, but against the 'wretched Jews' in Berlin. He appealed to them to stay calm and be patient, a new government was being formed at that moment in the next room, adding, in typical Göring style, 'Anyway, what are you worrying about? You've got your beer!'[8]

While Göring kept order in the Bürgerbräukeller, Scheubner-Richter took Hitler's Mercedes to collect Ludendorff, who was awaiting the call at his villa. Ludendorff later claimed that he had been taken completely by surprise and knew nothing of the *putsch*, though he had in fact been kept fully informed of the plot, and just happened to be wearing his full Imperial Army uniform.[9] Meanwhile, the code words 'Safely delivered' had been telephoned to police headquarters, where the head of the political police, Nazi Party member Wilhelm Frick, and former police chief Pöhner were waiting to take control – Frick had already ordered the police at the Bürgerbräukeller not to interfere, but simply to watch and report.

The message was also phoned to the other beer halls, including the Löwenbräukeller on the other side of the city centre, where Röhm and his men were waiting. On receiving news that the *putsch* was successful, Röhm formed up his men and marched them through the streets, with Himmler at their head carrying the old imperial banner, towards the Bürgerbräukeller. Halfway there, however, they were intercepted by a motor-cycle messenger with orders that they divert to the

Schönfeldstrasse, to seize and occupy the Bavarian War Ministry building, which housed Lossow's Reichswehr district headquarters. They took over the building swiftly and without incident, and secured it by throwing up a barbed wire barricade around it, behind which Himmler took up his post, still proudly holding the flag. But for some unexplained reason, Röhm failed to take control of the telephone switchboard, the communications hub of the various barracks and units throughout Bavaria, which also provided a direct connection to Seeckt's national headquarters in Berlin. It was the first in a series of fatal errors that night.

Back in the ante-room at the Bürgerbräukeller, Hitler, pale, agitated and sweating heavily, was waving his pistol about and declaring that 'no one leaves this room alive without my permission'. He told the triumvirate that he would head the new Reich government, but that there would be important posts for them: Lossow was to be Reichswehr Minister, Seisser Reich Police Minister, and Kahr Regent of Bavaria, with Pöhner as Minister-President. Ludendorff was to be chief of the new national army, incorporating the Kampfbund paramilitaries, and would lead the march on Berlin. Hitler apologised for having to act in this way, but said he had no alternative. If everything went wrong, he told them, he had four bullets left in his pistol – three for them and one for himself. Kahr, who had recovered his nerve, responded coolly that to die meant nothing in such circumstances, and asked for details of Ludendorff's part in all this. Hitler did not answer.[10] The noise from the main hall was building again, and he went to see for himself what was happening, leaving Graf to keep an eye on the prisoners.

Göring was finding it increasingly difficult to keep order, and when Hitler reappeared he had to threaten to put a machine-gun in the gallery before anyone would listen to him. When they did, he was able to work the old magic, 'turning that vast crowd inside out,' recalled the historian Professor Karl Alexander von Müller, who was part of it, 'as smoothly as one turns a glove inside out, with a few sentences.'[11] Putzi Hanfstaengl watched in admiration as Hitler transformed himself from an insignificant figure looking like a provincial bridegroom in his comical morning coat into a superman. 'It was like the difference between a Stradivarius lying in its case, just a few bits of wood and lengths of catgut, and the same violin being played by a master.'[12]

Hitler started by confirming what Göring had already said: that his actions were directed 'solely at the Berlin Jew government and the November criminals of 1918' and not against the army or the police.

Then he outlined his plans for new governments in Berlin and Munich, including Ludendorff as 'leader and chief with dictatorial powers, of the German national army', a choice that was greeted with great enthusiasm. 'In a free Germany,' he reassured the separatists among them, 'there is room for an autonomous Bavaria!' 'Out there,' he told his audience quietly, 'are Kahr, Lossow and Seisser. They are struggling hard to reach a decision. May I tell them that you will stand behind them?' The audience roared its approval. Hitler concluded with an emotional call: 'I can tell you this: either the German revolution begins tonight, or we will all be dead by dawn!'[13] The speech was, according to Müller, 'a rhetorical masterpiece', and although there were still many people in the hall who were not yet converted, the majority had been completely won over.[14]

Ludendorff arrived to a great reception amid cries of 'Heil', and joined Hitler and the triumvirate in the ante-room, where, perhaps overawed by his appearance and rank, they accepted his handshake and agreed to join the *putsch*. Hitler led them back on to the platform, where they pledged their support and promised to get rid of the Berlin criminals. There was much handshaking and smiling, and as each man made a short speech the audience cheered and shouted, climbing on their seats in their excitement. Hitler's face was a picture of delight – his fondest dreams were coming true. 'He had a childlike, frank expression of happiness that I shall never forget,' Müller wrote. His was inevitably the star speech, skilfully playing on every emotive chord: 'I am going to fulfil the vow I made to myself five years ago when I was a blind cripple in the military hospital: to know neither rest nor peace until the November criminals had been overthrown, until on the ruins of the wretched Germany of today there should have arisen once more a Germany of power and greatness, of freedom and glory.' As he finished, the whole hall burst spontaneously into *Deutschland über alles*.[15]

It seemed as though the *putsch* had succeeded. Göring, beaming happily, embraced and congratulated his SA commanders. With the Bavarian army and police on their side, they could overcome any resistance from Berlin. The future was theirs. He sent Hanfstaengl hurrying to Obermenzing to tell Carin the good news – even in his moment of triumph, he was still the devoted husband. Hanfstaengl returned with Carin's sister, Fanny, who told Göring Carin was still running a fever and was too ill to come, but had been revived by his message, which was a tonic in itself.[16]

Before anyone was allowed to leave the meeting, Hitler conferred with Göring and Hess and agreed that they should arrest the members of the existing Bavarian government who were present, together with other notables, as potential hostages and to prevent their causing trouble. The task was assigned to Hess, who stood on a chair and called out a list of names, including Minister-President Knilling, Police President Mantel and Crown Prince Rupprecht's chief adviser, Graf von Soden. All submitted meekly, and were herded off first to an upper room, and then to a safe house in the suburbs, guarded by Hess and a contingent of students.

The jubilation in the Bürgerbräu, however, soon proved to be premature. Things were already going badly wrong elsewhere in the city. None of the paramilitary units had succeeded in taking over any of the key points, apart from Röhm at the War Ministry, and Frick and Pöhner at police headquarters, where they were in any case soon ousted and placed under arrest. None of the government buildings, army or police barracks, the main railway station or the telegraph office were taken. And although almost the entire complement of 1000 officer cadets from the Infantry School had locked up their commanding officer and marched under the leadership of Rossbach, with swastika banners and a band, to join Hitler and Ludendorff, none of the senior officers in the army had gone over to the rebels.

The two most important military centres in the city, the barracks of the 19th Infantry Regiment and the Army Engineers, were proving particularly difficult. The commanding officers of both units were refusing to admit the rebels, or to hand over their arms and equipment. At the Engineers' barracks, 250 men of the Bund Oberland were taken prisoner. Hitler was incensed when he heard of this, and decided to leave the Bügerbräukeller and go there personally to sort things out. It was a serious error, exposing his lack of experience as a leader, whose place is at the centre.

Back at the Bürgerbräu, the crowd was breaking up and Göring was making arrangements to provide food and drink for his storm-troopers. Kahr, Lossow and Seisser approached Ludendorff, who had been left in charge, and said they needed to return to their offices to issue orders and make arrangements to implement the *putsch*. Accepting their word as officers, Ludendorff released them, and they scurried off. They did not return to their own offices, however, but to the 19th Infantry barracks, which had not been occupied by the Kampfbund. There, Lossow was greeted by the commander of the Munich garrison,

Lieutenant-General von Danner, who had been in the Bürgerbräu, with the cool question: 'All that was bluff, of course, Excellency?' Danner had already contacted Seeckt in Berlin, who had ordered him to tell Lossow that if he did not put down the *putsch* immediately, he would march south and do it himself. Thus encouraged, Lossow immediately reneged on the promises he had made in the Bürgerbräu and issued orders to garrisons throughout Bavaria to rush reinforcements to Munich. Kahr and Seisser naturally went along with him. Kahr had notices printed and posted up all over the city denouncing the *putsch*, declaring that the promises extorted from him and his colleagues at gunpoint were null and void, and that the Nazi Party, Reichskriegsflagge and Bund Oberland were dissolved. He then took off for the safety of Regensburg with the remnants of his government.

Throughout the night, more SA and other paramilitary units continued to arrive in the city, but they found only an absence of clear orders, and a confusion compounded by placards and posters pasted up everywhere, some proclaiming the revolution and naming Hitler as Reich Chancellor, others denying it and announcing warrants for the arrest of him and his co-conspirators. Hitler had counted on a bloodless *putsch* with the co-operation of the army and police, but from the moment he returned to the beer hall and discovered that Ludendorff had let the triumvirate go, he knew he had failed. His fears were confirmed by state radio bulletins issued by Kahr, Lossow and Seisser denouncing the *putsch* and confirming that all barracks and most key buildings were in the hands of the army and police. Röhm and his men still occupied the War Ministry, where Hitler, Ludendorff and Göring had visited them in the small hours of the morning for fruitless discussion about their next move, but at about 5 a.m. the building was surrounded by a cordon of Reichswehr troops. The only success of the operation was nullified.

As a bitterly cold morning dawned on 9 November, with snow and sleet blowing in the wind, the leaders were still trying to decide what to do. They had no contingency plans – which was hardly surprising, since their main plan had been sketchy to say the least. Should they simply disband? Should they withdraw to Rosenheim, some thirty-five miles to the south-east, to regroup? Both seemed cowardly options and were rejected. It was Ludendorff who suggested they march into the centre of Munich, and the others agreed, largely for want of any other ideas, though the aims of such a march were, like everything else at that moment, confused and uncertain. Ludendorff believed that with himself, the legendary war leader, at the head of the column, Reichswehr troops would never dare to open fire, and the citizens would join the marchers in a demonstration of overwhelming support, which would persuade the army and police to change their minds. After the briefest of discussions, it was decided that the march would start from the Bürgerbräu at noon.

In the meantime, Hitler sent a mutual friend as an emissary to Prince Rupprecht in his castle near Berchtesgaden, to try to persuade the prince either to change his mind and withdraw the condemnation of the *putsch* which he had issued during the night, or to intercede with Kahr and Lossow to obtain an honourable settlement. He also sent a squad of storm-troopers to the banknote printers to requisition bundles of 50-billion mark notes with which to pay his men. They collected 14,605,000 billion marks, for which they handed over a Nazi Party receipt. Göring, who did not share Ludendorff's confidence of his invulnerability, sent another squad to the city hall, to pick up more hostages. They grabbed the mayor and nine Socialist councillors, and dragged them, none too gently, back to the beer hall.

Shortly before noon, Göring assembled his SA men and the infantry cadets and made them swear an oath of allegiance to Ludendorff. Then he formed them into a column some 2,000 strong, and they began the march, behind two standard bearers carrying the flags of the Nazi Party and the Bund Oberland. Whatever the outcome, this was a moment to savour for Göring, as he found himself marching immediately alongside Ludendorff at the centre of the front rank, with Weber and Kriebel to his left. Hitler marched on Ludendorff's right, with Scheubner-Richter at his shoulder, then Graf and Ludendorff's aide, Major Hans Streck. The mood was sombre – one participant later described it as being like a funeral procession.[17]

The first obstacle facing the marchers was a cordon of green-uniformed state police armed with a machine-gun, blocking the Ludwig Bridge over the River Isar. Göring stepped forward and spoke to the police officer in charge, pointing out the hostages further back in the column, and warning that he had given orders to his men to shoot them if the police opened fire. The officer ordered his men to stand aside. The march proceeded towards to city centre, the mood lightening as the crowds on the pavements shouted their encouragement, many of them joining the marchers. The men began singing SA marching songs. In the Marienplatz, before the Gothic New City Hall with its elaborate carillon, they found a large crowd listening to a rabble-rousing speech from Julius Streicher, the violently anti-Semitic Nazi boss of Nuremberg, who had rushed to Munich to join in the fun. He broke off his speech and fell into line just behind Hitler, and most of those who had been listening to him followed on.

By now, the earlier despondency had given way to a heady triumphalism. The march passed through the Marienplatz and turned into the narrow Residenzstrasse, heading for the War Ministry to relieve Röhm and his men, who were still face to face with Reichswehr troops, neither side caring to fire on former friends and colleagues. But at the end of the street, in front of the Feldherrnhalle war memorial, a force of about 100 state police blocked the way, loaded rifles at the ready. Its commander, Michael Freiherr von Godin, had strict orders from Seisser not to allow the column to pass. This time it was Graf who went forward, shouting 'Don't shoot! His Excellency General Ludendorff and Hitler are coming!' Hitler called out 'Surrender!' The police did not heed either of them, and raised their weapons at an order from Godin. For a moment, there was a tense silence. Then a single shot. It has never been established who fired it – some eye-witness reports say it was Hitler himself, others credit Streicher or the police. And then both sides were shooting. Scheubner-Richter, marching arm-in-arm with Hitler, took a bullet through the head that killed him instantly. Hitler, with the instinctive reaction bred by four years in the front line, dived for the ground at the first shot or, as some reports have it, was dragged down by Scheubner-Richter as he fell. Either way, he felt a sharp pain in his shoulder which he believed was from a bullet but was in fact a simple dislocation. Göring was not so lucky: he was hit in the groin and hip, and fell to the ground seriously wounded and bleeding heavily. Ludendorff not only remained on his feet but, accom-panied by his aide, Major Streck, continued marching steadily towards the police rifles, impervious to the hail of bullets all around them, until, miraculously unscathed, they were arrested and led away into custody.

The gun battle lasted no more than half a minute, but by the time the shooting stopped fourteen *putschists* and four policemen had been killed. Two of Röhm's men were also shot dead as they tried to break through the army cordon around the War Ministry to join the battle. Hitler was the first to scramble away from the scene, picked up by the Munich SA medical officer, Dr Walter Schultze, in his car and driven off at speed, to find refuge in Putzi Hanfstaengl's country home at

Uffing, near the Staffelsee lake, south of Munich. There, he was nursed by Hanfstaengl's wife and sister – Putzi himself, like several other prominent Nazis, had fled over the border into Austria – until he was arrested two days later.

Göring was rescued by some of his SA men, who found a house with a doctor's nameplate and carried him there. According to Karl Bodenschatz, his past and future adjutant, 'The people on the ground floor threw him out, but there was an elderly Jewish couple upstairs and they took him in.' Frau Ilse Ballin, wife of a furniture dealer, and her sister had been trained as nurses during the war, and they tended Göring's wounds, cleaned them up and stanched the bleeding. They were well aware of who he was, and of his party's attitude to Jews, but they did not hand him over to the police. Instead, they kept him hidden until dark, when he could be moved to the clinic of Professor Alwin Ritter von Asch, a Nazi sympathiser, for more professional treatment. To his credit, Göring never forgot their kindness, and repaid his debt by protecting and helping them during the dark days of the Third Reich.

Safely in Professor Asch's clinic, Göring sent an SA man to tell Carin where he was. It must have come as a great relief to her, for although Fanny had seen the shooting, she had not been able to tell her what had happened to her husband. As soon as she received the news, Carin got up at once from her own sickbed, defying her doctor's orders by hurrying off into the bitterly cold night, to arrive at Göring's bedside within half an hour. She found him in considerable pain, and did what she could to comfort him. Fanny, meanwhile, was out and about in the city, trying to discover what was happening. What she found was not hopeful. The police were scouring the city hunting for members of the Nazi leadership. Lossow had personally signed a warrant for Göring's arrest, dead or alive. Certain that if he was captured he would face execution, Carin knew she had to get him out of Germany and that there was no time to lose.

'Every second is costly, Carin knows,' wrote Fanny, breathlessly dramatic. 'Plans must be made quickly, friends alerted. Hermann Göring must be got out of the city before daybreak, even at the risk of his life, even if the bleeding starts again and the pain is unbearable. Carin gives not a single thought to herself, to the fact that she is just out of a sick bed, feverish, her heart palpitating, her lungs choked! Now *his* heart has felt the dagger's stab, and will never be the same again. She must save him.'[18] And save him she did. With the help of his SA bodyguard, she drove him to the villa of a rich Dutch friend, Major Schuler van Krieken, in Garmisch Partenkirchen, a ski resort in the mountains about forty-five miles south of Munich. Unable to walk a step, he rested in bed, trying to regain his strength while she prepared to get him across the nearby border into Austria.

The next night, at 10 p.m., accompanied by a doctor, they drove to the frontier post at Griesen, hoping to slip across in the darkness. But the border guards had been warned to look out for them. They were stopped and escorted back to Garmisch, where Göring was placed in the local sanatorium to await a police officer from Munich with an arrest warrant. When the officer arrived, however, Göring had gone, spirited away through the back door with a fur coat over his night-shirt and driven away with the doctor, while Carin stayed behind as a decoy. They headed in the opposite direction from Griesen, to the frontier post at Mittenwald, and this time luck was with them. The striped barrier was up, and they were able to drive straight through. At the Austrian border post, Göring presented a passport borrowed from another doctor in Garmisch, and they drove on to Seefeld, where Göring was put to bed in the local inn. Next day, the driver went back for Carin, and on Monday 12 November they moved on to Innsbruck, and checked into the Hotel Tiroler Hof, which was owned by a Nazi sympathiser. But Göring was now running a high fever and was delirious with the pain from his wound, which was suppurating badly. He was rushed into hospital next day, in a critical condition.

Göring's revolution was over. He was exiled from his country, seriously wounded, a wanted man, separated from friends and associates, his dreams of glory as the leader of Germany shattered. He had lost everything, except Carin. It would be four years of hardship, pain and misery before he could return to pick up the pieces and start again.

PART TWO

THE YEARS OF STRUGGLE
1924–1933

V

REGROUPING

HITLER later claimed that the failure of the November *putsch* was 'the greatest stroke of luck in his life'. And so it was – but only after he had single-handedly turned a humiliating débâcle into a political triumph. At the time, things looked very black. His organisational and planning skills had been exposed as hopeless: with the forces at his disposal it should have been easy for him to seize control of Munich and indeed the whole of Bavaria, but he had not even been able to hold one single building for more than a few hours. His personal reputation for bravery was in tatters: he had been the first to dive for cover when the shooting started, while Ludendorff had not even broken step or lowered his head, and then he had deserted his men, running away and leaving them to the mercy of the police. His party had been banned, his associates put to flight, killed or arrested, and after two days of ignominious hiding he himself was imprisoned to await trial, possibly for his life. It should have been the end; instead, he turned it into a new beginning.

When he arrived in the fortress prison in the pretty little town of Landsberg am Lech, some forty miles west of Munich, the Nazi leader was received with respect and even adulation by the staff as well as the other prisoners. The previous star inmate, Count Anton von Arco-Valley, the man who had assassinated Bavaria's Socialist Minister-President, Kurt Eisner, in 1919, was moved out of the spacious cell number seven to make room for him. But he was deeply depressed and went on hunger strike for the first two weeks, regularly threatening to kill himself. Gradually, the clouds of despair lifted, and by the time he was brought to trial on 26 February 1924 he was back to his old self, and ready to come out fighting after ten weeks of preparation.

During that time, the political situation had changed out of all recognition. Kahr, Lossow and Seisser had been forced to retire, and a moderate BVP government had taken over in Munich and had begun to repair the relationship with Berlin. The national government, meanwhile, had reasserted its authority, brought inflation under control, and started making real progress in finding a solution to the reparations problem. There was still immense dissatisfaction in Germany as a whole and Bavaria in particular, and many tensions remained, but there were no more *putsch* attempts. The boil had been well and truly lanced outside the Feldherrnhalle on 9 November.

The trial of the principal conspirators lasted twenty-four days. With a fitting irony, it was held in the Infantry Officers' School whose 1,000 cadets had marched in support of the *putsch* – they had since been sternly disciplined and transferred to Thuringia. There were nine other defendants, including Ludendorff, Röhm, Pöhner, Frick and Kriebel, but from the start it was Hitler who dominated the proceedings. The Bavarian Minister of Justice, Franz Gürtner, a Nazi supporter, made sure he was given an easy ride by appointing judges, court officials and even prosecuting counsel, who were all sympathetic to the cause – the presiding judge was the same man who had given him the suspended sentence for breach of the peace in 1922. He was allowed to wear a suit, rather than prison clothes, appearing as a hero with his Iron Cross pinned on his breast, and with the active encouragement of the judge he used the courtroom as a political platform to brilliant effect.

His opening speech lasted four hours. Instead of denying his role in the failed *putsch* and pleading for mercy, he proudly claimed full responsibility, but refused to accept that he had committed high treason, since 'there is no such thing as high treason against the traitors of 1918'. If he had committed high treason, he went on, then why were those with whom he had consulted and conspired for months – Kahr, Lossow and Seisser – not with him in the dock? They had known everything and been involved in everything and what was more, he insisted, their pledges made to him in the Bürgerbräukeller had been genuine. Only later, under pressure, had they changed their minds and reneged. As for himself, he continued, 'I feel myself to be the best of Germans, who wanted the best for the German people.'[1]

As the trial progressed, he was allowed to interrogate the witnesses as he pleased, and to digress constantly into political diatribes. He reserved his sharpest attacks for the triumvirate, whom he tore into shreds, to loud and unchecked applause from the public gallery. Only

Lossow fought back, with all the contempt of a general officer for a presumptuous lance-corporal, describing him as fit only to be 'the drummer' and accusing him of overreaching ambition. But Hitler managed to have the last word, provoking Lossow into losing control and then demolishing him with the withering response, 'How petty are the thoughts of small men!'

Day after day, it was Hitler who made the front pages of all the newspapers throughout Germany. When the trial started he was barely known outside Bavaria. By the time it finished, he was a household name everywhere. Foreign papers gave the trial scant coverage, but this hardly mattered. Hitler had been able to hammer home his political message to his largest audience yet.

If the *putsch* had been a fiasco, the trial was a farce, and the last act delivered a suitably farcical denouement with the verdicts and the sentences. Ludendorff, as had been universally predicted – some reports say by the presiding judge himself before the trial even started – was acquitted, to his great disgust; he stomped out of the court swearing he would never wear his uniform again after it had been insulted in such a manner. Röhm was given fifteen months, less the time he had spent in Stadelheim prison awaiting trial, suspended on condition of good behaviour. He was released on 1 April. Hitler was given the minimum sentence of five years, less the time he had spent in prison on remand, plus a fine of 200 gold marks or an additional twenty days. He was assured of an early parole – this had apparently been the condition the lay judges insisted upon before they would agree to a verdict of guilty. A demand by the Minister of the Interior for his deportation to Austria was rejected on account of his war service in the German army. Weber, Kriebel and Pöhner received the same sentence as Hitler, the remaining defendants even less. The sentences were received with acclaim by the audience, which included many officers wearing full dress uniforms in honour of the occasion and of the former Quartermaster General, and all the defendants were garlanded with flowers and nationalist symbols. The court made no attempt to stifle these demonstrations of support.

Röhm's idea of what constituted 'good behaviour' was typically idiosyncratic. He still regarded the paramilitary side of the movement as its central core, with the party as little more than its political arm. Since both the SA and his own Reichskriegsflagge were banned, he immediately started trying to set up a new nationwide paramilitary organisation, which he called the Frontbann (Front Banner). This would incorporate the SA and the other banned units of the Kampfbund, and would be under the military leadership of Ludendorff. Believing himself to be in a position of strength, he wrote to Hitler setting out his terms: 'Party politics will not be tolerated in either the Frontbann or the SA . . . I categorically refuse to allow the SA to become involved in party matters; equally, I categorically refuse to allow SA commanders to accept instructions from party political leaders.'[2]

Hitler had no intention of losing control of the SA to Röhm. In any case, the failure of the *putsch* had proved how ineffectual the para-militaries were, and had convinced him that he could not achieve power in Germany by force, without the support of the army, which he could no longer expect. In future, the SA – *his* SA – would be confined to supporting the party in its political activities. It would revert to its original role as a strong-arm squad providing protection at meetings and fighting political enemies, notably the Communists, rather than the government. He rejected Röhm's terms out of hand, telling him he wanted to hear no more about the Frontbann. Röhm offered his resignation. Hitler simply ignored his letter, beginning an estrangement that was to grow ever wider over the following two years.

After the trial, Hitler returned to Landsberg prison, where he held court for the next nine months in surroundings akin to a decent offi-cers' mess, with some forty supporters attending to his every need. The dining-room where he presided each day was decorated with a large swastika banner. When he celebrated his thirty-fifth birthday on 20 April, his cell was swamped with flowers and gifts. For the first time in his life outside the army, he had no need to worry about finding the money for accommodation and food. He had plenty of time to think and to read, and no shortage of books, either from the prison library or sent to him by followers outside, which he consumed vora-ciously. He claimed later that Landsberg was 'his university paid for by the state' – but his choice of reading matter was limited to those authors and subjects that reinforced his own views, never those that challenged them. In Hitler's university, there were no arguments, no disputations, no polemics.

From reading, Hitler moved on to writing, contributing a stream of articles to the journals set up to fill the gap left by the banned *Völkischer Beobachter*. And in the summer he began work on a book, to which he gave the catchy title *Four-and-a-Half Years of Struggle against Lies*,

Stupidity, and Cowardice. Max Amman, who was to publish it, wisely decided to shorten this to *My Struggle – Mein Kampf*. Always happier with the spoken rather than the written word, Hitler decided to dictate the book, first to his chauffeur, Emil Maurice, and then to the better-qualified Rudolf Hess, who had been trained in commerce, including stenography, with the idea that he should join and eventually succeed his father in the family trading business in Alexandria, Egypt.

Always totally besotted, Hess had chosen to return from Austria and give himself up for trial in order to be with his idol in prison, an act of loyalty that Hitler never forgot. He had already earned Hitler's respect as a former front fighter: they had served in the same regiment, though Hess had been commissioned as a lieutenant in 1917, but they had never met during the war. Hess had been a good soldier, brave, disciplined and intensely patriotic. After receiving a serious chest wound in 1917, he transferred to the air force, but had only just qualified as a pilot when the war ended and he joined the ranks of embittered ex-servicemen convinced that they had been betrayed by the politicians and Jewish businessmen. His personal bitterness was increased by the British expropriation of the family business in Egypt.

Demobilised in Munich, Hess was dismayed by the general air of political disintegration and by the gangs of Red soldiers and sailors roaming the streets. He found refuge in the Thule Society, where he was soon drawn into extreme right-wing politics alongside future colleagues including Hans Frank, Rosenberg and Eckart, becoming involved in recruitment, procuring weapons and organising sabotage squads. Inevitably, in the spring of 1919, he joined Epp's Freikorps for the battles against the Räterepublik, proving himself a formidable street fighter capable of extreme and reckless brutality both then and later with the SA, despite being nicknamed 'Fräulein Hess' by fellow storm-troopers because of his devotion to Hitler.

Hess was an early and fanatical member of the party, falling instantly under Hitler's spell on his first visit to a meeting of what was still the DAP in May 1920. That night, he returned to his boarding house in Munich's bohemian Schwabing district in a state of high excitement, 'a changed man, alive, radiant, no longer gloomy and morose', as his then girlfriend and future wife, Ilse Pröhl, recalled. Bursting into her room, he blurted out: 'A man – I've heard a man, he's unknown, I've forgotten his name. But if anyone can free us from Versailles, then it's this man. This unknown man will restore our honour!'[3] It was a conviction he was never to lose. When he entered a competition at Munich

University for an essay on 'What must the man be like who will lead
Germany back to the heights?' he wrote a word portrait of Hitler –
and won first prize.

Like many ex-servicemen, including, of course, Göring, Hess had
enrolled at the University – where he formed a 100-strong SA troop
from his fellow students in February 1921 – to study history and
economics. But he was most interested in the lectures on geopolitics
given by Professor Karl Haushofer, a retired general who had developed the idea that a nation's ability to grow and prosper depended
largely on its living space, its *Lebensraum*. Hess embraced Haushofer's
ideas enthusiastically, and the professor took the brooding, introspective young man under his wing, welcoming him not only into his classes
but also into his home, where he 'became as one of the family'.[4] Hess
accepted his patronage gratefully: throughout his life, he always needed
a figure of authority on whom he could rely. He had fallen out with
his dictatorial father, because he refused to follow him into the business, and Haushofer seemed the ideal man to fill the gap.

In setting down Hitler's thoughts in *Mein Kampf*, Hess was clearly
far more than a mere amanuensis. Indeed, there is a good case for
regarding him as virtually its co-author: he not only edited and cleaned
up Hitler's poor grammar and vocabulary, but made his own contribution to the content of the book and its murky philosophy, especially
the 'science of German conquest' and the concept of *Lebensraum*. He
introduced Haushofer and his theories to Hitler, who was heavily influenced by them.

The months Hess spent with Hitler in prison cemented their close
relationship, and he emerged as the Führer's most intimate and trusted
confidant, though he always remained willingly subservient.
Emotionally – though not physically, of course – 'Fräulein Hess' became
'Frau Hitler', fussing over him, taking care of his every need, and
guarding his interests with a fierce jealousy. He became Hitler's secretary and then his deputy, but never his friend: how could he ever
presume to be a friend of his god, whom he worshipped?

Hess remained at the centre of the Nazi Party and its politics until
1941, playing a much more important role than most people realised,
since he was always content to live in Hitler's shadow. He was the perfect
back-room-boy, controlling the party's organisation, happily dealing with
all the details that Hitler with his Austrian *Schlamperei* found irksome
or was incapable of handling. At the same time, however, he revelled in
the show, the uniforms, bands and parades that captured the emotions

of so many Gemans. Although he was not a natural orator, he was quite capable of delivering powerful, rabble-rousing speeches expressing ideas that were as much his own as they were his Führer's – though Göring said Hess 'sweated blood' whenever he had to speak in public.[5]

Hitler was allowed unlimited visitors in Landsberg – during the first three months of his sentence he received at least 500. One of the earliest, on 5 April, was Carin Göring, who brought news of her husband and a request for money: their bank accounts in Munich had been frozen and their property, including the famous Mercedes 16 motor car, seques-trated. The man who had been so generous in helping to finance Hitler was himself now in dire need of funds.

The preceding four months had been a time of continuous trauma for Göring. In the Innsbruck hospital, weak from loss of blood and exhausted by his escape from Germany, he had lain in a critical condi-tion for weeks as his wounds festered around fragments of metal and stone and dirt from a splintered bullet that had ricocheted off the paving. Carin wrote to her sister on 8 December 1923, agonising over the fact that she could do so little to help as he suffered 'in body and soul'. 'The wound is nothing but pus over the whole thigh,' she wrote. 'It hurts so much that he lies there and bites the pillow, and all I can hear are inarticulate groans . . . Today it is just a month since they shot at him, and though they are giving him morphine every day now it does nothing to diminish the pain.'[6]

Carin had left the hotel and moved into the hospital two weeks earlier to be with her husband full time. She had also needed treat ment herself for a broken toe after being attacked in the street – although the Nazis had many supporters in Austria they also had many enemies. Life in Austria was not easy for the Nazi exiles. The Austrian authorities tolerated their presence only as long as they kept quiet and did not involve themselves in political activities. They were watched constantly, and their mail was opened. Göring, whose face was plas-tered all over Munich on 'Wanted' posters, received a steady flow of letters from Hitler by couriers crossing the mountains secretly, and more news from other exiles such as Hanfstaengl and Bodenschatz, who were among a group that had settled in Salzburg. He was also visited regularly by Hitler's sister, Paula, and by Hitler's lawyer, who came to consult him over the defence case he was preparing. He claimed later that he had offered to return to Germany to stand trial alongside

Hitler as soon as he was fit enough to walk, but was told he could be more valuable at liberty.

Gradually the infections reduced and the wounds healed, but the pain remained. The morphine injections were increased to two a day, continuing long after he was discharged from hospital on Christmas Eve, and Göring became increasingly dependent on the drug. It was a miserable Christmas for both him and Carin. He was still in a very poor state, both physically and mentally, thin, pale and trembling, hobbling around on crutches, deeply depressed and hardly speaking. At about 8 p.m. on Christmas night, Carin could stand it no longer. Having got him off to sleep at last, she flung a coat round her shoulders and left the hotel to walk aimlessly through the empty streets, oblivious to the heavy snow falling around her, until the sounds of 'Silent Night' drifting from an open window at last restored her spirits.

Carin's excursion had been a mistake – she had been badly chilled and by morning she was once again running a high fever. Her condition, aggravated by stress, did not improve until early February. By then, Göring's wounds had finally healed, but he still needed a stick to walk with, was still suffering severe pain, and still relying heavily on morphine. His depression was deepened by the fact that one of the bullets in his groin had damaged his testicles and left him impotent. The doctors could not say how long it was likely to be before he recovered his manhood, or indeed if he ever would – something he found very hard to accept.

He also found it hard to accept being penniless, and sponged shamelessly off friends and fellow exiles to maintain an ostentatious lifestyle that offended many of them. Carin's mother sent food parcels from Stockholm. The hotel proprietor gave them a thirty per cent discount on everything, and when they could not even manage that was happy to let them stay for free. Their maid and gardener back in Munich managed to get clothes and some personal belongings out of their villa in Obermenzing, and to have these smuggled into Austria, but there was no money. Göring began to make a little by speaking at Austrian Nazi Party meetings in Innsbruck, Salzburg and Vienna, at which collections were taken for him, but this was nowhere near enough for his needs or his tastes.

It was ironic that the main task Hitler set Göring, in addition to acting as his representative in Austria, was to seek out wealthy Austrians, especially those with interests in Germany, and charm them into contributing money to help pay for his defence. Hitler was still impressed by Göring's hero status and easy social skills, and regarded these as his main asset for the party. When Carin visited him in Landsberg on 5 April, he gave her only a signed photograph of himself, staring into the future in his tightly-belted trenchcoat, bearing the inscription: 'To the respected wife of my SA commander, in memory of her visit to Landsberg Fortress.' But according to Carin, he did give her a fresh assignment for her husband: he was to go to Italy as his plenipotentiary, make contact with Mussolini, propose an alliance with the German Nazi Party, and persuade him to loan it 2 million lire.

Carin's story about Hitler sending Göring to Italy may have been genuine, but it equally may have been something she invented as a way of saving face. What is certain is that by April the Austrian authorities were growing weary of Göring's increasingly aggressive political activities and outspoken attacks on the German government, and were making it clear that it was time for him to leave. Fascist Italy was the only country that would have him, and that he could afford to move on to. He and Carin arrived in Venice at the end of the month and, true to form, booked in at the luxurious Britannia Hotel on the Grand Canal, where the German proprietor was another Nazi supporter prepared to let them stay on credit. For a while, Carin told her mother, they lived 'as if Hermann had inherited a million'.

The Görings spent ten months in Italy, divided between Venice and a small pension in Rome, while Göring tried to obtain an audience with Mussolini. The Italian dictator, however, rejected all his approaches – he wanted nothing to do with Hitler, whom he saw as a hopeless nobody going nowhere. It seems that Göring could not bring himself to admit to his wife that he had failed; instead, he gave her accounts of non-existent meetings, which she faithfully included in her letters home, and even reported to Hitler during the two visits she made back to Munich. The Bavarian government had now released their property, though they still refused to grant Göring an amnesty, and she was able to sell the car and the house to raise much-needed cash. There was no money forthcoming from the party, though: she was distressed to discover that Göring's name had first been put on the non-active list, and then expunged completely from the membership rolls in what can only have been an act of petty spite by Alfred Rosenberg, who had often been the butt of Göring's sarcastic jibes and now found himself in a position to take his revenge.

*　　*　　*

Hitler had appointed Rosenberg as caretaker leader shortly before his arrest, in a hastily-scribbled pencil note: 'Dear Rosenberg, from now on you will lead the movement.' It was a move that surprised everyone, not least Rosenberg himself, for the self-styled party philosopher was probably the least decisive, least charismatic of all the inner circle. He had taken part almost by accident in the march of 9 November, simply because he had turned up at the Bürgerbräukeller to see what was going on. As a prominent party member he had been drafted into the second rank of the column, and had narrowly escaped being shot. But he could not in any way be described as a man of action, which was one of the reasons why Göring and many others despised him.

Rosenberg had been born into a well-to-do bourgeois family in Reval (now Tallinn), the capital of Estonia, on 12 January 1893, coincidentally the same day as Göring. He had studied architecture in Moscow, but had fled to Germany during the Russian Revolution. After a brief stay in Berlin he had gravitated to Munich, where he found his spiritual home in the pseudo-intellectual vagaries of the Thule Society, and employment as a researcher for several anti-Semitic publishers, including Dietrich Eckart, who introduced him to the DAP, which he joined before the arrival of Hitler. His claim to pure German ancestry was always dubious, his mother was recorded as Latvian, and indeed some of his many enemies accused him of having Jewish blood – the standard form of attack for any rival within the party – which they claimed was the secret shame that was the root of his virulent anti-Semitism.

Rosenberg was a sallow, unappealing man, whose physical appearance was as slipshod as his thinking. Dr Douglas M. Kelley, the American psychiatrist who examined him in Nuremberg in 1945, concluded that he was 'a relatively dull and a frightfully confused man. A large part of this confusion lay in the fact that he was unaware that he could not think straight, and he was further befuddled by the fact that he never realised his intellectual limitations.'[7] He was cold, arrogant, and boring beyond belief. But he had been a student of architecture, which commended him to Hitler, and could quote the literary classics and spout abstruse, half-baked ideas with total confidence, which led Hitler to revere him as an intellectual and a scholar. It was Rosenberg who brought from the Baltic the notorious fake 'Protocols of the Elders of Zion', detailing supposed Jewish plans for world domination and supposed atrocities committed by Jews against innocent Christians, all of which Hitler accepted unquestioningly.

Hitler was also impressed by Rosenberg's first-hand accounts of the horrors of the Bolshevik Revolution, and his belief that it had been caused by the same world conspiracy of international Jewry that had been responsible both for the start of the world war and for Germany's betrayal at its end. With Hitler so utterly in thrall to Rosenberg's thinking, it is hardly surprising that he should have appointed him editor of the *Völkischer Beobachter* in succession to Eckart, who was drinking himself to death. Making him acting leader of the party, however, was something else. It would have been hard to think of a less likely candidate, which was presumably Hitler's main reason for choosing him: Rosenberg presented no threat to his own position.

The universal doubts about Rosenberg's leadership were soon justified. He proved incapable of controlling the awkward personalities of Esser, Streicher and Amman, whom Hitler had nominated to support him, and still less the various factions into which the banned party was now splintering. Hitler did nothing to help sort out the mess. It suited him perfectly – while his subordinates and possible rivals were fighting among themselves, none of them could challenge his position, a tactic that he was to employ with great success for the rest of his life. Out of the confusion, however, a completely unexpected figure emerged who soon proved to be a genuine threat to Hitler's supremacy. He was Gregor Strasser, commander of the SA in Lower Bavaria.

Strasser was a large, bear-like man, with a balding, shaven head and powerful voice. He was primarily a man of action, who could brawl with the toughest and was quite ruthless in dealing with opponents and undesirables in his own party. But he was also capable of great warmth, humour and sensitivity, was cultured and well-read, mixed as easily with artists and writers as with politicians and paramilitaries, and enjoyed Homer and other classic authors. A close associate described him as an *Urbayer*, a genuine Bavarian,[8] and Kurt Ludecke wrote after first meeting him in 1924:

He seemed most genuine and of almost touching simplicity and modesty . . . He was an odd sight, this big man in his home-made breeches, black woollen stockings, and heavy shoes, with a little Tyrolean hat perched like a plate atop his head, completely out of harmony with his broad and massive features. But at the same time he impressed me with his calm strength, his pithy humour and robust health, suggesting at once something oaken and powerful.[9]

Strasser was born in the small Upper Bavarian town of Geisenfeld in 1892, the eldest of four sons and one daughter of a staunchly Catholic minor civil servant. The family was politically aware – his father wrote articles, necessarily under a pseudonym since he was a civil servant, calling for greater social justice for workers and condemning hereditary monarchy and capitalism. Gregor wanted to become a doctor, but his father could not afford the long training, so he became a pharmacist instead, starting with a three-year apprenticeship and then going on to Munich University. His studies were interrupted in 1914, when he volunteered for service in the First Bavarian Foot Artillery, seeing action in many important battles on the Western Front over the next four years. He was promoted from the ranks to lieutenant in the reserves in 1916, was severely wounded and won several decorations, including the Iron Cross First and Second Class.

He welcomed the fall of the old order in 1918, but regarded the new Republic as not a proper revolution but merely a revolt 'born out of cowardice, depravity, incompetence and treason', which 'betrayed, consciously betrayed, the national interests of the German people . . . [and which] must be thoroughly rooted out by a German revolution . . .'[10] His attitude to it was epitomised by an incident that occurred when he led his men back to the regiment's home town, Landshut, in December 1918. Entering the town, he was confronted by a representative of the local Soldiers' Council, who treated him to a long rant 'about the International, the victorious proletariat, the bloodthirsty generals and warmongers, the sweat-squeezing capitalists and stockbrokers'. Strasser sat on his horse, steadily edging the man backwards, saying nothing but collecting a whole mouthful of spit, until he finished with a cry of 'Give up your weapons! Tear down your flags and cockades! Vote for the Soldiers' Council!' Then, Strasser recalled, 'I let him have the whole mouthful of spit in the middle of his face. I flooded the rascal away. And then I gave the order, "Battery . . . trot!" And we marched back into Landshut the same way we had marched out in 1914.'[11]

Strasser resumed his pharmaceutical studies at Erlangen University, breaking off to join Epp's Freikorps as a company commander to take part in smashing the Räterepublik in Munich before returning to pass his finals with distinction in the spring of 1919 and find work as an assistant in a pharmacy. His younger brother, Otto, who had also served valiantly at the front during the war, interrupted his studies, too, to fight with Epp's Freikorps as a company commander, before continuing at the universities of Berlin, Munich and Würzburg, emerging in 1921 with a doctorate in national economic studies. The two brothers remained close, and were often regarded almost as a double act, but Otto was always the more intellectual of the two, with a more independent, questioning mind and leaning more to the left.

Gregor, meanwhile, had apparently begun to settle down as a respectable middle-class family man – his wife gave birth to twin sons in December 1920, and the following month he started his own pharmacy in Landshut. However, he had also become actively involved in paramilitary politics, leading the Landshut branch of a veterans' organisation formed by Erhardt, then moving into the Einwohnerwehr until that was dissolved. He joined the Nazi Party and the SA in the autumn of 1922, was soon commanding the Landshut SA company, and by March 1923 found himself in command of the SA in the whole of Lower Bavaria.

On 9 November Strasser answered the call to bring his unit to Munich, but did not take part in the march, being detailed to mount guard on the Wittelsbacher Bridge over the River Isar instead. He knew nothing of the events outside the Feldherrnhalle until late afternoon, when Ehrhardt arrived and told him to stand his men down. Prevented by the police from rallying to Hitler's aid, they marched back to the central rail station in good order, singing patriotic songs, and caught the evening train home. Back in Landshut, Strasser formed up his men outside the town hall, called for three rousing cheers for Führer and Fatherland before dismissing them, then hurried home, packed a bag and slipped away to stay with friends in north Germany.

At the turn of the year, preparations began for state Landtag elections between February and April, and the national Reichstag in May. Since the Nazi Party was banned, it could not take part officially, even if Hitler had wanted to, but the various *völkisch* groups held a meeting in Salzburg – where exiled Nazis could join in – at which Strasser proposed that they should sink their differences and unite against their common enemy, the Communists. At that time, Hitler still saw taking part in the parliamentary process as collaboration with the system he wanted to destroy, and therefore unacceptable. Strasser, more pragmatically, believed the best chance of destroying the hated Republic was from within. Defying Hitler, he took the lead in arranging an alliance between National Socialists and the Berlin-based DVFP, the

German People's Freedom Party, which had not been affected by the ban, to fight the elections as the Völkischer-Sozialer-Block, the V-S-B.

Although he had been interrogated by police about his part in the *putsch*, Strasser had not been charged with any offence connected with it. In mid February 1924, however, he was arrested for trying to recruit new members for the Nazi Party, one of whom turned out to be an undercover police officer, and was subsequently tried on a charge of aiding and abetting high treason. He was sentenced to fifteen months, joined Hitler in Landsberg, but was released almost immediately when he was elected as member for Lower Bavaria in the Landtag, where his twenty-two V-S-B colleagues chose him as their leader.

Riding high on publicity from the Hitler trial, the V-S-B had won by far the biggest vote in Munich, and seventeen per cent of the total vote in the rest of Bavaria, making it the second largest party in the Landtag. In the national elections a month later, the combined National Socialist-*völkisch* list received nearly 2 million votes, six per cent of the overall total – though in Franconia and the DVFP's stronghold in Mecklenburg the figure was more than twenty per cent – entitling it to thirty-two seats in the Reichstag. Among those elected were Röhm, Ludendorff, Feder and Frick.

On 7 July 1924, Hitler startled his followers by announcing his resignation as leader of the Nazi Party and his withdrawal from politics in general. The reasons he gave were 'general overwork', the fact that he found it impossible to accept responsibility for what was going on outside while he was in prison, and his need to concentrate on writing his book. The truth was that he wanted to distance himself from disagreeable developments in the *völkisch* movement, make a clean break with the past in order to start completely afresh in re-forming the party, and above all to ensure that nothing compromised his release on parole, which was due in October.

Immediately after Hitler had stepped down, Ludendorff and Albrecht von Graefe, head of the DVFP, formed a new party from the existing alliance, with themselves as joint leaders, 'until the liberated hero of Munich can again step into their circle as the third leader'. Logically, Rosenberg should have joined them as Hitler's stand-in, representing the Nazis and south Germany, but he had finally been forced to quit by Streicher and Esser. In his place, Ludendorff and Graefe invited Strasser to join them at the head of what was eventually named the Nationalsozialistische Freiheitsbewegung (the National Socialist Freedom Movement) or NSFB. Many Nazis in both north and south refused to accept Strasser's authority, which had not been confirmed by Hitler though he had at first agreed, resenting him as a usurper. Their hostility and distrust never really disappeared, festering, sometimes openly, at other times beneath the surface, over the next ten years. Nevertheless, for the moment at least, Strasser was very much in the ascendant.

It had been an amazing period for Strasser: eight months earlier he had been a small-time pharmacist running a chemist's shop in Landshut and commanding the local SA unit in his spare time. Since then, he had taken part in an abortive revolution, been on the run in north Germany, arranged an alliance with the DVFP, organised local and national elections, been arrested, imprisoned and released, been elected to the Bavarian Landtag, and finally found himself in partnership with the great hero Ludendorff as a national political leader. His workload was becoming impossible, so he decided he needed a secretary. He did not have to look very far – there was a suitable candidate in Landshut, a young man aged twenty-three who was unemployed, available, and a believer. His name was Heinrich Himmler.

Himmler had suffered the ignominy of simply being disarmed and told to go home after the failed *putsch* on 9 November. The putative siege of the Bavarian War Ministry had been the high point of his entire life until then: he even received 'fan mail' a few weeks later from a girl who knew his family, Mariele Rauschmayer, headed 'This letter is for my friend Heinrich. Let it be a small indication of our fervent gratitude and faithful memory of that deed which gave us a few moments when we learned to hope once more.' She enclosed a note scribbled in the excitement of the day itself:

Troops of the Reichskriegsflagge in front of the War Ministry, Heinrich Himmler at their head carrying the flag; one could see how secure the flag felt in his hands and how proud of it he was. I go up to him, incapable of speaking a word, but ringing in my ears is:

> Be proud I carry the flag.
> Have no cares, I carry the flag
> Love me, I carry the flag.[12]

No doubt Himmler took some comfort from this. He certainly needed any scrap he could get, from any quarter; he could hardly expect any from his family, having left home after quarrelling violently with his father. Turning to his substitute father, he visited Röhm in Stadelheim prison, taking him small presents: a copy of the *Grossdeutsche Zeitung* – a thinly disguised replacement for the banned *Völkischer Beobachter* under a different masthead – and some oranges. He was pleased to discover that: 'He still has his good sense of humour and is always the good Captain Röhm.'

Himmler's world had collapsed around him. He had no job and little chance of finding one. Along with the Nazi Party, the SA, and the entire Kampfbund, Kompanie Werner, on which he had pinned his last hopes of a military career, had also been dissolved. At the same time, his Catholic faith was fading fast – by summer he would have broken with the Church for ever, replacing the mysteries of the mass with the secrets and subterfuge of the revolutionary underground, into which he plunged with equally religious fervour. He still had the motorcycle he had bought during his first year of practical farm work as a student, so he could ride around the countryside as well as the city, carrying secret messages and keeping his former Reichskriegsflagge colleagues in touch with each other and with their leaders. Soon, everybody in the movement knew Heinrich Himmler. And what was more, they knew they could trust him.

Himmler threw himself into the election campaigns during the spring of 1924 with his typical obsessive thoroughness, riding tirelessly around the more remote rural constituencies. He began speaking at meetings, pushing an increasingly anti-Jewish line and appealing particularly to the farming community, whipping up their fears and problems which he understood so well. In what little spare time he had, he read, again obsessively, like Hitler confining his reading to a narrow range of authors who reinforced his prejudices. Many of them coincided with Hitler's choices, especially the works of Houston Stewart Chamberlain, an Englishman who had settled in Germany and become the arch prophet of German racialism. Before he lost his Catholic faith, Himmler had found vindication for his anti-Semitism in Chamberlain's assertion that Jesus was not Jewish, but the illegitimate son of a Roman centurion.

The offer of a job working for Strasser came as a godsend to Himmler, who was broke, homeless and almost starving, for it meant he could continue his political activities and get paid for them. Even though Strasser could only afford 120 marks (about £6 or $30) a month, which was hardly even a living wage, he also provided a sparsely furnished room above his shop in Landshut. Himmler was content. And so was Strasser: according to his brother Otto, he described his 'new adjutant' in glowing terms:

A remarkable fellow. Comes from a strong Catholic family, but does not want to know anything about the Church. Looks like a half-starved shrew. But keen, I tell you, incredibly keen. He has a motorbike. He is under way the whole day – from one farm to another – from one village to the next. Since I've had him our weapons have really been put into shape. I tell you, he's a perfect arms-NCO. He visits all the secret depots.[13]

Strasser was now travelling all over Germany, making speeches and liaising with other *völkisch* groups, particularly in the north. Consequently, Himmler found himself taking ever greater responsibility for day-to-day affairs in Lower Bavaria, gaining valuable experience of organisation and administration.

By the autumn, he was back on the hustings. The national elections in May had failed to produce a decisive result and the unstable Reichstag was dissolved on 24 October, with new elections called for 7 December. Himmler and his trusty motorbike swung back into action again, evangelising in the villages and hamlets where he preached the gospel of anti-Semitism and anti-capitalism, calling on the people to renounce the Jewish 'spirit of money' and exploitation of the workers in favour of a romanticised spirit of Germanic community. He followed the same line as Strasser, seeking an idealised form of Socialism that was national in character, quite different from the international, Jewish-Bolshevik version.

The elections in December 1924 were a disaster for the *völkisch* movement. The conditions that had boosted their vote in the spring, including the effects of the massive free publicity of the Hitler trial, had waned. The brilliant financial expert Hjalmar Schacht had succeeded in halting inflation by issuing a new mark based on gold, and on 16 August the French had accepted the American Dawes Plan for reparations payment and agreed to withdraw their troops from the Ruhr. Given the prospect of at least a measure of political stability and economic recovery, the German people turned away from the extremists at the polls. The *völkisch* vote dropped by fifty per cent to less than one million, cutting the allocation of seats from thirty-two to fourteen.

Strasser finished third on the NSFB list, after Ludendorff and Graefe, and was given one of the seats, representing Westphalia North. He could have continued to sit in the Bavarian Landtag, but wisely decided to step down in order to concentrate on his role in the Reichstag, which offered many advantages such as legal immunity, a comfortable salary and free first-class rail travel. He took full advantage of the travel concession, moving busily around north Germany building up contacts and support. Back in Landshut, Himmler was increasingly left alone to mind the store.

Hitler's parole had been delayed by various objections from the State Prosecutor's office, including, ironically, his suspected involvement in Röhm's Frontbann, which now had a membership of about 30,000, stretching from Austria to East Prussia. In October, Röhm had written to Ludendorff stating that the military wing of the movement was independent of the political wing and demanding its representation in the Reichstag. The NSFB leadership's response was to drop Röhm from its list for the December elections, publicly disowning him and pushing him further into the wilderness. With the elections over and his party in decline and disintegration, the authorities no longer saw Hitler as a threat. He walked free at 12.15 p.m. on 20 December 1924.

Now convinced beyond all doubt that he was the German Messiah, Hitler prepared to rebuild his fragmented party from scratch around the notion that he and the Nazi Party were one and indivisible. His first task was to have the ban on the party and its newspaper lifted. Early in the new year, in a series of meetings arranged with the help of his old ally Ernst Pöhner, he assured Bavarian Minister-President Held of his good intentions, promising to respect the authority of the state and to join it in its fight against Communism. He distanced himself from Ludendorff and his anti-Catholic ranting, which most Bavarians found offensive. And he gave his word that he would not take part in another *putsch* – an easy promise to make since the events of November 1923 had convinced him that the only sure way to power was through the ballot box not the gun. It worked – at least in part. The bans were lifted on 16 February 1925, but three weeks later, after delivering a provocative address to 4,000 supporters at his first revival meeting, held appropriately in the Bürgerbräukeller, Hitler was banned from speaking in public, a restriction that would last for three years.

On the same day that Hitler was gagged, Friedrich Ebert, who had been President since the Republic was founded, died suddenly, which meant yet another election. The Nazis were too insignificant to put up a candidate of their own, but they supported the nationalists' nominee, Ludendorff, who polled a humiliating 211,000 out of nearly 27 million, in the first round of voting. Ludendorff was dropped from the second ballot and replaced by his old chief, the seventy-eight-year-old Hindenburg, who scraped home for a seven-year term, largely due to the Communists splitting the Republican vote by insisting on fielding their own hopeless candidate rather than supporting the Socialist. It was the end of Hitler's bumpy relationship with Ludendorff.

On 17 February Hitler had a private meeting with Strasser, who had resigned from the leadership of the NSFB, which had been dissolved five days earlier. Strasser now agreed to join the new NSDAP, and was formally enrolled on 25 February as member number 9, pledging his support in reconstructing the party, but emphasising that he was joining Hitler as a colleague, not a follower. Such an implicit declaration of rivalry for the leadership was anathema to Hitler, but he needed Strasser, who had become a popular and respected figure in the movement as a whole.

Together, the two men worked out a deal, dividing the country between them. Strasser would work out of Berlin with a free hand to revive and reorganise the party in the north, capitalising on the contacts he had already made and on his position as a member of the Reichstag. Hitler, meanwhile, would concentrate on his own power base in Munich and the south. It was an arrangement that suited them both: Hitler hated Berlin and the Berliners, while Strasser enjoyed the capital's cosmopolitan atmosphere. The party's supporters in the industrialised north were mostly blue-collar Protestants, more tuned to Strasser's emphasis on the Socialist aspect of National Socialism; supporters in the south, however, tended to be bourgeois and petty-bourgeois Catholics, with more interest in Hitler's nationalist-racist policies. And for Hitler, the set-up had one great advantage – it kept Strasser away from Munich and the real centre of the party.

Although Strasser was now based in Berlin, he was appointed Gauleiter of Lower Bavaria. Hitler had divided the country into twenty-three districts – the number was later increased to thirty-two – roughly equating to the national electoral districts, to which he gave the old German name of Gau; each one was headed by a Gauleiter (Gau leader) who was in charge of all party affairs and answerable directly to him. Lower Bavaria had always been the party's heartland, and was therefore one of the most important – Ludecke described it as 'really the kernel of the new Hitler party, the nucleus of the second epoch of the Hitler movement'.[14] Strasser would inevitably be an absentee landlord for most of the time, but was too popular locally to be replaced. To provide cover, Himmler was made Deputy Gauleiter, his first official position in the party. With Strasser away most of the time, he was the *de facto* party chief in Lower Bavaria.

Himmler's new post was his springboard to prominence in the new Nazi Party. His Gau was close enough to Munich for him to have regular personal contact with party headquarters, so that those in positions of power and influence got to know him as a committed and diligent official. And through Strasser he built valuable contacts with leading Nazis in northern and central Germany. At the age of twenty-four, he was poised for rapid advancement within the party, even though that party had been reduced to little more than a splinter group on the edge of right-wing politics.

While Himmler was beavering his way happily forward, Göring seemed to have reached a dead end. After more than a year in Italy, he had still failed to reach Mussolini and his financial plight was desperate, exacerbated no doubt by his constant need of morphine. In the spring of 1925, they begged the money from Carin's mother to return to Sweden via Austria, Czechoslovakia, Poland and Danzig, and took a small flat in Stockholm.

It was a sad homecoming. Both Göring and Carin were in poor health. She had been ill in Italy, but her condition now deteriorated dramatically: her weak lungs became tubercular, her heart condition worsened, her blood pressure was low, and she developed what seemed to be epilepsy, suffering attacks of 'a sort of *petit-mal*', with sudden black-outs. She was advised to spend even more time resting in bed. He was still showing the effects of post-traumatic stress, had put on a great deal of weight, and was a morphine addict. He found a job as a pilot with a new airline operating between Stockholm and Danzig, but only managed to hold it for a few weeks. He and Carin had to pawn furniture to pay for her treatment and his drugs.

Göring's addiction made him dangerously unstable and prone to sudden violence. Fearful for their daughter's safety, Carin's family paid for him to enter Aspuddin Hospital for treatment. He went willingly, eager to kick the habit and regain his health and figure. But the treatment was brutal, little more than 'cold turkey', and after ten days he cracked, smashed open the locked drugs cabinet, attacked his nurses and threatened to kill himself. He was overpowered with the help of police and firemen, put in a straitjacket, and committed to Långbro Mental Asylum, where he suffered weeks of torture, complete with hallucinations and suicide attempts, before being declared clean on 7 October.

The medical reports during his treatment include such interesting comments as 'hysterical tendencies, egocentric, inflated self-esteem; hater of the Jews, has devoted his life to the struggle against the Jews, was Hitler's right-hand man . . .' He was also described as a weak character, a sentimental person, lacking in fundamental moral courage, but 'since he had been a German officer, he found it easy to obey'. Anxious that no one should suspect him of insanity because he had been a patient in an asylum, he was discharged with a certificate stating that he had not been suffering from mental illness.[15] He returned to Långbro the following May for a further detoxification cure for the use of Eukodal, a synthetic narcotic pain-killer based on codeine, and at the beginning of June 1926 was certified 'completely cured' from its use 'and free from the use of all types of opium derivatives'.[16]

Göring may or may not have been 'completely cured', as he and his doctors claimed – for the rest of his life there were conflicting reports on his drug habits. However, when he gave himself up to the Americans at the end of the war he had only paracodeine tablets with him, and he was painlessly weaned away from these within a few days. There was no evidence of morphine addiction, which would have involved a much more difficult withdrawal process. Cured or not, however, there was no way he could return to Germany in 1926 without facing arrest. He chose to stay in Stockholm, making a living of sorts as a salesman for BMW aero engines in Scandinavia. BMW had been taken over by an Italian Jew named Castiglioni, but Göring apparently did not mind this. A job was a job, and he had nowhere else to go.

VI

A STAR IN THE MAKING

THROUGHOUT 1925, Strasser took full advantage of his free travel concession as a member of the Reichstag – so much so, indeed, that he was reprimanded by the Reich President's office and fined 800 marks for spending too much time away from the chamber. Having delegated the general business of his own Gau to Himmler, he bustled around north and west Germany setting up new branches of the party, appointing Gauleiters and other officials, and booming out ninety-one public speeches, taking full advantage of another benefit of Reichstag membership – under parliamentary immunity he could say exactly what he liked, however scurrilous or inflammatory, without fear of arrest.

On 22 March 1925, Strasser called a meeting in the Hamburg industrial suburb of Harburg of all the potential leaders in north-west Germany. Most were former members of the Nazi Party, many of whom had followed him into the NSFB during the hiatus, so there was some existing framework on which to build in re-establishing the party in that broad region. But there was also a fair sprinkling of new blood, including a twenty-seven-year-old unemployed Rhinelander, Dr Joseph Goebbels, who had rushed to join the party immediately it was legalised again. On the recommendation of Karl Kaufmann, a bright young associate of Strasser who had made his mark organising sabotage attacks in the occupied Ruhr, Goebbels was given the job of business manager in the central office of the Rhineland North Gau. It was a small beginning, but one which the fiercely ambitious young doctor of philosophy could rapidly turn into a launching pad for a career.

Paul Joseph Goebbels was born on 29 October 1897 in the small industrial town of Rheydt, near Mönchengladbach, about fifteen miles west of Düsseldorf and barely twenty-five miles from the Dutch border.

With two older brothers and two younger sisters, he was the middle of five children of a devout Catholic father, Fritz, who had worked his way up from errand boy to clerk in the W.H. Lennartz wick factory, saving enough through hard work and thrift to buy a small, terraced house, where Joseph grew up. Fritz, the son of a poor labourer, became the firm's bookkeeper during the First World War and works manager in the 1920s, completing the family's rise from working class to the petty bourgeoisie. His wife, Katharina, the daughter of a village blacksmith, had been born in Übach just over the border in Holland though she grew up in Rheindalen, where she work as a dairymaid until her marriage.

The Goebbels were a close family, though Fritz, a man of 'Prussian integrity', ruled his wife and children with 'Spartan discipline'.[1] This was more than offset by the 'inexplicable unspoiled artlessness' of Katharina, who loved her children and lavished kindness on them all, but especially on Joseph, her favourite. She had nearly lost her life giving birth to him, and he was always a weak, sickly child in need of special care. He almost died of pneumonia when he was very small, and at the age of four contracted the bone marrow disease osteomyelitis, which affected his right leg and foot. Years of painful treatment culminating in a complex operation at the age of ten failed to alleviate the condition, and he and his parents had to accept that he would be crippled for life with stunted growth, a short leg and a club foot.

To the intensely religious Katharina, little Joseph's disability was a punishment inflicted on the family by God. She regularly took him to church to pray that God would give him the strength to fight off this evil, while pretending to neighbours that it had been caused by an accident. Not unnaturally in these circumstances, Joseph himself regarded his deformity with shame. It set him apart from other children, prevented him from joining in sport or games and turned him into a loner. 'The thought that the others did not want him around for their games,' he wrote in his autobiographical novel *Michael*, 'that his solitude was not his own choice, made him truly lonely. And not only lonely – it also made him bitter. When he saw the others running, jumping and romping about, he railed at his God for . . . doing this to him; he hated the others for not being like him; he even ridiculed his mother for being happy to have such a cripple.'[2]

There was no doubt that Joseph was clever, even precocious, but he was wilful and lacked application until at the age of ten, when he went into hospital for the last-chance operation on his foot, he discovered reading. One of the other pupils in his class at school, 'rich Herbert Beines', sent him a book of fairy tales as a present – clearly not all his school fellows despised him, though he hated their pity as much as their scorn. Fairy tales, or folk tales, as collected by Professor Jakob Grimm and his brother Wilhelm, were an important part of the romantic German nationalist movement in the nineteenth century; they also tended to be about poor boys overcoming seemingly insurmountable obstacles to achieve success – something that must have rung bells for Joseph. 'These books awakened my joy in reading,' he wrote later. 'From then on I devoured everything in print, including newspapers, even politics, without understanding the slightest thing.'[3]

As he came to realise the power of knowledge, Joseph's hatred for the 'common herd' turned to contempt. He compensated for his physical shortcomings by assuming a mental superiority, determined that he should always know more than his companions 'for he fully expected the others to be cruel enough to exclude him intellectually as well'.[4] With his new-found thirst for learning, he rose to the top of his class, and gained entrance to the local *Gymnasium*, where his two elder brothers were already pupils. Keeping three boys at the *Gymnasium* was a financial struggle for a humble clerk, and to make ends meet the family had to take on home work making lamp wicks for Fritz's factory. Firmly committed to an ethic of thrift and self-improvement, Fritz and Katharina believed it was well worth such drudgery to ensure a better future for their children.

There was never any problem motivating Joseph to work hard at the *Gymnasium* – he was determined 'to triumph over the classmates who had laughed at him and mocked him'.[5] Soon he was top in just about every subject, taking great satisfaction when other boys came to him for help with their work. He discovered talents for art, music and above all acting, and learned to play the piano on a second-hand instrument bought at great personal sacrifice by his father. He excelled in history and German, started writing romantic poetry and so impressed his German teacher that the man gave him special attention and extra tuition, and obtained work for him tutoring younger boys to help pay his fees when he failed to get a municipal scholarship to cover his final years at school. He also discovered religion, seriously considering the priesthood as a career, though he was attracted as much by the theatricality of the role as by its spiritual aspects. His parents, naturally, encouraged this, hoping the church would fund him to go on to university to study theology.

Goebbels's years at the *Gymnasium* proved happier than he had expected. He still had the chip on his shoulder, but as he progressed through school he learned how to relate to other people and even made two or three close friends. His achievements, not only academically but also on the stage, helped him come to terms with his physical disability, but he could never forget it completely. When he started to become sexually aware, he fixed his attentions on two women who were unattainable – the mother of a school friend, and the girlfriend of his brother – presumably subconsciously courting reasons for rejection other than his deformity. He was far from discreet, and both adventures ended in trouble, which may well have been what he intended. It was certainly a portent of things to come.

When war broke out in 1914, he presented himself at the recruiting office, though he knew he would be declared unfit for army service. This time, there could be no hiding the reason for his rejection, but he still had a fall-back excuse in the fact that he was too young at only sixteen. Desperately wanting to belong, he volunteered for alternative service, and spent a few weeks in the Reichsbank before being sent back to school. There, he threw himself eagerly into any activities that could be seen as contributing to the war effort, even if it was only packing and mailing Christmas presents for local lads at the front, or keeping a diligent eye open for enemy spies. For the rest of the time, when he was not struggling to control his sexual desires for his first real girlfriend, the beautiful but dim Lene Krage, he poured his patriotic feelings into a stream of emotional poems and compositions.

He ended his time at the *Gymnasium* with excellent results in his *Abitur* exams, and won the prize for the best essay, which entitled him to give the farewell speech for his class. Although it was well constructed, this first attempt at public oratory was an overblown melange of religiosity and extreme patriotism, which gave few clues to the incredible skills he would develop later.

In April 1917, Goebbels left home to study classical philology, German literature and history at Bonn University. The attractions of the priesthood had faded, as had a brief flirtation with the idea of medicine, but when his money ran out he still managed to get a scholarship from a church fund administered by the Albertus Magnus Association in Cologne. His parish priest vouched that his parents were good Catholics, and strongly commended Goebbels himself 'for his religious and moral conduct' – presumably Goebbels had not confessed to enjoying illicit sex with Lene in the local park. The scholarship was in the form of a loan, totalling nearly 1,000 marks over three years, which he neglected to repay until 1930, after the association had sued him several times. Even then, he only stumped up 400 marks, and that in instalments.

His inferiority complex fed not only by his small size and club foot but also by his working-class origins, Goebbels had been apprehensive about fitting in at university, knowing that most of the other students would be from upper and middle-class families. Sensibly avoiding the more elite and snooty student fraternities, he joined a modest but convivial Catholic association, Unitas Sigfridia, where he soon made friends and seems to have become a popular member. Despite this, and his success with a number of girls, he found it hard to settle. In May 1918, just as the German army's spring offensive on the Western Front was grinding to a halt, he left Bonn to continue his studies at Freiburg on the edge of the Black Forest, following his best friend, Pille Kölsch, who had moved there at the start of the previous term.

In Freiburg, Pille introduced him to Anka Stalherm, an attractive young woman from a wealthy family who was studying law and economics. Goebbels was completely bowled over by this girl with the 'extraordinarily passionate mouth' and 'dark blonde hair in a heavy coil on her marvellous neck', and he set about wooing her. Unfortunately, Anka was Pille's girl, and Goebbels was already involved with Pille's sister, Agnes, but as always when sex was on the menu, he was undeterred by such trivialities. He dropped Agnes, fell out with Pille, and went on pursuing Anka until they became a couple.

Goebbels later said that the summer term of 1918, spent with Anka in Freiburg, was the happiest time of his life. But he remained bitterly conscious of the social gap between them, and between himself and most other students. 'I was a pariah,' he wrote, 'an outlaw, one who was merely tolerated, not because I achieved less or was less intelligent than the others, but simply because I lacked the money that flowed so generously to the others from their fathers' pockets.'[6]

In the summer vacation, back home in Rheydt, he wrote his first play, *Judas Iscariot*, portraying Judas as an outsider who betrayed Jesus not for silver but in the hope of being able himself to take on the task of establishing the Kingdom of God on earth, rather than in heaven as Jesus promised. Although Goebbels claimed that he did not want to break with his religion, his play was a clear sign that he was losing faith in a church that could not deliver social justice here and now.

For the autumn term, Goebbels and Anka moved to the University of Würzburg in northern Bavaria, and it was there that he experienced the end of the war and the revolution. His reactions were not much different from most of his contemporaries – anger, disbelief, despair even – but he tended to internalise his feelings, relating Germany's fate to his own and indulging in a great deal of adolescent soul-searching. He finally turned his back on the Catholic Church in December, refusing to attend church or confession and staying away from Midnight Mass on Christmas Eve for the first time in his life. He no longer believed the Church could provide salvation, but he had not yet found a political alternative – in the Reichstag elections in Würzburg he voted for the BVP simply because his family traditionally supported the Centre Party, the organised political party of German Catholicism, to which it was affiliated. It was not until he returned home in January 1919 to find Rheydt occupied by Belgian troops who imposed a harsh regime of curfews and censorship that he began thinking seriously about the political problems of Germany's future.

His first thought, as usual, was to write another play, *Heinrich Kämpfert*, partly inspired by the problems and hardships of the workers he talked to in Rheydt, and heavily influenced by *Crime and Punishment*. There was, again as always, a strong element of autobiography in it: the hero was a working-class young man in love with a rich aristocratic girl, and much of the supposed drama consisted of the conflict between their contrasting backgrounds. It was naïve and immature student work, but an important step in developing his skills as a writer.

His political education, meanwhile, was taken in hand by an old school friend, Richard Flisges, who had won an Iron Cross and been wounded in the arm in the war. Flisges, a farmer's son, was keen to study German literature and Goebbels persuaded him to join him in Freiburg, where he and Anka intended to return for the summer term. Before then, the two young men walked and talked and put the world to rights as young men will, and even considered moving to India to seek the truth through eastern mysticism, forty years ahead of the hippy movement of the sixties. Flisges introduced Goebbels to the works of Marx and Engels. He read them avidly, but it was still Dostoevsky who exerted the greatest influence on his thinking. His next literary effort, apart from a number of romantic poems, was a fictionalised autobiography, *Michael Voormanns Jugendjahre* (*Michael Voorman's Youth*), a dark and deeply introspective work to which he returned several times over the next few years. As self-obsessed as ever, he was still more concerned with visions of his own future than that of Germany.

For the autumn and winter terms, Goebbels and Anka changed universities yet again, this time moving to Munich, despite the fact that the city council had banned non-Bavarian students. The Räterepublik was long gone, but the city was still in a state of turmoil. It was the time when Hitler had just joined the DAP and Himmler was starting his studies at the Technical High School, but Goebbels did not come into contact with either of them. He had no interest in right-wing political parties: he was still obsessed with trying to sort out his own confusion, which he described as 'chaos within me'.[7] His sympathies, however, were very much with the left: his next dramatic work, written over the Christmas vacation when Anka was away in the mountains with a group of affluent friends and he was too broke to go along, was entitled *Fight of the Working Class*. Set in a factory, the play was essentially a hymn to the power of hatred, and showed the combined influence of Richard Flisges and Karl Marx – which may be the reason why he fell out with Anka at this time. The quarrel was soon made up, but they were clearly drifting apart as they went back to their respective homes for the spring vacation.

Weakened by lack of food, Goebbels was sick again, both physically and psychologically. His mother's loving care helped to heal him, as did the fact that for once one of his brothers, Hans, who had just returned from three years as a prisoner of war with the French, was in a worse condition than himself and needed his support. Hans had been treated badly, and was so bitter that the family feared he might attack the Belgian occupation troops and cause trouble for them all, something they were desperate to avoid in their purposeful pursuit of respectability.

Goebbels found an added distraction from his own *Angst* in news of the Kapp *putsch* in Berlin, followed by the general strike and the battles between the Reichswehr and a 50,000-strong 'Red Army' of workers in the Ruhr which left 1,000 workers dead. Meanwhile, from Munich came news of the successful *putsch* that put Kahr in power for the first time. Goebbels wrote to Anka questioning 'whether a rightist government is a good thing'.[8] He was enthusiastic, 'at a distance', for the Red revolutionaries in the Ruhr, and poured his hopes into yet another naïve drama glorifying the workers' struggle, which he called *The Seed*.

Goebbels's dreams were Anka's nightmares, threatening her family, her class and her comfortable existence. She hated *The Seed*, and said so. After the vacation, she decided not to move on to Heidelberg with him, as they had planned, but returned to Freiburg. Alone in Heidelberg, he was soon hearing reports that she was being pursued by a fellow student and by a prosperous lawyer. He proposed marriage, and when she ignored him threatened suicide, wrote out his will, and staged a 'nervous breakdown'. His melodramatic gestures had no effect – Anka remained true to her class and married her lawyer, though she did not live happily ever after and later claimed that Goebbels was the only man she had ever loved, or who had loved her as she wished. Goebbels carried a torch for her for years, though this never stopped him being an inveterate womaniser, chasing every attractive skirt he could lay his hands on, and more.

He tried to dull the pain of parting, first with drink and then with work, but he could not shake off the black dog, wallowing self-indulgently in his hopelessness. A typically lugubrious diary entry of the time reads: 'Pessimism. Despair. I no longer believe in anything.'⁹ He did, of course, believe in one thing: himself. And once he had begun to come to terms with the loss of Anka he set about proving himself to the rest of the world. Instead of an ordinary degree, he would go for a doctorate, which was guaranteed to earn respect everywhere. Interestingly, his first choice as supervisor was a Jew, Professor Friedrich Gundolf, whom he described as 'an extraordinarily charming and agreeable man'. Gundolf was not available, however, and referred him instead to Professor Max von Waldberg, another Jew, who took him on, assigning him as a subject the work of an obscure early nineteenth-century romantic dramatist, Wilhelm Schütz.

Shutting himself in his old room in his parents' house, Goebbels worked solidly throughout the summer, completing his 214-page dissertation in four months flat. It was well received, and on 18 November 1921 he sailed through the oral examination to emerge as a doctor of philosophy. From then on, he insisted on being addressed as 'Herr Doktor' at all times; he developed an ostentatious signature complete with his credentials, and even initialled documents 'Dr G'. No one would ever be allowed to forget his achievement. It was an achievement, however, that did nothing to provide him with a living, something to which until then he had not given much thought.

Goebbels's sole ambition, unsurprisingly, was to become a writer, but he had not considered how to turn the hope into a reality that would relieve his proud but long-suffering parents from the burden of feeding and housing him. For weeks, he sat in his attic room, churning out poetry, essays and articles that no one wanted to read, until eventually an acquaintance helped him to place a series of six articles with the Cologne newspaper *Westdeutsche Landeszeitung*. During his low time following the break-up with Anka, he had been deeply impressed by Oswald Spengler's doom-laden book, *The Decline of the West*, which made the prognosis that the German Republic was in a state of terminal decay, which would lead inevitably to a dictatorship by a Caesar-like figure. Since then, however, Goebbels had moved on, and the articles were an attempt to refute Spengler's pessimism and offer hope for the future.

True to his unworldly views, Goebbels identified materialism as the cause of 'the political, intellectual and moral confusion of our time' and declared that it must be rejected and replaced with more spiritual values: 'Love of the fatherland,' he claimed, 'is worship of God.' He invoked the reawakening of the mystical 'German soul' as the key to recovery and called on Germans to reject 'everything foreign to our being' and look for salvation within their own selves and their own nation. For the first time, he had begun thinking and writing in *völkisch* terms, marking the start of a new phase in his beliefs, a turning away from Marxism into a new direction. He was still not entirely sure where that direction lay, but gave a clue in one of his articles: 'Sometimes,' he wrote, looking hopefully towards Munich, 'it seems as though a new sun is about to rise in the south.'

The articles led to a part-time job as a trainee on the cultural section of the *Westdeutsche Landeszeitung*, but this only lasted a few weeks. He subsisted on a bit of tutoring, and earned a few marks with a lecture at the School for Business and Trades on Spengler and German literature, but these provided meagre pickings. As the end of the year approached, he was becoming desperate. His new regular girlfriend, Else Janke, an elementary school teacher, came to the rescue by persuading a distant relative to find him a job. Goebbels was far from enthusiastic: the job was with the Dresdner Bank in Cologne, a 'temple of materialism' that was incompatible with his high ideals. But Else and his parents combined to pressure him into taking it, and on 2 January 1923 he took the 5.30 a.m. train from Rheydt to Cologne to start work.

Goebbels's time at the bank was not a happy one. Everyone thought he was lucky – banking was the most secure white-collar employment in Germany – but his pay barely covered the rent of the small room where he stayed during the week. He had little left over for food or other expenses – though he somehow managed to afford tickets for the opera, which had become a passion – so he was still dependent on hand-outs from his father, and from Else, whom he saw every weekend and as often during the week as she could get time off to spend the night with him in Cologne. He stuck with the job for several months, but his contempt for the capitalist system and all it stood for grew deeper every day as he was brought face to face with the realities of the financial world, particularly on the trading floor of the stock exchange, where he spent much of his time.

He had only been at work for a week when the reparations crisis erupted and French and Belgian troops marched into the Ruhr. Witnessing the hyperinflation that followed he was shocked at the way it wiped out the life savings of little people while wiping out the debts of rich landowners and industrialists, and allowed speculators to make fortunes out of other people's misfortunes. He was also shocked at the way his fellow bank employees shamelessly used their positions and inside knowledge to enrich themselves. 'This afternoon I told one of the young louts that I considered his actions a revolting swindle,' he told Else in a letter. 'He responded with nothing but a pitying shrug. And not one person among those who heard us spoke up for me.'[10]

Goebbels was filled with rage at reports that 'about a hundred children a month' were dying from starvation in Cologne, while the government debated the fine points of passive resistance and whether the Ruhr should be evacuated in stages. And any lingering respect for the Catholic Church was finally extinguished by the calculation that Cologne Cathedral's holdings, valued at 12 million gold marks, would be enough 'to send 560,000 starving children to the country or to a sanatorium for two months, thereby saving them for productive lives'.[11] His disgust at 'the hectic dance around the Golden Calf' was complete. 'You talk about capital investment,' he wrote in his diary, 'but behind these fine words lurks nothing but an animal greed for more. I say animal, but that is an insult to animals, for an animal eats only until it has had its fill.'[12]

By July, he could stand it no more and reported sick – though he had difficulty finding a doctor who would give him a certificate. He had threatened suicide shortly before, but once away from the bank on six weeks' sick leave, he recovered so quickly that he was able to go away with Else to Baltrum island in the Baltic, where they had first become lovers the year before. He wrote in his diary of 'golden days of peace', and of 'sweet afternoons in her room or in the dunes'.[13] The holiday, however, was interrupted by sad news: Goebbels's friend Richard Flisges, who had turned his back on university to seek truth in manual labour, had been killed in a mining accident. Goebbels was distraught, confiding to his diary that nothing made sense any more, and that he was 'alone in the world' – which says a great deal about his relationship with the ever-supportive Else.

As a memorial to the man who had been not only his friend but also his guide, Goebbels returned to his autobiographical novel, reworking it so that the hero became a composite of himself and Flisges, and changing its title to *Michael: Ein deutsches Schicksal in Tagebuchblättern* (*Michael: A German Fate in the Pages of a Diary*). The result was an inglorious hotchpotch of ideas from all his reading, expressed in purple prose and high-flown rhetoric, but from it emerged a new phase in his development. He still ranted and raged against the injustice of a cruel world, but he now looked for a human saviour to replace the Christian God he had rejected. Significantly, he had his hero conclude that belief is everything: 'What matters is not so much what we believe; only that we believe.'[14] Belief itself became his religion.

When he returned from Baltrum, Goebbels received another blow: a letter of dismissal from the bank, which drove him deeper into despondency, fuelling his need for something to cling to and reinforcing his bitter hatred of capitalism and all it stood for. He should not have been surprised – the supposedly secure world of banking shed 150,000 jobs in 1923[15] and his attitude can hardly have commended him to his bosses as someone to keep – but his sacking still seems to have come as a shock. He kept it secret from his parents, staying in Cologne during the week as though he were still working. But all the work he did was on his book and yet another self-searching drama, *The Wanderer*. He did not even bother to look seriously for a new job, though since he was not entitled to unemployment benefit, he was soon close to starvation. Else, 'good and willing like a child', gave him ten gold marks, but that would not last long, despite his reckoning that he could live for a week on one gold mark. Still he refused to admit the truth to his parents. Finally, at the beginning of October, he told them he was suffering from a nervous disorder, 'probably hereditary in origin', and his father, though indignantly refuting the idea of an inherited defect, sent him the money for a train ticket home.

*   *   *

Goebbels watched the mounting political chaos of the autumn of 1923 from the safety of his parents' house, convinced that he was witnessing 'the downfall of the Germanic ideal'. He wrote of indulging in 'wild days spent drinking, out of sheer despair',[16] presumably at his father's or Else's expense – he noted in his diary that one gold mark would buy fifty glasses of beer. The events in Munich on 8–9 November, however, made little immediate impact on him. He was more concerned with trying to find a new job and a new career in journalism or publishing, despite having every article he wrote rejected. He applied to the Berlin newspapers *Vossische Zeitung* and the liberal *Berliner Tageblatt* for an editorial position, and answered an advertisement by the Mosse publishing house for an editor. They all turned him down.

Bitter, angry and alienated, he poured out his spleen in his diary on the 'degenerate world' and the philistines who surrounded him in Rheydt, who were incapable of any intellectual conversation. He regarded them all with disdain, assuring himself that he was infinitely superior, refusing to surrender his independence of mind and descend to their level. Seeking an excuse for being rejected by the Berlin publishers, he blamed the fact that they were Jews, as were the bankers who had fired him. For some time, the entries in his diary had shown an increasing preoccupation with the Jews – the bald words '*das Judentum*' ('Jewry'), occur with depressing regularity whenever he refers to political discussions – and the more he dwelt on the thought, the more convinced he became that this was the answer. At last, he had found a focus for the hate that burned inside him like acid.

In the past, Goebbels had never been particularly anti-Semitic. Indeed, he had once told Anka Stalherm: 'You know, I don't really like this extreme anti-Semitism . . . I wouldn't describe the Jews as my best friends, but I don't think we'll get rid of them with insults or polemical attacks or even pogroms, and even if we could, it would be ignoble and unworthy of decent human beings.'[17] His family had no strong prejudices: they were proud to count a local Jewish lawyer, Dr Josef Joseph, as a friend, and Goebbels had spent many enjoyable hours as a schoolboy and as a student discussing literature and life with him. He had been happy to work under Jewish professors, and to top it all, Else Janke had a Jewish mother. It was Spengler's *Decline of the West* that first planted the seeds of racialism in his mind, his experiences with the bank in Cologne and the publishers in Berlin that fed and watered them, and another book, Houston Stewart Chamberlain's *Foundations of the Nineteenth Century*, that brought out their twisted flowers.

Goebbels had found a new Bible, and a new prophet to guide him on his quest for a new belief. When Chamberlain presented the so-called Aryan master race as 'the soul of culture' and the Jewish as the embodiment of all the evils of materialism, he could have been speaking directly to Goebbels, in his own language. Goebbels began to see evidence everywhere that the Jews were responsible for all the evils in the world, stemming from those two great pillars of materialism, communism and capitalism, both of which he saw as part of the international Jewish conspiracy for world domination.

Having found his new belief, Goebbels now needed to find his new Christ – or his Judas Iscariot as portrayed in his first play – to bring justice on earth. He did so between February and the end of March 1924, in the news reports from the improvised courtroom in Munich's former Infantry Officers' School. Day after day he avidly followed the progress of Hitler's trial, devouring the accounts of his evidence, swallowing his political assertions and relating to his creed. Hitler, he told the great man two years later, had spoken 'after my own heart', expressing

more than your own pain and your own struggle. You gave a name to the suffering of an entire generation who were yearning for real men, for meaningful tasks . . . The words you spoke there are the catechism of a new political faith amid the despair of a collapsing, godless world. You did not remain silent. God gave you the voice to express our suffering. You put our torment into words of redemption, formed statements of trust in the miracle to come.[18]

Eager to learn more about his new faith, Goebbels turned to another of his former school fellows in Rheydt, Fritz Prang, son of a local businessman, who had been a member of the Nazi Party before it was banned. Prang began taking him to meetings of the DVFP in Elberfeld, a district of Wuppertal south of the Ruhr. Goebbels was not impressed by what he saw. 'So these are the leaders of the *völkisch* movement in the occupied territory,' he wrote in his diary. 'You Jews and Frenchmen and Belgians have nothing to fear from these fellows. I have seldom attended a meeting at which so much drivel was uttered.'[19] And yet he managed to bite his tongue and refrain from treating the meeting to his usual cutting criticism.

One reason for his uncharacteristic reticence was that he saw an opportunity to shine in the future among such low-calibre leadership.

Another was that the local party leader, Friedrich Wiederhaus, whom Goebbels described as 'Wilhelminian, pot-bellied, with twisted moustaches, friendly, a good fellow, but not a man to impress the youth'.[20] Wiederhaus published a weekly paper, *Völkische Freiheit*, 'The Organ of the National Socialist Freedom Movement for an Ethnically Pure, Socially Just Greater Germany'. The paper had only four pages, but he had difficulty finding enough material to fill it every week. Goebbels leaped at the chance, and left the meeting with a commission for five articles. Before long, he was writing most of the paper, under a variety of pseudonyms, and by the beginning of October he was its managing editor, supervising its make-up, layout, production and distribution, invaluable experience that would serve him well in the future.

In August 1924, Prang took Goebbels to the grand meeting of all the *völkisch* groups and parties at which they cemented their alliance as the NSFB, the National Socialist Freedom Movement, and appointed a national leadership, following Hitler's announcement that he was withdrawing from politics. It was held in the National Theatre at Weimar – ironically the exact birthplace of the Republic and the constitution that they all abhorred. But it was also the home of Goethe, which for Goebbels far outweighed any subsequent aberrations. He was thrilled to be there alongside no less a personality than the great Ludendorff – this was, of course, some time before Ludendorff's credibility was destroyed by his disastrous defeat in the presidential elections. Presented to the general, Goebbels stood stiffly to attention: 'I speak. Describe the existing situation. He listens and nods approvingly. Acknowledges that I am right. Scrutinises me intently. A soul-searching look. He does not seem displeased.' Among the other nationalist leaders he met were Graefe, Streicher, Feder, the original co-founder of the Nazi Party, Koch, Reventlow and, by no means least, Strasser, 'the genial pharmacist from Bavaria, big, a little clumsy, with a deep Hofbräuhaus bass'.[21]

Stirred by the closing ceremonies and speeches and a march past with swastika flags flying, and filled by Ludendorff with 'firm, unshakeable faith', Goebbels had found his spiritual home. 'For me,' he wrote, 'the *völkisch* question is linked with all questions of the spirit and religion. I'm beginning to think in *völkisch* terms. This has nothing to do with politics; this is a philosophy of life.' The following day, he and Prang founded a Mönchengladbach chapter of the NSFB.

With nothing else to occupy his time, Goebbels threw all his energies into preaching his new faith, making speeches not only to his own party but to any discussion group or meeting where he could spread the word. The acting talent and stage presence he had displayed as a schoolboy blossomed as he discovered a gift for oratory and an ability to seize and hold an audience. According to Prang, his first effort was at a Communist meeting, and demonstrated the coolness, control and quick thinking that came to characterise his public appearances. After he had hobbled to the rostrum, an unprepossessing figure in his ill-fitting suit, he began by addressing his audience, provocatively, as 'dear fellow members of the *Volk* community'. In the uproar that followed, a man yelled 'capitalist exploiter!' Unfazed, Goebbels called the man up to the platform and invited him to show the contents of his wallet. 'We'll soon see who has more money!' he cried, emptying the pitiful few coins from his own on to the lectern. The audience was his. He continued his speech without further interruption.[22]

Goebbels had never heard Hitler speak, nor read anything he had written, but in his speeches he instinctively found himself following the path his idol had trodden. Like Hitler, he discovered that audiences used to the dry, text-based delivery of most German speakers could be electrified by a more dramatic style of oratory. Like Hitler, he practised regularly in front of a mirror: every speech was a theatrical performance, every gesture, every passionate peak consciously calculated and rehearsed for maximum effect. And like Hitler, he realised that style mattered more than content in rousing an audience, and truth not at all: what they wanted was not intellectual but emotional stimulation, feelings not facts.

Like Hitler, Goebbels kept his own emotions strictly under control while speaking, remaining cool and detached as he cynically manipulated his listeners. He soon discovered how easily he could whip an audience into a frenzy, and was rewarded when virtually every meeting he addressed ended in chaos and violence. From Rheydt, his reputation as a speaker spread quickly. Within a few weeks, he could write that he was known 'in all ranks of the followers of the National Socialist ideal throughout the entire Rhineland'.[23] His fame was purely local and he still had a great deal to learn about a movement he had only just joined, but to those who knew, he was clearly a star in the making.

Goebbels was among the first to join the new Nazi Party when the ban on it was lifted in February 1925. His job on the *Völkische Freiheit* had been in danger for some time because he had constantly filled its pages with praise for Hitler, and when Hitler was released and split his followers from the *völkisch* movement, Wiederhaus fired Goebbels and closed down the paper. Like Himmler in lower Bavaria, Goebbels was free to devote all his time and energy to the party – apart from that spent chasing women – though he had to wait nearly two months before Karl Kaufmann persuaded Strasser to appoint him business manager for the Rhineland North Gau's central office. Goebbels was happy to move to Elberfeld, which he described after his first visit as 'a pretty town, with a remarkable number of attractive women. Must be a good place to live!'[24]

It sounds like an amazingly rapid advancement to a grand position, but in fact the party desperately needed every member it could find and those who had no full-time job were particularly welcome – and assured of quick promotion. Apart from a tiny handful surrounding Hitler in Munich, and some Gauleiters in south Germany, all officials were unpaid, attending to party business in their spare time. The Gau's central office consisted of just three people: Goebbels, Kaufmann and the Gauleiter, Axel Ripke – yet another Baltic German writer with elevated ideas. There was no money for staff.

With no salary, Goebbels was forced to live as best he could on the few marks he was given as expenses, scraping along in a tiny rented flat in Elberfeld, always having to borrow money and never getting enough to eat. His physical hunger, however, was matched by his appetite for campaigning with both the spoken and written word. During the twelve months from October 1924, when he first discovered his gift for oratory, he made no fewer than 189 speeches as well as turning out a stream of leaflets, posters and a regular Gau newsletter and planning a major propaganda campaign.[25]

Goebbels's campaign was aimed at mobilising the masses of workers in the industrial Ruhr Valley and northern Germany, whose lives and needs were far removed from those of the bourgeois and petty-bourgeois citizens who were the party's main supporters in Bavaria and the south. Goebbels saw the ultimate enemy as international capitalism, and those who held power in Germany as its lackeys, betraying their nation for personal gain. These were the traditional targets of the Communists, of course, so the Nazis and the KPD, the Communist Party of Germany, were in direct competition for the same constituency, two rabid dogs fighting for one bone. It was only natural, therefore, that they should spend as much or even more time attacking each other as they did their common enemy. And Goebbels, who had so recently been happy to describe himself as a 'German Communist',[26] led the fight with all the intensity of a religious convert.

Goebbels saw the similarities between the Nazis and the Communists as clearly as he did the differences, which to his mind could be boiled down to nationalism as opposed to internationalism, that 'Jewish conspiracy'. 'In the final analysis,' he wrote in his diary later that year, 'it would be better for us to go down with Bolshevism than live in eternal slavery under capitalism.'[27] He took the 'Socialism' in National Socialism very seriously and felt enormous sympathy for the people of Russia and their struggles, claiming that Lenin understood them better than the tsars ever had. In an open letter to 'My Friend of the Left' he listed the many areas of agreement with the Communists in their shared 'fight for freedom' against the hated bourgeoisie. 'You and I,' he concluded, 'we are fighting each other but we are not really enemies. By doing so we are dividing our strength, and we shall never reach our goal. Maybe the final extremity will bring us together. Maybe.'[28]

This brought him into conflict with Ripke, who held very different views. Goebbels described him scornfully as 'really a bourgeois in disguise. With these fellows you can't make a revolution.' Ripke, however, could quote Hitler himself as his authority for his reactionary attitude – something that Goebbels, still starry-eyed about the hero he had not yet met, found impossible to stomach, trying to convince himself, in a revealing choice of phrase, that Hitler was 'on the way to class struggle'.[29]

Faced with the threat of being thrown out of the party by Ripke, Goebbels discovered another talent that he would develop and use throughout the rest of his career – a talent for intrigue. From his position as business manager, getting rid of Ripke proved to be remarkably easy. With the support of Kaufmann, another Socialist Nationalist, Goebbels first undermined Ripke by accusing him of disloyalty to Hitler over a minor matter of issuing membership documents locally rather than from Munich, then followed up with the more serious crime of embezzling party funds. The charge was never proved, but it was enough, especially since Strasser had always been suspicious of Ripke and seized the opportunity eagerly. 'Ripke is finished,' Goebbels crowed in his diary. 'Now we can get down to work.'[30]

The day after Goebbels wrote those words, Strasser visited him and Kaufmann in Elberfeld. Strasser was glad to be rid of Ripke not merely because of his suspected dishonesty but also because he represented the right-wing 'Munich clique', led by the odious propaganda chief

Hermann Esser and the arch Jew baiter Julius Streicher, who had hurled vitriolic abuse at him for his alliance with Ludendorff and Graefe the year before. Strasser had a plan to counter the 'harmful Munich direction', which he wanted to discuss with his two bright young allies, who were now the provisional leaders of the Rhineland North Gau. Strasser wanted to form all the north-western Gaue into one bloc, and at the same time launch a new 'intellectual leadership organ' for party officials, to be called the *NS-Briefe* (*NS-Letters*). The headquarters of the new bloc was to be in Elberfeld, putting Goebbels and Kaufmann at its very heart. And he offered the editorship of the new journal to Goebbels, at a salary of 150 marks a month. Goebbels grabbed the opportunity with delight – and presumably some relief – writing in his diary that the *NS-Briefe* would give him 'a weapon against the ossified bosses in Munich' and personal access to Hitler.[31]

Strasser may well have seen his proposed north-western bloc as a power base from which he could take over the leadership of the whole party, pushing Hitler upstairs as a sort of non-executive chairman or figurehead. He always maintained his loyalty to Hitler, however – after a top-level meeting in Weimar in July, at which Goebbels had probably seen and heard his Führer for the first time, he declared that Hitler alone was 'the engine that drove the party'. Like many others, though, he was exasperated by Hitler's organisational sloppiness, lack of firm direction and reliance on low-grade characters like Esser, Streicher and Amman. But any ambitions he might have harboured to replace Hitler were dispelled at the meeting of Gauleiters called to discuss his proposals on 10 September in Hagen, Westphalia.

Unfortunately, Strasser was unable to be at the meeting himself – his mother had been taken seriously ill and he had hurried south to her bedside. Without his unifying presence, the leaders of the eleven Gaue squabbled among themselves and shied away from anything that might hint at a palace revolution. They agreed only to form a loose association, the Arbeitsgemeinschaft der nord- und westdeutschen Gauleiter der NSDAP (Working Group of the North and West German Gauleiters of the NSDAP), known as the AG for short, under Strasser's direction and with a central office in Elberfeld. They did, however, agree to publish the *NS-Briefe* as a bi-monthly, with Goebbels as editor, so even though the so-called Socialist wing of the party had been shown not to exist as a body, it did at least have a mouthpiece.

A fortnight after the AG was set up, another meeting confirmed Kaufmann as Gauleiter of the Rhineland North, and Goebbels as its business manager. Almost immediately, they found themselves under continuous attack from the 'Munich clique', who saw them as part of a Strasser plot to remove Hitler and replace the original twenty-five-point party programme, drawn up by him with Drexler and Gottfried Feder in 1920, with more radical Socialist aims. This was at least partly true: Goebbels was already helping Strasser draft a new policy document. But he had no wish to see Hitler unseated. He had been studying the first volume of *Mein Kampf*, which had been published a few weeks before, and managed to convince himself that Hitler shared his hopes and beliefs, blinding himself to those parts of the book that strongly contradicted them. One small but significant doubt remained in his mind: 'Who is this man?' he asked in his diary. 'Half plebeian, half god! The real Christ, or only John?'[32]

Things began to move fast for Goebbels now. On 6 November he and Kaufmann were summoned to meet Hitler personally for the first time, when he visited Braunschweig. Goebbels expected to be grilled about his beliefs, and hoped somewhat ingenuously that he would be able to open Hitler's eyes to the malign influence of the Munich crowd on the party's true doctrine, and bring him over to 'our side entirely'. Hitler, however, had a different agenda. He had heard reports of the young firebrand with a talent rivalling his own for rousing an audience, and wanted to look him over and size up his potential. Such a gift was rare, and should be serving him, not Strasser, the rival who posed a threat to the absolute authority that he was determined to establish over the party.

Hitler was eating dinner when the two Rhinelanders arrived. 'He jumps up at once,' Goebbels wrote. 'Stands there before us. Squeezes my hand. Like an old friend. And those big, blue eyes. Like stars. He's glad to see me. I'm in heaven.' Hitler was turning on the charm at full power. He never mentioned policies or ideologies through the whole meeting, concentrating entirely on seducing the younger man. He talked 'with wit, irony, sarcasm, seriousness, fervour, passion', and Goebbels melted before him. 'This man has everything it takes to be a king,' he rhapsodised in his diary that night. 'The born tribune of the people. The coming dictator.'[33]

Two weeks later, they met again at a rally in Plauen, an industrial town in the southern corner of Saxony. It was a long way from home for Goebbels, showing just how far his reputation as a speaker had spread. And there, Hitler completed his conquest: 'Great joy! He greets me like an old friend! And looks after me. How I love him!' Hitler gave him a signed photograph, and asked him to convey his 'greetings to the Rhineland'. Recalling that cathartic day several months later, Goebbels wrote: 'Until then you were my Führer. There you became my friend. A friend and master with whom I feel bonded to the very end in a shared idea.'[34]

From Plauen, Goebbels moved on to Hanover for the second meeting of the AG, bearing Hitler's 'express authorisation' for its formation; no one had asked for his permission, but by giving it he was underlining his own supreme authority over all party affairs. The Gauleiters acknowledged it in the group's rule book, drawn up by Strasser and Goebbels and approved unanimously by their colleagues, committing themselves 'to work in a spirit of comradeship for the idea of National Socialism under their leader, Adolf Hitler'.[35]

Because Hitler had carefully avoided discussing policy issues with him, Goebbels still imagined they shared the idea of an anti-capitalist nationalist utopia. He continued working enthusiastically on the draft policy document, which called for such extreme measures as large-scale nationalisation of industry, worker participation in department stores and similar enterprises, and the expropriation of aristocratic estates. He named 'stock exchange capitalism' and its creature, parliamentary democracy, as the chief enemies of National Socialist freedom. He called for the creation of a European customs union that would form the basis of a United States of Europe with Germany at its heart. On foreign policy, he looked east, seeing a Russia that would 'one day awaken in the spirit of its greatest thinker, in the spirit of Dostoevsky . . . freed from Jewish internationalism' as 'our natural ally against the fiendish temptation and corruption of the West.'[36]

This was hot stuff, and the assembled Gauleiters argued fiercely over it at their next meeting, held at Hanover in January. The Gauleiter of Westphalia, Franz Pfeffer von Salomon, son of a high-ranking Pussian civil servant, an ex-officer and former Freikorps member who had marched in the Kapp *putsch* and been active in fighting the French in the Ruhr, poured scorn on the draft's 'liberal-egalitarian' nature and called for a more elitist, *völkisch* approach. Others criticised its Marxist character. Most were violently opposed to the orientation of its foreign policy.

Goebbels's fiercest critic was Gottfried Feder, who had come hotfoot from Munich after obtaining a draft and gatecrashed the meeting. Some reports say that Goebbels tried to get Feder thrown out, screaming 'We

don't want any stool pigeons here!' But in the democratic style of the
AG, a vote was taken and he was allowed to stay and take part in the
debate, which became increasingly heated. Eventually, Goebbels rose
to speak. 'Then I really let fly,' he recorded in his diary. 'Russia,
Germany, Western capitalism, Bolshevism – I speak for half an hour,
an hour. Everyone listens in breathless suspense. And then a storm of
approval. We have triumphed . . . At the end: Strasser shakes my hand.
Feder small and hateful.'[37]

Goebbels's draft was accepted, with only Feder and Robert Ley, an
alcoholic chemist who was Gauleiter of Cologne, dissenting, as was a
resolution to start a party newspaper for northern Germany, *Der
Nationale Sozialist*, from a new publishing house, the Kampfverlag,
with Strasser as editor-in-chief. Both newspaper and publishing house
were to be quite independent of the Munich party organisation, and
would clearly be in competition with and even opposition to the
Völkischer Beobachter.

There was more controversy when the meeting debated the question of expropriating the estates of the former princes and nobility
without compensation, on which the Communists and Socialists in the
Reichstag were demanding a referendum. Strasser, Goebbels and many
– though by no means all – of the AG members were strongly in favour.
Hitler and the Munich big-wigs were violently against – several nobles
and princes were among the party's biggest financial contributors, and
Hitler was getting three-quarters of his personal income, 1,500 marks
a month, from the divorced Duchess of Sachsen-Anhalt.[38] What was
more, he had no wish to lose the support of the rich industrialists who
were increasingly pitching in to the party's coffers, seeing it as a bastion
against Communism.

The arguments grew more and more acrimonious, with Feder, Ley
and others insisting that the meeting had no authority to decide
anything without Hitler's approval. Goebbels was later reported as
leaping to his feet and screaming: 'I demand that the petty bourgeois
Adolf Hitler be expelled from the Nazi Party!' – but this was written
many years later by Otto Strasser, who had an enormous axe to grind
and was never a very reliable witness at the best of times. In fact, the
resolution that was finally passed carefully avoided exacerbating the
conflict with Munich by stating that the AG had no intention of pre-
empting the party leadership's decision, and that in any case the question of compensating the princes was 'not an issue that touches on the
fundamental interests of the party'.[39]

Despite all the care taken by Strasser and Goebbels, Hitler was alarmed by the reports given to him by Feder, which to his mind revealed a clear threat to his position. For months he had done nothing. Now, he moved fast. At the beginning of February he met with Strasser and extracted a promise from him that the draft proposals would be withdrawn. Then he called a meeting of party leaders for Sunday 14 February. It was very short notice, especially for the unpaid northern Gauleiters, many of whom could not make it, and it was to be held in Bamberg, Upper Franconia, where Streicher ruled. There was no agenda. Hitler simply stated that there were some 'important unresolved questions' that he wanted them to discuss.

Goebbels went to Bamberg with Strasser 'full of good cheer', convinced that this was the time when he would finally win Hitler over to his point of view. 'In Bamberg we'll play the demure beauty and lure Hitler on to our terrain,' he noted in his diary. '. . . No one believes in Munich any more. Elberfeld will become the Mecca of German socialism.' In Bamberg, however, he was in for a very nasty shock.

Hitler had gone to great lengths to put on a show of strength, arriving in an impressive motorcade and ensuring that the local leaders plus Landtag and Reichstag deputies vastly outnumbered the few northern delegates. Goebbels and Strasser were virtually alone as supporters of the resolutions passed in Hanover. Since this was a private meeting, Hitler was able to speak, and speak he did, for at least two hours – some reports say it was four or five. Point by point he demolished everything that Goebbels and Strasser and the AG believed, tearing their draft programme to shreds. 'The programme of 1920,' he pronounced dogmatically, 'is the foundation of our religion, our ideology. To tamper with it would be an act of treason to those who died believing in our idea.' He utterly repudiated Goebbels's ideas on foreign policy. Above all, he reasserted his own dictatorial position in the party. His message was clear and unequivocal: the Nazi party was to be united under one Führer, or it was to be nothing.

Goebbels was devastated:

I feel battered. What sort of Hitler is this? A reactionary? Extremely awkward and uncertain. Russian question completely wrong. Italy and England our natural allies. Terrible! Our task is the annihilation of Bolshevism. Bolshevism is a Jewish creation! We must be Russia's heir! 180 millions! Compensation for the princes! Right must remain right. For the princes, too. Don't shake the question of private property! (*sic*!) Dreadful! Programme is sufficient! Content with it. Feder nods. Ley nods. Streicher nods. Esser nods. I'm sick at heart when I see you in such company!!! Short discussion. Strasser speaks. Hesitant, trembling, inept, the good, honest Strasser. God, how poor a match we are for those swine down there![40]

After Strasser's abject failure at the rostrum, the northern delegates waited expectantly for Goebbels, their star speaker, to challenge Hitler, but he dismayed them by remaining silent: 'I can't utter a word. I feel as though I've been hit over the head . . . Certainly one of the greatest disappointments of my life. I no longer have complete faith in Hitler. That's the terrible thing: my props have been taken away from under me.'[41]

Strasser had capitulated, but Hitler was too clever to rub his nose in the dirt. Such triumphalism would have alienated Strasser's considerable following, and he needed the northern members, including the little doctor whose promise he had noted. As soon as Strasser had finished speaking, Hitler went to him and put his arm round his shoulders in a public display of comradeship. Goebbels displayed his own loyalty by accompanying Strasser to the rail station at the end of the meeting.

Goebbels's disillusionment with Hitler lasted hardly longer than the overnight train journey back to Elberfeld. After a few hours of doubt, he concluded that Hitler was clearly still under the influence of the 'Munich clique', and he determined to continue the fight against them. 'Become strong. Let the Munich crowd have their Phyrrhic victory,' he wrote in his diary a few days later. 'Work, become strong, then fight for Socialism.'[42] As a first step, he and Strasser delivered 'a slap in the face' to Feder by telling him that the 'previous relationship of trust' was ended, and retracting the invitation to speak at a forthcoming rally in Essen. They also set about attacking Rosenberg, whom they saw as a particularly malign influence through his editorship of the *Völkischer Beobachter*.

Hitler continued his wooing of Goebbels, and his efforts to keep Strasser inside the party. He gave his approval to the new publishing house, and did not object when Strasser merged the two Gaue of Rhineland North and Westphalia into one powerful Ruhr Gau, with Kaufmann, Goebbels and Pfeffer as joint Gauleiters. And in April, after talking to Strasser, he removed Esser from the party's Reich leadership.

Although he worshipped Hitler, Goebbels was still Strasser's man and still wedded to the same Socialist ideals. Hitler's task of separating them was made easier when Strasser was confined to bed for several weeks with severe leg injuries after his car was hit by a freight train at a level crossing in Altenessen on 10 March. Hitler visited him at his home in Landshut, bearing sympathy and a giant bunch of flowers – then went to work on Goebbels, inviting him to speak, in his presence, in the movement's holy-of-holies, the Bürgerbräukeller.

Goebbels arrived in Munich on 7 April, together with Kaufmann and Pfeffer, to what he described as 'a grand reception'. The sun was shining, and Hitler's own car, a gleaming, supercharged Mercedes, was waiting at the station to drive them to their hotel through streets plastered with 'enormous posters' advertising Goebbels's appearance the next day. After a tour of the city, with a stop for wurst and beer in the Bratwurstglöckle, they returned to their hotel to find that Hitler had phoned to say he wished to welcome them personally. Goebbels phoned him from the coffee shop, and in a quarter of an hour he was there, 'big, healthy, full of life. His kindness in spite of Bamberg makes us feel ashamed.' He wished Goebbels well for his speech – and gave them his car again for an invigorating drive out to Lake Starnberg. Then it was time for the big event:

In the evening at 8 o'clock we drive to the Bürgerbräu. Hitler is already there. My heart is pounding so wildly it is ready to burst. I enter the hall. Roaring welcome. Packed shoulder to shoulder. Streicher opens. And then I speak for two and a half hours. I give it all I've got. The audience screams and shouts. At the end, Hitler embraces me. He has tears in his eyes. I am remarkably happy. Through the packed mass to the car. Shouts of 'Heil'. Hitler waits for me alone at the hotel. Then we eat together. He is the perfect host. And how great he is because of this.[43]

After the meal, Hess, Streicher and several other prominent members of the leadership joined them for a visit to a concert in the Reichsadler hall. Hitler kept Goebbels by his side the whole time, demonstrating his regard for his new young shooting star. That night, Goebbels found it impossible to sleep.

Kaufmann and Pfeffer were less impressed than Hitler by Goebbels's speech. To their ears, he had gone soft on the reactionary 'Munich clique' and they told him next day that his speech had been 'rubbish'. But Goebbels didn't care – all that mattered was that the Führer himself had praised him. Summoned to lunch alone with Hitler, all three were admonished for their part in the AG and the draft programme, before he gave them his absolution. 'In the end,' Goebbels wrote, 'unity follows. Hitler is great. He gives us all a warm handshake.' When Hitler treated them to one of his three-hour monologues, elaborating on his speech at Bamberg, Goebbels listened enraptured, seemingly unaware that Hitler was tailoring everything he said specifically to win him over. The views that had so depressed him before now seemed 'brilliant' and 'convincing':

I love him. The social question. A completely new insight. He has thought everything through. His ideal: a just collectivism and individualism. As to soil – everything belongs to the people. Production to be creative and individual- istic. Trusts, transport, etc, to be socialised . . . Taking it all round, he's quite a man. Such a sparkling mind can be my leader. I bow to the greater man, to the political genius.[44]

While the others returned to the Ruhr, Goebbels stayed in Bavaria with Hitler, getting to know the Munich big-wigs. He was dismissive of most of them; Hess, 'the decent, quiet, friendly, reserved, private secretary',[45] was the only one he really liked. He spent the weekend in Landshut, with Gregor Strasser and Himmler, whom he called 'a good fellow, very intelligent. I like him very much.' In between making speeches in Landshut itself and Dingolfing, he fell in love with Strasser's 'wonderful' extended family, whose warmth and comfortable good humour impressed him so much that he was moved to write in his diary: 'O, Gregor Strasser, how hard must the revolution be for you!'

Back in Munich, Hitler's seduction of Goebbels continued unabated. He spent hours talking to him about the politics of east and west and the problem of Russia. He invited him to dinner at his apartment – 'a darling young woman was there,' Goebbels noted – and took him on day-long sight-seeing tours through Bavarian beauty spots. He accom- panied him to speaking engagements in Stuttgart, sat with him on the platform, and when he had finished praised him and embraced him.

'I believe,' the besotted Goebbels wrote on 19 April, 'that he has taken me to his heart like no one else . . . Adolf Hitler, I love you because you are both great and simple at the same time. What one calls a genius.'[46] That night, he wrote a fulsome letter of greeting for Hitler's thirty-seventh birthday beginning: 'Dear and revered Adolf Hitler! I have learned so much from you . . .' The conquest was complete.

*   *   *

Goebbels's colleagues in the Ruhr naturally saw his change of direction as a betrayal of their Socialist principles, and his relations with Kaufmann in particular became strained. Both Kaufmann and Strasser accused him of kow-towing to Hitler, aptly labelling his conversion 'Joseph Goebbels's Damascus'. But he was unmoved. At the new party's first national rally on 3–4 July, held in Weimar since Thuringia was one of the few states where Hitler was not banned from speaking in public, he threw himself wholeheartedly behind the Führer principle, avoiding any controversial topics in his speech and abandoning the democratic procedures that had been such a feature of the party in the north.

Towards the end of the month, he was invited to join Hitler for a holiday in Berchtesgaden. The Führer had not yet bought the house on the Obersalzberg which was to become the Berghof, and was staying in the Hotel Deutsches Haus, working on the second volume of *Mein Kampf* and relaxing, protected by his secretary, Hess, his chauffeur, Emil Maurice, and his photographer, Heinrich Hoffmann. Interestingly, Strasser was also there. Goebbels, thrilled to be admitted to this intimate magic circle, joined them for scenic drives through the mountains and boat trips on the Königsee.

Wherever they went, they were treated to more of Hitler's rambling monologues as he poured out his thoughts on just about everything. Blinded by his infatuation, Goebbels saw him as 'The natural, creative instrument of a divine fate . . . Out of deep distress a star is shining! I feel completely bound to him. The last doubt in me has disappeared.' And a few days later:

He is a genius. The natural creative instrument of a fate determined by God. I stand shaken before him. This is how he is: like a child, dear, good, compassionate. Like a cat, cunning, clever and agile. Like a lion, magnificently roaring and huge. A fine fellow, a real man. He speaks of the state. In the afternoon, of winning the state and of the meaning of political revolution. Thoughts I may have had myself but not expressed. After supper we sit for a long time in the garden of the seamen's home, and he holds forth on the new state and how we will achieve it. It has the ring of prophecy. Above us in the sky a white cloud forms a swastika. A shimmering light in the sky that can't be a star. A sign from fate? We go home late! Far in the distance Salzburg shimmers. I am really happy. This life is worth living. 'My head won't roll in the dust until my mission is fulfilled.' That was his last word. That's how he is! Yes, that's how he is![47]

The following month, Goebbels broke publicly with Strasser and his associates, in an article in the *Völkischer Beobachter*. 'Only now,' he wrote, 'do I recognise you for what you are: revolutionaries in words but not in deeds.' He was hoping for a party position in Munich where he could be close to his idol – aiming high as usual, he even talked of being appointed secretary-general of the movement. But the Munich old guard, jealous of the attentions Hitler had lavished on this newcomer and suspicious of his sincerity, had other ideas.

Since June, there had been talk of sending him to Berlin, just about as far from Munich and Hitler as could be, to replace the Gauführer there, Dr Ernst Schlange, a Strasser protégé who had given up in the face of endless internal strife, particularly between the party and the SA. Goebbels had recently made a speech in the city and had been appalled by what he had seen. 'They all want me to go to Berlin as a saviour,' he wrote. 'Thanks for the desert of stone!'[48]

There were, however, compelling arguments in favour of Goebbels going to 'Red Berlin'. If the party was to become truly national it had to have a strong presence in the capital. 'Who has Berlin,' Hitler said, 'has Prussia, and who has Prussia has Germany.' But Berlin, the biggest industrial city in Germany, was the traditional heartland of Communist and Socialist support. The Social Democrats were the strongest party in the city, with seventy-four seats in the city council, followed by the Communists with forty-three. But with 250,000 members, 25 newspapers, 87 affiliated groups and 4,000 active political cells, Berlin's was the second biggest Communist Party in the world – only Moscow's was larger. Fighting it on its own ground was an almost impossible task. Goebbels was one of the very few in the party – maybe even the only one – who was equipped to tackle it.

Berlin was also the power base of the Strassers: the two brothers had set up the Kampfverlag there in March, with money Gregor had made by selling his pharmacy in Landshut, and were publishing *Der Nationale Sozialist* from it as a weekly with seven regional editions under local titles. In Berlin itself it was called the *Berliner Arbeiterzeitung*. Although the overall circulation was less than 8,000, the papers were a constant source of irritation to Hitler, since they inevitably peddled the Strassers' views rather than his. Otto, as always, leaned much further to the left than Gregor – Goebbels described him as a half Marxist and a fanatic[49] – and, unlike his brother, had not effected a reconciliation with Hitler. If anyone knew how to handle the Strassers, it had to be Goebbels, with his intimate knowledge of their thinking and methods.

For several weeks, Goebbels continued to resist. But at the end of August the party leadership asked him to take over the provisional direction of the Berlin Gau for four months, and he went to have a look three weeks later. The state of the party organisation was not encouraging, and he hated the city itself: 'Berlin by night. A sink of iniquity! And I'm supposed to plunge into this?' But a pilgrimage to Potsdam and the tomb of Frederick the Great – in the enticing company of Josefine von Behr, 'such a charming creature' – was 'one of the great moments of his life', and he began to weaken.

The existing officials in the Berlin office all did their best to persuade him, and when Emil Maurice told him, no doubt on instructions from Hitler, how much the Führer himself wanted him to take on this vitally important mission, he started to show some enthusiasm for the challenge. In any case, he was eager to move on from Elberfeld, where the atmosphere in the Gau office was growing increasingly sour and his personal relationship with Kaufmann more and more strained.

On 30 October, the day after his twenty-ninth birthday, he returned from yet another speaking tour to find a letter from Hitler confirming his appointment. 'Berlin is perfect. Hurrah!' he wrote. 'Now there's only one week before I'm in the capital of the Reich.' Convincing himself that his present life, with its constant round of speaking engagements and 'dreadful' experiences in places like Chemnitz, Plauen, Bochum, Zwickau, was 'so grey', he looked forward to 'saying farewell from Berlin'.[50] He swiftly cleared up his affairs in Elberfeld, dumped the 'half-breed' Else Janke, and bought a third-class rail ticket for Berlin.

VII

'CHIEF BANDIT OF BERLIN'

GOEBBELS arrived at Berlin's Anhalter station on Sunday 7 November 1926. He was met by Otto Strasser, who had arranged accommodation for him 'at an excellent price' with Hans Steiger, editor of the *Berliner Lokalzeitung*, and his wife in their spacious apartment near the Potsdamer Bridge over the Landwehr Canal. The Steigers were Nazi supporters and good friends of the Strassers – and so could be relied on to keep them informed about the activities of their new lodger. So, too, could the 'circle of intelligent and reliable friends of the party' who visited there regularly, and who helped to introduce him to the city. Frau Steiger took in other paying guests, all carefully selected, but she treated Goebbels as a friend of the family, giving him the run of the apartment and even providing a full-length mirror in his room so that he could rehearse his speeches in front of it.

In spite of his defection to the Hitler camp, the Strassers went out of their way to make Goebbels feel welcome – at least to begin with. No doubt they were aware of the special mandatory powers that the Führer had bestowed on him to do whatever he saw fit to clean out the Berlin party, and wanted to avoid antagonising him. But they must also have thought that at heart he still believed in the same philosophy as they did and could be a valuable ally. They certainly hoped that he would support them in their often violent squabbles with others in the local party, especially Kurt Daluege, who commanded the SA in Berlin. They may even have thought they could control him – Gregor, after all, had been his mentor before his meteoric rise. If so, they were in for a swift disillusionment.

For his first official appearance, at the memorial service on 9 November for those who had fallen in the Munich *putsch* three years earlier, Goebbels took a leaf out of Hitler's book, making his arrival late and in 'a particularly large and elegant taxi'. Otto Strasser, who was to introduce him, was annoyed on both counts. He told Goebbels that the members were all 'poor devils', who would be upset at such pretensions. 'You are absolutely wrong there, Strasser,' Goebbels replied with a contemptuous smile. 'You say I shouldn't take a taxi. On the contrary. I'd come in two cars, if I could. People must see that this outfit can make a good showing.'¹ He went on to prove his point with an electrifying speech that wowed his audience and turned his debut as their Gauleiter into a personal triumph.

The party that Goebbels took over was hardly even a splinter group on the edges of nationalist politics. With a mere 300 or so members – according to Goebbels – it was an irrelevance in a city of 4 million inhabitants, and even those 300 were more interested in fighting each other than in fighting the Communists and Socialists. Most of all, though, they fought with the SA, which overshadowed them with around 500 members in the city, and which Daluege insisted on keeping separate. Party headquarters was in a dingy, back-court basement at 109 Potsdamer Strasse, which Goebbels described as 'a kind of dirty cellar, we called it the opium den . . . It had only artificial light. On entering, one hit an atmosphere that was thick with cigar, cigarette and pipe smoke. Doing solid, systematic work there was unthinkable. Unholy confusion reigned. Any real organisation was practically non-existent. The financial position was hopeless.'²

The Munich mafia must have congratulated themselves on having the troublesome little doctor posted to the equivalent of Outer Mongolia filled with hostile natives who would surely dispose of him in double quick time. But Goebbels was a missionary, filled with zeal and strengthened by Hitler's blessing, and saw only the challenge and the opportunities. During his first week, he went through the local party like a whirlwind. His first directive on his first day in the office banned any further argument between the Strasser and Daluege camps, threatening expulsion from the party for anyone who disobeyed. He then appointed Daluege, a tall, beefy former sanitary engineer who rejoiced in the self-explanatory nickname 'Dummi-Dummi', as his deputy, thus tying him and the SA firmly into the party and sending an unmistakable message to the Strassers that he was his own man. He began looking for new premises. And he began tackling the party's poverty by setting up the NS Freedom Association, 'a circle of pledged donors' committed to making regular monthly contributions to party funds, which soon had more than two hundred members producing a total of 1,500 marks a month.

Goebbels was a young man in a hurry. On Sunday 14 November, exactly one week after he had arrived in Berlin, he led an SA propaganda march through the heavily Communist district of Neukölln. He was looking for trouble, and he found it: vastly outnumbered by the Communist Rotfrontkämperbund (Red Front Fighters), the pitifully small band of Nazis stood no chance when they were attacked with 'slingshots, blackjacks, sticks, and also pistols'[3] after he had made a deliberately provocative speech. They were beaten up so severely that they were forced to flee for their lives. Goebbels had made his presence in the city felt, and had posted notice of his future intentions. But for the moment, even he had to admit that he needed to spend more time preparing and strengthening his forces before launching any further actions.

Goebbels's move to Berlin was by no means the only significant organisational change in the Nazi Party in the autumn of 1926. Rudolf Hess's position was consolidated when he was made secretary of a new Reich party directorate, charged with setting up the bureaucratic framework of a state within a state, with departments for foreign affairs, agriculture, economic affairs, labour, the interior, and so on, as shadow ministries for all the main areas of government. There were also new auxiliary formations to bolster the party's ambitions of becoming a genuine mass movement: the Hitler Youth, the NS German Students' League, the NS Schoolchildren's League, and the NS Women's League, plus leagues covering the main professions: teachers, lawyers, doctors. The NSDAP may have been a small party, but it had big ideas.

While the foundations of a complex supporting structure were being laid, Hess was delighted to see Hitler tightening his grip on the leadership. He reminded Walter Hewel, who had been with them in Landsberg Jail, of the view Hitler had then expressed on the 'leadership principle': 'unconditional authority downwards, and responsibility upwards', which Hess saw as 'Germanic democracy' – a definition that would surely have pleased the Kaiser himself. Hess tellingly compared 'the great popular leader' with 'the great founder of a religion', who 'must communicate to his listeners a clearly established faith. Only then can the mass of followers be led where they should be led.'[4]

Like most extremist political organisations, the Nazi Party had been a snake pit of jealousy and personal animosity from its very beginning, its chieftains vying venomously for position and power. Hitler deliberately did little or nothing to discourage these petty rivalries, and indeed often positively encouraged them while maintaining the impression of Olympian detachment. He found it increasingly difficult to distance himself, however, when prominent members sought his intervention in their quarrels. To avoid this, he set up the party's own court, the USCHLA (Untersuchungs- und Schlichtungsausschuss – Committee for Investigation and Settlement) to maintain internal discipline and settle disputes without involving him. USCHLA's first head, retired General Bruno Heinemann, failed to understand that his role was not to judge crimes and pronounce punishments, but to hush them up and make sure no one challenged Hitler's authority. Heinemann, who was described by Goebbels as 'correct, asking stupid questions, in no way capable of serious thinking, a code of honour wandering around in human shape',[5] was swiftly replaced by the more compliant Major Walter Buch, and two assistants, Hitler's former bodyguard Ulrich Graf, and his lawyer, Hans Frank.

In September 1926, at about the time Goebbels was asked to take provisional charge of the Berlin Gau, Hitler put paid to what was left of Strasser's Greater Ruhr triumvirate by taking away Pfeffer von Salomon, and appointing him national commander of the reconstituted SA. He had started the process of re-establishing the SA at the Weimar rally, by officially creating eight new units to supplement the original four formed back in 1923. At the same time, a new SA formation, the Schutzstaffel (Protection Squad), known as the SS for short, a development of Hitler's original bodyguard, the Stosstrupp Adolf Hitler, had paraded for the first time. As a mark of its elite status, Hitler presented it with the 'Blood Banner' that had been carried at the head of the march to the Feldherrnhalle. Unlike the SA in general, there could be no doubt that the SS's sole loyalty was to Adolf Hitler personally.

Also in September, having completed the demolition of Gregor Strasser's potential power base, Hitler brought Strasser himself into the national leadership where he could keep a closer eye on him, appointing him Reich Propaganda Leader, the position that Goebbels had coveted. It was a decision that may have helped Goebbels make up his mind to accept the Berlin post. Strasser had pressed for the job, and he did it well, bringing to it an energy and professionalism that had been notably absent in the past. He worked tirelessly, touring the country to co-ordinate regional and local activities, drawing up lists of speakers, enthusing and organising party workers. It was Strasser, not Goebbels, who created the Nazi Party propaganda machine. But he did not do it alone: he took with him from Landshut to Munich his able deputy, Heinrich Himmler, who was officially appointed Deputy Reich Propaganda Leader.

It was Himmler, as always, who took care of the details and kept the machine running smoothly, while Strasser, as always, spent most of his time either in Berlin attending to his duties in the Reichstag and directing the Kampfverlag, or touring the country making speeches and rallying the troops. Himmler booked speakers, arranged their schedules, and organised their protection from attack by Communists. He gathered intelligence from many sources for use in propaganda – his room was crammed with newspapers, magazines and cuttings, and he received reports on rival political organisations and even went to their meetings to learn what they were about. He devised a new form of campaign that was soon adopted as standard Nazi Party procedure, in which selected areas were saturated with all forms of propaganda over a short period of time to achieve maximum impact.

Looking after speakers brought Himmler into contact with all the prominent members of the party, who came to know that they could rely on him to get things done, quietly and efficiently: '*Der Heini macht es schon*' ('Heini will see to it') became a catch-phrase that symbolised everyone's attitude to him, just as it had in his student days. Among those he worked with was Goebbels. Despite their different political and personal backgrounds, the two Young Turks – both were still in their twenties – found they shared many beliefs and got on well, meeting quite often for a gossip. At that stage, they regarded each other as allies against the uneducated philistines who made up most of the party leadership, rather than as rivals. And with all the energy of youth, they shared an amazing capacity for hard work, cramming their days full of activities that would have exhausted almost anyone. It was this as much as anything else that carried them both to the top.

Incredibly, even with all his other duties, Himmler still found time to go on speaking tours himself, as well as handling the printing and distribution of posters, leaflets and literature, and acting as assistant editor of the local *völkisch* paper, the *Kurier für Niederbayern* (Courier for Lower Bavaria). And he contributed regular articles to Goebbels's *NS-Briefe*. Like his speeches, these were almost always on the threat to German farmers from a supposed Jewish conspiracy to depress the value of agricultural land, buy it at 'junk prices' and then take it out

of production: 'When the catastrophe comes and a substantial proportion of German land is in Jewish hands,' he wrote, 'not a single stalk
of grain will grow on it. Then, without the protection of German agriculture, we will be entirely at the mercy of money-market foodstuffs.
These will then not be supplied at the current reduced prices, but food
prices will be driven up to exorbitant levels.'[6]

Although he now worked from an office in party headquarters in
Munich, Himmler still kept his job as Deputy Gauleiter, now not only
of Lower Bavaria but also of Swabia. One of his *ex officio* responsibilities was to organise and lead the SS in the Gau; his personal SS
membership number was 168. He was also Gauführer in Bavaria and
official party liaison man for the Artaman Society, an organisation
devoted to the *völkisch* ideal of renewing the pure Aryan German race
by reversing the flow of people from the land to the cities, those 'sinks
of iniquity', and directing them to settle the vast spaces in the East.
On an immediate and practical level, it sent young Germans to work
on the big estates of Saxony and East Prussia so that the land would
not be polluted by Polish workers. The Slav was Himmler's second
bête noir. 'Increasing our peasant population,' he wrote, 'is the only
effective defence against the influx of the Slav working-class masses
from the East. As it was six hundred years ago, the German peasant's
destiny must be to preserve and increase the German people's patri-
mony in their holy mother earth in battle against the Slav race.'[7]

Throughout 1927, Himmler beavered away in Munich, seemingly
content to be the perennial backroom-boy, accumulating brownie points
for diligence rather than brilliance. His commitment never faltered,
although the party itself was in the doldrums, with falling attendance
at meetings even when Hitler himself was the speaker – his public
speaking ban was lifted in Bavaria and most other states in March,
though in Prussia and Anhalt it remained in force until the autumn of
1928. There was only one place in Germany where interest in the party
was not in decline, and that was Berlin, where Goebbels worked frenet-
ically to breathe life into its moribund body.

Early in the new year of 1927, he found new premises for his central
office: four rooms with two telephone lines on the first floor front of
44 Lützowstrasse, above a motorcycle repair shop, a small café and the
Berlin Cremation Society's funeral parlour. He acquired a seven-seater
blue Opel landaulet car, which could be used as a speaking platform

and to ferry men rapidly to street fights, as well as his personal transport. He set up a training school for speakers. He formed a forty-
strong military band to lead Nazi marches. And he reorganised the
structure of the SA, splitting it into three 'standards' covering the inner
city, the suburbs and Brandenburg, each with up to twenty 'divisions'
of fourteen men, to enable it to react faster to opportunities for trouble.

Most SA men were unemployed toughs, always spoiling for a fight
– with each other if there was no one else available – and discipline
was a continuing problem, especially when it was the 'politicals' of the
party trying to impose it. During the first few weeks of his time in
Berlin, Goebbels spoke every single day at meetings of supporters or
SA men, preaching the Nazi gospel as though to an evangelical Bible
class where the faithful shouted 'Heil!' instead of 'Hallelujah!' In a
remarkably short time, his message began to bear fruit. At the same
time, he earned the respect of the SA by standing his ground fearlessly
on the platform during confrontations with the Communists, never
ducking or diving for cover when the beer mugs and chair legs started
flying. 'The oratorical gifts and organisational talent displayed by this
man were unique,' wrote the nineteen-year-old Horst Wessel, a university drop-out and Protestant pastor's son who had just joined the SA.
'There was nothing he couldn't handle. The party comrades clung to
him with great devotion. The SA would have let itself be cut to pieces
for him. Goebbels – he was like Hitler himself. Goebbels – he was *our*
Goebbels.'[8]

Goebbels knew it would take more than speeches to the faithful to
raise the profile of his party and attract new recruits. The answer lay
in publicity. 'Berlin needs sensation like a fish needs water,' he wrote
later. 'This city lives on it, and any political propaganda that does not
recognise this is bound to fail.'[9] For all his efforts, however, Berlin
remained largely unaware of the Nazi Party. The newspapers were not
interested in the clashes he staged between the SA and Communists.
Even fights with the police went largely unreported. Goebbels was
frantic. 'Let them curse us, libel us, fight us and beat us up,' he cried,
'but let them talk about us!'

To get people talking about them, Goebbels booked the Pharus Hall
in the Wedding district just north of the city centre for a rally, at which
he would speak on 'the collapse of the bourgeois class state'. It was a
brave and provocative move: Wedding was even more of a Communist
stronghold than Neukölln, and the Pharus Hall was the regular KPD
meeting place. To make sure his challenge was recognised he plastered

the streets with huge blood-red posters – a marked change from the small, cheap bills the party had previously used.

When Goebbels mounted the platform on 11 February, the hall was packed with an explosive mixture of supporters and opponents, though he had made sure that Nazis and SA men would be in the majority. Both sides had come armed with brass knuckles, sticks, chains and iron bars, and they pitched into each other ferociously, breaking noses and jaws and knocking each other unconscious until eventually the Communists were routed and forced to retreat under police protection. The SA recorded eighty-five Communists wounded against their own tally of three badly wounded and 'about 10–12 slightly'. Goebbels had the wounded men lifted on to the platform, proudly displaying their injuries as trophies. It was a notable victory. But the real success came next morning, when the Berlin newspapers all published graphic accounts of the 'Battle of Pharus Hall' and the Nazi Party was, if only for a day or two, the centre of that sensation Goebbels had sought to provide for the hungry city. When one paper called the Nazis bandits, Goebbels seized on it with delight and began billing himself as 'Chief Bandit of Berlin'.

The battle of Pharus Hall was, in Goebbels's own words, 'a good beginning'. It brought a wave of new recruits both for the party and for the SA, but he knew it was only a beginning. He needed to build on it, and he proceeded to do just that, inventing, lying, exaggerating with a cynical genius entirely untrammelled by conscience. Everything was grist to his propaganda mill: for a surprisingly long time he got away with implying that his foot had been crippled in the trenches, artfully dropping 'we who were shot up in the war', into speeches to establish a phoney rapport with veterans in the audience.

He gave the SA an ersatz dignity after Pharus Hall by creating a mythical hero, 'The Unknown SA Man', who was supposed to have fallen victim to 'Communist terror tactics'. He displayed healthy SA men swathed in bandages as though they had been attacked. He designated 19 March, the anniversary of the founding of the Berlin SA, as 'Mark Brandenburg Day', and put some 400 members on a train to the little market town of Trebbin, about twenty miles outside the city. There, he led them in a torchlight procession into the hills, where he staged a quasi-religious open-air memorial service to the 'victims of the movement' around a great bonfire.

Next day, after more speeches in the town square, the SA men boarded a train back to Berlin, on which happened to be a group of

Red Front Fighters, including a small shawm band. They started fighting on the journey and were pretty evenly matched. But when they reached the southern Berlin suburb of Lichterfelde East, the Nazis were joined by several hundred supporters gathered by Goebbels, who had driven back ahead of them in the Opel at top speed. The 'reception committee' swarmed on to the train and attacked the Communists, leaving sixteen wounded, six of them seriously, before Goebbels called them off. The day's sport, however, was by no means over. Goebbels formed his men into a column to march into the city centre behind the Opel, from which he directed them to smash Jewish shops and beat up anyone they spotted who looked Jewish. It was the first time anyone had turned the Nazis' verbal attacks on the Jews into physical action, a dreadful foretaste of the horrors to come.

Goebbels rounded off the Mark Brandenburg Day celebrations that evening with a closing ceremony on Wittenbergplatz in the centre of the smart West End, declaiming with breathtaking effrontery, 'We came openly into Berlin, at first with peaceful intentions. The Red Front Fighters' League has forced us to spill our blood. We will not allow ourselves to be treated like second-class citizens any longer!'[10]

Amazingly, though he was hauled in by the police for questioning, Goebbels was not charged with any offence over the day's events – he claimed in his statement that he had driven at the head of the march purely to study the reactions of people on the streets. Maybe the police realised how much he would have welcomed the publicity of a court appearance. He was rewarded in any case by extensive press coverage, and by another surge in membership: the police estimated that about 400 joined the Berlin party in March, bringing the total to about 3,000 – a ten-fold increase in barely five months under Goebbels's steward-ship. By any reckoning, and even allowing for the fact that he may well have been exaggerating in claiming there were only 300 members when he arrived, that was a remarkable achievement.

The result could not be questioned, but the methods used by Goebbels could be, and were, by many party members and most of all by the Strasser brothers, who had grown increasingly antagonistic to him since his arrival in Berlin. Gregor, although thoroughly anti-Semitic, always drew the line at physical violence, claiming later in a Reichstag speech 'We want no persecution of Jews, but we demand the exclusion of Jews from German life.'[11] The Strassers felt he had sold out, and was betraying their Socialist ideals. But mostly they felt the resentment and bitterness of rejected comrades-in-arms. They tried to undermine his position with scurrilous rumour-mongering against him and snide references and carping criticism in the *Berliner Arbeiterzeitung*.

Despite the Strassers' sniping, Goebbels felt strong enough by the end of April to invite Hitler to pay a 'royal' visit and make a May Day speech in the Clou dance hall on Mauerstrasser, between Friedrichstrasse and Wilhelmstrasse. It had to be a nominally private meeting, since the public speaking ban on Hitler was still in force in Prussia, but Goebbels managed to pack in an audience of several hundreds. To his dismay, however, the Communists refused to play ball: they kept away and kept quiet – and so did the press. With no disturbances and no violence to report, few papers bothered even to mention Hitler's visit. Goebbels, the prince of publicity, was mortified.

The aftermath of the May Day meeting, however, brought Goebbels a more newsworthy result than he had bargained for. Three days later, at a bigger event in the War Veterans Building, he tried to provoke the journalists who had ignored Hitler's visit by calling them 'Jewish swine' among other choice epithets. The journalists declined to rise to the bait, but one man in the audience did. Friedrich Stucke, who had wandered in from the street purely out of curiosity, was incensed by Goebbels's racist diatribe and yelled at him: '*Ja, ja*, you're the perfect Germanic youth, aren't you?' For once, Goebbels was too stunned to come back with a sharp riposte. As he howled with fury, his SA men set upon Herr Stucke and beat him up severely.

The incident was seen and reported by agents of the ever-present police political surveillance unit, but it would probably have remained just one of many on the files, except for the fact that Herr Stucke happened to be a Protestant pastor. Beating up Jews on the street was one thing, but beating up a Christian clergyman was going too far. Now the press went to town, and in the furore that followed, the Prussian government was at last forced to act. It proscribed the party and all its auxiliary formations in Berlin and banned Goebbels from speaking in public.

To his enemies both inside and outside the party, it looked as though Goebbels had finally shot his bolt, that his meteoric career was finished. A gagged Goebbels was a pinioned bird of prey, posing no threat to anyone. What was more, the party's finances would be severely hit, since the ticket money for entrance to public meetings made up a significant part of its income. The vultures gathered expectantly.

The Strassers were already running a vicious campaign against Goebbels in the *Berliner Arbeiterzeitung* which had peaked a week before the ban with an article entitled 'The Results of Miscegenation'. Published under the by-line of Erich Koch, a prominent party member in the Rhineland – who later vehemently denied authorship – the piece clearly implied that his club foot and 'repulsive ugliness' could only have come from a mixing of races. Actually written by Otto Strasser, it was simply the old Nazi custom of hurling the worst insult imaginable at party rivals by accusing them of having Jewish blood. But to Goebbels, with his lifelong sensitivity to his disability, it cut deep – no doubt the wound was still raw when Pastor Stucke mocked him. Both he and his supporters would have assumed that Stucke had been planted on the meeting by the Strassers, which would account for the savagery of their response.

Whatever his other faults, Goebbels was no quitter. He lashed out at the Strassers with charges that their mother and Gregor's wife were both Jewish, and pointing out that Otto had a distinctly Jewish appearance with his hooked nose and crinkly, gingery hair. After getting nowhere with appeals to Hitler, who sat on the fence as usual making sympathetic noises but doing nothing, he began his counterattack by hitting the Strassers where he knew it would hurt them most. Although he was not allowed to speak, he could still write: he could deliver his speeches in print. He would start his own Berlin newspaper, in competition with the *Berliner Arbeiterzeitung*, which was already struggling to survive in an overcrowded market – there were at that time around 130 other political journals published in Berlin.

Now, it was the Strassers' turn to run to Hitler crying 'foul'. They accused Goebbels of being a liar – which, of course, was no news to anyone – and of making false claims that he had been with Hitler from the very beginning and had been a Nazi leader of the resistance movement in the Ruhr. And they charged him with being entirely to blame for the ban on the party, which had been precipitated by his wild conduct. When Hitler took no notice, they started press rumours that he and Goebbels had fallen out.

Goebbels responded with great daring by giving Hitler an ultimatum: if the Führer insisted on his keeping quiet and not hitting back, he would ask to be relieved of his post as Gauleiter. He then called a special undercover meeting of the Berlin party and demanded a unanimous vote of confidence, failing which he would leave the city at once. The meeting gave him his vote – and agreed that Otto Strasser must have 'Jewish blood in his veins'. It also approved his plans for a new weekly paper, though some members were worried that it would damage the *Berliner Arbeiterzeitung*.

Since anything that weakened the Strassers suited Hitler perfectly, he gave Goebbels his blessing. At the same time, he issued a statement, which Goebbels had asked Hess to provide, dismissing the charges against him as inventions of 'the Jewish journalistic riff-raff', confirming that nothing had changed in their relationship, and concluding: 'As before, he enjoys my fullest confidence.'[12] Characteristically, what he did not do was to condemn the Strassers in any way.

Goebbels named his new paper *Der Angriff* (The Attack). The first issue hit the streets on 4 July 1977, after a short but typically brilliant advertising campaign. It started with blood-red posters simply stating 'Der Angriff' followed by a large question mark, then a second poster saying 'Der Angriff begins on 4 July'. There was no indication of what attack they were talking about, until the first copies went on sale. At first, *Der Angriff* was a disaster. Even Goebbels himself acknowledged this: 'Shame, desolation and despair swept over me as I compared this pale shadow of a paper with what I had really wanted to produce. A wretched provincial rag, printed slops! . . . Plenty of good intentions, but very little skill.'[13]

Much of the amateurish quality of the paper's make-up and production could be blamed on the fact that the experienced managing editor Goebbels had chosen, Julius Lippert, was serving a six-week jail sentence at the time of the launch. But the real blame lay not in the paper's appearance but in its editorial content, which was controlled by Goebbels himself. It was far too literary, too intellectual in its approach, too similar in feel to the *NS-Briefe*, to appeal to a broad readership. However, as he had so often proved before, Goebbels was a fast learner. He quickly changed his literary style to the coarse language of the gutter so that not even the meanest intelligence could find the paper too challenging, cleaned up the design and production and turned it into a brutally sharp tabloid.

Taking Hitler's dictum that the masses should only be presented with one enemy at a time, he concentrated entirely on attacking the Jews, unleashing torrents of hate in every issue. Reasoning that it was more effective to focus on individuals rather than generalities, he picked the Deputy Police Commissioner of Berlin, Bernhard Weiss, who had been largely responsible for the ban on the party, as his prime target. Labelling him 'Isidor', a name that he mistakenly believed was typically

Jewish, he turned *Der Angriff* into an 'anti-Isidor organ', mercilessly lampooning the unfortunate Weiss in scurrilous tales and vicious cartoons. When a friend remonstrated with him over the lies he was pumping out, reminding him that Weiss was a war hero who had won the Iron Cross First Class, he was completely unfazed. 'Propaganda,' he declared cynically, 'has absolutely nothing to do with truth.'

Fuelled by such sensationalism, sales picked up, and by the end of three months Goebbels could claim that the paper was breaking even. The claim was almost certainly another lie, but he could not have made it if the paper had not had a strongly visible presence, regularly selling out its print run of 2,000 copies. To boost circulation at the expense of the direct competition, the Strassers' *Berliner Arbeiterzeitung,* he used ruthlessly simple tactics. He denied his rivals access to party information, so that anyone who wanted to know dates, times and details of meetings and events could only find them in *Der Angriff.* And he employed SA men disguised as Communists to attack the newsvendors selling the Strasser paper and drive them off the streets.

As his own sales mounted, so the Strassers' slumped, and since there was money involved now, as well as ideology, their antipathy towards him increased. The row dragged on for the rest of that year, to the delight of the party's political enemies, with both sides trading insults for abuse until Hitler finally stepped in and forced Goebbels and Gregor to stage a public reconciliation on the platform of the Hofbräuhaus in Munich, in a show of shared loyalty to the common idea and the common leader in the person of Adolf Hitler.[14]

In the meantime, Goebbels was busy keeping his banned party alive. On the most straightforward level, he simply transformed all the various branches and formations into sports and social clubs, which had always abounded in Berlin. Members continued to get together in newly formed shooting, bowling and rambling clubs. In place of the forbidden brown uniform, the SA wore plain white shirts with the brown rubber seals from porcelain bottle tops wrapped around one button. At weekends, they took excursions into the Brandenburg countryside by train, with their uniforms in their haversacks. Once outside the city limits, they could put them on and march and parade and play soldiers to their hearts' content.

At the same time, to make sure everyone knew the party had not been buried, Goebbels organised a steady flow of SA men before the magistrates every day, some for wearing the forbidden brown shirt or the swastika badge, others for boxing the ears of 'impertinent and arrogant Jews', and so on. All in all, the ban proved to be a boon, taking members' minds away from their internal wrangling and uniting them in the shared buzz of clandestinity.

In August 1927, Goebbels organised a 450-strong Berlin contingent to attend the party congress, which was held that year in Nuremberg, the scene of the great German Day rally of 1923. For those who could afford it, he laid on four private trains at a special fare of twenty-five marks a head. But as a propaganda stunt, around fifty SA men agreed to make the 230-mile journey on foot, though in the event they hitched rides wherever possible, dismounting and forming up again to march through towns and villages. The long march took two weeks, with the press reporting its progress every day. On the outskirts of Nuremberg, those whose feet were too sore to march smartly fell out, leaving the others to process through the city to great acclaim, before joining up with their 400 comrades.

The Berlin contingent was a small one among the crowds of members assembled in Nuremberg for the most ambitious party rally yet. But their well-publicised march, together with the well-known tribulations the party had suffered in Berlin, raised them to heroic status, boosting Goebbels's own image within the party still further. And there was an added bonus still to come: when they returned in triumph to Berlin, Deputy Police Commissioner Weiss had all 450 arrested at the station and driven in open trucks to police headquarters on Alexanderplatz, where they were charged with belonging to an illegal organisation. Goebbels was delighted: Berlin was talking about them again.

The Nuremberg congress had in fact been a disappointment for the party as a whole, underlining how far it had to go if it was ever to achieve national importance. The *Völkischer Beobachter* claimed an attendance of 100,000 members, including no fewer than 30,000 SA men, but more realistic estimates put the total number at 15–20,000. Nevertheless, the elaborate staging and ceremonials offered a foretaste of things to come, and boosted the party's confidence and cohesion. One area that already had all the confidence it needed, however, was the SA, which paraded twelve new units before Pfeffer and Hitler for dedication at Nuremberg.

To Hitler, the SA's growing strength was a source not only of pride, but also of a certain unease. Most SA commanders, including Pfeffer himself, were former army officers and Freikorps leaders, loose cannons who still dreamed of seeing the SA incorporated in the Reichswehr, or even replacing it. There was still a degree of ambiguity in where exactly their loyalties lay. For one part of the SA, however, there was no ambiguity whatsoever: the Schutzstaffel was entirely devoted to Hitler. It was his praetorian guard, dedicated to serving and protecting him.

Since its formation in 1925, the SS had had a succession of commanders; the latest was Erhard Heiden, a man described by William L. Shirer as 'a former police stool pigeon of unsavoury reputation'.[15] Heiden was tough and doubtless loyal, but he was no organiser. If the SS was to be developed as a counterweight or even protection against the SA, it needed someone with a systematic brain and the ability to shape it up coherently. Someone like Heinrich Himmler, who had been quietly making his mark at party headquarters in Munich over the previous twelve months.

Himmler seemed destined to remain the perfect number two: he was already Deputy Gauleiter of Lower Bavaria and Swabia and Deputy Reich Propaganda Chief, and in early September he added the post of Deputy Reichsführer of the SS to his growing portfolio. The SS was still a small section of the SA, numbering hardly more than 200 – indeed, its size was carefully limited by the party rules to one officer and ten men in each local area. But this did not deter Himmler. He approached his new job with his usual energy and meticulous attention to detail, making his presence felt immediately. Once again, it was a question of 'Der Heini macht es schon'.

SS Order No 1, which Himmler promulgated on 13 September 1927, laid down strict regulations for dress and conduct. SS men were to wear uniform at all times when on duty or at meetings, with caps, breeches, ties and leather belts all in black to mark them out from the rest of the SA. If they saw any regular SA man wearing any part of the SS uniform, they were to report him immediately. They were to parade for a full inspection before every meeting, and were forbidden to smoke, interrupt or leave the room during the speeches. They were not to involve themselves in anything that did not concern them: 'The SS stands apart from all quarrels'. They were to be 'the most ardent propagandists for the movement', and were to hold regular propaganda marches in their areas.

Himmler's obsession with intelligence gathering and snooping was growing fast as he became more and more of a control freak. According to Otto Strasser, he was much taken with the secret police methods of Stalin's Cheka, and wrote a memo to Hitler proposing that the SS should take on this role within the movement, stressing that: 'They will be blindly devoted to you and continue the tradition of the Stosstrupp Hitler of 9 November 1923.'[16] Certainly in SS Order No 1 he confirmed that they were to carry out intelligence duties, reporting not only on the activities of political opponents like the Social Democrats, the Communists, Freemasons, and prominent Jews, but also on their own political leadership and the rest of the SA.

As important as intelligence gathering was – and Himmler recognised that the knowledge it provided was the passport to power – it was not his prime ambition for the SS. He had been reading about the Cheka, it is true, but he had been reading for much longer about other things, mostly to do with racial theories, the mystical relationship between blood and soil, and the ancient crusade of the Teutonic Knights carrying Germanic civilisation into the Slav wilderness. In pursuit of the supposed Aryan origins of the German race, he had studied the myths and legends of ancient India, and had been much taken with the Indian division of society into four basic classes or castes. The second of these castes, the Kshatriyas, particularly caught his imagination, for they were the noble warriors who had conquered India for the Aryans nearly 2,000 years before Christ. It was also, interestingly, the caste of princes and rulers, below the priestly Brahmans. 'Kshatriya caste, that is what we must be. That is the salvation,' he wrote.[17] In Himmler's mind, even at that early stage, the SS was to become the warrior elite, a mixture of Kshatriyas and Teutonic Knights who would bring his fantasies to life. The vision was his and his alone, certainly not Heiden's, and not even Hitler's, who wanted only a trustworthy bodyguard.

Surprisingly, in spite of all his duties, which still included dashing about the country visiting branches, making speeches, organising propaganda campaigns, inspecting local SS units, Himmler was somehow finding time to conduct a courtship, albeit mostly by post. The previous winter, while taking a short break in the Bavarian resort of Bad Reichenhall, he had literally bumped into an attractive woman in a hotel lobby while shaking the snow off his hat and on to her. Turning to apologise, he found himself looking at his vision of a Valkyrie, with clear blue eyes, blonde hair and a wide smile. Her name was Margarete Boden, Marga for short. She was the daughter of a German landowner in Gonzerzewo, West Prussia, had served as a nurse in the war and then settled in Berlin, where after a short-lived marriage she had used her father's money to open a private clinic for alternative medicine –

homeopathy, hypnosis, herbal remedies and the like – something which had fascinated Himmler since his childhood.

Marga was eight years older than Himmler, and much more versed in the ways of the world. There is little doubt that he was still a virgin when he met her, and it is generally accepted that she seduced him. 'And about time, too,' Otto Strasser ribbed him when he told him. Marga seems to have made most of the running, and although he was deeply in love with her, he hesitated for some time before introducing her to his parents: 'I would rather clear a hall of a thousand Communists single-handed,' he confessed to his brother Gebhard. She was, after all, a Prussian, a Protestant, and a divorcee, none of which would have pleased Professor Himmler. But eventually he took her home, and eventually the parents gave their approval, and the courtship continued throughout 1927 and into the following year.

On 2 October 1927, President Hindenburg celebrated his eightieth birthday. The nationalists celebrated with what the Nobel Prize-winning liberal journalist Carl von Ossietzky described as 'a gigantic jubilee of all the black-white-red'. A new memorial to the Field Marshal's great victory at Tannenberg was dedicated. And in the Reichstag the parties of the right combined with the Communists to vote through an amnesty for all those who had been imprisoned or forced into exile for political offences. Among those who returned to Germany shortly afterwards was Hermann Göring.

Leaving his ailing wife behind in Sweden, Göring hurried to Munich, to see Hitler and offer his services. But the welcome he received was decidedly cool. The party and Hitler had moved on in the four years Göring had been away. There could be no question of getting his old job back as commander of the SA, and all the other leading positions were filled by men who had emerged during that time, like Strasser, Himmler and Goebbels, or who had stayed to continue the fight and had not taken flight. Hitler had become a national celebrity in his own right, and no longer needed the glamour of a flying ace; and in any case a shadow had been cast over Göring's reputation by the Richthofen Veterans' Association, which had blackballed him over allegations of false claims for kills he had not made. Hitler had undoubtedly heard reports, too, about his drug problems, and had been fed poisonous gossip and rumour about him, especially by his arch-enemy Rosenberg.

Hitler could offer Göring nothing. He merely told him to 'keep in touch' and suggested that the best way he could serve the party – and so rehabilitate himself – would be to go to Berlin, get himself a job and build up his high society contacts again. Göring set about doing exactly that. He rented a room in a small hotel just off the Kurfürstendamm, and began working as an agent for BMW aero engines and the Swedish Tornblad automatic parachute, taking a slightly younger former artillery officer, Paul 'Pilli' Körner, whom he had known in the war, as his partner. Körner had a little money, hero-worshipped Göring and was happy to act as his unpaid chauffeur and secretary, driving him in style around Berlin in his smart Mercedes car.

Surprisingly, Göring seems to have made no effort to contact Goebbels, or Strasser or the underground Nazi Party in Berlin, or to become involved in politics again. He did, however, get in touch with as many wartime comrades as he could, starting with his old flying partner Bruno Loerzer. The magic of the *Pour le Mérite* had worked well for Loerzer. He was now involved with the Heinkel aircraft company and the fledgling Lufthansa airline, and had married a rich wife, who was able to give lavish lunch and dinner parties, where Göring could widen his circle of useful contacts.

Göring had not lost his social touch, and his circle of acquaintances grew rapidly. He used them, and his own *Pour le Mérite,* shamelessly to obtain new introductions and open new doors. Renewing his wartime friendship with Prince Philipp of Hesse, who was now married to a daughter of the King of Italy, gave him access to the very top levels of Berlin society, including the Crown Prince himself. He was flying high again, his drug problem was under control, and although he was no longer the slim young flying ace, much of his old ebullience returned.

Mixing with the very rich involved spending more money than he had, of course, but living well on tick was something Göring had had plenty of practice in, and in any case he saw it as a good investment. All this time, however, he was missing Carin dreadfully and worrying about her health. He hurried back to Stockholm to spend Christmas with her, but she was still not well enough to accompany him when he returned to Germany in the New Year.

The beginning of 1928 saw more changes in the party structure, as it became obvious that the strategy of wooing the urban working-class vote had not been a success. Hitler removed Gregor Strasser from his post as Reich Propaganda Chief, and made him Reich Organisation Leader, a job for which he was eminently suited and which he was delighted to take, regarding it as the top position in the party after Hitler. In fact, Strasser had been doing much of the organisational work already, since the man he was replacing, General Heinemann, had been pretty useless. Strasser had usually taken the chair at important party meetings, had been largely responsible for organising the party rallies at Weimar and Nuremberg, and had sorted out disputes between members in local branches and Gaue. Hitler took over the propaganda post himself, but kept Strasser's existing deputy – which meant that Himmler now found himself working directly for and with the Führer in the area that Hitler regarded as the most important of all.

At the end of March, the organisation and propaganda departments moved into top gear when new Reichstag elections were announced for 20 May. The Nazis decided to fight in all thirty-five electoral districts, with an overall list of thirty-six candidates, some of whom stood in several districts to improve their chances in the complex proportional representation voting system. Hitler was debarred from standing even if he had wanted to, because he was not yet a German citizen: he had renounced his Austrian citizenship in 1925 to avoid the danger of extradition, but had not obtained German citizenship, and was now officially stateless. The Nazi list was headed by General Franz Ritter von Epp, who had recently converted to the party from the BVP. Goebbels was on the list – the Berlin party had tried to divert him into the Prussian Landtag, but, as he wrote in his diary, 'I want to make a nuisance of myself to the gentlemen of the Reichstag.'[18] The others included Gregor Strasser, Feder, Munich's former political police chief Wilhelm Frick and, to many people's surprise, Göring.

Although he was not selling many parachutes, Göring's fortunes were improving, and so was Carin's health. With the income from other sources, including the agency for various other aviation products and a consultancy from the Heinkel aircraft company, he was able to rent a modest apartment at 16 Berchtesgadener Strasse, and bring Carin home, still delicate but at last able to travel. His spirits were rising, and he was ready to rejoin the action. As soon as he heard about the election, Göring decided he wanted all the benefits of Reichstag membership – free travel, a guaranteed income, daily allowances, political and social connections, legal immunity, personal kudos, and above all the opportunities for lucrative consultancies and backhanders.

There are conflicting accounts of how Göring came to be selected for the Nazis' electoral list. Carin told her son that one day while Hitler was in Berlin, staying at the discreet Hotel Sans Souci, 'the Führer asked to see his old comrade and welcomed him with open arms, happy to see how well and prosperous (!!) he looked. He asked him to take up the flag again on behalf of the party, and to fight for Germany's redemption at the elections in May.'[19] Carin, of course, could only know what her husband told her – and he was perfectly capable of deceiving her with white lies, as he had in Italy with stories of non-existent meetings with Mussolini. Those who support her version of events point out that Hitler needed Göring's social skills and high-level contacts to reassure the rich and powerful, who might be scared away by Goebbels's and Strasser's radicalism and the rough and tumble of the storm-troopers.

According to Putzi Hanfstaengl, however, who says he walked there with him but left him at the door, Göring went to see Hitler at his little flat in Thierschstrasse, Munich, not the Hotel Sans Souci in Berlin, at his own insistence, to demand a place on the list. In this version, he blackmailed Hitler by threatening to reveal the secret backers who were now financing the party, and to sue the party in the courts for the money he and Carin had poured into it in 1922 and 1923.

Bearing in mind Göring's awe of Hitler, it seems unlikely that he could ever try to browbeat him, even for so big a prize – or that Hitler would capitulate to such a threat. Göring would certainly have had to plead and perhaps argue with him, to convince him that he was fully rehabilitated, that he would be an asset to the party again, and that he deserved a place. He may well have hinted strongly that he knew about the secret backers, and that he wanted his money – that would have been perfectly in character. But he is more likely to have brought pressure to bear by reminding Hitler that he had marched alongside him in the November *putsch*, and had almost lost his life for the cause. He had been to hell and back during the past four years, and the party owed him something in return.

Hitler would have responded to such an appeal. He always had a soft spot for heroes, and Göring, with his *Pour le Mérite* and his wounds, was a hero twice over. What was more, Göring was clearly not a drug-crazed weakling as Rosenberg had made out, but a lively, energetic and ambitious individual who had put his life together again and was making a success of it. Whatever his reasons, Hitler was persuaded, though apparently only after three meetings – maybe the final one was in the Hotel Sans Souci. He included Göring on the list in eighth place. If the Nazis won the right to more than seven members, he was guaranteed a seat.

The election was a fairly dull affair in most districts, with increasing prosperity taking the heat out of the campaigns. Berlin was the exception. The ban on the party had been lifted on 31 March so that it could take part in the elections – Goebbels's speaking ban in the city had been raised at the end of the previous October, by coincidence on his thirtieth birthday – and it was formally reconstituted on 13 April, to go into battle against the Reds. 'They've already started shooting each other dead,' Carin wrote to her mother on 18 May. 'Every day the Communists with red flags and hammers and sickles on them range through the city, and they always clash with Hitler's men carrying their red banners with swastikas on them, and then there are fights, with dead and wounded.'[20]

Goebbels, meanwhile, was involved in a series of court cases, first on charges relating to the beating-up of Pastor Stucke and then for insulting Deputy Police Commissioner Weiss. When he was found guilty and given jail sentences, he appealed and managed to drag the proceedings out until he achieved Reichstag immunity. And all the time, he was writing furiously, pouring out a stream of pamphlets, posters, newspaper articles, and editorials, and charging about Germany making speeches: on 14 May, for example, he spoke twelve times in Munich alone.

Göring, too, proved one of the party's most popular speakers, able both to talk persuasively and quietly at businessmen's clubs and lunches, and to trade ribald jokes with workers at mass meetings. And while Goebbels, Göring, Strasser and Hitler himself were out on the campaign trail, behind the scenes Himmler was relishing the challenge of organising and co-ordinating the frantic schedules of all the party speakers, imposing discipline and order while keeping the propaganda machine turning at full speed.

For all their efforts, the results were profoundly disappointing. The time was not yet right for the Nazis, and they managed to poll only 809,771 votes nationwide, down 100,000 on the December 1924 election, a mere 2.6 per cent of the national total. In painful contrast, the

Communists had actually increased their vote by 500,000, to 3.25 million, while the Social Democrats had stormed home as the biggest party with over nine million votes. The Nazis were entitled to just twelve of the Reichstag's 500 seats. Two of them went to Goebbels and Göring.

VIII

'WE COME AS ENEMIES'

ON 13 June 1928, Göring and Goebbels both took their seats in the new Reichstag. Their intentions, however, were very different. Göring wanted to use the Reichstag, both for his own and the party's benefit; Goebbels wanted to destroy it. For months, Goebbels had sneered at the Reichstag in *Der Angriff*, changing his tune only slightly when the party decided to take part in the elections. Now he wrote equally scornfully to justify his membership. 'I am not a member of the Reichstag,' he declared, 'I am simply a possessor of immunity, a holder of a free travel pass. What does the Reichstag matter to us? We were elected to oppose the Reichstag, and we will indeed carry out the mandate in the way our voters intended.'[1] Two days later he underlined his message more brutally: 'We do not come as friends or as neutrals. We come as enemies. Like the wolf into the sheep flock.'[2]

Goebbels, ever the radical puritan, feared that he might be corrupted by the 'paid idleness' of the Reichstag. 'The whole business,' he wrote, 'is so rotten and crafty but also so sweet and seductive that very few characters can resist it. I am solemnly determined to stay strong, and I hope and believe that I will succeed.'[3] Göring had no such problems. He revelled in the opening ceremonies, enjoyed finding himself allocated a desk with Epp right at the front of the assembly, and was delighted by the many messages of congratulation he received, particularly one from Crown Prince Friedrich Wilhelm: 'Your extraordinary talent, your skill with words and your great physical strength are just what is needed for your new profession of people's representative.'

The Crown Prince had no great respect for the Reichstag, believing Göring would need his physical strength for the brawls and fist fights that were a regular feature of its sessions. Carin had told her mother with some dismay that at the opening session 'it was really dismal having to see so many Red Guards. They have made unheard-of progress and take up a colossal number of seats in the Reichstag. They were in their uniforms, wearing Jewish stars of David, red stars, it's all the same, and red armbands etc. Mostly young, and raring for a fight. And some of them absolute criminal types. How many in all these parties, except Hitler's, are Jews!'

Göring had no interest in punch-ups with the Communists in the Reichstag. In fact, he showed very little interest in the day-to-day business at all, making only one speech in the chamber during his first two years as a member. That speech was to demand higher subsidies for the Lufthansa airline, which 'had a great patriotic task to fulfil', and asking why there was no Secretary of State for Air – a position he naturally believed should be his. Apart from his personal interest in the airline as a covert means of developing a military air force, he was obligated to Erhard Milch, the commercial director of Lufthansa, who was paying him a retainer of 1,000 marks a month to lobby for the company.

As well as the Lufthansa money, Göring was also able to supplement his 750 marks a month salary as a Reichstag member with lucrative writing for newspapers, which clamoured for articles. And he was paid 800 marks a month by the party as a 'Reichsredner', a national speaker – the party had two lists of recognised speakers, those who were confined to their own Gaue and the select few, like Göring and Goebbels, star turns who were authorised to speak anywhere in Germany. Göring earned his money, dashing from one end of the country to the other addressing meetings, some with audiences of 20–30,000. But after years of scraping and begging, he was hungry for the taste of real money. Like a child let loose in a candy store, he took full advantage of the opportunities surrounding him.

Suddenly, money was coming from all directions. Göring's existing business was boosted by his new position, and BMW and Heinkel added substantially to what he made from their agencies with regular 'consultancy fees'. Other companies in the aircraft industry, such as Messerschmitt, paid him large occasional sums. Lufthansa agreed to cover the costs of his office, including the wages of Pili Körner and a secretary, and slipped him an extra 3,500 marks for the deposit on a luxury new apartment at No 7 Badensche Strasse in Berlin's smart Schöneberg district; the coal and steel magnate Fritz Thyssen paid for its sumptuous furnishings and decoration. And so it went on. One of the attractions of the new apartment was that it had an underground garage with a lift leading directly to Göring's lobby, so that guests could come and go discreetly, even secretly.

When the Deutsche Bank queried the amounts Lufthansa was paying him, Milch warned Göring that evidence of bribery could cause problems for him in the future and proposed a one-off payment of 100,000 marks, as an advance on his services for the duration of the present Reichstag. Göring accepted eagerly. That, he said, would suit him much better, adding, apparently ingenuously, that Thyssen had 'opened an account of 50,000 Reichsmarks for me. I can draw as much as I like . . . It will always be replenished.'4 The pattern was set for the rest of his life. Göring's days of penury and penny-pinching were over.

The Görings moved into their new apartment in November 1928, and began entertaining on a grand scale. Carin, despite her frail health, was an excellent hostess, 'radiating charm' according to Milch, who was a regular guest. Other regulars included royalty such as Prince August-Wilhelm, the Kaiser's second son, known to everyone as 'Auwi', and his younger brother Prince Eitel Friedrich, the Prince and Princess zu Wied, and leading politicians and businessmen. To their bemusement – and sometimes maybe amusement – these high and mighty guests would often find themselves sitting alongside humble farm workers from Bavaria, party members to whom Göring gave food and shelter when they visited Berlin. It was all part of the Göring image of good-hearted bonhomie, which he cultivated to mask his ruthless ambition and which did his reputation no harm whatsoever with the rank and file of the party or the rich and famous.

While Göring was feathering his nest and Goebbels was getting used to having enough to live on in reasonable comfort, Himmler was still struggling to get by on a party salary of 200 marks a month. Fortunately, Marga had a little money of her own, so they were able to get married on 3 July 1928. She sold her clinic in Berlin and bought a smallholding with a three-bedroom wooden farmhouse at Waldtrudering on the eastern outskirts of Munich, where they planned to start a chicken farm.

Himmler built a chicken-house, they bought fifty laying hens and planted herbs as a cash crop, but the project was doomed from the start. So, too, was the marriage, though they struggled on together for several years: Himmler's first love was the Nazi Party, and the party was a demanding mistress claiming both his thoughts and his time. Too busy to do anything at the farm, he left the running of it entirely to Marga, who had no experience or training. Money was a constant problem. Even after the best part of a year, she was writing to him: 'The hens are laying frightfully badly – only two eggs a day. I worry so about what we're going to live on and how we're going to save for Whitsun. Something's always going wrong. I save so hard, but the money's like everything else.'⁵ Things were so tight that when he missed sending his usual contribution home, Marga chided him that she wouldn't be able to collect his shoes from the menders.

On 20 January 1929, after exactly a year as deputy leader, Himmler was appointed Reichsführer of the SS. It brought him no extra money, and was not on the face of it a particularly important appointment – the SS was still only a section of the SA, consisting of a mere 280 men, scattered across Germany in seventy-five formations, *Staffeln*. The party at large regarded it as little more than a harmless canvassing organisation for the party press. But now that it was his to command, Himmler began shaping it into the instrument that would turn his boyhood dreams of crusading knights and orders of chivalry into reality. He began drawing up his plans to expand its size and refine its purpose into the elite force he had always wanted. By April, he had completed the draft regulations that would define the 'Order of the SS'. He submitted them to Pfeffer, his nominal chief, and to Hitler, who approved them, probably without too much thought and as an indulgence to his young assistant.

Once he had the go-ahead, Himmler set about his task with quiet determination and his usual meticulous attention to detail. 'We went about it like a nursery gardener trying to reproduce a good old strain that has been adulterated and debased,' he recounted later. 'We started from the principles of plant selection and then proceeded, quite unashamedly, to weed out the men we did not think we could use for the build-up of the SS.'⁶

The selection process for new members was based on strict racial and physical criteria, though the process was hardly scientific: 'I started with a minimum height requirement of 5 feet 8 inches,' Himmler told his officers later. 'I knew that men of a certain height must somewhere possess the blood I desired.'⁷ He personally scrutinised photographs of every applicant through a magnifying glass, to identify any suspect racial characteristics:

I used to think: are there any definite indications of foreign blood in this man? Prominent cheekbones, for instance, which might cause people to say 'he has a Mongolian or Slav look about him'? Why did I do that? Let me draw your attention to the lessons of experience. Think of the types who were members of the soldiers' councils in 1918 and 1919. Every one of you who was an officer at that time has personal experience of a large number of these people. You will therefore be able to confirm that, in general, they were people who somehow looked odd to Germans, who had some peculiar feature showing that there was foreign blood somewhere.[8]

Himmler's obsession with the physical appearance of his SS men throws doubt on a claim by Otto Strasser that he tried to recruit him as leader of the SS northern district, based in Berlin – as Goebbels had pointed out, Otto looked quite Jewish with his hooked nose and crinkly hair. There must be a tinge of doubt, too, in Otto's claim that Himmler told him: 'That Goebbels will be green and blue with rage. You would naturally be subordinate only to me, no one could interfere with you in any way. You could finally take your revenge on Goebbels.' Otto Strasser's rift with the Berlin Gauleiter was still not final in 1929, and Himmler still saw Goebbels as a friend and ally.

There is, however, a ring of truth in Otto's memory of Himmler telling him: 'The SS will be an Order sworn to the Führer. For him I could do anything. Believe me, if Hitler were to say I should shoot my mother, I would do it and be proud of his confidence.' This might well be the same man who could be seen speaking quietly to a picture of Hitler on the wall of his office, like an Orthodox priest communing with a holy icon. 'Heinrich, I shudder at you,' Otto says he replied. He added that afterwards the phrase became his regular greeting to Himmler: 'He always took it with a laugh, indeed he was flattered.'[9]

The exclusivity of Himmler's new order made it attractive, particularly to former Freikorps officers who wanted something better than the simple thuggery of the SA. Month by month, he made the entry requirements progressively stiffer, and the more difficult he made it, the more desirable it became. There was no shortage of men who wished to join, but Himmler had to move carefully to avoid alarming Pfeffer, who insisted on controlling all SS recruiting, fearful that it would cream off his best commanders – among those who had already moved across was Kurt Daluege, the founder of the Berlin SA, who was now commanding the SS in the city. The SS was still forbidden to act independently of the SA, but Himmler was content to bide his time, quietly building up its strength. By the end of 1929, membership had reached 1,000. His future power base was taking shape.

On a personal level, Himmler's life was less successful. The chicken farm was showing no sign of improvement and he was still having to scrape and scratch for every penny. He was pleased when Marga bore him a daughter, Gudrun, in the summer of 1929, but after that they lived apart. He was away so much on party duties anyway that she hardly noticed the difference.

Although they lived in the same city, Goebbels and Göring moved in totally separate orbits around the party and the Führer. On the opening day of the Reichstag, Goebbels's diary included Göring in a list of Nazi Deputies as simply 'Goering [sic]. Flyer captain. Rather bloated.' After that, there is no further mention until 12 April 1929, when he briefly notes a meeting at the Hotel Sans Souci with Göring, Hess and Hitler, saying they had a long discussion about a possible alliance with the right-wing veterans' paramilitary organisation, the Stahlhelm.

Goebbels and Göring shared a platform at a rally in Friedrichshain on 4 May, and afterwards enjoyed their first personal chat, with Göring waxing lyrical about Mussolini and his time in Rome. Goebbels described him as 'an exemplary officer'. But it seems from the diary that Goebbels did not get to visit Göring's home until 14 May 1929, when he records: 'The Deputies are invited to a small party. We enjoy ourselves very much. Thank goodness all the personal friction between us has now been eliminated. Goering [sic] has a wonderful house and as a rule is also a great guy.' The personal friction seems to have been within the group as a whole, rather than between the two of them, though a few weeks later Goebbels described a heated row in the Reichstag with Göring, 'who is becoming ever more of a parliamentary bastard. On this, he is thick as a post and foul as a toad. So far, he has treated the others as riff-raff, and yesterday he tried it on me. But then he put things right.'[10]

By the start of 1929, storm clouds were beginning to gather once more over the German economy. Germany was about to overtake Great Britain as the world's second biggest exporter, having concentrated on exports at the expense of the home market as the only means of meeting the huge reparations payments still being demanded by the Allies. But the recovery was a hollow one, propped up by short-term US loans: between 1924 and 1929, Germany ran up massive debts approaching 30 billion gold marks. The collapse in world food prices had plunged German agriculture into a critical condition, with farmers everywhere going bankrupt. Heavy industry in the Ruhr was also in a state of crisis, with the big employers locking out 230,000 iron and steel workers for several weeks after a wage dispute. The winter was a hard one and unemployment soared, reaching 3.2 million by February 1929, up by a million in less than a year. Discontent grew, and with it support for the extremist parties of both right and left.

The Nazis benefited from the country's woes, as people sought extreme solutions to extreme problems, but there was still a long way to go if the Nazis were ever to be more than a small part of the lunatic fringe of German politics. Hitler embarked on an aggressive propaganda campaign, organised and co-ordinated by Himmler, pouring out articles for the press and speaking to growing audiences all over the country. Goebbels joined in, blaming the 'international Jewish conspiracy' for Germany's plight and attacking the democratic system. Membership of the party rose to 108,717 by the New Year, but that was still tiny – not even half the strength of the German Communist Party, KPD, in Berlin alone.

Goebbels did more than his bit in Berlin, with a non-stop programme of speeches, marches and street battles as well as printed propaganda. But it was with the embittered peasants and small farmers in rural Germany that the Nazis began to make noticeable headway. In state elections in Saxony in May, after one of Himmler's saturation coverage propaganda campaigns that included four major speeches by Hitler, the Nazis won five per cent of the vote. A month later, in Mecklenburg they achieved four per cent – little enough, but double their local score in the Reichstag elections a year earlier. After another month they won control of the town council in Coburg in northern Bavaria; by October they notched up seven per cent of the vote in the state elections in Baden; two weeks later 8.1 per cent in Lübeck, and in early December 11.3 per cent in Thuringia, entitling them to six of the fifty-three seats in the Landtag. They even agreed to take part in the Thuringian state government, nominating Wilhelm Frick as Interior Minister.

In Berlin, meanwhile, they had received 5.8 per cent of the vote, disappointing on the face of it, especially when compared with a combined Communist and Socialist total of more than fifty per cent. But Goebbels could draw some satisfaction from the fact that it was almost four times the Nazis' total of 1928 and entitled them to thirteen seats on the city council, one of which he took for himself. It was all steady if unremarkable growth. A number of events, however, were about to combine to produce a sudden and dramatic change.

Foreign Minister and former Chancellor Gustav Stresemann had already failed to endear himself to the German right by ending passive resistance to the occupation of the Ruhr, accepting Germany's western frontiers as set at Versailles, and taking the country into the League of Nations in 1926. He had infuriated them by accepting the Nobel Peace Prize that year, in company with his French and British counterparts, Aristide Briand and Austen Chamberlain, and in 1928 by signing the Kellogg-Briand Pact outlawing war as an instrument of policy. In July 1929, following a new plan put forward by US banker and head of the General Electric Company, Owen D. Young, he had renegotiated Germany's crippling reparations payments, reducing them by seventeen per cent and rescheduling them to continue at a lower rate until 1988. The plan also provided for the withdrawal of Allied troops from the Rhineland five years earlier than the set date. By any normal standards, it was a diplomatic triumph, but to the far right parties it was a betrayal, signifying acceptance of Versailles and the *status quo*. They erupted in fury.

Hitler declared that the Young Plan, which had to be ratified by the Reichstag, would lead to the enslavement of the German people. Goebbels called it 'a death penalty passed on the unborn'. But the main opposition to the plan came from the DNVP, the German Nationalist People's Party, led by Alfred Hugenberg, a pig-headed former general manager of Krupp who had made a fortune out of the inflation and was now, at the age of sixty-five, the wealthy owner of a chain of newspapers, a leading news agency and the UFA film studio. To mount a powerful campaign against the plan, Hugenberg formed a committee that included men such as steel tycoon Fritz Thyssen, Stahlhelm chief Theodor Duesterberg, Heinrich Class, leader of the Pan-German League, and Hjalmar Schacht, the man who had stabilised the currency and defeated hyper-inflation. Though they were all influential in their own spheres, none of them had much appeal to the masses. The committee needed an injection of charisma – and Hugenberg, prompted perhaps by Thyssen, knew exactly where to find it. He invited Hitler to join the campaign.

The Nazis had been even more vociferous than the DNVP in their opposition to the Young Plan. But that did not change Goebbels's long-standing hatred of Hugenberg and his capitalist allies. Hitler had been toying with the thought of an alliance since the spring, and every time the subject came up it tested Goebbels's loyalty to its limit. Still seeing himself as a revolutionary, he was appalled at the idea of joining forces with the reactionaries who wanted to drag Germany back to the bad old days of the Hohenzollerns. His doubts about Hitler surfaced again – but as usual he blamed the Munich crowd for leading his idol astray. 'We still have too many philistines in the party,' he noted in April. 'Sometimes Munich's course is intolerable. I'm not prepared to go along with a corrupt compromise. I'll stick to the straight and narrow path, even if it should cost me my personal position.'[11]

Goebbels's personal position, however, was exactly the bait Hitler used to bring him back into line every time he tried to rebel. At the end of May, he sank his hook even deeper into the little Gauleiter's soul by offering him the prize he wanted more than anything except Hitler's love. Talking until 2 a.m. in his room at the Sans Souci, Hitler promised Goebbels that he would soon take over Reich propaganda. This would mean spending a couple of days every fortnight in Munich, where he would be provided with an office, staff, and a comfortable flat. Suddenly, Munich was attractive again. Now, Hitler won his support for an alliance with the DNVP by insisting that Goebbels should be in charge of all propaganda for the campaign. Hugenberg agreed, placing his press and film empire at Goebbels's disposal. Goebbels's objections suddenly evaporated.

This was the great opportunity Goebbels had been waiting for, a national platform encompassing genuinely popular newspapers, cinema newsreels and a news syndication agency, all entirely at his disposal and with no restrictions on costs. He seized it eagerly, turning the campaign against the Young Plan into a massive promotion exercise for the Nazi Party and an attack on the whole democratic system, branding the government as traitors willing to enslave the German people for the next fifty-eight years. 'Stresemann,' he shrieked, 'is not really an individual but the incarnation of everything rotten in Germany.' And when Stresemann obliged him by dropping dead on 3 October, he crowed that his death was 'execution by heart failure' and that 'a rock had been removed from the path to German freedom'.[12]

Three weeks after Stresemann's death, on 'Black Thursday', 24 October 1929, the American stockmarket crashed. The flow of dollars that had been financing German industry and reparations payments was abruptly cut off and short-term loans were called in, pricking the bubble of German economic recovery. Like a cartoon character running on air before plummeting into an abyss, the country continued to function for a while, but the fall was inevitable. When it came, it created the perfect conditions for the Nazi Party to take off in spectacular fashion.

The campaign against the Young Plan failed – the benefits to Germany, including an early withdrawal of foreign troops from the Rhineland, far outweighed the disadvantages of an extended payments schedule, and in a plebiscite in December 1929 only 13.8 per cent of the electorate voted against it. But for Hitler it had served its purpose wonderfully. It had given him publicity worth a fortune entirely at Hugenberg's expense, turned him into a national politician, and brought him into contact with a number of rich and powerful industrialists. When it failed, he blamed Hugenberg and the DNVP, and took the opportunity to break with them. But he did not break with the businessmen. He had wooed the most promising of them with invitations to that year's party rally at Nuremberg at the beginning of August, where they were duly impressed by the flags and banners and bands and the display of solidarity by some 40,000 of the party's 130,000 members. Some 25,000 SA men marched smartly through the city, together with a smaller SS delegation with Himmler at its head, and Hitler swore in twenty four new SA units. It was all heady stuff.

To the influential guests, the party and its SA army were the obvious answer to a Communist threat that was growing increasingly real – on May Day that year savage street battles in Berlin between the Red Front Fighters and police had resulted in 33 deaths, 198 civilians and 47 policemen injured, and 1,228 arrests, reviving fearful memories of the civil war of 1919. Goebbels had cleverly ordered his own men not to become involved.

One of the most important visitors to Nuremberg was Emil Kirdorf, the biggest coal and iron magnate in the Ruhr. Kirdorf had been making secret contributions to party funds for several years, but now he dipped even further into his deep pockets to provide most of the money to buy the impressive Barlow Palace, on Brienner Strasse and Königsplatz in Munich. Hitler renamed it the Brown House, and set about converting it into the party's new headquarters. As tastelessly grandiose as any ministry building, it was a clear statement of his intent to create an alternative government, ready to take over from the hated Republic.

On a personal level, on 10 September Hitler had moved into a luxury nine-roomed apartment in the Prinzregentenplatz, one of Munich's most fashionable squares, which he filled with heavy, dark furniture that had been specially designed for him by his favourite architect, Paul Ludwig Troost. He had also taken a lease for 100 marks a month on a modest alpine chalet, Haus Wachenfeld, on the Obersalzberg slopes above Berchtesgaden, his beloved holiday retreat. It was all a far cry from the seedy two rooms he had occupied on Thierschstrasse, and the time only five or six years before when he had relied on hand-outs from Göring for pocket money. The hand-outs he was receiving now were more substantial, but he still owed many of them to Göring's efforts in attracting and reassuring rich patrons. He also owed a great deal to Goebbels's work in promoting his and the party's image.

The Nazis' quadrupled vote in Berlin was due almost entirely to Goebbels's brilliant campaign. They had made scarcely any inroad into the Communist vote, which had been four times bigger, but he had succeeded in convincing the Communists that the Nazis were an enemy to be taken seriously. He no longer needed to go out of his way to provoke them or to provide fake casualties – indeed, he was lucky to escape with his own life when a bunch of Red Guards spotted him in his car near Görlitz station in Neukölln. 'Come on, proles!' he heard one shout. 'Here's Goebbels, the murderer of the workers! Now we'll put an end to him!' He recorded the encounter in breathless prose:

Before my eyes, clubs, daggers, brass knuckles appear. I receive a blow on my shoulder. As I drag myself aside, a Communist takes aim at me. A shot rings out. Stones fly. Tonak [Goebbels's driver] is already bleeding heavily. A wild volley of shots. Shots crackle from the car. The mob gives ground. I apply pressure to Tonak's wound. He starts the car and drives off, in full possession of his senses. White as a sheet, he grips the wheel. Over signs and kerbstones. Behind us stones fly, shots crack. We've escaped.[13]

As always, Goebbels made the most of every injured SA man, with lurid and bathetic reports of their suffering in *Der Angriff*, but there were so many now that they no longer had much impact. What he needed was something stronger, something with more dramatic potential. What he needed was a martyr. He had tried to create one at the end of 1928 with Hans-Georg Kütemeyer, an SA man whose body was found in the Landwehr Canal the morning after Hitler had spoken for the first time in the Sportpalast. Goebbels claimed that he had been murdered by Communists, but his old enemy 'Isidor' Weiss refused permission for a funeral procession, seized the excuse to search the party headquarters, turning up two pistols in the process, and pulled Goebbels in for questioning, in spite of his Reichstag immunity. The police then destroyed his martyrdom case by producing irrefutable evidence that Kütemeyer had committed suicide.

Undeterred, Goebbels continued his search. When nineteen-year-old Walter Fischer from Friedenau was killed in a fight with Communists towards the end of December 1929, Goebbels led an SA demonstration march to Fehrbelliner Platz, and three days later staged a memorial ceremony at the young man's graveside. The SA turned out in force, Prince August Wilhelm attended, and Göring, Goebbels and SA Sturmführer Horst Wessel made emotional speeches. Goebbels declared that the young man had been a 'blood sacrifice' and called for revenge against the 'red murder squads'. But Fischer was not the stuff of martyrs, and in any case had been made to resign from the SA by his Social Democrat father, an apothecary. Goebbels received 10,000 marks for the party and a further 100 for wounded SA men from Herr Fischer senior.[14] But he could not wring much publicity out of the death.

Returning to Berlin after spending Christmas in Rheydt with his family, mourning his father who had died on 7 December, Goebbels was immediately faced with another ceremonial SA funeral, this time for Horst Wessel's brother Werner, who had frozen to death after getting lost in the mountains while out skiing. Again, there was no mileage to be gained, but 500 SA men with flaming torches led the funeral procession past the Communists' headquarters, Karl Liebknecht House, in heavy rain.[15]

Coming so soon after his own father's death, which had affected him deeply, Goebbels found Werner Wessel's funeral emotionally shattering, and says he could hardly speak. Two weeks afterwards, late at night, he received news that Horst Wessel had been shot and was lying seriously wounded in St Joseph's Hospital in Friedrichshain. To his credit, Goebbels's first comment in his diary is 'The poor mother! So soon after her son Werner!' It was four days, however, before he visited Frau Wessel and then Horst himself, who was lying with 'his whole face shot away, disfigured. He looks at me, all rigid, then his eyes fill with tears and he murmurs: "One has to hold on! . . . I'm happy!"'[16] Goebbels said he was close to weeping. Wessel had been shot through the mouth and although they had been able to stop the bleeding, the surgeons were unable to remove the bullet, which had lodged in front of the cerebellum. There was little doubt that he would die. Goebbels had his martyr.

Horst Wessel had all the right qualifications. He was twenty-two years old, bright, good looking and idealistic. Far from being the typical mindless brown-shirted SA thug, he was the son of the Lutheran pastor of the ancient church of St Nikolas on the corner of the Alexanderplatz, and had been a promising law student at Berlin's Friedrich Wilhelm University before dropping out to devote himself to political activism, first with the Bismarck and Viking youth groups, and then the SA. His mother described his life to Goebbels as: 'Like a Dostoevsky novel: the idiot, the worker, the tart, the bourgeois family, the eternal torment of conscience, the eternal agony.'[17] He had been attracted to the Nazis by exactly the same things as Goebbels himself: a belief in social justice 'with the emphasis on Socialism' and the personality of Hitler. He had joined at about the time Goebbels arrived in Berlin, and had become his devoted follower.

Goebbels, recognising Wessel's leadership qualities, had earmarked the youngster for special treatment. For the first six months of 1928, he had sent him to Vienna, to study the methods and organisation of the Viennese party's highly successful youth group. Returning to Berlin, Wessel had been named leader of Storm Unit 5, the Alexanderplatz section, and had helped train Nazi Party cell leaders, despite the rule that SA members were not allowed to become involved in party affairs. When Goebbels started sending SA units to march and demonstrate in Communist districts after the May Day battles in 1929, with the intention of persuading Red Front Fighters to switch sides and become storm-troopers, Wessel was assigned to the notorious Fischerkiez slum area between his father's church and the Royal Palace. After a number of minor skirmishes, Wessel's unit was involved in a more serious attack on the Hoppe pub, which housed the local KPD headquarters, in which four Communists were seriously injured. Wessel became a marked man.

The Communists bided their time, waiting for the right opportunity to strike. It came in January 1930, when a widow named Salm asked the members of the Communist cell to which her late husband had belonged to help her with a Nazi lodger who was not paying his rent. The Communists were about to turn her away, since they knew she had betrayed the cause by giving her husband a Christian burial, but then she mentioned the man's name. It was Wessel. Now they knew where he was – and that there were no other SA men with him. A group of them went to the widow's house, and while some kept watch in the street, two of them went upstairs. One, Albert Höhler, had a pistol. He knocked on the door, and when Wessel opened it, shot him in the head. As Wessel collapsed at the feet of his girlfriend, a former prostitute whom he had rescued from the streets, the Communists ran for it.

The KPD's district headquarters spirited the killers out of the city, and instructed Frau Salm not to involve the party in any way. She was to tell the police that Wessel was a pimp and that the shooting had been part of a quarrel with another pimp over the girl whose earnings he was living on. They published that claim in their newspaper, *Die Rote Fahne*, denying that Höhler was a party member. Goebbels, of course, used *Der Angriff* to accuse the Communists of the crime and demand that the murderers be 'crushed to a pulp'.[18] When Höhler and his accomplices were picked up by the police after a tip-off on 3 February, their confessions confirmed that the attack had been political. The KPD and *Die Rote Fahne* were forced to retract, and Goebbels trumpeted a famous victory, though the myth of two pimps fighting over a tart lingers to this day.

Wessel took an agonising six weeks to die, during which Goebbels chronicled every aspect of his condition in *Der Angriff*, milking it for all it was worth and turning him into 'a Socialist Christ who had chosen to live among those who scorned and spat at him'. When he did eventually die, early on 23 February, Goebbels hurried first to the hospital, where he 'laid a few flowers on his bed' and comforted his grieving mother, before dashing off to meet with Göring and Dagobert Dürr, the editor of *Der Angriff*, to plan how they could best exploit the situation. They decided the Gau would go into deep mourning for fourteen days, during which party members were to abstain from all public amusements and honour his memory at every gathering. Parents were to tell their children to pray that all German youth should be filled with Horst Wessel's 'spirit of sacrifice'.

The funeral was a triumph for Goebbels, despite the police restricting the cortege to no more than ten vehicles. He claimed in his diary that there were 20–30,000 silent spectators lining the route from Wessel's parents' home to the St Nikolas cemetery. To his intense disappointment, however, Hitler chose not to come. Goebbels blamed Hess for keeping the Führer in Berchtesgaden; Hanfstaengl claimed it was Göring who persuaded him to stay away, fearful that he might become involved in the violence that was bound to erupt during and after the ceremony.

The first sign of trouble came in Bülowplatz, where 'The Internationale' sounded out from the KPD headquarters as the procession passed. Shortly afterwards, in Koblanstrasse, Communists broke through the police cordon, stones were thrown, shots fired and the hearse rocked. At the cemetery itself, which was packed to overflowing, the mourners were greeted by a message boldly daubed on the wall in white, 'To Wessel the pimp – a last Heil Hitler!' More stones flew over the wall into the crowd as the coffin, covered in a swastika flag, was lowered into the ground to the strains of the old song 'I Once Had a Comrade'. Two pastors and two students from Wessel's fraternities spoke briefly, and then Goebbels stepped forward and made 'the last roll call' – as he called Wessel's name, the assembled SA men responded 'Here!' Voice trembling with emotion, whether real or simulated, he launched into a eulogy, describing the dead man once again as 'a Christ-like Socialist' who had sacrificed himself for the movement.

The climax came with the singing, for the first time in public, of a song that Wessel himself had written and submitted to *Der Angriff* in March 1929. It was entitled 'Raise High the Flag', and was to be sung to a melody from a Communist songbook, which had itself been adapted from a Salvation Army hymn. The main refrain ran:

> *Die Fahne hoch! Die Reihen dicht geschlossen!*
> *SA marschiert mit mutig, festem Schritt.*
> *Kameraden, die Rotfront und Reaktion erschossen,*
> *Marschiern im Geist in unsern Reihen mit.*

> Raise high the flag! Close ranks up tight together!
> The SA march with bold and steady tread.
> Comrades shot by Red Front and reactionaries
> March with us in spirit in our ranks.

It was hardly poetry, and hardly great music. But it caught the imagination of the SA and the party, became the SA's most popular marching song, and for twelve years after 1933 was Germany's alternate national anthem, as 'The Horst Wessel Song'. Goebbels had created not just a martyr, but a national icon. It was one of his most successful confidence tricks, proving beyond all doubt his complete mastery of the black art of propaganda.

*   *   *

Since his first visit to his house ten months earlier, Goebbels's relationship with Göring had blossomed into a close friendship. His diary is smattered with complimentary references to Göring's character, especially in comparison with mutual enemies from Munich, as for example after sharing a speaking platform with Feder in Berlin:

With Göring to Viktoriagarten. Overflowing. Feder speaks. The old simpleton. Then I come on. I spend an hour on the automaton Hindenburg and call the lying press to account. Everyone very excited. . . . From there together with Göring and Feder. Göring is a good fellow, and very affectionate. Feder a conceited, vain, jealous dandy. I can't stand him.[19]

Goebbels was relishing his position as a Reichstag member and city councillor: although he rarely spoke in either, he put in an appearance most days at both the parliament and Berlin's 'Red Town Hall' – so called for the colour of its brickwork not its politics, though it had in fact always been dominated by the Socialists. Conscious of his new social status, he was rapidly acquiring a taste for the high life and high society that Göring enjoyed so much – though he always took good care to preserve his public image as an ascetic. As well as sharing speaking platforms and discussing party matters, he and Göring often dined and went to the cinema and theatre together, sometimes with Hans Schweitzer, a savagely anti-Semitic cartoonist whose work illustrated and complemented Goebbels's articles in *Der Angriff*, as well as appearing regularly in the *Völkischer Beobachter*. His diary entry for 20 January epitomises the new relationship:

To Göring's to eat. Then with him and Schweitzer to the Deutsche Theater. *The Kaiser from America*, with Werner Krauss. A fabulous evening . . . From there to the Schöneberger Ratskeller. Göring really carried on about Munich. Also about Hitler, in part with some justification. He works too little, too short, he is [word illegible]. And the women, the women! But against this stands an excess of ability and virtue, his charm, his goodness, his instinct, his human greatness. We are only glad that we have him and so put up with his weaknesses.[20]

The fact that they could criticise Hitler to each other shows the trust that had developed between them. They had become partners against the Munich crowd, and against the Strassers. Göring complained to Hitler that Otto Strasser's radical left-wing speeches and articles in the *Berliner Arbeiterzeitung* and its sister papers were constantly sabotaging his efforts to bring more rich industrialists and aristocrats into the party. Goebbels had a personal battle to fight against the Strassers, particularly Otto, and was grateful for Göring's support.

The simmering antagonism between Goebbels and the brothers had started to boil over in January 1930, when they had announced that they were to launch a new daily newspaper on 1 March. This was a blatant attempt to strangle his now twice-weekly *Der Angriff*, and was part of a general strategy to undermine his position as Gauleiter – 'an out-and-out stab in the back', he called it.[21] At the same time, Rosenberg and the Munich mafia mounted their own assault by announcing a daily Berlin edition of the *Völkischer Beobachter*. Goebbels appealed to Hitler for funds to turn his own paper into a daily, but Hitler prevaricated as usual and fobbed him off with yet another promise that he would soon be made Reich Propaganda Leader.

The two new dailies appeared on the day of Horst Wessel's funeral. Goebbels's pleas had gone unheeded. Göring had even gone to Munich on his behalf to try to persuade Hitler to stop publication, but had got nowhere. Goebbels was both furious and despondent, believing that Hitler had 'capitulated' to the Strassers. He railed bitterly against Hitler in his diaries and even considered resigning, but thought better of it, revenging himself by launching frenzied attacks on Otto Strasser in the columns of *Der Angriff*.

Eventually, after nearly a month of torment, Goebbels found some consolation when Hitler came to Berlin and, after listening patiently as he poured out all his resentments, told him and Göring that 'he was in a stinking rage against both Strassers' and that 'a curtain has come down between me and Strasser'. He said nothing about the promised role as Propaganda Leader, but as a sop asked Goebbels if he would like to be a minister in Saxony, where the party expected to score well in that year's local elections. Goebbels, though flattered, rejected the offer 'for the time being' – he had more urgent things on his mind in Berlin, including helping Hitler draw up a list of Reichstag candidates excluding the Strasser circle.[22]

Next day, Amman assured Goebbels that the Strassers would be destroyed. For the moment, however, it was vital that the party should present a united front as it prepared itself for new national elections, which everyone believed would come soon. This was why Hitler was in Berlin. Hindenburg had given formal approval to the Young Plan on 13 March, and Hitler now wanted to extricate himself from his alliance with Hugenberg and the DNVP, laying the blame on them for the failure of the campaign against it, before starting his election campaign.

The crumbling coalition government had finally fallen apart on 27 March, when its various partners could not agree on unemployment insurance contributions. Hindenburg refused to allow the Social Democrat Chancellor Hermann Müller to rule by emergency decree as the constitution allowed. But instead of dissolving the Reichstag and calling new elections, he appointed a new Chancellor, Heinrich Brüning, leader of the Catholic Centre Party, a desiccated, cautious politician who could be relied on to do as he was told and govern by presidential decree without involving the Reichstag. It was a significant moment, marking the end of democratic government in Germany and the beginning of fifteen years of authoritarian rule.

The ousting of Müller, and the choice of Brüning as his replacement, had been planned for some time, by a shadowy figure operating from an office in the Defence Ministry, Major-General Kurt von Schleicher. The bullet-headed Schleicher, whose name translates aptly as 'creeper' or 'intriguer', was a desk soldier whose job involved responsibility for the army's relations with other ministries and politicians. A man of considerable charm and high energy, he was a close friend of the President's son, Oskar von Hindenburg, and through him had become close to Hindenburg himself, whom he manipulated ruthlessly. He had used this friendship to have his own former mentor, General Groener, appointed Defence Minister, the first military man to hold the post in the Republic. In return, Groener had made him his right-hand man, ideally placed to carry out his devious designs.

Like Hindenburg, Schleicher was no lover of democracy: he believed the German people needed, and indeed wanted, government by a strong man, backed by the army. The archetypal *éminence grise*, he preferred to work behind the scenes, pulling the strings of power to achieve his aims. For years, he had been able to make or break the careers of officers at even the highest level – he had recently had the army's second-in-command, General von Blomberg, replaced by his own friend General von Hammerstein. Now, he had decided to turn his attention to politicians. The results were to prove disastrous for Germany, and eventually for the world.

While Brüning struggled to bring order to the German political scene, Hitler at last set about putting his own house in order. Otto Strasser had finally gone too far in April 1930, first by defying the Führer's strict orders and publishing details of his decision to break with Hugenberg, and then by using his papers to support a strike by metal-workers in Saxony which Hitler, under pressure from his big-business paymasters, had condemned.

Hitler called all the top party functionaries to a meeting in Munich on 26 April, to deal with the Strassers and their followers. Goebbels and Göring only just managed to make it – at Göring's invitation, Goebbels had spent Easter with him and Carin in Sweden for a week's holiday, setting the final seal on their close friendship. In spite of lousy weather, Goebbels had enjoyed every second, meeting Carin's son and all her family, visiting their homes and castles, and being entertained royally with excursions by car and boat and visits to the opera – he saw *Die Meistersinger*, which he thought was 'well and solidly played' – and the cinema, as well as all the best restaurants. He had ogled the beautiful blonde Swedish women and lusted after Carin's seventeen-year-old niece, who turned him on by riding her horse bareback. But all too soon, they had to return to Berlin, arriving back on 25 April, just in time to catch the train for Munich.[23]

The Munich meeting brought sweet satisfaction for Goebbels. After giving the despised Feder 'a terrible dressing down', Hitler turned on Strasser and presented him with an ultimatum: either finish with his newspapers or be fired from his post as Organisation Leader. He then spent two hours tearing into the Strasser group's policies and laying down his own line, which everybody was to follow. 'Bravo! Hitler is starting to lead again. Bravissimo!' Goebbels crowed to his diary. 'A complete reckoning with Strasser and the Kampfverlag, salon Bolshevism, everything.'

To crown Goebbels's day, Hitler ended by announcing his imme-diate appointment as Reich Propaganda Leader. 'Strasser is white as a sheet,' Goebbels wrote. 'He stammers out a couple of sentences to close, and then it's all over. We've triumphed all along the line. The opposition lies shattered on the ground. Strasser is destroyed. Now we shall see about the newspaper question. And now all these cowardly creatures will move over to me. That's the way men are.'[24]

With his new appointment, Goebbels was now established as one of the top three figures in the national leadership of the party. To cele-brate, he drove out in Hitler's car with Göring and Epp to lunch in brilliant sunshine by Lake Starnberg. Afterwards, before catching the overnight train back to Berlin, he had a short conference with 'my new secretary, Himmler. We are very quickly united. He is not excessively bright, but diligent and worthy. He seems to lean towards Strasser still. We'll soon knock that out of him.'[25]

On May Day, back in Berlin, Goebbels continued his and the party's remarkable rags-to-riches progress by moving into grand new offices at 10 Hedemannstrasse, just off Wilhelmstrasse and only a few hundred yards from the Reich Chancellery. With thirty light and airy rooms, the new headquarters was a far cry from the fetid 'opium den' he had inherited just three and a half years before and was a fitting symbol of the transformation he had wrought in the Berlin party's position, almost entirely through his own talent and energy. He was riding high now, but his victory was marred by the uncomfortable fact that Otto Strasser was still publishing his newspapers. Yet again, Hitler had failed to follow through on his promises to take action.

It was not until 21 May that Hitler spoke to Otto Strasser during a visit to Berlin, and even then he tried to avoid a confrontation by offering to have Max Amman buy the Kampfverlag on very generous terms. When Otto refused, he tried emotional appeals, the offer of a post as Reich press chief, and finally threats to drive him and his friends out of the party and ban members from any contact with him. Otto was unmoved, turning the conversation into an ideological argument over the nature of Socialism, driving Hitler into a fury with his rejection of the Führer principle, asserting that the Leader was nothing more than the servant of the Idea. At a second meeting next day, with Gregor Strasser, Hess and Max Amman present, Otto stuck to his radical anti-capitalist arguments, and demanded that the nationalisation of industry should be added to the party's programme. Gregor refused to support his brother any longer, siding now with Hitler, to whom he had renewed his public pledge of loyalty.

Hitler angrily labelled Otto Strasser 'an intellectual white Jew, totally incapable of any organisation, a Marxist of the first water'.[26] He promised Goebbels he would move against him – but not until after the state elections on 23 June in Saxony, where Strasser had many supporters. Even when the results were in, however, with the Nazis scoring what Goebbels described as 'a phenomenal victory', its percentage of the vote shooting up from 5 to 14.4 per cent, entitling them to 14 seats in the Landtag, he still did nothing.

Goebbels poured out his frustration in his diary, complaining bitterly that Hitler was always breaking his promises to him. He tried to pin him down by arranging for him to speak against Otto Strasser at a mass meeting of Berlin Gau members in the Sportpalast. But Goebbels knew he would duck out even then: 'He is backing away from the decision. So everything is turned on its head again. I'm sure he won't come on Monday. To avoid having to decide. That's the old Hitler! The procrastinator! Forever putting things off! That's what the movement has to deal with.'[27]

True to form, and to Goebbels's prediction, Hitler did indeed cry off. Instead of appearing in person at the planned showdown in the Sportpalast, he sent Goebbels a letter, giving him the go-ahead for a 'ruthless purge' of the party in Berlin: as he always had done, and always would do for the rest of his life, he was getting someone else to do his dirty work for him. Goebbels, with no such inhibitions, was delighted to do as he was asked. He started the purge with great relish at the beginning of July. Otto completed it for him by resigning, along with twenty-five of his followers, to found a new splinter party, the Union of Revolutionary National Socialists, later known as the 'Black Front', but it came to nothing. No one else defected, and there was no more trouble. Gregor resigned from the Kampfverlag and disowned his brother – to Goebbels's great regret, since he would have liked to see both of them removed. The brothers did not speak to each other again for three years.

On 17 July 1930, Goebbels was taking a short break with his latest girlfriend at Grumsin, about three hours' drive from Berlin. His pleasures were interrupted in the evening by a phone call from Göring: the Reichstag was challenging Brüning's right to impose a budget under presidential decree; there was to be an emergency debate next day. He dashed back to Berlin in the morning, arriving with just five minutes to spare before the vote. The result went against Brüning. But rather than submit to the will of the Reichstag, he announced that it was dissolved. There would be new elections on 14 September. The chamber erupted into mad chaos. The Communists sang 'The Internationale'. Everyone went wild. Goebbels was quite surprised that he and Göring managed to get out of the building unharmed. They decided they must go to Hitler immediately, and rushed off together to catch the night train to Munich.

Like all the leading Nazis, Goebbels was thrilled at the unexpected opportunity that the elections offered. The huge increase in the party's vote in Saxony boded well, and they had good reason to believe they could reproduce or even improve on it nationally – as the unemployment figures continued to rise, so did party membership, which had already reached 200,000 and was still growing fast. Goebbels could hardly believe his luck: barely ten weeks after his appointment as propaganda chief, he would be in charge of a national election campaign that had every chance of achieving major success. He was determined that this would be a campaign the like of which had never been seen before.

Oddly, in view of the excitement and the size of the task facing them, Hitler seemed to show no sense of urgency. While all the leading members of the party gathered to argue over strategy and the list of candidates, he took Goebbels off at midday to his favourite Café Heck, where Goebbels found the bourgeois atmosphere 'appallingly stuffy'. They then moved on to inspect progress on the new 'Brown House' – 'Pompous and large scale. Hitler is in his element.'[28]

Still avoiding getting down to work, Hitler spent the whole of the following day away from Munich, driving to Oberammergau, to see the famous Passion Play, accompanied only by his niece, Geli, and her mother, his half-sister Angela – and Goebbels. He could hardly have shown his favour to his new propaganda chief more clearly. Goebbels was 'pleasantly surprised' by the play. He thought parts of it were 'rather kitsch', but that on the whole it was all in 'decent folk taste'. The scene that made the deepest impression on him was the one with Pilate, which was 'very nearly a model lecture on the Jews. It was always that way, and still is today.'[29]

For the next week, Goebbels worked frantically on the election plans, drafting leaflets, fliers, posters, literature, as well as helping to finalise the list of candidates for approval at an all-day conference of Gauleiters. With this settled, he decided he could leave Himmler to get on with it, commenting rather patronisingly that now the groundwork was complete, all that remained to be done was technical. After the election, he noted, he would have to find another deputy: Himmler, as Reichsführer-SS, would be a member of the new Reichstag.

The campaign over the following six weeks was everything Goebbels had hoped for. Under the slogan 'Bread and Freedom', the party machine swamped Germany with millions of leaflets and posters, and produced a hundred authorised speakers to tour the country non-stop, addressing some 6,000 mass meetings, held in marquees and open-air arenas, often at night by the light of flaming torches, as well as conventional halls. The whole operation was masterminded by Goebbels, with Himmler attending to the details. Hitler himself made over twenty major speeches. Other stars like Göring, Goebbels and Strasser spoke several times a day. The number of smaller meetings in towns and villages across Germany reached an astonishing total of 34,000 during the last four weeks before the elections, completely dwarfing the efforts of all the other parties. To back this up, Goebbels supervised and co-ordinated the entire party press, ensuring that news reports were the same in all party newspapers. To ensure more general news coverage, the SA indulged in a constant stream of disturbances and vicious street battles with Communists and Socialists.

Throughout the campaign, both Göring and Goebbels were working under personal difficulties. Göring was worried sick over Carin, who had been taken ill again and was in a serious condition, but he did not let this interfere with his electioneering. Nor would she have wished him to: 'It is only when I think of how I can help him, or the Hitler movement, in some way or other,' she wrote to her mother, 'that strength seems to come to me from above.'[30] Göring took her to a sanatorium at Bad Kreuth, on the Tegernsee lake in Bavaria, and sent for Thomas, who was now eighteen, to come from Sweden to be with her while he was charging about the country.

The strain did affect Göring – according to Carin, he collapsed like a wounded animal after each speech – but he kept it well hidden, and his speeches were as boisterous as ever. A Munich police report on 8 August recounts that at the Circus Krone he called the Minister of the Interior 'a bottom spanker' and sneered that the only combat experience of Groener, the Defence Minister, was 'advancing from desk to desk'. To the delight of his audience, he said Groener should take the salute at the Constitution Day parade in two days' time 'with a slouch hat on his head and a peacock's feather sticking out of a certain part of his anatomy!'[31] This sally brought him roars of approval, and a 300-mark fine, which did nothing to moderate his knock-about style.

Goebbels, meanwhile, temporarily stripped of his immunity while the Reichstag was dissolved, was having to fight no fewer than five libel actions, one of them brought by Hindenburg. He relished the challenge they presented, and of course the publicity they brought. But in August, as the campaign approached its climax, he was faced with a more serious challenge from within his own organisation. For some time, unrest and discontent had been growing in the SA, with increasing demands for more money and more autonomy from the 'civilians' in the party offices. The SA was growing fast, as unemployed workers flocked to receive free handouts of food and shelter during the long days. Its membership had already swollen to more than 100,000, making it bigger than the Reichswehr, and its leaders were tired of being subordinate to the politicals.

There was considerable resentment, too, of the increasing affluence of the party bosses. 'We, the proletarian section of the Movement, are naturally delighted!' one of many anonymous pamphlets declared. 'We are quite happy to starve so that our dear "leaders" can enjoy themselves on their salaries of 2,000–5,000 marks a month. We were also overjoyed to hear that at the Berlin Motor Show our Adolf Hitler had spent 40,000 marks on a big new Mercedes.'[32] Goebbels was one of the targets of their anger, but Göring, with his blatantly opulent lifestyle, was not. Despite the difference in their backgrounds, it was always Göring who had the common touch, whose excesses were tolerated by the common people with a disbelieving smile. For most of their years of power, the jokes against Göring, even from the sardonic Berliners, were essentially good-natured, while those against Goebbels always had a bitter cutting edge.

On 7 August 1930, Goebbels had a long meeting at midday with a group of SA officers, led by their regional commander, former police and army officer Walter Stennes. Stennes, who had been a Freikorps leader and arms racketeer before joining the SA, had replaced Daluege in Berlin and was now an Oberführer (SA Brigadier), one of Pfeffer's seven senior deputies. He demanded that the SA should be given seats in the Reichstag, and said that if these were not forthcoming he would instigate a 'palace revolution'. He threatened to resign and take most of his men with him, warning that the strength of the SA in Berlin would fall from its present 15,000 to around 3,000. A courier had already gone to Munich to present their demands there.

After the meeting, Goebbels phoned Pfeffer, to find out what was going on. He found him 'very subdued'. Hitler had told him to 'get lost', and had called him a mutineer and a conspirator. That evening, after Goebbels had spoken at a meeting in Friedenau, two of Stennes's chief lieutenants came to him, looking very crestfallen. The accusations of mutiny had hit them hard, and they begged him to intervene with Hitler on their behalf. He promised he would.[33] The situation had been defused, at least for the moment, and he was able to concentrate once more on the election campaign and on his court cases.

The problems with the SA were far from over, however. They continued to rumble ominously for the rest of the month, until on 27 August, just as he was leaving Berlin for a speaking tour in Dresden and Hamburg, Goebbels heard news that the SA were planning a revolt. On arrival in Dresden, he telephoned his office and learned that the situation was even worse than he had thought: the SA leaders had all combined and were in open rebellion against his Gau and Munich. The SA medical officer, Dr Conti, confirmed the details, and left for Munich to report them as Goebbels completed his speech before hurrying back through the night to Berlin. Stennes confronted him there with an ultimatum: three seats in the Reichstag, more money, and political power – or the SA would walk out *en masse*. 'What an unbounded nerve!' Goebbels wrote in his diary. 'He is holding a pistol to my breast. Because we have the Sportpalast meeting tomorrow. But on 15 September we will have our revenge.'[34]

Before leaving for Hamburg, Goebbels called Munich, but – surprise, surprise – Hitler was not available: he was in Bayreuth at the Wagner festival. When Goebbels did manage to speak to him, he refused to take the SA threat seriously, insisting that he would not give them anything. He would send Otto Wagener, Pfeffer's Chief of Staff, to Berlin with full powers to sort everything out – Pfeffer, having lost both control of his men and Hitler's confidence, had resigned.[35] Back in Berlin the next day, Goebbels was shaken to discover that Stennes was not bluffing, when he withdrew the SA men who were supposed to be on duty at his Sportpalast meeting, leaving him without protection. Instead, they paraded in Wittenbergplatz, where they demonstrated against him. According to a report in the *Münchner Post*: 'There were loud cries of "Let Dr Goebbels come out and give an account of himself."' Some threatened to march on the Sportpalast and take the 'Goebbels rabble' apart.[36]

Goebbels had turned for protection, both against the Communists and the SA, to the SS under his own deputy, Daluege. They had managed the Sportpalast meeting well, and now posted guards on the Gau office, as Goebbels left for Breslau on the Saturday. Everything seemed to be under control, but at 2 a.m. the next morning he was woken up with a telegram from Berlin. The SA had stormed the Gau office and wrecked it, wounding two SS guards in the process. For a moment, Goebbels confessed, he lost his nerve. Then anger took over. There was no way he was going to let four years' hard work be destroyed in this way. He called in the despised police, who arrested twenty-five SA men, then telephoned Hitler in Bayreuth. This time, Hitler had to take the situation seriously. He left his bed and at first light hired a plane and flew to Berlin.

Goebbels met him there, with Göring, and told him the rebellion was spreading throughout Germany. If he did not make a settlement with the SA immediately, there would be a catastrophe. Hitler spent the day touring the city to talk to groups of SA men, and then met Stennes. They talked until 6 a.m. the next morning, without settling anything. But Hitler had an ace up his sleeve, and played it at a hurriedly convened meeting of some 2,000 storm-troopers: reminding his audience that Pfeffer had resigned, Hitler praised their achievements in the past, then announced that he was personally taking over as Supreme Commander of the SA and SS. They went wild with delight, as he ended with an emotional appeal for loyalty and capped it by wheeling out the eighty-year-old General Litzmann to make an oath on behalf of all SA men. Goebbels followed up with a short speech, and Stennes sealed the proceedings by reading out an order from Hitler authorising a substantial increase in the SA's funding.

The rebellion was over. After crashing out to recover from four nights with virtually no sleep, Goebbels returned to the hustings, raising the campaign to fever pitch during its final two weeks. On 14 September 1930, his hard work was rewarded when the German people went to the polls. At the start of the campaign, he had optimistically predicted a three-fold increase in the number of seats to around forty. When all the votes were counted in the early hours of 15 September, the results were better than his wildest dreams. The SA, no less, carried him shoulder high through the jubilant crowd in a packed Sportpalast, their recent quarrels with him all forgotten in the joy of the moment. With almost 6.5 million votes, the Nazi Party's percentage had rocketed from 2.6 to a staggering 18.3, overtaking the Communists who scored only 13.1 per cent. It was entitled to 107 seats, making it the second largest party in the Reichstag and headed only by the Social Democrats. Quite suddenly, the prospect of achieving power by legitimate means had ceased to be an impossible dream and had become reality. Faced with the disaster of the Depression, coming so soon after all their other misfortunes and hardships, the German people desperately needed some glimmer of hope and the Nazis, with their promise to change and revive Germany through strong government, seemed to offer the best prospect of a brighter future.

IX

'SS-MAN, YOUR LOYALTY IS YOUR HONOUR'

ONLY a week after the elections in September 1930, Hitler delivered a sharp rebuff to the radicals in the SA when he declared categorically that there would be no armed revolt. He was appearing as a witness for the defence in the trial of three young army officers charged with plotting high treason for trying to induce their fellow officers not to fire on Nazi rebels in the event of an armed uprising. As he had in Munich in 1924, he made the most of the public platform the trial provided. With the real prospect of power within sight, he needed to woo the generals, to persuade them that far from posing a threat to the army, the Nazis would in fact be its salvation, freeing it from the stranglehold of Versailles.

'I have always held the view,' he stated from the witness box, 'that any attempt to replace the army was madness. None of us have any interest in replacing the army. We will see to it when we come to power that out of the present Reichswehr a great army of the German people shall arise.' He assured the court that he and his party were committed to gaining power by purely constitutional means. When the presiding judge asked him what he meant, then, by talking about 'the German national revolution', he responded: 'That simply means the rescue of the enslaved German nation we have today. Germany is bound hand and foot by the peace treaties. The National Socialists do not regard these treaties as law, but as something imposed upon Germany by constraint . . . If we protest against them with every means at our disposal, then we find ourselves on the path of revolution.'[1]

The army was almost completely taken in by Hitler's assurances. Indeed, his old adversary General von Seeckt, who had been ousted as commander of the Reichswehr in 1926 and was now one of the newly elected members of the Reichstag, openly allied himself to the Nazis, at least for the time being. It was the SA that threatened to spoil everything. Hitler claimed in court that he expected to win a majority in the Reichstag after two or three more elections, and 'then there must come a National Socialist uprising and we will shape the state as we want to have it'. The hotheads in the SA, however, did not want to wait that long. They found it hard to understand his topsy-turvy idea of staging the revolution after achieving power, rather than achieving power by revolution; they still wanted to use their muscle to seize it by force and end what they saw as collaboration with the system they despised.

Now that he was so close to success, Hitler needed to keep the unruly elements of the SA in check and prevent their ruining his plan. It would not be an easy task. He intended to remain Supreme Commander of the SA himself, but to do the actual hard work – which was never his forte – he needed a Chief of Staff who could not only impose some much-needed discipline but would also command the respect of the hard-bitten storm-troopers. He needed someone who was not tainted by the factionalism that had caused so many problems within both the SA and the party, which ruled out most of Pfeffer's deputies and certainly the chief contender, Stennes, who was closely associated with Otto Strasser and his policies. In some desperation, he turned to a man who had absolutely no Socialist leanings, who had suitable experience and many of the right qualities, and who had been away from Germany for the past two years in South America as military adviser to the Bolivian army. He recalled Ernst Röhm.

Hitler and Röhm had been estranged since their disagreement over the Frontbann at the end of 1924, though Röhm is reputed to have told him as he departed: 'You have only to give me the word – "Be at the Siegestor at 6 a.m. on such and such a day with your men" – and I shall be there.'[2] Whether or not Hitler had stayed in touch with Röhm during his stay in Bolivia we do not know. But Himmler certainly had, keeping his old mentor informed of his progress. On 29 January 1930, for example, he wrote telling him: 'The SS is growing and by the end of this quarter should have reached 2,000,' adding proudly that 'as every month passes, service regulations and entry conditions are being tightened.'[3] With Himmler's help, the rift was healed and Röhm agreed to return.

What probably helped make up Röhm's mind was the assurance

Hitler had given the SA immediately after assuming the role of Supreme Commander that it would not only have 'special tasks' in the 'struggle for power', but that once power had been gained it would form the 'reservoir . . . for a future German national army'.[4] This was more or less what Röhm had always wanted, offering him a personal fast track to the highest reaches of the Reichswehr. He dropped everything in Bolivia and took the first available ship back through the Panama Canal. By 12 November, he was in the new 'Brown House', where he met Goebbels for the first time. 'He is very nice to me,' Goebbels noted, 'and I like him very much. An open, straightforward soldier. A character.'[5] It was agreed that Röhm would officially take up his new post on 5 January 1931.

Himmler must have been relieved at Röhm's return. After the incident at the Berlin headquarters in September, Hitler had redefined the role of the SS as 'primarily to carry out police duties within the party'. To underline this, he had given it greater autonomy from the SA, and had decreed that: 'No SA commander is entitled to give orders to the SS.'[6] At the same time, he had scrapped the restrictions on size, authorising Himmler to increase the strength of the SS to ten per cent of the SA's total. He had also agreed to a new uniform, all in black to emphasise the separation from the brown-shirted storm-troopers, and with a sinister death's head cap badge. The SS, however, was still nominally part of the SA, which meant that its Chief of Staff was Himmler's immediate superior. Himmler had every reason to believe that Röhm would be more sympathetic to his aims and ambitions than Pfeffer, who had jealously resisted his efforts to expand the SS. Now, he could set to and really start building his new order.

Göring would have dearly loved to have been the new chief of the SA – commanding more men than the Reichswehr generals would have given him immense satisfaction, not to mention considerable power. It would also have given him an official position within the party, something he had never had, and in fact never would have. Hitler, however, needed Göring where he was: associating him more closely with the anti-capitalist roughnecks of the SA would damage his valuable relationships with big business and the aristocracy. To ease his disappointment, he made him Vice-President, or Deputy Speaker, of the Reichstag, a position the Nazis, as the second largest party, were entitled to fill with their own nominee, placing him above not only Epp,

Goebbels and the leader of the Nazi caucus, Frick, but also Gregor Strasser, who was still the undisputed number two in the party itself.

On 13 October 1930, Göring led the other 106 Nazi members into the chamber, all wearing brown shirts and breeches in defiance of the ban on uniforms, while SA men put on a show of strength outside the building, on orders from Goebbels. Later in the day, also on the Gauleiter's instructions, SA men in plain clothes rampaged through the city smashing the windows of Jewish-owned stores and attacking anyone who looked Jewish. Both inside and outside the Reichstag, the Nazis were serving notice of their future intentions. That evening Göring proudly hosted a celebration in his apartment for Hitler and the leading members of the party, including Goebbels, Hess, Frick and Epp, with some of their principal backers, such as Prince August-Wilhelm, Prince and Princess Victor zu Wied, and Erhard Milch.

Carin's health was deteriorating again, but despite his romantic love for her, Göring's ambition was stronger than his concern for her well-being, and for her part Carin refused to give in to her illness, knowing that he needed her to entertain his colleagues and important contacts. Neither of them even considered easing up on their busy social schedule. On Christmas Eve, Carin had been running a temperature of 38°C (100°F), but still went ahead with the party they had planned.

'At eight o'clock Goebbels arrived to spend Christmas Eve with us,' she wrote to her mother.

He came loaded with presents for us all. For supper we had just cold meats and fruit. Then Goebbels played the harmonium, which I had brought into the living room for the holiday, while we all sang the old Christmas songs, 'Stille Nacht, heilige Nacht', 'O du fröhliche, o du selige', etc. Thomas and I sang in Swedish, Goebbels and Cilly [their maid] sang in German, and we harmonised. The fir tree was lit and the presents handed round. Then I got a shivering fit and it was so violent that I fell back on the sofa and had to be carried off to bed, with a fever and a bad headache.[7]

Even after her collapse, Carin still entertained sixteen guests to lunch on Christmas Day, including Goebbels again and the Princes August-Wilhelm and Victor zu Wied and their families, though she spent most of the day lying down and received two visits from her doctor. And still there was no let-up: only a few days later, on 5 January 1931, she and Göring gave a most important dinner party for Hitler to meet a select group of high-powered guests, including Thyssen and, most significantly, the former Reichsbank President, Hjalmar Schacht. The other guests included the ever-present Goebbels and, perhaps more surprisingly, Röhm, who had officially taken up his new post that day. Schacht was on good terms with Göring but had never met Hitler before, though they had both been involved in the campaign against the Young Plan. He was impressed by Hitler's ideas, which he thought were 'not unreasonable', and by his 'moderation' and his obvious anxiety 'to avoid anything that might shock us in our capacity as representatives of a more traditional society'.[8]

The introduction to Schacht scored another notable point for Göring, raising his standing with Hitler still further. It bore fruit almost immediately, when Schacht and Thyssen persuaded Brüning to meet with Hitler and Göring to discuss the Nazis joining a coalition government. They were unable to work out a deal, but it was clear that the party could not be kept out for much longer.

The seal was finally set on Göring's social position ten days after the dinner party with Schacht, when he and Carin travelled to Doorn in Holland to stay with the exiled Kaiser, at his personal invitation. 'We hope to profit by winning the Kaiser over to the party, the sort of thing Hermann is adept at,' Thomas von Kantzow wrote in his diary after seeing them off at the Zoo station. With three of his sons either members or supporters of the Nazi Party, the Kaiser must have been at least sympathetic, but that did not stop him losing his temper with the flying-ace-turned-politician, who was clearly not overawed by him. 'They flew at each other at once,' Carin wrote to her mother. 'They are both excitable and in many ways they are so like each other. The Kaiser has probably never heard anybody express an opinion different from his own, and it was a bit too much for him at times.'[9] The Kaiser was obviously not offended by Göring's outspokenness: at the end of dinner on the second day he toasted 'the coming Reich' – Göring responded tactfully with 'the coming king', without attaching a name. The visit must have been a success, for the Kaiser invited him back again the following year.

While their husbands were arguing about politics, the Empress was more concerned with Carin's delicate health. She was so shocked by her fragile appearance that she pressed money on her to pay for treatment at her favourite sanatorium at Bad Altheide in Silesia. Carin desperately needed treatment: a week later she was so ill that the doctors could not find a pulse and told Göring it was all over. She was revived with the aid of injected stimulants, but the prognosis for the future was not hopeful.

Inevitably, the strain began to show in Göring's behaviour, which became more erratic than ever. At the same time, partly because of this and partly because of jealousy, his relationship with Goebbels began to unwind, with a growing number of spats and disagreements. Increasingly, Goebbels's diaries include criticisms of Göring in place of the fulsome tributes of only a few weeks earlier. Goebbels was now moving more confidently in high society on his own account, and had less need of Göring's endorsement: he had acquired a wealthy and well-connected patron in Baroness Viktoria von Dirksen, stepmother of the then ambassador to the Soviet Union, who provided him with money, contacts and gossip. She told him Göring was back on morphine again,[10] and Goebbels was quick to report this to Hitler, ostensibly to discuss what they could do to help his friend, but subtly undermining his position with the Führer.

The division widened on 10 February 1931, when Goebbels persuaded the Nazi members to walk out of the Reichstag in protest at government plans to limit abuses of parliamentary immunity. Göring's was the only dissenting voice – Goebbels said he had developed in the wrong direction through his 'eternal negotiations'.[11] Goebbels had a personal interest in retaining immunity: he faced no fewer than eight prosecutions for various offences. But he also wanted to underline his view of the party as a revolutionary movement fundamentally opposed to the parliamentary system, and to dissociate it from the Reichstag, which he was still committed to destroying.

The cases against Goebbels had been mounting up since the previous summer. Before his immunity was renewed by the opening of the new Reichstag, he had dodged trial by consistently failing to turn up in court. When a judge issued a subpoena on the opening day of the new session, hoping the police would be able to catch him before he entered the building, he escaped arrest by hiding on the floor of a limousine with curtained windows and slipping in unobserved among the crowd. The Nazi members greeted him with loud cries of 'Long live the saviour of Berlin', and he taunted their opponents with 'You see, I'm sabotaging your bourgeois system!'[12]

The pending prosecutions did nothing to reduce Goebbels's manic determination to grab every opportunity of drawing attention to the party and himself in Berlin. When the American anti-war film based on Erich Maria Remarque's German novel *All Quiet on the Western Front* was premiered in Berlin, he organised a demonstration outside the Mozartsaal cinema while inside he and 150 SA men caused havoc

by shouting, whistling, releasing white mice and throwing stink bombs.
Over the next few days, thousands of storm-troopers paraded through
the streets singing the 'Horst Wessel Song' and starting fights with the
police, while Hitler, Goebbels and other prominent Nazis took the
salute. 'Over an hour,' Goebbels chortled. 'Six abreast. Fantastic! Berlin
West has never seen anything like it.'[13] The Berlin police finally countered by banning all outdoor demonstrations, rallies and processions,
but Goebbels recorded another victory when the Interior Ministry's
Film Board withdrew the film's certificate on the grounds that it was
'a threat to Germany's honour'.

As Goebbels whipped up the SA to ever greater excesses, pitched
battles with the Communists, both on the streets and in meeting halls,
became a daily part of Berlin life. Stabbings, shootings and other
serious injuries were commonplace. On New Year's Day there were
two deaths in the city; three weeks later more than 100 were injured,
many of them seriously, in a vicious brawl during a debate between
Goebbels and Walter Ulbricht, Chairman of the Berlin KPD, in
Friedrichshain Hall. There were more deaths and injuries in the
following days and weeks. Goebbels revelled in what he saw as the
prelude to revolution.

The SA were delighted with Goebbels's renewed radicalism, and he
was reconciled with Stennes, forming a friendship that supplanted his
waning relationship with Göring. He had recently moved into a smart
new apartment in the comfortable southern Berlin district of Steglitz,
and Stennes became a regular visitor there. Under his influence,
Goebbels reverted to his wild Socialist days, as they castigated the reactionary 'Munich tycoons' and plotted revolution. The only difference
between them was that Goebbels still clung to his delusion that Hitler
was a Socialist at heart, misled by the evil hangers-on who surrounded
him, while Stennes, whose eyes were not blinded by love for the Führer,
saw clearly that he was in fact the leading 'tycoon'.

With Goebbels's blessing, Stennes published a whole series of articles in *Der Angriff* advocating an armed uprising – in direct contradiction to Hitler's repeated declarations that he and the party were
totally committed to achieving power by legitimate means. On 21
February, Goebbels and Stennes decided that they were in total agreement on the political situation, and agreed to form an alliance to fight
for their opinions. 'SA + me. That is power,' he gloated in his diary.[14]

Göring had upset Goebbels by openly attacking *Der Angriff* for
supporting the Stennes line. Goebbels had confronted him about this,

insisting that the movement would only get on by strength and perseverance and accusing him of being too much of an optimist and relying too much on doing deals. He had got nowhere – there had clearly been a clash of monster egos. Göring, he fulminated, was suffering from delusions of grandeur, thought he was already Chancellor, and was 'an unrestrained opportunist'; everything stemmed from his morphine addiction. He should be put in a mental home, for his own good.[15]

The day before concluding his pact with Stennes, Goebbels had repeated his accusations to Hitler, claiming that Göring was making himself look ridiculous, 'a comic figure – like Falstaff', and had to take a drastic cure. He could no longer represent the party. As well as trying to destroy Göring's position with Hitler, Goebbels spread the rumour about his addiction through the party, adding such spicy tit-bits as the fact that Brüning, whom he claimed Göring idolised, had described him as 'all bottom'.[16] All Göring could do, when he and Goebbels met in mid March to thrash things out, was to deny that he was on morphine, reproach Goebbels for going over to Stennes and praising him too much in *Der Angriff*, and tell him he was surrounding himself with people who were 'all rubbish'. Goebbels responded by accusing him of being 'all business', and attacked the party's new draft economic programme, complaining that there was nothing left of Socialism. They parted, Goebbels noted, 'as half friends. But there still remains much between us.'[17]

By that time, it should have been clear to Goebbels that he was backing the wrong horse. Hitler did nothing about Göring, but was fast losing patience with Stennes, who was becoming more and more critical of his policies. Only five days after Goebbels had made his pact with Stennes, Röhm banned the SA from taking part in street battles and their leaders from speaking in public. This did not go down at all well with the SA in Berlin, or with Goebbels. An anonymous tip-off to the Berlin State Attorney's office led to the police discovering several letters from Röhm in the office of a doctor specialising in sexual disorders, complaining that he was having difficulty finding 'playmates'. No one ever found out who was responsible, but Goebbels certainly cashed in on the scandal within the party, passing on incriminating material and making jokes at Röhm's expense, trying unsuccessfully to get him dismissed. His liking for the 'honest, straightforward soldier' had lasted only a few short weeks before succumbing to his normal misanthropy. Röhm returned the compliment by spreading vindictive gossip about Goebbels.

Torn between his radical inclinations and his devotion to Hitler, Goebbels tried to mediate between Munich and Berlin. To promote loyalty to the party and goodwill towards the SA, he even organised a typical Goebbels stunt: a fake assassination attempt on himself with a parcel bomb that was 'heroically defused' by an SA man on the staff of *Der Angriff*. With Hitler's help, he managed to persuade Röhm not to dismiss Stennes, but his attempts to square the circle were doomed from the start.

The breaking point came on 28 March 1931, when Hindenburg issued an emergency decree requiring all political meetings to be registered, all posters and pamphlets to be subject to censorship, and giving Brüning wide powers to counter political excesses. Goebbels foresaw a ban on the party and the SA, and wanted to fight. To his dismay, however, Hitler ordered strict compliance with the law. 'Long live legality!' Goebbels snarled in his diary. 'Makes you want to vomit! Now we'll have to come up with new methods. That will be very difficult. Added to which the crisis with the SA and socialism. We have reason to be unhappy. We've made many mistakes, above all, too much dealing with the enemy. Now they have swindled us. That goes on Göring's account.'[18]

When Stennes refused to knuckle under, Hitler ordered Goebbels to meet him in Weimar, where he was holding a conference of party leaders. Goebbels went via Dresden, where he was scheduled to make two speeches, arriving worn out in Weimar at 5 a.m. on 1 April. Later that morning, somewhat fearfully since he knew his enemies in Munich were associating him with Stennes, he met Hitler and Röhm, who told him Stennes had been dismissed overnight. Before he had had a chance to digest this news, a telephone call from Berlin told him the SA had mutinied and had occupied his offices and those of *Der Angriff*. It was time to choose: Hitler or Stennes. For Goebbels there was no contest. Although his sympathies were entirely with the rebels, he had sold his soul to Hitler, and he could not deny him. Joining him on the platform to speak to the assembled leaders, he declared himself 'openly and unreservedly' his. Instead of rushing back to Berlin, he demonstrated his loyalty to Hitler once again by joining him in Munich, where they planned the counterattack together.

Hitler began by publishing a powerful editorial in the *Völkischer Beobachter* denouncing Stennes and his fellow rebels, declaring his determination to 'stamp out, root and branch, this conspiracy against National Socialism', and demanding that the SA men choose between

'Police Sergeant (ret) Stennes or the founder of the National Socialist Movement and the Supreme Leader of your SA, Adolf Hitler'. He condemned the slanderous rumours linking Goebbels with the rebels, and confirmed his full confidence in his Gauleiter.[19] He then gave Goebbels full power to purge the Berlin party of all 'subversive elements', assuring him in writing, 'Whatever you need to do to fulfil this task, I will back you.'

Goebbels had survived, but it had been a close-run thing. His relief, and his pleasure at finding himself still in Hitler's favour, was tempered however by news that in his absence from Berlin Göring had asked Hitler for authority to carry out a purge in the city. Not unnaturally, Goebbels saw this as a threat, with Göring trying to muscle in on his bailiwick. He reacted furiously. 'I won't forget that of Göring,' he wrote. 'It makes you despair of mankind. He's a heap of frozen shit.'[20] Hitler refused Göring permission to act in Berlin itself, but authorised him to take charge of a purge in the rest of Stennes's region, which included Brandenburg, Silesia, Pomerania and Mecklenburg, and bring it back into line. It was a typical Hitler ploy: the two former friends were now fierce rivals.

Stennes claimed he had taken over the party in the north and east, and announced that he had fired Goebbels as Gauleiter of Berlin. Goebbels countered at once by releasing SA men from their oath of loyalty to Stennes, and pressing ahead from Munich with his purge in Berlin, while Göring did the same in the wider area. Between them, they expelled some 500 SA men. All funding for the SA, which was handled by the various Gau offices, was cut off, and the rebellion collapsed within a week as the money ran out. Goebbels, who had taken a leaf out of Hitler's book by keeping out of the way and letting things take their course, returned to Berlin on 7 April, boosted by Hitler's call to party members to close ranks in unconditional loyalty behind his 'friend' the Gauleiter.

The Stennes crisis might have been a near disaster for Goebbels, but for Himmler it was a godsend, providing a vital plank in the construction of his own power base. His SS had distinguished themselves again by defending the Gau offices, standing firm under Daluege until they were overwhelmed by the sheer numbers of SA men. Although they had ultimately failed to halt the brown horde, the standing of the SS, and that of their Reichsführer, was greatly enhanced.

In the clear-out afterwards, Goebbels and Göring both relied on the SS for protection. To bring the SA to heel in the north and east, an SS man, Untersturmführer Friedrich-Wilhelm Kruger, was given Stennes's position as Gruppenführer East. Himmler was gratified when Hitler acknowledged the contribution of his black guards by writing to Daluege – almost certainly at Himmler's suggestion – using the phrase 'SS-Mann, deine Ehre heisst Treue' ('SS man, your loyalty is your honour'). It became the SS motto, engraved on every belt buckle from then on.

Himmler emphasised the importance of the concept two months later at a conference of northern SS leaders in Berlin, when he spoke on 'the purpose and goal of the SS', which was to be the elite guard of the nation and the race, as well as the Führer. 'We are not loved everywhere,' he lectured them in his prim, schoolmaster's voice. 'When we have done our duty we may be stood in the corner. We should expect no thanks. But our Führer knows the value of the SS. We are his favourite and most valuable organisation because we have never let him down.'[21]

With the mutiny crushed, and the mutineers scattered, Goebbels could start putting his Gau back in order again. It was a difficult enough job, made even harder by a number of personal problems. The Reichstag immunity vote that had given the Nazi members a reason for walking out in February had made him vulnerable to prosecution and he was now facing a growing number of charges. 'I'm reeling from anxiety, lack of rest, irritation, fury and indignation,' he wrote on 18 April. 'I'm nearly at the end with my nerves. These trials are killing me . . . My desk is piled high with summonses. It makes you puke! But I won't lose my nerve. That's what the enemy wants.'[22]

After the first few verdicts, all against him, he stopped fighting each case and concentrated on haggling and causing trouble over payment. This was only partly bloody-mindedness – although the individual fines were surprisingly moderate, they totalled 'huge amounts of money', which he soon found real difficulty paying.

What was causing Goebbels most Angst in April 1931, however, was not the money, or his quarrel with Göring, or even his health – he had been ill for several days with a high fever that he couldn't shake off. What was really worrying him was a woman. He had always been sex mad, chasing every available woman, with a surprisingly high success rate. In spite of his physical disability women found him attractive. He had 'come-to-bed' eyes, sensitive hands, and a voice that was a finely-tuned instrument played with the skill of a virtuoso, switching effortlessly from the strident tones of the public platform to honeyed softness in the bedroom. His seduction technique was obviously brilliant, enhanced perhaps by the hint of danger and the whiff of power that many women find irresistible. Others wanted to mother him. Since breaking up with Else, he had enjoyed an unending succession of girls, some quick one-night stands, some lasting weeks or months. He was even seeing his old love Anka from time to time in spite of her marriage. Usually, he had several women in tow at the same time, but for some weeks now there had been only one, and he was afraid he was losing her. Her name was Magda Quandt. She was twenty-nine years old, blonde, beautiful, elegant and sophisticated. She was divorced, but had a jealous lover, who threatened to shoot her rather than lose her to Goebbels.

Magda Quandt had been born Johanna Maria Magdalena Ritschel, in Berlin's Bülowstrasse, the daughter of a well-to-do engineer, a man of taste and learning with a particular interest in Buddhism, which his daughter later inherited. Her parents were divorced when she was three, but it was a civilised parting and Magda still saw her father regularly. After two years, her mother married a wealthy Jewish businessman called Friedländer, who became a loving and much-loved stepfather. When she was five, her father moved to Brussels, and shortly afterwards her mother and stepfather followed him to the Belgian capital, where they enjoyed a socially active life in a lovely period house.

Although her mother was a Protestant and her stepfather Jewish, Magda's father was Catholic and she was sent as a boarder to the Ursuline Convent of Sacré Coeur in Vilvorde, where despite a strict and even austere regime she seems to have been a model pupil, popular with both staff and girls. In the school holidays, her father and stepfather, both intelligent and cultured men, vied with each other to widen her education with trips around Europe, until the catastrophe of 1914 sent them all scurrying back to Germany, leaving behind their businesses and most of their personal possessions. Dr Ritschel still had his family business, based in Godesberg, and was not too seriously affected financially, but Friedländer had lost almost everything, and had to start again. His marriage to Magda's mother failed under the strain, and

they divorced. Magda attended a local high school as a day girl until
1919, when she was sent to a finishing school at Holzhausen, near
Goslar at the foot of the Harz Mountains.

While she was still at the finishing school – in fact, in the corridor
of a train taking her back to school from Berlin after a holiday –
Magda met the thirty-seven-year-old Günther Quandt, a seriously
wealthy businessman whose expanding empire already encompassed
textiles, chemicals and machine tools and would go on to include a
sizeable chunk of Daimler-Benz and a controlling interest in BMW.
Quandt, a widower with two young sons, pursued the beautiful
eighteen-year-old girl and persuaded her to marry him. She did so on
4 January 1921 and moved into his spacious villa at New Babelsberg,
on the banks of the River Havel between Berlin and Potsdam. On 1
November that year, she gave birth to a son, Harald. Shortly afterwards, Quandt took in the three orphaned children of a close friend,
so at the age of twenty Magda suddenly found herself looking after
six children and a large house. Over the next few years, Quandt bought
two more houses, one nearer the centre of Berlin, the other a country
manor house at Severin in Mecklenburg, some three hours drive from
the city. Despite her youth, Magda coped with the family and the
houses admirably.

Quandt and Magda travelled widely together, on business and
pleasure, to Britain, the French Riviera, the United States, Mexico,
Cuba and South America. Outwardly, it seemed a wonderful life, but
they gradually grew apart, separated by the difference in their ages and
their contrasting natures. Magda had been brought up by her father
and stepfather to be independent, strong-minded and cultured, with a
taste for the finer things of life. Quandt was a product of the Mark
Brandenburg and the Protestant work ethic, with the Prussian antipathy
for any form of ostentation or softness, either in business or private
life. He was used to having his own way and was inclined to be domineering. His lack of warmth eventually led Magda to take a young
lover. Quandt found out, threw her out of the house, and divorced her.

After Quandt had got over his initial reaction, the parting was
remarkably free of rancour. He gave her a very generous settlement of
50,000 marks to buy a house, plus 20,000 marks on deposit in case
of sickness, and a monthly allowance of 4,000 marks while she
remained unmarried. Harald was to live with his mother until he was
fourteen, unless she remarried. It is said that Magda only got such
good terms because she blackmailed Quandt by threatening to publish

certain documents – either letters from early love affairs or evidence of tax evasion. But since they remained on friendly terms – he even sent her a huge bouquet and took her to lunch at the exclusive Horcher's restaurant the day the divorce papers were signed – it seems most unlikely.

Magda bought a luxury, seven-room apartment on Reichkanzlerplatz, on the exclusive western fringes of Berlin, close to the Olympic stadium built for the cancelled 1916 games, and just round the corner from Quandt's house on the Frankenallee. Looking for something to relieve the boredom of being a free woman, she dropped in on a Nazi meeting in the Sportpalast during the 1930 election campaign. Goebbels was the main speaker, and as she listened she was caught up in the waves of emotion he unleashed in the packed hall. By the end of his speech, she was hooked on National Socialism. A day or two later, unable to clear his message from her mind, she called at his headquarters in Hedemannstrassse and joined the party.

Ignoring the warnings and objections of her family, friends, former husband and her lover, Magda threw herself wholeheartedly into the Nazi Party, starting with the local Berlin West End branch. She bought and actually read copies of Hitler's *Mein Kampf* and even Rosenberg's *Myth of the Twentieth Century*, and studied Nazi literature and news-sheets, swallowing them whole and coming to believe with total conviction that the Nazis were Germany's only possible salvation against destruction by the Communists. She was quickly made leader of the local NS Women's Organisation – her education and intelligence were far superior to most of the members, who tended to be petty bourgeois shop assistants, concierges and the like. But this was not enough to satisfy her, and she volunteered to help out in the head office of the Gau, where Goebbels soon singled her out for his special attention.

'A beautiful woman by the name of Quandt is making me a new private archive,' he noted casually in his diary. There was no *coup de foudre* as there had been for Göring when he first set eyes on Carin, and Magda scornfully denied that she found him personally attractive. Goebbels was not even distracted from his usual pursuits – immediately after that first reference to Magda, he went on to record that Ilse Stahl stayed with him until 6 a.m., describing her as 'An odd, good, beautiful, affectionate girl. And still quite innocent. I like her very much and think about her all morning.'[23]

The private archive that Magda was organising was Goebbels's collection of press cuttings and reports, his intelligence base for articles, speeches and campaigns. It was a vital part of his operation, so Magda's job brought her into ever-closer personal contact with him. For several weeks, their relationship remained professional and correct. Over Christmas, she was away looking after her ex-husband, who had fallen ill in Florence, taking him to recuperate in St Moritz. Quandt did his best to convince her of the true nature of National Socialism and the Nazis, whom he despised, but it was no use. She returned to work with Goebbels more eagerly than ever. Late sessions at the office soon became even later sessions in his flat. It was not long before she found herself under his spell, committed to him as much as to the party.

Goebbels could hardly believe his luck. This beautiful, charming, well-bred, well-travelled, sophisticated – albeit politically naïve – woman could be his answer to Carin Göring, who until then had been the party's favourite hostess. It rankled that Hitler always dined with the Görings when he was in Berlin, while he, Goebbels, was not in a position to offer similar hospitality in his own, more humble home. Magda Quandt, however, not only had experience in entertaining the rich and famous, she also had an apartment that was every bit as luxurious as Göring's, and in better taste, too. There was no doubt about it: Magda had class. To the poor boy from Rheydt, she was a catch worth sacrificing the joys of his harem for.

On 15 February 1931, he was able to report: 'In the evening, Magda Quandt came. And stayed a very long time. And blossomed in a bewitching blonde sweetness. How are you my queen? (1) A beautiful, beautiful woman! Whom I could well love. Today I am like in a dream. So full of satisfied bliss. It is truly wonderful to love a beautiful woman and to be loved by her.'24 The (1) seems to indicate that this was the first time they had sex – a month later, he was writing (8, 9) after describing how she 'gave love, a row, and love again'.25

Within weeks, Magda was travelling with Goebbels to meetings, as well as seeing him in the office and at his apartment. She even joined him in Munich when the Stennes revolt erupted in Berlin, staying with him in his hotel and giving him comfort and support during that trying time, though significantly he did not introduce her to Hitler. They were very much a couple, but her past life still got in the way. Back in Berlin she tried to extricate herself from her lover, who took a pistol and shot at her in her apartment when she ditched him in favour of Goebbels. She handled the distracted young man with great coolness, called the police and had him taken away, but was severely shaken and cut herself off for several days afterwards, while she took stock of her situation.

Goebbels, who knew nothing of Magda's drama, was plunged into deep despair, convinced he had lost her as she neither called him nor answered his calls. His anguish was compounded by the fact that he was ill and running what he said was a 40°C (104°F) fever, while trying to cope with the emotional turmoil of sorting out the after effects of the Stennes revolt and facing yet more costly court cases. To make things worse, he was under another public speaking ban, and had to sit by while Göring basked in the spotlight with the star speech at the Sportpalast on 20 April, to mark Hitler's forty-second birthday. 'All very nice,' he recorded with heavy irony. 'Göring treats me with honeyed kindness. I remain reserved. He is going to Munich and then to Rome. *Hans Dampf!* ['Johnnie Steam' – a character who is always rushing about] His departure will give the public a rest.'[26]

Eventually, Magda made her decision: breaking with most of her disapproving family and friends, she chose to commit herself to Goebbels. At Whitsun, they spent a passionate week's holiday together at Quandt's Severin estate, at the end of which they made 'a solemn promise' to each other: when the party had conquered the Reich, they would be married.[27] In July, without setting a date for the wedding, they went public and announced their engagement. It may be that Hitler had told Goebbels he must formalise his relationship – Röhm was getting his own back for Goebbels's earlier campaign against him by spreading scurrilous rumours about it, including the insinuation that it was really Magda's son he was interested in. Equally, it could be that Goebbels realised Carin Göring was failing fast and wanted to be ready to seize the opportunity when it came.

Once their betrothal was official, Goebbels was at last able to introduce Madga to the Führer, in the smart Kaiserhof Hotel in Wilhelmstrasse, opposite the Reich Chancellery and the Presidential Palace, where Hitler now based himself when he was in Berlin, having deserted the smaller, less ostentatious Sans Souci. Hitler was charmed by her, pleased by her keen interest in the party as well as by her elegance and good looks. There could be no doubt at all that she would be a great asset to Goebbels's career, and a worthy successor to Carin Göring.

Göring's trip to Rome in May 1931 had been a show put on to convince the Vatican, and southern Germany's Catholics, that the Nazi Party was not godless or opposed to the Church. Carin was not well enough to go with him; she went instead into the sanatorium in Bad Altheide which the Empress had recommended. He lied to her again about his time in Rome, just as he had in 1924. This time, he really did see Mussolini, and several other senior members of the Fascist government, but he was not, as he told her, the guest of the King for three weeks – though he had an introduction from his friend Prince Philipp of Hesse, who was married to the King's daughter – nor did he meet the Pope. The man Hitler had sent him to see was Cardinal Eugenio Pacelli, the future Pope Pius XII, who was then the Vatican's Secretary of State. It was a diplomatic mission that would pay off handsomely two years later, when Pacelli would travel to Germany as Papal Nuncio and conclude a concordat with the Nazis.

Returning to Germany, Göring was upset to discover that Hitler had asked Röhm to talk to Schleicher, who seemed to be coming round to the idea of including the Nazis in a right-wing coalition government backed by the army. Hitler wanted Schleicher to set up a meeting for him with Hindenburg. This was Göring's territory, and he was miffed at being bypassed, even suspecting that he had been sent to Italy to get him out of the way. As usual, Hitler was far ahead of him, shrewdly forestalling his indignation with the gift of a new motor car, 'a splendid specimen that was exhibited at the last Motor Show in Berlin,' Carin wrote to her mother. 'A Mercedes, grey on the outside, red leather inside, long, elegant, and stylish! They made only one of its kind.'[28]

Hitler's excuse for this blatant sweetener was that he had always felt badly about Göring's favourite car being confiscated by the Bavarian government in 1923, and was at last in a position to buy him a replacement out of the royalties he was earning from the soaring sales of *Mein Kampf*. It is more likely that the car was a gift to the party, or that it was paid for out of party funds, but Göring was happy to see it as a mark of Hitler's esteem. He accepted it with childish glee, and drove off at high speed to show it to Carin at the sanatorium. As soon as she was well enough, he whisked her away for a motoring holiday with her sister Fanny and Pilli Körner. Hitler, taking a few days break himself, underlined his personal regard by rendezvousing with the little party at their first stop, the Palast Hotel in Dresden.

Göring was so pleased with his new toy that he did not even pause to think that the two weeks leave he had been given by the party would keep him conveniently out of the way while Röhm continued to work on Schleicher. Aware that his time with Carin was limited, he drove her through the villages and little towns of Bavaria, and then into Austria, where they visited Ritter von Epenstein at Göring's childhood home, the castle in Mautendorf, before returning to Munich for the christening of his sister Paula's new baby daughter.

Apart from Göring himself, the star guest at the christening was one of his grand friends, the Duchess of Coburg. Hitler had been expected, but was in a state of shock after a personal tragedy, the apparent suicide in his apartment of his niece, Geli. Göring too was deeply upset by her death, and left the christening reception several times to phone Hitler at his publisher's house on the Tegernsee, where he was grieving inconsolably.

Geli, the twenty-three-year-old daughter of Hitler's half-sister Angela who kept house for him on the Obersalzberg, had been his constant companion for six years. It was a strange relationship that has never been properly explained, though it has been the subject of a great deal of prurient speculation over the years. What is certain is that Hitler was obsessively in love with her, despite or perhaps because of the twenty-year difference in their ages, that he was jealously possessive and refused to allow her any life of her own, which in the end made her intensely unhappy. He had given her a room in his new Munich apartment when he moved to Prinzregentenplatz, and it was there that she shot herself on 18 September 1931, after Hitler had left by car for a speaking engagement in Hamburg.

Hitler had stayed overnight in the Deutscher Hof Hotel in Nuremberg, and it was as he was leaving there the next day that he received a phone call from Hess, with the dreadful news. He rushed back to Munich, being stopped by the police for speeding after forcing his driver to go flat out. Back at his apartment, Hess, Amman, Party Treasurer Franz Xaver Schwarz, youth leader Baldur von Schirach and Gregor Strasser were waiting for him. Interestingly, it was Strasser who took charge and comforted him, and who by his own account stayed at his side over the next two days and nights, fearful that he might take his own life.[29]

Geli's mother took her daughter's body back to Vienna for burial, though Hitler could not attend the funeral. It is not clear whether this was because he was barred from entering Austria, or that he was afraid that, being stateless, he would be refused readmission to Germany if he left the country. Göring offered to go on his behalf, but Hitler refused, telling him to go back to Berlin and handle matters there. Interestingly, Hitler chose Himmler and Röhm to represent him at the funeral. A week later, when the spotlight had moved on, he slipped secretly across the frontier to visit the grave himself and to say his farewell. Then he picked himself up and returned to the struggle for power. He mourned Geli for the rest of his life, turning her rooms in Munich and in the Obersalzberg house into shrines. One odd effect of the tragedy was that he could never stomach meat again: 'It's like eating a corpse,' he told Göring.[30]

Barely a month after Hitler's trauma, Göring was suffering his own bereavement. Carin's mother died suddenly on 25 September and, ignoring her doctors' warnings, she insisted on going to Stockholm for the funeral. Göring reluctantly agreed to take her, but they arrived too late. That evening, Carin had a heart attack. The doctor doubted she would last the night, but once again she clung to life, and for the next four days and nights Göring never left her bedside except to shave or snatch a quick bite while she was unconscious.

On 4 October, a telegram arrived for Göring from Hitler, calling him urgently back to Berlin, where events were moving swiftly. The economic crisis was deepening by the day. Two major banks had crashed; the official unemployment figures had passed 5 million, with the real total at least two million more, and people were once again looking to the extreme parties for extreme solutions. Hitler had renewed his alliance with the DNVP and the Stahlhelm, to form a 'National Opposition' group ready to assume power, though he was careful to retain his independence. He had sent the Nazi members back into the Reichstag in September, where they were attacking the hapless Brüning government mercilessly. Aided by Schleicher, he had had further talks with Brüning, but still refused to co-operate with him. Now Schleicher had persuaded Hindenburg that he must consider asking the Nazis to form a new government, and Hindenburg had at last agreed to see Hitler.

Unfortunately, the President refused to see the man he called the 'Bohemian corporal' on his own; he had to be accompanied by someone respectable, preferably an officer. The obvious choice would have been Röhm – but although he was a former staff officer, he was hardly respectable. Hindenburg had heard the tales of his homosexuality, and refused to meet a man he considered to be a pederast and a pervert. He wanted Captain Göring, with his distinguished war record and his *Pour le Mérite*. And so the telegram was sent to Stockholm. For once, Göring put his wife before Hitler and the party: he refused to go, until Thomas told Carin about the telegram and she insisted he leave at once.

The meeting with Hindenburg took place on 10 October 1931, but was a total failure for the Nazis. Hitler was nervous, and Hindenburg did nothing to put him at his ease, receiving him with ill-concealed contempt and keeping him standing. Hitler responded by launching into one of his monologues, haranguing the President on the situation in Germany. Hindenburg was not impressed, and brought the audience to an abrupt close. He is said to have told Schleicher afterwards that he considered Hitler might be fit to be Minister of Posts, but Chancellor, never.

The day after the abortive meeting with Hindenburg, Göring went with Hitler to a massive rally of the National Opposition at Bad Harzburg, but neither of them had his heart in it and they left early, as soon as the SA had marched past and, rather pointedly, before the much bigger Stahlhelm paraded. Göring returned to the Reichstag, where he forced a vote of no confidence in Brüning, which failed by a mere fifteen votes. A motion by the National Opposition to dissolve the Reichstag and call fresh elections also failed by the narrowest margin. The Nazis' hour was approaching fast – rocketing party membership allied to massive gains in local elections in Hamburg boded well for their prospects nationally. But any jubilation Göring may have felt as he led his members in yet another walk-out from the Reichstag was squashed when he called Stockholm next morning to be told that Carin had died at 4.10 a.m. Utterly distraught, he left at once for Sweden, accompanied by his elder brother Karl and Pilli Körner.

Carin's body lay in an open white coffin in the Edelweiss Chapel at her parents' home, and Göring knelt beside it for hours, weeping and praying as he prepared to say his final farewell. She was laid to rest alongside her mother in the family vault at the little country church at Lövoe, near Drottningholm. Immediately after the funeral, Göring returned to Berlin, but he could not bear to stay in the Badensche Strasse apartment, with all its memories. He closed it up and moved into the Kaiserhof Hotel, where he would be immediately available to Hitler at all times.

The only way Göring could hope to dull the pain of his loss was by immersing himself in work. Hitler appreciated this and, as reassurance that Röhm was not taking his place as the party's arch wheeler-dealer in high places, fed his vanity by giving him a new title, 'Political Representative of the Führer in the Reich Capital'. As Göring himself later related:

The Führer said to me that he would very much like to have a direct representative who was independent of a party office and who could carry out political negotiations. This person was not to be tied to any particular party office. He asked me whether I would take over this function, especially as I was living in the capital of the Reich anyway.

I took over this commission – it was not an office, but rather a commission of a general nature. In a few sentences he gave me the liberty to negotiate with all parties from the Communists to the extreme rightists, in order, let us say, to undertake specific joint action in the Reichstag, or other suitable political steps. Naturally, also I was given in this connection the task of effecting the dissemination and the penetration of our ideals in all circles. To these circles belonged, as has already been mentioned, the industrial and intellectual groups. Since I had connections with and access to all these circles, it was quite natural that the Führer considered me specially suited for this task, as he could depend upon me absolutely in this respect and knew that I would use all my powers to advance our ideas.[31]

This was little more than formal confirmation of the role Göring was already playing, but it was more vital than ever at that time, as the political merry-go-round spun more and more dizzily, fuelled by hectic horse-trading and frantic finagling. Hitler had told a gathering of some 100,000 SA men in Brunswick in October 1931 that the party was 'within a metre of its goal', and this time he was not exaggerating. By the end of the year, party membership had reached a staggering 806,300,[32] and was still rising. In his New Year message, Hitler said that 1932 would be 'the hardest year of struggle that our movement has experienced', and went on to exhort: 'Let us have the courage today to ride like knights without fear and without reproach, through hell, death and the devil, to victory and liberty!'[33] Göring, Goebbels, Himmler and their colleagues could hardly wait to answer his call.

X

'NOW THE CHESS GAME FOR POWER BEGINS'

JOSEPH Goebbels married Magda Quandt on 19 December 1931 at a civil ceremony in Goldenbow, Mecklenburg, followed by a wedding in the little Protestant church at Severin. To Goebbels's great pride, Hitler himself was his best man, with General von Epp as his other witness. Apart from ten-year-old Harald, dressed in the uniform of the Nazi Party Youth Organisation, the only members of Magda's family present were her mother and her former sister-in-law, Ello Quandt. The reception afterwards was held in the Quandt manor house – in their divorce settlement, Quandt had given Magda permission to use the house whenever she chose. Nobody told him about the wedding reception, however – the estate manager, Walter Granzow, was a Nazi supporter, who was later made Minister-President of the state of Mecklenburg-Schwerin, partly as a reward for his co-operation.

It has been said that Goebbels and Magda abandoned their pledge to wait until the party had won power because she was pregnant. If she was, it could only have been by a few days, since their first child was born almost thirty-seven weeks later, which makes it virtually impossible for them to have known at the time of the wedding. It is far more likely that Goebbels wanted to put a stop to the spiteful gossip about his relationship with Magda and Harald, which Röhm had started. And it is even more likely that he felt the time was ripe for him to fill the vacuum left by Carin Göring's death and shift the social centre of the party elite in Berlin to Magda's elegant and spacious apartment in the Reichskanzlerplatz. He moved in with her immediately after the wedding.

Hitler soon found the Goebbels home a congenial place where he could relax in Berlin, away from the formality of the Kaiserhof. Goebbels and Magda both worked hard to please him: Magda baking the cakes and pastries he loved and Goebbels playing his favourite music on the gramophone, along with records of his most successful speeches. Both were prepared to listen to his interminable monologues with every appearance of being utterly entranced. Their shameless fawning paid off: Hitler became a regular visitor whenever he was in Berlin and his relationship with Goebbels grew into the nearest thing he could manage to a genuine personal friendship. But no matter how close they became, Goebbels still maintained a respectful deference towards his leader, always addressing him as '*Sie*' and never progressing to the intimate '*Du*' in their conversations. To have done so would have seemed like lese-majesty, going against the so-called 'Führer principle', something akin to the divine right of kings, under which all power emanated from the leader, who could do no wrong and was the embodiment of the state itself.

Because of their closeness, Goebbels hoped to influence Hitler towards his own brand of revolutionary National Socialism and against the 'reactionaries' in Munich. The hope proved to be a delusion, though Hitler, as always, seemed happy to encourage it. But Goebbels was able to influence him to take one momentous decision: in February 1932 he persuaded him, against the advice and the wishes of the Munich cabal, to run for election as President of Germany.

Hindenburg's term of office was due to expire on 5 May, but the idea of a presidential election at that time had little appeal for Brüning or Schleicher. Schleicher, devious as ever, came up with a plan to extend Hindenburg's term, ostensibly to spare the eighty-four-year-old President the stress of an election, but in fact so that Brüning would be able to go on ruling by decrees which he simply stuck under his nose for signature. The only problem was that this represented a constitutional change that would have to be approved by a two-thirds majority of the Reichstag. The Nazis' 107 votes would be crucial.

On 5 January, General Groener, who was not only Defence Minister but also acting Minister of the Interior, telegraphed Hitler asking him to come to Berlin for an urgent meeting. Hitler was in the editorial office of the *Völkischer Beobachter* in Munich with Hess, Rosenberg, and one of the paper's editors, Wilhelm Weiss, when the telegram arrived. He is said to have banged his fist down jubilantly on the message and exclaimed: 'Now I have them in my pocket! They have recognised that they have to negotiate with me!'[1] He travelled to Berlin, met Groener and Hindenburg's State Secretary, Otto Meissner, on 6 January and Schleicher and Brüning the following day. 'Now the chess game for power begins,' Goebbels noted with eager anticipation. 'Maybe it will last the whole year. A game that will be played with speed, intelligence and in part with cunning.'[2]

Contrary to his propaganda chief's hopes, however, Hitler played his opening moves with nail-biting indecision, despite being urged on by Goebbels, Röhm and Göring: the three rivals had put aside their personal differences to make common cause against the right-wing 'Munich clique' – so much so that Goebbels even managed a complimentary reference to Göring in his diary, saying he was 'a valuable help to the overburdened Führer'.[3] Goebbels's diaries for this period often need to be taken with a large pinch of salt, since the only version of them that we have was heavily edited by him for publication, appearing in German as *Vom Kaiserhof zur Reichskanzlei* in 1934, and in English translation as *My Part in Germany's Fight* a year later. All the same, he seems to have been happy to work alongside Göring again, capitalising on his popularity for the sake of the party.

For Goebbels himself, this was a period of some frustration. 'The press,' he noted, 'is wallowing in sensation. Would like to reduce our grand old man [Hindenburg] to an object for horse-trading.' But to his great disappointment, he could not join in the wallowing himself, because on 7 January Deputy Police Commissioner Weiss slapped yet another seven-day ban on *Der Angriff* for defaming the Jewish religion. And when he tried to address a meeting of 15,000 supporters in the Sportpalast that evening, the police closed it down, both because he was repeating the defamation and because the overcrowded audience was getting dangerously out of control.[4] To add to his woes, he was then banned for three weeks from public speaking in Berlin and Prussia, a gag that he found particularly irksome at this time of high excitement.

On 12 January 1932, Hitler rejected Brüning's plan to extend the President's term, then went over his head and wrote directly to Hindenburg, offering to support his candidacy if he would dismiss Brüning and call elections to the Reichstag and the Prussian Landtag. With the tide flowing more strongly than ever in their favour, the Nazis were confident that fresh elections would give them a commanding majority in both assemblies, albeit in partnership with the DNVP. When Hindenburg, to no one's surprise, rejected his offer, Hitler was faced with making the big decision: should he run for President against the Field Marshal?

The question split the party into two opposing camps. The Goebbels–Röhm–Göring faction believed that Hitler had no option but to run if he were to retain his political credibility. His followers, they argued, expected it and would be disappointed and disillusioned if he ducked the fight. The opposing group, led by Gregor Strasser, thought it would be equally damaging for Hitler to enter a hopeless contest: Hindenburg, the near legendary hero, could not be beaten, and Hitler's inevitable defeat would shatter the reputation of invincibility that he and the party had been successfully building.

Goebbels, more interested in the fight than the result, lashed out with his usual venom. 'There is one man in the organisation whom nobody trusts,' he told Hitler. 'There is a danger that he will disassociate himself from it at a critical hour, and cause us immeasurable and irreparable harm. He shows no solidarity and can be a true friend to no one. His name is Gregor Strasser.'⁵ Hitler listened, considered his options, and as usual did nothing, keeping everybody waiting for his decision.

Before taking his decision, Hitler wanted to size up the opposition outside the party and to gain the support of the powerful – and rich – capitalists and industrialists, without alienating the radical elements in the SA. This was a delicate balancing operation, needing great care and the support of Göring and Goebbels, who represented the two constituencies. He won the capitalists to his cause at the Industry Club in Düsseldorf on 27 January, with one of the most cleverly judged speeches of his entire life, reassuring them with sober, reasoned arguments and a total absence of histrionics, and promising to protect their interests against Communism and the trade unions. As he finished, the whole audience, which had initially been reserved and slightly hostile, rose to its feet, cheering wildly. A few days later Goebbels was able to note: 'Money affairs improve daily. The financing of the electoral campaign is practically assured.'⁶

While Hitler still vacillated, Goebbels was supremely confident of success. He was already making active preparations for the campaign, gearing up his department to produce 'masterpieces of propaganda on an unheard-of scale', and staging rehearsals of polling day with the SA and party members in Berlin. On 24 January he noted: 'The elections are prepared down to the minutest detail. It will be a struggle such as the world has never before witnessed.' And a week later: 'The lines of the election campaign are all laid down. We now need only to press the button to set the machine going.'⁷ Looking still further ahead, he was even talking to Hitler about his position in a Nazi government, discussing the role of his proposed department:

The idea is to organise a Ministry for the Education of the People, comprising control of the cinema, broadcasting, new educational establishments, arts, culture, and propaganda generally. This is altogether a revolutionary office, to be directed in general from the centre. Its object would be to set forth clearly the Idea of the Reich. It is a vast plan such as the world has not yet seen. I am already beginning to work out the basis of this ministry. It is designed for the intelligent support of the state, and to conquer not only the apparatus of government, but the people as a whole.[8]

On 15 February, Hindenburg finally fired the starting pistol by declaring that he would stand, and the Presidential Commission set 13 March as the date of the election. But Hitler still kept everybody waiting. In fact, he could do nothing else: he was not eligible for election, since he was not a German citizen. The press had cottoned on to this uncomfortable impediment at the beginning of February, running a story that Frick, while Minister of the Interior in Thuringia, had tried to resolve the problem in 1930 by appointing Hitler chief of police in an obscure little town in that state, thus qualifying him for automatic citizenship under the Weimar Constitution. Hitler had rejected the post as beneath him, but the matter had suddenly become urgent. Frick had since been ousted from his position in Thuringia, so it was arranged that a Nazi minister in Brunswick should provide him with a position as a government councillor, with the nominal job of representing that small state in Berlin. This would make him a civil servant and would give him the citizenship he needed, but it could not be done overnight – Hitler did not actually swear his oath of allegiance until 26 February. By 22 February, however, he could be sure that everything was in hand, and he authorised Goebbels to announce his candidacy that evening to a packed general party members' meeting in the Berlin Sportpalast. 'When after about an hour's preparatory speech I publicly proclaim the Führer's candidature, a deafening storm of applause rages for about ten minutes,' Goebbels recorded. 'Wild ovations for the Führer. They nearly raise the roof . . . People laugh and cry at the same time.'

'Late at night,' Goebbels gloated to his diary, 'the Führer rings me up. I give him my report and he comes over to our house. He is glad that the news of his candidature has been such a success.'[9] The men of the 'Munich clique' in the 'Brown House' were less pleased, however – neither Hitler nor Goebbels had bothered to tell them in advance.

They assumed Goebbels had gone out on a limb to force a decision, and immediately issued a denial to the press, which they then had to retract, to their chagrin and his great satisfaction. The newspapers naturally made the most of the schism. Goebbels feigned righteous indignation, while revelling in the impression the stories gave of his influence with Hitler. 'The press has insulted me,' he wrote. 'It declares it is I who have nominated the Führer, or even obliged him to come forward as candidate. How ill-informed it is; or better still, it acts as if it were ill-informed!'[10]

With his enemies in the party routed and his position established beyond all doubt, Goebbels threw himself into hectic, non-stop electioneering, with an energy that was truly phenomenal. As well as directing and co-ordinating the national campaign, he remained one of the party's star performers, along with Hitler himself, Göring and Strasser, who supported Hitler loyally once the decision had been taken. He spoke at no fewer than nineteen mass meetings in Berlin alone between 27 February and 13 March, plus nine others in cities as far apart as Breslau, Dresden, Magdeburg, Essen, Cologne, Hamburg and Nuremberg, and still found time to write articles and pamphlets galore, and to provoke constant brawls and disruptions in the Reichstag.

For the period of the election, Goebbels had moved the Propaganda Department from Munich to Berlin, and he shuttled back there each night, eating, writing, and snatching a few hours' sleep on trains. Couriers met him at intermediate stations to deliver packets of papers for him to work on while travelling. He had half a million posters printed and pasted up all over Germany, many of them designed by his friend Schweitzer, *Der Angriff*'s savage cartoonist. On the streets of Berlin, the SA were deployed to guard Hitler's posters as the Nazis and Communists fought to deface, paste over or rip each other's down.

To the traditional weapons of posters and mass meetings, Goebbels added the latest technological advances, in keeping with the image he was trying to create of a young, modern party, looking to the future. 'Fifty thousand gramophone records have been made, small enough to fit into an ordinary envelope,' he wrote on 29 February. 'The supporters of the government will be astonished when they place these miniature records on the gramophone. A film (of me) is being made and I speak a few words in it for about ten minutes. It is to be shown in the evening in all public gardens and squares of the larger cities.'[11] The message he pumped out constantly was of Hitler as the saviour of Germany, the prophet, the fighter, but above all the leader, the Führer, not only of the party but also of the German people as a whole.

The other three candidates, even the Communist leader Ernst Thälmann, could not hope to match the Nazi effort. The DNVP representative, the uninspiring Stahlhelm vice-chairman, Theodor Duesterberg, was completely wiped out. Hindenburg did not deign to campaign personally, delivering only one pre-recorded radio speech on the eve of polling day, though Brüning worked hard on his behalf, refusing to allow any other candidate air time on the state-controlled networks. Göring was given the honour of wrapping up Hitler's campaign with a bombastic speech in the Sportpalast on 12 March. 'Captain Göring speaks on top form,' Goebbels noted. 'He takes the System [the Weimar Republic] to account as never before. A magnificent end to the election fight in Berlin.'

Hitler chose to be in Munich for the results, while Goebbels held court in Berlin, with a party in his apartment. 'Everybody who has any legs to come on, young and old, seems to have turned up,' he wrote. Their mood was confident to begin with, but soon turned to depression as they listened to the reports on the radio, and it became clear that Hitler had failed. The final figures were both disappointing and encouraging. Hindenburg easily topped the list with 18,651,497 votes, to Hitler's 11,339,446. But the Communist Thälmann had only managed 4,983,341 and Duesterberg a derisory 2,557,729. Hitler had attracted a creditable 30.1 per cent of the total. Hindenburg, with 49.6 per cent, was only 0.4 percentage points short of the absolute majority he needed to return him to the presidential palace – but regarded it as a humiliation that the 'Bohemian corporal' had forced him into a run-off.

Goebbels made a show of intense disappointment, but in truth the result was very much what he and Hitler had expected, and they had already begun making plans for the second presidential campaign. The new polling day was to be 10 April, but Brüning declared an embargo on electioneering until 4 April, after Easter, so the new campaign would have to be condensed into less than a week. Goebbels accepted the challenge eagerly. But there was an alarming hitch on 17 March, when the Prussian police raided the SA offices in Berlin and discovered orders from Röhm, backed up by detailed plans and maps, for all SA and SS men to stand by in their barracks on the day of the first ballot, ready to carry out an immediate *coup d'état* if Hitler won.

This was a serious threat to Hitler's prospects – he could be charged with high treason if it was proved that he knew about the plot. Röhm hurried to reassure Schleicher, with whom he was now on close terms since the general, too, wanted to incorporate the SA into the army as a reserve or militia. Göring was given the job of refuting the charge to the public. He called a press conference at the Kaiserhof, where he underlined the party's commitment to legality with beaming, if tongue-in-cheek, affability:

It was most commendable of us to concentrate our 350,000 storm-troopers in their own quarters on election day. By so doing, we prevented bloodshed. As for the allegation of the police that we Nazis were preparing to surround Berlin, the whole idea is absurd. We are surely entitled to take our own measures for the evacuation from the city of our women and children so as to protect them from injury by government mobs, and that, in fact, is what we did. Why, heaven help us, we have so many former officers in our ranks that if we really wanted to stage a rising we could set about it in quite a different manner, I assure you, gentlemen.[12]

The threat was averted, for the moment, and Goebbels was able to go ahead with the new campaign with still greater ingenuity. Alongside the films and gramophone records he introduced another marvel of modern*technology, the aeroplane. Using a small Junkers passenger plane from the National Socialist Flying Corps, he sent Hitler on his first 'Germany Flight' from city to city under the slogan 'The Führer over Germany', adding a whole new dimension to the old concept of the whistle-stop tour. It created a sensation, not least because Hitler insisted on continuing to fly through bad weather and storms that grounded all other aircraft, enhancing his reputation for physical courage as he swooped down dramatically from the clouds. In seven days, he was able to address mass meetings in twenty different towns and cities from the Baltic in the north to Bavaria in the south, from East Prussia in the east to Westphalia in the west.

Goebbels's tactics paid off handsomely: Hitler added more than two million votes in the second ballot, raising his total to 13,418,547, almost 37 per cent. Hindenburg also increased his total, but by less than a million, to 19,359,983, or 53 per cent of the vote. Thälmann lost over a million, ending up with only just over a 10 per cent share. Hindenburg was returned to office, but he was old and increasingly infirm, and there was now only one successor waiting in the wings.

*   *   *

Even before the result of the presidential election was known, Goebbels was mobilising his forces again. The elections for the Prussian Landtag were scheduled for two weeks ahead, along with those for Anhalt, Bavaria, Hamburg and Württemberg. Together, they involved no less than four fifths of the population of Germany. 'We lose no time,' he wrote on presidential polling day itself, 'but proceed at once to plan our campaign for Prussia. At dawn I am still writing a leading article and proclamation to the Berlin party. They have fought stoutly. Now Prussia must be vanquished. That will be the next fortress to be assaulted. The second election has enormously enhanced our chances.'[13]

Goebbels organised the usual speaking tours, mass meetings and parades, plastered the country with yet more posters, and repeated the success of 'The Führer over Germany' with fresh flights. He himself spoke three or four times a night, as did Göring and other leading party orators. But they faced a serious handicap right at the beginning, when Groener persuaded a reluctant Hindenburg to ban both the SA and the SS throughout the country, after uncovering fresh evidence of plots to seize power by force. The police occupied Goebbels's headquarters in Berlin, and sealed the SA's offices. Schleicher had leaked an advance warning of the ban to the party two days before it was issued, so there was time to relabel SA units and reclassify the storm-troopers, who now numbered nearly 400,000, as regular party members. But the SA was an essential tool in any Nazi campaign, and Goebbels's task was made harder when its members were forced underground.

In the event, the SA ban hardly mattered. The state elections brought fresh triumphs for the party and fresh glory for Goebbels as the architect of what he described as 'a fantastic victory'. In Prussia, which covered two thirds of Germany, the Nazis received 36.3 per cent of the vote, increasing their number of seats from six to 162 to become by far the largest party, though still without an overall majority and unable to form a government. In Bavaria, Württemberg and Hamburg they did almost as well. And in Anhalt they achieved 40.9 per cent, enabling them to appoint their first Minister-President. But Goebbels's elation at the provincial results only increased his frustration at being no nearer to the national election he was now convinced the Nazis could win. 'We must come to power in the foreseeable future,' he wrote impatiently. 'Otherwise we're going to win ourselves to death in elections.'[14]

*　　*　　*

Ironically, it was the banning of the SA that finally unlocked the back door to power for Hitler and the Nazis. Schleicher was against the ban, since it interfered with his plan to merge the SA into the army, which would then back an authoritarian government that would to all intents and purposes be a military dictatorship, with the support of the Nazis. Furious that Groener and Brüning, whom he had regarded as his puppets, had gone against his wishes, he persuaded Hindenburg to write them an angry letter demanding to know why they had not banned the Reichsbanner, the Social Democrats' para-military organisation, as well as the SA. But this was only the opening shot. Schleicher was already having discussions with Röhm and Count Wolf von Helldorf, the dissolute son of an aristocratic racehorse owner and a former Freikorps leader, who had been given command of the SA in Berlin after the Stennes affair. Now, using Helldorf as a go-between, he invited Hitler for secret talks, during which he told him the army no longer supported Brüning or Groener. They would have to go.

This was the opportunity Hitler had been waiting for. He and Schleicher circled each other warily, each believing he could use the other to achieve his own aims. Hitler agreed to consider taking part in or at least supporting a nationalist government in return for the lifting of the ban on the SA and SS and a pledge to dissolve the Reichstag and call new elections.

Now the game was really afoot. Hitler and Goebbels both left Berlin for short holidays in Bavaria, to keep out of the way and avoid giving Brüning and his ministers any cause for suspicion as Schleicher prepared their downfall. Concentrating his fire first on the weakest link, Groener, he began the process of destroying him by spreading malicious rumours that he had become a Marxist and a pacifist, that his health was too poor for him to remain in office and that he had besmirched the honour of the army by marrying an unsuitable bride, who gave birth to a child born only five months after the wedding.

Hitler's and Goebbels's holiday in sunny Munich was interrupted by a phone call after a week. 'The bomb has exploded,' Goebbels noted dramatically. 'The Minister of Economics has tendered his resignation, and Groener and Brüning are tottering to their fall. The Führer must return to Berlin immediately.' They left on the night train. 'On the way, we scheme out daring things . . . We hold tremendous private confabulations in sleepers; how little the conductor dreams what they are about.'[15]

In Berlin the next day, Hitler had a 'decisive' meeting with Schleicher and 'a few gentlemen from the closest circle of the President'. Göring accompanied him. Goebbels, whom they disliked and distrusted, was kept well clear, but was told about it immediately afterwards by Hitler. 'Everything goes well,' he noted. 'Brüning will fall in a few days. The President will withdraw his confidence in him. The plan is then to install a Presidential Cabinet; the Reichstag will be dissolved, all coercive laws will be cancelled and we shall be free to agitate as we like and to deliver a masterpiece of propaganda.'[16]

Göring was chosen to strike the crucial blow in the Reichstag on 10 May. He tore into Groener with a powerful speech, beginning by taunting him over the ban on the SA:

Don't think that by removing his brown shirt you can take away the spirit of the SA man. While other parties change their policies like their shirts, for us spirit and policy remain the same in spite of prohibition and terror. Faithfulness and comradeship which to many of you have become a phantom, like your oath, for us are fundamental to the union of German men, who stand united for their country and their people . . . A government that, internally, externally, and in political economy, has lost every battle, can no longer ask for confidence. It has always been so in history. When a general has lost a battle, he has to go. Troops are not there to bleed to death for a general, and a people does not exist to be ruined by a government which cannot master the situation. And so we declare today that the Cabinet no longer enjoys the trust of the people. The people are clamouring for new men! . . . The Brüning Cabinet must go. It must go in order that Germany can live.[17]

Groener, sick with diabetes, tried to defend himself but was howled down and taunted with derisive laughter. Driven from the chamber, he was greeted by Schleicher, the former protégé whom he had regarded as a son, who told him coldly that he no longer had the support of the army. He clung on for another two days, during which Goebbels, Göring and the other Nazi members continuously disrupted the Reichstag in a concerted attempt to have the SA ban lifted. The government defeated them by thirty votes.

On 12 May, in the corridor outside the chamber, four hefty Nazis beat up a journalist who had published letters written by Röhm describing his homosexual tastes. The four refused to accept an expulsion order, sitting tight in their seats as their fellow Nazis, led by Goebbels and Göring, started a brawl, which got so out of hand that the police were called in to restore order. They were led by none other than Goebbels's personal *bête noire*, Deputy Commissioner Bernhard Weiss, giving Goebbels the opportunity for a fine display of feigned fury as he shrieked 'Isidor! Isidor! Out! Out!' Weiss calmly ignored the shouts, and arrested the four men.

Goebbels thought Weiss had done the party a great service. 'One has a vague feeling this may be the last great scene before the crash of the System,' he wrote. 'We can only be thankful. The more the parliamentary system exposes itself, the less need we have to do it for it!' At the end of this 'crazy day', Groener finally announced his resignation. 'That is the first result,' Goebbels crowed. 'Groener's fall is considered to be the beginning of the end. Late at night I give the Führer a description of the whole thing. He is extremely satisfied.'[18]

Schleicher, too, was pleased. The next day, he sent a message to the Nazi leadership saying things were 'progressing according to plan'. Indeed they were. The government was coming to pieces in Brüning's hands; ministers began baling out. When he asked Schleicher to take the post of Defence Minster, the withering reply was: 'I will – but not in your government.'[19] Schleicher knew the time of reckoning was close: with the help of the Prussian Junkers who had clubbed together to present the President with his estate at Neudeck, he had been destroying what little remained of Hindenburg's confidence in Brüning by persuading the old man that the chancellor was a closet Marxist intent on seizing the large country estates in a 'Bolshevist land settlement plan'.[20] Short of labelling him a pacifist, he could not have thought up a more damaging accusation.

Goebbels kept up his destabilising tactics in the Prussian Landtag, where he had taken one of the seats to gain extra immunity and escape a Supreme Court indictment for high treason. At its second session on 25 May, he led the 162 Nazi members in a pitched battle against the eighty Communists, using ink pots as missiles and chairs as weapons. 'It is short but conclusive,' he wrote. 'In three minutes we are alone in the chamber. The Communists have been driven out; the middle parties have taken flight. We sing the "Horst Wessel Song". Eight seriously wounded from the various parties. That should be a warning. It's the only way one can get respect. The council chamber is a scene of wreckage. We stand among the ruins as victors.'[21]

On 29 May, as the Nazis won their first absolute majority in Landtag elections in Oldenburg with twenty-four out of forty-six seats, Hindenburg summoned Brüning and gave him his marching orders. The next day, he received Hitler and Göring, and asked if they would honour the agreement Hitler had made with Schleicher to support the new government he was about to form, in return for the lifting of the ban on the SA and SS and the dissolution of the Reichstag. Hitler confirmed that he would. 'The bomb has exploded!' Goebbels wrote jubilantly. 'Von Papen is intended to be Chancellor. But that's of no interest now. Voting! Voting! Going to the people. We're all very happy.'[22]

Franz von Papen, the new Chancellor, was an urbane nonentity in his mid fifties, not over-endowed with intelligence or political experience, and with the face of a haughty baboon. He was a member of the Westphalian nobility, a former cavalry officer and noted gentleman jockey, who had married the daughter of a wealthy Saar industrialist. His only claim to fame was that he had been expelled from the United States, where he was military attaché before America entered the war, for clumsy attempts at espionage and organising sabotage. 'The President's choice met with incredulity,' wrote André François-Poncet, the French ambassador in Berlin. 'No one but smiled or tittered or laughed because Papen enjoyed the peculiarity of being taken seriously neither by his friends nor his enemies . . . He was reputed to be superficial, blundering, untrue, ambitious, vain, crafty and an intriguer.'[23] When Schleicher, who had of course chosen him for the position, was reminded that Papen lacked political experience and had no head for administration, he replied cynically: 'He doesn't need a head. His job is to be a hat.'

Papen belonged to Brüning's Catholic Centre Party, but was not a member of the Reichstag, having never got further than the Prussian Landtag. When he accepted the Chancellorship, the party promptly expelled him for betraying Brüning. This did not worry him much, since the President had instructed him to form a non-party government, and in any case, Schleicher, who of course had chosen him for the position, already had a complete list of ministers lined up. 'It's quite true,' an anonymous general in the Defence Ministry – we will call him General X for convenience – wrote incredulously in his diary after a conversation with Schleicher. 'The new Cabinet has been standing saddled in the stable for months. Everything was arranged to the smallest detail. A long time even before the Presidential election. Poor Brüning!'[24]

The new government was drawn entirely from the membership of the Herrenklub, the exclusive gentlemen's club in Vossstrasse, just around the corner from the Reichstag and the Wilhelmstrasse. Its ministers were a mixture of aristocrats and directors of large corporations, and were soon dubbed the 'Cabinet of Barons' by a public that regarded them as a very bad joke. The only serious politician among them was Schleicher himself, who Hindenburg insisted should come out of the shadows as Defence Minister. There were no representatives of the Nazi Party among them, though by this time Göring, Goebbels and Röhm were all members of the Herrenklub, but the Minister of Justice was Franz Gürtner, who had been Hitler's protector in the Bavarian government in 1923.

Hitler, staying on the Severin estate while electioneering for the Landtag elections in Mecklenburg, refused to give a written undertaking that he would work smoothly with Papen after the next general election, until his own conditions had been met. 'On the opposition side, there are men who need to be tackled with circumspection,' Goebbels wrote after long discussions with him. 'Intrigues are everywhere afoot. We are playing a risky game. So much the more must the dissolution of the Reichstag be a *sine qua non*.'[25]

Schleicher hurried out to meet Hitler secretly on a neighbouring estate, and reassured him that everything was still going according to plan. The next day, as Hitler and Goebbels motored back to Berlin after ending the Mecklenburg election campaign with speeches to a crowd of 30,000, Papen announced that the Reichstag was dissolved. The new national elections were scheduled for 31 July, the latest possible date, bad news for Goebbels, who was hoping it would be 3 July.

On the face of it, the situation looked promising for the Nazis. They had just achieved an absolute majority in Mecklenburg, and a similar result nationally seemed far from impossible. But the tactics invented by Himmler and honed to perfection by Goebbels were designed for short, concentrated campaigns, sweeping voters along in a rush of emotion. Spread over almost two months, the frenetic campaigning could pall. Election fatigue could set in, both in the electorate and in party workers. Worst of all, voters might have time to think. 'The longer the contest beforehand, the better for our opponents,' Goebbels grumbled. 'We shall have our work cut out to make up for this.'[26]

Any illusions Papen and Schleicher might have harboured about co-operation from the Nazis were shattered at the outset. 'We must dissociate ourselves at the earliest possible moment from the temporary bourgeois Cabinet,' Goebbels wrote on 5 June, and the following day launched an attack on them in *Der Angriff*. Understandably, Papen dragged his feet over lifting the bans on the SA and political demonstrations. Göring went to see the Interior Minister without success, and when Hitler met the new Chancellor for the first time on 13 June, he demanded immediate action to fulfil Papen's side of the bargain he had struck with Schleicher. At the same time, he made no bones about his own intentions telling him bluntly: 'I regard your Cabinet as only a temporary solution, and will continue my efforts to make my party the strongest in the country. The Chancellorship will then devolve on me.'[27]

When Papen still hesitated, Goebbels took matters into his own hands in typically aggressive fashion. The next evening, he led forty or fifty SA leaders in full uniform into a large restaurant on the Potsdamer Platz, the busiest square in Berlin, trying to provoke the police into arresting them. The police, however, failed to oblige, even after they had very deliberately sauntered across the square and up Potsdamer Strasse at midnight.[28]

The prohibition was finally lifted on 16 June, opening the way for a summer of mayhem unmatched since 1919. The Nazis, through the ever-willing SA, set out to provoke the Communists into violent battles intended to fill most Germans with the dread of the Bolshevik menace and drive them into the welcoming arms of the Nazi Party. The operation was orchestrated by Goebbels with cynical disregard for life or limb, including his own: he was often in the thick of the action, and was stoned in his home town of Rheydt and his old stomping ground in the Ruhr.

The summer of 1932 turned out to be a particularly hot one, and the heat served to exacerbate a situation that was already as unstable and explosive as a truck-load of nitro-glycerine on a bumpy track. By 20 July, there had been no fewer than 461 pitched battles on the streets of Prussia alone, in which eighty-two men were killed and 400 seriously wounded, with another eighty-two deaths in the rest of Germany, thirty-eight of them Nazis and thirty Communists. The worst single incident was in Altona, a workers' district of Hamburg, where the Nazis staged a march, escorted by police, on Sunday 17 July. The Communists took up the challenge, greeting them with a hail of gunfire from rooftops and windows. The Nazis responded with their own guns. Between them, they killed nineteen and wounded 285.

Papen's response to Altona's 'Bloody Sunday' was to ban all political demonstrations and parades for the remaining two weeks before the elections. But more importantly, he used it as an excuse to depose the state government of Prussia, on evidence provided by Schleicher that its Socialist ministers were in league with the Communists, and were therefore unable to maintain order. In its place, he imposed direct rule by the national government, under himself as Reich Commissioner. When the Prussian ministers resisted, he proclaimed martial law in Berlin and had the Reichswehr commander in the city, General Gerd von Rundstedt, send round a dozen men under a lieutenant to arrest them. To Goebbels's delight, they also arrested Police Commissioner Grzesinski and his deputy, Bernhard 'Isidor' Weiss, who were both dismissed. Weiss had recently filed his seventeenth charge of defamation against Goebbels; none of the outstanding cases ever came to court.

Papen's action, under emergency Presidential decree, was stretching the constitution to its limit. Its legality was dubious in the extreme, but no one raised a finger, or even a loud voice, to save the demo-cratically-elected state government. There was no call for a general strike, as in the Kapp *putsch*. All it had taken was a small squad of troops, without a tank or even an armoured car, to impose a dicta-torship on two-thirds of the country. It was a precedent that Hitler noted carefully.

Meanwhile, the election campaign – the fourth in as many months – was in full flow. By 1 July, reinvigorated by the challenge and the potential prize, Goebbels had everything prepared and was ready to plunge back into what had become an all-too-familiar routine. He managed to throw off his weariness, but the stress showed clearly in his diary entry for the opening day:

The travelling starts again. Work has to be done standing, walking, driving, flying. The most urgent conferences are held on the stairs, in the hall, at the door, or on the way to the station. You hardly have time to think. You are carried by train, motor car and aeroplane this way and that through Germany. You arrive at a town half an hour before the beginning of a meeting or some-times even later, go up to the platform and speak.

The audience generally has no idea of what the speaker has already gone through during the day before he delivers his address in the evening. Many of them, surely, imagine that he has nothing to do but make speeches! They misjudge him if he is tired and not quite in form. They regret that his oration leaves something to be desired, that he is not particularly witty, and that his choice of words is not happy. And in the mean time, he is struggling with the heat, with finding the right word, with the sequence of a thought, with a voice that grows hoarser and hoarser, with the cussedness of poor acoustics, and with the bad air from 10,000 tightly-packed people. . . . When the speech is over, you feel as though you've just been hauled fully-clothed out of a hot bath. Then you get back in the car and drive another two hours over bad roads.[29]

Goebbels once again deployed all the weapons in his armoury, plus one new one: on 18 July he spoke on the radio for the first time. It was not a happy experience – he was subjected to heavy censorship and felt that he ended up with 'mere words' and had not reached his audience – but he noted the medium's potential for the future. He shot more films, and persuaded Hitler to make his first gramophone record; labelled 'Appeal to the Nation', it lasted eight and a half minutes and sold 50,000 copies at five marks each.

Goebbels's high opinion of his own speeches was not shared by everyone. The anonymous diarist in the Defence Ministry heard him for the first time towards the end of the campaign and noted incredulously:

I believe there is nothing that the fellow can't twist to mean its opposite. Physically a dwarf, intellectually a giant. But a giant only in the art of pulling down, of destruction. A Mephistopheles! Such cripples should not be given power, otherwise they plunge the whole world into ruin simply to appease their accursed and suppressed complexes. They hate, and must hate, all that is sound and natural, simply because it has been denied them by fate. Herr Goebbels is a model example of this variety of man.[30]

During the last two weeks, Goebbels sent Hitler off on another 'Flight over Germany', this time covering an astonishing fifty-three towns and cities. For the first time, Hitler wore the brown shirt of the SA, with his medals pinned to his chest. His speeches concentrated on wooing the middle classes, promising that the Nazis would provide a better future for them – without in any way specifying how – and attacking the existing and previous governments. The campaign reached its climax on 27 July in and around Berlin, when he spoke to audiences of 60,000 in Brandenburg and Potsdam during the day and then a massive 120,000 in the Grunewald Stadium in Berlin, with another 100,000 outside, listening to him over loudspeakers.

When the results came in on the night of 31 July, the Nazi vote had more than doubled in the nine months since the last general election, to 13,745,000, a 37.3 per cent share of the total. However, this was only 300,000 more than Hitler had received in the presidential run-off – it looked ominously as though the period of rapid growth was levelling out. Nevertheless, with 230 seats the Nazis were easily the largest party in the Reichstag, and although they still did not have an overall majority in a house of 608, it would be impossible for any other party to govern without their co-operation.

'Now we must come to power and exterminate Marxism. One way or another! Something must be done,' Goebbels wrote in his diary the next day (he edited the entry heavily in the published version).

The time of opposition is ended. Now we go into action. Hitler thinks the same. Events have to sort themselves out, then we must take the decision. We shall not obtain an absolute majority this way. So we shall have to take another path. We face a hard conclusion . . . We will have a short breathing space, to consolidate our position, but then it will be power and what we can make of it! We must not be modest in our demands. Either sharpest opposition, or power. The middle way is death. That is Hitler's opinion, too.[31]

In fact, Hitler's opinion was not so clear. As usual, he was procrastinating, unable to make up his mind. After taking a couple of days' break to recover from the rigours of the elections, relaxing with Goebbels at two visits to the opera in Munich – *Die Meistersinger* and *Tristan und Isolde* – he conferred with his senior lieutenants by the lakeside on the Tegernsee in pouring rain. Together they talked over the alternatives: should they seek an alliance with the Centre Party, and accept partial power in a coalition? Or should they simply demand full power as the biggest individual party? Should they, indeed, abandon the policy of legality, now that it seemed to be failing them, and take the revolutionary path?

Röhm was naturally all for the military option, believing he could do a deal with Schleicher and the Reichswehr. Despite Papen's ban on marches and demonstrations, the SA had continued its violence to the very end of the electoral campaign, killing ten people and wounding eighty-three on polling day itself. Now it was on the alert, raring for a *putsch* and just waiting for the word to strike. Strasser and Frick, on the other hand, were in favour of a coalition: for some time Strasser had been actively discussing co-operation with the other parties, especially with the Centre Party and Brüning, who had become a close personal friend. To Goebbels and Göring, however, the idea of a coalition was 'unthinkable'. For them it was all or nothing.

Hitler listened to the conflicting opinions, and decided that what mattered most was that he should become Chancellor. He was prepared to accept a coalition, as a temporary expedient, but only under his control. On 4 August, he left Munich and hurried north for a secret meeting with Schleicher at the Fürstenberg army base fifty miles north of Berlin, to put his demands to the king-maker: Hitler himself as Reich Chancellor and Minister-President of Prussia, Frick as Interior Minister, Göring as Aviation Minister, the Labour Ministry for Strasser, and for Goebbels his projected Ministry for the Education of the People. Schleicher would remain Defence Minister. Hitler wanted total power, backed by an Enabling Act authorising him to rule by presidential decree, or everything was off.[32]

The negotiations with Schleicher took several hours. According to General X, Hitler complained 'almost despairingly' of the greed of his own people, worst of all Goebbels: 'He had already forced him to stand for the Presidency at the election, although he, Hitler, had explicitly refused. And now, too, Goebbels was against any understanding with Schleicher and any mere participation in the government.'[33]

Believing he had won Schleicher over, Hitler headed back to his anxiously waiting colleagues on the Obersalzberg, where the weather had miraculously changed from pouring rain to brilliant sunshine. Taking them on an outing to Salzburg, he told them everything had gone well and they could expect everything to 'burst out' in one more week. There were some changes to the line-up he had proposed: Strasser was to be given the Interior Ministries of both the Reich and Prussia, rather than the less important Labour portfolio, displacing Frick, who was to be State Secretary in the Reich Chancellery; the Nazis would nominate the Ministers of Justice, Economics and Finance, and Hjalmar Schacht would be put in charge of the Reichsbank again.[34] Göring was still to have Aviation – he was so pleased and so sure that he phoned his friend Erhard Milch at Lufthansa and invited him to be his State Secretary. Goebbels would be given the Prussian Ministry of Culture as well as his People's Education Ministry. 'A Cabinet of real men,' Goebbels exulted. 'If the Reichstag refuses to pass the Enabling Act it will be sent packing . . . We shall never give up power – they will have to drag us out as corpses . . . I still can't believe it. At the gateway of power. The great hour is here.'[35]

As it happened, the 'great hour' was still a little way off. The whole country, and Berlin in particular, was awash with rumours, but no one was taking any decisions. General X noted with relish that Brüning was trying to set up a coalition government with Hitler as Chancellor and himself as Vice-Chancellor and Foreign Minister, but that Hugenberg and the DNVP were 'trying to put a spoke in his wheel'. 'The reign of terror in the country grows from day to day,' he continued. 'A dozen dead has become a normal occurrence. A bad look-out for humanity in general if ever these Brown villains are let loose upon it!'[36]

Three days later, the general was writing that Hitler had sent Göring to Schleicher with a new plan, for which he begged his 'absolute discretion'. This proposed that the Nazis should try to make Schleicher Chancellor, and keep him there for at least two years, with three selected Nazis in his Cabinet. In return, Schleicher would do his best to persuade Hindenberg, 'who had grown impossible', to retire and put Hitler in his place as President. General X thought the plan would have been worth consideration, if they had not known Hitler would let them down. 'This certainty,' he wrote, '. . . made it easy for us to assume a role of moral indignation and reject the proposal. Herr Göring took himself off again.'[37]

As the days since the election passed, the 'Brown villains' of the SA were growing restive. While Goebbels was busy confirming that he would still retain his existing party positions as Gauleiter of Berlin and Reich Propaganda Leader alongside his new ministerial posts, he was concerned to receive a telephone call from Berlin saying that SA men were leaving their places of work to be ready for action. Helldorf had developed his own plans for the take-over of power. Party officials were ready for the 'great hour'. The whole city was in a state of high tension. 'If all goes well,' Goebbels wrote, 'then everything will be fine. If it goes badly, there'll be a terrible backlash.'[38]

Confusion was as rife in the higher echelons of the party as it was everywhere else. Strasser, Frick and Walther Funk, former editor-in-chief of the influential financial newspaper the *Berliner Börsen-Zeitung*, who had been brought into the party the year before by Strasser and was now his chief economic adviser, arrived from Berlin with disturbing news: the antics of the storm-troopers were making Funk's friends in business and industry nervous at the prospect of a Nazi government, and their support was wavering; the government was worried that Hitler was about to stage a *putsch* and was considering taking action against the SA; and to cap it all, Schleicher was reneging on his deal with Hitler.

Schleicher later said that he visited Hindenburg at his Neudeck estate, and put Hitler's demands to him, only to be met with a blank refusal.

It seemed that his influence with Hindenburg was waning, and that he was being supplanted by, of all people, Papen, who had wormed his way into the trust of the 'Old Gentleman' and become his favourite. Schleicher's belief that he could use the 'wooden-brained' Papen as his tool had backfired: Papen had discovered he rather liked being Chancellor, and saw no reason to step down, since Hitler could only command a majority in the Reichstag by joining forces with the Centre, which was unlikely, or the Communists, which was unthinkable. Papen did discuss with Hindenburg what might happen in the event of a Nazi–Centre alliance, but the President's reaction was utterly contemptuous: it would be a fine thing indeed, he declared, if he were to make 'the Bohemian corporal' Reich Chancellor.

After a long discussion with Hitler, Goebbels talked to Röhm about the situation in Berlin, and the SA was ordered to put on a show of force, deploying armed units around the government quarter. 'Makes the gentlemen very nervous,' Goebbels wrote. 'That is the point of the exercise.'[39] But it was not only the gentlemen in the Wilhelmstrasse who were nervous. The Nazis' nerves, too, were stretched to breaking point, and the next day Hitler set off once again for Berlin, travelling by car rather than train to avoid being seen. He spent the night with the Goebbels, not in their town apartment but in a cottage they had acquired in May in the lakeside village of Caputh, to the south-west of Potsdam, probably as a refuge for Magda, who was heavily pregnant with their first child. There he learned that Röhm had seen both Schleicher and Papen on his behalf during the day, but had got no further with either. The situation was looking grim.

Hitler saw both Schleicher and Papen the next morning. Both confirmed that there was no chance of Hindenburg's appointing him Chancellor, but Papen offered him the Vice-Chancellorship, plus the position of Prussian Interior Minister for Strasser. Hitler replied that that was not enough, and reminded them that he had 230 deputies in the Reichstag, to which Schleicher retorted drily: 'And we can dissolve the Reichstag and dissolve it again and again.'[40] Hitler lost his temper and began to shout, threatening to let his storm-troopers loose on the streets and to mow down the Marxists in a new St Bartholomew's Night massacre. Shocked by his uncontrolled rage, Papen brought the meeting to an end, saying the final decision must rest with the President. Hitler stomped off to Goebbels's Reichskanzlerplatz apartment, to await a call from Hindenburg's office, which came at 3 p.m. Goebbels answered the phone, and asked if there was any point in Hitler's coming, if the decision had already been taken. He was told the President wished to speak to Hitler before finally deciding anything.

Hitler's meeting with Hindenburg was famously described by the President's State Secretary, Dr Otto Meissner, in the formal language of an affidavit at the Nuremberg trials. But General X gives another version in his diary, which may be apocryphal and sounds suspiciously Chaplinesque, but is infinitely more entertaining. 'In the evening,' he writes, 'I was once more at the Herrenklub. Meissner described Hitler's debut in the palace. He almost burst with laughter, "it was so funny!"' He then goes on:

Hindenburg is waiting. Hitler enters, makes an abortive attempt at a profound bow, and fumbles with his hand behind his back to shut the door, which, of course, has already closed behind him. Then, noticing his lapse, he grows red in the face and makes with uncertain steps towards the Old Gentleman, who is standing in the middle of the room. But at the very start, he stumbles over the carpet, and, to judge from the furious glare he gives it, he is in urgent danger of flinging himself upon it and chastising it physically. Then, he laboriously continues his way and finds himself at last, at long last, before Hindenburg. Papen does the honours.

Then, said Meissner, came something supremely comical. Hardly had Hitler straightened himself from his devout reverence when he prepared to launch one of his great public speeches. But Hindenburg made a great sweep with his arm and Hitler collapsed in terrified silence. Into this silence, Hindenburg broke in a harsh voice: 'I have summoned you, Herr Hitler, in order to hear from you whether you are prepared to enter the Cabinet of Herr von Papen as Vice-Chancellor. Naturally, in that case, your party would be duty bound to support and assist the government to the full extent of its power.'

Hitler was taken aback, and could find no answer. Then Papen said, to make it easier for him: 'Of course, the composition of the Cabinet would be somewhat modified and your party asked to collaborate by being fully represented in it.' And Hindenburg went on very rudely: 'Yes, but the appointment of the Foreign Minister and the Minister of Defence shall remain exclusively my concern. Nothing will change that!'

Another silence. Then at last Hitler spoke: 'But, your Excellency, we must come to some agreement about the programme of this government first!' Hindenburg retorted: 'The government's programme? It is there. It is the programme of Herr Chancellor von Papen.' Hitler once more fell into an embarrassed silence. Then he ventured another question. 'And what, your Excellency, is to be done about Prussia?' Hindenburg, now visibly impatient, replied: 'I can't understand what you mean by such a stupid question! My Commissioner for Prussia is, and will remain, Herr von Papen. But please give me an answer to my first question, because of which I asked you to come here. This matter is not one that can be postponed.'

Then Hitler demanded 'full powers', *à la* Mussolini, and the Old Gentleman elegantly flung him out.[41]

Meissner's official Nuremberg account goes into much greater detail of Hindenburg's strictures on the behaviour of the Nazis, his attempts to persuade Hitler of the benefits of co-operation with other parties and his reasons for refusing him power. But the essence remains the same. Before Hitler left, Hindenburg reminded him that he was breaking the promise he had made before the elections to support a national government, and gave him a stern warning for the future. In the words of the brusque communiqué that Schleicher insisted should be issued immediately after the meeting: 'The President gravely exhorted Herr Hitler to conduct the opposition on the part of the NS Party in a chivalrous manner, and to bear in mind his responsibility to the Fatherland and to the German people.'

As Schleicher had intended, Goebbels was caught off guard by the speed with which the communiqué was issued, giving him no chance to get Hitler's version of events out first – indeed, it was so quick that one suspects it was already drafted before the meeting. For once, Goebbels had been beaten to the punch, and it hurt. He responded swiftly with a denial that Hitler had demanded 'entire and complete power in the state', as the communiqué claimed, but only the Chancellorship and a few ministries. But the general public preferred to accept Hindenburg's version, stating that he had refused to hand over power to 'a movement that intended to exercise it in a one-sided manner', and revealing that he had rapped Hitler over the knuckles for breaking his word. It was humiliating stuff, and did Hitler and the Nazis considerable damage. But it was not enough to sink them.

Hitler was back in Goebbels's flat within half an hour, still fuming and swearing vengeance, but still determined to achieve power legally. He called Röhm and the SA leaders to a meeting at the party offices, and spent some time persuading them that they must hold back their men and stamp out any idea of a *putsch*. 'It's most difficult for them,' Goebbels wrote. 'Who knows if their units can be held together? Nothing is harder than telling troops flushed with victory that victory has been snatched from their hands.'[42]

As a safety precaution, the SA and SS were sent on leave, for what was described in the *Völkischer Beobachter* as 'a short intermission in the struggle'. Mercifully, they obeyed, and the real possibility of civil war was averted. Goebbels and Hitler both took a break, too, Hitler retiring to lick his wounds on the Obersalzberg for a few days, Goebbels heading north to Heiligendamm, where the Baltic Sea sparkled in brilliant sunshine, leaving Magda in Berlin. 'Lovely leisure!' he wrote in his diary. He found it hard to escape completely, as dejected local party members besieged him with questions, but he was determined to enjoy a week's rest, with 'no politics, only sun, light, fresh air and peace'.

Hitler was back in action again after only a couple of days. Helldorf and Röhm persuaded him to receive a friend of Helldorf's, who had recently joined the party and who might be a useful and discreet go-between with Papen. The friend was Joachim von Ribbentrop, a successful wine merchant and determined social climber, who had served with Papen towards the end of the war in Constantinople, where he had been posted to a desk job after being invalided out of active service as a cavalry officer. Helldorf and Röhm reasoned that since hardly anyone knew of Ribbentrop's Nazi Party membership, he would be able to call on Papen, with whom he was still on good terms, without arousing unwanted speculation.

Hitler already knew Ribbentrop slightly, having dined at his house that spring, and regarded him – wrongly, as it turned out – as a sophisticated man of the world. But he rejected his view that Papen was a man of honour and far more trustworthy than Schleicher, with whom Ribbentrop said it would be impossible to work loyally. Hitler was still bitterly resentful and suspicious of Papen, whom he blamed entirely for his failure with Hindenburg. He held forth for two hours, but Ribbentrop refused to budge, telling him he was only prepared to act as an intermediary with Papen, and not with Schleicher. It was probably the only time in what was to be a long relationship that Ribbentrop openly disagreed with Hitler, and almost the only time he ever offered him good advice. Returning to Berlin, he reported to Papen that Hitler was adamant in demanding the Chancellorship or nothing. And with that, his mission ended.[43]

A few days later, Hitler repaid the SA for its obedience when five storm-troopers were sentenced to death for smashing their way into the home of a Communist miner in the Silesian town of Potempa on 9 August and kicking and shooting him to death in front of his mother. Forced to choose between offending pubic opinion and alienating the SA, he cynically chose the SA, and his lieutenants followed suit. Göring publicly praised the condemned men and sent money to their families.

Röhm visited them in prison. Goebbels, always ready to promote the radical line, lauded them as martyrs in *Der Angriff*, blaming everything on the Jews and ferociously attacking Papen; he received another one-week ban on the paper as a result. On 22 August, Hitler sent the men a telegram supporting them 'in the face of this most monstrous and bloody sentence' and promising that 'your liberation is from this moment a question of our honour. It is our duty to struggle against a government under which this was possible.'[44] Two days later, the death sentences were commuted. To many Germans who had been lulled into voting for him in February and July, Hitler's 'honour' in condoning such a brutal murder sounded like the honour of a gangster. Already sickened by the violence, they began deserting in their tens of thousands.

XI

THE TURNING POINT

THE opening session of the new Reichstag was set for 30 August 1932, and as that date approached so the political manoeuvring increased. 'It is quite impossible to see through all this intrigue,' Goebbels wrote. 'So many are pulling different ways that one cannot tell on the other side who is the betrayer or who is the betrayed.'[1] There was still an outside chance that Hitler could put together an absolute majority in the Reichstag by joining forces with the Centre Party, which would remove Hindenburg's excuse for continuing with a non-elected Presidential Cabinet. A coalition with the Centre was the last thing Hitler wanted, but the threat of it could be a useful bargaining tool. 'We have got in touch with the Centre, if only as a means of bringing pressure to bear on our opponents,'[2] Goebbels recorded after being called to Berchtesgaden by Hitler to discuss tactics.

Back in Berlin, Goebbels went to see Schleicher, to make sure he knew of the approach to the Centre, and came away convinced that 'although he outwardly betrays nothing, he is, in reality, in deadly fear of a possible union of the Führer with the Centre . . . He will accept a coalition, but not join it himself. His idea is a Presidential Cabinet; if it comes to nothing he will resign.' This sounded like good news, but Goebbels felt the same as Ribbentrop about the slippery general. 'I don't know if what he says is true or false,' he concluded. 'Either way, I have the impression that they want to lure us into a trap again. They are trying in a devious way to obtain the result they failed to achieve on 13 August. They believe they can scare us with the dissolution of the Reichstag – a little nationalist plan that we shall soon frustrate. I report by phone to the Führer; he agrees with everything.'[3]

Göring played his part, too, in the wheeling and dealing. When

Papen confirmed that he was only prepared to offer Hitler the Vice-Chancellorship, Göring told him baldly that

Hitler could become any number of things, but never Vice. If he were to be made anything it would naturally have to be in the highest position and it would be completely unbearable and unthinkable to place our Führer in any sort of second position . . . . I told him . . . that we would not only not support him, but we would also oppose his Cabinet in the Reichstag to the utmost, just as we would consistently fight every succeeding Cabinet which did not give us a leading influence in the Chancellery.[4]

Saying the party wanted nothing more to do with Papen, he met with Schleicher to discuss the programme for the new Reichstag, then returned next day to ask whether he would be prepared to join a 'Black and Brown' Cabinet – that is, a Centre and Nazi coalition. According to General X, who was present, 'Schleicher declined with thanks'.[5]

Using the Centre Party as a stalking horse may not have worked with Schleicher, but it did produce one positive result: when the Reichstag reconvened, the Centre deputies combined with the Nazis and the DNVP to elect a new Reichstag President, or Speaker of the House, Captain Hermann Göring. Göring, of course, was absolutely thrilled, bursting with pride – and with every reason. Barely seven years before, he had been a penniless exile, a helpless drug addict strapped into a straitjacket in a Swedish mental hospital. Now, at the age of thirty-nine, he held the third-ranking position in the Reich. He even had his own official palace – described by Albert Speer as 'an early twentieth-century building with strong elements of *nouveau riche* rococo'[6] – alongside the Reichstag and connected to it by an underground tunnel, to augment the new apartment he had recently moved into on the Kaiserdamm, just around the corner from Goebbels's. And, what was more important politically, he had automatic and direct access to Hindenburg.

Göring, according to Goebbels, took office 'with dignity and assurance', and made a restrained speech promising to fulfil his duties impartially, and to uphold the honour and dignity both of the house and of the German people. But he went on to emphasise that his election had proved that the Reichstag now had a working majority, and therefore there was no longer any excuse for an emergency government. This was a direct challenge to Papen and Schleicher, neither of whom was in the chamber. They were with Hindenburg, persuading him to sign an undated decree to dissolve the Reichstag whenever Papen chose and

– strictly against the constitution – to postpone new elections indefinitely because of national emergency. They intended to do away with 'party rule' for good, and replace it with an authoritarian regime backed by the army. Unfortunately for them, and ultimately for Germany and the world, Papen made one simple mistake: instead of hurrying round to the Reichstag and dissolving it immediately, he decided to wait until its next session, which Göring set for 12 September.

In the time before the Reichstag reconvened, the intrigues and horse-trading continued apace, within the Nazi Party as well as with Schleicher, Brüning and the other parties. Göring threw a glittering celebration party at his Kaiserdamm flat the evening after his election, which ended with his joining Hitler, Röhm and Goebbels in a secret conference lasting late into the night, to plot how they could drive Papen out of office. He then made full use of his access to Hindenburg to plead the Nazi cause, and his links to the other parties to persuade them to unite against the government.

Goebbels became a father on 1 September, when Magda gave birth to a daughter, Helga, but this did nothing to interrupt or slow down his non-stop round of speechmaking, writing and late-night meetings, interspersed with funeral ceremonies for murdered SA men. Within the party, he and Göring were working together again as a formidable partnership, undermining Strasser and his attempts to persuade Hitler to compromise. When Strasser suggested, at a meeting of Nazi leaders on 8 September, that they should join a Cabinet led by Schleicher, he was very firmly reminded that nothing short of Hitler heading a Presidential Cabinet would do. And Strasser suffered further significant defeats when Hitler agreed that Goebbels should take over Strasser's responsibility for everything to do with radio broadcasting, and that he could incorporate elements of Strasser's Organisation Department into his own Propaganda Department, which he was to reorganise as a model for his planned ministry.

The Reichstag's first working session on 12 September immediately turned into a farce, with Göring in the starring role. The agenda consisted of only one item: the government's programme for economic recovery. The Communists warned Göring in advance that they intended to call for an end to the state of emergency and a vote of no confidence in Papen and his government, an amendment to the agenda that could only go forward if it was accepted unanimously. The Nazis agreed to keep quiet. Everybody expected the DNVP to block the move by objecting, but when Göring put it to the house, neither they nor anyone else did so. Caught on the hop, he announced amid total confusion that the no confidence motion would therefore go ahead. Papen, furious at being baulked, would have used Hindenburg's dissolution order there and then – but he had not thought to bring it with him. Frick called for a half-hour adjournment. Göring approved this, then led Goebbels, Frick and Strasser through the tunnel to his palace for a hurried consultation with Hitler. They decided they could not miss the opportunity of both embarrassing Papen and sending a powerful message to the President by supporting the motion.

As the house reassembled, Göring saw Papen entering with the red dispatch box in which dissolution orders were traditionally carried. Pointedly ignoring him, and looking in the opposite direction when he tried to attract his attention, Göring announced that they would go straight to the vote on the Communist motion. The Chancellor had become the invisible man. When he tried to speak, Göring silenced him, saying the vote was in progress. Angrily, Papen strode up to the Reichstag President's chair, slapped the order down on his table, then marched out, followed by the other members of his Cabinet. Göring simply turned the paper face down, and read out the result of the division instead. The motion had been passed by 512 votes to 42, with five abstentions and one spoiled paper. All the major parties, including the Centre, had opposed the government. As the cheering died down, Göring 'noticed' Papen's dissolution order, turned it over and read it out. To roars of laughter, he declared that it was invalid, because the government had already been voted out. 'The Reichstag,' he announced, 'is not dissolved. The date of the next session will be made known to you by me.'[7]

Hitler, waiting in Göring's palace, was 'quite beside himself with joy'. So, too, were the other leading Nazis, who moved on to the Kaiserhof to continue their celebrations until well into the night. Of course, Göring's ploy had no chance of succeeding. The dissolution was confirmed the next day, and he had to write a letter of apology to Hindenburg, claiming that Papen, 'in his agitation' had laid the order on his table 'with the blank side upwards', so that he, Göring, had thought it was 'an unwritten sheet of paper'. 'A too blatant manoeuvre, genuine Göring!' commented General X.[8] But the blatant manoeuvre had done its job – Papen had been humiliated and discredited; clearly, he could not now govern indefinitely without the Reichstag, as he had planned, and was forced to call new elections, to be held on 6 November.

Goebbels faced the prospect of his fifth major election campaign of the year with mixed feelings, aggravated in the early stages by a severe bout of bronchitis. He sensed that the public, even more than the party workers, was growing weary of constant electioneering, and that voter apathy was the greatest danger to be fought. The desperation that had attracted people to the radical solutions promised by the Nazis was passing: the economic situation was at last showing signs of improving, unemployment was as bad as ever but was no longer soaring astronomically, and there had been good news a few weeks earlier when reparations payments were finally cancelled and the limitations on the army lifted – Brüning had negotiated this, but Papen had signed the agreement, which Hitler denounced as legitimising Versailles. All of this meant that the tidal wave of support for the Nazis had peaked and was now subsiding. They could not hope to build on, or even to maintain, their phenomenal success of July.

Although he refused to forecast the result, Goebbels believed that this would be the 'last confrontation' the party would have to face before coming to power, and this gave him the motivation he needed to start up the well-oiled machinery yet again. For a start, he moved the Propaganda Department back to Berlin. He organised Der Angriff to appear twice daily, to counteract the bourgeois papers, particularly those owned by Hugenberg, which were now totally hostile to the Nazis, except when they reported Strasser's speeches favouring co-operation with any other party – including Hugenberg's – that was prepared to work with the Nazis to save Germany. Then the circus hit the road again.

Goebbels's biggest headache was shortage of money. The continual campaigning had drained the party's funds, and Papen had used all his connections to persuade the big industrialists of the Ruhr, who were already cooling after the shenanigans in the Reichstag and the violence in the streets, to withhold their support. Somehow, the party managed to scrape together enough to pay for another vigorous campaign, including the aeroplanes needed for Hitler's fourth and biggest 'Flight over Germany', carrying him to no fewer than forty-nine towns and cities, but it was a close-run thing, and at times they had to resort to sending storm-troopers out on to the streets, with collecting boxes.

The cash flow problems, however, did nothing to damp Goebbels's pretensions. In the middle of the campaign, he dedicated new and grander offices for the party in Berlin in the heart of the government quarter. The building's refurbishment had been entrusted to a struggling young architect who had joined the party in 1931, Albert Speer, on the recommendation of Goebbels's organisation chief, Karl Hanke, for whom he had previously carried out a smaller assignment on a party villa in Grunewald. The results were obviously satisfactory, if not startling. 'What a long way we have come in six years,' Goebbels congratulated himself. 'From the basement in Potsdamer Strasse to the new district house in the Vosstrasse! Now we shall probably also succeed in crossing the last four hundred yards to the Wilhelmstrasse. The house is in perfect order. Dignified quarters for the work of a great movement.'[9] A few days later, he was celebrating his thirty-fifth birthday with four speeches before allowing himself 'a full night's rest by way of a birthday gift'.

As the campaign drew to a close, Goebbels plunged the party into fresh controversy by joining forces with the Communist leader Walter Ulbricht in backing a strike by Berlin's transport workers which was opposed by the trade unions and the Socialists. Inevitably there was considerable violence – on 4 November alone, three people were shot dead and nearly fifty seriously injured in clashes with the police – and inevitably the Nazis' political opponents made the most of their unholy alliance with the Communists. Alarmed middle-class voters were frightened away, and many party members had serious doubts about where this might be leading. But Goebbels rejoiced in the opportunity to restate his revolutionary credentials. 'There is wild fighting in the streets in Wedding and Neukölln,' he crowed. 'Traffic is at a standstill. Berlin is the picture of a dead city.' He claimed that the strike had improved the party's reputation 'brilliantly' among the workers, which was what mattered for the future. As far as he was concerned, it didn't matter if the party lost twenty thousand votes in the short term, because these had no importance in the revolutionary struggle.[10]

In the event, the party lost considerably more than twenty thousand votes on 6 November 1932. With 11,737,000 votes, it was down on its summer total by over two million, about the same as the fall in the national turn-out, reducing its Reichstag seats to 196. The second-placed Social Democrats scored only 7,248,000, a drop of three-quarters of a million, roughly the same as the Communists gained to reach six million and 100 seats. The DNVP, supporting the government, were the other winners, with an extra million votes, mainly taken from the Nazis, increasing their seats from 37 to 52. But this represented only 8.9 per cent of the total vote. With 33.1 per cent, the Nazis were by far the largest party, but they still did not have an overall majority.

Goebbels could console himself with the fact that the party's losses in Berlin had been proportionately less than in the rest of the Reich, down by only 2.4 per cent to 26.2 per cent of the total, and almost three per cent more than the Socialists. But his efforts to win the working-class vote had failed miserably: the Communists had for the first time become the strongest party in the city, with 31.3 per cent. The mood in the Berlin party slid from defiance to 'dull depression', exacerbated by its financial problems, which Goebbels described as hopeless: 'Nothing but debts and obligations, together with the complete impossibility of obtaining any reasonable sum of money after this defeat.'[11]

The transport strike that had cost the Nazis so much support collapsed the day after the elections, when the Communists pulled out. Still trying to justify it, Goebbels left Berlin that night for Munich, where Hitler told him and the other leaders that nothing had changed, that he was fully committed to continuing the fight, that there would be no reconciliation, no compromises: Papen must go, whatever the consequences. When news came from Berlin that Papen was putting out feelers to them, Göring issued a public statement saying the Chancellor did not have enough backing to open negotiations for a new government.

Göring's rebuff had little effect. 'Herr Papen is of course too innately thick-headed for that to keep him from trying to find a way of salvation in spite of everything,' General X wrote.[12] And indeed he did keep on trying, wheeling and dealing frantically in an attempt to put together some sort of coalition. Believing Hitler was now in a weaker bargaining position than he had been in August, he offered him nothing more than he had then. In fact, he needed Hitler far more than Hitler needed him, for without him he had no hope of forming a government backed by a majority in the Reichstag. Knowing this, Hitler kept his nerve and sat tight, replying only to impose impossible conditions for any co-operation.

Hitler knew, of course, that Papen had the option of dissolving the Reichstag yet again and calling yet more elections, in the hope that the Nazis' support would eventually collapse as quickly as it had risen. To forestall any such moves, he told Goebbels to start planning a new

propaganda campaign. Campaigns, however, cost money and the financial position of the party as a whole was just as precarious as that of
the Berlin Gau. With the big-business paymasters keeping their purses
buttoned, Göring bustled off to Rome, accompanied by Hjalmar
Schacht, to see if he could sweet talk Mussolini into making a loan.
He was actually sitting next to Mussolini at a banquet on the evening
of 17 November when he received a message that he must return to
Berlin urgently. Papen's Cabinet had resigned. Hitler had been
summoned by Hindenburg. He needed Göring at his side.

Papen, whom Schleicher had set up as his puppet, had cut his strings
and become a wilful and dangerous liability. Schleicher's patience had
finally snapped when Papen had started canvassing the idea of forcing
the Nazis to heel either by calling new elections in January with a
severely restricted franchise, or governing by a dictatorship. Either
course would have been unconstitutional, and likely to provoke a civil
war, with the Nazis and Communists joining forces, as the Berlin transport workers' strike had shown they could.

As Minister of Defence, Schleicher found the prospect of his 100,000-
strong Reichswehr facing well over half a million armed Nazis and
Communists on the streets of Germany too alarming to contemplate.
He had no difficulty persuading his fellow members of the Cabinet to
join him in resigning. Papen, isolated, was forced to follow suit – but
was confident that he would regain power when the President's negotiations with Hitler broke down, as they surely would, and that he
would then be in a stronger position to do as he pleased and move to
a dictatorship.

Cheered on their way by an excited crowd outside the Kaiserhof,
Hitler and Göring saw Hindenburg on 19 November. This time, the
aged President did not keep them standing while he leaned on his stick
but received them courteously, invited them to sit, and talked for over
an hour about Hitler's programme. And this time Hitler did not
harangue him but quietly outlined his policies, carefully tailored to fit
Hindenburg's prejudices, on strengthening the army, supporting big
business and above all not interfering with the big agricultural estates.
Partly reassured, Hindenburg said he would like to see Hitler taking
part in government, and asked him to go away and consult the other
parties, taking soundings on their willingness to join him.

It was clear to the Nazi leaders that Hindenburg was simply going through the motions, knowing full well that they would not be able to obtain a majority, and so giving him the excuse to reappoint Papen, his favourite. They spent hours talking about it in the Kaiserhof, before agreeing that Hitler should play what Goebbels called 'the chess game for power'. Göring was given the job of contacting the other parties. He quickly brought the Centre on board, but the DNVP refused even to talk.

The game continued over the next few days, in face-to-face meetings and a series of letters, with Hitler demanding a Presidential Cabinet under his Chancellorship with the same powers as Papen had enjoyed, and Hindenburg refusing, on the grounds that 'such a Cabinet is bound to develop into a party dictatorship and increase the state of tension prevailing among the German people . . . I cannot take the responsibility for this before my oath and my conscience'. The last government had fallen because it could not command majority support in the Reichstag. If he had to have another Presidential Cabinet, he preferred to have his friend Papen, who was a not a party leader, in charge of it. A flurry of discussions with the other parties led nowhere. By 24 November it was all over. Hitler was forced to concede, and break off negotiations. 'The revolution stands before closed doors again,' Goebbels noted bitterly.

Hitler and Goebbels left Berlin to concentrate on new state elections in Thuringia, but the game was still far from over. Papen naturally assumed he would simply resume office, but suddenly found himself fighting what Goebbels described as a rearguard action – not against Hitler but against Schleicher, who had decided his only sensible course was to go for the Chancellorship himself. He had already talked to the moderate parties, and now approached Strasser to ask if the Nazis would be prepared to join a government under his leadership.

Hitler kept Schleicher waiting, while he met with his four top lieutenants – Strasser, Göring, Goebbels and Frick – in Weimar, where they argued fiercely about what to do. Strasser believed, as he had done since the summer, that Hitler should take the Vice-Chancellorship and use it as a base from which to move on to ultimate power. Frick supported him. Goebbels and Göring, however, violently opposed any such move, urging Hitler not to weaken but to go on demanding all or nothing, and Hitler agreed with them. Göring called Schleicher and told him Hitler would not come to Berlin, but invited him to send an officer to Weimar to act as an intermediary. Schleicher sent his right-hand man, Lieutenant-Colonel Eugen Ott, who found himself subjected to a three-hour lecture from Hitler on why Schleicher should not become Chancellor. By the time he had finished and Ott could telephone Schleicher, it was too late: Schleicher and Papen had been to see Hindenburg that evening.

Papen, totally unaware of Schleicher's machinations, had assumed that his reappointment as Chancellor was a mere formality. He had started outlining his plans for ruling by emergency decree without benefit of the Reichstag until he could amend the constitution to change the electoral laws and re-establish a second chamber, the *Herrenhaus* (House of Lords), to restore power to the upper classes. In the meantime, he would use force to put down any attempt at a *coup*. He admitted that his proposals would involve Hindenburg breaking his oath to uphold the constitution, but assured him that he would be justified in placing the welfare of the nation above his oath, as Bismarck had once done.[13]

Schleicher interrupted to say that there was no need for the President to break his oath, since he believed he himself could form a new government backed by a Reichstag majority. He would achieve this by splitting the Nazi Party, detaching Strasser and at least sixty Nazi deputies from Hitler and combining them with the Centre Party, the Socialists and even the trade unions. Schleicher had delivered his masterstroke, but instead of being impressed, Hindenburg appeared shocked. Turning to Papen, he asked him to go ahead at once with forming a new government.

Papen's new tenure as Chancellor lasted less than twenty-four hours. As they left Hindenburg's office, he recalled, Schleicher gave him a warning, using the words spoken to Luther the night before he set out for the fateful Diet of Worms: 'Little monk, you have chosen a difficult path.' He followed up his threat at a Cabinet meeting the next morning by stating flatly that there was no chance of Papen's carrying out the President's directive, that any attempt to do so would result in chaos and civil war, and that the army could not guarantee to maintain law and order. To make doubly sure everybody had got the message, Schleicher then produced Lieutenant-Colonel Ott, who read out a report already prepared by the Truppenamt (War Office), which concluded that the army and police did not have the strength to defend the frontiers and maintain order against both Nazis and Communists.[14] With the army against him, Papen was done for.

With great reluctance, Hindenburg bowed to the inevitable – according to Papen's own memoirs, 'two great tears rolled down his cheeks' as he dismissed him. He sent him a signed photograph with the emotional inscription 'I had a comrade' and followed this with a letter repeating that his confidence in him 'remained unshaken'. He then appointed Schleicher as Chancellor.

Schleicher's first move as Chancellor was to try to make good his boast to Hindenburg by contacting Strasser and offering him the posts of Vice-Chancellor of Germany and Minister-President of Prussia. It was an attractive offer, made all the sweeter by Schleicher's programme to relieve unemployment and improve welfare payments, which he knew Strasser would find appealing. Strasser was tempted, both for his own ambition and for the party, which he thought was in danger of disintegrating – a fear that was heightened by the results that same day of the elections in Thuringia, where the Nazi vote dropped by a shattering forty per cent compared with 31 July.

Strasser did not accept Schleicher's offer, but nor did he tell Hitler about it until the following day, during a heated meeting of the party's big five at the Kaiserhof. Warning that morale among the membership was at an all-time low, that the party was on the verge of bankruptcy, and that fresh elections could be disastrous if Schleicher were to dissolve the Reichstag again, he pressed Hitler to accept a share of power by taking part in a broadly based government. In the argument that followed, he threatened to break away and form his own party for a new election, a move that Goebbels denounced as 'the worst bit of treachery the Führer and the Party have yet experienced'. With the backing of Goebbels and Göring, who, scenting blood, tore into Strasser mercilessly, Hitler refused to consider any compact with Schleicher except on his own terms. Sidelining Strasser, he sent Göring and Strick to present them to him.

Strasser was now reeling. After another stormy session with Hitler two days later, he fell, accepting that his position within the party was hopeless, and resigning all his offices. Before leaving to recuperate in Italy, he called together all the senior Gauleiters, apart from Goebbels, to explain his reasons, outlining his disagreement with Hitler's policies and tactics, and accusing him of wanting only to become Chancellor. He ended on an emotional note by attacking the 'game of intrigue' among those surrounding the Führer, which had increasingly excluded him from top-level discussions.[15] He told his brother later: 'I did not feel like playing second fiddle to Göring, Goebbels and Röhm . . . I regard that as a snub, as a personal humiliation.' Which, of course, is exactly what Goebbels and Göring intended: they had got rid of a dangerous rival.

For all the personal satisfaction it gave Göring and Goebbels, Strasser's departure caused a serious crisis within the party, and they were forced to spend the next few weeks on a massive damage-limitation exercise. To begin with, Hitler was upset by the break with Strasser, and worried that he might lead a breakaway or a revolt within the party. After receiving Strasser's letter of resignation, he called the same group of senior Gauleiters to his room and treated them to a two-hour speech demolishing Strasser's case without attacking him personally, speaking to them as their comrade as well as their leader, drawing them under his spell again, and ending by shaking each man's hand to cement the bond between them. But this success was not enough to lift the gloom of uncertainty. Afterwards, he spent the evening with the Goebbels. 'It is difficult to be cheerful,' Goebbels noted. 'We are all rather downcast, especially in view of the danger of the whole party falling to pieces and all our work being in vain.'

Hitler's mood was not helped by a phone call from Robert Ley at the Kaiserhof, reporting that the situation in the party was getting worse from hour to hour, and begging the Führer to return to the hotel at once. He did so, and at 2 a.m. sent for Goebbels, who found him closeted with Röhm and Himmler, having no doubt been preparing orders for the SA and SS in case of trouble. The *Tägliche Rundschau*, a newspaper that had always been sympathetic to Strasser, was carrying the full story of his resignation, describing him as the great man of the party and saying he should be its leader instead of Hitler. 'Treachery, treachery, treachery!' Goebbels exploded. Hitler, pacing up and down the room, struck a dramatic pose and declared: 'If the party once falls apart, I'll end it all in three minutes with a pistol shot.'

The good news was that Strasser had publicly announced that he was going away on leave, so he would not be around as a focal point for any insurrection. Nevertheless, there was no time to be lost in destroying his power base in the party. There and then, the four men analysed the situation and made the decisions. Strasser's Political Organisation was broken up into various pieces, with Goebbels taking over 'Popular Education'. Hitler appointed himself leader of the remaining core functions, with Ley as his chief of staff. Hess was promoted from Hitler's private office to be head of a new Central Political Commission. Known supporters of Strasser were to be purged.

Goebbels wrote a leading article for that afternoon's *Der Angriff*, denouncing him.

All party leaders and deputies were called to a meeting in Göring's presidential palace, at which Hitler worked his magic yet again, reducing many of them to tears with an emotional appeal for their loyalty. They rewarded him with a standing ovation and vows of absolute fidelity. 'Strasser,' Goebbels wrote, 'is now completely isolated. A dead man.' Hitler, he concluded with a note of personal triumph, had now, personally, done with him.[16]

To complete the process, Hitler and Goebbels each set off to make speeches to party officials in the districts where Strasser's influence had been greatest. Their theme was always the same: loyalty to the leader and to the 'Idea', a message that was underlined by Hitler on 15 December in a memorandum setting out guidelines for the reorganisation of the party and the reasons for dismantling the bureaucratic apparatus that Strasser had built up so carefully. 'For its dissemination,' he wrote, 'an ideology does not need civil servants but fanatical apostles.' The party's 'supreme and most sublime mission' was to spread the Idea, and its 'greatest and first task' was propaganda, as a means to obtain power.[17] Goebbels could hardly have wished for a greater accolade, a greater endorsement of his own value. His victory was complete. Neither Strasser nor his former supporters made any attempt to fight back, and by Christmas the party was stabilised again.

Göring spent Christmas with Emmy Sonnemann, a buxom blonde actress who had caught his eye earlier in the year at Weimar, where she was a member of the National Theatre company, playing romantic leading ladies. Emmy, who was born and raised in Hamburg, was a typical actress, with no interest in politics or very much else outside the theatre – at their first meeting, she was not even sure if she was with Goebbels or Göring. At thirty-nine years old, the same age as Göring, she was still an attractive, sexy woman, with an open, generous and happy nature. She had been married to an actor, but was amicably divorced. The relationship with Göring had blossomed quickly into a heady and joyful affair – one of the first things he did when he took possession of the Reichstag President's palace was to take a sheet of his headed notepaper and dash off a message to her, '*Ich liebe Dich, H*', which he despatched by messenger to Weimar with a large bouquet of flowers.

No matter how much he loved Emmy, however, she could not erase the memory of Carin, nor did she wish to, for she found his devotion to his late wife touching in its sincerity. Throughout their life together, she never showed any sign of resentment or jealousy. After spending Christmas with Emmy, Göring took the train to Sweden, to see in the New Year with Carin's family in Rockelstad castle and to take a much-needed rest. 'For hours every day,' he wrote to Emmy on New Year's Eve, 'I go for long walks in the most beautiful forest you've ever seen. I'm sleeping eight or ten hours a day; I just hope I can stay on a bit longer.'

While Göring was recharging his batteries in Sweden, Goebbels was having a miserable time back in Berlin. The stress of the previous weeks, following on the birth of their first child, brought on a recurrence of the heart condition Magda had suffered several years earlier, during her marriage to Günther Quandt. Returning home after the Gau Christmas party on 23 December, she had collapsed and was rushed into a private room at the University Women's Hospital, where she remained gravely ill for several days. Goebbels spent most of Christmas Day working, planning the campaign for local elections in the small rural state of Lippe-Detmold, midway between the Ruhr and Hanover, which were due on 15 January, before visiting Magda in the hospital. In the evening, he went to the cinema with Harald and his younger sister, Maria, who had come to Berlin to look after him and the baby.

Even though Magda was still seriously ill, Goebbels could not stay away from Hitler. As soon as Magda was off the danger list, he left her in hospital and set off for the Obersalzberg, taking Harald with him. Hitler had spent Christmas alone in his mountain retreat, mourning the absence of Geli, and no doubt pondering the fact that on 1 November her replacement, Eva Braun, had also shot herself, apparently trying to commit suicide for love of him. Aiming the gun at her heart, she had somehow managed to miss, and hit herself in the neck instead. The wound was not serious – she was able to telephone for a doctor herself – but it was enough to arouse feelings of guilt in Hitler, as well as memories of Geli's fate, and to bind him to her.

Joining Hitler on 28 December, Goebbels worked with him on preparing the Führer's New Year message, and planning for 1933. The prospects looked almost hopeless, with seemingly little chance of attaining power and the money situation so bad that the salaries of party functionaries had to be cut. There was only one glimmer of light: Ley brought news that Papen was trying to set up a secret meeting with Hitler. Goebbels thought this sounded hopeful: 'That would offer us a new opportunity,' he wrote. As things turned out, it would do far more than that.

Papen might have been sore with Hitler for turning him down, but he was irate with Schleicher, and determined to get revenge for his betrayal. His chance was not long in coming. Schleicher had broadcast to the nation on 15 December, and had managed to alienate just about everybody: big business by promising to restore the wage and welfare cuts imposed by Papen and to introduce strict price controls on essentials, starting with meat and coal; the farmers by declaring that he intended to scrap the agricultural subsidies on which they depended; the landowners by announcing a programme to nationalise vast tracts of land on bankrupt Junker estates in the east and hand them over to 25,000 peasant families. And worst of all, he offended Hindenburg, who saw his land proposals as nothing short of Bolshevism.

By coincidence, the Herrenklub honoured Papen with a dinner the next day, and he seized the opportunity to attack Schleicher in his speech to the 300 members present. He also indicated that the Nazi Party should be included in government. Afterwards, he was approached by one of the guests, Baron Kurt von Schröder, a banker in Cologne whom he had known for some time, who volunteered to broker a meeting between Papen and Hitler. Schröder was a leading member of a group of businessmen calling themselves the *Freundeskreis*, the circle of friends, of the Führer, formed under the aegis of Himmler by a small businessman called Wilhelm Keppler, which provided economic advice and some finance to the party. Schröder knew relations between Hitler and Papen were strained, but felt that he might be able to persuade Hitler to swallow his pride if there were a chance of destroying Schleicher. Papen agreed. Just before the end of the month, Schröder called him to ask if he would be free for a meeting at his house in Cologne early in January.

Hitler slipped quietly through the back door of Schröder's house shortly before noon on 4 January 1933, accompanied by Himmler, Hess and Keppler, in the best conspiratorial style. But their belief that the meeting was secret was shattered when Papen arrived at the front of the house, to be snapped by a waiting press photographer as he stepped out of his taxi. Schleicher's spies had worked well, and the next day the *Tägliche Rundschau*, the newspaper of the *Tat* circle, a conservative group whose members had introduced Strasser to Schleicher the previous summer, splashed the story that Papen was planning to use his good relationship with the President to bring about a Hitler government. Papen and Hitler were forced to issue a joint denial, claiming that all they had talked about was 'the possibility of a great national front of political unity'. For once, they were telling the truth.

Schröder, who sat in on the private discussion while Himmler, Hess and Keppler waited in another room, reported that Papen had originally suggested a Hitler–Papen government in which the two of them would be joint leaders. Hitler had rejected this, but said that if he were Chancellor he would include Papen's supporters as ministers, as long as they agreed with his basic policies of eliminating Social Democrats, Communists and Jews from prominent positions in Germany, and of restoring order in public life.[18] After two hours, they broke for lunch, encouraged by the progress both thought they had made, and agreeing to meet again in Berlin to thrash out further points.

The newspaper report in the *Tägliche Rundschau* was the first Goebbels heard about Hitler's meeting with Papen, for he had been deeply preoccupied during the first week of the year. After seeing in the New Year on the Obersalzberg with Hitler, shaking his hand at midnight and wishing him power in 1933, he had driven down to Berchtesgaden to call his sister, Maria, since the telephone line to Hitler's Haus Wachenfeld was down. She told him Magda was in a critical condition with a fever of 40.5°C (104.9°F), and said he should come at once. He and Harald left Berchtesgaden by the first train for Munich. Hitler, deeply concerned about Magda, followed by car. It being New Year's Day, there were no trains leaving for Berlin. Hitler tried to hire an aeroplane for Goebbels, but without success, and they were forced to wait for an agonising six hours, telephoning the hospital every ten minutes, until the night sleeper left at 9 p.m.

Arriving in Berlin at dawn, Goebbels rushed to the hospital. To his great relief, Magda's temperature had dropped and the crisis had passed. For the next few days, in between visits to the hospital, he submerged himself in work. In the published version of his diary, he claimed dramatically that Magda was still 'hovering between life and death'; the original diary, however, records that while he was still worried about her, she was improving steadily. She would not be well enough to return home, however, until 1 February. In the meantime, he found plenty to occupy his mind: the press was full of frenzied speculation as Strasser returned from Italy, met Schleicher and then Hindenburg, and apparently expressed his willingness to join Schleicher's government; a boy of the Hitler Youth and yet another SA man were murdered by the Communists, which gave Goebbels the opportunity for yet more spectacular funerals; the money situation was as bad as ever, and he was at full stretch trying to raise money and morale and to hold the Berlin party together; there were endless speeches to be made, articles to be written, and the election campaign in Lippe-Detmold to be organised.

Goebbels finally met up with Hitler on 9 January at Bielefeld, during a short break from the Lippe-Detmold campaign, when he learned the details of the meeting with Papen: 'Papen fiercely against Schleicher. Determined to get rid of him. Has the ear of Hindenburg, in whose house he is still living. Arrangements with us prepared. Either the Chancellorship or the powerful ministries. Defence and the Interior. That's still to be heard about. Schleicher does not have the order for the dissolution. He's on the downward path. Very mistrustful. Now much depends on Lippe.'[19]

Göring had by then returned from Sweden, refreshed and ready to pitch in to the battle again. Hitler and Goebbels gathered at his flat for a short meeting the next day, just the three of them, to discuss strategy. They all agreed that their principal enemy was Strasser, who was said to be considering not only entering Schleicher's Cabinet as Vice-Chancellor but also launching his own 'Social Nationalist Party', to fight the next Reichstag elections under the slogan: 'Against Göring and Goebbels!'

While Goebbels concentrated on the Lippe-Detmold election and Göring stepped up his efforts to persuade the other parties, particularly the DNVP, that Strasser was finished and they should back Hitler, Himmler played his part in the chess game by working quietly to facilitate a deal with Papen. Seeking a discreet location in Berlin, where there would be no repetition of the embarrassing leak over Schröder's house in Cologne, he and Keppler approached Joachim von Ribbentrop as an acceptable acquaintance of both Hitler and Papen, and asked if he would host a second meeting between them, at his luxurious villa in the leafy suburb of Dahlem. Ribbentrop was delighted. He sent his own chauffeur to collect Papen, while Hitler once again chose to slip in through the garden.

The meeting, during the night of 10 January, proved to be inconclusive. Papen reported that he had spoken to Hindenburg that afternoon, telling him Hitler was no longer demanding absolute power and was now prepared to serve in a coalition government with parties of the right. Hindenburg had told him to keep in touch with Hitler, but was still not prepared to appoint him as Chancellor. On hearing that, Hitler broke off the discussions until after the Lippe-Detmold elections.

After another hospital visit, Goebbels hurried back to Lippe-Detmold, where he set up his headquarters in a romantic moated castle, Schloss Vinsebeck, 'where neither telephone nor telegrams can disturb us', to press on with a saturation campaign. Money was still so tight that he depended almost entirely on the entrance charges to meetings to pay for everything – and in spite of raising the fees, he was several times on the brink of being unable to pay for the hire of halls. Nevertheless, he pulled out all the stops and wheeled in all the party's big guns: himself, of course, Göring, Ley, Frick, Prince Auwi, and Hitler, who spoke seventeen times in eleven days.

Lippe-Detmold was a tiny, rural constituency, with a total population of only 173,000, but a good result was vital for Hitler's negotiating position; there was still a great deal of hard bargaining to be done before he could hope to win the Chancellorship. On 15 January, he got that good result, when the party won almost forty per cent of the votes, an improvement of seventeen per cent on the last election in the state. Both the DNVP and the Communists had lost heavily, and though the Socialists had gained substantially, they were far behind the Nazis. This was the psychological boost the party needed, and it had come at exactly the right time: 'The party is on the march again,' Goebbels proclaimed joyfully.

While the voters were going to the polls in Lippe-Detmold, Schleicher was receiving the Austrian Justice Minister, Kurt von Schuschnigg, and telling him that 'Herr Hitler was no longer a problem, his movement had ceased to be a political danger, and the whole problem had been solved, it was a thing of the past.'[20] He had been lulled into this delusion by Papen, who had assured him that Hitler was no longer demanding the Chancellorship, but would be content with Defence, which of course Hindenburg would refuse him. Schleicher was led to believe that all he would then have to do was deliver the *coup de grâce* by having Strasser appointed Vice-Chancellor, and Hitler would be done for. It did not take long for him to discover just how much he had been misled.

With the election success under his belt, Hitler was free to turn his full venom on Strasser, and he did so with a vengeance the very next day, 16 January, at a conference of Gauleiters in Weimar. Gauleiter followed Gauleiter in denouncing Strasser as a traitor – 'Judas was better,' one declared – then Hitler tore him apart in a three-hour speech, at the end of which, Goebbels noted, everyone was raging against him. Schleicher's plan to split the Nazis and incorporate the Strasser faction in his government was dead in the water – if there ever had been such a faction it no longer existed, and Strasser himself had been driven out into the wilderness, totally isolated. When he tried to meet Hitler, to see if they could salvage anything of their relationship, his approach was icily rejected.

With none of the three main contenders, Schleicher, Papen and Hitler, able to form an acceptable government, there seemed to be a total stalemate in the contest for the Chancellorship. It was broken by the most unlikely agent: Ribbentrop, whose family, coincidentally, came from Lippe-Detmold, had taken to the role of go-between with enthusiasm, shuttling between Hitler and Papen during the final week of the elections, trying to persuade them to continue their discussions. Hitler would have done so anyway, as and when it suited him, but Ribbentrop was a convenient tool, and he seized on him with his usual opportunism. By this time he knew exactly how strong his position was, and he was working Papen with consummate skill, carefully manoeuvring him into a corner from which there was only one way out. Judging the time was right, he agreed to another meeting on 18 January.

This time, Hitler brought Himmler and Röhm to Ribbentrop's house, presumably to signal the Nazis' physical strength. His line had hardened since the last meeting, and he now demanded nothing short of the Chancellorship. When Papen, still reluctant to abandon his own hopes, responded that his influence with the President was not strong enough to achieve this, Hitler said in that case he saw no point in further talks, and left. Playing the reluctant bride, he allowed Ribbentrop to shuttle to and fro for another three days, before making his next move.

Ribbentrop always claimed that it was he who came up with the suggestion that if Papen felt he did not have enough influence with Hindenburg, they should bring in the only other men who had: Hindenburg's son, Oskar, and his State Secretary, Otto Meissner. Maybe he did suggest it, but considering what Hitler made of it, it is hard to believe he did not plant the idea in Ribbentrop's mind. In any case, it was to prove decisive.

The meeting took place late at night on Sunday 22 January, after an eventful day during which Goebbels had staged a massive demonstration in the streets of Berlin to mark the third anniversary of Horst Wessel's death. Hitler had marched at the head of the procession, had dedicated a memorial to the fallen storm-trooper in St Nikolas's cemetery, and had rounded off the day with a rousing speech to an overflowing Sportpalast before making his way to Dahlem at 10 p.m. To show he meant business, he was supported this time by his two most 'respectable' lieutenants, Göring and Frick, though Göring joined the meeting late – sensing the importance of the occasion, Hitler had called him back to Berlin from a speaking engagement in Dresden. Oskar von Hindenburg and Meissner had slipped out of the opera and taken a cab to avoid drawing attention to themselves. Papen was collected as usual by Ribbentrop's chauffeur.

The first hour of the meeting that night was taken up by a discussion between Hitler and Oskar, alone in a separate room. Hitler was well aware that the younger Hindenburg had consistently opposed his appointment, and that he was the man who had to be won round. There is no record of what passed between them in private, but it is generally assumed that Hitler used a mixture of threats and promises to get his way: threats to expose the Hindenburgs' involvement in tax evasion and the misuse of land subsidies; promises of more land for the family and army promotion to general rank for Oskar – both of which he received the following year. Whatever they talked about, when they emerged, a subdued Oskar raised no more objections to Hitler's appointment, and the meeting progressed.

Göring claimed later that 'in a rather lengthy conversation' with Oskar von Hindenburg:

I declared to the son that he should tell his father that, one way or another, von Schleicher would lead to shipwreck. I explained to him the new basic conditions for forming a new government, and how I had heard of the Field Marshal's willingness to entrust Hitler with the Chancellorship, thereby regarding the Party as a main basis for a future government majority if Adolf Hitler were also able to succeed on this occasion in drawing in the German Nationalists [DNVP] and the Stahlhelm – for he wanted to see a definite national basis . . . I told von Hindenburg's son that he could tell his father that I would undoubtedly bring that about, and the Führer gave me orders to undertake negotiations during the coming week with these parties on the one hand and with the Reich President on the other.[21]

Papen reported that Hindenburg was now prepared to accept Nazi participation in government, but was still refusing to make Hitler Chancellor. Hitler insisted that his party would co-operate only if he were Chancellor, but softened his previous line by saying that he would be satisfied with only two other Nazis in the Cabinet, Frick as Minister of the Interior and Göring as Minister without Portfolio. Papen finally agreed to recommend this to Hindenburg, on condition that he should be Vice-Chancellor.

The next few days passed in a whirl of frantic activity from all the main participants. Schleicher somehow got wind of the latest Dahlem meeting, and went to Hindenburg the next morning asking him to dissolve the Reichstag and postpone new elections indefinitely, leaving him in office as virtual dictator. Hindenburg refused, and with good reason – when Papen had tried to do exactly that at the beginning of December, Schleicher had used it to unseat him, warning it would lead to civil war. The same must surely apply now. If Schleicher wanted to continue as Chancellor, he would have to find majority backing in the Reichstag. Both men knew this was impossible, but still Schleicher twisted and turned, fighting desperately for survival.

By the Friday of that week, Hitler's nerves were stretched to breaking point. Göring had been haggling non-stop with the other parties, notably the DNVP, over the possible composition of a new Cabinet, but still there were no firm decisions. Papen was still havering, and when Hugenberg refused to accept either a Nazi Interior Minister or new elections, Hitler erupted angrily and threatened to leave Berlin at once for Munich. According to Ribbentrop, he and Göring had to calm Hitler down and persuade him to hang on. Ribbentrop recalled the scene in his memoirs:

I have never seen Hitler in such a state. I proposed to him and Göring that I should see Papen alone that evening and explain the whole situation to him. In the evening I saw Papen and convinced him eventually that the only thing that made sense was Hitler's Chancellorship, and that he must do what he can to bring this about. Papen declared that the matter of Hugenberg was of secondary importance, and that he was now absolutely in favour of Hitler becoming Chancellor; this was the decisive change in Papen's attitude . . . This recognition by Papen is, I believe, the turning point.[22]

The following day, 28 January, Schleicher admitted defeat, and when Hindenburg had once again rejected his request for dissolution of the Reichstag, offered his resignation and that of his entire Cabinet.

Hindenburg turned with obvious relief to Papen, and asked him to sound out the possibility of a Hitler Cabinet. All that he insisted upon was that Papen should be Vice-Chancellor, and that he, as President, should nominate the Foreign and Defence Ministers. As Foreign Minister, he wanted the current incumbent, Baron Konstantin von Neurath, a smooth and safe career diplomat. For Defence Minister, he chose General Werner von Blomberg, the army commander in East Prussia, currently advising the German delegation at the disarmament conference in Geneva. Hindenburg considered Blomberg to be thoroughly reliable and 'completely apolitical' – he did not know that, under the malign influence of his chief of staff, Colonel Walter von Reichenau, he had become a convinced Nazi supporter.

It looked as though Hitler was home and dry at last. But there were still several tricky moments before he could be sure. The DNVP's co-operation was put in doubt when Hitler rejected Hugenberg's demands for a share of power that was completely out of line with his party's thirty-six Reichstag seats. There was a brief impasse when Papen insisted on remaining Reich Commissioner for Prussia, instead of handing over to Hitler as the new Chancellor. After some argument, Göring and Ribbentrop managed to persuade Hitler to settle – 'with a bad grace' according to Papen – for the two Interior Ministries; Frick was to take the Reich ministry and Göring the Prussian, where he would be effectively Papen's deputy.

The show of 'bad grace' was, of course, entirely for the benefit of Papen and the other dupes who did not seem to realise that they had given the Nazis exactly what they wanted, what Göring later described as 'that instrument which at all times and in all nations is always the inner political instrument of power, namely, the police'.[23] As Prussian Interior Minister, Göring would control the police in three-fifths of Germany – the federal state of Prussia was still effectively the old Wilhelmine kingdom, including not only Berlin and Brandenburg but also the Rhineland, Hesse-Nassau, Westphalia, Hanover, Schleswig-Holstein, Lower Saxony, Pomerania, Silesia and East Prussia. As a bonne bouche, Göring was also to be Reich Commissioner for Aviation, then a relatively minor post within the Transport Ministry concerned solely with civil flying.

Even at this late stage, Schleicher had not completely given up the game, and still threatened to upset the rickety apple cart. On 29 January, having started rumours that Hindenburg was about to appoint Papen as a Presidential Chancellor, he invited Hitler to join him in putting

Hindenburg out to grass and allying the army and the Nazi Party in a military dictatorship. Hitler ignored him: he had overcome his nerves and was now supremely confident of achieving his goal legally. The one remaining obstacle was Hitler's insistence on new elections, which were opposed not only by Hugenberg, who feared that his party could be wiped out, but also by Hindenburg. After discussing the problem over lunch at the Kaiserhof, Hitler sent Ribbentrop to Papen with a message for the President saying that these would be the last elections – a promise that was to prove tragically prophetic.

With Göring putting the finishing touches to the deals with the other parties, there was nothing more for Hitler to do but wait, sitting in the Kaiserhof eating cakes and drinking coffee with a small group including Goebbels, who had no part to play in the negotiations and was forced to watch from the sidelines. Midway through the afternoon, Göring arrived, beaming broadly, to announce that 'everything was perfect'. The Führer would be appointed Chancellor next morning.

In the published version of his diary – though interestingly not in the original – Goebbels paid a fulsome tribute to the man he then regarded as his comrade-in-arms:

This is surely Göring's finest hour. And rightly so. He has diplomatically and skilfully prepared the ground for the Führer in nerve-racking negotiations for months or even years. His prudence, strong nerves and above all his firmness of character and loyalty to the Führer have been genuine, strong and admirable. His face was turned to stone when, in the very thick of the fight, his beloved wife was torn from his side by cruel death. But he did not flinch for a second. Seriously and firmly he went on his way again, an unshakeably devoted shield-bearer to the Führer . . .

This upright soldier with the heart of a child has always remained true to himself; and now he stands before his leader and brings him the greatest piece of news of his life. For a long time we say nothing; and then we rise and solemnly shake each other's hands.[24]

Even now, the drama was not over. At 10.45 p.m. that night, as the Nazi leaders were celebrating in Goebbels's flat, an emissary from Schleicher arrived with news that Hindenburg was, after all, about to appoint a Papen Cabinet. The army would not tolerate this, he said. Schleicher and the army's Chief of Staff, General Kurt von Hammerstein, had put the Potsdam garrison on alert, and were preparing to remove Hindenburg to his Neudeck estate and declare a military dictatorship. It was in fact a false alarm, though there can be little doubt that Schleicher was seriously considering such a move, but the Nazis were not prepared to take any chances at this late stage. Göring hurried off to alert Papen and Meissner. Hitler swung into action as he himself described:

My immediate reaction to this planned *putsch* was to send for the Commander of the Berlin SA, Count von Helldorf, and through him to alert the whole SA in Berlin. At the same time, I instructed Major Wecke of the police, whom I knew I could trust, to prepare for a sudden seizure of the Wilhelmstrasse by six police battalions . . . Finally, I instructed General von Blomberg to proceed at once, on arrival in Berlin at 8 a.m. on 30 January [from the disarmament conference in Geneva] direct to the Old Gentleman to be sworn in, and thus to be in a position, as Commander-in-Chief of the Reichswehr [*sic*], to suppress any possible attempts at a *coup d'état*.[25]

There were no more alarms, though the Nazi leaders sat up anxiously until 5 a.m. Blomberg was met at the station by Oskar von Hindenburg, who whisked him away from under the nose of Hammerstein's adjutant, who was waiting to take him to Schleicher. He was quickly sworn in as Defence Minister by the President, who informed him that it was his duty to stop Schleicher and keep the army out of politics.

At 10.30 a.m., Hitler and his Cabinet gathered in Papen's apartment and walked across the snow-covered rear gardens to the Chancellery complex, where Hindenburg was staying while his presidential palace was being refurbished. But they had still not found harmony and for a dreadful hour or so it looked as though the government might disintegrate before it could be sworn in. Hitler started complaining to Papen again about being denied the Prussian Commissioner's post, and at 11 a.m., the time of his appointment with the President, he was still squabbling furiously in Meissner's office with Hugenberg over his determination to call new elections. It was almost noon before Meissner ended the arguing by informing them that the President was not prepared to wait any longer, and managed to shepherd them into his presence.

Across the Wilhelmplatz in the Kaiserhof, Goebbels, Röhm and the other leading Nazis waited at the first-floor windows, anxiously watching the door of the Chancellery for Hitler to appear. 'We shall be able to judge from his face whether he has been successful,' Goebbels wrote. 'Torturing hours of waiting!' At last, accompanied by Göring and Frick, Hitler emerged from the Chancellery smiling, to be driven round the square through a wildly cheering crowd to the door of the hotel. Göring leapt out of the car first and strode up the steps bellowing out the good news at the top of his voice, preparing the way for his lord. Adolf Hitler had been appointed Chancellor. 'The final decision has been made,' Goebbels wrote. 'Germany is at a turning point in her history.'[26]

PART THREE

POWER AND REVOLUTION
1933-1936

XII

POWER

THE celebrations in Berlin on 30 January lasted throughout the day and well into the night, gleefully co-ordinated by Goebbels. On his orders, every SA and SS man in the city put on his uniform and took to the streets, to prepare for the great victory parade he had organised for that evening. While opponents of the Nazis shut themselves in their homes for safety, party members and supporters from all over Prussia, and indeed every other part of Germany within reach of the capital, swarmed into the city to swell the numbers. They gathered in the Tiergarten, where they were issued with torches, miraculously conjured up by Goebbels, which they lit as the march began at 7 p.m. Roaring out the 'Horst Wessel Song' and other fighting anthems, backed by the thunder of drums and the blare of military bands, they tramped in massed columns, sixteen-abreast, through the Brandenburg Gate and across Pariser Platz, where the French Ambassador watched from behind his embassy's curtains. 'These torches,' he wrote later, 'form a single river of fire, and the waves of this swelling river build up to advance with great power into the heart of the capital.'[1]

Wheeling right after passing the Adlon Hotel, which had been forced to lock its doors as every room was packed full, the marchers continued along the Wilhelmstrasse, past the British Embassy and the Presidential Palace to the Chancellery, where they paused to salute the old President, beating time with his stick as he watched from a window, apparently much moved. According to some reports, he remarked: 'If I'd known he could train troops like this, I'd have sent for the fellow long ago.' A few yards further on, they cast aside restraint and broke into wild shouts of acclaim and great cries of 'Sieg Heil!' for Hitler at another window, flanked by Hess and Göring wearing SA uniform.

The processions went on until well after midnight, throughout the city centre and beyond. In typical hyperbole, Goebbels claimed that a million people had taken part, but even the Nazi press reduced the figure to 500,000, while the British Ambassador estimated the numbers at ten per cent of that, and his military attaché reduced the figure to 'about 15,000'.[2] Everyone was agreed, however, that it was an impressive show.

This was Goebbels's finest hour, and he was determined to make the most of every second of it. Taking over the country's entire radio network, he broadcast a live commentary to the rest of the nation – where, according to British Ambassador Horace Rumbold, the news of Hitler's triumph had been received more phlegmatically than in Berlin.[3] When the stations in Stuttgart and Munich refused to carry the programme, Frick, as the new Interior Minister, issued a directive forcing them to comply. After a rousing introductory speech from Göring, Goebbels skilfully interlaced his commentary with 'vox pop' interviews with 'ordinary citizens' from every walk of life. The interviews, of course, were phoney: the participants were all party members and officials using false names. In his first act as the mouthpiece of the new regime, Goebbels was starting as he meant to continue – with a lie.

Despite receiving Hitler's plaudits for his efforts, Goebbels was denied a role in the government. He had made himself such a bogeyman during his turbulent six-year reign in Berlin that his inclusion would have panicked Papen and the conservatives, a risk that Hitler could not yet afford to take. Although he must have understood this, Goebbels still bitterly resented it, blaming the 'reactionaries' in the party for trying to 'slap him into the background'. Magda, every bit as ambitious for her husband as he was himself, fed his resentment by 'weeping with impatience' as he was passed over for positions they both felt should have been his. 'That's all I need!' he snarled to his diary when Bernhard Rust was made Prussian Minister for Education and Culture, and Walther Funk, the former editor-in-chief of the *Berliner Börsen-Zeitung*, was appointed as the government's press chief. Over the next few days, his black mood aggravated by yet another attack of flu with fevers of 39 and 40 degrees, he moaned that he was deeply depressed, had lost heart and was tired of living.[4]

Göring, meanwhile, delighted in being at the very centre of government and plunged into action immediately. At the first Cabinet meeting, five hours after Hitler had been sworn in as Chancellor, he gave clear notice of his intentions by warning that existing laws and police forces might not be strong enough to maintain order in the near future. For the present, he announced that he had already used his authority as Prussian Minister of the Interior to ban protest demonstrations in Berlin, planned for that evening by the Communists. He did nothing, however, to stop Nazis marching into Communist strongholds after the big parade that night with the deliberate aim of provoking trouble. And provoke it they did: in one bloody battle with Red Front Fighters in Charlottenburg's Wallstrasse, the leader of the notorious Murder Storm Unit 33, SA Sturmführer Hanne Maikowski, was shot dead, along with a police sergeant. For Goebbels, this was the icing on the cake: 'Maikowski shall be buried like a king,' he promised.[5] For Göring the deaths justified his heavy-handed approach and confirmed his dire warnings – which he took seriously enough to give Emmy Sonnemann, whom he had sent for from Weimar to share his triumph and watch the great parade from a room in the Kaiserhof Hotel, a loaded pistol for self-protection.

At that first Cabinet meeting, Göring demonstrated that he could lie just as successfully as Goebbels. Reporting that he had spoken on Hitler's behalf to the leaders of the Centre Party, whose support Hitler and Papen needed to form the Reichstag majority that they had promised Hindenburg, he said they were making 'impossible' demands as the price for their co-operation. He therefore proposed that the Reichstag should be dissolved and fresh elections called. That he had spoken to the Centre leaders was perfectly true; the rest was a fabrication – they had in fact done nothing more than open negotiations. Göring, however, knew that the DNVP's distrust of the Centre Party was so deep that they would believe his version without question; it would even outweigh their reluctance to agree to elections that might well give the Nazis an absolute majority with no further need of their support.

Hugenberg baulked slightly, suggesting that it would be simpler to outlaw the Communist Party: the removal of its 100 seats would give Nazis and DNVPs together a clear majority without the inconvenience and risk involved in elections. But Hitler was not prepared to go that far this soon; at this and other early Cabinet meetings he was the soul of responsibility, conducting business calmly, soberly and reasonably, always insisting on strict legality. It was his DNVP and conservative partners who made the extreme demands, while he, supported by Göring, presented a front of exemplary moderation. It was not Hitler but Papen who insisted that 'the coming election would be the last, and a return to the parliamentary system would be avoided for ever'.[6] Hitler, naturally, was more than happy to go along with Papen. He was even prepared to promise that existing Cabinet members would retain their positions in the new government, reinforcing their dangerous delusion that they had him in their pockets.

Papen's plan was that the Nazis and their allies, with the full resources of the state at their command, should make sure by hook or by crook of winning a two-thirds majority in the new Reichstag; they would then pass an Enabling Act giving the Cabinet full power to rule indefinitely without depending on either the Reichstag or the President's emergency powers. And it was on that basis, after Hitler had gone through the charade of talking personally to the Centre Party leaders the next day and making doubly sure they would not support him, that he, Papen and Göring called on Hindenburg and persuaded him to dissolve the Reichstag, for the last time.

In the coming elections, for which Hitler coined the slogan: 'Attack on Marxism', the cards were heavily stacked in the government's favour. To reduce the risks still further, however, Göring immediately called on the Cabinet to promulgate a decree, which had been prepared by Papen at the time of the Berlin transport strike but never used by him, giving them emergency powers to combat 'acts of terror' by the Communists. The ministers seized upon this eagerly as a valuable tool in suppressing opposition during the election. Its provisions, which needed only slight amendment, included press censorship, the power to ban political meetings, and an extension of 'protective custody' – in other words, arrest and imprisonment without charge or trial – for up to three months on the mere suspicion of planned criminal activities. The President signed the 'Decree for the Protection of the German People' on 4 February, in an almost casual move that marked the beginning of the end of civil liberty in Germany for over twelve years – and for much longer in East Germany.

The election date was set for 5 March, but Göring was not prepared to wait another month before starting the Nazi revolution. Added to his natural impatience was a genuine fear that the Communists would launch a counterstroke at any moment, a fear shared by most other leaders, including Hitler. While Goebbels was struggling out of his sick-bed to launch yet another election campaign, Göring seized his new ministry and the Prussian police forces by the throat, beginning the process of eliminating all dissent that was to escalate and spread across the whole of German society with incredible speed.

Alarmed, Papen briefed the press on 2 February with a reminder that as Reich Commissioner he was in charge in Prussia, and that Göring, as Police Minister, was subordinate to him. Göring, however, simply ignored him, greeting his protests and threats with the cheerful boast: 'You will only get me out of this room flat on my back!' That same day, after a search of the Communist Party's offices which according to a report in the *Vossische Zeitung* produced quantities of 'illegal literature', he banned all demonstrations throughout Prussia by the party and related organisations, and closed down its newspapers. Two days later, he dissolved the Prussian Parliament, and two days after that a further decree gave him virtually unlimited emergency powers in the state.

Those who complained in later years about Göring's laziness would have been hard pressed to recognise him now as he dived headlong into weeks of non-stop activity. After the first night, when he collapsed into bed alongside Emmy and asked her to buy flowers for the Führer next day – 'He will like that' – he worked literally day and night for the next two months, eating, sleeping, living in his new ministry at 63 Wilhelmstrasse. Emmy returned to Weimar, to play Margarete in *Faust*, seemingly unconscious of the ironic parallel with the role she was to play in real life. Had she stayed she would have seen little of her own Dr Faustus, though they did manage a few snatched meetings, mostly in the middle of the night.

On 31 January 1934, his first day in office, Göring called the entire staff of his ministry together for an introductory pep talk. Starting by reminding them that his own father had been a senior civil servant, he spoke of the 'new patriotic spirit' that they were to represent, and told them that their first duty was to eradicate any hint of Communism among themselves. He invited anyone who felt he could not work with him to resign at once. No one did – if there ever had been any Communists within the ministry, they had been cleared out during the previous few months by Papen. But this was not good enough for Göring: he intended to go further and root out anyone who might conceivably have left-wing or anti-Nazi tendencies. This was a major and urgent task in his eyes, since for years the Prussian civil service and police had been dominated by the ruling SPD, who had placed their own men in all positions of authority. To help locate the doubters, he sent for a thirty-two-year-old official in the political police department of the ministry, Rudolf Diels, who had co-operated with him as Reichstag President in identifying and combating the 'Red menace'.

Diels was not a Nazi Party member – indeed, the party refused him admission until 1937 – though he was what was known as a 'contributing member' of the SA, a sort of affiliate membership for people such as civil servants for whom full membership was illegal or professionally unwise.[7] The important thing was that he was violently anti-Communist. A reasonably handsome man, he bore heavy duelling scars from his student days as a member of a particularly rumbustious fraternity at Marburg, where he had distinguished himself by setting records for beer drinking, chewing drinking glasses, and womanising. After active war service on the Western Front he had fought with the Freikorps before joining the civil service, to the disgust of his former student brothers, who considered him an unprincipled opportunist for working under the Social Democrats.[8] They were right: he later proved his talent for opportunism by providing the falsified reports that enabled Papen to remove the Prussian SPD government from office in 1932.

Diels knew how the Interior Ministry worked. He knew where the bodies were buried, who was who, and who could be trusted. And he put his knowledge and experience at Göring's disposal, giving him expert advice on how to keep the machinery ticking over even while it was being dismantled and reassembled. He provided Göring with details from personnel and police files to enable him to purge all officials and officers who could be considered in any way doubtful. The police files he produced also included dossiers on all the Nazi leaders, including Göring himself, which the new Minister read with great enjoyment – though he was furious at a suggestion that he might be a suppressed homosexual because of his flamboyant dress style and apparent use of cosmetics.[9] There could be no denying the fancy clothes, but the make-up may have been explained by his habit of heavily powdering his face after shaving. Having destroyed his own dossier, Göring carefully stored those of his rivals for future use.

As a reward for his services, Göring promoted Diels to be head of Abteilung I, the political department of the Ministry's Police Division, with instructions to begin setting up a separate political police force. Until then, the political police in Prussia had been limited to intelligence gathering, under the control of regional officials and local police chiefs. Göring's new force was to be independent of the criminal police, answerable only to him, and would have the power to carry out 'executive functions' such as searches and arrests. He named it the Geheime Staatspolizei, the Secret State Police, a title that was abbreviated in the normal German fashion to 'Gestapo'.

By the end of his first week in office, Göring had enough information to start his purge in earnest. Outside Berlin, he fired the governors of all twelve Prussian provinces, thirty-one of the thirty-four district governors, all the police chiefs, and most of the mayors and county prefects, replacing them with Nazis – Gauleiters or prominent local 'old fighters' in the higher positions, local SA or SS commanders in the police and more junior posts.[10] To reassure the DNVP and conservatives in the government, he appointed a safe establishment figure, Dr Ludwig Grauert, as head of the Police Division of the ministry. Grauert, whom Göring later promoted to Under-Secretary, had been business manager of the heavy industry employers' association in Rhineland-Westphalia, where he had proved himself as a ruthless strike-breaker. It was believed that he had connived with Fritz Thyssen to bale out Hitler and the Nazi Party in 1932 by diverting some of the ample funds made available by the big employers for combating the trade unions and preventing strikes.[11]

Appointing Grauert was a masterly move by Göring in the party power game, cementing his personal relationship with the big guns of heavy industry. Equally masterly was his choice of SS-Gruppenführer Kurt Daluege as his own personal lieutenant in the Police Division, with the title Commissioner for Special Duties. Daluege was the man to whom Hitler had written 'SS-man, your honour is your loyalty', and he enjoyed the Führer's personal gratitude for combating the SA rebellions. He was now commander of the SS Group East, but operated virtually independently of Himmler, who saw him as his main rival for the leadership of the SS. He was also Goebbels's Deputy Gauleiter in Berlin, and in this role had many valuable political connections. At a stroke, Göring had bought a man with inside knowledge of Himmler's secretive SS, the inner workings of Goebbels's Berlin Gau, and the troublesome SA – Daluege had, of course, been the SA's first commander in Berlin before moving over to the SS. He might have been nicknamed '*Dummi-Dummi*', but there could be little doubt that he was a sharp operator with well-developed political instincts, who could be extremely useful to his new master.

Göring's purge was only the first step in his plan to transform the police into an instrument of the Nazi state. After issuing them with revolvers in place of their batons and rubber truncheons, which he considered 'undignified', he issued a directive on 17 February, setting out what he called his 'Manifesto'. It began by ordering the police to avoid 'even the appearance of a hostile attitude' towards the 'national' parties or their paramilitary wings, the SA, SS, Stalhelm and the smaller German Nationalist Kampfring, and instead to 'thoroughly support their activities and propaganda'. The 'Manifesto' continued in the most chilling terms:

On the other hand, the activities of organisations hostile to the State are to be checked by the strongest measures. With Communist terrorism and raids there must be no trifling, and, when necessary, revolvers must be used without regard to consequences. Police officers who fire their revolvers in the execution of their duty will be protected by me without regard to the consequences of using their weapons. But officials who fail, out of mistaken regard for the consequences, must expect disciplinary action to be taken against them . . . No officer should lose sight of the fact that failure to adopt a measure is more heinous than making mistakes in its application . . . [12]

Göring could hardly have put his message more plainly if he had simply said 'Shoot first and ask questions afterwards.' However, to make doubly sure the point was taken, he underlined it a few days later in a widely-reported speech to policemen in Dortmund that must have sent cold shivers through Papen:

In the future there will be only one man who will wield power and bear responsibility in Prussia – that is myself. Whoever does his duty in the service of the State, who obeys my orders and ruthlessly makes use of his revolver when attacked is assured of my protection. Whoever, on the other hand, plays the coward, will have to reckon on being thrown out by me at the earliest possible moment. A bullet fired from the barrel of a police pistol is my bullet. If you say that is murder, then I am the murderer . . . I know two sorts of law because I know two sorts of men: those who are with us and those who are against us.[13]

The immediate result of Göring's 'Manifesto' was that SA men throughout Prussia were able to do exactly as they pleased without fear of arrest or interference. He gave them even greater licence on 22 February, when he ordered that 50,000 of them and their fellow para-militaries should be recruited as auxiliary policemen, fearing that even with his brutally clear directives, the police would not be ruthless or strong enough in putting down the Communist backlash that he anticipated. The auxiliaries wore their own uniforms, with a simple white armband, and were paid the miserly sum of three marks a day. But there were many perks to be had: for a start, they could travel for free on public transport, and if they chose to help themselves from stores and markets, no shopkeeper or stallholder was going to be foolish enough to ask for payment. But best of all, they could settle old scores, both personal and political, with complete impunity.

Göring's fear of a Communist uprising was genuine enough, but he had other reasons for enlisting the SA men into his auxiliary police force. With its unruly violence, the SA was threatening to derail Hitler's legal revolution just as it was about to succeed. Göring hoped he could at least partially restrain the most active storm-troopers by putting them to work alongside and under the direction of the regular police. He intended to restrict their use to emergencies only, and to limit their numbers. And of course he hoped to bring them under his control, away from Röhm, whom he still saw as a dangerous rival. For once, however, he had seriously miscalculated. The SA auxiliaries refused to bow to any authority, including Göring's. They revelled in their new status, and went on a spree of beating, intimidation and murder while the police, whom they soon outnumbered, looked on helplessly. In the month leading up to the elections, fifty-one anti-Nazis were murdered by SA thugs; the Nazis claimed eighteen of their own people also lost their lives. Göring did nothing to restrain the killers.

Hitler approved of Göring's seizure of police control, but it aroused some resentment among his rivals within the party. In public, Goebbels was full of praise: 'Göring is setting things to rights in Prussia with splendid energy,' he wrote. 'He is the sort of man who does a thing radically, and his nerves are made to stand a hard fight.'[14] But in private he sang a different tune, complaining that Göring and Frick were 'leading everybody by the nose'. When told money was short again for the election campaign, he showed his true feelings in his unpublished diary: 'Fat Göring should go without his caviar for once. Makes me want to throw up!'[15] He was only partly mollified when Göring called the biggest industrialists, including the chairman of the Reich Association of German Industry, Gustav Krupp von Bohlen und Halbach, to a meeting in his palace with Hitler and, with the help of

Schacht, persuaded them to cough up three million marks to fund the campaign after promising them it would be the last for ten or even a hundred years.

Goebbels's reactions came entirely from personal jealousy. Frick and Himmler, on the other hand, felt aggrieved because they regarded themselves as the party's specialists in police matters. Frick, head of the party's legal division, had been a senior police official in Munich in 1923, and had been earmarked by Hitler for Police President of the city if the November *putsch* had succeeded. After the Nazis' electoral successes in 1930, when he had been made Interior Minister of Thuringia, he had begun Nazifying that state's police force, and indeed its entire civil service, with some vigour, before being forced from office by a vote of no confidence. Both he and Hitler had seen the 'experiment' in Thuringia as a practice run for the real thing once they had gained power in the Reich as a whole. His appointment as Reich Interior Minister should have given him control of all Germany's police forces. But the country's federal structure meant his control would remain purely nominal until that structure had been radically changed. In the meantime, Göring had outflanked him by grabbing real power in two thirds of the Reich, without bothering to consult him. Loosening Göring's grip on the Prussian police was not going to be easy, but Frick was determined to do it.

Himmler was still at least one level down from Göring and Frick in the party hierarchy, but he was gaining ground steadily in his usual quiet way, and he, too, had his eye on the police as his passport to personal power. He had refashioned the SS as the party's own internal security police, and so could claim some expertise in this area, backed by aides such as the head of the Police Division in the SS, Paul Scharfe, a vastly experienced fifty-nine-year-old former lieutenant colonel in the Schupo, the Prussian Security Police. Himmler had been concentrating for some time on recruiting former policemen, with some success. As early as July 1931, assuming that the SS would take over the police once the Nazis came to power, the leader in the Ruhr of the Association of Former Prussian Policemen asked him if his members could join the SS *en bloc*, estimating that some 40,000 would be ready to serve in the police of the Third Reich.[16] Himmler saw the Third Reich as a police state, with the police under the control of his SS. He would not easily be deflected from his vision.

*   *   *

Denied executive power, Goebbels poured his energies into his final election campaign. Once again, he flew Hitler around the country, but this time there was one important difference: the Führer only spoke in larger towns and cities with radio stations. With his passion for innovation, Goebbels had embraced the new medium of radio with great enthusiasm, secure in the knowledge that it could not be used by any of the Nazis' competitors. As a state-controlled service it was available only to the government – in the presidential elections a year earlier only Hindenburg had been allowed to broadcast; Hitler had been denied access to the airwaves. Now, the privilege was Hitler's as Chancellor, and he and Goebbels made the most of it. Every speech was transmitted to the nation, complete with a dramatic introduction by Goebbels, blocking off a whole evening of listening virtually every day during the campaign. The only non-Nazi politicians who were allowed to speak, as a special concession on 11 February, were their allies, Hugenberg, Papen and Franz Seldte, chief of the Stahlhelm.

Hitler's first broadcast was from the Sportpalast in Berlin on 10 February, starting with a twenty-minute lead-in from Goebbels building up to the moment of Hitler's arrival. Goebbels claimed an audience of twenty million. 'The whole of Germany was stood on its head,' he crowed. 'The masses were in senseless rapture.'[17] But when Hitler listened to a recording he was disappointed at the flatness and lack of colour in his delivery, and lamented to Goebbels: 'It seems to me that I am not exactly a radio personality.'[18] Undaunted, Goebbels called in the best audio engineers and went to work with them on improving the sound quality to add depth and flexibility to the Führer's voice and capture more of the atmosphere of the mass meetings. Using the very latest technology he managed to recreate something of the excitement of the live performance, and turned Hitler into a radio star whose voice was familiar in every household.

The constant theme of Hitler's speeches, and indeed of the whole election campaign, was the danger of Marxism – the general label under which he lumped together the Communists and the Social Democrats, who actually hated each other even more than they did the Nazis. To drive home the threat of revolution and ensure a landslide majority, the Nazis needed a Communist uprising, or at least some major outrage; but no matter how hard Goebbels and Göring tried to provoke one, the Communists refused to oblige. Even the elaborate funeral for SA-Sturmführer Hanne Maikowski passed without incident. The best Goebbels could do was to accuse them of cutting the main cable between the radio station and the stadium in Stuttgart on 15 February, so that part of Hitler's speech could not be broadcast. But this was no big deal – most listeners were probably very grateful for at least one evening's respite.

On 24 February, Göring ordered his political police to carry out another search of the KPD headquarters, Karl Liebknecht House, which the Communists had abandoned three weeks earlier when the President signed the 'Order for the Protection of the German People'. Stoking the fires of paranoia, he claimed in a press statement that they had found 'tons of seditious literature' in the cellars, calling for an armed revolution. This proved, he said, that Germany was about to be 'cast into the chaos of Bolshevism', with assassinations of political leaders, the murder of their families, and attacks on public buildings. But he did not disclose any hard evidence and the general public remained unimpressed. Goebbels played the matter down by giving it a bare nine-line mention in *Der Angriff* that evening, and only a single sentence the next day – he had, after all, run exactly the same story three weeks before. Hopes of a Communist rising before the elections seemed to be fading fast. Three days later, however, with less than a week to go, the ripest of plums suddenly dropped into the Nazis' laps, completely out of the blue.

On Monday, 27 February Goebbels spent the afternoon finalising details for 'The Day of National Awakening', which he planned for 4 March, the day before polling, as the culmination of his election campaign. His spirits had been lifted by hearing from Hitler that Papen had agreed to his new ministry, and by the arrival of a million marks from Göring's industrialist friends. That evening, in a mood for celebration, he and Magda entertained Hitler and a few other party leaders to dinner at their apartment. They were relaxing after the meal, listening to music and telling stories, when the telephone rang. It was Putzi Hanfstaengl, who had been unable to join them as he was confined to bed with a cold in the Reichstag President's palace, where he was staying as Göring's guest. Breathlessly, he demanded to speak to Hitler at once, and when Goebbels told him he could pass on any message, he said curtly, 'Tell him the Reichstag is on fire.' 'Is that meant to be a joke?' Goebbels asked. 'If you think it's a joke, come see for yourself!' Hanfstaengl replied, and hung up. Although he still thought it was 'a bit of wild fantasy', Goebbels started ringing round to see if it was true, before calling Hanfstaengl back and telling him the Führer wanted to know what was going on, 'and no more jokes'. Within minutes, Goebbels and Hitler were on their way, 'racing down the Charlottenburger Chaussee at 100 kilometres per hour'.[19]

Göring was working late in his ministry when he received the news. He immediately threw on his big camel hair coat, leapt into his car and drove the few hundred yards to his palace. The first firefighters and police were already at the scene, but there was little they could do. The Reichstag was well ablaze, a column of flames roaring towards the sky through the great glass dome, which had cracked and was acting as a chimney. Shouting 'We must save the tapestries!' Göring charged into the building, hoping to rescue the precious hangings. It was a hopeless task. The main debating chamber, with its oak panelling and upholstered seats, had become a furnace, sucking in air so fiercely that he found it hard to keep his feet. 'I was all but drawn into the flames by the hot draught,' he told American interrogator Dr George Schuster in 1945. 'Fortunately my belt snagged in the door [of a phone booth] and that stopped me toppling forward. Just at that moment, the huge cupola came crashing down.'[20]

When Goebbels and Hitler, wearing a flapping trench coat and a broad-brimmed black felt hat, entered the lobby, Göring waddled through the wreckage to greet them with the news that one arsonist had already been arrested, and that several Communist deputies had been in the building only minutes before the fire started. 'This is the beginning of the Communist revolt!' he cried. 'Not a moment must be lost.' Hitler was quick to agree. 'This is something really cunning,' he replied, 'prepared a long time ago.'[21] As he continued to take in the scene, Papen arrived, immaculate in evening dress from a dinner at the Herrenklub in honour of Hindenburg. Hitler grasped his hand and told him: 'This is a God-given signal, Herr Vice-Chancellor! If this fire, as I believe, is the work of the Communists, then we must crush out this murderous pestilence with an iron fist.'[22]

Rudolf Diels, who had rushed to the scene to supervise the police operation, hurried to report to Göring and Hitler that he had already interrogated the arrested suspect, a 'madman' who was solely responsible for the fire. But this was not what Hitler wanted to hear. Cutting Diels short, he insisted that the fire was a carefully-prepared Communist plot. Diels watched in amazement as he proceeded to work himself up into a fine rage before leaning over a balcony to 'shout uncontrollably, as I had never seen him do before':

There will no mercy now! Anyone who stands in our way will be mown down. The German people will not tolerate clemency. Every Communist functionary will be shot wherever he is found. The Communist deputies must be hanged this very night. Everybody in league with them must be arrested. There will no longer be any leniency for Social Democrats, either.[23]

After a hurried conference in the Prussian Interior Ministry with Hitler, Goebbels, Frick and Grauert, Göring swung into frenzied action in an atmosphere that Diels thought 'resembled a madhouse'. By chance, Göring had already had a list of Communists drawn up after the raid on Karl Liebknecht House, for arrest when the time was right. That time was now. He ordered Diels to carry out mass arrests of those on the list, who included all Communist officials and deputies – in total violation of their Reichstag immunity – plus prominent Social Democrats, trade unionists and left-wing intellectuals. He backed up the arrests by closing all Communist Party offices, banning all Communist and Social Democrat publications, and closing every castle and museum in Prussia, to highlight the danger of their becoming the targets for more arson attacks.

The round-up, carried out with unprecedented brutality mostly by the SA police auxiliaries, brought in around 4,000 prisoners that night, with truckloads of storm-troopers roaring through darkened streets to seize opponents from their homes and drag them off to SA barracks, where they were beaten and abused. There must have been some resistance: according to Goebbels, two SA men were killed in the process, but for once, apart from the ritual promise 'They will not go unrevenged', he made little of their deaths – there was simply too much going on. The action was to continue for over a month, by which time in Prussia alone some 25,000 opponents of the Nazis had been taken into 'protective custody' on Göring's orders.

This was the German people's first experience of Nazi government terror. Göring justified it with a lurid press statement, claiming – without producing a shred of evidence – to have proof that 'the burning of the Reichstag was to be the signal for a bloody insurrection'. 'Today,' he said, 'was to have seen throughout Germany terrorist acts against individual persons, against private property, and against the life and limb of the peaceful population, and also the beginning of a general civil war.'

This time, Goebbels supported Göring's claims to the full. After calling into the Gau office to make sure everyone was on the ball, he spent most of the night with Hitler at the editorial offices of the *Völkischer Beobachter*, composing inflammatory articles and proclamations for the morning edition, then returned to his own desk to dictate the lead story for *Der Angriff*. Communism, he declared, now had to be destroyed so completely that not even its name would remain: 'Now rise up, German nation! Rise up and cast your judgement! On 5 March let God's punishment smite the Red world plague! Hitler wants to act! Hitler will act! Give him the power to do so!'[24]

In fact, Hitler was given the power to act on 28 February, not by the popular vote but by an emergency decree, quickly drawn up by Frick, approved unanimously by the Cabinet, and signed without demur by Hindenburg. The 'Decree for the Protection of People and State to Guard Against Communist Acts of Violence Endangering the State' was the death warrant of democracy, and the charter for the coming Third Reich and all its iniquities. It was short and simple. Its first article removed at a stroke all the fundamental human rights enshrined in the Weimar constitution, specifically listing personal liberty, freedom of expression (including freedom of the press), rights of association and assembly, privacy of postal, telegraphic and telephonic communication, the need for warrants for house searches, and confiscation of property. The second article allowed the Reich government to take over the powers of the state governments to restore order, and a further article authorised the death penalty for violations of the decree, as well as for attempted assassination of members of the government, and for arson. It was the Nazis' passport to unfettered power.

The timing of the Reichstag fire was so opportune that it is hard to believe that the Nazis, and in particular Goebbels and Göring, had not set it up. They certainly had both motive and opportunity, and there can be no doubt that they were ruthless and devious enough. But in spite of the obvious suspicion, skilfully played on by the Communists' own propaganda machine which soon assembled a mass of mostly spurious circumstantial evidence, publishing it later that year in the *Brown Book of the Hitler Terror and the Burning of the Reichstag*, it is now accepted that the truth is much more mundane. The man who was arrested at the scene, a half-demented, twenty-four-year-old Dutch bricklayer called Marinus van der Lubbe, was responsible for the fire, just as he told his interrogators. His aim had been to stage a protest on behalf of oppressed workers. He was a former Communist, but he had acted alone. All that the Nazi chieftains were guilty of was seizing a fantastic opportunity and turning it to devastating effect.

Far from sounding alarm bells in the German populace, the emergency decree and the savage repression that followed were generally welcomed, and Hitler's popularity soared. Presented with such a wonderful gift, Goebbels turned the final run-up to the election into a triumphal progress. Göring did his bit as a speaker second only to Hitler in his celebrity, somehow finding time to dash around the country making rabble-rousing speeches such as one in Frankfurt am Main on 3 March, where he bellowed, to wild applause:

My measures will not be crippled by any legal considerations. I don't have to worry about justice; my mission is only to destroy and exterminate. Nothing more! . . . You may be sure I shall use the power of the State and the police to the utmost, my dear Communists, so don't draw any false conclusions; but the struggle to the death, in which my fist will grab your necks, I shall lead with those down there – the brown-shirts![25]

After mass meetings in Breslau, Hamburg and Berlin, Goebbels flew with the Führer to Königsberg in East Prussia for the campaign's grand finale. Königsberg may have seemed remote, but it was a brilliant choice. As well as having being severed from the rest of Germany by the hated 'Polish corridor' imposed by Versailles, it was the coronation city of the Prussian monarchs, the city where, in January 1701, the Elector Friedrich III had placed a crown on his own head and proclaimed himself King Friedrich I. The obvious allusion was not lost on the voters.

Goebbels had Hitler's final speech broadcast over the entire national radio network, with loudspeakers set up in the main streets and squares and beer halls of towns and cities throughout Germany. After exhorting his people to 'hold your heads high and proud once again', Hitler finished by describing how he, 'the simple soldier', had joined hands with the Reich President, 'who had released Prussia from the enemy as a field marshal'.[26] There was, according to Goebbels, 'a moment of solemn silence', then thousands of voices burst into the great Netherlands Hymn of Thanksgiving, 'Now thank we all our God', always associated with Friedrich the Great's victory over the Austrians at the battle of Leuthen in 1757. As the hymn reached its last verse, it was drowned out by the bells of Königsberg Cathedral, echoing across the country, giving the signal for the lighting of bonfire beacons, 'the fires of freedom', on mountains, hill-tops and all along the national frontiers. At the same time, SA bands struck up to start torch-lit marches in every city – in Berlin, they paraded through the Brandenberg Gate in an echo of the celebrations of 30 January.

Goebbels's 'Day of National Awakening' was a masterpiece of stage-management, as was the entire election campaign. When the votes were counted twenty-four hours later, the Nazis had scored over 17 million votes, an increase of 5.5 million compared with the previous November, which gave them 43.9 per cent of the total poll, entitling them to 288 of the 647 Reichstag seats. They had failed to win an absolute majority – something that was virtually impossible for any one party under the Weimar electoral system. But with the addition of the DNVP's 3 million votes and 52 seats, Hitler was able to set up a coalition government with the slim overall margin of 16 seats.

The majority, however, was narrow only on paper: the reality was quite different. Hitler and Göring had avoided banning the Communist Party itself when they closed its offices and publications, allowing it to fight the election and so register nearly 5 million votes that would have gone to other parties. The 81 deputies that this gave the Communists, together with six Social Democrats, were all either under lock and key or in hiding, and so could not vote in the Reichstag. A similar situation applied in the Prussian Landtag. In both parliaments, therefore, the Nazis had a clear majority. Hitler was now the undisputed and legitimate ruler of Germany, poised to seize absolute power. And the two men who had done more than any others to lever him into that position were his two chief lieutenants, Joseph Goebbels and Hermann Göring. They were fully entitled to feel pleased with themselves, and to look forward to the future with eager anticipation.

XIII

CO-ORDINATION

WITH Hitler firmly in place as Chancellor, the jockeying for position as his number two and therefore his heir took on a new edge, for now there was genuine power at stake. For the moment, there were five possible candidates – Göring, Goebbels, Frick, Röhm and Hess – but two of these could be discounted at once. Röhm was too much of a maverick, a dangerous loose cannon who would never be accepted by the army or the 'respectable' middle classes. Hess had considerable authority within the party, and indeed would be named Deputy Führer (for Party Affairs) on 21 April, but he was essentially a functionary with little practical experience as a political operator and was seen strictly as Hitler's deputy, never as his successor. Of the other three, Frick was a skilful politician already holding high office as Reich Interior Minister, nominally ranking higher in the government than Göring, and clearly enjoying Hitler's confidence. But he was lethargic and colourless, at heart a bureaucrat, lacking both the charisma and the ruthless drive of his two colleagues. And at fifty-six he was an old man by party standards – the average age of the party elite was only forty years: Hitler himself was forty-three, Göring had just celebrated his fortieth birthday, and Goebbels, proud to be the youngest minister in the Cabinet when he was officially sworn in by Hindenburg on 14 March, was only thirty-five. Himmler, who was still a second echelon figure, was younger still at a mere thirty-two. And so, until such time as any new contenders emerged, the contest was between Göring and Goebbels, the swash-buckler versus the Jesuit, the broadsword versus the stiletto. It promised to be a fascinating – and possibly bloody – match.

Göring was ahead in the government stakes: at the time of the elections he was a Cabinet minister, President of the Reichstag, Reich

Commissioner for Air and Prussian Interior Minister; but he held no appointments in the party. Goebbels held two vital party positions, as Reich Propaganda Chief and Gauleiter of Berlin, but although he was a Reichstag deputy, he was not yet a member of the government. That, however, would soon be put right, and he would shape up to his rival on more even terms as he was quickly rewarded for his part in the Nazi victory.

The day after the elections, Goebbels spent most of the afternoon with Hitler discussing the setting up of his new Ministry of Popular Enlightenment and Propaganda, for which he had waited so long. Both knew that this was the most controversial measure in Hitler's new government: leaving aside the principle of creating a ministry devoted to the indoctrination of the public, no one outside the party, and by no means all those inside it, trusted the man who was to run it, a man who had spent years building a reputation as an irresponsible and unscrupulous firebrand. Only now was Hitler strong enough to override all their objections, but he still hedged his bet by giving Goebbels his own Chief Press Secretary, Walther Funk, as Secretary of State.

The forty-three-year-old Funk, with his background in financial journalism, was one of Hitler's most influential economic advisers, and the Führer charged him with managing the finances, administration and organisation of the new ministry 'so that Goebbels will not have to bother' with these matters.[1] Hitler clearly intended Funk to be a restraining influence, keeping an eye on his hot-headed young genius; Goebbels didn't mind – it brought a potential rival under his control, where he could keep an eye on him. And despite his unprepossessing appearance – he was short, paunchy and ugly – and his known penchant for heavy drinking and homosexual debauchery, Funk was amusing company and had a sharp and ready wit. Over the next four years he proved to be Goebbels's most valuable aide and supporter, particularly in territorial disputes with other government departments, most notably Frick's Interior Ministry.

Like all the Nazi bigwigs, who collected titles and offices like decorations, Funk did not give up his existing job, but simply added a new one to his portfolio – he remained Chief Press Secretary until the end of 1937. Similarly, Goebbels was still Reich Propaganda Chief for the party, and Gauleiter of Berlin, though on 7 March he appointed a functionary called Sie Görlitzer to deputise for him in the Gau, while he concentrated on his new responsibilities.

Goebbels had decided his ministry was to consist – initially, at least

– of five main departments, covering press, film, radio, propaganda and theatre, each of which, he wrote, 'very much interests me personally, so for that reason alone I shall dedicate myself to them with zeal and joyful devotion'. It was to be housed in the Leopold Palace, conveniently situated just across the Wilhelmplatz from the Reich Chancellery. Originally built in 1737 and revamped a hundred years later by the great Berlin architect Karl Friedrich Schinkel, it was – and still is – one of the most elegant and charming buildings in the Wilhelmstrasse area. Goebbels admired the building's external beauty, but regarded the interior as hopelessly dark and old-fashioned, declaring that it would have to be extensively renovated before he moved in:

First, the masons and cleaners will have to be sent into the rooms, to strip all the stucco off the walls and pull down the heavy, stuffy, moth-eaten plush drapes, to let the sun shine in through the windows again. I cannot work in this twilight. I must have clarity, cleanliness and pure, uncluttered lines around me. I detest gloom. And just as the rooms need clearing out, so do the people. Yesterday's men cannot be tomorrow's pathfinders.[2]

The very idea of 'modernising' a Schinkel building was tantamount to sacrilege, and the old officials did their best to thwart Goebbels. After six years' experience of his direct-action methods on the streets of Berlin, they should have known better. In a chilling demonstration of his contempt for tradition, he simply gathered a crew of workmen who were members of the Berlin SA, and went in with them to knock off the plaster and tear down the panelling overnight. At the same time, they pulled old files, documents and newspapers from the shelves where they had lain, 'musty and dusty' for years, pitching them unceremoniously down the stairs into a giant heap of waste paper. 'Only clouds of dust attest the bygone splendours of bureaucracy!' he boasted to his diary.

When the 'worthy gentlemen' whom he was about to throw out appeared next morning, they were horrified at the chaotic mess. One put both hands to his head and stammered: 'Herr Minister, do you know you could go to prison for this?' Delighted to have shocked the prim civil servants, Goebbels sneered at him: 'Clear out, old man. In case you haven't heard, let me solemnly inform you that Germany is in the middle of a revolution and no ancient files are going to hold that revolution up.'[3]

Keeping things in the National Socialist family, Goebbels appointed Albert Speer, who had been responsible for refurbishing his Gau headquarters, to design and oversee the internal reconstruction. It was finished in record time, ready for him to move in on 22 March. Speer may not have been the world's greatest architect, but he was already demonstrating an impressive ability to get things done swiftly and smoothly. He did, however, make one grave mistake. 'I tried to carry out my assignment with due deference for Schinkel's interior,' he recalled later. 'But Goebbels thought what I had done insufficiently impressive. After some months, he commissioned the *Vereinigte Werkstätten* (United Workshops) to redo the rooms in "ocean liner style".'[4]

The building, of course, was not the ministry. The ministry was its people, and Goebbels's ideas on the people he wanted were as radical as his views on its architecture. This was the first ministry to be created by the Nazis, and he was determined it would be 'National Socialist by birth', recruiting his staff almost exclusively from party members – nearly 100 of his 350 officials and staff wore the golden party badge, an honour awarded for long and meritorious service to the party. A large number of them came from the party's propaganda department, so they were already well used to his aims and methods. Above all, he wanted them intelligent – more than half of them had university degrees, many of them doctorates – and he wanted them young. Few of those he chose were over thirty – his special assistant, Karl Hanke, was twenty-nine; an engineering graduate, he had been Goebbels's personal adjutant since 1932 and before that had worked with him as organisation leader for the Berlin Gau and bureau chief of the party Propaganda Directorate. As head of the important Propaganda Department, he appointed Wilhelm Haegert, who was only twenty-six. Youthful faces were everywhere. Goebbels believed his bright young men would make up in 'fervour, enthusiasm, untarnished idealism' what they lacked in experience or knowledge of official procedures.[5]

Goebbels made no secret of the purpose of his ministry. The official decree setting it up, which he himself had drafted with Hitler's approval, stated that it was 'to promote enlightenment and propaganda among the populace as to the policies of the Reich government and the national reconstruction of the German fatherland'.[6] At his first government press conference on 16 March, he put it more plainly: it was to make the people 'think uniformly, react uniformly, and place themselves at the disposal of the government, body and soul'. It was, in short, to be no less than the Ministry of Thought Control.

*   *   *

Backed by his young team, Goebbels threw himself into the task of convincing the German people that Hitler was indeed their saviour, the 'Führer' who would lead them back to their former greatness if only they would surrender themselves completely to him. Goebbels's choice of Königsberg for the culmination of the 'Day of National Awakening' had been inspired, but he followed it with an even more emotive reminder of Prussian glory, by persuading Hitler that he should hold the opening ceremony of the new Reichstag not in Berlin but in neighbouring Potsdam.

Potsdam was forever redolent of the Hohenzollern monarchy. Both the soldier king, Friedrich Wilhelm I, and his son, Friedrich the Great – Hitler's personal hero – were buried in the crypt of the Garrison Church, where the main ceremony would be held. The church itself had great resonance for the army – generations of guards officers had dedicated themselves there to serve God and the King – and choosing it served to reassure the present High Command of Hitler's respect. Hindenburg was particularly delighted, for the church had always held a special place in his affections: as a young officer returning from Bismarck's Austro-Prussian War in 1866, he had made a pilgrimage to it to give thanks for his survival, and for the victory that paved the way to a unified Germany under Prussian hegemony. He suggested the ceremony take place during the first week of April. Goebbels, however, was determined to milk the occasion of every drop of symbolism. He insisted it must be held on 21 March, which was not only the first day of spring, but also the anniversary of the opening of the very first Reichstag by Bismarck in 1871, after his victory in the Franco-Prussian War had finally clinched unification in the Second Reich.

The 'Day of the National Uprising', as Goebbels rather fancifully named it, was another demonstration of his flair for showmanship combined with meticulous planning of every tiny detail. It started with two services in other churches, one Catholic, one Protestant; Hitler attended neither. Eschewing religious observance, Goebbels took him instead to 'honour the fallen' at Berlin's Luisenstadt Cemetery, where several SA martyrs were buried. Hitler then swapped his party uniform for a top hat and cutaway morning coat and drove through cheering crowds to Potsdam, where he met the President, resplendent in his imperial field marshal's uniform and spiked helmet, on the steps of the Garrison Church, bowing obsequiously as he shook his hand. Together, the two men, one symbolising Germany's past, the other her future, processed down the aisle, the Chancellor following behind the aged

President in a calculated show of deference. The packed congregation of generals, princes, judges, diplomats, top civil servants, and Reichstag deputies dominated by the brown-shirted mass of Nazi members watched as Hindenburg paused before the empty chair set aside for the exiled Kaiser and raised his baton in salute.

In his speech, Hindenburg called for national unity and support for the new government. Hitler's response was a model of moderation, praising Hindenburg's 'great-hearted decision on 30 January . . . to entrust the leadership of the Reich to this young Germany'.[7] Goebbels claimed in his diary that everybody was greatly moved, and that he actually saw tears in Hindenburg's eyes as he listened, before rising to shake his Chancellor's hand.

After laying laurel wreaths on the kings' tombs to the thunder of a twenty-one-gun salute outside, the two present-day rulers emerged from the church to review a grand parade of the army plus, significantly, the SA, the SS and the Stahlhelm. Equally significantly, the flags that flew everywhere were not the black, red and gold of the Republic, but the Nazis' red, white and black, echoing the old imperial colours: Hitler had also prevailed upon the President ten days earlier to declare the swastika the official emblem of the nation. As the troops marched past, Hitler maintained the fiction of subservience by standing well behind Hindenburg and allowing the old field marshal to take the salute alone. But there could be no doubt in anyone's mind where the real power now lay.

Any doubts that may have lingered were soon dispelled when the new Reichstag convened that afternoon in the suitably theatrical setting of the Kroll Opera House, just across the Königsplatz from the burnt-out shell of the Reichstag building, swathed in swastika flags both inside and out and cordoned off by uniformed SS and SA guards. After re-electing Göring as its President, it adjourned for two days, reconvening on 23 March to pass the ironically-named 'Act for the Removal of Distress from People and Reich', the Enabling Act giving Hitler absolute power to rule for the next four years without reference to either itself or President Hindenburg.

Goebbels had made sure his message of the 'Day of the National Uprising' reached the whole of Germany and beyond by thoroughly briefing the national and international press and by making full use of his favourite ultra-modern media, radio and newsreel film, to achieve saturation coverage. In the following few days, he also had millions of postcards and posters printed, showing Hitler and Hindenburg shaking hands, personifying the reconciliation of the old Germany and the new, and promoting the image of Hitler as the Führer not only of the party but also of the nation. He needed to emphasise continuity with the glories of Germany's imperial past not only to comfort the middle classes and the army, but also to divert their attention from the revolutionary changes the Nazis were rushing through at a breath-taking pace.

After 5 March, the party embarked at once on an aggressive policy called *Gleichschaltung*, generally translated as 'co-ordination', a euphemism for forcing everything and everyone into line, or Nazification. It was the first step in the process of combining party and state into one indivisible whole, starting with the *Gleichschaltung* of all national institutions, organisations and associations, and spreading with incredible speed into virtually every corner of German life. Within a very few months, even the humblest village bowling or social club had placed itself under Nazi control, almost always voluntarily and usually enthusiastically. Goebbels's brainwashing was clearly working well.

A bigger and more revolutionary change was the *Gleichschaltung* of the federal states under a centralised national government – something that not even Bismarck or Wilhelm II had dared to contemplate. Amazingly, this abrogation of German constitutional history was accomplished in four days and with remarkably little protest. Those states that were not already under Nazi control were brought to heel with SA and SS marches and disturbances, followed by the imposition of a Reich Commissioner under the pretext of restoring order – the device that Papen had pioneered so successfully in Prussia a year earlier. In the following weeks, the centuries-old independence of the individual states was further eroded when Hitler changed the Commissioners into Reich Governors charged with carrying out his policies, and was finally destroyed in January 1934, when the states' autonomy in a federal system was officially abolished.

Most of the new Governors were senior Gauleiters. In Prussia, however, Hitler took the position himself, reviving Bismarck's tradition of combining the roles of Reich Chancellor and head of government of the largest state to underline the notion that Prussia and the Reich were synonymous. In doing so, Hitler automatically ousted Papen, who was still Vice-Chancellor, from his role as Reich Commissioner for Prussia. What he omitted to do, however, was to abolish the post of Prussian Minister-President, which had lain vacant since Papen's *coup* of the previous July. With his insatiable appetite for titles and positions, Göring wanted this one to strengthen his growing personal power base, and had been disappointed when Hitler had failed to give it to him immediately after the elections. Greatly daring, he proceeded to outflank the Führer by putting the matter on the agenda for the first meeting of the new Prussian Landtag, and getting himself duly elected; naturally, he still kept his responsibilities as Interior Minister. Hitler was forced to accept this *fait accompli* and confirm Göring as Minister-President of Prussia; shortly afterwards, on 25 April, he handed over the governorship, too.

Göring took great delight in signing himself 'Minister-President' – he soon dropped the words 'of Prussia' – tacitly implying that he was Prime Minister of all Germany. Again, Hitler made no objection. It seemed that he really was grooming Göring to be his successor, fulfilling the promise he had made way back in 1923 that the former air ace would one day be the leader of Germany. The understanding was that when Hindenburg finally died, Hitler would become President and Göring would take over as his Chancellor. In the meantime, a spell as virtual dictator over three-fifths of Germany would be a valuable preparation. It also provided yet another opportunity for self-aggrandisement: as Minister-President Göring saw himself as the legal successor to the King of Prussia, and the head of the Protestant Evangelical Church. He made this claim in an open letter to Bernard Rust, his Minister of Education and Culture, which he had published in the *Deutsche Allgemeine Zeitung* of 27 June. Expressing astonishment that a 'Reich Bishop' should have been appointed without his approval, he wrote: 'Until the revolution [of 1918], the King of Prussia was the *summus episcopus* of the Church of Prussia. In my opinion these prerogatives now devolve upon the Prussian State Ministry, i.e., upon the Prussian Minister–President.'

The Prussian positions were undoubtedly plums. But there was another appointment that for Göring was the icing on the cake: Goebbels's may have been the first new ministry to be created by Hitler after 5 March, but the second followed very shortly after, and covered an area that was as dear and as perfectly suited to Göring as Goebbels's was to him. His previous, rather nebulous office as Commissioner for Air within the Transport Ministry was transmuted into a full-scale Air

Ministry, with the secret task of creating and developing the world's biggest and most modern air force, from scratch. Unlike most air forces at that time, it would be an independent service, not subservient to either the army or navy, and with its own budget.

Back in February, at the very start of his Chancellorship, Hitler had made it plain to both the generals and the Cabinet that 'rebuilding Germany's defence capability' was to take precedence over every other consideration for the next five years.[8] Even the great work creation programme to eradicate the misery of six million registered unemployed was to be geared entirely towards rearmament.[9] And – sweet music to Göring's ears – money was to be no object. The financial picture became even more rosy in March, when the President of the Reichsbank, Hans Luther, was replaced by Göring's friend Hjalmar Schacht, who quickly devised an ingenious scheme of discounting government bills to produce vast sums of money outside the national budget. From then on, defence expenditure depended on only two factors: how much could be hidden from the Allied powers, and how much the military could spend. Hitler, in fact, chided the Defence Ministry for not asking for enough. He would never have that problem with Göring.

As his State Secretary, to run the ministry and plan and carry out the building of the new air force, the Luftwaffe, Göring chose Erhard Milch, the director of Lufthansa, whose experience in running the airline would be invaluable. Milch was a tough operator, every bit as ruthless as his boss, and almost as ambitious. He had never been a flier himself, having served as a front-line army officer during the war, and was not dazzled by Göring's glamorous record, or his *Pour le Mérite*. In any case, he had been handing out payola to him for years, and was not inclined to be subservient to him now, especially since he knew he was indispensable. It is said that he refused the appointment at first, and only allowed himself to be persuaded by Hitler himself, who told him it was not the party but Germany that needed him.

There was just one minor problem to be sorted out before the new State Secretary could be confirmed in the job: although his mother was a pure Aryan, his father, a pharmacist in Breslau, was a Jew. Göring was aware of this but, typically, was not bothered. He had a simple solution: Milch's mother was persuaded to sign a document 'confessing' that she had had an extra-marital affair with a certain Freiherr (Baron) Hermann von Bier, and that Erhard was the result. 'If we're going to take his real father away,' Göring is reported as saying, 'let us at least give him an aristocrat as a substitute.' A new birth certificate was issued, and Milch was in the clear. When anyone dared question this, Göring had a ready answer: 'It is I,' he thundered, 'who decides if someone is a Jew!' For cynicism, the two men were clearly well matched. Their turbulent relationship somehow survived for twelve years, possibly because in other respects they balanced each other out. Göring was the irrepressible man of vision, the dreamer of dreams forever making impossible demands; Milch was the practical engineer who turned those dreams into reality. It was Göring who, perhaps unfairly, took the credit for the Luftwaffe in its glory years; but by the same token, he also took the blame for its later disasters.

To counter Milch's hardness, Göring installed several of his old friends from the war in official positions in the Air Ministry. They included Karl Bodenschatz, the former adjutant of the Richthofen Squadron and now a full colonel in the regular Reichswehr, as his personal adjutant; Ernst Udet, one of the squadron's ace pilots who had been a companion on the barnstorming flying circuit, as a special adviser; and his old comrade and first flying partner, Bruno Loerzer, as head of pilot recruitment and training under the cover of two 'co-ordinated' bodies, the Reich Air Sports Union and the Reich Air Club, into which all the various flying and gliding clubs in Germany were amalgamated.

Surrounding himself with cronies in this way was another facet of Göring's unabashed corruptness: wearing his Prussian Minister-President's hat, he made his former business partner and unpaid chauffeur, Paul 'Pilli' Körner, his State Secretary, with an apartment in his official residence on Leipziger Platz to go with it. After all the years of depending on hand-outs from the rich and powerful, he thoroughly enjoyed being in a position to distribute a little largess himself – besides which, it bound people to him while fitting the image of *bonhomie* which he so liked to project.

Bonhomie was conspicuously absent from many of Göring's other activities. The round-up of opponents of the new regime, which he had initiated after the Reichstag fire, was soon producing so many prisoners that regular jails and police cells could not be expected to cope. As a solution, Göring ordered Diels and Daluege to open special jails to house the prisoners, plus 'concentration camps' (*Konzentrationslager*) based on those created by the British in South Africa to contain civilian prisoners during the Anglo–Boer War at the turn of the century – in later years, he was always at pains to point out that although he had created the camps, he had not created the name.[10]

Göring claimed later that he realised that if the SA were allowed to run the camps, 'the situation would conceivably not be a very pleasant one for the inmates. For this reason, I gave instructions that the guard, if possible to a large extent, should consist of police forces; only where these were not adequate should auxiliary forces be called.' The precaution, he admitted, did not always work. As he himself shrugged, 'You can't make an omelette without breaking a few eggs.' To the Nuremberg Tribunal after the war he confessed:

Of course, in the beginning there were excesses; of course, the innocent were also hurt here and there; of course, there were beatings here and there and acts of brutality were committed; but compared to all that has happened in the past and to the greatness of the events, this German revolution of freedom is the least bloody and the most disciplined of all revolutions known to history . . . I naturally gave instructions that such things should not happen . . . I always pointed out that these things ought not to happen, because it was important to me to win over some of these people for our side and to re-educate them.[11]

This, then, was Göring's justification for his camps: they were not supposed to be places of torment and torture, but centres of re-education and rehabilitation.

The SA, and to a lesser extent the SS, had no time for such hypocrisy. They were too busy settling old scores, dragging their captives back to their own barracks or to 'bunkers' in empty buildings, where they could indulge in sadistic orgies of beating, torture and murder without fear of interference. 'It was the duty of every good SA unit to have at least one of these [bunkers],' wrote Hans Bernd Gisevius, who became a Gestapo official later that year. 'The efficiency of a leader was judged by the number of his prisoners, and the reputation of an SA tough depended on the strength of arm with which he conducted a prisoner's "education".'[12] As the number of prisoners spiralled, they began following Göring's example and setting up larger, but unauthorised camps of their own, where they did as they pleased behind the locked gates.

Göring was horrified. This was the SA out of control again, threatening to cause great damage to his authority and his government. On 2 August, he disbanded the auxiliary police, thus removing the SA's official right of arrest, then turned his attention to the camps and 'bunkers'. He managed to close down the camp near Stettin, which was run by the Gauleiter of Pomerania, and one at Breslau, which had been set up by Edmund Heines, one of Röhm's closest collaborators. He had more difficulty dealing with a camp close to Berlin, run by Karl Ernst, chief of the Berlin SA, and was forced to swallow his pride and ask Röhm to order its closure. But the most troublesome was the SS camp at Papenberg, in the far west of his domain not far from the Dutch border, where the guards opened fire on his police when they tried to enter the camp, hitting one officer in the abdomen. This time Göring had to go directly to Hitler himself to get control of the camp. According to Diels – whose memoirs are often unreliable and at times downright mischievous – the Führer actually gave him army artillery to break up SS resistance.[13]

It took until the early autumn before all the 'wild' camps were either closed or taken over, by which time, according to Diels's estimate, at least 700 prisoners had been brutally murdered, chiefly by the SA. The surviving internees were transferred to four official, state-controlled camps, all to be staffed by regular Prussian police, under Göring's direction: Papenberg, near Osnabrück; Sonnenburg, near Frankfurt an der Oder; Lichtenburg, near Merseburg; and Oranienburg, just north of Berlin. Göring remained in charge of them until early in 1934.

Some time in February or March 1933, Göring acquired a wonderful new weapon against opponents of the regime when Diels drew his attention to a recently invented Swiss system for tapping telephone lines and recording conversations, telegrams and cables on a large scale. Diels presumably saw it as a useful tool for the Gestapo in identifying fodder for the concentration camps. Göring, however, was quick to realise the edge it would give him over his rivals if he could have reports of all their telephone calls, both private and official. He also spotted its potential for foreign as well as internal intelligence, all of which would serve to reinforce his personal power.

Göring knew that Hitler, like himself, did not trust human agents and would welcome an intelligence source that did not rely on spies and subjective reports that could be distorted or faked. When he proposed creating a secret agency to intercept calls and cables, Hitler agreed at once, and gave him the absolute monopoly that he asked for on wire-tapping within the Reich, a monopoly that Göring guarded jealously right through to the end. Every new wire-tap had to be approved by him, with a warrant initialled at its foot with his distinctive big 'G'. His approval was not given lightly and every request had to be justified, especially when it came from the Gestapo in later years.

Göring gave his new agency the innocuous title of Forschungsamt – literally, Research Office – generally shortened to FA. It began operating some time in March, in the attic of a defunct bank in Behrenstrasse, with a staff of four. By July, it had expanded to twenty, absorbing the Defence Ministry's existing Cipher and Monitoring Office; eventually, it employed about 3,500, housed in a converted residential complex in Schillerstrasse, in the smart district of Charlottenburg, churning out reports and transcripts on its distinctive brown pages which by the end of the Second World War would number nearly half a million. It became one of the most efficient and effective intelligence sources of the time, tapping not only German telephone lines but also every one of the many international cables that crisscrossed the country or passed beneath its coastal waters, and maintaining an obsessive secrecy that was never breached. The one official who tried to sell information about it was caught and executed.

Göring liked to start each day by reading a selection of FA brown pages, laid on his breakfast tray in a special red folder by his valet, Robert Kropp. They often gave him great amusement, especially when they revealed indiscretions of political rivals, or jokes against himself, which he liked to collect. But generally, the results were more serious in their nature. The first oblique reference to the FA's work can be found in the minutes of the Cabinet meeting of 29 March 1933, when Göring told Hitler of 'exaggerated' reports being filed by foreign newspaper correspondents on anti-Jewish atrocities in Germany. 'The atrocity reports were principally cabled to America by the Hearst Press representative here, Deuss. This has been established beyond doubt by tapping his telephone conversations.' As a result, Hitler agreed that Deuss should be deported.

The FA began life under the aegis of the Prussian Minister-President's office, and Göring put Pilli Körner in charge of supervising it. But as it grew, he switched it to the Air Ministry, away from prying bureaucrats and police officials, and out of the reach of Frick, who was intent on centralising all police work under his Reich Interior Ministry. By emphasising the FA's role in gathering military and foreign intelligence through intercepting and decoding embassy messages, Göring was able to disguise its domestic activities, fund it from the virtually unlimited defence budget, and make sure it stayed within his growing personal empire.

*   *   *

While Göring was busy defending the police elements of his empire from Frick and the Reich Interior Ministry, a new threat to them both was starting to take shape almost unnoticed in Munich. In spite of its role as the cradle and home of the Nazi movement, Bavaria had been the last of the German states to succumb to *Gleichschaltung*, and easily the most troublesome, due in large part to its historic antagonism to central control from Berlin. The Nazis had failed to win the state elections, and the Catholic Bavarian Peoples' Party under Heinrich Held had formed a government that leaned not only to separatism but even to the old dream of restoring the Bavarian monarchy. By 9 March, however, the local Nazis could not be held back any longer. SA and SS squads marched through the streets of Munich, seized government buildings and raised the swastika flag over the city hall. Meanwhile, Röhm, Himmler and Gauleiter Adolf Wagner arrived in Held's office and demanded that he resign and hand over power to General Ritter von Epp, the man who had crushed Munich's Räterepublik in 1919, as Reich Commissioner. Held tried to resist, but his protests to Hindenburg and Papen went unheeded, the army was ordered 'to stand at parade rest' and not interfere by helping him, and Epp was appointed over his head.

Epp's first move was to appoint Wagner as his Interior Minister, and give Röhm an undefined role as State Commissioner for Special Duties, a sort of minister without portfolio. On the face of it, this was something of a put-down for Röhm, who for several weeks had been angling for a role as General Commissioner for Public Security for the whole Reich – or at the very least for all the non-Prussian states – which would have given him control of all police forces. Himmler, too, was given what seemed a disappointingly minor appointment by Wagner: he was to be Acting President of Munich City Police.

It soon became clear, however, that far from being sidelined, Himmler and Röhm had co-operated on working out a joint strategy that would give each of them what he wanted, though the way in which this was achieved – quietly, via the back door – bore all the hallmarks of Himmler's devious mind rather than Röhm's more bull-at-a-gate approach. Since Röhm was still Himmler's superior, he would get the lion's share, but even this would prove to be illusory. Like a chess player sacrificing a piece to gain future advantage, the ever-patient Himmler was content to accept the smaller portion in Bavaria, knowing he was playing a much bigger game for a much greater prize.

Himmler's 'minor appointment' was in fact a key position, and would be the essential launching pad for his future career. The various county and municipal police forces throughout Bavaria were all under local control, but Munich City Police acted as a central co-ordinator for the whole state, especially in political police matters. These were handled by its Department VI, backed up in the northern half of the state by the equivalent department of the Nuremberg City Police. Department VI worked directly with the Interior Ministry – where Wagner made Himmler head of the Political Section, reporting directly to him. Like many others, Wagner was taken in by Himmler's inoffensive air as a perpetual subordinate who could be relied on to do as he was told. On 26 March, he made him Acting Police President of Nuremberg-Fürth, too.

Leaving Röhm and the SA to take control of the regular police throughout the rest of Bavaria, Himmler concentrated his attention on building a separate, centralised Bavarian Political Police, closely linked to his SS and its intelligence arm, the Sicherheitsdienst (SD). And to make doubly sure of maintaining both the link and his own authority, he appointed the chief of the SD, Reinhard Heydrich, as head of Department VI. Heydrich, who had only just celebrated his twenty-ninth birthday, had been a party member for less than two years, and an SS officer for barely eighteen months. But in that short time, he had established himself as one of Himmler's most trusted and significant lieutenants, and was already well on his way to becoming the Reichsführer's *alter ego*. One of his later associates, Walter Schellenberg, described him in words that would be hard to better:

He was a tall, impressive figure with a broad, unusually high forehead, small restless eyes as crafty as an animal's and of uncanny power, a long predatory nose, and a wide full-lipped mouth. His hands were slender and rather too long – they made one think of the legs of a spider. His splendid figure was marred by the width of his hips, a disturbingly feminine effect which made him appear even more sinister. His voice was much too high for so large a man and his speech was nervous and staccato and though he scarcely ever finished a sentence, he always managed to express his meaning quite clearly . . . He was inordinately ambitious. It seemed as if, in a pack of ferocious wolves, he must always prove himself the strongest and assume the leadership. He had to be the first, the best, in everything, regardless of the means, whether by deceit, treachery or violence. Untouched by any pangs of conscience and assisted by an ice-cold intellect, he could carry injustice to the point of extreme cruelty.[14]

This was the man Himmler would come to depend upon as his closest collaborator and most indispensable aide during the years ahead, and who would eventually become a dangerous rival.

Born in Halle, near Leipzig, on 7 March 1904, Reinhard Eugen Tristan Heydrich grew up in a cultured middle-class environment: his father, Bruno, a Wagnerian opera singer, was the founder and director of the Halle Conservatory of Music; his mother, the daughter of a court tutor, was an accomplished pianist. The young Reinhard himself trained seriously as a violinist – as an adult he held regular chamber music evenings at his home, impressing everyone with the warmth and sensitivity of his playing, especially of his favourite composers, Mozart and Haydn.

Bruno Heydrich was an easy-going, gentle man, dominated by his shrewish, arrogant wife. Young Reinhard clearly took after his mother, and seems to have spent most of his childhood seeking to win the love she was incapable of expressing, save through fierce discipline and frequent whippings. Bullied and teased at school because of his unusually high voice, devout Catholicism – Halle was a mainly Protestant town – and rumoured Jewish ancestry, he tried to prove himself by excelling at everything, both academically and on the sports field. He was undoubtedly clever, though by no means brilliant, was a good natural athlete, later becoming a champion fencer and an excellent skier, horseman, pilot and modern pentathlete. The taunts of Jewishness struck deep, even though they were based on a misunderstanding: Heydrich's paternal grandmother's second husband had been called Süss, a name that was usually Jewish, though in fact he was not a Jew. Despite his denials, and later even being cleared by Himmler's investigators, doubts lingered and the stigma of Jewishness plagued Heydrich throughout his career.

The Heydrichs, like many other middle-class families, suffered some hardship after Germany's defeat and the Revolution of 1918. And, again like many other middle-class families, they blamed Jewish financiers and revolutionaries for both, and developed a pathological fear of the 'Red menace'. In 1920, at the age of sixteen, fired with patriotic fervour, Reinhard joined the local Freikorps and several *völkisch* organisations, though he was not directly involved in any violent action. With his family unable to afford the expense of university, he looked around for some other means of further education, preferably free and with some prestige attached. He settled on the navy, and at eighteen succeeded in winning one of the few, prized places as an officer cadet at Kiel.

After initial training ashore, Heydrich was posted to the cruiser *Berlin*, a move that was later to foster various myths about his career, since the ship's first officer was Captain Wilhelm Canaris, who was to become head of the Abwehr, German Military Intelligence. Canaris had served as an intelligence officer during the war, first in Admiral von Spree's cruiser squadron and later running agents in Spain reporting on Allied shipping movements. Legend has it that he had continued his intelligence career as a staff officer immediately after the war, and had been involved in various shady operations, from the murder of the Spartacist leaders to the Kapp *putsch* and the funding of Captain Ehrhardt's murderous Organisation Consul. In 1923, however, he was back at sea in a conventional role, responsible among other things for the training of young officers, including Heydrich. Canaris is said to have taken a shine to the lanky young man, and to have made him his protégé. Perhaps he sensed that they were both outsiders: although he was fiercely nationalistic, Canaris did not conform to the conventional image of the Prussian officer, and was nicknamed 'the Levantine', both because of his Italian ancestry and his labyrinthine mind.

Heydrich was never popular among his colleagues, who taunted him as 'the nanny-goat' because of his high-pitched voice, or as 'Moses Handel' – the stigma of suspected Jewish blood had followed him into the navy and his refined musical tastes set him still further apart. His violin playing, however, served to bring him closer to Canaris, whose cultured wife, Erika, was delighted to find such a talented performer to enhance her musical evenings. The two men formed a lasting relationship before Canaris was posted back to a staff position in 1924.

It may have been at Canaris's suggestion that Heydrich decided to specialise in signals and wireless, with its obvious connections with intelligence work. After training at the Naval Signals School, he became signals officer of the fleet flagship, the *Schleswig-Holstein*, and from there moved on to various positions in the Baltic Naval Station, learning Russian and reaching the rank of lieutenant. Despite a harsh and overbearing manner that made him even more unpopular with the other ranks than with his fellow officers, it seemed that he was all set for a successful career in the navy. But in 1931, due entirely to the inherent faults in his own character, he threw it all away.

There was only one element in Heydrich's nature that matched his ambition, and that was his sexual appetite. During his years of Nazi power, he would habitually trawl the bars and brothels of Berlin, usually with a reluctant aide in tow, forcing himself on any woman who took his fancy. As a young naval officer, he had seduced a whole string of girls, including a young student at the Kolonialschule in Rendsburg on the Kiel Canal, where her father was director of a shipyard. Presumably Heydrich got her into bed with the promise of marriage, because when he announced his engagement to another girl, Lina von Osten, the nineteen-year-old daughter of a schoolmaster, whom he had rescued from the water after a boating accident, she angrily demanded that he keep his word. He refused. She told her father, who in turn told his friend, Admiral Erich Raeder, the Commander-in-Chief of the Navy.

It has never been clear whether the girl was pregnant by Heydrich, but the assumption must be that she was. However, no doubt under pressure from Lina, who had the same iron-willed personality as his mother and was determined to have him for herself, he still declined to marry her and was hauled before a court of honour consisting of four senior naval officers. Even then, he might have got away with it, had he shown the slightest sign of humility or regret. Instead, not only did he treat the court with such presumption that it reprimanded him for insubordination, but he also accused the girl of lying and tried to throw the entire blame on to her. This was not the honourable conduct expected of an officer and a gentleman, and in its report, the court questioned whether he could remain in the navy. Raeder delivered his answer at the end of April 1931: 'Dismissed the service for impropriety.'[15]

Apologists and conspiracy theorists have argued over the years that Heydrich's dismissal was a put up job, a smoke screen designed to cover the 'real' reasons, which range from Heydrich's over-enthusiasm for the Nazi Party to Raeder and Canaris arranging to infiltrate him into the SS intelligence service as an informer. None of these fanciful notions holds water, however, and as is usually the case, the more mundane explanation is the genuine one: Heydrich was drummed out of the navy in disgrace. With no pension and no prospects, he was forced to hunt for a job at the peak of the Great Depression, when unemployment was soaring. He was not a Nazi supporter – 'He was just a professional naval officer, wedded to his naval career,' Lina later wrote. 'His only other interest was sport. He knew nothing about politics, and had never shown any great interest in them.'[16] Lina, however, was a convinced Nazi and she persuaded him that the rapidly expanding party might offer him the sort of opportunity he needed.[17]

Heydrich joined the Nazi Party in Hamburg on 1 June 1931, and immediately wrote to an old family friend, Baron Karl von Eberstein, who was now an SA-Oberführer, a senior colonel, in Munich, giving details of his nine-year naval career and asking for his help in obtaining 'a major leadership position'.[18] Led to believe that Heydrich's experience as a signals specialist meant he had been involved in intelligence work, Eberstein passed his letter to Himmler, who he knew was looking for someone to take charge of his SS security intelligence section, Ic. Himmler, who had once dreamed of becoming a naval officer himself, was impressed by Heydrich's CV, and by his Aryan appearance in his photograph, but procrastinated as usual, until Heydrich, egged on by Lina, engineered a meeting at the chicken farm in Waldtrudering. After bluffing his way through a brief interview, Heydrich was given twenty minutes to draft a job description and orders for the running of a counter-espionage section. Himmler was suitably impressed with the result, and promptly took him on.[19] It would prove to be the most important appointment he would ever make.

Heydrich moved to Munich to start work as director of the Ic section on Himmler's staff in the 'Brown House' on 10 August 1931, with the rank of Sturmführer, an SS lieutenant.[20] It was a small beginning – he was, in fact, the only member of the section, his entire databank was contained in two files handed to him by Himmler, and he had to share an office and a typewriter with another SS officer. He was twenty-seven years of age, a newcomer both to the party and to security service operations – but he began to make his presence felt at once, and to display his talent for manipulation.

On 26 August, hardly more than two weeks after taking up his post, he addressed a meeting of senior SS commanders and presented them with a horrifying statement, which he claimed was based on solid research, that the Nazi movement had been heavily infiltrated by spies and agents for the police and rival parties. Warning them to be on their guard against these enemies in their midst who had to be rooted out at all costs, he left his audience in no doubt that he was the man for the job, and that he expected their full co-operation. Heydrich's warning may have been intended to boost his own position, but it was not entirely groundless – his confidential speech was fully reported in Munich police files the following day.[21]

Nine days after Heydrich had addressed the commanders, SS-Order No 43 informed all SS units that: 'With immediate effect, every Abschnitt (division) will set up an Ic desk to deal with all intelligence activities within the Abschnitt. Subsequently, an Ic desk is envisaged for every SS-Standarte (regiment).'[22] Intelligence work had formerly been a small part of the regular duties of every adjutant; in future, it was to be handled by specialist Ic officers, answerable to Heydrich. It was the first step in the creation of his own empire within Himmler's empire, the first step on the ladder that would lead him to personal power second only to that of Himmler himself.

The overbearing arrogance and ruthless ambition that had blighted his naval career were seen as desirable qualities in the SS, and Heydrich rose swiftly in the hierarchy, soon achieving ranks he could only have dreamed of at his age had he stayed in the navy. He was promoted to Hauptsturmführer (captain) on 1 December, the month in which he finally married Lina von Osten; a month later he became a Sturmbannführer (major), and by the end of July 1932 he was a Standartenführer (full colonel). But his progress was largely meaningless: he was still basically a staff officer, with no departmental budget, and his Ic section was insignificant by comparison with the two other intelligence services within the party, the Nachrichtendienst (ND), operated in each Gau by Goebbels's Reich Propaganda Department, and the SA's own substantial Ic section. Although he had moved out of the 'Brown House' into a two-roomed apartment early in the New Year, his entire staff still consisted only of himself and two or three assistants, operating under the cover of a press and information office, to which Himmler was officially entitled as a Reichstag deputy.

Because Heydrich's section was so small, and because the police, possibly influenced by an informer whom he had turned into a double-agent, seem to have accepted its cover as Himmler's press office, it survived intact when a series of police raids exposed and discredited the SA's Ic section. And when the SA and SS were banned in April 1932, Heydrich was able to continue his operations without interruption. By coincidence, Goebbels's ND organisation fell apart at this time, ravaged by incompetence and in-fighting, so that when Papen lifted the ban on paramilitary organisations in June 1932, Heydrich's SS Ic section was the party's only viable intelligence service.

Again by coincidence, the party leadership realised that if it was to control the increasingly powerful local barons in the party and the SA, it needed a centralised intelligence service to keep an eye on them and report their activities to the 'Brown House' so that any disloyalty or dissent could be stamped out. Himmler saw both the need and the opportunity, and set about fulfilling them by turning his Ic section into a new agency, the Sicherheitsdienst-SS (SS Security Service), known for short as the SD, under the direction of Heydrich and charged with discovering any threat to the party, whether internal or external. It was a natural development of the SS's role as the party's internal police force, and Rudolf Hess, as head of the party's Central Directorate, gave it his blessing: only the SS could be trusted completely to report on the SA and on party bosses. But what probably clinched matters for Hess was that, unlike Goebbels and Röhm, the other contenders for the security service, Himmler appeared to pose no personal threat to his own position in the party pecking order.

For the rest of 1932 and the early part of 1933, Heydrich devoted himself to recruiting personnel and establishing a network of SD officers and agents throughout Germany. Although his headquarters remained in Munich, Berlin was the essential fulcrum for any national operation, and he moved there towards the end of the year, with Lina, who was expecting their first child. Initially, Daluege, as commander of SS Group East, welcomed the newcomer and co-operated closely with him. But everything changed after Daluege became Göring's Special Commissioner and began setting up his own intelligence service in the Prussian Interior Ministry. Seeing Heydrich as Himmler's man and resenting his intrusion into his fiefdom, he put up the shutters and refused to talk to him. Heydrich suddenly found that he was *persona non grata* in Berlin, unable to get past Daluege's aides and receptionists. It was a slap in the face but by then it hardy mattered. Events were moving fast in Bavaria, and on 9 March 1933 Himmler called him back to Munich, where he had an exciting new job waiting for him.

At first, Heydrich failed to see the significance of his new post as head of Political Department VI of the Munich Police. He was more focused on extending his SD network and even tried to carry out his new role while commuting from Berlin. But by the end of the month, Himmler had relinquished his position as City Police President, handing over control of all regular police work to the SA in return for a separate Bavarian Political Police (BPP) independent of the regular police and under his personal control as Reichsführer-SS. The new BPP was the equivalent of Göring's Gestapo, and Heydrich was to be its chief.

Himmler's plan – the next stage in his overall grand design – was to repeat the Bavarian process in all the German states outside Prussia, with Heydrich's SD men taking charge of each new political police force. As members of the SS, they would, of course, all be answerable to Himmler, who would thus gain overall control of the entire non-Prussian political police apparatus. It would then only be a matter of taking the Gestapo away from Göring – admittedly not an easy task but by no means impossible – and Himmler would have under his command a unified Reich political police which would be synonymous with the SS. The real power this would give him in a police state was enormous, and Heydrich would enjoy a large share of it.

Himmler's SS empire was now expanding exponentially. Having delegated responsibility for political police work to Heydrich, he turned his attention to the SS as a whole, which was outgrowing even his legendary capacity for detailed administration. He needed a deputy, an adjutant, to relieve him of some of the burden, and the man he chose for this vital position was Karl Wolff, a bright and personable young officer, who exemplified Himmler's claims that the SS was an elite organisation. Six feet tall, with blue eyes and fair hair, he was the perfect Aryan specimen, with no Semitic skeletons in his cupboard and an impeccably upper middle-class background: his father was a district judge in Darmstadt, and he had been educated at the best *Gymnasium* in the city. Although only six months older than Himmler himself, he had served during the war in the prestigious Hessian Horse Guards Regiment 115, led by the Grand Duke of Hesse-Darmstadt in person, spending a year in action at the front, where he won promotion to lieutenant and the Iron Cross First and Second Class. After the war, he had married into a good family and following a number of jobs in banking and commerce had run his own advertising agency in Hamburg, until it was bankrupted by the economic collapse of 1931. Seeking a way out of the slough of despond, he turned to the SS, along with many other bitter and disillusioned young businessmen and professionals, including Heydrich, who joined at much the same time. Choosing Wolff as his adjutant was a wise move by Himmler, for he was intelligent, hard working, and moved easily in both army and big business circles. The two men soon developed a close relationship, and Himmler took to calling Wolff by the affectionate diminutive '*Wolffchen*' as a mark of his personal regard.

Once the Nazis had taken power in Bavaria, events there echoed those that had already taken place in Prussia, but with one or two significant differences. Wagner set up auxiliary police, just as Göring had done, but he divided them into two distinct branches: the Auxiliary Security Police, under the overall command of Röhm, drawn from the SA and Stahlhelm, and the Political Auxiliary Police, which was in effect the SS, commanded by Himmler as Reichsführer-SS. When the great wave of arrests of Communists, Socialists, and other opponents of the new regime flooded Bavarian jails, the SA and SS were empowered to imprison their opponents in officially approved camps, funded by the state.

Initially, there were camps run by the SA and SS in every sizeable town and city in Bavaria, but Himmler, with his obsessive concern with orderliness, moved quickly to bring them all under his centralised control. In marked contrast to the problems Göring faced, his deal with Röhm meant he had little trouble in removing the SA from the picture, and the SS were his own men anyway. On 21 March he announced to the press that he was opening a new main concentration camp in a disused former explosives factory near the village of Dachau, on the outskirts of Munich. It would hold up to 5,000 Communist and Social Democrat political prisoners.[23]

To emphasise the camp's legitimacy, Himmler first staffed it with policemen, under the command of a regular state police officer. But when this officer complained about conditions in the camp and questioned the legality of some arrests, he replaced him with SS-Obersturmführer Hilmar Wäckerle, and the guards with members of the Political Auxiliary Police – in other words, SS men. Under orders from Himmler, Wäckerle issued regulations stating that prisoners 'who made trouble' were to be executed, and within the next six weeks at least eleven men – all but one of whom were Communists or Jews – were either shot 'while fleeing or attacking guards' or 'committed suicide'. In the outcry that followed, Himmler's opponents within the Bavarian leadership, including Epp and the provisional Justice Minister, Hans Frank, began pressing murder charges. Himmler, however, asserted that since all the inmates of Dachau were political prisoners held under the emergency regulations, they were outside the normal judicial and criminal systems, and the charges were dropped. He quickly established the principle, which was later to be extended to the whole Reich, that 'protective custody' was the sole prerogative of the political police and anything connected with it was off limits to everyone else.

As a sop to his critics, Himmler fired Wäckerle. He then replaced him with the even more vicious Theodor Eicke, a forty-one-year-old former policeman and security officer with the giant IG Farben chemical trust, who had been in more or less constant trouble since leaving the army paymaster's department at the end of the war. Before he could take up his post, Himmler had to rescue him from a psychiatric hospital, to which he had been committed by an angry Gauleiter after he had led a local SA and SS revolt. It was a debt Eicke would never forget. Eicke took to his new job with enthusiasm as well as gratitude: he was to be the architect and chief of the Nazi concentration-camp system, founding the infamous Death's Head formations of camp guards and replacing the random brutality of the SA camps with disciplined, institutionalised violence and terror.

Himmler's growing power base rested solidly on the three elements, the SS, the Political Police and the camps, which were intertwined and interdependent, and yet kept strictly separate. What went on in the camps was entirely Eicke's preserve and he was answerable directly and only to Himmler. Heydrich was responsible for sending people to the camps, and for deciding if and when they should be released, but had no say whatsoever in what happened to them while they were inside. Similarly, Wolff had no jurisdiction over either the camps or the Political Police. By separating the authority of his three principal aides and restricting each to his own area, Himmler was making sure that none of them would be strong enough to threaten his own position.

During March, Himmler had strengthened his personal position, and that of the SS, by playing on Hitler's paranoia. Among the political prisoners he had arrested in Munich was Count Anton von Arco-Valley, the man who had murdered Bavarian Minister-President Eisner in 1919, and who had been moved from his cell in Landsberg to make room for Hitler in 1923. Himmler claimed that Arco-Valley had admitted to plotting a *coup* against Hitler.[24] Himmler duly claimed his brownie points for this, and for foiling an assassination attempt by three Soviet agents, who had 'placed three hand grenades near the Richard Wagner Memorial where Adolf Hitler's car was bound to pass'.[25] A few days later, he was warning the Führer: 'Through information from Switzerland we have, for several days, been aware that attacks on the Reich Chancellor, Adolf Hitler, and on leading personalities of the new state, have been planned by the Communists.'

Hitler needed little convincing that such threats were genuine. At virtually every Cabinet meeting he made some reference to them: 'The effect of a successful attack on me would be fearful,' he told ministers on 7 March. Even in the Chancellery he did not feel secure – the guards were provided by the army, and past experience had undermined his trust in the generals. There was, however, one man and one organisation he knew he could trust implicitly: the faithful Heinrich Himmler, always so concerned for his safety, and his SS. On his orders, Himmler provided 120 hand-picked men for his personal protection, under the command of a beefy Bavarian, SS-Gruppenführer Josef (Sepp) Dietrich. Later in the year, he gave this special unit the name Leibstandarte-SS Adolf Hitler, the Adolf Hitler Bodyguard.

Having gained Hitler's trust and with the three-part structure of his personal power base firmly established, Himmler was now poised to begin expanding his operations from Bavaria to the rest of the Reich. It would take the best part of a year, and it would of course be done quietly and unobtrusively, but once started his rise would be inexorable.

XIV

THE END OF THE BROWN REVOLUTION

WITH power secured and the Communists taken care of, Hitler and the Nazis could turn their attentions to their other enemies without fear of opposition, at least from inside Germany. These enemies included the Social Democrats, the trade unions, and even the Catholic Church, but at the top of the list were the Jews. The SA, of course, had been attacking Jews for years, insolently accepting the occasional arrest as part of the game, but after the March elections even the slightest chance of legal interference was removed. On 9 March 1933, Goebbels gave the nod to Berlin storm-troopers to begin an organised assault on the city's 160,000 Jews. Working in groups of between five and thirty men, they rampaged through the streets pouncing on any Jews they encountered. The *Manchester Guardian* reported that many were beaten 'until the blood streamed down their heads and faces, and their backs and shoulders were bruised. Many fainted and were left lying on the streets.'[1]

Over the following days and weeks, the attacks intensified and spread through other towns and cities. Those who had been brave enough to speak out in the past were singled out for especially savage treatment. In another report, the *Manchester Guardian* told how a Jewish businessman and money-lender in Straubing, Lower Bavaria, who had won a libel action against a Nazi deputy in the Bavarian Landtag, was dragged out of bed by four armed men who smashed their way into his home, drove him away in a car and shot him dead.[2] A young Jewish baker's apprentice in Berlin had previously brought charges of assault against SA thugs, who had been arrested and convicted. Now they took their revenge, dragging him off to their barracks, where they beat him to death. Before they threw his naked body on to the street from an upstairs window, they took their daggers and carved a large swastika into his chest. This time there were no arrests and no convictions.[3]

There was little mention of the attacks in the German news media, which Goebbels was already censoring, but he could do nothing about the foreign press. Around the world, indignation and anger mounted, especially in countries with significant Jewish populations like the United States, where the American Jewish Congress began campaigning for a world-wide boycott of German goods. Reaction in the party was swift: led by the arch anti-Semite Julius Streicher, Gauleiter of Franconia, the Nazi radicals screamed for a counter-boycott of Jewish shops, department stores and businesses in Germany. Goebbels had been pouring out anti-Semitic articles for the German press ever since the election, but now he did his best to place pieces in foreign papers, too, to counter what he called 'the Jewish horrors propaganda' abroad. On 26 March he noted smugly 'My article against horrors propaganda is published in the *Sunday Express*, and has a good effect. It makes things a bit easier for us in England.'[4]

When the *Sunday Express* article was published, Goebbels was in Berchtesgaden, summoned by Hitler, who had 'thoroughly thought over the situation in the solitude of the mountains'[5] and had decided what was to be done. Germany would mount its own boycott of Jewish businesses, starting on 1 April, to be organised and run by a central committee of thirteen party zealots under the leadership of Streicher. Göring, always ambivalent about anti-Semitism, was conspicuously omitted, as was Frick. But Himmler was one of the thirteen, and so, too, was Goebbels's protégé, twenty-eight-year-old Reinhold Muchow, who had been his organisation leader for the Greater Berlin Gau and who had pioneered the introduction of party cells in factories. Goebbels, though perhaps disappointed not to be put in overall charge, was to draft and publish the necessary proclamations and sell the operation not just to the party but also to the German public, which he did so successfully with articles, speeches and broadcasts that it was his name that was always associated with the boycott. The line he peddled, both nationally and internationally, was that actions against the Jews were defensive measures, which a reluctant Germany was forced to take to protect itself against the antagonism of international Jewry. 'The Jews of the whole world are trying to destroy Germany!' his posters shrieked across the nation. 'German people defend yourselves! Don't buy from the Jews!'[6]

In fact, the boycott was not a great success, except as an ominous warning to German Jews. The response from the general public in Germany was ambivalent, while the international outcry was so strong that Schacht and Foreign Minister Neurath pleaded with Hitler to call it off, fearing it would have disastrous results on the German economy and on the country's standing abroad. Some went even further, as Goebbels noted on 31 March: 'Many are downhearted and apprehensive. They believe the boycott might lead to a war.'[7] Hitler turned the situation to his advantage, telling the American, British and French governments that he would only postpone or call off the German boycott of Jewish businesses if they declared their official opposition to any boycott of German goods in their countries. To his surprise, they all caved in and rushed to appease him: his first attempt at international blackmail had worked.

In the event, the action went ahead – it would have been impossible to hold back the SA at that stage – but for one day only, on 1 April. Since that was a Saturday, many Jewish businesses were closed anyway, but the storm-troopers took to the streets in force, posting men outside Jewish-owned shops and department stores, holding placards telling people not to enter, daubing large yellow Stars of David and the single word 'Jude' (Jew) on the windows, along with anti-Jewish slogans. 'In many cases,' Lady Rumbold, the wife of the British Ambassador wrote to a friend, 'special notices were put up saying that sweated labour was employed in that particular shop, and often you saw caricatures of Jewish noses. It was utterly cruel and Hunnish the whole thing, just doing down a heap of defenceless people.'[8]

In general, there was little violence on the day. People thronged to the shops and stores out of curiosity, and many of them made a point of buying something, no matter what. The English novelist, Christopher Isherwood, for example, acquired a totally unnecessary nutmeg grater, the first thing he saw in the store he entered, and left twirling it in the face of the young SA man at the door, who responded with a wink.[9] Not everyone was so lucky, however – a lawyer in Kiel who dared to argue with storm-troopers was hauled off to SA headquarters and shot. This 'lynching' was headline news in most foreign newspapers, but Hitler simply ignored it, claiming in his next speech that 'the Jews of Germany had not had a hair of their heads ruffled'.[10] Goebbels was only too happy to share his Führer's selective blindness, describing the day as 'an impressive spectacle' and praising the storm-troopers' 'perfect discipline'.

Goebbels had a busy day of it, bustling around Berlin, making sure everybody saw him as the face of the regime. He spent the morning touring the main shopping streets of the West End; in the afternoon, he addressed what he claimed were 150,000 workmen in the Lustgarten, 'parading to unite their protest with ours against the horrors propaganda abroad'; in the evening he returned to the same spot to speak to 100,000 boys of the Hitler Youth, before dashing across the city to the Bismarck Tower on the Müggelberge hill in the Köpenick district, where a crowd of students were taking vows of loyalty to the Reich.[11] His speeches at the Lustgarten were broadcast to the whole nation – the day may not have been particularly successful as a boycott, but as a piece of self-promotion for Joseph Goebbels, it was a triumph.

A week later, on 7 April, Goebbels played a leading role in a six-hour Cabinet meeting which not only confirmed the end of Germany's federal system through a retrospective Law for the Co-ordination (*Gleichschaltung*) of the States within the Reich, but also began the process of legally excluding Jews and political opponents of the Nazis from public life. This was achieved with two measures: the euphemistically-named Law for the Restoration of the Professional Civil Service, and the Law on the Admission to the Practice of Law. Neither of the new laws specifically mentioned Jews, Socialists or Communists, speaking only of people who were 'not of Aryan descent' – defined as those who had even one 'non-Aryan' grandparent – and those who 'on the basis of their former political activities did not offer the assurance that they supported the national state without reservation'. Both categories were banned from the civil service – which included not only ministry and local officials but also teachers, academics and doctors in state hospitals – and from practising law. The only exceptions, at Hindenburg's insistence, were Jews who had served at the front in the First World War. There would be many further laws and decrees in the near future, but the groundwork was now firmly in place. 'One may well say that today history is being remade in Germany,' Goebbels rejoiced.[12]

That same marathon Cabinet meeting on 7 April also approved Goebbels's plan to make May Day a national holiday, a clever wheeze to steal the Communists' and Socialists' clothes and attract new followers among the workers. As a former Marxist himself, he well knew how thin the dividing line between the two philosophies was for them – indeed, large numbers of Red Front Fighters who enjoyed a good punch-up had already switched to the SA, where cynical Berliners nicknamed them 'beefsteak Nazis, brown on the outside, red on the inside'. He also knew how much they enjoyed the traditional gala atmosphere of May Day and how much they would miss it. Well, he would give them new galas, with the renamed 'National Day of Labour'. The idea was generally well received: Goebbels was both gratified and amused when the leaders of the Christian Trade Unions called on him to promise that their members would march with the Nazis in the parade, in return for what they called 'a fair deal'. 'Harmless, naïve souls!' he scoffed to his diary. 'As if we depended in any way on the Christian Trade Unions in our appeal to the whole German people! They do not yet seem to realise what is really going on. Within six months they will have been completely swept away, and will have no influence.'[13]

Goebbels ordered preparations to be started at once for the May Day celebrations, which were to culminate in the evening with parades and displays and speeches on Berlin's Tempelhof Field. His planning was meticulous, especially for the 'spontaneous' demonstrations of joy that he demanded. But the initial designs for the setting were less than inspiring. As Albert Speer, who happened to see them lying on his friend Hanke's desk while visiting the Propaganda Ministry, later recalled, they 'outraged both my revolutionary and architectural feelings'. 'Those look like the decorations for a rifle club meet,' he exclaimed. Hanke responded with a challenge: 'If you can do better, go to it.'[14] Speer could, and did. That same night, he sketched out his ideas for a huge speaker's platform backed by fifteen-metre-high red, white and black banners hanging vertically from wooden frames, interspersed with swastika banners, and illuminated from below by powerful searchlights shining straight up to the sky to create a 'cathedral of light'. It was pure melodrama.

Speer's boss in his day job at the Berlin Technical University, Professor Heinrich Tessenow, dismissed the designs as showy – 'They are big, that's all' – but Hanke thought they were terrific, and passed them to Goebbels, who in turn presented them to Hitler, who was delighted. Goebbels promptly claimed them as his own idea. The 'National Day of Labour' went ahead, with Speer's designs, and was a great success. The style had been set for future Nazi rallies, and Goebbels was happy to take the credit.

The next day, Goebbels's prophecy was fulfilled when the SA and

SS occupied trades union offices throughout Germany and the unions were all subsumed into one giant, compulsory organisation, the German Labour Front – apart from the Christian unions, which were allowed to survive until June. Other union leaders were arrested and imprisoned. The Labour Front was, of course, a subsidiary arm of the Nazi Party, and was under Robert Ley, the Gauleiter of Cologne. Although Ley was an habitual drunkard, he was an astute political operator and his new power base, backed by all the considerable financial resources he had grabbed from the unions, made him a potential rival, on whom Goebbels would have to keep a nervous eye.

Before the May Day festivities, Goebbels enjoyed two more triumphs, one in establishing Hitler's birthday, 20 April, as a national event with parades and bands and showers of presents, the other a much more personal affair. On 25 April he returned to his home town of Rheydt, to receive the freedom of the city. Only nine months before, he had been driven out by a stone-throwing mob; now, the town square was packed with a cheering crowd, he was fêted at his old school and honoured with special dramatic performances and public eulogies. He ended the day standing in an open car outside his mother's house with raised arm in the Hitler fashion, reviewing a torchlight procession of townsfolk. And to cap it all, Dahlener Strasse, where the house stood, was renamed Joseph-Goebbels-Strasse.

Goebbels could hardly have asked for a sweeter triumph – or for more convincing proof of the baseness of the humanity he so despised. The baseness of his own character is revealed yet again by his diary for that day. Claiming that he only 'put up with' the great reception for the sake of his mother, who had suffered 'calumny and persecution' for years because of him, he notes self-righteously: 'One knows what this sort of thing is like. To be a social outcast is to be mortally stricken . . . When one is defenceless as well as sensitive, one may break down completely under this kind of cruelty.' With unconscious irony, the entry for the day concludes: 'In Cabinet, the new law against the Jews is passed. A decisive step forward.'[15]

Goebbels was not the only one to be laying the ghosts of his past that April. Over Easter, Göring had returned to Italy, with its memories of heartbreak and frustration and, of course, of Carin. The contrast with those dark days nine years before could hardly have been more marked. Then, he had been a hunted, wounded outlaw; now he was a man of power and substance, on an official mission: Hitler had sent him as his special emissary to establish friendly relations with Mussolini, and to convince the Duce that Germany had no designs on Austria, which of course shared a border with Italy. He was also to disarm the Vatican by persuading the clerics that the Nazis were not as anti-Catholic as they were painted, but were the Church's ally in their determination to destroy its most deadly enemy, Communism.

Göring relished the idea of acting as an alternative Foreign Minister in place of the veteran diplomat Konstantin von Neurath, who was implacably hostile to the Fascist government. To impress the Italians with his current status, he had arranged that Hitler would telegraph an open message to him on the day of his arrival, 10 April, confirming his appointment as Minister-President of Prussia, despite the embarrassment this would cause Papen, who was accompanying him. The manoeuvre clearly worked, for he saw Mussolini at least three times, and went home with a sparkling Italian decoration to add to his war medals, the first of what would become a large collection.

He also met the Pope, though as a nominal Protestant he was happy to leave most of the talking to Papen, who was a Catholic. Papen's discussions with the Vatican marked a rapprochement with the Church authorities that was sealed in July by a Concordat, signed by Papen for the Reich and the Papal Secretary of State, Monsignor Eugenio Pacelli, former Papal Nuncio to Germany and the future Pope Pius XII, for the Vatican. Guaranteeing the Church's right 'to regulate its own affairs' in return for an undertaking not to interfere in political matters, this effectively silenced Catholic opposition in Germany. The head of the Church in Bavaria, Cardinal Faulhaber, who had been an outspoken critic of the Nazis, was now ready to turn a blind eye to their excesses and write a fulsome letter of congratulation to Hitler ending 'May God preserve the Reich Chancellor for our people'.[16]

For Göring, the most important meetings during his stay in Rome were with General Italo Balbo, the Minister of Aviation and a war hero like himself. The goatee-bearded Balbo was an even more flamboyant character than Göring, equally addicted to glitzy uniforms and grand gestures – he was for ever staging air shows, and enjoyed sending flights of huge aircraft across the seas to demonstrate the glories of Fascist aviation. In 1931, he had despatched a squadron of nine aircraft on a pioneering flight across the South Atlantic, which had considerably boosted Italy's prestige. Now, he was planning an even more spectacular triumph: in July 1933, he would lead a flight of no fewer than twenty-four Savoia Marchetti flying boats across the North Atlantic to land on Lake Michigan to a rapturous reception from the citizens of Chicago, whose population included some 300,000 Italian-Americans. Balbo was fêted like some conquering hero, even having a street renamed after him. And since the city was then hosting the World's Fair exposition, his fame became international, threatening to eclipse that of Mussolini himself. This, of course, was a grave mistake. On his return home, the Duce honoured him by promoting him to the rank of Air Marshal, then got him out of the way, removing him from office and sending him to govern Libya instead. The Italian Air Force, which had been one of the most advanced in the world, was allowed to wither into obsolescence. One of its first acts when Italy entered the Second World War was accidentally to shoot down and kill Balbo himself.[17]

In April 1933, however, Balbo was still literally flying high and still had much to offer the German fledgelings. Göring had taken Milch along with him, and between them they worked out the details of how Italy could help kickstart the new Luftwaffe behind the backs of the Allied powers. Initially, the most useful thing was the training of pilots, which Balbo agreed to provide. The first carefully selected contingent of German fliers included the young Adolf Galland, who was to become Germany's top fighter ace in the Second World War, and who later recalled that he returned from Italy in the autumn of 1933, 'an almost perfectly trained fighter pilot'. Nicolaus von Below, however, who was later to become Hitler's Luftwaffe adjutant, regarded his few weeks in Italy as 'unprofitable'. 'The Italian instructors,' he wrote, 'had no intention of being of any use whatever to us.' He thought he had learned more at Lipezk in the Soviet Union, where he had been one of ten 'Black Luftwaffe' trainees for five months back in 1929.[18] The following year, newly commissioned but still appearing as a civilian, Galland began training fighter pilots in secret at the German Commercial Flying School at Schleissheim.[19] Göring's future bomber crews, meanwhile, were practising long-distance night flying with an air parcels service between Berlin and East Prussia for the Reich railways.

Göring was in a hurry to get the foundations laid for his Luftwaffe. At the start of 1933, he had promised his old flying colleagues and the aircraft manufacturers that the German Air Force would be reborn; and now that Hitler had given him the green light, he had no intention of letting anything stand in his way. He was happy to leave Milch to handle the details – never his strong point anyway – but when his

State Secretary presented him with his schedule for setting up the complex infrastructure needed for the new air force, he simply laughed at him. 'You're planning to do all this over the next five years?' he scoffed. 'You've got six months!'

His attitude to the recruitment of senior officers was equally cavalier. With Hitler's backing, he cherry-picked the best officers from the army, over the protests of Defence Minister Blomberg. These included Colonels Walter Wever, who had been earmarked as a potential Commander-in-Chief, to be his Chief of Air Staff, Albert Kesselring, to be the head of administration, and Hans-Jürgen Stumpff as his personnel chief. Stumpff then took over recruitment, choosing 182 officers from the army and 42 from the navy's air service during the first year.

An air force, of course, is nothing without aircraft. Fulfilling his January promise to the manufacturers, Göring authorised Milch to issue contracts for the construction of 1,000 planes, backed by substantial government credits. They were to be prototype bombers, fighters and military transport planes masquerading as civilian aircraft, such as the Junkers 52, Heinkel 111, Focke-Wulf FW-200 and the Dornier flying boat. It was a tall order for an industry that then employed only 3,500 people nationally, but Göring was determined that it must grow, and grow fast. Quality might suffer at first as inexperienced men were recruited, but they could and must be trained: with six million unemployed, there were plenty of engineers and craftsmen to choose from who already had skills that could be swiftly adapted.

To lead the way, Göring nationalised the largest company, Junkers, which at the time had the capacity to build only eighteen Ju-52 transports a year, and poured money into it. Within months, it was employing 9,000 men in its assembly plants, with another 4,500 producing aero engines. At the same time, hundreds of thousands of men were put to work building airfields and barracks, ostensibly for organisations like the 'Reich Autobahn Air Transport Centre'. Although it was still strictly under wraps, the Luftwaffe was taking shape at Göring's usual breakneck speed.

As long as the development of the Luftwaffe remained secret, people could be deceived into thinking that Göring's position as Air Minister was merely a pleasant sinecure in recognition of his past and his special interest in flying. There was no such delusion about another position

Hitler gave him at that time, as Master of the German Hunt, to be followed shortly afterwards by that of Master of the German Forests. This was pure pleasure, but it was pleasure that he took extremely seriously.

Hunting had been a passion since boyhood, when he was given his first gun and his first lessons by his godfather, Epenstein, and he was proud of his ability as a first-rate shot. He spent as many weekends as possible stalking and shooting in the forests and heaths north of Berlin, particularly in the Schorfheide, a vast wilderness of woods, moorland and lakes that stretched away to the Polish frontier in the east and almost to the shores of the Baltic in the north. It was an area that he loved, and now that he was virtual dictator of Prussia, he made himself a present of a large chunk of it, persuading his government to set aside about 100,000 acres as his personal estate. At its centre, over-looking the Wackersee lake, he planned to build a hunting lodge to his own specifications, based on a Swedish lodge on the von Rosen estate. It was to be called Carinhall, as a memorial to his late wife. When her grave in Stockholm was defaced by anti-Nazi protesters while he was attending a family wedding that summer, he decided to build a granite mausoleum, facing the house across the lake, and to bring her body back to lie in it, waiting for him to join her.

The house was comparatively modest to begin with, though over the years it would expand into a grandiose Nordic palace fit for an emperor. It was completed in just ten months under the supervision of two young Prussian government architects, but it was entirely Göring's creation – he chose every fitting and feature himself, including designing what he regarded as suitably rustic outfits for the staff in green and gold – and it reflected his personality exactly: expansive, opulent, and filled with a strangely childlike delight in showy and often tasteless possessions. It also gave him yet another opportunity to dress up, this time in pseudo-medieval outfits of long leather jerkins, soft top boots, and voluminous silk shirts, and to march around his house and estate carrying a spear.

For all the grand reception areas, the sweeping staircases, the base-ment swimming pool and gymnasium, and the works of art that he crammed in everywhere, the most revealing room in the house was probably the eighty-foot-long space in the attic, where he installed a massive model railway layout, with straight runs of track stretching sixty feet and the finest locomotives and rolling stock money could buy. The whole thing was operated from a control panel installed beside a large red leather armchair, so that Göring, the eternal schoolboy, could play with his trains in comfort. At a later stage he introduced model aircraft on wires, which could swoop on the trains and drop dummy bombs on them, to add to the fun. Another source of innocent pleasure were the young lions he had taken to keeping as pets, and which had the run of the house and garden, to the consternation of many visitors. No doubt he kept them primarily for effect, but at the same time he treated them with genuine affection, which they seemed to return.

While Carinhall was being built Göring pressed ahead with turning the rest of his domain into a game reserve where he could entertain shooting parties of statesmen, kings, princes, industrialists and anybody else he wanted to impress. He restocked the forests with species of bird and animal that had been hunted almost out of existence, imported elk and bison from Canada, Sweden and East Prussia, reintroduced wild horses and rare varieties of deer, and instituted carefully controlled breeding programmes. He imposed new controls, at first in Prussia and then throughout the Reich, to regulate hunting, outlawing the use of poisons, lights, snares and steel traps, and fostering conservation measures that were decades ahead of their time, some of which have survived to this day. Hunters were tested to prove they could handle a gun before they were issued with a mandatory licence, were limited to strict quotas of kills, and had to have trained retriever dogs with them, so that wounded animals could be found and painlessly destroyed. And to reinforce his standing as an animal lover, he introduced a tough new law banning vivisection.

As Master of the German Forests, Göring's behaviour was equally admirable, instituting a number of reforms designed to combine the efficient exploitation of one of Germany's most important natural resources with far-reaching measures for conservation and renewal. He also inaugurated schemes for creating 'green lungs' around German cities that doubled as wildlife sanctuaries and recreation areas for the urban population, another surviving example of his few positive legacies.

Goebbels's pet loves were both more urban and more urbane than Göring's. His pleasures, apart from sex, were mainly intellectual, his interests cultural: he had been an avid opera-goer since his student days, he enjoyed good music, liked going to the theatre and was reasonably well-read; newspapers and journalism were an important part of his life, and he was excited by the potential of broadcasting; but his great passion was the cinema. He was a considerable film buff, and his diaries are full of cinema visits, sometimes several times a week, often accompanied by Hitler before the seizure of power. If Göring's idea of heaven was a wild heath stocked with an everlasting supply of happy, healthy game, Goebbels's was surely a darkened room pierced by a flickering beam of light projected on to a silver screen, preferably with a beautiful film actress by his side. In his new position, he realised that all this – film, broadcasting, theatre, music, books, the press – could be his to command. If he played his cards cleverly enough, he could become the absolute tsar of Germany's cultural life. No rejected writer could ever have hoped for so sweet a prize.

Throughout 1933, Goebbels worked assiduously to establish and extend his areas of control. It was not always easy. Most of them were the existing territory of other ministers, who were naturally reluctant to let go of anything that contributed to their own power, while others were coveted by his competitors in the Nazi rat race. His first task was to relieve Frick of the overall supervision of all things cultural, including the press, radio, music, art, films and theatre, which had traditionally been the preserve of the Interior Ministry. This could have been a problem, but Funk went to work at once and soon persuaded Frick that it was Hitler's wish that this role should be handed over to Goebbels. By 19 April, after spending Easter on the Obersalzberg with Hitler, Goebbels was able to write: 'I have now settled the areas of authority of my own ministry in connection with the other ministries concerned. The responsibilities of my department are defined in all directions. The entire cultural department of the Interior Ministry is now in my province.'[20]

The Interior Ministry was not Goebbels's only benefactor. The Economics Ministry had to hand over responsibility for all commercial promotion, exhibitions, trade fairs and advertising; the Transport Ministry gave him control of advertising on transport; and finally, after a bitter struggle, the Foreign Office was forced to relinquish all propaganda abroad, as well as art exhibitions, films and sports, and the Reich Government Press Office.

For Goebbels, the most important areas were radio and the press, the two most powerful and direct tools for controlling the flow of information and shaping public opinion. Even before he joined the Cabinet, he had begun the process of bringing them to heel, through

1. The young high flier: Göring became a fighter pilot in 1915, and scored his first kill that year. Shortly after this picture was taken, in 1916, he was himself shot down and seriously wounded. 2. 'Our successful combat flier, Oberleutnant Göring': by 1918, Göring had become a decorated war hero, displaying the coveted 'Pour le Mérite' in this patriotic postcard, and commanding the prestigious Richthofen Squadron. 3. Five years later, in 1923, he was commander of the Nazis' paramilitary SA – and still displaying his 'Pour le Mérite' as he posed for a different postcard. 4. Ernst Röhm ended the First World War as a regular army captain, his face bearing the scars of honourable wounds. But he soon became known as 'the machine-gun king', supplying weapons to revolutionary paramilitaries.

5. Rudolf Hess, seen here with Freikorps leader Gerhard Rossbach, relaxes happily outside the Munich Bürgerbräukeller on 9 November 1923, just before the start of Hitler's march on the city centre.

6. Behind the barricade outside the Bavarian War Ministry during the attempted *putsch*, Himmler holds the imperial banner.

7. The young firebrand: Goebbels, recently appointed Gauleiter of Berlin, makes one of his inflammatory speeches in March 1927. 8. In December 1931, Goebbels married Magda Quandt, whose son, Harald, accompanied them beneath the raised arms of an SA honour guard. Hitler, following behind them, was their principal witness.
9. Preparing for power: Hitler takes the oath of allegiance at a party meeting in Berlin in August 1932, flanked by (*left to right*), Göring, Frick, Gregor Strasser and Goebbels.

10. The gang's all here: Hitler and his chief lieutenants gathered in Berlin's Kaiserhof Hotel on 31 January 1933, to celebrate his appointment as Chancellor. *Left to right*: Frick (seated), Goebbels, Hitler, Röhm (who was airbrushed out of later prints of this picture), Göring, Rosenberg, Himmler and Hess. 11. The three top men in Germany: Göring revels in his position alongside Hitler and Hindenburg at the Tannenberg Memorial Parade in August 1933.

12. Precious intimacy: Goebbels demonstrates his close relationship with Hitler during a concert by the Italian tenor Beniamino Gigli in the Scala Theatre, Berlin, in November 1933. Magda watches them from the next row.

13. The rivals: in 1933, Hitler could still stand shoulder-to-shoulder with SA chief Röhm. Within a year, Röhm was eliminated.

14. Hail the conquering hero: Hess and Goebbels march alongside Hitler to an election rally in Berlin's Sportpalast in November 1933.

15. Local boy made good: Goebbels returns to his home town of Rheydt in glory, to be made an honorary freeman in 1934.

16. Glowing with pride and happiness, Göring celebrates his second marriage, to actress Emmy Sonnemann, on 10 April 1935, with Hitler's approval.

17. Hess and his deputy, Martin Bormann, leaving a meeting of Gauleiters and Reichsleiters in 1935. Hess controlled the party organisation until 1941, but Bormann was always at his shoulder, waiting his chance to take over.

18. Marking Göring's forty-fifth birthday, on 12 January 1938, Himmler leads his SS entourage in paying homage, including (*left to right behind Himmler*) Sepp Dietrich, Reinhard Heydrich and Karl Wolff.

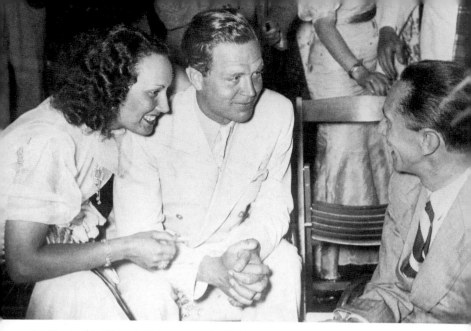

19. During his Olympic Games reception in August 1936, Goebbels chats with film stars Gustav Fröhlich and Lida Baarova. Within days, Goebbels would start a passionate affair with Baarova, which almost wrecked his marriage, and his career.

20. Goebbels enjoyed playing the movie mogul. Here, he shows off to Mussolini's son, Vittorio (*extreme right*). Immediately to Goebbels's left is his State Secretary, Karl Hanke, who had been Magda Goebbels's lover.

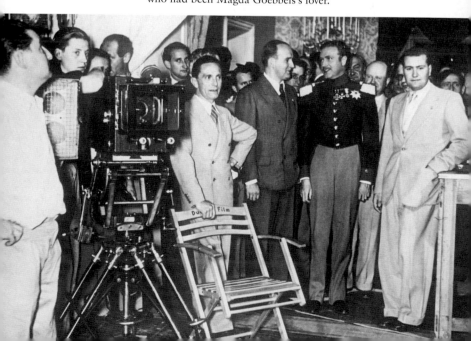

Interior Ministry decrees telling them what they must broadcast or must not print. As soon as his ministry was up and running, he moved swiftly to tighten his grip, starting with radio, which he thought 'automatically offers itself to the total state',[21] and which he regarded as the medium of the future, ideal for influencing the masses through the power of the spoken word. He had already demonstrated its potential with his coverage of Hitler's triumph on 30 January, and during the last election. Now he would show what he could do with it when he had total control. Appropriately, the first national event to be broadcast under his new management was the Day of Potsdam, his own creation.

Radio was easy to take over, partly because it was such a new medium but even more so because its organisation was relatively simple. It had, in fact, already been brought under state control by Papen in 1932 – another example of his paving the way for the Nazis. The network consisted of ten regional companies, owned and controlled by the National Broadcasting Company, which operated the transmitters and was itself owned and controlled by the Post Office. The Postmaster General was no match for Goebbels, and let go without a fight, including handing over the licence fees of two marks a month for each set, which made a useful addition to the ministry's finances.

Within a week of taking office, Goebbels announced that the Propaganda Ministry had acquired all the shares in the National Broadcasting Company, and called the general managers and directors of it and all the regional companies to Broadcasting House in Berlin, where he harangued them mercilessly. 'We make no bones about it,' he told them, thumping the lectern, 'the radio belongs to us and no one else! We will place the radio at the service of our idea, and no other idea will be expressed through it.'[22] Many of the pioneers of the medium, who were almost all still active since it was barely ten years old, were inevitably what Goebbels described scathingly as 'literary types, liberals, technocrats, money-grubbers and freeloaders'. They would all have to go. To remove 'the last remnants of Marxism' from broadcasting, he concluded ominously, there was to be a purge. Most of his audience, of course, would be among the victims, to be replaced by party men. Most were simply fired, but some, including the country's leading pioneer of live reporting and audience participation, Hans Flesch, were sent to concentration camps.

The only noteworthy opposition to Goebbels's plans came not from the men who were being ousted, but from Göring, jealously guarding every inch of his own fiefdom – which included the Prussian regional radio company. Reopening the cracks in their relationship, he wrote to several ministries and provincial governments soliciting support for his objections to Goebbels's centralisation of the system. It was, he said, not right for all broadcasting to be run by one agency: different regions had different interests and traditions, which needed to be catered for by the individual states, in close co-operation with the Reich, if they were to make the most effective use of the medium.[23] Goebbels was 'livid' at Göring's 'damned cheek', branding his move as 'the most stupid particularism' stemming from his 'lust for personal power'. He wanted to fly at once to Hitler, but decided instead to 'let matters ripen', convinced that the Führer was on his side.[24]

For Goebbels, there was more at stake in this squabble than control over the radio: Göring's main source of power lay in his role as ruler of Prussia, and anything Goebbels could do to undermine the autonomy, the 'particularism', of Prussia would weaken Göring's position and therefore improve his own prospects. Over the next month, he raised the matter several times with Hitler, until on 19 July he could claim victory, recording joyfully that Hitler had written to the state governors confirming his authority over all radio stations. 'Very good for me!' he crowed. 'Above all, against Prussia. Particularism must go!'[25]

Goebbels's mission was 'to create the first modern broadcasting system in the world', and he set about it with great drive, appointing one of his brightest protégés, a young journalist and propagandist called Eugen Hadamovsky, to carry out his wishes through the radio department of the ministry. It was a good choice; Hadamovsky fulfilled his brief with sickening efficiency. By August, he could declare: 'Party Comrade Dr Goebbels ordered me to purge the German radio of influences opposed to our cause. I can now report that the job has been done thoroughly.'[26]

At the same time, Goebbels ordered an immediate expansion of the system's hardware, ordering more transmitters and an increase in their power as a priority. And he began pressuring manufacturers to start mass producing cheap sets, the VE (*Volksempfänger*, People's Receiver) 301 – named for 30 January 1933, 'the most important day in Germany history'. They responded with a will, turning out over a million domestic sets in the following twelve months, to bring the total in use to more than 6 million. During the next five years the numbers continued to grow to 9.5 million, and before long still cheaper sets, the DKE (*Deutscher Kleinempfänger*, German Mini Receiver) meant that virtually every home in Germany had one. For special occasions, Goebbels had 6,000 loudspeaker columns installed in public places. He likened communal listening in schools, workplaces, public halls and squares to taking part in a church service, and issued edicts making it an offence to leave a public hall or to move away from one's workplace during a relayed party broadcast. And to make sure people listened, he appointed local 'wireless wardens' to report on audiences in their areas. Within two years he could claim audiences of at least 56 million for any Hitler speech.

Programmes were ruthlessly censored as the listening public was subjected to an unmitigated flood of blatant propaganda. In the early days, time was filled by broadcasting every word of every speech delivered by a party leader, punctuated by heavily slanted news bulletins. Relief came only with the safe option of hours of music – by good German composers, naturally. As the Nazi producers gained experience, skill and confidence, however, they were able to offer at least the appearance of a more varied diet, and listeners soon became so inured to the inbuilt messages that William Shirer, one of the most distinguished American radio journalists of that era, could write: '. . . As the years went by, Dr Goebbels proved himself right, in that the radio became by far the regime's most effective means of propaganda, doing more than any other single instrument of communication to shape the German people to Hitler's ends.'[27]

Taking over the press was a more complex matter. When Hitler first came to power, there were no fewer than 4,703 daily and weekly newspapers in Germany. Virtually every town, no matter how insignificant, supported a local paper, though in many cases circulation could be counted in hundreds rather than thousands. Most larger provincial towns had at least two or three, and each large city had several – Hamburg, for instance, had 10, Cologne 8, Berlin 20, and so on. And despite Goebbels's ludicrous claim that the press was dominated by Jewish interests, at least eighty per cent of all papers were owned by local German families, some of them Nazi supporters.[28] Nationalising them all would be virtually impossible, and in any case, there was no need. All Goebbels had to do was control their content, and this was something he and his ministry could achieve quite simply: any paper that stepped out of line would be shut down, either for a set period or permanently. The two hundred or so Social Democrat and the thirty-five Communist papers had already been put out of business and their plant and equipment either smashed or grabbed by the Nazi Party. It was a lesson other editors and proprietors could not ignore.

Leaving the papers in individual hands suited Goebbels's purpose. He was smart enough to realise that a totally uniform press would be counter-productive: it would be monotonous and boring and would quickly lose the credibility that was so essential if readers were to be duped into accepting his messages. Rather, he declared in a typical piece of pretentious gobbledegook, it had to be 'a piano, so to speak, in the hands of the government . . . uniform in principles but poly-form in the nuances'.[29]

The press might be a piano, but Goebbels provided the music. He turned the government press conference, at which accredited journalists had been admitted at noon each day to receive news and put questions to an official spokesman, into a daily session at which selected journal-ists were given instructions and directives by ministry officials or, on special occasions, by Goebbels himself. As a further way of controlling the flow of information, he took over the three existing news agencies and wire services– the Wolff Telegraph Bureau, Hugenberg's Telegraph Union and the Continental Telegraph Bureau – and merged them into a single state monopoly, the German News Service, DNB, to provide a single channel for news under his own supervision.

Goebbels, however, did not have things all his own way with the press. Following his habitual policy of divide and rule, Hitler had the party's press chief, Otto Dietrich, appointed chairman of the editors' and journalists' national association. Dietrich announced that member-ship was now obligatory, that 'Jews and Marxists' could no longer be members, and that all working journalists would be screened for 'racial and political reliability'. Anyone who wanted to continue working in the profession had to conform.[30] It was not long before Dietrich was issuing his own directives to editors, which inevitably became a source of friction with Goebbels.

As if Dietrich's intrusion was not enough, Goebbels also had to cope with the involvement of Max Amman, Hitler's own publisher, business manager and director of the party-owned Eher Verlag, in his dealings with the newspaper proprietors and publishers. Amman was made chairman of the German Publishers' Association, which became a state-controlled organisation to which all publishers had to belong. And once again, the message hammered home by Amman was 'toe the party line or shut down'.

Both Dietrich and Amman had direct access to Hitler, and could by-pass Goebbels as and when they chose. But in general, their aims were much the same as his, and he saw them as only minor irritants. Neither of them posed a real threat to his overall ambitions, and indeed he soon took Dietrich and his department into his ministry. The real thorn in his flesh, and one that would continue to gall him until the very end, was Alfred Rosenberg, the self-appointed keeper of the flame of National Socialism, who had always hated him as a closet Marxist. Rosenberg, as editor of the *Völkischer Beobachter*, saw himself as the party's expert on the press, and indeed on all things cultural, and never ceased sniping and griping at the rival who was always denying him his own place in the sun.

Goebbels's authority over the press, and his supremacy over Dietrich, Amman and Rosenberg, was finally confirmed in October 1933, with the passing of his Editors' Law. This removed responsibility for 'the total content and attitude of the textual part of the newspaper' from the publisher or proprietor and gave it to the editor, who became a state official answerable only and directly to the Propaganda Ministry. It became an offence punishable by a fine, imprisonment or cancellation of his licence for the publisher even to attempt to influence the editor in any way, and he could not fire an editor without the consent of the journalists' professional association. The muzzling of the press was complete. Amman and his friends could do what they liked on the business front, but Goebbels controlled every word published in every newspaper in Germany.

For all Goebbels's calls for 'polyform nuances', newspapers' editorial content inevitably became monotonous and boring. Circulations fell, advertising revenues shrivelled, and papers began failing: 1,600 went out of business in 1933. Nazi papers were not exempt from the general difficulties: Göring had to persuade a group of businessmen to join him in rescuing the ailing *National-Zeitung,* an ambitious semi-private venture founded by his friend Gauleiter Josef Terboven of Essen, which then became his personal mouthpiece, bringing him both profit and publicity.[31] At the same time, Jewish-owned papers and publishing houses were closed down or expropriated under the 'Aryanisation' process, most being bought at knock-down prices by Amman. The seizure that gave Goebbels greatest pleasure was the *Berliner Tageblatt,* owned by the Mosse family, which had turned down his job application ten years earlier. The great Ullstein publishing empire, meanwhile, went for one tenth of its capital value of sixty million marks to Amman and the party's Eher Verlag, which never actually paid the money. Later, the Eher Verlag bought up most of the regional Catholic papers, too. In the end, it owned no less than 82.5 per cent of the German press.[32]

On 10 May 1933, the same day that he recorded his victory over the Foreign Office, Goebbels took part in an event that was to do untold damage to the international reputation of the new regime. Despite the opposition of some leading party members, he was persuaded to make a speech at a symbolic book burning in Berlin's Opernplatz, directly facing the university and alongside the State Opera House and the National Library. The idea of publicly burning 'subversive writings' by Jewish, Marxist, and other 'non-German' authors at universities throughout Germany came not from Goebbels or his ministry, but from the German Students' Association. Goebbels himself was somewhat ambivalent about it. He had, after all, studied under Jewish professors whom he had admired, and there was always a danger that this might be brought out and used against him. When it came to it, though, he couldn't resist the opportunity to make a speech on intellectual matters, arriving at a rainy Opernplatz around midnight in an open car.

Some 20,000 volumes had been collected by students and storm-troopers from libraries and bookshops during the day, and were burning fitfully in a log enclosure – it was not a particularly impressive spectacle, and Goebbels's speech was 'not particularly enthusiastic', according to Golo Mann, who was there. Speaking in a 'rather civilised' tone, Mann recalled, he seemed to be trying 'rather to act as a brake than to incite',[33] an observation that was substantiated by his instruction to the press to report the event with restraint. Nevertheless, he still proclaimed it as marking the end of 'an era of Jewish hyper-intellectualism', branding the works on the pyre as 'intellectual filth'. Among the authors he condemned to the flames were obvious targets like Thomas and Heinrich Mann, Arnold and Stefan Zweig, Erich Maria Remarque, Sigmund Freud and Albert Einstein. But others were less understandable: why should they burn *Emil and the Detectives*, for instance, or *Bambi*, simply because their authors, Erich Kästner and Felix Salten respectively, were deemed unacceptable? And did Goebbels or anyone else know or care that one of the books consigned to the flames, written by Heinrich Heine in 1823, contained the sentence: 'Wherever they burn books, sooner or later they will burn human beings, too'? Supporting the book burnings was a grave mistake, which Goebbels would never live down.

Goebbels and Göring continued to vie for position throughout 1933, encouraged as usual by Hitler. Göring had scored a personal success with his official visit to Italy at Easter; at the end of May, Goebbels topped it with a week's 'state visit', accompanied by Magda, who completely captivated Mussolini and the rest of the Fascist government. Returning via Munich, they were so elated by Hitler's praise for their Roman conquest that they decided to have another child, 'This time a boy.'[34] Göring, however, did not give up. He regarded Italy as his own area of special interest, and made a further two visits during the year. In the end, however, he failed to convince Mussolini that Germany had no designs on Austria, and to his and Hitler's chagrin, the Duce signed a treaty with the Austrians which could only be seen as a hands-off warning to Germany.

A less serious area of competition between the two paladins was the splendour and number of their official residences. Göring already had his small palace as Reichstag President, and was probably entitled to another as Air Minister, though he never pursued this, preferring to go for the more significant establishment that was his due as Minister-President of Prussia. The existing Minister-President's residence on the Wilhelmstrasse, however, was a gloomy and undistinguished building, and Göring did not care for it at all, though he had moved Pili Körner into an apartment in the mansard roof. He had spotted something much better, a luxurious villa built shortly before 1914 for the Prussian Minister of Commerce, set in a large garden just off Leipziger Platz, on the angle of Stresemannstrasse and Prinz-Albrecht-Strasse, and shielded from the street by a high wall and a line of trees. It was almost next door to the Prinz Albrecht Palace, the former art school and museum where Rudolf Diels was establishing the headquarters of the Gestapo.

Summoning the chief architect of the civil service, Professor Heinz Tietze, Göring ordered him to rebuild and refurnish the villa in lavish style, turning it into a palace at the Prussian government's expense. Among the features he specified were a study based on Mussolini's in Rome, and a white alabaster staircase sweeping grandly from the entrance hall to the first floor drawing room, which was to be done out in red and gold and filled with paintings, tapestries and antiques 'loaned' by various museums. Pride of place went to Rubens's painting, *Diana at the Stag Hunt*, one of the most prized possessions of the Kaiser Friedrich Museum until Göring ordered 'his' director to have it delivered to his residence. The immense canvas was hung in the hall, where it could be raised to reveal a film projection room behind it. The house was also to have a spacious den for his pet lion cub.

Speer described Göring's new palace as 'a romantically tangled warren of small rooms, gloomy with stained-glass windows and heavy velvet hangings'.[35] The overall feeling was typically baronial, with heavy, ornate furniture large enough to take his growing bulk, brought on by a combination of high living and glandular imbalance. His weight would remain a problem until the end of his days, but he cheerfully accepted the nickname by which he was now generally known, '*Der Dicke*', the fat man. In a generous gesture, he gave the Wilhelmstrasse palace to Rudolf Hess, who had no house in Berlin. Hess had told him that he wanted to become a member of the government, and he had promised he would try to help him.[36]

Goebbels started at a disadvantage in the contest with Göring, having no ready-made residence to move into since his was a brand new ministry, but he soon turned this to good effect. He located the perfect house: the former palace of the marshals of the Prussian court, another elegant Schinkel building, set in a prestigious position in the most northerly of the ministry gardens, close to the Brandenburg Gate and convenient both for his office and Hitler's Chancellery. The only trouble was that it was occupied by Hugenberg, as Minister of Agriculture and Economics. That problem was solved on 26 June, when Hugenberg resigned from the Cabinet. Walther Darré, who replaced him as Minister of Agriculture, tried to move in but Goebbels swiftly warned him off, telling him the Führer wanted him 'close by'. Hitler supported Goebbels: 'The Chief is very good to me,' he noted on 29 June. 'I'm to get Hugenberg's official residence. Fabulous!'[37]

In a rush as always, Goebbels called in Albert Speer to refurbish the interior and add a large hall for receptions, demanding that the work be completed in eight weeks. Speer, 'somewhat recklessly', agreed. It was a decision that was to have a profound effect on his career. Many years later, he recalled:

Hitler did not think it would be possible to keep this deadline, and Goebbels, no doubt to spur me on, told me of his doubts. Day and night, I kept three shifts at work. I took care that various aspects of the construction were synchronised

down to the smallest detail, and in the last few days I set a large drying apparatus to work. The building was finally handed over, furnished, punctually on
the promised date.[38]

Hitler, with his passion for any sort of construction, had visited the
building every few days to see how the work was going, but Goebbels
had taken care to keep Speer away from him, wanting to take the
credit himself for beating the impossible deadline. He took possession
on Saturday, 15 July, delighted with the result. Magda had supervised
the furnishings, commissioning much of it from the Munich
Consolidated Workshops, and he raved about her 'fabulous taste'. That
evening, they proudly showed it off to Hitler, who was 'completely
and sincerely enthusiastic', agreeing that it was 'like a pleasure palace'.[39]
But he was sharply critical of a number of water-colours that Speer
had borrowed from the Berlin National Gallery. The artist, Emil Nolde,
was in fact a committed Nazi, but his painting style was expressionist,
far too modern for Hitler. Although Goebbels and Magda liked them,
they immediately kowtowed to his taste, sending for Speer and telling
him 'The pictures have to go at once; they're simply impossible.' Speer
replaced them without argument, wondering at 'this conjunction of
power and servility on Goebbels's part, which struck me as weird.
There was something fantastic about the absolute authority Hitler could
assert over his closest associates of many years, even in matters of taste.
Goebbels had simply grovelled before Hitler.' To his credit, Speer added:
'We were all in the same boat. I too, though altogether at home in
modern art, tacitly accepted Hitler's pronouncement.'[40]

Goebbels's joy at his new palace, and at Hitler's praise, was soured
a couple of weeks later, when Stresemannstrasse, the street on which it
stood, was renamed Hermann-Göring-Strasse. And to compound the
injury to his pride, Hindenburg then promoted Göring to the rank of
three-star General of the Infantry, backdated to 1 October 1931 in order
to give him seniority, presumably on the grounds that it was unthinkable for the commander-in-chief of the air force to be a mere captain.
As a quid pro quo, Göring 'persuaded' the Prussian government to present
the President with an estate in East Prussia, close to his existing estate
at Neudeck, plus the strip of forest that separated them – in his book,
favours always came at a price. Goebbels could hardly contain his rage
when he heard. 'The bastard!' he fulminated. 'He's going to be a general.
Why not go straight to a full field marshal? So, it's yet another new
uniform. Gets on my nerves. Such a show-off.'[41] He was right about

the uniform: Göring could hardly wait to shed the drab brown shirt of the SA for a smart new outfit in light blue, with an all-white version for warm weather. There was friction, too, in another area: Goebbels now had control over most of the theatres in Germany, but to his fury Göring refused to let go of the Prussian state theatres – which included jewels like the Opera House on the Unter den Linden. Despite his success in fighting Prussian particularism in radio, Goebbels was forced to accept defeat in this instance, railing helplessly against his rival's 'insolent pretensions' and accusing him of softness towards the 'reactionary nobility'.[42]

Later that year, Göring showed how he, too, could grovel. Hitler had commented unfavourably on his new residence: 'Dark! How can anyone live in such darkness? Compare this with my professor's work! Everything bright, clear and simple.' Göring had been extremely happy with his baronial hall, but he called in Speer, who was then working on refurbishing the Chancellery, and dragged him to the house. 'Don't look at this,' he told him. 'I can't stand it myself. Do it any way you like. I'm giving you a free hand; only it must turn out like the Führer's place.' Assured that money was no object, Speer went to work tearing down walls to make bigger rooms and adding a fine annexe in glass and bronze – a scarce metal in Germany at the time, the use of which was strictly forbidden for non-essential purposes. The work was completed early in 1934. Göring, Speer recalled, 'was rapturous every time he made an inspection; he beamed like a child on its birthday, rubbed his hands, and laughed.'[43]

Hugenberg's resignation from the government on 26 June 1933 was followed immediately by the final collapse of his DNVP; its paramilitary Stahlhelm had already been absorbed into the SA, and most of its senior members had defected to the Nazis. During the following few days, the other remaining parties all gave up and voluntarily dissolved themselves, too. The Communists, of course, had been banned long since; the Social Democrats had been banned on 22 June and all their assets confiscated. Germany was now a one-party state, a situation that was formalised on 14 July when the Cabinet passed the Law against the New Construction of Parties, which stated baldly:

The National Socialist German Workers' Party constitutes the only political party in Germany.

Whoever undertakes to maintain the organisational structure of another political party or to form a new political party will be punished with penal servitude for up to three years or with imprisonment of from six months to three years, if the deed is not subject to greater penalty according to other regulations.

The same marathon Cabinet meeting promulgated a string of other new laws, laying down the main planks of the regime. They covered among other things: 'the confiscation of property of the enemies of the people and the state'; the constitution of the Protestant Church; ratification of the Concordat with the Vatican; a 'law on the remoulding of the German peasantry', sanctioning rural resettlement; a compulsory sterilisation law 'For the Prevention of Hereditarily Diseased Offspring'; and laws permitting the revoking of German citizenship on racial grounds. In less than four months since the Reichstag had abdicated its responsibilities with the Enabling Act the totalitarian state was complete. The brown revolution, Hitler told his state governors, was over.

It was Goebbels's job to inform and convince the general public and party members, particularly the SA, of this, and at the same time to find ways of maintaining popular enthusiasm for the regime. Keeping the SA happy was a real problem, since whatever Hitler might say, Röhm and most of his men were intent on a second revolution, to create an SA state with Röhm as a parallel leader with Hitler, with real powers over the police, the military and even the civil administration, and the SA as an armed people's militia alongside the Reichswehr. Restraining the SA's ambitions was a hopeless task while Röhm was still in charge, but Goebbels did his best, despite the fact that he himself had initially shouted as loudly as anyone for the second revolution, which he said 'must come': 'The first revolution is not at an end,' he had written on 18 April 1933. 'Now we shall settle with the reactionaries. The revolution must nowhere come to a halt.'[44]

The SA was being denied its greatest pleasure – fighting, brawling and beating up opponents – but at least it could enjoy marching at the bigger, better and more frequent festivals and public holidays which Goebbels organised. The biggest of them all was the fifth party rally at Nuremberg that year, which was to be the grandest yet, a mammoth celebration of victory. Albert Speer, whose stock was still rising after the May Day rally in Berlin and his various work for Goebbels, was dispatched to Nuremberg to design something spectacular for the setting, which he duly delivered in the shape of a 100-foot-wide spread eagle mounted on a vast trellis, plus his trademark banners and columns of light that had worked so well at Tempelhof Field. Hitler gave his personal approval and Speer advanced a couple of more steps up the ladder, which suited Goebbels, who could claim him as his own discovery.

Soon afterwards, Hitler gave Speer's career another boost when he commissioned him to oversee the work of revamping the dilapidated Reich Chancellery. Although the designs were by Hitler's chief architect, Paul Ludwig Troost, who had rebuilt the 'Brown House', Troost and his staff were Munich-based and unfamiliar with Berlin firms and practices. Hitler recalled Speer's super-efficiency in the work he had done for Goebbels, as well as the May Day and Nuremberg rallies, and assigned him to aid them, which he did with conspicuous success. Speer was a personable young man, and Hitler took a liking to him, drawing him into his inner circle of regular luncheon guests. When Troost died in January 1934, Speer took his place, at the age of only twenty-eight.

The Nuremberg Rally was another triumph for the Propaganda Minister. During the opening speeches Wagner read out a proclamation from Hitler setting out 'very sharply' his fundamental policy on the states and particularism, 'above all on Prussia'. It was 'not to preserve, but to liquidate'. 'Göring,' Goebbels noted in his diary, 'went quite pale.'[45] In spite of this victory, however, Goebbels was still having to fight off rivals who threatened his position. He had 'almost panicked' in July when Ley came up with a plan to incorporate all the artists' professional associations into the Labour Front, which threatened his ambition to become the absolute tsar of Germany's cultural life. He hurried to see Hess for 'serious discussion' of Ley's intentions, warning him of 'Marxist tendencies' in the factory cell organisation[46] – ironically the same charge that was being levelled against himself by Rosenberg. Then he set about creating a formalised structure that would establish his control beyond all doubt.

Goebbels presented Hitler with a paper laying out his detailed proposals for the creation of a Reich Chamber of Culture in July. After a 'long discussion of basic principles' at Berchtesgaden, Hitler gave his approval on 24 August, whereupon Ley capitulated, saving face by withdrawing his union plans in return for Goebbels's support for his

Strength through Joy organisation. The chamber was officially inaugurated by a law passed on 22 September, which stated: 'In order to pursue a policy of German culture, it is necessary to gather together the creative artists in all spheres into a unified organisation under the leadership of the Reich. The Reich must not only determine the lines of progress, mental and spiritual, but also lead and organise the professions.' The chamber was to work in conjunction with Goebbels's Propaganda Ministry, and he was to be its president.

The Reich Chamber of Culture was an umbrella organisation covering seven individual chambers: of fine arts, music, the theatre, literature, the press, broadcasting and film. Everyone working in any of these fields, not only artists but also publishers, producers, radio-set manufacturers and so on, was obliged to belong to the relevant chamber, each of which had the right to expel or refuse admission to members for 'political unreliability'. This deliberately loose phrase meant that even those who were simply lukewarm about National Socialism, or who offended the apparatchiks who ran the chambers, if only through an ill-considered joke, could be deprived of the right to work in their chosen profession.

The emigration of writers, artists, musicians, thinkers, which had begun earlier in the year became a flood, led by Nobel Prize winner Thomas Mann. Some of Germany's most distinguished names departed for Paris, London, New York, Hollywood, each of them a warning beacon against the Nazi regime. Goebbels did his best to stem the flow, claiming that 'sniffing out ideologies' was not his intention, and that the government wanted only 'to be the good patron of German art and culture', putting an end to the 'heartless and bloodless dilettantism of an army of incompetents' and rooting out 'philistinism' and 'reactionary backwardness'. 'Only consecrated hands,' he declared, 'had the right to serve at the altar of art.'[47] A few prestigious names were persuaded by his high-flown words and stayed – the conductor Wilhelm Furtwängler, the composers Richard Strauss and Paul Hindemith, the pianist Walter Gieseking, the poet Gottfried Benn and the dramatist Gerhart Hauptmann, another Nobel Prize laureate, among them. But the majority realised that Goebbels's Ministry of Thought Control had become a reality, its tentacles stretching into every corner of German life. William Shirer observed, and later recorded, how effective it became:

No one who has not lived for years in a totalitarian land can possibly conceive how difficult it is to escape the dread consequences of a regime's calculated and incessant propaganda. Often in a German home or office or sometimes in a casual conversation with a stranger in a restaurant, a beer hall, a café, I would meet with the most outlandish assertions from seemingly educated and intelligent persons. It was obvious that they were parroting some piece of nonsense they had heard on the radio or read in the newspapers. Sometimes one was tempted to say as much, but on such occasions one was met with such a stare of incredulity, such a shock of silence, as if one had blasphemed the Almighty, that one realised how useless it was even to try to make contact with a mind which had become warped and for whom the facts of life had become what Hitler and Goebbels, with their cynical disregard for truth, said they were.[48]

On 24 September 1933, two days after the Chamber of Culture was established, Goebbels flew to Geneva, where he joined Foreign Minister Neurath to represent Germany at a League of Nations conference. The Foreign Office was terrified of what he might do, or, as Goebbels put it more graphically, was 'shitting its pants with fear'.[49] The diplomats need not have worried: according to their chief interpreter, Paul Schmidt, he conducted himself 'perfectly calmly . . . as though he had been a delegate to the League of Nations for years'.[50] He utterly despised the League and all the delegates and officials who attended it, but as one of the world's greatest liars, he had no difficulty in concealing his feelings and playing their game to perfection.

The trick he was asked to perform in Geneva was to fool the rest of the world into believing that Hitler and Germany genuinely wanted peace, and that their demand for parity in armaments was a reasonable request for purely defensive purposes. This was a hopeless task, particularly with the French, who resisted all his blandishments and refused to budge an inch. But he did succeed in surprising the international delegates – who knew of him only as a ranting revolutionary – with his charm, intelligence and correct behaviour, managing to convince many of them that the regime he represented could not be as black as it had been painted, and could be a valuable front-line ally in the battle against Bolshevism. This was a notable achievement. So, too, was his success in wooing the Polish Foreign Minster, Józef Beck, and the President of the Danzig Senate, Hermann Rauschning, away from dependence on France, and preparing the way to a pact of non-aggression and friendship with Germany, which the Poles signed on 26 January 1934.

Although the trips to Italy and Switzerland were the only times he had ever been out of Germany, they had whetted Goebbels's appetite and he began to harbour ambitions to add the Foreign Office to his portfolio. With that and the Propaganda Ministry, which of course he had no intention of giving up, he really would be able to challenge Göring for the undisputed second place in the Reich. Hitler, however, was far too shrewd to indulge this particular fancy, and Goebbels's dream was to remain unfulfilled, though he clung to it right to the end, using his control of propaganda and information services as an alternative Foreign Office.

For the moment, however, he had a more familiar task to perform. Convinced by his savagely derisive reports on his experiences in Geneva, Hitler decided to pull Germany out of the League of Nations and the Disarmament Conference. Hitler made the announcement himself on the radio on 14 October 1933, but it was left to Goebbels to deal with the press and the public, assuring them that Germany was still committed to 'a policy inspired by the most sincere desire for peace and international understanding', and accusing the other countries of using Germany as a scapegoat. 'We pulled out,' he told a packed Sportpalast meeting on 20 October, 'to clear the air, to show the world that things can't go on this way.'

To prove that the German people supported his actions, Hitler decided to hold a referendum, combined with new elections to tidy up the Reichstag. There would, of course, only be a single party to vote for, but Goebbels was to stage a full campaign, complete with mass rallies, speeches, posters and all the rest of the electoral machinery, all based on an emotive call for justice and freedom for the Fatherland. For what was positively the last time, he hit the campaign trail once again.

There was a brief distraction early in November when the trial of Marinus van der Lubbe for the Reichstag fire was held in Leipzig. In an effort to prove a Communist conspiracy, there were now four other defendants, the German Communist leader Ernst Torgler and three Bulgarian members of the Comintern (Communist International). The trial attracted a great deal of international interest, and did considerable damage to the Nazis' reputation, especially when Göring made a complete fool of himself as a witness, ranting and raving and arguing with the accused men, who ran rings round him in court with accusations of Nazi involvement. Goebbels appeared four days after Göring, and managed to restore some credibility by staying cool and completely in control. It was not enough to convince the judges, who found the Dutchman solely responsible and acquitted the others, but it allowed

Goebbels the pleasure of having scored a point over his blustering rival.

It was no coincidence that the referendum and election were held on 12 November, the day after the anniversary of the Armistice. And even allowing for a certain amount of manipulation and pressure, it was no surprise that the results of both were eminently satisfactory for the party: 96 per cent of the eligible population voted, and 95.1 per cent of these approved of the withdrawal from the League, while in the election 92.1 per cent voted for the single Nazi list. In the new Reichstag, there would be 639 Nazi deputies, plus twenty-two non-party 'guest' deputies, including Hugenberg. There would be no more parliamentary debates, only acceptance and acclamation of Hitler's policies by what was soon dubbed 'the Reich Glee Club', singing in unison under the baton of General Hermann Göring.

XV

NIGHT OF THE LONG KNIVES

THROUGHOUT 1933, along with all his other activities, Göring had played a skilful contest with Frick for ultimate control of Germany's police. As part of his plans for centralising the administration of the entire Reich, Frick wanted to bring all the sixteen state police forces under the control of his Reich Interior Ministry, starting with the biggest, Göring's own Prussian force. Göring agreed with the need for a strong, unified police force, and co-operated with Frick, even allowing his own police chiefs, Daluege and Diels, to be involved in the planning – which of course meant that he was fully informed of all that was going on. As always, he was looking for personal advantage, which in this case was simple: if there had to be a centralised national force, somebody had to be in charge – and who better than the man who was already running the country's biggest force? Chief of Reich Police was a title that would sit well with Göring's other appointments. It even held the promise of yet another uniform.

What mattered more than titles and uniforms, however, was power, and Göring knew that this lay not in control of the regular police but of the political police, epitomised by his own Gestapo. This above all was what he was determined to protect from Frick. He had already separated the Gestapo from the rest of the police force, placing it directly under his Prussian Interior Ministry. In November, when he heard that Frick was planning fresh centralisation moves that would bring all political as well as regular police under the control of the Reich Interior Ministry, he moved adroitly to frustrate him, transferring the Gestapo from his Prussian Interior Ministry and making it a separate agency directly answerable to the Prussian Minister-President. For the moment, the Gestapo was safe from Frick. But barely noticed by Göring or anyone else, a new challenge to his control of it was materialising in the unlikely shape of Heinrich Himmler.

While the two showmen of the party, Goebbels and Göring, basked in the spotlight, vying with each other for public attention and recognition, Himmler was more than happy to make progress unobtrusively. His private life was deliberately modest, and although he lived well, as befitted a Reichsführer-SS, he was scrupulously honest about his personal expenses, carefully keeping them separate from those incurred on party business. He had sold the chicken farm and bought a flat in Munich, not far from Hitler's, and near his parents, with whom he was now happily reconciled. He had also bought a villa called Lyndenfycht at Gmund, on the Tegernsee lake, where many of the party big-wigs had houses, but it was by no means a palace. Marga lived there with little Gudrun, now four years old, and a little boy the Himmlers had adopted since Marga could no longer have children. To all appearances, they were a happy family, and Himmler was a warm and devoted father, when he was there. Unfortunately for Marga and the children, this was not often, for he was more devoted to the party and his SS, and to his quiet quest for personal power, than he was to them.

Ever since taking over the Bavarian Political Police, Himmler had been moving quietly to extend his influence across the rest of the country, based on the understanding that the SS was the party's chosen security force. This had been reinforced by Göring's decision to draw his political police auxiliaries exclusively from the SS, a move that was copied in all the other state police forces, giving Himmler a foothold in each. In Prussia, Göring unwittingly opened the door in June 1933 by making him ministerial commissioner for auxiliary police personnel in the Gestapo office, at the same time giving Röhm a similar position for SA auxiliaries in the regular police, in the hope that the two leaders would take responsibility for disciplining their own men. Himmler had reacted positively, but as far as Röhm and the SA were concerned, it had proved to be a forlorn hope. When Göring and Frick officially disbanded the auxiliary police on 2 August 1933, the SA simply carried on in the same unruly fashion as before, arresting, beating and murdering opponents without hindrance. The SS, on the other hand, once again demonstrated its discipline by falling into line – apart from keeping on its notorious Columbia House interrogation centre.

All through the summer, Himmler shuttled tirelessly around the country, accompanied by Karl Wolff, visiting SS units, charming and disarming local political leaders, handing out honorary SS general ranks, helping other states to establish the SS–police–concentration camp power triangle that had proved so successful in Bavaria, and generally offering expert advice and guidance. All the political leaders, of course, were Nazis, and in many cases Himmler already had SS and SD men in positions of authority, which made his task easier. And when charm failed to work, he resorted to blackmail: Heydrich had an SD file on every prominent Nazi, detailing their peccadilloes, misdemeanours and misconduct, which could be used against them.

By the autumn, his efforts began to bear fruit, as one state after another offered him the command of their political police. It was a slow, patient process, a nibbling and gnawing rather than grabbing and gobbling, but by March 1934 Himmler had achieved the remarkable feat of commanding every single political police force in the Reich, with the exception of Prussia and the tiny enclaves of Lippe and Schaumburg-Lippe. Admittedly, some of them consisted of a mere handful of men, but others were more substantial; even though they remained individually separate, linked together under a single commander, they formed a significant power base. Himmler needed only the one missing card to complete his grand slam, and Göring was about to deal it to him.

At the end of March 1934, Göring suddenly opened negotiations with Frick on handing over the Prussian ministries to the Reich government. By mid April they had reached agreement. Göring's about-face may have seemed surprising at the time, but he had good reasons for it. To begin with, he was forced to recognise that once Hitler had publicly endorsed the 'liquidation of Prussian particularism', Frick's centralisation was unstoppable. For all his nimble footwork over the Gestapo, the best he could do for the rest of his Prussian empire was to salvage what he could through shrewd negotiation. In the end, he achieved a satisfactory result by hanging on to the two main levers of power – the secret police and finances – and keeping his treasured position as Minister-President, complete with official residence. His Interior Ministry was to be taken over by Frick, with Daluege remaining in command of the Prussian regular police and at the same time becoming head of the police department in the Reich Interior Ministry. In return, Göring kept the Gestapo.

The Gestapo, however, was in a mess. In less than a year, Diels had shaped it into the most sinister and feared agency of the state, but he had also allowed it to become a festering heap of internecine intrigues

– at one stage he had even fled for his own life to Czechoslovakia. If it was not to collapse altogether, Göring needed to replace its unstable and unreliable chief with someone who could impose order, discipline and authority on its warring factions. He did not have to look far to see that there was one outstanding candidate: Reichsführer-SS Heinrich Himmler. Himmler had been lobbying Hitler for some time to put him in charge of the Prussian Gestapo as well as the other political police forces. 'At that time I did not expressly oppose it,' Göring told the Nuremberg tribunal. 'It was not agreeable to me; I wanted to handle my police myself. When, however, the Führer asked me to do this and said that it would be the correct thing and the expedient thing, and that it was proved necessary for the enemy of the state to be fought throughout the Reich in a uniform way, I actually handed the [political] police over to Himmler, who put Heydrich in charge.'[1]

In spite of bowing to Hitler's wishes, Göring could hardly be expected to let go of such a powerful weapon as the Gestapo so easily, and nor did he. In fact, he remained in overall command, appointing Himmler as his Deputy Chief with the title Inspector of the Gestapo, and Heydrich, by now an SS-Gruppenführer (Major-General), as Chief of the Gestapa, the Gestapo Office. They moved in on 19 April, filling the Prinz-Albrecht-Strasse with Bavarians and starting to put their new house in order immediately. As head of section II 1A, responsible for Communism, Marxism and all affiliated organisations, trade unions and subversion, Heydrich installed one of his most trusted men from Munich, Heinrich Müller, a professional police officer with no real political or ideological commitment but a fanatical devotion to duty and efficiency. A man who lived for his work, he was to prove his worth many times over during the following eleven years, becoming known and remembered as simply 'Gestapo Müller'.

Initially, Himmler celebrated his success by rejoicing in the title: 'Reichsführer-SS and Political Police Commander of the States of Anhalt, Baden, Bavaria, Brunswick, Bremen, Hamburg, Hesse, Lübeck, Mecklenburg, Oldenburg, Saxony, Thuringia and Württemberg, and Inspector of the Gestapo in Prussia'. But even he couldn't get away with such a pretentious mouthful for long, and after Frick ridiculed him for it he shortened it to 'Political Police Commander of the States and Inspector of the Gestapo in Prussia'.[2]

Appointing Himmler meant not only that the Gestapo would be licked into shape and managed properly, it also meant that Göring could harness his nationwide secret police network and the SS to the dangerous task he was about to undertake: a deadly assault against Ernst Röhm and the SA. Göring had never liked Himmler, despising his priggish punctiliousness, but his SS was the only weapon capable of decapitating the SA without the risk of civil war; giving him the Gestapo was a necessary quid pro quo to ensure his support. Göring must also have hoped that by making him his subordinate, he would be able to control and use him: it was the same mistake that Papen, Hugenberg and the DNVP had made about Hitler.

Going after Röhm and his cohorts was a desperate measure to deal with a desperate situation, both for Göring himself and for Hitler. The SA had always been a destabilising, anti-government force – that was its *raison d'être*, and one which it found impossible to change, even though the party was now the government. Röhm and many of his SA members, including a hard core of leaders, took the 'socialism' in the party's title seriously, and wanted to destroy capitalism, big business, landed estates, the aristocracy, and the old officer corps in their 'the second revolution'. And if Hitler tried to stand in their way, then they would destroy him as well. 'The SA and SS will not allow the German revolution to go to sleep or to be betrayed at the half-way mark by the non-fighters,' Röhm proclaimed as early as June 1933 in the *Nationalsozialistische Monatshefte* (National Socialist Monthly). 'Whether they like it or not, we will carry on our fight. If they finally grasp what it is about, with them! If they are not willing, without them! And if need be, against them!'[3]

Hitler responded vigorously. On 1 July he told the SA and SS leaders: 'I will suppress every attempt to disturb the existing order as ruthlessly as I will deal with the so-called second revolution, which would lead only to chaos.'[4] Five days later, he called all the Reich Governors to a meeting in the Chancellery on 6 July and declared to them: 'The revolution is not a permanent state of affairs, and it must not be allowed to turn into one. The river of revolution that has been released must be diverted into the safe channel of evolution.'[5] The message could not have been clearer, but Röhm and his men refused to accept it, and simply continued making their own preparations. In August, Röhm warned: 'There are still men in official positions today who have not the least idea of the spirit of the revolution. We shall ruthlessly get rid of them if they dare to put their reactionary ideas into practice.'[6]

Göring had no doubt that he was at the top of Röhm's list, along with the heavy industrialists, financiers and aristocrats who were his friends and paymasters. The 'second revolution' was aimed at getting rid of these people, and bringing him down with them. All his new-found wealth, luxury and influence would disappear. He knew, too, that Röhm's ambition to take over the Reichswehr, subsuming it into a people's militia with himself as commander-in-chief, was still very much alive. To Göring, this was sacrilege – and anyway he had his own eyes set on the position of commander-in-chief. Röhm was already his only serious rival in terms of power as second man in the Reich, and for that reason alone Göring was intent on removing him. If he were to get control of the army, he would be virtually impregnable.

Any residual affection Göring might have had for the SA he had once commanded was destroyed in September 1933, when he had planned a grand parade in Berlin to mark the reopening of his Prussian State Council, culminating in the SA and SS marching past the Opera House, where he would graciously take the salute. Röhm and the commander of the SA in Berlin, Karl Ernst, were incensed by this obvious piece of self-aggrandisement, and gave orders that if the parade took place at all, their men should amble past the reviewing stand in such a slovenly manner that it would be a clear public insult. Göring found out, of course, and saved the day by inviting Röhm and Himmler to join him on the stand and share the honours. The parade passed off without incident, even goose-stepping smartly past the podium – but he neither forgot nor forgave the intended affront, and was determined to get his revenge.[7]

The greatest danger of an SA uprising was that it would unseat Hitler and tear the country apart again in a bloody civil war, since there was no way the army, itself under threat, could stand by and do nothing. The army numbered only 100,000 men, but they were all professional soldiers, well armed, well trained and well led. The SA included many former soldiers, but was largely an unruly, ill-disciplined mob of thugs and roughnecks. However, by early 1934, swollen by the incorporation of the Stahlhelm and other paramilitaries, it was 4.5 million strong – though only a third of the storm-troopers were Nazi Party members. It was also increasingly well armed as Röhm and his lieutenants made full use of their past experience to smuggle in illegal weapons, including a large number of heavy machine-guns. A direct head-to-head confrontation was clearly out of the question. Equally clearly, something had to be done, and Göring and Himmler, aided by Heydrich, would have to be the ones to do it. Frick could not be relied on for active help – he was far too much the bureaucrat, always concerned with the niceties of due process – but he could be asked to keep the uniformed police out of any conflict, and not to hinder or impede the SS, SD and Gestapo when the crunch came. The army, too, would agree to stand back and allow the plotters a free hand. And in party headquarters, they had a valuable ally in Hess, who would be glad to see the troublesome SA leadership cut down to size and subordinated to his Political Central Commission.

Göring had been gathering ammunition to use against Röhm and his clique for some time before he recruited Himmler to his cause: from early autumn 1933, he had been feeding Hitler selected Gestapo reports and FA telephone intercepts to warn him of the danger they posed. Hitler, however, procrastinated as usual, and even gave Röhm advancement on 1 December by appointing him to the Cabinet, along with Hess, as a Minister without Portfolio. Whether this was intended as a sweetener, or to deceive Röhm into a false sense of security, is impossible to say. Diels claimed later that he and Göring had provided Hitler with thick dossiers on SA misdeeds, including homosexual orgies involving the SA Chief of Staff and his lieutenants, and on their corruption of Hitler Youth members. After receiving one such dossier in mid December, Diels went on, Hitler turned to Göring and told him: 'This whole camarilla around Chief of Staff Röhm is corrupt through and through. The SA is the pacemaker in all this filth. You should look into it more thoroughly – that would interest me!'[8]

Despite his disgust, Hitler sent Röhm a warm letter on New Year's Day 1934, thanking him for 'the imperishable services that you have rendered to the National Socialist movement and to the German people'. He concluded by saying how grateful he was 'to be able to call such men as you my friends and fellow combatants'. Published in the *Völkischer Beobachter*, it was one of twelve such greetings to ministers and leaders but the only one to use the intimate '*du*' reserved for personal friends.[9]

Two weeks later, again according to Diels, Hitler was discussing with Göring 'the great traitors' who were leading lesser men in the party and the SA to revolt: General von Schleicher and Gregor Strasser, he said, were conspiring with Röhm and the SA leadership to topple the regime. He wanted those enemies of the state out of the way before they could attempt to seize power, adding, 'It is incomprehensible that Strasser and Schleicher, those arch traitors, should have survived until now.' Diels claimed that as they left the house on the Obersalzberg

Göring turned to him and asked, 'You understand what the Führer wants? These three must disappear, and very soon. They are downright traitors, I can assure you of that.' Diels said that when he asked if they could not be tried by a special court, Göring instantly slapped him down. 'The Führer's order means more than a court,' he responded, speaking 'urgently and forcefully, like a chained dog that has just been unleashed'.[10]

For all Göring's supposed urgency, Diels seems to have done nothing but carry on collecting information. Röhm, however, continued to dig his own grave by encouraging a personality cult among the SA that elevated him above Hitler, at the same time infuriating the army generals with strong hints that his Cabinet appointment might be the prelude to his taking over the Defence Ministry. On 1 February 1934, emboldened by an unshakeable belief that his friend Hitler really supported him, he came out into the open with a long Cabinet memorandum to Defence Minister Blomberg demanding that the defence of the country should be 'the domain of the SA' and that the Reichswehr be reduced to providing it with trained men. The memorandum, no copies of which have survived, apparently went on to propose that the SA should form the basis of a new 'People's Army', and that the armed forces – army, navy and air force – together with the SA, the SS and all veterans' organisations, should be under the control of a single Defence Ministry, with the clear implication that he would be in charge.[11] This really was dynamite, and Hitler would have to move swiftly to defuse it if it was not to blow up in his face.

The day after Röhm delivered his memorandum, Hitler told a meeting of Gauleiters that those who thought the revolution was not yet over were fools. Echoing his speech of seven months before, he said that there were people in the movement who thought revolution meant a permanent state of chaos. He called for stability, loyalty and blind obedience, with no internecine struggles. He stressed that there could only be one leader, that he, the first leader, had been 'chosen by destiny', but that the next leader must have the support of the entire movement and that 'no one could be selected who has a private power base'.[12] But that was as far as he could bring himself to go in condemning Röhm – or perhaps as far as he dared to go at that stage.

While Hitler was being mealy mouthed to his Gauleiters, Blomberg was being outspoken to his fellow generals. He related the contents of Röhm's paper, probably with some embellishment, to an urgently called meeting of army district commanders, who were understandably horrified by what they heard. Röhm's proposals left no room for compromise: whether he liked it or not, Hitler would have to choose between the army and the SA. In truth, there was really no choice: Hitler could not afford to alienate the army, especially when Blomberg and the new Commander-in-Chief, General Freiherr Werner von Fritsch, turned for support to Hindenburg, whose condition for giving Hitler the Chancellorship had been that he alone would appoint the Defence Minister. There was no way the Supreme Commander, whose antipathy to Röhm was well known, would ever agree to having 'that pervert' in charge of his beloved army.

The decisive factor for Hitler was that Hindenburg was growing increasingly frail and could not last much longer. Sooner rather than later, a new President would have to be chosen and Hitler was determined he would be the one: only the President stood between him and absolute dictatorship, including the supreme command of the armed forces. Still clinging to the illusion of legality, he wanted Hindenburg to nominate him as his chosen successor, but he knew that this was unlikely while he was linked to Röhm.

Hindenburg himself favoured a return of the monarchy, under a regent, as did many of the senior officers. So, too, did the conservative DNVP and Papen, the Vice-Chancellor, who still had a close personal relationship with Hindenburg. There were compelling arguments against the restoration of the monarchy, but it was by no means impossible. The Kaiser himself could never return, of course, but he could be represented by one of his sons, with 'Auwi', Prince August Wilhelm, the favourite – although this would raise an extra complication in that 'Auwi' was a senior officer in the SA. If Hitler was to avoid this and the various other possibilities – both Schleicher and Strasser were waiting menacingly in the wings, for instance – he would have to move with great skill. Röhm and the SA were useful scapegoats, who could be blamed for all the excesses of the regime while Hitler presented himself as the soul of reason and moderation, devoted to restoring Germany's strength, prosperity and pride, but eventually they would have to be sacrificed. The only question was when and how.

The army high command did not want to overthrow Hitler unless they were forced to do so. They knew that he was totally committed to rearmament and to strengthening the armed forces in every possible way, with the aim of expanding German 'living space' in the East, policies that few other politicians would have the nerve to carry through. He had pulled Germany out of the hated League of Nations and the Disarmament Conference, and on 29 January, two days before Röhm's memorandum, had announced plans for the reintroduction of compulsory military service and the creation of a new body, the Wehrmacht, to incorporate all three armed services. The army had also come round to the thought that although he had never been a commissioned officer, he had earned two Iron Crosses during his long service at the front and was a soldier at heart, and therefore one of them. Had he not proved this the previous July, by promulgating a new Army Law that denied the civil courts jurisdiction over military personnel and abolished the Republican practice of electing representatives of the rank and file, a throwback to the reviled soldiers' councils of the 1918 Revolution?

During February, Blomberg and Fritsch lobbied Hitler steadily, voluntarily making significant concessions such as adding the Nazi swastika to the army's official emblem, and applying the civil service 'Aryan clause', which barred anyone with even one Jewish grandparent from government service, to the officer corps, which led to the instant dismissal of some seventy officers. Fritsch justified these moves by claiming they would 'give the Chancellor the necessary impetus against the SA'.[13]

The generals' lobbying bore fruit on 28 February, when Hitler summoned the commanders of the army, the SA and the SS to a conference at the Defence Ministry on Bendlerstrasse to receive his guidelines for co-operation. These had in fact been drawn up for him by the army leaders, so it was not surprising that they completely rejected Röhm's plans for an SA militia, which Hitler said was not suitable for even minimal national defence. He intended, he said, to build up a well-trained 'people's army' in the new Wehrmacht, which would be equipped with the most modern weapons and was to be ready for all defensive operations within five years, and offensive operations within eight – his first overt admission that he was set on going to war to attain his territorial ambitions. The SA would be confined to minor military functions, such as border control and preliminary training under the control of the army, but its main role was to be the political education of the nation. 'The Wehrmacht,' he declared, 'must be the sole bearer of arms in the nation.'

It was a total defeat for Röhm, underlined by Hitler's threat to crush anyone who opposed him. If he had accepted it, all would have been well. But Röhm was never a man to accept defeat. He was forced to sign the agreement and shake hands with Blomberg, and then to host a 'reconciliation luncheon' at his own headquarters on Standartenstrasse, but after Hitler and the officers had left and the champagne had been swallowed, he exploded with rage. 'What that idiot corporal says means nothing to us!' he snarled. 'I have not the slightest intention of keeping this agreement.' In a thinly veiled threat, he added: 'Hitler is a traitor, and needs a long vacation . . . If we can't get there with him, we'll get there without him.'[14]

Unfortunately for Röhm, among those listening to him was SA-Obergruppenführer (Lieutenant-General) Viktor Lutze, Regional Commander in Hanover. Lutze, a former army lieutenant, regarded Röhm's rant as treasonous. Shortly afterwards, he travelled to Munich and reported it to Hess, who sent him on to see the Führer himself at his house on the Obersalzberg. To Lutze's surprise, Hitler received the news calmly. After talking for several hours, he told Lutze: 'We must let matters ripen.'[15] It was a typical Hitler response: 'Do nothing and see what happens,' or on a more hopeful note, 'Give them enough rope and they'll hang themselves.' But Lutze was worried that the renegade SA leaders might hang Hitler first. He took the first opportunity to confide in the head of Blomberg's Ministerial Office, Major-General Walter von Reichenau, an out-and-out Nazi supporter.

The army could not move against Röhm directly, but Reichenau was a highly political animal, and knew who would. He turned to the SS, and in particular to the cold-blooded and calculating head of the SD, Reinhard Heydrich, who had already decided that the only answer to the problem of Röhm was to liquidate him and his entire clique. Reichenau, who had come to the same conclusion, let him know that the army would not stand in his way.

When Göring gave Himmler and Heydrich the Gestapo, he expected them to be more effective against Röhm than Diels had been, and they did not disappoint him. Himmler, driven by his ambition to end his subservience to Röhm and make his SS an independent body, was as keen as Göring to get rid of the Chief of Staff. Although he had once hero-worshipped Röhm, his puritanical soul was now disgusted by his depravity. He did not want his noble SS order besmirched by association with the crude thuggery of the SA.

Heydrich, being completely amoral, was driven by ambition pure and simple, turning his considerable talents to preparing for the show-down that would open the gates to virtually unlimited power for Himmler and himself.

Göring's own dislike of the Chief of Staff had hardened into an implacable hatred fuelled by further slights to his *amour propre* and revealing intercepts by the FA. Röhm and Ernst, for instance, usually referred to him as 'that pig Göring', and Emmy as 'his sow'. At other times they called him '*Herr Reaktion*', and looked forward to 'The Day' when he would be swept away along with his big business friends. In January, Ernst had started posting armed SA guards outside Göring's home as an implied but calculated threat. Göring had had them removed, replacing them with men from the special uniformed police unit, the Landespolizeigruppe General Göring, that he had retained as his personal bodyguard, based in the former Prussian cadet school at Lichterfelde, his old Alma Mater, which it shared with Hitler's SS-Leibstandarte. An FA phone-tap recorded Ernst telling Röhm this was a pity, because the storm-troopers 'would have made it easy to blow the pig's brains out when the time comes'. Göring could hardly wait for the time to come when he would turn the tables and blow their brains out, but first he would have to persuade Hitler to stop prevaricating and take decisive action for once. It would not be easy, for Hitler still regarded Röhm as one of his few personal friends, and it might take a little time, but he would get there in the end.

Despite the 'agreement' foisted on them by Hitler, relations between the SA and the army deteriorated fast during the rest of the spring and early summer. As usual, Hitler tried to sit on the fence, leaving the two sides to fight it out between themselves. But in early April he received news that concentrated his mind wonderfully: Hindenburg's condition had deteriorated, and he was unlikely to last more than a few weeks. With no more time to lose, Hitler threw in his lot with the army, promising Blomberg and Fritsch that he would put a stop to Röhm's plans, cut the SA down to size, and guarantee the army's position, in return for their agreement to his becoming President. They accepted. What he did not promise was how he was going to deal with Röhm – because he simply didn't know. He hoped he could handle the matter peacefully, but deep down he must have realised that that was a very long shot indeed.

As spring moved into early summer, Heydrich and Himmler, aided all the way by Reichenau, continued gathering and concocting evidence against Röhm and his people. Göring, in overall charge of the operation, was consulted and informed, but was content to leave the details to Heydrich, at least for the time being. Soon, they started drawing up what they described as 'Reich lists of undesirable people', though they carefully avoided specifying what was to be done with these undesirables. While this was all going on, Göring made his own lists, and kept himself busy with his other interests, including the secret planning with Milch for the Luftwaffe, and his continuing ambitions as an alternative foreign minister. He turned his attention first to Poland, where he could combine diplomatic visits with hunting in the state forest of Bialowiéza: Józef Lipski, who was to become Polish Ambassador to Berlin later in the year, was another passionate huntsman and was delighted to arrange this, in return for invitations to join Göring on the Schorfheide. These shooting parties were an excellent way of forming and cementing personal relationships with Polish leaders.

In May, Göring extended his diplomatic activities with a ten-day 'vacation tour' of south-eastern Europe, accompanied by Milch, Körner, Prince Philipp of Hesse, and Emmy Sonnemann – whose presence created a minor scandal, as Goebbels was quick to inform Hitler. Göring's choice of destination was no coincidence. He had been offended by Mussolini's rejection of his assurances over Austria, and this was one way of getting back at him – the Italians regarded the mineral-rich Balkan states as their exclusive domain, and were likely to be upset by this high-profile intrusion. Aware of the potential threat to Italy of a resurgent Germany, Mussolini dreamed of creating a security zone through a south-central European confederation of Austria, Hungary, Yugoslavia and Albania, under Italian leadership.

To make his trip doubly offensive, Göring first announced that he would start his tour in Rome, then changed his mind just before his plane took off and headed for Budapest instead, leaving Mussolini's reception committee kicking their heels at the airport, a calculated snub that gave him great if childish satisfaction. Mussolini played tit-for-tat three weeks later when Hitler made his own first visit to Italy, by letting it be known through the Foreign Ministries that Göring would not be welcome.

Back home, Göring was putting the finishing touches to his new Berlin palace and Carinhall, cramming both with art treasures donated by galleries, museums, and people who recognised his growing lust for expensive gifts. Many of these were presented by local officials and businessmen when he descended on their towns and factories like a film star on tour, resplendent in white uniform and sparkling medals, to promote the regime and his own image. Carinhall was his particular pride, and with the first stage of the building complete, he could hardly wait to show it off. On 10 June 1934 he held a house-warming party for forty foreign diplomats, headed by US Ambassador Thomas Dodd, Italian Ambassador Enrico Cerutti and his wife, and the newly arrived British Ambassador Sir Eric Phipps, who wrote a long, acerbic account of the event as his first dispatch back to London.

The guests were assembled in a forest clearing to await their host, who arrived late in his two-seater sports car, dressed, according to Sir Eric, in 'aviator's garments of indiarubber, with top boots and a large hunting knife stuck in his belt'. He then lectured them, through a megaphone, on the natural history of the forest and his plans for breeding from the animals he had imported from East Prussia and elsewhere. To demonstrate this, he tried to get a bison bull from Canada to mate with one of its cows, but the result was disappointing. 'The unfortunate animal emerged from his box with the utmost reluctance,' Sir Eric recorded, 'and, after eyeing the cows somewhat sadly, tried to return to it.' Unabashed, Göring sped off back to the house, where the guests found him waiting for them on the steps, now wearing white drill trousers, tennis shoes, white flannel shirt and green leather jerkin, with the hunting knife still in his belt.

He led them on a tour of the house, 'displaying his vanity at every turn', according to Dodd, and 'often causing his guests to glance amusedly at each other', and carrying 'a curious, harpoon-like instrument' – it was actually a Scandinavian hunting spear, a gift from Count von Rosen, and Göring was looking for a suitable place to display it before Rosen arrived the next day. Emmy acted as hostess at dinner in the great hall – Göring introduced her as 'my private secretary', but gave the game away by repeatedly putting his arm around her waist and hugging her affectionately. The final part of the tour, after dinner, was a visit to the mausoleum across the lake, ready and waiting for Carin's sarcophagus, which was due to be interred ten days later. By this time, Phipps and Dodd had grown 'weary of this curious display', and slipped away back to Berlin.[16]

Carin's reinterment on 20 June was conducted with all the solemn pomp Göring could muster. Ranks of helmeted Reichswehr troops lined the route and a dozen of them carried the coffin to its final resting place, to the strains of the funeral march from *Götterdämmerung*. Party leaders, industrialists, diplomats and officials stood alongside members of Carin's family, including her son Thomas, and Hitler walked beside

Göring at the head of the cortège to honour the woman he had so admired. Once the sarcophagus was in place, the two men entered the mausoleum together, to stand alone in silent remembrance.

It was a moving and dignified ceremony, but signs of the mounting tension elsewhere still managed to intrude. Himmler arrived late, just as the ceremony was about to begin, pale and shaken, claiming he had narrowly escaped an assassination attempt. Drawing Hitler and Göring aside, he told them that someone had fired at his car. The bullets, he said, had passed through the windscreen and 'Providence alone' had saved him. At first, he blamed the Communists, and demanded that forty of them should be shot at once, but soon changed his mind and decided the SA were the culprits: the Berlin SA chief, Karl Ernst, he recalled, had regularly sworn to 'get that black Jesuit'. Only a few days before, Ernst had accused Himmler of trying to assassinate him when a workman had tossed a hand-grenade fuse into the Unter den Linden five minutes after he, Ernst, had driven past.[17] Daluege, who took charge of Himmler's car, soon came to the conclusion that the hole in the windscreen had been caused by a stone, thrown up by a car that had passed it at sixty-five miles an hour, but the theory of an assassination attempt was too convenient to dismiss.

Before Hitler left Carinhall after the ceremony, he talked privately with Göring and Himmler, who tried once again to convince him that the time had come to act. Hitler was well aware of the urgency: Hindenburg was fading fast, and at the same time tension was building everywhere amid mounting rumours and counter-rumours of an impending 'second revolution'. In addition, the first flush of enthusiasm among the German people for the new regime was cooling rapidly, as it failed to deliver on its promises of instant prosperity and above all the restoration of order which, with the Communists out of the picture, now hung on controlling the SA.

At the beginning of June, Hitler had ordered the SA to cancel its planned military exercises, partly to mollify the army but also to help persuade the Western powers to restart talks about rearmament. He had then spent five hours trying to persuade Röhm to abandon the idea of a 'second revolution'. But he does not seem to have issued him with any serious warning, and Röhm left convinced that when the crunch finally came, Hitler would support him against the generals and the reactionaries. Indeed, so confident was Röhm that he felt safe in announcing that on the advice of his doctor he was leaving for several weeks' sick leave – for iodine treatment for a rheumatic condition at the Bavarian spa of Bad Wiessee. The communiqué, which was published in the *Völkischer Beobachter* on 8 June, recommended SA leaders to begin organising their own summer leave. While a limited number should go away in June, it stated, 'for the majority, July will be a period of complete relaxation in which they can recover their strength'. Just in case anyone thought this was a total climb down, Röhm ended on a defiant note:

If the enemies of the SA delude themselves with the hope that the SA will not report back for duty after their leave, or only report back in part, we should leave them in their hopeful expectations. They will receive a fitting answer at the time and in the form which appears necessary. The SA is and will remain Germany's destiny.[18]

If the SS was to move against the SA it would have to be before July – it would be hard to charge them with plotting a *putsch* while they were away on leave. As Röhm left for his cure, Himmler and Heydrich ordered the SS and SD to stand by for action, and to intensify their surveillance of the SA. Heydrich identified four main areas – Bavaria, Berlin, Saxony and Silesia – which he claimed would be the main centres of the supposed SA uprising. Behind the wire in Dachau, Commandant Eicke held secret war games with his staff, preparing for strikes around Munich, Lechfeld and Bad Wiessee. Meanwhile, Göring and Heydrich began whipping up rumours and fabricating evidence of treasonous intrigues between 'dangerous' politicians, especially General von Schleicher and Gregor Strasser, two names guaranteed to fuel Hitler's paranoia, and Röhm and his SA leaders.

As it happened, it was not the SA that triggered the final crisis, but the conservatives. On Sunday, 17 June, three days before Carin's reburial, Papen made a speech to students at Marburg University, in which according to Hans Bernd Gisevius, 'he said openly what all decent Germans were feeling, all who were not in the grip of mass hysteria'. The speech had been written for him by a conservative thinker, Edgar Jung, and it is said that Papen did not see it until shortly before he was about to deliver it, which may account for his uncharacteristic courage in speaking out against the excesses of the National Socialist revolution, and the dangers of a 'second revolution'. It was time, he said, 'to silence the doctrinaire fanatics and put an end to the meddling with the serious work of serious men.' He attacked the 'selfishness, mendacity, beastliness and arrogance that are spreading under the guise of the German Revolution', and took hefty swipes at Goebbels and the creation of a 'false personality cult'. 'Great men are not made by propaganda, but grow out of their actions,' he stated, adding, 'No organisation and no propaganda, no matter how good, will suffice in the long run to preserve confidence.' The body of the speech continued:

The domination of a single party in place of the system of many parties, which has justly vanished, seems to me from the historical point of view a transitory phase which is justified only so long as it is necessary to safeguard the Revolution and organise the selection of government personnel . . . But no nation can afford an eternal revolt from below if that nation wishes to continue to exist as an historical entity. At some time the Movement must come to an end; at some time a firm social structure must arise and must be maintained by an incorruptible judiciary and an uncontested state authority. Permanent dynamism cannot shape anything lasting. Germany must not be a flashing meteor of which none can say where it will come to a stop.[19]

This was explosive stuff, and it was received with wild applause in the hall. Goebbels leapt on it at once and smothered it with a press and broadcasting ban – though not before the influential *Frankfurter Zeitung*, which he had allowed to survive as a token, only half-strangled, liberal voice for the benefit of foreign readers, had published extracts. Word of the speech and its tone, if not its exact contents, spread quickly through Germany, raising the temperature still further and bringing the crisis nearer.

Still a radical at heart, Goebbels was an eager advocate of a 'second revolution' and directed his venom not against the SA but against those he saw as the real enemy, the reactionaries. Knowing this, Göring and Himmler, and indeed Hitler, were careful to keep him in the dark about their plans: at this critical stage, they dared not trust him to keep quiet. Instead, they encouraged his rages against the reactionaries as a valuable smokescreen, lulling their victims into a false sense of security. Since early May, he had been touring the country making inflammatory speeches against 'alarmists and *Kritikaster* [a word made up by Goebbels, implying cranks who could do nothing but carp and criticise], the rumour-mongers and idlers, the saboteurs and agitators'. On 20 May, while enjoying a Whit Sunday cruise with him through Berlin's lakes on the smart motor yacht *Baldur*, which he had bought at Easter, Blomberg wound him up still more by feeding him the line that Papen had ambitious plans to step into Hindenburg's shoes when the President finally died. Goebbels took the bait. 'Absolutely out of the question,' he snapped into his diary. 'On the contrary, this mess must be cleared up first.'[20] Through May and into June, he redoubled his attacks, breaking off briefly when Hitler – perhaps to get him out of the way, perhaps to even the score in his personal competition with Göring – sent him on an official mission to Poland, to reaffirm the regime's peaceful intentions.

Papen's speech sent Goebbels into paroxysms of rage, and in a Sportpalast speech on 21 June he lambasted him and his fellow bourgeois conservatives as 'ridiculous twerps'. 'These people will not stop the progress of the century,' he yelled. 'We will trample them down as we march forward.' Coupled with his heavy-handed censorship, this was enough to provoke Papen into threatening to go to Hindenburg and resign as Vice-Chancellor. Hitler was horrified; he found it hard to believe that Papen would have spoken out so boldly without solid backing from the entire conservative and military establishment, and feared that he was about to lose the support of the army and the President. He managed to pacify Papen by disowning Goebbels and his criticisms, promised to have the ban on the speech lifted, and persuaded him to delay his resignation until they could visit the President together to discuss the entire situation with him – Hindenburg was no longer in Berlin, but had retired to his estate at Neudeck in East Prussia.

As soon as Papen agreed, Hitler immediately went behind his back and arranged an interview on his own with the President, ostensibly to inform him about his recent meeting with Mussolini in Venice, but in reality to test the water and check on the old man's state of health. He had been encouraged by a report from Walther Funk, who was staying at Neudeck, that the Field Marshal had barked: 'If Papen cannot stay in line, he will have to take the consequences.' At the door of Schloss Neudeck, he met Blomberg, who had been summoned by Hindenburg to discuss the crisis. Blomberg told him that unless he, Hitler, could restore calm in Germany, the President would declare martial law and hand power to the army. The President himself, according to a later account by his State Secretary, Meissner, told Hitler 'to bring the revolutionary troublemakers finally to reason'.[21] There was no more time for vacillation: now Hitler really would have to take decisive action, and fast.

*   *   *

The deadly end game was starting, and Göring, Himmler, Heydrich and Reichenau stepped up their moves to a frantic pace. While Hitler was still at Neudeck on 21 June, Göring had sounded the warning in the Prussian State Council, declaring: 'The first revolution was begun by the Führer. If the Führer desires a second revolution, he will find us ready and waiting. If he does not, then we are equally ready and willing to act against any man who dares lift his hand against the Führer's will.' The next day, Hitler made his first positive moves, ordering the arrest of Edgar Jung, the author of Papen's speech, and calling the man he had chosen to be Röhm's replacement, Viktor Lutze, from Hanover to stand by in Berlin and to take orders only from him. From then until the end of the operation, Lutze was constantly at his side.

Hitler told Lutze that Röhm had to be removed, since he intended 'to arm the SA and let it loose against the Reichswehr, in order to liberate him, the Führer, from the military, whose prisoner he was supposed to be'.[22] For the first time, he became directly involved in vetting the lists of those to be liquidated, discussing them with Lutze, who claimed that they started out with a mere seven names of the very top SA leaders, but that this was expanded by the 'wicked SS' first to seventeen and then to more than eighty, as they sought to settle personal scores.[23]

During the following week, both Hitler and Göring kept up a full programme of engagements, flitting from one end of the Reich to the other to give an impression that life was continuing as normal. Röhm was completely fooled, settling himself comfortably in the Hotel Hanselbauer at Bad Wiessee, dismissing all rumours that Hitler and the army were planning to move against him. His spirits were still high – the FA recorded a telephone conversation with Ernst back in Berlin, in which the two men fantasised about how they would deal with 'the pig Göring' when the 'due time' came. 'I will personally slice slabs of flesh off his fat body until he is half his size,' Ernst said. 'And only then will I stick my knife in his throat.' 'Do that,' Röhm chuckled. 'But don't eat any of the cuts. Forbidden meat!'[24] Such intercepts were guaranteed to raise Göring's hackles and harden his resolve still further, but at least they confirmed that the SA leaders were still unsuspecting. It is entirely possible, of course, that Röhm knew about the phone taps, and was deliberately making outrageous statements as a joke to wind up Göring. If so, the joke was on Röhm and it was Göring who would have the last laugh.

Heydrich was now in his element, concocting plots, fabricating evidence, starting rumours, all designed to convince both the army and Hitler that the SA really was about to stage a *putsch*. A man claiming to be an SA-Obergruppenführer (lieutenant-general) appeared in army district headquarters in Münster, asking for information on its organisation, since, he said, the SA would shortly be taking over the Reichswehr. Sepp Dietrich, commander of the SS-Leibstandarte, showed the Defence Ministry what purported to be an SA firing squad hit list that included virtually all army generals. In other districts, SS men produced SA plans for the dismissal of senior officers. An order signed by Röhm, ordering all SA units to arm themselves ready for an attack on the Reichswehr, mysteriously found its way on to the desk of Captain Patzig, chief of the Abwehr, military intelligence. Patzig showed it to Blomberg and Reichenau, who took it to Hitler, who was suitably impressed. And so it continued.

Though most senior army officers refused to take the rumours seriously, the fake evidence justified Blomberg and Fritsch putting all units on alert from 25 June 1934. Officers in headquarters and the Ministry were to keep loaded revolvers in their desks. Weapons and transport were to be made available to the SS, who were to be regarded as allies – as a relatively small force, concentrating on police work, they were not perceived as a threat. That same day, Reichenau had Röhm expelled from the League of German Officers, thus removing his protection as a member of the officer corps and making him fair game.

Also on 25 June, Hess, who was in on the conspiracy as leader of the Party Organisation and mentor of Himmler, went public with a broadcast speech designed to notch the temperature still higher. 'Woe to him who breaks faith in the belief that he can serve the revolution by revolt!' he warned. 'Adolf Hitler is the revolution's great strategist. Woe to him who plants his flat feet among the fine threads of the Führer's strategic plans, thinking to force the pace. He is an enemy of the revolution.'[25] Göring followed up with a blood-and-thunder speech of his own, roaring out the message: 'Anyone who erodes this confidence [in Hitler] is guilty of high treason. Anyone who wishes to destroy this confidence is a destroyer of Germany. Anyone who offends against this confidence will pay with his head.'[26]

The stage was now set. All that was needed was a word from Hitler. But Hitler still could not quite bring himself to give the order to eliminate his oldest friend, the man who had started him on his political career back in the dark days of 1919. The conspirators still needed to find something that would give him the final push. On 28 June, Göring persuaded Hitler to accompany him to Essen, first to visit the Krupp works and then to attend the wedding of Göring's friend and joint proprietor of the *National-Zeitung*, Josef Terboven, Gauleiter of Westphalia. Hitler later claimed that he had gone to Essen 'to present an outward impression of absolute calm and to give no warning to the traitors'. But Lutze, who went with him, saw things differently. 'I had a feeling,' he wrote, 'that it suited certain circles to aggravate and accelerate "the affair" just at the moment when the Führer was absent from Berlin and could therefore neither see nor hear things for himself, but was dependent on the telephone.'[27]

Lutze was quite right: Göring and Himmler had their double act worked out perfectly. The wedding reception had hardly begun when Himmler arrived from Berlin, bringing fresh revelations about the SA and the conservatives, which Göring backed up. When Himmler reported that Papen had arranged to see Hindenburg alone on 30 June, after hearing that Jung had been arrested by the Gestapo, alarm bells started ringing for Hitler. A wounded Papen was a dangerous animal, and he would undoubtedly try to persuade the President to take steps to limit the power not only of the SA, but also of Hitler himself. The *Reaktion* was on the march again; the prospect of martial law loomed. A pre-emptive strike was the only answer. Sending Himmler back to Berlin, Hitler left the reception and hurried with Göring to the Kaiserhof Hotel, where they were joined by Pilli Körner, who brought fresh news and a sheaf of brown pages from the FA, 'proving' that the SA was arming itself for a revolt throughout Germany. It was the vital last straw. 'I've had enough,' Hitler declared. 'I shall make an example of them.'

With no time to lose, the operation went into overdrive. Hitler telephoned Röhm's adjutant and ordered him to call all SA Obergruppenführer, Gruppenführer and inspectors to a meeting with him at Bad Wiessee in the late morning of 30 June. It was a brilliant idea – instead of having to risk rounding them up in their own territories across the length and breadth of the country they would all gather, voluntarily, in one quiet, fairly remote spot, far from their own supporters, where the SS could pick them up with ease. Hitler would supervise this himself. Göring would be in total charge of operations in the rest of the country, swinging into action as soon as he received the code word '*Kolibri*' (humming bird), to indicate that Röhm and his men had been successfully taken.

Göring flew back to Berlin at once with Körner and set up his operational control in his Leipziger Platz palace. The big danger was that the SA might not take the arrest of their leaders quietly. Göring brought in armed units of his personal police group to fortify the building and its approaches with sandbags and machine-guns. At the same time, he ordered Milch to deploy 600 troops who were being secretly trained for the Luftwaffe, to defend the Air Ministry building and Berlin's three airports. Himmler joined him in the palace, along with all essential staff, who were ordered to report at once with their toilet things and clean shirts for a three-day stay. Wolff spent virtually the whole of the seventy-two hours he was there on the telephone, making, according to his own account, over 7,000 calls mostly concerned with the names on the various lists. 'With almost every name,' he said later, '. . . it was a question of life and death.'[28] Heydrich shuttled to and fro between Göring's palace and his own Prinz-Albrecht-Strasse headquarters. Between them, they issued streams of orders to SS units throughout the country, calling them into barracks on full alert and sending sealed orders to commanders, which were not to be opened until Himmler, Heydrich or Göring gave the word.

The generals ordered all army units, too, to stand by in their barracks, and to start issuing weapons to the SS – to be returned as soon as the action was finished. Preparations went on all day, with Reichenau, Blomberg and other generals making regular appearances in the palace to consult with Göring. The *Völkischer Beobachter* that morning published a statement by Blomberg which made the army's position absolutely clear:

The Reichswehr considers itself in close harmony with the Reich of Adolf Hitler. The time has passed when people from various camps could pose as spokesmen of the Reichswehr. The role of the army is clearly determined: it must serve the National Socialist State, which it recognises. The hearts of the Reich and the army beat in unison . . . The Reichswehr wears with pride the symbols of Germany. It stands, disciplined and faithful, behind the leaders of the state, behind the Marshal of the Great War, President von Hindenburg, its supreme leader, and behind the Führer of the Reich, Adolf Hitler, who, coming from the ranks of the army, is and always will be one of us.[29]

Hitler, meanwhile, had flown to Bad Godesberg on the Rhine, keeping up the appearance of normality by fulfilling an engagement to visit a nearby Voluntary Labour Service camp and review a display in the grounds of one of his favourite hotels, the Rheinhotel Dreesen.

Nevertheless, the first thing he did when he arrived was to call Dietrich and Goebbels to fly to him from Berlin, leaving neither in any doubt that something momentous was about to happen. When Dietrich arrived, he was briefed fully then sent on to Munich, to take charge of two companies of the SS Leibstandarte who were on their way from Berlin by train to a small station near Landsberg, obtain weapons and transport from the army, and stand by for further orders.

Goebbels went to Godesberg with a light heart, full of eager anticipation, convinced that the Führer was going to deal with the hated *Reaktion* at last. 'So this is it!' he wrote in his diary before leaving. 'In the name of God. Anything is better than this terrible waiting. I am ready.'[30] The socialist revolution he had dreamed of for so long was about to be completed. It came as a nasty shock when Hitler told him what was really afoot. Once again, his idol had shown himself to be a reactionary at heart – and once again Goebbels turned an ideological somersault at his command. Hitler, ever the psychologist, told him he had proof that Röhm had been conspiring with Schleicher, Strasser and the French Ambassador, André François-Poncet, and that the situation was so serious that he had to act against Röhm and the SA rebels the next day. Instantly swallowing his own convictions, Goebbels begged to be allowed to take part, clearly nervous that he needed to remove any doubts about his own loyalty. To his delight, Hitler told him he wanted him at his side. Goebbels saw this as a mark of favour; but it is hard not to suspect that Hitler wanted him where he could see him, in case he was tempted to rebel and warn his friends in the SA, and also wanted him to be fully implicated so that he could not decry the action afterwards.

In the quiet of Godesberg, Hitler was once again conveniently divorced from the centres of activity, and once again dependent on the telephone, though Göring, more aware than anyone of the dangers of the phone, chose to communicate by sending Pilli Körner flying from Berlin carrying sealed messages. Most of those messages brought Hitler alarming news of threatened SA revolts and disturbances, some genuine, some fabricated, all grossly exaggerated. In Hamburg, a band of 'Old Fighters' had attacked and beaten the Portuguese Consul-General: that at least was true. It was also true that in various places scattered bands of storm-troopers had taken to the streets after hearing rumours that the army was about to move against them. It was not true, however, that there was any threat of an organised uprising. Nor was it true, as Himmler reported near midnight, that the SA in Berlin was ready to launch a *putsch*, starting at 5 p.m. the next day, 30 June, with the occupation of the government buildings. Karl Ernst, he said, had not left to join the other SA leaders in Bad Wiessee but had stayed behind in Berlin to direct the action in person. The truth was that most members of the Berlin SA had already gone on leave, and Ernst, who had been married a few days before – Göring had been his best man – was on his way to Bremen, to board a ship bound for Tenerife on a delayed honeymoon.

Hitler hardly had time to digest Himmler's news before an equally disturbing report arrived from Adolf Wagner, Gauleiter and Interior Minister of Bavaria, saying that the SA were marching through the streets of Munich. This was at least partly true: some 3,000 storm-troopers, alerted by anonymous, hand-written leaflets mysteriously circulated during the day, had indeed been rampaging through the city, chanting 'The Führer is against us. The Reichswehr is against us. SA out on the streets!' No one knew where the leaflets had come from – though Heydrich could probably have told them – and the regional SA commanders, Obergruppenführer August Schneidhuber, a former army colonel who was now also Chief of Police in Munich, and Gruppenführer Wilhelm Schmid, were quick to order their men to return home. But they were too late: the trick had worked. Hitler was incandescent at what he saw as this latest betrayal by Röhm. He could wait no longer – he decided to leave at once for Munich.

Hitler's tri-motor Ju52 landed at Munich's Oberwiesenfeld airfield as dawn was breaking. Glassy-eyed with fatigue and moving as though in a trance, he leapt from the plane and marched past the party offi-cials waiting to greet him, followed by his adjutants and Goebbels, Lutze and his press chief Otto Dietrich. Before leaving for Wagner's Bavarian Interior Ministry, he paused before two army officers whom he had summoned by radio, and told them: 'This is the blackest day of my life. But I shall go to Bad Wiessee and pass severe judgement. Tell that to General Adam.'[31]

At the Interior Ministry, Hitler had Schneidhuber and Schmid brought from their homes, screamed accusations of treason at them, tore the badges of rank from their uniforms, and informed them they were under arrest and would be shot. As they were led off to Stadelheim Prison, he ordered Wagner to send squads from the SS and Bavarian Political Police to arrest listed SA leaders and opponents of the regime. Then, without waiting for Sepp Dietrich and his Leibstandarte men, he headed for Bad Wiessee, with Goebbels and Lutze at his side, escorted by two carloads of SS men and Bavarian Political Police detectives.

Röhm was fast asleep when Hitler, pistol in hand, pushed open the door of his room at 6.30 a.m. He barely had time to get out a bemused 'Heil, my Führer!' before his Führer yelled that he was a traitor and was under arrest. Leaving two detectives to watch Röhm, Hitler moved on to bang on the doors of the other SA leaders who had already arrived at the hotel and repeated the process. Only one made any fuss – Edmund Heines, head of the Silesian SA in Breslau, who was found in bed with a fair-haired young man, to the great disgust of Hitler and Goebbels, who later described the scene as 'revolting – almost nauseating'.[32]

The whole thing was over in a few minutes, quickly, quietly and efficiently. The 'nest of conspirators' were all locked in the hotel's cellar, before being driven off to Stadelheim Prison in a hastily hired local bus. There was no bloodshed – that was to come later. There was one awkward moment when Röhm's heavily armed SA headquarters guard arrived belatedly in a lorry, but instead of turning nasty they obeyed Hitler's order to return to Munich without demur. Even the arriving SA leaders Hitler and his entourage met on the road as they drove back to Munich allowed themselves to be turned round and arrested without incident. Others were arrested equally calmly at Munich's main rail station as they stepped off their trains from various parts of the country. By mid morning there were some 200 of them awaiting their fate in Stadelheim.

At 10 a.m., back at the 'Brown House', Hitler gave Goebbels the honour of calling Göring in Berlin to tell him 'the majority of the criminals are now in custody' and give him the codeword 'Kolibri' to start the action across the rest of the Reich. Whatever misgivings he might have had, there could be no doubt now that Goebbels was in the affair up to his neck. Göring, who had been waiting impatiently in his ornate study, gave Himmler and Heydrich the go-ahead to unleash their SS and SD executioners. Throughout the country, sealed orders were opened to reveal lists of their victims, and the killing began.

In Berlin, squads of Göring's special police roared out of their Lichterfelde barracks in trucks and on motorcycles to surround and take possession of the city's SA headquarters. Once they were in position, Göring joined them to march into the building at their head and supervise the arrests personally. When they searched the building, he was gratified to discover an arms cache in the cellar containing, as he put it, 'more sub-machine-guns than the whole Prussian police had in its possession'.[33] Göring had meanwhile sent Bodenschatz for Papen, who arrived in his palace protesting loudly that as Vice-Chancellor he was in charge in Hitler's absence and should be responsible for any state of emergency. While he was arguing with Göring, Himmler calmly walked out to the ante-room, picked up a telephone and ordered 'You can go ahead now.' With Papen safely out of the way, an SS squad marched into his office and began searching it. His principal secretary, Herbert von Bose, tried to stop them, and was instantly shot dead. Shortly afterwards his other close confidant, Edgar Jung, was hauled out of Oranienburg concentration camp; his body was discovered in a ditch a few days later. Göring had Papen himself taken away and put under house arrest, guarded by SS men; Papen objected vigorously to this indignity, but later realised that Göring had saved his life. It was not, however, a humane gesture – Papen was simply too influential, and too close to the President, to be murdered.

As the day continued, the mood in Göring's palace became increasingly fevered. Hans Bernd Gisevius, a young police legal adviser who accompanied Daluege there during the morning, gave a vivid description of 'an atmosphere of hate, nervousness, tension, above all of blood and more blood'. The great hall was crowded with groups of officials and officers, talking urgently among themselves while liveried servants moved silently among them with trays of sandwiches. Messengers hurried in and out of Göring's study, where the 'execution committee' of Göring himself, Himmler, Heydrich and Körner conferred over the death lists, adding a name here, removing one there, all the time laughing and shouting exuberantly:

They do not appear to be in bad spirits. Göring exudes an air of cheerful complacency. He struts to and fro, an unforgettable picture: with his flowing head of hair, his white tunic, his grey-blue military trousers, his white boots reaching over his fat knees . . .

Things suddenly begin to get very noisy in there. Police Major Jakobi rushes out of the room in great haste with his helmet on and the chinstrap under his red face. Göring's hoarse voice booms out after him, 'Shoot them down. Take a whole company . . . shoot them down . . . shoot . . . just shoot them down . . . shoot!'[34]

And shoot they did. During the day, an estimated 150 SA leaders were dragged to the Lichterfelde barracks, stood against a wall and gunned down by sharpshooters from the SS and the General Göring Police Group. The unfortunate Karl Ernst was intercepted on the road to

Bremen. His chauffeur and his new wife were both wounded; he was pulled from the car and flown back to Lichterfelde for execution. In other parts of the country, and particularly in the SA stronghold of Silesia, the SS occupied regional SA headquarters and sent out orders for all SA officers with the rank of Standartenführer or above to report to their command posts. When they complied, those whose names were on the list were stripped of their insignia, packed into trucks and driven off into nearby woods, where they were shot, usually in the back of the head. Their bodies were left where they fell. Those who were not marked for execution were quick to affirm their loyalty and 'absolute obedience' to Hitler, and to repudiate the 'unheard of state of affairs' that had existed until then.

The SA men were far from the only victims that day. Göring and Himmler seized the opportunity to settle a few old scores. Schleicher was shot by SS men in plain clothes in his home in the fashionable Berlin suburb of Dahlem; his wife of eighteen months, who tried to intervene, was also killed. Major-General von Bredow, Reichenau's predecessor in the Defence Ministry and a close associate of Schleicher, was shot in his own home soon afterwards. Erich Klausener, head of Catholic Action and a former head of the Police Section in the Prussian Interior Ministry, met his fate in his office in the Transport Ministry as he washed his hands before lunch.

On Göring's personal orders, Gregor Strasser was picked up and taken to the Prinz-Albrecht-Strasse at about noon. Since his resignation from the government, Strasser had gone to great lengths to stay clear of politics, but just lately there had been signs that he and Hitler might be reconciled. On 23 June, Hitler had given him the golden party badge, bearing the membership number 9, and it was rumoured that he was thinking of making him Interior Minister. Even the hint of this was enough to seal his fate with Göring, who knew he could be a formidable rival. Himmler, an early protégé of both Röhm and Strasser, agreed. An eyewitness told Gisevius what happened when Strasser arrived in the Gestapo prison:

By that time some hundred arrested SA leaders were crowded together in one big room. These men had no idea why they had been arrested, nor did they know of the shootings that were going on in Munich and at Lichterfelde in Berlin. They were therefore inclined to look at the situation in its most humorous light, a mood which is common when people are arrested *en masse*. They cheered Strasser when he was brought in as a new comrade in misery.

Some hours passed and there was a great deal of coming and going. Then an SS man came to the door and called out Strasser. The man who had formerly been next in importance to Adolf Hitler in the Nazi Party was to be moved to an individual cell. No one thought anything of it as Strasser walked slowly out of the room. But scarcely a minute later they heard the crack of a pistol.

The SS man had shot the unsuspecting Strasser from behind and hit his main artery. A great stream of blood had spurted against the wall of the tiny cell. Apparently Strasser did not die at once. A prisoner in the adjoining cell heard him thrashing about on the cot for nearly an hour. No one paid any attention to him. At last the prisoner heard loud footsteps in the corridor and orders being shouted. The guards clicked their heels. And the prisoner recognised Heydrich's voice saying: 'Isn't he dead yet? Let the swine bleed to death.'

The bloodstain on the wall of the cell remained for weeks. It was the pride of the SS squadron, a kind of museum piece. These cut-throats showed it to all the terrified inmates and boasted that it was the blood of a famous man, Gregor Strasser. It was only after he had received numerous complaints that Heydrich ordered the bloodstains to be cleaned.[35]

Similar events were being repeated on a smaller scale throughout the Reich, as local SS men took the opportunity of settling personal grudges. In Breslau, a group of officers went out of control and murdered several Jews. In Bavaria, the former General State Commissioner who had foiled Hitler's 1923 *putsch*, Gustav Ritter von Kahr, now an old man of seventy-three, was taken from his home and murdered with an axe; his brutally hacked body was found a few days later in a swamp on Dachau heath, close to the concentration camp. Lesser victims included business rivals and, inevitably, several cases of mistaken identity where someone had a similar name to one on the list.

In the 'Brown House', Hitler called party chiefs and remaining SA leaders to the Senators' Hall and treated them to a furious tirade against Röhm and his accomplices. With gobs of spittle flying from his mouth, he accused them of 'the worst treachery in the history of the world', and claimed that Röhm had received bribes of 12 million marks from France, through Ambassador François-Poncet, to betray his country to its enemies and to have Hitler killed. The rant culminated in the announcement that Röhm and his principal co-conspirators were to be shot that very day – at which Hess leapt up and begged to be allowed to shoot Röhm, a request that he repeated later, almost quarrelling with Max Amman, who demanded the honour for himself. Returning to his own room, Hitler called for the list of the SA men being held in Stadelheim, and marked six names with a cross in green pencil, then dispatched Sepp Dietrich and a squad of selected marksmen to carry out the sentences. Strangely, Röhm's name was not marked – Hitler tried to cover his indecision with a claim that he had spared him because of his many earlier services to the movement, but no one was deceived.

Hitler flew back to Berlin that evening, arriving at Tempelhof at about 10 p.m. Once again, Gisevius gave a graphic description of the scene:

The plane from Munich was announced. In a moment we saw it, looming swiftly larger against the background of a blood-red sky, a piece of theatricality that no one had staged. The plane roared down to a landing and rolled towards us. Commands rang out. An honour guard presented arms. Göring, Körner, Frick, Daluege and some twenty police officers went to the plane. Then the door opened and Adolf Hitler was the first to step out.

His appearance was 'unique', to use the favourite word of Nazi commentators. A brown shirt, black bow tie, dark brown leather jacket, high black army boots – all dark tones. He wore no hat; his face was pale, unshaven, sleepless, at once gaunt and puffed. Under the forelock pasted against his forehead his eyes stared dully. Nevertheless, he did not impress me as wretched, nor did he awaken sympathy, as his appearance might well have done. I felt quite indifferent to him. It was clear that the murders of his friends had cost him no effort at all. He felt nothing; he had merely acted out his rage.[36]

Still on the runway, Göring reported to Hitler, who discovered for the first time how he had extended the operation on his own initiative. Himmler produced what was by now a rather tattered list, and Hitler ran his finger down it, pausing at one name, presumably Strasser's, before nodding and heading back to the Chancellery.

According to his own account, Göring only learned the full extent of the killing later that night. He said he went to Hitler at noon the next day, Sunday 1 July,

and asked him to issue an order immediately, that any further execution was under any circumstances forbidden by him, the Führer . . . because I was worried lest the matter should get out of hand – as, in fact, it had already done to some extent – and I told the Führer that under no circumstances should there be any further bloodshed. This order was then given by the Führer in my presence, and it was communicated at once to all offices.[37]

In his Nuremberg account, however, Göring failed to mention that there was one piece of bloodshed that he still desperately wanted. He and Himmler had both been dismayed to learn that Hitler had spared

Röhm, 'for old times' sake'. As Hitler acknowledged the cheers of crowds organised by Goebbels outside his Chancellery window that Sunday lunch time, and then hosted a garden party for party leaders, Cabinet ministers and their families, they worked on him, arguing that if Röhm were allowed to live, the whole operation would have been a waste of time. Eventually they wore him down, and he agreed – but insisted that Röhm should first be given the chance to take the honourable way out. On Himmler's orders, Theodor Eicke, the Commandant of Dachau, went to Stadelheim prison with two other SS officers, entered Röhm's cell and left him with a copy of the special edition of the *Völkischer Beobachter* giving details of his supposed plans for a *putsch*, and a pistol loaded with one bullet. When no shot had been heard after ten minutes, they had the pistol removed, then drew their own guns and returned, to find him awaiting them boldly, his chest bared. As he fell, his last words were 'My Führer, my Führer . . .' Hitler's official announcement was brief: 'The former Chief of Staff Röhm was given the opportunity to draw the consequences of his treacherous behaviour. He did not do so and was thereupon shot.'[38]

The action was complete. Göring ordered the police to burn all their records of it. As a result, it is impossible to say exactly how many people were killed, or who they all were. Göring himself admitted to 72 deaths; Hitler gave a total of 58 executed and a further 19 shot while trying to escape. But those figures include only victims on the 'official' lists. Gisevius, as a witness at Nuremberg in 1946, reckoned on between 150 and 200, taking into account Himmler's and Heydrich's subsidiary lists of enemies to be disposed of under cover of the purge. Other estimates, including those killed in local assassinations in various parts of the Reich, reach almost 1,000. And there are no figures at all for the hundreds, maybe even thousands, of SA men who were not killed but disappeared into concentration camps under 'protective custody'. As far as Göring and Hitler were concerned, the numbers were irrelevant. All that mattered was that the only threats to their positions had been removed, once and for all.

XVI

'WE ALWAYS APPROVE EVERYTHING OUR FÜHRER DOES'

By the time he called a halt to the killing on 1 July 1934, Hitler was both physically and emotionally exhausted. It was left to Goebbels to issue press statements and make a national broadcast telling the German people what had happened – or at least the party's version of it. He had already ordered the press not to publish death notices of the victims. Now, making great play of their degeneracy, and their 'shameful and repulsive sexual abnormality', he made sure they would not be mourned by decent Germans. He glorified Hitler as the 'saviour of the Fatherland', who, with his 'faithful followers' had refused to allow 'their constructive efforts, undertaken with great sacrifice by the entire nation' to be put at risk by 'a small band of criminals', in league with 'reactionary forces' and a foreign power. In an effort to save face after all his radical rhetoric, he described the action as the 'second revolution' but in a 'different form'. It was a chilling example of the double-think of which he was always capable – or maybe he was simply trying to convince himself.

Most of Goebbels's audience needed little convincing. The overwhelming reaction of the German public to the events of 30 June and 1 July was not one of horror but of relief. They were heartily sick of the SA's excesses, and if a few dozen leaders had been eliminated that was nothing compared to the thousands who had been murdered by the storm-troopers. When Göring's part in the operation became known, his popularity soared as Germans saw him as having removed the brutal menace of the SA from the streets and saving the nation from a bloody civil war. Even many foreign observers regarded him with a sort of grudging admiration. Soon after the purge, he turned up late for a dinner engagement with Sir Eric Phipps. Apologising profusely, he explained that he had just got back from shooting. 'Animals, I hope,' Phipps responded drily.[1]

Amazingly, the storm-troopers and their remaining officers accepted the emasculation of the SA without protest, and if it seemed a little odd that four million belligerent toughs who had supposedly been on the verge of an armed uprising should capitulate so quietly, no one thought to say so. Lutze immediately set about cleaning up the SA, purging the subordinate leadership and lower ranks of revolutionaries, troublemakers and 'degenerates', reducing the membership by forty per cent during the following year, and turning it into little more than a military-style sports and social club. It would never again pose any threat to Hitler and the party, or to middle and upper class society.

The army and the conservatives could hardly wait to show their support for the action. On 1 July, while the killings were still going on, Blomberg issued a statement to the armed forces praising the Führer's 'soldierly determination and exemplary courage' in crushing 'the traitors and mutineers' and promising that the army's gratitude would be shown through 'loyalty and devotion'.[2] Tellingly, he made no mention of the murder of two senior generals. That afternoon, the Berlin Guards Company paraded past the Chancellery in tribute, goose-stepping to Hitler's favourite Badenweiler March.

The ultimate accolade came the next day, in telegrams to both Hitler and Göring in the name of the Reich President – though there can be little doubt that they were written by his son, Oskar, and his State Secretary, Meissner. To Hitler, Hindenburg sent his 'profoundly-felt gratitude'. 'You have saved the German people from a grave peril,' the message said, adding the absolution 'He who wishes to make history must also be able to shed blood.'[3] The message to Göring read: 'Accept my approval and gratitude for your successful action in suppressing the high treason. With comradely greetings, Hindenburg.'

Two days later, Hitler presented an extremely succinct decree to Cabinet, casually included among some twenty minor edicts. It read, 'The measures taken on 30 June, 1 and 2 July to suppress treasonous assaults are legal as acts of self-defence by the state.' It was passed unanimously. And just in case there was anyone who had not got the message, he made it absolutely clear in his first speech after the event, made to the Reichstag on 13 July and broadcast live to the nation: 'In the state, there is only one bearer of arms, and that is the army; there is only one bearer of the political will, and that is the National Socialist

Party . . . Let it be known for all time to come, that if anyone raises his hand to strike the state, then certain death is his lot.'[4] The Nazi deputies packing the Kroll Opera House rose in acclamation – carefully ignoring the fact that no fewer than thirteen of their fellows had been among the victims of what came to be known as 'the Night of the Long Knives'. Göring as Reichstag President ended the session with an emotional endorsement. The entire German people, he declared, 'man by man and woman by woman' was united in a single cry: 'We always approve everything our Führer does.'[5]

Hindenburg's congratulatory telegrams to Hitler and Göring were virtually his last act as President; he died one month later, at 9 a.m. on 2 August. Hitler had visited him a few hours before, to pay his respects and try to obtain his blessing as his successor, but the old man was too far gone, drifting in and out of consciousness and addressing him obsequiously as 'Your Majesty'. Ignoring the fact that the Enabling Act, from which he derived his authority, specifically forbade any change in the institution of the Presidency, Hitler had taken the precaution the previous day of presenting another dubious piece of legislation to Cabinet, which combined the offices of President and Chancellor, to take effect on Hindenburg's death. Now, he automatically assumed the joint position, announcing that he wished to be known as 'Führer and Reich Chancellor', since the title 'Reich President' was too closely associated with the 'greatness' of Hindenburg for him to use.

Hitler was now unassailable: he was head of state, head of government, leader of the party, and Supreme Commander of the armed forces. As though this was not enough, Blomberg and Reichenau had – entirely on their own initiative – drawn up a new oath to be taken by every officer, soldier, sailor and airman, swearing allegiance not to the constitution or the Reich, but to Adolf Hitler in person, as the Führer. This was nothing new, but a throwback to earlier times, when recruits had pledged themselves to the king or the Kaiser, and as such was accepted with very little question.

The new oath was administered with indecent haste on 2 August, at ceremonies throughout the Reich. In the Air Ministry, Göring, wearing his new dress uniform, called a hundred of his officers together and told them the sad news of the Field Marshal's death. He then drew his sword. Milch stepped forward and rested his hand on the blade, while Bodenschatz read out the words of the new oath and the officers chanted them after him. At the end, Göring dramatically lifted the sword over his head and shouted 'Heil Hitler!' The officers raised their arms in salute and repeated the cry as one.

Hitler seemed to have forgotten his promise that when he became President Göring would be Chancellor, but if Göring was disappointed he never showed it, either at the time or later. He was in any case occupied with other things, most enjoyably with the development of the Luftwaffe. Hitler agreed with him and Milch that the bulk of the defence budget should go to building and equipping the new air force. Hitler needed little persuasion: he was an enthusiastic flier and there was a bonus in the need for a huge new ministry building, which would become a Berlin landmark, and which he could help to design. A 400,000-square-foot site was found off the Leipziger Strasse, conveniently close to Göring's palace, and plans were drawn up, with plaster models showing every sculptured detail for Hitler's approval. Grandiose enough to satisfy both men's megalomania, the new ministry was intended to house 4,000 civil servants and officers in 2,800 rooms, a mark of the scale of Göring's plans for his service.

In October, Göring seized another opportunity to needle Mussolini when King Alexander of Yugoslavia, along with French Foreign Minister Louis Barthou, was assassinated by a Croatian nationalist during a visit to Marseilles. The Yugoslavs suspected Italian involvement, and there were anti-Italian riots in Belgrade. Göring immediately saw the chance of getting back at the Italian leader for his condemnation of Germany's involvement in another assassination, on 25 July, of Austrian Chancellor Engelbert Dollfuss by Austrian Nazis, followed by a failed *coup*. Although Hitler had disowned the Austrian Nazis and tried to distance himself and Germany from the botched attempt to replace one fascist dictatorship with another, Mussolini had dispatched 40,000 troops to the Austrian border. He had recalled them three weeks later, but had joined Britain and France in reaffirming support for Austrian independence. Without consulting Hitler, Göring decided to go to the King's funeral as a representative of the German armed forces. Flying in Lufthansa's newest airliner, the Hindenburg, bearing a wreath inscribed 'To our heroic former enemy', and pointedly proclaiming that no German hand was to blame for the killing of King Alexander, Göring undoubtedly stole the show in Belgrade. According to British Ambassador Sir Nevile Henderson, he won the support of all Yugoslavs for Germany by being the only foreign visitor with the guts to ride in an open car in the funeral procession.[6]

The Foreign Ministry traditionalists in the Wilhelmstrasse were appalled as always by Göring's unconventional diplomacy, but Hitler was pleased, and that was all that mattered. A few weeks later, on 7 December, he gave him his reward for this, and above all for his handling of the Röhm affair, by signing two decrees, one appointing him as his deputy, 'in the event that I am impeded in the execution of the offices of Reich President and Reich Chancellor combined in my person', the other naming him as his successor. With Röhm dead and a shaken Papen retired as Vice-Chancellor and removed to Vienna as Ambassador, he was the undisputed second man in the Reich at last.

For Minister-President General Göring, 1934 had been quite a year. He celebrated on 11 January 1935 with his first annual winter ball in the State Opera House, a glittering occasion aping the Hohenzollerns' old court ball. The more radical party comrades sneered at his pretensions, but the ball soon became established as the social event of the season in Berlin, with Göring at the heart of high society, a position he enjoyed with unabashed delight.

1934 had been a remarkable year for Reichsführer-SS Himmler, too. He had completed his control of all the political police in Germany, formed an alliance with Göring, and disposed of the only men blocking his path to further power. A number of the SA leaders who had been eliminated had been police presidents, like Heines in Silesia, who had interfered with political police work; their removal gave him much greater freedom of action. But what really counted was that he had proved himself again to be Hitler's 'faithful Heinrich', and his SS had once more demonstrated its absolute reliability, obedience and discipline. By direct orders of the Führer, Himmler promoted all the senior SS men who had taken part in the purge, and honoured them with ceremonial daggers in a solemn ceremony. In contrast, Göring rewarded the Gestapo with a boozy party for Heydrich and his staff in the grounds of Carinhall, where he had a Bavarian-style beer garden erected for them.

Unlike Göring, who could shrug off murdering Röhm with a cheerful 'But he was in my way!', Himmler needed to justify himself with rationalisations and regrets. Speaking to all Gestapo officials in October, he described 30 June as 'the hardest day that can be visited on a soldier in his lifetime. To have to shoot one's own comrades, with whom one has stood side by side for eight or ten years in the struggle for an ideal, and who had then failed, is the bitterest thing that can happen to a man.' He followed this arrant humbug with the claim that the whole thing had been the fault of Jews, Freemasons and Catholics, who had infiltrated Röhm's entourage and 'driven him to catastrophe'. Their plan, he stated in all apparent seriousness, was 'no more and no less than the detonation of the National Socialist state from within, blowing it up with its own people. There would have been chaos, and it would have given a foreign enemy the possibility of marching into Germany with the excuse that order had to be created in Germany.'[7] This was either an utterly cynical invention or an astonishing piece of self-deception – unless, of course, Himmler himself had been deceived into believing it by the two men who were responsible for accumulating 'evidence', through the Gestapo, the SD and the FA, Heydrich and Göring. Either way, he used it as an excuse to order his detectives to concentrate on searching for the Jewish enemy that was behind all subversion, and the racial conspiracy underlying all crime.

Himmler's ultimate reward for his part in saving Germany from the dastardly Jewish–Catholic–Masonic plot came on 20 July, when Hitler removed the SS from its subsidiary status within the SA and declared it an independent arm of the party, with its Reichsführer answerable directly and only to him. Now, Himmler could really start building his empire, and indulging his fantasies. Ever the romantic, he believed he could now realise his vision of the SS as an order of chivalry through which he would revive what he saw as the ancient ideals of the Teutonic Knights, with himself as Grand Master. In the autumn of 1933, seeking a suitable seat for his order, he had discovered the ruined castle of Wewelsburg, the former stronghold of the soldier bishops of Paderborn, on a hill overlooking the Westphalian plain and the River Alme. On 27 July 1934, one week after the SS gained its independence, he took possession of it, leasing it from the local council for the nominal rent of 1 mark a year.

He planned to turn the castle into his own version of King Arthur's Camelot, complete with a round table for twelve 'knights' – carefully selected senior Obergruppenführer – where he could enact the mystic rituals of the order. It would double as an SS academy, and this was the purpose he gave to the Reich Minister of Economics when he asked for funds: 'I propose to develop Wewelsburg . . . as a Reich SS leaders' school and request the highest possible Reich grant to meet the building costs.'⁸ Other contributions came from the business contacts, mainly in the light industry and electro-chemical sector led by the IG Farben trust, which he had made back in 1932 to help finance Hitler's drive for the Chancellorship. Now that Hitler had access to all the resources of the state, the 'Friends of the Führer' had metamorphosed in the Freundeskreis RFSS (Circle of Friends of the Reichsführer-SS), pouring money into the SS. Himmler put the SS architect, Herman Bartels, in charge of restoring and rebuilding the castle, with the Labour Service doing the actual work. It was a project that would occupy him for several years.

On a more down-to-earth level, Himmler took another significant step on his climb to power when Hitler allowed him to form what amounted to a private army within the SS. To be known as the Verfügungstruppe (VT for short), which translates roughly as 'decreed force', it was to consist of three SS regiments and an intelligence department, and would incorporate the Leibstandarte and the small armed squads already maintained by each SS division. Blomberg and the army were persuaded that it was not in any way taking over from the SA, but was simply an extension of the SS's police function, and therefore posed no threat to them. Although they would provide it with military training, it would have 'no organisational connection with the armed forces in peacetime', but would benefit them by relieving the army of its responsibility for internal order, leaving it free to concentrate on preparing to face external enemies.

Blomberg acknowledged the new force in a secret memorandum to the service chiefs, plus Frick and Himmler, on 24 September, stressing that it was to be used 'for such special internal political tasks as may be assigned to the SS by the Führer', and in the event of war would be 'placed at the disposal of the armed forces'.⁹ On the face of it, it all looked innocuous. In fact, it was the foundation stone for the building of a new imperial guard, an elite military formation that would eventually grow into a parallel army, the Waffen-SS, with Himmler as its Commander-in-Chief.

Compared with Göring and the fast-rising Himmler, Goebbels found 1934 a difficult year in many ways. In their personal competition, Göring had streaked away with all the prizes, while he had been completely wrong-footed over the Röhm purge, only saving his position – and perhaps even his neck – by a swift volte-face. His *bête noire*

within the party, Rosenberg, had savaged him over his speech justifying the purge, which he said had made a 'catastrophic impression'
throughout the world, and accusing him of 'confusing the position of
a Reich minister with that of a small town rabble-rouser'.[10]

Hindenburg's death gave Goebbels the chance of re-establishing
himself as the voice of the regime, and at least partially redeeming
himself for his *faux pas* over the 'second revolution', but he was still
on very shaky ground. He made the first announcement of the death
of the President over the radio, in a suitably grief-stricken voice, and
then took charge of the arrangements for the official mourning and
the funeral. Hindenburg had wanted to be buried on his estate at
Neudeck, but Goebbels and Hitler decided there was much greater
propaganda value in laying him to rest at the Tannenberg memorial,
the site of his great victory over the Russians in 1914. Goebbels turned
it into a national event, mounting a monumental ceremony on 6 August
that emphasised the sense of political continuity, just as he had with
the Day of Potsdam the year before. The entire 65-mile route of the
funeral procession was lined with flaming torches.

The strains of 'Once I Had a Comrade' had scarcely died away before
he was back in the familiar routine of organising a massive propaganda
campaign for a national referendum on 19 August to confirm Hitler's
new position. Both he and Hitler were bitterly disappointed, however,
that although more than 95 per cent of the registered electorate went to
the polls, a mere 89.9 per cent of them voted in favour of the Führer.
Almost five million voted against Hitler.[11] Was Goebbels losing his touch?
One person who thought so was Rosenberg, who never missed an opportunity to put the boot in. In early August, he tried to gain control over
Goebbels's foreign propaganda role by demanding the authority to
oversee the movement's entire foreign policy. And when that failed, he
intensified his fight over cultural matters, informing Goebbels that Hitler
had authorised him to check out the political correctness of all organisations that had been 'co-ordinated'.

The Reich Chamber of Culture was at the top of Rosenberg's hit
list, and he immediately started attacking the leading figures in
Goebbels's Chamber of Music. He picked first on the composer Richard
Strauss, for having the libretto of his new opera, *Die schweigsame
Frau*, written by a Jew, and then turned on the modern composer Paul
Hindemith, for associating with Jews and writing music that Rosenberg
considered kitsch – Goebbels had praised Hindemith a few weeks earlier
as 'one of the strongest talents in the younger generation of German

composers'. Goebbels may have admired Hindemith's talents, but he could not afford to ignore the charge of associating with Jews, and he was forced to condemn him and proscribe his music.

The foremost German conductor and Vice-President of the Chamber of Music, Wilhelm Furtwängler, sprang to the defence of Hindemith with a major article in the *Deutsche Allgemeine Zeitung* attacking political interference in art. 'What should we come to,' he asked, 'if political denunciation be turned without check against art?'[12] Goebbels was furious, and the controversy quickly became a *cause célèbre*. That evening, Furtwängler was conducting at the State Opera, in front of Goebbels and Göring. When he appeared, the audience showed its support for him and hostility to Goebbels with tumultuous applause, a public display of disapproval that Göring took great pleasure in reporting to Hitler.

With his pride severely dented, Goebbels made the mistake of threatening Furtwängler, who promptly resigned both as Vice-President of the Chamber and Director of the State Opera and announced that he was joining the exodus to America. It looked like an outright victory for Rosenberg, until Furtwängler's plan was thwarted by his great rival, Arturo Toscanini, who blighted Furtwängler's US immigration prospects with outspoken criticism. The affair dragged on until the spring of 1935 before Goebbels was able, with Hitler's approval, to persuade the conductor to make a public apology. He had never meant, he said, to interfere in the cultural policy of the Reich, which should be made 'solely by the Führer, and the expert minister appointed by him'. 'A great moral success for us,' Goebbels told his diary. 'These artists are the oddest people in the world. Politically without a clue.'[13] As sour and prickly as ever, Rosenberg demanded that Furtwängler apologise to him and his NS Cultural Community, too, but Goebbels didn't mind. He had clearly won an important point in their vendetta. Furtwängler resumed his old positions, and the following year was appointed musical director of the annual Bayreuth Wagner Festival, a sure mark of Hitler's acceptance. Hindemith hung on for another two years, until his music was finally banned. He left Germany in 1938, and in 1940 settled in the USA, where he taught at Yale University.

The Nuremberg Party Rally in September 1934 confirmed Goebbels's reputation for spectacle with a bigger and more impressive setting than ever before. His protégé Speer developed the themes he had used in 1933, with 130 anti-aircraft searchlights, grudgingly loaned by Göring, pointing vertically to the sky after dark to create a 'cathedral of light' on the Zeppelin Field. Now that Hitler was the undisputed master of Germany, Goebbels could concentrate more than ever before on using the rally to pay homage to him and promote the Führer cult. Despite his adoration, however, he was miffed when Hitler personally commissioned the film director Leni Riefenstahl to make a documentary of the proceedings and ordered the Nuremberg authorities to give her virtually unlimited facilities, without reference to him or his ministry. Riefenstahl was a personal friend of Goebbels and Magda, but even so he was jealous at being bypassed and, Riefenstahl claimed later, tried to sabotage her work by having storm-troopers harass her cameramen. If this was true, he failed miserably, for the result was *Triumph of the Will* – the title was Hitler's suggestion – which was universally acclaimed as a technical masterpiece.

Hitler spoke several times at the rally, but his most memorable words came in a proclamation read out by Gauleiter Wagner: 'The German form of life is definitely determined for the next thousand years. With us, the unsettled nineteenth century has finally ended. There will be no other revolution in Germany for the next one thousand years!'[14] The myth of the 1,000-year Reich was born. It would have no more committed advocate than Goebbels.

Despite his ideological puritanism and the lip service he paid to the simple life – at Christmas 1933, for example, he hauled his brother Hans over the coals for driving a big limousine[15] – Goebbels's political insecurities during 1934 were amply compensated for by his growing affluence and the increasing luxury of his lifestyle. Under Magda's expert eye, his homes were furnished with elegant taste, he dressed in smart, custom-made suits, and entertained in style, often aboard his motor yacht *Baldur* on the Havel lake, where he rented a weekend house at the waterside. But the best perk of all was his involvement in the film industry. As President of the Reich Chamber of Culture, he was its undisputed tsar, to whom everyone, from producers to the lowliest walk-ons, had to make obeisance or risk never working again. He enjoyed his control of the theatre, press, publishing, radio and music, but none of them could match the movies for sheer magic – the others were tools, films were a passion.

Goebbels loved playing the movie mogul. He had a private cinema installed in his home and played films there every night, either classics or the latest releases not only from German studios but also from Hollywood: publicly, he might decry the American products – most of the studio heads were Jewish, after all – but privately he acknowledged their general superiority. In the other cultural areas under his control, he was mostly happy to delegate detailed supervision to his departmental heads, but in film he somehow found the time for a personal hands-on approach at every level and at every opportunity.

He set up the Film Credit Bank to provide finance, and no project could be green-lit until he had given his personal approval. He checked budgets and production schedules, agreed the choice of directors and writers, and read every script, regularly making alterations in his ministerial green pencil. He viewed rushes and interfered with shooting, dropping in unannounced on studios and locations. He exercised final censorship and decided on a film's quality rating, which was particularly important since each positive ratings point earned a tax rebate of four per cent. But the right that gave him most satisfaction was that of casting approval, with all that that implied.

Goebbels revelled in hobnobbing with the stars whom he had long admired as a besotted film buff. There were other bonuses, too, besides the boost to his ego of mixing with glamorous celebrities. He could enjoy lording it over them intellectually with no fear of his views being challenged or contradicted; and he could take his pick of pretty actresses and hopeful starlets, many of whom were only too happy to further their careers by gratifying his voracious sexual appetite on the casting couch. Göring spent many happy hours chuckling over the FA transcripts of his rival's amorous telephone conversations, and was not above drawing Hitler's attention to his activities.

Göring had always been a romantic in love, strictly a one-woman man, faithful unto death, and strongly disapproved of promiscuity. Goebbels, on the other hand, had been driven since his teens by an oversized libido, which he was incapable of controlling; as a bohemian and a revolutionary, he justified his adventures by despising bourgeois concepts of sexual morality. When Magda had discovered, very early in their marriage, that he was having an affair with an aristocratic lady, he shrugged off her anger by reminding her that he had never promised to be faithful.

By 1934, however, the Goebbels marriage was showing increasing signs of strain, aggravated not only by his constant infidelities but also by his unreasoning male chauvinism. When Magda gave birth to their second child on 15 April 1934 and it turned out to be another girl,

Hilde, and not the boy he had been hoping for, he blamed 'this misfortune' on her and refused to visit her at the clinic or even to send her flowers, until Hitler stepped in and made him see sense. It was not the first time Hitler had come to the rescue, nor would it be the last.

Magda had always been a great asset to Goebbels's career, supporting him with both her social skills and an enthusiasm for National Socialism that matched his own. Most important of all, she had a great rapport with Hitler, whom she adored and who in turn greatly admired her. But she had a stubborn streak of independence that did not sit happily with her husband's view that a woman's role in the National Socialist state was 'to be pretty and bring children into the world'.[16]

The first cracks in the marriage had shown up a year before, shortly after Goebbels had become a minister. He had been happy for Magda to broadcast the first Mothers' Day address on 14 May 1933, but had flown into a rage two months later when she wanted to chair a new German Fashion Centre. There had been 'loud scenes', which had escalated into a 'serious conflict' when she refused to go with him to the annual Wagner festival in Bayreuth. Hitler had been 'horrified' that Magda was not there, and had her flown in at once from Berlin. She arrived at the end of the first act of *Die Meistersinger*, 'radiant with beauty – the most beautiful of them all', but 'in very low spirits'. After they had sat late into the night with him, chatting with the performers from the opera, Hitler had made peace between them – 'He is a true friend,' Goebbels gushed in his diary. When Hitler agreed with Goebbels that women had no place in politics, however, the row flared up all over again. They made up their quarrel in bed, but although he noted the next day that she was 'sweet and good', and could be so loving, 'she made no apology in principle'.[17] The cracks had been papered over, but they were still there and would continue to widen over the coming years.

Hitler's growing international confidence was boosted in January 1935 with the first major removal of the provisions of Versailles since the crisis over reparations payments in 1923–4. In 1919, in addition to the ceding of the disputed provinces of Alsace and Lorraine, the neighbouring coal-rich area of the Saar had been placed under League of Nations control and the resources of its mines and factories handed over to France for a period of fifteen years. At the end of that time, the population was to be given the right to choose whether they should return to Germany, join France, or remain under League administration. The fifteen years were now up, and a plebiscite was due. Goebbels was called on to do his stuff again – it was small wonder that his New Year resolution for 1935 was 'Never to get weary'[18] – and he poured out the usual massive propaganda campaign. The result was a foregone conclusion, but even so the figures were a triumph for Goebbels and Hitler. Despite the fact that the vast majority of the Saar's population were Catholics and workers, 445,000 voted for reunion with Germany, 46,000 to continue the status quo, and a mere 2,000 for union with France. Goebbels trumpeted that that meant the Saarlanders, including former Communists and Socialists, had actively embraced National Socialism. When the Saar was returned to Germany on 1 March, its 'homecoming' was marked with the sounding of sirens and factory hooters throughout Germany, and Hitler's standing with the people rose still higher.

The implicit endorsement of his rule by the Saar plebiscite gave Hitler the confidence to go public with his rearmament programme despite the opposition of France and Britain, who were already well aware of it. The British, indeed, published their own arms plans on 4 March, based on 'the fact that Germany was rearming openly on a large scale, despite the provisions of Part V of the Treaty of Versailles'.[19] Sparked by this, Göring publicly revealed the existence of his Luftwaffe on 10 March. On 15 March the French announced that they were extending the length of compulsory military service from eighteen months to two years, thus significantly increasing the size of their armed forces. Hitler responded the following day – although he had taken the decision some days before, without consulting his generals – with the announcement that Germany would cast off the military restrictions of Versailles by reintroducing conscription and increasing the size of its army five and a half times, to 550,000 men, or thirty-six divisions.

The vast majority of Germans were delighted by what they saw as the restoration of their honour. On 17 March, designated 'Heroes' Memorial Day', cheering crowds gathered outside the Reich Chancellery and on the Unter den Linden to watch a great military parade. Marching alongside the army, navy, SS and SA were airmen of the new Luftwaffe, wearing the distinctive uniforms Göring had designed for them, including the innovation of collars and ties. Military traditionalists sniffily dismissed them as 'mufti-soldiers', but Göring was eager to emphasise his service's modernity, and anyhow the SS and party uniforms were both worn with ties. The next day, he had a squadron of bombers fly over central Berlin in perfect formation, their first public appearance.[20]

Any unease over rearmament evaporated within the next few days as it became clear that the Western powers would do nothing more than register formal protests. Hitler the gambler had called his opponents' bluff and got away with it again. Mussolini made the most noise, but in the end was reduced to impotent posturing as he realised he would get no support from Britain or France. Göring had made a vital contribution by playing on British and French fears of resurgent German air power. To make sure the world took it seriously, he had told the British Air Attaché that he already had 1,500 aircraft – the true number was about 800, many of which were obsolescent biplanes, but it suited no one to doubt his claims. When the suitably alarmed Attaché warned that there would be calls for an increase in the RAF, Göring replied that he would welcome that, since: 'In the next war we shall be fighting side by side to save Europe from Communism.'[21]

The fight against Communism conveniently embraced both the Jewish question – which Göring was always ambivalent about – and the plans for territorial expansion to the East at the expense of the Soviet Union – which he supported wholeheartedly. Unfortunately, the drive to the East would depend on finding a way through or around Poland, either by conquest or co-operation. Any attempt at conquest would almost certainly provoke Poland's ally and protector France into war in the West. Co-operation, on the other hand, would not only save money and blood but would also drive a wedge between France and Poland and break the threat of encirclement that always fuelled German paranoia, and which had just been raised further by a new treaty between France and Italy. Hitler gave the task of wooing the Poles to Göring, who accepted it with his usual ebullience.

Germans had viewed the Poles with resentment since they acquired large tracts of land from Germany when their country was reconstituted in 1919, including the hated 'Polish Corridor' cutting off East Prussia from the Fatherland. The distrust was mutual: the Freikorps had fought vicious battles over the frontier with Poland, passing the torch to the SA when they were disbanded – it was no coincidence that the split province of Silesia was the SA's most extreme stronghold. Winning over the Poles after a decade and a half of hatred would be a tricky task, but the brotherhood of the hunt gave Göring a huge advantage. Having entertained Lipski and other Polish notables at his shooting parties around Carinhall or at Rominten, another estate he had now bought in East Prussia, he accepted a reciprocal invitation to hunt wolves at Bialowiéza in January, in company with the Polish dictator, Marshal Józef Pilsudski.

During four strenuous but enjoyable days, Göring built a relationship with Pilsudski, working hard to convince him that the Polish Corridor need not be a contentious issue, and that both their countries could expand in the East, with a little collusion. In return for allowing Germany a free hand in the north-east of the Soviet Union, Poland could have the Ukraine. Assuring him that 'a common German–Russian frontier would be highly dangerous to Germany', he promised that Hitler would never do a deal with Stalin at Poland's expense. Göring's efforts to arrange a summit meeting between Hitler and Pilsudski foundered on the Polish dictator's pre-condition of a guarantee that Germany would not interfere in Danzig, the former German port on the Baltic which had been turned into a Free City by the Versailles Treaty. But the groundwork had been laid for future co-operation.

Göring's star status with ordinary Germans soared to new heights when, after heavy prompting from Hitler, he finally made an honest woman of Emmy. Their engagement in March 1935 coincided with the announcement of rearmament, and was received as part of the general mood of elation. Göring seized the excuse for a series of lavish parties and banquets, culminating in a grand gala reception in the State Opera House the night before the wedding, while squadrons of fighter planes flew in salute over decorated streets. The show did not go down well with everyone, however. 'Party people tell me Goebbels is in a rage at his arch-enemy's lavish displays, of which tonight was only one example, and that he's told the press it can comment sarcastically,' William L. Shirer noted in his diary, concluding: 'Not that many editors will dare to, I think.'[22]

Other Nazi chieftains might choose low-key secular weddings – though even Goebbels had found it hard to resist tradition altogether and had opted for a quiet country church after the civil ceremony – but Göring was incapable of doing anything modestly. He chose the Berlin Dom, the Hohenzollerns' ornate Protestant Cathedral on the Lustgarten, opposite the old Royal Palace – where else, after all, should the successor of the Prussian kings be married?

The wedding itself, on 10 April, was a truly regal affair: 'A visitor to Berlin might well have thought that the monarchy had been restored and that he had stumbled upon the preparations for a royal wedding,' Ambassador Phipps reported to London. 'The streets were decorated; all traffic in the interior of the city was suspended; over 30,000 members of the paramilitary formations lined the streets, whilst two hundred military aircraft circled in the sky, and at a given moment escorted the happy couple from the Brandenburger Tor to the Cathedral.' American correspondent Louis P. Lochner concurred: 'You had the feeling that an emperor was marrying,' he wrote. But it was Phipps who delivered the final observer's verdict: 'General Göring would thus seem to have reached the apogee of his vainglorious career. I see for him and his megalomania no higher goal, apart from the throne, unless indeed it be the scaffold.'[23]

At the reception in the Kaiserhof Hotel for 320 guests – Goebbels, for all his carping, was one of them, the others ranged from royal princes and ministers to young air force officers and Göring's valet, Robert Kropp, who was seated at the same table as the Führer – Hitler told Emmy she was now the first lady of the German Reich, and would have to assume the responsibilities of that position. Afterwards, the newlyweds went first with a small group of special friends to Carinhall, where Göring spent an hour alone in Carin's mausoleum. Emmy did not mind, indeed she seemed to find her husband's devotion to her predecessor endearing, and never showed any sign of jealousy. Equally, Carin's son Thomas never showed any resentment towards Emmy, attending the wedding and generously welcoming her as someone who would make his stepfather happy.

The Görings left the next day for a quiet honeymoon, first in the spa town of Wiesbaden and then in Dubrovnik, in a villa overlooking the Adriatic. Yugoslavia, of course, was one of Göring's areas of special interest, and choosing it helped to cement his relationship with its people and government. After the honeymoon, they paid visits to Belgrade, Sofia and Budapest, in each of which he was received like a head of state. Carin would have been proud of him and of what he had achieved since those terrible days in the Langbro Asylum for the Insane, barely ten years before; Emmy certainly was.

Coupled with his existing missions to Italy, the Balkans and Hungary, Göring's growing success in promoting German relations with Poland bolstered his position as Hitler's 'alternative foreign minister'. When Pilsudski died in May 1935, he was the automatic choice to represent Germany at the funeral ceremonies in Warsaw and Cracow, where he took the opportunity to meet the French Foreign Minister, Pierre Laval, and berate him for signing a pact with the Soviet Union. 'We know the Bolshevists better in Germany than you do in France,' he warned. 'You will see what difficulties your Paris Communists will cause you.' He went on to talk about rearmament and the need to improve relations between their two countries, and came away convinced that France genuinely wanted an understanding. In talks with the Polish leaders, and especially with Foreign Minister Colonel Józef Beck – another keen hunter – he was happy to find that his personal relationships with them were still close. But even with all his considerable charm, he could not persuade them to take a softer line over Danzig.

Reporting his visit to a secret Cabinet conference on his return to Berlin, Göring concluded that Germany would not be able to do anything about Danzig until she had become a great power once more, and that the prerequisite for this was 'the completion of our rearmament'. Unfortunately for him, there was one great obstacle to his plans for the Luftwaffe: money. Schacht and his Ministry of Economics had been told six months earlier to start making secret economic preparations for war, and he had used considerable sleight of hand to find the necessary funds so far. Along with a number of decidedly dodgy financial manoeuvres, he had been forced to create a siege economy, banning virtually all consumer imports and severely restricting foreign currency transactions. But he believed there were limits beyond which he dared not push the long-suffering German public. 'They are being starved of oil to cook with, butter for their bread, meat even for a Sunday dinner,' he told Göring. 'Soon there will be a black market, and then we will have to start shooting people. I simply cannot spare you any more money.'[24]

Schacht might have been one of the world's most brilliant economists, but he was no politician and knew little about ordinary people. Göring, on the other hand, knew nothing about economics, but everything about what the German people really wanted. For three weeks he worked with Pilli Körner on a major speech, which he then delivered with great panache to a mass rally in Hamburg, the city where the loudest complaints about austerity rations had been made. Wearing his Luftwaffe uniform and looking quite drawn after his latest bout of slimming, he began by outlining the tremendous progress that had already been made in restoring German pride through rearmament. He then moved on to remind his audience of the shaming restrictions still imposed on their country by Versailles. Only through strength, he told them, could Germany regain her rightful place in the sun.

Having softened the meeting up, he delivered the killer punch. 'I must speak clearly,' he cried. 'Some people in international life are very hard of hearing. They can only be made to listen if they hear guns go off. We are getting those guns. We have no butter, comrades, but I ask you: would you rather have butter or guns? Shall we bring in lard, or iron ores? I tell you, being prepared makes us powerful. Butter only makes us fat!' He slapped his hollow belly to emphasise his point, and the meeting erupted into roars of approval.[25] Radio listeners all over Germany joined in. Hitler sent him a telegram of congratulations. Schacht came up with the money for the Luftwaffe. The speech was reported around the world. The defining phrase, 'guns or butter' entered the international vocabulary. Göring, of course, never had to make the choice for himself – he could always have both. But no one ever mentioned that.

While Göring was away in eastern Europe, a new contender for the Foreign Ministry had entered the field, staking a claim to a place in Hitler's inner circle. For the moment at least, he was not a candidate for the succession, but for the rivals jostling and jockeying for position, his arrival on the scene was an unwelcome complication. Joachim von Ribbentrop, the man who had helped broker the Hitler–Papen alliance by hosting their secret meetings in 1932, had already been used by Hitler as his personal emissary to Britain and France, both of which he visited regularly in the course of his business. Now, in May 1935, he was being sent to London to negotiate a vital treaty. He had absolutely no experience in such matters, but Hitler seemed to regard this as an advantage rather than a drawback, since he disliked and distrusted the professional diplomats of the Foreign Ministry, rightly suspecting them of being unsympathetic to his revolutionary ideas. He wanted to bypass them and deal directly with foreign leaders, face to face, believing he could win concessions through the strength of his personality and the force of his arguments. To fix such meetings without the involvement of the Foreign Ministry, he needed a personal agent, reporting only to him. In a disastrous decision, he chose Ribbentrop.

Ulrich Friedrich Willy Joachim von Ribbentrop was just forty-two years old in May 1935. He stood about five feet ten inches tall and was quite handsome in a fleshy sort of way, but with cold, metallic eyes. He was intensely ambitious and hard-working but was totally under the domination of two people – his wife and Hitler. Papen described him in his memoirs as:

a man of markedly elegant appearance, always impeccably dressed, who spoke perfect English and French. Unfortunately, these qualities did not suffice to make him a statesman. Normally, a man of his education and background could have been expected to be a success in high office. In Ribbentrop's case there were insurmountable obstacles. He was immensely industrious, but devoid of intelligence; having an incurable inferiority complex, his social qualities never matured as they should have done.[26]

Papen was wrong about Ribbentrop's education, which was sketchy at best, and was possibly misinformed about his background, which was respectable but hardly outstanding. He had acquired the aristocratic 'von' by taking advantage of a Weimar law that allowed him to have himself adopted, as an adult in 1925, by a very distant relative who was entitled to it. This did not ennoble him, but permitted him to take her name, complete with particle; it meant nothing, but sounded good, a typical piece of Ribbentrop flummery. In return, he agreed to pay this 'aunt' 450 Reich marks a month for fifteen years, though he reneged after a short time and she had to sue him for the rest of the payments.

Ribbentrop's father, like several generations of the family before him, had been an artillery officer in the service of the Dukes of Brunswick, and had been stationed in Wesel, a Prussian garrison town on the lower Rhine near the Dutch border, when Joachim, his second son, was born in 1893. Soon afterwards, he was promoted to captain and posted to command the battery at the Palace of Wilhelmshöhe, outside Kassel, a summer residence of the imperial family, where Joachim, his elder brother Lothar and eventually their younger sister spent their early years in an atmosphere of military routines and court protocol. Captain Ribbentrop was a stern disciplinarian, and his sons found him a remote and forbidding figure. Their mother was gentle and loving, but contracted tuberculosis and died in 1902, shortly after their father had been promoted to the rank of major and posted to the important military city of Metz.

Three years later, Major Ribbentrop married again, to the daughter of a minor Prussian aristocrat – with a genuine 'von' – and the family moved into a fine villa in the centre of the city, where they enjoyed an active social life.[27] The young Ribbentrop attended the Kaiserliches Lyzeum, the best school in Metz, where he excelled at sport and music – he won a tennis tournament before he was fifteen, and became an accomplished musician, even considering a career as a concert violinist for a time. But he did less well academically, coming thirty-second in a class of fifty.

Metz was the capital of Lorraine, annexed by Germany only thirty years before, so Ribbentrop was exposed to French culture and the French language, which he soon learned to speak fluently. When his father inexplicably resigned his commission in 1908 and moved the family to Arosa in the Swiss Alps, the boys studied with English and French tutors, improving their language skills still further and revelling in the Alpine sports and cosmopolitan life of the resort, before setting off to spend a year in London, polishing up their English.

At the end of their year in London, the two boys sailed to Canada for a holiday with friends they had met in Switzerland. The short holiday turned into a four-year stay that might well have been permanent had it not been for the twin evils of war and tuberculosis. Joachim was seventeen when they arrived, Lothar one year older. They were due to inherit a modest amount of capital from their mother's estate when they were twenty, and passed the time until then in a series of jobs. Joachim worked in a bank in Montreal, and then as a construction worker on the Quebec Bridge and the National Transcontinental Railway. He seems to have been a popular, well-mannered and cheerful young man, always ready to entertain his workmates with music on his violin and showing little trace of the pomposity and arrogance of his later years.[28]

In the autumn of 1912, both brothers were struck down with TB. Lothar never shook off the illness, eventually dying in a Swiss sanatorium in 1918 after being repatriated on compassionate grounds at the outbreak of war. Joachim was luckier. His life was saved by the removal of a kidney, and though this was to have a marked effect on his health and behaviour in later life, he recovered so well at the time that he was able to resume his sporting activities, and even became a member of the Canadian ice skating team for the annual Ellis Memorial Trophy contest with the United States in February 1914. In the meantime, he had paid a brief return visit to Germany to claim his inheritance, and then spent a few months in New York, where he worked as a newspaper reporter for a while before settling in Ottowa and using his legacy to start a business importing German wines.

Ribbentrop might have settled in Canada had it not been for the war, but patriotism demanded that he return immediately to fight for the Fatherland. On 4 August he caught a train for New York, and sailed for Rotterdam on the 15th, full of fervour but not without regrets: 'I left behind my property, my brother who was seriously ill, the business prospects which had just opened up, many friends, and a young girl I wanted marry.'[29]

Ribbentrop had a good if unspectacular war with the Torgau Hussars, a famous cavalry unit in which his maternal grandfather had served, fighting on first the Eastern and then the Western fronts, winning a commission and the Iron Cross First Class, before being wounded in 1917 and invalided back to an office job in Berlin. Among the friends he made during his three years' active service was the lively young aristocrat, Count Wolf Heinrich von Helldorf, who was to play a decisive part in his life some fifteen years later. And when he was posted on attachment to the War Ministry Office in Constantinople in April 1918, he made the acquaintance of another dashing cavalry officer who was then Chief of Staff of the 4th Turkish Army, Franz von Papen.

Demobilised in the summer of 1919, Ribbentrop had to start his career all over again, this time with neither qualifications nor capital – he had lost everything in Canada and his father had meanwhile squandered the family fortunes and run up large debts. To his credit, the twenty-six-year-old Ribbentrop set about the problem energetically. He took a job as a commission agent in Berlin for a Bremen cotton importer, and on the side used his experience and contacts in the liquor trade to start supplying wealthy Berliners with fine wines and brandy smuggled from France, which were unobtainable through legitimate channels. By the end of the year, he had paid off his father's debts and made enough to set himself up as a registered wine merchant in Berlin.[30]

Ribbentrop was already doing quite well, but in July 1920 he set himself up for life by marrying Ann Elizabeth Henkell, an heiress to the famous sparkling wine firm, whom he had met while playing in a tennis tournament in Bad Homburg. As Goebbels remarked later, in a typically waspish put-down, 'he bought his title and married his money'. Anneliese, as she was known, was an attractive and intelligent young woman of twenty-four, but she was difficult and headstrong, and although her father disapproved of Ribbentrop, he was no doubt glad to get her off his hands. Recognising Ribbentrop as a fortune hunter, he refused to take him into the family firm, but used his influence to obtain a partnership for him with the Berlin wholesaler who handled Henkell wines.

However stupid Ribbentrop may have been in other areas, he was no fool in business. Making the most of his advantages, and with unstinting hard work and considerable acuity, he soon turned Schöneberg und Ribbentrop into one of the biggest import houses in Germany. By the end of 1924 – by which time he and Anneliese had produced two children, Rudolf, born in 1921 and Bettina in 1922 – he could afford to cock a snook at his father-in-law by dropping the Henkell agency to concentrate entirely on the lucrative import-export trade.

Still in his early thirties, Ribbentrop was a comparatively rich man in his own right, and he made sure the world knew it. He built a fine modern house to an arts and crafts design in the exclusive Berlin suburb of Dahlem, complete with a tennis court and swimming pool. He entertained lavishly there, with food as good as the fine wines he always served. He presented chamber music concerts, sometimes taking part on his violin, and became a prominent figure in the Berlin music scene. He collected modern art, becoming a patron of the French post-impressionist, André Derain.

Everything in Ribbentrop's immaculate, English-style garden was rosy. But the worm was already in the apple: his success had gone to his head and the eager, pleasant young man was fast becoming a pompous, self-important bore. Paul Schwarz, a diplomat who had known him in 1919 as a fellow member of a liberal weekly luncheon circle, was shocked at the difference he saw when he returned from a stint as Consul-General in Ceylon in 1928:

Nothing remained of the becoming shyness of bygone days, nothing of his cultivated, almost whispering, voice, and not a vestige of his excellent manners. Now he led his own society of *nouveaux riches* profiteers and impoverished gentry. Ribbentrop was virtual dictator of this group. He lectured his friends with unnecessary vigour on the dangers of Bolshevism . . . This was certainly not the cultured Ribbentrop I had known, but a loud, boisterous adventurer.[31]

To a large extent, the change in Ribbentrop's personality was brought about by Anneliese. His marriage to her may be seen as opportunism, but there can be no doubt that he was always devoted to her, so much so that he became to all intents and purposes her slave, completely dominated by her in every aspect of life. The American psychiatrist who interviewed him in Nuremberg after the war, Dr Douglas M.

Kelley, considered that she was a substitute for the mother Ribbentrop had lost at the age of eight, providing him with the emotional and material security he desperately needed. This may well be so, but what is certain is that she channelled her own ambitions through him, driving him relentlessly and interfering constantly, even insisting on being present at important meetings. The comparisons many people made in later years with Lady Macbeth were by no means far fetched, apart from the murder of the king.

It was Anneliese who pushed her husband into the arms of the Nazi Party – but not until it became clear that it was destined for power. Until then, apart from being violently against Bolshevism, he had shown no great interest in politics and none in National Socialism – he was by inclination a 'sentimental monarchist' and a moderate conservative. Many of his best customers and closest acquaintances were Jews, and he had never displayed any antipathy towards them or their race. His only connection with the party was his old army friend Helldorf.

Helldorf had become chief of the SA in Berlin, but Ribbentrop's contacts with him were purely social: Helldorf, for instance, had proposed him for membership of the exclusive Union Club, which controlled horse racing in Berlin. His seconder, incidentally, was Papen, one of the club's most distinguished members, but even so he had been rejected, largely, it is believed, because his use of the phoney 'von' marked him as a bounder. Although Helldorf was a nobleman, Anneliese refused for a long time to have him in her house, on account of his wild reputation as a hell-raiser. Eventually, however, it was Helldorf who convinced her that the Nazi bandwagon was really starting to roll, and that Ribbentrop had better jump aboard if he wanted to share in the spoils of its success.

Early in 1932, Hitler was a guest at one of the numerous dinner parties in the Dahlem villa, and afterwards had a long private chat with Ribbentrop, who impressed him with his knowledge of England and France. 'Hitler could not hear enough about England,' Ribbentrop recalled in his memoirs. 'Everything interested him: her way of life, parliamentary institutions, the city with its trade, and Empire policy.' For once, it seemed, Hitler was content to listen, and Ribbentrop was more than happy to oblige. 'What Hitler wanted above all else,' he wrote, 'was a permanent and clear settlement with Britain.' Ribbentrop agreed with him: 'It was the harmony of our views about England which on this first evening spent together, created the seed of confidence between Hitler and myself. At that time, however, I did not imagine that this was destined to lead to our later close collaboration in foreign politics.'[32]

Although Ribbentrop later claimed that he had been convinced at that first meeting that 'this man, if anyone, could save Germany from the great difficulties and distress which existed at that time',[33] he had not been struck by the *coup de foudre* that so many disciples experienced. It was Anneliese who was bowled over by Hitler and his vision, and who saw the chance for her husband to capitalise on his cosmopolitan polish and experience – she had no awareness of how shallow that experience was, or how deep his political ignorance. No doubt at her insistence, he joined the Nazi Party on 1 May 1932, as member number 1,199,927. He took care, however, to be listed in the local party in Rosenheim in Bavaria and not in Dahlem, in order to avoid drawing attention to something that might damage his business, of which he was now the sole owner. Anneliese herself joined the party later in the year.

Keeping his membership quiet was hardly the action of a totally committed convert, but as things turned out, it opened the door to great things for Ribbentrop. It was because no one knew he was a member that he was able to act as an intermediary between Hitler and Papen, and to host the critical secret meetings in January 1933 at which the deal was struck for Hitler to become Chancellor. And because of that, Hitler trusted him and chose him to be his unofficial personal adviser on Britain and France, foolishly believing his claims to be an expert.

At first, Ribbentrop simply did his best to sell the Nazi regime in Britain and France, and reported to Hitler on the general situation and attitudes in each country as he visited it. Then he started to get ideas. Trading on his connection with Hitler he managed to get interviews with political leaders, including the French Premier Edouard Daladier and Foreign Minister Joseph Paul-Boncour, and in Britain Prime Ministers Ramsay Macdonald and his successor Stanley Baldwin, Foreign Secretary Sir John Simon and Anthony Eden, trying to arrange private, face-to-face meetings for them with Hitler. None of them took him seriously, but both he and Hitler remained blissfully unaware of this, clinging to the delusion that he was a sophisticated man of the world able to deal skilfully with top French and British politicians. Nothing could have been further from the truth, but when Neurath complained about his bungling and the damage it was inflicting on Germany's reputation, Hitler was delighted to hear that Ribbentrop was upsetting the snooty, hide-bound professionals in the Wilhelmstrasse, and his opinion of him rose still higher.

By 1934, any lingering doubts Ribbentrop might have had about Hitler had disappeared, and he was totally in thrall to him. 'He was almost hypnotised by Hitler, like a rabbit by a snake,' wrote Werner Best, the SD's legal expert who later became Ribbentrop's agent in occupied Denmark. 'Of all the men who admired and feared Hitler and obeyed him unquestioningly, I would say from my own observation that Ribbentrop was the one most strongly under his spell.'[34]

For all his hero worship, Ribbentrop was irked by Hitler's failure to give him official recognition for his efforts, and badgered him regularly for a suitable appointment. He was a man who expected visible rewards – in February 1933 he had had the effrontery to approach Papen and ask for the post of State Secretary in the Foreign Ministry for his part in brokering the agreement with Hitler – and so far he had nothing to show for what he, if nobody else, regarded as important contributions to the cause. All that he had were an SS commission as a Standartenführer, given to him by Himmler in May 1933, and a Reichstag seat for Potsdam after the 12 November elections, probably fixed for him by Helldorf, who had become Chief of Police in Potsdam during Göring's Nazification of the Prussian police.

It was not until April 1934 that Hitler finally gave in to his importuning and persuaded Neurath to create a job and a title for him: Special Commissioner to the Reich Government for Disarmament Questions. The position carried the rank of Ambassador, responsible to the Foreign Minister, and he was given an office in the Foreign Ministry, with a bright thirty-one-year-old diplomat, Erich Kordt, as his assistant. Kordt, who had been secretary to the German delegation to the Disarmament Conference, was instructed to keep an eye on his new boss and report what he was up to, but not to save him from making a fool of himself, as Neurath was convinced he would.

Since Germany had pulled out of the Disarmament Conference six months before, Ribbentrop's new post was largely meaningless, except as an inadequate smokescreen for Hitler's true intentions. But it gave him ambassadorial status and therefore a high place in the order of precedence at dinner parties and receptions, which meant a great deal to him and even more to Anneliese. It also enabled him to approach foreign governments openly – though Neurath issued an order to all embassies that he was not to be allowed to talk to ministers without the German ambassador or his deputy being present. In keeping with his new position, he bought a fine eighteenth-century Schloss set in a large country estate some fifty miles east of Berlin, for weekend entertaining.

His sudden elevation did nothing to make Ribbentrop more popular. Sir Eric Phipps, as astute and acerbic as ever, reported to London: 'It is not only at the Foreign Ministry that Herr von Ribbentrop's advancement is resented. The true blue Nazis object to the allocation of plums to outsiders, while the Nationalists regard him as a renegade. The newspapers do not of course dare to criticise, but quote organs of the British press to show that the appointment has been received with astonishment in England.'³⁵ This was the only way Goebbels could undermine Ribbentrop without offending Hitler. Generally, however, Goebbels ignored Ribbentrop as an irrelevance at this time: he did not mention him once in his diaries for 1933 and 1934.

Ribbentrop's only friends in the upper reaches of the Nazi Party were Himmler and Röhm, to whom he had been introduced by Helldorf, and who was a regular dinner guest at Dahlem – the SA Chief of Staff was a noted gourmet and appreciated the excellent food and wines that were always served there. Ribbentrop claimed that they shared a common love of France and a desire to improve Franco–German relations. But it is a mark of just how much of an outsider he was in party circles that he seems to have been oblivious of the growing tensions between Hitler and Röhm. It came as a great shock to him when Himmler casually remarked while enjoying dinner with him and Anneliese on 29 June 1934 that Röhm was 'as good as dead', before leaving for urgent business with Göring. Entering his office in the Wilhelmstrasse the next day, Ribbentrop was greeted by one of Neurath's staff with the sardonic remark that he was glad to see he had not yet been arrested. To the delight of the diplomats and officials, he turned pale and fled. From then on, he began appearing in his SS uniform at every possible opportunity.³⁶

Soon after the death of Hindenburg, who had always regarded the Foreign Ministry as his preserve rather than Hitler's, Ribbentrop was allowed to set up his own private office, the Büro Ribbentrop. It was housed immediately across the street from the ministry's long, buff-painted, three-storey building, in number 63 Wilhelmstrasse, the former Prussian Minister-President's palace that Göring had rejected. The Büro began on a modest scale – it still had a staff of only fourteen by the end of the year – and although it was intended as an alternative foreign ministry, funded by the party rather than the government, neither

Göring nor Goebbels felt that it posed any serious threat to their own ambitions in that direction. The only person who was upset was Rosenberg, who was himself running the party's own foreign political department and who had always had his eye on the Foreign Ministry. But Rosenberg was so unpopular, especially with Goebbels over his interference in cultural affairs, that anything that spited him was regarded as a good thing. Hess in particular went out of his way to encourage and support Ribbentrop, if only to put Rosenberg's nose out of joint.

With the Büro as his base, Ribbentrop redoubled his efforts to improve Anglo–German relations, shuttling backwards and forwards between Berlin and London, making many contacts in the higher reaches of British society but irritating ministers with his clumsy pushiness, to the fury of Neurath and the German diplomatic establishment. They were even more furious when Hitler announced that Ribbentrop would lead negotiations with Britain for a bilateral agreement on naval rearmament, and appointed him Ambassador Extraordinary and Plenipotentiary on Special Mission. Certain that Ribbentrop would make a complete mess of things, Neurath made no complaint. But when Ribbentrop, flushed with this success, renewed his demand to be made State Secretary in place of the ailing Bernhard von Bülow, Neurath told Hitler he would resign if he appointed 'this total amateur, who has no idea at all of how the office is run'.[37] For once, Hitler sided with Neurath, knowing he could not afford to lose him just yet.

When the Naval Conference opened in the Foreign Office in London on 4 June 1935, it looked as though Neurath's hopes and fears would be realised at once. As soon as the opening speeches were finished, Ribbentrop delivered a bald ultimatum: either the British agreed to a German Navy of thirty-five per cent of the size of the Royal Navy, or the conference was off. Details could be discussed and negotiated, but the question of size was 'fixed and unalterable'. The negotiators on both sides of the table were aghast at his crudity. According to Paul Otto Schmidt, the experienced German interpreter, Sir John Simon, who was leading for Britain, 'flushed with anger. He replied with some heat: "It is not usual to make such conditions at the beginnings of negotiations." He then left the session with a frigid bow.' Schmidt started wondering what the weather would be like when they got back to Berlin.[38]

Incredibly, the British caved in the next day and agreed to Ribbentrop's demand. 'I scarcely believed my own ears when I heard this wholly unexpected statement,' Schmidt recalled in his memoirs.

The percentage, in fact, came as no surprise to the British, for Hitler had been canvassing it quite openly for some time, and they were aware that agreeing to it was probably their only chance of limiting German shipbuilding – if they could trust Ribbentrop's assurances that Hitler would honour it. The Conference resumed on 6 June, and continued for a further two weeks, with a break for Whitsun, before the agreement was settled by an exchange of notes on 18 June.

The Anglo–German Naval Agreement was an important milestone on Hitler's road to the renewal of German power, made all the more significant because the British had made it without reference to France or Italy, with both of whom they had agreed only two months earlier not to permit any further breaches of Versailles. The British government had changed during the course of the conference, with Ramsay Macdonald and Simon being replaced by Stanley Baldwin and Sir Samuel Hoare, respectively, and Hitler could well imagine that the agreement signalled a new phase in Anglo–German relations, perhaps even opening the door to the alliance he so fervently desired. Ribbentrop returned home in triumph. Hitler presented him with a signed photograph of the two of them together, Himmler promoted him to SS-Brigadeführer (Brigadier-General), and he was finally admitted into the leadership of the party with the rank of Amtsleiter (Departmental Leader) – lower than the top rank of Reichsleiter which he asked for, but none the less an official position. At the Nuremberg Rally in September, where he had previously been a nobody, he was treated as a hero. Hitler still did not see fit to make him Foreign Minister, and even turned down his renewed demand to be State Secretary, but he did hint strongly that he would succeed Neurath when the time was right. Much as Goebbels and Göring despised Ribbentrop as a none-too-bright Johnny-come-lately, an opportunist who had made no sacrifices and suffered no hardships for the party, they had to admit that he was a new player on the scene, who had the ear of the Führer and therefore had to be taken seriously.

Ribbentrop certainly took himself seriously. On the strength of his success in London, and his appointment as Ambassador Extraordinary, he decided to expand his Büro, changing its name to the more imposing sounding Dienststelle Ribbentrop and deliberately setting out to turn it into a rival foreign ministry. Hitler supported this folly, giving him a grant of ten million marks to expand it. At the time of the London negotiations its staff numbered about 30, by early 1936 it had grown to around 100, and by the autumn of 1936 it was over 150 strong.

The quality of the new recruits was another matter, however – they were mostly dubious characters, including many who had been rejected by the Foreign Ministry – and the organisation was chaotic in the extreme. For the most part, this did not matter, since despite Ribbentrop's efforts to muscle in on official diplomatic business he was little more than a sycophantic sounding board for Hitler's own ideas, which he absorbed and then parroted back to show how much in tune he and the Führer were. This was a game that most of the inner circle played, but to the dismay of Goebbels and Göring, Ribbenbtrop soon showed that he was even more skilled at it than they were.

XVII

THE FOUR-YEAR PLAN

By the middle of 1935, Goebbels's running battle with Rosenberg over cultural affairs had developed into a contest to prove which of them was the more radical anti-Semite and therefore the more politically pure. It was a contest in which Goebbels had an inbuilt advantage, not only as Propaganda Minister with control over the media, but also as Gauleiter of Berlin, where he could take direct action denied to Rosenberg. Even so, he still suffered an ignominious defeat when he was forced to fire Richard Strauss as President of the Reich Chamber of Music after Rosenberg discovered a letter Strauss had written saying he was merely going through the motions of supporting the regime. Goebbels might have been able to overlook the contents of the letter, but not the fact that it had been written to Stefan Zweig, a Jew.

Although discrimination against Jews was still growing, there had been relatively little physical violence against them since the later part of 1933, for fear of the damage to the economy and the country's international reputation. Now that the Röhm crisis, the announcement of rearmament, the return of the Saar and the Naval Treaty with Britain were all done with, it was time to get back to basics and fulfil one of the revolution's main promises: to remove the Jews from the life of Germany. There were also more cynical reasons for the timing. People were growing weary of the austerity and food shortages that they were being asked to endure for the sake of rearmament, and needed a distraction. And the disaffected storm-troopers of the SA needed something to take their minds off the aborted 'second revolution' and the excitement they had been cheated of. A renewed anti-Jewish campaign would do very nicely.

Goebbels led the way, whipping up hatred and demanding action both in speeches and in the pages of *Der Angriff*. Julius Streicher's poisonous paper *Der Stürmer* grew ever more rabid, while other Gauleiters screamed out their anti-Semitic tirades with fresh vigour. A new wave of violence began to spread through the country, along with a proliferation of 'Jews not wanted here' signs and banners at the entrances to towns and villages. In Munich, Wagner secretly organised anti-Jewish riots, then went on the radio to condemn the 'terror groups' he said were responsible.

To Goebbels's irritation, his own city, Berlin, was lagging behind in the persecution of the Jews, owing to the Police President's reluctance to turn a blind eye to thuggery. Retired Admiral Magnus von Levetzow was not a party member, but was a personal friend of Göring, who had appointed him and protected him earlier when he had complained about SA excesses. Goebbels decided Levetzow had to go. His opportunity came in mid July, while he was spending a few days' holiday with Hitler at Heiligendamm, his favourite resort on the Baltic coast. In the evening of Saturday, 13 July he received a telegram from Berlin telling him that a number of Jews had dared to stage a demonstration in a cinema showing one of his anti-Semitic films. He had complained to Hitler before about Levetzow's unsatisfactory attitude, but now insisted that this was the end. 'It is truly appalling,' he fumed in his diary, that he should have allowed such a thing to happen. Hitler promised to remove Levetzow, and issue a stern warning to Frick, who was now responsible for the police.[1]

By the following Wednesday, Hitler had still done nothing about Levetzow, and Goebbels had to nudge him into action with a staged riot on the Kurfürstendamm, in which Jewish shops were trashed and a number of Jews beaten up. 'Foreign press shrieks "Pogrom",' he noted in his diary. 'Now it's all up with Levetzow.' And indeed it was. The unfortunate admiral was removed from office the next day and replaced with Goebbels's own candidate, the Police President of Potsdam, Count Wolf Heinrich von Helldorf, who would enjoy dealing properly with the Jews. 'Bravo!' Goebbels wrote. 'Today a conference in Heilgendamm. With Daluege, Lippert and Görlitzer. Now we shall soon fix things. I rejoice over that. Helldorf entirely happy. In the evening we celebrate a little. With much laughter . . . We shall make Berlin clean again. With united forces.'[2]

Helldorf's first action on returning to Berlin was to close all Jewish stores on the Kurfürstendamm, Berlin's most fashionable shopping area; a few days later he banned all 'individual actions' against Jews in the city, blaming the earlier incidents on 'provocateurs'.[3] The general public, it appeared from Gestapo reports, was reacting badly to the renewed violence, though they had no great objections to discrimination – they did not mind what was done to the Jews, as long as it was done in an orderly, legalised way. The party itself was split between the radicals who wanted to drive the Jews out by force, and the more cautious conservatives, who wanted to use economic and legal methods.

The issue came to a head in September at the 1935 Nuremberg Rally. Hitler had decided the rally that year should be dedicated to the fight against Bolshevism, but for Goebbels, Jews and Bolshevism were synonymous, a point he hammered home in his keynote speech. Other speakers joined in, demanding immediate action, and building up towards a major row within the party, which was only averted by two hurriedly-drafted and draconian new laws. The first, and most important, deprived Germans with Jewish blood of their citizenship; the second, the Law for the Protection of German Blood and German Honour, made marriages or sexual relations between Germans and Jews illegal, and forbade Jews from employing Germans as servants.

As it happened, Reichstag members had been summoned for a symbolic session in Nuremberg to pass a law making the swastika banner the official and only flag of the Reich. The three laws were conveniently presented together, and duly passed. As President, Göring, whose idolised godfather had been a Jew with whom his mother had slept for many years, had the task of introducing and reading out the new laws that would have condemned them both as criminals, which he did in a dry voice completely devoid of emotion.

Goebbels was among the deputies voting for the new laws, but he had other things on his mind, apart from the sensation he claimed his speech had made in the world press: Magda, who was heavily pregnant with their third child, had been taken into the clinic during the day. He prayed that all would go well, and that it would be a boy. But it turned out to be a false alarm. It was another three weeks before police intercepted his car on the way to Hohenlychen for a showdown with Rosenberg and told him he must phone the clinic. The news was good. After an anxious ten-minute wait, the doctor told him he had a son. 'Indescribable!' he crowed. 'I dance for joy. We'll call him Helmut. Rejoicing without end. Return at a speed of 100 kph . . . With Magda. She bursts into sudden and anxious sobbing. The sweet dearest. You sweet, sweet thing . . . A boy! A boy!'[4]

*   *   *

Like all rushed legislation, the Nuremberg Laws, as they came to be known, were badly drafted and full of holes, which had to be filled in later. The most obvious of these was the lack of any definition of who or what was a Jew. Goebbels became heavily involved in the wrangles that followed for several weeks, arguing that anyone with any Jewish blood, and those married to them, should be driven out of Germany. In the end, he was forced to accept that the laws should apply only to 'full Jews', with four Jewish grandparents, and only in certain circumstances to 'half Jews', with two or more. To his disgust, 'quarter Jews' would not be affected. It was a compromise, 'the best possible', to avoid a permanent split in the party – 'For God's sake, it brings peace'. He was responsible for selling the revised laws to the public, noting that he would have to 'put them out in the press skilfully and unobtrusively, to avoid making too much fuss'.[5]

Göring, always the pragmatist, saw things very differently. He had been preoccupied during the summer with other matters, especially the build-up of the Luftwaffe, and his foreign missions, disguised as an extended honeymoon, had kept him out of the country for much of the time. He had not been party to the intrigues that led to the Nuremberg Laws, and Goebbels, still smarting at being kept in the dark about the Röhm purge, had taken care not to tell him. So the provisions of the new laws had come as a shock and it was only later that he could try to mitigate what he saw as their worst aspects. Back in Nuremberg in 1946 for trial as a war criminal, Göring told the International Military Tribunal:

The Nuremberg Laws were intended to bring about a clear separation of races and, in particular, to do away with the notion of persons of mixed blood in the future, as the term of half Jew or quarter Jew led to continuous distinctions and confusion as far as their position was concerned . . . I personally had frequent discussions with the Führer regarding persons of mixed blood and I pointed out to the Führer that, once German Jews were clearly separated, it was impossible to have still another category between the two which constituted an unclarified section of the German people, which did not stand on the same level as the other Germans. I suggested to him that, as a generous act, he should do away with the concept of the person of mixed blood and place such people on the same footing as the other Germans. The Führer took up this idea with great interest and was all for adopting my point of view, in fact, he gave certain preparatory orders. Then came more troubled times, as far as foreign policy was concerned . . . and the question of persons of mixed blood stepped into the background . . .[6]

The troubled times Göring spoke of were as much involved with domestic problems as they were with foreign policy. The harvest on German farms had been disastrous in 1934, leading to a shortfall in bread grain of at least two million tons; serious shortages of animal fodder had reduced livestock herds; food reserves, especially of grain, meat and fats, were almost all gone, and prices were rocketing while wages were falling. With the country's dwindling foreign exchange and currency reserves devoted entirely to buying raw materials for arms manufacture, there was none left for the import of foodstuffs. At the same time unemployment, which had been greatly reduced but by no means eliminated, was starting to climb again. A wave of discontent began to build.

Darré, the Food and Agriculture Minister, demanded a larger share of foreign exchange to buy vital foodstuffs, including several hundred thousand tons of fats. Schacht refused, provoking a bitter clash. Hitler, for once, intervened, ordering Schacht to release 12.4 million Reich marks to Darré to buy oil seed for margarine production. He then gave Göring the task of investigating the situation and arbitrating between the two ministers for the immediate future. It was a more complex problem than it appeared at first sight: without more food, the workers might well revolt or strike, harming the arms programme; but money spent on food could not be spent on raw materials, thus reducing armament production and increasing unemployment. To everyone's surprise, Göring chose butter (or at least margarine) over guns, and came down in favour of Darré.

Göring's decision was a shrewd political move, which eased the food crisis, but it was not enough in itself to restore the regime's sagging popularity. Something much bigger was needed, and it was Hitler, with his uncanny instinct, who spotted the right opportunity. He had already dismantled most of the provisions imposed by Versailles, but one still remained and it was a particularly emotive one. Since 1919, the entire territory on the left bank of the Rhine, plus a fifty-kilometre strip on the right bank, had been a demilitarised zone, which had been confirmed in 1925 by the Locarno Treaty guaranteeing the frontiers between Germany, France and Belgium. Germany was forbidden from constructing any fortifications, stationing any troops or making any military preparations in the area, a humiliation that all Germans felt deeply. Reclaiming the Rhineland would be even more popular than the return of the Saar.

There would be risks involved, especially from the French, who were still far stronger militarily. But the French would probably not move alone, without the backing of their allies, the British and Italians. The naval agreement had already driven a wedge between Britain and France, and Mussolini's invasion of Abyssinia in October 1935 had completed the break between the three powers. A little patient negotiation would be all that was needed to restore total German sovereignty in the Rhineland. In the diplomatic world, it was generally assumed that this was inevitable and that it could even be achieved by late 1936. But that was too low key for Hitler, and too late. He needed a spectacular triumph, a show of strength, and he needed it fast. In January 1936, the French provided him with a convenient excuse by signing a mutual assistance pact with the Soviet Union in violation of Locarno. At the same time, Mussolini, in need of new friends, suddenly changed his tune, indicating that German ambitions in Austria need no longer be a bar to friendship and that he would not support France and Britain in any action against Germany over Austria or the Rhineland.

The Olympic Games were held in Germany in 1936, and when Hitler opened the Winter Olympics at Garmisch-Partenkirchen on 6 February he must have been heartened to see that despite all the international vilification of his regime, none of the participating nations stayed away. This was a good sign, but there were still enormous dangers in assuming the French would accept a unilateral move, and both the Foreign Ministry and the generals were distinctly nervous – including Göring who, for all the big talk with which he was trying to scare the French, was aware of how weak his fledgeling Luftwaffe still was. Hitler spent most of February trying to make up his mind. Blomberg and Neurath urged caution; Ribbentrop, sensing what Hitler really wanted to hear, urged him to go ahead, assuring him that the British would not oppose him and would also restrain the French.[7] Goebbels, himself a Rhinelander, was all for action, but counselled him to wait until the French ratified their pact with the Soviets, which would give him an excuse.

The National Assembly in Paris ratified the Franco–Soviet pact on 27 February. On Monday, 2 March, after a weekend spent agonising with Goebbels in Munich, Hitler called Göring, Goebbels, Blomberg, Fritsch, Admiral Raeder, Commander-in-Chief of the Navy, and Ribbentrop to a meeting in the Chancellery and solemnly informed them that he had decided to go ahead. They were to start making their preparations at once. He would address the Reichstag the following

Saturday and proclaim the remilitarisation of the Rhineland, sugaring the pill with a simultaneous offer to rejoin the League of Nations, make an air power agreement and sign a non-aggression pact with France. The Reichstag would then be dissolved, so that the German people could show their approval in new elections 'with a foreign policy theme'.[8]

Now that he had finally made up his mind, Hitler was impatient to begin. But he kept the rest of his Cabinet in the dark until the evening of Friday, 6 March, when he presented them with his plan, which they naturally approved unanimously. Even as they were talking, troops of the Wehrmacht were already being transported towards the Rhine, disguised as SA and Labour Front detachments on an exercise. Goebbels rushed back to his ministry to continue his own preparations, confining his staff in the building overnight to prevent any leaks. At the same time, he invited the foreign correspondents to a hotel, where he shut them away with the promise of a major story the next day. At 2 a.m. everything was ready, and he crashed into bed, 'dead tired' but too excited to sleep. He was up again at 8 a.m., 'now completely calm', to start the great day.[9]

German newsmen had been summoned to the ministry at dawn, and they and their foreign colleagues were taken 'under tight security' to Tempelhof, where two aircraft were waiting for them. According to Goebbels, none of them had any idea what was afoot – one, he said, had even brought a naval almanac with him. Only when they were in mid-air were they told that they were on their way to Cologne, Koblenz and Frankfurt, to witness the Wehrmacht marching into the Rhineland. Goebbels himself stayed in his office, 'working excitedly', until it was time to go to the Reichstag at noon. Göring had entertained the deputies to a beer evening the night before, as a distraction, and Goebbels claimed none of them knew what was coming. They gave Hitler's speech a rapturous reception, which was echoed throughout the country, as the nation listened to it on the radio. Moments later, they were treated to commentary describing the troops marching across the Hohenzollern Bridge at Cologne to the left bank of the Rhine.[10]

A total of 30,000 soldiers, augmented by armed police units, took part in the operation, though only 3,000 of them actually crossed the river and their commanders had strict orders from a nervous Blomberg to withdraw at the first sign of opposition from the French. Göring, who admitted later to having 'moments of intense anxiety', managed to scrape together three fighter squadrons to put on a show of aerial support. Most of the aircraft were ancient biplanes, only one squadron was operational and even that had not had its guns calibrated, but they fulfilled their function. Göring had them flown around all the Rhineland airfields, having fresh insignia painted on them between flights to create the illusion of greater numbers.

'As a son of the Rhineland', Goebbels was given the honour of replying in Hitler's name to a message broadcast from the cathedral square in Cologne. The whole Rhineland, he reported, was 'a sea of joy'. His mother telephoned him, quite 'beside herself'. By the evening, it was clear that the rest of the world would do nothing: 'England is passive, France will do nothing alone, Italy is disappointed, America not interested.' At the end of a long and nerve-racking day, Goebbels could record: 'We have regained our sovereignty over our own land.'[11] Almost as one, the German people agreed with him, praising Hitler as the saviour who had dared all to restore their honour and their national pride. In the phoney election that followed on 29 March, Goebbels had little difficulty whipping up a staggering 98.9 per cent vote of support. Even allowing for vote rigging and intimidation, it was a remarkable achievement.

The man who gained the highest marks from Hitler over the Rhineland was not Goebbels or Göring but the upstart Ribbentrop. He had backed Hitler at every step, always telling him exactly what he wanted to hear and never expressing any doubts. When the Council of the League of Nations met in London on 14 March 1936, and invited Germany to send a representative to put its case, Hitler chose Ribbentrop, to the horror of the Foreign Ministry and particularly the Ambassador to London, Leopold von Hoesch, who utterly despised him.

It was inevitable that the League would condemn the remilitarisation, but Ribbentrop was shocked when it demanded that Germany withdraw its troops at once, admit an international force and refer the whole matter to the Hague Tribunal. He was even more shocked when Britain, France, Belgium and Italy announced military staff talks, with the implied threat of military action. But somehow, mainly through sheer obstinacy, he managed to drag out the discussions until all the heat had been taken out of the situation and the Allied powers were preoccupied with other international events.

Ribbentrop returned to Germany on 9 April, certain that the crisis had passed and that there was nothing more to worry about. Hitler received him warmly, more convinced than ever of his genius in foreign affairs, and invited him and his wife to celebrate at the Rheinhotel Dreesen, and afterwards on a memorable steamer trip up the Rhine. 'It was a perfect spring day,' he recalled in his memoirs, 'and all along the banks the people waved at us. The news of Hitler's trip had preceded our steamer, and more and more cheering crowds converged on the banks.' Ribbentrop's triumph was enhanced when he received news that Ambassador Hoesch, who had constantly derided and denigrated him, had died of a heart attack in London.

Hitler took his time in deciding on a successor to Hoesch. In the meantime, Ribbentrop shuttled to and fro between Berlin and London, acting as Hitler's personal representative, presenting a new 'peace plan' to the British government and trying once more to fix up a personal meeting between Hitler and Baldwin, at which he imagined all their differences could be talked away. But the canny Baldwin was not to be drawn, and Eden, who had now become Foreign Secretary, saw through Ribbentrop and his blatant attempts at splitting Britain and France. By mid June, it was clear that he had failed, and his stock with Hitler fell accordingly. Looking for some way of reviving it, he turned to the idea of an Anti-Comintern Pact with Japan, to the fury of Neurath, who had spent years carefully cultivating Japan's enemy, Chiang Kai-shek, and his Chinese Nationalist Government. Neurath complained to Hitler, who of course did nothing. Desperate to get rid of Ribbentrop somehow, Neurath then suggested that, 'with his special knowledge of the British', he would make a perfect Ambassador to London. As he told Papen: 'After three months in London, Ribbentrop will be done for. They can't stand him there and we will be rid of him for good and all.'[12]

Ribbentrop was horrified at the prospect of the London Embassy. The rebuff from Baldwin and Eden had taken the shine off his love affair with the British, and in any case he had no wish to move from Hitler's side and away from the centre of the Nazi power game. He did not want to give up the Dienststelle and be forced to concentrate entirely on relations with Britain rather than advising the Führer personally on all aspects of foreign policy. Worst of all, as Ambassador he would be working under Neurath. And to cap everything, the position he really wanted – failing that of Foreign Minister – suddenly became vacant when State Secretary Bernhard von Bülow died on 21 June. Once again, Neurath threatened to resign if Ribbentrop was given the job. Ribbentrop retaliated by threatening – but not to Hitler himself

– to resign as Hitler's adviser if he were not given it. He would, he declared, prefer to work with Himmler in the SS.

Hitler, as usual, kept everyone dangling. Finally, on 21 July at Bayreuth, he announced his decision. According to Ribbentrop, he offered him the post of State Secretary, telling him Neurath had agreed. Ribbentrop claimed that he had declined the offer and had begged to be sent to London, where he believed he could still achieve the rapprochement that Hitler had always wanted. But Erich Kordt gave the lie to this version in his own memoirs by recalling that he found Ribbentrop locked in his room afterwards, 'in a state of stunned depression'.[13]

To soften the blow, Hitler specifically stated in his letter of appointment that Ribbentrop could retain the Dienststelle and his interest in wider foreign policy, and that both in this and as Ambassador he would answer directly to him and not to Neurath. He also asked him to continue working towards the Anti-Comintern Pact with Japan. Ribbentrop could hardly wait to show the letter to Neurath – who promptly submitted his resignation and suggested Hitler take on the role of Foreign Minister himself. Hitler climbed down yet again, and agreed that Ribbentrop should be a regular Ambassador after all, answerable to Neurath in the normal way, and Neurath withdrew his resignation. As State Secretary, he appointed Hans-Heinrich Dieckhoff, a career diplomat who knew Ribbentrop from his Constantinople days and who was now his sister's brother-in-law.

Ribbentrop's appointment was unpopular with the Foreign Ministry, but that was as nothing compared with the reactions of the leading Nazis. Rosenberg, naturally, was insanely jealous and lost no opportunity of criticising him. Goebbels said little, though he believed Ribbentrop was too Anglophile. Göring warned Hitler that Ribbentrop did not really understand anything about foreign countries, that his knowledge of Britain was limited to whisky and of France to champagne. When Hitler said that Ribbentrop knew Lord Such and Such and Minister So and So, Göring retorted 'Yes – but the trouble is, they know Ribbentrop.'[14]

Goebbels celebrated the success of the Rhineland action by buying another house, a charming, vine-covered 'summer house' built in mellow red brick on the near island of Schwanenwerder, fronting the Havel Lake on the outskirts of Berlin. Schwanenwerder was one of the most exclusive locations around the city, where some of the wealthiest and most fashionable Berliners had homes, among them the film stars Gustav Fröhlich and his Czech mistress, Lida Baarova. Goebbels and Magda both fell in love with the house, but he had difficulty in raising the price of 350,000 marks. Hitler came to the rescue, ordering Max Amman, director of the party's publishing house, Eher Verlag, to 'be generous'. It was important, he said, for Goebbels to able to entertain in style in Berlin. If he had had the money himself, he would have given it to him, but Goebbels was one of Eher's best authors, which was why he was calling on Amman. Eventually, a deal was done whereby Amman bought the rights to Goebbels's diaries, with an advance on signature of 250,000 marks, followed by annual payments of 100,000 marks. And Magda then persuaded Hitler to increase her husband's ministerial salary.[15] As a thank-you, she fitted out a guest cottage in the grounds for Hitler, and he became a regular visitor, enjoying playing with the children as their loving 'Uncle-Adolf'.

As it happened, Goebbels was not the only one to have a new house that spring: Göring had built himself an alpine retreat on the Obersalzberg, very close to Hitler's, which had just been completely rebuilt to his own designs and turned into an imposing residence. It was no longer Haus Wachenfeld but the Berghof, literally, his 'mountain court'. By comparison, and by Göring's standards, his own new house was quite modest – no doubt he was careful not to overshadow the Führer's – but it was comfortable, tasteful and thoroughly Bavarian, and it had a large swimming-pool. It was a place where he could relax in *Lederhosen*, puff on his *Meerschaum* pipe, and enjoy the mountains that had always been so dear to him.

Throughout 1936, Göring continued to broaden his power base. On Hitler's birthday, 20 April, he was promoted to Colonel-General, level with the Commanders-in-Chief of the army and navy – a slight disappointment since he had been pressing for the new rank of Air Marshal, which Hitler rejected as un-German, but welcome nevertheless. Under his direction, the development of the Luftwaffe was roaring ahead, with new aircraft types as a priority. One of the most striking was the Ju-87, a dive-bomber based on the American 'Hell Diver' design, which Hugo Junkers was building at his plant in Sweden. Its potential had been spotted by Göring's former flying comrade from the Richthofen squadron and post-war barnstorming days, Ernst Udet, whom he had hired as a consultant to the Air Ministry in 1934. Udet personally demonstrated the prototypes to Milch and Göring – almost killing himself in the process when he crashed the first – and soon persuaded them that this was an exciting new weapon of war. Göring was impressed, but suggested that the plane's psychological effect would be even greater if it made a more terrifying noise than the howl of its engine as it dived on its prey. Udet agreed to fit a wind whistle, so that 'it'll scream like a demon out of hell when it dives down'.[16] Göring ordered that the new plane, the 'Stuka', short for *Sturzkampfflugzeug* (dive-attack aircraft), should go into immediate production, and appointed Udet as Inspector of Fighter and Dive-Bomber Aircraft.

The Stuka was by no means the Luftwaffe's only new aircraft. By the spring of 1936, test pilots were flying prototypes of the Messerschmitt 109 and 110 fighters, the Heinkel 123 dive-bomber, and the Dornier 17, Junkers 86 and Heinkel 111 medium-range bombers. Some German commentators considered that they had a lead of about two years over their international competition, but it is worth noting that in Britain both the Hawker Hurricane and the Spitfire Mark 1 were already flying – the Spitfire had made its maiden flight two days before German troops marched into the Rhineland – while in the United States the first Boeing Y1B-17 bombers, nicknamed 'Flying Fortresses', were rolling out of the Seattle factory.

Göring favoured the fighter plane; indeed he had originally envisaged a purely defensive air force composed entirely of fighters, but had soon realised that that was impractical and turned to developing medium-range bombers based on commercial aircraft. His Chief of Staff, General Wever, was intent on creating a strategic bomber fleet equipped with long-range, four-engined aircraft, but when Wever was killed in a plane crash at Dresden on 3 June, his policy died with him. Overriding Milch, Göring appointed Albert Kesselring, who until then had been in charge of administration, as the new Chief of Staff, and at the same time made Udet, an old fighter ace, Director of the Air Ministry's Technical Department, responsible for all forward planning. Both supported Göring's own preference. It was the end of the four-engined heavy bomber, a change that was to have a significant effect on the Luftwaffe's operations in the Second World War.

There were several reasons behind Göring's preference for smaller bombers. To start with, he still clung to his idea of the Luftwaffe as a defensive rather than an offensive weapon, and even in a war of aggression he saw Gemany's potential enemies as being in central and eastern Europe, and perhaps France. He did not foresee a conflict with Britain, for instance, where heavier bombers with a longer range might be an advantage. Milch later gave another explanation for the cancellation of the heavy bombers, claiming that Göring had told him: 'The Führer will only ever ask me how many bombers do you have? He will never ask me how big they are. For one four-engined job I can build two and a half medium bombers.'[17] At the Nuremberg Tribunal, Göring confirmed the question of numbers, but stated that his reasoning was that he was short of aluminium, 'and anyone only half an expert knows how much aluminium a four-engine bomber swallows up and how many fighters, that is, two-engine bombers, one can build with the same amount.'[18]

Aluminium was only one of the resources that were in short supply. Oil, rubber and iron ore were others, all of which had a serious effect on aircraft and other armaments production. All had to be imported, which left Germany vulnerable as always to strangulation by blockade. One possible remedy was to find synthetic substitutes, which could be manufactured by her advanced chemical industry, and Göring took a particular interest in this. As early as December 1933, he signed a contract with IG Farben for the manufacture of synthetic gasoline from coal. In the spring of 1935, he became responsible for the production of synthetic rubber, and a year later added Reich Fuel Commissioner to his collection of titles.

At about the same time Schacht, accompanied by Blomberg and Hans Kerrl, Minister for the Churches, came to him for help. Schacht, who was not a party member, was having difficulties with party leaders, who were refusing to accept his tough economic measures. The one person the party would always listen to was Göring, the charismatic 'Iron Man'. Would he agree to their asking Hitler to make him Commissioner for Raw Materials and Foreign Exchange, a permanent extension of the role he had played so successfully in resolving the food crisis a few months earlier? Hitler had in fact already asked him to work on ways of avoiding future economic crises, and was happy to formalise his new responsibilities. Göring himself described the outcome:

It was agreed that I should not function as an economics expert, which I was not; but someone was needed to take care of the difficulties due to shortage of foreign currency, which continuously arose because of our heavy demands, and at the same time to make available and to accumulate raw materials – someone who was capable of taking measures which would perhaps not be understood by many people, but would have the weight of his authority. Secondly, it was decided that in this sphere, though not as an expert, I should be the driving power and use my energy . . . Thus I entered the field of economic leadership.[19]

If Schacht had expected Göring to act simply as his mouthpiece, he was soon disillusioned as the new commissioner, ignorant of the accepted laws of economics, trampled roughshod over his theories and pursued his own aims and ideas. Relations between the two men became increasingly frosty, but there was little Schacht could do to bring Göring back under control. He had let the genie out of the bottle, and Göring had seized his opportunity with all his usual energy. When Schacht tried to persuade Hitler to limit Göring's authority, he was given short shrift and told to take the matter up with Göring himself. 'It won't go well for Schacht much longer,' Goebbels commented, after Hitler had told him about this during an excursion on the Propaganda Minister's boat. 'In his heart he doesn't belong with us. Above all in his speeches and writings. But Göring will find it difficult to deal with the questions of foreign exchange and raw materials. He doesn't understand too much about it, and will depend on advice.'[20]

Göring was well aware of what he needed. He set up a new agency, Minister-President General Göring's Raw Materials and Foreign Currency Unit, hand-picking experts from industry and the civil service to head the various departments and advise him. Then he roared into action as only he could. He gave tax breaks to stimulate domestic coal and ore production. He gave farmers cheap chemical fertilisers to boost food production. He called conferences, harangued top industrialists and negotiated barter deals with Romania and Yugoslavia to exchange armaments for foodstuffs, and with Spain, Turkey and Finland for vital metals. All through the summer, while other ministers and their staffs took vacations, he worked on in Berlin, using his Prussian State Council as an alternative to the Reich Cabinet, which was now virtually extinct, to rubber-stamp his decisions.

With his new responsibilities and opportunities taking up so much of his time, Göring allowed an old one to slip away without protest, content to retain no more than a nominal interest. On 17 June 1936,

Hitler decreed that, 'in order to ensure unified control of police duties in the Reich . . . the Deputy Chief of the Gestapo, Reichsführer-SS Heinrich Himmler is hereby appointed Chief of the German Police within the Reich Ministry of the Interior'. The qualification 'within the Reich Ministry of the Interior' was a sop to Frick, who had fought hard for control of a national police force with Daluege as its chief, but it was as meaningless as Himmler's subordination to Göring with the Gestapo had by now become. Heydrich had carried out the detailed negotiations with the Interior Ministry on Himmler's behalf, and he knew that they could safely ignore Frick and start the real business of merging the police into the SS to create a single instrument for turning Germany into a police state, under their control. Goebbels was among the radicals who understood and welcomed this development – and its added bonus of removing one element of Göring's personal power base – praising Himmler as 'energetic and uncompromising'.[21]

With his passion for organisation, Himmler had already worked out exactly what he wanted to do with the police, and he put his ideas into effect immediately. He began by dividing his new empire into two main departments: the Sicherheitspolizei, Security Police, bringing together the Gestapo and the Criminal Police, under the command of Heydrich, and the Ordnungspolizei, Order Police, commanded by Daluege, which included all uniformed police apart from traffic, which came under the Transport Ministry. The two departments were kept strictly separate, and each was responsible not to an overall police office but directly to Himmler and his personal office, controlled by Wolff. And Himmler, despite the nods to Frick and Göring in his titles, was answerable to no one but Hitler. There could be no doubt now that, at the age of thirty-five, and with the police, the SS and the concentration camps in his hands, he was a force to be reckoned with.

For two weeks at the beginning of August 1936, the Nazi leaders were concerned with less serious things as the Olympic Games were held in Berlin. The city had been selected in 1932, before Hitler came to power, and there had been serious doubts about whether the games would go ahead in view of the Nazis' racial policies, which were completely opposed to Olympic ideals. But the international community evaded confrontation once again. Hitler's own dislike of the Olympic movement had been assuaged by the assurance that the games represented a wonderful propaganda opportunity, and in any case gave him the chance to indulge his favourite interest by building the world's biggest sports stadium.

He also took the first step in his plans for the future of the entire city, widening the roads between the old Royal Palace at the top of the Unter den Linden and the stadium out to the west to create an eight-mile-long *via triumphalis* not just for sporting heroes but also for German armies returning victorious from war. The costs were enormous – the stadium alone took 77 million marks – but it provided work for thousands of unemployed men, and the foreign visitors who flocked to the games brought in half a billion marks in desperately needed foreign currency.

Sport came under the Propaganda Ministry, so Goebbels was responsible for staging the games, as well as for presenting an acceptable face of Germany to the world. For a brief period that summer, he swallowed his hatred of the Jews, had all the 'not wanted here' signs taken down, removed the brown, swastika-covered cabinets selling *Der Stürmer* from street corners, and instructed the press to tone down its anti-Semitism. A few books by forbidden authors such as Proust and Heinrich Heine reappeared in the shops. He even allowed two Jewish athletes to represent Germany. Forests of flags and banners blossomed everywhere, even on Jewish-owned department stores that were not allowed to fly the swastika but were now ordered to display the Olympic flag on their normally bare poles. Speer was called into service to design decorations for streets and buildings, draping the Propaganda Ministry and other palaces on the Wilhelmplatz in red velvet, green garlands and enormous gold ribbons. With all traces of institutionalised terror hidden away, it was a triumph of the propagandist's art at its most cynical.

Goebbels's organisation of the media coverage of the games themselves was also a triumph, easily surpassing anything seen at previous Olympiads. As well as the normal press facilities, he organised over 3,000 overseas radio broadcasts, in more than fifty languages – in the USA alone, they were relayed by more than 100 radio stations – and even succeeded in televising them to the Berlin area. Film newsreels carried pictures into every movie theatre at home and abroad, and these were followed by *Olympia*, another masterpiece by Leni Riefenstahl, who was contracted by the Propaganda Ministry but was answerable to Goebbels for the financial aspects alone and not the artistic content. Once again there were tales of his trying to sabotage her work, but his main objection to her was simply that she was a woman. When she complained of difficulties or made demands for more money, he dismissed her as 'a hysterical female. Not like a man!' And when his withering scorn drove her to tears, he sneered: 'It's impossible to work with these wild women . . . I stay cool to the core. She weeps. That's women's ultimate weapon. But it doesn't work with me any more.'[22]

For the two weeks of the games, Berlin enjoyed one enormous party. The most select occasion was a formal dinner given by Hitler for 150 guests in the refurbished state dining-room of the Chancellery, but the most eagerly anticipated events were the parties thrown by Göring and Goebbels, who could be relied on to compete with each other in the extravagance of their entertaining. There was a third entrant in the contest for the social highlight of the games: Ribbentrop chose to announce his new appointment at a gala dinner for 600 guests in the grounds of his Dahlem villa on 11 August. But although the food and wine were excellent, and the setting delightful – Ribbentrop congratulated himself that 'It all looked like fairyland' – it was utterly conventional. That was a charge that could never be made against either of the other two, and they both lived up to expectations.

Göring had an unfair advantage in being entitled to host three different parties in his capacities as Air Minister, Minister-President of Prussia and President of the Reichstag. He began with an exotic luncheon for the International Olympic Committee in the Reichstag President's palace. This was only a warm-up, however, for a dinner he gave in the State Opera House on 8 August, which rivalled Frederick the Great's celebration there of his victory over Austria in the First Silesian War in 1742, with which he had opened his new building. Göring transformed the majestic old theatre, bringing in tables and seating for 2,000 guests, who were entertained by singers and dancers from the Opera. Over 100 periwigged footmen in pink livery and knee-breeches lined the stairs, holding glass lanterns on long poles. The colour scheme for the evening was red and white, reflected in long banners hanging down all around the auditorium and stage. To maintain it, lady guests were asked to wear white, as did Göring himself, his dress uniform ablaze with decorations and gold braid. Berlin had known nothing like this since before the war.

Göring gave his third and final party in the grounds of his new villa, which he turned into a colourful Bavarian carnival, complete with carousels, sideshows, taverns and dance bands. The abiding memory for many visitors was of their host, riding round and round astride a carousel horse in his white dress uniform, 'wreathed in smiles and orders and decorations', backed by merry oompah music, waving gaily to hundreds of applauding guests.[23] It was a jovial and unthreatening image, presenting hundreds of foreigners with a benign face for the Third Reich.

In response, Goebbels took over the Pfaueninsel, Peacock Island, just below his new house on the Havel, for the final fling of the fortnight. Army engineers provided a pontoon bridge to link the wooded island with the shore. He called on all the resources of the film industry to decorate it from end to end and transform it into an enormous movie set, filled with pretty girls dressed as Renaissance pages in tabards and tights. The main entertainment was provided by the Berlin Philharmonic and dancers from the Berlin Opera in Charlottenburg, which came under Goebbels's control. This was followed by dancing to no fewer than three bands, and an enormous firework display over the lake. After that, the whole thing degenerated into something approaching an orgy, with male guests pursuing scantily-clad 'pages' through the undergrowth. The whole event could be seen as encapsulating the different aspects of Goebbels's character, just as Göring's did his.

Among Goebbels's guests at his party were his new neighbours on Schwanenwerder, the film stars Lida Baarova and Gustav Fröhlich. He spent much of the evening pouring on the charm for the beautiful twenty-two-year-old Czech girl, for whom he had developed a passion. She, dazzled by his position and flattered by his attentions, did nothing to discourage him. His relationship with Magda, who was incidentally three months pregnant with their fourth child, was very strained at that time. Shortly before the games he had discovered that she had been having an affair with a writer called Karl Lüdecke, and although he complained regularly about her refusal to accept or share his idea of an open marriage – which meant giving him *carte blanche* to sleep with anyone he chose – he was shocked and hurt when she took a leaf out of his book and did likewise. What made it worse was that the person who told him about it was Rosenberg, no doubt with malicious delight. Disregarding his own serial infidelities, he bullied her into a confession, then tore into her jealously, declaring that he would need a great deal of time to get over 'this great loss of trust'. But after sulking for several days, he made an uneasy peace after Hitler had praised her to him as the best woman he could possibly have found.[24]

Magda's fragile health was suffering under the strain, bringing a recurrence of her old heart problems, and she took refuge in more and more frequent stays in the fashionable White Stag clinic in Dresden. But her illnesses did nothing to prick Goebbels's conscience: even while he was castigating her he was wooing Baarova by arranging to stage the premiere of her latest film, *Der Verräter* (*The Traitor*) in Nuremberg to coincide with the party rally, and inviting her to the rally as his guest. The ploy paid off: Baarova was bowled over and succumbed to his advances. 'A miracle has occurred,' he purred to his diary that night. It was the beginning of a torrid affair that would eventually spin out of control and almost bring his career to an end.

Göring's entertaining during the Olympics had not been confined entirely to party-giving. On a smaller scale and with a different purpose in mind, he had looked after the American aviator, Charles Lindbergh, who arrived in late July at the invitation of the US Air Attaché, Major Truman Smith. Smith hoped that Lindbergh's fame as a pilot would enable him to get more detailed information out of Göring about the state of the Luftwaffe, and Göring was happy to oblige. He gave Lindbergh a warm welcome, and arranged various meetings and visits for him, including taking him to tea with the Crown Prince at the Cecilienhof Palace in Potsdam, lunch with the Richthofen Squadron, and tours of several aircraft factories and Luftwaffe installations. For the opening ceremony of the games, the American was Göring's guest in the Luftwaffe box. Nothing was too much trouble for this influential VIP.

Lindbergh was impressed with everything he saw – as indeed he was intended to be. 'We have nothing in America to compare with the Junkers factory,' he reported on 6 August, after a carefully stage-managed viewing. Smith had hoped that he would be able to uncover the Luftwaffe's secrets, not realising that these were concealing not its strength but its weakness. The Third Reich's international standing had been built on bluff, and the politically naïve Lindbergh swallowed the bluff whole. 'He admires Nazi Germany for its energy, masculinity, spirit, organisation, architecture, planning and strength,' the British diplomat Harold Nicolson noted after meeting him in London on his return from Berlin. 'He claims it has the largest air force in the world, with which it can destroy any other country.' Göring had done his work well. Now Lindbergh would carry his message around the world, and especially to the United States, where his views would help keep America out of any war with Germany.

A few days after the games closed, Göring joined Hitler on the Obersalzberg. His Olympic parties had been no more than brief interludes in his work with his team of economic experts, who by the end of the games had produced a detailed programme which he and Hitler discussed on long walks in the mountains. Göring had reported his progress on various occasions during the summer, notably at the Wagner Festival in Bayreuth, and Hitler had agreed that he should announce his plans in a major speech at Nuremberg. But now that he saw the enormous scope of Göring's proposals, and realised how they would dominate the rally, Hitler decided he would make the speech himself. That way, he would keep the starring role and at the same time silence any critics once and for all. Back at the Berghof, with Göring's help he dictated a detailed memorandum that was essentially a draft of his speech, outlining the new economic plan. Göring took two copies with him when he returned to Berlin, one for himself and one for Blomberg, his ally against Schacht and the Economics Ministry, who were strongly opposed to his plan to concentrate everything on rearmament, and wanted Germany to return to the international market economy.

The first Schacht and his supporters knew about the memorandum or Hitler's intentions was at a meeting Göring called on 4 September of the Prussian State Council, his 'Little Cabinet', when he read out the whole document. They were shattered. Göring's supporters, by contrast, were jubilant – Körner said this was 'the most beautiful day in our economic history'. In the memorandum, Hitler prepared the way for an all-out war against Bolshevism – in other words, with the Soviet Union – which he said was inevitable. 'A victory of Bolshevism over Germany,' he declared, 'would lead not to a Versailles Treaty but to the final destruction, indeed to the annihilation, of the German people'. He could not predict exactly when the crisis would come, but everything had to be subordinated to defending the nation against this danger. Germany's economic problems could be eased for the time being through partial self-sufficiency, he continued, but in the long term the only answer lay in expanding her 'living space'. In the meantime, in the next four years, the army had to be made ready for action and the economy prepared for war.[25]

Hitler's speech on 9 September was the sensation of the party rally. It was little altered from the memorandum, except that it gave a name to the operation, the Four-Year Plan, and named Göring as the man solely in charge of it. The appointment, which was confirmed on 18 October with a Führer decree, gave Göring immense and virtually untrammelled power over the entire economy, placing him above all ministers, including Schacht. There were a few who questioned his ability – Goebbels noted 'He has the energy. Whether he has the economic know-how and experience as well, who knows? Anyway, he'll make a lot of noise.'[26] Hitler seems to have imagined that he would work with a relatively small staff, co-ordinating the work of the existing ministries, but this was never Göring's way. He always wanted to be hands-on, and soon created a vast organisation with special commissioners for every area, each of whom set up his own sub-organisation and staff, overlapping and interfering with the work of the ministries. At its heart was the Office for the Four-Year Plan, based on his Prussian Ministry with the addition of another 1,000 or so civil servants, with his faithful sidekick Pilli Körner as its chief.

The Reich Labour Office was absorbed into the plan, and its chief was appointed General Plenipotentiary for the Allocation of Labour. His task, Körner later explained, was 'to regulate the allocation of labour and thus put an end to the great muddle on the labour market',[27] which sounded innocent enough, but had a sinister side, too, since one source of cheap labour that was increasingly exploited was the concentration camps. Some camps, for instance, were built close to quarries, to provide stone for building and aggregates for the construction of the autobahns and airfields. When there were not enough workers, the shortfall could easily be made up with more arrests, a practice that became increasingly common in future years.

Göring's responsibilities included total control of foreign currency, opening up undreamed-of personal opportunities that he was not slow to exploit. He revelled in his new authority and the rewards it brought him in bribes and inducements from industrialists, financiers and manufacturers and indeed anybody who was on the make. Money, jewels, fine furniture, priceless works of art poured into his lap from all quarters and he accepted them with unashamed delight. Sir Robert Vansittart, Permanent Under-Secretary at the British Foreign Office, observed dryly that Göring took to his new job 'with the gusto of Smith Minor, suddenly possessed of unlimited tick at the school stores'.[28] One of his most prized gifts came from the German

Automobile Manufacturers Society – a luxury motor yacht, *Carin II*, which to his satisfaction comfortably outshone Goebbels's boat.

One of the factors that had helped to concentrate Hitler's mind on the threat of Bolshevism was the situation in Spain, where the left-wing Popular Front had won the national elections in February 1936. The victory had been a narrow one, the right wing refused to accept it, and the threat of civil war loomed. Through the spring and early summer terrorist activity increased and political murders multiplied, against a background of horror stories of Communist violence against the Catholic Church. It seemed that the country was about to be taken over by Marxist revolutionaries. In July, the Commander-in-Chief of the army in Spanish Morocco, General Francisco Franco, led a rising of the garrisons there against the elected government, and prepared to march on Madrid. The only problem was that his troops were all in North Africa, and he had no means of getting them back to mainland Spain. The sailors of the Spanish navy mutinied when their officers tried to get them to ship Franco's men across the Mediterranean, and he had no suitable planes for an airlift. He turned to Fascist Italy and Nazi Germany for help.

Mussolini initially refused, and the German Foreign Ministry, unsurprisingly, reacted coolly. But Franco managed to get personal letters delivered to Hitler and Göring by two members of Rosenberg's Nazi Party Foreign Organisation, with the help of Hess. The emissaries arrived during the Wagner Festival in Bayreuth and put Franco's case: his fight against Bolshevism was hopeless without German aid. Hitler was acutely aware of the political dangers for Germany of a Bolshevik Spain, in league with the Soviet Union and no doubt France, which also had just elected a Popular Front government, under a Jewish Prime Minister, Leon Blum, but he still hesitated at getting involved. Göring was also cautious, but pointed out that although there were undoubted risks, they were outweighed by the economic benefits of the rich sources of raw materials that would become available to them if Franco succeeded. Hitler was swayed by this argument, and agreed.

Franco had asked for ten Ju-52 transport planes. Göring ordered Milch to send twenty, together with six Heinkel He-51s to provide fighter cover, and eighty-six Luftwaffe volunteers to fly and service them. By October, with Franco's forces firmly established back in Spain and the civil war blazing, he stepped up German assistance, sending fighters, bombers and a further 6,500 men, a force that would shortly become known as the Condor Legion. For Göring, this was a great opportunity to try out his Luftwaffe under combat conditions, and he ordered that personnel posted to Spain be rotated regularly so that as many as possible should gain valuable experience.

It was also a chance for him to foster his long-term ambition of improving relations with Italy, a hope that was soon realised. Mussolini had by this time decided on full support for the rebels, and was pouring vastly more men and money into Spain: Italian troops would eventually number between 60,000 and 70,000. German involvement alongside them was a major step in finally bringing about rapprochement. Hitler invited Mussolini to visit Germany the following year, and Mussolini sent his son-in-law and Foreign Minister, Count Galeazzo Ciano, to Berlin, where he signed a secret agreement on 23 October outlining a common foreign policy for their two countries. For once, Göring kept a low profile; there would be plenty of time in the future for him to make up for his offensive behaviour towards Italy the previous year.

Ciano returned home via Berchtesgaden, calling on Hitler, who received him effusively and declared that 'there was no clash of interests between Italy and Germany'. A week later, on 1 November, Mussolini publicly confirmed the new friendship in a flowery speech in the cathedral square of Milan, describing the line between Berlin and Rome as 'an axis round which all those European States which are animated by a desire for collaboration and peace can revolve'.[29] The term stuck – from then on, the alliance between the two countries was known as the Axis. Their desire for peace, however, was doubtful to say the least: German and Italian airmen were soon fighting side by side in Spain – in April 1937 they jointly bombed the defenceless Basque town of Guernica, leaving over 2,500 of its citizens dead or wounded.

Göring was flying high in October 1936, but Hitler had not forgotten Goebbels. On his thirty-ninth birthday at the end of the month, he sent him a personal standard and visited him at the Propaganda Ministry to demonstrate his friendship. 'We go into my room alone,' Goebbels recorded.

And then he speaks to me very kindly and intimately. About old times, and how we belong together, how fond he is of me personally. He is so touching to me. Gives me his picture with a glorious dedication. And a painting of the Dutch School. That was a wonderful hour alone with him. He pours out his heart to me. The problems he has, how he trusts me, what great assignments he still has in store for me. Göring was there, too. The three of us greet the thirty oldest members [of the Nazi Party]. That was a real treat.[30]

The next day, 31 October, Goebbels was even more ecstatic when he celebrated the tenth anniversary of his arrival in Berlin as Gauleiter. The local party mounted an exhibition in the City Hall with the title 'Ten Years of Struggle for Berlin'. *Der Angriff*, which was now published by Ley's German Labour Front, ran a special commemorative edition. He laid the foundation stone of the Dr Goebbels Home for 'poor and deserving party members and SA fighters', and established a benevolent fund in his name for actors in need – as long as they were not full or half Jews, married to Jews, or politically undesirable. The City of Berlin gave him a special birthday gift in the shape of a country house, 'a simple log cabin', at Lanke on the peaceful Bogensee Lake to the north of the city, where 'after the strain of his daily work serving the people and the Reich, he can find peace, relaxation, and a place to collect his thoughts'. The city put the house 'at the lifelong disposal of its honorary citizen, as a sign of its profound gratitude for his fruitful activity'.[31] He was to make good use of it in the coming year – though whether his activities there could be classed as fruitful is a matter of opinion.

The icing on the cake for Goebbels came that evening, with a packed rally in his honour at the Sportpalast that culminated in a Hitler speech praising him to the skies and then calling on the crowd to join in shouting 'Heil' to him. 'This I didn't expect,' he noted proudly. 'How grateful I am to him.' The rally, he said, 'ended with frenetic applause and unprecedented cheering.'[32]

No matter how popular Goebbels believed he was with the party, however, it was still Göring who was making the running. Two days before the Propaganda Minister had been fêted in the Sportpalast, Göring had himself been cheered by another packed meeting there when he called once more for 'guns before butter', and again at the State Theatre the next day when he launched the annual Winter Help Fund. He had then taken to the streets, shaking a collecting box at passers-by, and acknowledging their friendly shouts of 'Hermann needs a few coppers' with a happy grin. No other Nazi leader, and certainly not Goebbels, had such a warm rapport with the public. Hitler gave

Göring his unequivocal endorsement at a secret conference of leading industrialists on 17 December. 'Trust this man whom I have chosen,' he told them. 'He is the best man I have for the job.'[33] In his speech, Göring appalled Schacht by telling his audience to use any methods they could, legal or illegal, to bring in foreign currency, and to concentrate on production at all costs, regardless of profitability. He left them in no doubt about the meaning and purpose of the Four-Year Plan:

The battle we are now approaching demands a colossal measure of production capacity. No limit on rearmament can be visualised. The only alternatives are victory or destruction . . . We live in a time when the final battle is in sight. We are already on the threshold of mobilisation and we are already at war. All that is lacking is the actual shooting.[34]

PART FOUR

EXPANSION:
THE GREATER GERMAN REICH
1937–1939

XVIII

THE BLOMBERG–FRITSCH AFFAIR

'THE time of the so-called surprises is over,' Hitler told the Reichstag in his anniversary speech on 30 January 1937. And so it proved to be, at least for the rest of that year – the framework of the Nazi state was now in place and it was time to consolidate the gains already made. Germany had regained her self-respect and could take her place again among the great powers. In the same speech, he 'solemnly withdrew Germany's signature from the Treaty of Versailles', which was now finally dead and buried. To underline the fact that he was there to stay, he renewed the Enabling Act to extend his legal term of office indefinitely, and appointed Speer to the new post of Inspector-General of Building for the Reich Capital, with instructions to begin planning the reconstruction of Berlin as Germania, a thousand-year city for a thousand-year Reich.

With the Saar and the Rhineland safely back under German control, the next step in the Nazis' dream of a Greater Germany was to bring Austria back into the Reich, from which it had been excluded by Bismarck. But this would have to be handled with great care, if the newly cemented friendship with Italy was not to be destroyed. Despite, or perhaps because of, his own origins, Hitler was less bothered about annexing Austria than was Göring, who told the Nuremberg Tribunal how he first came to the idea:

In 1918 while in Austria for two days, having come by plane, I saw the revolution and the collapse of the Habsburg Empire take place. Those countries, with a predominantly German population, including Sudeten Germany, convened at that time in Vienna in the parliament. They declared themselves free of the dissolving Habsburg state and declared, including the representatives of Sudeten Germany, Austria to be a part of the German Reich . . . This statement by the representatives of the Austrian-German people that they wanted to be part of Germany in the future was changed by the peace treaty of St Germain and prohibited by the dictate of the victorious nations. Neither for myself nor for any other German was that of any importance. The moment and the basic conditions had of course to be created for a union of the two brother nations of purely German blood and origin to take place. When we came to power . . . this was naturally an integral part of German policy.

The assurances which Hitler gave at that time regarding the sovereignty of Austria were no deception; they were meant seriously. At first he probably did not see any possibility. I myself was much more radical in this direction and I asked him repeatedly not to make any definite commitments regarding the Austrian question. He believed, however, that he had first of all to take Italy into consideration.[1]

Göring could never shake off the nostalgic memories of his Austrian childhood in Mautendorf Castle. He still had family connections with the country: his two sisters, Olga and Paula, had both married Austrian lawyers and now had homes in Salzburg and Saalfelden respectively; his younger, anti-Nazi brother, Albert, had taken Austrian citizenship and worked in Vienna, managing the studios of the Tobis Sacha film company, where he made a point of employing German exiles. These, incidentally, included the actress Henny Porten, who had been forced out of the German film industry because she was married to a Jew. Emmy Göring was one of her best friends, and she persuaded Göring to call Albert, who arranged a contract for Henny. It was the first, but it would by no means be the last time Emmy would ask her husband to intervene on behalf of one of her many Jewish friends. Nor was it the only time Göring called on his brother for a favour. In November 1936, in return for allowing more Austrian films to be imported into Germany, he asked him for an informal, off-the-record introduction to the State Secretary in the Austrian Foreign Ministry, Guido Schmidt, a bright and boisterous thirty-six-year-old. Schmidt was another passionate hunter, and Göring hoped to use the 'green Freemasonry' to influence him and gain vital inside information while they were shooting together.

Göring's interest in Austria, however, was not simply a question of sentiment. He was coldly eyeing her gold and foreign currency reserves, and her extensive mineral resources, both of which would be invaluable assets to the Four-Year Plan. He also saw Austria as the gateway to Czechoslovakia, with its highly-advanced armaments industry and further mineral resources. Once Austria had been absorbed, Germany would surround the western half of Czechoslovakia on three sides – on the map it looked uncannily like a tasty mouthful in the open jaws of a lion. The next move would be to bring into the Reich the Sudetenland, the mountainous region around Czechoslovakia's north-western frontier, home to some 3.5 million Germans. This would strip the Czechs of their formidable border fortifications, and the jaws could snap shut. The eastern half of the country, the backward and mainly rural Slovakia, could be disgorged and left to its own devices.

For the whole of 1937, Göring's main preoccupation, after the Four-Year Plan itself, was preparing the ground for the *Anschluss*, literally the connection or joining together, of Austria and Germany. In this, it was he and not Hitler who was the driving force. When he visited Mussolini in Rome in January 1937, it was supposedly to talk about the situation in Spain, and indeed he started by criticising the Spanish tactics and giving details of how Franco's Moroccan troops were airlifted across the Strait of Gibraltar in German Ju-52s. 'Franco has much to thank us for,' he told the Duce. 'I hope he'll remember it later.' But he moved swiftly on to the subject of Austria, which his interpreter, Dr Paul Schmidt, thought was really the main purpose of the visit. 'Göring was very outspoken on this matter,' Schmidt recalled, 'frankly telling Mussolini that the *Anschluss* would and must come and that the event could not be delayed.' Mussolini's response was to shake his head vehemently, 'the only sign of opposition he gave on that day . . .'²

After his meeting with Mussolini, Göring slipped away for a few days' holiday on the Isle of Capri, part of which was spent with his friend Axel Munthe, the best-selling Swedish author, who offered to sell him his home there, the Castello di Barbarossa. Tempted as he was, Göring was unable to buy – he was in the process of adding major extensions to Carinhall, and in any case even he could not swing the foreign currency needed. He returned to Rome for a second meeting with Mussolini, taking the advice of German Ambassador Ulrich von Hassell to cool things over Austria by making the whole thing seem as long term as possible. He tried to soothe the Duce by promising that whatever happened, Germany would do nothing without consulting him. The only circumstances under which Germany might take action, he said, was if the Austrians tried to restore the Habsburg monarchy.

The Italians were only partly reassured, but Göring was unfazed, and went on working at the relationship, throughout the spring and summer, with further visits in February, April and May. His persistence paid off: Mussolini was gradually won over and finally accepted an invitation to pay a state visit to Germany in September, when he was given the full treatment with all the pomp and circumstance Hitler could muster. He was meant to be impressed, and he was – in spite of being half-drowned by a violent storm that almost stopped him making his principal speech to hundreds of thousands of drenched spectators on Tempelhof Field on 28 September.

Earlier that day, Göring had entertained Mussolini to a farewell luncheon at Carinhall, where he had had a large map of the Reich painted on one wall, illustrated with pictures in medieval style. Austria was included as part of the Reich, with no frontier marked. He walked the Duce casually past it several times, without getting any response, and eventually had to draw his attention to it. 'That gave me an excuse,' he recalled under interrogation, 'to talk bluntly about the two countries uniting.'[3] To Göring's intense frustration, Mussolini still refused to be drawn, but he chose to assume that because the Italian dictator had raised no objection, he would accept a German take-over in the end.

There was one cause for celebration that day: Emmy took the opportunity to announce that she was pregnant. It was an enormous surprise to everyone, including Göring himself, who had believed the wounds he had received in 1923 had made him sterile. The gossips and wits in Germany soon began speculating on whose baby it was – Mussolini and Count Ciano were the favourite candidates – but Göring himself never had any doubts over Emmy's faithfulness, and was ecstatically happy at the prospect of becoming a father at the age of forty-five.

Throughout 1937, Göring kept up his foreign interests, with more visits to the Balkans and shooting trips to Poland to build a relationship with Marshal Edward Smigly-Rydz, another hunting man who had succeeded Pilsudski as dictator. Göring took pains to assure him that Germany had no designs on the Corridor or any other Polish territory – keeping the Poles sweet was an important part of German strategy: they would need Polish compliance when they attacked Czechoslovakia. At home, he entertained a constant stream of foreign statesmen, diplomats and princes in Berlin, Carinhall and Rominten, among them Canadian Prime Minister Mackenzie King, Polish Ambassador Lipski, the Austrian Guido Schmidt, to whom he pointedly showed his famous map, the Duke and Duchess of Windsor, the former British Air Ministers, Lord Londonderry and Lord Lothian, and in November Lord Halifax, former Viceroy of India, currently Lord Privy Seal and President of the Council, and soon to be Foreign Secretary, who was Göring's guest at an international hunting exhibition that he staged in November.

One of Göring's most useful shooting guests was Sir Nevile Henderson, the new British Ambassador, sent by the new Prime Minister, Neville Chamberlain, to replace the sardonic Phipps in May. Henderson was a mediocrity, almost a caricature of the upper-class Englishman with his horsey face, beaky nose and moustache. He had previously served in Belgrade and Buenos Aires, but was considered a suitable choice for Berlin as he was more favourably disposed to the Nazi regime. He was certainly favourably disposed to Göring, whom he described as 'by far the most sympathetic' of all the Nazi leaders.

Yet another member of the hunting fraternity, Henderson earned Göring's approval by his skill and persistence in stalking stags, happy to ditch his dignity and crawl on his stomach through the under-growth to make a kill, and they built up a relationship that was to be invaluable over the following two years. While admitting that 'in any crisis, as in war, he [Göring] would be quite ruthless', Henderson went on:

He once said to me that the British whom he really admired were those whom he described as pirates, such as Francis Drake, and he reproached us for having become too 'debrutalised'. He was, in fact, himself a typical and brutal bucca-neer, but he had certain attractive qualities, and I must frankly say that I had a real personal liking for him . . . I liked Frau Göring as much as her husband, and possibly for better moral reasons. Absolutely unaffected, she was all kind-ness and simplicity.[4]

Praising Göring's organising and administrative qualities, Henderson said:

Those who worked with him commented upon his great ability to study files of documents and rows of figures and to extract out of them everything which was essential . . . He was a man to whom one could speak absolutely frankly.

He neither easily took nor lightly gave offence, and he was quick to seize the point at which one was driving . . . Very shrewd and astute, as fat men often are, his mind was simple and dealt only with essentials.[5]

Henderson noted with some surprise that 'however vain he may have been in small ways, and however much he loved pomp and uniforms and decorations, jewels and pictures, and the applause of his fellow men, he was quite without braggadocio over the big things which he had accomplished.' He was, Henderson said:

the absolute servant of his master, and I have never seen greater loyalty and devotion than his to Hitler . . . In all the very frank talks which I had with Göring, he never once spoke of himself or of the very great part which he had played in the Nazi revolution. Everything had been done by Hitler, all the credit was Hitler's, every decision was Hitler's, and he himself was nothing. Inasmuch as the enumeration of the posts which Göring filled in the Nazi regime took about five minutes to read, this self-effacement before his leader was all the more remarkable, particularly since, without Göring, Hitler would never have got where he was. Hitler's brain might conceive the impossible, but Göring did it.[6]

Alongside his regular dealings with Henderson, Göring also kept up a two-way channel of communication with the British aircraft industry and the RAF, regularly receiving visitors from Britain whom he could pump for information while trying to impress them with the Luftwaffe's growing strength. But he knew better than anyone that developing this latent strength depended on increasing industrial output, which in turn depended on increasing the supply of raw materials. The most crucial of these was iron ore. Germany, he had discovered, had sufficient iron ore of its own to produce about 14 million tonnes of pig iron a year, enough to provide for any wartime needs. But this source had not been exploited because German ore was acidic and difficult to smelt: it also contained only about 25 per cent iron, compared with 60 per cent in the high-grade ores of Sweden and Lorraine.

The steel barons of the Ruhr dismissed German ores as 'rubbish', and were understandably reluctant to get involved in such unprofitable working. Göring had urged them in 1936 to exploit local resources. He watched them impatiently as they dragged their feet for a year, then moved in himself. On 15 July 1937, he signed a contract with the H.G. Brassert Company of Chicago – whose boss, Hermann Alexander Brassert just happened to be his distant cousin

– to design and build furnaces capable of handling the low-grade ore. A week later he shocked the Ruhr industrialists by announcing that he was going to build the biggest integrated steelworks the world had ever seen, at Salzgitter, near Brunswick in Lower Saxony, over the Reich's largest ore deposits. The company was to be known as the Reichswerke AG für Erzbergbau und Eisenhütten Hermann Göring (the Hermann Göring Reich Works for Ore Mining and Iron Smelting), an unwieldy title that soon became simply the Hermann Göring-Werke, or HGW.

The steelmen, led by Krupp von Bohlen, squealed to Hitler, who simply referred them to Göring. Schacht complained bitterly to Göring himself over the costs involved. Göring ignored all their protests, and threatened to prosecute them for sabotaging the interests of the Reich. Krupp and his associates backed down. Schacht argued for a while, tried vainly to involve Hitler, then on 27 November resigned as Minister of Economics, saying it was not possible for his ministry and Göring to work side by side. Göring agreed, and promptly added the ministry to his portfolio, at least for the time being. Marching into Schacht's room, he snorted 'How can anyone have great thoughts in such a small room?' Then he grabbed the phone and called the Reichsbank – Schacht had remained its President and, for the sake of appearances, stayed in the government as Minister without Portfolio. 'Herr Schacht!' he bawled triumphantly, 'I am sitting in your chair!'

The HGW was the start of another mammoth empire for Göring, which over the following eight years was to spread across Germany, Austria, Czechoslovakia and south-eastern Europe, swallowing other companies wholesale, until it became by far the biggest industrial concern in Europe. It was not a state enterprise in the conventional sense, since it was not answerable to any ministry but to Göring personally, a fact that he underlined by appointing the ubiquitous faithful Pilli Körner as its Chairman.

Göring's business methods would have been the envy of any of the moguls, the Vanderbilts, Rockefellers, Astors, Guggenheims and their like, who had grabbed power and wealth in the nineteenth-century United States before they were shackled by anti-trust legislation. There was no such legislation to shackle Göring. He gave himself the right to confiscate or take shares in all iron ore deposits owned by his competitors, plus the coal mines and limestone workings needed for his steelmaking, paying not in cash but in shares in the HGW. He could also take a controlling interest in his competitors' businesses, and covered the huge deficits which the new HGW was bound to make in its early stages by forcing them to buy shares which they were later forced to sell back to him at a loss. For years, he had cultivated the big industrialists and capitalists as a supplicant. Now, he was not just one of them but on his way to becoming the biggest, most powerful and most ruthless of them all.

The ability to delegate responsibility was a vital part of Göring's success. He was a man who thought big, and as such only concerned himself with the big picture, leaving the detail to others. The down side of this was that the effectiveness and efficiency of the organisations he controlled, including the Luftwaffe and the Four-Year Plan, were smothered by a blanket of bureaucracy, as his subordinates sought to justify their actions and cover themselves against mistakes with a welter of forms and committees.

Even with proliferating legions of aides to do his bidding, however, the relentless pace and pressure of Göring's life took its toll. Amusements such as hunting, collecting works of art and fine jewels, playing with his train set or his pet lions, cruising the waterways of northern Germany in his motor yacht, all helped to relieve the strain, but it still showed through in things like his constant battle with his waistline. When he was under stress, he ate, often raiding the larder in the middle of the night to binge on cream-filled pastries and the like, and this combined with his glandular problem to send his weight soaring. He set himself a limit of 280 pounds, going on crash diets, sweating cures and exercise regimes whenever he reached it. He swam regularly in his private pools, and enjoyed playing tennis to his own rules, which involved his opponent always playing the ball to within his reach so that he did not have to run for it. 'Can't you see where I'm standing?' he would yell at anyone who transgressed.

Although he was concerned about his weight, a much more serious problem was his terror of succumbing once again to his morphine addiction, which he knew would destroy him and all he had achieved. To make sure that this did not happen, he seems to have undergone preventive treatment about once a year, in the strictest secrecy. Even so, every time he appeared tired or off-colour for whatever reason, there were rumours that he was back on the drug. The rumours were never substantiated: the popular image of Göring as a drug-crazed junkie is pure myth.

Göring did in fact develop a mild addiction around this time – to paracodeine pills, after they had been prescribed by his dentist as a painkiller. He was soon taking about ten a day, and continued to pop them until he was a prisoner in Mondorf after the war, by which time he was swallowing up to 100 a day with no ill effects. Paracodeine, which had just been developed by a German pharmaceutical firm, was a derivative of morphine, but contained so little of the drug that it was virtually non-addictive. The American psychiatrist at Mondorf, Dr Douglas M. Kelley, stated that Göring's normal daily dose of about twenty each morning and night was the equivalent of between three and four grains of morphine. 'This is not an unusually large dose,' he wrote. 'It was not enough to have affected his mental processes at any time.' Kelley decided that Göring took the pills as a habit much like smoking, partly to be doing something with his hands and mouth, and that he gained no particular stimulation from them. As proof of this, he weaned him off them quite painlessly in the course of a few days, simply by gradually reducing the dosage to zero,[7] something that would have been quite impossible with a genuine addiction, as Göring's own earlier experiences demonstrated.

Goebbels spent most of 1937 tightening his grip on Germany's cultural life. The press, broadcasting, publishing, music, the theatre, all were safely Nazified. He already had effective control of the film industry, but this was not enough: he wanted to own it, too. After bringing the Ufa film company to its knees through press attacks on its products, he forced its owner, Hugenberg, to sell his Babelberg studios and more than 120 cinemas to the government – in other words, to him. He then quickly mopped up the smaller film companies, and by May could boast: 'Now we are the masters of German film.' Having already eliminated Jews from the domestic industry, he could now remove them from all its foreign operations, by 'Aryanising' film export and distribution companies, along with the music recording business. Shortly afterwards he banned the showing of any old films with Jews in their casts.

In the world of the visual arts, he had already banned criticism, condemning critics as the 'disguised descendants of the Jewish critic-aristocracy', and part of the 'Jewish overrunning of German culture'. From now on, criticism was to be replaced by 'art reports' that simply catalogued pictures and sculptures and evaluated them in terms of the artists' 'purity of heart' and 'National Socialist intentions'. Any journalist daring to express an opinion was liable to instant dismissal, but some still managed to sneak in implicit criticisms between the lines of their reports. Moderate art journals were closed down, and replaced by Rosenberg's stultifyingly orthodox periodical, *Die Kunst im Dritten Reich* (Art in the Third Reich).

Rosenberg had been attacking modern art for years as 'cultural bolshevism'. Now Goebbels joined in, launching a massive assault on modern and especially expressionist and abstract works, which as a young intellectual he had always admired. Even as late as March 1934 he had been, along with Göring, the patron of an exhibition in Berlin of Italian Futurism. But now that Hitler had so clearly expressed his hatred of such art, Goebbels tried to outdo Rosenberg in condemning it. He appointed his old cartoonist from *Der Angriff*, Hans Schweitzer, as the arbiter of taste, with the ponderous title of Reich Plenipotentiary for Artistic Formulation. Schweitzer's opening shot was to close down the modern section of the National Gallery in Berlin and confiscate the pictures from it. He then headed a four-man commission to tour galleries and museums throughout the Reich, ordering the removal of offending works.

Altogether, the commission confiscated over 16,000 paintings, drawings, etchings and sculptures, mainly by German artists such as Nolde, Kokoschka, Barlach, Dix, Grosz, Kollwitz and Ernst, but also many by foreign masters such as Cézanne, Picasso, Matisse, Gaughin, Van Gogh, Braque, Pissarro, Dufy, Munch and Chirico. The commission's own tastes were epitomised by one of its members, Count Baudissin, director of the Volkswang Museum in Essen, who stated: 'The most perfect shape, the most sublime image that has recently been created in Germany has not come out of any artist's studio. It is the steel helmet.'[8]

To show the people what they should admire, in the summer of 1937 Goebbels and his underlings mounted a huge exhibition in the newly-completed 'House of German Art' in Munich, a monumentally boring edifice designed by Professor Ludwig Troost, who had been Hitler's favourite architect until his death in January 1934. Hitler took a personal hand in the final selection of 900 works from the 15,000 submitted, not only physically throwing out those he disliked but kicking holes in several of them. 'With the opening of this exhibition,' he promised in a high-flown speech at its inauguration on 18 July, 'has come the end of artistic lunacy and with it the artistic pollution of our people.' The result, according to William Shirer, was 'the worst junk I have ever seen in any country.'[9]

Outside, Munich was bedecked with flags, while carnival figures paraded through the streets to draw the crowds to the new gallery. Some 480,000 people visited it during 1937 – but over 2 million went to see another exhibition that Goebbels mounted simultaneously in a ramshackle gallery tucked away in a side alley. This was the 'Exhibition of Degenerate Art', intended to ridicule the works on show: pictures confiscated from other collections were jammed on the walls in a wild jumble devoid of any sense or order, without frames and labelled with crude and derisory titles. 'It contained,' said Shirer, 'a splendid selection of modern paintings – Kokoschka, Chagall and expressionist and impressionist works. The day I visited it, after panting through the sprawling House of German Art, it was crammed, with a long line forming down the creaking stairs and out into the street. In fact, the crowds besieging it became so great that Dr Goebbels, incensed and embarrassed, soon closed it.'[10] Even with its early closure, however, the 'Degenerates' proved to be the most popular exhibition ever staged in the Third Reich. After it closed, most of the pictures were sold abroad, to raise foreign currency for Göring and the Four Year Plan.

It was not just the showing of pictures that was strictly controlled, so too was their actual painting. Hitler laid down guidelines that could not be ignored, such as forbidding the use of any colour that could not be seen in nature by the 'normal' eye, and banning any depiction of human anguish, or ugliness in any form. Artists who insisted on flouting the rules – and there were several thousand who did – faced a number of sanctions starting with being barred from exhibiting, then from teaching, and finally from painting at all, even in the privacy of their own homes. Incredibly, Goebbels enlisted the Gestapo to make lightning raids on suspected transgressors, checking their brushes to see if they were still wet and preventing them from buying painting materials by issuing blacklists of proscribed painters to artists' suppliers.

Alongside culture, Goebbels was increasingly turning his attention to religion and the churches. Strictly speaking, this was the business of Hans Kerrl, a close personal friend of the Görings, who had been appointed Minister for Church Affairs in July 1935. But Kerrl was a moderate Nazi and not inclined to be too outspoken, and the role of chief persecutor of Christianity and the churches had been assumed by Rosenberg, something Goebbels could not possibly leave unchallenged. In spite of his pious upbringing and the fact that the Catholic Church had funded his higher education, since joining the Nazi Party he had consistently ranted against the churches and their influence on the people. His dream was to replace Christianity, with its Judaic foundations, with National Socialism as a religion worshipping the Führer as its god and saviour. Just lately, purely as a matter of expediency, Hitler had ordered him and the rest of the party to tone down their rhetoric. But that was about to change.

Late at night on 20 March 1937, Heydrich arrived at Goebbels's house on Hermann-Göring-Strasse, bringing a copy of a pastoral letter from the Pope that was to be read out from the pulpit of every Catholic church in Germany the next day, Palm Sunday. Entitled 'With Burning Concern', the letter condemned those who worshipped the idols of race, people, state, or the holders of state power, and was an obvious attack on the Nazi regime. Goebbels was furious, describing it as 'barefaced arrogance', and 'a provocation in the best sense of the word'. But he decided they should not tell Hitler until the morning, 'so that he would not be angry about it all night', and counselled Heydrich, who wanted to take strong measures, to 'play dead and ignore it'. They could deal with it, he said, by applying economic pressure, and in the meantime confiscating and banning every church magazine that published the Pope's message. Apart from that, he resolved to 'keep his nerve and wait until the hour comes to shake off these provocateurs.'[11]

At first, Hitler agreed with Goebbels's approach, but his patience soon gave out and he called for action against the Vatican, saying that since the clerics did not understand 'patience and mildness', they would have to 'find out how stern, tough and merciless we can be'. Goebbels started demonstrating this, seizing on 'the gruesome sex-murder of a boy in a Belgian monastery' to launch a violent press campaign smearing all ten thousand Brothers of Charity as homosexuals and paedophiles. 267 of Germany's 500 Franciscan friars were arrested and charged with offences against children in their care, many of them mentally deficient.[12] Many of the charges may have been true, each one representing an individual human tragedy, but Goebbels was concerned only with exploiting them to the full. He ordered all German newspapers to publish complete and unabridged reports supplied by his DNB news agency, in all their salacious detail, to shock and disgust their readers.

Soon afterwards he was delighted when Hitler chose him rather than Rosenberg to make a major speech that marked the climax of the campaign against the priesthood; Hitler even went through it with him after enjoying a boat trip with him and his family, 'giving him a few tips'. In the speech, delivered on 28 May at the Deutschlandhalle in Berlin and broadcast live across the nation, Goebbels spoke as a father, 'whose most precious treasure on earth' was his four children – Magda had presented him with another daughter, Holde, on 19 February. He raged against 'these preachers of morality' who were 'bestial and unscrupulous abusers of youth . . . a sexual plague that must be exterminated root and branch'.[13] He was in splendid form, and was rewarded afterwards with praise from Hitler, who 'pressed his hand' and told him 'he had listened to the whole speech on the radio and could not sit still for a moment'.[14]

Goebbels's championing of morality must have had the ring of hypocrisy for many of his listeners, who could not have forgotten the scandals of the Röhm purge and the number of active homosexuals in the upper reaches of the party, including his own State Secretary, Walther Funk. His own more orthodox sexual appetite, including his torrid affair with Lida Baarova, was also public knowledge. The affair was certainly no secret any more from Magda, particularly after Gustav Fröhlich had had a confrontation with her husband after catching him and Baarova together, and had then split up with Baarova and sold his house on Schwanenwerder. Undeterred, Goebbels continued to woo his mistress, making full use of his remote lakeside house on the Bogensee and vigorously promoting her film career, interfering constantly with every stage of production to make sure she received every advantage.

Although the Goebbels's marriage was close to breaking point, it somehow managed to survive, at least for the moment. Partly this was due to his failure to see why he could not have his cake and eat it: he could not resist the charms of Baarova, but he could not bear the thought of losing Magda and the children. His diaries are full of references to his playing happily with them, and on his stepson's birthday in November he took great delight in presenting him with a snazzy motor cycle.[15] Partly, though, he clung to his marriage because he was terrified of offending Hitler, who was displeased by the rash of divorces and separations among leading Nazi couples that year. Goebbels described this as 'a very serious problem' within the party. In his opinion, it was always the women who were to blame, for being 'too stupid and too awkward to hold their husbands'.[16] It was hardly surprising that when the puritans in the party wanted to make adultery an offence punishable by up to ten years in jail, he spoke out sharply against the proposal.

On 5 November 1937, Göring slipped away from his International Hunting Exhibition and changed into his Luftwaffe general's uniform to attend an important meeting with Hitler in the Chancellery. It was a small, extremely high-powered session: the others present were Raeder and Fritsch, Commanders-in-Chief of the navy and army, Blomberg, who was now both War Minister and Commander-in-Chief of the Wehrmacht, the combined armed services, and Neurath. The only other person there was Hitler's Wehrmacht adjutant, Colonel Friedrich Hossbach, who decided on his own initiative to take notes. Raeder had asked for the meeting, to thrash out the allocation of steel and other raw materials between the three services – typically, Göring was favouring the Luftwaffe over the army and navy. But before the showdown with Göring, which was all settled amicably, the meeting was treated to a four-hour monologue from Hitler on Germany's need and indeed her right to a greater living space than other peoples, and how this was to be won. 'The question for Germany,' he said, 'ran: where could she achieve the greatest gain at the lowest cost?'

'Germany's problem,' Hitler declared, 'could only be solved by means of force and this was never without attendant risk.' The extra living space would have to be in Europe, but there were 'two hate-inspired antagonists, Britain and France, to whom a German colossus in the centre of Europe was a thorn in the flesh'. Time, he said, was not on Germany's side: German strength would reach its peak by 1943–5, after which the other powers would start catching up. Germany had to strike before then, while her enemies were still preparing.

The first move, Hitler told his chiefs, must be the annexation of Austria and Czechoslovakia. This would secure Germany's eastern and southern flanks, free military forces 'for other purposes', gain enough extra manpower for twelve new army divisions, and, assuming the expulsion of three million non-Germans from the two countries, provide foodstuffs for five to six million Germans in the Reich. Britain and France, Hitler thought, had already tacitly written off Czechoslovakia, and would not interfere. In any case, he believed they would very soon be at war with Italy over her involvement in the Spanish Civil War, which Germany should do everything possible to prolong, and the probable Italian occupation of the Balearic Islands. If the British and French were to go to war with Italy, then he was 'resolved to take advantage of it, whenever it happened, even as early as 1938'. The descent upon the Czechs, he concluded, must be carried out with 'lightning speed'.[17]

The service chiefs and the Foreign Minister were 'shaken to the core' by this sudden revelation of Hitler's true intentions. To be sure, there was nothing new in what he said – the broad plan was all set down in *Mein Kampf* – but now he was saying it for real. He actually intended to start a war of aggression, as early as the following year. They had no objection to the idea of expansion, which was an aim they shared, or even to annexing Austria and Czechoslovakia, which they all took for granted would happen sooner or later. But they were horrified at Hitler's readiness to risk war with Britain and France, and began raising objections as soon as they had a chance to speak. Only Raeder, always the most coldly belligerent, said nothing.

Hitler listened to Blomberg and Fritsch with contempt at their faint-heartedness – 'Generals,' he believed, 'should be like a butcher's dog who has to be held fast by the collar because otherwise he threatens to attack anyone in sight.'[18] Before the meeting started, he had told Göring he wanted 'to light a fire' under them, because he was 'by no means satisfied with the rearmament of the army'. Their failure to respond finished them in his eyes. They, and the over-cautious Neurath, would have to go.

Göring, of course, was not taken by surprise: he and Hitler had talked the whole matter through for hour after hour in great detail. Much of what Hitler had to say about Austrian and Czech resources undoubtedly came from him, since it coincided so exactly with his own assessments, and his only proviso was that Germany should pull out of Spain before starting anything else. Hitler agreed, but said they should wait for 'a proper moment'. Göring was happy to do just that, in more ways than one.

The day after the generals' meeting with Hitler on 6 November, Germany's position was further strengthened when Italy joined the Anti-Comintern Pact, which Ribbentrop had signed with Japan a year before. Ribbentrop had at that time, incidentally, astounded foreign correspondents by declaring with perfect seriousness: 'Gentlemen, this pact means that Germany and Japan have joined together to defend Western Civilisation.'[19] While Göring, Goebbels and the other paladins welcomed Italy's entry as a sign of closer ties with Mussolini, they were less pleased to see Ribbentrop adding another feather to his cap. Like Neurath and the Foreign Ministry, they had hoped that his London mission would expose his failings and remove him from the scene, and had watched with barely disguised *schadenfreude* as he committed one gaffe after another, earning himself the nickname among the British establishment of 'Herr von Brickendrop'. 'Ribbentrop is making an utter fool of himself there,' Goebbels sneered. 'Above all, he is badly behaved and tactless. Yes, we made a bad casting mistake there. I must report this to the Führer.'[20]

Ribbentrop's ambassadorship had indeed been such a total disaster that the ridicule and denigration from the British Establishment had penetrated even his monstrous insensitivity. His reaction was that of a lover spurned, his Anglophilia souring into a bitter hatred that would colour all his advice to Hitler, with catastrophic results. But instead of being banished or at least withering away into insignificance, he had somehow managed to fool Hitler into accepting his credibility by a mixture of lies and shameless sycophancy. Terrified of being out of the Führer's immediate ambit, he had never stayed away from Berlin for long, spending as much if not more time there than in London – to the deep displeasure of both the German Foreign Ministry and the British government, as well as his rivals. He had maintained his Dienststelle, and even taken some sixty members of it to London with him. Now, his persistence and his alternative diplomacy had paid off with Italy, at exactly the right moment for the Nazi regime and for himself. Or so he thought.

When he reported his triumph to Hitler on 8 November, Ribbentrop was convinced that he was about to rewarded with Neurath's job. He was dumbfounded to find Hitler steaming with fury at his failure to obey orders and keep Neurath fully informed of his discussions in Rome. What was more, he had been boasting to everyone that he was about to be made Foreign Minister, something Hitler was not yet ready for. Hitler laid into him at the top of his voice, in full hearing of his aides. 'What do you think you are doing?' he yelled. 'I will not tolerate such behaviour!' Utterly shattered, Ribbentrop offered to resign, saying he would go as a volunteer to fight in Spain. Hitler waved aside this melodramatic gesture, and told him to get back to his post in London and stay there.[21] 'Ribbentrop is furious that he has not been a success in London,' Goebbels gloated. 'That comes in large part from his serious tactical errors. At least I can give the Führer another opinion now.'[22] Sadly, Hitler was not inclined to listen.

Ribbentrop scuttled back to London on 9 November much chastened. But his tribulations were by no means over. A week later Lord Halifax left for Germany, ostensibly to visit Göring's hunting exhibition in his role as Master of the Middleton Foxhounds, but in fact on a mission from Chamberlain to sound out Hitler and Göring on improving Anglo–German relations. The visit had been arranged by Henderson and Neurath, without consulting Ribbentrop: the British Foreign Office had specifically asked that he should have nothing to do with it, and Hitler had agreed. Ribbentrop was not even given a report on it afterwards by either side, and had to beg Neurath to tell him what had been said.

Halifax met Hitler at Berchtesgaden on 19 November, but their talk did not go well, with Hitler shouting angrily about the Western powers repeatedly obstructing his ambitions in south-east Europe.[23] It was left for Göring to repair the damage the next day, after lunch at Carinhall – which included, Halifax noted in his diary, 'some of the rawest beef I have ever seen'. Halifax was given the obligatory tour of the house and breeding grounds, and confessed in his diary to being 'immensely entertained', both by the house and by his host, whom he described as 'like a great schoolboy, full of life and pride in what he was doing, showing off his forest and animals and then talking high politics out of the setting of a green jerkin and red dagger'.[24]

Like two interrogators playing hard man, soft man, Göring counteracted Hitler's excitable harshness with what Paul Schmidt, who was the interpreter on both occasions, described as 'infinitely more diplomacy'. He covered exactly the same ground as Hitler, notably Austria, Czechoslovakia, Poland and Danzig, but spoke calmly, reasonably and with great charm, reassuring Halifax that 'Under no circumstances shall we use force,' adding with a smile that 'this would be completely unnecessary'; everything could be settled quite well by negotiation. Schmidt, who of course knew nothing of Hitler's revelations to his generals two weeks earlier, was convinced that 'this was in fact Göring's innermost conviction' and not an act. Maybe it was. Either way, it worked: 'We know from Chamberlain's diary,' Schmidt recalled admiringly in his memoirs, 'that Halifax went back with a favourable report – and I am convinced that this was mainly due to his talk with Göring at Carinhall.'[25]

* * *

Göring celebrated his forty-fifth birthday on 12 January 1938 with a luncheon in his Berlin mansion. Expensive gifts poured in from all directions; Hitler's was a painting of a falconer by the nineteenth-century German artist Hans Markart, neatly acknowledging Göring's passion for hunting without showing animals being killed, which was anathema to the Führer. Halfway through the party, Hitler and Göring surprised everyone by leaving the table and slipping quietly away. 'I'm off to a wedding,' Göring told Milch, with a wicked chuckle.

The wedding at which the two leaders were to be witnesses was a very quiet civil ceremony in the War Ministry building, between Blomberg and a young woman thirty-five years his junior, Erna Gruhn. It was an odd match: Blomberg was a widower nearing sixty years of age, with five grown-up children, a Field Marshal and an aristocrat; Erna was a shorthand typist in the Reich Egg Board, the daughter of a poor woman who took in ironing for a living. But she was bright, blonde and attractive, and Blomberg had fallen heavily for her, and she, it seemed, for him. There are conflicting versions of how they met. One is that they encountered each other while walking in the Tiergarten – which sounds suspiciously like a pick-up; the other is that they were introduced by the manager of a hotel in Thuringia where Blomberg was convalescing after an illness – which sounds suspiciously like pimping. Either way, they soon became lovers, and in no time Blomberg was besotted.

In mid December, Blomberg decided to marry his Erna – possibly because she had lied to him that she was pregnant.[26] Without mentioning this, Blomberg approached Göring as a fellow senior officer and asked his advice, saying that he planned to marry again, but that his bride-to-be was not only younger but also from a much lower social class. What did Göring think would be the reactions of the officer caste, and, more important, those of Hitler, whose approval he needed as Supreme Commander? Göring assured him that he need have no fears about Hitler, who would see his marriage to a girl of the people as a blow against the snobbery of the old order he so detested. When Blomberg confessed that Erna was also 'a lady with a past', Göring brushed this aside: 'What does it matter?' he responded. 'We are all men of the world!'[27]

Göring was right about Hitler. The Führer was delighted when Blomberg approached him after the state funeral of Ludendorff in Munich on 22 December 1937, and offered himself and Göring as witnesses. The only remaining obstacle was that Blomberg had a younger rival for Erna's hand; Göring took care of this, too, buying the man off with a well-paid job in South America. And so the marriage took place, and the newly-weds left for their honeymoon in Göring's favourite island, Capri, pausing on the way to visit the zoo in Leipzig, where they were photographed by the press in front of a cage full of monkeys – which struck Blomberg's Chief of Staff, General Wilhelm Keitel, as 'more than tasteless',[28] confirming his doubts about the match. Nine days later, an anonymous caller telephoned the Army High Command in Berlin, claiming to be a general, and demanding to speak to Fritsch. When he was refused, he shouted: 'Tell the general that Field Marshal von Blomberg has married a whore!' The secret was out.

Just how much Göring already knew about Erna's past, and how much he used that knowledge to further his own ends can only be a matter of speculation. There can be no doubt whatever of his ambition to scale the final pinnacle of his military career by becoming commander-in-chief of all the armed forces, or of his ruthlessness and cunning. Certainly, after Hitler's disillusionment with the generals at the 5 November conference, the time was ripe for Blomberg's removal. Equally certainly Hitler would have been looking for an excuse to sack him without provoking a clash with the army: Blomberg was a Field Marshal, he had been appointed by Hindenburg, and although the generals may have despised him as Hitler's stooge, they would still rally to defend him as one of their own. It is entirely possible that Göring deliberately drew him into a trap by encouraging him to marry, knowing through his own sources, including his FA phone taps, that Erna was, or at least had been, a prostitute and that Blomberg was infatuated with her. He could then, at the appropriate moment, discredit him, force his resignation, and take his place.

Within minutes of the anonymous telephone call, the FA transcript of it was on its way across Berlin to Göring. Whether it was planned or not – and who can say that he had not arranged the call – he took advantage of the situation immediately, asking the Berlin Police Chief, Helldorff, to investigate Frau von Blomberg's past. At 4.15 p.m., a 'very agitated' Helldorff was in Keitel's office with a police record card showing convictions for prostitution in seven different cities, plus distributing indecent photographs of herself and stealing from a client. He asked Keitel to identify her from the registration card for her change of address to Blomberg's apartment in the War Ministry building, and was surprised to discover that Keitel had never set eyes on the lady, even though his son was engaged to be married to Blomberg's daughter and the two men were therefore not just colleagues but almost family.

Blomberg had had to interrupt his honeymoon when his mother died, but was away in Eberswald sorting out her affairs, and could not be contacted. So Keitel referred Helldorff to Göring, who had been a witness at the wedding and must have met her. Göring, of course, identified her at once, and took personal charge of the matter, swearing the police to secrecy, saying he would speak to Blomberg the next day, and would also inform Hitler, who was away in Berchtesgaden.[29] He then ordered Helldorff to compile a complete dossier on Erna. When Hitler returned to Berlin, Göring was waiting for him, with a buff police file in his hand.

Hitler was shocked at the revelation, and furious at what he saw as the humiliation of having been conned into being a witness at the wedding and therefore a party to the scandal. He was incensed to hear about the pornographic photographs, which had been taken by a Czech Jew with whom Erna had been living at the time. He agreed that Göring should speak to Blomberg, and tell him it would be best for everyone concerned if he annulled his marriage immediately, so that the whole affair could then be hushed up. Blomberg refused.

Hitler spent a sleepless night, worrying about how he could avoid losing face. The next day, his adjutant Fritz Wiedemann saw him pacing up and down his room, shaking his head and muttering 'If a German field marshal marries a whore, anything in the world is possible.' At lunch, the atmosphere was tense, but Göring and Goebbels did their best to cheer him up. By next day, Goebbels had the whole story from Helldorff, and noted with some relish that Blomberg 'would have to say his goodbyes', adding 'Only the pistol remains for a man of honour . . . The Führer as a witness to the marriage. It's unthinkable. The worst crisis for the regime since the Röhm affair. I am shattered. The Führer looks like a corpse.'[30] On 27 January, Hitler had his final interview with Blomberg, and accepted his resignation. They parted on good terms, with Blomberg receiving a pay-off of 50,000 marks and keeping his full pay as a Field Marshal, on condition that he left at once for a world tour and stayed away from Germany for a year.

Returning to his office to clear his desk, Blomberg confided to Keitel that he blamed Göring for his departure: 'If Göring had not entertained hopes of becoming his successor, they would very easily have been able to cover up the whole affair with the mantle of true love.

He had known all along that his wife had lived loosely in the past, but that was no reason for casting a woman out for ever.'[31] Blomberg said he and Hitler had discussed the question of who should succeed him, but told Keitel that Fritsch, the obvious candidate, was not only out of the running but also on his way out altogether, 'as serious legal proceedings were pending against him of a kind that could not be set aside'. He did not elaborate, but told Keitel he was to report to the Chancellery in plain clothes at one o'clock, when Hitler would give him the details.

Keitel had hardly had time to change for his appointment with Hitler before Göring called him to his flat, wanting to know what Blomberg had told him, and asking if he had said anything about his successor. 'You are the only one in the running for that,' Keitel said, 'because you probably won't want to take orders from yet another army general.' That was exactly what Göring wanted to hear, and he confirmed it so readily that Keitel suddenly started wondering if he could be behind the mysterious business with Fritsch.[32]

Keitel's suspicions were well founded. The disposal of Blomberg could have been pure opportunism, but the assault on Fritsch was altogether murkier, with disturbing echoes of the framing of Röhm. When Göring presented Hitler with Helldorff's dossier on Erna von Blomberg, he gave him another file, on Fritsch, prepared by Heydrich and Himmler. Some two years earlier, Fritsch had been accused by a professional blackmailer, Otto Schmidt, of indulging in a homosexual act with a male prostitute called Sepp Weingärtner. Hitler and Göring had both been informed, but had decided to let the matter drop because the march into the Rhineland was about to happen. Schmidt had been turned over to the Gestapo for further questioning, and then interned in Papenburg concentration camp. Hitler had ordered the file on the case to be destroyed, and had then put it out of his mind.

Far from destroying the original file, however, Heydrich had kept it locked away in his safe, ready for use when the time was right. That time had now come. The partnership between Himmler, Heydrich and Göring, which had been so successful in disposing of Röhm and the other victims of the Night of the Long Knives was resumed in an action that bore all the hallmarks of a Heydrich deception. Himmler and Göring both had good reasons for wanting Fritsch removed: Himmler knew that Fritsch was an implacable opponent of any integration of the SS with the army, and would do everything he could to block it; Göring saw Fritsch as the only feasible rival to himself for Blomberg's

position. And so the game began again, but this time there was no
need for murder. All that needed to be destroyed was Fritsch's reputation, and that, for Heydrich, was child's play.

Towards the end of 1937, at the same time as Blomberg was confiding
his plans to Göring, the Gestapo started questioning Schmidt and
Weingärtner again. Schmidt was brought before Göring in his villa,
where he identified Fritsch from a photograph. On 25 January 1938,
Göring gave the file to Hitler. Fritsch learned about the accusations
later that day from Hitler's Wehrmacht adjutant, Hossbach. After
brooding angrily overnight, he demanded to speak to Hitler at once.
Hitler kept him waiting until the evening, while he conferred with
Göring, Himmler and the Reich Justice Minister, Franz Gürtner, before
seeing him in company with Göring.

'The Führer declared at once,' Fritsch wrote later, 'that I stood
accused of homosexual activity . . . If I confessed, he said, I should be
required to go away on a long journey and that would be the end of
it. Göring also spoke in this vein.' Göring then added that there could
be no doubt. 'This blackmailer,' he said, 'has consistently spoken the
truth in over a hundred other cases.' Certain of his ground, Fritsch
calmly denied everything. He was given the file to read. While he was
scanning it incredulously, Schmidt was brought into the room, looked
at him and said 'Yes, that's him.'[33] Göring marched out into the
adjoining room where Hossbach was waiting, and threw himself on
to a sofa, shouting breathlessly 'It was he! It was he!'

In fact, it was not he. The whole business was a case of mistaken
identity involving a retired cavalry captain named Achim von Frisch,
but by the time that was proved by a military court at which Göring
presided in March 1938, distinguishing himself by bullying the prosecution witnesses into confessing their perjury, it was too late. Fritsch
had been forced to resign, and Hitler, though offering him a handsome
apology, had no intention of reinstating him. Whether the mistake was
deliberate or accidental no longer mattered by then – it had done its
work, for Himmler, for Göring, and for Hitler, who had been given
an excuse to get rid of the difficult Fritsch.

For Göring, the result was a mixture of gratification and disappointment; gratification that Fritsch was no longer 'in his way', disappointment that despite his intensive lobbying he was not given the
overall command of the Wehrmacht as War Minister. Keitel had tried
twice to persuade Hitler to appoint him, but Hitler rejected this out
of hand, the first time 'saying there was no question of it as he had

given Göring the Four-Year Plan and he had to hang on to the Air Force as well, as there was nobody better for that than he; anyway, Göring had to gather experience in the affairs of state as his own predestined successor as Führer'.[34] The second time, after revealing why he could not appoint Fritsch, Hitler told him he had decided to take over the Supreme Command himself, with Keitel, like it or not, as his Chief of Staff.

Hitler abolished the War Ministry and in its place created a unified High Command of the Armed Forces, the Oberkommando der Wehrmacht (OKW), with himself as Supreme Commander and the three services reduced to its subsidiary arms. He chose Keitel as its Chief of Staff because he knew he was a pliable yes-man, who would do as he was told and tell him what he wanted to hear. Blomberg had dismissed Keitel as 'nothing more than the man who runs my office' when Hitler, who did not know him, asked about him as a possible replacement. 'That's exactly the man I am looking for,' Hitler had replied.[35]

To replace Fritsch as Commander-in-Chief of the army, Hitler chose General Walther von Brauchitsch, who promised to lead the army closer to National Socialism. Brauchitsch was respected as a soldier by his fellow generals, but was another spineless character when it came to standing up to Hitler. There was an unexpected hitch when it was discovered that he was in the process of divorcing his wife, raising the fear of yet another sex scandal. But it just so happened that his son Bernd was one of Göring's adjutants, and Göring dispatched him to talk to his mother and persuade her to go quietly, with the help of a generous financial settlement which Göring negotiated and Hitler provided, further obligating Brauchitsch to him. Hitler normally disapproved of divorces, but he seems to have welcomed this one, since both he and Göring knew that the new wife, Frau Charlotte Schmidt, was, as Ambassador Ulrich von Hassell said, 'a two hundred per cent rabid Nazi', who would make sure her husband toed the party line.

In other times and other circumstances, the removal of Blomberg and Fritsch might have been a minor scandal that would soon have been forgotten. Instead, it provided Hitler with the chance to make the third and final step in consolidating his absolute dictatorship: the Reichstag fire had provided the excuse for the Enabling Act; the Röhm purge had eliminated the threat of internal opposition within the party; now he used the Blomberg—Fritsch 'crisis' to emasculate the army, the only other power factor that could possibly threaten his position. On 20 February, when he made his annual Reichstag speech postponed from 30 January, he would be able to declare: 'There now exists not a single institution of this state which is not National Socialist . . . the greatest guarantee of the National Socialist revolution is the control we now have of all the institutions of the Reich, at home and abroad. The nation is protected, so far as the rest of the world is concerned, by our National Socialist armed forces from now on.'[36]

Goebbels, who claimed that Hitler's taking command of the Wehrmacht was his idea, also claimed to have thought up the way out of the crisis that was building rapidly as rumours of a political crisis at the highest level swept through Germany and the rest of Europe. On 31 January he spent two hours locked in private session with Hitler, who was calm again after the agitation of the previous few days, but was still 'very pale, grey and shaken'. After going over the situation they came up with a brilliant piece of political spin that would turn the whole thing to advantage: they would bury the firing of Blomberg and Fritsch as part of a major shake-up. 'In no way is the question to be presented as a triumph for the party,' Goebbels noted. 'And the true background must be obscured behind a smokescreen. I hope that the real motives will be drowned in the great reshuffle.'[37]

Hitler gave details of the great reshuffle to what was to prove to be the final Cabinet meeting of his rule on 4 February. Besides the departure, 'for health reasons', of Blomberg and Fritsch, it involved the compulsory retirement of sixteen senior generals, and the transfer of forty-four others who had shown a lack of enthusiasm towards National Socialism. The shake-up also extended to the other remaining bastion of conservative values, the Foreign Ministry: Neurath was relieved of his position as Foreign Minister and 'promoted' to head a new Privy Council of ministers – which was never to meet – and the ambassadors to Rome, Tokyo, London and Vienna were all replaced. Ribbentrop was to be the new Foreign Minister, to the disappointment and disgust of Goebbels, who noted that he had described him to Hitler 'all the time and with complete frankness' as 'a nobody'. Goebbels also lost his State Secretary, since Hitler made Funk Economics Minister – he had informed Funk almost casually when he met him by chance at the opera, saying Göring would tell him all about it. Goebbels moved his closest associate in the Propaganda Ministry, Karl Hanke, into the State Secretary's job.

Hitler made one more announcement at that last Cabinet meeting. Aware as always of the feelings of his paladins, he let Göring down gently with a juicy consolation prize: he promoted him to Field Marshal, making him the most senior serving officer in Germany.

XIX

ANSCHLUSS

At 11 a.m. on Thursday, 10 March 1938, General Field Marshal Göring took his seat in the Prussian Ministry building as president of the military court of honour to hear the case against Fritsch. He had barely opened the proceedings, however, before a messenger arrived with an urgent summons to the Reich Chancellery: Hitler needed him there immediately. Adjourning the court *sine die*, he hurried away, leaving the generals in suspense. Fritsch would have to wait a little longer for justice, while he and the Führer dealt with more urgent matters.

The more urgent matter, as Göring was already well aware, was Austria. The previous evening, the Austrian Chancellor, Kurt von Schuschnigg, had raised the temperature dramatically by announcing at a public meeting in Innsbruck that there was to be a national referendum the following Sunday, to vote on one emotionally loaded question: 'Are you in favour of a free and German, independent and social, Christian and united Austria; for freedom and work, and for the equality of all who declare for race and Fatherland?' The referendum was in breach of German–Austrian agreements and, according to Göring, heavily rigged: 'One could vote only by "yes",' he told the Nuremberg Tribunal. 'Every person could vote as often as he wanted, five times, six times, seven times. If he tore up the slip of paper, that was counted as "yes", and so on . . . That whole thing was a farce.' Göring's assumptions may or may not have been correct, but Austria's electoral rolls were certainly several years out of date, disenfranchising everyone under the age of twenty-four. There could be little doubt that the referendum would result in a massive 'yes' vote, which would completely undermine Nazi claims that the majority of Austrians wanted union with Germany.

The situation in the single-party, right-wing dictatorship in Austria had been volatile for some time. The Austrian Nazi Party and all its subsidiaries had been outlawed after the assassination by SS men of Schuschnigg's predecessor, Engelbert Dollfuss, during their bungled *putsch* attempt in 1934. Several thousand SS and SA men had fled into exile in Bavaria, where they formed an Austrian Legion, waiting impatiently for the call to return and fight. Many more went underground and kept up a campaign of violent demonstrations and terrorist activities, funded and encouraged by Germany, which increased steadily until in 1937 barely a day passed without a bombing taking place in some part of the country.

At the end of that year, Austrian police uncovered details of a plot to assassinate Schuschnigg, and in January 1938 they raided the headquarters of a Nazi cover organisation called the 'Committee of Seven', where they found documents signed by Hess outlining plans for an open revolt in the spring. These included the murder of Ambassador Papen by Austrian SS men disguised as members of Schuschnigg's Fatherland Front – a 'provocation' that had the fingerprints of Heydrich all over it – and would provide the excuse for the German army to move in, to prevent 'German blood being shed by Germans'.

In a personal meeting at the Berghof on 12 February, Hitler bullied and browbeat Schuschnigg into signing a two-page agreement drawn up by Ribbentrop, the main points of which were the removal of all restrictions on the Nazi Party in Austria, an amnesty for convicted Austrian Nazis, two Nazi supporters to be given key roles in the Austrian Cabinet – the intelligent and mild-mannered Viennese lawyer Dr Arthur Seyss-Inquart as Interior Minister with control over the police and security forces, and General Edmund Glaise-Hortenau as War Minister – and the start of preparations for economic and monetary union. To make sure the Austrian government ratified the agreement, Hitler ordered Keitel to move troops up to the frontier and start making obvious but fake preparations for an invasion. It was one more bluff that worked. The Austrian government capitulated, the Nazi ministers joined the Cabinet, and everything seemed to be going according to plan, until Schuschnigg dropped the bombshell of his snap referendum on 9 March.

Hitler was completely thrown when he heard of this 'extremely dirty knavish trick to make fools of Germany through a stupid, idiotic plebiscite'.[1] He immediately called Göring and Goebbels to the Chancellery, to discuss what they should do to counter this threat to their plans for a bloodless *Anschluss*-by-consent that would remove any reason for intervention by France, Britain or Italy. As usual, he dithered and vacillated, while Göring urged him to be decisive. By the end of the night he was, according to Goebbels, who stayed on alone with him until 5 a.m., 'in full swing' and 'in a wonderful fighting mood', though he still wanted to sleep on it before coming to any decision.

Göring had already started to take control of the situation. He knew that Glaise-Horstenau was visiting south Germany at the time, and as soon as he heard about the referendum he had him brought to Berlin to speak to Hitler and himself. He then had him flown to Vienna, with orders that he and Seyss-Inquart were to impress on Schuschnigg that Germany 'would never tolerate this provocation'.² The two Nazis were to demand that the referendum be called off at once, and that Schuschnigg should resign in favour of Seyss-Inquart.

Since Germany had been taken by surprise, some of the key players in any military action against Austria were absent: Milch was on holiday in Switzerland, Brauchitsch was away from Berlin on leave, General Walter von Reichenau, the Munich District Commander, was in Cairo at a meeting of the International Olympic Committee, and Ribbentrop was in London, presenting his letters of recall and saying his farewells. Göring called the two generals back, but left Ribbentrop where he was, telling Hitler he would be more useful there. To Ribbentrop's consternation, Hitler put Neurath back in temporary charge of the Foreign Ministry, working with the new State Secretary, Ernst von Weizsäcker.

When he arrived back at the Chancellery after adjourning the court of honour on 10 March, Göring found Hitler anxiously poring over maps. Goebbels joined them shortly afterwards, followed by Keitel, who had to admit that the army had prepared no plans for an invasion of Austria. The closest thing they had was 'Case Otto', the rough outline of a plan to counter any move to put Prince Otto von Habsburg on the Austrian throne. Hitler decided that Case Otto would have to do, and sent Keitel away with orders to prepare it, and to decide which army units could be ready to march in on the morning of 12 March, in two days' time. This time, the troop movements were to be real, not fake.

For the rest of that day, the Chancellery was abuzz with frenzied activity. Goebbels suggested that they should tell Seyss-Inquart and Glaise-Horstenau to demand that the referendum be postponed and held later under the same conditions as the Saar plebiscite. When Schuschnigg refused – as he undoubtedly would – the two Nazi ministers would resign, and 600–800 German aircraft would bombard Austria with leaflets, calling for the people to rise in revolt on Sunday, the day of the referendum, at which point the Wehrmacht and the Austrian Legion would march in to restore order. Göring thought this was pointless. He wanted to send the troops in on Saturday, to stop the referendum by force, and Hitler agreed with him. He sent for General Ludwig Beck, Chief of the Army General Staff under Brauchitsch, and, peremptorily brushing aside his objections, ordered him to have two army corps ready to cross into Austria in the morning. Weizsäcker suggested the two Austrian Nazi ministers could provide a quasi-legal pretext by making an appeal for German troops to go in, but Göring treated this with scorn, too. 'We don't need it,' he told Hitler. 'We're going in anyway, come hell or high water!'

Hitler's resolve was strengthened when a messenger arrived during the afternoon from London bringing word from Ribbentrop that he had seen Halifax, and that he was 'convinced that England of her own accord will do nothing in regard to it [the Austrian question] at present, and that she will exert a moderating influence on the other powers'. Britain's 'primary aim', he said, was to play for time while completing her own rearmament.[3] In fact, Halifax had given him a stern warning of the danger of war in Central Europe if Germany persisted in her aggressive attitude, adding that he 'attached the greatest importance to everything being done to ensure that the plebiscite was carried out without interference or intimidation'.[4] Ribbentrop, whose Anglophobia was now so deep that he welcomed the idea of war with Britain, chose not to report this. Halifax, suspecting he might not, sent a note of what he had actually said to Henderson, for him to pass on to Neurath, but by then it was too late.

With all the available telephone lines from the Chancellery being used to keep in touch with Vienna and Rome, Ribbentrop was out of touch and sidelined in London, having to rely on BBC news bulletins for information.[5] His own officials in Berlin could not help, since Göring had taken complete charge of events and was ignoring the Foreign Ministry. This did nothing to improve Ribbentrop's feelings for Britain, with whom he naturally associated this humiliation. He went ahead that evening with his grand farewell party at the Embassy, where he was seen by an incredulous British diplomat, Victor Cavendish-Bentinck, shamelessly chatting 'in the most affectionate manner' to the Austrian Minister, who was 'blissfully unaware' that the German army was poised to invade his country.[6]

Hitler's and Göring's biggest worry was how Mussolini would react. Göring was conscious that five divisions of the Italian army were stationed on the Brenner frontier, just south of Innsbruck, and was afraid that the Duce just might decide to take advantage of the opportunity to grab the eastern Tyrol, which he had long coveted. He needed to be discouraged from any such ideas, as did the Czechs, Hungarians and Yugoslavs, who all had greedy eyes on border provinces of Austria. Together Hitler and Göring drafted a cynical letter to Mussolini, explaining their hopes and fears and asking him to stand aside. Their tissue of lies and distortions started with the invented charge that the Austrians and Czechs were plotting together to restore the Habsburg monarchy and then attack Germany 'with at least twenty million men' – this despite the fact that Austria's entire population was barely seven million. The letter ended with an assurance that the frontier with Italy would remain at the Brenner Pass – in other words, that Germany would not pursue the return of the South Tyrol, known by the Italians as the Alto Adige, which had been awarded to Italy under the Treaty of St Germain in 1919. Göring dispatched his friend, Prince Philipp of Hesse, son-in-law of the King of Italy, to deliver the letter personally.

At 6.30 p.m., the OKW gave mobilisation orders to three army corps and the Luftwaffe. But it was not until 2 a.m. the next morning, after having changed his mind more than once during the day, that Hitler issued his Directive Number One for Operation Otto, ordering them to be ready to invade on 12 March by 1200 hours at the latest, 'if all other measures prove unsuccessful'. 'The behaviour of the troops,' he stated, 'must give the impression that we do not want to wage war against our Austrian brothers . . . If, however, resistance is offered, it must be broken ruthlessly by force of arms.' A supplementary order issued a few hours later stated that Czechoslovakian troops were to be regarded as enemies, but that the Italians were 'everywhere to be treated as friends'.

Goebbels spent most of the night at his ministry working on propaganda arrangements with his staff, none of whom were allowed to leave the building before the action started in Austria. By 8 a.m. he was back with Hitler, clearing the text of the leaflets with him. An hour later, Papen arrived from Vienna to find the Chancellery in a state of frenzy, with generals and officials milling around madly. Among them was Himmler, 'surrounded by a dozen giant SS officers', all wearing a new-style uniform, as were the SS troops on the frontier, their usual black and silver replaced by the army's traditional field grey, which was to be standard dress for foreign operations from now on. With no Frick or Blomberg to object, the SS Verfügungstruppe (VT) and armed Leibstandarte regiment were now linked to the army, and would go in alongside it. For Himmler, this was the fulfilment of the dreams of his youth, though he could scarcely have imagined then that he would be wearing a full general's uniform at the age of thirty-seven.

Himmler and his SS had been making preparations for the *Anschluss* for some time. Heydrich's SD staff had been working around the clock to compile a huge card index of Austrian personnel, while Keppler, founder of Himmler's Circle of Friends and Hitler's personal economic adviser, had been shuttling to and fro between Berlin and Vienna as the principal liaison with the Austrian Nazis. Himmler controlled the clandestine Austrian SS, led by Ernst Kaltenbrunner, which would be responsible for cleaning up and 'co-ordinating' the population, and he would of course be taking over the Austrian police.

With Hitler 'in a state bordering on hysteria', according to Papen, flying into sudden rages, giving and retracting orders continuously, creating misunderstandings and generally suffering from 'nerve-shattering tension',[7] it was Göring who came to the rescue again, directing events in Austria at long distance by telephone in an amazing twenty-seven calls during the afternoon and evening, all of which were recorded, transcribed and preserved by the FA, on his orders.[8] The first call, at 2.45 p.m., was from Seyss-Inquart in Vienna, reporting that Schuschnigg had cancelled the plebiscite but was refusing to step down and was insisting on imposing strict security precautions, including a curfew from 8 p.m. 'These measures of Chancellor Schuschnigg are in no way satisfactory,' Göring snapped, and put the phone down. His anger was purely for show, however. Schuschnigg had weakened. Göring the hunter had smelt blood, and was preparing to go in for the kill.

'At this moment,' he recalled at the Nuremberg Tribunal,

I had the instinctive feeling that the situation was now mobile and that now, finally, that possibility which we had long and ardently awaited was there – the possibility of bringing about a complete solution. And from this moment on I must take 100 per cent responsibility for all further happenings, because it was not the Führer so much as I myself who set the pace and, even overruling the Führer's misgivings, brought everything to its final development.

After a few minutes he called Seyss-Inquart again, giving the impression that he had consulted Hitler, though he was in fact acting entirely off his own bat. 'Berlin cannot agree in any way to the decision taken by Chancellor Schuschnigg,' he said. He demanded that Schuschnigg and his entire Cabinet should resign by 5.30 p.m., and added that if Seyss-Inquart was not appointed Chancellor by then, the German army would march into Austria. That morning, in deference to Hitler, he had sent Keppler to Vienna with the text of a telegram that Seyss-Inquart was to send to the Führer, asking for German assistance to put down disorder. Now, he told Seyss-Inquart to send the telegram.

For the moment, Schuschnigg still held out, desperately looking around for help from the three powers. The Italians forestalled him by sending a message saying they could do nothing, before he had even asked. The French were once again between governments – the Premier and his Cabinet had resigned the day before, and there was no one in Paris with the authority to act, even if they had wanted to. The British position was hardly more promising: Chamberlain had been distancing the British government from the problem ever since Hitler's Berghof ultimatum, blindly refusing to admit that Austria's independence was under threat. But they were Schuschnigg's last and only hope, and he had to try them. His appeal for help arrived at 10 Downing Street on Friday, 11 March while Chamberlain and Halifax were entertaining Ribbentrop to a farewell luncheon with a selection of leading British politicians. The lunch had not gone well. The atmosphere had been frigid. Frau Ribbentrop had snubbed Churchill when he expressed hopes for Anglo–German friendship, and Ribbentrop's response to Chamberlain's wish for an understanding was so discouraging that the British Prime Minister condemned him afterwards as 'so stupid, so shallow, so self-centred and so self-satisfied, so totally devoid of intellectual capacity, that he never seems to take in what is said to him'.[9]

When Chamberlain and Halifax tried to impress on Ribbentrop how seriously they viewed developments in Austria, he pleaded ignorance, and invited Halifax to call at the Embassy 'for tea' at 5.15 p.m. When Halifax arrived, Ribbentrop told him his ministry in Berlin knew nothing of any demands being made of Schuschnigg, and that he therefore supposed the reports to be untrue. His blustering indignation at Halifax's astute suggestion that maybe 'Herr Hitler had acted on his own without reference to the German Foreign Ministry' was punctured by the entry of his Counsellor, Ernst Woermann, to say that the BBC had just broadcast the news that Schuschnigg had resigned, under pressure.

Schuschnigg had been trying to resign all afternoon, but the Austrian President, Wilhelm Miklas, had refused to accept his resignation until 5 p.m. Göring was told that Miklas had appointed Seyss-Inquart as Chancellor and lifted the ban on the Nazi Party, and that the SA and SS had taken over police duties. But this turned out to be false: the Austrian President was digging in his heels and proposing to appoint one of his own people. Göring was furious at this display of obstinacy. His deadline of 7.30 p.m. for the order to the army to start moving tanks and troops into position for an invasion at first light was approaching fast. He roared down the phone at Seyss-Inquart:

Now remember the following. You go immediately with General Muff [the German Military Attaché in Vienna] and tell the Federal President that if the conditions which are known to you are not accepted immediately, the troops that are already stationed at or advancing to the frontier will march in tonight along the whole line, and Austria will cease to exist . . . Please inform us immediately about Miklas's position. Tell him there is no time now for any joke; just that, as a result of the false report we received before, action was delayed, but now the situation is that the invasion will begin tonight from all the corners of Austria. The invasion will be stopped and the troops will be held at the border only if we are informed by 7.30 that Miklas has entrusted you with the Federal Chancellorship . . . Then call out all the National Socialists all over the country. They should now be in the streets. So remember, a report must be given by 7.30 . . . If Miklas could not understand it in four hours, we shall make him understand it now in four minutes.

While he waited for Seyss-Inquart to report back, Göring busied himself with the composition of the new Austrian government. He had already given Keppler his list of ministers, but he called the embassy to confirm the names. It was symptomatic of the general confusion that the man he spoke to was not an official but an Austrian Nazi named Odilo Globocnik, who had been sent there by Seyss-Inquart to report progress, or rather the lack of it. Göring thought he was talking to someone called Dombrowski, but it made little difference. 'God knows who half the people rattling around in that embassy were,' he commented later. After he ordered Globocnik to get rid of the country's newspaper editors and replace them with 'our people', the conversation continued:

GÖRING: I want a report about the formation of the new Cabinet within an hour!
GLOBOCNIK: That is quite all right. Keppler has brought a list of nominees.

GÖRING: I want Fishbeck to get the Ministry of Economics and Trade.

GLOBOCNIK: Obviously.

GÖRING: Kaltenbrunner will be Minister of Security. And then Minister of Justice – that's quite clear?

GLOBOCNIK: Yes, yes.

GÖRING: Say the name!

GLOBOCNIK: Your brother-in-law, Dr Hüber, isn't it?

GÖRING: Of course.

At 6.34 p.m., Keppler called to say that Miklas still refused to appoint Seyss-Inquart. 'Well, then,' Göring exploded, 'Seyss-Inquart has to dismiss him. Just go upstairs again and tell him plainly that Seyss will call on the National Socialist guards, and in five minutes the troops will march in by my order.' Before he could say more, the telephone connection broke, as it frequently did that day.

Keppler and Seyss-Inquart trooped back to Miklas with the fresh ultimatum, but still the President refused to budge, insisting that Austria alone would determine who was to be head of government.

Seyss-Inquart reported the bad news to Göring, who agreed to wait a little longer while they went on trying to persuade Miklas. Schuschnigg, recognising the hopelessness of the situation, joined in, believing there was now no alternative to Seyss-Inquart, who at least 'had a good personal reputation as a practising Catholic and an honest man', but Miklas accused him of deserting him along with everyone else, and adamantly refused to appoint a Nazi as Austrian Chancellor. Outside, a Nazi mob was baying for Schuschnigg's blood. He decided to make a farewell broadcast, as a final act of defiance.

Schuschnigg's broadcast was brief, and emotional. He told the Austrian people that the German government had given President Miklas an ultimatum that if he did not appoint their nominee as Chancellor, German troops would invade. He declared that the German claims of disorder and violence were 'lies, from A to Z', but that the Austrian government had 'yielded to force since we are not prepared even in this terrible hour to shed blood', and had ordered its troops to offer no resistance. 'So I take my leave of the Austrian people,' he concluded, 'with a German word of farewell, uttered from the depths of my heart: "God protect Austria!"'

As Schuschnigg finished, Seyss-Inquart dashed to a telephone to report to Göring:

SEYSS-INQUART: Dr Schuschnigg has given the news over the radio that the Reich government has presented an ultimatum.

GÖRING: I heard it.

SEYSS-INQUART: And the government itself has abdicated . . . they are waiting for the troops to march in.

GÖRING: Did you dismiss them from office?

SEYSS-INQUART: No. No one was dismissed from his office, but the government has itself pulled out and let matters take their course.

GÖRING: And you were not commissioned? They refused?

SEYSS-INQUART: They refused now, as before. They are taking a chance with the invasion and hope that, if it actually takes place, executive power will be transferred to other people.

GÖRING: Right. I shall give the order to march in, and then you make sure that you get the power. Notify the leading people . . . that everyone who offers resistance or organises resistance will immediately be subject to our court martial, the court martial of our invading troops. Is that clear?

SEYSS-INQUART: Yes.

GÖRING: Including leading personalities. It doesn't make any difference.

SEYSS-INQUART: Yes. They have given orders not to offer any resistance.

GÖRING: Yes, that doesn't matter. The Federal President did not authorise you, and that also can be considered as resistance.

SEYSS-INQUART: Yes.

GÖRING: Well, now you *are* officially authorised.

SEYSS-INQUART: Yes.

GÖRING: Well, good luck. Heil Hitler.

A few minutes later, Göring was on the phone to General Muff, telling him the invasion was about to start and that Seyss-Inquart must stay in office and carry out the functions of government. They should try to avoid chaos, he said, adding that it would be best if Miklas were to resign.

'Yes, but he won't,' Muff replied. 'It was very dramatic. I spoke to him for almost fifteen minutes. He declared that he will not yield to force under any circumstances.'

'So! He will not give in to force?' Göring asked, incredulously.

'He does not yield to force.'

'What does this mean? He just wants to be kicked out?'

'Yes,' Muff said. 'He is staying put.'

Göring laughed. 'Well, I hear he has fourteen children. I'm not surprised he wants to stay put. Anyway, just tell Seyss to take over.'

Seyss-Inquart did so, but by now he, too, was showing signs of stubbornness. He made his own broadcast to the nation at 8 p.m., calling for calm and telling the Austrian people to offer no resistance to German troops. But he still refused to send the telegram appealing for their help, arguing that it was not needed, since there was no civil unrest. He went on until the early hours of the morning, with the support of Muff and Keppler, trying to persuade Hitler to call off the invasion and hold the troops on the border. But Göring was not prepared to do this. At 8.45 p.m., impressing on Hitler that he would lose credibility if he did not carry out his ultimatum, he got him to sign the executive order for the army to enter Austria at daybreak.

Three minutes later, he was on the phone to Vienna again, this time speaking to Keppler, who tried in vain to convince him that the invasion was unnecessary:

KEPPLER: The government has ordered the army not to put up any resistance.
GÖRING: I don't give a damn.
KEPPLER: Might I ask if a prominent personality in Berlin wants to add a few words for the Austrian people?
GÖRING: Well, I don't know yet. Listen, the main thing is that Seyss takes over all powers of government, that he occupies the radio stations and everything else . . .
KEPPLER: Well, we represent the government, now.
GÖRING: Yes, that's it. You are the government. Now listen carefully. The following telegram should be sent here by Seyss-Inquart. Write it down. 'The provisional Austrian government, which after the resignation of the Schuschnigg government considers it its task to establish peace and order in Austria, sends the German government the urgent request to support it in its task and help it to prevent bloodshed. For this reason it asks the German government to send German troops as soon as possible.'
KEPPLER: Well, the SA and the SS are marching through the streets, but everything is quiet.
GÖRING: Seyss-Inquart has to take over . . . and appoint a few people . . . the people we recommended to him. He should form a provisional government now. It is absolutely unimportant what the Federal President may have to say . . . Then our troops will cross the border today.
KEPPLER: Yes.
GÖRING: Look, he should send the telegram as soon as possible . . .
　　Well, he doesn't even have to send the telegram – all he needs to do is to say 'Agreed!'

An hour later, Keppler called back with a message: 'Tell the Field Marshal that Seyss-Inquart agrees.' Göring passed the text of the non-existent telegram to Goebbels, who had it blazoned across the front pages of all the newspapers the next day, and distributed throughout the world by his DNB news agency. When the British sent two strongly-worded but meaningless protests via Henderson, Neurath replied that relations with Austria were Germany's business and nothing to do with Britain, denied that there had been any ultimatum, and referred them to the telegram.

There was only one serious worry remaining, and that was relieved at 10.25 p.m., when Prince Philipp called at last from Rome. Hitler, his nerves still stretched to breaking point, grabbed the phone when he realised who it was. Göring's hard-worked FA technicians duly recorded his joyous babble, and the Prince's slightly embarrassed reactions, for posterity:

PRINCE: I have just come back from the Palazzio Venezia. The Duce accepted the whole thing in a very friendly manner. He sends you his regards . . . Schuschnigg gave him the news . . . Mussolini said that Austria would be immaterial to him.

HITLER: Then please tell Mussolini I will never forget him for this!

PRINCE: Yes, sir.

HITLER: Never, never, never, no matter what happens! I am ready to make a quite different agreement with him.

PRINCE: Yes, sir. I told him that, too.

HITLER: As soon as the Austrian affair has been settled, I shall be ready to go with him through thick and thin – through anything!

PRINCE: Yes, my Führer.

HITLER: Listen! I shall make any agreement. I am no longer in fear of the terrible position which would have existed militarily if we had gotten into a conflict. You may tell him that I do thank him from the bottom of my heart. Never, never, never shall I forget it.

PRINCE: Yes, my Führer.

HITLER: I shall never forget him for this, no matter what happens. If he should ever need any help or be in any danger, he can be convinced that I shall stick by him whatever may happen, even if the whole world gangs up on him.

PRINCE: Yes, my Führer.

Mussolini's acquiescence removed the last possible obstacle and sealed Austria's fate. There were still one or two loose ends to be tied up, but Göring could soon deal with the main ones. As it happened, one of the highlights of his social year was taking place that same evening, when he was due to host a gala reception for a thousand guests in the Haus der Flieger, the aviators' club he had set up in the old Prussian

Parliament building. The leading members of the diplomatic corps were all there – with the notable exception of the Austrian envoy and his military attaché – and he would take the opportunity of speaking to them then.

Like any event organised by Göring, the reception was on a grand scale, with music provided by the Luftwaffe band, followed by the orchestra, singers and dancers of the State Opera. It began at 10 p.m., in an electric atmosphere that was buzzing with one topic of conversation – which hushed suddenly when Ivone Kirkpatrick, the Counsellor at the British Embassy, gatecrashed to speak urgently with Henderson in private. He needed his approval of the formal note of protest that Halifax wanted him to send at once to Neurath. Henderson had reluctantly decided to attend the reception, only because 'it afforded me my only opportunity to see the Field Marshal'.

Göring arrived a little late, of course, and the operatic performance began almost as soon as he took his seat at the centre table. Henderson greeted him by shaking hands 'very curtly and coldly', which took Göring aback. 'As soon as we had sat down,' Henderson recalled in his memoirs, 'he tore off the blank half of his programme, wrote on it in pencil, "Immediately the music is over I should like to talk to you, and will explain everything to you," and handed it to me across the American Ambassador's wife. The last five words were underlined thrice, and in fact, when the performance came to an end, he got up hurriedly and waited for me outside.'

For three-quarters of an hour, in his private room, Göring treated Henderson to a diatribe against Schuschnigg, and a justification of the German action. Henderson tried to argue, but soon realised that it was hopeless. He was reduced to delivering a peculiarly English rebuke: 'After fighting Schuschnigg's battle for him to the bitter end,' he wrote, 'I finally said to Göring that "even supposing the Austrian Chancellor has been unwise, that is no excuse for Germany to be a bully". He followed this with an equally English appeal, urging Göring 'to do his utmost to see that the anti-Nazi Austrians were treated with the decency which their loyalty to their country merited'. Still unable to believe the worst of his host, he added in his memoirs: 'Had Göring been left to his own devices in Austria, I believe that he would have done his best to carry out such a policy.'[10]

Henderson was not the only diplomat who was still taken in by Göring. The Czech Minister in Berlin, Dr Vojtech Mastný, 'very excited and trembling', approached him as soon as he returned to the main hall, desperate to know what was happening and whether his country was under threat. Göring reassured him that it was not, that it was purely a 'family affair' with Austria and had nothing to do with Czechoslovakia, 'especially if you keep out of things altogether'. However, Göring said, he was concerned about rumours of a Czech mobilisation. Were they true? Mastný hurried off to the telephone, to find out. He returned soon afterwards, 'even more excited' according to Göring, who 'had the impression that in his excitement he could hardly understand me'. Göring, again by his own account, then told him: 'Your Excellency, listen carefully. I give you my personal word of honour that this is a question of the *Anschluss* of Austria only, and that not a single German soldier will come anywhere near the Czechoslovak border. See to it that there is no mobilisation on the part of Czechoslovakia which might lead to difficulties.'[11] Mastný agreed, and went off to report to his government in Prague that Göring had told him that 'Germany had no hostile intentions of any kind towards [Czechoslovakia], but on the contrary wished to continue advancing towards a rapprochement'.

Around midnight, the news that Göring had been waiting for finally arrived: Miklas had formally acknowledged Seyss-Inquart and his Nazi Cabinet as the new government of Austria. He collected Goebbels, who, elegant in tails, was holding court on his own table at the reception, and the two of them drove to the Chancellery to join Hitler in his study and listen with him as the 'Horst Wessel Song' was broadcast from Vienna for the first time. In barely nine hours since his first call, Göring's *coup* by telephone was complete. Austria's independence had been ended by remote control. There was just one more phone call that Göring had to make before he crashed into bed: hearing that Himmler and Heydrich were leaving at once for Austria, he sent an urgent message to Seyss-Inquart instructing him to take charge of the Austrian wire tapping service on his behalf. He intended to incorporate it into his FA, and needed to be quite sure that Himmler did not get his hands on it first.

Hitler flew to Munich in the morning of Saturday, 12 March, to drive from there to the Austrian frontier at his birthplace, Braunau am Inn, leaving Göring in Berlin as acting head of state. Goebbels stayed behind, too, to handle the media presentation of the *coup*, and to read on the radio the proclamation that Hitler had prepared before he left, justifying his actions and promising the Austrian people 'a real plebiscite' on their future. Himmler and Heydrich were already in Vienna, together with Wolff, Daluege, a small group of staff and an armed VT escort commando, having landed at the city's civil airport at 5 a.m. in two Ju-52s. They had been greeted by Schuschnigg's former Police Minister and a police guard of honour, before being whisked in convoy to the city centre, where Himmler took over the Hotel Regina for himself and his staff, and Heydrich commandeered the Hotel Metropole as his Gestapo headquarters. As they established themselves, reports from the frontiers told of German troops being greeted with flowers by wildly cheering crowds who had in many cases dismantled the barriers in readiness.

Kaltenbrunner, the tall, heavily-scarred Austrian SS chief who had been appointed Police Minister on Göring's orders, already had the security situation well under control, so Himmler could safely leave him in charge while he drove off with Wolff to wait for Hitler in Linz, the capital of Upper Austria, in company with Seyss-Inquart and Glaise-Horstenau. Hitler arrived later than expected, delayed on the roads from the frontier by rapturous crowds but also by stranded tanks and vehicles – Jodl reckoned that seventy per cent of the German armoured vehicles had broken down. The tank force commander, General Heinz Guderian, claimed the figure was only thirty per cent, but even that was a most unsatisfactory record of reliability, a symptom of the German army's rushed and inadequate preparation. But Hitler was unaware of these shortcomings as he made an emotional speech to vast and excited crowds in the city of his youth, and when he called Göring late that night, he could speak only of how beautiful his country was, how much his homecoming had affected him, and how grateful he was to Mussolini for not standing in his way.

Göring passed this on to Prince Philipp in Rome the next morning in a call from Carinhall, asking him to tell the Duce that Hitler would be writing to him and to reassure him that German troops had strict orders not to go beyond Innsbruck. The Prince was as excited as Göring and Hitler about the remarkable success of the operation. 'A swastika is already flying on the Austrian Consulate here,' he reported. 'And, incidentally, the King told me that Colonel Beck [the Polish Foreign Minister, who was visiting Rome] has told him that twenty-five thousand Jews have asked for passports in Vienna. The view here is that it would be best to open the frontier for a while, so that the whole scum can get out . . .' Göring, however, was concerned with the needs of the Four-Year Plan. 'All right,' he laughed, 'but not with any foreign currency. The Jews can go, but they will kindly leave behind their money, which they have only stolen anyway!'[12]

Göring's high spirits continued as he called Ribbentrop in London, ostensibly to fill him in on what was happening, but in fact for the benefit of the British government – he could not believe that the British would not listen in to all phone traffic to and from the German Embassy, in the same way that he used the FA. Ribbentrop's responses, and the comments he made about Halifax and Chamberlain, both of whom he hated and distrusted, clearly show that he was playing the game, too:

GÖRING: You know that the Führer has entrusted me with the conduct of the government while he is in Austria. I wanted to tell you there is indescribable jubilation in Austria. You can hear that over the radio.

RIBBENTROP: Yes, fantastic, isn't it?

GÖRING: Yes, the march into the Rhineland was nothing by comparison. The Führer was deeply moved when he talked to me last night . . . Apart from the Jews in Vienna and part of the black ravens, the Catholics, there is nobody who is against us. The Führer thinks that you should explain matters to the people over there. This story that we had given an ultimatum is completely false . . .

RIBBENTROP: I have explained that to Halifax and Chamberlain already.

GÖRING: The ministers asked us to back them up, so they would not be completely beaten up again and subjected to terror and civil war . . . Schuschnigg made speeches saying the Fatherland Front would fight to the last man, one could not know they would capitulate like that, and therefore Seyss-Inquart, who had already taken over the government, asked us to march in immediately . . . these are the actual facts, which can be proved by documents . . . the following is interesting, the absolutely total enthusiasm for National Socialism, which surprised even us.

RIBBENTROP: So the whole of Austria is for us?

GÖRING: Well, let me tell you, if there were an election tomorrow – I have already told Seyss-Inquart he should invite representatives of the democratic powers; they should convince themselves that this was really an election carried out on a democratic basis – and we should have ninety per cent of votes in our favour. Absolutely! . . . Responsible people from England and France should be asked to come over here and to watch what is actually going on . . .

RIBBENTROP: Göring, tell me, how is the situation in Vienna? Is everything settled yet?

GÖRING: Yes. Yesterday I landed hundreds of aeroplanes with a number of companies, in order to secure the airfield, and they were received with joy. The Austrian troops did not withdraw but fraternised immediately with the German troops, wherever they were stationed.

RIBBENTROP: That was to be expected.

GÖRING: The whole business is turning out as it was supposed to . . . In no way are we threatening the Czechoslovakian Republic, but now it has the opportunity of coming to a friendly and reasonable agreement with us . . . On condition France remains sensible . . . Naturally if France were now to organise a big mobilisation close to the frontier, it wouldn't be funny.

RIBBENTROP: I believe they will behave all right.

GÖRING: Our conscience is clear and that is a decisive factor. Before history, we have a clear conscience . . .

RIBBENTROP: I had a long, intensive conversation with Halifax, and I told him our basic conception also about the German–English understanding –

GÖRING: That was what I wanted to say. You know yourself, Ribbentrop, that I was always in favour of a German–English understanding. Anyone would be if he also recognised that we, too, are a proud and free nation. After all, we represent two brother nations.

RIBBENTROP: I can tell you one thing, Göring. The other day I spoke to Chamberlain . . . and I gained a very good impression of him . . . I don't want to speak over the phone, but I have the impression that Chamberlain, too, is very serious about an understanding . . . I also said to Halifax . . . that we honestly do want to come to an understanding and he replied that his only worry was the Czechoslovakian Republic.

GÖRING: No, no, that is out of the question . . .

RIBBENTROP: I told him then that we were not interested and we do not intend to do anything there . . . I got the best impression of Halifax as well as Chamberlain. He thought it would be a little difficult with public opinion because here it looks like force. I have the feeling that the normal Englishman, the man in the street, will say why should England bother with Austria? . . .

GÖRING: You can tell them that Schuschnigg wanted to rig the election. Seyss-Inquart has questioned officials, who said that even the number of yesses and noes were determined in advance . . . the most shameless manoeuvre ever . . . Conditions were grotesque! Imagine, only a few days ago there was a house search at my sister's, who's the wife of the new Austrian Minister of Justice. And they took pictures of the Führer from her, and of myself, her own brother. The British press has not written anything about that, has it?

The conversation continued for a full forty minutes, with Göring laying it on thick about Schuschnigg's vote-rigging and the difference there would be in the new referendum, talking about his plans for improving economic conditions in Austria, and praising the pro-Nazi articles written for the *Daily Mail* by Ward Price, a journalist whom Hitler and Goebbels regularly used to feed their views to British readers. As a parting shot for British listeners, Göring emphasised Hitler's strength of feeling over Austria:

GÖRING: Let me tell you this, confidentially. The Führer, who is usually well controlled, has his heart too much involved in all this, since it concerns his homeland. I believe if he receives any threat over the Austrian question he will never give in, and I have to make it clear, neither will the two nations. It would be a matter of fanaticism in Germany as well as in Austria.

RIBBENTROP: That's clear.

GÖRING: There can be no doubt. Whoever threatens us now will strike at both peoples and both will put up fanatical resistance . . .

Having played his part in London, Ribbentrop was desperate to get back to Germany now. 'My conferences here are at an end,' he told Göring, plaintively. 'And if I hang around here with no good reason, it might look "funny" . . .' Göring, savouring his power over him, gave him permission to return and then concluded: 'The weather is wonderful here. Blue skies. I am sitting on my balcony, wrapped in blankets in the fresh air, drinking coffee. Later on I have to drive in, I have to make a speech. The birds are twittering, and I can hear over the radio the enthusiasm which must be wonderful over there.'[13]

The plan had been for Austria to be merely associated with Germany, retaining a certain amount of autonomy with Hitler as President of both countries, until the promised referendum could be held on 10 April 1938. But the reception he received, when he crossed the frontier and drove to Linz on 13 March, with wildly cheering crowds chanting '*Ein Volk, ein Reich, ein Führer!*' (One people, one Reich, one leader!), made Hitler decide to go for full *Anschluss* at once. He sent for the official in Frick's Interior Ministry who was still hurriedly drafting legislation to make him President of Austria, and ordered him instead to draft a new law making Austria a province of Germany. The 'Law for the Reunification of Austria with the German Reich', which was to be signed for Germany by Hitler, Göring, Ribbentrop, Frick and Hess, was quickly drawn up in a Linz hotel, and the draft flown to Vienna for signature by the new Austrian government. Miklas refused, and resigned on the spot, handing over the presidency to Schuschnigg. But at that stage it was an empty gesture:

Austria had ceased to exist as a separate country. Its ancient name was changed to 'Ostmark' (Eastern Mark or Province), and even that was soon lost as it was split into seven Gaue, roughly corresponding to the former Austrian states.

Hitler's triumphal entry into Vienna was delayed for another day, while Himmler and Heydrich, with the Austrian police files at their disposal, finished cleaning up and making the city safe. To take care of this, standards of the VT, Leibstandarte and Death's Head concentration camp guards, plus some 40,000 armed police, had followed the army across the frontier in the second wave. They arrested between 10,000 and 20,000 'undesirables' and 'unreliables' in the first couple of days, a figure that would rise to 79,000 in Vienna alone over the next few weeks.

Göring, concerned as always to protect his friends, sent his private plane to collect Guido Schmidt, who had been promoted to Foreign Minister shortly before, and bring him to Berlin, to keep him out of the clutches of the Gestapo. The following year, he would appoint him to the board of the HGW, as an expert on the Balkans. Other Austrian ministers and notables were not so lucky. Schuschnigg was held under house arrest and subjected to continuous harassment and sleep deprivation for several weeks. He was then moved to an attic in Gestapo headquarters, the Hotel Metropole, where he was held in appalling conditions for a further seventeen months before being transferred to a series of concentration camps in Germany for the duration of the Second World War.

Initially, lesser political prisoners were shipped out to Dachau and other camps in Germany, but Himmler moved swiftly to find a suitable spot for a huge, purely Austrian camp, settling for a sloping site overlooking the Danube at the village of Mauthausen, near Linz. The attraction here was a number of quarries, which he could expropriate for a new commercial enterprise he was setting up, the German Earth- and Stonework Company – with a limitless supply of free labour, and free raw materials, it was bound to be a success. He ordered inmates to be brought from Dachau at once to start work on levelling and construction.

More immediately, Himmler unleashed the SS and SA throughout Austria to turn on the Jewish population with what William Shirer called 'an orgy of sadism', far worse than anything he had seen in Germany. It was particularly bad in Vienna, with its estimated 180,000 Jews, many of whom were forced to scrub pro-Schuschnigg slogans off walls and pavements. In some cases, they found that the 'water' in the buckets they were given turned out to be acid, which burned their hands. Others were forced to fasten their sacred prayer bands on their arms and then clean out unflushed public toilets and the latrines of SS and SA barracks. Meanwhile, their homes were raided and their possessions stolen or seized. In the provinces, more than seven hundred towns and villages where small numbers of Jews had lived raised white flags to indicate that they were now 'Jew-free'.[14]

The full range of German anti-Jewish laws and measures was introduced to Austria overnight: around 8,000 Jewish businesses were 'Aryanised', more than 30,000 Jews were thrown out of their jobs, Jewish doctors and lawyers were forbidden to practise, and 12,000 Jewish families were evicted from their homes.[15] Everywhere, they suffered physical abuse and indignities, all aimed at forcing them out of Austria. To help them on their way, Himmler set up the Central Office for Jewish Emigration in Vienna, headed by a promising thirty-two-year-old SS officer, Adolf Eichmann. It proved to be a great success – within weeks, some 98,000 Jews, nearly half of the country's total, had gone, leaving their money and possessions behind. Many others, unable to face the future, committed suicide.

Although Hitler was given a delirious reception in Vienna on 14 March, with all the Catholic churches ringing their bells and flying the swastika flag on the orders of the Primate of Austria, Cardinal Innitzer, he was keen to leave again as quickly as possible – the city held too many unpleasant memories for him. He slept that night in the best suite of the Imperial Hotel, where he claimed to have shovelled snow as a penniless down and out while the Emperor wined and dined inside, then reviewed a combined march past of German and Austrian troops, who had taken the oath of allegiance to him that morning. After addressing a vast crowd of some 250,000 people, he had a brief meeting with the Cardinal, who assured him of the support of Austria's Catholics, then flew out to Munich, to spend the night in his own apartment. He returned to Berlin the following day, to be greeted as a conquering hero by a reception committee at the airport, led by Göring, happily toting his Field Marshal's baton.

Göring had one small but significant piece of business to attend to before he could set off for Austria himself. The day after Hitler's return, he reconvened the court of honour to hear the charges against Fritsch, which he duly demolished with great gusto, though Fritsch afterwards commented that throughout the hearing he had been 'at pains to justify the conduct of the Gestapo'. Fritsch, however, blamed Himmler for everything: he even contemplated challenging him to a duel, but could find no army general willing to serve as his second, so was forced to let the matter drop and retire to his estate with a letter of apology from Hitler, but no suggestion of reinstatement. As a small consolation, he was made Colonel-in-Chief of his old artillery regiment: it was a purely honorary appointment, but when the Second World War began, he accompanied it to Warsaw, where a Polish machine-gunner gave him an honourable death in action as he deliberately exposed himself to fire.

The day after acquitting Fritsch, Göring presided over a hastily-called session of the Reichstag, at which Hitler gave the deputies his account of events in Austria, blaming Schuschnigg for forcing him to act by breaking his word with his 'election forgery'. He then announced new 'elections' for the whole of Germany, to be held at the same time as the Austrian plebiscite on 10 April. Goebbels went into his well-practised election routine, planning the campaign with great care to avoid voter fatigue. To deal specifically with Austria, he set up a satellite Reich propaganda office in Vienna, based in the former town house of a Jew who had fled, which he ostentatiously ordered to be fumigated before his staff moved in.[16]

Göring set off for his beloved Austria on 24 March, his first visit for several years. His popularity was as great there as it was in Germany, and he savoured every moment of it, driving through towns and cities in an open car, wearing his most dazzling uniforms, beaming and waving as he acknowledged the cheers. In his speeches, he promised the Austrians new industries, including a major steel plant in Linz as part of the HGW, autobahns, power stations, armaments factories, new inland harbours, a great Main-Danube canal to link Austria to the industrial regions of northern and north-western Germany, and new social measures. 'Unemployment will be completely banned!' he announced, then continued with a grin, 'But the time has come to finish all this Gemütlichkeit [easy-going way of life]. Now you must work hard!' In Vienna he struck a darker note. 'The city of Vienna,' he proclaimed, 'can no longer rightfully claim to be a German city. How can one speak of a German city where there are 300,000 Jews [sic]? Vienna must once more become a German city, because it has important tasks to perform for Germany's Ostmark, both culturally and economically. For neither of these can we make use of Jews.'

Presented with a report from *The Times* in London that 'since Hitler and his forces entered Vienna, some 7,000 Jews have committed suicide in that city alone,' Göring replied in a radio broadcast: 'We don't like Jews and they don't like us. We will make them glad to go away. I cannot help it if the Jews do away with themselves. I cannot put a policeman behind every Jew to prevent suicides!'[17] A day or two later, he made a sentimental return to Mautendorf, the castle where he had played so happily as a boy. There, he introduced the heavily pregnant Emmy to Ritter von Epenstein's widow, Lilli, who received them joyfully and told Emmy that the castle would some day be theirs, a bequest to Hermann from his loving Jewish godfather.

On 10 April 1938 the voters of the new Greater Germany went to the polls. Even allowing for the pressures and the vote rigging, the results were astonishing: 99.73 per cent of Austrians voted 'yes' to the *Anschluss*; in Germany as a whole, the single question 'Do you assent to the 13 March 1938 reunification of Austria with the German Reich, and do you vote for the list of candidates proposed by our Führer Adolf Hitler?' produced a 'yes' vote of 99.08 per cent. Goebbels congratulated himself and his ministry in his daily circular: 'Such an almost 100 per cent election result is a simultaneous page of glory for all election propagandists,' he wrote.[18] He and Göring had both done their jobs well, as too had Himmler and Heydrich in choking off any opposition in the new Ostmark. The way was now clear for the next great step forward.

One of the side effects of the *Anschluss* with Austria was that in a single day the Jewish population of Greater Germany was increased by over 190,000, almost exactly replacing those who had been forced to emigrate since Hitler came to power. The Jewish question, which had been allowed to simmer quietly since it had been put on the back burner at the time of the Olympics, was suddenly on the boil again, and the Nazi leaders were soon vying with each other to prove the strength of their anti-Semitic credentials.

Göring, as always, was more concerned with economics than ideology. He had nothing personally against Jews, as his famous saying

'I decide who is a Jew' clearly showed, and he was perfectly happy to buy jewellery or works of art from Jewish dealers in Germany or abroad. He had no qualms about helping individual Jews to escape the worst effects of laws for which he himself had been at least partly responsible. But he had no qualms, either, about grabbing their assets, to enrich both the state and himself. On 26 April, he decreed that all Jewish holdings valued at more than 5,000 Reichsmarks must be registered so that he would have a complete record of all Jewish wealth. Six weeks later, he ordered all Jewish businesses to be visibly marked and registered, so that they could be boycotted more effectively, and seized more easily when the time came.

Goebbels was encouraged by Göring's lists, which showed, he said, how many rich Jews there were, 'including quite a few millionaires', proving that 'any sympathy for them would be completely misplaced'.[19] With Hitler's blessing, he began a renewed campaign to drive the Jews out of Germany, and especially out of his own bailiwick of Berlin, where numbers were actually increasing as Jews forced out of small towns and villages sought refuge with their own kind in the big city. 'Is it not outrageous,' he screamed in his summer solstice speech to a packed Olympic Stadium, 'and does it not make one's face redden with anger, when one considers that in the last few months no fewer than 3,000 Jews have emigrated to Berlin? What do they want here? They should go back where they came from! They should stop provoking us!'[20] He instructed Helldorf to begin arresting them as 'work-shy and anti-social', telling a meeting of 300 officers that the police and the party must work hand-in-hand to force all Jews out of Berlin within the next half year – a tall order by any standards.

German Nazis and their supporters had watched with admiration as the Viennese mobs rampaged against the Jews during the first days of the new regime there. And they applauded as Eichmann and his team drove out over half of Austria's Jews within a matter of weeks, in many cases by physically bundling them over the borders into neighbouring countries, especially Poland, where many of them had come from. But there were still well over 400,000 in the Reich as a whole, and it was clear that far more drastic action was needed to get rid of them. For the storm-troopers of the SA, it brought a welcome revival of their heyday as they piled into orgies of intimidation and abuse in various cities. In Munich and Nuremberg, the local authorities joined in by demolishing the main synagogues, 'to clear space for new traffic schemes'.

In a more measured approach, Himmler had some 2,000 Jews arrested across the country on charges of 'race pollution', and sent to camps. He had recently opened a new concentration camp at Buchenwald, near Weimar, where prisoners were made to slave for fourteen to sixteen hours a day, breaking and hauling stones in the 'quarries of death', to feed Göring's construction programmes. Now, in preparation for a significant increase, those in Buchenwald and Sachsenhausen were put to work enlarging their camps, while at Dachau the workshops were turned over to sewing Stars of David on thousands of striped uniforms. The implications were obvious to anyone.

The pressure on the Jews continued unabated through the summer and autumn. On 17 August, a new decree ordered all Jews to take the names Israel or Sarah before their existing first names. On 27 September, Jewish lawyers were forbidden to practise in Germany. On 7 October, all German passports belonging to Jews – which already had to have a red letter J stamped on them – were withdrawn, to be replaced by special identity cards. This coincided with Polish measures to prevent the return of Polish Jews living in Germany.

Himmler immediately fired off a memo to Hitler, warning that 'In practice, this would mean that some 70,000 Polish Jews in Reich territory would have to be tolerated permanently in Germany.'

When the Polish government refused to change its decree, Himmler sent police to round up 15,000 Jews with Polish passports, load them on to special trains and transport them to the frontier. There, SS men took over, whipping and beating them to force them across the border – having first searched them to make sure no one was taking more than the permitted ten marks out of the country. Polish troops and border guards tried to drive them back again at bayonet point, but the SS stopped them, and for some time they were stranded in no man's land on the green frontier, giving the international press a field day, before they were finally allowed into Poland, where they were herded into primitive accommodation in barns and cattle sheds. For Himmler, the round-up and removal formed a valuable rehearsal for future operations on a grander scale.

XX

THE SUDETENLAND CRISIS

WITH the annexation of Austria, the open jaws of Greater Germany were set to close around Czechoslovakia, exactly as Göring and Hitler had planned. The Czechs, hostile, well-armed and protected by treaties with France and the Soviet Union, promised to be a much tougher mouthful than the Austrians, but there was a simple way they could be swallowed: in two bites. The first would remove the protective shell of the Sudetenland by taking it and its German-speaking population 'back' into the Reich. The fact that they had never been a part of it was immaterial – under the principles expounded by US President Wilson in 1918, which had formed the basis for the Paris Peace Conference, they were entitled to self-determination, and they were ethnic Germans. Stripped of its formidable defences, the body of Czechoslovakia would then be easy meat.

Only one thing militated against a two-bite approach: Hitler's desire to emulate his hero, Frederick the Great, by winnng territory through military conquest. There was no glory in a bloodless victory, and in any case he was eager to test his new Wehrmacht on the battlefield, under his own inspired direction. On his forty-ninth birthday, 20 April 1938, after the usual luncheon and the military parades and an effusive speech from Göring, he called Keitel into his study and ordered him to start preparing a revised version of Operation Green, a plan that had been prepared the previous year as a pre-emptive strike against Czechoslovakia to prevent its Soviet allies using it as a launch pad from which to attack Germany. That danger had passed. Now, he told Keitel, he saw Czechoslovakia as an obstacle to be removed before the time came for 'the big reckoning with the East, and by that he meant not just the Poles but particularly the Bolsheviks'. He said he had no intention 'of unleashing a war on the Czechs of his own accord', at least in the immediate future, but wanted to be ready, if the political need arose, 'to strike like lightning'.[1] It would take the French four days to mobilise, so an attack would have to succeed within that time in order to present the Western powers with a *fait accompli* in which it would be pointless for them to intervene.

For once, Göring was not directly involved in the political preparations. Although he desperately needed the Czech mineral and industrial resources for the Four-Year Plan, he had had little to do with the Sudetenland, or with Czechoslovakia as a whole. The Foreign Ministry had always handled relations with Prague, and despite its traditional caution had been secretly subsidising the crypto-Nazi Sudeten German Party for the past three years. Ribbentrop's arrival at the ministry immediately stepped up the pace and the pressure. Neurath had been a restraining influence on Hitler, but Ribbentrop was eager to impress him with his belligerence, and spurred him on with no regard for the risks involved.

The Sudetenlanders did have genuine grievances as an oppressed minority, and for some months the party's leader, a mild-mannered gymnastics teacher called Konrad Henlein, had been using these as the basis of a campaign of unrest, carefully orchestrated under Hitler's personal guidance. The *Anschluss* had given Henlein and his party a tremendous boost, and on 28 March 1938 he came to Berlin for meetings with Hitler and Ribbentrop, to receive his orders for his next moves. Without committing himself to a date, Hitler told him that when the time was right, a pretext would be created for the German army to march in to protect the Sudetenlanders. In the meantime, Henlein was to go on making increasing demands for concessions that the Czech government could not possibly accept, building up to calls for full autonomy and finally for separate German-speaking regiments within the Czech army.[2]

The next day, at the Foreign Ministry, Ribbentrop reminded Henlein that he must appear to be acting quite independently, and that the Reich government should not seem to be associated with his demands. He was, however, to maintain 'the closest possible contact with the Reich Foreign Minister': Ribbentrop was determined to make up for the ignominy of having been kept out of the *Anschluss* by ensuring that this time he alone would be at the centre, pulling the strings alongside Hitler.

For the next five months, Henlein played his hand skilfully, steadily escalating tensions with the secret help of the Abwehr and the Foreign Ministry. To maintain the fiction that Germany was not involved, Goebbels imposed a gag on the news media, forbidding critical reports on Czechoslovakia. When Henlein travelled to London in early May to talk to the British government, he was instructed to deny that he was receiving instructions from Berlin, and to tell the British that Czechoslovakia was disintegrating under pressure from the various minorities in its ethnic patchwork, who all resented Czech dominance.[3] The deception worked – the British and French applied increasing pressure on the Czechs to 'go to the utmost limit' to meet the Sudeten demands.

With no SS in Czechoslovakia, Himmler had no part to play in the build-up, except for making plans to take over the Czech police after the invasion. In any case, he was fully occupied with consolidating his position in the former Austria, raising new Totenkopf and VT units and absorbing the Austrian General SS into the Reich organisation. He was also busy expanding the SS in the Reich as a whole, creating a new department, the SS Ergänzungsamt, specifically to recruit men of 'good blood' not only in the Reich itself but also in the new territories it would soon acquire. Since the armed forces wanted such men, too, there was stiff competition here, especially as Himmler was doing everything he could to establish the SS, and particularly the VT, as a fourth military arm alongside the army, navy and Luftwaffe. Already, men enlisting in the armed VT – but not yet the Totenkopf concentration camp guards – were excused conscription for military service. To attract the recruits he wanted, he worked harder than ever on the elite image of the SS and the mystique of its secret rituals.

Heydrich, while supervising the establishment of the Gestapo in the Ostmark, was intent on developing a foreign intelligence role for the SD. For the moment, this was the sole prerogative of the Abwehr, the military intelligence service that was now commanded by his old mentor, the newly-promoted Vice-Admiral Canaris, with whom he had renewed his friendship. They were near neighbours in Berlin and rode out together in the Tiergarten most mornings, talking shop. One of the topics they must have discussed was the situation in Czechoslovakia, where Canaris was running undercover sabotage and subversion teams to back up Henlein's people and to set up secret arms and ammunition dumps. It would be Canaris's agents who would stage the inci-

dents needed to provoke an uprising and to justify German intervention: echoing the earlier plan to have Papen murdered in Vienna, Hitler
suggested that the assassination of the German Minister in Prague
during the course of an anti-German demonstration would do the trick.[4]
Heydrich's appetite was whetted, and he looked forward to the time
when he would be in charge of such clandestine operations against
Germany's enemies abroad, as well as within the Reich itself.

At the beginning of May 1938, Goebbels and Ribbentrop were among
a party of 500 who accompanied Hitler in three special trains on a
reciprocal state visit to Rome. Göring stayed behind in Berlin as acting
head of state once more, having been confirmed ten days earlier as
Hitler's designated successor in his political testament. In this capacity,
it gave him enormous pleasure to be able to receive the King of Sweden
on equal terms when he passed through Berlin on 3 May.

The Italian visit was a success for Hitler, despite his irritation at
finding he was officially the guest of the King rather than Mussolini,
and having to endure the insufferable snobbery of the royal court. He
was entranced by the beauty of Tuscany and Umbria and the fine buildings and works of art in Florence and Rome. And he amazed Foreign
Minister Ciano by turning the 'universal hostility' which greeted him
initially into sympathy and warmth through his conversations and
speeches, which included a public renunciation of all claims to the
South Tyrol that went down very well in Rome. More important for
Hitler was the deepening friendship of Mussolini, and the Duce's assurance that whatever happened over Czechoslovakia was of no interest
to him. That alone made the whole trip worthwhile.

Only Ribbentrop was seriously disappointed with the Italian visit. In
a clumsy and ill-judged attempt to gain personal kudos, he tried to get
the Italians to sign a treaty declaring eternal friendship, mutual support
and respect for existing boundaries. One secret clause went much further,
stating with undiplomatic baldness: 'If one of the contracting parties . . .
should be attacked by France and/or England, the other contracting party
will give it aid and assistance with all its forces.'[5] He sprang his draft
treaty on Ciano without warning while they were aboard the Italian
battleship *Cavour*, watching an impressive naval display in the Gulf of
Naples, where the highlight was eighty-five submarines diving and
surfacing in perfect synchronisation, then firing their deck guns in deafening unison. Although he was a notorious playboy and libertine, Ciano

had spent eleven years in the diplomatic service before his appointment as Foreign Minister and knew a few tricks. He neatly deflected Ribbentrop by returning an 'amended draft' which the interpreter Paul Schmidt described as 'a completely meaningless paper, whose emptiness amounted to a plain refusal'. When Ribbentrop tried to argue, Ciano crushed him with a sarcastic smile, assuring him that the solidarity between their two countries was so strong that they had no need of a formal treaty.[6] Ribbentrop never forgave Ciano this latest humiliation, and spent the next five years bitterly seeking revenge.

Ciano had nothing but contempt for his rival's ignorant amateurism, as he made clear to his father-in-law when reporting Ribbentrop's crude attempt to bounce Italy into a treaty. Mussolini, though he was not averse to the idea of an agreement in the long term, agreed, saying that Ribbentrop 'belongs to the category of Germans who bring misfortune to Germany. He talks left and right all the time about making war, without having a particular enemy or a clear objective in view.' He was not to be taken seriously.[7]

When Goebbels returned to shore from the *Cavour*, he found a messenger waiting for him with a personal telegram: Magda had given birth to their fifth child, another daughter whom they named Hedda. He was delighted with the news. Now that he had a son, he did not seem to mind daughters any more: when Emmy Göring also gave birth to a girl a month later he commented in his diary that Göring was right to be happy, since 'girls dote on their fathers more than boys, who at a certain age will detach themselves from the family'.[8]

In spite of his joy at the birth, all was far from well with Goebbels's marriage, as Magda understandably objected to his relationship with Lida Baarova and the way he was flaunting it in public. There were more and more of what he described as 'jealous scenes'. He had moved out of the main house at Schwanenwerder and into the guest house, but was spending an increasing amount of time in his log cabin at Lanke, with Baarova. It did not seem to bother him that his lover was Czech – perhaps it even added an extra piquancy to the affair.

Göring was awaiting the birth of his own child with some impatience, but found plenty to keep him occupied in the meantime. He was busy absorbing Austrian industry into the Four-Year Plan and the HGW, and setting up the new steel works he had promised near Linz, to exploit the high-grade iron ore. As a bonus, he was able to acquire the steel mills owned by Baron Louis de Rothschild, head of the Vienna branch of the Jewish banking and financial family, who was being held as a prisoner of the Gestapo alongside Schuschnigg in the attics of the Hotel Metropole. In exchange for his freedom to leave Austria, the Baron was persuaded to turn his mills over to the HGW. He was also forced, like other rich Jews, to leave behind his extensive collection of art and antiques. Such confiscated works were either exported for foreign currency, or sold at knock-down prices to privileged German buyers, including Göring, who was always first in the queue. His main rival was Rosenberg, who bought paintings and sculptures on behalf of Hitler for presentation to the House of German Art in Munich or the great new gallery he was planning for Linz.

Although he was ambivalent about military action against the Czechs, Göring was nevertheless involved in the preparation of the revised Operation Green, since any invasion would depend heavily on the Luftwaffe for its success. One essential consideration was the reaction of the Western powers, especially France, whose army with its 100 divisions still vastly outnumbered the Germans. Despite – or maybe because of – Ribbentrop's constant assertion that the French would do nothing, Göring was not convinced. Having persuaded Hitler that they had to protect their backs, just in case France decided to attack, he set off to inspect the West Wall, the line of fortifications along the length of Germany's western frontier, known to the outside world as the Siegfried Line.

Army engineers had begun work on the bunkers and forts of the West Wall in 1936 after the reoccupation of the Rhineland, but the schedule approved by Blomberg had envisaged an extended construction period of up to twenty years. It was hardly surprising, therefore, that Göring found that 'virtually nothing had been done, what had been done was inadequate, and there was barely the most primitive field defence system'.[9] His report to Hitler was damning. Hitler raged against the generals, accused them of sabotaging his plans, and removed them from all construction work, which he gave to Fritz Todt, the civil engineer who had masterminded the autobahn programme. The whole operation was to come under the Four-Year Plan, giving Göring yet another area of responsibility.

Hitler was spending even more time than usual on the Obersalzberg that year, since he had commissioned Speer to tear down the old Reich

Chancellory and build an enormous new one by the New Year, and the Wilhelmstrasse and Vossstrasse were a noisy construction site. On 20 May, Keitel sent the first draft of the directive for Operation Green to Hitler at the Berghof. With the generals almost unanimously against the entire scheme, the OKW had dragged its feet for four weeks, believing there was no great urgency. Bearing this out, the opening sentence echoed what Hitler had said to Keitel: 'It is not my intention to smash Czechoslovakia by military action in the immediate future without provocation, unless an unavoidable development *within* Czechoslovakia forces the issue, or political events in Europe create a particularly favourable opportunity which may perhaps never recur.'[10]

Somehow, the contents of the draft were leaked that same day and coupled with reports of German troop movements and word that Hitler had demanded details of German divisions on the Czech frontier that could be mobilised within twelve hours. In the general atmosphere of tension and mistrust, heightened by the fact that local elections were being held that weekend, the Czechs were taking no chances, and immediately ordered partial mobilisation of their army. By coincidence, two Sudeten German motor-cyclists were killed that morning in an incident involving Czech police, which did nothing to lower the temperature. Britain, France and the Soviet Union immediately confirmed their obligations to Czechoslovakia, and demanded to know what was going on. When the Germans denied the reports of troop movements, Henderson spoke to Weizsäcker in the Foreign Ministry, and asked him to get confirmation of this from Keitel, which Weizsäcker did at once by telephone.

In an effort to calm things down, Henderson released his findings to the British press, then, to make doubly sure, sent his two military attachés to tour the frontier districts of Saxony and Silesia the next day, looking for any signs of unusual military activity. They found none. By then, however, the affair had blown up into a full-scale international crisis, inflamed by Ribbentrop's hysterical rage that Henderson had contacted Keitel, 'behind his back'. Screaming at the Ambassador that he would make sure he was never again given any information on military matters, Ribbentrop refused to confirm that German troops were not about to invade Czechoslovakia, accused the Czechs of planning to massacre the Sudeten Germans under cover of a manufactured war scare, and threatened in 'the most reprehensibly bloodthirsty language' that if they persisted 'they would be exterminated, women and children and all'.[11]

Thoroughly alarmed by Ribbentrop's bellicose attitude, Henderson hurried back to the Embassy, reported his fears to London, and ordered his staff to prepare to send their families back to England. The British Cabinet was equally alarmed, not least because they were terrified of being dragged into a war they did not want, but instead of firing a warning shot across Hitler's bows, Halifax sent a half-hearted warning that if Germany attacked the Czechs, the French were bound to intervene and the Germans should not count on Britain standing aside.[12]

Halifax's warning may have been half-hearted, but it was enough to send Ribbentrop into another paroxysm of fury, though this time a sullen one. 'If a general war ensued,' he snapped at Henderson, 'it would be a war of aggression provoked by France, and Germany would fight as she had done in 1914.'[13] Declaring that threats of intervention left Germany 'completely cold', he went on to say that 'the Czechs were playing with fire if they relied on foreign aid, for before that aid arrived there would not be a living soul left in that state . . . If France were really so crazy as to attack us, it would lead to perhaps the greatest defeat in French history, and if Britain were to join her, then once again we should have to fight to the death.'[14] Halifax's personal response, which Henderson delivered later that evening to Weizsäcker, since to his relief Ribbentrop had gone haring off to report to Hitler at the Berghof, drew the Nazi Foreign Minister's attention to 'the danger of precipitate action leading to a general conflagration . . . which might prove to be the destruction of European civilisation.'[15]

The crisis evaporated as quickly as it had blown up, when it became clear to everyone that it had been a false alarm – the French and other embassies had sent their military attachés to the frontier regions, too, and they had all failed to find any action. Unfortunately, the Czechs could not resist thumbing their noses at Hitler, claiming loudly that he had intended invading but had been forced to climb down when they stood up to him, and the world's press took up the same mocking theme. Nothing could have been more calculated to harden his resolve. 'After 21 May,' he recalled later, 'it was quite clear that this problem had to be solved one way or the other. Every further postponement could only make the question more difficult and therefore the solution bloodier.'

For the rest of that week, Hitler shut himself away in the Berghof, brooding angrily, pacing the floor of his room at night, deciding what to do next. Then, his mind made up, he returned to Berlin and called his senior generals, Foreign Ministry officials and ministers to a conference on Saturday, 28 May 1938, which he opened with the words: 'I am utterly determined that Czechoslovakia shall disappear from the map.' Before the meeting, a worried Göring had taken aside Fritz Wiedemann, who had been Hitler's company commander during the war and was now his personal adjutant, and asked him: 'Does the Führer really imagine the French won't do anything if we weigh into the Czechs? Doesn't he read the FA intercepts I send over?' Warning that the army was not combat-ready, he promised to speak to Hitler about this. But Hitler had the bit between his teeth now, and there was no stopping him. No doubt to the relief of Göring and the generals, he did not envisage immediate action. But although he gave no actual date for an attack, he still wanted everything to be ready by the beginning of October. He accepted the draft directive for Operation Green, with only minor revisions, the first of which was the opening sentence, now turned on its head to read: 'It is my unalterable decision to smash Czechoslovakia by military action in the foreseeable future.'[16]

Apart from the readiness of the army for an attack in the East, the other factor that led Hitler to stay his hand was the lack of progress on the West Wall, which was in no state to delay the French, never mind keep them out. Göring was to see that Todt drafted in thousands of conscripts from the Labour Service – in the end more than 148,000 were employed, together with 50,000 army pioneers – to work flat out on building 10,000 substantial concrete structures within eighteen months. But 5,000 small bunkers and pillboxes to Hitler's own designs were to be ready by 1 October.[17] At the same time, the Labour Service workers were to be trained to use rifles, machine-guns and grenades, so that they could man the defences in an emergency.

Göring wasted no time in demonstrating once again the difference between the army generals, who were extremely reluctant to accept Hitler's orders, and his dynamic Luftwaffe. Immediately after the meeting, he hurried back to his office and called a conference of his senior generals for the very next day. They started operational planning for Operation Green at once, and within three days had issued complete orders for the construction of an Air Defence Zone (LVZ), a second defensive line behind the West Wall along the entire western frontier. This was Göring's own initiative, made, according to Nicolaus von Below, Hitler's Luftwaffe Adjutant, 'because the army did not want the West Wall or Siegfried Line and Göring saw the opportunity to put himself in Hitler's good books'. It consisted largely of 88mm flak guns set in concrete emplacements for a dual flak/anti-tank role, to the displeasure of the army chiefs, who regarded this as an unwarranted interference in its business. Göring rode roughshod over their objections, and by mid May 1939 the LVZ was already two thirds complete and 'easily a match for any French artillery and tanks of the time'.[18]

Having made up his mind to act, Hitler let Goebbels off the leash again. The ban on critical discussion was replaced by a campaign of black propaganda carefully planned to escalate steadily through the summer and reach a climax in the autumn. Goebbels issued daily bulletins to the press setting out how they were to deal with that day's 'incidents' in the oppression of the German minority, including fabricated atrocity stories which were authenticated with the help of general staff maps, telephone directories and electoral rolls. He was concerned, however, that even after three months of his campaign, the mood in Germany remained 'gloomy', with no enthusiasm for war, in marked contrast to the rejoicing of August 1914.[19]

On 2 June, Emmy Göring gave birth to a girl, whom they called Edda, after Mussolini's daughter. Göring's unbounded joy was a delight to see, and his popularity soared even higher – though it did not stop the rumours about the child's parentage or the speculation that she might have been conceived by artificial insemination, since it was whispered that Göring's wounds had made him impotent. But when Emmy took her child off to the peace of her cottage among the dunes on the holiday island of Sylt, he stayed behind in Berlin to work. It may well be that he thought they would be safer on the remote North Sea island than in the Reich capital at a time of such international tension, but in any case there was simply too much to be done for him to take a break at that moment.

The day before Edda's birth, the all-new Ju-88 bomber, which was to prove the most successful and versatile German aircraft of the Second World War, successfully completed its first test flights, and though it still needed a great deal of development, Göring ordered it to be put into production immediately. To step up aircraft production in general, he decreed that factories should start working ten-hour shifts, instituted new initiatives to train previously unskilled workers and apprentices, and even to employ women on the factory floor, a revolutionary proposal for Germany in general and the Nazi Party in particular. As the Luftwaffe's operational plans for Operation Green, including dropping paratroops from 250 Ju-52s into and behind the Czech frontier

fortifications, were completed, he called all the leading aircraft manufacturers to Carinhall for a pep talk, warning them of the coming
conflict with Czechoslovakia and then of wider war. Demanding greater
output and effort, he promised them that once the war was won
Germany would be the greatest power on earth, dominating world
markets. 'But we have to take risks to achieve this goal,' he told them.
'We have to stake something.'

Göring assured the aircraft manufacturers that neither Britain nor
France wanted war, and that they would not fight on behalf of
Czechoslovakia. But in private, he was not so sure, and began looking
to Germany's defences. He discussed plans for using the new autobahns as aircraft runways should airfields be attacked and damaged,
and for building air raid shelters and underground factories. He made
proposals for obtaining foodstuffs from Spain in return for arms shipments to Franco, to counter the effects of a possible blockade. And of
course he continued to push Todt to ever greater efforts on the West
Wall, authorising him to suspend work on autobahn construction and
all other building projects and switch the labour to the fortifications.

In an effort to avert war, he began putting out feelers to Halifax,
who had become Foreign Secretary in February, trading on the personal
relationship they had established the previous year. Carefully bypassing
Ribbentrop, he sent messages through various intermediaries, including
Wiedemann's girlfriend, Princess Stephanie von Hohenlohe, saying that
he would be interested in coming to London to discuss Anglo–German
relations. Briefed by Göring, but with Hitler's approval, Wiedemann
flew to London to talk to Halifax, stressing that Germany wanted a
peaceful solution to the Czech question. Halifax promised that Göring
would be made welcome if he came on those terms, but when
Wiedemann returned to Berlin, Hitler vetoed any visit by Göring, or
any further peace moves. Ribbentrop was furious yet again when he
discovered that he had been sidelined once more, and raised such a
fuss that Hitler fired Wiedemann as his adjutant and sent him to
America as Consul-General in San Francisco. And so, with Ribbentrop's
malign influence on the ascendancy, the crisis continued to deepen
throughout the summer.

The British continued to apply pressure on the Czechs to make
concessions to the Sudeten Germans, warning them that they could
only expect British support if they were prepared to listen to reason.
Henderson proposed to Halifax that he should invite Italy to join
Britain, France and Germany – but not Czechoslovakia – in a four-

power conference to impose a settlement, but Chamberlain rejected the idea because, as Henderson recorded, 'it would be difficult to exclude other powers from participating'.[20] The 'other powers', of course, meant the Soviet Union, which had a two-fold interest in the problem, first as a guarantor with France of Czechoslovakian independence, and secondly as Hitler's ultimate target. To the Western powers, Stalin was an even bigger demon than Hitler, and they wanted nothing to do with him. Instead of a conference, therefore, Chamberlain sent a former President of the Board of Trade, Lord Runciman, to investigate the problem and to mediate between the Czechs and the Sudeten Germans: in other words, to make the Czechs see sense.

While the international crisis over Czechoslovakia mounted, Goebbels found himself facing a personal crisis that threatened to destroy his career, as his infatuation with Baarova spun out of control. After spending what he described as 'a wonderful holiday, the most beautiful in my life' with her at Lanke,[21] at the beginning of August he finally came clean to Magda about how serious the affair had become. But instead of offering to leave her, he tried to persuade her to accept a *ménage à trois*, characteristically sending Baarova to prepare the ground before he dared broach the subject himself. After 'long discussions' that night and next day, he noted that it was 'not all settled yet, but very much clearer. I hope that we shall soon have set ourselves a new goal. I need it. This last month has really taken it out of me.'[22]

Amazingly, Magda seems to have agreed to her husband's suggestion, but when Baarova spent the next two weekends with them, Goebbels behaved so outrageously with his mistress in front of her and their other guests that she could stand it no longer. Goebbels wrote in his diary of a 'violent storm' during a boat trip on the Tegeler See on Saturday, 13 August – but it is not clear if he was writing about the weather or Magda. It could very well have been Magda, because that evening she turned up at the Görings' and poured out her heart to Emmy, asking what she should do about 'that devil in human form'.[23] Göring, of course, knew all about the affair, which he had been following through the FA intercepts, waiting for the moment when Goebbels would finally go too far and ruin himself. That moment had now arrived. He called Hitler at the Berghof, and told him Magda wanted to see him urgently as soon as he returned to Berlin.

Hitler had always had a soft spot for Magda, who had provided him with the closest thing he had ever known to a loving family home, and he was aghast at her demand to be allowed to divorce her husband. Politically, too, he found the idea unthinkable so soon after the scandal of the Blomberg marriage. And with the war of nerves with the Czechs approaching its climax he could not afford a major upheaval in the national leadership that might lose him his star propagandist. He refused to give Magda the permission she sought. Instead, he summoned Goebbels and gave him a severe talking to, like a heavy father, ordering him to drop Baarova immediately and warning him that his career depended on whether he could save his marriage.

Goebbels was 'shattered to the depths and thoroughly overcome', but capitulated immediately. Some reports say he offered to resign there and then and asked Hitler to send him as Ambassador to Tokyo, as far away from Berlin as possible, but this does not seem very likely – no matter how much he thought he loved Baarova, he loved Hitler, and his career, more. Wallowing in self-pity, he drove around 'in a dream' for an hour, before having 'a long and very sad telephone conversation' with Baarova. 'Life is so hard and cruel,' he wailed to his diary, words that he would repeat time after time over the next few days and weeks. 'But duty comes before everything. And in the most difficult hours one must obey its call. All else is temporary and transient. So I shall submit myself to it. Completely and without complaint. But I shall remain strong, even though my heart is breaking.' He concluded his diary entry with more melodramatic bathos: 'And now a new life begins. My youth is at an end.'[24]

Hitler had ordered Goebbels to patch up his marriage, but in the end the decision lay with Magda, and she, deeply wounded, took her time, letting him suffer while she twisted the knife. For days, they talked things out, with Hitler mediating between them but clearly favouring Magda as the injured party. Goebbels, with his incredible capacity for self-justification, seems to have felt no guilt over his behaviour, finding it hard to understand why Magda was being so 'hard and cruel' to him. He told Göring, 'tearfully', that he had to seek his pleasures elsewhere because Magda was so cold.[25]

He turned to his mother and sister Maria for support, and they responded loyally, listening to his interminable, childish complaints that this was the most difficult time of his life and that his 'heart was wounded unto death'. He had not eaten for three days, he moaned, and could only sleep with the help of powerful pills. His mother was ill, but he sat on her bed and listened to her wise advice to call a cease-fire with Magda until the end of September. 'In that time, many things can change,' he noted, 'for better or for worse. I only hope for the better. Grass must grow over the whole thing. And time must pass, which we all know heals everything.'[26]

Despite his anguish and sleepless nights, Goebbels continued working at full throttle, able to compartmentalise his private and public lives. He stepped up the press campaign against the Czechs, moved the ministry into war mode and integrated his new propaganda companies into the Wehrmacht. He conferred with Hitler virtually every day, but they talked only of business: 'Hitler's whole thinking at the moment is taken up with military questions,' he wrote. The warm relationship had become strictly professional, and even that was under threat. Goebbels was always aware that he was on probation, and that his political future lay entirely in the hands of Magda. If she were to insist on a divorce, he would be finished.

Göring was not well during August, suffering from his recurrent glandular disorder, but that did not stop him enjoying one of his favourite pastimes, fooling Germany's potential opponents, especially Britain and France, into believing his Luftwaffe was invincible. For the past year, he had been cultivating the Assistant Air Attaché in the French Embassy, Captain Paul Stehlin. His elder sister, Olga, had taken a shine to the Frenchman, an attractive man in his thirties, and with Göring's encouragement had developed a relationship with him. Stehlin, who as a schoolboy in Lorraine during the Great War had hero-worshipped the famous flying ace, could hardly believe his luck when he found himself drawn into his family circle, where he was privy to 'indiscretions' about air matters dropped by Göring. 'I had never hoped when I arrived in Berlin,' Stehlin naively recalled later, 'that I would learn, merely as a result of simple and straightforward conversations, in complete intimacy, what diplomats of high rank were desperately trying to find out . . . '

Stehlin was even happier when Göring invited him to learn more: 'Come out into the field,' he said. 'Come and see our exercises, look at our factories, I'll hide nothing from you, and you will get a more accurate idea of how it is with the Luftwaffe.'[27] The unsuspecting Captain was flattered to be given tours of airfields and factories and even completed sections of the West Wall, with guides as distinguished as Udet and Bodenschatz and sometimes Göring himself. Deeply impressed by German strength, he eagerly reported his findings to the French Air Ministry, convinced that he was not only serving his country's interests, but also his own – after all, how could such a *coup* fail to advance his career?

When the Commander-in-Chief of the French Air Force, General Joseph Vuillemin, accepted an invitation from Göring to pay an official visit to Germany in late August 1938, he had been well prepared by Stehlin's reports. Göring made sure he was not disappointed, calling on Milch and Udet to lay on an awe-inspiring show of aircraft and production capacity. Much of it was smoke and mirrors, with barely developed prototypes passed off as models already in mass production and planes hurriedly flown from one airfield to another to simulate greater numbers, but a great deal was genuine. To round it all off, Göring staged what Milch described as 'a grandiose spectacle' to demonstrate German air defence precautions and bombing capability which left the French general thoroughly shaken.

Vuillemin was right to be concerned by what he had seen, though not as much as he showed in his final report to Paris, in which he warned of the Luftwaffe's 'truly devastating power'. Göring had struck a decisive blow in the psychological war, which was reinforced shortly afterwards when Lindbergh came back to take part in an aviation congress in Munich, and was fed heavily inflated 'secret' aircraft production figures, which served to alarm Washington and London still further.

By the time of the Nuremberg rally in early September, the tension over Czechoslovakia was close to breaking point. The provocations organised by Henlein on Hitler's instructions were mounting every day, and Goebbels was making full use of them in his propaganda. The Czech President, Eduard Beneš, almost spoiled Hitler's party on 7 September by persuading his Cabinet to agree to almost all of Henlein's demands, and thus removing the excuse for an attack. But the Sudeten Germans managed to cook up a reason for breaking off negotiations, claiming that Czech police had harassed Sudeten deputies in Moravia. Operation Green was still on. Despite all the reservations and objections of his generals – the army Chief of Staff, Beck, had even resigned in protest, to be replaced by the more compliant General Franz Halder – Hitler had now set the date as 1 October. He was enjoying playing the warlord, constantly interfering in the plans at every level, and looking forward eagerly to turning them into action.

At Nuremberg, the British and French Ambassadors did their best to defuse the situation, but their efforts were useless. Henderson, who was forced to spend five days living in the special diplomatic train in the rail sidings, barely stopped talking the whole time. 'I had two long conversations with Göring, three with Goebbels, one or two with Ribbentrop, two or three with Neurath, half a dozen with Weizsäcker,' he wrote later. 'I conveyed, besides, an endless succession of warnings to a host of other Nazi personalities of scarcely lesser note, the cumulative effect of which, since talking there was almost the equivalent of broadcasting, I hoped would be useful.'[28] It was not. He may have talked, but no one was listening – apart from Göring.

Göring, unlike Hitler, was starkly conscious that neither the German economy nor the armed forces was in any condition to sustain a war. He wanted the Czech resources as much as anyone, but still hoped that he could get everything he needed without having to fight, and worked hard on Henderson towards this end. To bolster the illusion of a personal friendship and, no doubt, to show off at the same time, he drove Henderson out to his childhood home at Veldenstein, away from the raucous atmosphere of the rally. There, in the peace and quiet of the fairy-tale castle, he talked with his usual disarming frankness. He said that Hitler had asked him to inform the British government that if they allowed him to settle the Sudeten question, they would be surprised and gratified at the moderation of his other demands. He alerted the Ambassador of the danger of war being sparked by a Czech 'incident', such as the assassination of Henlein. He told him he planned to go hunting in Rominten at the end of the month, and 'hoped to goodness the Czechs wouldn't upset his shooting plans by starting trouble in the middle of them'. He then repeated an earlier suggestion that it would help if Chamberlain and Hitler were to meet.[29] Henderson, not having the resources of his embassy to hand in Nuremberg, hired a private plane to carry his handwritten report of all this back to London.[30]

The next day, Göring showed a different face to the world in his big speech at the rally. Still in pain from his swollen lymphatic glands but fortified by pills supplied by Hitler's physician, Dr Morell, he thundered a warning to the Western powers against interfering with Hitler's plans in the East. 'Our Rhineland frontier defences are impregnable!' he lied, and castigated Britain for complaining about 'German terror methods' while their 'whole colonial empire is held together only by the lash'. Turning directly to Czechoslovakia, he went on: 'An insignificant segment of Europe is making life unbearable for mankind. The Czechs, that miserable pygmy race without any culture – nobody even knows where they came from – are oppressing a civilised race, and behind them can be seen Moscow, and the eternal face of the Jewish fiend!'[31]

Hitler's closing speech on 12 September was restrained by comparison with Göring's. It was only after speaking for some time about the struggles of the party that he finally came to Czechoslovakia: 'I am in no way willing that here in the heart of Germany a second Palestine should be permitted to arise. The poor Arabs are defenceless and deserted. The Germans in Czechoslovakia are neither defenceless nor are they deserted, and people should take notice of that fact.' To everyone's surprise, he did not go on to demand the cession of the Sudetenland, nor even a plebiscite, but simply insisted on 'self-determination' for the Sudeten Germans. He ended rather weakly by saying that 'We should be sorry if this were to disturb or damage our relations with other European states, but the blame does not lie with us.'[32]

Göring was not at Nuremberg to hear Hitler's speech: his illness had worsened and he had retired to Carinhall to rest after delivering his broadside. But Ribbentrop stayed, fawning on the Führer and urging him on to war, repeating endlessly that Britain and France would never fight. When his four most senior ambassadors, Dirksen from London, Welczeck from Paris, Mackensen from Rome and Dieckhoff from Washington, joined together in appealing to him to persuade Hitler not to pursue a policy which they were convinced would lead to another world war, he banished them from Nuremberg, forbade them from speaking to Hitler, and sent them on compulsory leave for the rest of the month.

Hitler's Nuremberg speech may have been relatively anodyne, but it signalled a sudden change of gear on all sides. The Sudeten Germans erupted in a pre-planned programme of riots and violent incidents in which people on both sides were killed, the Czech government imposed a state of martial law, and the British and French panicked. Chamberlain had been considering for a little while whether or not he should meet Hitler; now he believed he had no choice. The stumbling block was Ribbentrop, who would be bound to block such a visit. But how could it be arranged without him? Henderson called Göring on 14 September and asked for his help. Göring needed no second bidding, and phoned Hitler at the Berghof immediately, to clear the way for a direct approach from Chamberlain. Hitler agreed. And so began two weeks of the most frantic shuttle diplomacy which ended by settling the fate not only of the Sudeten Germans but also of Czechoslovakia, and ultimately the rest of Europe.

Chamberlain telegraphed that evening, proposing that he should fly out the next day, which he did, accompanied by his chief political adviser, Sir Horace Wilson, a civil servant with even less experience of foreign affairs than himself, and Sir William Strang, head of the Central European Department of the Foreign Office. They were met at Munich airport at noon by Ribbentrop – it would have been impossible to keep him out altogether – who escorted them to Berchtesgaden on Hitler's private train. But once the introductions had been made at the Berghof, he was excluded as Hitler and Chamberlain retired to Hitler's study alone, accompanied only by the interpreter, Paul Schmidt, who wrote:

With Hitler's knowledge this had been settled between the English and the Germans beforehand, behind Ribbentrop's back. Both sides felt that our Foreign Minister would prove a disturbing element in any endeavour to achieve a friendly settlement between England and Germany. Hitler too had noticed the wounded vanity aroused by the English in his former London Ambassador. He had therefore agreed to the plan to exclude him, which had the approval of Henderson and Weizsäcker and the warm support of Göring. Ribbentrop therefore remained angrily in the background . . . [33]

While Ribbentrop sulked, Hitler treated Chamberlain to a lecture on the situation and listed his demands in a tone of rising indignation and excitement until the British Prime Minister pulled him up short. 'If I have understood you aright,' he said, 'you are determined to proceed against Czechoslovakia in any case. If that is so, why did you let me come to Berchtesgaden? Under the circumstances, it is better for me to return at once. Anything else seems pointless.' To Schmidt's surprise, Hitler retreated in the face of Chamberlain's firmness, and the discussion moved on to the subject of self-determination for the Sudeten Germans. After three hours of talk, Chamberlain announced that he would have to consult his Cabinet colleagues before going any further. Hitler agreed, and even promised that he would not attack the Czechs before they had met again, unless 'any particularly atrocious incident occurred' – which, of course, was no great concession since

Operation Green was not due to start until 1 October.

On that note, Chamberlain left to spend the night in his Berchtesgaden hotel, where Ribbentrop displayed his pique by forbidding Schmidt from giving him a copy of his notes on the conversation with Hitler. It was an unthinkable breach of diplomatic courtesy that did nothing to improve Ribbentrop's standing with either the British or his own staff. A few days later, Henderson asked Göring to help him obtain the notes. Göring had a serious word with Hitler about Ribbentrop's behaviour, and was able to tell Henderson that Chamberlain would be given a copy of the notes when he returned on 22 September.

Back in London, Chamberlain reported to his Cabinet, and to French Premier Daladier and Foreign Minister Bonnet, who hurried over from Paris. The two governments decided they would accept Hitler's demands for the cession of all territory with a German-speaking majority. The Czechs seemed to have no option but to agree to this, since it was obvious that neither Britain nor France was prepared to come to their rescue. Their only other hope, the Soviet Union, was ready and willing to fulfil its obligations. It had begun massing troops of the Red Army in the Ukraine – thirty infantry and ten cavalry divisions, one tank corps, three tank brigades and twelve air brigades were already along the frontier with Poland and another thirty infantry and ten cavalry divisions were in a state of readiness. But they had no common frontiers with Germany or Czechoslovakia and could not march against the Germans without permission from Poland or Romania to cross their territory. There seemed little hope of such permission being granted, since both had seized Russian territory in 1919 and 1920 and were understandably nervous of allowing the Red Army inside their frontiers.

The Romanians did agree to allow Soviet aircraft bound for Czechoslovakia to overfly their territory, and at the beginning of September some twenty Soviet bombers flew to join the Czech air force, the first of a total of sixty that the Soviets had promised. By 15 September, the Romanians had also withdrawn their objections to the transport of troops by the rail line across the Carpathian mountains. The Poles, however, were a very different case. Göring had promised them a share of the spoils if they collaborated with Germany, and they were moving their own troops up to the border with the northern Czech region of Teschen, or Cieszyn as they knew it, which was rich in iron and coal and had a minority Polish population that would provide an excuse for its seizure.

Soviet Foreign Minister Maxim Litvinov declared that his country would stand by its obligations to the Czechs, and called for staff talks with the French and an immediate three-power conference of Britain, France and the Soviet Union to decide on joint action, but his suggestion was ignored in both Paris and London. 'It is indeed astonishing,' Winston Churchill wrote later in his account of those eventful days,

that this public and unqualified declaration by one of the great powers concerned should not have played its part in Mr Chamberlain's negotiations, or in the French conduct of the crisis . . . They [the Soviets] were not brought into the scale against Hitler, and were treated with an indifference – not to say a disdain – which left a mark in Stalin's mind. Events took their course as if Soviet Russia did not exist. For this we afterwards paid dearly.[34]

Astonishing it may have been, but by the time Litvinov suggested a conference on 22 September, Chamberlain was already back in Germany, this time at Bad Godesberg, to inform Hitler that all his demands had been agreed.

To Chamberlain's astonishment, Hitler told him this was no longer enough. Reneging on his previous promises that he wanted nothing more than the Sudetenland, he made new and bigger demands, including the cession of territory to Hungary and Poland, together with an ultimatum: he would attack if Czechoslovakia did not comply by 1 October. Any plebiscites would now only be held after the event, under German occupation. In a state of shock, Chamberlain retired to his hotel across the Rhine to consider the new situation, but the next day returned to the Hotel Dreesen to meet Hitler again. While they were talking, the Czechs upset everything by announcing that they were mobilising, which gave Hitler the opportunity to put on a great show of rage, with Ribbentrop of all people appearing to calm him down and stop him declaring war there and then. Buttressed by the dictator's assurance that the Sudetenland really was the last of his territorial ambitions in Europe, and that he had no wish to include in the Reich people of other races than German, Chamberlain gave way again and promised to try to persuade the Czechs.

For the next seven days, the world was in a turmoil of tensions and uncertainty, whipped to ever greater heights by Goebbels's near-hysterical propaganda. War seemed inevitable. The British mobilised the Royal Navy, the French called up several categories of reservists and began a partial mobilisation, the Soviet Union also mobilised its fleet, as well as continuing to build up its forces on the frontiers – a fact that escaped the attention of most Western commentators. In London, gas masks were issued to the civilian population, sandbags were placed around government buildings and slit trenches dug in the parks. In Berlin, Göring kept the temperature up by having anti-aircraft guns mounted in prominent positions, including one on the roof of the IG Farben building in Pariser Platz, opposite the Adlon Hotel, where it could be clearly seen from the British and French Embassies. From across the Atlantic, President Roosevelt sent a stream of telegrams urging peace on everyone.

Göring, who had stuck by his intention of going hunting while the stags were still rutting, taking with him Körner, Udet, Loerzer and Tsar Boris of Bulgaria, reluctantly hauled himself back to Berlin. There he was dismayed to receive a report from his air staff that in spite of the panic in London the Luftwaffe still had no aircraft capable of operating effectively over Britain, and that a war of annihilation against Britain was therefore out of the question. Knowing he had to play for time, he fired off volleys of orders for yet higher production, more training for long-range operations over the sea, and strategic plans for future attacks, then set about redoubling his efforts to avoid war.

Meanwhile, the talking, and the shouting, continued. Sir Horace Wilson flew to and from Berlin carrying messages and an ultimatum from Chamberlain. Hitler set a new deadline of 2 p.m. on 28 September for the Czechs to submit to all his demands. On 26 September he made a bloodthirsty speech to the party faithful in the Sportpalast which brought them all to their feet and which was rounded off by Goebbels with the rousing cry 'Führer command – we will obey!' But the next day, when Hitler had a motorised division of the army drive through central Berlin to impress the foreign missions and journalists with German military might, the Berliners either ignored it or deliberately turned away. William Shirer, one of the journalists who was supposed to be impressed, noted in his diary that it was 'the most striking demonstration against war I've ever seen'.[35] Watching this marked lack of enthusiasm from his window in the Chancellery, a grim Hitler drew the appropriate conclusions, which were underlined at lunch the next day by Goebbels, who summoned up the courage to tell him, in a loud voice, that the German public as a whole was 'very much opposed to war'.

With Goebbels joining those who were urging caution, Ribbentrop was now the only one among the top leaders who was still banging the drum for war. The day before, he had enthusiastically ordered a special train complete with a supply of steel helmets, pistols and gas masks, for himself and his staff to use as a mobile headquarters when they accompanied Hitler to the battlefield.[36] Hitler himself was now having serious second thoughts – he had even sent what he considered to be a placatory letter to Chamberlain on the evening of 27 September. But as his deadline approached there seemed to be no way out without an unacceptable loss of face, and under the baleful influence of Ribbentrop he stuck defiantly to his hard line.

Salvation came with only three hours to spare, when an excited Göring burst in on Hitler and Ribbentrop, brandishing a brown FA transcript of a telephone conversation between Mussolini and his Ambassador in Berlin, Bernardo Attolico. Attolico was to tell Hitler that Chamberlain had been in touch with Mussolini asking him to take part in a four-power conference with Britain, France and Germany, to find a solution to the Sudetenland problem. Mussolini wanted Hitler to postpone German mobilisation for twenty-four hours, while he considered the proposal. Chamberlain had written to Hitler the night before, with proposals agreed with the French and sent to Prague pressing the Czechs to hand over the Sudeten territories by 1 October. The French Ambassador, François-Poncet, was on his way to see Hitler at that moment – a visit that Göring had fixed after François-Poncet had complained to Henderson that his request for an audience had been blocked. Henderson had called Göring, who had cut him short with: 'You need not say a word more. I am going immediately to see the Führer.'

Göring's feelers were finally bearing fruit. But even then, Ribbentrop tried to persuade Hitler not to agree to a meeting. Göring turned on him savagely, accusing him of being a warmonger and 'a criminal fool'. He shouted that he knew what war was, and he did not want to go through it again. But if the Führer said 'march' he would go in the leading aeroplane. The only thing he would insist on was that Ribbentrop should be in the seat next to him.

The conference opened in the newly-completed Führer Building in Munich shortly before 2 p.m. on 29 September, with Hitler, Chamberlain, Daladier and Mussolini sitting down together to dismember Czechoslovakia. There was no chairman and no agenda.

Ribbentrop, Wilson, Ciano and French Foreign Minister Alexis Léger took their seats behind them, and during the proceedings Göring, François-Poncet, Henderson, Attolico, Weizsäcker and various legal advisers, secretaries and adjutants came into the room to form an audience. The Soviets were not invited, and nor were the Czechs. Two Czech representatives did arrive, but were kept in a separate room to await the result without their being consulted or involved. In a fit of spite, Ribbentrop had tried to wreck things by drafting a proposed text that he knew would be unacceptable to the British and French, but he was outwitted by Göring who, together with Neurath and Weizsäcker, drew up a more suitable document which they gave to Attolico for Mussolini to present as his own. It was this draft that would form the basis of the agreement.

The conference went on until after 2 a.m. the next morning, with a break for dinner. The atmosphere was relaxed and amicable, and there were no serious problems in reaching a unanimous agreement. 'Actually, the whole thing was a cut-and-dried affair,' Göring told Dr Gilbert at Nuremberg in 1946:

Neither Chamberlain nor Daladier was the least bit interested in sacrificing or risking anything to save Czechoslovakia. That was clear as day to me. The fate of Czechoslovakia was essentially sealed in three hours. Then they argued for hours more about the world 'guarantee'. Chamberlain kept hedging. Daladier hardly paid any attention at all. He just sat there like this. [Göring slumped down and assumed a bored expression.] All he did was nod approval from time to time. Not the slightest objection to anything. I was simply amazed at how easily the thing was managed by Hitler. After all, they knew that Škoda, etc had munitions plants in the Sudetenland, and Czechoslovakia would be at our mercy . . . When he suggested that certain armaments which were across the Sudeten border should be brought into the Sudeten territory as soon as we take it over, I thought there would be an explosion. But no – not a peep. We got everything we wanted; just like that. [He snapped his fingers.][37]

The Czech representatives were finally informed of the terms of the agreement at about 2 a.m. on the morning of 30 September. They were to evacuate the whole of the Sudeten region, including all their border fortifications, starting on 1 October. They were to be out completely by 10 October, 'without any existing installations having been destroyed'. Everything was to be left behind – not only military arms and equipment but also all personal belongings: civilians would be allowed only the clothes they stood up in. They had to leave homes, furniture, household goods, the family horses and cows, everything. There would be no compensation paid by Germany, either to the Czech government or to individuals. When the final settlement was completed by a German-dominated 'International Commission' on 20 November, the Czechs had been forced to hand over 11,000 square miles of their territory, with sixty-six per cent of their coal, eighty per cent of their lignite, seventy per cent of their iron and steel, seventy per cent of their electric power, and forty per cent of their timber.[38] It was a wonderful bonus for Göring's resource-starved Four-Year Plan. No wonder he was able to tell Ciano, when he saw him and Mussolini on to their train in Munich, 'Now there's going to be a rearmament such as the world has never seen.'

The Munich agreement has gone down in history as a byword for short-sightedness, betrayal and cowardice, a triumph for appeasement and the policies of peace at any price. It undoubtedly opened the door to the Second World War, by handing Hitler a bloodless victory where in all probability, had the Czechs and their supporters chosen to fight, he would have suffered a bloody defeat. Hitler may not have fully realised this. Ribbentrop certainly did not. Göring, however, most certainly did and the outcome was a triumph for his tactics of scaring the Western powers so much that they simply did not dare to risk taking on his supposedly invincible Luftwaffe, nor even to throw the might of 100 French army divisions against Germany's five regular and seven reserve divisions manning her incomplete Western defences. When Chamberlain flew to Bad Godesberg for his second meeting with Hitler on 22 September, he had just received a letter from Lindbergh, written at the request of the American Ambassador in London, Joseph Kennedy, which said:

I believe that the German aircraft factories can produce 20,000 aircraft per year. Exact production figures at the moment are hard to determine. The most convincing reports I received are based on 500 to 800 aircraft per month. Germany now has the ability to destroy London, Paris, and Prague if it wishes to do so. England and France do not have enough aircraft for a counterattack or for defence. A major European war would, so I believe, permit Communism to overrun Europe.

I am convinced that it is wiser to permit Germany to expand in the East than to have England and France become involved in a war they are now unprepared for. For the first time in history, a nation has the power to lay waste the famous cities in Europe, or to spare them from this.[39]

Göring's deception campaign had been wonderfully successful.

Unfortunately for him, however, he had not only fooled the Western powers over the strength and capabilities of the Luftwaffe, he had fooled Hitler, too. The Führer's initial euphoria over the diplomatic rout started to wear off after only a few days, to be replaced by resentment, fed by Ribbentrop and Himmler, at being denied the satisfaction of a military victory. 'That fellow Chamberlain has spoiled my entry into Prague!' he complained angrily as he returned to Berlin. 'Next time,' he warned, 'I shall act so quickly that there will be no time for any old women to react.' Looking back on the result in February 1945, Hitler lamented:

I ought to have seized the initiative in 1938 instead of allowing myself to be forced into war in 1939 . . . It was the last chance we had of localising the war. But they gave way all along the line to our demands. At Munich, we lost a unique opportunity of easily and swiftly winning a war that was in any case inevitable . . . we ought there and then to have settled our disputes by force of arms and disregarded the inclination of our opponents to meet all our demands.[40]

In his ignorance of the realities in 1938, Hitler suspected his 'Iron Man' of going soft, a suspicion that Ribbentrop, still smarting over the slights he had suffered at Göring's hands, fostered assiduously, taking his revenge by pouring poison into Hitler's ear. Göring's influence with Hitler on matters of foreign policy would never be the same again. Over the coming months, Ribbentrop would supplant him completely, with catastrophic results.

XXI

KRISTALLNACHT

ALTHOUGH his standing in Hitler's eyes had been seriously damaged by his backing for the Munich agreement, Göring still persevered with his efforts to gain the rest of Czechoslovakia without a war. He was soon rewarded by promising signs. On 3 October, French Ambassador François-Poncet hurried back from consulting Daladier and Bonnet in Paris to tell him that the Franco–Czech alliance was finished and that France was eager to make a deal with Germany.[1] The new Czech President, Emil Hácha, who had replaced Beneš after Munich, could hardly wait to abase himself and his country by sending his Minister in Berlin, Vojtech Mastný to grovel to Göring, who noted in his diary for 11 October that Mastný offered:

most emphatic assurance that the new Czechia will realign her foreign policies: closest friendship with Germany. Assurance that internally the coming regime will lean to the extreme right. Liquidation of Communism. Fate and life of Czechia are in Germany's hands. He pleads that the country not be reduced to penury . . .

All this suited Göring's purposes perfectly. Having fatally weakened Czechoslovakia by carving off the Sudetenland, he aimed to complete the process by encouraging Slovakia and the other parts of the federation to break away, at which point Germany would simply pick up the pieces. The Czech heartland of Bohemia and Moravia, with its rich mineral deposits and industrial resources, could either be annexed or become a totally dependent German satellite. 'A Czech state minus Slovakia is even more completely at our mercy,' he noted to the Foreign Ministry, revealing his long-term aims by adding: 'Air base in Slovakia for operating against the East very important.' Pursuing this line, he had secret talks with Slovak leaders, who had already achieved autonomy immediately after Munich – the country's name had now been officially changed to the hyphenated Czecho-Slovakia – but now told him they wanted 'complete independence, with very close political, economic and military ties with Germany'. He interpreted this as a willingness to become a client state, and encouraged them by telling them that this was their only hope of fending off the predatory Hungarians, who were keen to annex large chunks of their territory.

As autumn turned to winter, Göring continued to hold secret talks with the Slovaks, Czechs, Romanians, Hungarians and, above all, the Poles. He invited Ambassador Lipski out to Carinhall to sound him out about his 'grand solution' of creating a German empire in the East, which he hoped to achieve with the help of a compliant Poland, acting as Germany's partner and receiving a share of the spoils in return. Like most Germans, he wanted to take back the formerly German land around Poznan, or Posen, which had been ceded in 1919, compensating the Poles with new territory to be taken from the Soviet Union on her eastern frontier, mainly from the Ukraine. War with Poland did not figure in his plans: he was convinced he could achieve all that he wanted through friendly persuasion, based on the personal relationships he had been nurturing for so long with the Polish leaders.

War with the Western powers did not figure in Göring's plans, either: he believed he could reach an understanding with Britain that would allow him to pursue his aims of expansion into south-eastern Europe unopposed. But in this he was directly opposed by Ribbentrop, who was grimly determined to have his revenge on the country that had rejected his advances. Hitler was going along with his Foreign Minister. When Ribbentrop travelled to Rome at the end of October, to try to persuade Mussolini to join a tripartite military pact with Germany and Japan, he told the Duce: 'The Führer is convinced that we must inevitably count on a war with the Western democracies in the course of a few years, perhaps three or four.' Carried away by his own belligerence, he boasted: 'The Czech crisis has shown our power! We have the advantage of the initiative and are masters of the situation. We cannot be attacked. The military situation is excellent: as from September [1939] we could face a war with the great democracies.'[2]

The Italians were unimpressed. 'What is he up to?' Ciano had wondered when Ribbentrop called to arrange the informal visit at short notice. 'I always distrust Ribbentrop's initiatives. He is vain, frivolous and loquacious. The Duce says you only have to look at his head to see that he has a very small brain. And he is very tactless.'[3] Ribbentrop's tactless and clumsy attempt to embroil the Italians in German war plans served only to alarm them, driving them to mend their fences with Britain, which had been damaged by the Italian adventures in Abyssinia and Spain. He was forced to return home empty-handed and seething yet again, niggled, among other things, by having discovered in Rome that Göring, without his knowledge but apparently with Hitler's blessing, had proposed a four-power consultation pact in the wake of Munich. He took steps to quash the idea at once.

Hitler's long-term ambition of finding *Lebensraum* in the East and smashing Bolshevism in the process, remained unchanged, and he, too, was looking to enlist the Poles as his allies. In the short term, he needed the alliance with them to safeguard his back during the showdown with Britain and France, which he now believed was necessary before he could safely move against the Soviets. In the meantime, there was still some tidying up to be done, and preparations to be made. After touring the Sudetenland, he inspected the captured Czech frontier fortifications, which were especially interesting as they had been constructed by French engineers and modelled on the Maginot Line. Once the inspection had been completed, they were used as targets for German guns, to test the best ways of smashing France's own defences when the time came. Hitler then moved on to a widely-publicised five-day tour of the West Wall, before returning to Munich on 14 October to receive the new Czech Foreign Minister, František Chvalkovský, with the threat that he would destroy Czecho-Slovakia in twenty-four or even eight hours if she ever stepped out of line.

While Hitler was browbeating Chvalkovský in Munich, in the Air Ministry in Berlin Göring was informing Germany's major arms manufacturers that the Führer had directed him 'to execute a gigantic arms programme beside which all our achievements up to now pale into insignificance'. The most important part of this was to be a five-fold increase in aircraft production. In fact, as Göring well knew but refused to acknowledge, his target of 19,000 aircraft, slightly more than half of which were fighter planes, would be impossible with the manpower and material resources available. Furthermore, putting them in the air would need eighty-five per cent of the world's output of aviation fuel. But this was only the start: according to Milch, the final programme called for 31,300 aircraft by April 1942, of which 7,700 were to be Ju-88 and He-177 bombers, neither of which was yet in production.[4]

A few days later, on 21 October, Hitler directed the OKW to secure the frontiers of Germany, including protection against surprise air attack, to be ready to liquidate the remainder of Czecho-Slovakia 'if her policy should become hostile towards Germany', and to annex the district of Memel, a Baltic seaport with some 40,000 mainly German-speaking inhabitants that had been cut off from East Prussia at Versailles and given to Lithuania, who knew it as Klaipeda.

That same evening, Magda Goebbels arrived at the Berghof, begging Hitler to allow her to divorce her husband. He refused, and sent for Goebbels. Two days later, he had a long talk with them both, said he wanted the marriage preserved 'for political reasons', and persuaded Magda to agree to a three-month trial period, on condition that Goebbels behaved himself impeccably. If they could not resolve their differences in that time, Magda could have her divorce, and Goebbels would have to resign. In an attempt to camouflage the rift, Hitler had his court photographer, Heinrich Hoffmann, take official pictures of himself with Goebbels and Magda, to demonstrate their togetherness. Unfortunately, their body language in the photographs told a completely different story: in the picture of the three of them that appeared on the front page of the *Berliner Illustrierte Zeitung* only Hitler was smiling.

News of the latest episode in the Goebbels scandal spread quickly through party circles, broadcast with malicious glee by Rosenberg and others. Himmler had fed Rosenberg with spicy details of 'dozens' of cases in the Gestapo files of women complaining about Goebbels's importuning and abuse of his position to demand sexual favours. He also passed some of the files to Hitler, as did Göring with transcripts of juicy telephone conversations. Baarova found herself the centre of much attention, but was ostracised by the film industry, her career in Germany abruptly terminated. Goebbels never contacted or spoke to her again. Aware that his own career was in serious danger of termination, too, he looked around frantically for something that would divert attention from his troubles. By an amazing stroke of fortune, he found exactly what he needed just two weeks later.

At around 10 a.m. on Monday, 7 November, a slight, seventeen-year-old Jewish refugee called Herschel Grynszpan walked into the German Embassy in Paris, pulled out a pistol and fired five shots at the Third Secretary, Ernst vom Rath. Three bullets missed, but two found their target and Rath collapsed, seriously wounded. The shooting was a personal gesture, protesting against the suffering inflicted on Herschel's own family, who were among those who had been expelled to Poland, but it gave the Nazis the excuse they had been waiting for to unleash a savage physical attack on the entire Jewish population of Germany. Goebbels seized upon it as an opportunity to restore his reputation as the most radical member of the party leadership, and to win back Hitler's favour.

Rath took two days to die, and when he did, it happened to be on the holiest day in the entire Nazi calendar. 9 November 1938 was the twentieth anniversary of the infamous 'stab in the back' by the 'November criminals' who had forced the Kaiser to abdicate, declared Germany a republic and agreed to sign an armistice. It was also the fifteenth anniversary of Hitler's failed *putsch*, and the 'old fighters' were congregated in Munich for their annual two-day commemoration, their emotions running high.

The night before, Himmler had kept up his bid to be the leader of the anti-Jewish pack, lecturing a meeting of his highest SS leaders in his toughest speech yet:

We must be clear that in the next ten years we will certainly face unprecedented critical conflicts. It is not only the battle against the nations which in this case are pushed forward simply as a front by our opponents, but it is the ideological battle against the entire Jewry, freemasonry, Marxism and churches of the world. These forces – of which I presume the Jews to be the driving spirit, the origin of all the negatives – are clear that if Germany and Italy are not destroyed, *they* will be destroyed. That is a simple conclusion. In Germany, the Jew cannot hold out. This is a question of years. We will drive them out more and more with unprecedented ruthlessness. Italy is going the same way and Poland does not want the Jews . . .

The other states, Sweden, Norway, Denmark, Holland, Belgium, are today not so naturally anti-Semitic but they will become so with time. We are sending our best propagandists in there . . . Furthermore, Czechoslovakia has become anti-Semitic, all the Balkans are anti-Semitic, the whole of Palestine is engaged in a desperate struggle against the Jews, so that some day there will be no place left in the world for the Jew. He says to himself, this danger will only be removed if the source, if the originating country of anti-Semitism, if Germany is burnt out and destroyed.

Be clear about it – in the battle that will decide if we are defeated there will be no reservation remaining for the Germans. All will be starved out and butchered. That is what will face every one, whether he is now an enthusiastic supporter of the Third Reich or not – it will be sufficient that he speaks German and had a German mother.[5]

Rath died at 4.35 p.m. but the news was not made public until the evening, when the 'old fighters' were gathered in the Old Town Hall for the final reception. Feelings were already running high. Goebbels conferred with Hitler there, the two of them speaking urgently but quietly about anti-Jewish riots that had taken place the previous night in Hesse and Magdeburg-Anhalt. Hitler, Goebbels said later, told him that although the party was not to organise such demonstrations, it should do nothing to stop them if they occurred 'spontaneously'. 'Hold back the police,' he told him. 'The Jews should for once get to feel the anger of the people.'[6] Others who were present heard Hitler say 'The SA should be allowed to have a fling.' He then left the reception without making his traditional closing speech. Whatever happened next, the head of state of the Greater German Reich could claim to know nothing, nor to have given any specific orders. That, together with the speech, was left to Goebbels – and Goebbels made the most of the opportunity.

'I have news for you here tonight,' he announced,

to demonstrate what happens to a good German when he drops his guard for one moment. Ernst vom Rath was a good German, a loyal servant of the Reich, working for the good of our people in our embassy in Paris. Shall I tell you what happened to him? He was shot down! In the course of his duty, he went, unarmed and unsuspecting, to speak to a visitor at the embassy, and had two bullets pumped into him. He is now dead.

Allowing the full effect of this news to sink in, he banged his fist on the table and raised his voice still further. 'Do I need to tell you the race of the dirty swine who perpetrated this foul deed? A Jew! Tonight he lies in jail in Paris, claiming that he acted on his own, that he had no instigators of this awful deed behind him. But we know better, don't we?' Pandemonium broke out in the hall, as the 'old fighters' yelled for vengeance. Goebbels quietened them, then continued: 'Comrades, we cannot allow this attack by international Jewry to go unchallenged. It must be repudiated. Our people must be told, and their answer must be ruthless, forthright, salutary! I ask you to listen to me, and together we must plan what is to be our answer to Jewish murder and the threat of international Jewry to our glorious German Reich!' The answer that Goebbels proposed was simple. There had already been anti-Jewish riots in various parts of Germany, he told his audience. Similar 'spontaneous' demonstrations must be organised immediately – but the party itself must not appear to be responsible.[7] The speech was received with 'storms of applause', according to Goebbels, then: 'Everyone tears straight off to the telephone. Now the people will act.'[8]

Goebbels had had two days to prepare an action, in concert with Heydrich, and it needed only a few telephone calls to put their plans into operation – though as it turned out they had slightly different ideas of what was to happen. On Goebbels's initiative, the Gauleiters and SA leaders were called to a meeting in the Hotel Schottenhammel where a member of the party's Reich directorate briefed them on what they were to do. Within half an hour, they were calling their Gaue to get things moving. Goebbels himself began issuing a stream of detailed instructions, shoring up Wagner, who was both Gauleiter and Interior Minister in Bavaria, when he lost his nerve after SA men began demolishing Munich's second synagogue, and giving direct orders for the destruction of the Fasanenstrasse synagogue in Berlin's West End.

From the Prinz-Albrecht-Strasse in Berlin, Gestapo chief Heinrich Müller sent an urgent teleprinter message to every state police bureau in the Reich, alerting them to the fact that 'demonstrations against the Jews, and particularly their synagogues, will take place very shortly'. The Gestapo were not to interfere but were to co-operate with the Regular Police to prevent looting 'and similar excesses'. They were also to secure any important archive material found in any synagogue – the Gestapo in Cologne were reminded that there was 'especially important material' in the main synagogue there, which was to be seized immediately – and to prepare for the arrest of some 20,000 to 30,000 Jews. Primarily, the order stated, '*well-to-do Jews* are to be selected'. More detailed instructions would be issued during the course of the night.

'If, during the actions about to take place, Jews are found in possession of *weapons*,' the final paragraph stated, 'the most severe measures are to be applied. The special task units of the SS as well as the general SS may be employed in all phases of the operation. Suitable measures are to be taken to ensure that *the Gestapo remains in control of the actions* under all circumstances . . . '[9]

The police had, in fact, already taken precautions to ensure that the Jews could not fight back effectively. They had begun disarming them on 8 November, removing anything that could be used for protection from every Jewish household. They claimed that their haul in Berlin alone already totalled 2,569 daggers and swords, 1,702 firearms and 20,000 rounds of ammunition.

While Himmler conducted the annual swearing-in ceremony for new SS men with Hitler at the Feldherrnhalle at midnight, watched by Goebbels and other party leaders, the pogrom was taking shape across the Reich. The further instructions that Müller had promised were put on the teleprinters to Gestapo and SD offices at 1.20 a.m. by Heydrich. The delay was due to his having to be roused from the Hotel Vier Jahreszeiten and then having to check with Himmler, who was closeted with Hitler and could only be reached through Wolff. Hitler gave his oral approval for the action, but stressed that the SS must not be seen to be part of the action, which was not its style, and that any SS men who were involved should wear civilian clothes.

Heydrich's orders confirmed the Gestapo chief's first message, and elaborated on the details:

FLASH MUNICH 47767 10.11.38 0120 SECRET
TO: ALL REGIONAL AND SUBREGIONAL GESTAPO OFFICES
TO: ALL SECURITY SERVICE DISTRICT AND SUB-DISTRICT HQs
FLASH URGENT SUBMIT AT ONCE!
SUBJECT: MEASURES AGAINST THE JEWS THIS NIGHT
On account of the attack on Legation Secretary v. RATH in Paris, demonstrations against the Jews are to be expected throughout the Reich in the course of this night (9–10.11.38). The following directives are issued for dealing with these events:

1. Immediately on receipt of this teleprint directors of Gestapo offices or their deputies must communicate by telephone with their regional party directorates – Gauleitung or Kreisleitung – and arrange a conference with them to discuss and agree upon the implementation of the demonstrations. The proper inspector or commander of the local police is to be called in. In the course of the meeting the political leaders are to be notified that the German police have received the following instructions from the Reichsführer-SS and Chief of Police and that measures taken by the political agencies are to be taken in accordance with them:
   (a) Only such measures are to be taken which will not endanger German lives or property (e.g., the burning of synagogues only to be carried out if there is no danger of the fire spreading to the surrounding district).
   (b) Businesses and residences of Jews may be destroyed but not looted. The police have been directed to supervise the execution of this order and to arrest looters.

(c) Particular care is to be paid in business streets that non-Jewish businesses are to be protected from damage under all circumstances.

(d) Foreign subjects are not to be molested – even if they are Jews.

2. Assuming that the directives given under No 1 are complied with, the demonstrations are not to be prevented by the police, but only watched to see that the directives are adhered to.

3. Immediately upon receipt of this teleprint, the police are to seize all archives from all synagogues and Jewish community organisations, to prevent them from destruction in the course of the demonstrations. This refers to material of historical importance, not to recent taxation lists, etc. The archives are to be handed over to the competent SD offices.

4. The direction of all Security Police measures with regard to the demonstrations against the Jews is in the hands of the Gestapo, insofar as the inspectors of the Security Police do not issue orders. Officials of the Criminal Police as well as members of the SD, the Special Task Units and the General SS may be brought in for carrying out the Security Police measures.

5. As soon as the events of the night make it feasible for the officials concerned, they are to arrest as many Jews – especially wealthy ones – in all districts *as can be accommodated in existing cells*. For the time being, only healthy male Jews of not too advanced age are to be arrested. After the arrests have been carried out, concentration camps in the region are to be contacted immediately, to make arrangements for the transfer of the Jews to the camps as quickly as possible. Particular care must be taken that Jews arrested on the basis of this directive are not mistreated.

6. The contents of this order are to be forwarded to the competent inspectors and commanders of the Regular Police as well as to SD district and sub-district HQs with the statement that the Reichsführer-SS and Chief of German Police has ordered these police measures. The Chief of the Regular Police has issued corresponding instructions to the Regular Police, including the Fire Fighting Police. The closest co-operation between the Security Police and the Regular Police must be maintained in carrying out the measures ordered.

Receipt of this teleprint is to be confirmed by the directors of the Gestapo or their deputies by teleprint to Gestapo Head Office for the attention of Standartenführer Müller.

Signed: Heydrich, SS-Gruppenführer[10]

All night the messages flashed to and fro to the SA, the SS, SD, Gestapo, Criminal Police, Security Police, Regular Police, party offices, all the complex components needed to keep the totalitarian machine running. The aim was clear: the Nazi state did not want the Jews, but it did want their remaining wealth. While the Jews were to be forced out, their businesses and property were to be preserved as intact as possible, ready for seizure. At 2.16 a.m., the Chief of the Security Police in Munich sent an urgent signal to Gestapo offices in Augsburg, Nuremberg and Würzburg:

Plain clothes agents of the Gestapo and Criminal Police are to move around in the demonstrations and are to prevent the permissible destruction of Jewish stores and apartments from leading to looting. They will remain with the groups of demonstrators and at the end of the demonstrations the uniformed Regular Police are to seal and secure the destroyed stores and apartments. Furthermore, in all police districts only existing places of detention are to be occupied by prisoners.[11]

Forty minutes later, Rudolf Hess joined in with an order to all Gauleiters stating that: 'On explicit orders from the very highest level, there is to be no arson against Jewish businesses or the like, whatsoever, under any circumstances.' Synagogues and Jewish community centres, it seemed, were to be burned to the ground wherever possible, but business premises and homes were to remain standing. However, while the police and the SD were under specific instructions on what they could or could not do, the SA were given no such orders. They were under the impression that they had a completely free hand, and acted accordingly.

The terror began in the early hours of 10 November, and spread rapidly throughout the length and breadth of Germany as party thugs, backed by ordinary Germans, went on the rampage. Otto Tolischus, for the *New York Times*, described it as a wave of destruction unparalleled in Germany since the Thirty Years War. The Berlin correspondent of the London *Daily Telegraph*, Hugh Carleton Greene, reported later in the day:

Mob law ruled in Berlin . . . and hordes of hooligans indulged in an orgy of destruction. I have seen several anti-Jewish outbreaks in Germany during the last five years, but never anything as nauseating as this. Racial hatred and hysteria seemed to have taken complete hold of otherwise decent people. I saw fashionably-dressed women clapping their hands and screaming with glee, while respectable, middle-class mothers held up their babies to see the 'fun'.

The 'fun' involved more than the wrecking of a few shops. During the twenty-four hours of Germany's first organised pogrom since the

Middle Ages, at least 7,500 stores, twenty-nine warehouses and 171 houses were destroyed; 191 synagogues were razed by fire and a further seventy-six physically demolished; eleven Jewish community centres, cemetery chapels and similar buildings were torched and another three gutted; at least 30,000 Jewish men were arrested and thrown into concentration camps, where they were subjected to indescribably sadistic torture. Seven Aryans and three foreigners were also arrested, 'for their own protection'.[12]

Heydrich reported to Göring on 11 November that the death toll was thirty-six, with the same number severely injured – all of them Jews. Not surprisingly, these figures had to be revised: by January 1939 it was admitted that the number killed during those twenty-four hours was officially put at ninety-one.[13] The true figure was at least 236, among them forty-three women and thirteen children, with more than 600 permanently maimed. Hundreds more, probably as many as 2,500, died appalling deaths in concentration camps during the following months.

As the violence finally exhausted itself, Goebbels called a halt with an official decree, and issued a statement to the world. The outrages, he said, were 'the justified and comprehensible indignation of the German people at the cowardly assassination of a German diplomat'. He denied that there had been any plundering or looting: 'In a few isolated cases, perhaps, old women made off with small trinkets or pieces of wearing apparel, to be used as Christmas presents. There was no robbery, or intention to rob.'[14]

Göring added his own touch of fantasy: 'No Jew had a hair of his head touched,' he claimed. 'Thanks to the outstanding discipline of the German people, only a few windows were broken in the riots.' Echoing the cynicism of their chieftains, the rank-and-file Nazis swiftly found a label for their night of vengeance. Mocking and belittling the terrible events that had taken place, they called it *Kristallnacht*, Crystal Night, the night of broken glass.

Göring had not been involved in the arrangements for the pogrom. He had been in Munich for the memorial march and dinner, but had avoided the reception, preferring to spend his time dealing with other business. By the time Goebbels was talking to Hitler, he was in his private train, heading back overnight to Berlin, unaware of what was being planned. As his train drew into the Anhalter Station the following morning, the conductor told him that he had seen fires blazing in Halle, some 130 kilometres south-east of the capital when they had passed through. Half an hour later, when he was dressed, he called his adjutant, who reported that there had apparently been riots during the night, that Jewish stores had been broken into and plundered and synagogues set on fire. Driving home through the streets, the extent of the damage quickly became clear, and Göring's temper began to flare. As soon as he arrived, he had a call put through to Gestapo headquarters and demanded a full report.

By the time he spoke to Hitler later in the morning, Göring was steaming. He had established Goebbels's part in the affair, and complained bitterly that the Propaganda Minister was sabotaging his efforts to prepare the economy for war. It was impossible, he told the Führer, for him to have such events taking place at such a time. He had been making speeches asking for 'every old toothpaste tube, every rusty nail, every bit of scrap material to be collected and utilised'. It was intolerable, he said, that 'a man who was not responsible for these things should upset my economic tasks by destroying so many things of economic value on the one hand and by causing so much disturbance in economic life on the other hand'.

Hitler, Göring testified at Nuremberg, 'made some excuses for Goebbels, but on the whole he agreed that such events were not to take place and must not be allowed to take place. I also pointed out to him, that in such a short time after the Munich agreement such matters would also have an effect on foreign policy.' Having unburdened himself to Hitler, Göring phoned Goebbels to give him a piece of his mind. He told him, he said, 'in unmistakable terms and in very sharp words, my view of the matter. I told him, with emphasis, that I was not inclined to suffer the consequences of his uncontrolled utterances, as far as economic matters were concerned.'[15]

Goebbels was totally unabashed by Göring's attack, just as he was by the criticisms that rained down on him from other ministers, notably Funk and Ribbentrop, who complained to Fritz Hesse, the Press Attaché in the London embassy: 'As for that little beast Goebbels, have you heard what his gangs have done everywhere? Those imbeciles have smashed up Jewish shops – which have long been Aryan property anyhow. They've spoiled my game for me. Yes, Goebbels smashes the windows, and I have to mend the foreign situation.'[16]

Over lunch with Hitler at the Ostaria Bavaria in Munich on 10 November, Goebbels defended his actions, insisting that the pogrom had shown international Jewry that the Reich was not to be trifled with, and Hitler was swayed by his arguments – he had, after all, given Goebbels his permission in Munich to let the SA loose. So when Göring spoke to Hitler on the telephone that afternoon, he found he had changed his attitude, and was now determined to introduce tough new economic measures against the Jews, waving aside his protests by telling him, perhaps only half joking, 'You had better be careful. People might get to know of your sympathy for the Jews.' Goebbels then joined the conversation, and at once started what Göring described as 'his usual talk: that such things [Rath's murder] could not be tolerated; that this was the second or third murder of a National Socialist committed abroad by a Jew'.

According to Göring, it was Goebbels who suggested imposing a fine – not on the rioters or the SA but on their victims, the Jews. He wanted this to be collected by each Gau, and 'named an almost incredibly high sum'. The two ministers argued, not about whether it was right to impose such a fine, but about who should collect it. Goebbels, as Gauleiter of Berlin, which had vastly more Jews than anywhere else, obviously stood to gain enormously from local fines. Göring, being responsible for the national economy as a whole, insisted that only the sovereign state had the right to take such measures.

Hitler finally resolved the squabble in Göring's favour, agreeing that such a fine was a matter for the national government. As for the amount, they settled on a nice round sum: one billion marks – at that time worth some US$400 million, or £85 million, the equivalent, at the beginning of the twenty-first century, of about US$4 billion or £2.6 billion. This massive payment, which became known as the Jewish Atonement Fine, represented about one fifth of all Jewish holdings, as registered under Göring's decree of 27 April. It came not a moment too soon, for the Reich Exchequer was in a critical condition: Göring's massive armaments drive had brought the country to the very brink of bankruptcy.

But Hitler was still not finished with the Jews. It was time, he told Göring, for what he described as 'the economic solution' to be carried through – in other words, for the Jews to be finally eliminated from the economic life of Germany. 'In order that there should be no further occasion for such events,' he continued, 'businesses obviously Jewish and known to be Jewish were first of all to be Aryanised.' This applied particularly, he said, to department stores, which were often a source of friction, since officials and staff of the ministries, who could only shop between the hours of 6 and 7 p.m., often used these stores 'and had difficulties'. After outlining what he wanted done, he ordered that a commission be set up at once to deal with it. To Göring's displeasure, he insisted that Goebbels should be a member, although, as Göring maintained, Goebbels 'had nothing to do with economic matters'.[17] Presumably, Hitler was afraid that Göring might be too soft on the Jews if left to his own devices.

Göring called a conference of all the ministries involved in the proposed commission at the Air Ministry the next day, Saturday, 12 November, at 10 a.m. It was a high-powered meeting: Goebbels brought along several subordinates from the Propaganda Ministry; Heydrich represented the SS, SD, Security Police and Gestapo, Daluege the Regular Police; the Foreign Ministry was represented by Ernst Woermann, head of the Political Department. Others present included Frick, Funk, Finance Minister Count Lutz Schwerin von Krosigk, Austrian Finance Minister Dr Hans Fishböck, and several other senior figures. All told, with aides and officials, there were around a hundred people present. As with all Göring's meetings, a stenographer took down every word for the record, much of which survived the war to be used as evidence at Nuremberg. It makes macabre reading.

Göring started by establishing that he was acting on Hitler's authority. 'I have received a letter,' he told the delegates, 'written on the Führer's instructions by Bormann, the Chief of Staff of the Führer's Deputy, asking that the Jewish question should now be co-ordinated and settled once and for all, one way or another. Yesterday, in a telephone call, the Führer reiterated that I was to co-ordinate the decisive steps.' Lambasting those responsible for the *Kristallnacht* pogrom, he complained that he had had enough of demonstrations that led nowhere:

They don't harm the Jews – they harm me, since I am the final authority for holding the economy together. If a Jewish shop is destroyed today, if the goods are thrown into the street, then the insurance makes good the damage to the Jew – he doesn't suffer at all. And furthermore, the goods that are destroyed are consumer goods, the people's goods!

In the future, if we consider it necessary for demonstrations to take place, I beg you to see to it that they are directed so as not to wound us, ourselves. Because it is insane to clear out and burn a Jewish warehouse and then have a German insurance company cover the damage – and the goods which I desperately need – whole bales of clothing and I don't know what else, are burned, while I need them everywhere. I might as well burn the raw materials before they arrive . . . I am not going to tolerate a situation in which German insurance companies are the ones to suffer. To prevent this, I will use my authority to issue a decree . . . But another problem immediately emerges: it may be that these insurance companies have reinsured in foreign countries. In those cases, I would not want to lose the foreign exchange they bring in. The matter must be looked into. For this reason, I have asked Herr Hilgard from the insurance companies to attend, to give us the best advice on the extent to which the companies are covered against such damages by reinsurance. I would not like to give this up under any circumstances.[18]

Stressing once again that the purpose of the meeting was not just to talk but to take decisions, Göring turned to the mechanics of grabbing Jewish businesses. Owners of larger businesses would be compensated at a valuation fixed by the state with 3 per cent government bonds. For smaller factories, only those he felt he needed would be handed over on those terms, while the rest would simply be shut down. Premises that could not be converted to another use would be demolished. The Foreign Ministry claimed the right to represent foreign Jews with holdings in Germany – Ribbentrop, who had been a successful businessman himself, clearly did not intend to miss an opportunity to enrich either himself or his ministry.

Characteristically, Göring also had his eye on works of art, jewellery, real estate and shares held by Jews. The question of exactly how their owners could be relieved of these desirable goodies should, he decided, be examined by a sub-committee under the chairmanship of Funk. Another, more sinister question that was also referred to a sub-committee was the idea of using the dispossessed Jews as a source of forced labour.

Goebbels was concerned with what was to be done with the sites of the burnt-down synagogues. Some towns might want to turn the sites into parking lots, he said, others might wish to erect new buildings. In any case, it was time for all synagogues to be dissolved. The Jews themselves, he proposed, should be made to pay for levelling and clearing the sites. Warming to his theme, he threatened to hijack the conference with a stream of proposals. 'I consider it necessary,' he announced, 'to issue a decree forbidding Jews from going to German theatres, cinemas and circuses. I have already prepared a decree, by the authority of the Reich Chamber of Culture . . . I am of the opinion that it is not possible for Jews to sit next to Germans in music halls, theatres and cinemas.

'Furthermore,' he continued, 'I advocate that Jews be banned from all public places where they might cause provocation. It is still possible for a Jew to share a sleeping car with a German. Therefore, the Reich Ministry of Transport must issue a decree ordering that there shall be separate compartments for Jews. If this compartment is full, then the Jews cannot claim a seat. They can only be given separate compartments after all Germans have seats. They must not mix with the Germans: if there is no more room, they will have to stand in the corridor.'

'I think it would be more sensible to give them separate compartments,' Göring interposed, irritated that Goebbels was shifting the subject away from the economy, and hoping to cut him off. But Goebbels refused to let go.

'Not if the train is overcrowded,' he replied.

'Just a moment,' Göring snapped. 'There will be only one Jewish coach. If that is filled up, the Jews will have to stay at home.'

'But supposing there are not many Jews going, let us say, on the long-distance express train to Munich. Suppose there are two Jews on the train and the other compartments are overcrowded. These two Jews would have a compartment to themselves. Therefore the decree must state that Jews may claim a seat only after all Germans have secured theirs.'

'I would give the Jews one coach or compartment,' Göring repeated, 'and if a case such as the one you mentioned should arise, and the train is overcrowded, then believe me, we won't need a law! He will be kicked out and he'll have to sit on his own in the toilet all the way.'

In front of all the assembled ministers, the two Nazi leaders went on squabbling like a couple of schoolboys.

'The Jews should stand in the corridor!' Goebbels shouted.

'They should sit in the toilet!'

Goebbels kept harping on, still not satisfied. Summoning up his authority as chairman, Göring thundered: 'I don't need a law. He can either sit in the toilet or leave the train!'

'I don't agree,' Goebbels grumbled. 'I don't believe in this. There ought to be a law! There ought to be a law banning Jews from beaches and resorts, too. Last summer . . .'

'Above all, here in the Admiralspalast [a Berlin musical theatre], there were really revolting things,' Göring interposed with heavy irony.

'And in Wannseebad [the bathing lido on the Havel],' Goebbels continued, impervious. 'A law – that Jews are absolutely banned from all German places of recreation.'

'We could give them their own,' Göring suggested.

'We will have to consider whether we should give them their own resorts, or place some German bathing places at their disposal – but not the best, or people might say "You are allowing the Jews to get fit by using our bathing resorts."'

There was no stopping Goebbels now, and for the moment all thoughts of economic matters were set aside as he ranted on. 'The question must also be considered whether it is necessary to ban the Jews from German forests. Herds of Jews are today running around in the Grünewald [a wooded area in west Berlin]. That is a constant provocation – we shall have constant incidents. What the Jews do is so provocative that it constantly comes to blows.'

'Well then,' Göring responded sarcastically, 'we shall have to give the Jews a certain part of the forest, and rangers will see that the various animals which are damnably like the Jews – the elk has a hooked nose, too – go into the Jewish enclosure and settle down among them.'

Stung by Göring's tone, Goebbels snapped back at him, saying he found his attitude provocative. 'What is more,' he went on, 'the Jews must not sit in German public parks. I am starting a whispering campaign about Jewish women in the gardens at Fehrbelliner Platz. There are Jews who don't look so Jewish. They sit down alongside German mothers and start to moan and grouse.' Jews would have to be banned from most parks, he insisted, but could have certain parks and gardens – 'not the prettiest, of course' – set aside for them. In others, there would be special benches where they were allowed to sit.

Finally, Goebbels turned to the question of schools. It was, of course, intolerable to him that Jewish children should be allowed to attend German schools and sit next to German children. He proposed putting an end to this situation by expelling all Jewish children, and decreeing that they should only attend their own, special Jewish schools. Segregation could never be too complete for Goebbels.

Göring finally put an end to Goebbels's diatribe by calling in Eduard Hilgard, head of the Insurance Companies' Association, to discuss the question of insurance. One of the biggest problems, it turned out, was that most of the property that had been damaged was only rented by Jews from Aryan landlords, who were responsible for buildings insurance. The replacement of all the broken glass that had given the pogrom its name would cost the insurance companies six million marks. But that was not the worst news for Göring: plate glass was only manufactured in Belgium, the quantity needed would take at least six months to produce, and it would have to be paid for in foreign currency.

Looting was another major headache for the insurers. Hilgard estimated the total cost of compensation at around 25 million marks – the stock of the Margraf jewellery store on Unter den Linden alone, which had been completely ransacked, was insured for 1,700,000 marks, he said. This hit a nerve with Göring, and he turned furiously to the police chiefs. 'Daluege and Heydrich,' he shouted, 'you must get me that jewellery back! Stage large-scale raids!'

'The order has already been given,' Daluege assured him. 'People are being searched and places raided all the time. According to my reports, 150 people were arrested yesterday afternoon.'

Heydrich added that there had been around 800 reported cases of looting throughout the Reich, but already over 100 culprits had been arrested. 'We are trying to get the loot back,' he said.

'And the jewels?' Göring demanded greedily.

'That's hard to say,' Heydrich replied. 'Some of the articles were thrown into the street and picked up. The same thing happened with the furriers. In the Friedrichstrasse, for instance, in Police District C, the crowd naturally rushed to pick up mink and skunk furs, and so on. It will be very difficult to recover them. Even children filled their pockets just for the fun of the thing.'

'The party should issue an order,' Daluege suggested, 'to the effect that the police must be notified immediately if a neighbour's wife – everybody knows his neighbour very well – has a fur coat remodelled or if someone is seen wearing a new ring or bracelet. We should like the party to assist in this matter.'

One bright spot for Göring was the hope that he could gain foreign currency from any reinsurance made abroad. When Hilgard tried to insist that the insurance companies must honour their obligations and pay out for the sake of their international reputation, Göring said that he would take care of that by issuing a government decree forbidding them from doing so. Heydrich came up with an answer: 'By all means let them pay the claims,' he interjected. 'But as soon as payment is made it will be confiscated. That way we will save face.' It was an ingenious idea, but Göring had an even better one. The insurance companies would pay out in full, not to the Jews, but directly to the Ministry of Finance.

Göring was unmoved by Hilgard's pleas that this would wipe out the whole year's profits for the insurance companies, and that many smaller ones would go bankrupt. But when Heydrich told him the state stood to lose more than 100 million marks in taxes on the materials and goods damaged or lost in the program, his temper began to rise again. And when Daluege pointed out that most of those goods were not the property of the Jewish shopkeepers but of Aryan suppliers, on consignment, and Hilgard said the insurers would have to pay for these, too, he blew up.

'I wish you'd killed 200 Jews instead of destroying such valuables!' he cried.

'Well, there were thirty-five killed,' Heydrich responded, as though this were a defence.

The prospect of being able to hold on to the payments, however, was clearly enough to pacify Göring. The process was completed for him, after a brief discussion of the foreign exchange question, by yet another bright thought: any of the jewels stolen from Margraf and other stores that were recovered by the police would not be returned, but handed over to the state. Not even Hilgard's insistent return to the profits that were to be lost could ruffle his good humour now.

'The Jew must report the damage,' he told him. 'He will get the insurance money, but it will be confiscated. The final result will be that the insurance companies will gain something, since not all the damage will have to be made good. Hilgard, you can afford to smile to yourself.'

'I have no reason to,' the insurance man replied, understandably bitter, 'if you describe the fact that we shall not have to pay for all the damage as making money.'

'Wait a minute,' Göring told him, thoroughly enjoying himself by now. 'If you are legally bound to pay five million, and suddenly an angel in my somewhat corpulent form appears before you and tells you you can keep one million, by thunder, isn't that making money? I wouldn't mind making a straight split with you, or whatever you call it. I only have to look at you – your whole body is smiling. You are getting a big rake-off!'

After dismissing Hilgard, Göring turned his attention to the remaining business of the meeting. The Foreign Ministry was concerned about foreign Jews in Germany, particularly those with American and British nationality, who had to be handled with care, and Polish Jews, who did not. Hitler, Göring said, was not happy that 'every dirty Polish Jew' had a legal position in Germany 'and we have to put up with it'. That, he said, had to stop. Hitler wanted to say to the Poles, 'You are doing things against your Jews in Poland, but the minute a Yid leaves Poland and arrives here, we have to treat him like a Pole. I'd like to have that reversed a little.'

Funk was concerned as to whether Jewish shops should be allowed to reopen. Fishböck, the Austrian Finance Minister, proudly reported that in Austria they already had a very complete plan. In Vienna, he said, there were 12,000 Jewish workshops and 5,000 Jewish retail shops. Even before the *Anschluss*, the Austrian Nazis had drawn up plans to close down 10,000 of the workshops and 4,000 of the retail stores, and to Aryanise the remaining 3,000 businesses. All they were waiting for was a law empowering them to withdraw business licences from whomever they chose, irrespective of the Jewish question.

'I shall have this decree issued today,' Göring promised. He was delighted to hear that the whole affair in Vienna, 'one of the Jewish capitals, so to speak', would be wound up by Christmas or the end of the year, which was wonderful.

Funk, eager not to be left out of the self-congratulations, said they could do the same thing in the old Reich: 'I have already prepared a law elaborating it. Effective 1 January 1939, Jews will be prohibited from running retail stores and wholesale establishments, as well as independent workshops. They will be further prohibited from keeping employees, or offering any ready-made products on the market, and from advertising or receiving orders. Where a Jewish store is open, the police shall close it down.' From the New Year, he went on to say, no Jew could be the head of an enterprise or hold a leading position, or be a member of a corporation. 'The competent ministers of the Reich,' he announced, 'are being authorised to issue the necessary provisions for execution of this law.'

'I believe we can agree with this law,' Göring declared. There was a great shout of 'Yes, indeed!'

Heydrich followed up by proudly reminding everyone that by setting up Eichmann's Central Office for Jewish Emigration in Vienna, he had been able to get rid of at least 50,000 Jews from Austria, while at the same time in the old Reich only 19,000 had been driven out. Göring was worried that there should be no repetition of the recent situation when thousands of Polish Jews were trapped between frontiers, but

Heydrich reassured him that at least 45,000 Jews had left the country by legal means. 'Through the Jewish societies,' he explained, 'we extracted a certain amount of money from the rich Jews who wanted to emigrate. By paying this amount plus an additional sum in foreign currency, this made it possible for a number of poor Jews to leave. The problem was not making the rich Jews leave, but getting rid of the Jewish mob.'

He warned that it would not be possible to maintain that level of emigration, and that it would take between eight and ten years to get rid of the remaining Jews, who in the meantime would be unemployed. If they were isolated, by wearing a badge or living in ghettos, they would be able to work for each other, in certain specified professions, as doctors, lawyers, hairdressers and so on. These ideas were enthusiastically received and discussed, but were shelved for the time being, though soon afterwards Jews would be forced to move out of Aryan tenement blocks and congregate in specified areas of the cities.

To round the meeting off, Göring came to the question of the Jewish Atonement Fine. 'How would you feel, gentlemen,' he asked, 'if I were to announce today that a fine of one billion marks is to be imposed on the Jews as their contribution?' Inevitably, the idea was received with enormous enthusiasm. Gratified, he declared: 'I shall decide on the wording – that German Jewry as a whole shall, as a punishment for the abominable crimes, etc, etc, make a contribution of one billion marks. That will do the trick! The swine won't be in a hurry to commit a second murder. For the rest, I must say, I would not like to be a Jew in Germany right now.'

The meeting broke up, in a mood of great satisfaction at 2.30 p.m. That same day, Göring issued his first three decrees: imposing the billion-mark fine, eliminating all Jews from the German economy by 1 January 1939, and laying down that Jewish property owners and tenants would have to make good the damage to their businesses and homes immediately and pay the costs themselves. In order to avoid any possible complications, he had one other decree up his sleeve, which he instructed the Justice Ministry to issue: all Jews of German nationality were barred from starting any legal proceedings in German courts over any matters arising from the events of the pogrom.

Goebbels followed with his decree banning Jews from theatres, concert halls, motion picture houses and exhibitions throughout Germany. And to round off the day's work, the meeting of ministers issued a statement promising 'further decisive measures to exclude

Jewry from German economic life and to prevent provocative activities', in the near future.

Goebbels had hoped that the *Kristallnacht* pogrom would restore his
position with Hitler; in fact, it almost finished him as the other ministers, scenting the blood of a rival whom they all resented, pounced on
him in a concerted attack. Polish Ambassador Lipski told the League
of Nations Commissioner in Danzig, Carl Burckhardt, that he had
heard 'from an eye-witness source' that 'a spontaneous anti-Goebbels
movement had taken place in the Reich Cabinet', and that 'the immediate dismissal of the Propaganda Minister had been demanded'.[19] The
demands were led by Himmler, who was furious that things had been
allowed to get so out of hand, tainting his sacred SS by involving it
in a mindless assault that was completely at odds with his own coldly
logical approach to the Jewish problem. As Heydrich had laid down
as early as 1934: 'The methods of "rowdy anti-Semitism" are to be
rejected. One does not fight rats with a revolver, but rather with poison
and gas.'[20] His approval for an action against the Jews had been on
the understanding that the conditions he had laid down through
Heydrich would be strictly adhered to, and that everything would be
done in an orderly fashion. Instead, there had been uncontrolled
disorder, which to him was total anathema.

Himmler asked Burckhardt to call on him at Prinz-Albrecht-Strasse
on 14 November, presumably to explain to him, and through him the
League of Nations, that the mob violence against the Jews was not
official German policy and that there would be no repetition of it either
in Germany or Danzig. But when Burckhardt arrived he was told the
Reichsführer-SS was ill as a result of the strain of the last few weeks.
He was seen instead by Wolff, who told him that Himmler condemned
the pogrom, and then began shouting angrily: 'The internal situation
in this country has become intolerable! Something must be done.
Goebbels is responsible for it all; his influence on the Führer is catastrophic. We had hoped to bring him down on the pretext of his propaganda during the Czech crisis and this time we definitely thought we
were sure of success. But once more the Führer has saved him. This
cannot continue; we shall have to act.'[21]

The Führer had indeed saved Goebbels. That morning he had called
on him and reassured him that he still had his complete confidence.
And in the evening he made a public display of his continued friend-

ship by going to the theatre with him. With Goebbels so clearly enjoying Hitler's protection, there was nothing Himmler or Göring could do. But to avoid any more internecine battles, Hitler banned Goebbels from any involvement in the Jewish question. Following his usual habit of playing his lieutenants off against each other, he decreed that Göring should 'concentrate the decisive steps under one central authority'. In future, Göring would be solely responsible for overseeing and co-ordinating all anti-Jewish policy and actions, a major addition to his already overstretched portfolio.

Göring took the first decisive step in his new role on 24 January 1939, when he ordered Heydrich to set up a Reich Central Office for Jewish Emigration in Berlin, based on the office he had set up in Vienna under Adolf Eichmann the previous year. Heinrich Müller of the Gestapo was put in charge, and wasted no time in getting things moving. Representatives of the Jewish community were forced to provide lists of seventy Jewish families a day who were prepared to emigrate. By the end of the year, they would have moved out 78,000 German and Austrian Jews, plus 38,000 Czech Jews. But by that time, the problem would have assumed a wholly new proportion.

XXII

'I'LL COOK THEM A STEW THAT THEY'LL CHOKE ON'

BY the beginning of 1939, Göring, Goebbels and Himmler were all showing signs of severe stress. For Goebbels personally, the last few weeks of 1938 had been horrendous. Rumours of his imminent fall from grace proliferated, despite Hitler's effort to camouflage the true situation by choosing to stay at Schwanenwerder for a couple of days in mid November, while Speer's builders made his living quarters in the Reich Chancellery temporarily uninhabitable. To make sure everyone got the message, Hitler called Göring, Keitel and Brauchitsch to the lakeside villa for meetings, as though there was nothing amiss. In reality, however, Goebbels's future was still uncertain as Magda stubbornly continued to refuse a reconciliation.

By mid December, the emotional strain was showing itself in physical symptoms, and Goebbels was admitted to the Charité Hospital suffering from unbearable stomach pains. The eminent Professor Sauerbruch was summoned from Dresden, and wanted to operate immediately – presumably on the assumption that Goebbels had a stomach ulcer – but Goebbels refused, 'for the moment', and the enforced bed rest seemed to do the trick. While he was in hospital, Magda had another meeting with Hitler. She did not tell Goebbels what had been said, but from the 'flood of reproaches' she rained down on him in his hospital bed she must have learned of the many complaints of sexual harassment collected by Himmler. When, after five days, he had recovered enough to go home to Schwanenwerder, she would not have him in the villa, and he was forced to spend a miserable Christmas and New Year on his own in the guest house, still far from well and spending most of his time in bed. The children visited him briefly, as did his mother and sister, but not Magda. His only outside visitors were Helldorf, who called twice, and Hanke, who came to report on 'an infamous attack that Speer is planning in the press against Lippert [the Lord Mayor of Berlin]. I make no secret of my feelings. That's right: too cowardly to attack him openly, so he stabs him in the back. Very nice! Nobody can get away with that sort of thing with me.'[1]

The meeting with Hanke was, Goebbels said, 'a frosty affair'. Apart from being his State Secretary, Hanke had been his closest confidant ever since he arrived in Berlin, and when the row with Magda first erupted Goebbels had asked him to act as go-between with her. Hanke's sympathy for Magda had deepened rapidly into love, and he had agreed to gather evidence for her to use in obtaining a divorce. It is hardly surprising that his relationship with Goebbels should have suffered, and that his reports had grown steadily cooler. But Goebbels did not appear to suspect the truth, believing that Hanke simply disapproved of his infidelities.

In the depths of his depression, Goebbels was relieved to receive a Christmas present of two books from Hitler, 'with very loving dedications', and a 'long, touching letter' for the New Year. He replied at once, setting out his situation 'very honestly', and dispatched Hanke of all people to deliver his letter personally to the Obersalzberg. Hitler solicitously invited him to join him at the Berghof, where he spent the next twelve days reading, talking, visiting the theatres in Salzburg, and discussing what he could do to save his marriage. Hitler told him he must clear up the situation soon, and promised to do all he could to help. But Magda kept finding new 'suspicions', and Goebbels had to confess that only time would tell if there was a way out.[2]

He returned to Berlin on the overnight train on 17/18 January, 'filled with burning anxiety'. The sun was shining when he arrived and everything seemed bright and cheerful, but, he said, for him 'there was only grief and bitterness'. Later, however, after another talk with Hitler, he sent his sister, Maria, to speak to Magda, who agreed to a meeting at Schwanenwerder the next day, where they finally managed to find themselves 'halfway in agreement'.[3] From there, things moved swiftly, with Hitler's encouragement. Magda had a lawyer draw up a marital contract, Goebbels accepted her terms without argument, Hitler made a few suggestions for improvements, and on 22 January, 'in a bleak mood', they signed. 'A new section of life begins,' Goebbels noted in his diary. 'I am still stunned by it all.'[4]

* * *

Himmler was another victim of stomach cramps, so severe that they almost knocked him out. The cramps were nothing new – he had been having them for years, together with blinding headaches – but they were worse now than they had ever been, and sometimes lasted for days without relief. They were not helped by his fear that they might be symptoms of the stomach cancer that had killed his father. Karl Wolff was seriously concerned for his chief, and suggested he consult Felix Kersten, a Swedish chiropractor based in Holland who was then enjoying great success in Berlin's high society.

Himmler now had a splendid villa close to Ribbentrop's in the fashionable Berlin district of Dahlem. Kersten visited him there, having first been sworn to secrecy to avoid unwelcome hints leaking out that the Reichsführer-SS was anything less than a perfect physical specimen, and was able to bring him almost instant relief. Himmler was so pleased he tried to persuade him to join his staff, to be on permanent call as his personal attendant. Kersten declined, but continued to visit him regularly until Holland was occupied during the war, when he finally agreed to devote himself exclusively to the Reichsführer. Kersten has been described as Himmler's masseur, and massage was certainly part of his technique, but in fact he practised a form of alternative medicine that perfectly suited Himmler's cranky beliefs. Their sessions together became his equivalent of psychoanalysis, when he could relax and speak his mind freely, secure in the knowledge that his confidences would be honoured in a doctor–patient relationship.

Himmler was helped by Kersten's treatment but he was clearly in need of a break. Not long after *Kristallnacht*, he took a long holiday in Italy, leaving Heydrich to deal with the aftermath of the pogrom and the establishment of the Gestapo and the SD in the Sudetenland. But he did not appoint Heydrich or anyone else to exercise overall control of the SS in his absence. That would have been far too risky.

Göring was also sick at the start of 1939, suffering from a recurrence of his glandular problems, general exhaustion, and depression. He spent more and more time away from his office, at Carinhall or Romintern, but for once his hunting and shooting trips failed to raise his flagging spirits. Although he had scored notable successes in securing the Sudetenland and in turning the disaster of *Kristallnacht* to economic advantage, he was still out of favour with Hitler and this weighed heavily on him.

On Hitler's instructions, he had convened a meeting on 18 November of the Reich Defence Council, or more properly the Ministerial Council for the Defence of the Reich, a super-committee under his chairmanship consisting of every minister and state secretary, plus Martin Bormann, Hess's deputy, on behalf of the party organisation, Himmler, Heydrich, the commanders-in-chief and their chiefs of staff. He had treated them to a three-hour speech setting out the need for a tripling of overall armaments, and warning them of the problems of achieving this with shortages of labour and raw materials, production capacity, and foreign currency. But the biggest problem of all was simply money. 'Gentlemen,' he told them gravely, 'the financial situation looks very critical.'[5]

Göring was not alone in worrying about the country's finances, and the inflationary consequences of filling the wage packets of the workers through the massive rearmament programme while at the same time choking off the supply of consumer goods. Early in the New Year, Schacht sent Hitler a memorandum signed by himself and all eight directors of the Reichsbank warning of the 'threatening danger of inflation' and calling for a reduction in spending. Hitler's response was to declare 'That is mutiny'. He sacked Schacht on the spot and replaced him as President of the Reichsbank with Walther Funk. Faced with such a reaction, there was no way Göring was going to put his own head on the block by telling Hitler of his concern and urging caution. He would simply have to go on living with his worries.

Ribbentrop played on Hitler's frustration at being denied the whole of Czecho-Slovakia, with its healthy gold and currency reserves that would have eased Germany's financial crisis, and persuaded him that Göring was to blame. Consequently, when Hitler invited the Polish Foreign Minister, Colonel Beck, to call on him at the Berghof on his way home after spending Christmas and the New Year in Monte Carlo, he asked Ribbentrop to join him and ignored Göring. On the face of it, the Foreign Minister was the proper and normal person to deal with his Polish opposite number. But Göring had worked so hard for so long at establishing a special relationship with the Polish leadership that cutting him out completely could only be seen as a calculated slight, which he felt deeply. It was also a grave mistake for which Germany, and the world, would pay dearly.

Hitler had invited Beck in order to broach the subject of Danzig and the Polish Corridor. This was an extremely delicate issue: the ancient port of Danzig, Gdansk to the Poles, at the mouth of the Vistula, had been Polish from 1466 until the second partition of Poland in 1793, but from then until 1919, when Poland was restored as an independent nation, it had been incorporated into East Prussia. Under the Versailles Treaty it had been turned into a free city under the sovereignty of the League of Nations, but effectively under Polish control. Together with the rest of East Prussia, it was separated from Germany proper by the so-called Polish Corridor, that strip of land extending north from Posen and West Prussia to provide Poland with her only access to the Baltic Sea. The return of Danzig, along with the other German port of Memel on the opposite side of East Prussia, was the next step in Hitler's progressive dismantling of Versailles. To go with it, he wanted a road or rail link across the Corridor, to provide Germany with access by land to Danzig and East Prussia.

The inhabitants of Danzig were overwhelmingly German, and their separation from the Reich was a running sore for all German nationalists. But Danzig was a highly emotive issue for the Poles, too, inextricably bound up with their pride as a newly-resurrected nation, and Beck insisted that public opinion in his country simply would not allow him to hand the city back to Germany. When Hitler tried to charm him into agreeing, he promised to reflect on the question, but would go no further. Ribbentrop accompanied him back to his hotel, and badgered him for several hours in his inimitable style, but for once he had met his match, as Beck stonewalled solidly and refused to give an inch. He did, however, agree to Ribbentrop's paying an official visit to Warsaw on 25 January, to commemorate the fifth anniversary of the 1934 non-aggression pact between the two countries, and Ribbentrop was able to present this as a sign of progress and of his personal success.

Ribbentrop was riding high now. Having already persuaded Hitler that he had been right in warning him that the Munich agreement would be a disaster, he had scored another success on 6 December, by signing a Declaration of Peace and Friendship with France, during an official visit to Paris which he had sprung on the French at the last minute, demanding that his reception must surpass that given to the King and Queen of Britain during their state visit the previous July. He claimed later that Bonnet had told him that France now accepted that Eastern Europe was a German sphere of interest. Bonnet adamantly denied this, but Hitler was convinced it was true, and Ribbentrop's stock rose accordingly.

The Franco-German Declaration was nothing but hot air, just like the Anglo-German Declaration, the infamous 'piece of paper' guaranteeing 'peace for our time' that Chamberlain had persuaded Hitler to sign, without Ribbentrop's involvement, before returning from Munich. But it rang alarm bells in Mussolini's ever-suspicious mind. His relations with France had never been good, but they had reached a new low during 1938, when deputies in the Italian parliament had screamed their claims to Corsica and Nice. The suggestion that Germany might be drawing closer to a genuine agreement with France was enough to persuade the Duce to make a swift about-face over the Tripartite Pact. On 1 January he told Ciano that he had decided after all 'to accept the proposition of von Ribbentrop to transform the Anti-Comintern Pact into an alliance. He wants the pact signed during the last ten days of January. He considers more and more inevitable a clash with the occidental democracies, and therefore he wishes to effect a military alignment in advance.'[6]

Ribbentrop was understandably delighted when Ciano gave him the news over a crackly telephone line the next day, in advance of an official letter. He plunged immediately into hectic diplomatic activity aimed at having the pact signed before Hitler's annual Reichstag speech on 30 January. To his dismay, however, the Japanese, who had been highly enthusiastic only a few weeks earlier, were now back-pedalling following another of their frequent changes of government. But he was still optimistic about bringing off what he was sure would be regarded by everyone as a major diplomatic triumph.

In his Reichstag speech on 30 January 1939, Hitler praised Göring for all that he had done. But Göring's pleasure was alloyed by the fact that the Führer also praised Ribbentrop, linked with Mussolini, before going on to his main topic, the Jews. In a two-hour tirade he blamed them for all Germany's ills, including her deteriorating international standing, and went on to issue a dire threat:

All my life I have been a prophet, and I have usually been laughed at for it. At the time of my struggle for power, it was mostly the Jewish people who laughed at the prophecy that one day I would attain the leadership of the state in Germany, and thereby of the entire nation, and that among other problems I would also solve the Jewish one. I think that the uproarious laughter of that time has since become stuck in German Jewry's throat. Today I want to be a prophet again: if international finance Jewry inside and outside Europe succeeds once more in plunging the nations into a world war, the result will

be not the Bolshevisation of the earth, and with it the victory of Jewry, but
the annihilation of the Jewish race in Europe.[7]

Göring was in the President's chair during Hitler's speech, and led the
applause and made the obligatory eulogy at the end. He was fully
aware of the implications, and of the prophetic threat of world war;
earlier in the month Hitler had clearly indicated that he had Britain in
his sights by giving priority to the expansion of the German navy at
the expense of the army and even the Luftwaffe in the supply of scarce
steel and labour. Göring had acquiesced in this – perhaps because the
programme for building six super battleships stretched over a period
of six years – but the idea of a major war filled him with dread.
Nevertheless, he was duty-bound to prepare the Luftwaffe for war, and
he put in hand a major reorganisation to ensure that it was.

The most important change was the creation of three air fleets, the
equivalent of armies, under commanders he could trust. Air Fleet 1
(East), was under General Albert Kesselring, Air Fleet 2 (North) under
General Helmuth Felmy, and Air Fleet 3 (West) under General Hugo
Sperrle, all highly competent officers. At the centre, Milch remained
in charge as Göring's deputy and State Secretary, with the young Colonel
Hans Jeschonnek as Chief of Staff, despite the fact that he and Milch
did not always get on well.

The vital post of Generalluftzeugmeister, literally General in Charge
of Flying Equipment, responsible for the development and supply of
just about everything, but above all of aircraft, went to Göring's old
crony, Ernst Udet. Udet, a heavy-drinking, hard-living womaniser, had
been an ace fighter pilot in Göring's Richthofen squadron in the First
World War, and a daredevil stunt flyer with him afterwards. No one
could doubt his bravery, or his popularity, but he was no administrator
and was completely lost as the general with the heaviest workload,
with no fewer than twenty-four departments reporting to him.

Udet was a prime example of Göring's weakness for looking after
his friends, regardless of their true abilities – Pilli Körner was another
whom he had promoted out of his depth in the Four-Year Plan. Both
were disastrous appointments. Milch would have been the ideal candidate for the Luftwaffe post, but he was ruthlessly ambitious, good at
his job, and refused to be subservient to Göring, who had come to
distrust him as a potential rival. Göring knew he couldn't do without
Milch, but was wary of increasing his power base in any way.

*   *   *

Ribbentrop had ousted Göring from dealings with the two countries, Italy and Poland, which he had come to regard as his personal spheres of interest, and it hurt, depressing him still further. Sir Nevile Henderson, returning to Germany in mid February after a four-month absence for a cancer operation, commented to him that Ribbentrop now seemed to have 'gathered all the threads of foreign policy into his own hands'. Göring growled back that there were 'certain countries such as Poland and Yugoslavia which remained his preserve', adding that Ribbentrop 'had instructions from the Führer to keep him informed at all times'.[8] But he knew very well that even had this been true Ribbentrop would not have abided by such instructions, and that he had to depend largely on the FA intercepts to keep himself informed.

As always when he was depressed, he sought comfort in food, with the result that his weight had rocketed past the critical 280 pounds, and his blood pressure soared dangerously. On doctors' orders he had embarked on another crash slimming course, aiming to lose sixty pounds. By mid February he was well on the way to his target, but Henderson was quite shocked to see the effects. 'Even if one weighs seventeen or eighteen stone, one cannot lose forty-two pounds with impunity,' he wrote. 'His heart had been affected by his treatment, and he told me that he was going to San Remo at the beginning of March for a long cure.' Revealing the depths of his weariness, Göring said that while he was away people could make what mistakes they liked – he wouldn't care.

Göring tried to convince the Ambassador that Germany's only reason for rearming was fear of British rearmament and what would happen if Chamberlain's government were to fall and be replaced by one under Churchill's leadership. Germany could not afford it, he complained, claiming that both he and Hitler would much rather spend the money on beautiful new buildings and improving social conditions for the people. Except for a few fools, he said, nobody in Berlin wanted a war of any kind. 'I believe,' the gullible Henderson reported to Halifax, 'that he would now like in his heart to return to the fold of comparative respectability. As the Field Marshal said to me this morning, tyrants who go against the will of their people always come to a bad end.'[9]

After reviewing an Air Force Day parade on 1 March, Göring set off in his special train for his much-needed holiday, accompanied by Emmy and Edda, with Carin Göring's sister Fanny, one of Emmy's nieces, Pilli Körner, and Göring's personal aide and 'court biographer',

Erich Gritzbach. They took a villa in San Remo on the Italian Riviera, where Göring could 'drop all business affairs', relax and indulge his passion for buying works of art and antiques from Italian dealers. But he could not forget politics entirely – he made a point of meeting and talking to 'many Englishmen' in San Remo, sounding them out about their attitude to Munich, which they accepted 'and even found satisfactory', and to developments in Czecho-Slovakia. 'Any other incidents, or demands on Czecho-Slovakia,' he discovered, 'would cause considerable excitement.'[10]

The peace of San Remo was interrupted in the late evening of 10 March, when Göring's chief intelligence officer, Colonel Beppo Schmid, arrived with a sealed message from Hitler informing him that the Czecho-Slovak state was breaking up, and that 'he could not let things go on as they were with impunity'. The situation, he said, was becoming 'an increasing menace to Germany, and he was determined to eliminate Czecho-Slovakia as a source of danger right in the centre of Germany, and was therefore thinking of an occupation.' A similar message had been sent to Milch, who was on holiday in Switzerland.

Göring would have packed up and hurried back to Berlin at once, but Schmid told him the Führer had specifically forbidden this, to avoid arousing international suspicion that something was going on. Göring suspected that Hitler's real reason was to keep him out of the way so that he could not argue against an invasion – which he promptly did by letter, warning that such an invasion might bring down Chamberlain, which would probably let in Churchill – 'and the Führer knew Churchill's attitude towards Germany'. He reasoned, as he had before, that there was no need for an invasion, with all its attendant risks. All they had to do was be patient, and they would get everything they needed to bind the Czechs to Germany, including a full communications, customs and currency union.[11] Göring sent Schmid back with his letter, but Hitler was in no mood to listen to reason.

Matters had come to a head in Czecho-Slovakia that morning, when Federal President Hácha had deposed the Slovakian government of Father Jozef Tiso in Bratislava and declared martial law. For some weeks, the Germans had been trying to stir up trouble between the Czechs and Slovaks, with Heydrich at last getting the chance to emulate Canaris and the Abwehr by using SD agents to carry out subversion and sabotage. Goebbels had played his part by beaming provocative radio coverage from Vienna into Czecho-Slovakia, while playing things down in the press in Germany. The results had been disappointing to say the least, with the Slovaks showing great reluctance to declare full independence and then call on Germany for protection.

Hácha's surprise move was a stroke of luck for Hitler, and he grabbed it eagerly. With Göring away, he conferred with Goebbels, Ribbentrop and Keitel, none of whom was likely to contradict him, and told them he had decided to march in and smash the rump Czech state in five days' time. The two ministers were jubilant. 'Our frontiers will stretch to the Carpathians,' Goebbels crowed. 'The Führer shouts for joy. This game is a dead certainty.'[12] The invasion would take place on the Ides of March (15 March), the date Keitel had privately 'put his money on', having noted that since 1933 this had always been the date on which Hitler had chosen to act. 'Was it always coincidence,' he wondered, 'or was it superstition? I am inclined to believe the latter, for Hitler himself often referred to it.'[13]

Unfortunately, even having their government unseated failed to rouse the Slovaks to the revolt Hitler needed. He had to have Tiso virtually kidnapped by Heydrich's men on 13 March and 'invited' to Berlin, where Hitler told him the Slovaks' historic hour had arrived, and that if they did not seize their moment, they would find themselves swallowed by Hungary, which was about to take over Ruthenia, also known as the Carpatho-Ukraine, the third and smallest segment of the federation, to the east of Slovakia. Chastened, Tiso returned to Bratislava the next morning and persuaded the Slovak Diet to declare independence. He did not, however, send the telegram that Hitler and Ribbentrop had thoughtfully prepared for him, calling for protection from Hitler, 'who had always supported freedom and self-determination of peoples'.[14] It took the arrival of German gunships on the Danube the next day, their weapons trained on the Assembly, to convince Tiso to send it. The Ruthenians were less reluctant, and sent a similar telegram without being asked – which was inconvenient for Hitler since he had already promised the Hungarians they could have Ruthenia. Ribbentrop had to tell the Ruthenians not to resist the Hungarian invasion.[15]

Hitler eventually summoned Göring to Berlin on the morning of 14 March, by which time all the important decisions had been taken without him. He arrived during the morning, and immediately presented the arguments against invasion that he had listed in his letter. Hitler said the situation had developed much more seriously than Göring realised, not only through the disintegration of Czecho-Slovakia with the secession of Slovakia. The decisive factor, he said, was intelligence he had received that there were Soviet aircraft and personnel at various Czech airfields, in breach of the Munich agreement. He feared that Czechia, especially without Slovakia, 'would be used as a Russian air base against Germany', and he was determined to eliminate this danger.[16] So there it was, Hitler had his excuse. There would be no turning back now.

For the past week, Goebbels had been having scare headlines splashed across all German newspapers, screaming that Moscow was arming the 'red underground' in Czecho-Slovakia, attacking German sports centres and generally committing unspeakable atrocities against ethnic Germans. Meanwhile, Wehrmacht and SS-VT units had been moving into preliminary positions a few miles from the Czech frontier, ready to carry out Operation Green as soon as the order was given.

Hitler told Göring that Hácha had asked for a meeting, and was on his way from Prague by train – he suffered from a weak heart, and could not fly. Hitler wanted Göring to be present for the meeting, to add his weight to the psychological pressure on the Czech President. When Hácha reached Berlin that evening, accompanied only by his Foreign Minister, Chvalkovský, his secretary and his daughter, he was met at the station by a guard of honour and a band, and by his Minister in Berlin, Mastný, who greeted him with the news that German troops were already crossing their frontier in Moravia-Ostrau, to prevent the Poles grabbing the steel works at Witkowitz. Hitler then kept him waiting nervously in the Adlon Hotel for hours, 'the old tested methods of political tactics', as Goebbels described it, before finally sending for him at midnight. To pass the time while Hácha was sweating it out, Hitler and his entourage watched a film entitled, appropriately, *Ein hoffnungsloser Fall,* (*A Hopeless Case.*)

Hácha is always described as frail and elderly. In fact, although he may have been frail, at sixty-seven he was only two years older than Winston Churchill, whose best years were still to come. But unlike Churchill, he was weak and nervous, with a retiring personality, and would have been no match for Hitler under any circumstances. In the situation he now faced, he was lost before he began. When he finally reached Speer's grandiose new Chancellery, Hitler continued with his mind games. Hácha was put through the ritual reception for a head of state, including inspecting the black-clad SS guard of honour which towered intimidatingly over his tiny figure, before being shown into

Hitler's vast reception study – his working study was a comparatively modest, much smaller room – where Hitler had assembled a sizeable group of Nazi notables, including Ribbentrop, Göring and Keitel, to overawe him.

Hácha had come to Berlin to talk, but he was only allowed to listen, as Hitler launched calmly into a torrent of accusations against the Czechs. The spirit of Beneš lived on, he said. Nothing had changed. He was convinced of Hácha's loyalty, but 'for the security of the Reich' it was necessary for Germany to assume a protectorate over the remains of Czecho-Slovakia. Hácha and Chvalkovský sat stony-faced. 'Only their eyes showed that they were alive,' wrote Paul Schmidt, the interpreter. 'It must have been an extraordinary blow to learn from Hitler's mouth that the end of their country had come.'¹⁷ Hitler went on to warn that German troops were already on the march and could not be stopped. Keitel, he said, would confirm that they would cross the frontier at 6 a.m. 'If you want to avoid bloodshed,' he concluded, 'you had better telephone to Prague at once, and instruct your Minister of War to order the Czech forces to offer no resistance.'

Hácha begged for a respite. He would have to speak to his government before agreeing to anything. Göring and Ribbentrop escorted him from the room, and while Schmidt tried vainly to get a telephone connection to Prague, and Ribbentrop fumed and raged, Göring went to work on him. Hitler had made up his mind, he said, and there was nothing that could be done to change things. He really must give the order at once to hold back his own troops, or there would be unnecessary bloodshed, which would be pointless as they could not hope to hold out for long. To drive his message home, he told Hácha his aircraft would appear over Prague at dawn, and he would be sorry if he had to bomb that beautiful city. He had no intention of bombing the Czech capital, which he considered quite unnecessary, and in any case his bombers were grounded by snow and bad weather. But as he put it at Nuremberg, 'a point like that might, I thought, serve as an argument and accelerate the whole matter'. In the event, it did more than that. To everyone's horror, Hácha turned pale and passed out cold.

Göring shouted for Morell, Hitler's doctor, to come at once. 'I hope nothing happens to him,' he said, terrified that if Hácha died in the Chancellery they would be accused of murdering him. 'It has been a very strenuous day for such an old man.' Morell arrived swiftly, examined the President, who by then had recovered consciousness but was breathing heavily, sitting in an armchair with his head back, and produced a hypodermic syringe. Morell's intravenous injection worked a miraculous transformation. Within moments, Hácha became 'fresh, alert' and ready to continue – Hitler later joked that he had become 'too lively' and that he 'was afraid he might not sign'.[18]

Morell later claimed that he had only injected vitamins, but there can be little doubt that the syringe had contained a powerful amphetamine, which the doctor had in his bag since he was regularly injecting Hitler with it as a stimulant and pain-killer. Some medical experts believe that this drug was responsible for Hitler's increasingly irrational behaviour around this time, since the acknowledged side-effects of amphetamine abuse include aggressiveness and willingness to take risks.[19] It could well be a factor in Hitler's refusal to listen any longer to Göring's reasoned arguments that they could get almost everything they wanted without going to war.

Hácha signed the prepared declaration at 4 a.m., 'confidently laying the fate of the Czech people and country in the hands of the Führer of the German Reich'. Two hours later, the first German troops – apart from those who had already occupied the area around the Witkowitz works – crossed the frontier in a snow-storm, and three hours after that, the advance units entered Prague. There was no resistance.

Hitler left for Prague at midday on 15 March in his special train, taking Ribbentrop with him to share in the glory as a reward for his support. Completing the journey by road, to allow him to show himself to Czechs and his own army columns, Hitler spent the night in the Presidential Palace, Prague's historic Hradschin castle. When Hácha arrived back several hours later – his train having been delayed in Germany to allow Hitler time to install himself – he was dismayed to find himself driven not to the front door but to the servants' entrance at the rear, a move that symbolised the position the Czechs were to have from now on in what had been their own land.

The next day, speaking from the balcony of the castle, Hitler proclaimed to a shocked and sullen populace that their country no longer existed. It had been replaced by the Protectorate of Bohemia and Moravia, to be governed by a Reich Protector who would be appointed by himself, as would his State Secretary and Head of the Civil Administration. He chose Neurath as Protector, with the Sudeten leader Henlein as administrative head and his former deputy and bitter rival, Karl Hermann Frank, as Secretary of State, thus guaranteeing the perpetual internal friction that Hitler liked to generate among his subordinates.

Himmler and Heydrich had entered Prague with Hitler, and immediately began setting up the apparatus of the police state in what was now becoming a well-practised routine. Heydrich commandeered a large bank as his Gestapo and SD headquarters, from which task groups comprised of security police, Gestapo and SD officials began rounding up suspected opponents of the regime, using lists already prepared from the great SD card index in the Prinz-Albrecht-Strasse. As his Chief of Police in the Protectorate, Himmler appointed Frank, who was a protégé of Heydrich and the SD, and who had been a fairly notorious small-time gangster and head of the Sudeten Nazi Party.

Goebbels stayed behind in Berlin to handle the press announcements, and Göring once more assumed the role of acting head of state. He told the Nuremberg Tribunal that he had not accompanied Hitler because he was 'rather annoyed' that 'the whole matter had been carried out more or less over my head'.[20] His resentment, however, did not prevent his leading the reception committee that welcomed Hitler back at the Görlitzer Station, his moon face beaming cherubically, brandishing his Field Marshal's baton like a club, and making a truly sickening eulogy of the all-conquering hero, with 'tears in his eyes' according to Goebbels.[21]

Goebbels organised a spectacular show in the city, with thousands of cheering supporters braving the snow and ice to line the route as Hitler drove along the Unter den Linden through a great tunnel of light formed by searchlights, and a massive fireworks display to follow. But in the country as a whole the celebrations were decidedly muted: in marked contrast with Austria and the Sudetenland, Hitler had not brought Germans back into the Reich, but had subjugated an alien people.

Even more than the horrors of *Kristallnacht*, Hitler's naked aggression and breach of trust over Czecho-Slovakia marked the start of disillusionment for many ordinary Germans. Doubts began to grow, together with fear that he was leading them deliberately into war. For foreign governments, especially those of Britain, France, the Soviet Union and Poland, it was the decisive turning point. On 17 March, while Hitler was still in the Protectorate, visiting Brno, Polish Ambassador Lipski had hurried to see Göring, complaining that he had been trying for five days to see either Ribbentrop or Weizsäcker but had been constantly fobbed off. He was deeply concerned about what had happened to

Czecho-Slovakia, and particularly by the military occupation of Slovakia, which meant that there were now German troops on three sides of Poland's frontiers. Göring calmed him down, reassured him that Hitler wanted to maintain friendly relations with Poland, and promised that no German troops would be stationed on the Polish–Slovak border.

Four days later, Lipski finally got to see Ribbentrop – who promptly undid all Göring's efforts by warning that if the Poles did not accept his earlier offer to guarantee Poland's existing borders and give her a free hand in Slovakia and a share in the Ukraine, in return for Danzig and a road and rail link across the Corridor, there would be trouble, starting with a propaganda war 'in which our relations would be reduced to nil'.[22] He then invited Beck to Berlin – which in view of what had happened to Hácha only a week earlier sounded suspiciously ominous. The Polish government's immediate reaction was to put its forces in the Corridor on alert and call up reservists.

Over the next few days, the political temperature soared with threat and counter-threat as Ribbentrop tried to bully the Poles into submission, and the Poles refused to be intimidated. All Göring's careful work over the previous years was destroyed, and Poland was driven into the arms of the British, who had finally seen the light. On 15 March 1939, Chamberlain had astonished the House of Commons by refusing to accept that the Czech invasion was a breach of the Munich agreement and declaring that he would not be deflected from his course: 'We will continue to pursue our policy of appeasement.' Two days later, however, in a speech in Birmingham Town Hall, he abruptly changed his tune – if he had not done so, Göring's prophecy would have come true and he would have been unseated. 'Is this the last attack upon a small state,' he asked, 'or is it to be followed by another? Is this, in fact, a step in the direction of an attempt to dominate the world by force?'

The answer to Chamberlain's first question came with disconcerting speed. On 20 March, Ribbentrop presented Lithuania with an ultimatum demanding the immediate cession of Memel and its hinterland, adding with his usual delicacy that if the Lithuanians did not agree, their capital city, Kaunas (Kovno) would be bombed. Without waiting for an answer, Hitler embarked on the cruiser *Deutschland*, to sail into Memel harbour at the head of a German naval squadron and take possession of the city for the Reich – because of the Polish Corridor, the only way to get there without the unthinkable humiliation of having to ask Polish permission to cross her territory was by sea.

Hitler was a poor sailor, and the weather was rough; he was violently seasick for the whole of the voyage. His temper was not improved by the fact that the Lithuanians had the temerity to resist his demands, while they cried for help to the British, French and Polish military attachés in Berlin. But no one was interested. Alone and friendless, the Lithuanians finally capitulated at 1.30 a.m. on Wednesday, 23 March, after Ribbentrop had warned that the German warships would shoot their way in.

Looking pale and drawn after his ordeal at sea, Hitler rode into Memel at the head of his troops at 2.30 p.m. that afternoon. He delivered the usual rousing speech welcoming the population back 'into an even mightier Germany', and made a tour of the city before flying back to Berlin with another bloodless triumph under his belt, the second within a week, both taking him ever nearer to his ultimate goal, the Soviet Union. This time, he decided to forgo the hero's welcome in Berlin.

The seizure of Memel served to concentrate Polish minds wonderfully. But being Poles they refused to be cowed by the German pressure. When Ribbentrop lost his temper and screamed at Lipski that any Polish action against Danzig would be treated as aggression against the Reich, the Ambassador simply retorted that any further moves by Germany to take back Danzig would result in war. Beck confirmed this to the German Ambassador in Warsaw, who protested: 'You want to negotiate at the point of a bayonet!' Unfazed, Beck shot back: 'That is your own method!'[23]

While Ribbentrop had been trying to intimidate the Poles, Beck had been sounding out the British about a bilateral pact. Chamberlain and his Cabinet responded positively, and on 31 March the Prime Minister, looking tired and ill, announced to cheers in the House of Commons that Britain would offer unconditional support to Poland 'in the event of any action which clearly threatened Polish independence'. The French, he added, had authorised him to say that they joined Britain in these assurances. Beck would be arriving in London on 4 April to discuss the details of a mutual-assistance pact covering any attempt to undermine Polish independence, economically or in any other way.[24]

This was precisely what Hitler had been trying to avoid, and he 'flew into a passion' when he heard. Canaris, who had brought him the news, gave his associates a graphic description of the scene: 'With features distorted by fury, he stormed up and down his room, pounded his fists on the marble table-top and spewed forth a series of savage imprecations. Then, his eyes flashing with an uncanny light, he ground out the venomous threat, "I'll cook them a stew that they'll choke on!"[25] The next day, launching Germany's second new battleship, the *Tirpitz*, at Wilhelmshaven, he made a biting speech attacking Britain and her 'encirclement policy' and issuing threats against both Britain and Poland. Before setting out for what he described as the first holiday of his life, aboard the cruise ship *Robert Ley*, one of two owned by the Nazi Labour Front's recreational organisation, 'Strength through Joy', he ordered Keitel to draw up plans for an invasion of Poland, Operation White, to be ready to start by 1 September.

Göring was not consulted about Operation White, nor had he been involved in the decision to seize Memel. Still deeply wounded at the way he had been eclipsed by the odious Ribbentrop, he had left Berlin on 21 March to resume his interrupted holiday in San Remo, leaving Milch to run the Luftwaffe and Körner the Four-Year Plan. He had agreed with Milch that they should take over the Czech Air Force and all its planes and equipment and form a new Air Fleet 4, to cover the south-east, under the Austrian Air Force's General Löhr, but took no part in carrying it out. He also left it to Körner and Funk to start organising the rape of the Czech economy by seizing its gold and currency reserves and 'buying' control of the major industrial and arms-manufacturing concerns, such as Škoda, Brno Weapons, Poldi Ironworks and Witkowitz Steel, for the HGW.

Though he was pleased to have the immediate financial problems surrounding the rearmament drive solved, and to add the Czech companies to his portfolio, Göring had no desire to go and see them for himself, and in fact never did set foot in the former Czecho-Slovakia, until 21 April 1945, when he drove through Pilsen on his final journey to the Obersalzberg. He did, however, appoint his younger brother, Albert, who had been running the Tobis Sacha film studios in Vienna, as export director of Škoda. For once, it was a suitable appointment: Albert was a qualified engineer who had previously worked as a sales representative for the heating division of Junkers. He also, incidentally, bore a striking resemblance to Ritter von Epenstein, Göring's mother's Jewish lover, and spent much of his time, both then and right through until 1945, doing what he could to help individual Jews to survive, often with his brother's collusion.

For the rest of March and the first week of April, Göring rested quietly in San Remo with his family and friends, before taking up an offer to visit Libya made by his friend Marshal Balbo at Carinhall the previous autumn – when Balbo had earned his undying devotion by presenting him with a magnificent star decoration of black and white diamonds. They sailed from Naples to Tripoli aboard the Hamburg-America-Line ship *Monserrat* on 7 April. Balbo pulled out all the stops to entertain them royally. Two Italian navy destroyers escorted them into Tripoli, where the whole town was bedecked with flags and welcoming banners. They stayed in Balbo's summer villa by the sea – where they froze – and were treated to a series of parties, camel rides in the desert, a tour of the Roman remains at Leptis Magna, and impressive military parades and mock battles in the desert with live ammunition.[26]

Balbo's grand reception in Libya quite restored Göring's spirits, at least for the time being. The Italians had invaded Albania on 7 April, and he seized the opportunity of scoring over Ribbentrop by calling on Mussolini to congratulate him on his success. Taking care not to inform the German Foreign Office until everything was arranged, he arrived in Rome on 14 April, to be greeted by Ciano and put up in the official government guest house, the Villa Madama. With much of his former ebullience, he regaled the Italian Foreign Minister on the journey from the station with his views on the 'formidable' power of the Axis, and surprised him with a harsh attack on Poland.

It was quite like old times, meeting the Duce the next day, reaffirming Germany's friendship and telling him Hitler had asked him by phone to express his 'extraordinary pleasure' at Mussolini's Albanian triumph. This was an outright lie – he had not spoken to Hitler, but he was eager to re-establish his own position and to restore German–Italian trust, which had suffered after Hitler had invaded Czecho-Slovakia without warning his ally. 'Every time Hitler occupies a country, he sends me a message,' Mussolini had complained glumly when Prince Philipp of Hesse had informed him orally after the event.[27] His Albanian adventure was an attempt to emulate Hitler's successes, and he had deliberately not consulted him in advance.

Making the most of his time back in the sun, Göring talked to Mussolini about strengthening the Axis through the proposed bilateral military pact. He stressed how well prepared Germany was for war, saying that although his own bomber fleet was not yet fully equipped, the British could not hope to catch up before 1942, and that in any case he still hoped to persuade them to change their anti-German policies. And he floated the idea of approaching the Soviet Union 'though certain intermediaries', with a view to a rapprochement, in order to scare the Poles into seeing sense. 'The Duce,' Göring reported, 'welcomed this idea most warmly', but said they would have to consult Japan before seeking a rapprochement between the Axis powers and the Soviets. 'If Japan had no objections,' Mussolini concluded, 'this rapprochement could be effected with comparative ease.'[28]

Göring had two more long conversations with Ciano, one of them in the Armed Services Ministry, promoting closer co-operation, before he left, well satisfied. 'He is rather pleased with his stay in Rome,' Ciano noted after seeing him off at the station, 'for it has given him contacts with me and with the Duce. Generally speaking, the impression is that even Germany intends to keep the peace. Only one danger: Poland. I was impressed not so much by what he said, but by the contemptuous tone he used in talking of Warsaw.'[29]

From Rome, Göring headed straight back to Berlin, to help celebrate Hitler's fiftieth birthday on 20 April. He arrived back at 6 p.m. on 18 April, looking bronzed, fit and happy, but when he joined Hitler for dinner that evening he was immediately deflated when he learned for the first time about Operation White and Hitler's plans to recover Danzig by force. Being kept in the dark about something so important came as a serious blow, made even worse by Hitler's turning on him and accusing him of acting like a woman when he tried to counsel moderation.[30] Clearly, the combination of Ribbentrop's thirst for blood and Dr Morell's amphetamines, backed up by the eagerness of the army generals for a war with the Poles, whom they hated and despised, had completely wiped out Göring's appeals to reason.

Goebbels had also been away, from 28 March, on a grand tour of Hungary, Yugoslavia, Greece, Egypt and Turkey, which was partly holiday and partly a series of semi-official visits when he could try his hand at foreign affairs and boost his belief in his own importance. He stopped first in Budapest for two days in pouring rain, toured the city, saw all the sights, listened entranced to Gypsy music – 'which went straight to my wounded heart. Oh, God, oh, God!' – and watched a ballet in the Opera House. But he also visited the film studios and had talks with the Culture Minister, 'who talked twaddle about the Jewish question', and had meetings with both the Minister-President, Count

Teleki, and the Regent, Admiral Horthy, who thanked him for German help over Czecho-Slovakia, 'which was all that Hungary could have wished for'. While he was in Budapest, he heard the news that the Spanish Civil War was over, with the fall of both Madrid and Valencia, which he regarded as a victory for Germany, too. 'We have every reason,' he wrote in his diary, 'to celebrate ourselves.'

From rainy Budapest, he flew to Greece, stopping off briefly in Belgrade, where the Yugolavs were friendly, but worried. By Salonika the weather had cleared, and Athens was bathed in warm spring sunshine as he viewed the Acropolis – 'Oh, what a moving show! The cradle of Aryan civilisation!' – and other temples and sites. He called on the ageing dictator, General Ioannis Metaxas, and tried to persuade him that Greece would be better off aligning herself with Germany than with either Britain or Italy. But Metaxas refused to be drawn, declaring that Greece would remain neutral whatever happened. Later in the day, he had a meeting with the Anglophile King George II, exchanging platitudes and pious hopes, and assuring him that Germany was leading the fight against Bolshevism, but would not go to war, except for her rights.

Goebbels was disturbed by the news about the Polish situation, but decided that Hitler would call for him if he needed him, and in the meantime he could carry on with the rest of his holiday. After looking at the rest of the ancient monuments in and around Athens, he flew on to Rhodes, which had been occupied by Italy since 1912, and then to Egypt, where he marvelled at the 'indescribable sight' of the pyramids, before returning to Rhodes to spend a lazy Easter on the beach. It was an unfortunate coincidence that on the day he arrived in Cairo the Italians invaded Albania, and on the day he left Rhodes Britain and France gave Greece and Romania guarantees similar to that given to the Poles.

Istanbul was last place on his itinerary, with more sightseeing, shopping for presents in the bazaar, and a sombre visit to the German military cemetery, where he pondered on how great the Reich had been at the time of the last war. He had no political talks with Turkish leaders, which was perhaps just as well: while he was there, Canaris's intelligence agents discovered that Turkey and Britain were negotiating a defensive alliance, which they hoped to extend to the whole of the Balkans. Hitler quickly sent a new Ambassador to Turkey: Franz von Papen, who had been a secret agent there during the First World War and could be relied on to intrigue with the best – which he did for the next five years.

Goebbels flew home on 14 April, stopping briefly *en route* in Belgrade, for a chat with the Yugoslav Foreign Minister, who gave him a guided tour of the city while his plane was refuelling and told him German prestige in the Balkans had risen enormously, while Italy's had dropped sharply. He arrived at Tempelhof at 5 p.m. It had been, he wrote, 'a wonderful journey, rich in great and deep impressions'. But he was glad to be back in Berlin, where 'everybody is so nice and so friendly to me – perhaps I am also nice, because I am relaxed'. He plunged into work at once with Hanke, who filled him in on the thousands of minor organisational and personal matters that had come up during his absence.[31]

What Hanke did not tell him was that he had been bombarding Magda with love letters while she had been away on her own holiday for three weeks, touring under a false name with the Speers and three other couples through Sicily and southern Italy. Speer knew all about Hanke's infatuation, and had invited Magda to join the group to escape from his attentions. According to Speer, she had been 'firm in her refusal',[32] but in fact she was beginning to respond to Hanke's wooing, and a new crisis would soon erupt in the Goebbels marriage.

The celebrations for Hitler's fiftieth birthday on 20 April were yet another triumph for Goebbels's flair and stage-management skills. But he was upstaged by Speer, who impressed Hitler with his efficiency as well as his flair by completing the first stage of the great East–West Axis, the great new triumphal boulevard running from Unter den Linden to the Olympic stadium, exactly on schedule, just as he had the new Chancellery on 9 January. And although Goebbels gave the Führer a spanking new fast car as his gift, Speer topped this with a fifteen-foot high model of the proposed victory arch for the planned new city, which proved to be easily his favourite present. To Goebbels's intense chagrin, Speer was fast becoming Hitler's Benjamin. The old order was changing, but it was still Goebbels who broadcast the obligatory speech to the nation on the eve of the birthday, and Göring who made the obligatory speech to Hitler on the day itself.

The centrepiece of the whole show was a massive, five-hour-long parade of troops and military equipment, including tanks and the newest heavy guns, on display for the first time, designed to impress and intimidate potential enemies and victims alike. Hitler's guest of honour, seated alongside him on the rostrum, was Hácha. Hitler had ordered Ribbentrop to invite 'as many cowardly civilians and democrats as possible', but the Poles stayed away and the ambassadors of Britain, France and the United States were also missing, having been recalled by their governments after the occupation of Czecho-Slovakia. Goebbels captured the occasion for posterity, by commissioning a special Ufa newsreel documentary, for which twelve cameramen shot some 28,000 feet of film and which was finally edited down at a ratio of 20:1 to create another masterly portrayal of power. Dubbed with solemn classical music over a sententious commentary, the film was primarily intended for domestic consumption, to create confidence among the German people for the coming battles.

By now, it was becoming clear to Göring that, although Hitler spoke constantly of a war in two or three years' time, the battles were likely to come a great deal sooner than that. Faced with Hitler's determination to fight, the British attitude was hardening rapidly. In February the government had started issuing free corrugated-steel air-raid shelters, known as Anderson shelters, to individual households in areas most likely to be bombed; on 27 April, they switched from such purely defensive measures when Chamberlain introduced military conscription, for the first time ever in peacetime Britain. Fully briefed by Jeschonnek on Operation White, Göring ordered Luftwaffe preparations to go ahead at full speed. He also ordered Jeschonnek and Milch to start staff talks with Italy, to co-ordinate joint action.

On a more personal level, he sent Bodenschatz to Munich to find the Jewish Ballin sisters, who had saved his life after the 1923 *putsch* attempt. He told Bodenschatz to tell them he had made arrangements for them to leave Germany immediately, for their own safety. They were to go to the Argentine consulate-general, where they would be given visas. As a special mark of his concern, they would be allowed to take all their money with them. Even more personally, another person who decided to leave Germany was Epenstein's widow, Lilli, who was terrified of facing another war. Again, Göring arranged an exit permit for her, and an entry visa for the United States, where she had relatives in Chicago. Before she left, she made Veldenstein over to him and baby Edda, with the promise that he would also have Mautendorf, when she died. As things turned out, he did not have long to wait. She did not care for Chicago, was homesick for Mautendorf, and returned later that the summer. She died from a heart attack on 1 September.

Göring was forced to stay in Berlin after Hitler's birthday celebrations to perform various official functions, the most important of which had been to preside over the Reichstag on 28 April, when Hitler had made an important speech lasting two hours and twenty minutes. Hitler's main purpose had been to respond to a letter that President Roosevelt had sent him two weeks before, appealing to him to give assurances to thirty-one states in Europe and the Middle East that he would not attack any of them over the next twenty-five years. This was a gift to the Führer, and he seized on it with delight. Ribbentrop had contacted all the named states, asking each of them directly if they felt threatened in any way by Germany. Since it would have been unthinkable for any of them to answer yes, Hitler was able to read out a long list of countries that had said no. With withering sarcasm, he poured scorn on Roosevelt and tore his appeal to shreds, roared on by the cheers and laughter of the Nazi deputies.

What was more significant in the speech, however, was that Hitler renounced the 1934 Non-Aggression Pact with Poland, and the 1935 Naval Agreement with Britain, leaving Germany free to build as many warships as he chose. He blamed Britain for forcing him into this, though he went out of his way to express his admiration for the British Empire, and his desire to reach an understanding. He attacked the Poles venomously, but carefully avoided any criticism of the Soviet Union, something that had been a feature of almost every major speech of his career. Göring instructed Bodenschatz to point this out to the French when he sent him to talk to Stehlin a few days later, knowing that it meant Hitler was thinking of a rapprochement with the Soviets, to give him a free hand in attacking Poland. 'There will be no war on two fronts this time,' he warned.[33]

Still sick at heart at his loss of favour, Göring returned to San Remo again on 3 May, to nurse both his wounded pride and his collapsing health. Bodenschatz told the Polish Military Attaché that 'there was no hope of restoring Göring's health, and his political eclipse at the hands of Ribbentrop was now complete'. The Attaché passed the gossip on to the British Embassy, who relayed it to London. Henderson, concerned at the implications, did a little research of his own and came up with the conclusion that the rumours were exaggerated. Göring, he reported, had 'a form of diabetes' but was improving under medical care in San Remo. 'There is, on the other hand,' he concluded, 'no doubt that he is out of favour with Hitler at the moment.'[34]

Göring and Goebbels may both have been out of favour, but Himmler – coincidentally Ribbentrop's only friend in the inner circle and equally bellicose – was climbing steadily in Hitler's estimation. From 14 to 20 May, he and Wolff accompanied Hitler on a tour of the West Wall fortifications, which Hitler had decided to inspect without consulting Göring. On their way back to Berlin, they stopped at the army training grounds near Münster where Himmler had laid on a demonstration by the SS-VT 'Deutschland' regiment, designed to show that the VT were no longer ill-trained amateurs playing at soldiers. Besides Hitler, Himmler had invited several army generals to watch the exercise, which consisted of an infantry assault on wired and entrenched positions, using live ammunition and grenades, and preceded by an army artillery barrage using live shells.

As the exercise showed, the VT units were turning swiftly into efficient military formations, under the direction of a former East Prussian army captain, Felix Steiner, who had developed his own revolutionary ideas on the use of elite troops, based on his experiences in the field with the original *Sturmabteilung* units at the end of the First World War. The traditionalist officer corps rejected his theories, but the VT provided him with the perfect opportunity to put them into practice, and he had trained his men for a new, completely mobile style of warfare.

The demonstration was a great success – only two men were wounded. The generals were impressed, and so was Hitler, who gave Himmler the permission he had sought for so long, but which the army and OKW had always refused, to form a full SS-VT division which could fight alongside those of the army. This would require its own artillery regiment, and Hitler ordered Keitel to make the necessary guns and equipment available. For Himmler, this meant that the foundations were now in place for the creation of his true party army, the Waffen-SS.

While Himmler was climbing higher up the ladder, Göring was digging himself deeper into the mire. Before he left Berlin, he had spotted an opportunity to show the world that he still counted, and at the same time score a point over Ribbentrop. With the end of the war in Spain, he would trade on the debt owed to him by Franco by paying him a visit, on which he would be received with all the splendour he felt he deserved. He had ordered his Four-Year Plan representative in Spain, Johannes Bernhard, to make arrangements with the new Spanish government without involving or informing the German Ambassador, claiming that the visit and the talks he hoped to have with Franco were concerned with military matters, and no concern of the Foreign

Ministry. Franco at first agreed to meet him, then changed his mind. After several days of haggling, the meeting was on again, but there was disagreement about the location. Franco insisted on the inland city of Saragossa, Göring wanted the seaport of Valencia, and sailed there from Italy on the Hamburg-America Line ship *Huascaran*, escorted by no fewer than four German destroyers.

Unfortunately, by the time Göring reached the Spanish coast, Ribbentrop had got to hear about the excursion, and had called off the meeting. When Hitler sent a signal forbidding him from going ashore, Göring had no option but to turn around and sail back to Italy, deeply humiliated. Ribbentrop composed a sixteen-page letter of rebuke, complaining not only of the Spanish trip but also of his unauthorised state visit to Mussolini the previous month. For some reason, the letter was never delivered, but was filed away in the Foreign Ministry archives. But there can be little doubt that Ribbentrop made sure Göring was aware of its contents.

Göring's humiliation at the hands of Ribbentrop was still not complete. Dragging himself back to Berlin, he discovered that Mussolini had decided to go ahead with the bilateral pact, which Hitler now wanted as a response to the agreement signed by Britain and Poland. For the time being, Ribbentrop had been forced to abandon his dream of including Japan in the formal military alliance, and had only managed to win the Italians round by lying to them about the time scale for any hostilities, promising Mussolini that Hitler had no intention of going to war with anyone for at least three and possibly five years. Göring attended the ceremony at the Chancellery on 22 May to witness Ciano and Ribbentrop putting their signatures to what was dubbed the 'Pact of Steel', but balked when Ribbentrop invited him to stand behind him for the official photograph. He was the second man in the Reich, he snorted, and if he did pose for the photographers and newsreel cameramen, he would sit down and Ribbentrop could stand behind him.

His chagrin became almost unbearable at the banquet held that evening in the Italian Embassy. The future Italian Ambassador to Berlin, Dino Alfieri, was amused to spot him slipping into the dining-room and surreptitiously switching his and Ribbentrop's place cards, so that he would be on Ciano's right and Ribbentrop on his left. But what came next, in Alfieri's words, was 'a tragedy in miniature'. Returning to the reception, he was just in time to see Ciano conferring on Ribbentrop Italy's most exclusive honour, the bejewelled Collar of the

Order of the Annunciation, which officially made him a cousin of the King.[35] Göring was so upset by this, according to Alfieri, that 'it was only with great difficulty that [he] was restrained from leaving the Embassy immediately'.[36] Ciano observed that he 'had tears in his eyes when he saw the collar of the Annunziata around the neck of Ribbentrop. Von Mackensen [the German Ambassador to Rome] told me that Göring had made a scene, complaining that the collar really belonged to him, since he was the true and only promoter of the alliance.'[37] Ciano took pity on Göring, and promised he would try to get another collar for him. He was as good as his word, but it took until May 1940 before he could prise one out of a very reluctant King Victor Emmanuel III, and the affair rankled with Göring for all that time. He never forgave Ribbentrop.

Hitler called a meeting of his commanders-in-chief and their chiefs of staff on the day after the signing of the Pact of Steel. Significantly, Himmler and Wolff were among those present, but Göring could not face it. At the last minute, he took off to lick his wounds in the peace of Carinhall, sending Milch to stand in for him. But when Milch asked if he should report on the meeting to Göring, Hitler said no, he would do that himself. Hitler laid out his plans for attacking Poland at the first opportunity. Danzig might be the excuse, but it was not the issue, he told them. 'What matters for us is expanding our living space in the East and securing our food supplies.' Poland must be isolated from the West, he said. He still believed that Britain and France would keep out of things for the moment, but that a showdown with Britain was inevitable in the long run, and if it came sooner it would have to be faced. 'England is our enemy,' he declared, contradicting all his previous expressions of regard, 'and the showdown with England is a matter of life and death.' He warned his commanders to be prepared for a long war, possibly lasting for ten to fifteen years.[38]

XXIII

'I HAVE THE WORLD IN MY POCKET'

ALL through the summer of 1939, the German war machine was being geared up for action as international tension stretched ever tighter. Amazingly, Hitler spent most of this time away from Berlin, either shut away at the Berghof or travelling around the country, leaving his ministers and generals to carry out his wishes. On 15 June, Brauchitsch delivered the completed plans for the invasion of Poland to him. A week later, Keitel submitted a timetable for the operation, which was limited by two factors: it had to start late enough for the harvest to have been got in, and early enough for victory to be achieved before the autumn rains turned the Polish plains into a quagmire. The latest date for a decision on starting deployment was 12 August.

The attack on Poland was to be a blitzkrieg, a lightning war. To achieve it the entire resources of the nation would have to be mobilised, which was Göring's responsibility. To plan and co-ordinate this, he called a second meeting of the Reich Defence Council on 23 June, at which the main topic was manpower. Some seven million men were to be called up on mobilisation, he told the meeting, and these would have to be replaced somehow in industry and agriculture.

Göring's solution to the manpower shortage amounted to the introduction of slave labour: some of the shortfall, he said, particularly in agriculture, would be made good by employing 'hundreds of thousands of workers from the Czech protectorate' to work in Germany 'under supervision and housed in hutments'. In addition, Funk was to arrange what work could be given to prisoners of war and the inmates of jails and concentration camps, which Himmler said 'would be put to much greater use in wartime'. The other main problem, apart from the chronic shortage of coal and raw materials, was transport. The German transport system,

Göring concluded, after hearing a damning report from the army General Staff, was not ready for war. He ordered that it should be improved at once, in case of 'an unexpected call, at short notice' for military action.[1]

His appetite for power and influence revived, even though his health was still far from perfect, Göring set about impressing Hitler with his achievements in developing the Luftwaffe, which by September would number twenty-one squadrons, with 260,000 men. Considering the problems with obtaining raw materials, this was a commendable feat, but it was still well short of the target he had set, and many of the squadrons would not be up to full strength. To show Hitler what they could achieve, Göring and Udet laid on a display of new aircraft and equipment under development at Udet's research and testing establishment at Rechlin, on 3 July. Hitler marvelled especially at the rocket-boosted take-off of an overloaded He-111 bomber, and the maiden flight of the He-176, the world's first jet-propelled aircraft, which reached the phenomenal speed of 850 k.p.h. in a short hop.

The demonstration was a great success – too much so, in fact, since Göring failed to explain properly to Hitler that most of what he had seen would not be ready to enter squadron service until 1942 or 1943, the time that Hitler had always given for the showdown with the West. Eager to please his Führer, and nervous of seeming negative or over-cautious, Göring promised him that everything he admired would be delivered soon. This was a great mistake. Even though his Luftwaffe adjutant, Nicolaus von Below, tried to warn him that what he had seen was 'music for the distant future', Hitler felt confident that if it became necessary he could face a major war with such an air force at his command.[2]

It would naturally suit Hitler best if the showdown with Britain could be delayed until a time of his own choosing, after he had finished with Poland. With Ribbentrop still insisting that Britain would not go to war for the Poles, and that he could press ahead with impunity, he took care not to provoke Britain in other ways, constantly praising the British Empire and stressing that he had no wish to attack Britain's position in the world outside Europe. This was a line that Goebbels found hard to follow – for all his mastery of the German popular imagination, his one great failing as a propagandist was that he never understood the British psyche, nor indeed that of other countries outside the

Reich. He never appreciated that his threats and bombast were counter-productive, driving the British to greater determination rather than frightening them off.

After the show of strength at Hitler's birthday parade, and the signing of the Pact of Steel, Goebbels concentrated his propaganda on the threat of Britain's supposed 'encirclement' policy, attacking the evil, capitalistic designs of her 'plutocrats', hiding behind the 'self-righteous phrases' from the 'rather elderly moralistic auntie of Europe'.[3] Hitler had to restrain him, instructing him to promote moderation and self-control. For the moment, he was also to play down incidents in Danzig, to avoid inflaming popular passions too early. He was allowed to make one provocative speech on 17 June in Danzig, condemning supposed ill-treatment of ethnic Germans by the Poles and demanding the Free City's return to the Reich, but this was purely to test reactions in Britain, which were predictably outraged. Apart from that, everything was to be kept 'simmering'.

At about that time, Goebbels had the welcome distraction of moving back into his official residence on Hermann-Göring-Strasse, which had been knocked down and rebuilt on a suitably grander scale over the previous year, not by Speer this time but by the architect of the new Berlin City Opera, Professor Paul Baumgarten. The costs had escalated enormously during the project, far outstripping the budget, because Goebbels – spurred on by his need to compete with Göring – had insisted that he needed somewhere 'on a generous scale' in order to fulfil his growing obligations to entertain guests. Only the finest materials could be used, and he engaged the Consolidated Workshops of Munich once again to design and furnish the interior. His study was done out all in red, producing the effect, according to his aide Wilfred von Oven, of 'a certain macabre splendour'. The wall behind his desk was almost entirely filled by a full-length portrait of Hitler, flanked by a portrait of Hitler's great hero, Frederick the Great. Oven counted six pictures of the king in different parts of the building. By the time everything was completed, the cost had reached 3.2 million marks, 1.2 million more than the original estimate. It was all a very far cry indeed from the asceticism of Goebbels's early days.

Only one thing was missing from the grand new residence – its mistress. Although they were formally reunited, relations between Goebbels and Magda remained cool, and he suspected that she was still seeing Hanke. He had still not recovered his place as the Führer's most intimate confidant – he had been excluded from all the top-level secret meetings that year, and so had played no part in deciding policy – and suspected that his estrangement from Magda was the reason. He feared that if he lost her to Hanke, Hitler would cut him off completely. With the annual pilgrimage to Bayreuth approaching, he was becoming desperate that they should join Hitler there as a couple. Dropping everything, he followed her to Bad Gastein, where she was recuperating after another bout of illness, and spent three days arguing incessantly with her in her hotel. She finally capitulated when he threatened to take the children away from her unless she returned to him and vowed never to see Hanke in private again.

In Bayreuth, Goebbels and Magda joined Hitler in the spacious wing that Winifred Wagner had built specially on to her Haus Wahnfried for him and his guests, and that evening sat with him, Winifred Wagner and the Speers in the big central box at the opera. Unfortunately, the opera they saw was the tragic love story *Tristan und Isolde*. It was all too much for Magda, who wept silently through the performance, and sobbed uncontrollably in a corner of the salon during the interval, to the consternation of her husband and the bemusement of Hitler. The next morning, Speer explained everything to Hitler, who sent for Goebbels and, according to Speer, 'informed him in a few dry words that it would be better if he left Bayreuth immediately with his wife. Without allowing him to reply, or even shaking hands with him, he dismissed the Propaganda Minister and turned to me: "With women Goebbels is a cynic."'[4]

Goebbels and Magda went back to Berlin, to try to patch up their marriage, but it was not until late October, after she had suffered more sharp problems with her heart, that they began to get it all together again. Hanke left the Propaganda Ministry at the end of July, and joined the army, to serve with the *Panzerlehrregiment* (Panzer Training Regiment), fighting with it in Poland.

While Goebbels was trying to sort out his marital problems, and being kept largely in the dark about the march to war, Göring was trying to find ways of keeping Britain and France out of the conflict, opening secret lines of communication to Chamberlain using his invaluable Swedish connections. In May and June the head of the Electrolux corporation, Axel Wenner-Gren, who had been introduced to him in 1936 by Count von Rosen, had conversations on his behalf with Chamberlain and his advisers, trying to find some sort of common ground. Wenner-

Gren even drew up an outline programme for a twenty-year peace treaty between the two nations, but the conditions he considered Britain would need to confirm Germany's good faith, including an end to racial persecution and the closure of the concentration camps, were too drastic for Göring to pursue.[5]

From his own Four-Year Plan office, Göring sent one of his top economists, Helmut Wohlthat, who had already been in touch with Chamberlain's adviser, Sir Horace Wilson, on previous visits to London. To avoid Ribbentrop finding out and interfering, neither side wanted to involve its Foreign Office. Wohlthat was a good choice: he was always travelling around on banking and trade business of one sort or another, and could make trips without arousing suspicion – the visit in June had been as a delegate to the International Committee on Jewish Emigration, and on 17 July he was ostensibly attending the International Whaling Conference. He discovered that Chamberlain was as desperate as Göring to find a way out, and that being essentially a businessman with his roots in Birmingham trade, the British Premier believed Hitler could be bought off, if the deal was good enough.

Wohlthat was astonished to be given a long memorandum, which Wilson and Chamberlain had written together, outlining proposals for the closest possible alliance between Britain and Germany, covering political, military and economic areas. Britain's guarantee to Poland would be ditched as 'superfluous'; Danzig would be relegated to being no more than a minor problem; economic co-operation between Europe's two greatest industrial nations would create 'an unprecedented economic boom' throughout the world. The question of colonies was covered by a plan for what was described as a 'colonial condominium', a 'large, integrated territory, which would embrace the larger part of tropical and sub-tropical Africa'. Although the other European colonial powers would be involved, Britain and Germany would be in control. Having reported back to Göring personally, Wohlthat had a second secret meeting in London three days later, this time with Robert Hudson, Minister for Overseas Trade, who came up with another effort to buy Hitler off with a financial package worth a staggering £1 billion.[6] Göring could have laid this before Hitler with some confidence, but unfortunately before he could do so details of the financial part of the offer were leaked to French Intelligence, some say by Hudson himself. A furious Daladier made sure the British press got the story, which was splashed across the front pages under the headline 'The Biggest

Bribe in History', and the immediate furore in Parliament torpedoed the deal completely.

Even with Wenner-Gren and Wohlthat out of the game, Göring was still active, through another Swedish businessman whom he had known for several years, and who approached him with an interesting proposition. Birger Dahlerus was a machine-tool manufacturer who had lived and worked in the English industrial midlands for some time in his youth and had recently completed another business trip to the region. A friend of Göring's stepson, Thomas von Kantzow, he loved both Britain and Germany, and was horrified at the thought that they might soon be at war with each other. Dahlerus was deeply concerned that Hitler did not realise that the British government would keep its word to go to war over Poland. He believed he could convince Hitler of this by bringing to Germany a group of his British business friends – men who were not politicians and had no part in government, but who could speak for the people. With Hitler's approval, Göring agreed to meet Dahlerus's friends on behalf of the Reich, and on the strength of this, Dahlerus spoke to Halifax, who said he would be interested in receiving a full report from the Englishmen after the meeting. If it was positive, it could pave the way for a conference with authorised delegates, on neutral territory such as Holland or Sweden.[7]

The meeting eventually took place on 7 August, in a remote farmhouse belonging to Dahlerus's wife on the west coast of Schleswig-Holstein, under elaborately secret arrangements. Thomas von Kantzow accompanied Dahlerus, and seven British businessmen, led by Charles Spencer, a director of the John Brown engineering and shipbuilding group, took part. As briefed by Halifax, they stressed that although Britain would stand by the guarantee to Poland, the British government was still more than willing to talk and to listen. Göring for his part warned that if Germany failed to reach an understanding with Britain, she did have another option. 'It is still open for us to negotiate with Russia,' he told them.

Göring seemed to regard an agreement with the Soviets as a fallback position to keep Britain out of the war. Poland would be wrapped up within a couple of weeks, before the British could even start moving troops into France, and if the Red Army was neutralised, the Wehrmacht would be freed to concentrate entirely on defending Germany's western frontiers. Surely, this would be enough to deter Britain from a pointless intervention? The day before his meeting with the Englishmen, he had called Milch, Udet and Jeschonnek to his yacht to receive fresh orders for the Luftwaffe. Turning his previous policy on its head, he ordered them to start building it up as an offensive force, with thirty-two new bomber wings consisting of 4,330 aircraft, including 2,460 Ju-88 dive-bombers, by April 1943. He said confidently that there would be no war with Britain until then.[8]

The Soviet Union was the key to the whole situation in the summer of 1939. At the current stage of German military development, the Wehrmacht was easily capable of crushing the Polish army on its own, but if the Red Army joined in on Poland's side, it could be a very different story, particularly if the British and French were to attack simultaneously in the West. Although the Red Army was in no fit state for war after Stalin's savage purges of the previous two years had virtually wiped out its leadership, it was still a formidable force of well over five million men. And even though both Britain and Germany tended to underestimate its power, neither of them could think of war in Poland without considering it.

Throughout much of 1939 both sides had been flirting with the idea of making a pact with Stalin, the West to make sure he would join in any war against Germany, the Germans to make sure he stayed out. In fact, the only people who never even considered opening negotiations with the Soviet Union were the Poles, who may have had most to gain but also had most to lose. Both sides viewed an alliance with Stalin with great distaste. But Hitler, being totally amoral, had the advantage of having absolutely no scruples. While the British and French agonised and dragged their feet, he quietly got on with preparing the ground, sending a steady stream of tacit signals to Stalin, and biding his time until the moment was right.

Hitler was supported with great enthusiasm by Ribbentrop, who liked to claim the idea of a rapprochement as his own, and by Göring, who had his eyes on the Soviets' vast resources of raw materials, which he could tap by bartering finished goods and machinery without the need for foreign exchange. Even Keitel and the generals were not averse to the idea, remembering with a certain nostalgia the ways in which the Soviets in the 1920s had helped them to circumvent the restrictions of Versailles with secret training facilities for the 'Black Reichswehr'. There was also a military tradition of co-operation with Russia, going back to Frederick the Great.

Stalin desperately needed a protective agreement. He could be under no illusions about Hitler's ultimate aim: the Nazi leader had never made a secret of his intention to smash Bolshevism, and therefore the Soviet Union. Stalin's fear was that once the Wehrmacht had smashed its way through Poland, which it would surely do with ease, it would charge on into Belorussia and the Ukraine and then into Mother Russia itself. Taken in like the German generals, Göring and the Italians, Stalin had believed he would have two or three years to rebuild both the Red Army and the political leadership before Hitler launched his major war. Suddenly, however, he realised that German sabres were not merely rattling in their scabbards, but were being drawn in earnest.

And then, on 15 May, two days after anti-Polish riots in Danzig had raised Stalin's alarm in the West, Germany's Anti-Comintern partner Japan had attacked his Far Eastern frontiers between Mongolia and Manchuria, or Manchukuo as the occupying Japanese had rechristened it. This was only the latest clash in a conflict that had been dragging on for years, but it promised to explode into something far more serious. Stalin had already been forced to commit at least twenty-four divisions of his best troops to the area, and was now faced with the potential nightmare of having to fight on two fronts, with his ill-prepared forces split between the two extremes of his huge empire. In Mongolia, he could expect no help from anyone, but in the West he had two options: he could form an alliance with the Western powers against Hitler, or he could sign a pact with the devil and buy Hitler off, at least for the time being.

Initially, Stalin favoured the Western alliance, but throughout the late spring and summer carefully kept the door ajar to Hitler through protracted negotiations for a trade agreement, with the understanding that once the price had been settled a political and military agreement could follow swiftly. The negotiations were conducted for Germany by the Foreign Ministry expert, Karl Schnurre – Ribbentrop kept Göring well away from them, though he was the minister most affected. Skilfully and infuriatingly playing the two sides off against each other, Stalin allowed the trade negotiations to reach the final stages, while at the same time welcoming an Anglo–French mission to Moscow to negotiate a mutual assistance pact. Like scorpions about to mate, the two dictators circled each other warily, both refusing to commit themselves until the last possible moment. By August, with Hitler's deadline for Operation White approaching fast, that moment could not be delayed much longer.

*   *   *

On 10 August, the fuse was lit in Danzig, as the German and Polish governments faced up to each other for the first time over the administration of the Free City, and the Nazi Gauleiter, Albert Forster, emulated Henlein in the Sudetenland with an inflammatory public speech to a wildly cheering crowd. Their next rally, he told them, would take place after Danzig's annexation by the Reich. Hitler let Goebbels off the leash again, and under his direction the German newspapers exploded into an orgy of anti-Polish propaganda, all screaming that it was Poland that was disturbing the peace of Europe, Poland that was threatening to invade Germany.

That same day, Admiral Canaris flew to Salzburg for a conference with Keitel and Hitler's OKW adjutant, Lieutenant-Colonel Rudolf Schmundt, to discuss sabotage and subversion operations behind Polish lines during Operation White. When he had finished talking to Keitel, Canaris was driven to a meeting with Ribbentrop at nearby Schloss Fuschl, the Foreign Minister's latest acquisition, which he had moved into on 9 July. Schloss Fuschl was an elegant four-storey former hunting lodge dating from the fifteenth century, beautifully located on the shore of the lake of the same name, and came complete with a large estate and the neighbouring village. For Ribbentrop, however, its main attraction was that it was within an easy forty-minute drive from the Berghof. It was the ancestral home of an Austrian nobleman, Gustav von Remnitz, a strong advocate of Austrian independence, whom Ribbentrop had persuaded Himmler to arrest and throw into Dachau concentration camp after the *Anschluss*. He had then requisitioned the house and all its contents, having Frau von Remnitz and her young son evicted in the middle of the night by SS men. Ribbentrop had in fact had the castle and its owner in his sights for some time, ever since Remnitz, a close friend of Annaliese von Ribbentrop's brother, Stefan-Karl Henkell, had snubbed him by not inviting him to the dinners he held there every year for distinguished visitors to the Salzburg Festival.

Ribbentrop gave Canaris orders for his part in a special operation, code-named 'Canned Goods', organised by Himmler and Heydrich, which would provide the final 'provocation' for war with Poland. It consisted of two separate but co-ordinated incidents, both of which involved the use of condemned men from concentration camps – the actual 'canned goods' – together with special SS squads masquerading as Polish troops. Canaris was to provide back-up, including 150 Polish army uniforms and assorted Polish small arms from the Abwehr's stocks.

The first incident was to be led by one of Heydrich's toughest intellectual gangsters, thirty-nine-year-old Alfred Naujocks, who had studied engineering at Kiel University, joined the SS in 1931, and had been a member of the SD since its formation in 1934. He specialised in undercover assignments, such as disposing of enemies of the Nazis both in Germany and elsewhere, and had been responsible for running arms and explosives into Czechoslovakia during the Sudeten crisis. 'On or about 10 August 1939,' Naujocks told the Nuremberg Tribunal,

the chief of the SD, Heydrich, personally ordered me to simulate an attack on a radio station near Gleiwitz, near the Polish border, and to make it appear that the attacking force consisted of Poles. Heydrich said: 'Practical proof of these attacks by the Poles is needed for the foreign press as well as for German propaganda.'

My instructions were to seize the radio station and to hold it long enough to permit a Polish-speaking German who would be put at my disposal to broadcast a speech in Polish. Heydrich told me that this speech should state that the time had come for fighting between Germans and Poles.

The second incident was to be more complex and even more provocative. A group of Polish-speaking troops, also wearing Canaris's uniforms and using the weapons he was to supply, was to attack and seize a German customs post at Hochlinden, engaging SS troops in a mock battle. Genuine Polish troops garrisoned just across the border at Rybnik would be ordered into the fight by a Polish officer who had just defected to Germany.

In both cases, there were to be 'Polish' bodies – which was where the concentration camp prisoners came in. They were to be supplied by Gestapo Müller. As Naujocks said in his affidavit: 'Müller stated that he had twelve to thirteen condemned criminals who were to be dressed in Polish uniforms and left dead on the ground at the scene of the incident, to show that they had been killed during the attack. For this purpose, they were to be given lethal injections by a doctor employed by Heydrich. They were then also to be given gunshot wounds. After the incident, members of the press and other persons were to be taken to the spot.' Naturally, the corpses would all have Polish army passbooks in their pockets, to confirm their identities, in addition to their uniforms and weapons. Heydrich was proud of his scheme. 'Up to now,' he told Naujocks in his briefing, 'the idea was mine and I've prepared it without the Führer's knowledge. But now the Führer has endorsed the plan.'[9]

* * *

The following day, 11 August, Ribbentrop received another visitor at Fuschl: Ciano. The Italians had realised at last that Ribbentrop had duped them into signing the Pact of Steel with false promises that there would be no immediate war, and Mussolini was close to panic at the thought of being dragged into a conflict for which he had no appetite, and for which his armed forces were by no means prepared. Having failed to persuade Hitler to meet him at the Brenner Pass for a face-to-face discussion, he dispatched Ciano to talk to him about his idea for a world peace conference. 'The Duce is anxious,' Ciano wrote in his diary, 'that I prove to the Germans, by documentary evidence, that the outbreak of war at this time would be madness.'[10]

Ribbentrop, of course, did not agree with Mussolini's assessment. As he and Ciano walked in the garden at Fuschl before lunch, the Italian asked him: 'Well, Ribbentrop, what do you want? The Corridor or Danzig?' To his horror, Ribbentrop, 'gazing at [him] through his cold, metallic eyes', replied, 'Not that any more. We want war!' He announced what Ciano described as 'the German decision to set a match to the European powder keg . . . in much the same tone that he would have used about an inconsequential administrative detail'.[11]

The atmosphere during their ten hours of talks that day was icy. Ciano could get nothing definite out of Ribbentrop about German plans. 'His conscience bothers him,' he noted. 'He has lied too many times about German intentions towards Poland not to feel uneasy now about what he must tell me and what they are getting ready to do.'[12] His distrust of Ribbentrop was so great that he ordered the crew of his aircraft to stay with it all night in the hangar at Salzburg airfield, fearing sabotage. And when he discussed the day's conversations with Ambassador Attolico and Counsellor Magistrati, from the Italian Embassy in Berlin, he insisted on talking in the bathroom with all the taps running, to foil the bugs that he was sure had been planted in his room.

All Ciano's arguments, both to Ribbentrop and to Hitler over the following two days at the Berghof, made absolutely no impression on their closed minds. 'I am unshakeably convinced,' Hitler told him, 'that neither England nor France will embark upon a general war.'[13] Ribbentrop was so sure that 'both France and England would remain passive during the slaughter of Poland', that over dinner he insisted on making a bet with Ciano: 'If England and France remained neutral, I would give him an Italian painting. If those powers intervened, he would give me a collection of old armour.'[14] Needless to say, Ribbentrop never honoured the bet. Ciano left for Rome on 13 August, 'completely disgusted with the Germans, with their leader, with their way of doing things. They have betrayed us and lied to us. Now they are dragging us into an adventure which we have not wanted and which might compromise the regime and the country as a whole.'[15]

Ciano's meeting at the Berghof on 12 August had been interrupted in late afternoon by the arrival of two messages, which lifted Hitler's mood dramatically. Suddenly full of smiles and good humour, he suggested that they leave the rest of their talks till next morning, and invited Ciano to accompany him for tea in the pavilion perched on a nearby rocky peak that Martin Bormann had had built for him as a surprise present for his fiftieth birthday. Poor Ciano was forced to accept, despite hating heights and disliking tea, since Hitler was clearly intent on celebrating the news he had just received: the two messages, Ribbentrop explained, were from Moscow and Tokyo. 'The Russian government,' Hitler announced, 'has agreed to open political negotiations, and has asked for a minister to be sent.'

Ciano remained silent, suspecting that the 'messages' were nothing more than a typical theatrical device designed to impress him as part of Hitler's efforts to inveigle Italy into a disastrous military partnership. And he was partly right. The message from Tokyo had in fact been received the day before, and contained little more than a list of the problems the Japanese War Minister was having in trying to persuade his colleagues in government to support Germany. Hitler and Ribbentrop said nothing about its contents. The message from Moscow was actually from Schnurre in Berlin, reporting that his opposite number in the Soviet Embassy had called him that morning on instructions from his Premier and Foreign Minister, Vyacheslav Molotov, to say that the Soviets were interested in discussions not only of economic matters, but also political matters, including the question of Poland.

On the face of it, Schnurre's news did not look particularly exciting, but it was the sign Hitler and Ribbentrop had been waiting for, and its timing was significant: the Anglo–French military mission had arrived in Moscow the previous morning, to begin negotiations for a mutual assistance pact. The composition of the team did not inspire confidence in Stalin that the British and French were really serious. It was led by a British admiral whose only claim to fame was an acquired name so pretentious it put Ribbentrop's phoney 'von' completely to shame: the Honourable Sir Reginald Aylmer Ranfurly Plunkett-Ernle-Erle-Drax had been born plain Reginald Plunkett, second son of John William Plunkett, heir to the Irish title Baron of Dunsany. He had added the other names by royal decree after the death of his mother, whose first name was Ernle. Erle and Drax were the names of former owners of the beautiful Dorset mansion he inherited from her. The French side was led more credibly by General Joseph Edward Doumenc, an artilleryman and tank warfare expert who, at sixty, was the youngest general in the French Army. There was no minister, even below Cabinet rank, from either country, and the mission chose to travel not by air, since Doumenc did not like flying, but by slow steamer to Leningrad and thence by train to Moscow. The whole journey took six days, and when the talks began at 10.30 a.m. on Saturday, 12 August, it was discovered that Drax had no written credentials and therefore, as far as the Soviets were concerned, no authority to negotiate.

It was small wonder that Stalin chose to cover himself by inviting the Germans to talk at the same time. Well aware of the urgency for Hitler, he put on a show of nonchalance, suggesting that progress could only be made 'by degree'. Growing increasingly anxious, Hitler wooed Stalin for the next few days, while the Soviet leader continued to play it cool, insisting that they could not move on to military and political talks until the trade agreement was settled. On 14 August, on Hitler's instructions, Ribbentrop offered to travel to Moscow himself, emphasising the marked difference between the German and the Anglo–French approaches. And as a clincher, he offered to carve up Poland and eastern Europe between Germany and the Soviet Union, something the British and French could never do.

That same day, Hitler called his three commanders-in-chief, Göring, Brauchitsch and Raeder, to the Berghof, together with their chiefs of staff and Dr Todt. He said nothing to them about the negotiations with the Soviet Union, but after telling them he was certain that Britain and France would not fight, he outlined his plans for the coming campaign, and ordered them to begin the countdown to the invasion of Poland. None of them raised any objections. They left to start issuing the necessary orders: Brauchitsch and Göring to begin moving troops and equipment towards the Polish border, Raeder to deploy the pocket battleships *Graf Spee* and *Deutschland* to the shipping lanes in the Atlantic, and twenty-one U-boats to stations to the north and north-west of the British Isles, all ready to attack British shipping.

For the next few days, Stalin and Molotov played Ribbentrop like a fish that has taken the bait and is firmly on the hook. The text of the trade treaty was agreed on 18 August: Germany would provide the Soviet Union with manufactured goods worth 200 million marks a year, in exchange for foodstuffs, oil and raw materials to the same value. But when Ribbentrop, through Schnurre, asked if the agreement could be signed that same day, the Soviets told him that formal approval by their government might take a little time. And when he asked if they could now move on to the Non-Aggression Pact, Molotov pointed out that the trade treaty had not yet been signed. A few hours later, he changed his mind, said the treaty could be signed the next day, and handed over his draft for the Pact. He said Ribbentrop could come to Moscow on 26 or 27 August – knowing full well that the 26th was the date Hitler had set for the invasion of Poland.

Göring, meanwhile, was still fretting about Britain. He had received no response to the meeting with the seven businessmen, nor to the suggestion he had floated to them of a four-power conference. Now he sent a personal message to Halifax, via the British Secret Service, saying he wanted to visit England to see Chamberlain on 23 August. Suprisingly, Chamberlain agreed, and arrangements were put in hand. 'The idea,' Halifax recalled in his memoirs, 'was that he would land at some disused aerodrome, be picked up in a car and taken directly to Chequers [the Prime Minister's official country residence in mid Buckinghamshire], where the staff would have been given *congé*.'[16]

The British had not given up making their own secret advances: Sir Horace Wilson was still trying to find some way of handing over Danzig to the Reich in return for nothing more than an assurance from Hitler that this would finally satisfy his territorial demands. While Göring was arranging to fly to Britain, Wilson was busy suggesting to Ribbentrop's London Press Attaché, Fritz Hesse, that he might fly to Germany to talk directly to Hitler. Ribbentrop, naturally, squashed the idea at once.

As the days passed and the deadline for war approached, Ribbentrop grew increasingly hysterical at being kept dangling by the Soviets. Hitler, too, seemed on the verge of a nervous breakdown, but after more frantic bargaining he decided to cut across all diplomatic conventions and wrote a personal letter to Stalin, accepting the Soviet draft of the Pact, and assuring him that 'the substance of the supplementary protocol desired by the Soviet Union can be cleared in the shortest possible time if a responsible German statesman can come to Moscow himself to negotiate'. Stressing the urgency of the situation, he pleaded with him to receive Ribbentrop on Tuesday, 22 August, or Wednesday the 23rd at the latest.[17] Stalin kept him waiting for another twenty-four hours, which Hitler later described as the most agonising of his life. His doctors waited anxiously, on stand-by in case they were needed. In the middle of the night he phoned Göring, who was sound asleep in his Obersalzberg chalet, to complain about the delays, generally let off steam, and talk about the contingency plan of Göring's proposed visit to London and ideas for securing Danzig.

The next day, Göring went to see Hitler, with Brauchitsch and Himmler, to discuss the problems of stopping the Poles blowing up the two vital bridges across the Vistula into Danzig, each a mile long. Aerial photographs taken by Luftwaffe reconnaissance planes clearly showed demolition charges already in place. Göring had the answer: his Stukas would attack the Polish guard posts at the ends of the bridges and the local power station, knocking them out with the precision bombing that only the Ju-87s could guarantee, while Luftwaffe paratroopers destroyed the cables to the electric detonators. An innocent-looking freight train would arrive at the last minute from East Prussia, carrying concealed assault troops and sappers to back up the aerial assault. Simultaneously, the Luftwaffe would hit the Polish naval base at nearby Gdynia. Göring, the leader of the anti-war faction in the government, would be responsible for striking the first overt blows in the war. His health and vigour restored, he was back in Hitler's favour, his 'Iron Man' once more.

It was not until 8.30 p.m. on Monday evening that Ribbentrop received the news by phone at Fuschl that Molotov had agreed to see him in Moscow on the 23rd. 'Marvellous! I congratulate you,' Hitler cried when he called him, ignoring the fact that it was his own intervention that had clinched things. None of the courtiers around Hitler had ever seen him so elated. The photographer Heinrich Hoffmann, hurrying in to record the historic moment on film, saw him slap his knee in delight. Walther Hewel, his Foreign Ministry adjutant, recorded that he hammered his fists on the wall in jubilation, 'uttering incoherent cries', then bursting out triumphantly: 'I have the world in my pocket!'[18]

All the proposed flights to and from Britain were cancelled. Ribbentrop hurried to agree the text of the announcement of his impending visit and its purpose, which Stalin and Molotov wanted to release at midnight, and to inform the Italians and Japanese. Neither was happy. Ciano had been trying to hustle Ribbentrop into a meeting at the Brenner Pass, to tell him that Mussolini would denounce the Pact of Steel unless the Germans abided by its conditions and consulted their partner before taking any military action. He knew that once they had signed a pact with the Soviets, they would no longer need Italian support and there would be little the Italians could do to hold them back. He noted with somewhat grudging admiration: 'There is no doubt that the Germans have struck a master blow.'[19]

The Japanese, who had recently fought and lost a major battle with the Red Army in Manchuria, losing 20,000 men, were considerably more upset at not even being consulted. The Japanese Ambassador in Berlin, General Hiroshi Oshima, who until then had been Ribbentrop's closest friend in the diplomatic community, reacted angrily when the Foreign Minister telephoned him with the news late on 21 August. The next day, he drove to the airport in Berlin to confront him on his way to Moscow, angrily denouncing the forthcoming Nazi–Soviet Pact as a betrayal of his country and a violation of the 1936 Anti-Comintern Pact. Refusing to have his party spoiled by an unpleasant scene, Ribbentrop told him he did not have time to explain everything then, and passed him to Weizsäcker, who tried in vain to placate him.[20] Oshima resigned, and was recalled to Tokyo the following month. He was, however, reappointed a year later, and served in Berlin until the end of the war.

The news of the Pact came as a tremendous shock to Goebbels, who until then had been told nothing about any deal with the Soviet Union. Having been convinced for so long that the destruction of Bolshevism was the great mission of National Socialism, he was unnerved and uneasy about this *volte-face*. But he quickly convinced himself that this 'brilliant propaganda *coup*' was one more example of the Führer's genius, and issued instructions to the German press that it was to concentrate on this 'sensational turning point' in European politics. He specifically forbade, however, any discussion of 'the ideological differences between the two nations, either in a positive or a negative vein', or any mention of the embarrassing subject of the Anti-Comintern Pact.[21]

The editors responded with a will – William Shirer described the German press the next morning as 'wonderful to behold', as the dailies competed with each other to give the biggest welcome to the news.

The prize, perhaps inevitably, went to *Der Angriff*, with the unwieldy and hardly accurate headline blazoned across its front page: 'The world is faced with a towering fact: two peoples have established a common foreign policy after a long and traditional friendship which has produced the basis for mutual understanding'.[22] Sharing the front pages and the headlines, as if to underline the import of the Pact, were stories of 'unbelievable atrocities' being committed by the Poles against their German minority. There was no mention anywhere that war was imminent, but for Goebbels, the propaganda countdown had begun.

Before he left for Berlin and Moscow on 22 August, Ribbentrop attended the start of a conference at the Berghof, to which Hitler had called his fifty most senior commanders three days earlier, immediately after sending his personal letter to Stalin. They were to be prepared to make detailed presentations of their operational plans, down to army level, for a campaign in Poland. In an effort to disguise the military purpose of the conference, Hitler had instructed the generals and admirals and Obergruppenführers not to wear uniform but to dress informally, in plain clothes, to avoid attracting attention. 'He particularly wants the conference to remain absolutely secret,' the summons read, 'and no word of it whatever to leak out to the foreign press.' No one was to make any record of what he said.

Göring had taken the informal dress instruction literally, greeting his fellow commanders on the terrace wearing, according to Admiral Boehm's description, 'a soft-collared white shirt under a green elkskin jerkin adorned with big buttons of bright yellow leather, grey shorts and grey silk stockings that displayed his impressive calves to considerable effect. This dainty hosiery was offset by a pair of massive laced boots. To cap it all, his paunch was girded by a scarlet sword belt, richly inlaid with gold, from which dangled an ornamental dagger in an ample sheath of the same material.'[23] General Erich von Manstein is said to have called out on seeing him: 'Field Marshal! Are you the bouncer?'[24]

Shortly before noon, the officers took their seats in rows of chairs arranged in a half circle in the great hall, with Göring at the centre, flanked by Brauchitsch and Raeder. Hitler entered, with Ribbentrop and Keitel at his side, laid his notes on the grand piano and began to speak. There were no official minutes, but at least three members of the audience, Canaris, Halder and Admiral Boehm, took surreptitious notes. 'I have called you together,' Hitler told them, 'to give you a picture of the political situation, in order that you may have some insight into the individual factors on which I have based my decision to act, and in order to strengthen your confidence. After this we shall discuss military details.'

The main purpose of Hitler's speech was to prepare his generals for war with Poland, to convince them that it was both just and necessary, to quell their fears of its spreading into something they could not control, and then to motivate them into tackling it with enthusiasm and determination. Naturally, he laid all the blame for the current situation on the Poles, who could if they had chosen have been Germany's accomplices in his expansionist schemes. 'In the beginning,' he said, 'I wanted to establish an acceptable relationship with Poland in order to fight first against the West. But this plan, which appealed to me, could not be put into effect because the essential points changed. It became obvious that in the event of a conflict with the West, Poland would attack us.'

He spoke for some time about the differences between his new Germany and the 'rotten democracies', claiming that there was no outstanding personality in either Britain or France who could compare with him or Mussolini: 'Our enemies are inferior men, not men of action, not masters. They are little worms!' Warming to his subject, he poured more scorn on Germany's potential enemies throughout Europe, then raised his voice for the first time: 'All these fortunate circumstances will not prevail in two or three years. No one knows how long I shall live. I am now fifty and at the height of my powers. It is best that war should come now, rather than in five years' time, when both I and Mussolini will be five years older. Therefore, the showdown had better come at once!'

As the generals gasped, Hitler went on, attacking Britain, France and Poland and explaining why he believed the Western powers would not intervene, particularly now that he had come to an understanding with the Soviet Union. 'I have struck this weapon from the hands of these gentlemen,' he declared dramatically. 'Now I have Poland where I want her! We need not be afraid of a blockade: the East will supply us with grain, cattle, coal, lead and zinc.'

Allowing the implications of his statement to sink in for a moment, Hitler looked around at his audience, then launched into a typical, rousing finale: 'It is a mighty aim, which demands mighty efforts. My only fear is that at the last moment some *Schweinehund* will come along with another proposal for mediation. We have made a start on the destruction of England's hegemony. Now that I have made the political preparations, the way is open for the soldiers!'[25]

The room erupted in applause, led by Göring, who leapt to his feet, bounced up the three shallow steps to the highest level in front of the doorway, and made a brief speech thanking the Führer and assuring him that the armed forces would do their duty. The conference broke for lunch, and Ribbentrop left for Munich airport, where Hitler's new personal plane, a four-engined Focke-Wulf Condor, waited to fly him first to Berlin and then on to Moscow, via East Prussia.

In the afternoon, proceedings resumed with the generals' presentations of their operational plans, before Hitler wrapped things up with another, hour-long speech designed to send them away fired with the conviction that he was right. After a great deal of rhetoric, he wound himself up to an emotional climax:

As regards our conduct of the war – close your hearts to pity! Act brutally! Crush every living spark! Eighty million people must get what is justly theirs. Their existence must be made secure! Might is right – so we must act with the greatest harshness. You must take decisions swiftly, and always have faith in the German soldier. Any failures will be due solely to leaders having lost their nerve!

The wholesale destruction of Poland is the military objective. Speed is the main thing. You must pursue them until they are completely annihilated. I am convinced that the German Wehrmacht is equal to all demands. I will give you the order for the start of hostilities later. It will probably be for Saturday morning.[26]

Ribbentrop's negotiations in Moscow on 23 August were simple and swift. Since Hitler had already accepted the principles of the Soviet draft of the main Pact, all that needed to be discussed were minor details and the secret protocol that was to be attached, defining 'spheres of interest' in eastern and south-eastern Europe and the Baltic. This was Stalin's price, and he was determined to exact it in full, negotiating it personally. The main points were all settled within three hours, before the break for dinner. Poland was to be carved up between the two powers, with Stalin taking back the areas of Belorussia and the Ukraine that the Poles had grabbed from the infant USSR in the war between them in 1920, plus a considerable chunk of Poland proper.

With the German zone ending at Warsaw, the canny Stalin had created a broad buffer zone that would keep the German armour well clear of Moscow. He also demanded Bessarabia, which had been given to Romania in 1918. The Baltic States were slightly more complicated. Hitler wanted Lithuania and part of Latvia, up to Riga, but was willing to give Stalin the remainder of Latvia, plus the whole of Estonia and Finland.

At this point, Ribbentrop discovered, as he put it, 'how hard Soviet diplomacy could be'. Stalin was unhappy at losing Lithuania, since that would deprive him of ice-free ports – the Gulf of Riga was frozen in winter, but the Baltic coast remained clear. He wanted the small ports of Libau and Windau (now Liepaja and Ventspiels) on the Baltic, which would mean redrawing the line south of Riga to include the rest of Latvia, and he was not prepared to settle for less.

Ribbentrop, in theory, had a completely free hand to negotiate and agree anything, but he was unwilling to give anything away without authorisation from his Führer. During the adjournment for dinner, he sent a short message to Hitler reporting on progress and asking his permission to give Stalin the two ports. Hitler, waiting impatiently in the Berghof, sent an orderly for an atlas, and when the man returned with an ordinary schoolbook, put on his spectacles and merely glanced cursorily at the Baltic coastline. The message he sent back to Moscow must rank as one of the shortest in the history of diplomacy. It read, quite simply: 'Yes, agreed.'

Ribbentrop and Molotov signed the Nazi–Soviet Non-Aggression Pact at 2 a.m. on the morning of 24 August. After an hour of toasts and celebration, Ribbentrop returned to the German Embassy and telephoned Hitler at the Berghof, to confirm the news personally. Hitler was ecstatic. 'That will hit them like a bombshell!' he exclaimed. Ribbentrop told him that there was now no chance of Britain and France going to war over Poland, and that he expected the Chamberlain government to fall within a day. With his nerves now restored, Hitler gave the order for Operation White to start at 4.30 a.m. on 26 August.

XXIV

'IF WE LOSE THIS WAR, THEN GOD HAVE MERCY ON US'

GÖRING flew back to Berlin on 23 August, while Ribbentrop was still on his way to Moscow, and called a meeting of ministers at Carinhall. He told them in strict secrecy that Hitler had decided to attack Poland in three days' time, and assured them that the conflict would not escalate into a world war, then asked them all about their departments' war preparations. He was pleased to hear from the Minister of Food and Agriculture, Darré, that although general food rationing would be necessary at once, bread and potato rationing could be postponed for four weeks thanks to prudent stockpiling. For all his optimism, however, he had workmen busy disguising the house with camouflage netting as he spoke.

Still clinging to the hope that he could find a way of keeping Britain and France out by driving a wedge between them and Poland, he had called his friend Dahlerus in Stockholm that morning and asked him to come to see him at once. Although Hitler had vetoed his own visit to London, he had agreed that he could send Dahlerus in his place. Göring briefed the Swede to say that he was confident he could persuade Hitler to be satisfied with Danzig and access across the Polish Corridor, and to ask if Britain would put pressure on the Poles to enter into direct negotiations with Germany. He repeated his and Hitler's offer of German military aid to defend the British Empire, and suggested that the British send a top general such as Sir Edmund Ironside to talk to him man to man. Driving Dahlerus back to Berlin in his own two-seater sports car, he was delighted when he was spotted and cheered by people in the street as they stopped at traffic lights, confirming that his personal popularity was as high as ever. An hour later, he was meeting Polish Ambassador Lipski, trying to persuade him that there were no major differences between their two countries, and that the main problem was the Poles' alliance with Britain.

At about the same time that Göring was talking to Lipski, Hitler was receiving Henderson at the Berghof. The Ambassador had brought a letter from Chamberlain, warning that Britain was determined to fulfil its obligations to Poland, but was still ready to talk, and wanted to see direct discussions between Germany and Poland on reciprocal treatment of ethnic minorities. Hitler already knew the contents of the letter, by courtesy of Göring's FA intercepts, and had prepared himself for a theatrical performance designed to bully the British into dropping Poland. 'At my first interview with him that day,' Henderson wrote with his usual understatement, 'Hitler was in a mood of extreme excitability. His language as regards the Poles and British responsibility for the Polish attitude was violent, recriminatory, and exaggerated.' When Henderson reiterated that Britain was bound to honour her obligations, he snapped back: 'Then honour them! If you write out blank cheques, you must expect to have to pay out on them.'[1]

Hitler sent Henderson away, thoroughly shaken, promising to have a written reply ready for Chamberlain in two hours. In fact, the reply was already written, but he wanted to make the Ambassador sweat a little longer. As soon as Henderson had left the room, he slapped himself on the thigh, laughed, and said to Weizsäcker, 'Chamberlain won't survive that conversation! His Cabinet will fall this evening.'[2] Weizsäcker tried in vain to persuade Hitler that his actions would have precisely the opposite effect, strengthening rather than weakening Chamberlain's position so long as he stood firm, but it was no use – Ribbentrop's insidious influence had done its work too well. When Henderson was called back to receive the written reply, he found it and its author utterly intransigent, and though Hitler had calmed down, he blamed Britain for everything. Henderson left with tears in his eyes, saying how bitterly he regretted that his mission had clearly failed.[3]

Hitler flew back to Berlin to give Ribbentrop a hero's welcome. He greeted him in front of his assembled courtiers as 'a second Bismarck', then took him off to his study with Göring and Weizsäcker, to hear the details of his trip and analyse the situation. Ribbentrop had reached the apex of his career and was riding high on his success. It was not to last. Next day, 25 August, as appeals for peace continued to pour in from all directions – President Roosevelt, the Pope, the rulers of Belgium, the Netherlands, Luxembourg, the Scandinavian countries, Canada – Hitler was stunned by the news that Chamberlain had not only survived but had also repeated the British commitment to Poland in Parliament, adding that it would be 'a dangerous illusion' for Germany to think that the Nazi–Soviet Pact would change anything.

Hitler called for an explanation from Ribbentrop, who still insisted the British were looking for a way out and would back down when they were presented with one. With this in mind, Hitler postponed the deadline for issuing the code-word for the invasion for one hour, and called Henderson to the Chancellery. With Ribbentrop in silent attendance, he promised 'a large and comprehensive offer' to Britain, once the Polish problem had been solved. He would guarantee to defend the British Empire even against his own allies, the Japanese. Convinced by Ribbentrop that the new offer would give Chamberlain the excuse to do nothing on the grounds that he needed time to consider it, he made his personal Condor aircraft, in which Ribbentrop had flown to Moscow, available to fly Henderson to London.

After Henderson had left, Hitler spent fifteen minutes alone with Ribbentrop, strengthening his nerve. There is no record of what was said, but it is fair to assume that Ribbentrop was still playing the same tune as he had two days earlier when Weizsäcker had told him that the British would still come to the aid of Poland but that Italy would leave Germany in the lurch. 'I disagree with you 100 per cent!' he had stormed. 'Mussolini is far too great a man to do that!'

After talking with Ribbentrop, Hitler called Keitel and gave the order for Operation White. The attack on Poland was to begin at 4.30 the next morning. The OKW issued the code-word to every service. By cable, telephone, teletype, it was passed on down the line until it had reached the unit commanders of more than half a million troops, five armies poised ready to charge into Poland from north, west and south. In Silesia, Pomerania, East Prussia and Slovakia, ammunition was broken out, engines tested, fuel checked. The great advance towards the frontier would start rolling at 8.30 that evening. In Berlin, Hitler's newly completed special train, *Amerika*, was brought out of its shed at the Tempelhof depot and made ready to take him to the front. Telegrams were sent to every Reichstag deputy, ordering them to attend an emergency session at 5 a.m. the next morning. All telephone lines to France, Britain and Poland were cut.

Two hours later, Hitler was screaming 'Stop everything!' He had received two disturbing messages in quick succession. The first was that Britain had signed a mutual assistance treaty with Poland and was now firmly committed to come to her aid; in addition, the French Ambassador, Robert Coulondre, had confirmed that France would also stand by Poland. The second was that while Mussolini was ready to support Germany in a localised conflict with Poland, he could not join in a war with the Western powers, because of the 'present state of Italian war preparations of which we have repeatedly and in good time informed you and Herr von Ribbentrop. At our meetings, war was envisaged for after 1942, and by that time I would have been ready.' Mussolini's message concluded by saying that he could do nothing to help now unless he was provided with large quantities of raw materials and armaments.[4]

Ribbentop had been 100 per cent wrong, and now had to face the consequences. He had misled the Italians and misread the British and French, with the result that Germany now faced the war he had always wanted without a major ally. And to complete the disasters of the day, Japan broke off negotiations for a tripartite alliance, in protest at the Nazi–Soviet Pact. From being the Führer's golden boy, he was suddenly plunged into the depths of disgrace, and there he stayed for the next seventy-two hours, distraught and hysterical, barred from Hitler's presence. For advice, Hitler telephoned Göring, his 'Iron Man', who had counselled a negotiated settlement from the start and was still actively trying to avert war with the West.

Göring, who had purposely stayed away from the mob in the Chancellery that day, responded cautiously to Hitler's news of halting the invasion.

'Is this temporary,' he asked hopefully, 'or for good?'

'Just for four or five days,' Hitler told him. 'I shall have to see whether I can eliminate British intervention.'

'Will four or five days be enough?' Göring responded.[5]

Göring hurried to the Chancellery, where he found Hitler in a state that Halder described as 'pretty broken up'. He advocated a compromise, suggesting they try for another Munich, and reminded him that he already had an emissary in London. His emissary, Dahlerus, managed after great difficulties to reach him by telephone while he was still with Hitler, to say that he had seen Halifax, who had thanked him for his efforts but had then told him Henderson would be flying in from Berlin the next morning, with a message from Hitler. Since normal diplomatic channels were now open again, there was no further need for Dahlerus's amateur services. Göring did not agree, knowing that 'normal diplomatic channels' meant involving the Foreign Ministry, and therefore Ribbentrop, who would do everything in his power to sabotage his peace efforts – as indeed he did over the next few days, refusing even to reply to offers of mediation from Italy, Belgium and the Netherlands. Göring told Dahlerus that things had deteriorated because of the signing of the Anglo–Polish Treaty, and that war might break out at any moment. Only a top-level personal meeting could save the peace.

The next morning, Saturday 26 August, Halifax invited Dahlerus for another meeting, having consulted Chamberlain in the meantime. Dahlerus told him that he believed Göring was 'the only man in Germany who might prevent a war', and persuaded Halifax to write a personal letter to him, with Chamberlain's approval, confirming Britain's wish to reach a peaceful settlement.[6]

Back in Berlin, Goebbels had been playing his usual role in preparing the German public for an act of aggression by blaming the victim, and his well-orchestrated press campaign was reaching its climax. That Saturday, the normally staid *Börsen-Zeitung*'s headlines proclaimed: 'COMPLETE CHAOS IN POLAND – GERMAN FAMILIES FLEE – POLISH TROOPS PUSH TO EDGE OF GERMAN FRONTIER!' The *12-Uhr Blatt*'s read: 'THIS PLAYING WITH FIRE GOING TOO FAR – THREE GERMAN PASSENGER PLANES SHOT AT BY POLES – IN CORRIDOR MANY GERMAN FARMHOUSES IN FLAMES!' The *Völkischer Beobachter* on the Sunday carried the banner: 'WHOLE OF POLAND IN WAR FEVER! 1,500,000 MEN MOBILISED! UNINTERRUPTED TROOP TRANSPORT TOWARDS THE FRONTIER! CHAOS IN UPPER SILESIA!'

All this was a skilful blend of half-truths and blatant lies: no planes had been shot at, no farmhouses deliberately burnt down at that time, but Germans were certainly fleeing for safety and troops were on the move. The *Völkischer Beobachter*'s 'uninterrupted troop transport' referred only to Polish troops, who were being rushed to defend their frontiers – but failed to mention German troop movements or mobilisation. There was a significant increase in the territory now being publicly demanded: not only Danzig and a corridor across the Corridor, but everything in the East that Germany had lost in 1918, meaning the whole of Silesia and Posen.

Goebbels also made full use of cinema newsreels – a valuable source of information for the general public in those days before television brought instant pictures into the home. Former Ambassador Ulrich von Hassell recorded the results in his diary a few days later: 'Last night I saw in the movies a disgusting example of how human misery is exploited for purposes of propaganda. Weeping women and children are shown and in voices choked with tears they describe their sufferings in Poland.' But Hassell also noted that the German public was growing used to Goebbels's techniques: 'The audience remained completely passive; there was only very weak applause at the showing of military pictures, not taken up by the bulk of the audience.'[7]

Göring arrived at the Chancellery at midday on Saturday 26 August, dressed to dispel any thought of pessimism in an all-white uniform, white socks and shoes, and around his neck a black silk cravat passed through a gold ring set with diamonds, rubies and sapphires. The previous evening he and Hitler had decided to call Mussolini's bluff by asking him what he would need to bring his forces up to strength. The Italian demands had now arrived, and they sat down with Keitel, Brauchitsch and Milch to discuss them, along with the general situation.

It was an impressive list, 'enough to kill a bull, if a bull could read', Ciano noted gleefully in his diary, having specifically compiled it as something Germany could not possibly provide.[8] It included seven million tons of oil, six million tons of coal, two million tons of steel, one million tons of timber, impossibly large quantities of other metals, minerals and rubber, and no fewer than 150 fully-equipped anti-aircraft batteries to protect Italy's industrial centres. Ambassador Attolico had tried to make it look even worse by adding, on his own initiative, a demand that everything had to be delivered before operations could begin.

It was clearly a try-on, but Hitler was unfazed. He immediately began dictating a reply, agreeing to all the Italian demands, plus, to Göring's further horror, not just the anti-aircraft batteries Mussolini had requested, but 150 full battalions – three times the number of guns. When Göring protested that this was totally out of the question, he replied grimly: 'I'm not concerned with actually making the deliveries, only with depriving Italy of any excuse to wriggle out of her obligations.'

But his temper soon cooled, after Milch suggested that Germany might even be better off without the Italians, provided they made enough warlike noises to keep the British and French occupied. Their 'benevolent neutrality' would deny the enemy access to the Reich through Italy, while Germany could keep all her precious materials and supplies for her own use, and even obtain more from Italy if need be. Hitler was delighted at the idea – it was reported that he slapped his thigh yet again – cancelled his angry response and wrote an 'understanding' letter to Mussolini, who accepted the let-out gratefully with extravagant promises about the number of divisions he would station along his frontiers.

The next day, Hitler called in another favour from the Duce. 'In this difficult struggle,' he wrote, 'you and your people can best help me by sending me Italian workers, both for industrial and agricultural purposes . . . In specially commending this request of mine to your generosity, I thank you for all the efforts you have made for our common cause.'9 It was a request that was almost certainly inspired by Göring, since it addressed one of his most pressing problems, finding replacements for the men from factories and farms who had been drafted into the armed services. All in all, things could hardly have worked out better.

Dahlerus arrived back from London that evening, and was driven to join Göring, who was on his special train on his way from Carinhall to his underground operational headquarters, code-named Kurfürst, at Wildpark on the outskirts of Potsdam, near Frederick the Great's San Souci Park and Palace. As the train moved off again, he handed over the letter from Halifax. Göring snatched it from him, tore it open with trembling fingers, and tried to read it. But his English was not good enough, and he thrust it back to Dahlerus, asking him to translate it with care, bringing out every shade of meaning. The letter was fairly anodyne, and full of platitudes, according to Halifax, but when Dahlerus had finished reading it out, Göring rang the bell for his aide, Lieutenant-Colonel Konrad, and ordered: 'I want the train stopped at the next station. Have a car waiting for me there.' Turning back to Dahlerus, he said: 'We are going back to Berlin. The Führer must be told about this letter.'

It was midnight by the time they arrived, and Hitler, for once, had gone to bed early, exhausted by his dealings with Mussolini, to say nothing of the other events of that hectic day. Göring sent Dahlerus back to his hotel, the Esplanade, to wait until called, while he marched into the darkened Chancellery and had Hitler woken up. When he was collected about fifteen minutes later and ushered into Hitler's study, Dahlerus found Göring beaming with satisfaction alongside the Führer, who stood in one of his favourite poses in the centre of the room, legs apart, arms behind his back, a scowl on his face.

The interview that followed was one of the strangest ever recorded with a head of state. For all the supposed importance of the letter from Halifax, Hitler made no reference to it. He started with his standard lecture on the history of the party and its policies, growing steadily more excited and moving into a diatribe against Britain. When Dahlerus managed to get a word in, saying that he had lived in Britain as a working man, and could not agree with Hitler's bad opinion of the British, Hitler seized eagerly on this and questioned him for half an hour on his experiences, demanding more and more information and refusing to listen to anything else.

Eventually, and with obvious reluctance, Hitler turned to the present situation – and immediately flew into a rage. Stomping round the room with strange, jerky movements, his eyes glazed, he poured out a tirade of invective against his enemies and boasts of German strength. Dahlerus pointed out, speaking slowly and quietly 'to avoid irritating him unnecessarily, since his mental equilibrium was patently unstable', that Germany's enemies had also strengthened their armed forces. This produced another excited outburst, with Hitler declaring that Germany was irresistible and could defeat her adversaries by means of a rapid war. Then he suddenly stopped, stared into space, and began talking as though in a trance: 'If there should be a war, then I will build U-boats, build U-boats, build U-boats, build U-boats, U-boats, U-boats . . .' It was like a record that had stuck, his voice becoming more indistinct as it died away. Then a sudden spasm shook his body. He raised his arms into the air and began to shriek, as though addressing a huge audience, but still staccato and disjointed: 'I will build aircraft, build aircraft, aircraft . . . And I will destroy my enemies! War does not frighten me! The encirclement of Germany is impossible now. My people admire me and follow me faithfully. If there are privations ahead for the German people, then let it be now – I will be the first to starve and set my people a good example. My sufferings will spur them on to super-human efforts.'

Dahlerus was horrified by the spectacle. He turned to see Göring's reactions – and was equally horrified to see that he did not seem at all perturbed. And then, as suddenly as it had begun, the trance evaporated. Hitler began pacing the floor again, as though regaining his senses. Turning to Dahlerus, he spoke calmly, seriously: 'Herr Dahlerus, you who know England so well – can you give me any reason for my perpetual failure to come to an agreement with her?'

Dahlerus hesitated, then answered honestly that in his opinion the difficulty lay in the lack of confidence in Hitler and his government. At this, Hitler struck his chest with his hand. 'Idiots!' he cried. 'Have I ever in my life told a lie?' His composure restored, he told Dahlerus: 'You have heard my side. You must go at once to England and tell it to the British government. I do not think Henderson understood me, and I really want to bring about an understanding.'[10]

Hitler gave Dahlerus a list of six points, which he was not allowed to write down but had to memorise, to take back to London. They confirmed that Hitler wanted a pact or alliance with Britain, and in return for British help in obtaining Danzig and the Corridor, plus the former German colonies, he would guarantee the new Polish frontiers and pledge Germany to defend the British Empire. When the Swede asked for specific details of the territory Germany wanted in the Corridor, Göring called for an atlas, marked the relevant map in red then tore out the page and gave it to him to put in his pocket. It was almost 5.30 a.m. when Dahlerus left the Chancellery to fly to London. While he was in the air, Hitler told the Abwehr and SD to stand by to carry out their 'provocation' attacks on 31 August. He had provisionally rescheduled the invasion to start on 1 September.

Dahlerus was back in Berlin, reporting to Göring in his Leipziger Strasse villa, at 11 p.m. on Monday, 28 August with the news that while the British would stand by their commitment to Poland, they were prepared to talk about a possible pact, as suggested by Hitler. They were, moreover, prepared to instruct the Poles to start direct negotiations with Germany – which was exactly what Hitler was after. His plan was to create a situation where Germany would appear to be reasonable and the Poles obstructive, so that he could blame them for the ultimate breakdown and hopefully persuade Britain to abandon them. The next four days on the diplomatic front would be spent entirely on that, while the mobilisation of the Wehrmacht galloped ahead at full pace. One advantage of the delayed start to Operation White was that it allowed the build-up of strength to continue for almost an extra week, by which time the twenty-seven divisions already in position near the frontiers had grown to sixty, and the total number of men under arms had reached two million.

Henderson flew back to Berlin on 28 August, and handed Hitler the official British reply to his 'offer' at 10.30 p.m. that evening. Since this was a formal occasion, Ribbentrop was back at Hitler's side, with Paul Schmidt standing by to interpret. Hitler received Henderson calmly and politely, in a 'friendly atmosphere', and was not angered by what he read – which is not surprising since Dahlerus, on Göring's instructions, had spent half the previous night at the British Embassy helping to draft it for the Foreign Office. The document added little to what Dahlerus had said, but it did confirm that Colonel Beck had actually agreed to begin negotiations with Germany. Promising to give his official written reply next day, Hitler handed the note to Ribbentrop, telling him – no doubt with sly amusement – to discuss it with Göring.

After Henderson had gone, Hitler and Ribbentrop joined Göring, Himmler, Hess, Bodenschatz and Weizsäcker in the conservatory. The Führer was in a good mood, joking and displaying his gift for mimicry by imitating Henderson's English-accented German as he recounted what had been said. He even welcomed the British idea of an international guarantee for Poland's frontiers: 'I like it. From now on I shall only do things on an international basis. International troops shall go in – including Russians! The Poles will never agree to that.'

Himmler's record of that night's conversation can be found in a rare surviving fragment of his diaries:

We have to aim a document at the British (or Poles) that is little less than a masterpiece of diplomacy. He wants to spend tonight thinking it over; because he always gets most of his best ideas in the small hours between 5 and 6 a.m.

At this, Göring inquired, 'My God, don't you get any sleep, even now? Or have you got insomnia again?' The Führer replied that he often dozes from three to four o'clock in the morning and then suddenly wakes up to find the problems arrayed in pristine clarity before his eyes. Then he jumps up and jots down a few key words in pencil. He himself doesn't know how it happens – all he does know is that in the wee small hours of the morning everything that might confuse or distract disappears.[11]

'Tonight,' Hitler promised, 'I'm going to hatch something diabolical for the Poles, something they'll choke on.' Göring warned him to be cautious: 'We should stop playing *va banque*.' But Hitler would have none of it. 'I have played *va banque* all my life,' he replied.[12]

When Henderson returned to the Chancellery at 7.15 p.m. on 29 August to receive the written reply, Hitler was playing the hard man again. With a well-simulated display of rage, he accused the Poles of 'barbaric acts of maltreatment against the German minority' – there had been reports in the midday press of the alleged murder of six German nationals in Poland, together with news of Polish general mobilisation. As he moved on, it was soon clear that he had had his moment of inspiration in the wee small hours. While accepting the British proposals, he told Henderson, and agreeing to enter into direct nego-tiations, he had two new provisos: the Soviet Union must be involved in any territorial guarantees, and a Polish emissary, 'with full powers', must come to Berlin within twenty-four hours. Henderson said that sounded like an ultimatum, and lost his temper when Hitler accused him of not caring how many Germans were slaughtered in Poland. The interview blew up into a shouting match, ending with what Henderson described as 'a harangue' by Hitler on his genuine wish for friendship with Britain. But, he added, he did not intend to sacrifice 'vital German interests' for this. When Henderson asked what he meant by 'vital German interests', he said his government would draw up a list of acceptable proposals for a solution of the problem, and would show these to the British government before the Polish negotiator arrived.

Henderson left the Chancellery 'filled with the gloomiest forebod-ings'. When he had protested again about the twenty-four-hour time limit for the arrival of a Polish plenipotentiary, Hitler had told him the General Staff were pressing him for a decision:

His army and air force were ready to strike, and had been since 25 August. They were telling him that one week had already been lost, and that they could not afford to lose another, lest the rainy season in Poland be added to their enemies. When I passed through the ante-room on my way back to my car, it was full of army officers, Keitel and Brauchitsch among them. Meeting them there did not tend to dispel my apprehensions.[13]

Unnerved by Henderson's sudden show of spirit, Hitler feared he might not present the German case to the British government with sufficient sympathy, and asked Göring to dispatch poor Dahlerus to London yet again. Göring marked up a copy of Hitler's latest proposals, heavily underlining the important points, and stressed the urgency of his mission: 'With sixty divisions – about one million men – not counting the Soviet divisions, confronting Poland, anything may happen. The Poles are mad . . .' Once again, he tore a page from an atlas to show the territories Germany wanted, and then he sent Dahlerus on his way – but not before thanking him for all that he had done, in case they never met again, warning him that 'certain people', meaning Ribbentrop, were determined to prevent Dahlerus 'getting out of this alive'.

Hitler spent much of the day on 30 August working on the German proposals for an acceptable solution that he had promised Henderson. On his instructions, the Foreign Ministry drew up a list under sixteen heads, ostensibly to have them ready for presentation to the Polish negotiator, should one come. In fact, despite British pressure, the Poles had no intention of being caught like Hácha and the Czechs, and the Germans knew this, through Göring's FA intercepts of conversations and cables between Warsaw and the Berlin Embassy. So Hitler was able with complete confidence to draw up a list of proposals that was so reasonable, not to say generous, that the whole world must surely condemn the Poles for refusing to consider them. At the same time, he gave Albert Forster, the Gauleiter of Danzig who had been unilater-ally declared Head of State in the Free City a week earlier, instructions on what he was to do when the invasion started.

During the day, Hitler boosted Göring's position with yet another appointment, as Chairman of a Ministerial Council for the Defence of the Reich, with wide powers to promulgate decrees. In effect, he was putting Göring in charge of running the country in order to leave himself free to concentrate on running the war. Unlike the old Reich Defence Council, it was a compact body. Its other members were Hess, as Deputy Leader of the party, Frick as Plenipotentiary for Reich Administration, Funk as Plenipotentiary for the Economy, Lammers, the Head of the Reich Chancellery, and Keitel, as Chief of the OKW. It looked like a war cabinet, but in the event was never able to operate as one without Hitler, and it withered away within a few months.

Henderson called at the Foreign Ministry at midnight, the deadline for the arrival of a Polish negotiator, to collect Hitler's promised sixteen points and to deliver yet another British note appealing to both sides to stop all troop movements to clear the way for real negotiations.

Hitler could not be bothered to see him, leaving Ribbentrop to deal with him – which he did in no uncertain way. Paul Schmidt, the only other person present, described the meeting as the stormiest that he ever experienced during his twenty-three years as an interpreter. 'Ribbentrop,' he said, 'had come straight from the Chancellery, and was obviously in a state of almost shivering excitement . . . with a pale face, set lips and shining eyes.' His first question, after greeting Henderson 'with an icy expression and stiff formality', was 'Where's the Pole your government was supposed to provide?'

When Henderson asked why the German proposals could not be given to the Polish Ambassador in the normal way, Ribbentrop lost all control and began shouting. Henderson tried to carry on in his normal calm way, but was soon on his feet, too, shouting back and giving as good as he got. He reprimanded Ribbentrop like a naughty schoolboy for using bad language, which only made matters worse. Schmidt kept his head down and scribbled furiously in his notebook, afraid that the two men would come to blows. 'The least that can happen now,' he thought, 'is that the Foreign Minister of the Reich will throw His Britannic Majesty's Ambassador out of the door.'

Fortunately, the storm passed, and, as Schmidt put it, 'it did not come to wrestling'. But when Henderson asked for Hitler's proposals, Ribbentrop read them to him in German, gabbling so fast that the Ambassador could not follow, and then refused to follow the usual practice and give him a copy – Hitler had in fact explicitly forbidden him to do so, to make sure they were not given to the Poles who might spoil everything by accepting them. Henderson, thinking he had misheard, asked again, and Ribbentrop refused again, throwing the document down on the table and saying it was out of date anyhow, since the Polish envoy had not appeared. Silently, Schmidt willed Henderson to ask for a translation, which he would have given slowly enough for him to make notes, but he seemed too shocked to say anything.

'There was nothing left for me to do,' Schmidt wrote, 'but to make a thick red mark in my book at the place where I had jotted down Ribbentrop's refusal, as a sign that in this hour the die was cast for war.'[14]

Amazingly, Henderson was still prepared to go on trying to avert the catastrophe – and so, it seemed, was Göring. Dahlerus had returned from London again, and was with him on his train. Desperate to know how the British had reacted to Hitler's sixteen points, Göring asked him to call the Embassy. When the First Secretary, Sir George Ogilvy-Forbes, told him about the disastrous meeting, both men were aghast. Göring had a copy of the sixteen points, and had Dahlerus dictate them to the Embassy over the phone. Henderson called Lipski, gave him the details, and begged him to arrange an immediate meeting between the two Field Marshals, Göring and Smigly-Rydz, adding that there would be no hope of negotiations succeeding if Ribbentrop were involved. Lipski said he would put the suggestion to Warsaw, but 'not tonight'. It was too late, he said. And with that he went to bed.

It was indeed too late. All the desperate diplomatic activity on 31 August, all the hurried meetings and telephone calls and cables flashing to and fro made no difference. At 6.30 a.m. Hitler gave the order for the attack to start the next day, 1 September, at 4.45 a.m. – Göring had persuaded him to move it back from the originally planned time of 4.30, to give his aircraft more light to take off and attack. At 12.40 p.m. he signed his Directive No. 1 for the Conduct of the War, which began: 'Now that every *political possibility* has been exhausted for ending by peaceful means the intolerable situation on Germany's eastern frontier, I have determined on a *solution by force* . . . In the *West*, it is important that the responsibility for the opening of hostilities should be made to rest squarely on Britain and France.'[15]

Still Göring continued working on the British. To make quite sure they had the sixteen points, he had sent Dahlerus to the Embassy at 10 a.m. with a typed copy. Soon afterwards, he invited Henderson and Ogilvy-Forbes to tea that afternoon, for what turned out to be two hours of fairly meaningless talk about 'the iniquities of the Poles and his own desire for friendship with England'. The Ambassador 'augured the worst from the fact that he was in a position at such a moment to give me so much of his time'. He deduced, correctly, that this meant that 'everything, down to the last detail, was ready for action', and that there was nothing left for Göring to do except to make 'a forlorn effort to detach Britain from the Poles'.

To demonstrate the Poles' bad faith at this critical hour, Göring showed Henderson a copy of an intercepted message from Warsaw to Lipski, in which Beck instructed the Ambassador to play for time and 'not under any circumstances to enter into any concrete discussions'. Was Britain still prepared to go to war for such people? He told him how much he would hate to bomb Britain. In this, at least, Henderson could agree with him. 'What if a bomb should accidentally hit my own person?' he asked. 'Then I shall send a special plane to drop a wreath at your funeral,' Göring replied, in all sincerity.

Henderson asked Göring to do his best to prevent the text of the sixteen points being published, since in his view this would 'probably and finally wreck the last prospect of peace'. Göring told him there was nothing he could do; the German government – meaning, presumably, Hitler – 'felt obliged to broadcast their proposals to the world in order to prove their "good faith"'.[16]

Goebbels did exactly that at 9 p.m. that evening. All German radio broadcasts were interrupted for an announcer to read out the text of Hitler's proposals, to demonstrate to the German people and the rest of the world how reasonable they were, and how unreasonable the Poles were being in rejecting them. Naturally, the statement did not mention that the proposals had never actually been put to Poland, or that they had been set an impossible time limit for sending a representative.

An hour before, Alfred Naujocks and his disguised SS men had staged their attack on the radio station at Gleiwitz, fired a few pistol shots, broadcast an inflammatory proclamation in Polish, and left behind the dead concentration camp victims as mute evidence. They had been carried there in trucks, alive but drugged unconscious by powerful injections, and shot on site in order to spill the right amount of blood. Shortly afterwards, the other frontier incidents planned by Heydrich were carried out near Kreuzburg and Hochlinden.

At dawn on 1 September, sixty German divisions began rolling across the Polish frontier, the massive guns of the old battleship *Schleswig-Holstein* opened fire on the Polish garrison in Danzig harbour, and Göring's Stukas howled down on their targets, their banshee wails heralding the explosions of their bombs as they destroyed Polish air bases and planes on the ground. The war had begun.

Shortly before 10 a.m., on a heavy, overcast morning, Hitler drove through almost deserted streets to the Kroll Opera House to address the Reichstag. No one cheered as he drove past. The few people who were on the streets were faced with the ominous sight of five heavy anti-aircraft guns which had been set up overnight along the East–West Axis in the heart of the city, to augment the lighter 88-mm guns that had been hoisted on to the roofs of buildings like the Adlon Hotel.

Göring had boasted many times that no British bomber would ever reach Berlin, and that if any did, 'You can call me Meier!' But he was taking no chances.

In place of his usual brown jacket and swastika armband, Hitler wore a new field grey tunic, with a small SS eagle high on the left sleeve, which his SS aides had had tailored for him without his knowledge. About one hundred deputies had been called up for military service, but Göring, who presided as normal, had made sure there were no empty seats by having party functionaries drafted in. Ribbentrop, back in favour having triumphed over Göring by blocking all his efforts to prevent war, sat in the prize position on Hitler's right, with Hess on his left. Hitler's speech was not one of his best – Shirer, listening in from a radio studio as he relayed it live to the USA for CBS, thought he sounded hesitant and unsure of himself, and strangely on the defensive, as if he was 'dazed at the fix he had got himself into and felt a little desperate about it'.[17] He described the assault on Poland as a counter-attack, blamed Poland for everything, and trotted out the usual fantastic farrago of lies, self-justification and braggadocio.

Not until he neared the end did he speak the truth: 'I am asking of no German man more than I myself was ready to do throughout four years . . . From this moment, my whole life shall belong more than ever to my people. I now want nothing more than to be the first soldier of the German Reich. I have once more put on this uniform, which is most sacred and dear to me. I will not take it off again until victory is ours – or I shall not live to see the end.' In case of such an eventuality, he named Göring as his successor.

There was no immediate declaration of war from either Britain or France, mainly because of confusion over the facts. Göring had sent a message to Henderson at 6 a.m. to tell him that the Poles had started the war by blowing up the bridge over the Vistula at Dirchau – the aerial and paratrooper operation to prevent this had been foiled by early morning fog. He said that Hitler had given orders for Polish forces to be driven back from the frontier and their forward air force destroyed after he had heard of this and the attack on the radio station at Gleiwitz. During the day, however, Chamberlain and Halifax steadfastly refused all approaches – mainly made through the indefatigable Dahlerus – to talk while German troops remained on Polish soil. At the same time, Hitler, equally steadfastly, rejected all Mussolini's offers

to mediate: the Italian leader tried to persuade him to call a temporary halt to the fighting, to be followed immediately by a five-power
conference, but Hitler would have none of it.

By the evening, the truth was becoming clear, and Henderson and
Coulondre were instructed to deliver notes warning that unless the
Germans suspended all aggressive action and gave satisfactory assur-
ances that they would withdraw their forces from Polish territory,
Britain and France would fulfil their obligations to Poland. Ribbentrop,
po-faced, received each of them without comment except to say that
Poland was the aggressor and that he would pass on their notes to the
Führer. Neither of the notes specified a deadline, and therefore neither
was an ultimatum as such. Seizing on this as confirmation of his blind
belief that Britain would not fight, Ribbentrop invited Sir Horace
Wilson to Berlin for talks. The response shook him: Wilson told Hesse,
who had approached him on Ribbentrop's behalf, that there could be
no talks until Germany withdrew from Poland. He went on to say that
Chamberlain's delay in declaring war 'had excited the most violent
indignation in the House of Commons and in the Cabinet', and that
Germany could expect an ultimatum the next day.[18]

When Hesse's report of this response arrived, Ribbentrop was in the
Chancellery with Hitler and Göring, both of whom read the telegram.
Hitler angrily reproached Ribbentrop, asking 'What's this?' and Göring
could not resist rubbing it in. Ribbentrop gritted his teeth and replied
defiantly, 'I still believe I am right, my Führer.'[19] But when the British
Embassy called the Foreign Ministry after midnight to make an appointment for Henderson to present a note at 9 a.m. the next morning, he
decided he could not face him, and ordered Schmidt to receive it in
his place. The next morning, Göring once again offered to fly to
London, and even ordered a plane to be prepared. But he was rebuffed
with the now familiar response: no talks without withdrawal. Time
had finally run out.

The British note, as expected, was an ultimatum, stating that: 'If
His Majesty's Government has not received satisfactory assurances of
the cessation of all aggressive action against Poland, and the withdrawal of German troops from that country, by 11 o'clock British
Summer Time, from that time a state of war will exist between Great
Britain and Germany.' Henderson, a gentleman to the last, told Schmidt
he was sorry to be handing such a document to him in particular, 'as
you have always been most anxious to help'.

Schmidt hurried across to the Chancellery, where most of the senior ministers and leading party members were crushed into the ante-room. He pushed his way through and into the study. Hitler was sitting at his desk, and Ribbentrop stood by the window. Both looked up expectantly, and listened as Schmidt slowly translated the ultimatum. When he had finished, there was complete silence. Hitler sat motionless, staring ahead. Finally, after what seemed to Schmidt like an age, he turned to Ribbentrop, who had remained standing by the window. 'What now?' he asked, with a savage look 'as though implying that his Foreign Minister had misled him about England's probable reaction.'

Ribbentrop answered quietly: 'I assume that the French will hand in a similar ultimatum within the hour.'

His duty done, Schmidt backed out of the room with some relief. In the ante-room he announced the news to the crowd. It was greeted once again with complete silence. 'Everywhere in the room,' Schmidt recalled, 'I saw looks of grave concern even amongst the lesser party people.' He noticed Goebbels standing in a corner, 'downcast and self-absorbed, looking like the proverbial drenched poodle'.

The silence was finally broken by Göring. 'If we lose this war,' he said, 'then God have mercy on us.'[20]

PART FIVE

WAR: GERMANY TRIUMPHANT

XXV

BLITZKRIEG

HITLER'S special train, *Amerika*, pulled out of Berlin's Stettiner Station at 9 p.m. on Sunday, 3 September, heading east. Completed only days before, the train consisted of a steam locomotive (a second was added later, to work in tandem) hauling fifteen armour-plated cars, protected at front and rear by banks of 2-centimetre quick-firing anti-aircraft guns, mounted on flat cars and manned by a crew of twenty-six. Hitler's own Pullman car, number 10206, was at the front, immediately behind the first flak car and a car containing baggage and a power generator. It contained his sleeping compartment, bathroom and drawing-room, plus accommodation for his Chief Wehrmacht Adjutant, Colonel Rudolf Schmundt, his Chief Personal Adjutant, Wilhelm Brückner, and a valet. It was followed, in order, by a conference-car with a communications centre with several teletype machines, a car housing the 22 SS and SD men of his escort, a dining-car, two sleeping-cars for the rest of his personal entourage plus any guests, a bath-car, a staff dining-car, two cars for secretaries, aides, cooks and signal-corps men, a car for Press Chief Otto Dietrich, with a 700-watt short-wave radio transmitter, and finally another baggage and generator car before the rear flak car. Hitler's Pullman, the main dining-car and the sleeping-cars could be connected with the postal telephone network during stops.[1]

Amerika was the first of a long series of Führer headquarters that Hitler would occupy for most of the Second World War, preferring the cramped and inconvenient accommodation of rail cars and damp concrete bunkers to the luxury of his new Chancellery. If they wanted to remain close to him – and most of them were terrified of being far from his side – his lieutenants had to follow suit. Shortly after *Amerika* steamed out of Berlin, it was followed by two others: *Atlas*, which was used by the OKW's General Staff, and *Heinrich*, which housed such civilian notables as Himmler – hence the train's code-name – Chancellery Chief of Staff Lammers, and Ribbentrop. *Heinrich* at that time consisted of an amazing collection of cars which, according to Paul Schmidt, who accompanied Ribbentrop, was made up of 'almost every variety of model which had ever rolled on German tracks', from ancient, decorated carriages to Ribbentrop's newly-built streamlined saloon. The passengers, jammed together in discomfort, were as ill-matched as the rolling stock. Schmidt commented wryly on the situation in his memoirs:

Had this arrangement gone on, conditions would have been impossible, owing to the continual friction between Himmler, Ribbentrop and Lammers. If the three had in later years to travel together the train would doubtless have exploded from the internal stresses, if the conflicting views of its occupants about the political and geographical routes they wanted to travel had not already wrenched it to pieces. In the early period, however, they were all more or less going in the same direction, and even used to pay visits in the evenings to each other's saloons.

Ribbentrop's staff lived in a Mitropa sleeping-car and worked in one of the elderly wooden restaurant-cars, whose accumulators were so weak with age that when the train stopped the lights faded and they had to resort to candles stuck in empty bottles. The Foreign Minister himself sat in his saloon-car, directing operations. 'This,' Schmidt said, 'took the form mostly of hour-long telephone conversations with the Foreign Office in Berlin, in the course of which he became wildly excited. His yells resounded far across the lonely railway siding on to which we were usually shunted . . . A rain of "cowards", "lazybones", "dunderheads" and "people who don't seem to know there's a war on" came from the Minister's coach.'[2]

Goebbels and Göring both sensibly stayed behind in Berlin to get on with their own jobs. Göring supervised Luftwaffe operations through the Air Ministry and, revelling in his role as pseudo Prime Minister, convened almost daily meetings of the Defence Council, restoring a semblance of Cabinet government to the Reich. He was completely back to his old self, vital, vigorous, and, according to Darré, who was one of several ministers regularly co-opted to the Council, 'every inch a soldier'. 'What a guy!' Darré noted after one meeting. 'Hess sends his stooge as usual: what a zero, he can't stand up to Göring. Thus the dwindling party is gradually frozen out.'[3] Somehow, Göring also found time to make morale-boosting visits to airfields and munitions factories, where he told the workers that Germany was still willing to make 'an honest peace' with the Western powers, but that if British or French planes tried to bomb Germany they would suffer fearful retaliation. The day before, still putting out hopeful peace signals, he had phoned Dahlerus in Stockholm and told him that he would not make the first move against Britain.

Goebbels, who had shared Göring's anti-war feelings, took refuge in self-deception, convincing himself against all the evidence that whatever Hitler did must be right, and that when it finally came to it Britain and France would not actually fight. To stop them convincing the German public otherwise, or sowing doubts by contradicting the German version of what was happening, one of his first acts was to draft a decree forbidding any unauthorised persons from listening to foreign broadcasts or spreading news picked up from them. The penalty was imprisonment in a concentration camp or even, 'in particularly serious cases', death. Conveniently, he already had the mechanism in place for enforcing the new law: the existing network of 'radio monitors' set up to ensure that people listened dutifully to party broadcasts.

The Wehrmacht had gone into battle accompanied for the first time ever by integrated propaganda units, so that a 'war of words' would be conducted at the same time as the 'war of weapons'. Although these units came under Wehrmacht operational control, their aims and material were provided by Goebbels. He was naturally pleased by the new status this gave him, but his success in the military field was offset by a reverse in the area of foreign propaganda, which he had taken over from the Foreign Ministry in 1933.

Since becoming Foreign Minister, Ribbentrop had been irked by this encroachment on his territory, and for the last two years had been 'nibbling away' at Goebbels's authority. Goebbels had naturally resisted any attack on his empire, particularly from a man he so despised, and during the summer they had had several 'very ugly confrontations', culminating in a physical battle for control of an overseas broadcasting station set up by Ribbentrop in Charlottenburg. Goebbels had been furious about this incursion into not one but two areas of his authority – foreign propaganda and radio – and he had sent a gang of Berlin SA men to seize the station. Ribbentrop had sent his bodyguard to take it back, and the SS had had to be sent in to stop the fighting. To Goebbels's chagrin, Hitler had ruled in favour of Ribbentrop then, and now, on 8 September, he did so again, albeit ambiguously. Taking advantage of being at his side, Ribbentrop had persuaded Hitler that he should be responsible for deciding policy on foreign propaganda during the war. His victory was only qualified, however: the practicalities were still to be handled by the Propaganda Ministry, working to his directives.

Once again, Hitler had ensured that his subordinates would be kept busy competing with each other. He even declared that they were not to approach him again about their differences, unless they were prepared to face him side by side.[4] And so the differences – and the competition – continued. They both set up press clubs for foreign correspondents in Berlin, and their ministries both held press conferences for them at 11 a.m. each day. To ensure that journalists attended, their food ration coupons were issued fortnightly at the end of a conference; Goebbels scored a notable point by arranging for 'his' correspondents to receive the bigger rations normally reserved for heavy industrial workers.

By the time the special trains pulled out of Berlin heading for the front, Göring's Luftwaffe had already virtually destroyed the Polish Air Force in a series of devastating raids on airfields and defensive installations, and had disrupted communications with attacks on roads and railways. Although what remained of the Polish Air Force fought valiantly, most of its planes were obsolescent and no match for the German Me-109s and Stukas, which soon gained total air supremacy.

The new concept of blitzkrieg depended on tight co-ordination between ground and air forces, and the Luftwaffe played its part to the full, strafing and dive-bombing Polish troops and creating further confusion by bombing towns and cities. This was an essential role, for despite the legend that has since grown up that everything was mechanised or armoured, the bulk of the German army still moved on foot or by horse: on 1 September 1939, German ground forces possessed well over half a million horses. Of the sixty German divisions involved in Poland, only five were armoured, each with about 300 tanks, five were 'light' divisions with fewer tanks, and only five of the forty-two infantry divisions were motorised. The Poles, however, had only two mechanised brigades.[5] Stories of Polish cavalry hopelessly charging German tanks with lances is a myth, originally created by Goebbels's propaganda companies to sap Polish morale, but they might just as well have been true. Outnumbered, outmanoeuvred and outgunned, and with no air support, their forces, no matter how bravely they fought, were doomed from the start. After only five days, the Polish army had been cut to shreds, though it continued to resist for another three weeks.

With the Wehrmacht closing in on Warsaw, the Polish government fled to Brest-Litovsk on 6 September. Two days later, 60,000 Polish troops were surrounded near Radom, to the south of Warsaw, and the 4th Panzer Division smashed its way into the suburbs of the capital itself. From his railway siding in Pomerania, Ribbentrop called on the Soviet government to send in the Red Army to grab its agreed share of the country, but Stalin and Molotov temporised: Stalin had no intention of getting involved in any actual fighting. He preferred to wait until Warsaw had fallen, so that he could claim that the Polish government had ceased to exist and that he was sending in the Red Army to restore order and to aid the Ukrainians and Belorussians who were being 'threatened' by Germany. He also had some unfinished business in the Far East, where his troops under Marshal Zhukov were locked in a decisive battle with the Japanese.

To put pressure on the Soviets, Ribbentrop directed Canaris, with Hitler's consent, to stage an uprising of Ukrainian nationalists in eastern Poland, with whom the Abwehr's subversion agents had been working for some time, 'aimed at the extermination of Jews and Poles'. 'All Polish farms and dwellings should go up in flames,' he said, 'and all Jews killed.'[6] The uprising began, but Stalin and Molotov were unmoved, and continued to bide their time.

Hitler's panzer commanders, meanwhile, were discovering that tanks were not suited to street fighting. When they were driven back from the suburbs of the city, he turned to the artillery and above all the Luftwaffe to bombard Warsaw into submission. The Luftwaffe distinguished itself, and therefore brought fresh kudos to its Commander-in-Chief, by the ferocity and accuracy of its bombing, but even so it took some days to accomplish the task, by which time there was not a single building left undamaged. Ribbentrop told Molotov on 16 September that the city would fall the next day, and the Red Army began moving into eastern Poland at dawn – Stalin had, coincidentally, signed a cease-fire that day with the defeated Japanese in Mongolia.

To Ribbentrop's fury, Schmidt had failed to wake him at 5 a.m. to tell him it was happening. Standing in his underpants, face lathered, brandishing his razor, he yelled angrily: 'The German and Russian armies are rushing towards each other – there may be clashes – and all because you were too slack to waken me! You have meddled with the course of world history! You have not enough experience for that!' Schmidt tried to calm him by reminding him that there was an agreed demarcation line and that the two armies were in direct communication with each other, but it was no use. What had really infuriated Ribbentrop was that Goebbels had heard the news first, and it had therefore been released through the Propaganda Ministry rather than the Foreign Ministry Press Office.[7]

In the event, Warsaw held out until 27 September, by which time the Soviets had taken possession of their share of the country, with disgruntled Wehrmacht commanders, who knew nothing of the secret protocol, having to pull back from ground they had conquered. And Ribbentrop was flying back to Moscow to sign the German–Soviet Boundary and Friendship Treaty formalising the new frontiers – at the time he received the news of the fall of Warsaw he was eating a quick lunch at the Park Hotel in Königsberg, where his plane had landed to refuel. In Moscow, he was discomfited to find that Stalin had changed his mind about the division of the spoils. He did not want the areas of central Poland that had been specified in the Pact, only the regions of the Ukraine and Belorussia that the Soviets had lost in 1920. To Stalin, Poles always meant trouble, and never more so than when they were divided, and he was happy to let Hitler have them all. In exchange, he wanted Lithuania, to complete his set of Baltic states.

Ribbentrop tried to negotiate, but was completely out of his depth with Stalin, who had almost certainly planned the whole thing all along, knowing that Hitler might initially have dug in his heels over Lithuania, with its strong ethnic German connections. When the Nazi leader now agreed to hand it over without a fuss, Stalin was heard to tell Molotov that he had in effect declared war on the Soviet Union – the only reason he had given Lithuania away was because he intended to take it back again as soon as the time was right. Oddly, this does not seem to have occurred to Ribbentrop, who flew home after being fêted with a magnificent twenty-four-course banquet in the Kremlin, and enthused to Hitler over his reception, saying how much he had felt at home in Moscow, 'as though among old party comrades'. His remark did not go down well with the genuine old party comrades, who had never accepted him as one of them.

*   *   *

After making a triumphal progress through the streets of Danzig on 19 September, Hitler had spent the last week of the Polish campaign in the comfort of the Kasino Hotel in the nearby seaside resort of Zoppot. From there he made two flights to the outskirts of Warsaw, where he enjoyed a grandstand view from the tower of a sports stadium of the planes and guns pulverising the city before his eyes. Satisfied that his aim of permanently obliterating the Polish capital was proceeding according to plan, he boarded his train again on 26 September and headed back to Berlin.

That evening, Göring brought Dahlerus to see him, and together they briefed the Swede and sent him back to London to talk to Halifax and Chamberlain yet again. 'The British can have peace if they want it,' Hitler told Dahlerus. 'But they will have to hurry.'[8] They would indeed – only a few hours later, Hitler called his commanders-in-chief to a meeting and ordered them to prepare 'Operation Yellow', the attack on the West. It was to begin at the end of October, while the world was still in awe of German military might and before Britain could finish building up her strength.

Göring did not demur. Like Hitler, he still hoped that they might reach an accommodation with Britain, if need be after defeating France: Hitler told the commanders-in-chief that his aim for the attack in the West was 'to destroy France and bring Britain to her knees'.[9] Throughout the Polish campaign, Göring had tried to keep his connections with London alive through various channels, and had even made contact with Roosevelt in the United States, though these approaches had all eventually come to nothing. Now, he held out the possibility of setting up what was left of Poland as a new, independent state with which Germany could sign a peace treaty, thus letting Britain off the hook and opening the door to an armistice.

On 6 October, Hitler spoke to the Reichstag lauding the Wehrmacht's victory: 'In all history there has scarcely been a comparable military achievement . . . ' He lambasted the Poles and made much of his new alliance with the Soviet Union, which had enabled him to complete the dismantling of the Versailles Treaty. And then he spoke of his desire not merely for an understanding with France and Britain but for friendship. 'I believe,' he went on, 'even today that there can only be real peace in Europe and throughout the world if Germany and England come to an understanding . . . Why should this war in the West be fought? For the restoration of Poland? The Poland of the Versailles Treaty will never rise again. This is guaranteed by two of the biggest states in the world.'

He proposed a four-power conference to solve the problems of European peace and security, saying 'it would be more sensible to tackle the solution before millions of men are first sent uselessly to their death'. But he finished on a warning note: 'If, however, the opinions of Messrs Churchill and his followers should prevail, this statement will have been my last. Then we shall fight, and there will never be another November 1918 in German history.'[10] It amounted, in Ian Kershaw's graphic phrase, to 'an olive branch clenched in a mailed fist'.

Goebbels seized eagerly on the propaganda opportunity, directing the German press to play up the speech for all it was worth, ignoring the fact that as a serious peace proposal it was worthless. The *Völkischer Beobachter* headlines next day led the way: 'HITLER'S PEACE OFFER. NO WAR AIMS AGAINST FRANCE AND BRITAIN. REDUCTION OF ARMAMENTS. PROPOSAL OF A CONFERENCE'. But Chamberlain and Daladier were unimpressed by such vague promises. The British Prime Minister had finally learned that Hitler's word meant nothing, and on 12 October he rejected the supposed offer in a national broadcast, and turned away Göring's back-door peace feelers – Dahlerus had been shuttling to and fro again, and was then in the Hague, waiting for a reply to a letter from Göring which he had delivered to the British Ambassador to Holland, reiterating what Hitler had said in his speech.

Hitler promptly cashed in on Chamberlain's refusal, blaming him for 'rejecting the hand of peace and deliberately choosing war'. Leaping in ahead of Goebbels, Ribbentrop had his press department issue a circular to all foreign stations denouncing Chamberlain's response as 'an outrageous affront'. Göring told Dahlerus the German government would make no reply to Chamberlain's statement, which he described as a declaration of war, and called him back to Berlin. He kept up his approaches to London, while still trying to persuade Hitler to postpone the attack, but his chances of success dwindled steadily, and the military build-up continued apace.

Goebbels had started the war with a lie, by condemning the 'Polish terrorist attacks on German soil' at Gleiwitz and Hochlinden, and now followed it up with another, even bigger one. On 3 September, some two hundred miles west of the Hebrides, a German U-boat had sunk the British passenger liner *Athenia*, carrying mostly women and children evacuees to Canada and America. 112 of the 1,400 passengers, including twenty-eight Americans, died. With memories of how the sinking of the *Lusitania* had been one of the factors that had brought America into the First World War, the Germans had vigorously denied that any of their submarines was involved. Since the U-boats were operating under strict radio silence, the truth could not be known for sure until they had all returned to base. The *U-30*, which had been responsible, did not dock until 27 September, when her captain claimed that he had mistaken the liner for an armed merchant cruiser, which would have been a legitimate target. With Hitler's blessing, Rear-Admiral Doenitz, the Commander-in-Chief of U-boats, ordered this to be deleted from the *U-30*'s log and kept secret. But after Britain had rejected Hitler's new peace offer on 7 October, Goebbels was allowed to use the sinking in a ploy that was exceptionally cynical even by his own standards. On Sunday, 22 October he went to the microphone and broadcast an accusation that Churchill, as First Lord of the Admiralty, had personally ordered a time bomb to be planted in the *Athenia*'s hold, so that he could blame Germany for the sinking. The next day, the *Völkischer Beobachter* carried the story on its front page under the unequivocal headline 'CHURCHILL SANK THE ATHENIA'.[11]

Brauchitsch and the army generals objected vehemently to Hitler's plans for a quick attack on the West, despite the fact that the troop trains had been rolling westwards at full capacity ever since the fall of Warsaw, redeploying the fighting divisions to the French and Belgian borders. According to Keitel, who shared the generals' reservations, 'they considered that the army was as yet not capable of launching any fresh assault after its Eastern campaign, without a pause to recover, to regroup and remobilise, to finish its training and to complete its re-equipping. Particular doubts were expressed about winter warfare, with the fog and rain, the short days and the long nights, which made mobile warfare virtually impossible.'[12] But when first Keitel and then Brauchitsch pressed their views on Hitler, he flew into such violent rages that they both offered their resignations – which he refused, saying 'he would prefer not to have such requests made to him in future'. He said, Keitel wrote later, that 'it was his prerogative to tell me when he had no further use for my services, and until then I was to do as I was told in the office to which he had appointed me.'[13]

Göring felt just as strongly as the generals – the Luftwaffe had used up half of its entire stock of bombs in Poland, 189 aircrew had been killed and 285 aircraft lost, mostly during low-level attacks on Polish anti-aircraft batteries, and he still had few planes capable of attacking Britain from airfields in Germany. But he knew better than to argue with Hitler. Instead, he ordered the Luftwaffe to prepare for action in the West, while he continued with his peace efforts until the end of the year, through intermediaries as diverse as the King of Sweden, the European President of General Motors, and an American oil million-aire, William Rhodes Davis, as well as the dogged Dahlerus.

Göring's peace efforts, and his known opposition to war with the West, led him into an ambivalent and potentially dangerous situation at this time. When he returned from London at the beginning of October, Dahlerus had brought the difficult message that the British would only negotiate with a new German government, one not led by Hitler. The clear implication was that Göring should be its leader. After discussing this in the garden at Carinhall, where Dahlerus had asked him point blank whether his loyalty was to Hitler or Germany, Göring arranged for him to meet Canaris, who he knew was critical of Hitler. Whether he also knew that the slippery spymaster was involved in a conspiracy to overthrow the Führer is impossible to say. Such conspir-acies certainly existed; there were several disparate opposition groups, each with its own programme, but the most important was led by Colonel-General Beck, who had resigned as Chief of the Army General Staff in 1938. Halder, who had succeeded Beck, was another promi-nent member among the generals, and the civilians included former Ambassador Ulrich von Hassell and Carl Friedrich Goerdeler, who had resigned from his post as Mayor of Leipzig in protest against Nazi anti-Semitic measures.

Meeting on 11 October at the Continental Hotel in Munich, Goerdeler asked Hassell whether he thought Göring could be a possible leader. 'In spite of serious doubts,' Hassell recorded in his diary, 'he had come to the conclusion that Göring was the only solution – temporarily, of course. Beck also had finally come to that conclusion. I agreed with this view.' Goerdeler then went on to say that 'high functionaries from Göring's entourage had sounded him out as to whether we might be inclined to use Göring to put things in order'.[14] According to Goerdeler, Göring's unnamed 'high functionaries' had agreed to the conspirators' conditions, which centred around a return to the rule of law, but nothing more seems to have come of the approach. The plotters were indecisive talkers not doers, and it would be another four and a half years before they would find the courage to take any action, by which time Göring no longer figured in their plans, nor they in his.

Halder, Beck and the other generals, including Brauchitsch, had decided they would arrest Hitler as soon as he gave the final order for the attack in the West to begin. However, although he was constantly updating his orders, he was also constantly having to put back the date for one reason or another, initially because of a shortage of spare parts for the tanks, later because of bad weather. The havoc wreaked by the Luftwaffe on the Polish Army had impressed him so deeply that he refused to launch his attack without the assurance of several days' clear flying weather to allow Göring's aircraft to do their stuff again. In the absence of such an assurance, he postponed and rescheduled the attack no fewer than fourteen times between November and January, denying the conspirators the excuse they needed for his arrest and Göring's promotion.

The success of the Luftwaffe, plus his energetic efforts to keep Britain out of the war, had restored Göring to favour and confirmed his position as the second man in the Reich. But the man who benefited most from the Polish campaign was undoubtedly Himmler, who seized every opportunity to extend his own power base. At the beginning of the war, he had taken another step towards his planned integration of the SS and police into a State Security Corps by putting the Gestapo, the Kripo (Criminal Police), the Sipo (Security Police) and the SD under a single Central Office for Reich Security, the Reichssicherheitshauptamt, known as the RSHA. The SD, which was still a party agency, became a state organisation too, funded by the state and so freed from interference from jealous party rivals like Rosenberg. One of the benefits of the new body to Himmler was that it moved the Gestapo further away from Göring, who was still its nominal chief.

While Himmler was officially head of the RSHA, it was managed by Heydrich, as his Deputy Director. Under its umbrella, Heydrich formed five SD Einsatzgruppen, Special Task Forces, one to accompany each German army into Poland. Each Einsatzgruppe was divided into four Kommandos of 100–150 men, which were attached to army corps. They wore the army-style uniforms of the SS-VT, with the SD diamond on the left sleeve, and were officially charged with 'the suppression of all anti-Reich and anti-German elements in rear of the fighting troops, in particular counter-espionage, arrest of politically unreliable persons, confiscation of weapons, safeguarding important counter-espionage material, etc.'[15] This sounded like a normal military policing assignment, but the Einsatzgruppen had other purposes that were kept from the officers and men of the army: they were to decapitate Poland by liquidating aristocrats, intellectuals, teachers, doctors, priests, landowners, businessmen – all those capable of providing leadership or forming a new ruling class. An even more unsavoury task was to provide beds for wounded German soldiers by removing patients from mental hospitals in Pomerania and West Prussia and killing them with a single shot in the back of the neck. They were also, of course, to start rounding up and removing Jews.

When the Einsatzkommandos went into action with pre-prepared lists of victims, shooting or hanging them in their thousands without trial or ceremony and in full view of soldiers and civilians, some shocked generals complained. The arbitrary killings, they protested, were affecting the morale of their troops, who were 'especially incensed that instead of fighting at the front, young men should be demonstrating their courage against defenceless civilians'.[16] They also pointed out that the actions were seriously damaging the economic productivity of the conquered lands, and demanded that the 'housecleaning', as it was called, 'should be deferred until the army has withdrawn and the country turned over to civil administration', which they envisaged for early December.[17]

Brauchitsch, as spineless as ever, declined to condemn the activities of the Einsatzgruppen. According to Halder, who raised the matter with him, he limited himself to saying that 'Nothing must occur which would afford foreign countries an opportunity to launch any sort of atrocity propaganda based on such incidents. Catholic clergy! Impractical at this time.'[18] Hitler was unmoved by moral or propaganda arguments but decreed on 21 September, presumably after conferring with Göring, that economic needs were more important than ideology, at least for the moment, and that all racial measures should be postponed until the end of military operations.

Heydrich put his own interpretation on Hitler's decree. Presenting it to a meeting of his SD and Sipo departmental chiefs and Einsatzgruppen commanders on the day it was issued, he told them that while the order for executions had been withdrawn, nothing could be allowed to interfere with measures against Polish aristocrats, priests and teachers, who had no significant economic importance. Those in the western provinces were to be arrested at once, and either sent to a concentration camp or deported to what he called 'the foreign-speaking Gau' to the east. Actions against the Jews were also to continue. Large areas of western Poland were to be cleared completely of Jews, while elsewhere all Jews living in the countryside were to be moved into ghettos in cities situated at railway junctions, 'so that future measures may be accomplished more easily'. Farmland belonging to Jews was to be expropriated, and 'entrusted to the care' of German 'or even Polish' peasants. Over the next twelve months, they were to be transported by goods trains into central Poland, together with Jews from the Reich, and 30,000 gypsies.[19]

The division of Poland was completed on 8 October when Hitler and Göring jointly signed an order annexing the western provinces of Poland into Germany, under the new name of the Warthegau. In the east, Stalin tried to give his seizure of the Ukrainian and Belorussian provinces a semblance of legality by waiting until elections could be staged – in both senses of the word – some three weeks later, for 'peoples' assemblies' which instantly proclaimed Soviet power and asked the Supreme Soviet of the USSR to 'admit' their territories into the Soviet Union. But Hitler was in too much of a hurry for such formalities.

Like Stalin, Hitler did not want troublesome Poles within the Reich, and he designated the central region of the former country as the 'General-Government of Poland', with Cracow as its capital, to be ruled directly by Germany but not to be part of it. As Governor-General, he appointed Hans Frank, his and the party's legal adviser, former Minister of Justice in Bavaria, and President of the German Bar Association. Frank had always seemed to be a civilised and reasonably cultured man, described by William Shirer as 'one of the least repulsive of the men around Hitler'.[20] But the mask was stripped away immediately with his first public pronouncement after his appointment: 'The Poles,' he declared, 'shall be the slaves of the German Reich.' And he went on to match his words with deeds in the most bloodthirsty way. Later, when he heard that Neurath, who had been appointed 'Protector' of Bohemia and Moravia, had put up posters announcing the execution of seven Czech university students, Frank boasted: 'If I wished to order posters to be put up about every seven Poles shot, there would not be enough forests in Poland to make the paper for them.'[21]

Göring needed to start exploiting Polish resources as soon as possible, to feed the war machine. There was no problem with the annexed provinces, where everything automatically became German, but in the General-Government he expected Frank to extract food, raw materials, machinery and forced labour for the Reich. Frank was also expected to accommodate, in one way or another, the millions of people who were to be poured into the General-Government like waste into a sink. These fell into two categories: Jews from all parts of the Reich, and Poles from the Warthegau. These unfortunate souls, whose families had often lived in the region for centuries, were to be evicted and moved east of the Vistula, to be replaced with German settlers and *Volksdeutsche*, ethnic Germans who were to be 'repatriated' from the Baltic states, outlying parts of the old Poland, and the new Soviet areas.

Hitler gave the job of removing and replacing Jews and Poles to the man he knew would put his heart and soul into the task, Heinrich Himmler. As head of the SS, Himmler was already committed to the purification of the German race, and during 1939 had taken direct control of the multifarious agencies dealing with racial matters, which had proliferated in the usual Nazi way in a welter of overlapping and competing bureaucracy. Now, with Hitler's blessing, he set up a new organisation, the Reich Commissariat for the Consolidation of German Nationhood, the RKFDV, which was to be the supreme office for all racial matters, ranging from the repatriation and resettlement of all ethnic Germans from other countries to the elimination of 'all foreign elements within the Reich which represented a danger to the German state and people'.

In these matters, Himmler was given authority over all other Reich offices and all administrators in the occupied territories.[22] This was a massive strengthening of his position, though Hitler, typically, left room for friction by not rescinding the overall responsibility for Jewish matters in the Reich that he had given to Göring back in 1938. Preoccupied with his war in the West, Hitler was happy to leave Himmler to do as he pleased in Poland, and Himmler took full advantage – though he was careful to clear all his actions with Hitler first, so that he could silence opponents or critics by saying 'I do nothing that the Führer does not know about'.[23]

Poland offered Himmler the opportunity at last to start realising his youthful dreams of a new Teutonic empire in the East, populated with pure German settlers contentedly working the land and raising generations of Aryan children along with their crops. He had tried to make a start in the Czech lands earlier in the year, but had been thwarted by the needs of the German armaments manufacturers for Czech industry and labour and their fears of the upheavals that would be created by mass deportations at such a critical time. In the former Poland, there were no such obstacles; there was even somewhere to put the dispossessed.

He started by ordering the relocation to the General-Government of 550,000 of the 650,000 Jews in the annexed provinces, together with all Poles considered unfit for 'assimilation'. Within a year, 1,200,000 Poles and 300,000 Jews had been cleared out, though only 497,000 *Volksdeutsche* had arrived to take their places. The expulsions began on 7 November, with forced marches over frozen ground and slow rail journeys in unheated box cars. For those who survived the journey, Himmler provided no housing or shelter, in spite of the fact that the winter was one of the harshest in living memory. The weather proved an excellent ally for the Nazis in their 'cleansing' mission: it killed more Poles and Jews than the German execution squads accounted for.[24]

Himmler had added an important extra strand to his tangled web of control at the beginning of the war through a new rank of police and SS officer, the Höherer SS- und Polizeiführer, or HSSPF. These officials, one for each military district both in the Reich and in the conquered territories, were to take overall command on his behalf of all his forces – the regular SS, VT, and all police – co-ordinating their activities and moving towards ever-closer integration. As his personal representatives, they were responsible for all matters of security and race, a definition that could be stretched to cover just about everything. In theory, they were subordinate to the military or civilian heads of the occupation governments – the generals and Gauleiters, and the Governor-General – but they took orders from them only 'in so far as these did not conflict with the orders of the Gestapo or higher authorities' – in other words, Heydrich and Himmler. Their ambivalent status inevitably caused confusion and conflict, especially with the military governors: already sickened and infuriated by the activities of the Einsatzgruppen, the generals could hardly wait to hand over to the civil authorities and turn their backs on the whole unpleasant business, which they did on 26 October.

By the time the new civil administrations took over the conquered territories from the military, the Einsatzgruppen had been turned into regional sub-divisions of the Gestapo and SD, answerable to the HSSPFs, and through them to Himmler. They formed the bases of alternative, SS governments, a sure source of internecine disputes over precedence, which started to erupt almost at once and continued throughout the life of the regime.

Not content with the powers he had acquired as Reich Commissar for the Consolidation of German Nationhood, nor even as Reichsführer-SS and Chief of the German Police, Himmler went on obsessively adding new pieces to his complex bureaucratic apparatus. His subsidiary offices concerned with racial control already included the Central Office for Race and Resettlement, the Ancestral Heritage Office to investigate the credentials of Germans who were to be resettled, the Lebensborn programme which initially provided orphanages for the illegitimate children of SS men but which was fast developing into an SS human stud farm, and the Liaison Office for Ethnic Germans. In October, he set up a Central Land Office, to handle the sequestration and redistribution of property, and a Central Immigration Office to deal with the repatriation of *Volksdeutsche*, especially those from the Baltic states. This had to be balanced by a Central Office for Evacuation, and by a new department in the RSHA under the direction of Adolf Eichmann to specialise in evacuating Jews. Added to these were agencies to handle and manage confiscated property.

The list – and the Himmler empire – simply went on growing. But it did not do so without opposition. Frank, of course, objected to having so many Jews and Poles dumped in his fiefdom, refused to allow in transports, and threatened to have Eichmann arrested if he ever set foot in the General-Government. Albert Forster, whom Hitler had appointed Gauleiter of the new Gau of Danzig–West Prussia, flatly rejected Himmler's orders to accommodate German Balts from Estonia: puffed up by the role Danzig had played in the Polish conflict, he saw himself as a contender for the succession and Himmler as a hated rival, and obstructed him whenever he could. Erich Koch, Gauleiter of the enlarged New East Prussia, which included large areas of formerly Polish territory, was equally adamant that he would not allow repatriated immigrants to be settled there. The squabbles over jurisdiction dragged on and on, delaying and threatening Himmler's Arcadian vision.

To add to Himmler's problems, Göring suddenly muscled in by setting up the Haupttreuhandelstelle Ost (HTO), the Main Trust Office for the East, to grab all confiscated Polish-Jewish property for the Four-Year Plan. This would completely block the work of Himmler's Central Land Office in redistributing property to *Volksdeutsche* settlers, but when he complained, Göring pulled rank and simply referred him to the head of the HTO. After a great deal of haggling, Himmler was allowed to have agricultural land, but all industrial and urban property was to go to the HTO. It was a salutary reminder that Göring was still at the top of the pecking order after Hitler. When Darré, the Minister of Agriculture, set up his own office for the management of sequestered Polish estates, he placed it under Göring's HTO, even though he had always shared Himmler's Utopian dreams.

Göring's immediate concern was to exploit the former Polish lands to the full. On 19 October he issued a directive for the 'complete incorporation' of the industries of the annexed provinces 'into the Greater German economic system at the earliest possible time', and the removal from the General-Government of 'all raw materials, scrap materials, machines, et cetera, which are of use for the German war economy. Enterprises which are not necessary for the meagre maintenance of the bare existence of the population,' he ruled, 'must be transferred to Germany.'[25] But he wanted more than machinery and materials: he demanded that Frank provide 'at least one million male and female agricultural and industrial workers to the Reich – among them at least 750,000 agricultural workers, of which at least 50 per cent must be women, in order to guarantee agricultural production in the Reich and as a replacement for industrial workers lacking in the Reich.'[26] Frank was more than happy to lose a million Polish mouths from the General-Government, and started transporting them early in 1940.

The task of justifying the savage treatment of the Poles to the German people naturally fell to Goebbels, who approached it with his usual zest, concentrating on atrocities they had supposedly committed against the ethnic German minority. There had undoubtedly been many genuine cases, including evictions, beatings, forced marches and shootings, culminating in a bloody massacre in Bydgoszcz (Bromberg). All told, a probable total of around 4,000 ethnic Germans were killed. But this figure was inflated in Goebbels's propaganda first to 5,400, and later to an incredible 58,000. The German public as a whole had no difficulty in accepting the charges: they had been brainwashed for years into believing the Poles, as Slavs, were an inferior race. Hitler certainly believed this. When he returned from Warsaw after taking the salute at the great victory parade on 5 October, he told Goebbels they were 'more animal than human, completely apathetic and amorphous . . . the filth of the Poles is unimaginable. And their ability to make judgements is nil.'[27]

Hitler told Goebbels he did not want Poles to be assimilated. He wanted the General-Government to be simply a reservoir of slave labour, and Goebbels was to be responsible for their 'obedience training'. He was given charge of all propaganda in the territory, and set up branch offices of his ministry in the Governor-General's office and in the four administrative districts of Cracow, Lublin, Radom and Warsaw. But he did not realise the immensity of his task until he visited Poland for the first time at the beginning of November, to check over his new outposts of public enlightenment and to see conditions in the country for himself, and was deeply shocked by the 'oppressive despair' that he found there.

His first stop was Lodz, a city that was to be 'Germanised', cleansed of its 'Polish and Jewish trash' and turned into Litzmannstadt. Seyss-Inquart met him off the plane and gave him a short report before he met Frank for a discussion of the situation, in which they agreed that they could not allow any new cultural life for the Poles, since this would provide a focal point for a revival of Polish nationalism. Touring the Jewish ghetto afterwards he got out of his car to make a thorough inspection. 'Indescribable!' was his disgusted reaction. Echoing Hitler, he wrote in his diary: 'These are not human beings any more, they are animals. So this is not a humanitarian task, but a surgical one. One must operate, and radically. Otherwise, Europe will be destroyed by the Jewish sickness.' He did not have much time for the Poles, either. After viewing the Polish streets, he decided that Asia started here. And in Warsaw, which he described as 'hell', he noted without pity the way the population, 'apathetic and shadowy' – another direct echo of Hitler's words – 'crawled through the streets like insects'.[28]

Goebbels backed up his newspaper coverage of Poland with film, but to his dismay, Hitler was scathing of the quality of the newsreels he pumped into the cinemas every week. Goebbels blamed the 'unimaginative' Wehrmacht cameramen attached to the propaganda companies, but when Hitler went on to complain in a twenty-minute tirade that he was not making any truly Nazi films he could only stutter in his defence that the films he was making were nationalistic. He hurried to put things right with a violently anti-Semitic feature film, *Jud Süss*

(*Jew Süss*), and a major documentary, *Der ewige Jude* (*The Eternal Jew*), which aimed to counter the civilised image of Western Jewry by showing Jews in their 'original state' in the Polish ghettos, in 'pictures that cannot lie'. The final sequence, which women were not allowed to see, showed scenes of the ritual slaughter of animals by a kosher butcher. When Goebbels first saw the footage, he took grim satisfaction in describing it as 'so gruesome and brutal in its details that one's blood runs cold'. 'These Jews,' he concluded with breathtaking hypocrisy, 'must be exterminated.'[29] Hitler agreed with him completely – but not yet. While there was still some hope of coming to terms with the Western powers, he would hold on to the Jews as a bargaining counter.

XXVI

'YELLOW'

WHILE Poland was being dismembered and plundered, the planned attack in the West was being rescheduled every few days. This may have been unnerving for everyone concerned, but the first of the fourteen changes was responsible for saving Hitler's life, possibly twice over. He had reluctantly abandoned his first choice of 25 October as the start date, after finally accepting that the Wehrmacht simply could not be ready by then, but after an acrimonious conference with Brauchitsch and Halder on the 27th, he overrode all their objections and ordered that it would definitely begin on 12 November. Halder alerted his fellow conspirators that their moment had arrived – whereupon they promptly panicked. The great generals' plot collapsed. To their relief, the weather intervened on the 7th. After receiving a bad forecast, Hitler postponed the attack for three days, saying he would confirm the new date at 6 p.m. on 9 November.

The annual reunion of the old fighters in the Bürgerbräukeller was scheduled, as always, for the evening of 8 November. Hitler travelled to Munich to make his regular speech, but because he needed to be back in Berlin the next day to take the vital decision on Operation Yellow, he spoke for a shorter time than usual – Göring claimed that he had called Hitler's adjutant, Julius Schaub, and told him to put a note on the lectern, reminding the Führer to cut his speech short. Whether acting on Göring's instructions or his own initiative, Schaub put several reminders in front of Hitler, who left early to board his special train. Ten minutes later, a bomb exploded in a pillar immediately behind the speaker's position, killing eight people and injuring sixty-three others, sixteen of them seriously.

The bomb had nothing to do with the generals, or with the British

Secret Service, whom Goebbels blamed in the next morning's newspapers. It was in fact the work of a lone assassin, a thirty-six-year-old joiner called Georg Elser, with no particular political affiliations but a quiet, personal determination to put a stop to the madcap rush into war in the only way possible. When the bomb went off, he was already heading for the Swiss frontier, where he was picked up in a routine arrest for trying to enter Switzerland illegally. The contents of his pockets, which included a postcard of the Bürgerbräukeller, gave him away, and when he was taken in for questioning, he confessed readily.

Elser was not executed, or even put on trial, but interned in Sachsenhausen concentration camp, where he was treated as a privileged prisoner until the last days of the war when the Gestapo murdered him. The reason for this was that Hitler and Himmler planned to stage a show trial, at which they would 'prove' that he had been acting for the British Secret Service. Himmler, conveniently, already had his eye on two British agents who could be blamed. For the last month, even while they were occupied with events in Poland, he and Heydrich had been working on an elaborate sting to entrap MI6's Head of Station in The Hague, Major Richard H. Stevens, and his colleague, Captain Sigismund Payne Best, an agent of the Z Organisation, MI6's doubly-secret back-up network. Using one of Heydrich's brightest young SD men, Walter Schellenberg, posing as an anti-Nazi army officer representing a fictitious group of conspirators, they hoped to uncover the identities of the real conspirators.

Stevens and Best were the ideal patsies to take the rap for the assassination attempt, and Himmler ordered Schellenberg to lure them to a café on the German–Dutch border at Venlo. As the two Britons sipped aperitifs on the terrace, Alfred Naujocks and a band of SD heavies crashed through the barrier in a big black car, with sub-machine-guns blazing in the best gangster-movie style, and kidnapped them. They, too, ended up in concentration camps, but were never brought to trial. They had served their purpose, however, by casting the British as ruthless villains and boosting Hitler's popularity, at a time when he needed to convince the German public and military that he was right to attack the West. For Himmler, his success in capturing them had the added benefits of increasing his prestige and at the same time distracting attention from what had been a serious lapse in security in the Bürgerbräukeller – which was, of course, his responsibility.

*   *   *

Early in the New Year, the weather Hitler had been waiting for finally appeared, with a forecast of a period of crisp, cold, dry conditions, ideal for flying. On 10 January 1940, he consulted with Göring and set a new date for the attack in one week's time, on 17 January. The revised plans were updated and distributed. One set, however, for a paratroop division in Cologne, never reached its destination. The Luftwaffe officer detailed to deliver it missed his train on the morning of 11 January after a boozy night out, and hitched a ride, against all regulations, in a light aircraft. Unfortunately, the pilot lost his way, ran short of fuel, and made a forced landing – in Belgium. The officer reported, through the German legation, that he had succeeded in burning the papers 'to insignificant fragments, the size of the palm of his hand' before Belgian soldiers managed to grab them. The Brussels newspapers, however, carried a story that a Belgian officer had managed to salvage them virtually intact.

As Commander-in-Chief of the Luftwaffe, Göring carried the ultimate responsibility for this catastrophe, and he was 'beside himself for several days'.[1] How much had the Belgians learned? Had the officer really managed to burn enough of the documents to make them illegible? Göring experimented by trying to burn a similar packet of papers, but only succeeded in scorching his hands when he tried to pull them out of the stove. In desperation, he consulted a professional clairvoyant used by Emmy, who told him that the documents had been completely destroyed.

Hitler was not reassured by this, but according to General Student, remained calm while Göring raged, knowing that his reputation had been severely damaged. That evening at dinner, however, Hitler had plenty to say about 'the negligent manner in which even the most sensitive files were handled by the Luftwaffe'.[2] The offending officer committed suicide while still in Belgium. Göring fired the Commander-in-Chief of Air Fleet 2, General Felmy, and replaced him with Kesselring, who had commanded the Polish campaign. But he himself remained very much in the doghouse.

Whether or not the Belgians had actually been able to read the plans, the element of surprise had certainly been lost, and Hitler had no option but to cancel Operation Yellow until late spring. He was also forced to rethink the plans themselves, on the assumption that enough of the captured documents could have survived to give the enemy a clear idea of the German strategy. In fact, he welcomed the opportunity to recast them, having always regarded them as far too conventional, based as they were on the First World War Schlieffen Plan: outflanking the Maginot Line with a great sweep through Belgium to the coast, then turning south and advancing on north-west France on a broad front. It was the natural – and obvious – way of attacking France, and the Allies were bound to be prepared for it.

In Poland, Hitler had restrained himself from interfering, but now he seized the chance to play the warlord to the full, brushing aside the cautious generals and imposing his own gambler's instincts, going *va banque* yet again. He would still attack France through Holland and Belgium, to outflank the Maginot Line, but instead of putting the main emphasis on a drive from the north, he would allot the main effort to a drive through the hilly, wooded terrain of the Ardennes, which was supposedly impassable to tanks. This would be followed by a swift dash to the Channel coast behind the Allied armies, cutting them off in the rear as they advanced to face the German army group in the north. Labelled Sichelschnitt (Sickle Cut), it was indeed a bold and daring concept, which Hitler claimed as his own, though it had coincidentally been thought up by Major-General Erich von Manstein, the brilliant commander of XXXVIII Corps, who had been Rundstedt's Chief of Staff in the Polish campaign.

While the new plans were being developed for Operation Yellow, Hitler and the OKW were preparing for another attack, much further north, to which they gave the innocuous-sounding code-name Weserübung (Weser Exercise). Stalin had used the Nazi–Soviet Pact to force Lithuania, Latvia and Estonia to accept Red Army garrisons, but when he tried to bully Finland into handing over a broad strip of territory in the south, plus a number of islands in the Gulf of Finland, to improve the defences of Leningrad, the Finns refused. Stalin sent in the Red Army on 30 November. The Finns defended themselves vigorously. The 'Winter War' had begun. To everyone's surprise, the Finns proceeded to give the Soviets a very bloody nose, inflicting defeat after defeat and dragging out the war well into 1940, when they were finally overcome by sheer weight of numbers. War in Scandinavia posed a threat to the vital supplies of high-grade iron ore that Germany was obtaining from northern Sweden, which were delivered by rail to the Norwegian all-weather port of Narvik for shipment to Germany by sea. There was a strong possibility that Britain and France would seize the ore fields under the pretext of sending troops through Norway to aid the Finns.

Or they might simply choose to ignore Norwegian neutrality and seize Narvik, to cut off the supply route. Grand Admiral Raedar had been pressing Hitler for some time to occupy Norway and Denmark, to provide bases from which the German Navy would be able to protect the ore carriers and launch attacks on British shipping in the North Atlantic. On 12 December, after introducing him to the Norwegian fascist leader, Vidkun Quisling, a protégé of Rosenberg, Raeder persuaded Hitler to commission an exploratory study by the OKW.

Hitler remained unconvinced of the need to occupy Norway until 16 February, when the German supply ship *Altmark*, carrying 300 British seamen taken prisoner from the nine ships sunk by the pocket battleship *Graf Spee* in the South Atlantic before her ignominious end in Montevideo, tried to sneak home through Norwegian waters. The British destroyer, *HMS Cossack*, brushed aside both diplomatic protests and Norwegian naval vessels to pursue the *Altmark* into Jossing Fjord, board her and rescue the prisoners. The British justified their incursion by claiming that the Norwegians had failed to prevent a breach of their neutrality by the Germans. It was enough to alert Hitler to the seriousness of the danger, and he immediately set about preparing for an invasion. Significantly, he did not inform Göring about the possibility of an attack on Scandinavia, even though he had such a deep personal interest in the region.

Hitler had reacted to the security lapse of the Luftwaffe courier by issuing an order restricting the distribution of information on military operations on a strictly need-to-know basis. The order, which was to be displayed in every military office, stated: 'No one: no office, no officer, may learn of something to be kept secret if they do not absolutely need to have knowledge of it for official reasons.' In a clear expression of his lack of trust, he decided that Göring did not need to know about Norway, or about the new ideas for Operation Yellow, at least for the moment. Göring was not alone. Hitler also excluded – with perhaps more justification – Brauchitsch, Halder and the Army General Staff, together with the Luftwaffe Staff. He confined all planning entirely to himself, three staff officers from the OKW under Keitel and Jodl, and the general he chose to command the operation, General Nikolaus von Falkenhorst.

Hitler had never met Falkenhorst, who was currently a corps commander in the West, but appointed him at the suggestion of Jodl, who recalled that he had served in Finland at the end of the First World War and so had some knowledge of Scandinavia. Hitler was so obsessed with secrecy that he did not even consult Brauchitsch before making the appointment, and forbade Falkenhorst from obtaining maps or documents on the area from the Army General Staff. The bemused general had to go out and buy a Baedeker tourist guide to Norway, and then lock himself away in a hotel room with it to draw up an outline plan, which Hitler approved that same afternoon. Eight days later, Falkenhorst presented him with a complete operational plan for the occupation not only of Norway but also of Denmark, in order to provide secure lines of communication between Germany and Norway.

Keeping Göring in the dark was made easier by the fact that he had withdrawn from Berlin as he was having problems with his health again: his glands were playing up, his weight had climbed to its maximum, and his old wound from 1923 had become inflamed. Having sent Emmy and Edda to live in the safety of the Obersalzberg and Veldenstein, he made his headquarters in Carinhall, which was being extended yet again, despite the national shortage of men and materials for the war effort.

This incredible disregard for wartime priorities was endemic in the Nazi leadership, as they continued to jockey for position and prestige. At the same time as Göring was enlarging Carinhall, Ribbentrop and Goebbels both had costly building projects under construction. Goebbels, who had finally managed to repair his relationship with Magda the previous autumn, was creating a luxurious complex of low, farmhouse-style buildings to rival Carinhall, near the 'simple log cabin' at Lanke which the Berlin authority had given him, and where he had enjoyed many of the steamiest moments of his affair with Lida Baarova.

The Lanke project had originally been banned by the local authority, prompted by the jealous Rosenberg, on the grounds that it was in a nature reserve, but Göring, in his capacity as Reich Chief Forester, had overridden their objections, and decreed that 'the construction should not be hindered in any way'.[3] The main house in Goebbels's new rural retreat was to have twenty-one rooms, including five bathrooms, and a cinema. Imitating Hitler's Berghof, it had huge picture windows looking out across the Bogensee lake, which could be raised and lowered electrically, as could the bar. The adjoining service building had a further twenty-seven rooms, all furnished to the highest standards. When it was finished in November 1940, it would cost 2.26 million marks – Goebbels had worried about the bill, but in the end Göring came to the rescue again and arranged for it to be picked up by the Reich Trustee of Funds in the name of the German film industry.

Ribbentrop, meanwhile, was trying to keep pace with Göring and Goebbels by having a grandiose new official residence created out of the old Reich President's Palace at 73 Wilhelmstrasse, which was being extensively rebuilt and extended to his own and his wife's specifications, by Speer. When the building was almost complete, Hitler inspected it and, in Speer's own account, 'showed dissatisfaction':

Hastily and recklessly, Ribbentrop thereupon ordered the new annex torn down and rebuilt. Probably in order to please Hitler he insisted on clumsy marble doorways, huge doors, and mouldings which were unsuitable for rooms of middling size. Before making the second inspection, I begged Hitler to refrain from making negative comments, or else the Foreign Minister would order a third rebuilding. Hitler actually held his tongue, and only later in his intimate circle did he make fun of the building, which to his mind was an utter failure.[4]

There is no record of what Hitler thought of the extensions to Carinhall, or even of whether he ever saw them, but Göring's architectural taste, though always monumental, was much more secure than Ribbentrop's. He justified the expense to the state, which funded the work, by announcing that when he reached sixty years of age, he would give Carinhall and all its contents to the nation, as the Hermann Göring Museum.

Göring's penchant for castles was in evidence again in the new field headquarters that Speer was constructing for him on an old feudal estate at Kransberg in the Taunus Mountains near the French border, in preparation for Operation Yellow. He was delighted with the result, in marked contrast to Hitler, who rejected the similar headquarters that Speer had constructed for him at nearby Ziegenberg, despite the immense cost and effort that had been expended on it. Instead, he demanded something 'small and simple', on the grounds that 'It is not fitting that I revel in luxury while my soldiers live in dugouts.'[5] Göring had no such inhibitions – even his special train, *Asia*, was fitted out to the height of luxury, including an immense bath that could have graced the villa of a Caesar.

At Carinhall, during the first three months of 1940, Göring called a constant stream of visitors to a packed schedule of meetings. After the débâcle of the lost plans, he had vowed to act as 'Commanding General of the Luftwaffe' and now held regular detailed discussions on operations for Yellow with the chiefs of his Air Fleets. On 9 February, he met with the principal armaments manufacturers, to try to find ways of urgently boosting production on a short-term basis. Telling them that he did not expect the war to last longer than 1941, he ordered them to concentrate all their energies on the immediate needs of the armed forces. All long-term projects, apart from the production of synthetic fuels, were to be held over. Following this order, Milch cancelled development work on the Jumo 004 jet engine, the fuselage for the Me-262 twin-jet fighter, and an anti-aircraft rocket.

For all Göring's exhortations, there were still delays and bottlenecks, exacerbated if not caused by the burden of bureaucracy, in the production and supply of munitions to the army. In an effort to improve the situation, Göring called in Fritz Todt, the mastermind behind the autobahns, who quickly realised that the main problems were red tape and interference by the Army High Command, the OKH (Oberkommando des Heeres), in production methods. Todt had already scored over the army when he took over the building of the West Wall from the army's engineers. On 17 March he took over the manufacture and supply of weapons from the army's Ordnance Office when he was appointed Reich Minister for Armaments and Munitions. It was another slap in the face for Brauchitsch and the generals, and another triumph for Göring, who gained the overall control he had long wanted.

Wearing his economic dictator's hat, Göring held conferences to supervise the absorption into the Reich of the new territories in the East, and to plan the incorporation of those about to be conquered in the West. He told General Georg Thomas, Chief of the OKW's War Economy and Armaments Office, not to worry about using up Germany's reserves, since they would soon be masters of France, Belgium and Holland. 'The decision follows,' he said, 'to exploit everything of ours to the utmost in 1940, and to exploit the raw materials reserves at their expense in later years.' The army would be responsible for plundering the captured territories of all valuable raw materials, shipping them to the Reich 'trainload upon trainload'.[6]

For the East, he called a conference of all the generals involved, plus Himmler in his new role as Reich Commissar for the Consolidation of German Nationhood, Frank, and the Gauleiters of the annexed provinces, to discuss the best ways of exploiting the former Czechoslovakia and Poland. The conquered lands, he told them, must become the granaries of the Reich. They should be stripped of all scrap metal, including church bells, and useful materials such as leather and rubber.

At the same meeting, he told Himmler to suspend the movement of Jews into the General-Government, because of the adverse publicity that was being generated, particularly in America, by news reports of the appalling hardships and cruelty they were suffering. Sadly, through a combination of inefficiency and infighting, the response to his order was slow. He had to repeat it on 23 March, and even then it did not become fully effective until May, by which time thousands more had perished.

The adverse foreign reports had been partly responsible for bringing an American peace envoy, Under-Secretary of State Sumner Welles, to Berlin at the beginning of March, when he talked separately to Hitler, Ribbentrop and Göring on three successive days. Hitler had issued a written directive to both of his ministers, saying that Welles should be allowed to do most of the talking, but Ribbentrop obviously found this impossible. After receiving him coldly, without a word of greeting, never mind a welcoming smile, Ribbentrop refused to admit that he understood English and called on Schmidt to interpret as Welles outlined his mission from President Roosevelt to seek a basis for peace. Welles recalled the rest of the interview with astonishment:

Ribbentrop then commenced to speak and never stopped for well over two hours . . . [he] sat with his arms extended on the sides of his chair and his eyes continuously closed. The pomposity and absurdity of his manner could not be exaggerated. One could only assume that he envisioned himself as the Delphic oracle . . . [7]

Göring received Welles in a much more civilised manner on 3 March – Schmidt thought his handling of him was most skilful – though he followed Hitler's instructions by insisting that Germany had never wanted war, which had been forced upon her. 'But what was Germany to do,' he asked plaintively, 'when the others wanted to destroy her?' He blamed Britain and France for their obduracy, emphasising the efforts he personally had made to ensure peace. When Welles told him that the American people were 'profoundly moved' by the plight of the Jews in Germany, he was quick to remind him of the American attitude to their own coloured and native races. Welles was more impressed by Göring than he had been by the other Nazi leaders – he had spoken to Hess as well as Hitler and Ribbentrop. Though he found him just as ruthless and untouched by human feelings, he felt that unlike the others he was capable of taking a wider view of Germany's relations with the rest of the world.

Noting Göring's 'monstrous girth', Welles was also intrigued by the high colour in his cheeks and at first assumed, as did so many others on various occasions, that he was using rouge. But as the day wore on and the colour drained from Göring's face, he realised that it was due to some sort of 'physical maladjustment'. Göring proudly showed off his house and treasures, including the young lion that had the run of the house, but the patrician New Englander was unimpressed, writing afterwards that 'it would be difficult to find an uglier building or one more intrinsically vulgar in its ostentatious display'.[8] Surprisingly, for such a normally generous host, Göring offered Welles nothing to eat during the several hours he spent at Carinhall – presumably because he was himself on a starvation diet and could not bear the sight of food.

The day before his meeting with Welles, Göring had been shocked to receive Hitler's directive for the invasion of Denmark and Norway, the first he had heard of the secret plan. Furious that he had not even been consulted, and that the directive put the Luftwaffe under the control of Falkenhorst, he stormed off to complain loudly to Hitler. According to Below, he was 'disappointed if not actually offended that Hitler had not entrusted the mission to him'.[9]

One of his main concerns, apparently, was that he had given a personal guarantee only a few days earlier to the King of Sweden, via his stepson Thomas, that Germany would always respect Swedish neutrality. But since Sweden was not mentioned in Hitler's directive, his worries on this score appear to have been groundless. The subordination of the Luftwaffe to Falkenhorst was much more serious, and he refused to sanction it. The Army High Command was also in a state of 'fury', because the troops demanded for the northern operation would have to come from those already earmarked for the revised 'Yellow'. To resolve the squabbles, Hitler called the commanders-in-chief of all three services to the Chancellery on 5 March, where, according to Jodl, Göring 'vented his spleen because he was not consulted beforehand. He dominates the discussion and tries to prove that all previous preparations are good for nothing.' Hitler managed to mollify Göring, and preparations went ahead, with greater involvement from the Luftwaffe, which in the event was to prove decisive.

Both men were preoccupied with the approaching attack in the West, and as it approached Hitler was concerned to make sure he had Mussolini on side. German–Italian relations had been cool since the previous December, when Mussolini had been angered by Hitler's support for the Soviets against the Finns, whom the Italians saw as heroes. In a biting speech to the Italian Chamber, Ciano had attacked Germany in general and Ribbentrop in particular for breaking their promise not to go to war for three years, and for signing the pact with Stalin. And Mussolini had followed this up with a New Year letter to Hitler urging him to restore the Polish state and seek a mediated peace with the Western powers, whom he said the Germans had no hope of defeating. Hitler had shown his displeasure by not replying, but now needed to mend fences, and quickly. Sumner Welles had visited Mussolini before coming to Berlin, with the intention of trying to split the Italian dictator from the Axis alliance, and was due to return to Rome in mid March. To forestall him, Hitler sent Ribbentrop to see Mussolini, carrying a long letter in which he reaffirmed his determination to fight and played on Mussolini's hunger for historic glory. 'Sooner or later, Duce,' he wrote, 'I believe that Fate will force us after all to fight side by side.'[10]

Ribbentrop hammered home the message that the Wehrmacht had proved its awesome power in Poland and was now invincible, and delivered an invitation from Hitler for a face-to-face meeting at the Brenner Pass. Mussolini swallowed the bait, aided by pique that the British had just started a naval blockade of German coal shipments to Italy. Hitler promised to deliver a million tons of coal a month by rail instead, and even to cover the transport costs. The meeting took place on 18 March, in falling snow on the little Brenner railway station. Nothing new was said. Hitler did not tell Mussolini anything about his decision to invade Norway and Denmark, nor any details about his plans for the attack in the West. And Mussolini in turn merely reaffirmed that he would enter the war on Germany's side, but not until he was ready. Nevertheless, Ribbentrop, who had accompanied Hitler, claimed it as another feather in his cap.

*   *   *

At precisely 5.20 a.m. German Summer Time on 9 April 1940, one hour before dawn, the German ministers in Norway and Denmark handed notes from Ribbentrop to their host Foreign Ministers, informing them that their countries were being taken under German protection for the duration of the war. The notes stated that this was entirely the fault of the British and French, who had started everything by 'unleashing this war of aggression, which they had long been preparing, against the German Reich and the German people'. 'The Reich government,' they went on, 'has resolved, from now on, to protect and definitely assure peace in the north, with all its power, against an English–French attack.' It was true that the British and French were preparing to occupy Narvik, against the Norwegians' wishes. Ribbentrop had played on this four days earlier by having his Minister in Oslo, Curt Bräuer, invite members of the Norwegian government and other dignitaries to the Legation to watch a special film show. What they saw was Goebbels's film of the Polish campaign, which culminated in a sequence showing the destruction of Warsaw in horrific detail, with a caption reading: 'For this they could thank their English and French friends.'[11] But Ribbentrop's assurances that the German troops did not come as enemies, and that Germany had no intention of infringing the two countries' territorial integrity and political independence were undermined by his going on to declare that 'any resistance would be broken by all possible means . . . and would therefore lead only to absolutely useless bloodshed.'[12]

The Danes, after some heart-searching, capitulated under protest. To aid their decision, a squadron of Luftwaffe bombers flew low over the centre of Copenhagen as a warning, while German paratroops secured the airfields. Aware that their flat little country was completely defenceless, the Danes could only watch helplessly as the German tanks and guns and troops on bicycles rolled in. The seventy-year-old King Christian had no time to flee, and decided to stay with his people. By lunch-time it was all over: the German army had taken control of every key point and the Luftwaffe had occupied all the airfields, filling them with planes to be used against the Norwegians, should they choose to cause trouble.

The Norwegians did indeed choose to cause trouble, though they were severely hampered by having no standing army: mobilisation papers had to be sent out by post that morning. Their government's immediate response to the German note had been: 'We will not submit voluntarily: the struggle is already under way.' The outraged Ribbentrop

wired back telling Bräuer, 'You will once more impress on the government there that Norwegian resistance is completely senseless.' But he
was too late. The mobilisation notices were in the post and the king
and his government had left Oslo by special train to seek safety in the
mountains, followed by a fleet of twenty-three trucks carrying secret
papers from ministries and the gold from the Bank of Norway.

The navy played the principal role in the invasion of Norway, using
virtually the entire German fleet to carry troops to all the main ports.
But it suffered severely at the hands of Norwegian shore batteries and
British ships, submarines and carrier-based aircraft, which were already
in Norwegian waters in strength, in preparation for an Anglo–French
occupation of Narvik planned for 10 April. When Germany's latest
heavy cruiser, the 10,000-ton *Blücher*, led an impressive naval force
towards the capital along the fifty-mile-long Oslo Fjord she dealt easily
with the two flimsy minesweepers and a whaler which bravely opposed
her, but was then sunk by a shore battery. The ship was torn apart
when her ammunition blew up, and some 1,000 men lost their lives,
among them Himmler's Gestapo officials and administrators who were
to arrest and replace the Norwegian government. The rest of the force,
including the pocket battleship *Lützow* (the former *Deutschland*,
hurriedly renamed after the loss of the *Graf Spee*, since Hitler could
not countenance the possibility of a ship with that name being sunk)
which had also been hit by the shore guns, turned tail and retreated
ignominiously to the sea. German honour was saved by the pilot of a
single Messerschmitt fighter, who was bold enough to capture the
unprotected Oslo airport by landing there. Others followed swiftly,
taxiing into position to ring the runway so that troop transports could
fly in safely. By noon, eight companies of infantry had been landed,
and 1,500 men were formed up behind a military band to march cere-
moniously into the centre of the city.

Long before then, all the other airfields in the country had been seized
by Luftwaffe paratroops, to achieve complete air supremacy. In the hope
that the Norwegians would see sense and acquiesce in a peaceful occupation, Hitler had ordered that no towns or cities were to be bombed.
Of the 1,008 aircraft that Göring deployed, almost half were Ju-52 transport planes to ferry troops by air. There were comparatively few fighters,
since there was little or no aerial opposition, but as Norwegian resistance grew, and the Allies made landings in the centre and north of the
country, the Luftwaffe was forced into a more active role, bombing and
strafing enemy forces. Göring took advantage of this to remove the

Luftwaffe in Norway from Falkenhorst's control, sending Milch to Oslo to organise a new air fleet of some 600 fighters, bombers and reconnaissance aircraft.

While Falkenhorst in Norway and Hitler in Berlin lost their nerve over Allied landings and the heavy losses by the German navy – Jodl was appalled by Hitler's loss of control, noting in his diary 'The hysteria is frightful' – Milch stayed cool. The Luftwaffe acquitted itself well, and was largely responsible for driving the Allies out of everywhere but Narvik by the end of the month. To Hitler's displeasure, King Haakon VII refused to co-operate or even to negotiate, destroying his hopes of a compliant puppet regime like the one in Denmark. Although this was largely due to his own miscalculation by trying to insist on the king's appointing Quisling as Prime Minister, he blamed Ribbentrop. Closing down the Legation in Oslo and dismissing the senior diplomats involved, he banned him and the Foreign Ministry from any connection with Norway for the rest of the war. Instead of a Reich Plenipotentiary running the country from the Legation, he appointed Göring's friend and newspaper partner, the Essen Gauleiter Josef Terboven, to rule as a dictator, with the title of Reichscommissar.

The Narvik operation dragged on through May, with the German occupiers under constant pressure from the Allies. Despite the best efforts of Göring and Dahlerus, the Swedish government refused to compromise its neutrality by allowing even non-military supplies to be transported overland through Sweden to the beleaguered troops. As the situation worsened, Dahlerus offered to negotiate an armistice at Narvik, under which the area would be demilitarised and placed under Swedish control, but this came to nothing. The mixed British, French and Polish force was finally driven out in early June, suffering heavy casualties, mainly from Luftwaffe attacks.

The occupation of Denmark had cost Hitler only twenty casualties, killed in minor skirmishes with troops who had not received the surrender order in time. But Norway had proved considerably more expensive. In addition to 1,317 men killed, 1,604 wounded and 2,375 missing or lost at sea, his already small fleet had been decimated. Three cruisers and ten destroyers – half of the navy's destroyer strength – were lost, two heavy cruisers and one pocket battleship were severely damaged and put out of action for several months. In the summer of 1940, apart from U-boats, the German navy was virtually non-existent, comprising only one 8-inch cruiser, two light cruisers and four destroyers, a factor of considerable importance in the war against Britain. The Luftwaffe, by contrast, emerged almost unscathed and ready for the battles that lay ahead.

As dawn was breaking on 10 May, Hitler arrived at his new field head-quarters, a converted anti-aircraft artillery site blasted out of a wooded mountaintop at Rodert, near Münstereifel, forty-five kilometres by road from the Belgian frontier. Setting a precedent for fanciful code-names that he would follow for the rest of the war, he called it 'Felsennest', 'Rocky Nest' or 'Eyrie'. Even as he inspected the bare concrete bunker that was to be his home for the next few weeks, its furnishings minimal, its soundproofing so poor that Keitel, who was given the cell next to his, would be able to hear him turning the pages of a newspaper, the air was filled with the roar of engines as wave after wave of Göring's bombers swept overhead. They were on their way to attack more than seventy airfields in Belgium, Holland and northern France, destroying between 300 and 400 planes on the ground and so ensuring air supe-riority for Hitler for the vital next two weeks.

Some of the aircraft carried paratroops, to be dropped in Holland at strategic points deep inland. The Dutch, well aware that an attack was imminent, had opened the sluices to flood the water barriers which formed their chief lines of defence, and hoped these would hold back the invaders. Göring's paratroops leapfrogged these and landed in the rear of the Dutch forces to seize the three most vital bridges at Moerdijk, Dordrecht and Rotterdam before the defenders could blow them up. Others attacked airfields unprepared for such surprise tactics, and secured them so that air transports could land conventional troops. One company was landed on the river near Rotterdam by obsolescent seaplanes.

Dutch forces resisted bravely and strongly, holding back the German advance in several key places, especially in Rotterdam, where they succeeded in sealing off the northern end of the bridges. By 14 May, a frustrated Hitler consulted Göring, who suggested they bomb the city into submission. Hitler agreed, and Kesselring was ordered to send in the bombers. The result was one of the most controversial opera-tions of the war in the West. The entire centre of Rotterdam was destroyed in the raid, with terrible loss of life – initial estimates, exag-gerated by fear and confusion, gave a figure of some 25–30,000 deaths, but the final toll was between 800 and 980, with 78,000 people made homeless. What made the raid so notorious, however, was not the casualties but the fact that the bombers struck while negotiations for the surrender of the city were taking place.

Göring, who was in constant touch from his train, parked at Luftwaffe headquarters at Wildpark, denied at Nuremberg that the raid was a deliberate terror tactic. He claimed that it was directed at Dutch gun positions, and had been called for by radio and ground signals by General Student, commander of the paratroops, who was trapped with his men on the city side of the bridge by heavy machine-gun and artillery fire. The paratroops themselves had no artillery or heavy weapons: 'Bombing was the only sort of artillery available for the parachute troops,' Göring said, 'and I had assured my parachutists before the venture that they would under all circumstances receive protection from bombers against heavy fire.'

Göring ordered Kesselring to use one squadron of bombers, which attacked in three groups of up to 36 aircraft. By the time the first group arrived over the target, surrender negotiations were already in hand, but it was too late to inform the pilots – at that stage of the war, ground-to-air radio communication was cumbersome and slow. As Göring stated: 'There was no radio connection between Rotterdam and the planes. The radio connection went by way of my headquarters, Air Fleet 2, to the division, from division to squadron ground station, and from there there was a radio connection to the planes . . .' The best Student and his men could do was to send up red flares, the signal to abort. Unfortunately, the first wave of aircraft either did not see or did not understand them, and pressed home the attack, exactly on target. The second and third groups saw and understood, and pulled out without dropping any bombs. But it was too late. A tragic trail of events had already been triggered.

In itself, the strike was not particularly heavy – as Göring told the Nuremberg Tribunal: 'If I remember the figures correctly, there were at the most 36 twin-motored planes which released mainly 50-kilo bombs.' The terrible destruction was caused not by high explosives but by fire. One of the buildings hit was a margarine factory, from whose ruptured storage tanks poured a blazing river of oils and fats that became a sea of fire engulfing surrounding buildings and quickly spreading throughout the city. It was the war's first example of a phenomenon that was later to bring savage retribution to several German cities, the firestorm. Ungallantly and incorrectly, Göring blamed the Rotterdam fire department, which was itself a victim of the blaze, for failing to prevent its spread.[13]

The destruction of Rotterdam marked the end of the fighting in the Netherlands. At dusk that same day, General Winkelmann, the Commander-in-Chief of the Dutch forces, ordered his men to lay down their arms. Queen Wilhelmina and her government were evacuated by two British destroyers, to continue their war defiantly from London. Though it never managed to crush the Dutch people's spirit, the Wehrmacht had taken just five days to crush Holland – and there could be no doubt where the main credit lay. The Luftwaffe was the star of the show, and Göring could bask happily in its success.

There was further glory for the Luftwaffe, and therefore for its Commander-in-Chief, in Belgium. Its most spectacular success came on 11 May with the capture of the Belgian Fort Eben Emael, a great mass of concrete and steel on the German frontier, commanding the bridges over the River Meuse and the Albert Canal near Maastricht, protecting the city of Liège, and blocking the Wehrmacht's route to the coast. Manned by 700 defenders, Eben Emael was reputed to be the most powerful fortress in the world, capable of withstanding the heaviest pounding of bombs and shells and of holding out indefinitely against any attack. Hitler, however, had other ideas. Aware of the necessity of knocking out the fortress before any advance could proceed, he had spent many hours studying a scale model of it in the Chancellery and had come up with a typically unconventional plan. The fort had a vast flat roof, on which gliders filled with shock troops and engineers were to land and capture the fort from there. In the event, nine gliders landed successfully, carrying seventy-eight men who attacked the gunports at close quarters with grenades and flamethrowers, shattered the armoured gun turrets with new hollow charge explosives that spread flames and gas in the chambers below, and blew up the ventilating system. Within an hour, at a cost of six killed and nineteen wounded, those seventy-eight men had neutralised 700 defenders, trapping them inside their own impregnable fortress; after Stuka attacks and hand-to-hand fighting in the underground tunnels, they surrendered the next day, when conventional German troops arrived.[14]

With the guns of Eben Emael silenced, more airborne troops landed and seized the bridges. The door was open for the advance into central Belgium. Hitler literally hugged himself for joy when he heard of this – but there was even better news to follow: the British and French were advancing at full speed from France into Belgium to meet his armies. 'I could have wept for joy!' he recalled later. 'They'd fallen right into my trap! It was a crafty move on our part to strike towards Liège – we had to make them believe we were remaining faithful to the old Schlieffen Plan.'[15]

Behind the Allied armies' backs, the panzers of Rundstedt's Army Group A were already powering their way through the forests and hills of the Ardennes. On the vital left flank, the most southerly, the XIX Panzer Corps was led by Lieutenant-General Heinz Guderian, the creator of the theory of blitzkrieg. Known as 'Hurrying Heinz', he amply justified his nickname now. The staff planners had allowed nine days for the panzers to cross the Ardennes and reach the Meuse. Guderian said he could do it in four. In the event, he reached it in two, his tanks rolling through Luxembourg without opposition and into south-east Belgium, their drivers threading their unwieldy vehicles through the 'impassable' forests by sheer nerve and driving skill, backed up by impeccable preparation and maintenance, with teams of mechanics riding with each column ready to deal with any breakdowns on the spot. At 1500 hours on Monday, 13 May, the first troops crossed the Meuse and established a bridgehead. At dawn the next day, Guderian's tanks started pouring across. By 15 May, his way was clear and he swept on across France, ignoring orders to halt, first from Rundstedt and then from Hitler himself, who had once again lost his nerve, unable to believe his good fortune and fearful that lines of communication would become overstretched.

Guderian was untroubled by such worries. For mile after mile, his tanks sped on, still almost unopposed, racing towards the coast over open roads to the rear of the Allied armies. When they ran short of fuel, they simply stopped at roadside filling stations and used the pumps, for free. From time to time, some stopped for their crews to take on human fuel by milking cows in the fields. They reached the Channel coast at Noyelles, near Abbeville on the mouth of the River Somme, on 20 May, having covered 200 miles in ten days in a giant, deadly sickle cut. With the rest of Army Group A also powering its way west, the Allied armies, including the whole of the British Expeditionary Force, were cut off from their supply lines in the south. The trap had snapped shut.

The amazing advance had been supported all the way by the Luftwaffe's fighters, bombers and Stukas, which successfully beat off opposition both on the ground and in the air. The disparity between the Allied and German air forces was starkly demonstrated as the obsolescent aircraft of the French air force were overwhelmed and the

RAF lost 100 of its French-based bombers, mainly Fairey Battles and Bristol Blenheims, in three disastrous days as they tried to attack German troop concentrations. By 14 May, the RAF had only 206 serviceable aircraft left in France, out of an original total of 474.[16]

RAF bombing raids were equally ineffectual at this time. Winston Churchill, who had taken over from Chamberlain as British Prime Minister on 10 May following the débâcle in Norway, ordered the first strategic air raids on Germany that same night, when eight Whitley bombers attacked communications targets near the Dutch frontier. The next night a larger force of eighteen Whitleys and eighteen Hampdens attacked roads and rail facilities in Mönchengladbach. Damage was light, and three RAF bombers were shot down. It was the first major attack by either side on a centre of population, though twenty-four civilians, thirteen of them children in a kindergarten, had been killed in an air raid on Freiburg in the Black Forest on 10 May. The Freiburg bombs turned out to have been dropped by three German He-111s whose pilots thought they were over Dijon, 140 miles away in France: Göring was distraught – but Goebbels was quick to make capital out of the tragedy by blaming the French. On 15 May, in retaliation for the Rotterdam raid, Churchill sent ninety-nine aircraft to bomb oil and steel facilities in the Ruhr, but again the results were negligible, and served only to highlight the superior destructive power of the Luftwaffe.

While the fires were still raging in Rotterdam on 15 May, Göring ordered his train to carry him west to join Hitler, in anticipation of the great victory that was surely coming. *Asia*, lengthened by the addition of more coaches for a number of new young aides under the command of his chief adjutant, Major Bernd von Brauchitsch, the son of the Army Commander-in-Chief, who was responsible for briefing him on events, arrived in the Eifel the next morning. It was parked at the mouth of a tunnel, in which it could take cover from any air attack, conveniently close to Hitler's 'Felsennest'. The Air Staff, under Jeschonnek, parked nearby in their own command train, *Robinson*.

Ribbentrop, who had trailed after the Führer with Himmler and Lammers on board *Heinrich*, was less fortunate. Hitler had no time for the Foreign Minister's pompous verbosity, and ordered him to remove himself and his headquarters to a new location, some sixty-five kilometres away. The rebuff was just the latest blow to Ribbentrop's pride. Still in Hitler's bad books over the business with the King of

Norway, he was already smarting from what Paul Schmidt described as 'a major battle in his private war' with Goebbels. He had gone to elaborate lengths to maintain secrecy while drafting the announcement, which followed the now normal line that the Germans had been forced to move into the two countries to protect them against the British and French, who were about to violate their neutrality and use them as bases from which to launch an attack on Germany. He had intended to hand copies of this to the Belgian Ambassador and the Dutch Minister personally, before reading it out on the radio, but Goebbels had spiked his guns by getting in first with a dawn broadcast of the complete text. 'While through the loudspeaker in the background the mellifluous tones of his arch-enemy could be heard reading out the fateful memorandum,' Schmidt recalled, Ribbentrop had been beside himself with fury, screaming: 'My whole broadcasting section is dismissed without notice for inefficiency!'[17]

Ribbentrop was further put out on 19 May, when the new Italian Ambassador, Dino Alfieri, who had previously been Mussolini's Propaganda Minister, arrived from Rome with a special gift for Göring: the coveted Collar of the Order of the Annunciation, which Ciano had finally prised out of King Victor Emmanuel. He presented it to him in a brief ceremony under the camouflage netting of the special train, and Göring put it on immediately and paraded it before his staff, beaming with delight. In his eyes, an injustice had been remedied.

By 24 May, the Germans began tightening the vice on the Allied armies caught in its trap. Guderian's tanks, driving northwards, had captured Boulogne and surrounded Calais, and were lined up along the Aa Canal between St Omer and Gravelines, twenty miles from the only remaining port, Dunkirk, while the Sixth and Eighteenth Armies were pushing down from the north-east. British and French counterattacks had failed, and they began pulling back towards Dunkirk, the French to set up a stronghold, the British to begin evacuation. At this point, Hitler's nerves got the better of him again. When Rundstedt halted his panzers, in spite of protests from some of the commanders on the ground and many of the General Staff, Hitler supported his decision. He considered, as did Rundstedt, that the exhausted men and machines needed time to regroup before beginning the final assault on troops who were likely to turn and fight when their backs were to the sea.

There are three enduring myths about Dunkirk. One is that Hitler deliberately halted the advance for sentimental reasons, to allow the British, whom he admired, to escape in the hope of forming a grand Anglo–German alliance to carve up the world. The second is that it was Göring's idea, and that he persuaded Hitler to hold back the ground forces to let the Luftwaffe take the glory for finishing off the Allies in the pocket. The third is that the RAF stayed at home in Britain and failed to protect the Allied troops during their withdrawal. None of them is true.

In the first place, it was Rundstedt who ordered his armour to halt, until more infantry could be brought up. Hitler endorsed his decision for good reasons: the Allied armies in the north were defeated and going nowhere, but there were still powerful French forces further south and there was no point risking the valuable tanks that he would need for the battles still to come. On the same day that he issued the halt order, he issued his directive for the next stage of his strategic plan, Operation Red, the battle for France. In this, he said that the Luftwaffe's present task was to break the remaining resistance of the encircled enemy, and prevent any British forces from escaping across the Channel. As Jodl told his staff when they questioned the decision: 'The war is won. It just has to be ended. There is no point sacrificing a single tank if we can do it much more cheaply with the Luftwaffe.'[18]

That was a sentiment with which Göring agreed wholeheartedly. Seizing his opportunity, he promised Hitler that his Luftwaffe could do the job, and Hitler accepted his offer gratefully – to the disgust of the Army General Staff, particularly Halder, who told William Shirer after the war that he had made it 'for a reason which was character-istic of the unscrupulously ambitious Göring. He wanted to secure for *his* air force, after the surprisingly smooth operations of the army up to then, the decisive final act in the great battle and thus gain the glory of success before the whole world.'

Ignoring the crucial role of the Luftwaffe, including its airborne troops, in the campaign, Halder went on to say that Milch and Kesselring had told Brauchitsch in Nuremberg Jail in January 1946 that Göring played on Hitler's contempt for the army generals by persuading him that 'the prestige of the Führer in the German home-land would be damaged beyond repair' if they were allowed to claim the credit for the great victory, and that the only way of preventing that was for the Luftwaffe and not the army to fight the decisive battle.[19] Such convoluted reasoning may sound far-fetched now, but at that time it was all too symptomatic of the jealousies and paranoia that characterised the Nazi regime; the accusations could well be true, but they could also be yet another symptom of the same complaint.

Unfortunately for Göring, things did not go according to plan. Bad weather and low cloud grounded his planes for the next two days, giving the British and French forces time to set up a defensive perimeter. The first things his reconnaissance planes saw when they were able to fly were thirteen British warships and nine troop transports taking men aboard in Dunkirk harbour. Realising for the first time that the British were seriously intending to evacuate, Hitler rescinded the stop order, but only allowed his armour to make limited advances, preferring to bring up artillery to supplement the air attacks. In any case, the tank crews were now resting and overhauling their vehicles, and could not leap back into action immediately.

Göring was still totally confident that his planes could keep the Allies pinned down; so much so that he moved his train back to Wildpark and took time out to fly over Rotterdam in a Ju-52 to survey the damage, before continuing to Amsterdam for a little fine art shopping, in company of his old friends Loerzer and Udet. Returning to France, he flew into Felsennest in a light aircraft and boasted ebulliently to Hitler that his aircraft had the British and French troops around Dunkirk pinned down: 'Only fishing boats are getting through. Let's hope the Tommies can swim!' The 'fishing boats' and other small craft – yachts, motor cruisers, paddle steamers, pleasure boats and working boats, almost everything that could float, a total of between 850 and 950 assorted vessels – were to fling his words back in his teeth over the next nine days as they chugged back and forth across the sea, laden to the gunwales with British and French soldiers plucked from the beaches under the noses of the Germans. After the disasters in Norway, there was no German navy to stop them.

For much of the time, bad weather again prevented the Luftwaffe planes from flying, and when they did, they received a shock: the RAF Spitfires and Hurricanes, flying from British bases that were in many cases nearer than the Luftwaffe's in Germany, quickly proved more than a match for Göring's Me-109s and Stukas. Between 27 and 30 May the RAF shot down 179 aircraft for the loss of only twenty-nine. But since most of the aerial dogfights took place above the thick cloud layer, the men on the ground and in the sea were unaware of them – hence the belief among so many that the RAF had deserted them.

Despite the weather and the RAF, Göring's planes did wreak considerable damage to the port and to the escaping men and their ships and boats. On 1 June they sank four destroyers and a passenger ship and severely damaged four other ships, causing Vice-Admiral Ramsey, controlling the operation from a room sunk deep in the cliffs of Dover, to ban daylight sailings. By the time the evacuation finished on 3 June, between 10,000 and 15,000 men lay dead on the beaches, around the harbour and in the streets of the blazing town. Around 40,000 French troops who had not got away were taken prisoner. The British had been forced to leave behind all their transport and heavy arms and equipment, including virtually all the army's latest 25-pounder field guns, and they had lost 177 precious aircraft. 232 of the rescue vessels had been sunk. But no fewer than 338,226 British, French and Belgian soldiers had been rescued, and the Luftwaffe's and Göring's reputations had been severely dented.

Churchill stood up in the House of Commons in London on 4 June, the day the Germans broke into Dunkirk, to 'lay the full story' before Parliament. His speech that day is remembered for his famous rallying cry, 'We shall fight on the beaches, we shall fight on the landing grounds, we shall fight in the fields and in the streets, we shall fight in the hills; we shall never surrender.' But before ending on that great growl of defiance, he had paid tribute to the men and machines that had made it possible:

We must be careful not to assign to this deliverance the attributes of a victory. Wars are not won by evacuations. But there was a victory inside this deliverance, which should be noted. It was gained by the air force.

. . . This was a great trial of strength between the British and German air forces. Can you conceive a greater objective for the Germans in the air than to make evacuation from these beaches impossible, and to sink all these ships which were displayed, almost to the extent of thousands? Could there have been an objective of greater military importance and significance for the whole purpose of the war than this? They tried hard and they were beaten back; they were frustrated in their task. We got the army away; and they have paid fourfold for any losses which they have inflicted . . . All our types and all our pilots have been vindicated as superior to what they have at present to face.[20]

Churchill's words must have been bitter gall to Göring, but he put a brave face on things, leading his staff through the smouldering ruins of Dunkirk the next day and gleefully inspecting the huge piles of abandoned weapons and equipment. Milch joined him later in his train, now parked near the coast, and proposed that they should immediately drop airborne troops across the Channel to seize airfields and set up a bridgehead for an invasion of Britain. But Göring told him this was not possible, since he only had one airborne division available. After the war, he claimed that if he had had four divisions, he would have gone ahead, but that sounds like wishful thinking after the event. It was certainly not what Hitler wanted at the time, when he was more concerned with completing the defeat of France, after which he still believed he could make peace with Britain.

The Belgians had surrendered on 28 May, without consulting their allies, and as soon as Dunkirk had fallen Hitler moved his headquarters from the Eifel to the Belgian village of Brûly-de-Pesche, on the border with France to the south of Namur, which had been cleared of its inhabitants to accommodate him and his staff. He gave it the romantic code-name 'Wolfsschlucht', 'Wolf's Gorge'. With the British gone he was free to turn his entire fighting strength, some 136 divisions plus the Luftwaffe, against the forty-nine battered divisions still left of the French army.

The French soldiers fought hard, but they could not hope to hold the rampaging Wehrmacht. The Germans broke through their defences after two days and swept down on France, fanning out in all directions. The French leaders panicked. Defeat turned into total collapse. The government fled, first to Tours and then to Bordeaux, abandoning Paris and declaring it an open city to prevent its destruction. German troops entered it without opposition on 14 June, and marched victoriously through the Arc de Triomphe and down the Champs-Élysées. General Bock, commander of Army Group B, flew into Paris airport unhindered to take the salute, then paid a visit to Napoleon's tomb and took lunch at the Ritz Hotel before shopping for luxuries in the city's exclusive stores.

Mussolini, meanwhile, had entered the war on 10 June, desperately anxious that it would all be over before he had a chance to claim either glory or spoils. He had informed Hitler on 30 May that he would be ready to attack the French on 5 June, but Hitler had asked him to postpone this for a week, to give the Luftwaffe time to finish off the remainder of the French Air Force first. Mussolini's poorly prepared and unenthusiastic forces only managed to advance a few hundred metres along the Riviera into Menton, however, before they were halted by French troops whom they outnumbered by three to one. On the

Alpine frontier, they made no headway whatsoever.

To the German Army, the Italian intervention was a total irrelevance – they were still swarming across France as fast as they could go. On 16 June, the Reynaud government collapsed; Marshal Pétain took over and sued for peace. Hitler declared that he needed to consult his Italian ally before settling the terms for an armistice, and met Mussolini in Munich on the 18th, with their Foreign Ministers. There was, in fact, very little consultation – Hitler simply wanted to tell Mussolini what he was doing, and try to keep him in his place by leaving him to negotiate his own, separate armistice with the French.

Ciano was wryly amused when he asked Ribbentrop the same question that he had put to him at Fuschl, 'What do you want – war or peace?', and this time received the opposite answer: 'Peace'. He deduced, rightly, that Ribbentrop was parroting Hitler's views as usual and refused to be drawn any further, 'because he does not know as yet the precise ideas of Hitler'.[21] Instead, he told Ciano of his scheme, originally dreamt up by his former furniture remover, Martin Luther, whom he had put in charge of 'Jewish affairs' in the Foreign Ministry, to ship the half million Jews in Western Europe to the French colony of Madagascar. It was a harebrained idea, which had been mooted and dismissed by the Polish government three years earlier, but having been excluded from the East by Himmler and Frank, Ribbentrop felt he had to show Hitler that he was making some contribution to solving the great problem.

The armistice with France was signed on 21 June, in the same railway coach as the 1918 armistice – German Army engineers knocked down the wall of the museum that had housed it ever since, dragging it out and positioning it on the exact spot in the forest at Compiègne that it had occupied then. The night before, a minor Foreign Ministry official, Erich Tuch, had chanced upon Hitler, all alone in the forest clearing, rehearsing his entrance and going through his act in careful detail, working through every gesture, every contemptuous expression. On the day, his performance was perfect. Accompanied by his entourage in strict order of precedence – Göring, Ribbentrop, Hess, Raeder and Brauchitsch – he stepped out of his car at exactly 3.15 p.m. and walked 'with the springy step of the triumphant conqueror' towards Marshal Foch's old railway car, pausing on the way to inspect the great granite block commemorating the earlier occasion, and its inscription, in

French: 'HERE ON THE ELEVENTH OF NOVEMBER 1918 SUCCUMBED THE CRIMINAL PRIDE OF THE GERMAN EMPIRE – VANQUISHED BY THE FREE PEOPLES WHICH IT TRIED TO ENSLAVE'.

William Shirer, who was among the international journalists invited to witness the event, noted in his diary:

Hitler reads it and Göring reads it. They all read it, standing there in the June sun and the silence. I look for the expression on Hitler's face. I am but fifty yards from him and see him through my glasses as though he were directly in front of me. I have seen that face many times at the great moments of his life. But today! It is afire with scorn, anger, hate, revenge, triumph.

He steps off the monument and contrives to make even this gesture a masterpiece of contempt. He glances back at it, contemptuous, angry – angry, you almost feel, because he cannot wipe out the awful, provoking letters with one sweep of his high Prussian boot.[22]

Hitler aimed to humiliate the French delegates with the ceremony, in repayment for the humiliation heaped on the German generals in November 1918, and he did so by choosing this location, without warning them in advance. He did not even stay to witness the signing – as soon as the preamble had been read out by Keitel, he left, with Göring, Brauchitsch, Raeder, Ribbentrop and Hess. But he chose not to humiliate them with the armistice itself, the terms of which were hard but surprisingly magnanimous. The Germans would occupy only the north and the west coast of France, leaving two fifths of the country 'free' under its own government headed by Pétain. France would retain her colonial empire, and part of her navy to protect it, with the rest of her ships simply being put out of commission. He did not want to encourage the French to continue the war from North Africa, or with the fleet. And above all, he hoped his apparent moderation would persuade the British to accept his offers of peace, putting an end to the short war he had planned in the West and leaving him free to concentrate on preparing for his real crusade.

In the early hours of 25 June, Hitler proclaimed the end of the war as 'the most glorious victory of all time' and ordered that bells should be rung in Germany for a week, and flags flown for ten days. He ordered the partial demobilisation of the army, reducing it from 160 to 120 divisions, in order to return men to industry, though it was symptomatic of the German refusal to commit to a total war economy that most of them went back to manufacturing consumer goods. A few days earlier, he had told Halder and the Army General Staff to start planning the transfer of troops to the East. Initially, this was to involve only fifteen divisions, but now he ordered the number to be increased to twenty-four, six of which were to be armoured and three motorised infantry. This was to be disguised as a normal redeployment or as preparation for an attack on British positions in the Middle East. But in truth it was the start of the build-up for the invasion of the Soviet Union.

XXVII

EAGLES AND SEA LIONS

WITH France defeated and the British driven from the continent of Europe, the Nazi leaders relaxed for a few days in a holiday mood. Hitler fulfilled a lifetime's ambition by visiting Paris on 23 June 1940, but chose to fly in at the curious hour of 5.30 a.m., taking with him a small group, including Keitel, two architects, Speer and Hermann Gieseler, and his favourite sculptor, Arno Breker. In a whirlwind sightseeing tour, they visited the Opera, the Eiffel Tower, La Madeleine, the Tomb of the Unknown Soldier under the Arc de Triomphe, Napoleon's tomb in Les Invalides, and finally the church of the Sacré Coeur on the heights of Montmartre, before heading back to the airport. Their visit had lasted barely three hours.

Hitler told Goebbels later that he had found Paris 'very disappointing'[1] but to Speer he showed much greater enthusiasm. 'Wasn't Paris beautiful?' he asked, then went on, 'But Berlin must be made far more beautiful. In the past, I have often considered whether we would not have to destroy Paris. But when we are finished in Berlin, Paris will only be a shadow. So why should we destroy it?' He told Speer to draw up a decree in his name, ordering full-scale resumption of work on rebuilding Berlin. 'Berlin,' he declared, 'is to be given the style commensurate with the grandeur of our victory.'[2] Speer was delighted to take him at his word, and Göring was soon releasing funds and scarce materials for the great project. It says a great deal about Hitler's confidence that he does not seem to have even considered the possibility that the new buildings might be bombed by the RAF.

Besides Berlin, Hitler's building programme also covered Nuremberg, Munich and Linz; in the autumn he added, by personal decrees, another twenty-seven 'reconstruction cities'. The horrified Speer estimated that the cost of party buildings alone in those cities would be between 22 and 25 billion marks. By April of the following year, Göring was assigning no less than 84,000 tons of precious iron and steel a year to the projects, and contracts worth 30 million marks were awarded to granite companies in Norway, Finland, Italy, Belgium, Sweden and Holland. Incredibly, a special transport fleet was created, with ship-yards set up in Wismar and Berlin to build 1,000 boats with a cargo capacity of 500 tons each. The reconstruction programme was to be complete by 1950, Hitler decreed, and nothing must be allowed to stand in its way.

As Speer left Brûly, he overheard Hitler, 'in radiant good humour', discussing the invasion of the Soviet Union with Keitel and Jodl. But for the moment, Hitler had other things on his mind. Accompanied by his First World War comrades Max Amman and Ernst Schmidt, he became a tourist for a few days, visiting the battlefields where they had spent four years in the trenches, and paying homage to the dead in the German war cemeteries. Göring, having assured his own staff that nothing would happen before Hitler had made his victory speech to the Reichstag in two weeks' time, went his own way, returning first to Amsterdam and The Hague and a few days later to Paris, on shop-ping expeditions to acquire more works of art for his rapidly expanding collection.

Goebbels also took the opportunity to go sightseeing in Holland, Belgium and France, and to talk to German soldiers, who were all eager to go to England to finish the job. Following faithfully in Hitler's footsteps yet again, he made his own day-trip to Paris, taking in the same guidebook sights but also going on to Versailles, 'where Germany was condemned to death'. Buoyed up by victory and utterly convinced of Hitler's infallibility, he could hardly wait for the great showdown: 'I hope Churchill doesn't give in at the last minute,' he wrote. Churchill had become his *bête noire*, impervious to his jibes and so dangerous that 'Germany would not stand where it does today if he had taken the helm in 1933.' But even while he took every opportunity to deni-grate the British Prime Minister, he could not help feeling a grudging admiration for 'the scintillating style' of his oratory and had to admit that 'the old fox' was 'a man of great gifts',[3] and a worthy opponent in their battle of words.

Throughout the short war in the West, Goebbels had used every trick he could think of to drive a wedge between Britain and France, and to undermine the morale of French troops through devices such as leaflets suggesting that while they were fighting at the front, their womenfolk were being seduced by their allies. This was no longer propaganda or indoctrination, but psychological warfare, with radio messages urging French soldiers to desert, and rumours that the Germans intended to confiscate all private bank accounts, designed to cause panic withdrawals. Now, he turned his attention entirely against Britain, ordering his ministry to step up the psychological war in preparation for the invasion that he was sure was about to be launched.

He was taken aback, therefore, when Hitler summoned him to his new headquarters, near Freudenstadt on the Kniebis mountain in the Black Forest, code-named 'Tannenberg' (Pine Mountain), to which he and his staff had moved on 28 June, and told him to ease up on the propaganda blitz on Britain. Hitler had called him to discuss arrangements for his triumphal return to Berlin, and the big victory speech he was to make to the Reichstag, in which he said he intended to offer Britain 'one last chance'.

Goebbels was back in favour these days after patching up his marriage – as living proof, Magda was five months pregnant with their 'reconciliation baby'. Pathetically grateful for Hitler's approval, he was more in thrall to him than ever, describing him as a 'historical genius, towering above all others' – but he was still excluded from his full confidence, especially in military matters. Knowing nothing of the plan to invade the Soviet Union, he found Hitler's attitude to Britain hard to understand, and equally hard to sell to the German public, but he blindly accepted that whatever the Führer said or did had to be right. He told his staff that while they must keep up the existing level of hatred for Britain, they had to 'tread water' for the moment, 'for we must not anticipate the Führer's actions'.[1] He kept up the personal attacks on Churchill, but reined in any criticisms of the British people.

Goebbels was on more familiar ground with organising Hitler's return to Berlin as a conquering hero, and pulled out all the stops to make it a memorable occasion. Arriving at 3 p.m. on Saturday, 6 July at an Anhalter Station bedecked with flowers and flags, 'the greatest warlord of all times', as Keitel dubbed him, was welcomed by Göring and driven to the Chancellery through streets packed tight with wildly cheering crowds. But there was a giant shadow looming over the celebrations: the war was not actually over. The day before, the British had demonstrated that they had no intention of pulling out when the Royal Navy attacked and destroyed the French fleet in harbour at Mers-el-Kebir in Algeria, killing some 1,200 French sailors. Hitler had said that the ships would take no further part in the war, but Churchill dared not trust his word. 'It is impossible for us to allow your fine ships to fall into the hands of our German or Italian enemies,' he told the French, offering them a choice of sailing either to Britain to join forces with the Royal Navy, or to the French West Indies, where they would stay neutral, out of German reach, or of scuttling their ships where they lay. When the French refused all three options, the British struck, displaying a ruthless determination that came as a shock to the Führer.

This setback to his hopes upset all Hitler's calculations. He postponed the speech he had been planning to make in the Reichstag on the Monday, and after a brief meeting with Ciano travelled south to Munich and then to the Berghof. The British insistence on continuing the fight came as a bitter disappointment to him, and called for serious thought. His ultimate goal was unchanged: to attack and destroy the Soviet Union, and with it Bolshevism, at the same time providing the living space he wanted for the expansion of the German people in the East. If the British would only accept this and leave him to pursue it unhindered, all would be well. If not, he would be faced with the dreaded prospect of a war on two fronts, which could only be avoided by knocking out one opponent before the other had time to start.

Convinced that Britain was only holding out in the hope that the Soviets would come to her aid, he believed that knocking them out in a swift blitzkrieg would force Churchill to give up and sue for peace. After his amazing success in the West, he saw no reason why he could not defeat the Red Army equally quickly, maybe even in one month. On the other hand, the British were still reeling after their comprehensive defeat in France, their army shattered, stripped of its equipment and heavy weapons, leaving them, he believed, demoralised and easy meat for the power of the Wehrmacht in an equally quick campaign. These were his two main options: a land and air invasion of the Soviet Union, or a sea and air invasion of Britain. There was a third, aimed at strangling Britain by sealing off the Mediterranean at Gibraltar and Suez and cutting her lifeline across the Atlantic with U-boat attacks on her shipping, but this would take far too long and he never seriously considered it.

Hitler vacillated and procrastinated for several days, before making his decision. Once the Soviet Union had been dealt with, he reasoned, there would be no more trouble from Britain – therefore, worries about Britain should not prevent Germany attacking the Soviet Union. At the same time, he still clung to the possibility that if he kept up the direct pressure on Britain she might see sense in any case. So, on 16 July, with marked lack of determination, he issued his Directive No. 16 for the preparation – but not yet the execution – of an invasion, under the code-name 'Sea Lion'. Everything was to be ready by mid August, and everything was to be done ostentatiously. 1,000 heavy barges were to be taken from Germany's inland waterways and a further 900 from Holland and Belgium. They were to be assembled on the French coast, in full view of the British. The fact that this would cripple the German transport system and bring large sections of the economy to a grinding halt was less important than putting on a sufficient show of strength. No doubt Hitler believed he would soon be able to return the barges safely to their normal work.

Whether he seriously intended to launch a cross-Channel invasion is open to doubt. Certainly, most of the army and Luftwaffe generals regarded it as a giant bluff. Jeschonnek, for instance, told the liaison officer between the Air Staff and the OKW that in his opinion the Führer had not the slightest intention of crossing the Channel: 'There isn't going to *be* any "Sea Lion",' he said. 'And I haven't got time to concern myself with it.'[5] Rundstedt, Commander-in-Chief in the West, could not even be bothered to attend the amphibious landing exercises. Encouraged by Göring, Hitler believed the clear threat of invasion, coupled with air attacks on the ports and shipping on which Britain depended for her very life, would be enough to bring Churchill to his senses at last. With this in mind, he allowed Göring to start small-scale bombing raids on British ports and coastal installations, but strictly forbade any attacks on inland towns and cities.

Göring finally convened the Reichstag to hear Hitler's twice-postponed speech in the evening of 19 July. The auditorium of the Kroll Opera House was packed, with Reichstag deputies in the orchestra stalls, generals and admirals in the dress circle, and diplomats in the theatre boxes. Six empty seats on the front row of the stalls bore wreaths in memory of deputies who had been killed in action. Every nook was filled with flowers, and medals glittered on hundreds of gold-braided dress uniforms. Göring outshone everyone else in a brand-new uniform that he had designed himself for this day, a dazzling creation in pale pearl-grey – prompting his own officers to grumble that he had chosen to stop wearing Luftwaffe uniform.

Göring knew what they did not – that 'as a reward for his mighty contribution to victory' he was to be promoted that day from Field Marshal to Reich Marshal of the Greater German Reich, making him a six-star general and the most senior officer not only in Germany but in the entire world. It was a rank that had been held only once before, by the Austrian Prince Eugene of Savoy, victor over the Turks back in the early eighteenth century. Hitler was also to present 'the creator of the Luftwaffe' with the Grand Cross of the Iron Cross, a decoration awarded only once in the First World War, to Hindenburg, and the only one to be awarded during the Second World War.

William Shirer, watching from the press gallery, was amused at the way Göring 'acted like a happy child playing with his toys on Christmas morning . . . chewing his pencil, and scribbling out in large, scrawly letters the text of his remarks which he would make after Hitler finished.'

He chewed on his pencil and frowned and scribbled like a schoolboy over a composition that has got to be in by the time class is ended. But always he kept one ear cocked on the Leader's words, and at appropriate moments he would put down his pencil and applaud heartily, his face a big smile of approval from one ear to the other.

He had two big moments, and he reacted to them with the happy naturalness of a big child. Once when Hitler named two of his air force generals field marshals, he beamed like a proud big brother, smiling his approval and his happiness up to the generals in the balcony and clapping his hands with Gargantuan gestures, pointing his big paws at the new field marshals as at a boxer in the ring when he's introduced. The climax was when Hitler named him Reichsmarshal. Hitler turned around and handed him a box with whatever insignia a Reichsmarshal wears. Göring took the box, and his boyish pride and satisfaction was almost touching, old murderer that he is. He could not deny himself a sneaking glance under the cover of the lid. Then he went back to his pencil-chewing and his speech. I considered his popularity – second only to Hitler's in the country – and concluded that it is just because, on occasions like this, he's so human, so completely the big, good-natured boy. (But also the boy who in June 1934 could dispatch men to the firing squads by the hundreds.)[6]

Göring's elevation to Reich Marshal was necessary to keep his pre-eminent position, for Hitler created no fewer than twelve new field marshals during his speech: Keitel, Brauchitsch, Rundstedt, Bock, Leeb, List, Kluge, Witzleben and Reichenau from the army, and Milch, Kesselring and Sperrle from the Luftwaffe. Such wholesale largess was in marked contrast to the Kaiser's promotions during 1914–18, when he created only five field marshals during the whole war. But there was cold calculation behind Hitler's generosity. The honours he bestowed so freely, together with the financial rewards attached – Göring's new rank brought him 20,000 marks a month in tax-free salary, enough to fund most of his fine art shopping expeditions – were calculated to make the recipients more than ever beholden to him, reinforcing their oaths of loyalty.

The non-military disciples did not fare nearly so well in Hitler's speech. Ribbentrop, who had spent days at Hitler's request preparing a draft of the speech for him, was disappointed to find that his work had been totally discarded. As consolation, he was given a back-handed compliment for 'putting into effect my directives in the field of foreign politics in faithful, untiring and self-sacrificing work'. Goebbels, who had welcomed the local 218th Infantry Division back to Berlin the day before with a rousing speech in Pariser Platz amid such flag-waving and bell-ringing as had not been seen since Bismarck's formation of the German Reich in 1871, received only a brief mention, as the director 'of a propaganda the excellence of which becomes apparent through a comparison with that of the World War'. Himmler, who had just returned from his own short break touring with Wolff in Burgundy, where he dreamed of creating an autonomous SS state under his own rule, was given an equally brief mention for 'his services in organising the security of our Reich' as well as the Waffen-SS (Armed SS), as the VT field units were now known. He was gratified, though, when six of his Waffen-SS commanders were awarded the Knight's Cross.

The main point of Hitler's speech, however, as he had told Goebbels earlier that day, lay in making a final peace offer to Britain. After vilifying Churchill as 'this type of unscrupulous politician who wrecks whole nations' he concluded:

In this hour I feel it to be my duty before my own conscience to appeal once more to reason and common sense in Great Britain as much as elsewhere. I consider myself in a position to make this appeal since I am not a vanquished foe begging favours, but the victor, speaking in the name of reason. I can see no reason why this war need go on. I am grieved to think of the sacrifices it must claim . . .[7]

His crocodile tears failed to impress anyone in Britain. Within the hour, the BBC and the press were rejecting his so-called offer without even waiting for the government's reaction. The official rejection came three days later, when Halifax contemptuously 'brushed aside' Hitler's 'summons to capitulate to his will', and declared that 'we shall not stop fighting until freedom is secure'.[8]

Goebbels was quick to seize the opportunity to make capital out of this. As Shirer commented the next day: 'The press campaign to whip up the people for a war with Britain started with a bang this morning. Every paper in Berlin carried practically the same headline: "CHURCHILL'S ANSWER – COWARDLY MURDERING OF A DEFENCELESS POPULATION!" The story is that since Hitler's Reichstag "appeal for peace" the British have answered by increasing their night attacks – on helpless women and children.'[9] Details of British air raids that had been kept strictly secret were suddenly trotted out. All were clearly against military objectives. 'But according to Goebbels's lies,' Shirer wrote, 'only women and children were hit.'

The British refusal to admit defeat was a nuisance to Hitler. He wanted to invade the Soviet Union, not Britain, for which he had made no plans and for which the Wehrmacht was ill-equipped: witness the fact that no one had even considered building landing craft, for instance, to transport troops across the Channel. Both he and Göring continued to hope for a diplomatic solution, and Göring put out yet more peace feelers through Holland and Sweden, but they knew these were unlikely to succeed. Undeterred by his failure at Dunkirk, Göring still believed he could bring Britain down by an air war alone, making an invasion unnecessary. But whatever happened, the RAF had to be beaten first. Neither a seaborne invasion nor unrestricted terror bombing of British cities would be possible without control of the air.

On 1 August, after hearing from Raeder that the earliest possible date the navy could be ready for an invasion of Britain was 15 September, Hitler gave Göring the go-ahead he had been seeking for the full-scale air offensive, code-named Operation Eagle, to start four days later. But he still expressly forbade the terror bombing of cities without his personal approval. His Directive No. 17 stated that 'the Luftwaffe must cut down the British air force as soon as possible with all the means at their disposal', which fitted well with Göring's regular strategy of starting any campaign with attacks on enemy airfields and facilities. Unfortunately for him, bad weather forced him to postpone 'Eagle Day', the start of the Battle of Britain, until 13

21. Ernst Udet, another much-decorated air hero, was one of Göring's closest friends and colleagues – until Göring drove him to suicide.

22. 'Can't you see where I'm standing?' Göring had his own rules for playing tennis – and his own dress code, including hair net.

23. Göring's other relaxations included keeping pet lions in his house …

24. … and hunting in the forests of northern Germany, always his favourite pastime.

25. But his pleasures also included building a massive industrial empire, exemplified by this model of a giant new steelworks for Austria.

26. The setting in the Kroll Opera House on the sixth anniversary of the Nazi seizure of power, with Göring enthroned as President, highlights the theatrical nature of the Reichstag.

27. Welcomed by Italian Foreign Minister Ciano as he arrives in Rome for talks with Mussolini, Ribbentrop cannot hide his delight.
28. But the pinnacle of his career comes on 23 August 1939, when he signs the Non-Aggression Pact with the Soviet Union, and is greeted 'like an old comrade' by Stalin.
29. Once the war had begun in 1939, Ribbentrop followed Hitler into Poland, conducting the foreign affairs of the Reich from a stool by the railroad track.

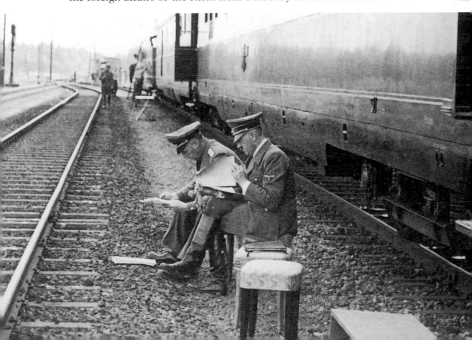

30. Himmler took pride in the activities of his SS-Leibstandarte Adolf Hitler in the 1939 Polish campaign. Here he talks to Sepp Dietrich at the front.

31. Even as his murder squads continue to rampage through Poland in 1940, he finds time to play Bavarian happy families with his wife Marga and daughter Gudrun.

32. Still believing his Luftwaffe will crush the RAF, Göring talks to a young pilot during the Battle of Britain. 33. Desperately trying to reinforce the Luftwaffe, Speer and Milch watch a demonstration of new weapons and aircraft in September 1943. 34. 'My Führer, my God'. Goebbels shows his utter devotion on the Obersalzberg during a respite from the Eastern Front in 1943.

35. Even in winter snow, Himmler uses a
country walk in March 1944 to press his
plans on Hitler.

36. The whole Goebbels family together for what may have been the last time. Magda's son, Harald, was the only one to survive, as a prisoner-of-war of the British. Magda poisoned the other six children.

37. As the final catastrophe loomed, Goebbels took on the role of Defender of Berlin. His troops included old men and young boys, such as sixteen-year-old Willi Hübner, whom he presented with the Iron Cross.

38. The moment of surrender: Göring, wearing a white armband, gives himself up to American forces at Fischhorn, accompanied by his adjutant, Berndt von Brauchitsch.

39. 'I feed my dogs better than this'. In captivity at Nuremberg, Göring is reduced to basic prison food – and loses a great deal of weight.

40. Masterful to the end, Göring dominates the trial proceedings with his confident, relaxed manner, in marked contrast to Ribbentrop, who becomes a pitiful wreck.

August, and even then the attacks by Air Fleets 2, 3 and 5, from Northern France, the Low Countries and Scandinavia, were disrupted and badly co-ordinated.

This was the first time Göring had mounted a completely independent campaign – his previous spectacular successes had been working in close support of ground forces. It was also, apart from the brief engagement over Dunkirk, the first time the Luftwaffe had faced an opponent that was its equal in equipment and skill. On the face of it, the Germans appeared to have a significant advantage, with battle-hardened pilots, experienced commanders and vastly superior numbers: 1,260 long-range bombers, about 320 dive-bombers, 800 single-engined and 280 twin-engined fighters, plus a number of reconnaissance aircraft, against the RAF's 900 fighters, of which no more than 600 could be in the air at any one time.[10] But the distance Air Fleet 5 had to cover from Denmark and Norway meant its fighters could provide no cover for its bombers, and even in the south, flying from bases in France and the Low Countries, the Me-109s of Air Fleets 2 and 3 did not have the range to stay in British air space for more than a few minutes of combat, while the twin-engined Me-110s were too slow and unwieldy against the RAF Spitfires and Hurricanes. The Stukas, which had wrought such havoc elsewhere, were even slower and more vulnerable, and proved to be such easy meat that they were soon withdrawn from the battle. The Heinkel 111 and Dornier 17 medium bombers could not carry enough bomb loads to inflict serious strategic damage, and the Junkers 88 was still unreliable. In terms of numbers, the Luftwaffe still had the edge over the RAF, but it was by no means a decisive advantage.

The British, moreover, had two secret weapons that made all the difference: radar and Ultra. The Germans knew a little about radar – they had their own version – but they never realised how much more advanced the British system was, and therefore failed to concentrate enough effort into knocking out the chain of stations around the English coast. They knew nothing about Ultra, the intelligence derived from cracking the supposedly unbreakable German Enigma codes. The first brilliant success in this area had been achieved only weeks earlier, and although there were still large gaps, particularly with German naval codes, by a happy chance the Luftwaffe codes had been the first to be broken, enabling British intelligence to read encoded radio messages at all levels, from Göring and Jeschonnek down to individual groups, from 21 May onwards.

The radar stations gave early warning of enemy aircraft as they crossed the Channel towards Britain; vital as this was, it alerted the RAF control rooms only minutes before an attack. Ultra, on the other hand, allowed the RAF to know German orders for an attack at almost the same time as they were transmitted to the Luftwaffe. In the end, of course, victory depended on the pilots in the air, on their machines and on the organisation on the ground. But Ultra warnings helped to level the playing field by giving the RAF a chance to be prepared for battle. It was one of the reasons why Göring's planned three-day hammer blow failed to achieve its object of 'wiping the RAF from the skies'.

On 15 August, the Luftwaffe flew 1,786 sorties against British airfields, but the RAF was ready for them, fighting back with determined ferocity. By the end of the day, the Germans had lost 75 aircraft, while downing only 32 RAF fighters. It was a pattern that was to be repeated every day over the next five weeks, and as German losses mounted the shortcomings of Udet's technical operations became glaringly apparent. With an output of only 375 planes a month, the factories could not keep pace with the need for replacements, while repair facilities were inefficient and badly organised. Although aircrew losses were heavy – so much so that Göring had to order that crews must never include more than one commissioned officer – there were times when he had more pilots than machines.

Day after day, the battle raged, with each side overestimating the damage it was inflicting. This was serious for the British, but catastrophic for the Germans. By 19 August, when bad weather forced a lull in operations, the Luftwaffe believed it had reduced RAF frontline fighter strength to about 300 planes. When flying resumed on 24 August, Göring directed his planes to concentrate during the day on targets the RAF was bound to defend, particularly airfields, in the belief that this would draw the few remaining Spitfires and Hurricanes into battles with superior numbers of German fighters, which could then wipe them out. Meanwhile, German bombers would attack at night, without escorts, to keep up the pressure. In fact, the RAF still had around 600 front-line fighters, so although Göring's tactic did begin to produce results, it was not the immediate success he had hoped for. The balance of kills swung in Germany's favour for the first time, but no matter how many Spitfires the Messerschmitts shot down, there always seemed to be enough left to continue the fight.

The unescorted night bombers did produce an immediate result, but it was not what had been planned. On the first night, they began attacking RAF bases and other targets in Portsmouth and the London area. Ten bombers sent to attack the Thameshaven oil storage installations some twenty-five miles downriver from Central London lost their bearings and managed to drop their bombs right in the heart of the City, destroying many historic buildings including the church of St Giles, Cripplegate, built by Christopher Wren.

Over a month earlier, Churchill had told his Secretary of State for Air, Sir Archibald Sinclair, that if the Germans bombed London, 'it seems very important to be able to return the compliment next day upon Berlin', and asked if this was possible.[11] Sinclair had replied that it was certainly possible, given twenty-four hours' notice. The German bombers had hardly left London in the early hours of 25 August before the order to retaliate was given. That night, 103 twin-engined Hampdens, Wellingtons and Whitleys took off to bomb Germany; 81 of them headed for Berlin.

Because of persistent cloud and a lack of sophisticated navigation equipment, only 29 bombers reached Berlin – over a 580-mile outward trip, the 20 mph cross wind they encountered could blow a bomber off course by as much as 66 miles. When they got there, they found the city masked by thick cloud, which made accurate bombing impossible. Fortunately it also prevented the German searchlights picking up the aircraft, and the flak gunners could only fire wildly in the direction of the engine noise as planes flew over them.

According to German newspaper reports, which Goebbels limited to his six-line official communiqué, the only bombs that fell within the city limits were a handful of incendiaries which destroyed a wooden summerhouse in the northern suburb of Rosenthal, slightly injuring two people. But many Berliners plainly heard bombs exploding in the city centre, and the next day three streets were roped off to keep people from seeing the damage. In addition to 22 tons of bombs, many with delayed-action fuses, the British planes also dropped leaflets, saying that 'the war which Hitler started will go on, and it will last as long as Hitler does'.[12]

The RAF hit Berlin again on the night of 28–29 August, killing ten people and injuring twenty-nine, and returned thirty-eight more times between then and the end of October. The damage they caused was slight – one of the worst casualties was Göring's pride, as Berliners, with typical black humour, renamed his Air Ministry 'the Meier Ministry', as a reminder of his boast that if the RAF ever flew over

Berlin they could call him Meier. Hitler, however, regarded the raids as a calculated insult that must be repaid with interest. On 4 September, in a speech at the Sportpalast inaugurating that year's Winter Relief campaign, he ranted against 'the cowardly RAF' and vowed he would 'answer' the British raids 'night for night'. For every two, three or four thousand kilograms of bombs they dropped on Germany, he promised, 'we will in one night drop 150, 230, 300 or 400 thousand kilograms! When they declare that they will increase their attacks in our cities, then we will raze *their* cities to the ground!'¹³ The next day, he called Göring and rescinded his ban on the bombing of towns and cities, ordering a massive attack on London to begin immediately.

Göring set off at once from Paris to the Channel coast in *Asia*, to brief his three field marshals on this sudden change of plan, and to oversee operations personally. He claimed later that he had tried to persuade Hitler to let him knock out the airfields around London first, but that Hitler had 'insisted that he wanted London itself attacked for political reasons, and also for retribution',¹⁴ though this may well have been wisdom after the event. At the time, the Luftwaffe High Command, and therefore Göring, believed that such raids would compel the British to throw their last reserves into the defence of London, enabling them finally to break RAF Fighter Command and with it British resistance. Either way, the raids on London went ahead and the vital fighter airfields, which were on the verge of destruction, were saved.

In the late afternoon on Saturday, 7 September Göring stood on the clifftop at Cap Gris Nez watching the first wave of 320 bombers roar overhead in massed formation while he broadcast to the German nation, bragging that he had taken personal command of the air war against Britain. 'This is the historic hour,' he pronounced, 'when our air force for the first time delivers its blows right into the enemy's heart.' That first day and night, 625 bombers supported by 648 fighters struck at the capital, in the heaviest air raids ever known at that time, causing immense damage and heavy casualties in London's East End and docks. The next day, the raiders flew in again, guided by the still-burning fires, to pound the area mercilessly. During those two days and nights, they killed 842 people and injured 2,347, and that was only a fore-taste of what was to come. By the end of the month, the figures would have reached about 7,000 dead and 9,000 injured, but the spirit of the Londoners remained unbroken.

The first raid had caught the RAF by surprise. For some reason, perhaps because the orders from Göring and his commanders were delivered by hand or land-line rather than by radio, Ultra does not seem to have warned them of the switch and they were still expecting attacks on airfields. By the second raid, they were ready *en masse* to make a fight of it, and started to inflict casualties on the Germans. For the next week, the battle raged furiously. Buckingham Palace and St Paul's Cathedral were both hit on 11 September. Confident that the RAF was on the ropes – at an Air Ministry press conference the next day, foreign correspondents in Berlin were told that 'the RAF will not be able to hold out for more than two weeks' – Göring launched what he believed would be the killer punch with another huge raid on 15 September. But the RAF had perfected its tactics and was waiting in strength, to intercept the Luftwaffe planes long before they got near London, the Spitfires and Hurricanes swooping like hawks to disperse and destroy them. A second, bigger attack two hours later was dealt with even more decisively, with the RAF putting every single fighter in the air, leaving nothing in reserve. The RAF claimed to have shot down 185 German planes that day, at a cost of only twenty-six. In fact, the true total of kills was no more than sixty, of which thirty-four were bombers, but it was enough. The Luftwaffe had lost around 175 aircraft in the past week, bringing the total since 'Eagle Day' to a staggering and unsustainable 1,294. RAF losses amounted to around 788.[15] The Battle of Britain was over. Operation Sea Lion was called off on 17 September.

Dunkirk had been a setback for Göring. The Battle of Britain was a decisive defeat. He had not only failed to neutralise the RAF fighters over Britain and the Channel, he had also failed to prevent the bombing raids on Berlin, the Ruhr, Hamburg and other ports and cities, which the British had been mounting throughout the battle. And he had failed to protect the barges and boats assembled on the coast for Sea Lion, which had been regularly attacked by fast, light Blenheim bombers. Although the ageing Blenheims were desperately vulnerable – 147 of them were shot down in August and September – they managed to destroy 360 barges, and killed many troops when they hit a full-scale embarkation rehearsal. It was another reason for abandoning the invasion.

Whether or not Sea Lion had ever been a serious proposition, its cancellation was another dent in Göring's reputation. But he still insisted to Hitler that he could force Britain to her knees through air power alone, and stepped up the bombing offensive accordingly. On the day the invasion was called off, the Luftwaffe struck London with the fiercest raid yet, causing some 10,000 casualties in twenty-four hours. The Battle of Britain had metamorphosed into what Britons called 'the Blitz'; from then until 13 November, the Luftwaffe pounded London on every single night but one with between 150 and 300 bombers, including some Italian planes based in Belgium, dropping at least 100 tons of high explosive every time, plus raids on Birmingham and Bristol.

Initially, the night raids were augmented by daytime attacks with fighter-bombers, but these were stopped in mid October, when the losses became too great. By mid November, when the offensive was switched to various other cities, including Plymouth, Southampton, Liverpool and Coventry, the Luftwaffe had dropped over 13,000 tons of high explosives and over a million incendiaries on London, at a cost of less than one per cent of its aircraft. The raid on Coventry on the night of 14–15 November was one of the most controversial of the war at that stage. As well as twelve armaments factories, much of the ancient centre of the city, including the fourteenth-century cathedral, were destroyed, 380 people were killed and 865 injured.[16] Göring felt no guilt, and was quite happy to accept personal responsibility:

Although the Führer wanted, now as before, to see London attacked, I, acting on my own initiative, made exact preparations for the target of Coventry because, according to my information, there was located in and around Coventry an important part of the aircraft and aircraft accessories industry. Birmingham and Coventry were targets of the most decisive importance for me. I decided on Coventry because there the most targets could be hit within the smallest area.

I prepared that attack myself with both air fleets . . . and then with the first favourable weather, that is, a moonlit night, I ordered the attack and gave directions for it to be carried out as long and as repeatedly as was necessary to achieve decisive effects on the British aircraft industry there . . .

That the city itself was greatly affected resulted from the fact that the industry there was widely spread over the city, with the exception of two new plants which were outside the city, and again the damage was increased by the spreading of fire. If we look at German cities today, we know how destructive the influence of fire is.[17]

The morning after the Coventry raid, Göring left for his hunting lodge at Rominten in East Prussia with Emmy and Edda and his immediate entourage, handing over command of the Luftwaffe to Milch and direction of the Four-Year Plan and the economy to Körner. He was both physically and emotionally exhausted, depressed by Hitler's displeasure at his failures, and in need of several weeks' rest. For months he had been struggling with heart and glandular problems, consulting a string of doctors and relying on his nurse, Christa Gormanns, who had been his full-time attendant since 1937, to administer his numerous treatments and medications. He was now taking around thirty paracodeine pills a day, popping a couple like jelly beans every time he felt stressed – which was often.

Göring's previous six months had been hectic by any standards. As well as directing the air war against Britain, he had kept up a busy schedule of meetings on all the other subjects for which he was responsible. Hitler, obsessed with his role as supreme warlord, had more or less given up running the country, leaving day-to-day affairs to him as his quasi Prime Minister. The lean Ministerial Defence Council met only a few times as a form of War Cabinet, but became unworkable as more and more ministers and officials insisted on joining in. Göring, who had always been impatient with bureaucracy, soon abandoned it and reverted to his habitual autocratic style, issuing edicts and decrees and leaving others to sort out the administrative chaos that often ensued.

He had found occasional relief in hunting – he had even had a stag transported to France from Carinhall shortly before the armistice so that he could shoot it, but had fallen asleep on his stand by the time it came into sight. In late September, when the rutting season had begun, he had spent a long weekend at Rominten, shooting and talking with fighter ace Adolf Galland, who had just been decorated by Hitler with the Oak Leaves to his Knight's Cross after his fortieth victory over the Thames Estuary. But he had hurried back to France after receiving news of disastrous losses to the daytime bombing fleet. He had also indulged his passion for collecting, basing himself in Paris, where he took over a complete floor of the Ritz Hotel, while he drooled over the pictures in the Louvre and acquired the choicest works of art that had been confiscated from French Jews and were now displayed in the Jeu de Paume gallery. In between the haggling, he shuttled back and forth in *Asia* between Paris and the Luftwaffe General Staff's headquarters train, code-named *Robinson*, which was parked at Le Déluge, near La Boissière in north-western France.

In October, he invited Goebbels to visit Paris as his guest, gave him tea at the Palais Rothschild, took him to art exhibitions and galleries, strolled with him along the banks of the Seine, and treated him to an evening in the Casino de Paris night club, where he could forget the war amid 'many beautiful women and disarming nudity'. Guided by Göring the art connoisseur, Goebbels bought a beautiful Aubusson carpet as a wall hanging for his house at Lanke, for 26,000 marks. Clearly, relations between the two men had improved now that Goebbels was reunited with Magda – it was around this time that Göring took care of his worries over paying for the house.

Goebbels took advantage of his visit to Paris to investigate the French film business. He was intent on extending his control of film making and distribution throughout Europe, both as a means of propaganda and indoctrination and also as a lucrative source of income – in 1940, his cinematic empire would bring in a clear profit of 70 million marks. To keep this out of the hands of the Finance Ministry, he allocated most of it to a special fund for the construction of new cinemas, but curried favour with Hitler by making donations of 5 million marks to the Führer's culture fund and 1.5 million to the social fund of the Winter Relief programme.[18]

At the beginning of November, Göring was back in Berlin for a conference of the commanders-in-chief with Hitler, to be briefed on the outcome of a series of disappointing meetings the Führer had just had with Franco, Pétain and Mussolini. He was dismayed to hear Hitler savagely criticising the Luftwaffe for the first time, accusing him of exaggerating RAF losses and claiming that he had more accurate figures. Göring's failures over Britain, Hitler charged, had made it doubtful that Spain would now enter the Axis alliance. When Hitler talked of switching the war to the East with an attack on the Soviet Union, Göring did his best to dissuade him, just as he had in August, when he had spent three hours arguing fiercely against any such a move before Britain was knocked out. He believed it would be folly to risk a war on two fronts, and in any case he still needed the grain, oil and raw materials that the Soviets were punctiliously providing under the trade treaty.

Göring did not believe the Soviets were anywhere near ready to launch their own attack on Germany, which made a German invasion in the East less urgent and gave time for a fresh approach to the problem of removing Britain first. He wanted to seal off Britain's lifeline to the Middle East and the Empire through the Mediterranean by grabbing Gibraltar at one end and the Suez Canal at the other, in joint actions with the Italians and the Spanish. For once, he was in agreement with Raeder, who had drawn up a similar plan of his own, partly, no doubt, because it would lead to a bigger and more powerful navy. But even faced by the two commanders-in-chief, Hitler refused to commit himself entirely to the Mediterranean option, telling the commanders that 'everything must be done to be ready for the great showdown' with the Soviet Union.

The Mediterranean option, in fact, was seriously flawed. The assault on Gibraltar was not possible without Spanish involvement, and Franco's price for co-operation was deliberately pitched too high. The North African operation was in the hands of the Italians, who had some 230,000 men in Libya facing 31,000 British and Indian troops in Egypt, but they were ill-equipped, ill-prepared and unenthusiastic. The Italian Tenth Army had invaded Egypt on 13 September, but three days later, after advancing barely fifty miles, had stopped at Sidi Barrani, halfway to the British lines, to await supplies. It was still waiting.

Mussolini was suffering even worse ignominy in Greece, which he had invaded on 28 October without warning Hitler – and indeed very much against his wishes – in a fit of pique after Hitler had moved a German division into Romania without warning him, ostensibly to help train the Romanian army but actually to safeguard the Ploesti oilfields on which Germany relied for sixty per cent of her petroleum needs. 'Hitler always faces me with a *fait accompli*,' the Duce complained to Ciano. 'This time I am going to pay him back in his own coin. He will find out from the papers that I have occupied Greece. In this way the equilibrium will be re-established.'[19] The result was an even greater humiliation than the fiasco in the Western Desert as the Greeks rallied to the defence of their country and drove out the invaders within days, with heavy losses. Mussolini's ill-conceived venture succeeded only in draining strength from his North African campaign, and providing a perfect excuse for the British to base troops and planes in mainland Greece and occupy the strategically important islands of Crete and Lemnos.

Shortly afterwards, twenty Swordfish aircraft from the British carrier *Illustrious* torpedoed Italian ships at anchor in Taranto, seriously damaging three battleships and two cruisers and putting almost half of the Italian battle fleet out of action for most of the war. And within another three weeks, the British army in the Western Desert launched its first offensive, recapturing Sidi Barrani and taking 38,000 Italian and Libyan prisoners at a cost of 624 British casualties. Far from being able to rely on Italian support, the Wehrmacht would have to come to their rescue.

Göring's Mediterranean plan was in tatters, but he still had high hopes of the Blitz on Britain, sending the Luftwaffe to bomb cities, factories, communications and above all ports most nights from mid November until May 1941. Despite rapidly improving British defences, the raids caused enormous damage, not least to housing, killing more than 43,000 civilians and injuring another 139,000, for the loss of some 600 bombers, about 1.5 per cent of all sorties flown. But British aircraft and arms production was hardly affected, and the spirit of the people was strengthened rather than broken. The air offensive had completely failed to bring Britain to her knees.

While Göring was opposed to a war with the Soviets for entirely prag-matic reasons, Ribbentrop's objections were personal and emotional. He regarded the Nazi–Soviet Pact as his greatest achievement, a natural continuation of Bismarck's eastern policy, and he did not want to do anything to undermine it. Indeed, he hoped to extend it, and even to draw the Soviets into a grand alliance. His hatred for Britain was as strong as ever, and he still saw her, rather than the Soviet Union, as Germany's real enemy.

Perhaps the most bizarre manifestation of Ribbentrop's obsession with Britain came in late July 1940, when he hatched a plot to kidnap the Duke of Windsor, the former King Edward VIII, from Portugal, where he was waiting to sail to the Bahamas to take up his new appoint-ment as Governor. Ribbentrop believed that he could use the Duke as a rallying point for the anti-Churchill, pro-German faction which he imagined still existed in the British Establishment, and persuaded Heydrich to send Walter Schellenberg, who had masterminded the kidnapping of the two British Secret Service officers at Venlo, to Portugal to seize him. Well aware that there was no fifth column in Britain, Heydrich instructed Schellenberg to make sure the Duke boarded his ship safely and sailed away before he could become an embarrassment, which he duly did. Ribbentrop, thwarted, turned back to his long-term aim of fostering friendship with the Soviet Union.

The German–Soviet relationship on which Ribbentrop set such store had been under strain from both sides during the summer. Hitler had been irritated by the Soviet annexation of the Baltic states in the north and Bessarabia in the south, though both had been allocated to them in the Pact. Stalin had been upset when Hitler had started supplying arms to Finland again, then signed an agreement allowing German troops to cross Finland *en route* for northern Norway, and to station troops to protect the route. He had also been annoyed when Ribbentrop, without consulting him, imposed a settlement on Romania of long-standing border disputes with Hungary and Bulgaria, and had then guaranteed Romania's new frontiers. This had led to the abdication of King Carol of Romania, in favour of his young son, Michael, with the authoritarian former War Minister, General Ion Antonescu, as Regent. Antonescu was strongly pro-German and anti-Soviet, and invited Wehrmacht troops into his country as a protection against Soviet incursions: Hitler sent a motorised division, augmented by tanks and backed up by Luftwaffe squadrons, which Stalin naturally saw as a threat.

Stalin was even more suspicious of Ribbentrop's next diplomatic triumph on 27 September, when Japan, greedily eyeing the Far Eastern empires of France, the Netherlands and Britain, finally joined Germany and Italy in signing a Tripartite Pact. The Pact recognised German and Italian hegemony in 'the establishment of a New Order in Europe' and Japanese leadership in Greater East Asia, and the three powers agreed to come to each other's aid if any of them was attacked 'by a power not at present involved in the European war or the Sino-Japanese conflict'.[20] Ribbentrop only informed Soviet Prime Minister and Foreign Minister Vyacheslav Molotov of the Pact the day before it was signed, but he assured him that it was 'directed exclusively against the American warmongers', and even contained a clause specifically stating that it did not 'in any way affect' existing relations with the Soviet Union. Two weeks later, he wrote an inordinately long letter to Stalin, officially inviting Molotov to visit him in Berlin.

Any doubts Hitler might still have had about attacking the Soviet Union were finally removed when he met Molotov on 12 and 13 November. The Soviet Premier, who had already endured a morning of Ribbentrop's vacuous speechifying, was at his most frosty, refusing to be fobbed off with the broad generalities and sweeping gestures that were Hitler's stock-in-trade. After listening impassively, he proceeded to ask detailed and pointed questions about the Tripartite Pact, the precise meaning of phrases such as 'Greater East Asia' – which of course had never been clearly defined – and German intentions regarding Finland, Romania, Turkey, Bulgaria and the Balkans. He refused to accept that Britain was already defeated, and was unimpressed by offers of the Soviet Union being given a free hand to move south, towards India and other British possessions. He wanted concrete concessions now, not vague promises for the future. Hitler had never been cross-questioned so sharply or so relentlessly, but he controlled himself and answered as well as he was able, until growing darkness outside gave him the excuse to end the conversation. 'I fear we must break off this discussion,' he said, rising from his armchair. 'Otherwise we shall get caught by the air-raid warning.'²¹

Later that evening, Ribbentrop held a reception for Molotov at the Kaiserhof Hotel. The security precautions were the most elaborate ever seen in Berlin, with the entire area sealed off by the SD, who were terrified there might be an assassination attempt. With the aid of the Gestapo, all politically suspect persons were screened, and Russian émigrés removed from the city and sent to stay in distant hotels, at government expense. Molotov's own security men worked closely with Heydrich's men, under the overall control of Himmler. Every side door and tradesmen's entrance to the hotel was hermetically sealed and guarded.

Everyone who was anyone in Berlin was there, with one notable exception – Hitler did not attend. Göring and Hess deputised for him, Göring making up for the Führer's absence by his size and splendour – according to Valentin Berezhkov, Molotov's interpreter, he was wearing a uniform of silver-thread fabric, his chest covered from shoulder to waist in medals and decorations, and his fingers jammed with rings sparkling with precious stones.²²

The next morning before lunch, Molotov called on Göring at his Air Ministry office, to discuss the state of trade between Germany and the Soviet Union. Molotov wanted answers again: why were German deliveries falling so badly behind schedule? Göring turned on his jovial charm and refused to be ruffled, as Hitler and Ribbentrop had been, by the Soviet leader's hard line. As a result, the atmosphere stayed friendly, though neither man gave an inch. The problem, Göring explained, was entirely of the Soviets' own making: their orders were concentrated in a very narrow range of commodities, chiefly machine tools and armaments, which were in unusually great demand in Germany itself. Molotov countered by saying that surely Germany now had greatly increased resources after occupying so many foreign territories, and so should have no difficulty filling Soviet orders.

Göring had a ready answer to that, too. Only a few days before, he said, he had been complaining to Hitler that the new lands were proving to be a strain on Germany, that economically they were more of a burden than a benefit. He then returned to the attack by complaining about the amount of technical aid being asked for by the Soviet Union. Some of this, he said, amounted to demands for industrial secrets. The encounter ended in a draw.

After lunch with Hitler in the private dining-room in his residence, Molotov returned to the attack. The arguments became more ill-tempered and abrasive, particularly over Finland and Romania and by the end of the day Hitler was glad to see the back of his difficult guest. Despite the sour feeling of the talks, Molotov went ahead with the reception and dinner he had planned at the Soviet Embassy on the Unter den Linden. Göring, never one to miss out on a feast, was there again, as was Hess and, of course, Ribbentrop, leading a good turn-out of top personalities and officials. But again, Hitler did not attend. He stayed in the Chancellery, sulking over his failure either to hypno-tise or bully Molotov into compliance.

The food and drink were as sumptuous as at any Kremlin celebra-tion. There was Crimean champagne for the start of the reception, and the dinner itself included all the very best Russian produce, with lash-ings of caviar and vodka. It was, said Paul Schmidt, 'a very good party'. But it was brought to an abrupt halt by the arrival of unwelcome gate-crashers – the RAF. 'We had heard of the conference beforehand,' Churchill wrote later, 'and though not invited to join the discussion did not wish to be entirely left out of the proceedings.'[23] Molotov had just made a short speech proposing a toast to Hitler, and Ribbentrop had just risen to reply when the air-raid sirens sounded. Trying to appear nonchalant, he said sarcastically, 'Our British friends are complaining that they have not been invited to the party. But we shall not let their fireworks interfere with us in any way. We shall continue in the air-raid shelter.'

The Embassy, however, did not possess its own shelter. Everyone headed for the doors as fast as they could, with Göring and Hess leading the way. Once they had been driven off at high speed, the other guests poured out of the building and hurried to find protection else-where. Ribbentrop took Molotov to his own shelter, beneath his new residence just around the corner, where he began his final attempt to stave off the rupture in German–Soviet relations which by now was looking more and more certain. But from his opening words it was obvious that he had learned absolutely nothing from the previous three sessions. Trapped in the underground bunker with him, Molotov was forced to sit and listen for two and a quarter hours to a dreary rehash of empty phrases.

At one point, with his usual maladroitness, Ribbentrop suddenly drew from his pocket a draft agreement admitting the Soviet Union to the Tripartite Pact, but even this was vague and imprecise, skirting round all the issues to which Molotov had already demanded detailed answers. Molotov ignored it, and returned to the attack with a new wave of tough questions which he asked Ribbentrop to comment on. Ribbentrop did his best, but it was clear he was floundering. Like a drowning man he sought something to cling to – and found it in Britain. Blaming Britain for everything that was happening, especially in the Baltic, the Balkans and the Black Sea, he found his way on to what seemed to be the firm ground of the dissolution of the British Empire. Inviting the Soviet Union once again to participate in this, he ended with a confident flourish by reminding Molotov that he had not yet answered his question about whether the Soviet Union was interested in obtaining an outlet to the Indian Ocean.

Molotov's answer must surely rank among the most cutting ripostes in the history of diplomacy. The Germans, he said, were assuming that the war against Britain had already been won. If therefore, as Hitler had said earlier when asked about delays in the delivery of goods to the Soviet Union, Germany was waging a life-and-death struggle against England, he could only construe this as meaning that Germany was fighting 'for life' and England 'for death'. And when Ribbentrop, completely missing the heavy sarcasm, continued to reiterate that Britain was indeed finished, Molotov wearily delivered his final thrust. 'If that is so,' he said, 'then why are we in this shelter, and whose are those bombs that are falling?'[24]

Molotov and most of his advisers – with the exception of several who stayed behind to place further orders for machinery, arms and aircraft – left Berlin the next morning at 11 a.m. and headed home again. They had been in the city for exactly forty-eight hours. At the Anhalter Station, the only leading Nazi to see them off was Ribbentrop. Göring was busy organising the raid on Coventry, which was to take place that night, and preparing to travel to Rominten the next day for his much-needed rest and recuperation.

At noon, Hitler told his daily war conference that he had never expected much from the discussions, but that they had shown which way the Russians' plans were lying. 'Molotov has let the cat out of the bag,' one of his adjutants recorded him saying. He was greatly relieved that this 'would not even have to remain a marriage of convenience'. After months of indecision, Hitler had finally made his mind up: he would attack the Soviet Union in the spring of 1941.

XXVIII

'THE WHOLE WORLD WILL HOLD ITS BREATH'

WILLIAM Shirer, that most astute observer of the Nazi scene, had been based in Berlin since 1934. He had witnessed the regime's evil flowering and its malign effects on the people of Germany with an acerbic eye, and had worked tirelessly trying to inform and warn his native United States, and indeed the rest of the world, of its dangers. By the beginning of December 1940, however, worn down by the constant battle with censorship and obstructionism, he had had enough, and decided to return home. In his diary for 1 December, he summed up the situation he was leaving behind, including his view of the relative positions of 'the really big shots' around Hitler.

Looking at the 'jungle struggle' for the succession, there was no doubt in his mind that Göring was 'very definitely the Number Two man in Germany and the only Nazi who could carry on the present regime were Hitler to pass on'. Noting that Hess 'lacks the strength, the ambition, the driving force and imagination for the job of top man', he turned to the other contenders:

Goebbels, who used to be Number Three, has lost ground since the war, partly because he has been swept aside by the military and the secret police, partly because he has bungled his propaganda job at crucial moments, as when he ordered the press and radio to celebrate the victory of the *Graf Spee* the day before it was scuttled.

Goebbels's place as the third man in Germany has been taken by Heinrich Himmler, the mild-mannered little fellow who looks like a harmless country schoolteacher, but whose ruthlessness, brutality, and organising talents have landed him in a key position in the Third Reich. He's important because he has whipped the Gestapo into an organisation which now watches over almost every department of life in the country and which keeps for Hitler and the politicians a watchful eye on the army itself. Himmler, alone among Hitler's lieutenants, has power of life and death over all citizens of Germany and the occupied lands, and it is a rare day when he does not take advantage of it. The evidence you find buried daily in the back pages of the newspapers in the little notices which read: 'SS Chief Himmler announces that Hans Schmidt, a German (or Ladislav Kotowski, a Pole), has been shot while offering resistance to the police.'

. . . Ribbentrop, a vain and pompous man, thoroughly disliked in the party and by the public, is still in favour with the Führer because he guessed right about England and France (Göring guessed wrong and as a result suffered a temporary eclipse) at Munich. The fact that he guessed wrong in September 1939, when he assured Hitler the British wouldn't fight, has not affected his standing at the Chancellery. Hitler has recently taken to calling him 'a second Bismarck', though men like Göring, who despises him, can't understand why.[1]

Shirer was right about Himmler's advance to the number three position, though at the time he could not have known the full extent of the Reichsführer's expanding authority. With the internal security of the Reich firmly under his control, Himmler had spent most of 1940 developing two other areas of his growing power: his private army, the Waffen-SS, and the police and SS apparatus in the eastern territories where he planned to establish his personal empire. He had to face considerable opposition – from the army in one case and Göring, the Gauleiters and governors in the other – but when it came to political infighting, no one could match him for tenacity and ruthlessness.

The Waffen-SS had officially come into existence at the end of October 1939, when the various armed formations of the SS had been amalgamated under the leadership of Himmler's recruitment chief, SS-Obergruppenführer Gottlob Berger. A brash, loud-mouthed Swabian, the son of a saw-mill owner, Berger had been seriously wounded as a second lieutenant in the First World War, and had been one of the earliest recruits to the Nazi Party. After a rumbustious period in the SA, where he made more enemies than friends, he had joined the SS in 1934, and had become Himmler's éminence grise in military matters, feeding his ambition to turn the Verfügungstruppe into a self-contained army.

In the Polish campaign, the SS-VT troops had both impressed and horrified the Wehrmacht commanders. Fighting alongside regular army units, they had distinguished themselves by their élan and their conspicuous bravery; but they had appalled the generals by their reckless disregard for their own lives and the high casualty rates which they courted as a badge of courage. The generals complained, too, that besides failing to protect their men, the SS officers were not properly trained for complex operations and that their units did not integrate well with the divisions to which they were attached. Himmler responded by persuading Hitler to allow him to form completely separate SS divisions, under their own commanders, a major step towards his ambition of a self-contained private army.

Himmler and Berger formed three divisions from the three main elements that were incorporated into the Waffen-SS. The existing VT regiments, 'Deutschland', 'Germania' and 'Der Führer', were combined to form the motorised SS-Verfügungs Division (its name was changed later to 'Das Reich'); the 'Totenkopf' Division was formed from the Death's Head units, made up of Eicke's concentration camp guards, who had been replaced in the camps by men who were either too old, too young, or unfit to fight; the third division was created from the armed Order Police, though this did not formally become a part of the Waffen-SS until 1942. Sepp Dietrich's Leibstandarte remained as a separate motorised infantry regiment within the Waffen-SS – it was to form the nucleus of a new division two years later. The two Junker cadet schools and the replacement units completed the new body.

The SS divisions fought with all their usual fervour in Holland, Belgium and France – the first Iron Cross of the campaign was won by SS-Obersturmführer Kraas of the 'Leibstandarte' in Holland. Unlike the situation in Poland, there were no *Einsatzgruppen* following the Wehrmacht troops in the West, but there were still dark portents of things to come. As the British were starting their withdrawal from France on 27 May, a unit of the 'Totenkopf' Division accepted the surrender of about 100 men of the 2nd Royal Norfolks in a farm at Paradis, near Béthune, after some of the heaviest fighting of the campaign. They disarmed them, then slaughtered them with machineguns. Those who were not killed instantly were finished off with pointblank shots or bayonets.

This atrocity might have been explained away as the work of Eicke's brutalised concentration-camp thugs – but the very next day a company of the elite 'Leibstandarte' herded a similar number of British prisoners into a barn at Wormhoudt, then threw in hand grenades and opened fire on the defenceless men, killing all but sixteen.[2] The army was outraged by such blatant disregard of the rules of war, but despite the generals' protests no member of the Waffen-SS was court-martialled

or disciplined in any way – indeed, the company commander responsible for the Wormhoudt massacre went on to command an SS division later in the war. It is hard to imagine Göring condoning such
behaviour – he would have had the offenders shot. But Himmler apparently saw nothing wrong with it.

Himmler had been recruiting furiously ever since the Waffen-SS was
formed. At the start of the Polish campaign, he had had some 23,000
SS soldiers, in the VT and the Death's Head units; by the start of the
war in the West, he had more than 100,000. Compared with the army's
three million, it was so tiny it should have been insignificant, but the
generals quite rightly saw this upstart rival as a threat to the Wehrmacht.
Hitler tried to calm their fears by insisting that the Waffen-SS divisions
must remain under the operational command of the army and be
attached to different army corps. He forbade the formation of an SS
corps, and ruled that the size of the Waffen-SS was not to exceed 5–10
per cent of the peacetime strength of the army. And in a secret decree
issued on 6 August 1940, he made it quite clear that he did not see it
as the alternative army the generals feared, but as 'an armed state
police capable, whatever the situation, of representing and enforcing
the authority of the Reich in the interior of the country'.[3]

The generals were still suspicious, however, and continued to place
every obstacle they could in the way of the Waffen-SS's expansion,
starving it of men and arms and equipment – especially heavy weapons
and tanks, which could be decisive in any internal power struggle once
the war was over. Himmler tried to find a way around this by doing
a private deal with Fritz Todt, using the output of the concentration
camp quarries and the SS building materials companies, which the Todt
Organisation needed for its construction projects, plus the promise of
20,000 Polish slave labourers, as bargaining counters to bypass the
army and receive direct supplies of arms from Todt's Ministry of
Munitions. But the arrangement was short-lived: the generals blocked
it after only six weeks, and reasserted their control.

The Wehrmacht was even tougher over the question of manpower,
refusing to allocate conscripts or even more than a third of volunteers
to the Waffen-SS. Göring supported the army generals, 'because this
creaming off of the best voluntary material meant that men of that type,
who would have made equally good officers, were partly lost to the
army and the air force, and therefore they opposed this expansion'.[4]

Himmler's answer, which clearly indicated where his ambitions lay, was to turn to sources of recruits where he was not in competition with the Wehrmacht: ethnic Germans outside the Reich and the 'Germanic' elements in the conquered lands. To begin with, there were large ethnic German communities in many of the Balkan states, notably in Romania, where, conveniently, Berger's son-in-law, Andreas Schmidt, was their leader. Schmidt, a fanatical Nazi supporter, soon recruited around 1,000 eager volunteers, whom he had to smuggle out to evade the strict ban on any Romanian fit for military service leaving the country.

While ethnic Germans were filling the gaps in the regular Waffen-SS formations, the victories in Scandinavia and the Low Countries opened the door for Himmler to expand further by forming his own Foreign Legion. He moved fast. Denmark had capitulated but fighting was still going on in Norway when he visited the Chancellery on 20 April 1940 for Hitler's fifty-first birthday celebrations and got permission to raise the first non-German Waffen-SS regiment, SS-Standarte Nordland, from volunteers among the pure-blooded Nordic men of Norway and Denmark. A few weeks later, after victory in the West, he added the 'Germanic' Dutch and Flemish, and opened a training centre for them all at Sennheim in Alsace, which was as much concerned with indoctrination as arms drill.

In those early days, there was no shortage of young men dazzled by German successes and seduced by the dream of becoming modern Teutonic knights lording it over the sub-human Slavs in the East. By the spring of 1941 Himmler and Berger would have recruited enough men from those four countries to form a whole division, the SS-Wiking Division, under German commanders and NCOs. As the swastika spread its shadow further and further, they opened recruiting offices in all the occupied countries in northern and western Europe, with equal success. The SS-Wiking was the first of twenty-one divisions made up largely or entirely of foreigners, along with seven comprised mainly of ethnic Germans, out of a grand total in 1944–5 of thirty-eight SS divisions. By 1945, more than 800,000 men would have served in the Waffen-SS – but by that stage by no means all of them were willing volunteers.[5]

While his Waffen-SS was fighting and murdering so savagely in the West, Himmler still found time to think about his plans for the East. On 25 May, when he visited Hitler at Felsennest to obtain permission to start recruiting Dutchmen and Belgians, he presented him with a six-page memorandum under the heading 'Some Thoughts on the Treatment of Foreign Populations in the East'. The title may have been bland, but the contents were diabolical. The different races that had made up the population of Poland – Poles, Jews, Ukrainians, White Russians, and various smaller groups – would be 'broken up into the largest possible number of parts and fragments' in order to destroy their national consciousness. 'Racially valuable elements' – people with German blood – were to be extracted and brought to Germany for 'assimilation', while the rest were left to wither away. The Jews were barely mentioned: they were to be 'completely eliminated by means of a large-scale emigration to Africa or some other colony'.

'If these measures are consistently carried out,' Himmler wrote, 'the population of the General-Government will be reduced over the next ten years to a remnant of substandard beings. It will consist of a leader-less labour force, capable of providing Germany with a work force of annual itinerant labourers and the manpower for special tasks (streets, quarries, construction).' Education of children was to be limited to the most basic requirements: 'how to count up to a maximum of 500, how to write one's name, that it is a Divine Commandment to obey Germans, and to be honest, industrious and trustworthy. I do not consider reading to be necessary.'

One of the most chilling parts of the document stated that brighter children who were judged to be 'racially immaculate' would be removed to Germany to be brought up as Germans, 'so that the danger of these sub-human peoples of the east obtaining a leadership stratum of equal strength to us through such people of good blood will be removed'. 'Cruel and tragic as this may be in each individual case,' Himmler wrote, 'if from inner conviction one rejects the Bolshevik method of physical extermination as un-German and impossible, then this method is still the mildest and best.'[6] Over the next two to three years, tens of thousands of fair-haired youngsters were torn from their homes and parents and placed with families in Germany, to help boost the population.

Himmler's rejection of the 'Bolshevik method of physical extermina-tion' did not extend to those who were not fit, healthy and racially pure. He had no compunction in sanctioning the murder of thousands of mental patients in order to clear their hospitals for wounded soldiers.

And he raised no objection to the so-called 'euthanasia' of babies and young children born with deformities of any sort, both physical and mental. The killing of the children was carried out by regular doctors in hospitals and institutions, under rulings from the Health Ministry and the Führer's Chancellery, and although the SS chief physician, Dr Ernst Robert von Grawitz, was one of the panel who selected the doctors authorised to carry it out, Himmler had no direct involvement.

Himmler was involved, however, when the 'euthanasia' project was extended from children to adults. Questionnaires were sent to all asylums and mental institutions in October 1939, calling for exhaustive details of every patient in one of four categories, who were all to be killed. The instruction sheet listed these as:

1. Patients suffering from the diseases enumerated below and who within the institution can be occupied not at all or only at the most mechanical work (picking, etc): schizophrenia, epilepsy, senile disorders, therapy-resistant paralysis and other syphilitic disorders, retardation from whatever cause, encephalitis, Huntington's chorea and other terminal neurological conditions; or
2. have been continuously in institutions for at least five years; or
3. are in custody as criminally insane; or
4. do not possess German citizenship or are not of German or related blood, giving/designating race and nationality.

In a helpful note, 'race' was defined as 'German or related blood (German blooded), Jew, Jewish *Mischling* [mixed race] 1st or 2nd class, Negro, Negro *Mischling*, Gypsy, Gypsy *Mischling*, etc.'[7] All patients in this category were to be exterminated regardless of what condition they were suffering from, simply because they were Jews or blacks or gypsies.

The adult 'euthanasia' programme, code-named T4 after the address of the responsible Chancellery department, Tiergarten 4, was again carried out by regular doctors. But the buses that carried the doomed victims were provided by the SS and were manned by SS personnel wearing medical white coats over their jackboots and uniforms. And the attendants inside the centres were all SS men.

Himmler was also deeply involved in the methodology of the killings, through his overall command of the Criminal Police, the Kripo. A Kripo chemist called Dr Albert Widmann had been asked to find a less wasteful method of killing than a shot in the back of the neck and had suggested gassing with carbon monoxide. Another Kripo official,

Criminal Commissar (and SS-Obersturmführer) Christian Wirth from Stuttgart, had built a prototype gas chamber in a disused prison at Brandenburg, and conducted experiments to compare results with lethal injections. The gas emerged as the clear winner, disposing of eighteen to twenty victims at a time with perfect simplicity.

To avoid the inconvenience that might be caused by panic, Wirth hit on the ingenious idea of disguising the gas chamber as a communal shower room complete with benches, and pumping in carbon monoxide through perforated water pipes. Two SS chemists with doctoral degrees watched through a peephole with great satisfaction as the naked victims 'toppled over, or lay on the benches . . . without scenes or commotion'. After five minutes, the room was ventilated and SS men cleared the corpses using special trolleys to load them into cremation ovens without the need for physical contact. Four killing centres were set up immediately in old hospitals or castles, all with high walls and in remote locations, under conditions of great secrecy.[8]

In East Prussia, a *Sonderkommando* (special task unit) commanded by Dr Rudolf Lange operated a mobile variation of the gas chambers, using specially adapted air-tight vans where the vehicle's exhaust could be switched into the vehicle to provide the carbon monoxide. Between 21 May and 8 June 1940, Lange's unit disposed of 1,558 mental patients in this way.[9] Although the 'euthanasia' programme was an end in itself, it also proved to be a valuable rehearsal for the much larger operation that was to start the following year.

On 14 June 1940, as German troops marched in triumph down the Champs-Élysées in Paris, the first official concentration camp in Poland was opened in a former cavalry barracks at Oswicim in Upper East Silesia, a town of some 12,000 inhabitants known to the Germans as Auschwitz. The new camp, under the command of Rudolf Höss, a convicted murderer who had served five years in prison before learning his craft as a jailer under Eicke at Dachau, was intended to house 10,000 Polish political prisoners, who were to be treated with particular harshness. There were some Jews among them, but very few – although many Jews were in brutal labour camps, they were not yet being sent to concentration camps simply for being Jewish. Instead, throughout the year Himmler's men were busy isolating them, herding them into ghettos in Polish towns and cities where they could be dealt with more easily when the time was right – Heydrich suggested dealing with those in the overcrowded and sealed-off Warsaw ghetto by starting a deadly epidemic there, but nothing came of it.

At Auschwitz, the prisoners were put to work building a plant next to the camp where IG Farben would use their slave labour to produce synthetic rubber and oil from Silesian coal, for Göring's Four-Year Plan. Himmler had an additional role in mind for Auschwitz: he intended to set up a centre for agricultural research with huge laboratories and breeding stations for animals and plants, as part of the German Research Institute for Nutrition and Foodstuffs, the SS company he had set up at Dachau in 1939 for the production of herbs and spices. For the moment, he had no plans to turn it into an extermination centre.

Himmler's business interests were now growing even faster than his military empire. At about the same time as the first prisoners were arriving at Auschwitz, he was opening other new camps in various locations, to increase production of building materials for his SS Earth and Stone Works Company. At Neuengamme, near Hamburg, for instance, he extended the existing camp, a satellite of Sachsenhausen, to house Scandinavian, French, Dutch and Belgian political prisoners engaged in making bricks. A new camp near Natzweiler in Alsace provided French and German labour for stone quarries. And at Gross Rosen in Lower Silesia, Polish prisoners from the annexed territories were worked to death in a granite quarry.

Besides the Earth and Stone Works and the Nutrition and Foodstuffs Institute, Himmler formed two other major companies based on the camps: the German Equipment Company, which owned all the plants and ran a number of trades, from baking bread to cutlery manufacture, woodworking and iron foundries; and the Company for the Utilisation of Textiles and Leather, which used the women prisoners of Ravensbrück to make uniforms for the Waffen-SS. All four companies were set up with a normal business structure, in which SS interest was carefully concealed, and their administration was kept strictly separate from that of the camps. They were controlled by a holding company, Deutscher Wirtschaftsbetrieb (German Industrial Concern) known as DWB, run by SS-Obergruppenführer Oswald Pohl, head of the Economics and Administration Main Office of the SS, a bull-necked, shaven-headed former captain in the navy's paymaster branch. With the exception of Heydrich, Pohl had become the most powerful of Himmler's lieutenants, with authority over a wide range of areas, including all finances. Imitating the Nazi state itself, Himmler had set up the various 'main offices' of the SS like government ministries, with overlapping and often vaguely defined responsibilities, so that their chiefs were in constant competition with each other, both for power and for Himmler's favour.

Himmler's hopes for the early realisation of his dream of settling his warrior-peasants in the Eastern territories had been thwarted by his rivals for power there, the Wehrmacht, the Gauleiters, and Governor-General Hans Frank, who all refused to knuckle under to his HSSPFs. He would have to bide his time until the boundless spaces further east, in the Soviet Union, became available. He would not have to wait long. On 18 December 1940, Hitler issued his Directive No. 21. It began:

The German Wehrmacht must be prepared *to crush Soviet Russia in a quick campaign* (Operation Barbarossa) even before the conclusion of the war against England.

For this purpose the *army* will have to employ all available units, with the reservation that the occupied countries must be secured against surprises.

For the *Luftwaffe* it will be a matter of releasing such strong forces for the Eastern campaign in support of the army that a quick conclusion of the ground operations can be counted on and that damage to eastern Germany by enemy air attacks will be as slight as possible.

At the same time, the directive continued, 'offensive operations against England, particularly her supply lines, must not be permitted to break down'. To that end, 'the main effort of the *navy* will remain unequivocally directed against England even during an Eastern campaign'.

The attack must be swift and daring, aiming to destroy the Red Army in the West. Soviet units must be cut off and prevented from fleeing into the vastness of Russian territory. The aim of the whole operation was to conquer Russia as far as a line drawn from the Volga in the south to Archangel in the north. Once the Luftwaffe had destroyed the Red Air Force, it would then be free to turn its attention to bombing the remaining Soviet industrial centres in the Urals.

The directive went on to set out the grand strategy for the operation, and the help that could be expected from the 'probable allies', Romania and Finland, on its two wings. Secrecy was to be preserved at all costs, with the whole operation disguised as *'precautionary meas-

ures for the possibility that Russia should change her present attitude towards us'.[10]

Preparations for Barbarossa were to be completed by 15 May 1941, but before then there were things to be taken care of in North Africa and the Balkans. Göring had interrupted his sick leave at Rominten on 3 December to receive Milch and the Deputy Chief of the Air Staff, General Hoffmann von Waldau, who had brought him the plans for moving an air corps to southern Italy and Sicily, to support the Italians with attacks on Alexandria, the Suez Canal, Malta and the straits between Sicily and North Africa. The order for the move was issued on 10 December, the day after the start of the battle of Sidi Barrani, and the Luftwaffe units, linking up with the Italian air force, were soon making themselves felt with attacks on British shipping and the beleaguered island fortress of Malta.

Hitler had already issued a directive for Operation Marita, the invasion of Greece to drive out the British forces which could use the mainland and the islands of Lemnos and Crete as bases for bombing raids on the vital Ploesti oilfields. But to get to Greece, German forces would need to pass through Romania, Bulgaria and possibly Yugoslavia – and there were problems with all three countries. Ribbentrop had managed to persuade Romania, along with Hungary and Slovakia, to join the Tripartite Pact in November, but Bulgaria and Yugoslavia, both of which were also being wooed by Stalin, held out stubbornly.

Romania was proving to be Germany's most enthusiastic and reliable ally. Antonescu had hit it off splendidly with Hitler in Berlin in November, and he cemented their friendship on 14 January when he visited him again at the Berghof and agreed to allow more than half a million German troops to assemble in his country, to prepare for Marita. In return, prompted by Ribbentrop, Hitler agreed to support Antonescu in his internal struggle with the Iron Guard, the military wing of the Romanian Fascist movement, which had helped him to power but was now threatening his position.

Less than a week after Antonescu arrived back in Bucharest, the Iron Guard staged a revolt, seizing all government buildings apart from the dictator's palace and the Foreign Ministry. When Antonescu appealed for German aid, Ribbentrop agreed immediately, telling him he should crush the Iron Guard as ruthlessly as Hitler had crushed the SA in 1934. German tanks moved in, and the Iron Guard surrendered to government troops, who followed Ribbentrop's advice by massacring most of them. The few leaders who survived were rescued by the SD, which had been sponsoring the Iron Guard for some time and had been behind the attempted *coup*. They were hidden in safe houses, then smuggled out of the country in ambulances, dressed in German uniforms.

Furious at what he described as 'a gigantic conspiracy against the official foreign policy of the Reich', Ribbentrop seized the opportunity to strike at his SS rivals, convincing Hitler that it was not just Heydrich and the SD who were involved, but the entire hierarchy of the SS. Himmler was personally implicated by letters from him to the Iron Guard leader, Hora Sima – who had been hidden from the police in the house of Andreas Schmidt, Berger's son-in-law. For once, Hitler backed Ribbentrop, flying into an almighty rage and screaming that he would 'smoke out the black plague' if it did not toe the line.[11]

Gratified to discover that the SS and SD were not invulnerable after all, Ribbentrop went on the offensive, having all the SD agents in Romania brought back to Germany, where some of them were arrested and imprisoned. With Hitler's approval, the SD was forbidden to interfere in the internal affairs of other countries, and all the SD 'police attachés' in German diplomatic missions were placed under the authority of the head of mission, to whom they were obliged to show all their correspondence with the RSHA. It was a notable victory, which Ribbentrop celebrated by ceasing to wear the SS uniform of which he had previously been so proud, and forbidding his officials from doing so either. Shortly afterwards, he began replacing German heads of mission in south-eastern Europe with leading SA members, who had no diplomatic experience or ability, but who could be relied on to keep the SS and SD in their place.

Ribbentrop was less successful in trying to persuade Hitler not to go ahead with Barbarossa, but to form a deeper alliance with the Soviet Union instead, regularly reminding him of Bismarck's eastern policy. He only discovered the plan on 9 January 1941, when he joined the operational chiefs of the three services and the OKW for the final session of a three-day council of war, and must have been horrified by what he heard. After running through the position of Britain, France, Spain, the Balkans and Italy, Hitler went on to present the defeat of the Soviet Union as the answer to all Germany's problems. Even if it did not force Britain to capitulate, it would release the full power of the German forces to finish her off. In addition, it would keep America out of the war by allowing the Japanese to turn the full power of their forces against her in the Pacific. Therefore, 'Russia must be smashed', and soon.

Hitler repeated the strategic objectives he had outlined in his Barbarossa directive, dismissing the vast distances as being 'no greater than those which have already been mastered by the Wehrmacht', and even added a new goal – the oilfields of Baku, on the Caspian Sea. His fantasies flowered as he built up to the climax of his long speech, concluding with the promise: 'The gigantic territory of Russia conceals immeasurable riches. Germany must dominate it economically and politically, without annexing it physically. Thus we will have everything we could possibly need to wage war in the future even against whole continents, if need be. We shall be invincible. When we fight this campaign, let Europe hold its breath!'[12]

Ribbentrop must have found it especially galling to hear Hitler deriding Stalin as 'a clever fellow . . . [who] will not hesitate to tear up every written treaty if it suits his purpose'. For at that very moment Karl Schnurre was in Moscow finalising a whole raft of new treaties, centred around a revised trade agreement providing for increased deliveries of raw materials, including petroleum, copper, tin, nickel, tungsten, manganese and molybdenum, plus 2.5 million tons of grain a year. There were treaties covering the resettlement of Germans from the Baltic states, and a lump sum payment for private German property there. There was also an agreement on the new boundary between Germany and Lithuania, with compensation of 7.5 million gold dollars from the Soviet Union for an extra piece of territory known as the Lithuanian Tip, which had been the cause of bitter recriminations when Stalin had grabbed it in 1939. Ribbentrop was specially excited by this – when Schnurre returned to Berlin he eagerly asked to see the gold, and was most disappointed when Schnurre patiently explained that this was a paper transaction, which simply halved the German trade deficit.[13]

Notwithstanding Hitler's comments on Stalin's probity, Ribbentrop issued a jubilant and typically wordy circular to all embassies and missions describing the package as settling all the questions pending between Germany and the Soviet Union. Economically, he claimed, the trade deal meant the final collapse of the British blockade and refuted the 'malicious expectations which our enemies expressed upon the conclusion of the first economic agreement that Soviet promises would exist only on paper'. 'The Soviet Union,' he went on, probably with more than an eye on Hitler, 'has delivered everything that she promised. In many fields she has delivered more than had originally been agreed upon. In the organisation of the huge shipments, the Soviet Union has performed in a really admirable manner.'[14]

For once, Göring was in agreement with Ribbentrop. The benefits of the trade agreement were at the top of the arguments that he continued to press on Hitler over the next few weeks, as he, too, took every opportunity to try to dissuade him from continuing with Barbarossa. He was so persistent, indeed, that Hitler actively discouraged him from attending conferences and saw as little as possible of him. Göring later told Emmy that Hitler had said to him: 'I refused to see you, Göring, because I knew you would do all you could to talk me out of it.'

On 24 January, however, Hitler called Göring to the Berghof, together with Jeschonnek and his Parachute Division commander, General Kurt Student, who had just recovered from a serious head wound caused by a stray bullet during the battle for Rotterdam, where his life had been saved by the skill of a Dutch surgeon. Hitler's purpose was to discuss Luftwaffe operations in Greece, and in particular Crete, where Student was to lead an airborne invasion under Göring's overall command. On the train journey from Berlin, however, the main topic of conversation had been Göring's opposition to Barbarossa, and when they arrived at the Berghof at midday, he closeted himself alone with Hitler until 8 p.m., arguing desperately. According to Student, Hitler emerged 'sunk deep in thought', and Göring believed he had succeeded. 'Thank God, no war with Russia,' he told his two generals. Two days later, however, Hitler phoned Göring in Berlin and told him he had changed his mind: 'We shall attack in the East.'[15]

Hitler confirmed his decision to Göring in another meeting, this time back in the Reich Chancellery on 28 January. Göring, who was immersed at that time in a series of top level conferences on raw materials supplies, broke the news to his arms and economic experts the following day. They all agreed that a war with the Soviet Union was 'economically unthinkable', though one, his Russian-born agriculture specialist Herbert Backe, commented that conquering the Ukraine would solve Germany's chronic grain shortage. To Göring, this was small comfort, and after ordering General Georg Thomas, the chief of the OKW's economics and armaments branch, to prepare a study of the problems, he took himself off next day on a consolation shopping trip to The Hague and Amsterdam, followed a few days later, after a brief stopover at Luftwaffe forward headquarters at Le Déluge, with a three-day binge of art plundering in Paris.

He was not present, therefore, at Hitler's conference with his generals on 3 February, to hear and discuss the army's operational directive for the campaign in the East. Based on inadequate and erroneous intelligence of Soviet capabilities, the plan was wildly over-optimistic. Although some of the problems with transport, communications and fuel supplies were highlighted, Hitler heard nothing to dent his belief in a quick victory. He ended the conference on an even higher note than he had sounded on 9 January: 'When Barbarossa starts,' he proclaimed, 'the whole *world* will hold its breath and say nothing.'

Between the two conferences with his generals, Hitler had summoned Mussolini and Ciano to the Berghof on 19 and 20 January for a meeting that the Duce was dreading. He was convinced that Hitler would humiliate him over his failures in Greece and North Africa, where the British, now strengthened by the arrival of Australian troops, were advancing fast and already attacking the defences of Tobruk. Hitler, however, was consideration personified, going out of his way to be tactful and sympathetic. He offered to augment the help already coming from the Luftwaffe with two armoured divisions and one of light infantry, and Mussolini accepted gracefully. In return, Hitler asked the Duce to do his best to persuade Franco to join the Axis, so that the Germans could attack Gibraltar through Spain.

Unfortunately, Ribbentrop insisted on taking a hand with Franco, to deny the Italians the kudos of bringing Spain into the war. But his hand was so heavy, and his personal message so much like an ultimatum, that the Spanish dictator took umbrage, and told the Italians that owing to a food crisis in Spain it would be impossible for him to join in the war. It was the end of Göring's Mediterranean option against Britain.

Hitler had talked to Mussolini about the coming campaign in Greece, and had inveighed at some length against the Soviet Union – but he had made no mention whatever of Barbarossa. Having no need of Italian support in the East, he was determined to keep them in the

dark until the last possible moment, partly for reasons of security –
he was convinced that the King of Italy told the British everything –
and partly because he did not want to share the spoils of victory with
them.

In North Africa, the Italians were facing disaster. By 6 February, the
British and Australians had completely destroyed the Italian Tenth
Army, captured Benghazi and were on the point of completing the
occupation of the province of Cyrenaica. If there was to be a rescue
operation, it would have to be soon. Naming General Erwin Rommel
as commander of the Afrika Korps, Hitler dispatched him to Tripoli
so quickly that he did not even have time to pack his bags. The next
day, the first of the promised German forces, the 5th Panzer Regiment,
sailed from Naples.

For the Führer, however, North Africa was nothing more than a
sideshow. His attention was firmly focused on his preparations for his
great campaign in the East. By the end of the month, he had persuaded
King Boris of Bulgaria to join the Tripartite Pact by offering to provide
him with an outlet to the Aegean, and during March some 680,000
German troops moved from Romania into Bulgaria, over three great
bridges swiftly erected across the Danube by army engineers, to be
ready for the drive into Greece.

Yugoslavia proved a more difficult nut to crack. Throughout March
Ribbentrop continued to work on the Yugoslav Regent, Prince Paul,
with alternate threats and bribes, ignoring warnings from his own
Foreign Ministry experts and the SD that the Serbian people and army
would not accept an alliance with Germany. Disregarding the fact that
he had wooed Hungary, Italy and Bulgaria with the promise of juicy
pieces of Yugoslavia, he promised Prince Paul that Germany would
guarantee Yugoslavia's frontiers, and offered him part of Greece,
including Salonika. Finally, on 25 March, the Yugoslavs succumbed,
agreeing to join the Pact but with secret provisos relieving them of any
military obligations.

The Premier and Foreign Minister were smuggled out of Belgrade
in a plain car to avoid the wrath of their own countrymen, slipped
over the frontier and whisked off to Vienna, where they signed the
Pact and met Hitler in the Belvedere Palace, where he confirmed the
offers Ribbentrop had made and promised not to send German troops
through their country. They departed for home again swearing to repay
his kindness and understanding with feelings of loyalty and devotion
towards Germany.

Hitler's elation over Yugoslavia's accession was short-lived. There was outrage in Belgrade, the ministers were abused and spat on when they arrived back the next day, and that same night Prince Paul and his government were overthrown in a popular uprising led by senior army and air force officers, with the support of the British SOE (Special Operations Executive), a secret service organisation devoted mainly to sabotage and subversion. The seventeen-year-old King Peter, who escaped from his uncle's minders by climbing out of a window and sliding down a drainpipe, announced that he had ascended the throne. The new government was led by the air force chief, General Dusan Simovic, who immediately refused to ratify the Tripartite Pact, and offered instead to sign a simple non-aggression pact with Germany, thus avoiding either alliance or dependence and completely ruling out all possibility of allowing German troops to cross the country.

When Hitler received news of the *coup* at noon on 27 March, in a telegram saying the former government ministers had been arrested, he thought at first it was a joke. When he realised it was true, he flew into one of the most violent rages of his life. Screaming that he had been personally insulted, he sent for Ribbentrop, Göring, the army and Luftwaffe commanders, and the Hungarian and Bulgarian envoys. Ribbentrop was called from a meeting with the Japanese Foreign Minister, Yosuke Matsuoka, who had arrived on an official visit the previous evening and was due to meet Hitler at 4 p.m. that afternoon. Göring was closeted with Birger Dahlerus, whom he had just warned about Barbarossa.

Hitler stormed through the Chancellery to the conference room where Keitel, Jodl and the adjutants were waiting for the daily briefing. He brandished the telegram at them, 'bursting out spontaneously', as Keitel himself recalled, 'that he had no intention of standing for that: now he would smash Yugoslavia once and for all; never mind what the new government might tell him, he had been disgracefully betrayed, and a declaration of loyalty now would only be a feint, a ploy to gain time.' He intended, he declared, to order immediate concentric attacks on Yugoslavia from the north and east. Brushing aside Keitel's protests that they could not mount such attacks now because they were locked into the carefully planned timetable for Barbarossa, he stormed 'Some solution will have to be found. I intend to make a clean sweep in the Balkans – it is time people got to know me better. Serbia has always been a state prone to *Putsche*, so I am going to clean her up.'[16]

When the military chiefs had all arrived, Hitler treated them to a diatribe against the Serbs and Slovenes, and told them he was determined to smash Yugoslavia both militarily and as a state. There would be no ultimatum, no diplomatic approach. When Ribbentrop tried to suggest one, Hitler turned on him. 'The Yugoslavs,' he spat, 'would swear black is white. Of course they will say they have no warlike intentions, and when we march into Greece they will stab us in the back!'[17] Blaming Ribbentrop for not having anticipated the *coup*, he told him he 'never wished to see him again'. Shattered, the Foreign Minister took to his bed for several days, suffering from a minor breakdown.[18]

Göring had no such problem. His Luftwaffe would be at the forefront of the operation, charged as usual with preparing the ground for the rest of the Wehrmacht by wiping out the Yugoslav air force on the ground and totally destroying Belgrade. And at dawn on Palm Sunday, 6 April, it began doing just that. Göring claimed at Nuremberg that the targets in Belgrade were 'the War Ministry, the railroad station, the General Staff building, and one or two other ministries'. But since these were 'spread about within the city', he said, the city itself 'was also affected by the bombardment'.[19]

Göring's self-justifying version of the attack on Belgrade was entirely at odds with the truth – which must cast doubt on his account of other events, most notably the destruction of Rotterdam. In fact, Hitler had been most specific in ordering him 'to destroy Belgrade in attacks by waves', underlining his intentions by labelling the attack 'Operation Punishment'. 300 bombers of VIII Air Corps, under General Wolfram von Richthofen, flew more than 500 bombing raids at rooftop level over the defenceless city, reducing it to rubble, killing over 17,000 civilians and wounding many more.

Belgrade fell on Easter Sunday, 13 April, and four days later the Yugoslav army surrendered. The assault on the Greek mainland, which had started simultaneously, took only a little longer. The British had pulled four divisions, around 53,000 men, out of North Africa and hurriedly shipped them to Greece to strengthen the small force already there, but they and the Greeks were soon overwhelmed by the fifteen divisions of Field Marshal List's Twelfth Army, four of them armoured, and the superior power of the Luftwaffe, with some 1,000 planes to the RAF's 100. There was no bombing of Athens, however – Hitler had strictly forbidden it. By 21 April, the bulk of the Greek army had surrendered and the British, Australian and New Zealand troops were being evacuated by sea. By the time the withdrawal ended on 30 April, about 50,000 men had been shipped out, mostly to Crete, but once again their heavy equipment and vehicles had to be destroyed or left behind, together with some 12,000 prisoners.

The Luftwaffe had once again played a vital role in the German successes in Yugoslavia and Greece, where in addition to the usual bombing and strafing, paratroops had been used to seize the Isthmus of Corinth after a British rearguard had destroyed the bridge over the deep gorge of the canal. Göring needed the boost to his reputation – it had been badly dented on the night of 9–10 April, when the RAF struck Berlin with the heaviest of a continuous series of raids that had started a month earlier. That night the British bombers devastated the heart of the old city, hitting the State Library, the Crown Prince's Palace, the University, and many other buildings for several blocks on either side of the Unter den Linden. Worst of all, the State Opera House was gutted. Its massive exterior walls were left standing, but direct hits by about thirty incendiary bombs created an inferno that reduced the auditorium to a mess of burnt timbers and twisted girders. In retaliation, Göring ordered a heavy raid on London in which St Paul's Cathedral was damaged, but it came too late to assuage Hitler, who blamed him for the failure of the Luftwaffe to protect the Reich capital.

In an angry exchange, Hitler took the opportunity to castigate Göring over Luftwaffe equipment failures, especially the Ju-88, which the bomber squadrons were complaining was 'useless' – they wanted to have the old but well-tried He-111 back again. Göring stood his ground, admitting that the existing Ju-88 had its faults – it had, after all, been forced into production before its development was complete – but claiming that these had now been dealt with and that the latest model, already coming off the production lines with more powerful new engines, would prove to be a success, as indeed it was.

Hitler commissioned Speer to reconstruct the Opera House at once, but Göring had more urgent tasks for the builders. After the first heavy raid in March, Berlin's police chief, Helldorf, had called on Goebbels in his capacity as Gauleiter to tell him how worried he was about the city's ability to withstand really heavy bombing. There were, he said, simply not enough adequate public shelters. Goebbels, who had always regarded Helldorf as a pessimist, listened impatiently. 'What London can put up with,' he told him, 'Berlin will also have to bear.' Göring was less complacent. He had always resisted the idea of purpose-built air-raid shelters in Berlin as an admission of failure, but now he was forced to order a crash programme of public shelters, plus three massive 'flak towers'.

The flak towers were great concrete structures 120 feet or more in height and bristling with anti-aircraft guns, one at the Zoo, in the heart of the West End, one in Humbolthain Park, due north of the Unter den Linden, and one in Friedrichshain Park, east of Alexanderplatz. Designed by Speer to look like medieval fortresses, with walls of reinforced concrete eight feet thick, they were proof against bombs or shells. With their own water and electricity generators and their own hospitals, they were kept stocked with enough food and ammunition to sustain a twelve-month siege. They provided secure storage facilities for the treasures from the city's art galleries and museums, emergency studios and accommodation for the staff of the national broadcasting service, and air-raid shelters capable between them of holding close on 50,000 people. Two years earlier, such a provision, tacitly admitting the possibility of an enemy invasion of Berlin, would have been considered as unthinkable defeatism. Now, it was a sensible precaution.

The flak towers were at the centre of a vast new anti-aircraft system, controlled from the Zoo tower, which ringed the city with searchlights and flak batteries, while the city itself was packed with fortified gun emplacements, with every landmark heavily camouflaged. For the first eighteen months of the war, Berliners had tended to regard the flak defences of their city as a joke: 'Hermann's sleeping battalions' they called them. Suddenly, they were no longer a joke, but a formidable weapon capable of inflicting serious harm on any attacker. It was all a far cry from the days when Göring had boasted that no enemy aircraft would ever fly over Berlin.

Fortunately, after the six-week spring onslaught on Berlin, the RAF turned its attentions elsewhere, to concentrate on attacking the bases of the U-boats and long-range Focke-Wulf 200 Kondors that were sinking thousands of tons of British merchant shipping in the Battle of the Atlantic. For several months British bombers were directed against targets like Kiel, Hamburg, Bremen and Bordeaux, giving Berlin – and Göring – a much-needed respite.

The Luftwaffe for its part kept up its raids on British cities at full power until mid May, when the Blitz was wound down as the air fleets were moved to the east. The last big raid on London before a lull of ten weeks was on the night of 10–11 May, and it was the heaviest and most deadly of the war, killing 1,436, injuring 1,792, damaging Westminster Abbey and the British Museum and destroying the House of Commons, among other historic and important buildings.[20] During the nine months of the campaign, Göring's bombers had killed more than 43,000 civilians throughout the country, injured another 139,000, and caused enormous damage to the country's infrastructure and housing, all for the loss of some 600 bombers.[21] But even this had failed utterly to bring the British to their knees, or to have any great effect on aircraft and arms production. Göring's contention that he could win the war by air power alone had been proved wrong again.

At about 11 p.m. on 10 May, just as the big raid on London was starting, a lone Me-110 long-range fighter crashed in the lowlands of Scotland, not far from Glasgow. Though he had never used a parachute before, its pilot had bailed out, injuring his leg as he landed awkwardly. When he was picked up by a local farmhand, he gave his name as Captain Alfred Horn, and said he had an important message to give to the Duke of Hamilton. It did not take long to establish the true identity of 'Captain Horn': he was in fact Rudolf Hess, and he had come on a crackpot personal mission to persuade Britain to make peace.

Hitler did not learn of the flight until late the following morning at the Berghof, when two of Hess's adjutants arrived with a letter from Hess, explaining what he had done and why. A long memorandum from Hess had in fact been delivered the previous evening, but Hitler had not bothered to open the envelope, assuming it was routine party business. Now Hitler was shattered by what he saw as the 'disloyalty' of the most slavishly devoted of all his devoted followers. According to Paul Schmidt, 'he was as appalled as though a bomb had struck the Berghof'.[22] Speer, who had just arrived in the house with sketches of yet more grandiose buildings for Germania, suddenly heard 'an inarticulate, almost animal outcry' from his study, followed by a roar: 'Bormann at once! Where is Bormann?'[23]

Göring, troubled once again by heart problems, was at Veldenstein Castle, which he was in the process of restoring. Hitler telephoned him there with a terse message: 'Göring, get here immediately. Something dreadful has happened,' before slamming down the phone without further explanation. Ribbentrop was summoned from Fuschl equally abruptly. His first concern was fear that Hess might actually succeed in his aim of persuading the British to overthrow Churchill and make peace, but his expert on Britain, the former Press Attaché in London, Fritz Hesse, managed to reassure him that that was totally impossible. Hitler's main worry was the effect Hess's flight might have on Stalin and the Japanese, who to his chagrin had just signed a non-aggression pact. 'Who will believe me,' he asked, 'when I say that Hess did not fly there in my name, that the whole thing is not some sort of intrigue behind the backs of my allies?'[24]

Göring did not arrive at the Berghof until 9 p.m., by which time Hitler had calmed down. Handing him Hess's letter, Hitler asked if Hess could have managed to fly an Me-110 to Scotland. Göring thought it unlikely, confirming what Udet had already told Hitler on the phone. 'If only he would drown in the North Sea,' Hitler moaned. 'Then he would vanish without a trace, and we could work out some harmless explanation at our leisure.' Galland claimed later that Göring called him at this point and ordered him to send out fighter aircraft to intercept Hess's plane, but since it was more than twenty-four hours since Hess had left, that seems most unlikely. It may be that Göring wanted them to search for any signs of wreckage in the sea – itself an almost impossible task – or more probably that he was trying to show Hitler he was doing everything he could, knowing that the Luftwaffe, and therefore he, would be blamed for allowing Hess to fly. Galland put up a token flight, which of course found nothing.

After another day of agonising silence, Hitler instructed his Press Secretary, Otto Dietrich, to issue a statement that was read out over national radio that evening. It said that Hess had been suffering from 'a worsening illness', and that the letter he had written showed 'in its confused ravings traces of mental disintegration' that suggested he 'had fallen prey to delusions'. It concluded by saying that, sadly, it had to be assumed that 'Hess has crashed or had an accident somewhere'.[25]

The statement was the first Goebbels had heard of the crisis, and he was disgruntled that he had not been consulted, especially since he thought the approach was a mistake. 'What a spectacle for the world:' he noted in his diary, 'a mentally-deranged second man after the Führer.' Summoned to Berchtesgaden along with all the other Gauleiters, he was shown Hess's letter and memorandum, which he thought was 'a confused mess – schoolboy dilettantism'.[26]

On the morning of 13 May, the BBC ended the suspense by announcing that the Deputy Führer was in Britain – and in good health.

As soon as Hitler's meeting with the Gauleiters was over, Goebbels hurried back to Berlin, to set about repairing the damage, doing his best to divert attention from Hess and pushing the line that he had made the flight under the influence of astrologers and occultists. Ironically, he was not so far from the truth: after the war, in Spandau prison, Hess told Speer 'in all seriousness that the idea had been inspired in him in a dream of supernatural forces'.[27] Hitler sent Ribbentrop flying off to Rome with the unenviable task of explaining the situation to Mussolini, who thoroughly enjoyed watching him squirm – just for once, Göring was pleased to leave dealing with the Italians to the Foreign Minister.

With Hess out of the game for good, Hitler moved swiftly to avoid any power struggle developing within the party. He told the assembled Gauleiters that he would not appoint a replacement for Hess as Deputy Führer, that Hess's office would be known in future as the Party Chancellery, and that it would come under his personal direction. It would be run, as before, by party comrade Martin Bormann, the one man Göring, Goebbels and Ribbentrop did not want to see as Hess's successor.

Known as the party's 'brown eminence' and 'Hitler's evil spirit', Bormann lived his life in the shadows, unseen and unknown by the general public in Germany, but feared, distrusted and hated by all the leading Nazis. While they all sought what he described as 'public notoriety', he deliberately avoided it; while they made speeches and wrote articles for the people, his instructions went only to the party leadership; while the others gloried in a plethora of imposing titles, he was content to be simply 'Leader of the Party Chancellery', and 'the Führer's secretary', though this appointment was not formalised for another eighteen months or so. He was never concerned with appearances, only with realities.

Goebbels dismissed the faceless bureaucrat in the ill-fitting uniform contemptuously: 'Bormann is not a man of the people. He has always been engaged in administrative work and therefore has not the proper qualifications for the real tasks of leadership.'[28] But Goebbels was, untypically, missing the whole point of what made Bormann dangerous – twenty years earlier, Russian Bolsheviks had said much the same thing about their party functionary, Josef Stalin. Fortunately or unfortunately, however, Hitler did not follow Lenin's example of leaving the field clear with his early death, so Bormann's full potential in a power struggle was never put to the test. But that potential was always there, and the others knew it, if only instinctively.

Outwardly, Bormann was totally unprepossessing. Albert Speer described him accurately: 'He was a short, stocky man with rounded shoulders and a bull neck. His head was always pushed forward a little and cocked slightly to one side, and he had the face and shifty eyes of a boxer advancing on his opponent . . . The contrast between him and Himmler was really grotesque. If I thought of Himmler as a stork in a lily pond, Bormann seemed to me like a pig in a potato field.'

Speer spoke for all the disciples when he said of Bormann: 'A few critical words from Hitler and all his enemies would have been at his throat.'[29] But Hitler never uttered one critical word of his amanuensis, preferring instead to endorse his loyalty and usefulness. 'I know,' he said,

that Bormann is brutal. But there is sense in everything he does and I can absolutely rely on my orders being carried out by Bormann immediately and in spite of all obstacles. Bormann's proposals are so precisely worked out that I have only to say yes or no. With him I deal in ten minutes with a pile of documents for which I should need hours with anyone else. If I say to him, remind me about such and such a matter in half a year's time, I can be sure that he really will do so.[30]

Seven years younger than Göring, three years younger than Goebbels, and the same age as Himmler, Bormann was born in 1900 in Halberstadt, Saxony, the son of a postal clerk who had previously been a trumpeter sergeant-major in the army. Like Himmler, he joined the army too late to see action, but served as a gunner in a field artillery regiment for a year before returning to the hardships of civilian life in post-war Germany. Having studied agriculture for a year before his call-up, he managed to find work as a trainee farm manager on the estate of an extreme right-wing aristocrat in Mecklenburg, where the labourers turned out to be members of the banned Freikorps Rossbach, a bunch of tough mercenaries employed to protect the farm and the district from any Communist troublemakers.

Bormann became the Rossbach group's treasurer, bringing much needed order to its chaotic affairs. Later, he was involved in the kangaroo court murder of a schoolmaster suspected of being a Communist spy and in sympathy with the hated French occupiers. The teacher – who, incidentally, had taught Bormann at elementary school

– was beaten to death by half a dozen members of the group – the fatal blows being struck with an uprooted sapling by a man called Rudolf Höss, who was later to distinguish himself as the commandant of Auschwitz. Typically, Bormann took no part in the actual murder, only providing the transport for the killers in the shape of a horse and cart from the farm. Nevertheless, he was sentenced to twelve months' imprisonment for his complicity.

Bormann's time in jail continued his political education. On his release, he returned for a while to his old job, but found it increasingly irksome working as a servant of the aristocracy. The Rossbach group had crumbled and died – most of its members were still in jail – but in its place he joined a new paramilitary organisation, the Frontbann, which had just been set up by Ernst Röhm. When he decided to make use of his experience as Rossbach's treasurer by going into politics as an organiser, it was a short step from the Frontbann to the NSDAP. On 17 February 1927, he became member number 60,508, and went to work in the party's head office in Munich.

Bormann's progress within the Nazi Party was by no means spectacular: like the man himself, it was painstaking, thorough and inconspicuous. He worked as a regional press officer, district leader and Gau general secretary in Thuringia, before joining the staff of the SA headquarters in Munich. There he met and married Gerda Buch, the twenty-two-year-old daughter of Major Walter Buch, a former regular army officer, friend of Hitler, and the party's chief judge. It was a good move – two of the witnesses at the wedding were Rudolf Hess and Adolf Hitler. Shortly afterwards, Bormann was put in charge of the party *Hilfskasse* (welfare fund), which provided financial help for members who were in distress, particularly those who were injured in the increasing number of street battles with the Communists and Socialists.

The new job suited Bormann's talents perfectly, and he handled it with great skill, reorganising the fund's chaotic administration and bringing much-needed financial probity to its accounts. During the three years in which he ran the fund, he gained more than the quiet respect owed to a skilful book-keeper: he also earned the gratitude of hundreds of rising party officials to whom he dispensed aid. And as an added bonus, the fund also provided Hitler with additional money when finances were tight. Over the years, Hitler developed such faith in Bormann's ability and reliability that he entrusted him with the management of all his personal finances – right to the end, Hitler's properties in the Obersalzberg and elsewhere were registered in Bormann's name. And it was Bormann who conceived the notion that Hitler was entitled to a royalty every time a postage stamp bearing his image was sold, and who collected and administered the huge sums that this brought in, together with royalties from *Mein Kampf* and other publications.

It was Bormann who handled the purchase of Haus Wachenfeld and its rebuilding as the Berghof. It was Bormann who bought up the rest of the Obersalzberg, evicting peasants and farmers, tearing down centuries-old farms and inns, a children's sanatorium and sailors' rest home, to turn the whole mountainside into a secure party compound, including a large house for himself and his family midway between Göring's house and the Berghof.

Bormann would go to any lengths to ingratiate himself with Hitler. He restricted himself to strictly vegetarian food when he was in his company, though he enjoyed bloody steaks and chops when he was out of his sight. Hitler once complained that a peasant farm further down the mountain spoiled the view from the terrace of the Berghof; twenty-four hours later, it had completely disappeared. And when Hitler mentioned that he was tired by standing in the sun in front of the Berghof greeting the adoring followers who were allowed to file past to pay homage, a large shade tree appeared overnight, as if by magic. For Hitler's fiftieth birthday, Bormann had a large, stone 'teahouse' constructed nearby on the peak of the 6,000-feet high Kehlstein mountain, which could only be reached by a specially-constructed road ending in a 136-yard-long tunnel leading to a vertical elevator drilled out of the solid rock; it involved 3,000 workers slaving night and day for thirteen months and cost around 30 million marks. Ironically, Hitler barely ever used it.

Six months after the Nazis came to power, Hitler rewarded Bormann's bureaucratic skills by appointing him Chief of Staff to Hess at party headquarters, with the top party rank of Reichsleiter, and a seat in the Reichstag. For the next eight years, he worked ostensibly under Hess, all the time insidiously extending his own power and influence. Like Hitler, Hess was never keen on paperwork and as he became increasingly obsessed with mysticism and astrology he was happy to leave organisational matters to his Chief of Staff. It was a fatal mistake. Soon, Bormann had supplanted him in all but name.

Alfred Rosenberg described the situation vividly:

Whenever I visited Hess, he [Bormann] was often present; later on, almost always. When I had dinner with the Führer, Bormann and Goebbels were usually there. Hess obviously got on the Führer's nerves, and so Bormann took care of the queries and orders. Here is where he began to make himself indispensable. If, during our dinner conversations, some incident was mentioned, Bormann would pull out his notebook and make an entry. If the Führer expressed some displeasure over some remark, some measure, some film, Bormann would make a note. If something seemed unclear, Bormann would get up and leave the room, but return almost immediately – after having given orders to his office staff to investigate forthwith, and to telephone, wire or teletype.[31]

From the start, Bormann began taking hold of the strings of power within the party, making sure that all promotions, demotions and appointments were in his hands alone. While Hess had been content to be informed of committee decisions after the event, Bormann managed to persuade Hitler that his office should be represented at all important committee meetings. Hess, of course, was usually too busy to attend; Bormann was never too busy, nothing was ever too much trouble. Before long he was not merely part of the decision-making process, but was making almost all the decisions on behalf of other officials, who, like Hess, could not be bothered.

When Hess flew to Britain, his two adjutants, who had brought his letter to the Berghof, were arrested, heavily interrogated and thrown into a concentration camp for not stopping him. Bormann, however, his right-hand man and Chief of Staff, came up smelling of roses, though to some the smell was of something less innocent, as Albert Speer recalled:

At the time it appeared to me that Bormann's ambition had driven Hess to this desperate act. Hess, also highly ambitious, could plainly see himself being excluded from access to and influence over Hitler. Thus, for example, Hitler said to me some time in 1940, after a conversation with Hess lasting several hours: 'When I talk with Göring, it's like a bath in steel for me; I feel fresh afterwards. The Reich Marshal has a stimulating way of presenting things. With Hess, every conversation becomes an unbearably tormenting strain. He always comes to me with unpleasant matters and won't leave off.' By his flight to England, Hess was probably trying, after so many years of being kept in the background, to win prestige and some success. For he did not have the qualities necessary for survival in the midst of a swamp of intrigues and struggles for power . . .[32]

There could be not the slightest doubt that Bormann had those qualities in abundance, and that he was now in a position to start making the fullest use of them.

Göring was uncomfortably aware that Hess's flight could be seen as another black mark against the Luftwaffe, even though Hess had obtained the Me-110 direct from the manufacturer, Willi Messerschmitt. He hoped to rebuild his prestige, however, with the invasion of Crete. Urged on by Student, he had persuaded Hitler to allow him to mount an airborne operation to capture the great island and drive out the British, who could use it as a base not only for bombing Ploesti but also for protecting the approaches to the Suez Canal and to attack Axis shipping in the eastern Mediterranean. This applied particularly to the supply routes to North Africa, where Rommel had been on the offensive since mid March, taking advantage of the withdrawal of some 60,000 British and Commonwealth troops for the Greek campaign.

Hitler agreed, somewhat reluctantly, to what was code-named Operation Mercury. Halder noted acidly in his war diary: 'Operational control for Crete. Reich Marshal will have overall responsibility. Ground forces will operate under him to the complete exclusion of Army High Command. Dangerous business!'33 It was indeed dangerous. Communications in Greece had been so disrupted that all German orders had to be given by radio, using Luftwaffe Enigma ciphers which the British were able to read. The element of surprise was missing, therefore, and when the first paratroops dropped over Maleme Airfield on 20 May, they met stiff resistance. The British and Commonwealth forces were still disorganised and poorly armed after their evacuation from the Greek mainland, and were completely without air support, but they fought fiercely for ten days until they were forced to admit defeat and pull out, leaving some 5,000 men behind as the Luftwaffe sank three cruisers and six destroyers and damaged seventeen other British ships. The Stukas which had been so badly mauled in the Battle of Britain came into their own again with no Spitfires to oppose them.

It looked like another triumph for Göring and the Luftwaffe: over 5,000 Iron Crosses were awarded to those who had taken part, and the survivors were entitled to wear a special cuffband embroidered with the word 'Kreta' in gold and white. Goebbels made great propaganda out of what he described as a smashing victory and the capture of a key strategic position in the eastern Mediterranean. 'Our operations on Crete have been greeted enthusiastically all over the world,' he crowed. 'Deservedly so. We are keeping this subject on the boil.'

But the victory was a costly one, with 6,698 casualties, including 3,352 dead, out of a total force of less than 18,000. 1,653 of the dead were paratroops.[34] More than 200 Ju-52 transport planes were lost. Many senior officers were highly critical of Student's invasion plan, which they thought was badly botched. It was a tarnished triumph for Göring, which did little to restore his reputation. Shocked by the high casualty rate, Hitler decided that he would never again allow a major airborne operation against enemy-held territory.

XXIX

'THE GREATEST DECEPTION OPERATION IN MILITARY HISTORY'

AFTER the conquest of Crete, there were no more distractions and the build-up for Barbarossa could go ahead at full speed. The operations in the Balkans, however, had delayed everything by five vital weeks: instead of invading in mid May, as Hitler had originally intended, he now confirmed the date for the invasion of the Soviet Union as 22 June, leaving the Wehrmacht barely four months to achieve victory before the Russian winter set in. In fact, although he later tried to use the Yugoslav diversion as his excuse for failure, he could not have started much earlier, since unusually heavy rainfall during the spring produced a vast sea of mud, in which tanks and vehicles would have been hopelessly bogged down. At the time, however, Hitler was quite unfazed by the postponement, still supremely confident that he could knock out the Soviet Union in a matter of weeks. Even Göring, now accepting that there was nothing more he could do to prevent the attack, assured his air force generals that the Soviet Union would 'collapse like a house of cards' – the Führer himself had told him so, he said, and 'the Führer is a unique leader, a gift of God. The rest of us can only fall in behind.'

Privately, Göring was far less sanguine, partly no doubt because of alarming reports about Soviet arms production, particularly in tanks and aircraft, which he had received from his technical experts who had visited the Soviet Union as part of the trade deal. He chose to disbelieve them so that he could disregard them, and said nothing to Hitler for fear of being regarded as a defeatist. Concealing his own doubts and fears, he put on a show of enthusiasm for the campaign in the East. 'The Luftwaffe,' he told his fighter chief, Galland, 'would win new laurels. The Red Air Force was numerically strong, but hopelessly inferior in machines and personnel. It would only be necessary to shoot down the leader of a unit for the remaining illiterates to lose themselves on the way home. We would shoot them down like clay pigeons.' When Galland asked him what would happen to the fight against Britain, Göring replied that 'in two, or at the most three months, the Russian colossus would be crushed. Then we would throw all our strength against the West, enriched by the inexhaustible strategic resources of Russia.'[1]

Göring was especially interested in the Soviet resources. He had persuaded Hitler to give him total economic control of all conquered territories in the East, and he intended to strip them of everything he could lay his hands on to bolster Germany's own war economy. To carry out the plunder, he set up a new agency, Wirtschaftsstab Ost, Economic Staff East, setting out its objectives in a stark memorandum on 2 May, which began:

1. The war can only be continued further if the entire armed forces can be supplied with food by Russia in the third year of the war.
2. There is no doubt that as a result millions of people will starve if we take the things we need from the country.[2]

As Göring's plans developed in all their dreadful detail during May and June, further directives and memoranda followed, grouped together in what came to be known as the 'Green File'. All foodstuffs and raw materials from the south and south-east of the Soviet Union that were not needed by the Wehrmacht, or to provide the barest essentials for the local people producing them, were to be removed to Germany. The rest of the Soviet population, plus those in the northern industrial areas and the cities, including Moscow and Leningrad, who normally depended on food supplies from the south, were to be systematically starved to death. All industries in the northern areas were to be permanently destroyed, so that the remaining population would be completely dependent on Germany for their consumer goods.

To make sure there could be no misunderstanding, the main directive of 23 May continued:

It follows . . . that the German administration in those territories may well attempt to mitigate the consequences of the famine which will undoubtedly take place and to accelerate the return to primitive agricultural conditions. An attempt might be made to intensify cultivation in these areas by expanding the acreage under potatoes or other important food crops giving a high yield. However, these measures will not avert famine. Many tens of millions of people in this area will become redundant and will either die or have to emigrate to Siberia. Any attempt to save the population there from death by starvation, by importing surpluses from the black soil zone, would be at the expense of supplies to Europe. It would reduce Germany's staying power in the war and would undermine Germany's and Europe's power to resist the blockade. This must be clearly and absolutely understood.[3]

By the time Crete fell, most of the formations used in the Balkan campaign had been moved back north for Barbarossa. At the beginning of June the army already had 129 divisions, only twenty short of Hitler's final target, standing ready for the short move into their start positions along an immense line stretching from the Baltic to the Black Sea. Göring's aircraft, of course, did not need to fly east until the last possible moment, but airfields and ground support organisations had to be prepared in advance. Throughout the spring, while commanding the Balkan operations, making plans for the economic exploitation of Soviet territory, stiffening the anti-aircraft defences of the Reich, continuing the blitz on Britain, running the Four-Year Plan and his expanding HGW industrial empire – plus, of course, buying works of art, completing the latest extensions to Carinhall and starting the renovation of Veldenstein – Göring had overseen preparations on a scale large enough to cope with nearly two thirds of the entire Luftwaffe strength: 2,770 aircraft out of a total of 4,300.

Concealing these activities from Soviet aerial reconnaissance, and from spies and agents on the ground, was difficult but vital: not only were the aircraft to be spread thinly over a front stretching for some 950 miles, but they were also faced with an estimated Soviet strength of between 8,000 and 10,000 aircraft. Although these were thought to be mainly inferior or obsolete types, their sheer numerical superiority could prove to be a great problem. For all Göring's upbeat statements to his generals, he knew that the only way the Luftwaffe could be sure of knocking out the Red Air Force was to do it at the very beginning, if possible on the ground, making use of all the hundreds of reconnaissance flights and aerial photographs they had been taking of Soviet airfields over the past few weeks.

The enormous size of the Red Army posed similar problems. Every fresh intelligence report confirmed the fact that even though they formed the biggest invasion force in history, German troops would face considerably larger Soviet forces, so here, too, surprise was not just desirable but essential. With such massive troop movements, and the presence of over three million men under arms, concealment was impossible. What had to be done, therefore, was to conceal not their presence but their purpose, through a vast deception.

Hitler had ordered the deception operation for Barbarossa at the same time as he made the very first announcement of his intention to attack the Soviet Union, on 31 July 1940. The build-up in the East was to be passed off as training and preparation for attacks on Gibraltar, North Africa and England, in areas out of reach of British air strikes. As the plans matured, every possible means was used to create a huge double-bluff, by presenting Barbarossa itself as 'the greatest deception operation in military history', aimed not at the Soviet Union but at Britain, and this remained the principal cover story right up to the end.

Preparations for the abandoned Operation Sea Lion went ahead at full strength during the spring of 1941, and elaborate rehearsals were staged for other invasions from Norway to Scotland and from the coast between Rotterdam and Cherbourg to eastern and south-eastern England. The Lufwaffe made ostentatious and intensive reconnaissance flights of possible landing sites in England. Handbooks were printed on the British way of life, ready for distribution to invading troops. In Berlin, several dummy ministries were set up to take charge of the administration of a conquered Britain, though for the most part these remained as names only.

Although the deception operation as a whole was in the hands of the OKW, under the control of Canaris, Goebbels joined in enthusiastically with the Propaganda Ministry. 'I am having an invasion of England theme written,' he wrote in his diary, 'new fanfare composed, English speakers brought in, setting up propaganda companies for England, etc . . . The coming weeks will be very nerve-racking. But they will provide further proof of the supreme skill of our propaganda. The other civilian ministers have no idea what is going on. They are working towards the apparent goal of England. I am eager to see how long it will be until things really take off.'[4] At the beginning of June, he called a meeting of specially selected senior staff in his ministry. 'Gentlemen,' he told them, 'I know that some of you think that we are going to fight Russia. But I must tell you today that we are going to fight England. The invasion is imminent. Please adapt your work accordingly.'[5]

To Goebbels, the airborne invasion of Crete was a godsend. With Hitler's full approval, and backed by Göring boasting loudly that 'No island is now safe', he wrote a major article for the *Völkischer Beobachter*, headed 'Crete as an Example'. Much of it was concerned with describing the technical details of the operation and praising the troops and the Luftwaffe. But the heart of the piece was a warning to Britain. 'If the British today are excitedly discussing the fall of Crete,' he wrote, 'all you have to do is substitute England for Crete, and then you will know why they are so frantic. If the Churchill clique in England doesn't discuss the theme of invasion publicly, it is not because they do not fear an invasion, but precisely because they do fear it . . . The Führer himself has coined the phrase that there are no more islands.'

The article was published on 13 June, in the Berlin edition of the paper – which was then 'seized' at 3 a.m. and withdrawn from circulation, 'at the request of the Wehrmacht', as soon as copies were known to have reached the foreign correspondents and embassies in the city. Goebbels then placed himself in public 'disgrace', to complete the illusion that he had committed a grave indiscretion.

The article worked like a bombshell, he wrote in his diary the next day. 'Everything goes without a hitch. I am very happy about it. The big sensation is under way. English broadcasts are already claiming that our troop movements against Russia are sheer bluff, to conceal our plans for an invasion of England.' The next day, he was still congratulating himself and blowing up the effects of his article out of all proportion. 'At home, people regret my apparent *faux pas*, pity me or try to show their friendship despite everything,' he gloated, 'while abroad there is feverish conjecture. We stage-managed it perfectly. Only one cable got through to the USA, but that is enough to bring the affair to the attention of the whole world. We know from tapped telephone conversations between foreign journalists working in Berlin that all of them fell for the decoy.' [6]

A more plausible explanation for the presence of some of the troops in the East was that they were there as protection against the Soviet Union. Indeed, this was included in the Barbarossa directive itself, which laid down that 'All orders to be issued to Commanders-in-Chief . . . must clearly indicate that they are *precautionary measures* against the possibility that Russia should change her present attitude to us.' This was also the fiction that was fed to all Germany's allies, right up to the very last moments. Mussolini was unwittingly pressed into service on 2 June, when he met Hitler at the Brenner Pass again for hurriedly-arranged talks, the purpose of which were a mystery to him. Hitler waffled for two hours without mentioning Barbarossa. He wept when he spoke of Hess's defection, and gave the impression that he had no precise plan of action but would welcome a compromise peace with Britain.[7] Ribbentrop dropped a broad hint to Ciano the following week, when he visited him in Venice to celebrate the accession to the Tripartite Pact of Croatia, which had been given nominal independence from the dismembered Yugoslavia. But Ciano failed to pick it up, and it was not until 3 a.m. on 22 June, a bare half hour before the attack, that Hitler finally let his closest ally into the secret with a last-minute letter.

Hitler's 'precautionary measures' claim was backed up on the ground by the construction of strong defensive fortifications in the most likely places for a Soviet attack and, as an extra piece of bamboozlement, in those areas where the main centres of the German attack were planned. This line of deception was particularly valuable in implying that Germany would react only to Soviet moves, and even convinced many senior German officers that Hitler's decision to invade the Soviet Union was made under the threat of a Soviet attack on Germany. It also persuaded Stalin that Hitler was about to make fresh economic and territorial demands on him during the summer of 1941, and that he could therefore expect to receive some sort of ultimatum on which he could negotiate, before any attack. This expectation was strengthened by rumours assiduously spread by Goebbels and Ribbentrop in their respective foreign press clubs. The most notable of these listed the actual conditions that Hitler was to demand, which according to Goebbels included a ninety-nine-year lease of the grain-producing Ukraine.

Göring played his part in the deception in mid June, immediately after his conference with his generals at Carinhall, by telling his old friend Birger Dahlerus, in the privacy of his private train, that he had personally drafted a list of demands to ensure the steady supplies of food and oil which Germany needed from the Soviet Union in order to continue the fight against Britain. These included demobilisation of the Red Army, the establishment of a separate government in the Ukraine, control of the Baku oilfields, and a guaranteed outlet to the Pacific. Dahlerus, always notoriously indiscreet, hurried off to Stockholm and told the British Minister and the American Embassy. So convincing was this information that when it reached the State

Department in Washington, Sumner Welles told Lord Halifax, who was now British Ambassador to the USA, that this was part of Hitler's pressure tactics, and that he thought Stalin would agree to almost everything, except Soviet demobilisation.[8]

Other officially-started rumours were designed to strengthen the impression that negotiations were still possible between Germany and the Soviet Union, and that all would soon be well between them. In Rome, the state radio broadcast a story that they had already signed a full-scale military alliance. And Ribbentrop is believed to have been responsible for the rumour that swept Berlin at the end of May that Stalin himself was about to arrive in an armoured train for talks with Hitler in Berlin or Königsberg. This story was supported by various arrangements that were made in Berlin. The management of the Bellevue Palace was told at the end of May to prepare for a visit by Soviet dignitaries, and the Anhalter railway station was closed to the public at the beginning of June while decorations with red banners and a huge electric red star were tried out. In both cases, the staff were given strict orders not to talk about what was going on – with the inevitable result that they all talked like mad and the story spread swiftly throughout the city.

Other rumours were started at lower levels, one source being a member of the Wehrmacht staff disguised as a porter in the Berlin fruit and vegetable market, meeting place for hundreds of shopkeepers and merchants. Another useful starting point was the newspaper distribution centre, where newsagents collected their papers every morning. These stories were usually simple and direct, talking of improved deliveries of grain from the Soviet Union, the possibility of Stalin's taking a four-week rest cure at Baden-Baden, the stopping of all leave for troops in the West, and the 'fact' that there were to be no more through trains to the West.

Such rumour-mongering helped to create confusion and 'noise' – the swamping of genuine intelligence information with a mass of disinformation, distortions and half-truths. Stalin received the correct information that Barbarossa would start on 22 June, but he was also given other dates ranging from 6 April right through May and up to 15 June, and as each one proved wrong, it became less likely that he would accept the true version for what it was.[9] Werner Wächter, a senior official at the Propaganda Ministry, later explained Goebbels's technique in admirably simple language. The preparations for Barabarossa, he said, were accompanied by so many rumours, 'all of which were equally

credible, that in the end there wasn't a bugger left who had any idea
what was really going on'.[10]

The strain of preparing for Barbarossa was taking its toll on Himmler,
triggering the worst stress symptoms he had ever suffered and bringing
him to the brink of collapse. His old gastric pains had returned, accompanied by literally blinding headaches, which tested the skills of Felix
Kersten to the limit. 'I've repeatedly told him he is trying his nervous
system too severely,' Kersten noted.[11] But there could be no let-up for
Himmler now; there was too much at stake.

Alongside Kersten's ministrations, Himmler could at least find some
sexual and emotional relief in his domestic life, for he had now left
the domineering Marga and was living with his secretary, an attractive young woman twelve years his junior, Hedwig Potthast, known
as 'Häschen' ('Bunny'). It was, by all accounts, a genuinely loving
relationship which survived until the end of his life, but Himmler
never divorced Marga – Lina Heydrich claimed that it was Häschen
who stopped him, for the sake of Marga and his daughter Gudrun,
to whom he always remained a good and caring father. While this is
possible, it is more likely that he was concerned with maintaining a
public image of respectability for the leadership – he had already
refused Wolff permission to divorce his wife and marry his mistress,
who had borne him two children – that was curiously at odds with
the obscenities they practised in their political lives. And, of course,
there was the overriding factor that Hitler hated divorce. Himmler
had no intention of following the path that had almost ended
Goebbels's career, especially now that he was on the brink of fulfilling
his greatest dreams.

Himmler's main role in Barbarossa was confirmed by an instruction
that Hitler added to his Barbarossa Directive on 13 March:

The Reichsführer-SS has been given certain special tasks by the Führer in
preparation for political administration which results from the necessity finally
to settle the conflict between the two opposing political systems. Within the
framework of these tasks, the Reichsführer-SS acts independently and on his
own authority.[12]

As in Poland, the 'special tasks' started with Heydrich's Einsatzgruppen,
which would follow the army to deal mercilessly with political

leaders and Jews, a task 'so difficult that it cannot be entrusted to the military'.

Heydrich met Göring two weeks later, to present his plans for this operation, which would be so savage that the previous year's actions to eliminate Polish leaders would pale by comparison. All officials of the Communist Party and the Comintern, all captured Red Army political commissars, all Jews in the service of the state or party, all gypsies and other 'anti-social elements', all saboteurs, propagandists and other extremist elements, were to be executed immediately, without trial. Göring gave his approval, with a few minor amendments, and told Heydrich to prepare a three- to four-page set of directions for the army 'about the danger of the GPU [Soviet Secret Police, later known as the KGB], the political commissars, Jews, etc, so that they would know whom to put up against the wall'.[13] He also approved Heydrich's proposals for 'the solution of the Jewish Question', which involved clearing all the Jews from the whole of Europe and dumping them in the wastes of the Soviet Union, where they could be left to die – which accorded perfectly with Göring's own plans.

Having obtained Göring's blessing, Heydrich started recruiting his new, larger Einsatzgruppen in April, from the SD and the various police departments of the RSHA. Finding suitable volunteers was not an easy task – the senior and middle-ranking officers of the RSHA prided themselves on being the intellectual elite of the party, and were not eager to dirty their hands with such direct horrors. Most came from respectable professions such as the law, academia or the civil service, and had to be pressed reluctantly into leading the murder squads. Even the rank and file had to be dragged out of the Gestapo, Kripo and SD offices, with men from the regular Order Police and the Waffen SS making up the numbers to the 3,000 mark.

Heydrich formed them into four Einsatzgruppen of about battalion strength, each of which was divided into a number of *Einsatzkommandos* or *Sonderkommandos* of about 70–120 men and sub-commandos of about 20–30. He then subjected them, and particularly their 120 leaders, to an intensive course of training and indoctrination. By mid June, they were ready. Any who were still squeamish salved their consciences by reminding themselves that they were acting on the orders of their supreme commander and head of state, and therefore had no option but to obey.

They were given their perfect excuse – as were the generals – by what became known as the 'Commissar Order', issued on Hitler's behalf by the Army High Command on 6 June, but stemming from a speech he had made to his commanders-in-chief and generals at the end of March. 'The coming struggle in Russia,' he had declared, 'was the clash of two ideologies and the product of racial differences, and would have to be fought with unprecedented, unmerciful and unrelenting harshness.' Political commissars, he said, were not soldiers but 'criminal villains' and must be exterminated. 'I insist absolutely that my orders are executed without contradiction . . . German soldiers guilty of breaking international law will be excused. Russia has not participated in the Hague Convention and therefore has no rights under it.'[14]

Clearing out the Jews, commissars and subversives was only the first stage of Himmler's grand design. His plans for planting his warrior-peasant settlements in Poland and the Warthegau had been baulked by Göring, Frank and the Gauleiters, but the great empty spaces of the former Soviet territories would be his promised land, where he would be free to do exactly as he pleased. In the apt setting of the SS Order's castle at Wewelsburg, he told Heydrich, Wolff, Daluege, Berger and the SS generals who were to command the Einsatzgruppen or be his HSSPFs in the new areas, that he aimed to eliminate thirty million Slavs to make room for his new empire.

He ordered his Race and Resettlement Office, the RuSHA, to draw up a master plan for the East, in which a huge area bounded by Leningrad and Lake Ladoga, the Valdai Hills, Bryansk and the River Dnieper was to be settled by Germans – and ruled by Heinrich Himmler. Fourteen million inhabitants were to be deported to make room for them; another fourteen million would be allowed to stay, but must be 'Germanised' within thirty years. The General-Government and the Baltic states were to be completely 'repopulated'. It was a vision of breathtaking presumption, marred only by Hitler's choice of Rosenberg to head the civil administration in the East. But even this had its compensation: Rosenberg's appointment came as a devastating blow to Ribbentrop, who had been so convinced that he would be given the job that he had even set up a Foreign Ministry committee to form the nucleus of the government that he would head. He was so shocked by the snub that he took sick for most of April. Himmler was not unduly put out – he thought so little of Rosenberg that he would simply ignore him, as would Göring.

Before any plans could be put into effect, of course, the Soviets had to be defeated, but Himmler had no doubts on this score. He was looking forward to sharing in the glory through the Waffen-SS. His divisions had distinguished themselves again in the Balkans by spearheading the attacks in Yugoslavia and Greece: the 'Leibstandarte' had broken through from southern Serbia into Albania, rampaged through Thessaly and joined Göring's paratroops to force the passage into the Peloponnese; in central Serbia, 'Das Reich' had played a major part in capturing Belgrade. Now they were ready to take their places in the great campaign. The 'Leibstandarte', now a full division, and the 'Wiking' were allotted to Army Group South, 'Das Reich' to Army Group Centre, and the 'Totenkopf' and Police divisions to Army Group North.

Athough the Waffen-SS divisions all came under army command during operations, Himmler still saw them as the nucleus of his private army, and now that they numbered 160,000 men he felt the need to establish his own headquarters staff, in parallel with the OKH (Ober Kommando des Heeres, High Command of the Army) and OKW. Among other things, the Headquarters Staff Reichsführer-SS was responsible for Waffen-SS units that he intended to keep away from the army under his personal control, for use against Jews and partisans behind the front. At the same time, he enlarged the Waffen-SS by including various other units and formations, notably the concentration camp guards, who from now on would wear Waffen-SS uniforms and carry Waffen-SS paybooks.

The concentration camps were becoming more prominent in Himmler's planning at this time. Paying his first visit to Auschwitz on 1 March, to inspect progress, he dismissed Höss's complaints about the overcrowding, lack of facilities and constant epidemics due to inadequate sanitation, and his plea for a halt to deliveries of prisoners. Instead, he ordered him to expand the camp to accommodate 30,000 prisoners, and to start building a vast new compound for 100,000 prisoners of war, two miles west of the main camp around the deserted village of Brzezinka, known in German as Birkenau, where he intended to establish an armaments manufacturing centre to take advantage of the unlimited supply of cheap labour.

Hitler held his final briefing conference for Barbarossa with his commanders-in-chief and generals on 14 June 1941, the day after Goebbels's 'indiscretion' over Crete. He listened to their plans carefully, with few interruptions, then gave them an hour-long pep talk stressing that this was a war against Bolshevism, and that once the Soviet Union had collapsed, Britain would come to terms. Warning that the Russians would fight hard and make heavy air attacks, he continued:

The Luftwaffe will win quick successes and thus lighten the load for the army groups. The worst of the fighting will be over in six weeks. But every soldier must know what it is we are fighting for. It is not the territory that we want, but rather that Bolshevism is destroyed. If we lose this war with Russia, then all Europe will become Communist. If the British cannot see that, they will lose their leading role in world affairs and with it their Empire. To what extent they will trust themselves to the hands of the Americans remains to be seen. But the Americans are interested in this war only for what they can get out of it.[15]

At 6 p.m., Göring briefed Hitler on his own about Luftwaffe plans, but according to his Deputy Chief of Air Staff, Waldau, he appeared to be unenthusiastic and barely interested, and the next day, when he called his senior Luftwaffe commanders to Carinhall for his own planning conference, Milch, too, thought he seemed depressed. The stress of his enormous responsibilities was clearly taking its effect. A few days earlier, General Josef Kammhuber, the commander of the night fighter squadrons in Holland, had visited him at Veldenstein and been shocked by his appearance, noting that his face was very red, that there were deep rings under his eyes, and that he seemed tired to the point of exhaustion. At dinner, he had merely picked at his food, and hardly touched his wine.

At that meeting, Göring had briefly revealed his true feelings when ordering Kammhuber to transfer half of his aircraft to the East. When Kammhuber objected, saying he did not have enough planes to combat the RAF bombers as it was, Göring rounded on him angrily. 'Look, Kammhuber,' he snapped,

I do not want this war against Russia. I am the one who is against it. So far as I am concerned, it is the worst possible thing we could do. It is economically mistaken, politically mistaken and militarily mistaken. I have argued against it until I am blue in the face, but they won't listen. Now I'm washing my hands of the whole business – the whole war. Do what you can. Get half of your night fighters transferred. I just can't be bothered about what happens any more![16]

Goebbels was summoned to the Chancellery in the afternoon of 15 June, using a back door rather than the main entrance, to perpetuate the myth that he was in disgrace over the Crete article. Hitler greeted him with 'great warmth' and then gave him a detailed briefing on the situation, telling him the attack would begin as soon as all the troops were in position, which should be in about a week. 'It will be a mass attack in the grandest style, the mightiest history has ever seen,' he said. Goebbels had always regarded co-operation with the Soviet Union as 'a blot on our escutcheon', and was thrilled that the moment had come at last to 'wash it away' by 'exterminating Jewish Bolshevism'.

With his unlimited capacity for self-delusion, Goebbels needed little persuasion to accept Hitler's preventive war argument. 'We have to act,' he noted in his diary that night. 'Moscow wants to keep out of the war until Europe is exhausted and its life-blood sucked dry. Then Stalin would act to bolshevise Europe and impose his form of rule.' When he left the Chancellery, having had the registration plates on his car changed to make it less conspicuous, he had his chauffeur drive him through the streets so that he could observe the people 'walking innocently in the rain. Happy people who know nothing of our cares and live only for the day. It's for all of them that we work and struggle and take every risk. So our people may live!'

Goebbels was already hard at work on propaganda material for the invasion: he had noted on 12 June that he had 30 million leaflets ready for distribution to the German public. Now he set the presses rolling to produce great quantities – one diary entry gives the number as 200,000, another as 800,000 – of the Führer's personal message to the troops. Comprising four closely-printed pages, this was rushed to the front in great secrecy on 20 June, and distributed to every company and platoon to be read out to the men by their officers on the night of 21 June. Halder dismissed it as 'a long-winded manifesto'. It was certainly way above the head of the average soldier, consisting mainly of a review of German foreign policy since 1939, and the political reasons why Hitler felt he had to attack the Soviet Union.

It ended, however, with an emotional rallying cry: 'German soldiers! You are about to join battle, a hard and crucial battle. The destiny of Europe, the future of the German Reich, the existence of our nation, now lie in your hands alone. May the Lord God help us all in this struggle.'

*   *   *

Hitler spent the afternoon of Saturday, 21 June composing another proclamation, this time to the German people as a whole, which was to be read out over the radio by Goebbels at 5.30 the next morning, and choosing between musical phrases suggested by Goebbels for use as fanfares. He settled on a few bars of the 'Horst Wessel Song' to introduce the first proclamation, but had more difficulty deciding on the right music to precede the announcement of victory in the East. He also wrote long letters to Mussolini and Admiral Horthy, the Regent of Hungary, at last telling them what was happening, and laying all the blame on the Soviet Union. Claiming he had clear evidence that the Soviets were about to attack Germany, he told Mussolini that he had decided 'to put an end to the hypocritical performance of the Kremlin'.[17]

In the evening, after dinner, he took a short drive through Berlin before settling down with Goebbels to go through the text of the proclamation for the last time and then to spend a whole hour choosing fanfares. Goebbels noted in his diary that Hitler looked completely exhausted when he returned from his drive, but that this changed as the time for the attack grew nearer: 'The Führer seems to lose his fear as the decisive moment approaches. It is always the same with him. He relaxes visibly. All the exhaustion seems to fall away.'

It was 2.30 a.m. when Goebbels drove back to his ministry, to spend a hectic hour giving his staff their final instructions. He withdrew to his room at 3.30 a.m., just as the invasion began. 'Now the guns are thundering,' he wrote in his diary. 'May God bless our weapons! . . . I pace restlessly back and forth in my room. The breath of history can be heard. Great, wonderful time in which a new Reich is being born. In the midst of pain, it is true, but it is emerging into the light.'[18]

Two hundred metres along the Wilhelmstrasse, the Foreign Ministry was ablaze with lights as Ribbentrop waited to receive the Soviet Ambassador, Vladimir Dekanozov, in Bismarck's old room, to which he had returned for this special occasion. Dekanozov had been phoning every hour during the Saturday, trying to see him to deliver an urgent note, but had been fobbed off with the excuse that the Foreign Minister was out of Berlin. Then, in the middle of the night, he had been summoned peremptorily to appear at 3.30 a.m. Dr Hans Strack of the Foreign Ministry's Protocol Department, accompanied by a young interpreter, Erich Sommer, had been dispatched with an official car to bring him to the Ministry, where Ribbentrop waited, with Paul Schmidt at his side. Schmidt recalled the scene vividly in his memoirs:

I had never seen Ribbentrop so excited as he was in the five minutes before Dekanozov's arrival. He walked up and down his room like a caged animal. 'The Führer is absolutely right to attack Russia now,' he said to himself rather than to me; he repeated it again and again as though he wanted somehow to reassure himself. 'The Russians would certainly themselves attack us, if we did not do so now.' He went on walking up and down the large room in a state of great excitement, his eyes flashing, and kept repeating these words. At the time, I attributed his attitude to the fact that he looked on himself as the creator of Russo–German understanding, and now found it harder to destroy his own work. Today, I can almost believe that on that day he felt, subconsciously at any rate, that disaster would result from the decision he now had to communicate to the Russian Ambassador.[19]

Photographers, film cameramen and reporters, sent by Goebbels to preserve the occasion for posterity, swarmed around Dekanozov and his First Secretary, Valentin Berezhkov, as they stepped out of the car in front of the Foreign Ministry and passed between the two stone sphinxes flanking shallow steps, carpeted in vivid red, leading to the entrance hall. Uniformed adjutants stood to attention and raised their arms in stiff Nazi salutes, while their chief led the way through the glass-panelled doors to the office where Ribbentrop was waiting, standing beside the ornate antique desk with its marble top.

As the tiny Dekanozov advanced towards him, Ribbentrop stepped forward and greeted him silently, with a formal handshake, adopting, as he later told Italian Ambassador Alfieri, 'his most freezing manner'. Dekanozov, with Berezhkov translating, started to read out the note from Moscow, which he had brought with him. Ribbentrop, stony-faced, held up his hand to stop him.

'That is not the question now,' he said. 'The Soviet government's hostile attitude to Germany and the serious threat represented by Russian troop concentrations on Germany's Eastern frontier have compelled the Reich to take military counter-measures. As from this morning, the relevant counter-measures have been taken in the military sphere.' With that, he signalled to Schmidt, who stepped forward and began to read out a many-paged document. After a general preamble accusing the Soviet Union of enmity to Germany, and of breaking the terms of both the Non-Aggression Pact and the Friendship Treaty, the note proceeded to list a number of grievances and border incidents stretching back over the whole twenty-two months of the Pact. These, plus the overflying of German territory, the note declared, were 'unambiguous proof' that the

Soviet Union was about to 'stab Germany in the back during her battle for her very existence'.

Berezhkov had started translating for Dekanozov, whispering in his ear as Schmidt read. But after the preamble, when the note began listing incidents and the dates of alleged frontier violations, the Ambassador could see where it was leading, and waved him to stop. Berezhkov, at a loss, stood in silence, running the fingers of his right hand through his thick dark hair. Sommer, standing two steps behind them, watched fascinated as the back of Dekanozov's bald head gradually turned lobster-red, and his hands, which were straight down by his sides, clenched tightly.

The reading of the note took some twenty minutes of the thirty that had been allotted for the interview. While it continued, Ribbentrop stood leaning against Bismarck's desk, looking, to Sommer, as though a heavy load had been lifted from his shoulders. When it was finished, he nodded his approval, and Schmidt handed the bulky document to Dekanozov, who stood in a state of shock, repeating over and over in Russian, 'I deeply regret this . . . I deeply regret this.'

Pompously, Ribbentrop proclaimed that he, too, regretted that all his efforts to reach an understanding with the Soviet Union had proved unsuccessful. But Dekanozov had recovered his composure, and was not prepared to accept this final iniquity. 'It is entirely due to the non co-operative attitude adopted by the German government,' he snapped. 'Under the circumstances, there is nothing more for me to do but make the necessary arrangements with your *chef de protocole* for the transport home of my mission.' With that, he gave a curt bow, and departed, without offering to shake hands.[20] At the same time, the German Ambassador in Moscow, the courtly Count Werner von der Schulenburg, was delivering an identical note to Molotov, whose stunned reaction was to ask if this was supposed to be a declaration of war. Describing the German action as a breach of confidence unprecedented in history, he concluded bleakly 'Surely, we have not deserved that?'

As Dekanozov left the German Foreign Ministry, Alfieri arrived, the first of a procession of friendly or neutral ambassadors and ministers to be informed of the war. Alfieri was allotted ten minutes, the others five minutes each, with a pause in the schedule at 6 a.m. There had been the usual wrangle between Ribbentrop and Goebbels over who should make the official announcement, which was settled with a compromise: Goebbels broadcast Hitler's proclamation from the

Propaganda Ministry at 5.30 a.m., watched by the press, who then crossed the Wilhelmplatz to the Foreign Ministry, where at 6.00 a.m. Ribbentrop read a formal statement declaring war, and gave a brief press conference.

By a sad irony, the scenes with Dekanozov and the other envoys, which marked the final demise of Bismarck's eastern policy of maintaining good relations with Russia, were the last official acts ever to take place in the Iron Chancellor's old office. Although he was pleased to be called a 'second Bismarck', Ribbentrop never used the room again.

XXX

BARBAROSSA

IN his proclamation to the troops on 21 June, Hitler had described the build-up in the East as the biggest front line in history, and for once he was not exaggerating. Between the Baltic and the Black Sea, the German forces were arranged in three massive army groups, comprising seven armies, four Panzer groups and three air fleets. Poised on the frontiers, waiting for dawn to break after the shortest night of the year, were no fewer than 3,200,000 men – 148 divisions, including nineteen Panzer divisions and twelve motorised infantry divisions, with 600,000 trucks, 650,000 horses, 3,580 armoured fighting vehicles, 7,184 artillery pieces and over 2,700 aircraft.[1]

On the two wings, to north and south, the Finns and Romanians added another 400,000 men, extending the entire front to the Arctic Ocean, a total length of 1,800 miles. It was indeed an awesome array of force – by comparison, the Allied invasion of Normandy on 6 June 1944 landed a first wave of six seaborne divisions and three airborne, a grand total of nine divisions containing some 75,000 British and Canadian troops and 57,000 Americans, along a front of less than fifty miles.

Unlike the other countries that Hitler had attacked since 1939, the Soviet Union was, on paper at least, militarily stronger than Nazi Germany. Official Soviet figures give the total size of the Red Army in June 1941 as 5,373,000 men, of whom 2,680,000, making up 170 divisions, were facing the Germans in the West. They were armed with 37,500 field guns and mortars (Soviet figures do not differentiate between the two types of weapon), 14–15,000 tanks, and 8–9,000 fighter planes, 1,540 of which were modern types.[2] Bearing in mind the old military dictum, strictly adhered to by Allied commanders of the day such as General Bernard Montgomery, that a numerical superiority of 3:1 is necessary to ensure the success of any attack, the Red Army should have had no difficulty in holding off the Wehrmacht. The fact that it did not is down to various factors, but the most prominent are the success of the deception campaign, coupled with Stalin's refusal to believe countless warnings, and the role of the Luftwaffe in gaining immediate and total supremacy in the air. What makes this all the more remarkable is that the Luftwaffe actually deployed less aircraft than it had in the campaign in the West.

Zero hour for the invasion was dawn, which varied between 3 and 3.30 a.m. along the immense front. The German guns opened up their preliminary barrage fifteen minutes earlier, but by then Göring's aircraft had already crossed the frontiers over Belorussia at high altitude, unseen and unheard in the darkness. At first light they began swooping down on the sixty-six airfields of the region, which had all been thoroughly reconnoitred in advance, to wipe out the Soviet fighters, most of which were neatly positioned in full parade formation in the open. Many were actually pegged down to the ground, so that they could not be easily moved, and very few were either armed or fuelled, following the normal Soviet precaution to prevent pilots deciding either to abscond or to pose a threat to the regime.

The result was that when the Germans dived down from the skies, not only were the Soviet planes sitting ducks, most were also unable to take off to defend themselves or their bases. By noon, the Luftwaffe had destroyed some 1,200 Soviet aircraft, at least 800 of them on the ground. Within forty-eight hours the number was being estimated at 2,500, a figure so impressive that Göring questioned it, only to be told after it had been carefully checked by reconnaissance flights that the true figures were in fact 200–300 more. The Red Air Force in the West had been annihilated. At the same time, the bombers struck at Soviet towns, cities, communications centres and other selected targets, bringing further confusion and paralysing much of the Soviet response. On the ground, the German armies smashed their way forward unhindered by Soviet air attacks and backed by close air support from their own fighters and Stukas in true blitzkrieg style. Göring may have been opposed to the attack, but his Luftwaffe had covered itself in glory yet again, and he was riding high on its back.

Hitler left Berlin in *Amerika* at midday on 23 June, for his new field headquarters in the East which, with his usual taste for the melodramatic, he had named 'Wolfsschanze', 'Wolf's Lair'. The location, hidden among dank and dismal woods in an area of swamps and lakes about eight kilometres from the small town of Rastenburg in East Prussia (now Ketrzyn, in Poland), had been chosen for him by his adjutants the previous November, and constructed over the winter and spring by Todt. It was dank, dismal and plagued by swarms of voracious mosquitoes that made life miserable for everyone, but especially for the two women secretaries, whose arms and legs were not protected by high boots and long sleeves.

The central complex, Security Zone One, consisted of ten heavily reinforced and camouflaged concrete bunkers, with Hitler's at the northern end, and which also housed Otto Dietrich, Bormann and Keitel, with adjutants, aides, secretaries, servants and security staff. The Wehrmacht Operations Staff under Warlimont were in an adjoining complex, Security Zone Two, while Brauchitsch and the Army High Command were about eighteen kilometres away in their own complex, 'Mauerwald', built on higher, drier ground.

Göring had no bunker in the area, only a siding where he could park his special train, Asia, and an office set aside for his use in Wolfsschanze. The Luftwaffe High Command moved Robinson, its mobile headquarters, to the shore of Lake Goldap, conveniently close to Göring's favourite hunting lodge at Rominten, and he chose to stay either aboard Asia or at Rominten, about one hour's drive from Wolfsschanze.[3] For the first week of the new campaign, however, he stayed away from the front at Carinhall. When he finally visited Wolfsschanze, on 29 June, Hitler rewarded him – perhaps to reassure him that Bormann was not usurping his position – by publicly confirming his status with a signed decree: 'Based on the law concerning the successor of the Führer and Reich Chancellor of 13 December 1934, and repealing all former decrees, I appoint Reich Marshal of the Greater German Reich Hermann Göring as my successor.'[4]

With more immediate effect, Hitler also issued a decree giving Göring, as Plenipotentiary of the Four-Year Plan, the power to take all necessary measures for the maximum exploitation of the conquered territories. For this purpose, all officials in the East, both military and civil, were subject to his orders. This meant that Göring alone had the right to make decisions on economic policy in the East, and that he alone was responsible for allocating assets to other Reich agencies, which had to channel all economic requests through his office. To make quite sure that he retained control of the essentials, at the end of July he followed the precedent he had established with the Hermann Göring Werke and set up a number of giant monopoly companies: the Zentralhandelsgesellchaft Ost (Central Trading Company East), responsible for the production, collection and distribution of all agricultural products; the Kontinentale Öl Aktiengesellschaft (Continental Oil Company) for the extraction, refining and sale of petroleum products; and similar monopoly companies for iron and steel, mining, textiles, leather goods and tobacco, all to be under his central direction.

Like Göring, Himmler had no permanent quarters at Wolfsschanze, and until September operated from his train in a siding a few kilometres away. As it became clear that the campaign in the East would not after all be a short one, he found a farmhouse nearby for his personal use, and had a more permanent field command post, 'Hochwald', built around the rail siding, with barracks, garages and full service facilities. For the next few months, he became Hitler's most regular visitor: they had much to discuss, in strict privacy.

Ribbentrop, terrified as always of being out of reach of his Führer, hurried after him, but was shunted off to another rail siding some forty kilometres away, to keep him out of Hitler's hair. Indulging his taste for grand houses, however, he soon found himself a castle to requisition at Steinort, a mere eight kilometres from Wolfsschanze, as his personal residence, and moved in in July, bringing with him a trainload of fine wine, most of the ornate furniture from the former German Embassy in Warsaw, and a large personal staff. Unlike Gustav von Remnitz at Fuschl, the owner of Schloss Steinort, Count Heinrich Lehndorff, was allowed to keep one wing for himself and his family. Most of Ribbentrop's office staff, however, lived and worked in a hotel some distance away, so that a great deal of their time was wasted shuttling between the two.

Ribbentrop only returned to the Wilhelmstrasse twice during the rest of 1941, and was barely seen there over the next three and a half years. While this was in many ways a great relief to the officials in the Foreign Ministry, it was also a great inconvenience, for with his usual lack of consideration and ignorance of how a department was run, he would summon them from Berlin for the most trivial reasons and then keep them hanging around for days with nothing to do.

Foreign ambassadors, too, were often summoned for no good reason. And when Hitler moved for a while to a new headquarters at Vinnitsa in the Ukraine the following year, the situation became even more fatuous. As Paul Schmidt, who had to accompany those who needed an interpreter, recalled, a special sleeper train left Berlin every evening, arriving at Warsaw the next morning, Brest-Litovsk at noon, and the former Russo–Polish border in the evening:

From there on, because of the partisans and frequent damage to the track, this luxury train proceeded at a snail's pace to Vinnitsa, where it arrived the following morning. But the foreign diplomats had to turn out at Berdichev, at three in the morning, and make a two hours' drive to Ribbentrop's field headquarters. He received them at eleven o'clock, lunched with them at noon, and flew with them at one o'clock to Hitler's headquarters. Here the conversation took place at about three or four o'clock and lasted an hour or two. They then had to return by car to Ribbentrop's field headquarters, where they dined, leaving at midnight for Berdichev and catching the Service Train back to Berlin at 2 a.m. They arrived back in Berlin at 8 a.m. two mornings later. This, for a short discussion with Hitler, on what were nearly always trivial or irrelevant matters, ambassadors or other important persons spent three days and four nights travelling. This example is characteristic of the methods favoured by Hitler and Ribbentrop.[5]

Goebbels remained in Berlin, trying to overcome popular dismay at the opening of the Eastern Front, with its bitter echoes of the First World War. For the first week of the campaign, Hitler forbade the Wehrmacht from releasing any hard news about the progress of the troops in the East, and Goebbels could do nothing but pump out anti-Bolshevik propaganda and try to convince the German people that Hitler had had no option but to launch a preventive war. Then on 29 June, Otto Dietrich issued twelve special bulletins to be broadcast at fifteen-minute intervals from 11 a.m., each preceded by the Russian fanfare based on Liszt's *Hungarian Rhapsody*, and each announcing a different victory.

First came the announcement of air supremacy. Then a parade of captured cities – Grodno, Brest-Litovsk, Vilnius, Kaunas, Dünaburg, Minsk, the list went on and on – followed by news that two Soviet armies were encircled at Bialystok and that the Soviets had lost 2,233 tanks, 4,107 aircraft, and huge numbers of men taken prisoner. It was an impressive tally, but the sheer repetition was counter-productive. People soon grew bored with hearing it and began questioning how much was propaganda. Goebbels was appalled at the way the reports were crammed together, which he described as 'laying it on too thick'.

He was forced to accept it as Hitler's decision this time, but vowed never to let it happen again.[6]

As the spectacular advances of the Wehrmacht continued, the German leaders were convinced that complete victory was within their grasp. Indeed, as early as 3 July, Halder noted in his diary: 'It is probably no exaggeration to say that the Russian campaign has been won in the space of two weeks.'[7] Although he qualified this by acknowledging that 'the sheer geographical vastness of the country and the stubbornness of the resistance, which is carried on with all means, will claim our efforts for many more weeks to come,' he had no doubts that it would all be over, as planned, before winter set in. Halder's optimism was shared by Hitler and all the generals, and seemed to be amply justified by the estimated Soviet losses: eighty-nine of out 164 divisions wiped out and more than 7,500 aircraft already destroyed. Only nine of the Red Army's twenty-nine tank divisions were thought to be still fit for combat.[8] How could any army survive such depredation?

In fact, the writing was on the wall if Hitler and his generals had chosen to read it; for no matter how many machines they knocked out, or how many Soviet soldiers they killed or captured, there always seemed to be more to take their place. A combination of arrogance and poor intelligence had led to a gross underestimation of Soviet resources and production capacity – to say nothing of the sheer determination of the Red Army troops – which in the end would prove fatal.

In mid July, 1941, however, Hitler had not realised the uncomfortable truth. 'By 15 August,' he told Ambassador von der Schulenburg, who had just arrived back in Germany, 'we shall be in Moscow. By 1 October the Russian war will be over.' On 15 July, he ordered arms manufacturing priority to be switched away from the army, to the Luftwaffe and the navy, in preparation for renewed action against Britain, and decreed that the strength of the army 'could be considerably reduced in the immediate future'.[9] And the following day, as the major city of Smolensk, a mere 350 kilometres from Moscow, fell he held a five-hour conference with Göring, Bormann, Lammers, Keitel and Rosenberg to discuss the exploitation of the conquered territories, and the establishment of permanent German rule. They must keep their ultimate aims secret, Hitler said, in order to avoid making 'premature enemies', and would present themselves as liberators. But there must be no doubt in their own minds that they would never again leave these territories. 'Basically,' he continued,

it is a matter of cutting up this giant cake so that we can first rule it, secondly administer it, and thirdly exploit it. The Russians have now given the order for partisan warfare behind our front. This partisan war has its advantages: it gives us the excuse to exterminate anything opposing us. Pacification of the conquered territory can best be achieved by shooting dead anyone who even looks at us the wrong way. As a basic principle, no military power must ever again be possible west of the Urals.[10]

Significantly, Ribbentrop was not invited to the conference. He had exasperated Hitler by constantly trying to involve him in his squabbles with Rosenberg over Foreign Ministry representation in the East, and as a result ended up with nothing – Hitler agreed with Rosenberg that 'the internal organisation of the newly-acquired areas was no concern of the Foreign Ministry'. In contrast with the earlier idea of dividing the region into small, nominally independent states with which Germany would have diplomatic relations through the Foreign Ministry, it was now to be simply a German empire, with Rosenberg in charge as head of the newly-created Reich Ministry for the Occupied Eastern Territories.

Rosenberg's remit, however, excluded any control over the three main power bases: the army, Göring's Four-Year Plan Organisation, and the SS, all of whom went their own ways. Rosenberg, who had been born in Estonia and educated in Moscow, had a vision of winning over some of the nationalities, especially the Ukrainians, as allies against their former Russian masters. But Göring had no time for this soft approach. He was interested only in exploiting the Ukraine as a source of food for Germany, and was ready to let 20–30 million natives die of starvation. With Bormann's backing, he easily overrode Rosenberg's objections and persuaded Hitler to appoint his own protégé, Erich Koch, the exceptionally brutal Gauleiter of East Prussia, who could be relied on to carry out his wishes with maximum harshness, as Reich Commissar of the Ukraine.

Göring's plans for the economic exploitation of the conquered regions suffered a major setback on 3 July, when Stalin, in his first speech to the Soviet people since the invasion, ordered a scorched-earth policy. Where the Germans were advancing, he said, nothing must be allowed to fall into their hands:

not a single locomotive, not a single rail car, a single kilogram of grain or litre of fuel. Collective farmers must drive off all their cattle and turn over their grain to the state authorities for safe keeping. Anything of value that cannot be removed, including ferrous metals, grain and fuel, must be destroyed, without exception. Nothing must be left to the enemy. And in those areas that he has already occupied, guerrilla units must be formed. Their tasks will be to blow up bridges, roads, stores, set fire to the forests, disrupt communications and so on. Conditions must be made unbearable for the enemy.[11]

Added to the scorched-earth policy, which included the destruction of mines, and the blowing up of dams and oil wells, the Soviets physically removed whole industries out of the combat areas even as the German Panzers advanced. The speed of the German advance meant the Soviets could not move everything: for example only seventeen out of sixty-four steel works in the Donets Basin and one third of the factories producing ammunition were relocated, the remainder either being destroyed or falling into German hands. Nevertheless, between July and November 1941, a total of 1,523 complete installations, 1,360 of which were major facilities directly involved in armament production, were dismantled, transported to safety east of the Ural mountains on the equivalent of a million and a half freight cars, and reassembled. Ten million workers were shipped out to man them. Long before the end of the year, many of the factories Göring had hoped to capture and turn to his own use were back in production and sending increased numbers of heavy tanks, guns, aircraft and other weapons to the front.[12]

By the end of July, Göring was facing more immediate problems with the Luftwaffe. Aircrew who had been flying and fighting without a break since 22 June were exhausted, and the organisational defects in servicing and replacing their aircraft had become obvious. As well as losses to enemy action, hundreds of aircraft had been damaged or destroyed by crashes on poor airfields, so that he now had only 1,045 serviceable planes to cover the whole immense front. When Hitler demanded air raids on Moscow, there were simply not enough bombers available to make any impression on the city. The problems were compounded by the demands of the other theatres of operation, notably in North Africa, where the overstretched Luftwaffe was unable to provide adequate support for ground forces or protection for the supply convoys, even with the help of the Italian air force.

The fault lay with Ernst Udet, whose administrative incompetence had dragged the Technical Office and indeed the entire German aircraft industry into a state bordering on total collapse. Manufacturing and development programmes were in chaos, new aircraft models were years behind schedule, and production figures had been totally falsified to show some 1,500 more planes delivered than had actually been made. Göring had been aware of Udet's inadequacies for some time, but had turned a blind eye, refusing to condemn his old friend or to face up to the uncomfortable truth. Now, however, things were so bad that he could no longer avoid taking action – his own position was under threat. Under pressure from Milch and Jeschonnek he summoned Udet and lambasted him mercilessly as a bungling liar. But he did not fire him. Instead, he authorised Milch to sort out the mess.

Udet and Milch were as incompatible as oil and water: Udet was a warm, happy-go-lucky character, popular with everyone for his wit and good humour, while Milch was so unemotional and businesslike that Jeschonnek once commented that 'when Milch pisses, ice comes out'. Udet was deeply unhappy at being put under Milch's control and effectively sidelined, but Göring, anxious to save face, refused to let him stand down. According to the aircraft manufacturer Ernst Heinkel, Göring several times told Udet: 'You have to stay on. You have to work together with Milch. If I relieve you, the whole world will realise that there is something wrong.'[13]

As the First World War ace increasingly took refuge in drink and drugs, Milch swept into action, installing management controls in the Technical Office, firing the cronies and drinking partners with whom Udet had surrounded himself, and drawing up new production plans to solve the supply problems. He assembled teams of skilled engineers and fitters and flew with them to the Eastern Front, driving them mercilessly to repair everything in sight, until the crisis had been averted. 'This was just one of those "heroic orders" that were later to become the norm and only blinded vision to hopeless reality,' wrote Heinkel. 'In Hitler's eyes, the deed made Milch seem the coming man.'[14]

By late August, Udet was on the verge of a complete breakdown. Göring invited him to Carinhall for rest and recuperation, but soon realised that he needed more than that and persuaded him to check into the Luftwaffe's central clinic for treatment. When Udet discharged himself prematurely, Göring took him away to the Sternberg hunting grounds in East Prussia, where they took carriage rides and boating trips together for a week. It cannot have helped, however, that Milch was also there for some of the time, along with Jeschonnek and Adolf Galland.

For the next few weeks, Göring was too busy to see much of his old friend, who was still going rapidly downhill. He was not present at a conference in the Air Ministry when Messerschmitt executives produced damning documentary evidence of Udet's falsification of figures and orders and his attempts to cover up his misdemeanours and incompetence. Milch claimed afterwards that he tried to help Udet by inviting him to join him for a couple of days in Paris, where they could resolve their differences. But for Udet it was too late. He spent the weekend in a drunken party in his apartment. At 9.30 a.m. on the Monday morning, 17 November, he telephoned his current mistress and asked her to tell Pili Körner to look after his will. While she was still on the line, he shot himself. When she and Körner arrived at the flat, they found him lying dead across the bed, with two empty brandy bottles and his revolver on the floor. On the wall behind the bed, he had scrawled two messages in red crayon: 'Iron Man, you have deserted me' and 'Why did you put me in the hands of that Jew Milch?' An unsealed envelope in his safe contained a letter to Göring accusing him of conspiring against him, and ranting on against Milch.

Udet had been one of Göring's oldest and dearest friends, and he was shattered by his death. But although he was racked with guilt, his first instinct was to save himself embarrassment and blame, and to avoid any hint of scandal. To be charitable, he also probably wanted to preserve Udet's reputation by hushing up his suicide, and the reasons behind it – which, of course, would also reflect badly on himself and his service. Through his doctor, he instructed Milch to issue an official statement from the Air Ministry: 'While testing a new type of aircraft on Monday, 17 November 1941, Generalluftzeugmeister Colonel-General Udet suffered such a serious accident that he died of his injuries on the way to hospital. The Führer has ordered a state funeral for this officer, who died in such tragic circumstances in the execution of his duty.'

The following day, all flags in Berlin flew at half-mast. The funeral took place three days later, in Hitler's presence, and was attended by every Luftwaffe holder of the Knight's Cross, with the most famous of the current aces, Galland and Mölders, the General of Fighters, among the pall bearers. Göring walked behind the gun carriage bearing the coffin to the Invalidenfriedhof, the military cemetery, and gave the only address. In a voice choked with emotion, he intoned 'I can only say that I have lost my best friend'.

The day's drama was not yet over, however. On his way back from the funeral, Mölders was killed when the He-111 in which he was a passenger developed engine trouble and crashed into a factory chimney in Breslau. Göring appointed Galland in his place, and added Udet's position to Milch's existing responsibilities, the only good to come out of the whole sorry business: Milch immediately set about doubling aircraft production for the coming year, with further increases to follow as efficiency improved.

Himmler had no problems with his principal subordinates, perhaps because, obsessed with control, he kept them on a tighter reign than Göring. Constantly vying for personal advantage, they all carried out their duties with fanatical zeal, and none more so than Heydrich, as he supervised the activities of the Einsatzgruppen, and their co-ordination with the armies to which they were attached. The sheer scale and barbarity of their operations as they followed hard on the heels of the armies is too horrific to recount in detail here. But there are countless harrowing reports from shocked eye-witnesses of hellish scenes as they murdered Jews, partisans, state and party functionaries in their tens of thousands. Initially, most of the victims were shot, usually on the edge of pits which they or other Jews had dug in the earth, usually having been duped into believing they were about to be transported to some other location. Stripped of their clothing and belongings, they included men, women with babies in their arms, and children. Many were not killed outright but buried alive.

One witness was Karl Wolff, who accompanied Himmler on a behind-the-lines inspection tour of the various Einsatzgruppen. Einsatzgruppe B, attached to Army Group Centre, was under the command of Arthur Nebe, the head of the Kripo, and had its head-quarters in Minsk, the capital of Belorussia. As well as assembling all his officers and NCOs to be addressed by Himmler, Nebe had laid on a demonstration for Himmler's delectation: the execution of some 200 Jews, described by Wolff as 'spies and saboteurs'. Himmler, according to Wolff, was pleased to watch: 'It is as well that I can see it for myself for once.' The demonstration took place in a nearby field, where two pits had been dug, each some twenty-five feet long, six feet wide and six feet deep, with a twelve-man firing squad standing at the ready. The victims, mostly young men but also including some women and children, were driven up in trucks and made to lie face down on the bottom of the pits. Himmler positioned himself on the edge of the first pit, where he had a good view and watched, arms folded across his chest, lips tightly pursed, as the police captain in charge gave the order to fire.

It was the first time Himmler had seen anyone killed. Wolff said that he jerked convulsively, passed his hand across his face, and staggered, his face turning green. Again according to Wolff, he took out a handkerchief and wiped away pieces of brain that had splashed on to his cheek and coat, heaving as he turned away. That may or may not be true – Wolff was writing after the war, and was not above embroidering his memories for effect. In any case, Himmler stayed while the next batch of prisoners was dispatched, and afterwards gave a speech to the men to stiffen their resolve. 'I can tell you that it is hideous and frightful for a German to have to see such things,' he told them. 'It is so, and if we had not felt it to be hideous and frightful we should not be Germans.' Saying that they would no doubt have seen how he 'hated this bloody business', he reminded them that they must all do their duty, however hard it might be.[15]

His experience in Minsk shook Himmler, and he told Nebe that they would have to find another method of killing. This, of course, was out of consideration not for the victims, but for their executioners. The more brutalised among them were able to carry on killing, day after day, apparently with no more emotion than butchers in an abattoir. Others, however, were not so lucky. Many cracked under the strain and could only continue with the help of alcohol. Some suffered breakdowns, some committed suicide. The constant fear of Himmler and his commanders was that discipline would break down and the men would run amok in an uncontrolled orgy of sadistic slaughter.

The immediate solution was to use the gas vans already developed for the T4 euthanasia programme, which had proved so successful in mental hospitals that Himmler had extended it to the concentration camps, where prisoners who were seriously ill, either physically or mentally, were weeded out, along with Jews, gypsies, homosexuals and other unwanted elements. He had also promoted, and provided premises at Auschwitz for, experiments in cheap, non-surgical mass sterilisation for Jewish women through phenol injections, developed at his suggestion by a distinguished gynaecologist and reserve SS-Gruppenführer, Professor Carl Clauberg – though this was necessarily a very long-term solution. There were an estimated 5 million Jews in the western Soviet Union, plus nearly 3 million in the former Poland and another 3 million in the rest of Europe. To exterminate them all within a reasonable time would need more than vans or bullets or hypodermic syringes.

There was a great deal of confusion and disagreement among the Einsatzgruppen chiefs and the HSSPFs as to what should be done with the Jews. Some still believed they should be deported to some unspecified territory in the East, where they could be left to die of starvation and neglect; some wanted to exterminate them on the spot. Others favoured concentrating them in one huge camp in the coal-mining region, where they could be worked to death while at least making some economic contribution. But whatever happened, it was clear that a definite plan had to be made, and quickly.

'There is a danger this winter that the Jews can no longer all be fed,' the head of the SD in Posen, SS-Sturmbannführer Rolf-Heinz Höppner, wrote to Adolf Eichmann, now head of Gestapo Desk IVB 4, the department in the RSHA responsible for Jewish affairs, on 16 July. 'Serious consideration must be given as to whether the most humane solution might not be to finish off those Jews not capable of work by some sort of swift-acting preparation. This would be more pleasant than letting them starve . . . This may to some extent sound fantastic, but would in my view be quite possible to implement.'[16]

There could no longer be any doubt what the ultimate outcome was to be; the only question was how it was to be achieved. During five days that he spent at Wolfsschanze from 15 to 20 July, Himmler had several private meetings 'under four eyes' with Hitler at which they discussed the problem at some length. Like all conversations on this most sensitive subject, no record was made, but there can be no doubt that Hitler gave Himmler the go-ahead to deal with it radically and urgently. Himmler immediately briefed Heydrich, who called Eichmann into his office and told him: 'The Führer has ordered the physical extermination of the Jews.' He then, according to Eichmann, 'quite contrary to his habit, paused for a long time as if he wanted to test the effect of his words on me.' It took a moment for the full implication to sink in, 'but then I understood, and said nothing further because there was nothing more I could say.'[17]

Eichmann was ordered to draft an authorisation document, which Heydrich presented to Göring – who was still nominally in charge of Jewish policy as Chairman of the Reich Defence Council – on 31 July. It read:

Complementing the task that was already assigned to you on 24 January 1939, to solve the Jewish problem by means of emigration and evacuation in the best possible way according to present conditions, I hereby charge you with making all necessary preparations in regard to organisational, factual and material matters for a total solution of the Jewish question within the area of German influence in Europe. Should these come within the competence of other government departments, then such departments are to co-operate.

I charge you, furthermore, to send me, before long, an overall plan concerning the organisational, factual and material measures necessary for the accomplishment of the desired final solution of the Jewish question.[18]

By the time Göring signed Heydrich's document, Himmler was already taking steps to put the 'desired final solution' into effect. He called Höss from Auschwitz to his office in Berlin, where he told him: 'The Führer has ordered the final solution of the Jewish question and we – the SS – have to carry out this order.' Because the existing liquidation facilities in the East were inadequate, he had decided to use Auschwitz for the task, and Höss would be in charge. Eichmann would come to see him 'in the near future', to give him the details, after which he was to send Himmler his plans for the proposed plant immediately. He was not to breathe a word to anyone, not even his superiors, about the order.

Eichmann visited Höss at Auschwitz a few days later, when they calmly discussed the mechanics of the operation. Agreeing that gas was the only practical method of killing such large numbers, they chose a suitable site for a new facility, on the edge of the proposed new camp at Birkenau, where they planned to build gas chambers capable of handling 800 people at a time. Eichmann said, however, that the carbon monoxide used in the vans and the T4 programme was not entirely satisfactory, and promised to find something better.

In fact, it was not Eichmann but Höss's deputy at Auschwitz, SS-Hauptsturmführer Karl Fritsch, who found something better a few weeks later. Batches of Soviet prisoners for liquidation under Hitler's Commissar Order were regularly sent to the camp, where they were shot in a nearby gravel pit. Fritsch had the bright idea of using them as guinea pigs on whom he could try out a commercial fumigant already used extensively in the camp to kill rodents, lice and other vermin. Marketed as rapidly-evaporating crystals, its name, Zyklon (Cyclone) B, was a play on its major constituent, hydrogen cyanide, Zyanid in German. Fritsch had the windows and all ventilation to the cellars of Block II closed off, and herded in some 600 Soviet prisoners plus 250 patients from the camp hospital for good measure. An SS-man trained in pest control and wearing a gas mask scattered the lethal crystals then locked the sealed doors. The results were highly satisfactory, though it seems that a few prisoners managed to survive the first effort, and the quantities of crystals had to be worked out by trial and error during a series of experiments under Höss's direction, until the executioners got it quite right.[19]

Himmler and Heydrich now had the means to carry out the 'Final Solution'. The use of Zyklon B in fake shower rooms would not become standard, however, until late 1942, by which time a string of new extermination camps would have been set up to supplement the 'throughput' of Auschwitz-Birkenau. Until then, the carbon monoxide vans and static chambers would continue to ply their vile trade but the bullet would remain overwhelmingly the main means of murder. At the end of September, shortly after the Germans had taken Kiev, the capital of the Ukraine, in one of the bloodiest battles of the war, Einsatzkommando 4a, part of Einsatzgruppe C, shot no fewer than 33,771 Jews in a ravine called Babi-Yar, on the outskirts of the city.[20]

The massacre at Babi-Yar was supposedly a reprisal for a number of bomb attacks by partisans, including one that destroyed the hotel being used as German headquarters, killing hundreds of soldiers. But the self-congratulatory report on the incident paints a different picture. 'The Jewish population was invited by poster to present themselves for resettlement,' it states. 'Although we had initially only counted on 5,000-6,000 Jews reporting, more than 30,000 Jews appeared; by a remarkably efficient piece of organisation, they were led to believe in the resettlement story until shortly before their execution.' The same report also includes details of the slaughter of an even larger number of Jews and Communists – 35,782 – in the Black Sea ports of Nikolayev and Kherson.[21]

The Einsatzgruppen were augmented by regiments of Order Police under the direct control of Himmler's HSSPFs in each of the conquered regions, together with roving Waffen-SS detachments, which had been reinforced with half-trained auxiliary volunteers from the local populations in the Baltic states and the Ukraine. Their job was to mop up any Jews or partisans missed by the Einsatzgruppen, and a fierce competition soon developed between the two forces over who could kill more. Hitler followed their progress all the way: on 1 August, the day after Göring signed the 'Final Solution' document, Gestapo chief Heinrich Müller sent a secret order to each of the four Einsatzgruppen commanders: 'Continual reports from here on the work of the

Einsatzgruppen in the East are to be presented to the Führer.'²² He must have been well pleased with the results. By the end of 1941, the Einsatzgruppen claimed to have disposed of more than 300,000 out of some 500,000 murdered Jews.

At the same time as his thugs were massacring the Jews of Kiev at Babi-Yar, Heydrich was given a new assignment. He and Himmler had spent two days at Wolfsschanze, talking to Hitler and Bormann about the Protectorate of Bohemia and Moravia, where the vital armaments industry was facing serious problems of sabotage, strikes and low work rates. The blame for this was laid on Neurath, whose moderation as Reich Protector had been constantly criticised by the party zealots in his administration. Hitler decided to send the former Foreign Minister on sick leave and replace him with Heydrich, whom no one could ever accuse of moderation, with the title of Deputy Reich Protector and the brief to crush all Czech resistance without mercy.

Following the usual Nazi custom, Heydrich did not relinquish any of his other responsibilities, remaining chief of the RSHA and continuing to dispose of Jews at the same time as Czech patriots. Although his new position was essentially an extension of his role as a super policeman, it marked a considerable step forward in his career; for the first time, he was not subordinate to Himmler, and he had direct access to Hitler. Well aware of Heydrich's overweening ambition, Himmler must have started looking over his shoulder with extra care.

Goebbels paid his first visit to Wolfsschanze on 18 August, where he was shocked to find Hitler, at loggerheads with his generals and recovering from a severe attack of dysentery and a worsening heart condition, still unwell and 'very irritable'. Although the Wehrmacht had scored a stunning string of victories, these had not been achieved without cost: German casualties for the first six weeks included an estimated 30,000 dead. Hitler admitted that he had been astounded by the ferocity of the Soviet resistance, and even more so by its size and equipment. As Halder noted in his war diary on 11 August: 'The whole situation makes it increasingly plain that we have underestimated the Russian colossus. At the outset of the war, we reckoned with about 200 enemy divisions. Now we have already counted 360.'²³

Goebbels, ever the hawk, thought it was a good thing that they had not been 'clearly aware of the dimensions of the danger', and 'had absolutely no conception of a whole series of their armaments, especially their heavy weapons.' Not only would this have given Hitler months of 'much greater worries', it might even have caused him to shy away from confronting the question of the East and of Bolshevism, which had to be resolved. Hitler admitted that had he known the true situation, his decision to attack would have been much more difficult, but he assured Goebbels that the war in the East would still be over by winter.[24]

Goebbels was anxious to re-establish his position in the hierarchy, having been sidelined by his chief rivals during the campaign in the East. He had at least scored a victory over Ribbentrop, by persuading Hitler that he and not the Foreign Ministry should be responsible for propaganda in the East designed to undermine the Red Army. But Ribbentrop was out of favour anyway, after an amazing quarrel with Hitler on 28 July. This had started from the trivial matter of gallantry decorations for diplomats and had then escalated into a blazing row over Hitler's entire reasoning behind the war in the East, which Ribbentrop had always opposed, and culminated in his offering his resignation. Hitler had then become wildly excited and had collapsed into a chair with an apparent seizure that had frightened the life out of the Foreign Minister, who grovelled and begged forgiveness until Hitler finally agreed to let him stay in his post, as long as he promised never to cross him again. Slinking back to Steinort, Ribbentrop took to his bed in a darkened room for several days, and may even have suffered a slight stroke himself – from then until his death he suffered splitting hemi-cranial headaches and occasional paralysis of his right arm and leg.[25] He never dared to disagree with Hitler again.

Ribbentrop's fall from grace may have been gratifying for Goebbels, but it did little to ease his chagrin over the fact that Göring and Himmler were notching up tangible successes while his own efforts to win over the populations of the 'liberated' territories through propaganda had failed to produce results – even though this was largely due to the activities of Himmler's murder squads. Desperate not to be left behind in the contest for personal credibility, he turned to his other role, as Gauleiter of Berlin, and his eternal obsession, the Jews. In his eyes, it was a 'scandal' that while Himmler was concerning himself with the Jews in the East, there were still 75,000 Jews 'roaming around' the Reich capital, of whom only 23,000 were working while the rest were living as 'parasites' – as if they had a choice. They spoiled both the appearance and the atmosphere of the streets, he complained, and must be removed from among the German people, despite the 'powerful bureaucratic and sentimental opposition' he would have to overcome. He would not rest, he declared, until 'we have drawn the final consequence for Jewry', and he begged Hitler to make this soon.

Hitler promised him that as soon as transport was available, the Berlin Jews would be the first to be removed to the East. However, with the army alone needing 120 trainloads of supplies every day,[26] and the available rolling stock reduced by half due to the time it took to cover the enormous distances to and from the Eastern Front, not to speak of breakdowns and partisan actions, there was simply no transport to spare.

In the meantime, to increase pressure on the Jews in the Reich, Goebbels proposed a list of measures, most of which Hitler approved. While he was still at Wolfsschanze, he discussed them with Heydrich, who had been appointed Acting Reich Protector that same day, and they were put into effect during the following month. The most visible of them was that all Jews had to wear a yellow cloth Star of David with the word 'Jude' (Jew) written across the centre, sewn on to their clothing to make them easily identifiable. Covering or concealing the star was strictly forbidden. Jews were banned from moving out of the district in which they lived without first obtaining police permission, and were banned from using public transport except, as a special concession, to travel to and from work, and even then were not allowed to sit down.

Other regulations stopped Jews buying clothes, smoking tobacco, using public telephones, keeping pets, having their hair cut by an Aryan barber, using the services of 'German' tradesmen, owning any electrical appliances, gramophones, typewriters, bicycles or hand mirrors, all of which had to be handed in. Their rations were reduced, and monthly support payments 'rigorously limited', 'so that the Jew cannot buy off Germans of weak character'.[27] A thorough 'combing out' of any who could not be used for essential war work would determine those who were 'ripe' for transportation to the East.

Incredibly, within a few weeks, trains were found, and on 14 October Goebbels's friend Kurt Daluege, as Chief of the Order Police, signed a directive for the first deportation of Berlin Jews. Speer, who as General Building Inspector was responsible for taking over Jewish-owned or occupied apartments to accommodate bombed-out Berliners, had already warned the Jewish community leaders that he would shortly begin a further 'resettlement', but this time the resettlement took a different form. On 15 October, as darkness fell, two Gestapo men arrived at each apartment to be vacated and ordered the family to pack one suitcase with essentials. They took them to the remains of the synagogue on Levetzowstrasse, still in ruins since it was burned down during *Kristallnacht*. There, they were kept for three days before being marched in a long procession through the city to the Grunewald rail station. Young children and the sick were driven in trucks. On 18 October, the first train left, its doors locked and windows barred, carrying 1,000 Berlin Jews to be dumped in the working ghetto at Lodz in the Warthegau, the annexed territory around Posen in the west of what had been Poland.

Nine more trains followed in the next few weeks, together with others from Luxembourg, Düsseldorf, Cologne, Hamburg, Munich, Prague and Vienna, delivering Jews to Lodz, Minsk, Kaunas and Riga. Goebbels exulted in his success, crowing his satisfaction in a virulent article for his 'serious' weekly, *Das Reich*, entitled 'The Jews Are to Blame', in which he proclaimed that Hitler's prophecy was coming true and the war which the Jews had started was resulting in their extermination. Their fate, he wrote, was 'harsh but more than deserved', concluding that 'pity or regret is completely out of place here'.[28]

Goebbels and Hitler discussed one other major concern during the four hours they spent talking while walking in the woods on 18 August: the need to mend fences with the churches. While both men were vehemently anti-Christian, they also recognised the danger of alienating millions of believers during the critical time of war. Bormann, however, seemed blind to the threat. One of his first moves after being confirmed as head of the Party Chancellery at the beginning of June had been to issue a secret circular to all Gauleiters on 'The Relationship of National Socialism to Christendom'. It was an uncompromising blast against organised religion, beginning 'National Socialist and Christian concepts are irreconcilable' and going on to claim that 'our National Socialist ideology is far loftier than the concepts of Christianity, which in their essential points have been taken over from Jewry. For this reason we do not need Christianity . . . All influences which might impair or damage the leadership of the people exercised by the Führer with the help of the NSDAP must be eliminated. More and more, the people must be separated from the churches and their organs, the pastors . . . '[29]

There was already considerable friction between the Catholic Church and the party, exacerbated by various actions ranging from the removal of crucifixes from Bavarian schools and attempts to stop morning prayers, to bans on church publications and the closure of monasteries.

Now it seemed that Bormann, who for once had spoken without Hitler's authority, had effectively declared war on the Church. Goebbels had been extremely annoyed, especially when he learned that the secret memorandum had been leaked in full to the Church authorities. 'Why does Bormann have to release a pronouncement on the church question at this time anyway?' he complained. 'It is not a problem of any decisive importance in winning the war.'

The damage to the party's image had been severe, and it continued through the summer, when the euthanasia programme became public knowledge. After a period of pussyfooting around the subject – a pastoral letter from German Bishops in early July merely hinted at the truth by declaring it was wrong to kill except in war or self-defence – the Catholic Bishop of Münster in Westphalia openly denounced what was happening. In a forthright sermon on 3 August, thousands of copies of which were printed and circulated clandestinely, he linked the T4 killings to recent heavy air raids on Münster, implying that these were the punishment of God for breaking the sixth commandment. With no conscious irony, he called on Hitler to protect the people from the Gestapo.

Party hotheads demanded that the Bishop should be hanged, but even Bormann now realised that this was impossible – or at least that Hitler would never sanction it. Goebbels agreed, warning that if they took any action against the Bishop they would forfeit the support of the population of Münster and Westphalia for the rest of the war. Despite the fact that he had commissioned a film, *Ich klage an* (*I accuse*), justifying the euthanasia programme, which was almost ready for release, he told Hitler during their long talk that they should not encourage public discussion over the subject. 'Such a debate,' he believed, 'would only inflame feelings again. In a critical period of the war, that would be extremely inadvisable. All inflammatory matters should be kept away from the people at present. People are so preoccupied with the problems of the war that other problems only arouse and irritate them.'[30] Hitler took his advice, and officially cancelled the T4 programme on 24 August – though the killings continued in secret. Goebbels released his film five days later.

The German offensive in the East had paused at the end of July for refitting and repair. Göring had seized the excuse of a Luftwaffe staff conference at the Quai d'Orsay in Paris to indulge in a three-week shopping spree, buying more diamonds from Cartier, raiding the Jeu de Paume again and helping himself from a newly discovered cache of Rothschild art treasures, including eighteenth- and nineteenth-century Dutch and French paintings. When he returned to Wolfsschanze, he found Hitler locked in a bitter dispute with his army generals over strategy.

The generals wanted to launch a massive attack by Army Group Centre to destroy the main Soviet armies ranged around Moscow, which was not only the capital and nerve centre of the Soviet Union but also its communications hub and a major arms-producing area. Hitler, however, was intent on mounting a two-pronged attack on the wings first, aimed at Leningrad and the Baltic states in the north, and the Donbas region in the south, to capture all the industrial and agricultural wealth of the Ukraine and open the way to the oil-rich Caucasus. Göring naturally sided with Hitler, quarrelling so violently with Brauchitsch that the army commander suffered a mild heart attack. Göring's own heart thumped so hard he had to call his personal physician, Dr von Ondarza.

Hitler, as always, imposed his will on the generals, lambasting them savagely in a memorandum on 22 August for failing to carry out his operational plan. He accused Brauchitsch of lack of leadership, contrasting it with Göring's firm leadership of the Luftwaffe. Göring did not have long to bask in Hitler's praise, however – less than a month afterwards he too suffered the lash of the Führer's tongue. Hitler demanded that he mount the greatest attack in the history of aerial warfare by assembling the Luftwaffe's entire bomber strength for a series of raids that would utterly destroy both Leningrad and Moscow, leaving not a single building standing or an inhabitant alive – which in his view would be better than leaving the populations to starve, since it would be impossible to feed them.

Bodenschatz wrote later that he was proud of Göring at that moment:

He began very politely by saying that while he found the Führer's project worth studying, his immediate reaction was that it would be a most difficult operation to carry out. When Hitler harshly asked him why, he became bolder and said outright that it would be the height of folly to withdraw the Luftwaffe from all other fronts just for one operation. What about the attacks on London? Had the Führer not demanded that they must be continued with unremitting force? It would be dangerous to stop, because it would give the British people respite. Their factories would open again, their aircraft industries get under way, and before they knew it the British RAF would be as strong as Germany.

All the warmth Hitler had been showing to Göring vanished instantly. He screamed that he knew why he was opposing his plan: the Luftwaffe was afraid, just as he had always suspected. It was made up of cowards. They did not want to attack Leningrad because they were afraid of its anti-aircraft defences.

'Göring could have told him what everyone else in the room knew,' Bodenschatz continued. 'That Leningrad's defences were nothing like as fearsome as London's, over which our fliers had been operating for months. But instead, he said: "It is impossible, my Führer. It cannot be done." Hitler looked at him coldly for a moment, then turned his back on him and ignored him for the rest of the conference.'[31] Such a point-blank refusal from anyone else would have resulted in instant dismissal. Hitler accepted it from Göring, albeit with very bad grace, but some observers believed he never forgave him, and that the incident marked another significant step in the decline of his influence. Nevertheless, the concerted air raids on Moscow and Leningrad were never attempted.

The great new offensive opened on 23 August 1941, with more instant successes for the Wehrmacht in both the north and south. Army Group North scythed through the Baltic states to cut off Leningrad on 8 September and start the longest siege in modern history, lasting 900 days, as Hitler decided not to storm the heavily defended city but to starve it to death. On the same day, Army Group South reached Kiev, which it captured on 18 September, by which time its Panzers had completed a giant pincer movement to encircle four entire Soviet armies. The Germans claimed to have taken some 665,000 prisoners; the Soviets admitted losing 527,000 men wounded and captured during the previous week's fighting. Either way, it was a staggering result, the biggest single capitulation of the war.

The Wehrmacht's victorious progress persuaded Hitler to change his mind about the drive for Moscow, and he authorised a major operation, code-named 'Typhoon', to start as soon as possible. 'In a few weeks,' he declared confidently, 'we shall be in Moscow. I shall raze that damned city and in its place build an artificial lake with central lighting. The name of Moscow will disappear for ever.'[32]

Hitler's optimism was not universally shared in Germany, where much of the population, especially in rural areas, could not see the point of the war in the Soviet Union and the sacrifices it was demanding of them. Even before the battle of Kiev, the Eastern armies had lost some 400,000 casualties, each of them a tragedy for a family back home. Goebbels, with the responsibility of maintaining popular morale, was intensely aware of the growing discontent, which was aggravated by Hitler's absence: he had not spoken directly to his people since 4 May, and had not been seen in public since the start of Barbarossa. Goebbels paid his second visit to Wolfsschanze on 23 September, to urge him to return to Berlin to address the nation and lift people's spirits as only he could.

Hitler agreed to make a speech in the Sportpalast on 3 October to open that year's Winter Aid campaign, but he was preoccupied with preparations for the attack on Moscow, which was due to start on the 2nd, and prevaricated until literally the last minute. Not until the evening, after Typhoon had been successfully launched, did he confirm that he would come to Berlin the next day. Even at such short notice, Goebbels was able to fill the streets with crowds to cheer their leader on his way, and to pack the Sportpalast to the rafters with the faithful, to give him and his message a reception as rapturous as those of the heady days in the run-up to power in 1933. Hitler delivered the goods, blaming the war entirely on the British warmongers and international Jewry, and justifying the attack on the Soviet Union as preventive, stressing the enemy's 'gigantic preparations' and the 'immense danger' they had posed. 'We have escaped the annihilation not only of Germany, but of the whole of Europe, only by a hair's breadth,' he declared, before going on to reassure his audience: 'I can say today that this enemy is already broken and will not rise to his feet again.'[33] Goebbels was delighted with the speech, noting that it would be a great help in his propaganda.

Hitler left Berlin at 7 p.m., and was back in Wolfsschanze first thing the following morning, to receive the latest reports from the front. The news was good: the German Panzers were overwhelming the Soviet defences once again. By mid October, they had captured Orel, and completed another vast encirclement of around 500–600,000 men at Vyazma and Bryansk, on the highway to Moscow. Jodl reported: 'We have finally and without exaggeration won the war!' And Otto Dietrich announced to the press: 'For all military purposes Soviet Russia is done with.' Goebbels, jealous of Dietrich anyway, was furious and protested to Hitler that his statement was injudicious and might lead to a terrible let-down over the next few days. But Hitler silenced him with the reply that it had been a political chess move, aimed at inducing Japan to enter the war against the Soviet Union.[34]

On 16 October, with German advance units only sixty miles from Moscow, the Soviets could only muster a total of 90,000 men, all that were left of the 800,000 on the front at the start of the German offensive. 250,000 civilian Muscovites, seventy-five per cent of them women, were drafted to dig trenches and anti-tank ditches, as the government evacuated the city in great panic, though Stalin himself remained at his desk in the Kremlin. It looked as though Hitler's boasts were about to be made good – until the intervention of three great Russian generals: General Mud, General Winter and finally General Zhukov. The mud brought the German advance to a halt in late October, when the heavy autumn rains turned the dirt roads and indeed the whole countryside into a quagmire, bogging down men and machines and preventing fuel and supplies reaching the tanks and other tracked vehicles which could traverse the sodden terrain. With the frosts of November, the ground hardened again, and the assault on Moscow could be continued. But by then the Red Army had been able to bring up reserves and reinforcements, and to prepare the city's defences in depth.

By the time the Wehrmacht was ready to start hurling itself at Moscow again, winter was closing in. Without adequate clothing – Hitler had been so confident of a quick victory that he had made no provision for it – the German troops began freezing to death. The Waffen-SS had been equipped with furs, seized by the methodical Himmler from Jewish ghettos, but they made up only a small proportion of the army. Soon, General Guderian, leading the charge, was losing 1,200 men a day to frostbite, and any wounded who were not carried into cover within minutes had no hope of survival. Guns and equipment jammed as the lubricating oils froze solid – the Red Army, by contrast, had long ago developed oils that could resist the cold. Fires had to be lit under tanks to thaw out their engines, turrets and tracks in temperatures which according to German sources plummeted to an awesome -52°C – though the Soviets dismissively said they were no worse than the normal 30–40° below zero. And the over-extended supply lines, stretching back 1,000 miles to Germany, failed to deliver as, in addition to the breakdown of road transport, the railway system came to a complete standstill when German locomotives, and their water towers, froze solid.[35]

On 6 December, their latest assault battered to a freezing halt by grimly determined defenders less than fifteen miles from the Kremlin itself, the Germans suddenly found themselves facing a third and even more fearsome enemy when Zhukov, Commander-in-Chief of the Soviet front, unleashed his great counterattack. For five and a half months, the Germans had rampaged through the Soviet Union, killing and capturing and destroying. They had taken more than three million prisoners, created hundreds of thousands of casualties and destroyed or captured vast quantities of weapons and equipment. Although they were themselves almost exhausted, they were entitled to expect that the Red Army must be at its last gasp. And yet, suddenly, they found themselves facing powerful new armies, well equipped, warmly clad, tougher even than Himmler's elite Waffen-SS divisions.

To the reserves he had dredged up from new conscripts and the remnants of the Western armies, Zhukov had been able to add massive reinforcements from the Far East, battle-hardened Siberian troops to whom the Moscow temperatures seemed like a mild spring day. The Japanese, still smarting from the defeats inflicted on them by Zhukov himself with these very troops, and bound by a treaty they had signed with Stalin on 13 April 1941 after receiving confused messages from Ribbentrop, had decided not to enter the war against the Soviet Union. The Soviet master spy in Tokyo, Richard Sorge, in his last *coup* before he was discovered and arrested in September, had informed Moscow that they had nothing to fear from Japan that year. Stalin had promptly transferred half the entire strength of the Far Eastern Command to the defence of Moscow, some ten rifle divisions, plus 1,000 tanks and 1,000 aircraft. Zhukov was therefore able to hit the Germans with three fresh armies made up of over a million men, including some of the toughest fighters in the world. Within three weeks he had driven the enemy back nearly a hundred miles.

'The Miracle of Moscow' was Hitler's first major defeat on land, shattering the myth of the invincible Wehrmacht, and changing everything. Meanwhile, on the other side of the world, another event was taking place that would make his ultimate defeat inevitable. Zhukov's counteroffensive had begun on 6 December. A few short hours later, at 7.30 a.m. local time, the Japanese attacked the US Pacific Fleet in Pearl Harbor. The European conflict had become a world war.

PART SIX

WAR: DEFEAT

XXXI

THE FINAL SOLUTION

THE attack on Pearl Harbor came as a shock to Hitler, and to Ribbentrop, who had spent much of the previous year vainly trying to persuade the Japanese to attack the Soviet Union. When Ribbentrop staged a European Foreign Ministers' Conference in Berlin on 25–27 November 1941, to renew the Anti-Comintern Pact for a further five years and add another eight signatories – Bulgaria, Croatia, Denmark, Finland, Hungary, Romania, Slovakia and Spain – Japan was the only country to have given Germany no support in her Eastern war. By that time, however, Ribbentrop had become convinced that war with the United States was inevitable, and had begun urging the Japanese to move against the Americans instead.

Two days later, after telling Ambassador Oshima that 'he did not believe that Japan could avoid a showdown with the United States, and that the situation could hardly ever turn more favourable to Japan than it did now,' he assured him that Germany would join in immediately should Japan go to war with America.[1] He had no idea that the Japanese fleet had already sailed from the isolated Tankan Bay in the Kurile Islands heading for Hawaii – the Germans were being kept in the dark, just as they had always kept their allies in the dark over their own invasions.

When he was woken in the small hours of 8 December to be given the news of Pearl Harbor, Ribbentrop was 'extremely angry' at being disturbed for what he thought was 'probably a propaganda trick of the enemy's for which my Press Section has fallen'. Only after it had been confirmed by further investigation did he believe it.[2] He claimed at his Nuremberg trial that it had been an unpleasant surprise, and that 'we never considered a Japanese attack on the United States to be to our advantage'.[3] But when he telephoned Ciano during that same night, he was in high spirits: 'He is so happy, in fact,' Ciano wrote, 'that I can't but congratulate him, even though I am not so sure about the advantage.'[4]

Drawing on an understanding of 'the American soul' which he claimed to have gained during the four years he had lived there, Ribbentrop was scathing about the United States' military potential. Repeating the grave miscalculation he had made of Britain's will to fight, he now wrote off the Americans – their weapons, he claimed, were 'junk', and they would never be able to fight in Europe – and encouraged Hitler to declare war on them at once, to pre-empt America getting in first. 'A great power doesn't let itself have war declared on it, it declares war itself,' he told Ernst Weizsäcker.[5] At noon on 11 December, he had the pleasure of doing so. He summoned the American Chargé d'Affaires, Leland Morris, and, keeping him standing, read out a formal statement accusing President Roosevelt of inciting war through repeated violations of neutrality, belligerent attacks on German U-boats, and overt acts of war. Then, with a 'sweeping gesture' he handed over the document and dismissed Morris, 'who obviously felt his position keenly', with a stiff bow.[6]

Immediately after Morris had left, Ribbentrop welcomed the Japanese and Italian Ambassadors, to sign an extension of the Tripartite Pact stating that none of them would make a unilateral peace with Britain or the USA. For Ribbentrop, this was the apogee of his career to date, now that the Nazi–Soviet Pact was buried and forgotten: his brainchild had become a full-scale military alliance. It was also his last significant diplomatic success: from then on, he became increasingly marginalised, and indeed over the next ten months did virtually nothing of note.

As soon as he had told his entourage at the Wolfsschanze about the Japanese attack, Hitler had telephoned Goebbels, who was delighted by the news. 'The United States,' Goebbels wrote, 'will no longer be able to provide England so rashly with aircraft, weapons, and shipping capacity, since it can be assumed that they will need all that for their own war with Japan.'[7] Hitler told him he was returning to Berlin the next day, and asked him to convene the Reichstag. For the last few weeks, he had been thinking of making a speech outlining the events of the year, but had put it off as the Soviet campaign had turned sour.

Now he could use the declaration of war against the United States to give him a more positive angle.

In a long talk in the Chancellery on 9 December, Hitler agreed that this was the propaganda line that Goebbels would follow, believing the new challenge would raise morale. They also agreed that he would blame the weather alone for the Wehrmacht's difficulties in the East, playing down any suggestion that they had underestimated Soviet strengths, but admitting that there were problems. Having noted how effective Churchill's 'blood, sweat and tears' approach had been in stiffening British resolve, Goebbels had decided it was time to start giving the German people a certain amount of bad news. What the British could take, he thought, so could the Germans. He had even admitted to his senior staff that suppressing bad news had been a 'basic mistake', making people 'oversensitive'. What he did not say was that he had little option, since with the enormous casualty figures affecting almost every family it was impossible to keep them secret any longer.

One other piece of bad news that could not be kept secret was the disastrous failure to provide the troops with winter clothing, which was causing serious resentment among their families. But Goebbels managed to turn this to good effect, mounting a massive Winter Aid operation that successfully mobilised the home front by calling on people to donate not money but ski wear and similar clothes. In a national radio broadcast to launch the appeal, he declared that 'people at home would not deserve a moment's peace if a single German soldier was exposed to the harshness of winter without articles of warm clothing'.[8] He sent film, theatre and sports stars around the country to drum up support, which they did so successfully that the campaign, which was due to end at Christmas, had to be extended until 11 January 1942. Although an incredible 67 million articles were collected, it was essentially no more than a hollow and cynical PR exercise, of little benefit to the troops since there was no means of transporting and distributing them in time for them to be of any use. It was, however, a brilliant psychological move, diverting attention from the true reasons behind the problem by involving people in a whirl of activity that led them to believe they were providing a solution.

Hitler arrived back at Wolfsschanze on 16 December to find his armies on the brink of total disaster in the face of the great Soviet counter-attack. As they were forced back, the spectre of Napoleon's fate before

Moscow in 1812 loomed ominously over them. 'If they had once begun a retreat,' one divisional commander, General von Tippelskirch, recalled later, 'it might have turned into a panic flight.' That it did not was due entirely to Hitler, who flatly refused to allow any further withdrawals. He had already dismissed Rundstedt, Commander-in-Chief of Army Group South, after he had captured and then withdrawn from Rostov, on the Don, replacing him with Reichenau, the most rabid Nazi of all his generals, who died of a stroke in January. Now, any general or field marshal who even argued for a planned withdrawal to a better defensive position was instantly dismissed. The Commanders-in-Chief of the other two army groups, Centre and North, Field Marshals von Bock and von Leeb, were both replaced. The Panzer wizard Guderian was another victim, together with fellow Panzer commander Erich Hoepner, who was dismissed, stripped of his rank, uniform, decorations and pension rights. At a slightly lower level, some thirty-five corps and divisional commanders were sacked during the winter of 1941–2.

Göring, always happy to see the army generals suffering, gave Hitler his full support, especially since the Führer had only praise for the Luftwaffe leaders like the hard-nosed air corps commander, Colonel-General Wolfram Freiherr von Richthofen, who had learned his craft in Spain, bombing Guernica. So when one of Göring's own paratroop commanders, Lieutenant-General Hans Graf von Sponeck, who had been awarded the Knight's Cross for his role in leading the airborne landings at The Hague the year before, pulled back one division of his force in the Crimea after Soviet troops had landed by sea behind it, he came down on him hard. He court-martialled him, stripped him of his rank, and bulldozed the court into imposing the ultimate penalty. 'The Reich Marshal,' Himmler asserted later, 'had the utmost difficulty in getting his fellow judges – all generals – to agree to sentence this coward to death.' Even Hitler felt this was going a little too far, and commuted the sentence to fortress imprisonment. But Sponeck did not survive the war: he was executed in 1944, in the wake of the bomb plot of 20 July.

The most high-profile and significant departure was of Brauchitsch, the Commander-in-Chief of the Army himself. Having been treated with increasing contempt by Hitler and suffering a severe heart attack in November, Brauchitsch was already a broken man by the time the Red Army launched its counteroffensive. He tried to persuade Hitler to agree to a general withdrawal around Moscow to avoid disaster, only to receive screaming abuse in reply. Despite his suffering further heart attacks, Hitler refused his repeated attempts to resign, perhaps because he could not decide on a possible successor. On 19 December, however, Hitler found the right man, indeed in his eyes the only man, for the job – himself. Why should he not be Commander-in-Chief of the Army, as well as Supreme Commander of the Wehrmacht? 'This little matter of operational command,' he told Halder, whom he kept on as his Chief of the General Staff, 'is something anyone can do. The task of the Commander-in-Chief of the Army is to train the army in a National Socialist way. I know of no general who could do that, as I want it done.'[9]

Throughout the rest of December and January, the Soviets hammered at the German lines, particularly in the centre, forcing them back but failing to break them. After long arguments, Hitler grudgingly allowed Field Marshal von Kluge, the new Commander-in-Chief of Army Group Centre, to make tactical withdrawals, 'step by step in order to protect his communications', but the general order of 'no retreat' still stood. Casualty figures continued to climb: by 20 February, when the Soviet offensive ground to a halt, total German losses since the start of Barbarossa, not counting Hungarians, Romanians and Italians, would pass the million mark, thirty-one per cent of the entire force, including 199,448 dead, 708,351 wounded, 112,627 cases of severe frostbite, and 44,342 missing.[10]

If he was to mount a renewed offensive in the spring, Hitler would need more replacements than he could raise from Germany alone. He sent Keitel to Budapest and Bucharest to wheedle more divisions out of the Hungarians and Romanians, and at the end of the month Göring, never averse to a trip to Rome, set off to convince Mussolini that the setbacks on the Eastern Front were only temporary. His message was that the Soviet Union would be defeated in 1942, with Italian help, and Britain 'would lay down her arms' the following year. As a sweetener, he told the Duce that the Luftwaffe was about to start an all-out aerial assault on Malta, which the British were using as a base from which to attack Italian supply routes to North Africa. Mussolini promised to send another two divisions of Italian troops to the East in March, if the Germans would give them artillery.

Göring was clearly in good form. Ciano, who felt slighted at being kept out of the discussions, described him as 'bloated and overbearing' when he finally had lunch with him on 2 February, and added a memorable description of the dinner they had at the Excelsior Hotel two days later, before he left for home on *Asia*:

During the dinner Göring talked of little else but the jewels he owned. In fact he had some beautiful rings on his fingers. He explained that he bought them for a relatively small sum in Holland after all jewels were confiscated in Germany. I am told that he plays with his gems like a little boy with his marbles. During the trip he was nervous, so his aides brought him a small vase filled with diamonds. He placed them on the table and counted them, lined them up, mixed them together, and became happy again. One of his high officers said last evening: 'He has two loves – beautiful objects and making war.' Both are expensive hobbies. To the station he wore a great sable coat, something between what automobile drivers wore in 1906 and what a high-grade prostitute wears to the opera. If any of us tried a thing like that we would be stoned in the streets. He, on the contrary, is not only accepted in Germany but perhaps even loved for it. That is because he has a dash of humanity.[11]

Göring had hardly arrived back in East Prussia when he received startling news. Shortly before 8 a.m. on Sunday, 8 February, Fritz Todt had been killed when the plane returning him to Berlin after a visit to Hitler crashed while taking off from the Wolfsschanze airstrip. Göring had been increasingly at loggerheads with Todt for some time, and had in fact been intriguing for two or three months with Himmler, Heydrich, Goebbels and even Bormann, to oust him from office in a *coup* reminiscent of the removal of Blomberg and Schacht. He had gone so far as to prepare a draft of a Führer decree extending his own control over the economy and appointing him as Minister for War Production with power over all the armed forces, but was not quite ready to present it to Hitler. As soon as he heard of Todt's death, he rushed to Hitler's HQ, to persuade the Führer to let him take over his responsibilities. But quick as he was, he was too late. He was staggered to find that Hitler had already appointed Albert Speer, who was with him when Göring arrived, as Todt's successor in all his capacities.

Speer, who the evening before had accepted Todt's offer of a lift back to Berlin in his plane but had changed his mind at 3 a.m., deciding he was too tired after a long session with Hitler, was still coming to terms with his good fortune, not only for his narrow escape but also for his elevation. He had expected to be given Todt's role as construction chief, but was as surprised as Göring when he was given the

Armaments Ministry as well. For all his professed modesty, Speer was in fact intensely ambitious, and was thrilled to find himself raised to Cabinet level at the age of thirty-six. As an instinctive politician and a gifted manipulator, his first action was to cover his back by persuading Hitler to make his appointment an order.

Göring had no option but to accept the situation with as good grace as he could muster, but he recognised that Speer was a potentially dangerous rival, and set about clipping his wings. The day after Todt's funeral on 11 February, he invited him to his Berlin villa, where he received him cordially, saying how he hoped the harmony that had always existed between them while Speer was working as his architect would not change. 'When Göring wanted to,' Speer recalled in his memoirs, 'he could display a good deal of charm, hard to resist if somewhat condescending. Then he came down to business.'[12] Still exuding *bonhomie*, he told him that he had had a written agreement with Todt, defining the boundaries of his responsibilities. He was having a similar document prepared for Speer, stipulating that in his procurement for the army he could not infringe on areas covered by the Four-Year Plan. Realising that any such agreement would tie his hands completely, since the Plan covered the entire economy, Speer said nothing, and the meeting ended as cordially as it had begun, with smiles and handshakes.

Despite the smiles, Göring soon discovered that he had met his match, as Speer moved fast and with characteristic skill to outflank him, aided by the formidable combination of Hitler and Milch, with whom he had developed very good relations through his work on Luftwaffe construction projects. Milch had invited Speer to a conference in the Great Hall of the Air Ministry the next day, when representatives of the three services were to try to thrash out the problems of their conflicting armament demands with top industrialists. Sensing that this would be a trial of strength, and that he would have to stamp his new authority on everyone involved, Speer took the precaution of going to see Hitler, who was still in Berlin. Hitler had promised him that he could call on him at any time if he felt he needed his support, and he was as good as his word. 'If any steps are taken against you, or if you have difficulties,' he told him, 'interrupt the conference and invite the participants to the Cabinet Room. Then I'll tell those gentlemen whatever is necessary.'[13]

Having tipped off Milch in advance, Speer did just that. After the normal preliminaries at the meeting, Albert Vögler, General Manager of the United Steelworks, declared that the only way of resolving the chaos was by giving one man the sole power of making decisions. The industrialists didn't care who it was. No one suggested Speer. After the army and navy representatives had made their cases, Funk, acting on Göring's orders, nominated Milch, but to everyone's surprise, Milch said that although he was greatly honoured, he could not accept. Speaking for the first time, Speer played his ace by telling the delegates Hitler wished to speak to them in the Cabinet Room at the Chancellery. The conference would reconvene, he said, on the 18th – in his ministry, with himself in the chair.[14]

Hitler kept his promise to Speer, talking for about an hour and leaving no one in any doubt as to who was now in charge. Göring, he said, could no longer look after armaments within the framework of the Four-Year Plan. This task had to be separated from the Plan and handed over to Speer. This clearly amounted to stripping away an important part of Göring's authority, but that was the way it had to be: 'A function was given to a man and then taken away from him again; such things happen. The capacity for increased production was available, but things had been mismanaged.' After listing and praising Speer's abilities and achievements, he ended by telling the delegates that he expected them to co-operate fully with him and to treat him fairly: 'Behave towards him like gentlemen!' he exhorted, using the English word. With Hitler's endorsement still ringing in their ears, the delegates to the resumed conference were quick to declare their support, and to add their signatures to a document confirming Speer's full authority.[15]

Göring was livid when he found out what had happened. He summoned Speer to Carinhall, where he kept him waiting for an hour before appearing in what Speer described as a flowing green-velvet dressing gown and greeting him coolly. He complained bitterly that he had not been invited to the meeting with Hitler, and then, 'with an agility I would not have thought so fat a man capable of, he leaped to his feet and began pacing the big room, frantic with agitation'. Raging against his deputies, he said that by signing Speer's document they had made themselves his underlings for all time to come, and without even asking him. He ended by declaring that he could not accept 'such nibbling away at his power' and threatening to go to Hitler at once and resign as head of the Four-Year Plan.

Speer thought such a resignation would have been no great loss, 'for although at the start Göring had pushed the Four-Year Plan with great energy, by 1942 he was generally regarded as sluggish and distinctly averse to work', as well as increasingly unstable. Unfortunately, Hitler would not have accepted his resignation, but would have dodged the issue by finding some sort of compromise that would have done nothing but create fresh complications for everyone. Speer knew that he could only head Göring off by presenting him with some way of saving face. He assured him that the new arrangement would not impinge in any way on his position, and that he was prepared to work within the framework of the Plan, as his subordinate.[16] A few days later, on 1 March, Göring signed a decree drafted by Speer, appointing him 'Chief Representative for Armaments within the Four-Year Plan', and authorising him 'to give armaments . . . within the whole of the economy the priority which is appropriate for them in wartime'.

Göring was still not entirely won over, grumbling that foreign press reports that he had been downgraded were undermining his prestige with German industry. Speer was quick to realise that what Göring was really worried about was that any such loss of standing might well affect the vast amount of bribes, presents and inducements he received from industry to fund his lavish lifestyle. Demonstrating his acute psychology once again, Speer suggested inviting the top industrialists to a meeting, at which he would make it clear that Göring was still in overall charge. Göring was delighted, and immediately ordered some fifty businessmen to come to Berlin, where Speer kept his promise. 'Thereafter,' Speer wrote later, 'thanks to Göring's lethargy, I was able to work freely and unhampered. No doubt he was often jealous of my successes with Hitler; but during the next two years he hardly ever tried to interfere with anything I was doing.'[17] Over those two years, Speer, working closely with Milch, succeeded in increasing arms production in general, including aircraft, by 300 per cent, and of tanks by 600 per cent. Göring might have been jealous, but he would have been a fool to interfere.

Speer's advancement at his expense was followed swiftly by further blows to Göring's authority. His control of manpower resources was given to Fritz Sauckel, a short, stolid man with a bald head and a minimal toothbrush moustache, who had been Gauleiter of Thuringia since 1926. Speer had wanted Karl Hanke, the man who had given him his first architectural commission for the party in Berlin and who was now Gauleiter of Lower Silesia, to get the job, but this had been blocked by Bormann. Showing his muscle as party boss, he said Hanke had not been a Gauleiter long enough. Hanke's old love affair with

Magda Goebbels may have counted against him, but the real reason for his rejection was undoubtedly that he was Speer's friend, and his loyalty would have been to him rather than to Bormann and the party organisation.

To make doubly sure that Sauckel would not be in Speer's pocket, Bormann persuaded Hitler to make the new commissioner responsible for finding and deploying labour – chiefly from the Ukraine and the Eastern territories – not simply for armaments production but for the whole of German industry. For the sake of appearances and Göring's battered pride, Sauckel was given the title of General Plenipotentiary for the Mobilisation of Labour within the Four-Year Plan, but he was no more answerable to Göring than was Speer: he was directly and only responsible to Hitler, through Bormann.

Accepting the situation, Göring wound up his own labour deployment section, for once voluntarily shedding part of his power – though his decision may have been prompted by foreseeing nothing but trouble ahead. Speer had hardly been confirmed in his new post before Keitel demanded the immediate release for front-line duties of a quarter of a million army troops who had been made available for munitions production. 'That,' Keitel recalled, 'was the beginning of the struggle for manpower, a struggle that was never to end.'[18]

The army's desperate need for men was good news for Himmler, giving him the chance he had been waiting for to expand the Waffen-SS. With Brauchitsch gone and Hitler himself as Commander-in-Chief, the army could no longer block recruitment or equipment: indeed, it was now the Waffen-SS that had priority in both areas, as Keitel complained:

Compared with the Army, the fresh manpower requirements of the navy and air force were minimal, while that of the Waffen-SS rose in a steeply climbing curve, an insatiable siphon skimming the cream of German youth. With the Führer's support, the Waffen-SS had enticed the most valuable sections of German youth into its ranks by means of open and concealed, legal and illegal propaganda methods, and by indirect pressure tactics, too; the best elements of youth, who would have been perfect future commanders and officers for the army, were thereby lost to us.

All my protests to the Führer were in vain; he refused to have anything to do with my arguments. Merely to mention the subject resulted in an angry outburst from him: he knew our distaste and dislike for his Waffen-SS because it was an elite, he said, an elite which was being politically trained in the way he had always had in his mind, something which the army had refused to do; but it was his unalterable intention to channel as many of the finest young men of the whole country into the Waffen-SS as volunteered for it – there would be no limit on the number of volunteers.[19]

Hitler allowed Himmler to form a new SS division, the 'Prinz Eugen', composed mainly of Croat volunteers, and to expand the ethnic German SS cavalry brigade into the 'Florian Geyr' Division, with more to follow. At the same time, he finally granted the Waffen-SS's dearest wish, by converting the four existing formations – the 'Leibstandarte', 'Das Reich', 'Totenkopf' and 'Wiking' – into Panzer divisions, to make up the first SS Panzer Corps.

Himmler's delight at this success was enhanced by a more personal achievement – his mistress, Häschen, gave birth to a son, whom they called Helge, on 15 February. This meant that he had to provide her with a home, since Marga and Gudrun continued to live in his houses in Dahlem and on the Tegernsee. Unfortunately, he had no capital – unlike some other Nazi chieftains he had always been scrupulously correct in his personal finances, living entirely on his salary. Eschewing the easy option of dipping into SS funds, he approached Bormann for a loan of 80,000 marks from the party, and with his help built a new house, whimsically named 'Haus Schneewinkellehen', at Schönau on the Königsee, the neighbouring village to Berchtesgaden.[20] Since spending so much time at Wolfsschanze, Himmler had become close to Bormann, and their friendship deepened as Gerda Bormann, who of course lived on the Obersalzberg, took Häschen under her wing.

By the end of March 1942, after ten weeks of continuous, bitter fighting, the Soviet counteroffensive finally exhausted itself. The Wehrmacht had been driven back up to 100 miles in places, but the line had not broken, and as the spring thaw turned the ground back into a quagmire, both armies were forced to pause. In the West, however, the war in the air was picking up again. At the same time as he was coping with Speer's and Sauckel's inroads into his position, Göring faced a renewed threat from the RAF. The British had stopped their bombing raids the previous November, after suffering unacceptable losses to German flak and night-fighters, but now, under pressure from Stalin to try to divert Luftwaffe resources from the Eastern Front, they started again, strengthened by their new generation of four-engined heavy bombers. On 3 March they struck at the Renault factory on the outskirts of Paris, though most of their bombs landed on workers' houses, killing 623 and injuring 1,500. Five days later they started their new campaign proper with the first of eight raids on Essen, each employing between 100 and 200 aircraft. Essen was heavily defended, and the raids were largely ineffectual. At the end of the month, the British decided to try out the new tactic of area bombing, sending 234 aircraft to fire-bomb the medieval town of Lübeck, to the north of Hamburg, and following this with similar raids on Rostock, with its Heinkel factory, Essen, Hamburg and Dortmund.

Apart from the one on Lübeck, which burnt out the heart of the town, none of the raids was particularly effective, but they did achieve one major objective by tying down an estimated 10,000 anti-aircraft guns which could otherwise have been used in the East. Nevertheless, the Luftwaffe defenders on the ground and in the air were holding their own, and Göring could feel confident again. By way of retaliation for the destruction of Lübeck and Rostock, he ordered a series of raids on English cathedral cities, starting with Exeter and continuing with Bath, Canterbury, Norwich and York, labelled the 'Baedecker raids' after a Foreign Ministry spokesman announced at a press conference that the Luftwaffe would bomb every English building marked with three stars in the Baedecker guidebook.

Göring's confidence was not to last. On 31 May, while he was at Veldenstein, he received an irate call from Hitler saying the RAF had raided Cologne with a massive force of 'hundreds' of bombers; the local Gauleiter had called him personally, and so had Goebbels, who put the number at 250–300. Göring dismissed the reports, saying it was impossible, and that no more than 70 planes had taken part, 44 of which had been shot down – which would have been a superb result. But the true number of attackers had been not just hundreds, but almost 1,000, as Churchill himself announced in London.

Nothing like it had ever been seen before. The recently-appointed Commander-in-Chief of RAF Bomber Command, Air Marshal Arthur Harris, had dredged up virtually every airworthy bomber in Britain, from every possible source, including training establishments and Coastal Command. 1,046 had taken off from 53 different airfields; 39 were shot down, mostly by night-fighters, but about 910 reached and bombed the target. The city was devastated, but not destroyed; amazingly, thanks to excellent shelter provision, only 469 people were killed,

though more than 45,000 were rendered homeless. But the psychological and political damage was enormous.

The Cologne raid was another nail in Göring's coffin. Hitler blamed
him personally for his failure to protect the Reich, complaining to his
adjutant, Nicolaus von Below, that the Luftwaffe had never given the
flak the attention it needed. 'This was the first time I had heard him
criticise Göring,' Below wrote later. 'Hitler never regained absolute
confidence in the Reich Marshal.'[21]

While Göring was recovering from the shock of the 1,000-bomber raid,
Heydrich was fighting for his life. On 27 May, as he drove from his
estate outside Prague to his office in Hradschin Castle, three Czech
agents ambushed his unescorted, open-topped, unarmoured car as it
slowed to take a hairpin bend in the city suburbs. The first man levelled
a Sten gun at him, but it jammed, twice. Instead of hitting the accel-
erator, Heydrich's terrified driver hit the brake, giving the second
assassin time to lob a grenade, which exploded under the car. Heydrich
leaped out, firing his revolver after the fleeing agents, unaware that he
had been wounded until he suddenly collapsed. The explosion had
damaged his spine and driven fragments of metal, leather, horsehair
stuffing and pieces of uniform into his abdomen. He was rushed to
hospital, where Czech surgeons operated to remove the debris from
his internal organs. But the damage was severe, the wounds became
infected and septicaemia set in: in those days before antibiotics, this
meant almost certain death.

Himmler is said to have wept when he heard the news in his field
headquarters. But it was five days before he travelled to Prague to visit
his stricken colleague in hospital, fuelling speculation that he was not
entirely heartbroken at the prospect of losing him. Even when he
dispatched one of the most eminent surgeons in Germany, his friend
Professor Karl Gebhardt, to tend Heydrich, there were many who
wondered if the doctor's mission was not to save him but to make sure
he died, as he did on 4 June after nine days of agony. Heydrich, they
said, had become too powerful, too much of a threat to Himmler, especially now that he had direct access to the Führer. He was said to have
bragged while drunk that he planned to become Minister of the Interior,
taking the RSHA with him and leaving Himmler with an SS shorn of
police, SD and Gestapo. He had even speculated that he rather than
Himmler or Göring might become Hitler's successor, after using the

Reich Protector's job to demonstrate his ability to govern a country. Could it be, the rumour-mongers asked, that Himmler had actually ordered the killing?

In fact, the murder had been ordered by the Czech government-in-exile in London, and the killers had been trained, equipped and parachuted into Prague by the British SOE. The reason was not that Heydrich had inflicted a brutal regime of terror on the people of the Protectorate, but that he had been too soft on them and was winning their support. He had started his rule with all the harshness that was expected of him, earning the nickname 'the Butcher of Prague'. Within hours of his arrival he had arrested the Czech premier, Alois Elias, dragged him through a rigged trial and sentenced him to death, while his Gestapo commandos moved to smash the underground Home Army, arresting everyone who was even suspected of belonging to the resistance, or any opposition group. In two weeks, the Czech resistance movement had been virtually destroyed.

After the stick came the carrot. Heydrich turned off the terror as quickly as he had started it, and proceeded to woo the Czech workers and peasants, whom he needed to increase industrial and agricultural output, with increased wages and rations, supplies of scarce clothes and shoes, holidays in luxury Bohemian spa hotels, and a vastly improved social security system. The policy worked: production increased rapidly and active opposition to German rule all but ceased – to the horror of the government-in-exile. The only way to revive it was to provoke the Germans into a new wave of terror and repression.

Heydrich's assassination was specifically intended to incite the most savage German reprisals, and it succeeded. After conferring with Hitler, Himmler ordered the arrest of 10,000 Czechs as hostages, including the entire intelligentsia as listed in Heydrich's card-index. 100 of these were to be shot that night, along with all political prisoners. Even though the assassins, together with another 120 members of the resistance, were killed in a gun battle in a Prague church after being betrayed by a fellow agent for a large reward, the reprisals went ahead. According to a Gestapo report 1,331 Czechs, including 201 women, were executed immediately. The mining villages of Lezáky and Lidice, the names of which had been found among the dead agents' belongings, were razed, all their adult male inhabitants shot, and the women transported to Ravensbrück concentration camp in Germany. The children were examined by Himmler's racial experts, thirteen of them were selected for

'Germanisation' and taken to a Lebensborn home for adoption by German couples; the rest were shuffled around from camp to camp until they had all died, from disease, starvation or exposure.[22] All told, about 5,000 people were executed in revenge for Heydrich's death. Additionally, 3,000 Czech Jews were pulled out of Theresienstadt model concentration camp and put on trains for 'resettlement' at an extermination camp.

The extermination camps were Heydrich's legacy: after his death, their creation and deadly purpose were given the code-name 'Aktion Reinhard' in his memory, but he had started planning the operation several months earlier. The day after receiving Göring's signature on the document of 31 July 1941, he had informed Himmler: 'It may be safely assumed that in the future there will be no more Jews in the annexed Eastern Territories . . .'[23] It was a bold promise, but it raised two very important questions: where were they to go to, and what was to be done with them when they got there? Heydrich had his eyes on the gulag, the ready-made network of prison and labour camps in Siberia, which accommodated an estimated ten million Soviet citizens. 'As soon as we have reached a clarification of the military situation in the East,' he told Goebbels in the convoluted jargon of the Third Reich, 'they should all in the end be transported into the camps established by the Bolsheviks. These camps had been set up by the Jews. What was more fitting, then, than that they should now also be populated by the Jews?'[24] It was a logical conclusion – the only trouble was, the Germans had to win the war before they could get at the gulag.

The problem was compounded as the year wore on by the start of the evacuation of Jews from the old Reich. Swollen by the trainloads of those deported from the Reich, and with no exits, the already over-crowded ghettos were soon becoming unmanageable. By the time of the annual November gathering in Munich, it was agreed that something drastic would have to be done. On 11 November, Himmler called his newly-appointed HSSPF for North Russia, SS-Obergruppenführer Friedrich Jeckeln, and instructed him to exterminate all the Jews in the Ostland, as the Baltic states had been renamed, 'down to the very last one'. 'Tell Lohse [the Reich Commissar Ostland] it is my order,' he said, 'which is also the Führer's wish.'

Lohse was horrified at the prospect of killing valuable workers and irreplaceable craftsmen, and asked for a ruling from Rosenberg's ministry. 'Were all Jews to be killed,' he asked, 'regardless of economic considerations?' Heydrich had already foreseen the argument that many Jews were essential to the war industries, and dismissed it. There was a risk, he had stated on 4 October, that 'primarily on economic grounds many a claim will be made that the Jews are an indispensable labour force and that no one will make any effort to obtain alternative labour to take the place of the Jews.'[25] Lohse was told that economic considerations did not apply to Jews.

The liquidation of the Riga ghetto began on 30 November. 14,000 Latvian Jews were taken out into the forest and shot, following exactly the same routine as at Babi Yar, Minsk and scores of other murder sites. A planned holding camp outside Riga for 25,000 German Jews *en route* for the East had barely been started, and when the first 1,000 arrived they were simply marched off into the woods and shot alongside the Jews from the ghetto. Five following trains were diverted to Kaunas in Lithuania, but the fate of their passengers was just the same: they were taken out and shot by the local *Einsatzkommando*.

Jeckeln reported the complete liquidation of the Riga ghetto by phone to Himmler, who said he was 'satisfied with the results' and that more trainloads of Jews would be arriving in Latvia shortly. These were also to be liquidated, though he was not yet sure whether he wanted them shot or driven into the swamps to perish: the psychological effects of the mass shootings were causing serious problems of morale and discipline in the *Einsatzkommandos*, and rumbles of protest from the army. New, less stressful – and less public – methods would need to be found, and they soon were.

Even before the trains began bringing thousands of Jews from all over the Reich, there were already well over 100,000 packed into the ghetto at Lodz – renamed Litzmannstadt by the Germans – and the local authorities were vehemently opposed to taking any more. Indeed, the Reich Governor of the Warthegau, SS-Gruppenführer Arthur Greiser, was keen to get rid of those he already had, in any way he could. Unlike Lohse in the Ostland, Greiser had absolutely no scruples where Jews were concerned. He asked Himmler to provide trained executioners to help him liquidate all 100,000 as quickly as possible. The enormous numbers involved ruled out shooting, and Heydrich turned instead to SS-Hauptsturmführer Rudolf Lange and his T4 vans, following the advice of the Chief Medical Officer of the SS, Dr Ernst von Grawitz, that poison gas was the most efficient and humane method.

Lange made his headquarters in an old mansion near Chelmno

(Kulmhof), in the General-Government some forty miles north-west of Lodz, with three vans. He started operations on 8 December with the first consignment of some 700 Jews, who had been driven there from the ghetto on the pretext that they were to be resettled for work in the East. He used the same deception that had worked so well with the euthanasia victims, persuading them to undress and enter the vans in the belief that they were being taken to showers before being issued with new clothes. The vans, with their exhausts diverted into their rears, then drove off to a clearing in the woods a few miles away where pits had been dug. By the time they arrived, the occupants would be dead and could be unloaded directly into their mass graves by a detachment of selected Jews, after they had been searched by Germans and Ukrainians for rings, valuables hidden internally, and gold teeth, which were yanked out with pliers. Jews were not the only ones to die at Chelmno: among the first victims were 5,000 gypsies who had been deported from Germany to the ghetto in Lodz. Once they had been dealt with, Lange's men began systematically removing 700 Jews a day from Lodz to Chelmno.

Unfortunately, Lange's system was never as efficient as it was intended to be, and there were frequent breakdowns. Death was supposed to take no more than fifteen minutes, but it sometimes took hours; often some victims were still alive when the doors were opened. Eichmann, sent by Gestapo Müller to inspect the operation, was deeply shocked by what he saw and – so he later said – rushed away in his car, speechless with horror. After receiving Eichmann's report, Himmler called in Kripo Commissar Christian Wirth, the man who had set up the first experimental gas chambers in Brandenburg for the euthanasia programme, and who had created the idea of disguising them as shower facilities. Himmler ordered him to start equipping a string of new camps with permanent gas chambers in the Lublin region of the General-Government, under the overall supervision of the local HSSPF, Odilo Globocnik – the Trieste-born Austrian Nazi who had taken Göring's phone call in Vienna about government appointments during the *Anschluss*. All the personnel involved were sworn to strict secrecy by Himmler, who told them 'he was making a superhuman-inhuman demand on them, but it was the order of the Führer'.[26]

On 29 November 1941, as the slaughter in Riga was starting, Heydrich had invited a number of state secretaries and SS representatives to a conference in a villa in the lakeside Berlin suburb of Wannsee, at the southern end of the Havel only a few hundred yards from Goebbels's home at Schwanenwerder. The conference was to have been held on 9 December, but with the news of Pearl Harbor, he postponed it until 2 January 1942, and then again until 20 January, by which time more than 40,000 Jews and gypsies had been murdered at Chelmno.

The Wannsee conference was not concerned with policy – this had already been decided: the Jews were to be removed and exterminated, and there could be no argument or discussion about it. The conference was called to deal with the practical problems of putting this into effect, and the participants were not ministers but bureaucrats, most of them lawyers, trained to handle details dispassionately and thoroughly. The fourteen high civil servants and party officials represented all the government departments involved: the East Ministry, the Interior Ministry, the Justice Ministry, the Four-Year Plan, the General-Government and the Foreign Ministry, plus the RSHA, the Race and Resettlement Main Office, the Security Police, the Party Chancellery, and the Reich Chancellery. Eichmann acted as secretary, taking the minutes with a stenographer. It was all very calm, orderly and matter-of-fact.

Heydrich began by establishing his own authority, announcing that Göring had appointed him 'Plenipotentiary for the Preparation of the Final Solution of the European Jewish Question', and had charged him with producing 'an overall plan concerning the organisational, factual and material measures necessary' for the desired final solution. Such a plan, Heydrich explained, required 'prior joint consultation' of all the agencies involved, 'in view of the need for parallel lines of action', and that was the purpose of this conference. Himmler, he said, would hold overall responsibility for the operation, regardless of geographic boundaries. He then reminded the meeting that all emigration to foreign countries had been banned, and replaced by evacuation to the East. This, however, was 'merely a matter of expediency', which would provide valuable experience for the 'approaching final solution of the Jewish problem'.

The solution, Heydrich declared, concerned the whole of Europe, not just Germany and the conquered territories. There were only 131,800 Jews left in the old Reich, but there were 5 million in the Soviet Union, 2,994,684 in the Ukraine, 2,284,000 in the General-Government, 742,000 in Hungary, 700,000 in unoccupied France and her North African possessions, 58,000 in Italy, and so the catalogue continued. Even Britain and Ireland were included in the list, with 330,000 and 4,000 respectively. All told, including the neutral countries, the total according to the RSHA came to about 11 million. To dispose of them, 'Europe will be combed from West to East'.

Jews capable of work in the East, Heydrich declared, would be 'separated by sex and led in large labour columns to build roads, whereby a large proportion will no doubt fall away through natural reduction'. In the perverted Darwinism that informed Nazi thinking, he warned that those who survived would have to be 'dealt with appropriately', since they would be the 'toughest elements' who would form 'the germ cell from which the Jewish race could regenerate itself'.

Sitting around the polished table in the comfortable villa, normally used as a rest and recreation home for SS personnel, the officials worked steadily through the day, meticulously co-ordinating and planning the great forced exodus, and addressing such intractable problems as defining the status of part-Jews, and those in mixed marriages. Only as the meeting drew to its close was there any direct discussion 'of the various types of solution possibilities', though Eichmann's carefully oblique minutes do not go into any detail.[27]

When the conference was over, Heydrich relaxed for a little while, pleased that everything had gone so well. 'I remember,' Eichmann recalled later, 'that . . . Heydrich, Müller and myself sat very cosily near the stove and then I saw Heydrich smoke for the first time, and I thought to myself, "Heydrich smoking today": I'd never seen him do that. "He is drinking brandy": I hadn't seen him do that for years. . . . We all sat together like comrades. Not to talk shop, but to rest after long hours of effort.'[28]

The first of the new camps, built specifically as extermination centres using carbon monoxide, opened on 17 March 1942 at Belzec, on the Lvov–Lublin rail line. It had six gas chambers, designed to look like 'a sort of bath house', with 'geraniums, then a little stairway and then, on each side, three rooms 16 feet x 16 feet x 6 feet with wooden doors like a garage. The rear wall was formed by large wooden folding doors. As a "thoughtful little witticism" a Star of David was painted on the roof.'[29] For all their friendly appearance, those six rooms were capable of killing 15,000 people a day. The production line for murder was in business. A second camp, at Sobibor, some 100 miles east of Lublin, was opened in April with a capacity of 20,000 a day, and a third, at

Treblinka, seventy-five miles north-east of Warsaw, started work three months later and soon had no fewer than thirty gas chambers capable of dealing with 25,000 a day. In the autumn, gas chambers were introduced to the existing concentration camp at Lublin, which was later known as Majdanek.

Auschwitz was also pressed into service during the spring, with a special extension to the main camp, across the railway line in the birch wood known as Birkenau. Following his success with Zyklon B on Soviet prisoners of war, camp commandant Höss had refined the process through further experiments using several hundred Jews from various cities in Upper Silesia, conducted in a converted farmhouse in Birkenau. Now, he was told to construct large new gas chambers to use Zyklon B, and authorised to order crematoria to dispose of the bodies, rather than burying them, which was becoming a problem at all the camps. In some, the decomposing bodies had swelled and forced open the tops of the burial pits, emerging from the ground like accusing zombies. Obsessed with the need for secrecy, Himmler ordered that the mass graves be exhumed and the bodies burned on great pyres, with any remaining bones ground to dust, so that there could be no chance of counting them. The resulting ash and powder were sold as agricultural fertiliser and bone meal.

Unlike the other locations, Auschwitz was not a remote village in the wilds of eastern Poland but a sizeable town in what was now part of the Reich, and at a major rail junction. While the other three camps were intended to dispose of the Jews in the General-Government, the new facility at Auschwitz was to deal with those from further afield, including Western Europe. The first arrivals, on 26 March, were 999 Slovak Jewish women. They were followed every few days for the next month by further transports of men and women from Slovakia. In the meantime, on 30 March, 1,112 Jews arrived from Paris, mainly Polish Jews who had fled to France at the start of the war, and who had been rounded up and held in a detention camp at Compiègne.

Auschwitz was also different from the four new camps in several other respects, the most important of which was that it was not solely dedicated to death but was primarily a slave labour camp for Poles and Soviet prisoners of war. The new extension at Birkenau, however, covering a vast area of more than 175 hectares divided into sections by electrified barbed-wire fences, was reserved entirely for Jews. It accommodated 100,000 people in crude wooden barracks, while in Auschwitz itself there were only 18,000. Auschwitz was built originally to serve the IG Farben industrial complex at Birkenau and other works in the surrounding districts of East Upper Silesia: coal mines, synthetic fuel and rubber factories, and several hundred other military and industrial plants, which had relocated to the area from Germany, attracted by substantial tax breaks and the opportunity to make great profits through the use of cheap labour. By the end of 1942, there would be thirty-nine labour sub-camps in the area to supply it.

Jews deported to Auschwitz-Birkenau were not automatically killed. On arrival, old people, children and the sick were sent straight to the gas chambers, but men and women judged fit for work were marched away, tattooed on the arm with a serial number, and housed in barracks from which they would be sent each day to their allotted jobs, hired out to industry at three marks a day. Consequently, although the death rate was inevitably high due to bad conditions, lack of food, maltreatment and overwork, several thousand Auschwitz prisoners managed to survive until the end of the war. From the four other camps combined, the total of survivors was only 109. The final tally of deaths at Auschwitz-Birkenau would reach between 1.2 and 1.5 million, of whom about 800,000 were Jews. During the fifteen months following the first killings at Chelmno, the four other death camps accounted for some 2 million victims. At least another million, meanwhile, were slaughtered by the *Einsatzgruppen*.

Heydrich's death at the beginning of June 1942 did nothing to delay or disrupt Aktion Reinhard, which by then had developed its own deadly momentum. The 'Jewish question' had always been at the heart of Himmler's whole philosophy. The elimination of all Jews from the region was a vital first step in clearing the East for the great German settlement programme that he envisaged, with himself as the liege lord, for which he had set up a special department that had spent the first five months of 1942 preparing a detailed grand plan. With Heydrich gone, he simply stepped up his personal involvement, especially in the death camps.

In mid July, he paid a visit to Auschwitz, touring the various sections, inspecting the farm and the agricultural laboratories and plantations with their breeding and growing experiments, and the herb gardens, and going over the plans for future development with Höss. In the hospital block, he was briefed on the progress of the medical experiments, including sterilisation of Jewish women by injection and the castration of men by X-ray, to both of which he had given his approval a few days before. But when Höss and his camp doctors complained about the high illness and mortality rates among prisoners caused by overcrowding, lack of nourishment and poor sanitation, Himmler showed no sympathy. 'For an SS-Führer there are no problems,' he told Höss. 'His task is continually to remove problems himself immediately they appear! Over the *how*, *you* blow your brains out, not I!'[30]

The highlight of the trip was undoubtedly the visit to Birkenau, to inspect the existing gas chamber and the construction site for a combined 'underground changing room–gas chamber–crematorium' complex. Satisfied with this, Himmler was then taken to Auschwitz rail station, to view the arrival of two trains bringing the first Jews deported from Holland. The spur taking trains directly into Birkenau had not yet been built, and the selection process by an SS doctor took place on the platform itself. The able-bodied men and women were lined up and marched off to their barracks; the rest were loaded into trucks to be driven to the 'shower room'.

Himmler and his entourage followed, so that he could watch the entire grisly process from beginning to end, watching impassively as the naked women's heads and bodies were shaved and the hair packed into sacks to be taken away and sold as stuffing for luxury mattresses. As the doors of the gas chamber were closed and sealed, he looked though the observation window at the packed mass of humanity screaming, clawing, vomiting, shitting and wetting themselves as they died. It took twenty minutes. 'The screaming, the elderly, the ill, the frail and children collapsed first,' Höss wrote afterwards. 'He [Himmler] viewed the extermination process in complete silence, saying nothing at all. Several times he watched me unobtrusively and the Führers and Unterführers taking part.'[31] No doubt he was comparing the effect this method of killing was having with the traumas caused by shooting.

Himmler himself appeared to be less affected than he had been by the shootings at Minsk. After inspecting the IG Farben 'Buna' synthetic rubber and oil plant, he joined the camp's officers in the mess for dinner, chatting amiably with them about their families and careers, apparently quite unconcerned by what he had witnessed during the day. And when dinner was over, he and his entourage, together with Höss and his wife, accepted an invitation from the Gauleiter of Upper Silesia to visit his residence in Kattowitz, where according to Höss, he was 'in best sparkling form'. He charmed the two ladies present, and led the conversation in a variety of innocuous topics, ranging from children's education, new houses, books and pictures, to his personal experiences of visits to the front with the Führer. He even drank a glass of red wine and smoked a cigar, with evident enjoyment.

The next day, it was back to business. With his old-world attitude to women, Himmler had decreed that only he could authorise corporal punishment for them. A professional prostitute in the camp had been caught stealing, and Himmler decided she should be beaten in his presence, so that he could see the effect for himself. The woman was brought out, strapped across a vaulting horse, and given five lashes across her bare backside. Himmler watched, but again said nothing. He completed his tour by inspecting the camp's domestic arrangements, and the section devoted to sorting the belongings of the dead Jews, again without showing any emotion. Complimenting Höss on his work, he promoted him to SS-Obersturmbannführer (lieutenant-colonel), and told him Auschwitz was to become a major centre for SS armament manufacture. He ordered him to exterminate all gypsies not capable of work, warned him to expect increased numbers of Jews and said that he must speed up the building of the crematorium complexes. Then, switching on the charm again, he called on Höss's wife to pay his respects and chat to her and the children before he left.

The two trainloads of Jews watched by Himmler at Auschwitz-Birkenau marked the start of the assault on Western Jewry proper. It was somehow fitting that they came from Holland, where the Reich Commissioner was Arthur Seyss-Inquart, the man who had delivered his fellow Austrians to Hitler in 1938. He had been promoted to the rank of SS-Obergruppenführer (lieutenant-general), for his role in the *Anschluss*, and despite his mild and intelligent manner was as zealous as any other SS general in pursuing the Nazi dream. He had imposed the wearing of the yellow star on Dutch Jews in May, and began deporting them in mid July, with a cold efficiency that eventually sent 110,000 to Auschwitz and later Sobibor, of whom only 6,000 survived. Soon afterwards, the Jews of the rest of Western Europe – Belgium, France, Scandinavia – and then the Balkans, followed.

There was no let up, meanwhile, in the Eastern carnage. On 19 July, the day after his visit to Auschwitz, Himmler wrote to Friedrich-Wilhelm Krüger, his HSSPF East in Cracow, using the familiar euphemism but making his meaning quite clear: 'I command that the resettlement of the entire Jewish population of the General-Government shall have been carried out and completed by 31 December 1942.'[32]

The largest group of Jews in the General-Government were herded together in the ghetto of Warsaw – some 400,000 souls crammed into an area approximately two and a half miles long by one mile wide, a district that had previously housed 160,000, and penned in by high walls. On 22 July, their 'resettlement' began. The head of the Jewish community, Adam Czerniakow, was ordered to assemble 6,000 people a day for deportation, and told that if he failed, his wife would be shot. The next day, he committed suicide. But the deportations continued. Over the following ten weeks, 310,322 Jews were 'resettled' to Treblinka, the camp that had been built especially for this purpose. As Himmler's industrialised death factories got into their terrible stride, the numbers became incomprehensible in their obscenity.

XXXII

THE BEGINNING OF THE END

HITLER summoned Goebbels to the Wolfsschanze on 19 March 1942, to discuss the announcement of cuts in the food rations, something that needed to be handled with great care if public morale was not to be severely damaged. Deprived of his daily conversations with the Führer, the Propaganda Minister was eager to re-assert his position as his most radical lieutenant – no easy task when the opposition included Himmler and Bormann, both of whom were in regular attendance. He wanted to unburden himself of a long list of concerns, which he felt had been neglected because of Hitler's absence from Berlin and his obsession with the war in the East. Civilian morale, Goebbels believed, had deteriorated to such an extent that it could only be restored by truly radical measures, but his efforts in this respect were being frustrated by people with vested interests. All his old socialist instincts came flooding back as he accused the rich of using the black market to avoid the hardships being suffered by the rest of the population. But when Göring, of all people, had introduced a stringent law banning the black market, Funk, as Economics Minister, had intervened to soften its impact.

Goebbels had been scandalised to see soldiers returning to duty on the Eastern Front having to stand in the corridors of trains, 'while fine ladies, returning suntanned from holiday, naturally had their sleeping compartments'. He hoped to obtain the support of Bormann and the party to persuade Hitler that they should introduce tough new measures, including a law under which 'all offences against known National Socialist principles of leadership of the people in times of war will be punished with appropriate retribution'.[1]

Above all, Goebbels wanted to introduce total mobilisation of the home front, with every single aspect of life geared to the war effort – too many inessential consumer goods were still being produced, taking up precious manpower and resources. And on the question of manpower, he believed much of the chronic labour shortage could be solved by introducing compulsory war work for women, who had made a notable contribution to the German munitions industry during the First World War. In both Britain and America, women were filling the factories, while in the Reich they were still largely confined to the home.

When he brought his worries to Hitler, who was looking grey and old after the strains of the winter, he found he was pushing at an open door on most of the issues. Hitler shared his concern about the problems of morale on the home front, and his contempt for a legal establishment that constantly obstructed the radical approach that was needed. A surprising amount of the traditional German legal system still survived – judges, for instance, still enjoyed a great deal of freedom and could not be removed, even by the Führer. And Hitler had been deeply rankled when Colonel-General Hoepner, whom he had dismissed in January along with Guderian, took the government to court for the restitution of his pension rights, and won.

Goebbels complained that the acting Justice Minister, Franz Schlegelberger, a civil servant who had filled the post temporarily since the death of Franz Gürtner the previous year, often blocked his requests for action against the Jews, on the grounds that they were not covered by any existing law. This even extended to their removal to Auschwitz, since the camp was located within the Reich – though there seemed to be no legal obstacle to their deportation to territories that had not been incorporated.

Playing on Hitler's annoyance over the Hoepner affair and other cases where judges had imposed sentences that he believed were too light, Goebbels attacked the 'failure' of the judicial system and pressed him to appoint a new Justice Minister. He pushed for Otto Thierack, the hanging judge who was currently presiding over the notorious People's Court, trying cases of treason and other serious offences against the regime. Thierack was an SA-Gruppenführer and, Goebbels said, 'a real National Socialist'. Hitler took his time, as usual, but finally appointed Thierack in August. By then, however, the role of Justice Minister was largely academic.

On Sunday, 26 April, Hitler had the Reichstag convened for his final assault on the legal system, in which he demanded the right to dismiss anyone from office, including judges 'who visibly fail to recognise the demands of the hour'. It was left to Göring, as Reichstag President, to propose a decree granting Hitler, as 'Leader of the Nation, Supreme Commander of the Wehrmacht, Head of Government and Supreme Holder of Executive Power, as Supreme Law-Lord, and Leader of the Party', the power, 'without being bound by existing legal precepts', to remove from office and to punish anyone, of whatever status, failing to carry out his duty, without respect to pension rights, and without any stipulated formal proceedings'. The resolution was, of course, approved unanimously. It was the last ever to be passed: the Reichstag never met again. From then on, Hitler was not simply above the law, he was the law. His orders had the strength of law, and his first order was to remove Hoepner's pension, retroactively.

The only one of Goebbels's proposals which Hitler did not agree with was the employment of women, which went against Nazi principles. Goebbels was not the only one seeking to change this: Speer was also keen to tap into this readily available source of labour for his munitions factories, but when he suggested this to Sauckel at the beginning of April, the new Labour Commissioner reacted with horror. Speer managed to persuade him to take the question to Göring for a decision, but was disappointed again at Carinhall. 'I was scarcely allowed to advance my arguments,' Speer recalled. 'Sauckel and Göring continually interrupted me. Sauckel laid great weight on the danger that factory work might inflict moral harm upon German womanhood; not only might their "psychic and emotional life" be affected, but also their ability to bear. Göring totally concurred. But to be absolutely sure, Sauckel went to Hitler immediately after the conference and had him confirm the decision."

To add insult to injury, Sauckel then informed all his fellow Gauleiters – who of course included Goebbels – of his victory over Speer, and rubbed it in by announcing a further concession that he had obtained: 'In order to provide the German housewife, above all mothers of many children . . . with tangible relief from her burdens, the Führer has commissioned me to bring into the Reich from the Eastern territories some four to five hundred thousand select, healthy, and strong girls.'[3] Most of these half million girls went to the households of party functionaries, adding to the incredible number of 1.4 million domestic servants still employed in the Reich in the middle of the war.

*　　*　　*

When 'Operation Blue', Hitler's second summer offensive against the Soviet Union, opened on 28 June 1942, the German war machine was riding high again. Preliminary offensives had secured the Crimea and the Kerch Peninsula, and this had been followed by a major victory in countering a Soviet move to recapture Kharkov, the Soviet Union's fifth largest city and the main administrative and rail centre of the eastern Ukraine: in a fierce battle, the Red Army had lost more than a quarter of a million men and 1,200 tanks. On the Leningrad front, the Germans surrounded and destroyed all nine divisions of the Second Shock Army, under Lieutenant-General Andrei Vlasov, who was captured and changed sides, disgusted at the lack of support he had received from Stalin. In North Africa, Rommel, whose force included eight Italian divisions as well as the two armoured divisions and one motorised infantry division of the German Afrika Korps, had captured Tobruk and pushed forward to El Alamein, a mere sixty-five miles from Alexandria. Although he was in fact at the end of his strength, he seemed poised to capture Egypt and the Suez Canal and sweep on to the oilfields of the Middle East before linking up with the German armies already advancing towards the Caucasus. A jubilant Hitler promoted him instantly to Field Marshal, even though he was only commanding a corps. At sea, U-boats and aircraft were taking a heavy toll of Allied convoys carrying vital aid to the Soviet Union, and sinking 700,000 tons a month of British and American shipping in the Atlantic.

Despite its successes, the Wehrmacht did not have the strength to attack along the whole front this time: Hitler had less than half the number of men that he had had for Barbarossa, even with 52 divisions provided by his allies: 27 Romanian, 13 Hungarian, 9 Italian, 2 Slovak and 1 Spanish. Instead, he concentrated on the southern part of the front, with the strategic objectives of destroying Soviet reserves, taking Stalingrad, and capturing the oilfields of the Caucasus. 'If I do not get the oil of Maikop and Grozny,' he told General Friedrich Paulus, commander of Sixth Army, 'then I must end this war.'[4]

Goebbels enthusiastically joined in a deception exercise to persuade Stalin that the German attack would be aimed at Moscow. He placed articles in newspapers such as the *Frankfurter Zeitung*, with its sizeable foreign circulation, and sent a publisher, Otto Kriegk, first to the centre of the Eastern Front and then to Lisbon, that hive of Allied intelligence agents, where he pretended to get drunk in bars and indulged in apparently loose talk. Goebbels's activities in this field were characteristically naive, and probably achieved little, since Stalin was already convinced that Moscow would be the German target – indeed, when the real plans fell into his hands after a German aircraft carrying them crashed behind Soviet lines, he believed they were a plant and refused to be fooled. But Goebbels's efforts did bring him praise from Hitler, which for him at least made them worthwhile.

Operation Blue started splendidly. By 6 July Fourth Panzer Army had captured the city of Voronezh and Sixth Army had reached the River Don, with negligible losses. Two days later the second phase began, and the campaign as a whole was soon a whole month ahead of schedule. Much of the credit for this was due to the Luftwaffe, which was performing brilliantly – although it was vastly outnumbered, it was flying up to 3,000 sorties a day, ten times as many as the Red Air Force – and Göring's stock rose accordingly.

To be nearer the action, Hitler moved his headquarters on 16 July from Wolfsschanze to a collection of log huts at Vinnitsa in the western Ukraine, code-named 'Werwolf'. The site was as ill-chosen as Wolfsschanze, for it was hot, humid and swarming with malarial mosquitoes, and Hitler complained that it gave him a permanent headache. Nevertheless, the whole circus was forced to move there, though no one outside of Hitler's immediate entourage had regular quarters in the area, since the location was only intended to be temporary. Göring parked *Asia* at Kalinovka, about half an hour's drive away, but spent as little time there as possible.

One of Göring's more pressing reasons for spending time in Berlin was to talk to oil experts, discussing how to bring the Soviet oilfields back into production once they were captured. The experts were not optimistic, assuming that the retreating Soviets would have destroyed the well-heads – and they were right. When First Panzer Army advanced to take Maikop on 9 August, they were guided by the flames and dense black smoke of the burning wells. Even when the fires were put out, the Germans would need at least 120 rigs to drill new wells. They had none, and Göring had not allocated enough steel to build them.

Stalin needed the oil as much as Hitler. He still had Grozny and the immense fields at Baku, but he needed a clear passage up the Volga River from the Caspian Sea to get it to the central Soviet Union. If the Germans took Stalingrad, they could block the Volga and at the same time cut the road and rail links between the Caucasus and central Russia, and all would be lost. On 21 August, after destroying most of the Soviet Fourth Tank Army, Paulus launched Sixth Army from the

Don towards the Volga, covering the 90 kilometres in a two-day dash, behind waves of dive-bombers. On the afternoon of 23 August, his troops arrived on the west bank of the Volga in the northern suburbs of Stalingrad, and his guns began shelling the city.

Much of Stalingrad was already in ruins. Earlier that day General von Richthofen, now Commander-in-Chief of Göring's Fourth Air Fleet, had sent 600 bombers – Ju-88s, He-111s and Ju-87 Stukas – in wave after wave to pulverise the city in a demonstration of carpet bombing that more than matched the British attack on Cologne. Hitler himself had decreed that Fourth Air Fleet's entire strength was to be concentrated on the Stalingrad front for the beginning of the offensive, so that when it began it would be supported by 1,200 aircraft, half of them fighters in a ground-attack role. The bombers flew a total of 1,600 sorties that first day, dropping 1,000 tons of bombs for the loss of three aircraft. They returned every day for a week, by which time they had killed 40,000 people and created vast fields of ruins and rubble which provided perfect cover for determined defenders.

Once they had reached the Volga, there was in fact no need for the Germans to occupy Stalingrad itself, but for Hitler the city held an almost mystical significance. Originally known as Tsaritsyn, it had been held for the Reds in the Russian Civil War of 1918 by Voroshilov, Budenny and Stalin. All three claimed credit for the victory, but when Stalin assumed absolute power he rewrote the history books to give himself all the honour, renamed the city and turned its defence into a Soviet military legend. Along with Leningrad, Stalingrad was one of the two 'holy cities' of Soviet Russia. If Hitler could capture it, he believed, he would destroy Stalin as well as achieving an immense prestige victory in the eyes of the rest of the world.

The battle for Stalingrad began in earnest on 13 September, and quickly developed into a savage struggle through streets, houses and factories. For two months the two sides fought with guns, grenades, bayonets, knives and even sharpened shovels. At first, it seemed the Germans must prevail. But the city was held by the Soviet Sixty-Second Army under a new young general, Vassili Chuikov, whose tactical flair was matched by an unbreakable nerve. Even when his front was reduced to a few hundred yards, with entire divisions reduced to barely 500 men, his determination never flagged. Nor did that of the men under his command, men like Sergeant Pavlov of the 13th Guards Division, who crammed sixty soldiers with rifles, mortars, heavy machine-guns and anti-tank weapons into a four-storey house and held it against every assault for an incredible fifty-eight days. Or the eighteen survivors in 138th Divisional HQ, who took on seventy German tommy-gunners in hand-to-hand fighting and successfully beat them off.[5]

Enraged by his armies' failure to score more quick victories in either the Caucasus or Stalingrad – though in both cases this was due to his own orders – Hitler lashed out at his subordinates as usual, dismissing generals left, right and centre. He fired Field Marshal List from Army Group A in the Caucasus, and took command himself. He fell out with Jodl and Keitel, and would have replaced them with Paulus and Kesselring, but decided the military situation in Stalingrad and North Africa was too bad for such a change in the OKW leadership at that time. But Halder was not so lucky. His attempt to tell Hitler that the Soviets were producing at least 1,200 new tanks a month, and could raise around 1.5 million fresh troops led to a blazing row in front of the headquarters staff and on 24 September Hitler told him he had to go. 'Half of my nervous exhaustion is due to you,' he told him in parting. 'It is not worth going on. We need National Socialist ardour now, not professional ability. I cannot expect this of an officer of the old school like you.'[6]

Halder was replaced by the forty-seven-year-old Major-General Kurt Zeitzler, Chief of Staff to Rundstedt in the West, who was not only eleven years younger than Halder but also more dynamic, and a firm believer in Hitler. Keitel did not think he was the right man for the job, but Göring was prominent among those who supported his appointment. Unlike Halder, Zeitzler had no difficulty in passing on Hitler's orders forbidding Paulus from attempting to withdraw his exhausted men from Stalingrad.

The autumn of 1942 was a bad time for the Germans altogether as many of their earlier successes were reversed. In the Battle of the Atlantic, the dominance of Dönitz's U-boats was broken by improved Allied convoy tactics, by new developments in radar and high frequency radio direction finding gear, and by the introduction of very long range aircraft, notably specially equipped Liberators, to patrol what had been the 600-mile gap in air cover in mid ocean. In October, more U-boats were sunk than were launched – thirteen against eleven – while for the first time the Americans and British built more ships than were sunk. The great sea battle was by no means over, but the Germans no longer had things all their own way.

With the build-up of Allied strength in Britain, the threat of a cross-Channel invasion had been highlighted on 19 August, when a Canadian and British force mounted a large-scale raid on Dieppe. Although the operation had been misconceived and totally botched, it did serve to remind Hitler of the danger. Shortly afterwards he called Göring and Speer to a meeting with a small group of generals, and ordered them to start constructing an Atlantic Wall with 15,000 bunkers to defend the French coast.

The Mediterranean, however, was the area of the most immediate concern. Malta had withstood a fearsome and sustained aerial bombardment, and had been reinforced by sea convoys bringing supplies, and the US aircraft carrier *Wasp*, from which sixty-one precious Spitfires flew into the island to drive the Luftwaffe bombers from the sky. Guided by intelligence supplied by the Enigma cipher-breakers under the code-name 'Ultra', ships and planes based in Malta were able to cut German and Italian supply lines to North Africa, sinking three-quarters of all their ships. Meanwhile, the British had appointed two new generals – Bernard Law Montgomery to head the Eighth Army in the Western Desert and Harold Alexander as Commander-in-Chief Middle East – who between them put new heart into the British and Commonwealth troops and fresh purpose into the planning of a new offensive. On 23 October, Montgomery launched his attack on the newly renamed German–Italian Panzer Army at El Alamein.

Rommel was recuperating from illness in Germany, where Goebbels had pressed him into PR service, including appearances at Sportpalast rallies. He flew back at once to Egypt, but by the time he arrived at El Alamein, the battle was already lost to Montgomery's vastly superior forces, backed by the RAF's total command of the air. The fighting continued for several days, but on 2 November Montgomery's infantry and armour broke through the German–Italian lines. True to form, Hitler ordered Rommel to stay put: 'In the situation in which you now find yourself, there can be no other consideration save that of holding fast, of not retreating one step, of throwing every man and every gun into the battle . . . It would not be the first time in history that the stronger will prevailed over numerically stronger enemy battalions. But you cannot show your battalions any other way than that which leads to victory or death.'[7] Rommel obediently if reluctantly halted the withdrawal he had already begun. However, he sent a messenger, the former director of Goebbels's Press Department, now attached to the Afrika

Korps, Alfred-Ingemar Berndt, to explain the situation to Hitler, who had moved back to Wolfsschanze at the end of October. With Goebbels's help, Berndt managed to persuade him to revoke his order, and the Afrika Korps was saved, but only for the moment.

On 5 November, as the Eighth Army broke through Rommel's fall-back defence line at Fuka, Montgomery announced that the British and Commonwealth forces had won a complete and absolute victory in Egypt, and that the Afrika Korps was in full retreat. Rommel's second-in-command, General Ritter von Thoma, was one of nine generals among the 10,000 Germans and 20,000 Italians taken prisoner. All over Britain, church bells sounded in celebration, ringing for the first time since 1940, when their use was reserved for raising the alarm in case of invasion. Churchill, speaking from the Lord Mayor of London's Mansion House a few days later, delivered one of his most memorable and prophetic sentences. 'This is not the end,' he intoned. 'It is not even the beginning of the end. But it is, perhaps, the end of the beginning.'

In Berlin, Göring received reports that Luftwaffe reconnaissance planes had spotted a great Allied armada passing through the Straits of Gibraltar, heading into the Mediterranean. With no real idea of its destination, he presumed that it was carrying fresh forces to Libya, and called Kesselring, who was now based in Rome as Wehrmacht Commander-in-Chief South-West, to tell him it must be stopped as soon as it came within range of his aircraft. 'If the convoy should be beaten, decimated, destroyed, dispersed,' he said, it would reduce the importance of Rommel's defeat at El Alamein to no more than a tactical breakthrough. The Führer, he continued, had asked him to tell Kesselring that attacking this convoy must be given absolute priority:

Tomorrow, you are to deliver an appeal to your men stating that their actions, their capacity for sacrifice, their courage, their stamina, will redound to the glory of the German Luftwaffe. Tell them that I expect every German airman to do his utmost, even to the supreme sacrifice. The convoy is to be attacked without pause, day and night, wave after wave.

When the airmen load their bombs, tell them their job is to attack the aircraft carriers so that the planes can't land or take off. Next, hit the troop transports: *matériel* without men is worthless.

No other operations are to take place beside those against this convoy. It

is the most important convoy. It is Number One. You are to direct the operations against it in person.[8]

While the Allied convoy steamed on, Göring kept busy with the
normal duties of his multifarious roles. Stung by insinuations that he
was losing his hold on the economic sphere, he had delivered a rebuke
to Speer on 5 November. 'For the sake of historical truth,' he wrote,
'I should like to make it absolutely plain that I have not relaxed my
grip on the essentials of the Four-Year Plan for one instant. A glance
at the dates of the conferences and sessions, at their minutes, at the
decrees, laws, and ordinances that I have issued throughout this war,
should satisfy you immediately that I continue to shape the crucial
affairs of the Four-Year Plan despite my preoccupation with the
Luftwaffe.'[9] A glance at his office diary for 7 November is enough to
give the lie to those who accused him of indolence: he had twenty-
four appointments that day involving fifty-two people, including
Himmler, Sauckel, Ley, Milch, Rust and Mölders's widow, followed by
a board meeting of HGW-Romania.[10]

The next morning, there was further news of the Allied armada –
and it was not good. The ships had not come within range of
Kesselring's aircraft in the eastern Mediterranean but had made instead
for Algeria and French Morocco, where they had started landing the
first of 100,000 American and British troops under the command of
General Dwight D. Eisenhower. The Americans were now involved in
the European land war, as well as fighting the Japanese in the Pacific.

Incredibly in view of the situation in North Africa and the Soviet Union,
Hitler had taken time out from his duties as Supreme Commander of
the Wehrmacht, Commander-in-Chief of the Army and Commander-
in-Chief of Army Group A, to meet up with his old comrades from
1923 for their annual beer fest in Munich. At dawn on 8 November,
his train was stopped at a small station in the Thuringian Forest for
him to be given a message from the Foreign Ministry, informing him
of the Allied landings in North Africa.[11]

At Bamberg, a little further down the line, the train stopped again
to take on board an agitated Ribbentrop. He had been making a rare
visit to Berlin, believing it was safe to be out of touch with his Führer
during the Munich reunion, which as a Johnny-come-lately he was not
entitled to attend, but had flown down immediately he heard the news.

Without waiting to consult him, Hitler had already sent a telegram to Otto Abetz, the Nazi Ambassador to the Vichy government in Paris, instructing him to demand that the French government should break off relations with Washington, provide the Luftwaffe with facilities in North Africa, declare war on the Allies and fight the invasion along-side the Germans.

Ribbentrop, utterly failing to read Hitler's intentions and still clinging to his belief that Britain was the real enemy, tried to take advantage of the situation by remounting the hobby horse that Barbarossa had forced him to abandon eighteen months before. If, as seemed prob-able, they could not expel the British and Americans, he said, then Africa and the Axis forces there were lost, the Mediterranean would be wide open to the enemy, and Italy would be in trouble. The Führer, he continued, needed to make 'a decisive reduction of his war commit-ments', and he asked for permission to contact Stalin through the Soviet Embassy in Stockholm to begin negotiating a peace settlement. He believed this could be achieved, though 'if need be, most of the conquered territories would have to be given up'.

It would have been glaringly obvious to anyone except Ribbentrop what Hitler's reaction would be. But the obtuse Foreign Minister was amazed when he became 'hysterical': 'He flushed, jumped to his feet and told me with indescribable violence that all he wanted to discuss was Africa – nothing else.'[12] What was truly amazing was that Ribbentrop survived – had he been a general, he would have been sacked on the spot, without a pension.

In Munich, Hitler delayed his speech to the 'Old Fighters' until the evening, while he conferred in the 'Brown House' with Goebbels, Himmler, Ribbentrop and Keitel on what to do about France and Italy. The French Premier, Pierre Laval, had immediately agreed to Hitler's first two demands – breaking off relations with Washington and providing facilities for the Luftwaffe – but was havering on the other two, and there were serious doubts about the attitude of French forces in North Africa, who might well choose to join the Allied invaders rather than resisting them. Hitler resolved to occupy the rest of France, in order to forestall any possible Allied invasion in the south, and summoned Laval to come at once from Vichy to Munich. He also invited Mussolini, who pleaded illness and sent Ciano in his place.

In his delayed speech to the 'Old Fighters', Hitler made no mention of the Allied landings, and airily dismissed Rommel's defeat at El Alamein as nothing more than a brief hiccup. Stalingrad, he told them, was all over apart from a little mopping up: 'I wanted to take it and, you know, we are modest: we have it. There are only a few tiny places there.' He was taking his time, he said, because he did not want another Verdun.[13]

In France itself, there was no chance of another Verdun. On 11 November, with Laval being kept safely out of the way by Ribbentrop and told nothing, German and Italian troops moved in to occupy the whole of southern France apart from the Toulon naval base, where there might have been resistance – indeed, when German tanks finally moved in on 27 November, the French navy promptly scuttled all the ships anchored there and blew up their munitions dumps, oil storage tanks, all stores of value, and coastal batteries. Ribbentrop, meanwhile, had asserted himself by procuring changes in the French constitution to strip President Pétain of most of his already limited powers, and handing Nice, Corsica and Tunisia to the Italians.

From Munich, Hitler moved to the Berghof on 12 November, for a few days' rest. According to Below, he was depressed by the Anglo–American moves, worried by the problems of supplying the forces in North Africa, and had lost faith in the Italians, who he thought were pro-British – unaware that the British were reading Enigma codes, he even believed that the Italians were feeding them with information on German transports. He was also critical of Göring, and the Luftwaffe. 'Göring had also been in Munich,' Below recalled, 'and it struck me then that Hitler and Göring no longer talked together as they had done previously. Hitler said that Göring did not keep himself properly informed, and Hitler preferred to talk with Jeschonnek for that reason.' He disparaged the air defence of the Reich: they needed more flak, because there were never enough fighters, and those they had were always in the wrong place, or the weather was too bad. On the Eastern Front, he hoped there would be no new surprises, but suspected that the winter would bring a new Russian offensive.[14]

One week later, the dreaded Russian winter arrived, and with it came the new offensive. While Chuikov, at his last gasp and almost out of ammunition, had been holding the Germans locked in the carnage of Stalingrad, Zhukov was preparing for battle on a grand scale. Zhukov had been appointed Deputy Supreme Commander under Stalin at the end of August, and had immediately flown from Moscow to take personal command of the Stalingrad front. For weeks he had struggled to build up his forces. Then, on 19 November, in temperatures as low as -30°C, he launched his counterattack, 'Operation Uranus', with an unbroken eight-hour artillery barrage before unleashing sixty divisions in a huge pincer movement to encircle the German armies around the city and their Italian, Romanian and Hungarian allies. Ignoring the advice of his generals and advisers, including his new Chief of Staff, Hitler once again forbade any withdrawal to safety.

Hitler failed to realise exactly how serious the threat was until it was too late. On 20 November he discussed it on the telephone with Göring, who was at Carinhall, but neither of them was unduly alarmed. Göring stayed put, but later that day Jeschonnek arrived at the Berghof with a skeleton staff, and it was with him that Hitler discussed the possibility of supplying Paulus and his army by air, should they be surrounded. Jeschonnek assured him that the Luftwaffe could do the job, using transport planes and bombers if need be, and the next day Hitler ordered Paulus to stand firm 'despite the danger of temporary encirclement'. He would continue to be supplied by rail, but if and when that became impossible there would be an airlift.

Only after he had made this promise to Paulus did Hitler call Göring, who was in the middle of a meeting in Berlin, blasting the oil experts for not getting the sabotaged Maikop wells back into production. Göring promised that the Luftwaffe would do what it could – as Chief of Staff, Jeschonnek should know its available resources, and if he said it could manage, then it must be able to. Richthofen, the general on the ground, was sure it could not, both because he did not have enough aircraft and because of the atrocious weather conditions. He called Göring and told him so, and sent the same message to Zeitzler and to the Commander-in-Chief of Army Group B, General Maximilian von Weichs. Milch, however, assured Göring that they could do it, and with that advice Göring ordered every possible transport, including his own courier plane, to be made available for an airlift. Then he boarded *Asia* and set off for Berchtesgaden, attended by a personal retinue that included not only his valet and nurse but also a heart specialist.

When he arrived at the Berghof, he found that Jeschonnek had already given Hitler a plan for the operation of an airlift between German lines and Stalingrad. He told Pili Körner a few days later that when Hitler questioned him about its feasibility, he could only say, 'My Führer, you have the figures. If these figures are right, then I am at your disposal.' Unfortunately, the figures did not add up, even for

a short period. Jeschonnek had miscalculated the carrying capacity of
the aircraft, and made no allowances for breakdowns or bad weather.

Even by the most optimistic estimates, around 800 fully-laden
Ju-52s would need to fly in every day to keep Sixth Army alive – and
after the disastrous losses at Crete the Luftwaffe now only had a grand
total of 750, at least 100 of which were in North Africa, while many
others were unserviceable. And the Ju-52, while it was a sturdy and
well-proven workhorse, was a lumbering machine that was easy prey
to Soviet flak and fighters. Other planes, such as the larger four-engined
Condor and the new Junkers 290, could carry greater loads but were
far less rugged. Bombers could be adapted but were not really suitable
for cargo carrying. The other great shortcoming was on the ground;
Richthofen warned that he would need six full-sized airfields within
the Stalingrad cauldron instead of the two he had, and properly trained
ground crew, which he did not have. Göring claimed after the war that
he had given these figures to Hitler, who had simply replied: 'I want
everything, everything, committed, do you hear? If you use enough
planes, we can easily keep Stalingrad supplied until the spring.'[15]

That evening, Hitler decided to move back to Wolfsschanze. He was
actually aboard his train when the news came through that the trap
had closed around Stalingrad: in just four days, Zhukov had completely
encircled the Sixth Army, trapping up to 290,000 men.[16] Hitler's long
drive to the East was finally over.

The journey to East Prussia took twenty hours because of frequent
stops for Hitler to telephone Zeitzler, who begged him continually to
allow Sixth Army to fight its way out. Hitler was adamant: Paulus was
to stand fast and wait to be relieved by Fourth Panzer Army, which
was positioned to the south-west of Stalingrad. It would be ten days
before the relief operation could be mounted, but in the meantime, he
would be supplied with food, ammunition and fuel by air.

Perhaps to forget the awful prospect of what was happening at
Stalingrad, perhaps because he genuinely believed it was only a temporary hitch, Göring headed for Paris and a three-day shopping spree –
some of it with Jewish dealers – at the end of which no fewer than
seventy-seven crates of artworks and antiques were loaded aboard *Asia*
for shipment to Carinhall. When he returned to Wolfsschanze, the talk
was all about North Africa. Rommel suddenly appeared in person, to
beg Hitler's permission to pull out of Libya altogether, before he was

crushed between Montgomery's Eighth Army from the east, and Eisenhower's forces from the west. Hitler would have none of it. 'Abandon Tripoli?' he shouted. 'Never, never, never! Not if it costs a hundred thousand lives!' In a three-hour conversation with Rommel and Göring, he argued that Italy would probably defect if the Axis lost North Africa. In any case, with the Allies already in French Morocco and Algeria, it was vital to stop them building up bridgeheads from which they could launch an invasion of Europe via the south of France or Italy. He finally agreed, however, to allow Rommel to pull his forces back into Tunisia and to establish a new front at Gabès, to deny the Allies a jumping off point for an invasion of Sicily.

The next day, a chastened Rommel promised that his troops would fight to the death, but said that would only be possible if he received fresh supplies of tanks, guns and armaments. Hitler turned to Göring, and told him to give Rommel everything he needed. 'You can pile it all on my shoulders,' Göring replied at once. 'I shall attend to it all myself.'[17]

Whatever the Germans did in North Africa would obviously have to be agreed and co-ordinated with the Italians, and Göring set off for Rome in *Asia*, taking Rommel with him. Rommel described the two-day journey as one of the most exasperating experiences of his life, as he tried to pin Göring down to discussing his military problems, only to have to listen to endless chat about the Reich Marshal's art collection and animals. Like most army generals trained in the austere philistinism of the Prussian officer corps, he despised Göring's flamboyant foppery and self-indulgence. According to Rommel's own account, Göring showed no interest in Africa, except where there might be a chance of winning laurels for himself through the performance of the Luftwaffe or his own 'Praetorian Guard', the Hermann Göring Panzer Division, which he had already committed to the fight and which was then on its way to Tunis.

Emmy was accompanying her husband to Rome, and Rommel's wife, Lucie, joined the train at Munich. Frau Rommel had never met Göring before, and was even more disapproving than her husband of his appearance and behaviour. She thought he was a megalomaniac, was appalled at Emmy's slavish devotion to him, and noted with great disdain his emerald tie clip, his watch-case studded with more emeralds and his enormous diamond ring. 'You will be interested in this,' he told her, 'it is one of the most valuable stones in the world.'

At the Excelsior Hotel, where they all stayed in Rome, he continued his ceaseless babble about pictures and sculpture, to the despair of Frau Rommel, who was seriously worried about her husband's depressed state over the threat to his army. Instead of offering Rommel reassurance and support, Göring spent all the time he could away from conferences searching for pictures and boasting about beating down dealers. 'They call me the Maecenas of the Third Reich,' he said proudly to the Rommels, who both thought his 'antics' made him more like a Nero fiddling while Tripolitania, if not yet Rome, was burning.[18]

At the hurriedly-called conferences with Italian General Staff officers, Göring was busily stirring things up – as Hitler had ordered him to – trying to push the Italians into making more of an effort. After their heavy losses in Libya, and recent heavy bombing of their northern cities including Milan, Turin and Genoa by the RAF, their appetite for the war was diminishing fast. The day before, Churchill had publicly reminded them that the Allies were holding 300,000 Italian prisoners, including 100 generals. Göring's approach was brutal; according to Paul Schmidt, translating yet again, 'he ranted and threatened. He showed very little psychological insight, for he alienated the Italians by his crude insensitive behaviour and my impression was that he left them still less inclined to make an effort than they had been before.'[19] He also managed to upset Rommel again by dropping his support for the withdrawal to Gabès, under pressure from Kesselring and the Italian commander in Libya, General Ettore Bastico. Milch, who arrived from Berlin as the conference ended, found Rommel in an upstairs room weeping with rage at Göring.[20]

Göring had long talks with Mussolini, who was ill with a stomach complaint, trying to stiffen his resolve. He promised him that in addition to the 10th Panzer Division which was already in Tunisia, Germany would send the Hermann Göring Division which was on its way, and the Adolf Hitler and Deutschland Panzer Divisions, 'three names that mean much to German honour',[21] to make up a new Fifth Panzer Army under General von Arnim, while Rommel and his German–Italian Panzer Army tried to hold the line in Tripoli. By early December, 50,000 German troops and 18,000 Italians were being rushed to occupy Tunisia.

In no hurry to get back to Germany, Göring stayed in Italy for several more days, holding conferences both with the military and with civilians. Prince Otto von Bismarck, Counsellor at the German Embassy, mischievously whispered to Ciano's secretary that he was only there to save Rommel's face, that he knew full well that there was nothing more to be done in North Africa, and that all his promises 'are bound to be left up in the clouds'. His principal aim, therefore, was 'to create confusion and to give documentary proof that the blame for everything rests on our poor organisation of transport, ships, railroads, etc.' Bismarck added that 'the military technicians of the Embassy are surprised at the amount of nonsense which the Reich Marshal has been capable of putting together'.[22]

The bad impressions Göring was creating were not limited to the embarrassed German Embassy; Colonel Montezemolo, who acted as secretary for the top-level meetings of the four marshals – Göring, Kesselring, Rommel and Cavallero, Chief of the Italian Supreme Command – said that he was surprised by his 'proud ignorance'. For Ciano, the last straw came when Göring took off to Naples, 'declaring that he intends to appoint "as Superintendent of Transportation the secretary of the party in Naples, who is a young and active man, and who thinks as he does".' 'Can it be,' Ciano asked waspishly, 'that Göring is really thinking of appointing himself the Reich Protector of Italy?'[23]

Göring arrived back at the Wolfsschanze on 11 December, to report to Hitler that Rommel had completely lost his nerve, and that Mussolini was urging him to make a settlement with the Soviet Union, or at the least to set a defensive line that could be held with small forces. When Ciano and Cavallero arrived a week later, they repeated this advice to Hitler, with the backing of Göring and Ribbentrop, who were for once singing from the same song sheet. The Italians' appeal for an end to the senseless fighting in the East had been given extra urgency the day before when their Eighth Army, on the Don front west of Stalingrad, had collapsed with heavy losses after putting up a stiff fight. But Hitler refused even to discuss the possibility of stopping.

There was no avoiding the subject of Stalingrad now, as the Soviet garrotte tightened inexorably, and the Luftwaffe struggled more and more to airlift supplies in and wounded men out. When the airlift had first been mooted, Sixth Army had said they needed 700 tons of supplies a day. Göring had immediately scaled this down to 500 tons; his transport staff reckoned they could move 350, but even this proved wildly optimistic. Faced with virtually insuperable problems of ice and snow and freezing fog, to say nothing of enemy action, the very best they managed was on 19 December, when 154 aircraft landed with 289 tons, but this was exceptional: the overall daily average by the end of the operation was 116 tons. As the days became weeks, increasing numbers of planes were shot down or crashed and the airfields captured or destroyed. By mid January, those planes still flying were reduced to dropping meagre supplies by parachute or simply tipping them out of the doors. Deprived of ammunition, fuel or food, the men on the ground were dying from freezing or starvation as much as from enemy bullets and shells.

While the soldiers and airmen were dying in Stalingrad, Göring celebrated Christmas and New Year with Emmy and Edda at Carinhall, with no shortage of goodies. Goebbels, celebrating more abstemiously with his family, had organised a special radio programme on Christmas Eve linking troops on all the fighting fronts, including Stalingrad, to sing carols and send messages to their loved ones at home. The relay of a choir singing 'Silent Night' supposedly 'on the Volga front' came as a surprise to those men actually on the Volga front – 1,280 of whom died that Christmas Day – since it was staged in a studio in Berlin. Unaware of this, most families found some seasonal comfort in it, and Goebbels was pleased with the result of his deception. He was more ambivalent, however, about his present from the Führer: an armoured Mercedes with bullet-proof windows, an uncomfortable reminder that there had been an attempt on his life at the beginning of the month.

Göring was looking forward to receiving a host of gifts on 12 January, his fiftieth birthday, and he was not disappointed. Expensive presents poured in from all directions, including two more decorations from Italy and a golden sword from Mussolini personally – it had originally been intended for General Franco, just as the Star of San Maurizio, presented to him by Ciano, had been intended for King Zog of Albania, but what did that matter? Keitel, on behalf of the Wehrmacht, gave him a solid gold, jewel-encrusted casket in which to keep the parchment confirming his appointment as Reich Marshal. Hitler ordered a public celebration and sent him a personal, handwritten letter of congratulation, which he kept as one of his most treasured possessions. In the evening, he had the State Opera House, which like all Berlin theatres had been closed, opened for a gala performance consisting of music by Handel and Gluck, followed, intriguingly, by scenes from the English play *A Midsummer Night's Dream*.

For once, the celebrations had a hollow ring for Göring, who by then had realised that the war was lost, and his own position with it.

The next day, he took to his bed with heart palpitations, as Hitler appointed what became known as the Committee of Three, the closest he was prepared to go to an inner War Cabinet, to co-ordinate and manage 'total war' measures on the home front. In a severe blow to his standing, Göring was not included. But nor was Goebbels, the main advocate of total war, or Speer, who had joined Goebbels in presenting Hitler with the plan for such a committee three months earlier. Instead, on the advice of Lammers, Hitler had chosen the heads of the three main arms of his personal authority, the OKW, the Reich Chancellery and the Party Chancellery: Keitel, Lammers himself, and Bormann, the three men who were constantly at his side. None of them could possibly pose any threat to his own position; none of them was ever likely to argue with him.

Goebbels had spent months pressing Hitler to declare total mobilisation of the home front, and had enlisted Speer, Funk and Ley to help him draft his proposals to shut down everything that was not essential for the war effort. The people would have to accept a lower standard of living, with Goebbels's hated 'upper 10,000' having to make 'particular sacrifices'. Meeting in private at Schwanenwerder the four men had worked out the details, the most important of which was that anyone not serving in the forces would be conscripted to work on producing armaments and food – and that included women between the ages of seventeen and fifty. They estimated that this would release between half and three-quarters of a million men for the front within three months.

Speer and Goebbels had presented their plan to Hitler at the beginning of October. He had listened, and promised to issue the decree they sought, but had done nothing. Goebbels had approached him again two months later, but it was not until after the New Year holiday that he finally reacted, sending Bormann and Lammers to talk to him. Bormann agreed with Goebbels's ideas, and commissioned him to draft a decree 'on the comprehensive deployment of able-bodied men and women for the defence of the Reich', to be ready for Hitler to review as quickly as possible. Goebbels, Speer and Funk went through the draft with Bormann, Lammers and Keitel on 8 January, and Hitler signed the decree on 13 January. But he did not appoint the committee until the 18th, and when he did Goebbels was bitterly disappointed. He had expected to be put in charge, with the power to make radical changes to the whole of life in the Reich. Now, he was not even a member of the committee. When he tried to get in touch with Hitler to persuade him to change his mind, he was blocked by Lammers. Hitler finally saw him on 22 January, and soft-soaped him by saying he had not wanted to burden him with administering such an immense programme. Instead: 'He would like me to take on the role of the moving force behind the whole thing.'[24] Easily seduced by Hitler, as always, Goebbels allowed himself to be fobbed off, at least for the moment.

Hitler had bypassed Göring on 14 January 1943 by ordering Milch to take personal command of the Stalingrad airlift. Milch had flown out at once to the Don front, which was being pushed steadily further back, increasing the distance to the Stalingrad pocket until it was at the extreme range of the heavily laden aircraft. But, as one of his senior transport officers wrote, 'one look at the actual situation was enough to convince them that nothing more could be done with the inadequate resources available'.[25] Milch had hardly arrived before Hitler came through on the telephone, demanding an increase in airlifted supplies. Shortly afterwards Göring phoned, forbidding him from flying into the cauldron to see conditions for himself. Göring had at last woken up to the reality of the disaster, and spent more and more time with Hitler at Wolfsschanze, attending his daily conferences and sending streams of frenzied telegrams to Milch, who was doing everything he could with great energy and ruthless determination, but it was hopeless. On 22 January, as Hitler was deflecting Goebbels, Paulus requested his permission to capitulate. Hitler replied that surrender was 'out of the question'. Sixth Army was to 'stand fast to the last soldier and the last bullet'.[26]

On 30 January, with Hitler still holed up in the safety of the Wolfsschanze as his troops perished a thousand miles away, Göring marked the tenth anniversary of Hitler's accession to power with a broadcast speech from his office in the Air Ministry. Comparing the Sixth Army in Stalingrad with the ancient Spartans at Thermopylae, he told the nation, and those men crouched among the ruins of the city itself: 'In years to come, it will be said of the heroic battle on the Volga: when you come to Germany, say that you have seen us lying at Stalingrad, as our honour and our leaders ordained that we should, for the greater glory of Germany.' As the doomed troops listening in their dug-outs realised only too clearly, it was their funeral oration. Just as Göring began his speech, the sirens wailed over Berlin and flights of RAF Mosquito fighter-bombers roared low over the rooftops in a perfectly-timed attack, the city's first full-scale air raid in daylight. Goebbels was due to deliver Hitler's own speech immediately after Göring, but because of the raid this had to be postponed until later in the day. It made only one brief mention of Stalingrad, and that was a tacit admission of failure. 'The heroic struggle of our soldiers on the Volga,' Goebbels pronounced on Hitler's behalf, 'should be an exhortation to everyone to do his maximum in the struggle for Germany's freedom and our nation's future, and in a wider sense for the preservation of the whole of Europe.'[27]

The Mosquitoes returned twenty-four hours later, to disrupt the celebration of Luftwaffe Day. The De Havilland Mosquito, with twin Rolls Royce Merlin engines and a plywood frame, was a remarkable aircraft. It was as fast as a fighter, with a top speed of over 400 miles per hour, and although it was a small aircraft it could carry two-thirds of the bomb load of the B-17: 4,000 lb of high-explosive bombs or a load of small incendiaries, either of which it could plant on target with great accuracy. And because it could fly fast and low in loose formation, unlike the lumbering heavy bombers, a flight of Mosquitoes was extremely difficult to detect or intercept. The Luftwaffe had nothing like it, and its appearance over Berlin was a painful reminder to Göring of the continuing shortcomings of German aircraft production as well as the gaps in his air defences.

Shortly after the Mosquitoes had struck for the second time, the news arrived that the drawn-out agony of Stalingrad was over. Despite being promoted to Field Marshal the day before, Paulus had finally surrendered. The remnants of six divisions trapped in a smaller pocket held out for another two days, but by 2 February all was silent. 91,000 men, all that remained of the 290,000 who had been encircled ten weeks before, shuffled off into captivity, from which a mere 6,000 would return at the end of the war. In the Stalingrad campaign as a whole, Germany and her allies had lost around half a million irreplaceable men, and all their tanks, guns and equipment. In addition, the Luftwaffe had lost 488 transport planes and bombers, and large numbers of fighters and Stukas, the equivalent of an entire air fleet, plus a complete flak division.

Goebbels presented the defeat as a heroic sacrifice, orchestrating the media with a stream of detailed instructions on how they were to handle the news. In the official communiqué, which he broadcast as a special announcement on 3 February, he implied that the Sixth Army had fought to the last man, with no surrender and no prisoners: 'They died so that Germany might live.' But no matter how hard he tried to spin, there was no way he could disguise the size of the disaster. El Alamein might have been the end of the beginning for Churchill, but for Hitler, Stalingrad was definitely the beginning of the end.

XXXIII

'DO YOU WANT TOTAL WAR?'

'THE chief influence on the Führer, at least up till the end of 1941 or the beginning of 1942, was exerted by me,' Göring told the Nuremberg Tribunal. 'From then until 1943 my influence gradually decreased, after which it rapidly dwindled.'[1] His powers had been reduced during 1942 by Speer's and Sauckel's appointments, and by the setting up of a Central Planning Committee consisting of Speer and Milch, with Pili Körner included as a sop to him, to oversee the provision and distribution of essential raw materials. There had also been a crisis in his HGW industrial empire, which by then included 176 factories, 69 mines and metallurgical companies, 46 transport companies, 156 trading companies and 15 building firms.[2] Under pressure from a group of senior managers, it had been forced to divest itself of all its armament manufacturing, leaving it to concentrate on its original core business of iron and steel production. Göring had objected strongly, declaring that he wanted 'nothing to do with this jumble sale' when a list of arms firms to be sold back to the private sector had been drawn up, but he had been outflanked again by Speer, who had already persuaded Hitler that it was necessary.[3] Although they were technically independent, most of the companies involved now came under the control of Speer's ministry.

Despite these depredations, Göring was still the undisputed second man in the Reich at the end of 1942, enjoying wide powers over the economy, and responsible for making policy decisions on taxation, prices, food and agriculture, foreign trade and most industrial production apart from weapons. He still retained at least nominal control over transport, essential raw materials, fuel, synthetic rubber and oil, and even managed to cling on to the production of aircraft and air armaments until well into 1944. And of course, he was still Commander-in-Chief of the Luftwaffe and the highest ranking officer in the Wehrmacht. The reasons for his rapid decline in 1943, however, are not hard to find. If only to avoid blaming the true culprit – himself – for the disaster of Stalingrad, Hitler needed a scapegoat and Göring was the obvious candidate, sharing with Paulus the brunt of Hitler's anger. Deeply upset, and fearful of facing Hitler, Göring made himself scarce, keeping well away from Führer Headquarters for several days, most of which he spent at Emmy's bedside in hospital, where she was recovering from a sinus operation.

But no matter how much he ranted against him in private, Hitler was careful never to criticise Göring in public. 'I alone bear responsibility for Stalingrad,' he told Field Marshal von Manstein on 6 February. 'I could pin the blame on Göring, but he is my designated successor, so I can't.'⁴ To the party leadership, the Gauleiters and Reichsleiters whom he had called to the Wolfsschanze next day, he said he had believed Stalingrad could be supplied by air, but that 'dreadful weather conditions' had made it impossible. He blamed the catastrophe itself on the 'complete failure' of his allies, the Romanians, Italians and Hungarians. It was their collapse, he said, that had made it necessary for him to order the Sixth Army to stand fast and tie up the Red Army, 'to prevent the catastrophe engulfing the entire Eastern Front'. 'The Caucasus army,' he told them, 'had been saved through the sacrifice of the Sixth Army in Stalingrad.'⁵ None of the Gauleiters questioned Hitler's excuse for condemning 290,000 men to death or captivity. 'I was astonished,' Below noted, 'at how this approach convinced them.'⁶

Göring, too, blamed Germany's allies when he called his senior Luftwaffe generals to Rominten between 15 and 17 February for a situation conference and a pep talk. But he added his own cruel indictment of Sixth Army:

If the men had fought harder, particularly in Stalingrad itself, we should still have the city today and it would not have been captured. Paulus was too weak, he didn't turn Stalingrad into a proper fortress. Thousands of Russian civilians were fed along with his troops. He should have sacrificed them ruthlessly so that his soldiers had enough to survive. And that goes for the hopelessly injured – they shouldn't have been dragged along but allowed to fade away. The Paulus army just relied on the Luftwaffe and expected miracles from it . . . And then this army's Chief of Staff, General Schmidt, has the gall to say, 'The Luftwaffe has committed the biggest treachery in history because

it could not manage to supply the Paulus army.' The army lost its airfields –
how on earth was a mass airlift supposed to be possible after that?[7]

Göring was already in trouble with Hitler for failing to protect the
Reich against Allied air attacks, and his reputation had taken further
knocks during January. On the 16th, the RAF had returned to Berlin
for the first night raid in many months, with 201 heavy bombers
catching the complacent defenders completely by surprise – Wing-
Commander Leonard Cheshire, a future winner of the VC who was
on his sixth visit to the city, reported seeing only one small searchlight, and described the flak as 'negligible'. The bombers killed 198
people, including 53 prisoners of war – 52 of them French – and five
foreign workers. Only one aircraft failed to make it home. The
following night, they struck again, with 187 planes, though this time
the gunners were on the alert. Together with the night-fighters along
the bombers' route, they shot down 22 RAF aircraft, a devastating
success rate but still not enough to save Göring from obloquy.

The new raids marked the beginning of an ominous new phase in
the air war, with a dramatic increase in Allied strength. During 1942,
the British had brought a whole new generation of heavy bombers into
service: Stirlings, Halifaxes, and above all the superb Lancasters, four-
engined aircraft with a longer range and higher ceilings than the old
Wellingtons and Hampdens, and with the capacity to carry much
greater bomb loads. On the first raids of the new campaign, many
were carrying 8,000lb bombs, the heaviest yet dropped on Berlin. They
were also equipped with on-board radar, H2S, which displayed a map-
like picture of the ground below, even through heavy cloud and in
complete darkness. H2S was still fairly rudimentary and not entirely
reliable, but it was a vast improvement on previous aids to navigation
and bomb aiming. Its discovery on a bomber shot down over Rotterdam
on the night of 30 31 January did nothing to lighten Göring's gloom,
which had been deepened three days before by the first large-scale
daylight raid on Germany by B-17 Flying Fortresses and B-24 Liberators
of the US Eighth Army Air Force, on the Wilhelmshaven naval base.

With the Americans bombing by day and the British bombing by
night, the outlook for Germany – and for Göring – was bad. When
Hitler called for retaliatory raids on Britain, he simply did not have
the aircraft to do it effectively. He had taken the decision back in 1937
not to develop a four-engined, long-range heavy bomber, and it was
too late to start now. And too many of his existing medium bombers

lay wrecked on the frozen steppe around Stalingrad. His helplessness
increased his depression and accelerated his physical and mental decline,
which was caused mainly by exhaustion and not, as most people
thought, by drug addiction. Along with a cocktail of other medication
for his various ailments, he certainly gobbled more and more paracodeine pills, but as the doctors at Nuremberg discovered, these
contained only minute quantities of morphine. There were no signs of
multiple injections anywhere on his body, and no hypodermic syringe,
or any other drugs, in his belongings. The pills were clearly a habit
and not an addiction: when he was weaned off them in 1945, he
suffered no obvious withdrawal symptoms. This was in marked contrast
to the violent reactions that had put him into a straitjacket in a Swedish
mental hospital twenty years before, an experience that he would surely
never have risked repeating. Nevertheless, because of his history, the
rumours that he was a morphine junkie proliferated – it was a handy
explanation for his wild mood swings and increasingly erratic behaviour, such as abruptly falling asleep while speaking, as happened on
more than one occasion.

Goebbels subscribed enthusiastically to Hitler's notion that the 'heroic
sacrifice' of the Sixth Army had somehow purified the German nation
and prepared it for greater things to come. At the safe distance of
1,000 miles from the frozen hell of Stalingrad, he condemned Paulus's
failure to do the honourable thing and fall on his sword, 'choosing to
live fifteen or twenty years longer rather than to gain eternal life of
several thousand years [sic] in unfading glory'.[8] With a blind cynicism
as great as his master's, he calculated that he could exploit the disaster
to impose on the home front the 'total war' he had wanted for so long.
He had announced measures towards this in the speech he made on
30 January, and since then had started to introduce them in his own
Gau, Berlin.

He had already combed out three hundred men from his ministry
for military service, replacing them with women. Now, he shut down
all businesses in the city that were not contributing to the war effort
in some way. He closed jewellers and other luxury shops, banned
fashion magazines, and even started a campaign against fashion itself,
declaring that women did not need to dress up since they would please
'victorious, homecoming soldiers just as much in patches'. He was
forced to qualify this, however, when Hitler, with his decided views on
women's duty to look good, objected. 'There is no need,' Goebbels

announced, 'for a woman to make herself ugly.'

He allowed only two nightclubs to stay open, but these were restricted to soldiers in transit who had nowhere else to go between midnight and 5 a.m., and dancing was forbidden. He had most of Berlin's prostitutes rounded up and sent to the Eastern Front to serve the troops there. And with typical Jacobin zeal he ordered the closure of luxury restaurants, where the rich had been able to eat without ration cards provided they could afford to pay from fifty to a hundred marks a head. This brought him into direct conflict with Göring, who ordered his favourite restaurant, Horcher, in which he was believed to have a financial stake, to stay open. Goebbels sent round a squad of SA men to hurl stones at the restaurant's windows until it complied, whereupon Göring reopened it under the guise of a club for Luftwaffe officers, which as a service establishment could not be touched. Other restaurants were eventually allowed to reopen, on condition that they served 'field kitchen dishes' to show their support for the soldiers at the front.

At a conference of Gauleiters in Posen on 6 February, and again when they reassembled before Hitler at the Wolfsschanze next day, Goebbels tried to persuade his fellow leaders to give him control of the implementation of total war, which would have made up for his disappointment over the Committee of Three. But Bormann outsmarted him yet again, restricting him to propaganda and public relations and giving him specific instructions not to treat it as a 'class warfare' issue. Bormann also blocked his efforts to promote a change of policy in the East, where he believed that the constant threat from partisans could be countered by treating the people more humanely, in order to contrast the 'bestiality of the Bolshevik system' with the hope of a better life under 'civilised' German rule. Since this involved suppressing any hint that their lands were to be seized for German settlers – a suggestion that struck at the very roots of *Lebensraum* – it was not likely that Hitler would ever agree. Nor did he.

With his latest bid for power quashed, Goebbels concentrated on what he did best, making rousing speeches to the nation. Under the heading 'Do You Want Total War?' he spoke to workers in Düsseldorf on 15 February as a rehearsal for a great rally in the Berlin Sportpalast three days later. There, under a giant banner reading 'Total War – Shortest War!' he gave one of the performances of his life to an arena packed with the party elite, and to the rest of the country through a live radio broadcast. Film cameras recorded his every word, and every reaction from ministers and celebrities, for newsreels that would be rushed out to every cinema in the country within the next few days. For such a vital occasion, he was determined not to miss a trick – supporting him from the gallery were Magda and their two eldest daughters, ten-year-old Helga and Hilde, who was almost nine, wheeled out in public for the first time.

Goebbels's speech was a call to arms in a holy war against 'the hordes from the steppe', the Soviet divisions bearing down on the glorious German troops, behind whom were the 'Jewish liquidation squads'. And behind them were 'terror, the spectre of famine, and unbridled anarchy in Europe'. Summoning up all his considerable powers of description and oratory he painted a lurid picture of the dangers they all faced, steadily building the tension and the fear, and the excitement. Terror, he proclaimed, had to be answered with counter-terror. 'Bourgeois squeamishness' had to end. The audience was enraptured, approaching hysteria as he handled them like a virtuoso musician playing on a responsive instrument. When he reached his climax, he paused dramatically. Then, after an electric silence, he boomed the question: 'Do you want total war?' 'Yes, yes,' they cried, applauding. 'Do you want total war?' he repeated. 'Do you want it, if necessary, to be even more total and more radical than we can ever imagine today?' The crowd erupted in a thunderous roar of 'Ja!' 'Do you accept the fact,' he shouted, 'that anyone who detracts from the war effort will lose his head?' The response was even bigger, even louder, even more emphatic. Nodding at them, emotionally drained, he raised his hands for silence and then declaimed the great war-cry of the movement to free Prussia from Napoleon's occupation in 1812: 'Now, people arise, and let the storm break loose!'9 And the storm did break loose, at least in the Berlin Sportpalast, with scenes that it had not witnessed even in 1933. The radio stayed on air for another twenty minutes, broadcasting the sounds of stamping and cheering to homes and work-places across Germany.

After the speech, Goebbels invited a selected group back to his residence on Hermann-Göring-Strasse, where in the interests of fuel economy he had closed off the larger rooms and removed many light bulbs. In the gloom, Speer was amazed to hear him analyse his perform-ance, which Speer had assumed to be 'a purely emotional outburst', like an actor after a first night. Even the carefully selected audience had been part of it, like a studio audience in a modern TV or radio show. 'Did you notice?' Goebbels asked. 'They reacted to the smallest nuance and applauded at just the right moments. It was the politically best-trained audience you can find in Germany.'

The speech had been directed to the wider public listening on their radios, and beyond that, with its stark reminder of the dangers of Bolshevism, to the rest of the Western world. Goebbels was delighted by the praise it received in the German press – even though editors had been given detailed instructions on what to say. But he was more pleased by the favourable reactions of some of the foreign press to his anti-Bolshevik line. Speer believed that this was because he had his eyes set on becoming Foreign Minister, and was using 'all the eloquence at his command . . . to turn Hitler against Ribbentrop'. For a while, Speer noted, he seemed to be succeeding, but just as he thought he had won, 'Hitler unexpectedly began praising Ribbentrop's excellent work and his talent for negotiations with Germany's "allies".' 'You're altogether wrong about Ribbentrop,' he told Goebbels. 'He is one of the greatest men we have, and some day, history will place him above Bismarck. He is greater than Bismarck.'[10]

Hitler then crushed Goebbels's hopes in this direction altogether, by forbidding him to extend any more feelers towards the West, as he had done in his Sportpalast speech. Churchill and Roosevelt had met at the end of January at Casablanca in newly liberated French Morocco with their Combined Chiefs of Staff, to plan future strategy, and Roosevelt had declared the doctrine of demanding Germany's unconditional surrender. There was therefore no point in even thinking about negotiations; the war would have to be fought to the finish.

The fear of the advancing hordes from the East added fresh urgency to Goebbels's determination to cleanse his Gau of Jews once and for all, and on Saturday, 27 February he made his move. At 6 a.m., lines of army trucks with grey canvas covers began roaring through the streets, escorted by armed SS men. They stopped at factory gates, in front of private houses and apartment blocks, to load up with human cargo. Men, women and children were herded and penned like animals destined for the stockyard, and driven to the sidings at Grunewald rail station, to be loaded into box cars and carried to Auschwitz. The whole operation was run with deadly bureaucratic efficiency. In spite of the desperate shortage of locomotives and rolling stock for the war in the East, and the depredations of the RAF on communications, the transports ran strictly to schedule. The paperwork was immaculate: if a consignment was for 1,000 Jews, then there would be 1,000 Jews on board, not 1,001, never 999, but exactly 1,000.

There was, however, an unexpected hitch in Goebbels's plan. During the initial round-up, some 6,000 Jewish men who were partners in mixed marriages were segregated from the others, and taken to a building in the Rosenstrasse, not far from SS headquarters. On the Sunday morning, their non-Jewish wives descended on Rosenstrasse and crowded round the building where their husbands were being held. There they stood, refusing to leave, shouting and screaming for their men, hour after hour, throughout the day and the night and into the next day, until the worried SS officials, no doubt with the approval of Goebbels and Himmler, finally gave way. Rather than machine-gun 6,000 German women, they released their husbands, designating them as 'privileged persons' who were to be 'incorporated into the national community'.

To add to Goebbels's fury, some 4,000 other Jews managed to avoid the round-up. He assumed they had been tipped off. 'The better circles,' he complained, 'particularly the intellectuals, do not understand our Jewish policy, and partly side with the Jews . . . But we'll catch them yet. Whatever happens, I won't rest until at least the capital has become completely Jew-free.'[11] What he did not understand was that most of those he sought, and more, had gone into hiding long before, to live as 'U-boats' in the slang of the time. Some 5,000 survived until the end of the war, protected by sympathetic Berliners. In the pretence that they did not exist, on 19 May Goebbels declared his city to be Jew-free, something he saw as his 'greatest political accomplishment'.

With his Sportpalast speech, Goebbels had staked his claim once again to take charge of the war on the home front, but he would need allies to overcome the Committee of Three. He had already recruited the small group of 'intellectuals' in the Reich leadership – Speer, Funk and Ley, the only others beside himself at Cabinet level with a university education – and they now started meeting over tea and Cognac to plot ways of sidelining Bormann, Lammers and Keitel and thereby cutting through the bureaucracy that was stifling the war effort. It did not take them long to realise that there was a ready-made instrument in the Ministerial Defence Council, which Göring had used so success-fully as a War Cabinet in September 1939, but which had fallen into disuse when Hitler returned to Berlin from the Polish front. It had never been rescinded, and as its head, Göring had extremely wide-ranging powers, including the right to issue decrees without Hitler's approval. 'Bormann and Lammers,' Speer wrote, 'would have to bow to this existing authority, whose potentialities had so far gone untapped because of Göring's indolence.'[12] They would need Göring as nominal head of what would in effect be a domestic government, leaving Hitler free to concentrate on the military direction of the war. But the plan was for Goebbels to be named as Göring's Deputy, in which position he could chair the weekly meetings and control everything.

Göring was barely on speaking terms with Goebbels at that time because of the Horcher affair, so Speer was deputed to approach him first, to sound him out and prepare the ground. Göring, deeply depressed over Hitler's disfavour and his own awareness that the war could no longer be won, had retreated to his house on the Obersalzberg, where he received Speer amicably in his Renaissance prince mode, wearing a dark green velvet dressing gown adorned with a huge ruby brooch. His fingernails were lacquered, and Speer thought his cheeks were rouged, though this may have been simply the high flush that he often showed. They talked for about five hours, and according to Speer their conversation was 'friendly and unconstrained'. Göring listened quietly to the proposal: 'As he sat, he occasionally scooped a handful of unset gems from his pocket and playfully let them glide through his fingers. It seemed to delight him that we had thought of him.'[13]

For someone who liked to describe himself as a political novice, Speer handled Göring with great skill, clearly knowing exactly which buttons to press, though it is hard to believe that Goebbels would not have advised and even rehearsed him in what to say. Göring's deep dislike of Bormann was no secret – he hated him for his unctuous personality, his boorish ways and above all for his malign influence on Hitler. Two examples of his personal behaviour had particularly offended Göring: he had moved his mistress into his house, forcing his wife to accept a *ménage à trois*, and once when a stray dog had attacked his own pet, he had doused it with petrol, set it alight, and roared with laughter as he watched it run away in flaming agony.

Defiling the marital bed and cruelty to animals were two of the most heinous sins in Göring's eyes, but there was an even worse offence: an attack on his personal position. Strolling together on the mountainside, Speer told him how Bormann was using every opportunity to undermine his prestige. He had watched how Bormann operated at Hitler's teatimes, which Göring did not attend:

He never worked by direct attack, I said. Instead, he would weave little incidents into his conversation which were effective only in their sum. Thus, for example, in the course of the teatime chatter Bormann would tell unfavourable anecdotes from Vienna in order to damage Baldur von Schirach, the Hitler Youth leader. But Bormann carefully avoided agreeing with Hitler's subsequent negative remarks. On the contrary, he thought it prudent to praise Schirach afterwards – the kind of praise, of course, which would leave an unpleasant aftertaste. After about a year of this, Bormann had brought Hitler to the point of disliking Schirach and often feeling outright hostility towards him. Then – when Hitler was not around – Bormann could venture to go a step further. With an air of casually dismissing the matter but in reality annihilating the man, he would remark contemptuously that of course Schirach belonged in Vienna since everybody there was always intriguing against everybody else. Bormann would be playing the same sort of game against Göring, I added in conclusion.[14]

As a final clincher, Speer told Göring he had evidence that Bormann was planning to supplant him as Hitler's successor, and presented him with a number of examples to prove it. As Speer himself put it, 'That certainly activated his juices!'[15] After that, Speer had no difficulty in persuading him to forget his quarrel and invite Goebbels to fly down to the Obersalzberg so that they could discuss their plans in detail together.

Göring was due to leave shortly for Italy, where the Fascist regime was facing serious internal trouble. At the end of January 1943, in the wake of the disasters in Stalingrad and North Africa, Mussolini had dismissed Marshal Cavallero as Chief of the High Command, and a few days later had fired most of his Cabinet ministers, including Ciano, who opted to become Ambassador to the Holy See, coincidentally alongside Ernst von Weizsäcker, who had finally managed to escape from Ribbentrop and obtain a similar posting. Mussolini took over the Foreign Ministry himself, assuming, as the official announcement put it, 'the entire burden for the conduct of political and military operations in the delicate stage of the conflict'.[16]

What little enthusiasm remained in Italy for the war and the Axis alliance was fading rapidly, and her strained relations with Germany were damaged still more when Ribbentrop visited Rome during the last four days of February. Instead of offering support, he offended Mussolini by lecturing him on the need to continue the war in the East, and attacking his protection of Italian Jews and his support for the Chetniks in Croatia. Göring's visit was to inspect the tenuous supply lincs to the Luftwaffe units operating out of Italy, but he now also had the task of undoing some of the damage caused by Ribbentrop, and bolstering the Duce's sagging confidence. Before he left, however, he wanted to talk 'urgently' to Goebbels, who crowed expectantly to his diary: 'If I should succeed in winning Göring over completely to the new war policy, that would be a positive achievement.'[17]

Goebbels's restored affection for Göring even extended to his appearance as he greeted him and Speer at the door. 'He was wearing a somewhat baroque outfit,' he wrote, 'which, if one didn't know him, one would have found a bit comic. But that's the way he is, and one must put up with his idiosyncrasies. They even have a certain charm . . .'[18] Having successfully buried their hatchets for the time being, Göring and Goebbels talked solidly for several hours, with Speer encouraging them. Goebbels flattered Göring, but at the same time chided him for allowing the Ministerial Defence Council to fall into disuse. Because of Hitler's obsession with military matters, there was 'a total lack of a clear leadership in domestic and foreign policy'. Both men were concerned about the Führer's health: Göring commented that in three and a half years of war, he had aged by fifteen years, that he shut himself away too much and was living a very unhealthy lifestyle.[19]

Though neither of them ever said it out loud, they clearly acknowledged that Hitler's state of health made the question of the succession more urgent. Goebbels may have had his differences with Göring, but they had been through a great deal together and, what was more important, he believed he could manage Göring should he become leader. He could not say the same for Bormann, or for that matter Himmler. Himmler could not be sidelined, so he would have to be brought into the revived Defence Council, where they could at least keep an eye on him. Bormann would have to be cut down to size, and quickly. Carefully emphasising that everything they planned was out of loyalty to the Führer and their desire to help him by relieving him of some of his burdens, they prepared their plans against the Committee of Three, whom Göring referred to disparagingly as 'the three kings'. Goebbels also targeted Ribbentrop, whom he was still hoping to replace as Foreign Minister, and Göring joined in eagerly. The war, he charged, was Ribbentrop's doing: he had never made any serious attempt at a *modus vivendi* with Britain, simply because he had an inferiority complex.[20]

'While talking,' Goebbels recorded in his diary,

I gained the impression that Göring was visibly stimulated by what I said. He became very enthusiastic about my proposals and immediately asked how we were to proceed specifically. I suggested that he make a number of nominations and I would try to win over the rest. We won't tell them about our real intentions – gradually to freeze out the Committee of Three and transfer its powers to the Ministerial Council. That would only cause unnecessary trouble. We have no other ambitions but to support each other and to form a solid phalanx around the Führer.

They agreed they would have to choose their moment carefully to put the proposal to Hitler, with Goebbels and Speer preparing the ground in advance. They would meet again in two weeks' time, with Funk and Ley, after which they would proceed against Bormann and his clique. 'We would stand together,' Speer recalled later, 'supporting each other in the decisive meeting with Hitler. All was agreed: a small conspiracy.'[21]

In the event, the 'small conspiracy' came to nothing. The RAF chose the very day Goebbels, Göring and Speer met on the Obersalzberg to launch its most devastating raid on Berlin to date, with 302 heavy bombers carrying mostly incendiaries, plus 4,000lb and 8,000lb high-explosive 'cookies'. The damage that night was enormous. At Tempelhof, 20 acres of the railway repair shops were destroyed, while elsewhere 20 factories were badly damaged and 875 buildings, mostly domestic dwellings, reduced to rubble. The Prager Platz, half a mile south of the Zoo, was completely flattened, the Foreign Ministry Press Office was destroyed, and there was considerable damage all along the Unter den Linden. Over 700 people were killed and 64,909 made homeless. Göring's stock sank again with Hitler, and plummeted three days later when massive attacks on Essen signalled the start of the Battle of the Ruhr, which continued solidly from then until 10 July. It was not a propitious time for proposing fresh powers for the Reich Marshal.

Goebbels and Speer had travelled to Vinnitsa, where Hitler had temporarily returned to direct the new spring campaign in the East, to broach the subject, but Hitler had raged so violently against Göring and the Luftwaffe that they decided it was not worth trying, especially when news came through of a heavy raid on Nuremberg. In Göring's absence in Italy, Hitler had Bodenschatz roused from his bed to be given a roasting. Goebbels intervened to defend Göring and rescue Bodenschatz, but there was little he could really do to mollify Hitler's fury. 'Göring now knows it is the eleventh hour for him,' he noted. As though to confirm this, Hitler ordered Göring to leave Rome at once and return to Vinnitsa to give an account of himself.

Göring arrived at Vinnitsa in the afternoon of 11 March, at about the same time as Rommel, who had just been relieved of his army group command in North Africa after losing the battle of Medenine, which he had been forced into fighting against his will. His removal was being kept secret, however, for fear of the effect it would have on morale, and he was officially being sent on sick-leave. The two men were able to commiserate with each other before Göring faced the Führer at 9.30 p.m. for a severe tongue-lashing. Hitler demanded retaliation raids on British cities, 'terror from our side', as the best way of preventing German cities being reduced to heaps of rubble. Inveighing against the Luftwaffe generals, living lives of luxury in French châteaux and showing no interest in attacking Britain, he made it clear that the only way Goring could regain his confidence was to take control of the Luftwaffe again. Göring responded during the rest of that spring and summer with a stream of invective towards his pilots, accusing them of cowardice and incompetence. But he knew that the real problem was shortage of aircraft. Between them, Milch and Speer were achieving miracles of reorganisation in the aircraft industry, and had already improved output to about 2,000 planes a month despite the damage to factories caused by Allied bombing. The planes they were turning out, however, were obsolescent and Germany was falling further behind in new technology.

Smarting from Hitler's vitriolic censure, Göring called all the aircraft manufacturers – Messerschmitt, Heinkel, Dornier, et al – to Carinhall and vented his anger on them in turn. 'I have been deceived,' he cried theatrically, 'on a scale to which I was previously accustomed only in the variety acts of magicians and conjurors!' There were some things, he shouted, which he was told before the war were completely ready, but which were still not even ready today! Where was the heavy bomber he had been promised? Why was the much-vaunted He-177 suffering catastrophic losses caused by crashes, not enemy action? Why could the enemy jam German radar, while the Germans could not jam his? Why can they 'drop their bombs through cloud cover into a pickle barrel in a railroad station, but our gentlemen "can't quite find London"?'[22] On and on he raged – the transcript of his speech covers 100 pages. He might have been no better informed than usual, but there could be no doubt that, for the moment at least, he had recovered his energy to the full.

* * *

The day before he delivered his harangue to the aircraft manufacturers, Göring had presided over another secret meeting of the conspirators, in his Leipziger Platz palace, to discuss further tactics for, as Speer put it, 'recapturing Hitler for ourselves'. It was agreed that at the first suitable moment, Göring himself should make the proposal to Hitler for reviving the Ministerial Defence Council, with Speer and Himmler included in its membership. The right moment seemed to have come when a conference was arranged to challenge Sauckel's claims on labour supply figures, which he was exaggerating to Hitler by as much as a million workers. Sauckel, of course, was Bormann's protégé, and an attack on him would therefore be an attack on Bormann, too.

The conference was called for 12 April, at the Chancellery secretariat building on the Obersalzberg, since Hitler was spending a few days at the Berghof. Before it started, Milch joined Speer in reminding Göring what they wanted, and he rubbed his hands and said 'that will soon be taken care of'. But it soon became clear that things were not going as planned. For a start, the conspirators were surprised to discover that Himmler, Bormann and Keitel had joined Sauckel at the table. Then a message arrived from Goebbels, saying he had been taken ill on his way to the Obersalzberg. He was lying in his car with 'an attack of renal colic', he said, and would not be able to attend the meeting. He had presumably been got at by Bormann or Himmler – or perhaps he had heard the news that Bormann had just been officially appointed Secretary to the Führer, and decided it was time to change horses. From that time onwards, his attitude to Bormann changed, mentioning him in glowing terms in his diary, and noting that whatever his faults, he had been 'extraordinarily loyal' to the Führer.

When the meeting started, Sauckel simply denied everything, and claimed he had already delivered the workers Speer and Milch wanted. This was the moment when Göring was expected to wade into him, demanding evidence and accusing him of lying. Instead, he launched into an attack on his own deputy, Milch, accusing him of making difficulties for 'our good party comrade Sauckel, who was exerting himself to the utmost and had achieved such successes'. 'It was,' according to a shattered Speer, 'as though Göring had picked out the wrong phonograph record.' Himmler, who was providing large numbers of slave labourers from his concentration camps, produced a horribly plausible explanation for the discrepancy in the figures: 'Isn't the most likely explanation of the missing million bodies,' he suggested calmly, 'that they are dead?'[23]

With the defection of both Goebbels and Göring, the conspiracy had collapsed. It is likely that Göring's change of heart had come with Himmler's entry into the game at Bormann's side: Göring was concerned for a number of reasons with improving relations with Himmler and the SS. Another possible reason for his sudden *volte-face* emerged after the meeting, when he took Speer aside and told him: 'I know you like to work closely with my State Secretary, Milch. In all friendship I'd like to warn you against him. He's unreliable; as soon as his own interests are in question, he'll trample over even his best friends.' Speer passed this on to Milch, who laughed and told him Göring had said exactly the same thing about him. Speer thought this was Göring's attempt to sow distrust, and that 'the sad fact was that our circles were so infected by suspicion that friendship was felt to be a threat'.[24] It seems more likely, however, that Bormann was playing his usual game. He would only have had to persuade Göring that Milch was trying to supplant him as Commander-in-Chief of the Luftwaffe, and that Speer was intent on usurping his role as Hitler's chosen successor, to set him against his collaborators. There is, of course, no evidence for this. There is evidence, however, that at about that time, Bormann gave Göring some six million marks from the Reich Fund, to finance his art habit.

Göring's art mania was showing no signs of easing: indeed, that same month he demanded two million marks from Finance Minister Count Schwerin von Krosigk for yet more extensions to Carinhall, to house his growing collection. Göring was by no means alone in using precious resources for his private building projects, though by this time most other Nazi big-wigs were more concerned with their safety. Goebbels, while thriftily removing light bulbs, was having a deep air-raid shelter built in the garden of his official residence, at a cost of 350,000 marks and enough material, the architect complained, to build 300 working-class homes.[25] And in the grounds of the Reich Chancellery a new underground bunker with eighteen rooms was being built for Hitler, at a cost of 1.4 million marks.[26] Harsh reality was intruding at last into the Führer's fantasy world.

Göring was not the only one of Hitler's paladins to feel the rough edge of his tongue at that time – Hitler was ill, deeply depressed and subject to even more violent mood swings and sudden rages than usual. Himmler had suffered a severe dressing down in January for some unknown reason, possibly his failure after seven months to appoint a successor to Heydrich as head of the RSHA – shortly afterwards he made the surprise choice of Ernst Kaltenbrunner, the little-known HSSPF Vienna, bypassing all the obvious candidates like Gestapo Müller and the SD's foreign intelligence chief, Schellenberg, to avoid any of them acquiring too much personal power. It is more likely, however, that Hitler's displeasure sprang from a flood of complaints about the Inland SD, which, although it was forbidden to interfere in internal party matters, regularly sent in highly critical reports on local leaders from its spies and informers. Whatever the reason, Himmler's petulant reaction revealed an enormous inferiority complex. Bormann told his wife in a letter that Himmler was 'deeply offended, and apparently not just since yesterday', complaining that Hitler had treated him unjustly for years; while others had been favoured, he had only been considered good enough to raise divisions for the Führer.

If Hitler's criticism was about the activities of the SD, then it would have been instigated by Bormann, protecting the interests of his Gauleiters and party officials. It was typical of Bormann's manipulative methods that he then tried to comfort Himmler, reminding him he had to set this rare criticism against the way that Hitler was always praising him to other people. Himmler, however, refused to be mollified. 'H[einrich] H[immler]'s criticism was so bitter, and at times so acid,' Bormann wrote, 'that in other circumstances I should have had no choice but to get up and say: "I am sorry, but I must take my leave of you, and take off your uniform. The Führer is the Führer, and he is beyond all criticism."' He did not leave, or discard his SS uniform, because, he said, he made allowances for the nervous strain Himmler was under and the distorted view of things that this produced. But, he wrote, he found Himmler's 'chilly way of criticising unpleasant'.[27]

By the spring of 1943, such unpleasantness was forgotten, and Himmler's star was rising fast once more. He had pleased Hitler by reporting that up to the end of 1942, his extermination camps had already disposed of at least two million Jews, and those figures would soon increase dramatically: the four new destruction-line complexes of underground changing room–gas chamber–electric lift–crematorium ovens just coming into service at Auschwitz-Birkenau, would be capable of disposing of 20,000 Jews a day.

Apart from the extermination camps, Himmler now ruled over twenty officially designated concentration camps and 165 affiliated labour camps, mostly located in the Reich itself, plus thousands of smaller camps set up by local SS and police chiefs.[28] The nature of these camps had changed considerably since the start of the war, when they were mainly used for preventive detention, with inmates being put to work in quarries and other traditional prison occupations. Now, under the direction of Oswald Pohl, the head of the Economics and Administration Department of the SS, their main purpose had become the manufacture of a wide range of products in SS enterprises, and above all the supply of workers to labour-starved industries.

This meant that the prisoners now had to be seen as an economic asset, in much the same way as slaves on American cotton plantations or in West Indian sugar fields. Although Himmler and the new Minister of Justice, Thierack, had agreed that certain categories of prisoners could be worked to death, numbers had suddenly become important. Nevertheless, the death rate in the 'regular' camps was still running at around sixty per cent. At the end of 1942, Pohl complained that out of 136,870 new arrivals in concentration camps between June and November, 70,610 were already dead: this, he pointed out, 'seriously reduced the numbers available for armaments work in the concentration camp factories'.[29] Such losses not only harmed the war effort, they also reduced SS profits, which Pohl's office had worked out in meticulous detail:

The hiring of concentration camp inmates to industrial enterprises yields an average return of 6 to 8 RM, from which 70 pfennig must be deducted for food and clothing. Assuming an inmate's life expectancy to be 9 months, we must multiply this sum by 270. The total is 1,431 RM. This profit can be increased by rational utilisation of the corpse, i.e. by means of gold teeth fillings, hair, clothing, valuables, etc, but on the other hand every corpse represents a loss of 2 RM, which is the cost of cremation.[30]

Control over this important labour source at a time when eleven million German men had been removed from the economy to serve in the armed forces, gave Himmler enormous leverage in the struggle for power, as well as impressing Hitler. And when Hitler agreed to his setting up his own armaments factories, he moved a significant step forward towards his dream of an integrated, self-contained SS state within a state.

The main beneficiary of Himmler's labour supply was Göring's Reichswerke: by the end of 1942 it was obtaining between eighty and ninety per cent of its 600,000-strong workforce from the camps, while for the rest of German industry, the ratio was around twenty per cent.

This was, of course, one of the prime reasons why Göring needed to keep in with Himmler, and why he co-operated with the SS in obtaining non-Jewish slave labour from the occupied countries. He also co-operated in some of the experiments carried out on prisoners in the camps, especially those concerned with exposure to extreme cold and high altitude, which were relevant to Luftwaffe survival techniques. Like the SS doctors involved, he seems to have had no problems with killing prisoners in the name of science.

Hitler may have been impressed by Himmler's concentration camp programme, but what had really earned his approval was the perform-ance of the Waffen-SS in the East. As the Red Army ground forward in its great counteroffensive after Stalingrad, Hitler had sent in the three original elite SS units, the 'Leibstandarte', 'Das Reich' and 'Totenkopf', which had just been refitted in the West and equipped with the latest armoured fighting vehicles and artillery, including the new Panther medium tank and an updated version of the Tiger heavy tank. Redesignated SS-Panzergrenadier divisions, they were formed into the II SS-Panzer Corps. When two Soviet armies crossed the River Donets east of Kharkov on 11 February 1943, Hitler ordered them to hold the city as a fortress, which in his terms meant to the death. On 16 February, encircled and threatened by an uprising in the city itself, they disregarded his order and broke out, leaving Kharkov to the Soviets. Having driven 184 kilometres (115 miles) south to join up with General Hermann Hoth's Fourth Panzer Army, they were soon back again and eager to restore their honour. Disobeying another order, this time from Hoth to bypass the city, they charged straight in and in three days of extremely vicious fighting succeeded in taking it. The victory, and the savagery with which it was won, was enough to make Hitler forgive the insubordina-tion, and he had nothing but praise for his brave SS warriors. As the spring thaw and Soviet exhaustion brought the fighting in the East to a temporary halt again, he began planning a new campaign using Kharkov as the anchor, in which they would play a prominent role.

Gratified – and no doubt relieved – by Hitler's praise, Himmler visited his men in Kharkov later in April, to congratulate them and remind them of their duty as racial warriors:

We have only one task, to stand firm and carry on the racial struggle without mercy . . . We will never let that outstanding weapon, the reputation for horror and terror that preceded us in the battles for Kharkov, fade, but will constantly add new meaning to it. They can call us what they like in the world; the main thing is that we are the eternally loyal, obedient, steadfast and unconquerable fighting men of the Germanic people and of the Führer, the SS of the Germanic Reich.[31]

By this time, Himmler was finding it difficult to keep personal control of the Waffen-SS, which was becoming increasingly independent, but he was happy to accept the kudos it earned him. Hitler had already agreed to the formation of two new SS-Panzergrenadier divisions, the 9th and 10th; now he authorised two more, one by merging Norwegian and Danish volunteer regiments into the 11th Nordland Division, the other, the 12th SS-Panzerdivision 'Hitlerjugend', made up of seventeen-year-old volunteers from the Hitler Youth. More new divisions were formed during the summer and autumn – the 16th Panzergrenadier Division was named the Reichsführer-SS – but recruitment was becoming ever more difficult, and was only achieved with coercion and conscription, both of which negated the idealistic SS fanaticism.

SS fanaticism was nowhere more evident that spring than in Warsaw. The clearing of the huge ghetto had begun in earnest the previous July, when Himmler had issued orders that the occupied Eastern Territories were to be completely cleared of Jews by the end of the year. A fresh wave of slaughter had swept across Poland, Belorussia and the Ukraine, as 400,000 Jews were murdered during the month of August 1942, and still the massacres continued, supplemented by trainloads of Jews from France, Belgium, Holland and Norway. Some 265,000 Jews from Warsaw had been carted off to the gas chambers of Treblinka during August and September, the largest slaughter of a single community in the whole of the Second World War. About 50,000 remained, and Himmler had been infuriated to discover that 32,000 of them were 'so-called armaments workers', mainly producing clothing, boots and furs for the Wehrmacht, plus parts for machinery and aircraft, for private firms in competition with his own enterprises. He had ordered that these workers and their equipment should be transferred to concentration camps, and that the Wehrmacht should then place its orders for uniforms and equipment with the SS.

By this time, however, the Warsaw Jews had learned the truth about the 'deportations' and the real purpose of Treblinka. With nothing to lose, they had decided they would no longer go quietly. They formed a Jewish Fighting Organisation, known by its Polish initials ZOB

(Zydowska Organizacja Bojowa) and began collecting and making what weapons they could – initially they only had two pistols between them but they gradually acquired more, plus seventeen rifles and several thousand grenades. They also started fortifying buildings and constructing underground bunkers and tunnels connected to the sewer system. When the HSSPF East, Friedrich Wilhelm Krüger, sent special SS squads into the ghetto on 18 January 1943 to carry out Himmler's order to close down the private firms and round up more Jews for Treblinka, they met with stiff resistance, as 1,000 Jewish fighters threw grenades and shot at them with pistols, killing twelve. The fighting continued for three days, until the Germans withdrew, bewildered and humiliated. They did not return until the morning of 19 April, the Jewish festival of Passover, by which time they had prepared their operational plan and increased the size of their force to about 3,000 men, equipped with heavier arms, including a tank, an armoured car, several artillery pieces, heavy machine guns and flame throwers.[32]

Even with this strength, the Germans failed at the first attempt, and were driven out of the ghetto by a hail of Molotov cocktails, grenades and bullets. Himmler, kept informed by telephone, swore furiously, dismissed the commander of the force on the spot, and ordered his replacement to begin a new attack in two hours' time. The battle raged for four weeks, with the Germans burning and demolishing buildings block by block, and the Jews, both men and women, fighting stubbornly to the death. It was not until 16 May that SS-Brigadeführer Jürgen Stroop, the commander of the operation, was able to report by teleprinter to Krüger and Himmler: 'The former Jewish residential quarter of Warsaw has ceased to exist. The Great Action was ended at 20.15 with the blowing up of the Warsaw synagogue. Total number of Jews dealt with: 56,065, including both Jews caught and Jews whose extermination can be proved.' 631 bunkers had been destroyed. Around 20,000 had been killed in the ghetto, and 36,000 sent to the gas chambers of Treblinka. Stroop reported that German losses amounted to 16 killed and 90 wounded, but this was no doubt to please Himmler; the true figures were estimated at 400 and 1,000. As a souvenir, Stroop proudly compiled all his reports into a handsome volume bound in black pebble leather, under the title 'There is no longer a Jewish residential district in Warsaw', and illustrated with 54 photographs.[33] He had three copies made, one for himself, one for Krüger, and one for Himmler, who rewarded him with the Iron Cross, First Class.

On 19 June, Himmler visited Hitler at the Berghof and reported that the clearing of the General-Government was well on the way to completion. He did not tell him, however, that the news of the revolt in Warsaw had inspired Jews in other ghettos, most notably in Bialystok, and even in the Treblinka and Sobibor death camps, to fight with equal ferocity. Expressing his satisfaction, Hitler told him that 'the deportation of the Jews must go on, regardless of any unrest it might cause during the next three to four months, and that it must be carried out in an all-embracing way'.

By 1943, the Western powers knew of the Final Solution, though there was precious little they could do about it. Goebbels, still hoping that it might be possible to split Britain and America away from the Soviet Union and draw them into the fight against Communism, was trying to find ways of distracting them from the Jewish question. Similarly, as whispers about the extermination camps began to spread among the German people, stemming in part from secretly-heard broadcasts by the BBC in London and the Soviet information service in Moscow, they too needed to be diverted. In early April, he found a way of doing so, at least for a little while, with the news that a number of mass graves had been discovered in the forest of Katyn, near Smolensk, containing the bodies of thousands of Polish officers, who had been taken prisoner by the Red Army in 1939.

There were in fact some 4,500 bodies, most with their hands tied behind their backs and killed with a single shot in the back of the neck.[34] They had clearly been murdered by the Soviets. In an astonishing display of hypocrisy, Goebbels seized avidly on this atrocity, inflating the number of dead to 10–12,000 and ferrying groups of journalists to the site, to see and report on the horrors for themselves. They were followed by delegations from neutral and occupied countries, including Poland – though he must have had difficulty finding Polish priests, scholars and writers after the activities of the *Einsatzgruppen*, which of course were never mentioned. Nor were the extermination camps, who counted their victims in millions.

Goebbels's campaign was a great success. The exiled Polish government in London accepted both the figures and the charge that the Soviet Union was responsible, and demanded an investigation by the Red Cross. Stalin responded by breaking off diplomatic relations with the 'bourgeois' Poles, and Goebbels whooped with delight. 'All enemy broadcasting companies and papers are unanimous,' he wrote in his

diary. 'The break is to be seen as a complete triumph for German propaganda, especially for me personally. People admire the extraordinary
skill and cunning with which we linked a highly political issue to the
case of Katyn. Suddenly cracks are appearing in the Allied camp.'

It was just as well that Goebbels had such confidence in his skill
and cunning – he would need every ounce of them over the next three
months, if he was to maintain morale among the German people as
one disaster followed another. On 12 May 1943, the exhausted Axis
forces in North Africa finally surrendered; more than 238,000 German
and Italian soldiers were taken prisoner. Goebbels suppressed the
figures, treating the defeat like a victory and Rommel as a hero, who
had reluctantly been sent home on sick-leave.

There was more bad news at sea, where the month was labelled
'Black May'. Grand Admiral Karl Dönitz, who had taken over as
Commander-in-Chief of the Navy at the end of January while still
remaining Commander-in-Chief of U-boats, had had a good winter. By
early March, he had around 435 U-boats in his fleet, with more than
100 at sea each month; they were locating every Allied convoy, attacking
half of them and sinking twenty-two per cent of the ships. The high
point was reached between 16 and 18 March, in a running battle
between 38 U-boats and two convoys, in which they sank 21 merchant
ships and a naval escort vessel, for the loss of one U-boat. From then
on, however, Allied countermeasures began to bite, with fresh break-
throughs in Ultra intelligence, backed up by improved electronic equipment, more very long range Liberators, and aircraft operating from
carriers, and the situation was soon reversed. During the first four
months of 1943, about 50 U-boats were sunk; in May alone, however,
47 were destroyed, one third of all those on station. Dönitz withdrew
all his boats from the North Atlantic and repositioned them south of
the Azores. The long Battle of the Atlantic had ended in a decisive
defeat.

Goebbels could keep the disaster at sea largely invisible from the
German people. The battle in the air, however, was impossible to hide,
as Germany's industrial centres were pounded night after night and
day after day by the RAF and the USAAF. Between March and July,
the RAF concentrated no fewer than forty-three major raids on the
Ruhr, including one on the night of 16–17 May, when the Lancasters
of the RAF's 617 Squadron threaded their way through mist, hills and

flak to breach the Möhne and Eder dams with Barnes Wallis's ingenious 'bouncing bombs', causing vast floods in the industrial valleys and putting a vital hydro-electric power station out of action. Göring, who was recuperating at Veldenstein from yet another illness that had put him in bed at the end of April, was angry and humiliated. 'My people tell me "We're not sure we can find London at night,"' he complained later. 'But their guys fly over to a dam that's socked in with fog, and whack right into it.'[35]

The day before the Dambusters raid, the Americans had caused serious damage to the navy's installations at Kiel. 'If this continues,' Goebbels wrote gloomily, 'we shall have to face serious consequences which in the long run will prove unbearable.' It did continue, especially in the Ruhr. A week later, the RAF hit Dortmund with over 2,000 tons of bombs in the heaviest raid of the war to date, and he recorded that the reports he received were 'pretty horrible . . . Industrial and munitions plants have been hit very hard . . . Some eighty to one hundred thousand inhabitants without shelter . . . The people in the west are gradually beginning to lose courage. Hell like that is hard to bear . . . Destruction is virtually total. Hardly a house is habitable.'[36]

Goebbels took control of the situation by setting up a new Interministerial Committee for the Relief of Air Raid Damage with himself as chairman, travelling from city to city, inspecting the ruins and talking to the people, who received him warmly everywhere. 'These suffering people felt that at least someone cared about their fate,' his aide, Rudolf Semmler recorded.[37] To the disgust of Goebbels and many others, neither Hitler nor Göring visited the bombed cities at that time, Hitler because he simply could not stand the sights and in any case was preoccupied with planning his new summer campaign in the East, Göring because the burden of guilt laid on his shoulders was too much to bear.

In fact, for once Göring had little to be guilty about, for no one could have done any more to protect the Reich in the face of overwhelming numbers. As any Allied aircrew member would testify, German air defences were now formidable both by day and by night, with chains of radar stations from the western coast to the heart of the Reich picking up intruders and guiding flak and fighters on to them. Ironically, the H2S radar which had infuriated Göring was a great help to the defenders, for its distinctive signal could be easily picked up and tracked, pinpointing the bombers' positions from take-off to target, for both fighters and radar-controlled flak. The night-fighters, successfully adapted versions of the Me-110, Ju-88 and Do-217, each with its own onboard radar, provided fearsome opposition, flown by young men defending their homeland with just as much determination as the RAF pilots in the Battle of Britain. By the beginning of July, the German air defences were knocking out between five and six per cent of enemy planes on every raid. Between 11 June and 9 July the RAF lost over 100 heavy bombers, a rate of loss that could not be sustained, and Air Marshal Harris was forced to admit defeat and call off the Ruhr offensive.

The Battle of the Ruhr was a victory for the Luftwaffe, but no one was under any illusion that it could bring anything more than a brief respite. Smaller raids continued against other targets, and then, on 24 July, the bombers turned their attentions to Hamburg. The RAF committed over 3,000 aircraft to four massive night raids on the city over a ten-day period, with additional nuisance raids in between, while the USAAF launched daytime raids on the 25th and 26th. Demonstrating its strength compared with Göring's fading bomber arm, the RAF managed to slip in a return raid on Essen on the night of 25–26 July, with 627 planes dropping over 2,000 tons of bombs and putting the Krupp works out of action.

The British attacked Hamburg almost without opposition, having completely disabled German defences by the simplest of all devices – code-named 'Window', it consisted of clouds of aluminium foil strips scattered across the sky to blind and confuse the radar on which searchlights, flak and night-fighters were totally dependent. On their second visit, they added a hail of incendiaries to the 8,000lb, 4,000lb and 1,000lb high explosive bombs, and started firestorms, and panic. 'The scenes of terror which took place in the firestorm area are indescribable,' Major-General Kehrl, the Hamburg Civil Defence chief, reported. 'Children were torn away from their parents' hands by the force of the hurricane and whirled into the fire. People who thought they had escaped fell down, overcome by the devouring heat, and died in an instant. Refugees had to make their way over the dead and dying. The sick and infirm had to be left behind by the rescuers as they themselves were in danger of burning.'[38] An estimated 44,600 civilians and 800 servicemen had been killed, at least one million people had fled; half the city, an area covering 8.5 square miles (22 square kilometres) had been reduced to rubble, and 580 industrial and war production firms destroyed or seriously damaged.[39]

The destruction of the mighty city of Hamburg struck as heavy a blow to German morale as Stalingrad. 'A wave of terror radiated from the suffering city and spread throughout Germany,' Adolf Galland recalled later. 'Appalling details of the great fires were recounted, and their glow could be seen for days from a distance of 120 miles. A stream of haggard, terrified refugees flowed into the neighbouring provinces. In spite of the strictest reticence in the official communiqués, the terror of Hamburg spread rapidly to the remotest villages of the Reich. Berlin was evacuated with signs of panic.'[40] Once again, the blame fell on Göring.

The Hamburg raids came at the end of a month of unremitting disaster for the Germans. On 5 July, after several weeks of delay, Hitler had launched his new offensive in the East, 'Operation Citadel', aimed at cutting off five Soviet armies in a massive bulge around the important rail junction of Kursk, midway between Kharkov and Orel. It started well, but soon ran into trouble as the well-prepared Soviet forces held them in fierce fighting and then counterattacked. With 2,700 Soviet tanks facing an equal number of German Panzers, it was the biggest tank battle in history, and it raged with unprecedented ferocity for a whole week.

While the fighting at Kursk was at its height, news came that US and British paratroops had landed in Sicily on 9 July, followed by a full-scale invasion two days later, clearly a prelude to an attack on mainland Italy itself. Hitler, deeply alarmed, called off Citadel and ordered the II SS Panzer Corps, which he claimed was as good as twenty Italian divisions, to be redeployed to Italy. With Kesselring and Jodl both declaring that Sicily could not be held, Hitler flew off to see Mussolini at Feltre, near Belluno, in northern Italy, to try to put fresh heart into him. He took Göring with him, but not Ribbentrop, who was in disgrace for being absent from his post during the invasion of Sicily – he had in fact been in bed with pneumonia, and was probably still not well enough to travel, but that was small consolation. It was a wasted journey. The Duce, who had been ill for some time with a stomach ulcer, looked considerably older than his sixty years and had clearly lost the will to go on. Göring does not seem to have played any significant part in the meeting, which turned into the usual monologue by Hitler to a dejected Mussolini. His efforts to raise the Italian leader's spirits were not helped by reports of the first heavy air raid on Rome, which came in just as they began to talk: carefully avoiding the historic centre, 500 bombers of the US Nineteenth Air Force had dropped 1,000 tons of bombs on the city's rail marshalling yards and airfields.

Roosevelt and Churchill had issued a joint message to the Italian people three days earlier, concluding that they would have to choose whether to 'die for Mussolini and Hitler – or live for Italy and civilisation'. They chose to live. On 24 July, the Fascist Grand Council, including Ciano, voted to give the King full powers to seek ways of saving Italy from destruction. The next day, the King dismissed Mussolini and appointed Marshal Badoglio in his place. Mussolini was placed under house arrest on the Mediterranean island of Ponza.

The Battle of Kursk, enlarged by the Soviets with fresh offensives around Orel and Kharkov, ended at the beginning of August with the Wehrmacht's greatest ever defeat. Stalingrad had been traumatic: Kursk was catastrophic. It was without doubt the single most important battle in the European war, and the decisive turning point on the Eastern Front. Although the Germans lost only 20,000 men, what counted was that the strength of the Panzers had been broken. However hard the bomb-battered German factories worked, German armour could never regain its numerical superiority over a Red Army backed by an arms industry that was only now getting into its awesome stride behind the Urals, out of reach of a Luftwaffe that still had no long-range heavy bombers. While Hitler and his generals counted the cost of their failure, the Red Army was poised to begin rolling inexorably forward, smashing its way across 1,000 miles of devastation to its ultimate target: Berlin. The tide had finally turned.

XXXIV

'CALL ME MEIER!'

THE fall of Mussolini unnerved Hitler and his paladins more than the failure of Citadel, for it brought not only the danger that Italy would defect from the Axis, but also the uncomfortable thought that what had happened in Rome might possibly happen in Berlin. Hitler heard about it during his noon conference with his generals on 25 July 1943, while they were discussing the first, terrible air raid on Hamburg the previous night. He immediately began raving that he wanted German troops to occupy Rome, depose the new regime, and bring Mussolini to safety in Germany. Forgetting that he had just been lambasting Göring and the Luftwaffe, he turned at once to his most trusted lieutenant, phoning Göring and telling him to come at once to the Wolfsschanze. To the astonished generals he explained:

The Reich Marshal has been through many crises with me. In a crisis he stays completely cool. One cannot have a better adviser in times of crisis than the Reich Marshal. In times of crisis the Reich Marshal is both brutal and ice-cool. When it's make or break, I've always seen how he's the ruthless one, as hard as iron. So, you won't find a better man, there isn't a better man around. He's been with me through every crisis, the most difficult crises, and he's always been ice-cool. Whenever things got really bad, he became ice-cool . . .[1]

Next, he sent for Himmler, Goebbels and Ribbentrop, to complete the magic circle of his closest associates, and had Rommel called back from Salonika, where he had been sent to deal with the mounting partisan problem and prepare for the defence against the Allied invasion that Hitler had anticipated would take place in Greece. The new situation meant Italy had become the prime target, and Hitler intended to switch Rommel to take overall command there. Hitler had no doubt that

Badoglio, no matter how much he protested Italy's loyalty, would come to terms with the Allies and take Italy out of the war. Until then, German plans to occupy the country as a whole would have to remain on hold. He still wanted to send crack troops into Rome to take over the city, and even the Vatican, but Goebbels and Ribbentrop, joining forces for once and backed by a cautious Rommel, managed to dissuade him. Instead, he ordered Himmler to find out where Mussolini was being held, so that he could be rescued and brought to Germany.

While the agonising was still going on over Italy, the heart-searching began over the tragedy that was still taking place in Hamburg. Göring had sent Bodenschatz to the city to talk to Gauleiter Karl Kaufmann and get accurate information, and he had returned with the appalling details. When he saw them, Göring issued orders that from then on priority was to be given to the defence of the Reich by producing more fighter aircraft, something with which all his generals agreed whole-heartedly, even those of the bomber arm. By concentrating on stopping the raids, they believed they could give the aircraft industry time to regenerate, after which they would be able to start striking back.

'Never before and never again did I witness such determination and agreement among the circle of those responsible for the leadership of the Luftwaffe,' Galland wrote later. 'It was as though under the impact of the Hamburg catastrophe everyone had put aside either personal or departmental ambitions . . . to do everything in this critical hour for the defence of the Reich, and to leave nothing undone to prevent a second national misfortune of this dimension.'² Fired up by this united mood, Göring left the generals and went to see Hitler, to obtain his approval. He did not get it. He emerged from the Führer's bunker in a state of shock, walked past his generals without speaking or looking at them and closeted himself in an adjoining room. After a while, he called in Galland and the General of Bombers, Dietrich Peltz, who were staggered to find him completely broken down, his head buried in his arms on the table, moaning incomprehensibly. They stood, embarrassed, while he gradually pulled himself together enough to tell them they were seeing his 'deepest moments of despair'. The Führer had lost faith in him, he said. Hitler had rejected their proposals for all-out defence, and given the Luftwaffe what he described as one last chance to restore its honour with large-scale bombing attacks on England instead. Terror, Hitler had insisted yet again, could only be smashed by counter-terror.

Wiping the tears from his eyes, Göring straightened and declared that Hitler had made him realise his mistake: 'The Führer is always right. We must deal such mighty blows to our enemy in the West that he will never dare to risk another raid like Hamburg. General Peltz, I hereby appoint you assault leader against England.'[3] Peltz did his best with the limited resources at his disposal, but the series of raids he mounted on England resulted in unacceptable losses with little to show for them: British civilian casualties during the last three months of 1943 were 247 killed and 561 injured.

Meanwhile, the bad news continued to pile up during August, reaching a climax on the 17th, when the battle for Sicily ended after thirty-nine days. 40,000 German and 62,000 Italian troops were safely evacuated to the mainland, with all their arms and equipment,[4] but the Axis forces had suffered 167,000 casualties, 37,000 of them German, during the campaign.[5] On that same black day, 571 RAF bombers dropped 1,937 tons of high explosive bombs on the secret weapons research and construction site at Peenemünde on the Baltic, setting back production of the V-1 flying bomb and V-2 rocket by weeks, while 315 American planes hit the ball-bearing plants at Schweinfurt and then the Messerschmitt works at Regensburg, both in deepest Bavaria, before flying on to land in North Africa.[6] This was the USAAF's first strategic raid, and although the Luftwaffe brought down no fewer than sixty aircraft, this was not enough in German eyes to outweigh the fact that it killed 400 Messerschmitt workers and reduced German ball-bearing production by thirty-eight per cent.

For some time, Göring had been offloading the guilt for the Luftwaffe's defensive failures on to Jeschonnek, along with most of its other problems. As the relationship had spiralled downwards, Jeschonnek had tried in vain to move from his position as Chief of Staff to the active command of an air fleet, but Hitler had refused to sanction it. The abuse that both Hitler and Göring heaped on him after the 17 August raids was the final straw and the next day he followed Udet's example and shot himself, leaving a note saying he could no longer work with Göring. The official announcement stated that he had died from a stomach haemorrhage. In his place, Göring appointed General Günter Korten, an efficient, reliable officer who brought fresh purpose to the Luftwaffe over the next year, aided by his new deputy, the stolid Bavarian Lieutenant-General Karl Koller.

While Göring was falling further and further from grace, Himmler

was rising fast. On 20 August, Hitler appointed him Minister of the
Interior, in place of Frick, who he thought was 'old and worn out' at
sixty-seven, and against whom Goebbels had been intriguing for several
months. Events in Italy had forced Hitler to concede that he needed
to take a tighter grip on the home front to prevent any subversive
action, and Himmler was clearly the man to do just that. Himmler's
police state was complete: instead of the Interior Ministry controlling
the police, the police now controlled the Ministry, the SS controlled
the police – and Himmler controlled them all.

On 23 August, as the Red Army re-took Kharkov for the final time,
the RAF returned to Berlin with 727 Lancasters, Stirlings and Halifaxes,
plus a scattering of Mosquitoes acting as pathfinders. As they
approached the city, they found themselves facing a new threat: Berlin
was now defended by night-fighters as well as its formidable flak
batteries. Until then, German fighters had kept away from the cities,
where they were just as vulnerable to flak as were the British bombers.
They had operated only along the routes from the coast, guided to
their targets by ground-based radar. With the collapse of the radar-
controlled system after the introduction of Window, Major Hajo
Herrmann, a bomber expert, had come up with a risky but effective
tactic, which he christened 'Wilde Sau', 'Wild Boar'. This involved
committing fighters to a wild free-for-all in the skies over the cities,
where their pilots could rely on visual contact to find and attack enemy
bombers caught in searchlight beams or the light of flares, or silhou-
etted against the glow of burning buildings on the ground. Because
they were not relying on radar, conventional night-fighters with crews
of two or three – a gunner and radar operator as well as the pilot –
could be supplemented by faster, more manoeuvrable, single-seater
aircraft. They aimed to catch the raiders in the middle of their bombing
runs, when they were at their most vulnerable. Unable to change course
until their bomb bays were empty, they provided relatively easy targets
for daring young Luftwaffe pilots.

It was hazardous – the fighters were at risk from their own flak as
well as from the bombers' guns and the danger of mid-air collision –
but it worked. The RAF lost sixty-two aircraft on 23 August, the heaviest casualties ever sustained in one night. The Luftwaffe, on the other
hand, could regard their night's work as eminently satisfactory. They
had lost nine aircraft, but only four aircrew. The RAF were back on

25 August, and again on 31 August and 3 September, but with fewer aircraft each time – the success of the flak and the night-fighters was steadily reducing the number of planes available to Air Marshal Harris.

After 3 September, Harris called off the attack on Berlin. It was a victory for Göring and the Luftwaffe, but it was an unseen triumph, and it was overshadowed by the landing of the British Eighth Army at Reggio di Calabria on the toe of mainland Italy. That same day, the Italians signed an armistice with the Allies, though it was kept secret until 8 September, to avoid the Germans seizing control of the country before the Americans and British had landed in force, which they did the next day.

Hitler had just returned from a flying visit to Army Group South's headquarters at Zaporozhye on the Eastern Front, where he had been forced to agree to a full-scale retreat, and was in no mood to accept the Italians' defection. He had already moved sixteen German divisions into Italy, including the Leibstandarte SS-Panzergrenadier Division switched from the East – he had changed his mind over the other two Waffen-SS divisions, Das Reich and Totenkopf, and kept them in the East – and they were primed to take control in central Italy. German troops marched into Rome on 10 September, forestalling an Allied airborne invasion by seizing the airports. 650,000 Italian soldiers were forcibly disarmed and taken into captivity, 300,000 of them sent to the Reich as forced labour. Resistance was put down with ruthless savagery: 6,000 Italian soldiers were killed in one division that held out for two weeks. Along with the air force, most of the Italian fleet escaped and sailed to Malta to join the Allies, but Luftwaffe planes intercepted and sank the battleship *Roma* and seriously damaged her sister ship, the *Italia*.

On 12 September, the SS distinguished itself in Hitler's eyes yet again with the audacious rescue of Mussolini – though Göring's paratroopers shared in the glory of an operation reminiscent of the capture of the Belgian fortress of Eben Emael. Himmler's men had discovered that the Duce was now being held in a remote ski hotel, 6,500 feet up on Monte Corno, the highest mountain in the Abruzzi. The task of recovering him from this inaccessible spot was given to SS-Obersturmbannführer Otto Skorzeny, head of special commando units in the RSHA, who landed twelve gliders carrying ninety of Student's paratroopers on the steep slope right outside the hotel door. Aided by the Italian General Spoleti, they overpowered the Carabinieri guards, released Mussolini, and flew him out in a Fieseler Storch, which

Student's personal pilot, Captain Gerlach, somehow managed to land and take off again from a tiny open space, though heavily overloaded with Skorzeny and Mussolini as passengers.

After a hair-raising flight through the mountains, Mussolini was taken to meet Hitler at Wolfsschanze. He did not stay long. Hitler was 'extraordinarily disappointed' by his broken-down appearance and defeated attitude, and sent him off to Munich after three days to start forming a new government. 'He left without a spring in his step,' noted Below. 'His time had run out.'⁷ Hitler's decision to restore him to power, if only nominally, was prompted by Ribbentrop, who argued for this rather than regarding Italy as an occupied enemy state like France, since it was the only way in which he, Ribbentrop, could still have some involvement in Italian affairs. Under German tutelage, therefore, Mussolini set up the Italian Social Republic, but the area he supposedly governed from a villa on Lake Garda was strictly confined between Rome, where the SS held sway, and the northern frontier areas, which were under German military control. Even his nominally independent republic came under a German Commander for Upper Italy, and the SS had a free hand everywhere.

Himmler appointed Karl Wolff, his former Chief of Staff and liaison officer at Führer Headquarters, as his personal representative in Italy, with the title of Highest (as opposed to the usual Higher) SS und Polizeiführer. Wolff was convalescing after a serious operation for the removal of a kidney stone, but was in Himmler's bad books for going over his head to get Hitler's permission to divorce his wife and marry his mistress, after Himmler had refused it. The new appointment was a way of moving him away from the centre of things at Führer Headquarters, but Wolff was delighted at having his first independent command. Himmler replaced him at Führer Headquarters with SS-Brigadeführer Hermann Fegelein, a former SS cavalry officer with a dubious past and a winning manner, who was to marry Eva Braun's sister the following year.

One of Wolff's first actions was to order the round-up of Italy's 37,000 Jews, which Mussolini had always resisted, and the burning of their synagogues. A few hundred Jews in the north managed to escape over the mountain passes into Switzerland, while several thousand more found refuge in Catholic homes and institutions. Ribbentrop persuaded Hitler to decree that Rome's 6,730 Jews should be taken to Mauthausen concentration camp in Austria as hostages, but when the round-up started only 1,015 could be found. Although he failed to speak out and condemn the action – which might have prevented it – the Pope had personally ordered his clergy to open the Church's sanctuaries to non-Aryans in need of refuge. 4,805 were taken into monasteries, convents and other religious institutions in Rome and the Vatican itself, while most of the remaining 910 were hidden in private homes. The 1,015 that were found were not taken to Mauthausen, but to Auschwitz. Sixteen of them survived the war.[8]

Someone who did not survive was Ciano. Under threat of prosecution from the Badoglio government for corruption, he and his wife had fled to safety in Bavaria. When Mussolini reluctantly agreed to set up a special tribunal in Verona to try as many of the 'traitors' who had voted to oust him as he could lay hands on, the vindictive Ribbentrop had Ciano deported at once, without waiting to be asked. He was executed on 11 January 1944, to Ribbentrop's great satisfaction.

Throughout the autumn of 1943, Germany's position continued to deteriorate. In the East, the Soviets pushed inexorably forward with more than two and a half million men against barely half as many Germans and their allies, taking back the Donbas and reaching the Dnieper by the end of September. They took back Smolensk on 25 September and Kiev on 6 November, and advanced through Belorussia towards Minsk. By the beginning of December, the Soviet High Command had completed plans for a great winter offensive to start at the end of the year and go on non-stop until the invaders had been driven back across the Soviet frontiers.

Meanwhile, in Italy on 13 October, Badoglio declared war on Germany, and those Italian units that had escaped now joined the Allies, to fight as 'co-belligerents'. The Western Allies were making slow progress against determined German defence, but they had established their hold on the southern part of the country, from which American bombers could reach Austria, southern Germany and the Balkans, including the Romanian oilfields at Ploesti. In the Balkans, where German troops had taken over from Italians, partisan activity increased until it became a real problem, tying down large numbers of men.

Although the British air raids on Berlin had been suspended, attacks on other targets continued relentlessly, by day and by night. On 14 October, 291 Flying Fortresses took off from bases in England heading for the ball-bearing factories of Schweinfurt again. They were protected by their own fighter escorts as far as Aachen, but after that were left to defend themselves with their own armament. Only three failed to make it to the target, but those who did were torn apart by Luftwaffe fighters under orders from Göring to risk everything in close-quarter attacks, emptying their magazines, then landing to refuel and reload, before returning swiftly to the fray. The Luftwaffe lost fourteen fighters, but claimed jubilantly to have knocked out 121 B-17s. The true score was 60 shot down, with 17 sustaining heavy damage and another 121 less seriously damaged, but it was still an impressive tally. Including kills during four earlier USAAF raids, the Luftwaffe had brought its total in that one week to 148.[9] The Americans retired, hurt; there would be no more daylight raids until the New Year.

For some months, Göring had avoided public appearances, his confidence sapped by Hitler's constant criticism. Rudolf Semmler, Goebbels's aide, had noted in his diary on 10 August: 'Politically, Göring might as well be dead. Rumours have already made him out to be dead. Hitler, with whom Göring surprisingly enough still stands high, has therefore advised that the Reich Marshal should be seen again among his people, to win back his popularity.'[10] Göring obliged reluctantly with a walkabout in the Berlin markets, accompanied by a staff of bemedalled officers. Semmler reported that he had been greeted with whistles and cat-calls of 'Herr Meier!' No doubt with a certain amount of *Schadenfreude*, Goebbels commented that Göring had been unwise to keep out of the public eye for so long, and that it only encouraged rumours. He came to the rescue with a special press campaign to boost Göring's image. But after his Berlin appearance, Göring withdrew once more into his own world until the victory at Schweinfurt persuaded him that it was safe to come out again.

This time, he did it properly, touring the shattered towns and cities of the Ruhr and the Rhineland, seeing for himself the devastation and the efforts to carry on regardless, and above all meeting the people. He had already stopped wearing his medals as a token of solidarity with their suffering, and was dressed more soberly than usual. To his relief – and amazement – he found that he had not lost his touch. Everywhere he stopped he was mobbed by cheering crowds, and the shouts of 'Call me Meier!' were good-humoured, the sort of ribbing one exchanges with a friend, which he could respond to with a self-deprecating grin. It was almost too much for him. 'I'm human, too,' he said afterwards in a speech to his airmen in the canteen at Arnhem-Deelen airbase, 'and I would have understood if these people who had just ruins around them – just rubble to the left and right of them – upon seeing a brass hat go by (and the one responsible for the whole mess, at that, or at least responsible for their defence) – might, well, not exactly toss rotten eggs at me, but at least throw the odd scowl or shout "You fat old lump!" What a welcome! I could have cried.'[11]

Göring's relief after Schweinfurt was short-lived. On the night of 18 November 1943, 411 RAF Lancasters roared over Berlin at the unprecedented rate of twenty-seven bombers a minute, dropping 1,593 tons of bombs in just sixteen minutes of hell. On 22–23 November, they were back again, with no fewer than 775 bombers. The Chancellery was among many government buildings seriously damaged, along with the Kaiserhof Hotel and Göring's Forschungsamt, which was completely wrecked. Harris had launched his Battle of Berlin in earnest. It continued over the next four months, with sixteen major raids on Berlin and nineteen on other towns and cities by way of diversion – and so did Hitler's tirades against Göring. Göring, in turn, lashed out at his staff, bullying and threatening them mercilessly, demanding ever more from pilots and production staff, castigating aircraft manufacturers and designers.

Output from the aircraft factories had increased dramatically despite the damage and disruption caused by the bombing, but it was still not enough. There were dozens of new designs in development, some weird and wacky, many of them technically advanced, as well as a constant stream of improvements to existing models. The tried and tested Me-109 in all its varied configurations had been joined in service by an even better fighter, the Focke-Wulf FW-190, but most of the new designs could not be ready in time to make any real difference.

To save his reputation – and Germany – Göring needed the 'wonder weapons' that Goebbels regularly hinted at in his efforts to raise public morale. There was a host of ideas, many of them harebrained, but three were viable, genuinely effective, and in an advanced state. One, a long-range rocket with a one-ton warhead, code-named A4, was being developed by the young scientist Wernher von Braun under the aegis of the army. The second, effectively the first cruise missile, was a small, pilotless aircraft with a range of up to 200 kilometres (125 miles), powered by a simple pulse-jet engine and also carrying a one-ton warhead, which became known as the Flying Bomb, or V-1 – the V standing for *Vergeltungswaffe*, reprisal weapon. The V-1 was the Luftwaffe's weapon. It was well advanced before the raid on Peenemünde, which only delayed its final development by a few weeks, and by the beginning of November the first sixty-three concrete launching ramps were being built near the Channel coast, pointing towards London. Göring issued a contract to the Fieseler company to start mass production of the bombs in January 1944.

The delays caused by the Peenemünde raid to Braun's rocket, soon to be known as the V-2, which was in any case much more complex and expensive to produce than the flying bomb, were more serious. Himmler and the SS came to the rescue, with Pohl's Works Department creating a huge underground factory in a cave complex near Nordhausen in the Harz Mountains, complete with the most basic living quarters for prisoners who had until then been producing components in the secrecy of Buchenwald concentration camp. Code-named 'Dora', the new workshops were prepared and equipped in the remarkably short time of two months, but large-scale production did not start until May 1944, and it was September before the first operational rockets were fired.

The third new project was ready to be rushed into production by the end of 1943, and would undoubtedly change everything, given the chance. Unfortunately, Hitler denied it that chance. The Me-262 twinjet fighter was the furthest advanced of various German jet aircraft designs: its first test flight had taken place on 25 March 1942, with a second four months later. Galland had flown a new model in May 1943, and had reported enthusiastically on its performance to Göring. He had reached the unheard-of speed of 520 miles per hour (830 kph), 130 mph (210 kph) faster than the Me-109, making it easily the fastest plane in the world. Göring immediately ordered top priority for its manufacture, with the first production model planned for January. The Me-262 was clearly capable of outflying any enemy aircraft, but it was a fighter, and Hitler, still wedded to the belief that attack was the best form of defence, was interested only in bombers. Without even informing Göring, Milch or Korten, he discussed the new plane with the designers and engineers, then cancelled its production and ordered more prototypes and testing. Göring was naturally upset at this undermining of his authority, but there was worse to come.

In an attempt to restore Hitler's faith, Göring ordered a display of the Luftwaffe's latest planes and equipment at Insterburg airfield in East Prussia near the Wolfsschanze, on 26 November. Pride of place in the long line of planes, many of which were prototypes and nowhere near ready for service, went to the Me-262, which Hitler was seeing for the first time. He was very impressed by its appearance, called Willi

Messerschmitt over, and asked him pointedly if it could be built as a bomber. To the horror of Göring, Milch and Korten, Messerschmitt, always eager to please, said it could and that it was capable of carrying two 250-kilogram bombs in racks under its wings. Hitler was delighted. This, he declared, was the fast bomber he had been waiting for, and overriding Milch's protests he ordered that it should be built exclusively as such.

Göring tried in the next few days to persuade Hitler to change his mind, but he was sharply rebuffed, and failed yet again to stand up to the Führer. When he went to Paris on 6 December, to supervise 'Operation Capricorn', a planned campaign of retaliatory raids on London, he left written orders with Milch that the Me-262 was 'to be regarded only as a jet *bomber*'. It soon became obvious that it was impossible to convert the Me-262 into a pure bomber, but efforts to accommodate Hitler's obstinate demands by turning it into a fighter-bomber delayed production for several vital months.

Operation Capricorn had been directly ordered by Hitler, but Göring quickly discovered that the Luftwaffe simply did not have the resources to mount it with any chance of real success, and postponed it. After tasting the delights of Paris for a few days, and acquiring a few more works of art from museums and dealers, he rolled back to Carinhall to spend Christmas and New Year with his family.

At Carinhall, he received a surprise present for his fifty-first birthday that embarrassed even him. It came from the Hermann Göring Parachute Division and consisted of sixteen crates of the rarest art treasures, which the troops had 'rescued' from the mountain-top Benedictine monastery of Monte Cassino in central Italy, where the Italian government had stored 187 crates of art and antiquities, mostly from museums and galleries in Naples. When the Hermann Göring Division took over the building, to create a virtually impregnable strong point dominating the Allied line of advance, they offered to transport the crates and their contents to the Vatican for safety. Only 172 crates arrived in Rome. The rest, containing the most delectable works, including pictures by Titian, Van Dyke, Raphael, Claude Lorraine, Tiepolo, Brueghel the Elder and other masters, plus antique gold and silver objects and bronzes from Pompeii and Herculaneum, were sent to Carinhall. It was a breathtaking haul, and must have been an immense temptation, but for once, Göring's conscience overcame his greed. He reprimanded the Hermann Göring Division, but he did not send the treasures back to Italy. After consulting Hitler, he had them packed up again and sent to the salt mines at Alt Aussee in the Alps, 'for safe keeping'.

The heavy raids on Berlin brought fresh challenges and opportunities for Goebbels. He had been called the 'Conqueror of Berlin', now he proclaimed that he wanted to earn the title 'Defender of Berlin'. He took personal charge of the whole situation, directing the emergency services from the luxurious bunkers excavated under the Wilhelmplatz for the Kaiserhof Hotel, which he had requisitioned as his command centre. When the raiders left, he toured the battered and burning city, comforting and encouraging the people, making impromptu speeches, supervising the distribution of food and drink, and generally showing his face everywhere. His popularity soared, even among workers in the industrial suburbs, where his storm-troopers had taken so many beatings in the early years of the Nazi struggle. After taking part in serving hot food in 'Red' Wedding after a raid on 29 November, he recorded in his diary with some pride: 'The men and women workers received me with an enthusiasm as unbelievable as it was indescribable.' A packing case was found for him to stand on, and he was 'forced' to make yet another speech.[12]

He had already evacuated hundreds of thousands of old people, children and non-working women to safer parts of the country: 400,000 children had been sent to foster homes or school camps in Austria or Silesia in August, leaving their mothers free to work in the city's munitions factories. In late November and early December, he ordered a fresh evacuation to the countryside around Berlin, from where people could commute to work in the city. His own children had been evacuated to the Obersalzberg in 1941, but had returned to the city during the lull in the RAF raids. Now he moved them to the safety of Lanke, but he himself remained in the city centre, ostentatiously sharing the dangers faced by his Berliners and working flat out to maintain morale.

This, Goebbels felt, was his great chance to implement total war in his own city – and he succeeded. There was virtually no absenteeism in the factories, and output remained high. Being Berliners, they indulged in a great deal of black humour, but they kept working, and there were none of the rebellious demonstrations calling for an end to the war that he had feared. Hitler rewarded him on 21 December by appointing him head of the newly-formed Reich Inspectorate of Civilian Air Protection Measures. Goebbels responded with gushing gratitude for the Führer's demonstration of trust, telling him how happy he was to be able to bear 'a little of the gigantic burden of care that lies upon you', and assuring him that he could count on him 'in any and every situation'.[13]

The New Year of 1944 brought little cheer to Germany and its leaders. Civilian morale came close to breaking point as the RAF continued to rain high explosives and incendiaries on Berlin and other cities. On 20 January, for instance, they dropped 2,400 tons of bombs on Berlin, while Göring's Operation Capricorn, which started the next day, barely scratched London. Göring claimed that between 300 and 400 German bombers had taken part in the raid; the British estimated the number as around thirty. Galland, admittedly not an impartial witness, reckoned that during the whole of January and February no more than 275 tons of bombs were dropped on London. However, the 'Little Blitz', as it became known, accounted for 1,086 killed and 1,972 injured during that time, so it was by no means completely ineffectual.

By early February, Göring had a new factor to contend with in the defence of the Reich as the Americans resumed daylight raids, with the big bombers protected by fighters. During the pause after the disasters of Schweinfurt, they had developed long-range versions of the P-51 Mustang, fitted with the Merlin engine and drop tanks under the wings holding enough fuel to escort the B-27s and B-24s right into the heart of Germany, as far even as Berlin. Now there was nowhere in the Reich where Luftwaffe fliers were secure from attack by the skilled and highly aggressive American pilots. When Göring was first told of the appearance of single-engined, single-seater fighters in German air space, he refused to believe it, but he was soon forced to accept it as real.

In sharp contrast to the RAF's Bomber Harris, the newly appointed commander of the US Strategic Air Forces in Europe, General Carl Spaatz, believed that the way to shorten the war was to destroy the Luftwaffe rather than the cities, and on 20 February 1,000 of his bombers began their 'Big Week', accurately pounding every important target of the German aircraft industry and dropping 10,000 tons of bombs during five murderous days. They then turned their attentions to Berlin, with 590 planes scoring 75 direct hits on the Erkner ball-bearing works in a precision-bombing raid on 8 March, and putting it out of action for some time. Thanks to the Mustangs, the American loss rate, though still heavy, was less than a third of what it had been in October 1943, and German aircraft production was severely hit.

Although the US Air Force was winning the daytime war, the Luftwaffe's night-fighters claimed significant successes against the RAF when it attacked Leipzig on 19–20 February, losing 78 out of 816 bombers, and Nuremberg on 30–31 March, with 96 planes of 795 shot down and 71 badly damaged. The Nuremberg raid was the RAF's equivalent to Schweinfurt; after it, Harris stopped sending his bombers on mass raids on distant targets. It was another notable victory for the Luftwaffe, but it was so heavily overshadowed by the death and destruction on the ground that it did little to restore Göring's failing reputation or halt the flood of criticism against him. Hitler, according to Below, launched 'a blistering tirade at the Air Defence Organisation and the Luftwaffe', and, completely overlooking 'the courageous engagements by our numerically inferior fighter force . . . demanded that higher numbers of aircraft be destroyed'.¹⁴

After the disasters of 'Big Week', which killed thousands of aircraft workers and wrecked factories and half-completed planes, it was clear that without drastic action the air war was lost. Recognising this, Göring was forced to relinquish part of his power, allowing Milch to set up a special Fighter Aircraft Staff in partnership with Speer's ministry to co-ordinate all aspects of production and cope with the crisis, under the direction of Speer's energetic and ambitious deputy, Karl-Otto Saur. It was the first step in handing over responsibility for all aircraft production to Speer, something that Göring had always refused even to consider. He retired to Veldenstein to lick his wounds and rest.

Hitler had left the Wolfsschanze at the end of February, while work was in progress to reinforce the headquarters with tons of concrete against Soviet air attack. But instead of sharing his people's suffering in Berlin, he chose to base himself in the safety of the Berghof, which was swathed in camouflage netting to merge into the mountainside. Göring followed him to the Obersalzberg towards the end of March, after a brief respite at Veldenstein, to be on hand to counter the influence of Bormann in his own domain. It was there that he received another sharp reminder of his diminishing influence when he learned of the murder of fifty British and Commonwealth RAF officers, prisoners of war who had been among seventy-five or eighty who had tunnelled their way out of Stalag Luft III at Sagan in Silesia, which was technically an air force establishment and therefore under his command.

Some of the escapers were caught by the camp guards before they had got far, and were taken back inside unharmed. Some fifty others managed to cover some distance before they were recaptured by police and SS. Without consulting Göring, Hitler ordered Himmler to have these prisoners shot by the SD. Göring was horrified when he found out. He went first to Himmler, who confirmed that the men had been shot, and said that he had received the order directly from the Führer. Himmler claimed, Göring said later, that he had opposed this but that Hitler had 'absolutely insisted on it, since he maintained that escapes to such an extent represented an extreme danger to security'. Göring told the Nuremberg Tribunal that he had then talked to Hitler about the matter:

I explained to him why this order . . . was completely impossible and what repercussions it would cause with regard to my airmen employed against the enemy in the West. The Führer – our relations were already extremely bad and strained – answered rather violently that the airmen who were flying against Russia have to reckon with the possibility of being immediately beaten to death in case of an emergency landing, and that airmen going to the West should not want to claim a special privilege in this respect. I then told him that these two things really had no connection with each other.

Then I talked with the Chief of my General Staff and asked him . . . to write to the OKW and say that I was now requesting, that the air force was requesting, that these camps be taken from our control. I did not want to have anything more to do with prisoner-of-war camps in case such things should ever happen again.

With a breathtaking lack of sensitivity – and perspective – Göring solemnly concluded: 'I myself considered it the most serious incident of the whole war.'[15]

The murder of escaped prisoners by the SS was echoed by a growing number of attacks by civilians on Allied aircrews who had baled out of their aircraft. Their anger at the destruction of their homes and loved ones was increased as Mustang fighters began shooting up trains, trucks and even civilians on the ground, as well as military targets, while escorting the big bombers. All Allied airmen were dubbed 'terror fliers' and were liable to be lynched or shot by the police when they parachuted to earth. As feelings ran ever higher, any parachutist was in danger, even German airmen, who were attacked on several occasions.

Göring did his best to stop the lynchings, but was blocked by

Bormann, who ordered the police not to intervene. Hitler was firmly behind Bormann, raging at Göring and demanding to know the names of officers who had protected airmen from the population and what punishment they had received. 'I did not have these people searched for or arrested,' Göring said at Nuremberg, 'nor did I have them punished.' He kept on insisting that lynchings and beating must be stopped, until Hitler cut him short by saying he knew that 'both air forces have come to a mutual agreement of cowardice'. Incensed by such an accusation, Göring snapped back: 'We have not come to an agreement of cowardice, but somehow we airmen have always remained comrades, no matter how much we fight each other.'[16]

In Italy the military situation had deteriorated into a bloody stalemate during the early months of 1944. Helped by the hilly terrain and relative narrowness of the front, the German armies had halted the Allied armies, but could not drive them back again. On 22 and 23 January, when Allied troops landed at Anzio, south of Rome, the German commanders' swift reaction prevented a breakout from the beachhead, but the two sides remained locked in savage combat for four long months. There was deadlock, too, in central Italy, most notably around Monte Cassino, where the paratroops and Panzergrenadiers fought a grim defensive battle from the fortified town and hill – though not, until it had been bombed by the Allies, from inside the monastery itself, having promised the Vatican they would not use it. They held out until 17 May.

On the Eastern Front, the war had become a catalogue of death and disaster as the Soviet juggernaut ground relentlessly forward. On New Year's Eve, the Red Army captured Zhitomir, and three days later crossed the pre-war Polish frontier. On 27 January the siege of Leningrad was finally broken after two years and four months. During the first seventeen days of February, twenty-five German divisions were wiped out in the Ukraine. On 15 March, the Red Army crossed the River Bug, the main start-line for Barbarossa in 1941. By 18 March, as the spring thaw brought a pause in the fighting, Soviet troops reached the Romanian border. After two and three-quarter years of savage fighting and appalling losses, the German army was back where it had begun.

Fearful that the Hungarian government was about to follow the Italian example and desert him, allowing the Red Army to roll unhindered across their country and into Austria, Hitler invited the Regent, Admiral Horthy, to visit him at Klessheim Castle, the former residence of the Archbishops of Salzburg. When Horthy arrived, on 18 March, Hitler accused him of negotiating with the Allies to take Hungary out of the war and tried to browbeat him into signing a document 'inviting' Germany to occupy his country the next day. Unlike Hitler's previous victims, Schussnigg and Hácha, however, the seventy-five-year-old Admiral objected strongly and tried to leave. He was prevented, ludicrously, by a mock air raid staged by the SS guards, complete with a dense smoke screen around the building, and when he tried to telephone his government he was told the raid had severed the lines and it was impossible to get through. Eventually, with pressure from Ribbentrop and threats to his own family, he was persuaded to accept a temporary occupation of Hungary, until a new government had been installed, and he was allowed to leave, accompanied, significantly, by Kaltenbrunner, Heydrich's successor as head of the RSHA. His train was delayed on its journey while four German battle groups moved into Hungary. With them went Adolf Eichmann and a special Einsatzkommando to begin rounding up and deporting Hungary's 750,000 Jews, who until then had not been harmed.

Within days the first ghettos were set up in brickyards, timber yards and abandoned barracks but the first trains did not leave for Auschwitz-Birkenau until 29 April. Between then and early July, 437,402 Hungarian Jews were transported to the labour camps and the gas chambers, which were so overwhelmed by the arrival of as many as 12,000 a day that they and the cremation ovens could not cope and Höss's men had to resort to the old *Einsatzgruppen* methods of shooting and burning in open pits. Under pressure from the King of Sweden, the Pope, the International Red Cross and the British and American governments, Horthy had the deportations stopped on 8 July.

Himmler, meanwhile, had sent a Hungarian Zionist Jew called Joel Brand to Istanbul on one of the most bizarre errands of the war: to negotiate with the Allies the exchange of a million Jews for foreign currency, various commodities, and 10,000 trucks, 'for use only on the Eastern Front'. The offer was accompanied by the threat that if the Allies did not agree, all the Jews remaining in Hungary, Poland, Romania and the Protectorate would be annihilated.[17]

It is hard to fathom Himmler's motives in making such an approach not long after he had told his senior SS officers and the Gauleiters that not only Jewish men but also all Jewish women and children must be killed without mercy to prevent any revival of their race, and the children's survival as avengers. It may be that he could see the writing on the wall and wanted to set himself up with the Western Allies as the Nazi leader with whom they could negotiate. It is also possible that he was trying to drive a wedge between the West and Stalin, seeing an Allied split as Germany's only hope of avoiding total defeat; like Hitler and Goebbels, he still clung to the delusion that Britain and America could eventually be made to see sense and join Germany in the fight to keep Bolshevism out of Western Europe. This was certainly how London saw it: 'a sheer case of blackmail or political warfare' intended to cause trouble by leading the Soviet government to believe that the British and Americans were negotiating with the enemy. The Americans, a little more cynical perhaps, thought that maybe Himmler and Eichmann were trying to line their pockets with foreign currency for their personal use after Germany's defeat. Either way, nothing came of it. The British and Americans informed the Soviets, who refused to countenance any dealings with 'Hitlerite Germany'. The Western Allies, however, strung Himmler along for several months, in the hope of delaying further killings.

Himmler had in fact been putting out feelers to both the West and the Soviet Union for some time, probably since 1942, through Walter Schellenberg, the head of the Foreign SD, and certainly since August 1943, when his chiropractor Kersten had made contact on his behalf with Roosevelt's special representative in Stockholm, Abram S. Hewitt. He had followed this by sending a personal friend, the lawyer Karl Langbehn, with Schellenberg, first to Stockholm and then to Switzerland, to sound out each side on the possibility of a separate peace, using the conquered territories and the Jews as bargaining counters.[18] He had also had secret contacts with the conservative opposition in Germany itself, partly no doubt to keep an eye on them but presumably also hoping to stake his claim to a place either within or even at the head of a new government, should Hitler fall. None of these moves came to anything, but he was careful to keep the channels open against future contingencies, and to foster the belief that he was the only man with enough power to negotiate a peace settlement on the basis of a change of leadership in the Reich.

During the spring of 1944, Himmler had spread his tentacles still wider by fulfilling his long-held ambition to take over the Abwehr, the OKW's intelligence and counter-espionage organisation. The Gestapo had suspected for some time that the Abwehr was harbouring a nest of enemies of the regime, and since the death of Heydrich with his close personal relationship with Canaris, the little admiral had been living on borrowed time. A Gestapo investigation into breaches of currency regulations by members of his staff had provided the opportunity Himmler had been waiting for when it revealed that the men responsible were not only smuggling Jews out to Switzerland, but were part of a ring plotting to overthrow Hitler and – horror of horrors – negotiate a separate peace with the Allies. Three of the conspirators, lawyer Hans von Dohnanyi, his brother-in-law Pastor Dietrich Bonhoeffer, and an army officer, Lieutenant Josef Müller, were arrested, and Canaris's Chief of Staff, Major-General Hans Oster, was cashiered.

Even before the dust had settled, Gestapo Müller and his men had discovered another resistance ring involving members of the Abwehr, which weakened Canaris's position still further. The final blows came in early February, when the Abwehr representatives in the vital posts in neutral Switzerland, Sweden and Turkey all defected to the enemy, and Abwehr agents in Spain blew up a British ship loaded with oranges, even though Hitler, after complaints from Ribbentrop, had ordered an end to all acts of sabotage there. Hitler had raged against Canaris, whereupon Hermann Fegelein, as though joking, suggested that the 'whole business' of the Abwehr should be handed over to the Reichsführer-SS. Hitler seized on the idea, sent for Himmler, and ordered him to merge the SD and Abwehr into a unified intelligence service, under his command.

Himmler now had fresh channels of communication with foreign governments – all secret services talk to each other as part of the great game, and the Abwehr was no exception, so it had contacts with Allied and neutral services, which Himmler took over and exploited. He gave command of the new super secret service to Schellenberg, who had already proved that he knew what to do with it. Apart from purely military intelligence and some sabotage functions, the whole Abwehr organisation, including its foreign outstations and agents, became part of Schellenberg's Department VI of the RSHA on 14 May, after weeks of negotiation with the OKW. Canaris was initially held under house arrest, but in June he was rehabilitated and given a meaningless post as head of the OKW's Special Staff for Trade and Economic Warfare, no doubt so that Himmler and Schellenberg could use his knowledge and his contacts.

*　　*　　*

Two important pieces of information that the new intelligence service failed to provide were the date of the Allied invasion of north-west France, code-named 'Operation Overlord', and where it would take place. The Germans had been nervously anticipating this since the beginning of the year, when Rommel was moved from Italy to supervise the strengthening of the Atlantic Wall and take command of Army Group B, comprising Seventh and Fifteenth Armies. The defeat of the U-boats in the Atlantic had allowed the build-up of men and *matériel* from North America to continue almost without hindrance during 1943 and the first half of 1944; by June four million men and 280 million tons of arms and equipment had been shipped from the United States and Canada to join British, other Commonwealth and exiled European troops in a massive invasion force. Their presence could hardly be kept secret, but the timing and direction of the invasion could, and was, aided by the tightest of security and a wonderfully effective campaign of disinformation and deception.

In April, Göring's reconnaissance aircraft spotted the huge armada of landing craft and support vessels being assembled at Portsmouth, Southampton and the Isle of Wight. He reported this to Hitler, and they agreed – against the opinion of most of the generals – that the invasion was most likely aimed at Normandy or the Cherbourg Peninsula, but there was still no real indication of when it would take place. On 25 April, Göring sent bombers to attack the landing craft, but did not have the strength to do them much harm. He sent two of his best divisions of ground troops, the 91st Airborne and the 5th Paratroop, to the Cherbourg Peninsula, but could not move the bulk of his aircraft out of the Reich, where they were needed in the desperate fight against the Allied bombers, which had ominously switched the focus of their attacks to the destruction of the vital synthetic fuel plants and the disruption of communications and transport.

A large number of Göring's aircraft were also tied down in Italy, where the Allies had finally broken the stalemate and were fighting their way slowly northwards. On 4 June, Hitler ordered all German forces to leave Rome, and declared it an open city. On the 5th, the US Fifth Army moved in. Around midnight that same day, 23,400 paratroops and glidermen in three airborne divisions, two American and one British, descended on the flanks of the invasion beaches in Normandy, while a fleet of nearly 7,000 landing craft and ships stole silently through the darkness towards the French coast. At 6.30 a.m. on 6 June, 'D-Day', the first wave of troops hit the beaches. The invasion had begun. By the end of the day, the Allies had landed 75,512 British and Canadian troops and 57,500 Americans, and had established four beachheads.[19]

The element of surprise had played perhaps the major part in the success of the landings – Rommel was so sure that no attack was imminent that he had even gone home to Ulm for a few days' leave with his family – but almost equally important was the total command of the air. Eisenhower, the Supreme Allied Commander, had 7,500 aircraft immediately available for direct support, and could call on 3,500 bombers that were continuing to blast Germany and communications to the invasion zone through France; on D-Day itself, they flew 10,585 sorties. Opposing them, the Luftwaffe had just eighty fighters based in Normandy.[20] On the first day, the Allies recorded only thirty attacks by German aircraft, involving 319 fighters, bombers and ground attack planes. The OKW and Hitler, still believing the invasion was not the real thing but a feint, refused to allow Göring to start transferring squadrons from the Reich until late on 7 June, by which time the airfields they were supposed to land on had been bombed virtually out of existence.

Göring still had one chance of salvaging any of his reputation, and he grabbed at it, with Hitler's backing. The V-1s and their launching sites were fortuitously almost ready for use, and after six days of frantic effort the first ten flying bombs were catapulted up their ramps on 12 June. First results were hardly encouraging: four crashed on take-off, one failed to cross the Channel, five reached London but caused little damage and failed to create the mass panic that Hitler had forecast. Furiously, he almost cancelled production, but was persuaded to give the missiles one more chance, and three days later 244 were successfully launched When Otto Dietrich, his Press Chief, brought him British newspaper reports of fear and confusion in the British capital, he was convinced that his 'wonder weapons' would indeed force Britain to sue for peace, even at this late stage. Goebbels, who was much more doubtful, had to beg him not to raise the German people's hopes that the war would now be over within days, for fear of a backlash against the government when it did not happen.

Göring, who according to Speer had tried to blame Milch for the earlier fiasco with the V-1, now eagerly claimed the credit for its success. For the moment at least, his stock rose again, but it could not last. In the month of May, for the first time in four years, there had been no British air raid casualties; in June the V-1s killed 1,935 and injured 5,906, and in July 2,442 and 7,107 respectively.[21] But after that the figures fell rapidly – in September only 190 were killed – as the RAF learned how to deal with the 'doodlebugs', as the British chirpily dubbed them. Although they inflicted serious damage on London, it became clear that they would not deliver the hoped-for knock-out blow.

As the Allies broke out of their beachheads and forced their way across Normandy, their bombers were able to turn their attentions back to Germany again, destroying even more of the dwindling stocks of fuel oil and the hydrogenation plants, until there was barely enough to keep the Luftwaffe planes in the air. On 21 June, they hit Berlin with the heaviest raid yet, with 1,000 bombers escorted by 1,200 fighters. 184 B-27s and Mustangs flew on to land at Poltava, in the Ukraine. They were trailed by an He-177, which reported their destination back to the headquarters of Colonel-General Robert Ritter von Greim's Lutflotte 6 in eastern Poland, and that night, on Göring's orders, Greim sent a strong force of German planes to bomb Poltava. They destroyed 43 B-17s, 15 Mustangs and scores of Soviet aircraft, plus 450,000 gallons of aviation fuel.

But any jubilation Göring may have felt was tempered the next day by other news from the Eastern Front. It was 22 June, three years exactly since the start of Barbarossa, and Stalin chose that day to open a massive summer offensive along the whole front. By 3 July, the Red Army had encircled Army Group Centre in Belorussia, destroying twenty-eight German divisions comprising 350,000 men. It was a similar story in the north and south, in Poland, Lithuania, Estonia, Latvia and the Ukraine. In six weeks, they advanced more than 300 miles and cleared the Germans from the whole of Soviet territory. By the end of July, they were only 400 miles from Berlin.

XXXV

LAST THROW OF THE DICE

AT 12.42 p.m. on Thursday, 20 July 1944, during Hitler's daily conference in the Wolfsschanze, a bomb exploded under the table in front of him. It had been planted by an army staff officer, Colonel Count Claus Schenk von Stauffenberg, a decorated war hero who had been severely wounded in Tunisia, losing an eye, the whole of his right hand and two fingers of his left. Stauffenberg was the leader of a conspiracy of army officers and some politicians and diplomats who had determined to assassinate Hitler and form a new government. The key to their plan was the Replacement Army, the home-based organisation consisting mainly of recruits under training before they were deployed to active service units. The Replacement Army alone had the men, the weapons and the organisation to take control – indeed, there was a ready-made official plan, approved by Hitler himself, for the Replacement Army to impose martial law in the event of a civil uprising or a revolt by foreign workers. Code-named 'Valkyrie', it was perfect for use by the conspirators after they had disposed of the Führer.

Stauffenberg had managed to get himself appointed Chief of Staff to the Commander-in-Chief of the Replacement Army, Colonel-General Fritz Fromm, a man of huge physique but doubtful moral strength. The plotters knew that he was not unsympathetic to their cause – few generals were – but they could not trust him to instigate anything. However, as his Chief of Staff, Stauffenberg was entitled to issue orders to the Replacement Army in his name, and would therefore be able to put Valkyrie into operation. What was more, he had regular access to the Führer, and regular opportunities to kill him.

Because of his disabilities, Stauffenberg could not use a pistol, so he decided that the best means of killing Hitler would be a time bomb.

Twice, on 11 and 15 July, he had attended Führer briefings with a bomb in his briefcase. Twice, he had aborted the operation – first, because he hoped to get Himmler and Göring at the same time and Göring did not turn up, the second time because Hitler unexpectedly ended the briefing early. On that occasion, the order for Valkyrie had already gone out, and the Replacement Army had swept from its barracks to take up positions to control the 'emergency'; the conspirators had passed it off as a practice drill, something they would not be able to repeat if anything went wrong the next time. On 20 July, Stauffenberg decided he could not wait for Göring and Himmler, and went ahead, placing his briefcase under the table near Hitler then leaving the room on the pretext of making a telephone call. When the bomb went off, he was in an office about 200 yards away with another member of the conspiracy, General Erich Fellgiebel. They watched with a mixture of horror and satisfaction as the hut exploded in smoke and flame and bodies and debris were flung through the open windows. Convinced that Hitler was dead, Stauffenberg left Fellgiebel to telephone Berlin with the signal to activate Valkyrie, while he and his aide-de-camp bluffed their way out of the compound and dashed to the airfield, where their He-111 plane was waiting.

Hitler, however, was not dead. Another officer had moved the briefcase to the other side of a stout, solid oak table support, which had protected Hitler from the immediate effect of the explosion. The open windows and wooden walls of the guest barracks where the conference was being held instead of in the underground concrete bunker that was still being reinforced, had done the rest, the walls being blown outwards, lessening the blast. Several of the officers in the room had been wounded, some mortally, among them Hitler's army adjutant, Schmundt, and Göring's Luftwaffe Chief of Staff, Korten, who had been skewered by a jagged piece of wood. But Hitler had survived, relatively unharmed. With a communications blackout imposed, Stauffenberg continued on the two-hour flight to Berlin unaware of what had happened – or rather, what had not happened.[1]

Göring was not at Hitler's briefing – he avoided them wherever possible, finding them too painful – but he was at the Wolfsschanze, ready to meet Mussolini, who was arriving that afternoon. When the bomb went off he was in his own office there, arguing fiercely with Greim's Chief of Staff over the continued failure of Air Fleet 6 to bomb Soviet power stations beyond the Urals. Summoned by Below, he rushed to Hitler, who was sitting in his bunker, his tunic torn, black trousers and long white underpants in shreds, being tended by Dr Morell. Hitler's ear drums were burst, and his right arm was swollen and painful, but apart from lacerations and slight burns to his hands, legs and face, he was uninjured and could walk without help. Göring's hour had not yet arrived. He would not even need to deputise for Hitler in greeting Mussolini – but he would, as always, be at his side.

Himmler was at his own field headquarters, Hochwald, where he was alerted by Below. He called Kaltenbrunner in Berlin and ordered him to collect a team of detectives and fly to the Wolfsschanze at once, then he called for his car and escort and hurried to congratulate Hitler on his miraculous escape. According to Kersten, who was with him, he was electrified by the news. 'Now my hour has come,' he told him. 'I will round up all the reactionary gang and have already given orders for the traitors' arrest.' Kersten ventured to ask whether Hitler's escape was really a good thing for Germany. Himmler had no doubts. 'What's that you're saying, Kersten? Is that your real opinion? You ought not even to think that, let alone say so,' he replied. 'By preserving the Führer, Providence has spared him to us so that we may bring the war to a triumphant conclusion under his leadership.'[2] 'Providence', the closest the Nazis could bring themselves to saying 'God', was the word on everyone's lips over the next few days.

This was clearly a tricky moment for Himmler. Why, with all the resources of the police state at his disposal, had he failed to uncover such a plot – if, indeed, it was a plot and not the work of a single man – and why had he failed in his most basic and overriding duty, to protect Hitler? Even now, there was confusion. The first suspects were Speer's forced labourers from Eastern Europe, engaged on reinforcing the bunkers, but as more details emerged attention quickly turned to Stauffenberg. He was known to be flying back to Berlin, but Himmler did nothing to have him arrested on his arrival, and does not seem to have realised at that stage that he was part of an attempted *coup*. He was well aware of two other groups of plotters, whom he had been watching for some time, and whom he may have been planning to use for his own devious ends. But the Gestapo and SD were barred from interfering with the army, which was still quite literally a law unto itself, as it always had been, and so knew nothing of Stauffenberg's group of officers in the Bendlerblock, the army headquarters building in the Bendlerstrasse. Fortunately for Himmler, and for the regime, the officers turned out to be the most inept and halfhearted bunch of revolutionaries imaginable, who had not taken even the most basic steps needed to seize power, such as taking control of radio stations and the communications network.

Mussolini's visit went ahead as planned that afternoon. Arriving by train at 3 p.m., accompanied by Marshal Graziani, Karl Wolff, as Himmler's and the Reich's representative in northern Italy, and Eugen Dollmann, the former Gestapo chief in Rome, he was greeted by Hitler, pale, shaking, his hair singed and with his right arm in a sling. Göring, Himmler, Ribbentrop and Dönitz were there in support. After inspecting the wreckage of the conference room, they moved into the teahouse to talk. Mussolini had come to discuss the situation in Italy, the use of Italian prisoners-of-war in Germany and four 'republican legions' that had been formed from their number, which Mussolini wanted to defend his shrunken state; Hitler agreed to their use, but only against Italian partisans.[3] He assured the Duce that the war would soon turn back in Germany's favour. Production of fighter aircraft would soon be more than 5,000 a month, he said, and no fewer than 1,200 of their new jets would drive the Allies out of Normandy, leaving him free to concentrate on winning back the Eastern Front.

Inevitably Hitler's escape dominated the conversation, and frayed nerves soon showed as the Germans began squabbling amongst themselves, blaming each other for the war and for the fact that it had not been won. Hitler, his ears plugged with cotton wool, popping different coloured pills and lozenges, took little notice. Then someone mentioned the Röhm affair, and the purge that had followed it. The effect was electric. According to Dollmann, Hitler leapt to his feet, 'in a fit of frenzy, with foam on his lips', shouting that he would have his revenge on all traitors. 'Providence had just shown him once again,' he was reported screaming, 'that he had been chosen to make world history; and he ranted wildly about terrible punishments for their women and children – all of them would be thrown into concentration camps – an eye for an eye and a tooth for a tooth – none should be spared who set himself against divine Providence.' He raged for a full half-hour, before ending with the megalomaniac cry: 'I'm beginning to doubt whether the German people are worthy of my great ideals!'[4]

In the hubbub that followed, with everyone trying to outdo everyone else in their protestations of loyalty, Göring and Ribbentrop almost came to blows. Göring called Ribbentrop a 'dirty little champagne salesman', told him to 'shut your damned mouth' and threatened him with his heavy marshal's baton. Ribbentrop was heard shouting back petulantly: 'I am still Foreign Minister, and my name is *von*

Ribbentrop!'[5] With the two men still shrieking at each other, Dollmann quietly led the Italians out and back to their train.

The remarkable afternoon was by no means over, yet. Hitler was roused to fresh fury when Himmler brought news that orders for a military take-over had been issued from the Bendlerstrasse in Fromm's name. There and then, he appointed Himmler to replace Fromm as Commander-in-Chief of the Replacement Army and Chief of Army Armaments. Wolff recorded that Göring suggested Hitler should not stop there but should make Himmler War Minister as well, at which Himmler said in a small, hesitant voice, 'My Führer, I can manage that as well.' Hitler, however, was not prepared to give him that much power. He told him to fly to Berlin at once, and deal with everything at the source. 'You have full powers,' he said. 'Go to it!'[6]

'My Führer,' Himmler replied proudly with the old mantra that had first made his name, 'leave everything to me.'

When they learned of Hitler's survival, the conspirators panicked. Unfortunately for them, the Gauleiter of Berlin did not. Goebbels was in his ministry study talking to Funk and Speer about the problems of implementing his total war provisions when he received a telephone call from Otto Dietrich at Führer Headquarters informing him of the failed assassination attempt. He said later that he had felt 'as though the ground beneath his feet was quaking', but after being assured that Hitler was not seriously hurt, he ate lunch normally if somewhat more quietly than usual, and then took an afternoon nap. He was woken about an hour later, to be presented with a terse statement from Führer Headquarters, supposedly dictated by Hitler himself, to be broadcast at once. Unhappy with the wording, and perhaps even wanting to hedge his bets until he knew exactly what was happening, Goebbels held on to the statement and carried on with his routine work. It was around 5 p.m. before he was galvanised into action by a phone call from Hitler himself, telling him that a full-scale military *putsch* was under way throughout the Reich.

Goebbels's first move was to call Speer and tell him to drop everything and come at once to his residence – he said he needed his calm head to balance his own impetuosity, though Speer later wondered if he had wanted to have him there so that he could keep an eye on him. At that point, no one was above suspicion. Himmler, whom Goebbels could not locate, was high on his list – several times throughout the evening, according to Speer, 'he expressed his distrust of the Reichsführer-SS and Minister of the Interior'.

Speer had not long arrived in Goebbels's second-floor office when he looked out of the window and saw troops of the Guard Battalion Grossdeutschland in full combat gear surrounding the building and taking up positions to close off the Brandenburg Gate. Goebbels took one look, then disappeared into his adjoining bedroom, and took a handful of cyanide capsules from a pill box, slipping them into his jacket pocket, 'just in case'. Then he sent for the commander of the troops surrounding the house, Major Otto Remer, after confirming his loyalty with Lieutenant Hans Hagen, a political officer from the Propaganda Ministry who happened to have delivered a lecture on National Socialist principles to Remer and his men earlier that very afternoon.

Remer, a thirty-two-year-old fanatical Hitler supporter, had been told by the Commandant of the Berlin Garrison, Major-General Paul von Hase, who was one of the leaders of the conspiracy, that Hitler had been assassinated and the SS were attempting a *putsch*. He had been ordered to seal off the Wilhelmstrasse area and arrest various ministers, including the Propaganda Minister. Remer was a loyal soldier. His duty, he insisted, was to obey the orders of his superior officer without question. When Goebbels reminded him of his oath of personal loyalty to the Führer, he replied that the Führer was dead.

'The Führer is alive,' Goebbels retorted. 'He's alive. I spoke to him myself a few minutes ago. An ambitious little clique of generals has begun this military *putsch*. A filthy trick. The filthiest trick in history.' The silver-tongued Propaganda Minister worked coolly to persuade Remer that destiny had afforded him a tremendous opportunity, and then he played his trump card. 'I am going to talk to the Führer now,' he told him, 'and you can speak with him too. The Führer can give you orders that rescind your general's, can't he?'

Within seconds, the connection had been made on Goebbels's direct line to Führer Headquarters, and Hitler himself was on the phone. Remer snapped to attention on hearing the familiar voice, responding with a smart '*Jawohl, mein Führer!*' as Hitler promoted him to colonel on the spot and commanded him to crush the rebellion in Berlin. He was to obey only the orders of Goebbels, Himmler and General Reinecke, who was being put in charge of all troops in the capital. Remer left Goebbels's office to switch his battalion over to the defence of the Nazi government, and to hunt down the ringleaders of the *putsch*.

Goebbels took advantage of the plotters' inexplicable failure to seize the radio stations, and broadcast the announcement of the attempt on Hitler's life, stressing that he had suffered only minor abrasions and had been well enough to receive Mussolini that afternoon. Then he had Remer assemble about 150 of his men in the garden of his residence, so that he could address them personally. 'Once I convince them,' he told Speer, 'we've won the game. Just watch how I handle them!' Illuminated only by the light falling on him through an open door, Goebbels put on a show of quiet confidence. He made no commands or threats, but appealed to the unquestioning loyalty that had been instilled in them over the years. And it worked. They moved off afterwards, determined to do their duty against the traitors, come what may.[7]

Even in the Bendlerblock, the revolt had collapsed. General Fromm, who had been locked up in his adjutant's office – albeit with sand-wiches and a bottle of wine to keep him comfortable – broke out with the help of a group of loyal Nazis. There was a brief shoot-out, in which the only casualty was Stauffenberg, who was hit in his good arm. The arrival of Guard Battalion troops finally settled the matter, as the conspirators were rounded up and placed under arrest. Eager to save his own skin by disposing of anyone who might reveal that he had known about the plot for several weeks but had done nothing to stop it, Fromm appointed himself supreme judge and jury, and condemned the ringleaders to immediate execution. Shortly after midnight, Stauffenberg and his colleagues were marched out into the courtyard and lined up against a wall. In the light from the hooded headlamps of a row of army vehicles, they faced a firing squad. Stauffenberg died proudly, standing straight and unbowed, crying 'Long live our sacred Germany!'

As the echoes of the shots died away, Fromm sent a teleprinter message to Führer Headquarters: 'Attempted *putsch* by irresponsible generals bloodily crushed. All ringleaders shot.' As he marched across the yard to inspect the firing squad, Speer arrived in his white sports car, with Remer in the passenger seat. They were halted outside the gates by Kaltenbrunner, who was standing in the shadow of the trees with Otto Skorzeny, surrounded by SS men and Gestapo officers, watching quietly, almost surreptitiously. When Speer explained that he and Remer had come to stop Fromm's summary court martials, Kaltenbrunner told him that he and the SS did not want to get involved, and would certainly not interfere, since this would only cause fresh trouble with the army. He had forbidden his men from entering the

Bendlerblock. 'In any case,' he said, no doubt having heard the volley of shots, 'the summary court martial has probably taken place already.'

At that moment, Fromm appeared, on his own. Leaving the SS officers under the trees, Speer and Remer approached him. Full of self-justification, Fromm complained about the treatment he had received, and informed them that the leaders of the *putsch* were dead. Speer and Remer were not pleased. Dead men could not talk, could not provide names and details. Fromm asked to be taken to Goebbels's residence, which had become the central command post for the operation, so that he could telephone Hitler to clear his name. Goebbels had him placed under arrest instead. At about this time, Himmler appeared at last, and issued orders in his capacity as Commander-in-Chief of the Replacement Army, that there should be no more summary executions.

Goebbels had spent much of the evening trying to persuade Hitler that he must speak to the nation – and indeed the world – on the radio, but it was not until after midnight that everything was ready and the broadcast began. He said he was speaking to let the German people hear his voice and to know that he was uninjured and well, and to tell them about 'a crime without parallel in German history'. A conspiracy to eliminate him had been hatched, he said, by 'a tiny clique of ambitious, irresponsible, and at the same time criminal officers. I was spared a fate that holds no terror for me, but would have had terrible consequences for the German people. I regard this as a sign that I should continue the task imposed on me by Providence.' The criminals, he promised, would be ruthlessly exterminated.

When he had finished speaking, Hitler invited Dönitz and Göring to address the nation – in that order, which must have given Göring pause for thought. Turning up for the midday conference two days later, he made a brief speech to Hitler, giving thanks once again for his survival and proposing 'as a visible token of the Werhmacht's gratitude for his miraculous escape, the Hitler salute be introduced immediately throughout the armed forces'. He produced an order already prepared, which Hitler signed, 'whereupon,' the stenographic record states, 'all those present spontaneously saluted'.[8]

Zeitzler had cracked under the strain of working with Hitler and had suffered a nervous breakdown at the beginning of the month. Hitler had continued without an Army Chief of Staff for three weeks, but on the day after the bomb had turned to Guderian, whom he had recalled from disgrace in March 1943 to be Inspector-General of Armoured Forces, effectively head of Panzer Command. Guderian's loyalty had been demonstrated during the emergency, when a tank unit had driven into central Berlin to support the Guard Battalion. His first Order of the Day as Chief of Staff renewed the army's pledge of loyalty, and made the Nazi salute compulsory 'as a sign of the army's unshakeable allegiance to the Führer and of the closest unity between army and party'. A week later, he issued another order stating that:

Every General Staff officer must be a National Socialist officer-leader not only by his model attitude towards political indoctrination of younger commanders in accordance with the tenets of the Führer . . . I expect every General Staff officer to declare himself immediately a convert or adherent to my views, and to make a public declaration to that effect. Anyone unable to do so should apply for a transfer from the General Staff.[9]

With the threat from the army completely removed, Himmler shifted his clean-up operation into top gear. Suddenly, the Gestapo was everywhere, questioning everyone, searching homes and offices, hauling people off for interrogation. No one was safe. The General Staff was decimated as hundreds of officers were arrested, while others whose involvement could not be proved but who were considered unreliable were replaced. Many committed suicide, among them Rommel, who had been in hospital at the time of the bomb, having been shot up in his car by an Allied fighter plane. He was flushed out several weeks later and given the chance of an 'honourable' death by poison rather than the traditional pistol shot, to allow his death to be passed off as the result of his earlier wounds.

On 23 July, by pure chance, a series of diaries was discovered in the ruins of a bombed house, which incriminated Canaris and other senior officials. The former spy chief was arrested at once, and the Gestapo searchlight turned towards the Abwehr and then into diplomatic and political circles as it became clear that the conspiracy stretched far beyond the Bendlerstrasse. Some of the names were long-standing conservative or liberal opponents of the regime. Others were more surprising: both Hitler and Goebbels were incensed to find Count Helldorf, the Police President of Berlin, an 'Old Fighter' and former SA leader, prominent among them. Others included Schacht, Halder, and Göring's Prussian Finance Minister, Johannes Popitz.

Hitler had sworn he would show no mercy to any of the conspirators, and Himmler took care to make sure this was no idle threat.

Those who found themselves in the Gestapo cellars in Prinz-Albrecht-Strasse were subjected to the most horrific tortures. One who somehow survived the experience, Lieutenant Fabian von Schlabrendorff, soon realised that the object of the exercise was not primarily to extort a confession. What Himmler and the Gestapo wanted was names, and they were prepared to use any means to extract them. Spikes were driven into Schlabrendorff's fingertips, his legs were encased in metal tubes lined with yet more spikes, which could be screwed slowly into the flesh, while his head was enclosed in a sort of metal helmet covered with a blanket to muffle his screams.[10]

After the first wild reaction, Himmler's men settled down to a deliberate and methodical investigation. He took the opportunity to spread his net over all opponents of the regime, whether or not they were connected in any way with the bomb plot, and over a period of several weeks around 7,000 arrests were made, many of them, no doubt, as a result of denunciations made through jealousy or spite. Most ended up in concentration camps, but the principal conspirators were tried in the notorious People's Court by Roland Freisler, the rabid 'hanging judge'; the army officers among them had first been dismissed the service by an honour court presided over by Rundstedt and including Guderian and Keitel.

Himmler had persuaded Hitler not to hold great show trials, at which the accused men would have had chance to air their views, but to confine them to the People's Court, where Freisler would ride roughshod over the legal niceties, in front of small, carefully chosen audiences. Goebbels ordered that the trials were to be filmed, to be shown to the troops and the general public as an example, and the whole thing was as carefully staged as any Hollywood movie. Freisler wore a magnificent blood-red robe, and the court was hung with great swastika flags, behind which the cameras were concealed. They were started and stopped by signals from Freisler, who conducted the proceedings virtually single-handed. Once the cameras were running, he screamed and shouted at the accused, aiming to show them as little more than common criminals.

The men, however, all behaved with great composure in spite of the fact that they were kept unshaven and had been dressed in old clothes taken from concentration camp victims. The most senior of them, retired Field Marshal Erwin von Witzleben, looked especially pitiful, since his false teeth had been taken away and his unsupported trousers were far too big, so that he had to keep grabbing hold of them to stop them falling down. As he did so, Freisler screamed at him: 'You dirty old man! Why do you keep fiddling with your trousers?'[11]

All the defendants in the first trial were condemned to death by hanging – as traitors they were denied the 'honour' of being beheaded. They died that same day, 8 August, at Plötzensee Prison in the north-west of Berlin. Since hanging was not the normal method used in Germany, the prison had no scaffold. Instead, eight large meat hooks had been fixed at intervals along a roof beam. The nooses used were shaped like a figure eight, with two loops, one for the victim's neck, the other to go over the hook. They were mostly made of hemp rope, but in some later cases piano wire was used. With no drop, the condemned men were not killed instantaneously by having their necks broken, but more slowly, by strangulation. Some took up to twenty minutes to die in agony.[12]

Goebbels sent cameramen to film the whole process, so that the Führer could be sure that his orders had been carried out that 'They must all be hanged like cattle'. But after recording the first two execu-tions, the two cameramen assigned to the task could not face any more, and refused to continue. The executioners, however, did not stop – they were kept busy until the very last days of the war. Even as the Allied armies closed in on Berlin, there was no let-up in the hangings, as the death toll mounted to nearly 5,000 souls.

As part of his vengeance, Himmler moved against the families of the conspirators, especially the aristocrats among them, invoking what he claimed was the ancient Teutonic punishment of *Sippenhaft*, 'kith and kin detention', or *Blutrache*, 'blood-vengeance'. 'You only have to read the Germanic sagas,' he told a meeting of the Gauleiters in Posen Castle on 3 August. 'When a man was outlawed, it was said: this man is a traitor, his blood is bad, it contains treason, it will be extermi-nated . . . the family of Count Stauffenberg will be wiped out down to its last member.'[13] The Gauleiters applauded.

The bomb plot marked a watershed for Hitler. In some respects, it was the culmination of the Nazi revolution, finally breaking the power of the army and the old aristocracy. From then on, he believed he could rely on the party alone, and he shut himself off from anyone whose loyalty could not be traced right back to the old time of struggle. After 20 July, the only three men who counted at the top were Bormann, as the party boss, Himmler and Goebbels. They formed a tight ring around the Führer, working closely together but watching each other jealously, and freezing out the three who had never been really accepted by the party: Göring, Ribbentrop and Speer.

Göring and Ribbentrop were easy targets. The Luftwaffe's failures had already discredited Göring in Hitler's eyes, and the continuation of his sybaritic lifestyle at a time when the rest of the country was enduring the harshest privations, was enough to damn him. Hitler had lost all confidence in his abilities, though he still retained a personal attachment to him. Few others did, however – Himmler ordered the Gestapo to investigate any possible connections Göring may have had with the conspiracy, and told Dönitz that if Hitler had been killed: 'It is absolutely certain, Grand Admiral, that under no circumstances would the Reich Marshal have become his successor.' Ribbentrop, for his part, had been sidelined by events: with fewer and fewer countries maintaining diplomatic relations with Germany, there was virtually nothing left for a Foreign Minister to do, apart from seeking a peace settlement, which was taboo.

Speer's star had risen fast and flared brightly, until in late 1943 Hitler could greet him and Himmler as 'you two equals' – something that must have rankled with the Reichsführer-SS. Now it burnt out just as quickly. For twelve months, Speer had been seen as a serious contender, perhaps even the favourite, for the succession. But at the start of 1944 he had made the mistake of falling sick and being out of circulation for four months, as a knee operation in Himmler's SS clinic at Hohenlychen, sixty kilometres north of Berlin, went drastically wrong. He almost died from a severe pulmonary embolism, which was misdiagnosed and badly treated by Himmler's close friend, Dr Karl Gebhardt, and he had to spend some time even further out of the loop convalescing in the Tyrol. During his illness, there was a genuine attempt from within his own ministry to unseat him, but he was more concerned with a paranoid fear that Himmler was trying to get rid of him for good by having him killed.

If Speer's fears had been justified, Himmler's failure would have shown remarkable incompetence, for surely nothing could have been simpler than to dispose of a critically-ill patient who was in the care of SS doctors in an SS hospital. What was simpler still, however, was character assassination, and with Speer away from the court, Himmler and his ally Bormann had no difficulty in dripping poison into Hitler's ear and destroying his faith in his former Benjamin.

Speer had gone on running his ministry from his sick bed, and he continued to work wonders in armaments production, which reached an all-time high in July in spite of the air-raid damage and shortages of materials. Soon after returning to his office in May, he had scored a victory over Göring by finally taking over all responsibility for aircraft production; Milch, carrying the can for Hitler's Me-262 fiasco, was given the meaningless title of Inspector-General of the Luftwaffe, and retired to his hunting lodge north of Berlin. But even with this increase in his authority, Speer was no longer in the contest for the succession – he had no power base in the party, and the party was all that mattered now. Indeed, he had antagonised the Gauleiters by trying to override their control over industry in their own districts, and antagonising the Gauleiters meant antagonising Bormann, which was a fatal mistake.

Speer's one close ally at this time was Goebbels, whom he supported wholeheartedly in his increasingly desperate attempts to turn his vision of total war from words to action, lining up with him against Bormann and Himmler. Goebbels had formed an unofficial committee of like-minded ministers and top officials, including Funk, Ley and Sauckel as well as Speer, which met every Wednesday evening to discuss ways of moving things forward, but although they were among the most influential men in the Reich, controlling industry, the economy and labour, they could do nothing without Hitler's consent – and their access to Hitler was barred by Bormann.

Goebbels had finally managed to penetrate the barrier by convincing Hitler's Wehrmacht adjutant, Schmundt, that time was running out, and persuading him to pass this on to Hitler. On 21 June, Hitler had called Goebbels to the Berghof, to talk about his ideas. He had listened carefully, but refused to accept that the moment had come for total war, and sent him away disappointed yet again. The next day, the great Soviet summer offensive had begun, but even that had done nothing to change Hitler's mind, and as the weeks went by and the position on both fronts grew steadily worse, Goebbels had grown more and more frantic.

Speer, anxiously watching his fuel supplies and factories being systematically destroyed, promised to prepare a paper proposing that Goebbels should take over responsibility from 'the incompetent Committee of Three' for 'rallying all the home front forces behind the war effort'. Goebbels himself wrote a long memorandum to Hitler setting out in detail what needed to be done, and promising that the measures he was advocating would release enough men to create fifty new divisions within three to four months. The memorandum was dated 18 July.[14]

The shock of 20 July finally concentrated Hitler's mind – or, as Goebbels put it more earthily to his aide, Rudolf Semmler, 'It takes a bomb under his arse to make Hitler see reason.'[15] When he joined the other top Nazis at the Wolfsschanze two days later, Goebbels had every reason to believe that he had impressed Hitler with his decisive handling of the crisis in Berlin and would be rewarded at last, and this time he was not disappointed. He found Lammers ready to propose, no doubt on the Führer's instructions, that the Committee of Three be disbanded, and Goebbels given the powers he had asked for to reform the state and public life. At the same time, Himmler would be given 'extensive authority' to reorganise and reform the Wehrmacht. With a fitting show of reluctance, Goebbels declared that he would accept the new duties solely because the Reich's perilous position called for 'major measures', and Hitler had to be 'relieved of all petty details'.[16]

Hitler confirmed Goebbels's appointment as Reich Plenipotentiary for the Total War Effort the following day in front of all the leaders, including Göring, who was most put out that he had not been given the job, since he was chairman of the Ministerial Defence Council. To save Göring's face, Goebbels suggested that Lammers should word Hitler's decree to say that the Reich Marshal had proposed the appointment in his official capacity, and Hitler happily went along with this, reluctant as always to do anything in public to damage Göring's prestige. The device fooled no one, least of all Göring, who stomped off to Rominten in a tantrum that lasted five weeks, emerging only to deliver the eulogy for Korten's funeral at Tannenberg on 28 July, then disappearing again claiming to be ill with a throat abscess. In the meantime, he had surprised everyone by appointing the mild-mannered and delicate Head of Flying Training, General Werner Kreipe, as his new Chief of Staff, over the head of Karl Koller, Korten's deputy who had been filling the post since his death. However, since he refused to return to the Wolfsschanze to introduce Kreipe to Hitler, he ordered Koller to carry on, and for six weeks there were effectively two Chiefs of Staff, a bizarre set-up that did nothing to ease the general state of confusion in the Luftwaffe.

Goebbels took to his new task, which he described to his staff as giving him 'practically full dictatorial powers' within the Reich, with grim satisfaction and boundless energy. 'We are actually in a position,' he told the German people in a broadcast announcing his appointment and his aims, 'to turn the fortunes of war in our favour. All that is needed to bring this about is there for the taking. Let's take it! Never again will the Almighty reveal his presence to us as clearly as when he worked a miracle on behalf of the Führer, saving his life.'[17]

At last, he had the recognition he had always craved, with the right to issue directives to ministers and the highest-ranking government authorities, and he meant to make the fullest use of it. Unfortunately, there was a catch – there was always a catch in the Nazis' byzantine world of jealously guarded status symbols. He was entitled to issue directives to the ministers and officials, but it was up to them whether or not they acted on them. Mostly they did, but there was no guarantee. And there were limits to his powers where they infringed on the territories of the other satraps: they did not apply to the party and its organisation, which was Bormann's domain; they did not apply to the Wehrmacht, where Himmler now held sway; and they most definitely did not apply to the SS. Nevertheless, he could justifiably claim to be 'the dictator of the home front'.

The most urgent need was for men at the front: in the three months following the D-Day landings the German armies on all fronts lost some 1.2 million men, dead, wounded or missing, and the losses continued to mount. Goebbels's first move was to order the call-up for full military service of boys aged between sixteen and eighteen, and men between fifty and sixty. He scoured schools, colleges, offices and factories for recruits, conscripting tens of thousands of men in reserved occupations. Starting with his own Propaganda Ministry, he demanded a thirty per cent reduction in government staffing levels. To balance this, he extended the standard working week to a minimum of sixty hours – except, of course, for forced labour, which was already working seventy-two. He raised the upper age limit for women drafted into war work from forty-five to fifty, and ordered school holidays to be extended 'indefinitely', so that twelve- to fourteen-year-old children could work in light industry, releasing women and the few remaining men for the heavier work.

This drive produced 451,800 men by October, enabling Himmler to create twenty-five new divisions designated as Volksgrenadiers, to differentiate them from the old army. Although many regular army divisions had been reduced to little more than battalion strength, Hitler decided that they should not be restored. He believed that troops who had suffered severe defeats no longer had the morale to fight effectively, and such divisions should be left to 'bleed to death', while still existing on paper as full divisions in the German order of battle to create an illusion of greater strength.

For those already in the armed forces all leave was cancelled, and men previously considered unfit for active service were routed out of administrative posts and sent to the front. Goebbels had whole battalions formed of men suffering from stomach troubles, ear problems, rheumatism, and gall and kidney stones. He proudly informed the Gauleiters that he had sent 79,874 such men to the front from Military District VIII alone. 'The physician in charge of this military district reckons that in the Reich as a whole one could recruit enough men suffering from these ailments to form one hundred such special battalions,' he told them, 'all in all around two million men fit to be dispatched to the front. We are taking the view that, for instance, a chronic stomach ailment cannot be regarded as a life insurance, and that it could hardly be the aim of this war to send the fit to die while the ailing are preserved.'[18]

Goebbels's concentration on sending men to the front brought an end to his close alliance with Speer, and at the same time confirmed Speer's fall from the very highest level. Speer saw the labour needs of his factories as equally important to those of the armed forces, which after all could not fight without weapons and ammunition, and when Goebbels demanded 100,000 recruits from the armaments industry he went over his head to Hitler on 21 September. Trying to use his personal relationship with the Führer to ignore the ban on criticising Goebbels, he presented him with a long letter of complaint, demanding an end to his interference and that of the Gauleiters. Hitler, who was ill for most of September with high blood pressure, heart problems, stomach cramps and jaundice, simply passed him and his letter to Bormann and Goebbels, who happened to be in the Wolfsschanze that day. Between them they made short work of the Armaments Minister, and Bormann forbade his raising the matter with Hitler again.

To drive home the reality of his total mobilisation to the country at large, Goebbels closed most theatres, concert halls, drama schools, *conservatoires* and art schools. Orchestras were shut down, as were many newspapers when paper and printing were still further restricted. Firms producing non-essential goods such as toys or fashion items were shut. Public transport services were cut drastically, and film production and broadcasting – two activities that he had always maintained as essential morale boosters – were considerably reduced. The nature of the films that were still being made was changed, too – gone were the supposedly realistic war dramas, to be replaced in the main by frothy light comedies designed to raise audiences' spirits. One exception, on all counts, was a lavish colour film, *Kolberg*, a period piece showing the epic defence of the small Baltic town of that name against Napoleon in 1803, for which 187,000 soldiers were withdrawn from active service to work as extras, on Hitler's orders, along with 4,000 sailors and 6,000 horses. He and Goebbels were both 'convinced that such a film was more useful than a military victory' in propaganda terms.[19]

Throughout July and August 1944, the invaders closed on Germany from east, west and south. In the East, the Red Army scored a series of spectacular victories on all fronts from the Baltic to the Black Sea, trapping fifty German divisions in the Baltic states and destroying Army Group Centre in Belorussia, advancing 400 miles in six weeks before halting only ten miles from Warsaw on 31 July. On 24 July they had liberated the first extermination camp, Majdanek, discovering thousands of charred corpses and seven gas chambers, which they displayed to war correspondents from all the Allied armies. When horrific photographs of the remains were published around the world, Hitler exploded in fury at 'the slovenly and cowardly rabble who did not erase all traces of the camp in good time'.[20] Meanwhile, other Soviet armies were grinding their way through northern Poland and Lithuania. Shortly before dawn on 17 August, the first Soviet infantrymen splashed across the River Sheshupe, the border of East Prussia, and planted their section's red battle flag alongside frontier marker number 56. Soviet soldiers were on German soil at last.

Away to the south, three days later, other Soviet forces crossed into Romania and captured the Ploesti oilfields, Germany's last major source of natural oil. The Romanians swiftly changed sides, declaring war on Germany on 25 August. The next day, as Hitler ordered the withdrawal of all German troops from Greece, Bulgaria deserted the Nazi fold. On 29 August there was an armed uprising in Slovakia. A few days later, Finland too jumped ship, accepting Soviet armistice terms and turning on the German troops still in the country.

In Italy, meanwhile, the British Eighth Army entered Florence, where the retreating Germans had destroyed all the bridges across the Arno apart from the fourteenth-century Ponte Vecchio which could not carry heavy traffic, and the Allies continued to fight their way north against fierce opposition. In France, the fighting in Normandy had been savage since the landing, but on 30 July the tanks of the newly-formed US Third Army, under the inspired leadership of General George S. Patton, finally broke out and roared towards Le Mans and Orléans, then turned east towards the Seine. By the time they had reached the river on either side of Paris, there had been a second Allied landing in the south of France, between Cannes and Toulon, and American and Free French forces were advancing fast up the Rhône valley.

On 25 August, General Jacques Leclerc's French 2nd Armoured Division, followed by units of the US 4th Infantry Division, rolled into Paris to be greeted by the men and women of the Resistance, who had risen against the remaining German troops to liberate their city after four years of enemy occupation.

Hitler refused to allow his generals to withdraw their battered forces from France, insisting that they fight on. Still deeply distrustful of the General Staff, he prepared a detailed plan himself, though he was 1,000 miles away from the front lines and had little idea what was really going on. The result was to turn defeat into disaster. Within days the entire German force in France, hopelessly short of fuel and ammunition, was routed, forced to retreat into Germany as fast as it could go.

The Allied armies pursued the fleeing Germans at full speed. The Canadian First and British Second Armies under Montgomery covered 200 miles in four days, leaping from the lower Seine right into Belgium. They liberated Brussels on 3 September, the fifth anniversary of Britain's entry into the war, and Antwerp the following day. To their south, the US First Army, under General Courtney H. Hodges, moved equally fast to reach south-eastern Belgium and capture the fortresses of Namur and Liège. Patton's Third Army, meanwhile, was powering its way east to reach the Moselle river and link up with General Alexander Patch's French–American Seventh Army, which had fought its way north from the Riviera.

Only when they reached the German frontier were the Western Allies forced to halt their furious progress as they ran out of steam – or rather, out of fuel and ammunition as their lines of supply became overstretched. At 6.05 p.m. on 11 September, the 85th Reconnaissance Squadron of the US 5th Armored Division, an advance unit of the First Army, crossed the frontier into Germany, near Stalzenburg. But that was as far as anyone went for the time being.

The respite was badly needed and vitally urgent for the Germans: they had to start from scratch, hurriedly preparing the defence of the Fatherland. Since 1940, Hitler had always refused even to consider such a possibility, so there was no master plan and the fortifications of the West Wall were unmanned and had largely been stripped of their guns. Now they had to be re-equipped and reorganised. It seemed an impossible task, and one for which Hitler had absolutely no enthusiasm: as always, he believed that attack was the best form of defence, and rather than digging in behind the barricades, he began to plan a great counteroffensive, imagining he could still drive the Allies back to the sea.

While the Allied armies were closing the ring around Germany during August and September, Himmler was occupied with a battle on a smaller scale in the city of Warsaw. The Warsaw Uprising started at 5 p.m. on 1 August, when 37,000 men and women of the underground Polish Home Army led by Tadeusz Komorowski, who used the *nom de guerre* 'General Bór', opened fire on the German occupiers.

Bór-Komorowski had deliberately triggered the rising in advance of the arrival of the Red Army, which was halted only ten miles away, within artillery range, fearing the consequences for Poland if the Soviets liberated the capital. By the end of the day, most of the Old Town was in the hands of the insurgents, and they were preparing to drive out the hated Germans and welcome the advancing Soviets into a free city. They had bargained for a battle lasting from seven to ten days, with aid from the Soviets. Stalin, however, had no interest in helping Bór-Komorowski and his people, whom he regarded as the army of the anti-Communist Polish government-in-exile in London. If the city was to be liberated, it would be by the Red Army. Ignoring all their pleas for aid, he ordered the Commander-in-Chief of the Belorussian Front, Marshal Konstantin K. Rokossovsky, to sit back and wait while the Home Army was annihilated by the Germans.

There were good military reasons to back up Stalin's political inaction. Marshal Rokossovsky had already lost 123,000 men in the approach to Warsaw, and rightly feared a German counterattack from the south on his exhausted troops. He knew that two crack SS-Panzer divisions, the Wiking and the Totenkopf, plus the Hermann Göring Division and the 19th Panzer Division, were being rushed to the defence of the city. Moreover, he was acutely aware of the difficulty of trying to take a large city whose defenders were prepared to contest every street, every building – the memory of Stalingrad cast a very large shadow.

Hitler was determined to hold Warsaw against the Soviets, but to do so he needed to put down the uprising. He gave the job to Himmler, who saw it as a great opportunity to complete the job started in 1939, and erase Warsaw from the map for ever. As he told a meeting of army officers in September:

When I heard the news of the rising in Warsaw, I went immediately to the Führer. I should like to tell you this as an example of how one should take news of this kind quite calmly. I said, 'My Führer, the time is disagreeable. Seen historically, however, it is a blessing that the Poles are doing it. After five, six weeks we shall leave. But by then Warsaw, the capital, the head, the intelligence of this former 16–17 million Polish people will be extinguished, this *Volk* that has blocked us in the east for 700 years and has stood in our way ever since the first battle of Tannenberg. Then the Polish problem will no longer be a large problem historically for our children who come after us, nor indeed for us.'[21]

In overall command of the operation, Himmler put the head of his anti-partisan squads, SS-Obergruppenführer (Lieutenant-General) Erich von dem Bach-Zelewski, who mobilised the most notorious units in the entire SS. These included the Dirlewanger Police Brigade, composed almost entirely of criminals, court-martialled service- and SS-men, and foreigners on probation for the Waffen-SS, and the even more brutalised Kaminski Brigade, made up mainly of former Ukrainian prisoners-of-war who hated the Poles even more than they hated the Russians. By mid August he had assembled 21,300 troops, equipped with an impressive array of weaponry including tanks, artillery, flame-throwers, heavy mortars, gas generators and the like, and the battle proper began.

Himmler ordered that all Poles, whether or not they were insurgents, were to be shot, and some 40–50,000 were massacred during the first five days. By the time Bór-Komorowski was forced to surrender on 1 October, more than 15,000 of his fighters and between 200,000 and 250,000 civilians, out of a population of 1 million, had been killed. Bach-Zelewski reckoned his casualties as 10,000 dead, 9,000 wounded and 7,000 missing. The capitulation agreement recognised Bór's insurgents as combatants, to be treated as prisoners-of-war rather than partisans. It also called for the complete evacuation of the city. In an unprecedented move, all the surviving civilians were moved out, mostly on foot, the able-bodied to forced labour in the Reich, the old, very young and infirm to camps and the gas chambers. To complete Himmler's promise to eradicate Warsaw, eighty-three per cent of the surviving buildings were then destroyed.[22]

The horrors inflicted on the Poles in Warsaw had been so unspeakable that when Guderian heard the details he went to Hitler and demanded that the two SS brigades should be removed at once from the Eastern Front. Hitler gave in to him. Before they were withdrawn, Bach-Zelewski had Kaminski shot – 'as a possibly dangerous witness', according to Guderian.[23] The other brigade commander, however, Dr Oskar Dirlewanger, was rewarded with the Knight's Cross. Himmler sent him straight from Warsaw to help crush the uprising in Slovakia, which was achieved by the SS once more, again with maximum barbarity.

While the Poles and Slovaks were being slaughtered on his orders, Himmler managed to find time to spend a day in his house near Berchtesgaden, with Häschen Potthast and their two children – she had given birth to a daughter, Nanette Dorothea, in Hohenlychen Clinic on, of all days, 20 July. The child, according to Martin Bormann's wife, Gerda, looked 'ridiculously like her father' and had grown big and sturdy. Himmler took no phone calls or messages, but devoted the whole day to 'hanging pictures, doing things about the house and playing with the children'. The cosy domestic scene was deceptive, however. While the baby gurgled happily in her basket and her brother Helge played with toy carts and a blue wheelbarrow made by wounded SS troops in Hohenlychen, Himmler had more sinister toys in his 'special lair' in the attic.

Bormann's son, Martin Junior, told Gitta Sereny in 1991 of visiting the house in 1944, when he was fourteen, and being shown Himmler's 'special collection' by Häschen:

When she opened the door and we flocked in, we didn't understand what the objects in that room were – until she explained, quite scientifically, you know . . . It was tables and chairs made of parts of human bodies. There was a chair . . . the seat was a human pelvis, the legs human legs – on human feet. And then she picked up a copy of *Mein Kampf* from a pile of them – all I could think of was that my father had told me not to bother to read it as it had been outdated by events. She showed us the cover – made of human skin, she said – and explained that the Dachau prisoners who produced it used the *Rückenhaut*, the skin of the back to make it.[24]

Himmler's peaceful interlude with his second family could only be brief. Along with all his other duties, he was faced with another international crisis when he learned that Horthy had been negotiating with the Allies to take Hungary out of the war. Hitler turned to the SS once again, to deal with the threat, and Himmler sent in Bach-Zelewski and Skorzeny, who resolved things in typical gangster fashion by kidnapping Horthy's son under fire from Hungarian guards, rolled up in a carpet, and flew him out to Mauthausen concentration camp. Threatened that if he did not co-operate his son would be shot, Horthy still broadcast an announcement to his countrymen of the separate peace he had concluded with the Soviet Union. But as soon as he had finished speaking the radio station was seized by men of the Hungarian Fascist Party, the Arrow Cross, who declared that Hungary would continue the war against the Soviet Union as Germany's ally. After further threats by Bach-Zelewski and Skorzeny, Horthy gave in and agreed to leave for Germany, escorted by Skorzeny and armed German guards, to spend the rest of the war as 'Hitler's guest' in a Bavarian castle. Himmler's SS had saved the day once more.

The deportation of Hungary's remaining Jews, which Horthy had stopped in July, was resumed, but with a difference. Himmler was ending the killings in the death camps, but decided he could make use of the Hungarian Jews as slave labour in the SS cave workshops building the V-2 missiles. Since he could not spare any fuel or transport, they would have to travel on foot. Tens of thousands were rounded up and began the long forced march, but so many Jewish women died on the way that by mid November the Arrow Cross leader, Ferencz Szalasi, called a halt. 70,000 Jews were left crammed into the ghetto in Budapest, waiting helplessly for the war to end and dying in their thousands.

In the West, the Allies tried to break through the defensive positions which Rundstedt, brought back from retirement to reassume command, had established to hold them on the German frontiers. In a bold bid to outflank the Westwall and open the way for a drive on the Ruhr, Montgomery launched 'Operation Market Garden', in which some 20,000 American and British troops were landed by parachute and glider behind German lines between Eindhoven and Arnhem in the Netherlands. Their aim was to capture three bridges over the Meuse,

Waal and Lower Rhine respectively, but they ran into bad weather and two SS Panzer divisions, which happened to be refitting right on the spot. Montgomery, in fact, had been given incontrovertible intelligence, from Ultra and photographic sources, of the presence of the Panzer divisions, but refused to change his meticulous plans and insisted on going ahead.[25] The result was a disaster for the Allies, who were forced to withdraw with heavy losses, and a great victory for the Germans. Hitler, however, chose not to see it that way. He was furious at the failure of the Luftwaffe to prevent the landings in the first place, and blamed Göring entirely.

Hitler's patience with Göring had been wearing thin for some time, and Market Garden was the final straw. He sent for Greim, the Commander-in-Chief of Luftflotte 6 in the East, and told him he wanted him to take command of the Luftwaffe. Greim, a First World War flying ace, had been a fervent Nazi since the 1920s, and had been the pilot for Hitler's first flight. He was eminently suited for the job – he had started the war as the Luftwaffe's personnel chief, and had commanded a number of fighter groups before distinguishing himself as a Luftflotte chief. Hitler told Greim that despite Göring's many faults and failings it would be politically impossible to sack him at that time, so although Greim would have full operational control, Göring would remain Commander-in-Chief, though in name only. Greim was no fool, and he knew Göring. It would be an impossible situation. Somehow, he managed to avoid a decision, and strung Hitler along until early November, by which time Göring had got to hear of the proposition and had made his feelings known so strongly that Hitler gave up on the idea, at least for the moment. He consoled himself by insisting that Göring get rid of the lugubrious Kreipe as Luftwaffe Chief of Staff, and replace him with Koller, the tough Bavarian.

There was some better news for Göring at that time. Speer had ignored an angry order from Hitler to stop all fighter aircraft production and concentrate entirely on flak guns, and pushed ahead with the reforms he had been working on to increase production. He had delivered a record 2,878 fighters in September,[26] so that Göring and Galland now had about 3,700 available for action. The first Me-262s were entering service, albeit as fighter-bombers, and creating havoc and consternation among Allied planes and troops wherever they appeared. But there were still not enough of them to be really effective, and although they were virtually untouchable in the air, they were vulnerable on the ground. They needed much longer runways than conventional aircraft, and these gave away their locations to Allied attackers, who sought them out and destroyed them and the runways. Above all, their use was limited even more than piston-engined aircraft by the acute fuel shortage, as the enemy bombers specially targeted the refineries producing the precious jet kerosene. The same problems applied to a second jet aircraft, this time one designed as a fast bomber, the Arado 234, which was just starting to come into operation. Göring did manage at last to persuade Hitler to allow him to form an experimental squadron of fifty Me-262 fighters, which went into action in mid October with some success. But fuel was so short that pilots could not be adequately trained, and the fastest planes in the world were often towed on to the runways for take-off by teams of oxen, since the thirsty Me-262 used 200 litres of kerosene to taxi into position.

The V-1s had not produced the collapse of Britain, but they were still droning their way across the Channel and causing some harm to people and property. To try to counter Allied bomb damage to the fixed launching sites, Göring had a number of He-177 bombers modified to carry V-1s on their backs, for air launches. More severe results were achieved by the army's V-2 rockets, the first of which were launched against London and the Belgian city of Antwerp, which the Allies were clearing to use as their major supply port.

On 18 October 1944, the 131st anniversary of the defeat of Napoleon at the 'Battle of the Peoples' near Leipzig, which had finally liberated the German states from the French invaders, Himmler broadcast to the nation from East Prussia, to announce the formation of a citizens' militia to help defend the Fatherland, to be known as the Volkssturm. He reminded his listeners how the Prussian Landsturm had been raised in the spring of 1813 from ordinary citizens 'armed with every variety of weapon from flintlocks with and without bayonet, spears, axes, pitchforks, swords, scythes . . . etc'. 'With the words "Fatherland! Fatherland!"' he continued, 'the Landwehr [territorial reserve] and Landsturm attacked the better-armed, -trained and battle-hardened enemy in all regions, and over the course of months accompanied by many reverses, drove the French enemy from the Prussian lands.'27

The formation of the Volkssturm was the culmination of the doctrine of total war, and Goebbels believed it would come under his jurisdiction. He had suggested forming civilian border protection units as early as mid July, when the Red Army entered Lithuania. But Bormann had proposed a more general call-up immediately after 20 July, primarily as a way of arming party functionaries against internal unrest, and it had, therefore, become a party matter. Bormann had turned to Himmler and they had agreed to divide responsibilities between them, drafting a decree together during August, which Hitler signed on 26 September. Every remaining male between the ages of sixteen and sixty and not serving in the armed forces – an estimated six million men – was to be drafted into service to defend the Fatherland in the final emergency. Volkssturm units were to be raised in each Gau by the Gauleiter, under the political and organisational control of Bormann, on behalf of Hitler. Himmler, as Commander-in-Chief of the Replacement Army, was in charge of arming, training and deploying them.

Goebbels was left to command only the Berlin Volkssturm, as Gauleiter. He called its members to take their oath, each promising unconditional loyalty to Hitler and swearing that he would never surrender, at a parade in the Wilhelmplatz, in front of the Propaganda Ministry, on 12 November. By an ironic coincidence, it was the day after its British equivalent, the Home Guard, had held its farewell parades as it was disbanded.

There were no uniforms for the Volkssturm – a matter of great regret to many men in a society that traditionally valued the uniform so highly. The only standard issue was an armband. Individual units did what they could to improvise some form of common outfit from what was available, including in some instances captured British battledress. Most men at the Berlin oath-taking had managed to get hold of steel helmets.

Far more serious was the lack of weapons. There were two levies of Volkssturm, the first supposedly armed and the second intended as a replacement. But there were virtually no weapons even for the first echelon. In one battalion, for instance, the first company was given only two rifles, the second company several Italian rifles but only a few rounds of ammunition, and the third some machine-guns, an old anti-tank gun, and a few Italian rifles. There was a reasonable supply of hand grenades and the new hand-held *Panzerfaust* anti-tank rocket, a crude but highly effective weapon that actually performed better than the American bazooka on which it was based.[28]

Himmler had chosen East Prussia to launch the Volkssturm because it had already been invaded by Soviet troops and the Gauleiter, Erich Koch, had started forming his own units. Indeed, the situation there looked so black by mid October that Göring had all the furniture and effects from his hunting lodge at Rominten removed and shipped back to Carinhall, where Emmy distributed them among friends and acquaintances who had lost their own in the bombing. Göring then gave orders for a flight of three FW-190s from the forward airfield at Gerdauen to destroy the lodge itself with bombs and rockets, to prevent its falling into Soviet hands. He shook the hands of the young pilots when they returned, and presented each of them with the Iron Cross, First Class.

As it turned out, Göring had been premature in destroying the lodge at Rominten – the Soviet advance was halted until the New Year, fittingly by the Panzer Corps Hermann Göring – but he knew more than anyone that the end was inevitable. When the three pilots asked him about the state of the war, he told them frankly that it was lost, and that there were no 'wonder weapons'. They were impressed by his honesty. But it was an honesty that was tearing him apart as he struggled to continue a fight that he no longer believed in.

He was still as flamboyant as ever, but it was an increasingly hollow show. When he visited Peenemunde on 30 October to see the latest experimental anti-aircraft rockets, he appeared, according to General Dornberger, the army chief of the station, in 'bright red, soft morocco leather riding boots with silver spurs . . . wearing an amply cut thick fur coat of Australian opossum, the fur outwards'. But when he was asked to decide on which rockets should be developed further, he clearly knew that it was all pointless. 'He pretended to be studying the drawings on the walls,' Dornberger wrote,

but he was no longer looking at them. He was totally disinterested . . . About every five minutes his eyes started to turn until one could only see the whites. He staggered, reached into the pocket of his coat, and swallowed a small, round, rose red pill. Instantly he straightened and appeared to be quite normal again. After five minutes, the same process . . . When he climbed the stairs to the roof of the small tracking building of the 'Waterfall' project, he pulled a heavy revolver out of its holster, threw it up into the air several times and caught it again. His adjutant took the weapon away from him with the remark that it was loaded and not on safety.[29]

Göring, Goebbels, Himmler and even Ribbentrop – though, interestingly, not Bormann – had all done their best to persuade Hitler to sue for peace, either with the West or the Soviets. But Hitler, always the gambler, was as determined as ever to go for broke, and was planning one last throw of the dice. During his illness in September, he had lain in his cot, thinking hard, and had come up with a plan. While the Soviets were held in the East, he would surprise the Western Allies with another blitzkrieg, just like the old days in 1940. And just like in 1940, he would strike through the Ardennes, where they were least expecting it, split and encircle the American forces – there were only four weak US divisions in the area – and power across to the sea, to take Antwerp and cut off their main supply and escape route.

Through October and into November, the plans were hurriedly prepared for what was originally code-named 'Operation Watch on the Rhine' – the name was later changed to 'Operation Autumn Mist'; the Americans would call it the Battle of the Bulge. On 20 November, Hitler left Wolfsschanze for what would be the last time, travelling to Berlin for a minor operation to remove a polyp from his vocal chords, delighting Goebbels by visiting him and his family on 3 December for tea, the first time he had done so for five years. The occasion was only slightly marred by the fact that he brought his own tea in a thermos flask, and his own cakes in a sealed bag.[30] He also brought a small bunch of lilies of the valley for Magda, saying they were all he could get, since her husband had closed down all the florists in Berlin.[31]

Himmler rose yet higher in Hitler's favour in November, when he was appointed Commander-in-Chief Army Group Upper Rhine, using his Volksgrenadier, Volkssturm and flak units to bolster the Nineteenth Army and protect the frontier from the Swiss border to the Saar, during the Ardennes offensive. Fortunately for everyone, the Allies chose not to attack in that sector, so General Himmler's military command skills were not tested in battle, for the moment. His four Waffen-SS Panzer divisions, the 'Leibstandarte', 'Das Reich', 'Hohenstaufen' and 'Hitler-jugend', now formed into the Sixth SS-Panzer Army under Sepp Dietrich, were given the key role at the centre of the Ardennes offensive. And at the start of November he was given the honour of deputising for the Führer at the annual celebrations with the 'Old Fighters' in Munich. Göring had hopes of a revival of his fortunes, too, since he could now provide over 3,000 aircraft for the operation, at least on paper.

Hitler took up residence in a new field headquarters, Adlerhorst (Eagle's Nest), near Bad Nauheim in the Taunus, on 10 December. The offensive began on the 16th, and at first all went well. The element of surprise was complete – the foggy weather was too bad for the Allied aircraft, which had a considerable advantage in numbers despite Göring's extra planes, to attack the German columns, which made significant advances. Goebbels trumpeted the news on the radio and in the press, claiming one of the great victories of the war. But after seven days, the skies cleared and the Allied air forces roared into the counterattack, with 2,000 aircraft at a time hammering German troops and supply lines, and destroying their planes on the ground and in the air, before armoured forces from Patton's Third Army arrived to relieve and reinforce the American troops on Christmas Eve.

Inexperienced and poorly trained pilots were no match for the battle-hardened Americans and British, and they were wiped out in large numbers. The final crunch came on New Year's Day, 1945, when Göring put up every available plane, around 800 fighters and bombers, for early morning mass attacks on Allied airfields in northern France, Belgium and Holland. They destroyed 156 planes, but in the process lost more than 300 themselves, many of them to their own flak around the V-2 launch sites, who had not been warned that they were coming. Co-ordination had not been helped by the fact that a few weeks earlier Hitler had removed control of the flak from Göring and the Luftwaffe and given it to Himmler.

By 3 January, Hitler was forced to admit that the battle had been lost. It dragged on until 16 January, by which time the Germans were back where they started. 'The fighter arm received its death blow during the Ardennes offensive,' Galland wrote later. It was an accurate assessment, and not only for the fighters. The Luftwaffe and indeed the Wehrmacht as a whole never recovered, having lost 100,000 of the 500,000 men involved, and nearly all their tanks and aircraft.[32] Hitler had gone for broke for the last time. Now, he was bankrupt.

For Göring, the Ardennes catastrophe brought a fresh challenge, when his leading fighter pilots rebelled. He had tried to pin the blame for the Luftwaffe failures on Galland, firing him for insubordination and using the wrong fighter tactics, but the pilots objected vociferously. After five top aces, led by Colonel Günther Lützow, had tried to persuade Greim to go over Göring's head to Hitler and demand his replacement, Göring agreed to meet them and hear their grievances. But when Lützow presented him with a long and detailed list, including sore points such as the priority being given to the bomber arm and the misuse of the Me-262, he blew up.

'What you are offering me here, gentlemen,' he roared, 'is high treason, is mutiny! You, Lützow, you . . . I will have you shot!'[33] He did not carry out his threat, sending him to an air staff post in Italy instead and forbidding him from returning to the Reich. But nor did he recall Galland, putting him under house arrest in the Harz

Mountains. In his place as General of Fighters, he was forced by Hitler to appoint Colonel Gordon Mac Gollob, who had been recommended by Himmler as politically reliable.

The 'mutineers' could consider themselves lucky. At exactly the same time, Göring was reasserting his authority by imposing a whole string of death sentences on junior officers and NCOs for a variety of offences ranging from trading petrol for liquor to fleeing their posts under fire. He also ordered the execution of General Waber for using Luftwaffe trucks to transport 'extraordinary quantities' of loot, including cigarettes, champagne, spirits and coffee, from the Balkans to his homes in Bavaria and Breslau. 'From one private house in Serbia,' Göring announced indignantly, 'he stole valuable works of art: a watercolour, a carpet, and two vases.'[34]

Galland was deeply depressed by his dismissal, by criticisms of his licentious lifestyle, and by an investigation being conducted into his affairs by the Gestapo on Gollob's orders. When he began talking of shooting himself, Milch intervened with Göring, telling him he could not stand a third scandal after Udet and Jeschonnek, and reminding him that he had enough dirt on the Reich Marshal to have him court-martialled.

Göring came up with a brilliant solution to the whole problem. He promoted Galland to Lieutenant-General and gave him a new assignment, to form an elite fighter squadron from the mutineers and other crack pilots, based at Munich-Riem airbase. They were to fly the Me-262 jet fighters, and would be reporting directly to Göring himself, bypassing Gollob.

The special squadron, Jagdverband 44, acquitted itself well over the next three months, but it was yet another case of too little, too late, at a time when Luftwaffe generals were being retired because there was nothing for them to do. The bravery and skill of the jet pilots, and those of all the other units, was not enough to hide the fact that the Luftwaffe, like its Commander-in-Chief, was a spent force.

XXXVI

GÖTTERDÄMMERUNG

EVEN before the Ardennes defeat was completed, the Soviets opened their greatest offensive of the war, intent on steamrollering their way right into the heart of the Reich. Hitler had been told it was about to happen, but refused to believe it – when Guderian presented the intelligence reports, he flew into a rage and declared that the man responsible for them must be mad and deserved to be locked up in a lunatic asylum. Himmler, who was with him, agreed. 'It's all an enormous bluff,' he stated confidently.[1]

On 12 January, as Göring was visiting Adlerhorst to receive Hitler's felicitations on his fifty-second birthday – the Nazi leaders all set great store on birthday celebrations – Marshal Ivan Stepanovitch Koniev launched his First Ukrainian Front in a massive attack to the south of Warsaw, heading for Cracow and then the industrial wealth of Silesia. Two days later, Zhukov unleashed his First Belorussian Front, spearheaded by the Eighth Guards Army under Chuikov, the hero of Stalingrad, across the Vistula north and south of Warsaw, which they took on 17 January. Still further north, Rokossovsky aimed his armies at East Prussia and the Baltic coast. Between them, Zhukov and Koniev disposed of two and a quarter million men and about 6,500 tanks, giving them a five to one superiority in men and armour over the Wehrmacht overall, while in artillery, they had seven times as many guns. In the crucial Vistula sector, the imbalance was at its greatest, with eleven to one in infantry, seven to one in tanks, and twenty to one in guns.

Guderian had warned Hitler: 'The Eastern Front is like a house of cards. If the front is broken through at one point, all the rest will collapse.' He was proved absolutely right. Cracow and Lodz were both taken on 19 January, and by the next day the Soviets had broken through along a line of 350 miles, from East Prussia to the Carparthians. The German armies were in full retreat everywhere, and alongside them, fleeing for their lives, were the ethnic German settlers planted in the region by Himmler. In Hungary, the Soviets surrounded Budapest on 18 January and Hitler, to Guderian's disgust, chose to send Sepp Dietrich's Sixth SS-Panzer Army there rather than to the north, hoping to defend the Hungarian oilfields, Germany's last source of fuel.

Hitler left Adlerhorst, his last field headquarters, on 15 January, arriving in Berlin by train early in the morning of the 16th. He was driven straight to the Chancellery, the blinds on the windows of the car pulled down as usual to shut out the unwelcome sight of the destruction he had brought upon the city. The Chancellery was even more badly damaged than when he had last seen it a month before. Every window had long since been shattered, but now only the ground floor and cellar were habitable. His large study, where he had held his daily conferences while in Berlin, was one of the few rooms that remained undamaged, but the west wing of the old Chancellery building, which had housed his private apartment, had collapsed. He moved his office and residence into the barely completed bunker deep under the Chancellery garden. For some time, when no daylight raid was expected, he continued to hold daily conferences in his old study, but more and more he was forced to stay underground, in what the wags among his entourage called his 'cement submarine', eighteen rooms of bare concrete.

It would have made more sense had Hitler gone to the OKW bunker in Zossen to the south of the city, which was both more roomy and fully equipped as a military headquarters, and was out of the target zone of the constant air raids. As Supreme Commander he would have been in direct contact with his General Staff, who were all based there, and would have saved Guderian three hours spent commuting to and from the Chancellery each day. Zossen also possessed the most modern communications systems, while the bunker had only a fairly small telephone switchboard, of a type designed by Siemens for use by one operator in a divisional headquarters or a medium-sized hotel. It did have an army radio transmitter, but this worked only on medium and long waves and needed an external aerial that had to be jury-rigged using a length of wire suspended above the bunker by a balloon. As the situation continued to deteriorate, many people tried to persuade him to move to Zossen or, failing that, to the big Luftwaffe bunker at Wannsee. But he refused, claming that he was doubtful about the strength of 'army concrete'. The truth was, of course, that since 20 July he no longer felt safe among army officers. In the Führer bunker, he was surrounded at all times by Himmler's hand-picked SS guards.

By this time, Hitler himself was a wreck, both physically and mentally. He had developed a marked tremor in his left hand after the bomb attempt, but this shaking had now spread to the whole of his left side, and his gestures were slow and jerky, like a man in an advanced stage of Parkinson's disease. He had taken to keeping his hand in his pocket, so that the shaking would not be seen, or using his good right hand to hold his left arm against his body. He had become stooped, almost hunch-backed, with a sagging pot belly. He walked with an awkward shuffle, dragging his left leg a little, and had to have his chair pushed under him when he wanted to sit down. With his ashen complexion, he looked like an old man in his seventies, rather than a mere fifty-five. But his pale blue eyes, though tired and bloodshot, could be as hypnotic as ever, and he still retained the unmistakable aura of power, and the ability to switch on a commanding presence that could still inspire a certain awe.[2]

Despite his exhaustion, Hitler insisted on running every detail of the war. Indeed he even increased his involvement: one of the first directives he issued from Berlin, on 21 January, ordered all commanding generals down to divisional level to inform him in advance of every operational movement from their units. 'They must ensure that I have time to intervene in their decisions if I think fit,' he declared, 'and that my counter-orders can reach the front-line troops in time.'

Hitler's interference brought more clashes with Guderian. He was furious when General Friedrich Hossbach pulled his Fourth Army out of East Prussia, after it had been overrun by Rokossovsky. Hossbach was intent on saving as many of his men as possible and was also trying to keep an escape corridor open for half a million East Prussians fleeing on foot and in horse-drawn wagons. He had cleared the withdrawal with his immediate chief, Colonel-General Hans Reinhardt, Commander-in-Chief of Army Group North, but not with Guderian or the Führer. Hitler summoned Guderian, himself an East Prussian, and ordered him to dismiss both generals immediately, together with their staffs. 'They deserve to be court-martialled!' he raged, accusing the two men of treason.[3] Guderian protested that he did not consider either man a traitor, but Hitler ignored him and replaced Reinhardt with Colonel-General Lothar Rendulic, a committed Nazi noted for his advice to his cornered troops: 'When things look blackest and you don't know what to do, beat your chest and say "I'm a National Socialist – that moves mountains!"'

Hitler had also ignored Guderian's violent objections when he replaced the Commander-in-Chief of Army Group Centre, on Rendulic's right, with another of his Nazi favourites, Colonel-General Ferdinand Schörner. In despair, Guderian approached Ribbentrop on 24 January, told him the war was already lost, and asked him to try to get an immediate armistice in the West so that troops could be transferred to face the Soviets. Ribbentrop still favoured seeking peace in the East, and during the last six months had joined with Ambassador Oshima in trying to persuade Hitler to agree to Japanese mediation; at the beginning of the year he had also, with Hitler's permission, put out feelers to the Americans, through the OSS chief in Switzerland, Allen Dulles, but had been firmly told that the only way to end the war was by unconditional surrender. Nevertheless, having sworn Guderian to secrecy, he hurried to snitch to Hitler about his suggestion, provoking a new row between the two men. 'In the future,' Hitler screamed at his Chief of Staff, 'anyone who tells anyone else that the war is lost will be treated as a traitor, with all the consequences for him and his family. I will take action without regard to rank and reputation!'[4]

Guderian weathered the storm, and once again swallowed his anger at Hitler's irrational meddling. But there was worse to come. On 24 January, as convoys of trucks began moving government documents from Berlin to Bavaria for safe keeping, the Führer approved Guderian's proposal to form a brand-new emergency army group in the East, to be rushed into the gap between Army Groups North and Centre in a last-ditch effort to stem the flood tide of Zhukov's advance. However, he rejected Guderian's choice of Field Marshal Baron Maximilian von Weichs, a brilliant and daring field commander then in charge of German forces in Yugoslavia, as its commander. Instead, Hitler decreed that the new force, to be known as Army Group Vistula, should be commanded by Heinrich Himmler.

Guderian exploded at the idea of 'such an idiocy being perpetrated on the unfortunate Eastern Front'. Himmler's only previous military experience, apart from a brief period as a cadet during his youth, had been with Army Group Upper Rhine, where he had not distinguished himself with a poorly executed attempt to recapture Strasbourg. Encouraged by Bormann, who was eager to see his rival fail, Hitler insisted that the Reichsführer-SS was a great organiser and adminis-trator, and that his very name would inspire the troops to fight to their last breath. Besides, he went on, as Commander of the Replacement Army, Himmler was the only man who could instantly form a new force. When Guderian tried to provide Himmler with at least minimal General Staff support, Hitler overrode this, too.

Convinced that his hour of glory had come at last, Himmler accepted enthusiastically, and set off at once for the front, near Danzig. As his Chief of Staff, he chose SS-Brigadeführer Heinz Lammerding, a brave Waffen-SS tank general, but one with little staff experience. He was armed with one outdated situation map, had only a handful of SS offi-cers, and his new army group barely existed on paper. But as new divi-sions arrived from the reserves, he began forming them into a defensive line. Incredibly, this ran not from north to south but from east to west, from the northern Vistula to the Oder, offering no protection to Berlin and little more to Pomerania in the north. Zhukov more or less ignored it, sweeping around it to the south on 29 January to reach the Oder. Himmler launched his best SS units in a despairing counterattack, but they were easily beaten off.

'By 27 January,' Guderian recorded, 'the Russian tidal wave was rapidly assuming for us the proportions of a complete disaster.'[5] Coincidentally on that day, in the middle of a snowstorm at about 9 a.m., a lone Soviet scout from Koniev's 100th Infantry Division walked into a nightmare as he entered a compound containing a group of wooden buildings, about seventeen miles south-east of Katowice in Upper Silesia. The place was called Monowitz, and it was part of the vast Auschwitz-Birkenau complex. The Germans had started pulling out of Auschwitz eleven days before – for all his brave words to Hitler, Himmler had no illusions left about the situation in the East. He had ordered the gas chambers and crematoria to be closed down nearly three months before, on 2 November, and since then his men had set about destroying the evidence, carefully dismantling everything, including the factories, and setting fire to the barracks, many of them with the prisoners still inside. But even then, Himmler had not released or even abandoned those prisoners who were still capable of working. Over five days, starting on 17 January, 56,000 of them had been lined up and sent westwards on foot, on a 150-mile forced march through the snow and ice of winter, to the subterranean SS factories. Those who were too sick or too weak to walk were shot, as were thousands who dropped out along the way. The same tragic scenario was played out at most of the concentration camps in the East as they were overrun.

The lone Soviet soldier had entered the grounds of the Monowitz prison infirmary. When the main force of the 100th Division arrived about thirty minutes later, they found nearly 600 sick and dying men and women, out of 850 who had been left behind. The soldiers distributed their bread among them, and later that day a Red Army doctor and medical staff arrived to tend them.

The rest of Auschwitz-Birkenau fell to the Soviets that afternoon after the camp guards had killed 231 Red Army men in a brief but bloody fight. After they had cleared the mines from the surrounding area, the troops were able to enter the death factory, where they found some 5,000 surviving prisoners who had escaped the transports. They also found mountains of clothes, all neatly sorted and baled – 368,820 men's suits and 836,244 women's dresses – grotesque pyramids of dentures, spectacles and shoes, and, perhaps most ghastly of all, seven tons of women's hair.[6] The world had been shocked by Maidanek, but this was almost too terrible to comprehend. Koniev did not visit the camp personally. He felt it was more important that he retain his objectivity than rage at the horrors that had been discovered. In military matters, he believed, it was vital to preserve a cool head – but there could be little hope of mercy for the men who were responsible.

Having got Hitler back in Berlin at last, Goebbels worked hard to restore some of the personal intimacy that had previously existed between them, trying to make up for lost time by visiting him in the Chancellery or the bunker as often as possible, and joining his late-night tea parties to fawn on him. He did his best to strengthen Hitler in these awful times, sending him quotations from works of history on ancient Rome, Alexander the Great and, of course, their shared hero, Frederick the Great of Prussia, showing how they had triumphed after all appeared lost. It seemed to have worked, when on the black day of 27 January, Hitler told him that he wanted 'to show himself worthy of the great examples of history. He would never be found to waver in the face of danger.'[7]

Goebbels tried once again that day to persuade Hitler to sack Ribbentrop and give him the Foreign Ministry, but without success. He presumably thought that he could negotiate a separate peace with the West, still blindly believing that it was only a matter of time until the Allied coalition fell apart as Britain and America took fright at the Soviet penetration into Europe. He was not alone in clutching at this last straw, the only hope – apart from miracles and 'wonder weapons' – that anyone could still have.

Göring had played the same tune to the Führer at that day's situation conference, saying that the British would not like to see a Soviet invasion of Germany. 'They certainly didn't plan that we would hold them off while the Russians conquer Germany,' he said. 'If this goes on we shall get a telegram in a few days.' Hitler responded that he had deliberately set out to frighten the British and Americans with rumours that that was the Soviet plan. Goebbels may have convinced himself that this was true, but Göring certainly did not believe it. He had started packing up his works of art in Carinhall some weeks before and sending them south, to Veldenstein and the Obersalzberg. And when a Soviet armoured scout car was seen in the Schorfheide near Carinhall on 29 January, he ordered Emmy to leave next day for the Obersalzberg with Edda and the rest of the womenfolk. He agreed that on the way she should collect her friends who were still in the city and take them with her.

After the conference on 27 January had broken up, with not a single decision having been taken concerning the critical situation east of the Oder, Hitler had received a telephone call from Schörner at Army Group Centre. Hitler had consistently forbidden any retreat in the industrial and mining region of Silesia, but Schörner now told him he had ordered its evacuation. Hitler said nothing. Schörner continued: 'These troops have been fighting a heavy battle for two weeks, and now they're finished. If we don't relieve them, we're going to lose the whole Seventeenth Army, and the road to Bavaria will be wide open. We're moving back to the Oder, and there we will stop.' The silence at the other end of the line continued. Then, after what seemed an eternity, Hitler replied, in a weary voice: 'Yes, Schörner. If you think it's right, I'll have to agree.'[8] For once, and possibly the last time, Hitler had listened to reason.

For Speer, the loss of Upper Silesia marked the end of all hope. He had already prepared a farewell memorandum to his staff, and ordered his assistants to collect photographs and records of his architectural projects and store them in a safe place – as if such a thing existed in Berlin. Now he prepared a note for Hitler on the hopeless situation for armaments production. Deliberately disregarding the warning he had heard Hitler deliver to Guderian six days before, he began his report unequivocally: 'The war is lost.' He went on to detail falling production figures and to forecast what might be possible in the coming three months. Silesia had been providing sixty per cent of Germany's coal supplies. Now there were only two weeks' stocks to fuel factories, railways and power plants. 'After the loss of Upper Silesia,' he concluded, 'the German armaments industry will no longer be able even approximately to cover the requirements of the front for ammunition, ordnance and tanks . . . From now on, the material preponderance of the enemy can no longer be compensated for by the bravery of our soldiers.'[9]

Hitler was not impressed, but nor did he fly into one of his ungovernable rages. He pointedly ignored Speer for two days then called him to his study and calmly admonished him. 'You are perfectly entitled to let me know your estimate of the armaments situation,' he told him, '. . . but as for your last paragraph,' and here, Speer says, his voice became cool and cutting, 'you cannot write that sort of thing to me. You are to leave to me the conclusions I draw from the armaments situation.' Speer recalled in his memoirs that Hitler said all this 'very softly, without any sign of excitement, whistling somewhat between his teeth. The effect was not only much more definite but far more dangerous than one of his furies, for whatever he said in a rage could easily be taken back the next day. Here, I felt quite distinctly, I was hearing Hitler's last word on the subject.' Hitler dismissed him curtly.[10]

For Speer the love affair was ended. He had for some time been secretly disobeying Hitler's orders to destroy all industrial plant and communications in areas about to be taken by Allied forces, and to divert transport used to carry food to the civilians in the West to carry armaments, leaving the population to fend for themselves. Now his disillusionment was complete. He began planning how he could introduce tabun poison gas into the bunker's ventilation system to kill Hitler, and with him Bormann, Goebbels and Ley during one of their nocturnal chats, since he considered those three could be even more dangerous with Hitler gone. In the event, however, his assassination plan proved impossible, and he did not have the nerve to try any other way. 'Quite aside from all question of fear,' he wrote, 'I could never have confronted

Hitler pistol in hand. Face to face, his magnetic power over me was too great up to the very last day.'[11] He confined himself instead to frustrating Hitler's scorched-earth orders.

Goebbels scored a small success with Hitler by managing to persuade him to broadcast a speech to the nation on 30 January, the first time he had done so for two years, to mark the twelfth anniversary of his seizure of power. Goebbels believed making the speech would be good both for Hitler and the German people, but it turned out to be little more than a hollow rallying cry, barely mentioning the catastrophes taking place to East and West. 'We are going to force a turn of the tide,' Hitler declared. 'However grave the crisis may be at the moment, in the end it will be mastered by our unalterable will, by our readiness for sacrifice and by our abilities. We will overcome this emergency. And in the struggle it will not be the interior of Asia that will win, but Europe, represented by that nation which for fifteen hundred years has defended and will always defend Europe against the East, our Greater German Reich, the German nation!'[12] Germany, he said, would never surrender. Germany would fight on to the last. Hitler expected every man to do his duty, even the sick.

Goebbels gained another title that day, when Hitler named him 'Defender of Berlin'. Less than twenty-four hours later, he faced his first test in his new role. With Silesia cut off and advance units of the Red Army already crossing the Oder, a sudden panic gripped the city with the rumour that Soviet tanks had reached Strausberg, only eleven miles from the city boundary and less than twenty from the centre. Goebbels put the Volkssturm on the highest alert. All over the city, men disappeared from their homes. Most reported to their units to receive what few arms were available – at a roll call of 1,000 men a short time before, for example, only eighteen had rifles. Then, fearful but determined, they piled into the trenches they had been digging for weeks, or went to work building makeshift barricades in the streets of the eastern districts. Other men, far too many to be counted, simply disappeared. Knowing that resistance was pointless, they were not prepared to face almost certain death to prolong Hitler's regime for a few more hours or days; all that mattered to them was that the war should be lost as quickly as possible.

Police on the beat were ordered to wear steel helmets and carry carbines – but they were clearly meant to keep the population in order rather than fight the Soviets. Foreign workers were locked in their camps, with armed guards at the gates in case of trouble. There were few regular troops anywhere near Berlin now: Himmler had taken all the remains of the Replacement Army to form his new army group. To strengthen the Volkssturm, Goebbels had Luftwaffe anti-aircraft units with their 88-mm guns hurriedly brought into the city from nearby regions.

The panic faded as quickly as it had started, when it was confirmed that the Soviet armies were still only at the Oder. The government was not evacuated, party officials were not called up, Volkssturm units were stood down. Boys and elderly men clambered out of their trenches and left the uncompleted barricades, to drift thankfully back to their homes. But they hardly had time to enjoy their relief when the city was hit by a fresh catastrophe.

On Saturday, 3 February, at 10.45 a.m., the first of a giant armada of American bombers appeared overhead. For one and three-quarter hours they filled the sky in a non-stop tidal wave, nearly 1,000 Flying Fortresses and Liberators dropping 2,267 tons of bombs, the heaviest single raid yet. The central districts and the government quarter got the worst of it. The Chancellery was the bull's-eye, and suffered a number of direct hits. Bormann described the results in a letter to his wife, his 'beloved Mummy-girl', at home on the Obersalzberg:

The Reich Chancellery garden is an amazing sight – deep craters, fallen trees, and the paths obliterated by a mass of rubble and rubbish. The Führer's residence was badly hit several times; all that is left of the winter gardens and the banquet hall are fragments of the walls; and the entrance hall on the Wilhelmstrasse, where the Wehrmacht guard was usually mustered, has been completely destroyed . . .

In spite of it all, we have to go on working diligently, for the war continues on all fronts! Telephone communications are still very inadequate, and the Führer's residence and the Party Chancellery still have no connection with the outside world . . .

And to crown everything, in this so-called government quarter we still have no light, power or water supplies! We have a water cart standing in front of the Reich Chancellery, and that is our only supply for cooking and washing up! And worst of all, so Müller tells me, are the water closets. These *Kommando* pigs use them constantly, and not one of them ever thinks of taking a bucket of water with him to flush the place . . .[13]

The Propaganda Ministry was hit twice in the raid and Goebbels moved staff into the basement and senior officials into his residence, which he turned into an annexe of the Ministry. Gestapo headquarters in Prinz-Albrecht-Strasse was damaged so badly that prisoners had to be moved out to the comparative security of the Flossenbürg and Buchenwald concentration camps. The People's Court was also hit, with one unlamented casualty: Judge Roland Freisler was killed as he ran across the courtyard to the shelter.

Throughout the raid, not a single Luftwaffe fighter appeared over Berlin. A frantic Göring called his headquarters demanding to know why, and was told that every last fighter was in the air counterattacking the Soviets on the Oder. Since this was where the action was, Göring started taking himself off there, to talk not only to the airmen but also to army and SS officers like Skorzeny, glad of any excuse to escape from Hitler and the dreadful atmosphere in the Führer bunker. 'For a long time,' Speer recalled later, 'he had been made the scapegoat for all the failures of the Luftwaffe. At the situation conferences, Hitler habitually denounced him in the most violent and insulting language before the assembled officers. He must have been even nastier in the scenes he had with Göring privately. Often, waiting in the ante-room, I could hear Hitler shouting at him.'[14]

Seeking an ally, Speer called on Göring at Carinhall a few days after his meeting with Hitler. Göring made him welcome, and they settled down comfortably by the fire to talk, over a meal of cold venison and 'an excellent Rothschild-Lafite'. Speer spoke candidly of his disillusionment with Hitler. Göring sympathised, saying he understood perfectly, and indeed often felt the same. It was easier for Speer to break free, he continued, having joined Hitler much later, but he could not. He had been with him for so long, and shared so many years of struggle and so many experiences that he was bound to him, come what may.

As the Americans blasted Berlin from the air, the Red Army was perilously close to the city on the ground: Chuikov, with a bridgehead across the Oder at Küstrin, was just forty-three miles from the Wilhelmstrasse and the Führer bunker. But the Soviet advance had been so fast that the forward units had once again outrun their supplies and support. They were desperately short of fuel, ammunition, spares and above all men – the great advance had taken a terrible toll in casualties. Although both Zhukov and Koniev were eager to regroup and rearm fast before charging forward again on what had become a personal race, they were forced to pause while they gathered their strength again. On 6 February, Stalin phoned Zhukov from Yalta in the Crimea, where he was in conference with Churchill and Roosevelt, and ordered him to postpone the attack on Berlin. 'We must consolidate on the Oder,' he told him, 'and then send all the forces you can to Pomerania, to join with Rokossovky and smash the enemy's Army Group Vistula.'[15]

This was bad news for the Commander-in-Chief of Army Group Vistula, who was already in serious trouble. On the afternoon of 13 February, the day after the communiqué at the end of the Yalta Conference had confirmed Allied insistence on unconditional surrender, punitive reparations, the demilitarisation and division of Germany into occupation zones, the trial of war criminals and the abolition of the Nazi Party, Guderian arrived at the Chancellery prepared for a show-down with Hitler over Himmler's performance. On the way in from Zossen for the daily Führer conference, he told his Chief of Staff, Lieutenant-General Walther Wenck, 'Today, Wenck, we're going to put everything at stake, risking your head and mine.'

At the conference, in front of Bormann, Göring, Keitel, Jodl, Dönitz, Himmler, Fegelein, and Kaltenbrunner among others, Guderian was as good as his word. After quickly describing the situation in the East, he demanded that the counterattack against Rokossovsky begin in two days. Himmler stammered a protest. It could not be done, he said. The front-line units needed more ammunition and more fuel. Agitated, he took off his glasses and began polishing them. Guderian turned back to Hitler.

'We can't wait until the last can of petrol and the last shell have been issued!' Guderian shouted. 'By that time the Russians will be too strong!'

'I will not allow you to accuse me of procrastination,' Hitler snapped back, clearly stung.

'I'm not accusing you of anything,' Guderian retorted. 'I'm simply saying that there's no use in waiting until the last lot of supplies has been issued – and the favourable moment to attack has been lost.'

'I've just told you that I won't allow you to accuse me of procrastinating!'

Guderian brushed the attempted rebuke aside, and went on. 'I want General Wenck at Army Group Vistula as Chief of Staff. Otherwise there can be no guarantee that the attack will be successful.' He glared at the hapless figure of Himmler. 'The man can't do it. How could he do it?'

Hitler rose to his feet. 'The Reichsführer is man enough to lead the attack on his own,' he declared.

'The Reichsführer doesn't have the experience or the right staff to lead the attack without help. The presence of General Wenck is absolutely necessary.'

'How dare you criticise the Reichsführer! I won't have you criticise him!'

Guderian remained unbowed, repeating his demand. 'I must insist that General Wenck be transferred to the staff of Army Group Vistula to lead the operation properly.'

With neither man prepared to give ground, the argument became more and more heated. One by one, the other men around the table slipped unobtrusively away to the ante-room, until only Hitler, Himmler, Guderian, Wenck and their adjutants remained. Guderian himself described what happened next, as he continued to argue for a counterattack, to be masterminded by Wenck:

His fists raised, his cheeks flushed with rage, his whole body trembling, the man stood there in front of me, beside himself with fury and having lost all self-control. After each outburst of rage, Hitler would stride up and down the edge of the carpet, then suddenly stop immediately before me and hurl his next accusation in my face. He was almost screaming, his eyes seemed to pop out of his head and the veins stood out on his temples.

After two hours of this, with Guderian still refusing to budge, Hitler suddenly gave way. 'Well, Himmler,' he said, stopping in front of the Reichsführer's chair, 'General Wenck is going to Army Group Vistula tonight, to take over as Chief of Staff.' Turning to Guderian, with his most charming smile, he told him: 'Now let us please continue with the conference. Today, Colonel-General, the General Staff has won a battle.'[16]

Wenck took up his post that night and immediately set about organising the counterattack. Himmler, pleading an angina attack, checked himself into Hohenlychen – he had relocated his field headquarters to an SS mansion at Birkenhain, near Prenslau, conveniently close to the hospital – and left him to it.

That night, the RAF turned its attention to the city of Dresden, in response to a Soviet request to paralyse rail junctions and communications centres and so prevent or at least hinder the eastward movement of German troops. The RAF sent in some 800 heavy bombers in two waves, dropping incendiaries and high explosives, and the USAAF followed up the next day with over 400 bombers. The entire centre of the ancient city, some 1,600 acres, was completely destroyed in a vast and terrible firestorm in which at least 35,000 people died.

Himmler, obviously not too ill to fulfil his duties as Interior Minister, was informed by the Dresden police chief, but did not take his report seriously at first. 'The attacks were obviously very severe,' he responded to SS-Obergruppenführer Ludolf von Alvesleben's agonised message, 'but every first air raid always gives the impression that the town has been completely destroyed. Take all necessary steps at once . . . All the best.' The next day, when the extent of the tragedy was clear, he made his priorities plain, telling Alvesleben that he could relocate his office, but only to the suburbs of Dresden. 'Any further,' he said, 'would make a rotten impression. Now is the time for iron steadfastness and immediate action to restore order. Set me a good example of calm and nerve!'[17] Coming from a man who had just run away from the battlefield, his exhortation had a certain ironic twist.

Goebbels, in angry tears at what he heard, demanded Hitler's permission to shoot '10,000 or more English and American prisoners-of-war' as a reprisal, one for every German citizen killed in air raids. Hitler, equally emotional, was prepared to agree, even though it would have meant abrogating the Geneva Convention. He even saw an advantage in provoking retaliation from the Allies, which might deter German soldiers on the Western Front from giving themselves up knowing they would be treated well as prisoners. Fortunately, Keitel, Jodl, Dönitz and even Ribbentrop combined to persuade him not to do so. Significantly, Göring was not included in those whom he asked for advice.

Goebbels rushed to pour blame on Göring, accusing him of being solely responsible for the Allied terror raids, and said he would haul him before the People's Court if he could. 'What a burden of guilt this parasite has brought on his own head, for his slackness and interest in his own comfort,' he told his aides. 'Why didn't the Führer listen to my earlier warnings? But I was always called a pessimist and an ignorant civilian, who could not understand military matters.'[18] All his old hatred of Göring the 'sybarite' surfaced again, wiping from his memory the many times he had praised him as a friend. 'Fools covered with medals and vain, perfumed fops have no place in the conduct of a war,' he wrote in his diary. 'Either they change or they must be eliminated.'[19]

* * *

With Hitler's mental and physical condition getting worse by the day, the question of the succession was now becoming urgent. Goebbels believed he could eliminate Göring and Ribbentrop without much bother, but Himmler and Bormann were another matter entirely. Knowing he would have to reach an understanding with them, he drove out to Hohenlychen on 14 February to see Himmler. Although the front was in a state of crisis, the Commander-in-Chief of Army Group Vistula was neither too busy nor too ill to talk to him about more urgent matters, and listened attentively as he outlined his proposals for a new government intended, he said, to lighten Hitler's burden. Hitler would perform the role of Head of State, Goebbels would be Reich Chancellor and Foreign Minister, Himmler would be War Minister in command of the Wehrmacht, and Bormann would be Party Minister.[20] Himmler was non-committal and Goebbels returned to Berlin, where he continued his efforts to enlist Himmler's support for another week.

Himmler, however, had his own fish to fry. When Goebbels had talked about the possibilities of saving the Reich through a separate peace, and said that he felt it was 'more likely that something could be accomplished in the East' with the 'more realistic' Stalin, he had dismissed the idea. He believed Britain would still 'come to its senses', and that this was the route to follow. What he did not tell Goebbels was that he was already involved in negotiations with the West, and was about to receive an intermediary, Swedish Count Folke Bernadotte, a nephew of the King of Sweden and Vice-Chairman of the Swedish Red Cross, at Hohenlychen. Himmler had been nurturing contacts with the West since 1941, mainly through Schellenberg, but more recently using his masseur, Kersten, as well, working mainly through Stockholm and Switzerland, convinced that the West would eventually agree to negotiate a separate peace with him. Utterly blind to his image outside Germany, he fondly imagined that the Western leaders would find him more acceptable than Hitler. He was right, however, in assuming that they knew he was the only man, apart from Hitler, who had the power to make any settlement work, and so he persevered in the vain hope of saving his own skin and position.

Bernadotte arrived in Berlin on 17 February, with the official purpose of negotiating the repatriation of Swedish-born women who had married Germans but were now either widowed or deserted. In fact, he hoped to achieve the release of all Scandinavian prisoners, and others if possible, from the concentration camps. Himmler covered himself by making sure the Swede met Ribbentrop and Kaltenbrunner first, before visiting him at Hohenlychen on 19 February. Bernadotte was impressed by his ordinariness – he thought he looked like 'quite an unimportant official, whom one would hardly have noticed if one had met him on the street', and by 'the lack of anything diabolical in his appearance'. Himmler, he wrote later, 'seemed strikingly and amazingly obliging'.[21]

Their discussion was amicable, though Himmler insisted that Germany would not give up the struggle, and that he personally could never go back on his oath and betray Hitler. He decided he was not prepared to release Scandinavian concentration camp prisoners unless Bernadotte could guarantee in return that Danish and Norwegian resistance fighters would cease harrying the Germans. Since Bernadotte could not make deals on behalf of the resistance movements in other countries, the whole negotiations were in the verge of collapse until Schellenberg persuaded his chief to agree that the prisoners could all be transferred to one camp, where they could be looked after by the Red Cross.

Bernadotte was now willing to co-operate, since he had achieved part of what he had come to Berlin for, and Himmler authorised Schellenberg to draw up terms which the Swede could pass to Eisenhower as the basis for negotiation. According to Schellenberg, Himmler changed his mind again the next day. He had realised that the only way they could proceed was if they staged an SS *putsch* against Hitler and the crew of the 'cement submarine'. In the end, he decided he could not bring himself to betray his Führer – at least not on his own doorstep. For at that same time, Wolff was in Berne, the capital of Switzerland, negotiating on his behalf with Allen Dulles for an armistice in Italy that would allow troops to be withdrawn to fight in Germany.

While Himmler was skulking in Hohenlychen, Wenck was organising his army group's counterattack, launching the Third Panzer Army in a powerful thrust against Zhukov's exposed right flank that sent the Soviets reeling. But two days later, driving back to the front at dawn on 21 February after spending all night briefing Hitler in Berlin, Wenck took over the wheel of his staff car from his exhausted driver. Before long, he too fell asleep, and the car smashed into the side of a railway bridge, trapping him inside as it burst into flames. He was pulled out just in time, but his injuries included a fractured skull and five broken ribs. Deprived of his leadership, the counterattack fizzled out, and with it Himmler's standing in Hitler's eyes.

Only a few weeks earlier, Himmler had seemed to be indisputably the second most powerful man in Germany, but now the ground was crumbling beneath his feet, as his influence slipped away. Even the RSHA, the engine-room of his power, was being run as a personal fiefdom by Kaltenbrunner, reporting directly to Hitler and spending most of his time in the Chancellery, where he had formed a close friendship with Bormann. It is tempting to credit Bormann with engineering Himmler's slide. Presenting him with the poisoned chalices of the two army group commands may or may not have been Bormann's idea, but there can be no doubt that he encouraged Hitler to do so. And it is fair to assume that he realised the task would be beyond Himmler's capability, and that it would keep him away from Führer Headquarters, leaving him, Bormann, free to machinate and manipulate. If he had counted on Himmler falling flat on his face as a general, he was very quickly rewarded.

Rokossovsky launched his major attack northwards through Pomerania on 24 February, and Zhukov joined in on 1 March. Himmler, along with the General Staff, had expected the main assault to be directed towards Berlin, and was taken completely by surprise. By 1 March, the Soviets had reached the Baltic at Kolberg, the setting of Goebbels's epic colour film – he got round the embarrassment by suppressing the news. Himmler took refuge in his hospital bed, claiming to be suffering from angina again. Lammerding reported that he had flu. According to Kersten, his highly nervous state was aggravated by an order he had just received from Hitler to destroy the concentration camps and exterminate all the prisoners to avoid their falling into enemy hands[22] – which would remove another major pillar of his power base.

Himmler had recovered sufficiently to travel to Berlin for an interview with Hitler on 15 March. For some days, Hitler had been ranting against him in his absence, blaming him for the military collapse in Pomerania, and accusing him of disobedience and of letting him down by 'falling prey to the General Staff'. Now it was Himmler's turn to experience what Göring had suffered so often, as Hitler gave him 'an extraordinarily severe dressing-down'.[23] To Himmler's own failures Hitler added his fury at the news that Sepp Dietrich had ordered his Sixth SS-Panzer Army, including the four crack Waffen-SS divisions, one of which bore Hitler's own name, to withdraw from Budapest.

Hitler forced Himmler to issue his order to Dietrich that the divisions must remove their 'loyalty is my honour' armbands as a mark of disgrace.

On 20 March, Guderian finally managed to persuade Himmler that he must give up his army group command, for the sake of his health – though the Chief of Staff thought he had nothing worse than a slight head cold. Nevertheless, Guderian offered sympathy, and suggested that perhaps he had been overworking, reminding him that as well as being Commander-in-Chief of Army Group Vistula he was also Reichsführer of the SS, Chief of all German police, including the Gestapo, Minister of the Interior, and Commander-in-Chief of the Replacement Army. Such a portfolio, he said, would surely 'tax the strength of any man'. Why not give up one of them – such as the army group? Himmler seized on this possibility. Yes, he told Guderian, it was only too true that his many positions really taxed his endurance. 'But how can *I* go and say that to the Führer?' he asked. 'He wouldn't like it if I came up with such a suggestion.'

'Would you authorise me to say it for you?' Guderian asked quickly. Himmler nodded his agreement. Guderian then began sounding him out on the need for an immediate armistice, but although he listened carefully, Himmler refused to be drawn.

Guderian sped back to Berlin, where Hitler agreed – 'but only after a lot of grumbling and with obvious reluctance' – to relieve the overworked Reichsführer. As a replacement, Guderian suggested Colonel-General Gotthard Heinrici, who was then commanding the First Panzer Army in the Carpathians, in eastern Czechoslovakia. Hitler, inevitably, opposed the idea of Heinrici, a cousin of Rundstedt, but Guderian persevered. Heinrici, he insisted, was the one man for the job. 'He's especially experienced with the Russians,' he said. 'They haven't broken through him yet.' Finally, Hitler was convinced, and a telegram was sent to Heinrici informing him of his new appointment.

Meeting Himmler for the first time the next day, for the hand-over of command, Heinrici found him more concerned with treating him to an interminable speech of self-justification than with giving him details of the forces under his command or a proper assessment of the situation. The monologue had gone on for forty-five minutes and showed no sign of abating when the telephone rang. Himmler paused to answer it, listened for a moment in silence, then handed it to Heinrici. 'You're the new commander,' he said. 'You'd better take this.'

Heinrici took the telephone and introduced himself. On the other end was General Ferdinand Busse, commander of the Ninth Army, facing Chuikov at the fortress town of Küstrin, which controlled the only bridges across the Oder and Warta rivers in that area. 'The Russians have broken through,' Busse reported, 'and have enlarged their bridgehead near Küstrin.' Heinrici relayed the information to Himmler, who shrugged nervously.

'Well,' he said, 'you're the new commander of Army Group Vistula. Issue the proper orders.'

Heinrici glared at him. 'I don't know a damn thing about the army group. I don't even know what troops I have or who's supposed to be where.'

Himmler said nothing. Clearly, Heinrici could expect nothing from him. Turning back to the telephone, he asked Busse what he proposed.

'I'd like to counterattack as soon as possible, to restabilise my forces around Küstrin,' was the reply.

'Fine. As soon as I can I'll come to see you and we'll both look over the front lines.'

As Heinrici replaced the receiver, Himmler started talking again as though nothing had happened. The general cut him short. It was vital, he said, that he should have the Reichsführer's considered opinion of the overall situation, and of Germany's war aims. Himmler pulled a disagreeable face, then said, conspiratorially, 'I want to tell you something personal.' Leading Heinrici to a couch on the other side of the room, where the stenographer who had been noting down the conversation could not hear, he told him, 'I have taken the necessary steps to negotiate a peace with the West.'

'Fine,' Heinrici responded. 'But how do we get to them?'

'Through a neutral country,' Himmler told him. 'I'm telling you this in absolute confidence, you understand?' He did not enlarge upon this statement any further. All he wanted to do now, it seemed, was to get away as quickly as possible.

'He was only too happy to leave,' Heinrici told his former Chief of Staff in the Carpathians in a telephone call that night. 'He couldn't get out of here fast enough. He didn't want to be in charge when the collapse comes. No – he wanted just a simple general for that, and I'm the scapegoat.'[24]

Guderian met Himmler at the Chancellery the next day, walking with Hitler. He asked to speak to him in private and Hitler, no doubt believing it was to do with the handover of command, left them to it. But the Chief of Staff had other things on his mind, and plunged into the heart of the matter at once, picking up the question of peace where he had left off the previous day.

'The war can no longer be won,' he told Himmler. 'The only problem now is finding the quickest way of putting an end to the senseless slaughter and bombing. Apart from Ribbentrop, you are the only man with contacts in neutral countries. Since the Foreign Minister is reluctant to ask Hitler to open negotiations, you must go with me to Hitler and urge him to arrange an armistice.'

Again, Himmler appeared receptive and interested, but again he refused to commit himself, or to offer support. If he had been scared of trying to resign, he was terrified at the prospect of telling Hitler the war was lost. He would have him shot, he said, if he were even to approach him with such a proposal. Despite his apparent sympathy – and the fact that he was, of course, busily trying to arrange peace negotiations on his own account – he seems to have faithfully reported the conversation to Hitler. That evening, after a blazing row over the loss of Küstrin that dwarfed all their previous altercations, the Führer cut short his situation conference and asked Guderian to stay behind.

'I understand that your heart condition has taken a turn for the worse,' he said coldly. He ordered Guderian to take sick-leave, with immediate effect.[25]

By the beginning of March, the British, Canadian and American armies of Montgomery's Twenty-First Army Group had occupied the entire west bank of the Rhine from Nijmegen to Düsseldorf. Against surprisingly fierce opposition, they had shattered nineteen German divisions, which had lost 90,000 irreplaceable men. To their south, General Omar Bradley's US Twelfth Army Group was busy clearing the eighty miles of west bank from Düsseldorf down to Koblenz. Lieutenant-General Courtney H. Hodges's US First Army, fighting alongside the Ninth, captured Cologne on 7 March. That same day, by a great stroke of luck, part of Hodges's army, the 9th Armoured Division, found the railway bridge across the Rhine at Remagen undestroyed. The advance guard charged over it, others followed swiftly and before long there were four divisions across the river, establishing a bridgehead several miles deep. The following day, Patton's Third Army also reached the Rhine, only three days after launching its attack from the Moselle. Another 49,000 German soldiers had been removed from the war during Hodges's advance, captured when they were immobilised by lack of fuel. By 21 March, when the West Wall was completely cut off, the tally of German prisoners taken since the beginning of the Allied offensives in February had reached more than 280,000, and overall German losses to 350,000 men. Eisenhower's forces were lined up on a broad front, ready to advance from the Rhineland right into the heart of Germany.

The capture of his native Rhineland was an emotional blow to Goebbels, the more so when he learned that his home town of Rheydt had capitulated to the Americans without a fight. The thought of a white flag flying over his parents' home was unbearable, as was the US plan to set up 'a so-called free German newspaper' there, which he saw as a deliberate insult to him. 'I'll find ways of restoring order in Rheydt at least,' he promised himself in his diary, and began making elaborate plans to send in an undercover squad of Berlin party members 'already trained in such acts', to assassinate the mayor, who was willingly collaborating with the Americans.[26]

He was even more moved on 13 March, the twelfth anniversary of his appointment as Minister of Propaganda, when he received what he described as 'the worst conceivable omen for the next twelve years': in the daily Mosquito raid that evening, his already damaged ministry building was totally destroyed by a bomb. He was at home when it happened, but drove to the Wilhelmplatz immediately to survey the damage. He had taken great pride over the years in restoring the old palace, and for once was genuinely upset. 'One's heart aches to see so unique a product of the architect's art, such as this building was, totally flattened in a second,' he wrote in his diary. The building was still blazing when he got there, and he was terrified that 500 Panzerfaust missiles stored in the basement would explode.

At home later, he passed what he described as 'a somewhat melancholy evening' with his family. 'Slowly one is beginning to realise what this war means for us all,' he wrote – an astonishing admission after nearly six years of slaughter. Equally astonishing was his refusal to accept defeat: 'We had all taken the ministry so much to our hearts. Now it belongs to the past. I am firmly convinced, however, that when this war is over, not only shall I reconstruct a new monumental ministry – as the Führer says – but restore the old ministry in all its glory.'[27]

*   *   *

In spite of all Goebbels's bluster, Magda knew the end could not be far away. She feared not only for her husband but also for herself and their six children. Goebbels suggested she take the children and move out westwards, where she might find shelter with the British, but she refused to leave him. Without telling him, she went to Dr Morell and asked him to provide her with enough poison to kill herself and the children when the time came. She had gone to the right man – for nine years, Morell had fed the Führer mysterious cocktails of pills and potions, including vast doses of amphetamines that were contributing significantly to the tremors that affected him so badly. He had grown rich on the proceeds of treating Hitler and his top associates and their families, and had set up his own pharmaceutical company. He was happy to provide her with what she needed to end her children's lives.

'When I think that in a few weeks' time I may have to kill these innocent creatures,' she told Rudolf Semmler, 'I go nearly crazy with grief and pain. I am always wondering how I will do it when the time comes. I cannot talk about it with my husband any more. He would never forgive me for weakening his resistance. As long as he can go on fighting, he thinks that all is not lost.'[28]

That may have been what Goebbels told his wife, but with his staff he kept discussing different scenarios for the end, always looking for the most dramatic and Wagnerian last act. One of his ideas was to lead his long-suffering staff in a fight to the finish in the Zoo flak tower, blowing it up in the final stage of the battle with himself and everyone else inside it. In another vision, he saw himself dying a hero's death on the barricades, swastika in hand. His staff were less inclined to indulge in such theatrics. Few of them had any appetite for suicide: they saw themselves as civil servants, not samurai warriors.

Goebbels, as Defender of Berlin, was intent on turning the entire population into samurai warriors, but was still a little vague about exactly how. When Lieutenant-General Helmuth Reymann took up his post as military commander of the city on 5 March, he could find no sign that his predecessor, who had been taken sick, had actually done anything to prepare the city against attack. This was perhaps understandable, for Hitler and Goebbels had until very recently still insisted that any suggestion of the Soviets being able to reach the city was defeatist talk, punishable by death.

Nothing had been done to protect the civilian population from ground attack, or to evacuate the remaining children, or the sick and elderly. There were not even any plans, let alone stocks of food, for feeding them under siege conditions. The barricades, road blocks and improvised tank traps that Berliners had started to erect in their near panic at the end of January remained unfinished. A 'Fundamental Order for the Defence of the Reich Capital' was issued at last on 9 March, and although it contained a fair amount of practical detail it also included a great deal of wishful thinking, and bore the unmistakable stamp of Goebbels's hysterical prose. Much of it was typically grandiose, imprecise and emotional, a scenario for *Götterdämmerung*:

The capital will be defended to the last man and the last bullet . . . The struggle must be conducted with
  Fanatical resolution
  Imagination
  Every means of *deception, artifice and cunning*:
  Stratagems of all kinds, devised in advance or on the spur of the moment
  on
  above and
  beneath the ground
. . . It is a condition for the successful defence of Berlin that
  Every building
  Every house
  Every floor
  Every hedge
  Every shell crater
  Be defended to the utmost!
It is not nearly so important that those defending the capital have a detailed knowledge of the mechanics of their weapons; *what matters is that*
  every man
  be inspired and suffused with a
  fanatical resolve
  with a WILL TO FIGHT
  realising that the world is watching us with bated breath and
  that the struggle for Berlin may decide the war.[29]

Goebbels still refused to consider evacuating any of the 3 million civilians remaining in the city, even the 120,000 children under the age of ten. And when Reymann asked what provision had been made to provide infants with milk if the city were cut off, Goebbels told him, quite wrongly, that he had enough canned milk in store to last three months. When he received Reymann's first report on the army's stocks of food, fuel, weapons and ammunition, and on how many fit men were available, he calculated that they had enough of everything to hold out for eight weeks under siege. 'Taken as a whole,' he noted with astonishing complacency, 'the situation is extraordinarily satisfactory. Eight weeks is a long time, during which a lot can happen. In any case, we have made excellent preparations and above all it must be remembered that, if the worst should happen, an enormous number of men with their weapons would flow into the city and we should be in a position to use them to put up a powerful defence.'[30]

Reymann was unconvinced by any of it, but worked night and day to do what he could to prepare some sort of defences. He needed Goebbels to provide him with men and materials, asking for a minimum of 100,000 men a day. He got fewer than 30,000, and many of those were wasted as the chaotic bureaucracy ordered men from Spandau on the city's western edge to work at Karlshorst, way over to the east, while sending men from Tempelhof to work in Spandau. With most transport services at a standstill, and those trains that were running disrupted by air raids, much of the labour force spent all day struggling to and fro across the ruined city. And when they got there, they had no tools or equipment.

Even if Reymann could achieve the impossible and get the defence lines into a reasonable state before the Soviet assault, he was faced with the still bigger problem of who was to man them. In ideal circumstances he would need at least 200,000 well-trained and well-armed men to defend the city. After doing his first sums he estimated that he would have no more than 125,000. In fact, including the last-ditch levies he had as few as 94,000, 60,000 of whom were untrained Volkssturm members who came under the jurisdiction of the party, not the army. Most of these had no weapons, but when Reymann raised the matter with Goebbels, he was told that the arms factories were working flat out to supply the armies on the Oder front, but if the city was encircled then they would be able to provide adequate quantities to the defenders. Knowing that when the city was surrounded there would be no factories still working, Reymann was not reassured.

By the end of the month, although the Soviets still had not attacked, the situation in Berlin was truly parlous. Virtually all the anti-aircraft artillery, including the versatile 88-mm guns, had been moved to the front, together with the last units of the Replacement Army and the

entire complement of the military training establishments. Soon there
would be nobody left but the Volkssturm.

Reymann returned to the question of evacuating the civilians, particularly the children, but again got short shrift. Under pressure, Goebbels
admitted that an evacuation plan did exist, prepared earlier by the SS
and the police. It turned out to consist of one small-scale map, on
which possible evacuation routes through the city to the south and
west had been inked in. The idea, it seemed, was for evacuees carrying
only hand luggage to make their way on foot for up to twenty miles
along the chosen routes to suburban rail stations. There was no provision for sanitation stations, food distribution points, or transport for
the old and sick. Nor was there any indication of where the trains to
carry them to safety would come from.

Accepting that there was little chance now of organising an orderly
evacuation, and that he would be stuck with millions of civilians when
the Soviet attack came, Reymann turned to the problem of feeding
them – by now, he knew Goebbels had lied about stocks. Where was
the food to come from? How were babies to be provided with milk?
Goebbels referred him to the mythical three months of canned milk,
but then produced a more imaginative solution.

'How will we feed them?' he asked, rhetorically. 'We'll bring in livestock from the surrounding countryside, that's how we'll feed them!'

The thought of bringing cattle into the middle of a battle zone,
where they could not be fed, herded, milked or protected, struck
Reymann as ludicrous. He returned to the attack on evacuation. 'Surely,
we must consider an immediate evacuation programme,' he pleaded.
'We cannot wait any longer. Each day that passes will multiply the
difficulties later on. We must at least move the women and children
out, before it's too late.'

Goebbels did not answer for a moment. Then he said, mildly, 'My
dear General, when and if an evacuation becomes necessary, *I* will be
the one to make the decision.' His voice hardened as he concluded:
'But I don't intend to throw Berlin into a panic by ordering it now!
There's plenty of time! Plenty of time!'

Reymann knew there was not plenty of time. By now, surely, not even
Goebbels could doubt that a Soviet attack was imminent. At 11 a.m.
that morning, shortly before 600 US bombers hit industrial installations at Siemensstadt and Marienfelde, knocking out the Daimler-Benz
factory among others, the city had been taken completely by surprise
by an unusual low-level aerial attack. The aircraft, mostly fighters,

strafed the streets with cannon and machine-gun fire for about twenty minutes. They came not from the West but from the East, bearing the red star of the Soviet Air Force.

On 18 March, a beautiful, sunny Sunday, 1,250 American bombers supported by 700 fighters had pounded Berlin in yet another destructive daylight raid. They were opposed by Me-262s, flying in significant numbers for the first time: 28 jets shot down 15 US planes, but neither they, nor the flak, which accounted for another seven, could prevent the bombers bringing the city to a standstill. The Luftwaffe was so short of fuel, aircraft and pilots that to all intents and purposes Berlin had become an open city to attack from the air.

Hitler was concerned about the state of the city, and telephoned Goebbels for a situation report as soon as he rose at midday. But he was also prepared to destroy Berlin to deny it to the Soviets – his scorched-earth policy was to apply to the whole country, including the capital. Speer tried to dissuade him, taking the risk of presenting him with another report that afternoon giving a truthful assessment of the country's position: the final collapse of the economy was certain within four to eight weeks, after which the war could not be continued. Appealing to Hitler's humanity, he said that they had to do what they could to maintain at least the basics for the survival of the people.

'At this stage of the war,' he wrote, 'it makes no sense for us to undertake demolitions which might strike at the very heart of the nation . . . it cannot possibly be the purpose of warfare at home to destroy so many bridges that, given the straitened means of the postwar period, it will take years to rebuild the transportation network . . . Their destruction means eliminating all further possibility for the German people to survive.' Turning specifically to Berlin, Speer wrote: 'The planned demolition of the bridges in Berlin would cut off the city's food supply, and industrial production and human life in the city would be rendered impossible for years to come. Such demolitions would mean the death of Berlin.'

Hitler rejected Speer's pleas with contempt. 'If the war is lost, the nation will also perish,' he told him. 'Besides, those who remain after the battle are only the inferior ones, for the good ones will all have been killed.' The next day, 19 March – which happened to be Speer's fortieth birthday – he issued his 'Nero Order', for the destruction of all industrial plants about to fall into enemy hands, all important electrical facilities, water works, gas works, food and clothing stores, all bridges, all railway and communications installations, all waterways, all ships, freight cars and locomotives.

Speer set about sabotaging Hitler's order, and another calling for the entire civilian population of areas threatened by the enemy in the West to be evacuated, on foot if necessary. There were no provisions for transporting, feeding or housing them. Sick to death of the war, the people in small towns and villages were doing their best to prevent the Wehrmacht defending them. All they wanted was to get it over with as quickly and as painlessly as possible. For the next month, Speer dashed about the country talking to Gauleiters and generals, frantically trying to persuade them not to carry out the order, with a great deal of success. He continued to stick his neck out by arguing with Hitler, refusing to go quietly when Hitler tried to get rid of him in his usual way by sending him on sick-leave. 'I am not sick!' Speer insisted. If Hitler wanted to be rid of him he would have to dismiss him publicly, something he was loath to do. Speer survived, and even managed to persuade Hitler, at the end of March, to modify the order and give him full responsibility for implementing it, tacitly acknowledging that he never would.

Time was rapidly running out for Speer in stopping the destruction in the West, as the British and American armies smashed their way forward, after crossing the Rhine in strength on 23 March. By 1 April, the US First and Ninth Armies had surrounded the Ruhr, trapping the whole of the German Army Group B, with two Panzer armies, twenty-one divisions, plus two corps of Army Group H, amounting to almost 325,000 men. This was a staggering loss to Germany, leaving a gap 200 miles wide in the Western Front, with only a few disorganised divisions standing between the Ruhr and Berlin. On all the other fronts, the picture was similar. In the Netherlands, where conditions had been appalling throughout the winter, the Germans finally began withdrawing, though there was still some bitter fighting ahead. In Hungary, Austria and East Prussia, the Red Army drove on relentlessly, and all the time Zhukov and Koniev continued to build up massive strength on the Oder and Neisse, ready to crash forward as soon as the spring floods subsided.

As well as trying to organise the defence of Berlin, Goebbels was working on plans to activate partisan groups supposedly set up in the occupied territories by the SS under the code-name 'Werwolf'. On 1 April, he began broadcasting a stream of typical rhetoric, calling for suicidal resistance, under the regularly repeated slogan: '*Besser tot als rot*' ('Better dead than red'). But with all that was on his plate, he still found time to go on fighting his private battles for power and planning elaborate new projects for the future. He achieved a small but highly satisfying victory over Göring by persuading Hitler that the entire organisation of the Luftwaffe should be simplified, and that he should be given the authority to carry out the operation.[31] He also managed, after years of intrigue, in getting Hitler to dismiss his rival, Otto Dietrich, from his post as Reich Press Chief.[32] But he failed yet again in renewed efforts to get rid of Ribbentrop.

Bormann, too, was feverishly planning for the future, issuing more decrees and orders than ever – over 400 between January and April – and making provisions for restructuring the party to control the new Reich that would emerge at the end of the war. His wife shared his faith: 'One day,' she wrote to him in February,

the Reich of our dreams will emerge . . . In some ways, you know, this reminds me of the *Götterdämmerung* [the twilight of the Gods] in the Edda [the ancient Norse saga] . . . The monsters are storming the bridge of the Gods . . . the citadel of the Gods crumbles, and all seems lost; and then, suddenly, a new citadel arises, more beautiful than ever before . . . We are not the first to engage in mortal combat with the powers of the underworld, and that we feel impelled, and are also able, to do so should give us a conviction of ultimate victory.[33]

The *Götterdämmerung* was being invoked more and more often in those traumatic days. Speer had it included in the programme of the final concert by the Berlin Philharmonic Orchestra on 12 April, as a signal to the musicians that this was their last performance. Music had always played a large part in Speer's life, and throughout the war he had hardly ever missed a Philharmonic concert. Goebbels had considered the orchestra such a vital morale booster that he had exempted all its 105 musicians from military service. Now, however, he had decreed that they would all be included in the final draft for the Volkssturm. When Speer protested, Goebbels, not surprisingly, was unsympathetic.

'I alone raised this orchestra to its special level,' he told him. 'My initiative and my money have made it what it has become, what it represents to the world today. Those who follow have no right to it. It can go under along with us.'

It was unthinkable to Speer that this unique ensemble should perish pointlessly on the barricades. He had the musicians' papers extracted from the draft board files – a trick Hitler himself had used at the beginning of the war to save his favourite artists from call-up. Then he formulated a plan to spirit the entire orchestra away from the city at the last minute before the Soviets attacked it. The first part of the plan had gone into effect on 28 March, when he had had most of the orchestra's library of scores, together with its pianos, harps and Wagner tubas, and the musicians' dress suits, loaded into trucks and driven away for safe storage at Plassenberg, a small town near Bayreuth. Now with the Soviet forces poised to attack, he decided it was time to evacuate the musicians themselves.

He sent word to the orchestra's manager, Dr Gerhart von Westermann, that the advertised programme for that day's concert should be changed. It should open with the finale from Wagner's *Die Götterdämmerung*, which depicted the destruction of Valhalla, the death of the Gods, and the end of the world. This would be followed, less melodramatically, by Beethoven's Violin Concerto, played by the orchestra's leader, the brilliant twenty-three-year-old Gerhard Taschner, and then Bruckner's Romantic Symphony. The music was the signal to the musicians that after the concert there would be a bus waiting to take all those who wished to leave the city to safety in the Kulmbach-Bayreuth area, which was about to be taken by the Americans. The concert began at 5 p.m., as planned. But there was no bus waiting outside – the musicians had voted to stay in Berlin. Only Taschner had chosen to leave, with his wife and two children and the daughter of another musician. They were driven south in Speer's own car, escorted by his adjutant.[34]

Returning to his office from the concert, Speer was called at once to the Führer bunker, where Hitler rushed towards him, animatedly waving a newspaper clipping. 'Here, read it! Here! You never wanted to believe it. Here it is!' His words, said Speer, came in a great rush. 'Here we have the miracle I always predicted. Who was right? The war isn't lost. Read it! Roosevelt is dead!'[35]

Among the works of history with which Goebbels had been trying to hearten the Führer during the last few weeks, his favourite had been Thomas Carlyle's *History of Frederick the Great*. He had read aloud to him from the chapter that told of the turning point in the Seven Years War in 1762, when Prussia faced overwhelming odds against an alliance of Russia, Austria and France. Frederick had almost given up hope, and said he would give up the fight and commit suicide if things had not improved by 15 February. Goebbels had read Carlyle's apt and dramatic words with relish: 'Brave King! Wait yet a little while, and the days of your suffering will be over. Already the sun of your good fortune stands behind the clouds, and soon it will rise upon you.' Shortly afterwards, the 'miracle of the House of Brandenburg' had come to pass. Tsarina Elizabeth of Russia, Frederick's most deadly enemy, died suddenly; her successor made a separate peace, to become an ally, and Prussia went on to victory. Hitler had seen the parallel at once, and his eyes, Goebbels said, 'were filled with tears'.

Goebbels had been visiting the front near Küstrin when the news of Roosevelt's death broke, and he did not learn of it until he returned home just after midnight. Trembling with emotion, he called for the best champagne. 'This is the turning point!' he exclaimed, as he telephoned Hitler, to congratulate him. 'It is written in the stars that the second half of April will be the turning point for us,' he told him, referring to a horoscope he had unearthed shortly before. 'This is Friday the thirteenth! Providence has struck down your greatest enemy. God has not forsaken us. Twice he has saved you from savage assassins. Death, which the enemy aimed at you in 1939 and 1944, has now smitten your most dangerous enemy. It is a miracle! It is like the death of Tsarina Elizabeth.'[36]

For the moment, Hitler was buoyed up by the news, though Speer describes him sitting exhausted, 'looking both liberated and dazed as he slumped in his armchair. But I sensed that he was still without hope.'[37] When Ribbentrop visited him the next day, however, he found him, he said, 'in seventh heaven'. At the daily conference, his mood was still ecstatic – not even the news that Vienna had fallen to the Red Army could lower his spirits. He announced that the war would be won in Berlin: units falling back from the Oder front would form a hard nucleus that would draw the Soviet troops towards it. German armies would then be able to attack from the outside, to destroy the enemy in a decisive battle. He would remain in Berlin, to inspire his forces to victory.

His generals were less than convinced by this strategy, and several tried to persuade him to leave the city and go south, to the comparative safety of Berchtesgaden. But he refused even to consider it, and when they had gone he began drafting a new proclamation to the troops, so bombastic that even Goebbels thought it too far-fetched, and held off distributing it until the Soviet attack began. He did not have long to wait. At exactly 3 a.m. on 16 April, Zhukov's artillery opened up with a terrifying barrage. Koniev's followed suit shortly afterwards, to the south, and Rokossovsky's to the north.

Between them, the three Soviet fronts had about 2.5 million men, 41,600 guns and mortars, 6,250 tanks and self-propelled guns, more than a million multiple rocket launchers, and 7,500 aircraft. The First Belorussian Front alone had a stockpile of 7.147 million shells. Heinrici's Army Group Vistula, by comparison, had at the very most 250,000 poorly armed men, with about 850 tanks, 500 anti-aircraft batteries serving as artillery, and 300 aircraft that had virtually no fuel.[38]

This time, there was to be no miracle.

XXXVII

THE END OF THE ROAD

ON the eve of Hitler's fifty-sixth birthday, Goebbels broadcast a rambling and emotional panegyric to him as the saviour of his people, whom they should follow 'faithfully, without reservation . . . trusting in the lucky star that looks down on him and all of us now as before.' With all his usual empty verbosity, Goebbels called on the German people 'on no account to give a gleefully watching world the satisfaction of witnessing the spectacle of belly-crawling submission, but proudly to unfurl the swastika in the face of the enemy instead of the white flag of surrender he is expecting to see.' After ranting against the 'flood of Bolshevism' and international Jewry, who wanted to see the world destroyed, he promised that 'God will throw back Lucifer, as he has done before when the dark angel stood before the gates of power, back into the abyss from whence he came.' He concluded with a final, pointless piece of bombast: 'Germany is still the land of loyalty; in the hour of danger she will celebrate her greatest triumph. Never shall history say that the people have abandoned their Führer, or that the Führer has abandoned his people. And this means victory!'[1]

Maybe Goebbels still believed the nonsense he was spouting, even though Roosevelt's death had not produced a breach in the enemy alliance. Certainly none of the other paladins did, as they gathered in the ruins of the Chancellery the next day, 20 April, waiting in line to pour their ritual congratulations on the deranged dictator. Hitler slept late – he had not gone to bed until 9.00 that morning. After breakfasting and playing for a few minutes with his German shepherd Blondi's puppy, he started the day in the wrecked garden by inspecting delegations from the Courland Army in Latvia and the SS-Division 'Berlin', and pinning medals on twenty young boys from the Hitler

Youth, who had performed exceptionally bravely against the Soviet tanks and on anti-aircraft and rescue operations. Göring, Goebbels, Himmler, Speer, Dönitz, Ribbentrop, Keitel, Kaltenbrunner, and General Hans Krebs, Guderian's former deputy who had taken over as Army Chief of Staff, led the line-up, followed by various other generals. They all offered their congratulations and swore their undying loyalty, but they must have realised that this was the last time they would all be together. Most of them could hardly wait to leave.

Göring was perhaps the most eager of them all to be on his way, to be clear of the madhouse. He intended to leave as quickly as possible for Berchtesgaden, and in an attempt to look less conspicuous was wearing a new uniform, having discarded his dove-grey outfit with its elaborate gold epaulettes in favour of plain khaki drill, with his gold Reich eagle pinned on each shoulder. Some of the officers present commented that it made him look suspiciously like an American general, but it was in fact the new summer uniform that was already being issued to the army.

The previous day, with Soviet forces perilously close to the Schorfheide, he had finished packing up at Carinhall, loading twenty-four cars and lorries with files and equipment, plus the remaining treasures that had not been included in the two trainloads he had already sent south. He had then taken his hunting rifle for the last time and gone into the breeding grounds, calling his last four bison to him by name and then shooting them, so that they would not fall into the hands of the Soviet troops. He ordered their carcasses to be distributed to help feed the endless columns of refugees trailing past his estate. In the early morning, he made his last visit to Carin's mausoleum, kneeling alone beside her sarcophagus to say his farewells. He had had the buildings on which he had lavished so much care laced with demolition charges, and his last act before driving out of the gates was to press the plunger on the detonator to blast them all into rubble. He parked his lorries under guard at the Luftwaffe headquarters at Werder, while he drove into the city to give Hitler his greetings and attend his last Führer conference.

Before the conference began, he took Keitel aside to get his support for moving his operational headquarters to Berchtesgaden, now that Carinhall was no more and signals contact with Werder was becoming sporadic. Since there was now only one main road to the south still open between Halle and Leipzig, there was no time to lose. Keitel agreed to propose to Hitler that he should go, in what he described as 'my own absolutely firm belief at that time that the Führer and the OKW staff would . . . also be transferring their supreme command to Berchtesgaden'. Keitel put the proposal to Hitler, who he says agreed 'and went so far as to suggest this himself to Göring'.[2]

Everyone at the Führer conference tried to persuade Hitler to move south to the Obersalzberg. Over the previous ten days, everyone who was not absolutely vital to the Führer Headquarters had been sent there in special trains and convoys of lorries, together with advance contingents from the staffs of the OKW and OKH. Planes were standing by to fly out the final top brass, including Hitler, Keitel and Jodl, at a moment's notice. But Hitler refused to commit himself. He would go no further than confirming the instructions he had given on 14 April that if the Soviets and the Americans cut the country in two, the fight would be continued under separate commands for the north and south. For the northern half, he now formally transferred command of the armed forces to Dönitz. Kesselring had been named as Supreme Commander in the south, but Hitler refrained from handing over to him, keeping open the option of taking command himself in the so-called 'Alpine Redoubt': 'I shall leave it to fate whether I die in the capital or fly to Obersalzberg at the last moment.'[3] Until then, Göring was to be in charge.

Before leaving the bunker, after a perfunctory farewell from Hitler, Göring cornered Himmler for a private chat about making contact with the Western Allies. In a bugged conversation with Lammers recorded while they were prisoners in ASHCAN, Göring said that Himmler told him he had already been in touch with Bernadotte, and was in fact due to meet him again that very evening. Taunting Göring, he said: 'You know, he must be the man sent by Eisenhower to negotiate.' Göring did not rise to the bait. 'I can't believe that,' he said. 'Don't take offence, but I doubt that they'll find *you* acceptable as a negotiating partner.'

'Sorry to contradict you,' Himmler responded infuriatingly. 'But I have incontrovertible proof that I am considered abroad to be the only person capable of maintaining order.'

Göring was stunned into silence, broken only by Himmler asking if he would appoint him Chancellor should anything happen to the Führer. He could only say that that would not be possible, since the offices of Führer and Chancellor had been combined by law. But Himmler persisted, perhaps deliberately needling him. 'Herr Reich Marshal,' he continued, 'if anything should prevent you from succeeding the Führer – say you are eliminated – can I have the position?'

'My dear Himmler,' Göring replied, 'we shall have to wait and see. That will depend upon circumstances. I can't for the life of me see what might prevent me from taking up the office.'⁴

Himmler and Göring went their separate ways from the Führer bunker. Göring set off for Werder, but was caught in an air raid by RAF Mosquitoes and forced to take refuge in a crowded public shelter, where he entertained the people with jokes against himself, playing up his jovial image to the last and successfully testing his continuing popularity with ordinary folk. Then, as he himself put it, 'we headed for the hills'. Picking up his convoy at 2.20 a.m., he hit the one remaining road to Bavaria at top speed, not even pausing to acknowledge the farewell salute of Koller, left behind to cope alone with Hitler on behalf of the Luftwaffe.

Himmler headed north for Ziethen Castle, on the Baltic coast east of the Gulf of Lübeck, where Schellenberg waited to bring him up to date on the latest state of their treasonous peace negotiations. Speer sped north to Hamburg, where, with the aid of the sympathetic Gauleiter Kaufmann, he recorded a radio speech calling on the people to give up the fight now and to resist all efforts to put Hitler's Nero Order into operation, and forbidding all Werwolf activities. It was never broadcast. In the end, he got cold feet about betraying Hitler publicly.

Back in the Chancellery, Bormann joined Eva Braun and the Führer's secretaries and personal entourage in celebrating Hitler's birthday. With the Mosquitoes departed, Eva led everyone upstairs to the living room of Hitler's private apartment. The room was empty apart from a large circular table – all the other furniture had been moved down into the bunker. Someone brought a wind-up gramophone, but there was only one record, a pre-war hit called 'Red Roses Bring You Happiness'. They played it over and over again, while they drank champagne and danced – even Bormann and fat Dr Morell joined in. Outside, there was the constant rumble of Soviet guns. Suddenly there was a heavy explosion close by. A telephone rang and someone hurried to answer. The party atmosphere evaporated, and people began to return to the bunker.

While Göring was driving south, and Bormann was dancing in the ruined Chancellery, Himmler spent a hectic night driving back and forth across north Germany. When he arrived at Ziethen Castle after a drive of some 130 miles from Berlin, Schellenberg was waiting to take him to Kersten's country home, Hartzwalde, for a meeting with a representative of the World Jewish Congress, Norbert Masur. Kersten had persuaded Masur to take his life in his hands and fly from Sweden to Berlin, knowing that Himmler was desperate to gain credit with the West. He sat down with this Jew at 2 a.m., drinking coffee with him, Kersten, Schellenberg and his private secretary, Dr Rudolf Brandt, and started on a long-winded justification of Germany's actions against the Jews. Somehow, after about forty-five minutes of this, Kersten and Schellenberg managed to get him to talk business, and eventually he confirmed that his promises that no more Jews would be killed and that the camps would be handed over intact to the Allies would be honoured. Meanwhile, he would allow the fifteen thousand women prisoners still in Ravensbrück concentration camp, half of them Jewesses, to be released and taken by Red Cross transports to Sweden. Masur was understandably dubious about Himmler's promise, but he kept it and the women were released two days later.

After leaving Masur and Kersten at about 5 a.m., Himmler, Schellenberg and Brandt drove non-stop to Hohenlychen, where Bernadotte was waiting for a meeting over breakfast, when they discussed more details about the release of concentration-camp prisoners. Himmler was exhausted and highly nervous, and could not bring himself to talk about peace negotiations. It was left to Schellenberg, as he drove the Swede back to the airport in Berlin, to suggest that he set up a meeting between Himmler and Eisenhower. Bernadotte, however, said he needed to hear it officially from Himmler himself before he could make any approach to the Americans.

The RAF and US Eighth Air Force made their last raids on Berlin during the night and early morning of 21 April. From then on, the Soviets would take over, not only with the Red Air Force, but also with artillery, for Chuikov's heavy guns were within range of the city centre, at Marzahn, a mere nine miles away. At 11.30 a.m., they opened up. Salvo after salvo poured into the heart of Berlin. Around the Wilhelmstrasse, shells were landing at the rate of one every five seconds. The Brandenburg Gate was hit, and one of its wings collapsed, the ruined Reichstag building burst into flames once more, the Unter den Linden erupted all along its length, the old Royal Palace, already little more than a battered hulk, blazed again.

The explosions even rocked the deep Führer bunker, which was normally cushioned by the soft alluvial soil around it. Hitler, no doubt reminded of his days in the trenches during the First World War, telephoned Koller in the absence of Göring, to get something done to silence the Soviet guns. Koller told him he was already using the guns on the Berlin flak towers to engage the enemy batteries near Marzahn.

For the rest of the day, Hitler's mood swung from one extreme to the other, buoyed up by a massive amphetamine injection from Morell and a large dose of the drops that had been prescribed the previous year for a mysterious eye complaint. That day he told his valet, Heinz Linge, to increase the dose from one drop to five. Their main constituent was cocaine. In a state of high excitement, Hitler poured out streams of irrational orders, screaming furiously as his impossible demands were not implemented. He called Koller demanding to know why there was no air cover. Where were the much-vaunted jet fighters? Koller told him the planes were all grounded by lack of fuel and enemy attacks on the airfields. 'Then we don't need the jets any more,' Hitler snapped back. 'The Luftwaffe is superfluous. The entire Luftwaffe leadership should be hanged straight away!'[5]

Later in the day, believing there was the possibility of a counterattack, he called Koller again and ordered him, on pain of death, to send all available Luftwaffe personnel, including Göring's private army of paratroops defending Carinhall, to join new formations being scraped together. The 'private army', which had once comprised a whole division armed with a double complement of modern weapons, had long since been dispersed, and there was now barely a battalion left guarding the ruins. During the night, Koller managed to scrape together 12–15,000 ground staff, the equivalent numerically of a division, but untrained of course and mostly unarmed. When he reported this to Hitler, somewhat fearfully, he was surprised that there was no outburst of rage at the other end of the line. Instead, the Führer spoke encouragingly, full of optimism: 'You will see, the Russians will suffer the greatest defeat, the bloodiest defeat in their history, at the gates of Berlin.'[6]

The next day, Hitler had come down from his euphoria and was suffering the reaction. He may also have been suffering drug withdrawal symptoms, without his daily dose of amphetamine: he had dismissed Morell from the bunker that morning, after the doctor had offered him an injection of morphine to calm him down. In his paranoia he had suspected Morell of wanting to knock him out so that he could be removed from Berlin and flown to Berchtesgaden. When Keitel arrived at 3 p.m. for the daily conference, he sensed at once that 'leaden clouds lay heavily over the atmosphere'. Hitler's face was a yellowish grey, his expression was stony. He was nervy and unable to concentrate; twice during the conference he got up and wandered into his private room next door.

Hitler seemed barely to listen as Krebs delivered his grim situation report, showing the noose tightening around them every minute. But when he reported that SS-Obergruppenführer Felix Steiner had refused to give the order for a counterattack north of the city, he was ominously silent. Then he went berserk. He leapt to his feet, and began to rant and rave. His face turned white and then purple, his limbs shook uncontrollably. The men with him had seen him angry before, but they had never seen him like this. His voice cracked as he screamed and cursed them all for cowardice, treachery, incompetence, insubordination, disloyalty. Even the SS now told him lies. At the climax of his wild outburst, he yelled: 'The war is lost! Everything is falling apart.'

Regaining some control, he cried that he would stay in Berlin, with the Berliners. He would lead the final battle himself, in person – and when the last moments came, he would shoot himself. 'Alive or dead, I shall not fall into the hands of the enemy,' he declared. 'I can no longer fight on the battlefield; I'm not strong enough. I shall shoot myself.' Then, quite suddenly, his rage evaporated and he began to crumple. Slowly, he sank back into his chair, collapsing into himself. Shrunken, deflated, he began to cry like a small child. 'It's all over,' he sobbed. 'The war is lost. I shall shoot myself.'

For almost five minutes the others stood watching him, silent and embarrassed. Then, incredibly, they tried to persuade him that there was still hope, that he must remain in charge of the nation, that he must move out of Berlin to Berchtesgaden and continue directing the war from there. He rejected their appeals. They could leave him, he said bitterly, they could all leave Berlin but he would stay. 'I order an immediate radio proclamation to the people of Berlin,' he continued, 'of my resolve to remain with them to the end, whatever happens.'

Hitler ordered Bormann, Keitel and Jodl to fly out that night. Keitel was to take command of the armed forces in the south, with Göring acting as Hitler's personal deputy. All three refused to go.

'In seven years, I have never refused to obey an order from you,' Keitel said, 'but this is one order I shall never carry out. You cannot and should not leave the Wehrmacht in the lurch at a time like this.'

'I am staying here,' Hitler replied obdurately. 'And that is that. Göring can take over the leadership down there. If there has to be any negotiating with the enemy, as there has to be now, then Göring is better at that than I am. Either I fight and win the Battle of Berlin – or I am killed in Berlin. That is my final and irrevocable decision.'[7]

Word of Hitler's outburst and collapse had been passed swiftly to all the Nazi chieftains not in the bunker. In telephone call after telephone call during the afternoon and evening they all spoke to Hitler, entreating him to fly out to the south, to save both himself and Berlin. Dönitz phoned from his new headquarters at Plön, some fourteen miles south-east of Kiel, promising to send more naval troops to help defend Berlin. Ribbentrop called to offer hope of a great diplomatic *coup* that would solve everything, even then. Himmler made an impassioned speech over the phone, and then sent Dr Gebhardt to assure Hitler of his support and to offer him his personal SS escort squad of 600 men. But Himmler did not go himself. 'They're all mad in Berlin,' he declared. 'What am I to do?' He answered his own rhetorical question by dispatching Schellenberg to Lübeck, to see Bernadotte and tell him that he, Himmler, was ready to ask him officially and in his own name to approach Eisenhower on his behalf with an offer of surrender in the West.[8]

Albert Speer, despite all his later protestations, was still under Hitler's spell. When he heard about the collapse he did not reach for the telephone but set off at once from his estate at Bad Wilsnack, sixty miles north-west of Berlin, to see his idol for one last time. It took him ten hours. He started by car, on roads jammed solid with refugees, but had to abandon that as hopeless. Then, in spite of the desperate shortage of fuel, he persuaded Luftwaffe contacts to supply him with a plane and a fighter escort to Gatow, from where he flew on in a Fiesler Storch to put down on the improvised airstrip on the East–West Axis before the Brandenburg Gate. There was no useful purpose to the trip. It was purely personal – Speer could not bear the thought that Hitler would die without his having said a proper farewell. He also felt the need to confess his sins in sabotaging the Nero Order, and in publicly stating that the war was lost. He felt the trip was worthwhile when Hitler apparently forgave him, and he flew out again, gratified by his absolution.

* * *

The one paladin who did not seek to persuade Hitler to leave was Goebbels. Consumed as always by his thirst for the grand dramatic gesture, he was resolved that the Führer should go out, literally, in a blaze of glory like a mythical Nordic warrior. And he would go with him, for he was determined to die in Berlin, the city he believed he had made his own. He planned the same fate for Magda and the children. 'My wife and family are not to survive me,' he had told Speer earlier. 'The Americans would only coach them to make propaganda against me.' Knowing this, Hitler now invited Goebbels and his family to move into the bunker with him. They arrived that afternoon, in two limousines, each of the six children clutching the one toy they had been allowed to take.

Magda and the children were given Dr Morell's suite of four small rooms in the upper bunker, while Goebbels had a room in the deep bunker, alongside the Führer. The children regarded the whole thing as a huge adventure. They liked 'Uncle Adolf' and were delighted when his secretary Traudl Junge took them upstairs into the ruins of the Chancellery building, to find the boxes of presents that had been sent to Hitler on his birthday. They were allowed to pick out what they wanted, and take things back downstairs.

Koller called Göring, who had reached the Obersalzberg at 11.00 that morning, to tell him of Hitler's breakdown and his insistence on staying in Berlin. Göring told him to leave Berlin and come to him, which he did, flying south and arriving at noon on 23 April. Before leaving, Koller had spoken to Jodl, who had given him the full details of Hitler's outburst, including his statement that Göring was to take over the leadership in the south and conduct negotiations with the enemy. Koller reported all this to Göring, who said he regarded Hitler's behaviour as 'a mean trick', which put him in a difficult position. He asked for a report on the military situation, which Koller gave him with the help of maps.

'Then,' Koller recalled later, 'he asked me whether I thought that Hitler was still alive or whether he had, perhaps, appointed Martin Bormann as his successor. I told him Hitler was alive when I left Berlin.' It was up to Göring to act now, he said. Philipp Bouhler, head of the Führer Chancellery, the man who had been in charge of the T4 euthanasia programme, and a close friend of Göring, agreed.

This was the moment Göring had been waiting for since 1923, the moment when he would take over the leadership of Germany, as Hitler had promised him when he first joined the party. But did he dare to seize it? He agonised. 'Bormann is my deadly enemy,' he said. 'He is only waiting to get at me. If I act, he will call me a traitor. If I don't, he will accuse me of having failed at the most difficult hour.'

He called for the steel box in which he kept Hitler's decree of 29 June 1941, confirming him as his successor, took out the document and read it aloud. It seemed quite clear: 'Should I have my freedom of action curtailed or be otherwise incapacitated, Reich Marshal Hermann Göring is to be my deputy or successor in all offices of State, Party and Wehrmacht.' But Göring was still nervous, and called in Lammers for his opinion as State Secretary of the Reich Chancellery. Lammers had no doubts. 'The law of 29 June 1941 is valid and legally binding,' he confirmed. 'The Führer has made no other order. If he had, I would have known. He could not have changed the decree legally without me.'

Still Göring hesitated before taking such an enormous step. Koller suggested he send a message to Hitler, seeking his approval. Göring agreed at once, and drafted a careful note, with the help of Lammers and Koller. It read:

My Führer,
Since you are determined to remain at your post in Fortress Berlin, do you agree that I, as your deputy in accordance with your decree of 29.6.41, assume immediately total leadership of the Reich with complete freedom of action at home and abroad?

If by 2200 hours no answer is forthcoming, I shall assume you have been deprived of your freedom of action. I will then consider the terms of your decree to have come into force and act accordingly for the good of the people and the Fatherland.

You must realise what I feel for you in these most difficult hours of my life, and I am quite unable to find words to express it.

God bless you and grant that you may come here after all as soon as possible.

Your most loyal Hermann Göring

Speer was still in the bunker when Göring's message arrived, and he followed Bormann when he took it in to Hitler, claiming that Göring was staging a *coup d'état*. 'Perhaps,' Speer pondered later, 'this was Bormann's last effort to induce Hitler to fly to Berchtesgaden and take control there.' If so, it failed, as Hitler remained apathetic. But a second radio message, addressed to Ribbentrop and with a copy to Keitel, gave Bormann fresh ammunition, and he leapt on it eagerly. It read:

To Reich Minister von Ribbentrop:
I have asked the Führer to provide me with instructions by 10 p.m. 23 April. If by this time it is apparent that the Führer has been deprived of his freedom of action to conduct the affairs of the Reich, his decree of 29 June 1941 becomes effective, according to which I am heir to all his offices as his deputy. [If] by 12 midnight, 23 April 1945, you receive no word either from the Führer directly or from me, you are to come to me at once by air.

'Göring is engaged in treason!' Bormann cried. 'He's already sending telegrams to members of the government and announcing that on the basis of his powers he will assume your office at twelve o'clock tonight, my Führer!'

This time, Hitler listened.

'An outburst of wild fury followed,' Speer wrote, 'in which feelings of bitterness, helplessness, self-pity and despair mingled. With flushed face and staring eyes, Hitler ranted on as if he had forgotten the presence of his entourage: "I've known it all along. I know that Göring is lazy. He let the air force go to pot. He was corrupt. His example made corruption in our state. Besides, he's been a drug addict for years. I've known it all along."' Then he fell back abruptly into his apathy. 'Well, all right,' he said. 'Let Göring negotiate the surrender, it doesn't matter who does it.'[9]

At about 5 p.m., Göring received his answer:

The decree of 29.6.41 only comes into effect on my explicit agreement. There can be no talk of lack of freedom to act. I forbid you to take any steps in the direction you have indicated.
    Adolf Hitler.
    Heil Hitler
    Signed, Martin Bormann

Göring immediately sent signals to Ribbentrop and Keitel cancelling his previous message. But it was too late, the damage had been done. A second signal from Bormann in Hitler's name arrived shortly afterwards, stripping him of his right of succession. Because of his long service to the party, it said, he would be spared the death penalty, and any further measures, as long as he resigned all his offices on the grounds of ill health. Within half an hour, he had done so, and was stripped of all his positions – even, as Bormann boorishly interjected into a telephone conversation he was listening in to between Keitel and Krebs a couple of days later, his Reich Chief Huntsman's job.[10]

Bormann had taken it upon himself to order the two SS chiefs on the Obersalzberg, Frank and Bredow, to arrest Göring for high treason and to confine him and his staff, plus Koller and Lammers, in 'honourable custody'. Well aware of the delicacy of the situation, and Göring's overpowering personality, he added: 'You will answer for this with your lives.' Frank and Bredow took a squad of thirty SS men to Göring's villa, and placed him under house arrest, confining him to his room and preventing any contact with Emmy or his staff. For the moment, that was as far as Bormann dared to go, knowing that Hitler would never sanction the ultimate penalty. But he also knew beyond doubt that Hitler would not last much longer, and he was determined to exact his full measure of spite, even if it were from beyond the grave. He sent Frank and Bredow a further order: 'The situation in Berlin is becoming ever more tense. Should Berlin fall and we go down with the capital, then the traitors of 23 April must be liquidated. Men, do your duty! Your lives and your honour are at stake!'[11]

By the time the RAF blasted the Obersalzberg on 26 April, however, destroying the Berghof and wrecking Göring's villa among other damage, Göring had got to work on the SS men, and they were having considerable doubts about their mission. He had little difficulty in persuading them that they should all move to his castle at Mauterndorf. They were making their way there along the icy mountain roads when the radio announcement of his 'illness' was broadcast:

Reich Marshal Hermann Göring has been taken ill with his long-standing chronic heart condition, which has now entered an acute stage. At a time when the efforts of all forces are required, he has therefore himself requested to be relieved of his command of the Luftwaffe and all duties connected thereto. The Führer has granted this request. The Führer has appointed Colonel-General Ritter von Greim as the new Commander-in-Chief of the Luftwaffe while simultaneously promoting him to Field Marshal.

The news of Hitler's breakdown on 23 April had triggered Himmler, too, to take action. While Göring was being falsely accused of treason, he was committing actual treason by meeting Bernadotte in the Swedish consulate in Lübeck. As he explained to the Swede, he had previously been unable to break his oath to the Führer, but the situation was now changed: if Hitler was not already dead, he soon would be, and he, Himmler, had a free hand therefore in preventing further bloodshed by capitulating to the Western Allies, in order to allow them to advance unhindered to the East. He asked Bernadotte to pass this message to the Swedish government, for them to convey to Eisenhower.

Bernadotte knew that Himmler was seriously deluded in thinking the Western Allies would even consider separate peace talks. But he took advantage of the situation by extracting a promise from Himmler to include Norway and Denmark in the capitulation, and to allow the Scandinavian prisoners already concentrated in Neuengamme to be taken to Sweden by the Red Cross, as the price for passing the message to his government. Himmler agreed, and wrote a short note for Bernadotte to give to his Foreign Minister. Then he left to drive back to Hohenlychen to start planning his government.

When Speer called on him there the next day, and filled him in on what had been going on in Berlin, Himmler maintained that Göring's fall from grace meant nothing. 'Göring is going to be the successor now,' he said. 'We've long had an understanding that I would be his Premier. Even without Hitler, I can make him Head of State.' With what Speer described as a conniving smile and without the faintest embarrassment, he added:

You know what he's like – naturally, I'll be the one to make the decisions. I've already been in touch with various persons I mean to take into my Cabinet. Keitel is coming to see me shortly . . . Europe cannot manage without me in the future, either. It will go on needing me as Minister of Police. After I've spent an hour with Eisenhower, he'll appreciate that fact. They'll soon realise that they're dependent on me – or they'll have a hopeless chaos on their hands.

After describing his dealings with Bernadotte, he hinted that there might be a place for Speer as a minister. Speer mischievously offered him the use of his plane to make a farewell visit to Hitler, but Himmler waved it aside. He had no time, he explained, calmly: 'Now I must prepare my new government. And besides,' he added in all seriousness, 'my person is too important for the future of Germany for me to risk the flight.'[12]

News of Himmler's treachery exploded like a grenade in the Führer bunker at about 7 p.m. on Saturday, 28 April. Heinz Lorenz, the official in the Propaganda Ministry responsible for monitoring foreign news sources, hurried in with a sensational piece of news. He had just picked up a broadcast from the BBC in London, confirming a Reuters report that Himmler had offered the Western Allies an unconditional surrender on behalf of all German troops. There had been a rumour about this earlier in the day, but Himmler had denied it categorically to Dönitz. Now it was clear that he had lied. What was more, the report stated that he had assured the Allies that he could implement and support an unconditional surrender – implying that he had the powers of a head of state. Hitler was utterly shocked, far more deeply than he had been over the supposed treachery of Göring. He had always regarded Himmler as his most trustworthy and loyal follower, but now his 'trusty Heinrich' had gone behind his back over the most important issue of all. This, he shouted wildly in what was fast becoming a repetitive cliché, was the most shameful betrayal in human history.

When he had regained some control, he shut himself away in the conference room with Bormann and Goebbels, leaving everyone else to wait in the ante-room. No doubt his two heirs apparent were delighted to see yet another arch rival disposed of. And no doubt they were only too happy to suggest a way Hitler could satisfy his thirst for revenge: Himmler was out of reach for the moment, but his representative was in the bunker, and under arrest.

Hermann Fegelein, Eva Braun's brother-in-law, had tried to escape the 'Valhalla stuff' as he called it the day before, and had been picked up in his apartment in Bleibtreustrasse, just off the Kurfürstendamm, with his mistress, drunk, in civilian clothes, and with a suitcase stuffed with money, jewellery and false passports. He had been taken back to the bunker, stripped of his rank and locked up, to be dealt with when he was sober enough to stand trial. Fegelein would make an excellent scapegoat for the sins of his master. Although he denied any knowledge of Himmler's treasonable activities, Hitler, Bormann and Goebbels were determined someone should pay. Fegelein was taken out into the Chancellery garden and shot.

In a state of near hysteria, Hitler rushed into the sick-room, to speak to Greim, who was nursing a bullet wound in one foot, sustained when he and his mistress, the famous woman pilot Hannah Reitsch, had flown in two days before at Hitler's command, to receive his appointment as Göring's successor. There had been no need for him to make the dangerous flight – Hitler could have dealt with him over the telephone – and now he ordered him to make the even more dangerous take-off from the East–West Axis, to fly to Plön, where he was to put Himmler under arrest. 'A traitor must never succeed me as Führer,' he yelled. 'You must get out to make sure he doesn't.'

Soon afterwards, the two flyers were driven to the airstrip in an armoured car. Reitsch, who wanted to stay and die with the Führer, was in floods of tears. She carried with her various letters from people in the bunker, including a farewell from the Goebbels to Magda's son Harald, who was a prisoner-of-war with the British, and one from Eva Braun to her sister Gretl, in which she made no mention of Fegelein and his fate. The little plane was tossed around like a leaf in a gale of shellfire, but finally climbed out of it to 20,000 feet. Below, Reitsch and Greim could see nothing of the centre of Berlin but a sea of flame. Setting course for Rechlin air base, they flew safely on their way.

Back in the bunker, Hitler's wild behaviour subsided. All the excitement of the previous two hours had drained away completely, and he withdrew to his private quarters without another word, his face an expressionless mask. Himmler's defection was the final betrayal. There was nothing left now but to end it all.

The situation in Berlin, as in all of Germany, was hopeless. The American and Soviet armies had met at Torgau on the Elbe on 25 April, cutting Germany in two, and the Americans had halted, leaving Berlin to the Soviets. The city was completely surrounded and though the German armies and units of the Volkssturm continued to resist bravely and stubbornly, they were being cut to shreds everywhere. The armies that Hitler constantly called to rescue him and the city were largely phantoms, or already encircled and out of the game. Soviet troops were already in Alexanderplatz and Potsdamer Platz, only a few hundred yards from the bunker.

Shortly before midnight, Hitler called his youngest secretary, Traudl Junge, to his study to take dictation. She was puzzled to see that the room was arranged as if for a party. The table was covered with a crisp white cloth, embroidered with the initials AH, and on it stood the silver dinner service and eight champagne glasses. Hitler winked at her then led her through into the conference room. Standing at the map table, staring down at its bare, polished surface, he began to dictate his last will and testament.

'More than thirty years have passed,' he began, 'since I made my modest contribution as a volunteer in the First World War, which was forced upon the Reich. In these three decades, love and loyalty to my people alone guided me in all my thoughts, actions and life . . .' He covered the old familiar ground in the old familiar manner, claiming yet again that he had never wanted war, but that it had been forced upon the world by the machinations of international Jewry. The sole responsibility for all the subsequent death and horror – including the death of so many Jews – lay with the Jews themselves. But now that the end had come, now that he had decided to remain in Berlin, 'I die with a joyful heart in the knowledge of the immeasurable deeds and achievements of our peasants and workers and of a contribution unique in history by our youth which bears my name.' He reserved some of his bitterest comments for the German officer corps who, unlike himself, 'had failed to set a shining example of faithful devotion to duty, unto death.'

Turning to more practical matters, he officially pronounced anathema upon both Göring and Himmler, expelling them from the party and stripping them of all their offices. They had brought, he said, 'irreparable shame on the whole nation by negotiating with the enemy without my knowledge and against my will'. He named the members of the government that was to take over when he was dead. Grand Admiral Dönitz was to become President of the Reich and Supreme Commander of the Wehrmacht, but would not inherit the title of Führer. Goebbels was to be Reich Chancellor, Bormann Party Chancellor. There was no place for Speer, nor for Ribbentrop, no doubt dropped at the behest of Goebbels, who in company with Bormann kept bringing Traudl Junge fresh names to add to the list. Seyss-Inquart was to be Foreign Minister. A variety of party hacks and nonentities were named for the other offices of state. To ensure that the new government was injected with the virus of anti-Semitism, he urged his successors 'to uphold the racial laws to the limit and to resist mercilessly the poisoner of all nations, international Jewry'.

Finally, he came to personal matters. 'During the years of combat,' he declared, 'I was unable to commit myself to a contract of marriage, so I have decided this day before the end of my earthly life to take as my wife the young woman who, after many years of faithful friendship, has of her own free will come to the besieged capital to link her fate with my own. She will, according to her own wishes, go to her death as my wife. For us, this will take the place of all that was denied to us by my devotion to the service of my people.'

It was the first that Traudl Junge had heard of his intention to marry

Eva Braun. She started to look up at him, but he was still dictating. He ended with a typically Wagnerian flourish: 'My wife and I choose to die in order to escape the shame of flight or capitulation. It is our wish that our bodies be burned immediately, here, where I have performed the greater part of my daily work during the twelve years I have served my people.'[13]

Oddly, Traudl Junge did not weep. But Goebbels did. She had returned to her office and was typing out the document when he suddenly appeared, distraught, and with tears streaming down his face. Hitler had ordered him to leave Berlin. 'But I don't want to run away and leave the Führer,' he wailed, like a child being sent away to school. 'I am the Gauleiter of Berlin and my place is here. If the Führer dies, my life has no meaning. He even said to me, "Goebbels, I didn't expect this from you! You refuse to obey my last orders!"' Then, not to be outdone, Goebbels started dictating his own will to Junge, which he ordered to be attached to Hitler's as an appendix.

'For the first time in my life,' he dictated, 'I must categorically refuse to obey an order of the Führer.' He continued by saying that his wife and children joined him in this, and that he would lose all self-respect were he to leave the Führer alone in his hour of greatest need. 'In the delirium of treachery,' he went on, 'there have to be a few who stay unconditionally loyal to him, even unto death'. He and his wife and children (who, were they old enough, to judge, would agree) were firmly resolved not to leave the Reich capital, but rather 'to end a life which for me personally has no further value if it cannot be used in the service of the Führer and by his side.'[14]

In the midst of all the hysteria, a purely practical matter suddenly intruded: no one in the bunker was legally empowered to perform a marriage ceremony. Without some appropriate official to declare them man and wife, Hitler's last act would be nullified. Goebbels had the answer. As Gauleiter of Berlin he knew of someone authorised to act as a registrar of marriages who was still in Berlin, fighting with the Volkssturm. He was a municipal councillor and his name was Walter Wagner. A group of SS men was dispatched across the city, to bring him back alive.

The ceremony took place in the conference room, with Goebbels and Bormann as witnesses. Afterwards, the newly-weds led the way into the study to share their wedding feast of champagne and sandwiches with their guests. Eva sent for the wind-up gramophone with its single record, 'Red Roses', to provide a sentimental musical background, and went into the corridor outside the room to accept the congratulations of staff not invited to the private party. She was relaxed and smiling, every inch the gracious hostess.

The following day, 29 April, the mood in the bunker was black. Three messengers were sent out to try to find a way through the Soviet lines to deliver copies of Hitler's testament to Dönitz, General Schörner, and the 'Brown House' in Munich. As the Soviet troops started a concentrated attack on the last pocket of resistance around the bunker, three of the younger aides were given permission to try their luck at breaking out. Shortly afterwards, Below followed them, carrying a letter to Keitel, who was with the rest of the High Command, outside the city. To add to Hitler's gloom, he received news that confirmed his determination to avoid falling into the hands of his enemies, dead or alive: Mussolini had been captured and executed by Italian partisans; his body, and that of his mistress, Clara Petacci, had been taken to Milan, hanged upside-down in a square, and stoned by a mob. What Hitler did not know that day was that the German forces in Italy had surrendered.

Himmler had provided Hitler with a collection of cyanide capsules in brass cartridge cases a few days before. But Himmler was no longer to be trusted. Did the capsules contain genuine poison, or a drug that would allow him to be captured and handed over alive to the Soviets? To make sure, Hitler had one tested on his German shepherd bitch, Blondi, perhaps the only living being that he felt genuine affection for. She died instantly.

While Hitler was checking that Blondi was dead, Goebbels was giving a party for nurses and children, about forty people in all, in one of the cellars under the Chancellery building. It was, he said, the last farewell to Berlin for himself, his wife and their children. Everyone sat around a long oak table, while a fifteen-year-old Hitler Youth played an accordion and sang songs like 'Die Blauen Dragoner' (The Blue Dragoons). In the next cellar, Professor Ernst-Günther Schenck, one of Hitler's doctors, had set up his emergency casualty station. As the Hitler Youth sang his cheery songs, Schenck, 'up to my elbows in entrails, arteries and gore', continued with some of the 370 major operations he had carried out over the last week on men and boys, some even younger than the singer, seriously wounded in the streets. As well as an acute shortage of bandages, drugs and all but the most basic equipment, Schenck had to cope with two personal problems: he was not a qualified surgeon, but a nutrition expert, and he was almost insensible for lack of sleep. The nine senior SS officers who shared a room with him were now permanently drunk and noisily enjoying the favours of equally drunken women determined to make the most of their last hours.

The next day, with all hope of relief finally gone, Hitler sent for Bormann at around noon, and told him the time had come. He took lunch as usual around 1 p.m. with his secretaries and his dietician. Eva Braun did not join them. After the meal, Hitler had all the staff lined up in the corridor outside his room, where he shook hands with each of them, and murmured a few words, so softly that they could not make out what he was saying. Eva was with him, looking her best, with her hair carefully done up and wearing Hitler's favourite dress, black with pink roses on either side of a square neckline. She embraced Traudl Junge. 'Please try to get out of here,' she said. 'You might make it. Give my love to Bavaria.' The she turned and followed her husband into his room.

SS-Sturmbannführer Otto Günsche, Hitler's SS adjutant and body-guard, took up his post outside the door. His orders were to let no one in until it was all over. But he was unable to stop a distraught Magda Goebbels, who came rushing down the corridor and forced her way in. She emerged again almost immediately, weeping – Hitler had not wanted to speak to her. Junge remembered that in all the drama no one had thought to feed the six Goebbels children. She found them, took them along to the dining room and sat them down at the big round table. She found some fruit and ham, and was just making sandwiches when she heard a shot.

Outside Hitler's room, Günsche waited a few moments before entering. He found Hitler on the sofa, his body crumpled over the arm, his head hanging down towards the floor. Blood was dripping on to the carpet from a bullet hole in his right temple. His 7.65-mm Walther pistol lay on the floor beside his foot. Eva was curled up at the other end of the sofa, her legs tucked under her. On the small side table lay her own pistol, which had not been fired, and a square of pink silk chiffon. There was a strong smell of bitter almonds about her body.

The casing of the cyanide capsule lay on the floor, like an empty lipstick tube. A vase of flowers had been knocked over. Automatically, Günsche picked it up.

After checking that Hitler and Eva were both dead, Günsche called in the guards. They wrapped the bodies in blankets and carried them up to the surface, where they laid them in a shallow trench already scraped out for the purpose. Erich Kempka, Hitler's chauffeur, arrived with three or four soldiers hauling about forty gallons of petrol in jerrycans and poured it over the bodies. Goebbels, Bormann, Krebs, Heinz Linge, and General Wilhelm Burgdorf, Hitler's Wehrmacht adjutant, joined them and watched as they tried to set fire to it. It refused to catch. They tried again, growing more frantic as shells hurtled around them, many landing uncomfortably close. Eventually, Kempka wound a piece of paper into a torch, lit it, and tossed it into the trench from a safe distance. At last there was a whoosh as it caught light. Flames blazed up and black smoke rose into the foul air, to mingle with the pall lying over the city. Everyone around the pathetic little funeral pyre raised their arms mechanically in a final Nazi salute, then scurried back underground.

The new Reich Chancellor held his first and only situation conference that evening. After some opposition from Bormann, who had the crazy notion that they could use the 300 to 500 troops around the bunker to break through the Soviet lines and make their way to Dönitz, Goebbels broke his promise to Hitler and decided to try to seek a truce with Stalin. Krebs, who had served in Moscow as acting Military Attaché and spoke good Russian, volunteered to act as his envoy, and Goebbels wrote a letter for him to carry to Zhukov, together with a copy of Hitler's testament naming the new government, under a white flag.

At considerable risk of being shot by their own side as much as by the Soviets, Krebs and two other officers eventually arrived at the Soviet command post and were received by Chuikov, who then phoned Zhukov, who called Stalin, waking him up at his dacha outside Moscow. Krebs did his best to engineer a cease-fire, after which there could be peace talks with Dönitz, but it was soon clear that the Soviets would accept nothing but an unconditional surrender, and he was forced to send word back to the bunker via Colonel Theodor von Dufving, Weidling's Chief of Staff, who made a hair-raising return under fire, unreeling a telephone line as he went.[15]

Back at the bunker, Goebbels was still very calm. Bormann, on the other hand, appeared to be very frightened. Dufving explained that the Soviets were demanding unconditional surrender. 'I shall never, never agree to that,' Goebbels responded in his best Hitler style. He asked if Dufving thought that it was still possible, from what he had seen, to break out of Berlin. Dufving's answer was 'Only singly, and in civilian clothes.' Goebbels said he would not make a final decision until he had spoken to Krebs. If the telephone line did not work, then Dufving would have to bring Krebs back.

The telephone link with Chuikov's command post proved to be erratic – the line was constantly being cut by bullets. Three times Dufving ran back and forth under fire, trying to lay new cable, but each time it was quickly broken. He then resorted to running across carrying written messages, but this was generally unsatisfactory. For one short period, the connection was established, and Krebs was able to talk to Goebbels, who insisted that he return to the bunker for further discussions. Krebs left the Soviet command post at 1.08 p.m. As soon as he and his party were safely back on the German side, Chuikov ordered every gun and rocket-launcher in his command to open up with maximum intensity fire.

Krebs reiterated that the Soviets would accept nothing short of unconditional surrender, which Goebbels and Bormann both rejected. 'The Führer forbade capitulation,' they declared.

'But the Führer is dead!' General Weidling exclaimed.

'The Führer always insisted on carrying on the struggle to the end,' Goebbels repeated, 'and I do not want to surrender.'

Weidling, thoroughly exasperated, reminded them that resistance was no longer possible. Then he left, to return to his own headquarters. Taking his leave of Krebs, he invited him to go with him, but Krebs told him: 'I shall stay here until the last minute, then put a bullet through my brain.'[16]

With his one attempt at international negotiations an abject failure, Goebbels prepared for the end. He sent a signal to Dönitz, giving him details of Hitler's death and the composition of the new government – Bormann had previously informed the Grand Admiral that Hitler had named him the new President but with typical deviousness had not said anything about Hitler's death. Then he withdrew to his study to finish writing his diary: what mattered now was the image he would leave to posterity – over the last few weeks he had

had all his diaries photographed on to glass plates and carefully stored away as his memorial.

Goebbels finished writing at about 4 p.m. As evening approached, Magda got her children ready for bed, in their long, white nightgowns. She brushed each child's hair carefully, then gave each of them a mug of drinking chocolate, which had been spiked with a powerful soporific drug called Finodin. In her last letter to her son, Harald, she had told him: 'I shall give my darlings sleeping potions and then poison, a soft and painless death.' Once they were deeply asleep, she planned to crush a cyanide capsule into each of their mouths.

No one knows for sure what took place in the children's rooms. Perhaps everything did work out according to Magda's plan. Certainly, all the children died that night, but when their bodies were found, Helga's had several black and blue bruises on it. Perhaps the dose of Finodin had not been enough to sedate the child, the eldest of the six. Perhaps Magda had had to force to cyanide down her daughter's throat. Either way, it did not look as if Helga had had a soft and painless death.

An hour after murdering her children, Magda was seen playing solitaire in her husband's study, pale, red-eyed, stony-faced and smoking endlessly. Later that evening, the Reich Youth Leader Artur Axmann came to say goodbye to Goebbels. He found the couple sitting at the long table in the conference room with several of the bunker personnel. Goebbels was pleased to see him, and talked nostalgically about the early days of the movement – street fighting in Wedding, beating up Communists and Socialists, winning over the workers to National Socialism. That was the real triumph, he said: to have won the hearts of the German workers. Throughout his monologue, Magda sat like a silent Medea, sipping champagne and smoking. Someone whispered to Axmann not to ask after the children.

At 8.15 p.m. Goebbels informed the SS guards that he and his wife intended to commit suicide out of the bunker in the open air. At least, he joked blackly, it would save the guards the trouble of having to carry the bodies upstairs. He put on his hat, scarf, long greatcoat and kid gloves, then offered his arm to his wife. Together they mounted the stairs to the bunker entrance. They planned to die in the same way as the Führer; both had cyanide capsules, and Goebbels carried a Walther P-38 revolver. They stood together. Magda bit her capsule and slid to the floor. Her husband delivered the *coup de grâce*, shooting her in the back of the head. Then he bit on his own capsule, pressed the Walther's muzzle to his temple and fired.

The SS guards doused the bodies with petrol and set fire to them. They burned through the night, but were only partly destroyed – there had not been enough petrol left to do the job properly.

As soon as the bodies were alight, the escape parties gathered their things and rushed for the exit, in a mad scramble led by Bormann. Soon, there were only three people left: Krebs, Burgdorf and the commander of the SS bodyguard, Hauptsturmführer Schedle. They had all decided to shoot themselves. Those who left met with mixed fortunes. A few, including the three secretaries, managed to make their way safely to the West. Some were captured by the Soviets, and spent years in harsh captivity. Most were killed, including Bormann, who only got as far as the Lehrter rail station on Invalidenstrasse before he and his companion, Dr Stumpfegger, came under fire and ended their lives with their cyanide capsules to avoid being captured. Their bodies were buried under the rubble and were not discovered and identified until many years later.

The official government of the Reich was now under Dönitz, at Plön, near Kiel in Schleswig-Holstein – though it was quickly moved to bigger and more secure quarters in the nearby naval base at Flensburg – and it was a magnet for the surviving top Nazis. First on the scene, quick as always to seize an opportunity, was Speer, who had been holed up in the area in a caravan on Lake Eutin. He attached himself to the admiral at once, moving into a room in his headquarters and effectively appointing himself chief adviser. Dönitz gave him the title Minister of Economics and Production. His first act was to persuade Dönitz to sign an order to his friend Gauleiter Kaufmann authorising him to thwart the local party fanatics by surrendering Hamburg without a fight – the British had threatened that if there were resistance they would bomb the city into submission, as they had done a few days earlier with Bremen. On 2 May, he flew with the order to Hamburg, where he made a live broadcast to the nation, abandoning the speech he had recorded earlier and making a more general exhortation against any further demolition.

For the next few weeks, Dönitz solemnly ran what Speer described as his 'operetta government', with daily Cabinet meetings and detailed discussions on administration. The only meaningful acts he performed were to agree to a surrender of forces in north-west Germany to Montgomery on 4 May, and then the unconditional surrender of all German forces on 7 May, taking effect the following day. Speer found himself comfortable accommodation in Glücksburg Castle as the guest of the Duke of Mecklenburg and Holstein, from where he was driven to Cabinet meetings each day at 10 a.m. He was also able to visit his family several times, at their hideaway some twenty-five miles away. When Allied intelligence officers arrived to request his co-operation with the United States Strategic Bombing Survey, to help with the air war that was still continuing against Japan, he was happy to oblige, impressing them with his knowledge. The relaxed regime lasted until 23 May, when the British finally got around to arresting him and carting him off to captivity and more rigorous questioning.

Almost as quick off the mark as Speer was Himmler, still utterly convinced that he was indispensable, and that he would be the new leader of Germany. He drove over to Plön with a heavily armed escort, but was shocked to find Dönitz had been named as the new head of state, and even more shocked when Dönitz turned down his offer to become his number two – by which he clearly meant Reich Chancellor. Until the surrender, Dönitz still needed Himmler and his SS and police, so took care not to antagonise him, even though he tried to behave as though he were Chancellor. But after 7 May, with the Allies in total charge and the SS banned, Himmler was of no further use and he told him to go. Himmler's world had finally collapsed.

Himmler was prepared for this. Two days earlier, as the Western cease-fire was signed, he had called his SS chieftains together for a farewell address. Even then, he could not cast off the fantasy world altogether, hinting mysteriously that destiny had a great new task for him. It was a task that he would have to undertake alone, he said, though a few of them might accompany him. The basic message, however, was *sauve qui peut*. They had all been furnished with false papers, showing them to have served in various arms of the legitimate forces – members of the Concentration Camp Inspectorate were all supposed to have been in the navy. They had also been provided with cyanide capsules.

Himmler had papers showing him to be Sergeant Heinrich Hitzinger of the Field Security Police – a real person, who had been executed for defeatism – and two phials of poison. He set off shortly afterwards with two adjutants, also posing as Field Security Policemen in the appropriate uniforms – to maintain the hierarchy, both were dressed as privates. As a further disguise, Himmler shaved off his moustache and wore a black patch over his right eye. His intention was to join other SS men in the Bavarian mountains, where he would set up the 'Werwolf' resistance movement. Unfortunately, the Field Security Police was a bad choice of cover: it was one of the organisations on the Allied blacklist. Himmler and his companions were spotted and picked up at a British control point midway between Hamburg and Bremen, as normal routine arrests.

Although he was in British captivity, Himmler had not been recognised, and was bundled into trucks and shifted from camp to camp along with a motley collection of other prisoners. Eventually, it seems, he found the indignity too much to bear and he revealed his true identity, perhaps hoping to receive the special treatment he felt was his due. Still clinging to delusions of his importance, he said he wanted a meeting with Montgomery or even Churchill, to offer them his organisation and experience to help them in the coming fight against the spread of Bolshevism in Europe. No one took him seriously.

He was taken to Second Army headquarters outside Lüneberg, where he was strip-searched. Two brass tubes were found, one containing a glass phial of what Himmler said was medicine for stomach cramps, the other empty. Having already had one suicide by poison, the interrogators had little doubt what it really was, and that he probably had the phial from the empty case secreted in his mouth. But when the army doctor opened his mouth, saw the end of the capsule in a hollowed tooth and tried to get it out, Himmler suddenly yanked his head free, flicked it loose and bit it.

The doctors and interrogators leaped on him and tried to save him, grabbing his throat and turning him upside down, but the cyanide had done its work. After fifteen minutes of frantic effort, they had to admit defeat. He was certified dead at 11.04 p.m., on 23 May. Two days later, a British sergeant-major wrapped his corpse in camouflage netting, tied it with telephone cable, and dumped it in the back of a truck. He drove out alone into the wilderness of Lüneberg Heath, dug a hole and pitched the body in, filling it and disguising the spot before driving away. The second most powerful man in the mighty Third Reich had come to an ignominious and anonymous end.

*   *   *

Ribbentrop had also been an early arrival at Plön, having set up his own headquarters nearby on 30 April. Dönitz ignored him at first, and only contacted him to see if he knew where Neurath, Ribbentrop's predecessor in the Foreign Ministry, could be found, as he wished to offer him the post of Foreign Minister. Ribbentrop could hardly believe what he was hearing, and demanded a personal interview. When he saw Dönitz late on 1 May, he was still shocked at the slight, and insisted, according to Dönitz, 'that he had a legal right to be appointed Foreign Minister and was, indeed, the right man for the task, for . . . the British knew him and had always been pleased to deal with him'.[17] Dönitz, who regarded him as an idiot, was unmoved. Eventually, he appointed Count Schwerin von Krosigk, who had been Finance Minister since the Papen government of 1932, to the meaningless post.

Ribbentrop slunk away to Hamburg, where he found lodgings in a rooming house in the suburbs run by 'an attractive brunette', passing his time for the next six weeks endlessly writing and rewriting a rambling letter to the British government. By the time he was discovered after a tip-off to the British Field Security headquarters on 14 June, the letter, attempting to justifying himself and Hitler, had reached 5,000 words. Because the tip-off came late in the evening, the senior officers had all departed for the day, leaving a young Scot, Lieutenant J.B. 'Jimmy' Adam, in charge. When Adam and three NCOs arrived at the rooming house, the door was opened by the brunette, wearing a diaphanous dressing gown. They found Ribbentrop asleep in a single bed, wearing pink and white pyjamas. He began mumbling nervously in German as they woke him, but switched to perfect English when he realised what was happening. 'The game is up,' he said, in an obviously rehearsed speech. 'I congratulate you. You know who I am. If you had come two days later, I would already have given myself up voluntarily.'[18] Next day, he was flown to Mondorf-les-Bains, to join the other prominent Nazis in ASHCAN.

Göring was in Mauterndorf when he heard the announcement of Hitler's death on the radio. Distressed in spite of all that had happened recently, he hurried to give the news to Emmy, who was in bed with sciatica. 'He's dead, Emmy,' he blurted out, near to despair. 'Now I'll never be able to tell him that I have remained loyal to the end.' He was so distraught that Emmy feared he was losing his mind, and to distract him she complained of severe heart pains. He sat by her bed to comfort her, and gradually regained control of himself.

By that time, he had succeeded in winning his SS guards round, and the danger of their shooting him was receding. Koller, back in Berchtesgaden, was concerned for Göring's safety, despite receiving abusive messages from him demanding to know why he had not come to his rescue. He was, however, in a tricky situation: he knew by now of Bormann's order to the SS guards to 'exterminate the traitors of 23 April', and feared that he might be counted as one of them. When SS-Standartenführer Brause, who was in charge of the guard detachment at Mauterndorf, arrived on the evening of 1 May after a long and diffi-cult journey, Koller was relieved when the SS man said he had become friendly with Göring and wanted to release him, but needed higher authority to do so. Koller referred the question to Kesselring, who had now taken command of southern Germany, but Kesselring, aware that Kaltenbrunner was still alive and active, was evasive.

There are several conflicting versions of what happened next. General Paul Deichmann, commander of I Air Corps based at Linz, said that Brause contacted Kesslering asking if he still had to carry out Bormann's order to shoot Göring, his family and staff. Kesselring forbade this, and ordered him to move out with his unit, leaving Göring and his entourage to themselves. Göring could no longer do any harm, he said. While the SS squad was leaving, Göring was in the castle grounds, saw a Luftwaffe signals unit passing the gate and waved to them, beck-oning them to come to him. Recognising him, they responded, entered the grounds and formed up. 'It was one of the most beautiful moments of my life,' he said afterwards, 'to stand there in front of my troops and see them present arms to their Commander-in-Chief.'

The first thing Goring did when he was released on 6 May was to send a message to Dönitz complaining of Bormann's intrigues against him and offering to go and negotiate with Eisenhower 'as one marshal to another', pointing out his success 'in all the important negotiations abroad with which the Führer always entrusted me before the war'. 'Moreover,' he added, 'both Great Britain and America have proved through their press and radio, and in the declarations of their statesmen over the last few years, that their attitude towards me is more favourable than towards all other political leaders in Germany.' Dönitz never replied. But it did not matter – Göring was back, as ebullient as ever.

Koller had requisitioned a castle for his use at Fischhorn on Lake Zeller – it belonged, ironically, to Hermann Fegelein's brother, who had snootily refused to have Göring as his guest. Before leaving Mauterndorf for Fischhorn, Göring sent his adjutant, Berndt von Brauchitsch, ahead to contact the Americans under a white flag and deliver two letters, one to the nearest divisional commander, the other to Eisenhower, asking for a meeting. A detachment of American soldiers was dispatched to collect him, but he was delayed by heavy refugee traffic on the road, and after waiting at the castle for some time, they drove off to search for him. They found him in the middle of a traffic jam, beaming at crowds of German troops who had jumped from their vehicles to greet and salute him and shake his hand.

The war was over, but Göring still believed he was a plenipotentiary about to negotiate the terms of an armistice, rather than a prisoner, and for the first few days in American custody, there was nothing to disabuse him of this. He was treated royally, first at Fischhorn, where he wined and dined with Brigadier-General Robert J. Stack, then at the headquarters of the US Seventh Army at Kitzbühel, where he drank champagne and talked flying with General Carl Spaatz, Commander-in-Chief of the US Strategic Air Forces. But when Eisenhower saw pictures and stories of the reception in the press he was aghast, and ordered him to be taken at once to the Seventh Army Interrogation Centre at Augsburg, where he was to be treated like any other prisoner.

When he arrived in Augsburg, there was no reception committee to greet him, he was brusquely relieved of his medals, his solid gold epaulettes and Reich Marshal's baton, and the enormous diamond ring he was wearing, so that he could not use any of them as bribes. He was housed, to his dismay, in a block of workers' apartments, and fed on basic army C rations. He cheered up, however, when invited to the officers' mess for cocktails the next evening, where he chatted freely and even joined in a sing-song. The lively and relaxed conversation was intended to mask its real purpose as part of a 'carrot and stick'-type interrogation, but Göring was not fooled, and the Americans understood this. Major Kubala, the camp commandant, reported on 19 May:

He is by no means the comical figure he has been depicted so many times in newspaper reports. He is neither stupid nor a fool in the Shakespearean sense, but generally cool and calculating. He is able to grasp the fundamental issues under discussion immediately. He is certainly not a man to be underrated. Although he tried to soft-pedal many of the most outrageous crimes committed by Germany, he said enough to show that he is as much responsible for the policies within Germany and for the war itself as anyone in Germany. Göring took great pride in claiming that it was he who was responsible for the planning of the paratroop landing in Crete, that it was he who had drawn up plans for a capture of Gibraltar . . . that it was he who was responsible for the development of the Luftwaffe. On the other hand, he denied having anything to do with the racial laws and with the concentration camps, with the SS and the atrocities committed both in Germany and outside. Göring is at all times an actor who does not disappoint his audience . . .

The cause for which Göring stood is lost – but the canny Hermann, even now, thinks only of what he can do to salve some of his personal fortune, and to create an advantageous position for himself. He condemns the once-beloved Führer without hesitation. Up to now, he has not made a plea for any of his former henchmen, alive or dead. Yet, behind his spirited and often witty conversation, is a constant watchfulness for the opportunity to place himself in a favourable light.[19]

On 21 May, Göring was moved from Augsburg and flown to Luxembourg in a four-seater Piper Cub aircraft, accompanied by his faithful valet, Robert Kropp – he had been told he could take only one aide with him, and he chose Kropp over Brauchitsch or any of his adjutants. They were delivered safely to the Palace Hotel, Mondorf – ASHCAN.

'When Göring came to me at Mondorf,' Colonel Burton C. Andrus, the stiff-necked commandant of ASHCAN, wrote later, 'he was a simpering slob with two suitcases full of paracodeine. I thought he was a drug salesman. But we took him off his dope and made a man of him.'[20] In fact, the credit for weaning Göring off his pills, and for rebuilding his confidence, was the US Army psychiatrist, Douglas M. Kelley, who decided that he used them as a habit, like chewing gum or smoking cigarettes, and treated him accordingly. 'I used a simple, straight withdrawal method,' he wrote in his memoirs, 'cutting down the dosage each day until no more drug was allowed. Throughout Göring had no special complaint other than occasional pains which were easily relieved with mild sedatives.' Kelley also played on his vanity to persuade him to lose weight. He weighed in at 280 pounds when he arrived at Mondorf; by the time he left he had shed 80 pounds and was in better physical shape than he had been for twenty years, though he still suffered occasional minor heart attacks.

During the four months he spent at Mondorf, Göring dominated the other prisoners, by the force of his personality, and his assurance that he was Hitler's rightful successor – as far as he was concerned, the orders stripping him of his positions and appointing Dönitz Head of State had been issued by Bormann, not Hitler, had not been signed by the Führer, and so were invalid. He was a model prisoner, enjoying the interrogation sessions, co-operating willingly with his questioners, and – as always – winning over his guards with charm and genial good humour. Even the Soviet interrogation team who arrived grim and threatening, were soon heard roaring with laughter and parted from him with smiles, handshakes and back-slapping. However, he failed to seduce Colonel Andrus, who carried his antipathy on to Nuremberg, where he became prison commandant, or Dönitz, who remained as cold and haughty as ever.

The other prisoners at Mondorf were split into two camps by the ridiculous contest for supremacy and precedence between Göring and Dönitz. But when they were all moved to Nuremberg Jail in September, there was no longer any question of who was the more important. Göring's name headed the list of defendants in the indictment for trial before the International Military Tribunal. He was the undisputed number one at last.

For the month before the trial started, the defendants were confined to their one-man cells in the prison wing of the Palace of Justice, under a rigorous regime. The interrogations continued with greater intensity. There were regular searches of cells, when they were stripped naked while bodies, clothes and furnishings were checked with minute thoroughness – Andrus was determined that none of them, and especially Göring, would use a cyanide capsule to escape the hangman. The precautions were stepped up even more when Ley managed to strangle himself in his cell with a torn up towel that he fastened to the toilet pipe. They were moved frequently and without advance warning to other cells. Once a day, they were allowed to exercise for thirty minutes, alone, in a prison courtyard. And they were allowed to choose defence counsel from approved lists, with whom they could spend lengthy sessions of preparation. Göring chose a staid, seventy-year-old former patent and labour lawyer from Kiel, Otto Stahmer.

The indictment was divided into four counts:

1. The formulation or execution of 'a common plan or conspiracy'.
2. 'Crimes against peace'.
3. 'War crimes', covering violations of the laws or customs of war, defined

as 'murder, ill-treatment or deportation to slave labour or for any other purpose of civilian population of or in occupied territory, murder or ill-treatment of prisoners of war or persons on the seas, killing of hostages, plunder of public or private property, wanton destruction of cities, towns and villages, or devastation not justified by military necessity'.

4. 'Crimes against humanity', an innovative charge, seen as an extension of Count 3 and defined as encompassing 'murder, extermination, enslavement, deportation, and other inhumane acts committed against any civilian population before or during the war, or persecutions on political, religious or racial grounds . . .

Each of the accused was tried under at least two of the counts. Most, including Göring, were charged with all four.

When the trial began, on 20 November 1945, Göring was seated in the principal position in the dock, at the right-hand end of the front row, and from there he watched and listened. Seated next to him, Hess and Ribbentrop cut sorry figures by comparison – Hess confused, vacant, maintaining a show of amnesiac innocence; Ribbentrop looking shattered, dejected, utterly defeated. Refused permission to make a carefully prepared statement, Göring was allowed only to respond to the charges against him by pleading 'Not guilty' – to which he added quickly 'in the terms of the indictment'. It would be another four months before he was called, on 13 March 1946, but even while he was forced to sit silently as other witnesses and defendants were questioned, he made his presence felt.

Sir Norman (later Lord) Birkett, the alternate British judge, recorded in the private notes he made at the time:

Göring is the man who has really dominated the proceedings, and that, remarkably enough, without ever uttering a word in public up to the moment he went into the witness box . . . He has followed the evidence with great intentness when the evidence required attention, and has slept like a child when it did not, and it has been obvious that a personality of outstanding, though possibly evil qualities, was seated there in the dock.

Once he was called to speak, on 13 March 1946, he dominated everything even more, as he held the spotlight for nine days of examination and cross-examination, during which he was taken through the entire history of the Nazi Party, the Third Reich, and the part he had played in both. He made no excuses, no apologies, accepted full responsibility for all his actions and justified them wherever it was possible. Far from being ashamed of anything he had done, he was openly proud of his achievements. This was his last appearance in a starring role, and he made the most of every moment. As Birkett noted:

Nobody seems to have been quite prepared for his immense ability and knowledge, and his thorough mastery and understanding of the detail of the captured documents. He has obviously studied them with the greatest care and appreciated the matters which might assume the deadliest form . . .

Suave, shrewd, adroit, capable, resourceful, he quickly saw the elements of the situation, and as his confidence grew, his mastery became more apparent. His self-control, too, was remarkable and to all the other qualities manifested in his evidence he added the resonant tones of his speaking voice, and the eloquent but restrained use of gesture.[21]

In boxing terms, the prosecution never laid a glove on Göring during his cross-examination. Worse, he even scored a technical knock-out over the chief American counsel, Robert Jackson, who ended up by tearing off his earphones and throwing them down in exasperated frustration. But it was all hopeless, as Göring and everyone else knew. The guilty verdict on all four counts delivered on 1 October had always been a foregone conclusion, and came as no shock. What did come as a shock to Göring was the sentence of death by hanging. 'At least I should be spared the ignominy of the noose,' he complained to Gustave Gilbert, the German-born US psychologist who had tended to his mental welfare in the prison. 'I am a soldier. I have been a soldier all my life, always ready to die by another soldier's bullet. Why shouldn't a firing squad of my enemies dispatch me now? Is that too much to ask?' Evidently, it was. His formal request to the Tribunal was rejected.

He was allowed one last meeting on 7 October with Emmy, who had been imprisoned for a short period but was now living with Edda in a hut on Göring's Veldenstein estate. They had spoken to each other through a wire-reinforced glass partition, watched by guards. Emmy told him he could die peacefully knowing he had done all he could at Nuremberg. She would think that he had died for Germany, and asked if they would really shoot him. 'You may be sure of one thing,' he replied. 'They won't hang me . . . No, they won't hang me.' Nor did they.

The hangings of all the condemned men – Göring first, followed by Ribbentrop, Keitel, Kaltenbrunner, Rosenberg, Frank, Frick, Streicher, Jodl and Seyss-Inquart – were scheduled for 2 a.m. on 16 October. At 11.44 p.m. on the 15th, Göring lay on his bed in his cell and bit into a cyanide capsule, which he had somehow managed to secrete or have smuggled in despite Andrus's security measures. By the time the guard watching through the observation flap noticed anything was wrong, he was already dead.

The others were executed on schedule, with Ribbentrop moved up into first place – his hanging was botched, and he took some twenty minutes to die, but the others passed off without a hitch. Göring's body was added to the others as they were photographed, wrapped in mattress covers, sealed in coffins then driven off in army trucks with a military escort to a crematorium in Munich, which had been told to expect the bodies of fourteen American soldiers. The coffins were opened up for inspection by American, British, French and Soviet officers, before being loaded into the cremation ovens. That same evening, a container holding all the ashes was driven away into the Bavarian countryside, in the rain. It stopped in a quiet lane about an hour later, and the ashes were poured into a muddy ditch. Göring, like the other disciples, had come to the end of the road.

ACKNOWLEDGEMENTS

I am grateful to the following publishers and copyright holders for permission to use quotations from the books listed:

Don Congdon Associates, Inc., for *Berlin Diary* (© 1941, renewed 1968) and *The Rise and Fall of the Third Reich* (© 1959, 1960), both by William L. Shirer.

Curtis Brown Group Ltd, on behalf of the estate of H. Montgomery Hyde, for *Lord Birkett*.

Hodder and Stoughton Ltd, for *Failure of a Mission*, by Sir Nevile Henderson.

Macmillan Publishers Ltd, for *Albert Speer: His Battle with Truth*, by Gitta Sereny (UK & Commonwealth rights).

Orion Publishing Group, for *The Ribbentrop Memoirs*, by Joachim von Ribbentrop; *The Bormann Letters*, edited by Hugh Trevor-Roper; *Inside the Third Reich*, by Albert Speer (UK & Commonwealth rights).

Random House Inc., for *Albert Speer: His Battle with Truth*, by Gitta Sereny, and *Panzer Leader*, by Heinz Guderian (North American rights).

In a very few instances, despite my best efforts, I have been unable to trace the current copyright holders of books published many years ago, from which I have made quotations. To these, and anyone I may have inadvertently missed, I offer my apologies and thanks.

For permission to reproduce illustrations I wish to thank the following:

akg-images (2, 3, 8, 13, 17, 18, 20, 23, 24, 27, 29–31, 37)

Hulton Getty (1, 4–6, 10–12, 16, 21, 22, 25, 26, 28, 36, 38–40)

Popperfoto (9, 32)

Ullstein (7, 14, 15, 19, 33–35)

Anthony Read
July 2003

NOTES

Abbreviations:

AA	Auswärtiges Amt (German Foreign Ministry)
AdR	Akten der Reichskanzlei (Reich Chancellery Files)
BA, BAK	Bundesarchiv (German Federal Archives)
BA-MA	Bundesarchiv-Militärarchiv (German Federal Military Archives)
BDC	Berlin Documents Centre
DBFP	Documents on British Foreign Policy
DGFP	Documents on German Foreign Policy
DRZW	*Das Deutsche Reich und der Zweite Weltkrieg*
FO	British Foreign Office document, in PRO files
IfZ	Institut für Zeitgeschichte, Munich
IMT	Proceedings of the Trial of the Major War Criminals before the International Military Tribunal, Nuremberg
IWM	Imperial War Museum, London
MK	*Mein Kampf*
NA	US National Archives, Washington, DC
NCA	*Nazi Conspiracy and Aggression*
ND	Nuremberg Document
OKW KTB	Oberkommando der Wehrmacht, Kriegstagebuch
PRO	British Public Record Office, Kew, London
USAMHI	United States Army Military History Institute
VB	*Völkischer Beobachter*
VfZ	*Vierteljahreshefte für Zeitgeschichte* (History Quarterly)

Prologue
1. Andrus, pp. 22–3.
2. Ibid., p. 29.
3. Ibid., p. 27.
4. IMT, vol. 29, ND 2233-PS.
5. Goebbels, *Tagebücher*, 6 November 1925.
6. Ibid., 25 November 1925.
7. Strasser, *Mein Kampf*, p. 45.
8. Ibid., p. 35.
9. Andrus, pp. 29–32.
10. Ibid., p. 38.
11. Quoted in Sereny, p. 558.
12. Andrus, p. 113.
13. Hyde, *Lord Birkett*, pp. 510.
14. Kelley, p. 47.
15. Ibid., p. 59.
16. Ibid., p. 54.

I: 'Our time will come again'
1. Ferguson, p. 289.
2. Hitler, *Mein Kampf*, pp. 89–90.
3. Keegan, p. 368.
4. Ibid., p. 433.
5. Herwig, p. 404.
6. Shirer, *Rise and Fall*, p. 49.
7. Keegan, p. 296, quoting Halpern.
8. Hitler, MK, p. 91.
9. Channon, pp. 148–55.
10. Ritchie, p. 300.
11. Hitler, MK, p. 92.
12. Bodenschatz, quoted in Mosley, p. 41.
13. Ibid.
14. Ibid., p. 44.
15. Kelley, p. 45.
16. Berlin Handbuch, p. 408.
17. Frischauer, p. 23.
18. Mosley, p. 9.
19. USAMHI: HG's travel journal.
20. Quoted in Irving, p. 33.
21. IMT, vol. 9, p. 292.
22. Gritzbach, p. 143.

II: 'If only there could be fighting again'
1. Frischauer, *Himmler,* p. 17.
2. Shirer, p. 78; Hanser, p. 184.
3. Hanser, p. 184.
4. Maser, p. 159; Kershaw, p. 121; Hanser, p. 186.
5. Himmler Diary, 11 November 1919.
6. Ibid., 24 September 1919.
7. Ibid., 15 December 1919.
8. Ibid., 28 November 1919.
9. Ibid., 1 December 1919.
10. Hanser, pp. 224–5.
11. Central Archives of NSDAP, Microfilm 98: Receipt dated 16 May 1920 from No. 14 Alarm Company.
12. Bullock, *Hitler*, p. 63; Hanser, p. 258.
13. Himmler Diary, 19 February 1922.
14. Ibid., 11 June 1922.
15. Ibid., 26 June 1922.
16. Röhm, p. 86.
17. Ibid., p. 115.

III: Fighting the November Criminals
1. Bodenschatz, quoted in Mosley, p. 53.
2. BA-MA file MS1g, 1/13.
3. *Carin Göring*, by Fanny Countess von Wilamowitz-Moellendorff, quoted in Mosley, p. 56.
4. Ibid., quoted in Frischauer, p. 44; Manvell and Fraenkel, p. 23; Irving, pp. 39–40.
5. Ibid., quoted in Mosley, p. 56.
6. AA file Referat Deutschland, Pers.1: Dispatch by German Legation, Stockholm, 28 Sept 1938.
7. IMT, vol. 9, p. 236.
8. Jäckel and Kuhn, p. 679.
9. Kelley, p. 46.

10. Ibid., pp. 46–7.
11. IMT, vol. 9, p. 236.
12. Ibid.
13. Trevor-Roper (ed.), *Hitler's Table Talk*, 3–4 January 1942.
14. Kelley, p. 53.
15. Lüdecke, p. 129.
16. Kelley, p. 53.
17. Jäckel and Kuhn, pp. 923–4.
18. IMT, vol. 9, p. 237.
19. *Carin Göring* by Fanny Countess von Wilamowitz-Moellendorff, quoted in Mosley, pp. 70–1.
20. Trevor-Roper (ed.), *Hitler's Table Talk*, p. 168.
21. Jäckel and Kuhn, pp. 781–6.
22. Bennecke, pp. 54, 61.
23. Carin Göring letters, USMHI, quoted in Irving, p. 47.
24. Quoted in Irving, p. 46.
25. The Treason Trial of Adolf Hitler, NA films T84/1, quoted in Irving, p. 47.
26. Irving, p. 48, quoting Göring correspondence with Dr Leo Negrelli, and Giuseppe Bastianini's *Memoirs* (Milan, 1959).

IV: Beer Hall Revolution

1. Deuerlein, pp. 181–2.
2. Padfield, p. 63, quoting Smith.
3. Carin Göring's letter to her son, Thomas, quoted in Mosley, p. 75.
4. Gordon, p. 243.
5. Deuerlein, pp. 505–6; Bracher, p. 150.
6. Stachura, p. 24.
7. Deuerlein, pp. 192–3; Müller, pp. 160–6; Gordon, pp. 287–8.
8. Hanfstaengl, p. 134; Deuerlein, pp. 193–4.
9. Gordon, pp. 259–60; Kershaw, *Hubris*, p. 205.
10. Jäckel and Kuhn, p. 1053.
11. Müller, p. 162.

12. Hanfstaengl, p. 100.
13. Jäckel and Kuhn, pp. 1054–5.
14. Müller, p. 162.
15. *Der Hitler-Prozess*.
16. Mosley, p. 81.
17. Frank, p. 61.
18. *Carin Göring* by Fanny Countess von Wilamowitz-Moellendorff, quoted in Mosley, p. 88.

V: Regrouping

1. *Der Hitler-Prozess*, pp. 18–28.
2. Röhm, pp. 313–14.
3. Knopp, pp. 221–2.
4. Kelley, p. 17.
5. Ibid., pp. 17–18.
6. Carin Göring letters, quoted in Mosley, pp. 90–1.
7. Kelley, p. 32.
8. Stachura, p. 30.
9. Ludecke, p. 226.
10. Strasser, 'Von der Revolte zur Revolution!', *Berliner Arbeiter-Zeitung*, 6 November 1927, quoted in Stachura, p. 14.
11. Albert Krebs, *Tendenzen und Gestalten der NSDAP: Erinnerungen an die Frühzeit der Partei* (Stuttgart, 1959), quoted in Stachura, pp. 15–16.
12. NA Microfilm T-175, Roll 99, Frames 2620049, 2620053.
13. Strasser, *Mein Kampf*, p. 15.
14. Ludecke, p. 259.
15. IfZ, Hermann Göring collection, ED. 180, quoted in Irving, *Göring*, p. 88.
16. BA, NS 26/vorl. 1225.

VI: A Star in the Making

1. Goebbels, *Tagebücher*, 8 and 11 December 1929.
2. Goebbels, *Michael* (1919).
3. Goebbels, *Tagebücher*, IfZ 1:2.
4. Goebbels, *Michael*.

5. Ibid.
6. Oven, p. 287.
7. Goebbels, *Tagebücher*, IfZ 1:16.
8. Letter to Anka Stalherm, 13 March 1920, BA, NL 118/110.
9. Goebbels Diaries, IfZ 1:21.
10. Goebbels, 'Aus meinem Tagebuch', BA, NL 118/126.
11. Ibid.
12. Ibid.
13. Goebbels, *Tagebücher*, August 1923 in Baltrum.
14. Goebbels, *Michael*.
15. Burleigh, p. 77.
16. Goebbels, *Tagebücher*, IfZ 1:28.
17. Letter to Anka Stalherm, 17 February 1919, BA, NL 118/126.
18. Goebbels, *Die zweite Revolution*, p. 7.
19. Goebbels, *Tagebücher*, 30 June 1924.
20. Ibid.
21. Ibid., 19–20 August 1924.
22. Fraenkel and Manvell, *Goebbels*, pp. 71ff.
23. Goebbels, *Tagebücher*, 27 September 1924.
24. Ibid., 30 June 1924.
25. Reuth, pp. 62–3.
26. Goebbels, *Tagebücher*, IfZ 1:27.
27. Ibid., 23 October 1925.
28. Goebbels, *Die zweite Revolution*.
29. Goebbels, *Tagebücher*, 28 May 1925.
30. Ibid., 19 August 1925.
31. Ibid., 21 August 1925.
32. Ibid., 14 October 1925.
33. Ibid., 6 November 1925.
34. Goebbels, *Die zweite Revolution*, p. 8.
35. Jochmann, p. 213.
36. Goebbels, *NS-Briefe*, 15 October 1925.
37. Goebbels, *Tagebücher*, 25 January 1926.
38. Bullock, *Hitler*, p. 137.
39. Ulrich Wörtz, 'Programmatik und Führerprinzip', p. 85, quoted in Reuth, p. 69.
40. Goebbels, *Tagebücher*, 15 February 1926.
41. Ibid.
42. Ibid., 22 February 1926.
43. Ibid., 13 April 1926.
44. Ibid.
45. Ibid.
46. Ibid., 19 April 1926.
47. Goebbels, *Tagebücher*, 24 July 1926.
48. Ibid., 10 June 1926.
49. Ibid.
50. Ibid., 30 October 1926.

VII: 'Chief Bandit of Berlin'

1. Otto Strasser, *Mein Kampf*, p. 30.
2. Reimann, p. 69.
3. *Spandauer Volksblatt*, 15 November 1926.
4. Albrecht Tyrell, *Führer befiehl . . . Selbstzeugnisse aus der 'Kampfzeit' der NSDAP*, quoted in Kershaw, *Hubris*, p. 295.
5. Goebbels, *Tagebücher*, 13 April 1926.
6. 'Die Lage der Landwirtschaft', *NS-Briefe*, 1 April 1926.
7. Himmler, *Völkische Bauernpolitik*, NSDAP Central Archives, Microfilm 98.
8. Horst Wessel, 'Notes on Politics', 1929, quoted in Reuth, p. 82.
9. Goebbels, *Kampf um Berlin*, p. 28.
10. Goebbels's statement to police, 21 March 1927: Landesarchiv Berlin, Rep. 58, Zug 399, no. 302, vol. 1.
11. Strasser Reichstag speech, 17 October 1930: BA ZSg 103/831.
12. VB, 25 June 1927.
13. Goebbels, *Kampf um Berlin*, p. 209.

14. Albrecht Tyrell, *Führer befiehl . . . Selbstzeugnisse aus der 'Kampfzeit' der NSDAP* (Düsseldorf, 1969), quoted in Kershaw, *Hubris*, p. 296.
15. Shirer, *Rise and Fall*, p. 153.
16. Strasser, *Mein Kampf*, p. 45.
17. Himmler reading list, number 235.
18. Goebbels, *Tagebücher*, 3 May 1928.
19. Letter from Carin Göring to Thomas von Kantzow, quoted in Mosley, pp. 110–11.
20. Letter from Carin Göring to her mother, quoted in Mosley, p. 112.

VIII: 'We come as enemies'
1. *Der Angriff*, 28 May 1928.
2. Ibid., 30 May 1928.
3. Goebbels, *Tagebücher*, 15 June 1928.
4. Irving, *Göring*, p. 96.
5. NSDAP Central Archives, microfilm 98.
6. 'Die Schutzstaffel', address of 18 January 1943, RFSS Microfilm 155, quoted in Höhne, p. 52.
7. IMT, vol. XXIX, p. 208.
8. Ibid., pp. 208–9.
9. Strasser, *Mein Kampf*, p. 45.
10. Goebbels, *Tagebücher*, 27 June 1929.
11. Ibid., 5 April 1929.
12. Reuth, p. 108.
13. Goebbels, *Tagebücher*, 23 September 1929.
14. Ibid., 15 and 23 December 1929.
15. Ibid., 29 December 1929.
16. Ibid., 19 January 1930.
17. Ibid.
18. *Der Angriff*, 21 January 1930.
19. Goebbels, *Tagebücher*, 18 January 1930.
20. Ibid., 20 January 1930.
21. Ibid., 24 January 1930.

22. Ibid., 1 April 1930.
23. Ibid., 17–25 April 1930.
24. Ibid., 28 April 1930.
25. Ibid.
26. Ibid., 22 May 1930.
27. Ibid., 29 June 1930.
28. Ibid., 20 July 1930.
29. Ibid., 21 July 1930.
30. Carin Göring letter, Wilamowitz-Moellendorff, p. 130.
31. Files of Hans Frank, NA, NL 110/AH.2, quoted in Irving, *Göring*, p. 97.
32. Anonymous leaflet in NSDAP Central Archives, microfilm 17.
33. Goebbels, *Tagebücher*, 8 August 1930.
34. Ibid., 30 August 1930.
35. Ibid.
36. *Münchner Post*, 4 September 1930.

IX: 'SS-Man, your loyalty is your honour'
1. Hitler, *Reden, Schriften, Anordnungen* (RSA), vol. III, Pt. 3, p. 439–41.
2. Heiden, p. 198.
3. Letter from Himmler to Röhm, 29 January 1930, NA Group T-175, RFSS Microfilm 199.
4. Peter Longerich, *Die braunen Bataillone: Geschichte der SA*, p. 107, quoted in Kershaw, *Hubris*, p. 348.
5. Goebbels, *Tagebücher*, 12 November 1930.
6. Höhne, p. 57.
7. Carin Göring letter, Wilamowitz-Moellendorff, pp. 138–9.
8. Schacht, *My First Seventy-Six Years*, pp. 279–80.
9. Carin Göring letter, Wilamowitz-Moellendorff, p. 142.
10. Goebbels, *Tagebücher*, 4 January 1931.

11. Ibid., 11 February 1931.
12. Ibid., 29 September and 13 October 1930; *Vossische Zeitung*, 14 October 1930, quoted in Reuth, p. 123.
13. Goebbels, *Tagebücher*, 9 December 1930.
14. Ibid., 23 February 1931.
15. Ibid., 18 and 20 February 1931.
16. Ibid., 21 February 1931.
17. Ibid., 16 March 1931.
18. Ibid., 29 March 1931.
19. VB, 5–7 April 1931.
20. Goebbels, *Tagebücher*, 4 April 1931.
21. Berlin Document Centre, Microfilm 87, Leaders' Conference SS Group East, 13–14 June 1931.
22. Goebbels, *Tagebücher*, 18 April 1931.
23. Ibid., 7 November 1930.
24. Ibid., 15 February 1931.
25. Ibid., 26 March 1931.
26. Ibid., 20 April 1931.
27. Ibid., 31 May 1931.
28. Carin Göring letter, Wilamowitz-Moellendorff, p. 143.
29. Shirer, *Rise and Fall*, p. 167.
30. G. M. Gilbert, p. 69.
31. IMT, vol. 9, p. 242.
32. Hauner, p. 76.
33. VB, 1–2 January 1932.

X: 'Now the chess game for power begins'

1. Heiden, *Der Führer*, p. 342.
2. Goebbels, *Tagebücher*, 7 January 1932.
3. Ibid., 11 January 1932.
4. Ibid., 7, 8, 9, 10 January 1932.
5. Ibid., 6 January 1932.
6. Ibid., 8 February 1932.
7. Ibid., 24 January, 4 February 1932.
8. Ibid., 22 January 1932.
9. Ibid., 22 February 1932.
10. Ibid., 23 February 1932.
11. Ibid., 29 February 1932.
12. Manvell and Fraenkel, *Göring*, pp. 61–2.
13. Goebbels, *Tagebücher*, 10 April 1932.
14. Ibid., 23 April 1932.
15. Ibid., 6 May 1932.
16. Ibid., 8 May 1932.
17. Blood-Ryan, pp. 155–6.
18. Ibid., 12 May 1932.
19. Wheeler-Bennett, quoted in Shirer, *Rise and Fall*, p. 205.
20. Klotz, p. 50.
21. Goebbels, *Tagebücher*, 28 May 1932.
22. Ibid., 30 May 1932.
23. François-Poncet, p. 23.
24. Klotz, pp. 30–1.
25. Goebbels, *Tagebücher*, 2 June 1932.
26. Ibid., 6 June 1932.
27. Papen, p. 162.
28. Goebbels, *Tagebücher*, 14 June 1932.
29. Ibid., 1 July 1932.
30. Klotz, p. 127.
31. Goebbels, *Tagebücher*, 1–2 August 1932.
32. Ibid., 5 August 1932.
33. Klotz, p. 142.
34. Goebbels, *Tagebücher*, 7 August 1932.
35. Ibid.
36. Klotz, pp. 136–7.
37. Ibid., pp. 140–1.
38. Goebbels, *Tagebücher*, 9 August 1932.
39. Ibid., 11 August 1932.
40. Klotz, pp. 147–8.
41. Ibid., pp. 150–2.
42. Goebbels, *Tagebücher*, 13 August 1932.
43. IMT, vol. 10, p. 227; Bloch, pp. 27–8.
44. Baynes, p. 166.

XI: The Turning Point

1. Goebbels, *Kaiserhof*, 25 August 1932.
2. Ibid.
3. Ibid., 26 August 1932.
4. IMT, vol. 9, pp. 243–4.
5. Klotz, p. 156.
6. Speer, p. 73.
7. IMT, vol. 9, p. 244; Goebbels, *Kaiserhof*, 12 September 1932; Klotz, pp. 165–6.
8. Klotz, p. 168.
9. Goebbels, *Kaiserhof*, 17 October 1932.
10. Ibid., 4 November 1932.
11. Ibid., 11 November 1932.
12. Klotz, pp. 188–9.
13. Papen, pp. 216–17.
14. Ibid., p. 222.
15. Stachura, pp. 112–14.
16. Goebbels, *Tagebücher*, 10 December 1932.
17. BA Koblenz, NS22/10, quoted in Kershaw, *Hubris*, pp. 403–4.
18. NCA, vol. II, pp. 922–4.
19. Goebbels, *Tagebücher*, 10 January 1933.
20. Kurt von Schuschnigg, *Farewell Austria* (London, 1938), pp. 165–6, quoted in Shirer, *Rise and Fall*, p. 227.
21. IMT, vol. 9, pp. 245–6.
22. Ribbentrop, pp. 24–5.
23. IMT, vol. 9, p. 254.
24. Goebbels, *Kaiserhof*, 29 January 1933.
25. Hitler, *Secret Conversations*, p. 404.
26. Goebbels, *Kaiserhof*, 30 January 1933.

XII: Power

1. François-Poncet, p. 48.
2. DBFP, 2nd series, vol. iv, 402.
3. Ibid., 401.
4. Goebbels, *Tagebücher*, 6, 10, 11 and 13 February.
5. Ibid., 1 February 1933.
6. AdR, Reg. Hitler, 6.
7. Browder, *Foundations*, pp. 55–6.
8. Gisevius, pp. 39–40.
9. Mosley, p. 150.
10. Browder, *Foundations*, p. 52.
11. Gisevius, pp. 37–8.
12. Heiden, p. 216.
13. Ibid.
14. Goebbels, *Kaiserhof*, 13 February 1933.
15. Goebbels, *Tagebücher*, 13 Febrary 1933.
16. Browder, *Foundations*, p. 46.
17. Goebbels, *Tagebücher*, 11 February 1933.
18. Riess, p. 126.
19. Goebbels, *Kaiserhof*, 27 February; Hanfstaengl, p. 294.
20. US Army Historical Commission interrogation, 20 July 1945.
21. Hans Mommsen, 'Der Reichstagsbrand und seine politischen Folgen', *VfZ* 12 (1964), pp. 351–413.
22. Papen, p. 268; Delmer, pp. 188–9.
23. Diels, p. 194.
24. *Der Angriff*, 28 February 1933.
25. NCA, vol. IV, p. 496 (ND 1856-PS).
26. Goebbels, *Kaiserhof*, 4 March 1933.

XIII: Co-ordination

1. IMT, vol. 13, p. 106: Funk's testimony.
2. Goebbels, *Kaiserhof*, 11 March 1933.
3. Ibid., 13 March 1933.
4. Speer, p. 59.
5. Goebbels, *Kaiserhof*, 18 April 1933.
6. BAK, R 43 II/1150a.
7. Domarus, vol. 1, pp. 227–8.

8. AdR, Reg. Hitler, 50–1.
9. Ibid., 62–3.
10. IMT, vol. 9, p. 257.
11. Ibid.
12. Gisevius, p. 104.
13. Diels, pp. 190–3.
14. Schellenberg, pp. 29–30.
15. Aronson, pp. 25–35.
16. Wighton, p. 35.
17. Heydrich, p. 28.
18. Aronson, pp. 35–7; BDC/SSO, Heydrich, NSDAP No. 544,916.
19. Aronson, pp. 37–8, quoting Eberstein.
20. BDC/SSO, Heydrich: RFSS to SS-Sturmführer Reinhard Heydrich, 10 August 1931.
21. Police Report No. 748: HA/28A/1773, quoted in Browder, *Foundations*, p. 27.
22. Aronson, p. 87.
23. Buchheim et al, p. 405.
24. Tobias, p. 135.
25. Ibid., p. 136.

XIV: The End of the Brown Revolution

1. *Manchester Guardian*, 27 March 1933.
2. *Manchester Guardian*, 16 March 1933.
3. Marley, p. 238.
4. Goebbels, *Kaiserhof*, 26 March 1933.
5. Ibid.
6. Marley, pp. 262–3.
7. Goebbels, *Kaiserhof*, 31 March 1933.
8. Lady Rumbold letter of 2 April 1933, quoted in M. Gilbert, *Holocaust*, pp. 34–5.
9. Isherwood, p. 183.
10. VB, 7 April 1933.
11. Goebbels, *Kaiserhof*, 1 April 1933.
12. Ibid., 7 April 1933.

13. Ibid., 11 April 1933.
14. Speer, p. 59.
15. Goebbels, *Kaiserhof*, 25 April 1933.
16. Alfons Kupper (ed.), *Staatliche Akten über die Reichskonkordatsverhandlungen 1933* (Mainz, 1969), pp. 293–4, quoted in Kershaw, *Hubris*, p. 488.
17. Brendon, pp. 122–5.
18. Below, p. 12.
19. Galland, p. 17.
20. Goebbels, *Kaiserhof*, 19 April 1933.
21. Goebbels, *Revolution der Deutschen*, p. 157.
22. Heiber (ed.), *Goebbels Reden 1932–1939*, pp. 87, 89, 106, quoted in Reuth, pp. 176–7.
23. Joseph Wulf, *Presse und Funk im Dritten Reich: Eine Dokumentation*, p. 292, quoted in Reuth, pp. 184–5.
24. Goebbels, *Tagebücher*, 17 and 20 June 1933.
25. Ibid., 19 July 1933.
26. Riess, p. 135.
27. Shirer, *Rise and Fall*, p. 308.
28. Hale, p. 3.
29. Wulf, *op. cit.*, pp. 85ff., quoted in Reuth, p. 174.
30. Hale, pp. 81–3.
31. Ibid., pp. 56–7.
32. Burleigh, p. 208.
33. Haarman et al, *Das war ein Vorspiel nur*, quoted in Reuth, pp. 182–3.
34. Goebbels, *Tagebücher*, 6 June 1933.
35. Speer, p. 72.
36. IWM, FO 645, Box 157.
37. Goebbels, *Tagebücher*, 29 June 1933.
38. Speer, p. 60.
39. Goebbels, *Tagebücher*, 16 July 1933.
40. Speer, pp. 60–1.

41. Goebbels, *Tagebücher*, 23 August 1933.
42. Ibid.
43. Speer, pp. 72–3.
44. Ibid., 18 April 1933.
45. Ibid., 2 September 1933.
46. Ibid., 7 and 11 July 1933.
47. Goebbels, *Signale der neuen Zeit: 25 ausgewählte Reden von Dr Joseph Goebbels*, Munich, 1934.
48. Shirer, *Rise and Fall*, pp. 308–9.
49. Goebbels, *Tagebücher*, 23 September 1933.
50. Schmidt, p. 283.

XV: Night of the Long Knives
1. IMT, vol. 9, p. 259.
2. Frick to Himmler, 10 January 1935, NA, T-175/70/2587696–97.
3. *Nationalsozialistische Monatshefte*, no. 4 (1933), pp. 253–4.
4. Baynes, vol. I, p. 287.
5. Ibid., pp. 865–6.
6. Shirer, *Rise and Fall*, p. 256.
7. Manvell and Fraenkel, *Göring*, p. 108; Gisevius, pp. 107–8; Browder, *Foundations*, p. 85.
8. Diels, p. 379.
9. Domarus, vol. 1, pp. 338–42; Baynes, vol. I, p. 289; VB, 2 January 1934.
10. Diels, p. 386.
11. Karl Dietrich Bracher, Wolfgang Sauer, Gerhard Schultz, *Die nationalsozialistische Machtergreifung*, p. 904, quoted in Höhne, p. 96; Kershaw, *Hubris*, p. 504; Fest, *Hitler*, pp. 453–4; Shirer, *Rise and Fall*, p. 267.
12. NSDAP/HA, Reel 54, Folder 1290.
13. Fest, *Hitler*, p. 454.
14. Ibid., p. 455; Höhne, p. 96; Kershaw, *Hubris*, p. 505.
15. Höhne, p. 97; Fest, *Hitler*, p. 455; Kershaw, *Hubris*, p. 505.
16. Phipps dispatch: DBFP, vol. VI, pp. 749–51.
17. Gisevius, p. 129.
18. Noakes and Pridlam, *Documents on Nazism*, p. 208.
19. Papen, p. 309; Gisevius, pp. 126–7; Fest, *Hitler*, p. 459.
20. Goebbels, *Tagebücher*, 21 May 1934.
21. Otto Meissner, *Staatsekretär*, p. 363, quoted in Kershaw, *Hubris*, p. 511.
22. Lutze's diary, quoted in *Frankfurter Rundschau*, 14 May 1957, quoted in Höhne, p. 105.
23. Lutze's diary, quoted in Fest, *Hitler*, pp. 460–1.
24. FA intercepts in AA Political Archives, quoted in Mosley, p. 191.
25. VB, 26 June 1934.
26. Ibid., 27 June 1934.
27. Lutze's diary, quoted in Höhne, p. 110.
28. J. von Lang, *Der Adjutant – Karl Wolff: Der Mann zwischen Hitler und Himmler*, p. 3, quoted in Padfield, *Himmler*, p. 157.
29. VB, 29 June 1933.
30. Goebbels, *Tagebücher*, 29 June 1934.
31. Munich Provincial Court I, 4 July 1956, case for the prosecution against Josef Dietrich and Michael Lippert, p. 77; *Süddeutsche Zeitung*, 8 May 1957. Quoted in Höhne, p. 113.
32. VB, 3 July 1934.
33. IMT, vol. 9, p. 266.
34. Gisevius, pp. 215–16.
35. Ibid., pp. 157–8.
36. Ibid., p. 160.
37. IMT, vol. 9, p. 267.
38. Domarus, vol. 1, p. 404.

XVI: 'We always approve everything our Führer does'

1. Ivone Kirkpatrick, *The Inner Circle*, p. 90, quoted in Large, p. 132.
2. Domarus, vol. I, p. 405.
3. Ibid.
4. Ibid., p. 421.
5. Fest, *Hitler*, p. 471.
6. PRO, FO 434/1, Sir Nevile Henderson's dispatch of 29 October 1934.
7. NA Microfilm, T-175, Roll 89, Frs 1536 ff.
8. Höhne, p. 153.
9. IWM F2, AL 2704, E313.
10. Rosenberg, *Das politische Tagebuch*, p. 39, quoted in Reuth, p. 210.
11. Domarus, vol. I, p. 444.
12. Shirer, *Nightmare Years*, p. 158.
13. Goebbels, *Tagebücher*, 2 March 1935.
14. VB, 6 September 1934.
15. Goebbels, *Tagebücher*, 27 December 1933.
16. Ibid., 19 August 1941.
17. Ibid., 20, 21, 22 July 1933.
18. Ibid., 1 January 1935.
19. British White Paper, Cmd 4827, 1935.
20. Shirer, *Berlin Diary*, p. 35.
21. Interrogation of Lt-Gen Ulrich Kessler, NA, RG238, box 210, quoted in Irving, *Göring*, p. 155.
22. Shirer, *Berlin Diary*, p. 36.
23. DBFP, vol. XII, no. 285.
24. Schacht, *Account Settled*, quoted in Mosley, p. 203.
25. Mosley, pp. 203–4, quoting various contemporary newspaper accounts.
26. Papen, p. 373.
27. Ribbentrop, pp. 2–3.
28. Bloch, pp. 6–7.
29. Ribbentrop, p. 12.
30. Paul Schwarz, *This Man Ribbentrop*, pp. 55–6, quoted in Bloch, pp. 11–12.
31. Schwarz p. 17; Bloch, p. 15.
32. Ribbentrop, pp. 27–8.
33. IMT, vol. X, pp. 227–8.
34. Bloch, p. 46.
35. DBFP 2/VI, no. 407 of 26 April 1934.
36. Bloch, pp. 58–9, quoting Erich Kordt, *Nicht aus den Akten*.
37. Ibid., p. 68, quoting John L. Heineman, *Hitler's First Foreign Minister: Constantin Freiherr von Neurath, Diplomat and Statesman*, p. 131.
38. Schmidt, pp. 33–4.

XVII: The Four-Year Plan

1. Goebbels, *Tagebücher*, 15 July 1935.
2. Ibid., 19 July 1935.
3. Kershaw, *Hubris*, p. 562.
4. Goebbels, *Tagebücher*, 3 October 1935.
5. Ibid., 15 November 1935.
6. IMT, vol. 9, pp. 273–4.
7. Ribbentrop, p. 52.
8. Goebbels, *Tagebücher*, 4 March 1936.
9. Ibid., 8 March 1936.
10. Ibid.
11. Ibid.
12. Bloch, pp. 96–7; Papen, pp. 372–5; Kordt, p. 146.
13. Bloch, p. 97; Kordt, p. 148.
14. Kelley, p. 82; Shirer, *Nightmare Years*, p. 198.
15. Goebbels, *Tagebücher*, 17, 22 and 29 March, 8 and 9 April, 22 October 1936.
16. Mosley, p. 206.
17. Paul, p. 161, quoting Paul Deichmann.
18. IMT, vol. 9, p. 280.
19. Ibid., p. 282.

20. Goebbels, *Tagebücher*, 3 May 1936.
21. Ibid., 19 June 1936.
22. Ibid., 6 August, 6 November 1936.
23. Rhodes James, p. 111.
24. Goebbels, *Tagebücher*, 2, 4 and 7 August 1936.
25. DGFP, C/V, Doc 490.
26. Goebbels, *Tagebücher*, 20 October 1936.
27. IMT, vol. 9, p. 151.
28. Vansittart report of 10 September 1936, Vansittart Papers, Churchill College, Cambridge, quoted in Irving, *Göring*, p. 167.
29. Ciano's diplomatic papers, 60, quoted in Kershaw, *Nemesis*, p. 26.
30. Goebbels, *Tagebücher*, 30 October 1936.
31. *Der Angriff*, 31 October 1936.
32. Goebbels, *Tagebücher*, 31 October 1936.
33. Domarus, vol. II, p. 658.
34. IMT, TWC vol. 12, pp. 460–65; ND NI-051.

XVIII: The Blomberg–Fritsch Affair
1. IMT, vol. 9, p. 292.
2. Schmidt, pp. 63–4.
3. Irving, *Göring*, p. 187; Kershaw, *Nemesis*, p. 68.
4. Henderson, pp. 80, 83.
5. Ibid., pp. 87, 91.
6. Ibid., p. 84.
7. Kelley, p. 46.
8. Paul Ortwin Rave, *Kunstdiktatur im Dritten Reich*, p. 50, quoted in Grunberger, pp. 534–5.
9. Shirer, *Rise and Fall*, p. 304.
10. Ibid.
11. Goebbels, *Tagebücher*, 21 March 1937.
12. Grunberger, pp. 557–8.
13. VB, 29 May 1937.

14. Goebbels, *Tagebücher*, 29 May 1937.
15. Ibid., 2 November 1937.
16. Ibid., 11 February 1937.
17. IMT, vol. 25, pp. 402–13, Doc 386-PS; DGFP series D, vol. 1, from Neurath to Ribbentrop.
18. Fabian von Schlabrendorff, *Offiziere gegen Hitler*, p. 60, quoted in Fest, *Hitler*, p. 541.
19. Shirer, *Nightmare Years*, pp. 198–9.
20. Goebbels, *Tagebücher*, 27 October 1937.
21. Reinhard Spitzy, *So haben wir das Reich verspielt*, pp. 185–9, quoted in Bloch, p. 143; Kordt, pp. 171–4.
22. Goebbels, *Tagebücher*, 16 November 1937.
23. Schmidt, pp. 76–7.
24. Halifax Diary, PRO FO371/20736.
25. Schmidt, pp. 77–8.
26. Irving, *Göring*, p. 195.
27. Frischauer, p. 149, interview with Erna von Blomberg.
28. Keitel, p. 43.
29. Ibid., pp. 43–4.
30. Goebbels, *Tagebücher*, 26 and 27 January 1937.
31. Keitel, p. 45.
32. Ibid., p. 46.
33. Fritsch private papers, quoted in Irving, *Göring*, p. 199.
34. Keitel, pp. 47–9.
35. Warlimont, p. 13.
36. Domarus, vol. II, pp. 796–7.
37. Goebbels, *Tagebücher*, 1 February 1938.

XIX: *Anschluss*
1. *Der unbekannte Dr Goebbels: Die geheimen Tagebücher 1938*, ed. David Irving, entry for 10 March 1938, quoted in Kershaw, *Nemesis*, p. 74.

2. IMT, vol. 9, p. 295.
3. DGFP, D/I, no. 146.
4. Ibid., no. 145.
5. Bloch, pp. 171–2.
6. Ibid., p. 171.
7. Papen, p. 428.
8. The transcripts of all Göring's telephone conversations quoted here are to be found in ND2949-PS, IMT, vol. 31, pp. 368ff.
9. Chamberlain letter to his sister Hilda, Chamberlain Papers, Birmingham University, 18/1/1041, quoted in Bloch, p. 172.
10. Henderson, pp. 124–6.
11. IMT, vol. 9, pp. 299–300.
12. IMT vol. 31, pp. 368ff, ND2949-PS.
13. Ibid.
14. Martin Gilbert, p. 61.
15. Ibid., pp. 62–3.
16. Goebbels, *Tagebücher*, 19 June 1938.
17. Frischauer, p. 155; Manvell and Fraenkel, *Göring*, p. 171.
18. BA, R55/445, Rundspruch Nr. 69. Tagesparole vom 11 April 1938.
19. Goebbels, *Tagebücher*, 31 August 1938.
20. *Deutsche Allgemeine Zeitung*, 23 June 1938.

XX: The Sudetenland Crisis

1. Keitel, pp. 62–3.
2. DGFP D/II, no. 107.
3. Ibid., pp. 273–4.
4. Ibid., no. 133.
5. D.C. Watt, 'An Earlier Model of the Pact of Steel', *International Affairs*, vol. 33, pp. 185–97, quoted in Bloch, p. 180.
6. Ciano Diaries, I, 5 May 1938; Schmidt, pp. 83–4; DGFP D/I,

no. 759.
7. Ciano Diaries, I, 6 May 1938.
8. Goebbels, *Tagebücher*, 3 June 1938.
9. Keitel, p. 64.
10. IMT, vol. 28, p. 357.
11. Henderson, pp. 135–6; DGFP, D/II, no. 184; DBFP 3/I, nos. 249, 252; Schmidt, pp. 84–5.
12. DBFP 3/I, nos. 250, 264.
13. Henderson, p. 137; Schmidt, p. 85.
14. DGFP D/II, no. 186.
15. Henderson, p. 137; Schmidt, p. 85.
16. IMT, vol. 25, pp. 433–4, ND 388-PS.
17. Keitel, p. 65.
18. Below, p. 21.
19. Goebbels, *Tagebücher*, 1 September 1938.
20. Henderson, pp. 141–2.
21. Goebbels, *Tagebücher*, 2 July 1938.
22. Ibid., 6 August 1938.
23. Hassell, p. 37.
24. Henderson, 16 August 1938.
25. Hassell, p. 37.
26. Goebbels, *Tagebücher*, 16–21 August 1938.
27. Srehlin, *Témoignage pour l'Histoire*, quoted in Mosley, pp. 222–5.
28. Henderson, p. 146.
29. DBFP, II, no. 257.
30. Henderson, p. 145.
31. Shirer, *Nightmare Years*, p. 337; Toland, p. 472; Frischauer, p. 160.
32. Domarus, vol. II, pp. 900–5.
33. Schmidt, p. 91.
34. Churchill, *The Gathering Storm*, pp. 274–5.
35. Shirer, *Berlin Diary*, pp. 142–3.
36. Helmuth Groscurth diary, 26 September 1938, quoted in Bloch, p. 195.

37. G. M. Gilbert, p. 88.
38. Shirer, *Rise and Fall*, p. 515.
39. Paul, pp. 174-5.
40. F. Genoud (ed.), *The Testament of Adolf Hitler: The Hitler–Bormann Documents, February–April 1945, pp. 67, 95-7*, quoted in Hauner, p. 133.

XXI: *Kristallnacht*

1. Göring Diary, I, *Besprechungen*, published in London *Daily Herald*, 7-14 July 1945.
2. Ciano Diary, I, 28 October 1938.
3. Ibid., 23 October 1938.
4. Paul, pp. 176-7.
5. NA Microfilm T-175, roll 90, quoted in Padfield, *Himmler*, pp. 238-9, and Kershaw, *Nemesis*, p. 130.
6. Goebbels testimony to party inquiry, IMT 3063-PS; Goebbels, *Tagebücher*, 10 November 1938.
7. *Der Stürmer*, 15 November 1938.
8. Goebbels, *Tagebücher*, 10 November 1938.
9. IMT 374-PS.
10. IMT 3063-PS.
11. Ibid.
12. IMT 1816-PS.
13. IMT 3058-PS.
14. FO371/21637.
15. IMT, vol. 9, pp. 275-6.
16. Hesse, pp. 59-61.
17. IMT, vol. 9, pp. 276-7.
18. The incomplete stenographic record of the meeting on 12 November 1938 is in IMT, vol. 27, 1816-PS.
19. Burckhardt, p. 228.
20. Burleigh, p. 316.
21. Ibid., p. 230.

XXII: 'I'll cook them a stew that they'll choke on'

1. Goebbels, *Tagebücher*, 1 January 1939.
2. Ibid., 3, 4, 8, 11, 15, 17 January 1939.
3. Ibid., 18, 19 January 1939.
4. Ibid., 23 January 1939.
5. ND 3575-PS.
6. Ciano Diary, II, 1 January 1939.
7. VB, 31 January 1939; Domarus, vol. II, p. 1058.
8. Henderson to Foreign Office, 18 February 1938, FO371/22965.
9. Henderson, p. 188; Henderson to Halifax, 15 and 22 February 1938, FO800/315.
10. IMT, vol. 9, p. 301.
11. Ibid.
12. Goebbels, *Tagebücher*, 11 March 1939.
13. Keitel, p. 78.
14. DGFP series D, IV, no. 209.
15. Ibid., no. 237.
16. IMT, vol. 9, p. 302.
17. Schmidt, p. 124.
18. Hoffmann, p. 94.
19. Heston, pp. 127-9.
20. IMT, vol. 9, p. 303.
21. Goebbels, *Tagebücher*, 20 March 1939.
22. Lipski, *Papers and Memoirs 1933-1939*, no. 137, quoted in Bloch, p. 219; DGFP D/VI, no. 61.
23. Polish White Book, no. 64.
24. DBFP, series 3, IV, no. 582.
25. Gisevius, p. 363.
26. British Consul in Libya's report, FO371/23808.
27. Ciano Diary, II, 15 March 1939.
28. DGFP, series D, VI, no. 211.
29. Ibid., 17 April 1939.
30. Henderson to Halifax, 3 May 1939, FO800/315.
31. Goebbels, *Tagebücher*, 28

March–15 April 1939.

32. Speer, pp. 214–15.

33. French Yellow Book, no. 123.

34. DBFP, series 3, V, nos. 377 and 510.

35. Bloch, p. 227.

36. Alfieri, *Dictators Face to Face*, p. 25, quoted in Manvell and Fraenkel, *Göring*, p. 193.

37. Ciano Diary, II, 23 May 1939.

38. IMT, vol. 37, pp. 546–56; DGFP, series D, VI, no. 433; Domarus, vol. II, pp. 1196–1201.

XXIII: 'I have the world in my pocket'

1. NCA, VI, pp. 718–31, ND 3787-PS.

2. Below, p. 24.

3. VB, 27 May 1939.

4. Speer, pp. 219–20.

5. FO371/23020.

6. Read and Fisher, *Deadly Embrace*, pp. 106–9; DGFP, series D, IV; FO317/22990.

7. FO800/316.

8. Paul, p. 191.

9. NCA, VI, pp. 390–2, ND 2751-PS.

10. Ciano Diary, II, 9 August 1939.

11. Ibid., final entry, 23 December 1943.

12. Ibid., 11 August 1939.

13. Schmidt, p. 132.

14. Ciano Diary, II, 23 December 1943.

15. Ibid., 13 August 1939.

16. Halifax, p. 209.

17. DGFP, series D, VII, no. 142.

18. Ribbentrop, pp. 92–3; Heinrich Hoffmann, p. 102.

19. Ciano Diary, II, 22 August 1939.

20. DGFP, series D, VII, nos. 183, 186; Weizsäcker, p. 201.

21. Propaganda Ministry Confidential Bulletin No. 188/39, BAK, Oberheitmann Collection, ZSg 109, quoted in Reuth, pp. 252–3.

22. Shirer, *Berlin Diary*, 24 August 1939.

23. IMT, vol. 41, pp. 16–30.

24. Irving, *Göring*, p. 258.

25. IMT, vol. 41, pp. 16–30; DGFP, series D, VII, nos. 192, 193.

26. Ibid.

XXIV: 'If we lose this war, then God have mercy on us'

1. Henderson, p. 256; DGFP, series D, VII, no. 200; DBFP, series 3, 161–3.

2. Weizsäcker, p. 252.

3. Henderson, p. 257.

4. DGFP, series D, VII, no. 271.

5. Göring's interrogation, 29 August 1945. NCA VIII, p. 354, ND TC-90.

6. Dahlerus, pp. 53–6; FO371/22982 and 22991; FO800/316.

7. Hassell, p. 64.

8. Ciano Diary, II, 26 August 1939.

9. DGFP, Series d, VII, no. 272.

10. Dahlerus, pp. 55–66.

11. Himmler Diary, quoted in Irving, *War Path*, p. 256; Bullock, *Hitler and Stalin*, pp. 694–5.

12. Weizsäcker Papers, diary entry for 29 August 1939.

13. Henderson, pp. 264–7.

14. Schmidt, pp. 150–3; Henderson, pp. 269–72.

15. IMT, vol. 34, pp. 456–9, ND C-126; NCA VI, pp. 935–9.

16. Henderson, p. 275.

17. Shirer, *Rise and Fall*, p. 722.

18. DGFP, series D, VII, no. 558; Fritz Hesse, *Hitler and the English*, pp. 83–7, quoted in Bloch, pp. 259–60.

19. Franz von Sonnleithner, *Als Diplomat im Führerhauptquartier*, p. 13, quoted in Bloch, p. 260.

20. Schmidt, pp. 156–8.

XXV: Blitzkrieg

1. Peter Hoffmann, p. 67.
2. Schmidt, pp. 159–61.
3. Irving, *Göring*, pp. 273–4.
4. DGFP, series D, VIII, no. 31.
5. Paul Latawski, in Dear and Foote, pp. 903–6.
6. IMT, vol. 2, pp. 446–7, 477; vol. 3, pp. 20–5.
7. Schmidt, p. 162.
8. DGFP, series D, VIII, pp. 140–5.
9. Halder, *Kriegstagebuch*, 27 September 1939.
10. Domarus, vol. III, p. 1393.
11. Canaris Diary, unpublished, p. 767.
12. Keitel, p. 99.
13. Ibid., p. 101.
14. Hassell, 11 October 1939.
15. Helmut Krausnick, 'Hitler und die Morde in Polen', *VfZ*, April 1963, p. 108, quoted in Höhne, p. 298.
16. 14th Army Operations Section, quoted in Höhne, p. 302.
17. Halder, *Kriegstagebuch*, 19 September 1939.
18. Halder, *Kriegstagebuch*, 20 September 1939.
19. IMT, ND 3363-PS.
20. Shirer, *Rise and Fall*, p. 795.
21. IMT, vol. 1, p. 297.
22. Ibid., vol. 26, pp. 255–7, ND 686-PS.
23. IfZ, ZS 627 (General Wilhelm Ulex) Fol. 124, quoted in Kershaw, *Nemesis*, p. 248.
24. Shirer, *Rise and Fall*, p. 797; Read and Fisher, *Deadly Embrace*, pp. 359–60.
25. IMT, vol. 4, p. 547, ND EC-410.
26. Ibid., p. 543, ND 1375-PS.
27. Goebbels, *Tagebücher*, 10 October 1939.
28. Ibid., 2 November 1939.
29. Ibid., 17 October 1939.

XXVI: 'Yellow'

1. Hassell, p. 102, quoting Ilse Göring.
2. Below, p. 50.
3. BAK, R55/422, quoted in Reuth, p. 280.
4. Speer, pp. 243–4.
5. Ibid., p. 244; Sereny, p. 216.
6. IMT, ND EC-606.
7. Welles, p. 75.
8. Ibid., pp. 76–8.
9. Below, p. 54.
10. DGFP, series D, VIII, no. 663.
11. Churchill, *Gathering Storm*, p. 531.
12. Ibid., IX, no. 53.
13. IMT, vol. 9, pp. 337–9.
14. Dear and Foot, p. 318; Shirer, *Rise and Fall*, p. 870.
15. Hitler, *Secret Conversations*, p. 94.
16. Churchill, *Finest Hour*, p. 38.
17. Schmidt, p. 176.
18. Jodl Diary, unpublished. In Imperial War Museum, London, 24 May 1940.
19. Shirer, *Rise and Fall*, pp. 879–80.
20. Churchill, *Finest Hour*, pp. 102–4.
21. Ciano Diary, II, 18–19 June 1940.
22. Shirer, *Berlin Diary*, 21 June 1940.

XXVII: Eagles and Sea Lions

1. Goebbels, *Tagebücher*, 3 July 1940.
2. Speer, pp. 248–9.
3. Goebbels, *Tagebücher*, 13 and 23 June 1940.
4. Willi A. Boelcke (ed.), *Kriegspropaganda 1939–1941: Geheime Ministerkonferenzen im Reichspropagandaministerium* (Stuttgart, 1966), p. 417, quoted

in Reuth, p. 273.

5. Karl Klee, *Dokumente zum Unternehmen Seelöwe*, p. 296: letter from Major Freiherr Sigismund von Falkenstein to General Otto Hoffmann von Waldau, 25 June 1940, quoted in Irving, *Göring*, p. 292.

6. Shirer, *Berlin Diary*, 19 July 1940.

7. Domarus, vol. III, pp. 1540–59.

8. Churchill, *Finest Hour*, pp. 229–30.

9. Shirer, *Berlin Diary*, 23 July 1940.

10. Malcolm Smith, in Dear and Foot, p. 159.

11. PRO, Premier Papers, 3/14/2.

12. Shirer, *Berlin Diary*, 26 August 1940.

13. Domarus, vol. III, p. 1580.

14. IMT, vol. 9, p. 340.

15. Malcolm Smith, in Dear and Foot, p. 163.

16. Alfred Price, in Dear and Foot, pp. 138–9.

17. IMT, vol. 9, p. 340.

18. Goebbels, *Tagebücher*, 29 March and 1 April 1941.

19. Ciano Diary, II, 12 October 1940.

20. DGFP, series D, vol. XI, no. 118.

21. Schmidt, p. 215.

22. Berezhkov, p. 28.

23. Churchill, *Finest Hour*, p. 516.

24. Nazi–Soviet Relations, pp. 218ff.; Churchill, *Finest Hour*, pp. 512–18; Berezhkov, pp. 33–18; Schmidt, pp. 209–20.

XXVIII: 'The whole wold will hold its breath'

1. Shirer, *Berlin Diary*, 1 December 1940.

2. Dear and Foot, p. 1288; Höhne, p. 462; Padfield, *Himmler*, p. 300.

3. Hans-Günther Seraphim, 'SS Verfügungstruppe and Wehrmacht', in *Wehrwissenschaftliche Rundschau*, 12 (1955), quoted in Höhne, p. 457.

4. IMT, vol. 9, p. 415.

5. G.H. Stein, *The Waffen SS*, table reproduced in Dear and Foot, pp. 1047–8.

6. Helmut Krausnik et al, 'Denkschrift Himmlers über die Behandlung der Fremdvölkischen im Osten (Mai 1940)', *VfZ* 5 (1957), pp. 194–8.

7. Instruction sheet from Heyde Trial Documents, pp. 210–11, reproduced in Lifton, p. 69.

8. Lifton, pp. 71–2, Heyde Trial Documents, in Lifton, pp. 293–5.

9. Lifton, pp. 78–9.

10. Nazi–Soviet Relations, pp. 260–2; IMT, vol. 26, pp. 47–52.

11. Schellenberg, p. 179.

12. Domarus, vol. III, pp. 1652–3.

13. Schnurre, personal interview with the author.

14. DGFP, series D, vol. 9, no. 640.

15. Combined Services Detailed Interrogation Centre, GRGG 354, quoted in Irving, *Göring*, p. 312.

16. Keitel, pp. 138–9.

17. DGFP, series D, vol. 12, nos. 383–5; IMT, vol. 15, p. 422, Jodl testimony; IMT, vol. 9, pp. 333ff, Göring testimony.

18. Bloch, p. 323.

19. IMT, vol. 9, p. 336.

20. Goralski, p. 158.

21. Alfred Price, in Dear and Foot, p. 140.

22. Schmidt, p. 233.

23. Speer, p. 250.

24. Ibid., p. 251.

25. Domarus, vol. III, p. 1714.
26. Goebbels, *Tagebücher*, 14 May 1941.
27. Speer, p. 253.
28. Goebbels, *Tagebücher*, 6 March 1943.
29. Trevor-Roper, *Last Days of Hitler*, p. 45.
30. Heinrich Hoffmann.
31. Rosenberg, *Letzte Aufzeichnungen*, quoted in Fest, *Face of the Third Reich*, p. 198.
32. Speer, p. 252.
33. Halder, Kriegstagebuch, 8 May 1941.
34. MacDonald, p. 301; Dear and Foot, pp. 275–7.

XXIX: 'The greatest deception operation in military history'

1. Galland, *The First and the Last,* quoted in Mosley, pp. 272–3.
2. IMT, vol. 9, p. 349; ND 2718-PS.
3. IMT, vol. 4, pp. 4–7; ND EC-126.
4. Goebbels, *Tagebücher*, 31 May 1941.
5. Semler, p. 39.
6. Goebbels, *Tagebücher*, 14 and 15 June 1941.
7. Ciano Diary, II, 2 June 1941.
8. Read and Fisher, *Deadly Embrace*, pp. 598–9, quoting Dahlerus and Welles.
9. Berezhkov, p. 72.
10. Whaley, p. 179; Read and Fisher, *Deadly Embrace*, pp. 598–9, quoting Wheatley.
11. Kersten, p. 173.
12. Warlimont, p. 123; Halder, 13 March 1941; IMT, ND PS-447.
13. Götz Aly, *'Endlösung': Völkerverschiebung und der Mord an den europäischen Juden* (Frankfurt am Main, 1995), quoted in Kershaw, *Nemesis*, p. 354.
14. Halder, *Kriegstagebuch*, vol. 2, pp. 335–7 (30 March 1941); Warlimont, p. 162; IMT, vol. 7, pp. 396–7.
15. Below, p. 102.
16. Mosley, pp. 274–5, interview with Kammhuber.
17. DGFP, series D, vol. 12, no. 660.
18. Goebbels, *Tagebücher*, 22 June 1941.
19. Schmidt, p. 234.
20. Ibid., pp. 234–5; Read and Fisher, *Deadly Embrace,* pp. 637–9; Sommer, *Das Memorandum,* pp. 164–9, 245–66, and personal interviews; Berezhkov, pp. 76–9.

XXX: Barbarossa

1. Erickson, *Road to Stalingrad*, p. 98; Dear and Foot, p. 109; DRZW, vol. IV, p. 72.
2. Kershaw, *Nemesis*, p. 393; Read and Fisher, p. 7; Dear and Foot, p. 109–10.
3. Peter Hoffmann, pp. 216–31.
4. Paul, p. 219.
5. Schmidt, pp. 248–9.
6. Goebbels, *Tagebücher*, 30 June, 1, 5, 30 July 1941; Domarus, vol. III, p. 1740, n. 323.
7. Halder, *Kriegstagebuch*, pp. 446–7, 3 July 1941.
8. *OKW KTB*, vol. I, p. 1021; DRZW, vol. IV, p. 487.
9. IMT, vol. 34, pp. 298–302; ND C-74.
10. IMT, vol. 38, pp. 86–94; ND L-221; DGFP, series D, no. 114.
11. Erickson, *Road to Stalingrad*, pp. 138, 141–2; Read and Fisher, *Deadly Embrace*, p. 648.
12. Read and Fisher, pp. 650–1.
13. Ernst Heinkel, *Stürmisches*

Leben, quoted in Paul, p. 222–3.

14. Ibid.

15. K. Wolff, 'Eichmanns Chef Heinrich Himmler', Neue Illustrierte, 23 April 1961; case for the prosection against Karl Wolff, Provincial Court Munich II, reference 10a Js 39/60, quoted in Höhne, pp. 365–6; Padfield, Himmler, pp. 342–3.

16. Noakes and Pridham, Nazism, vol. III, no. 824.

17. Ibid., no. 826.

18. Ibid., no. 825; IMT, vol. 9, pp. 517–20, ND 710-PS.

19. Höss, pp. 207–8.

20. Kershaw, Nemesis, p. 468; IMT ND NO-3137.

21. Ibid.; Martin Gilbert, pp. 201–6; Höhne, pp. 360–1; Goralski, p. 176.

22. Gerald Fleming, Hitler und die Endlösung (Wiesbaden/Munich, 1981), p. 86, quoted in Kershaw, Nemesis, p. 464.

23. Halder, Kriegstagebuch, p. 506, 11 August 1941.

24. Goebbels, Tagebücher, 19 August 1941.

25. Bloch, p. 338.

26. Keitel, p. 177.

27. Goebbels, Tagebücher, 18, 19, 20 August 1941.

28. Das Reich, 16 November 1941.

29. McGovern, pp. 65–6.

30. Goebbels, Tagebücher, 15 August 1941.

31. Mosley, pp. 277–8, quoting Bodenschatz; Paul, pp. 221–2.

32. Bullock, Hitler and Stalin, p. 810, quoting A. Zoller (ed.), Hitler Privat (Düsseldorf, 1949), p. 160.

33. Domarus, vol. III, pp. 1759–63.

34. Goebbels, Tagebücher, 10 October 1941; Semmler, p. 56.

35. Keitel, p. 166.

XXXI: The Final Solution

1. DGFP, series D, no. 512.

2. Schmidt, pp. 236–7.

3. IMT, vol. 10, p. 297.

4. Ciano Diary, II, 8 December 1941.

5. Weizsäcker, p. 328.

6. Schmidt, pp. 237–8.

7. Goebbels, Tagebücher, 8 December 1941.

8. Goebbels, Das eherne Herz: Reden und Aufsätze aus den Jahren 1941/42, pp. 134f., quoted in Reuth, p. 301.

9. Halder, Hitler als Feldherr, p. 45.

10. Goralski, pp. 204–5.

11. Ciano Diary, II, 4 February 1942.

12. Speer, p. 283.

13. Ibid.

14. Ibid., pp. 283–5.

15. Ibid., pp. 285–6.

16. Ibid., pp. 288–90.

17. Ibid., pp. 290–1.

18. Keitel, p. 168.

19. Ibid., pp. 168–9.

20. Schellenberg, p. 358.

21. Below, p. 148.

22. Dear and Foot, pp. 690, 279; Foot, SOE, pp. 200–1.

23. Martin Gilbert, p. 177.

24. Goebbels, Tagebücher, 24 September 1941.

25. Höhne, p. 378.

26. IMT, vol. 42, p. 546.

27. IMT, ND NG-2586-G; Noakes and Pridham, Nazism, vol. III, no. 849.

28. Eichmann pre-trial interrogation, used in the Eichmann Trial, 20 June 1961, session 75, quoted in Martin Gilbert, p. 283.

29. SS-Obersturmführer Kurt Gerstein, quoted in Höhne, pp. 375–6.

30. Padfield, pp. 389–95; Höss, pp. 207–8.

31. Höss, pp. 207–8.
32. NA, T-175, RFSS Microfilm 122.

XXXII: The Beginning of the End

1. Goebbels, *Tagebücher*, 19 March 1942.
2. Speer, pp. 308–9.
3. ND 016-PS.
4. IMT, vol. 7, p. 260.
5. Zhukov, pp. 388–424; Erickson, *Road to Stalingrad*, 430–72; Read and Fisher, *Fall of Berlin*, pp. 98–9.
6. Halder, *Hitler als Feldherr*, pp. 50–2.
7. Domarus, vol. III, p. 1931.
8. Telephone conversation tapped by Italians: Ugo Cavallero, *Diario* (Rome, 1948), quoted in Irving, *Göring*, pp. 365–6.
9. Ibid., p. 366.
10. NA film T84/6/5269 and 5870ff., quoted in ibid., pp. 366 and 536 (notes).
11. Below, p. 157.
12. Ribbentrop, pp. 168–9; NCA, Supplement B, pp. 1203–4, 1241; Bloch, p. 361.
13. Domarus, vol. III, p. 1938.
14. Below, pp. 157–8.
15. Mosley, p. 295, quoting record of interrogation of Göring by US Military Intelligence at Augsburg interrogation centre, May 1945.
16. Beevor, Appendix 1, pp. 439–40.
17. Rommel pp. 366–9; Young, pp. 179–80; Mosley, p. 292; Manvell and Fraenkel, *Göring*, p. 254.
18. Ibid.
19. Schmidt, p. 260.
20. Milch Diary and handwritten note, quoted in Irving, *Göring*, p. 373.
21. Ciano Diary, II, 1 December 1942.
22. Ibid., 2 December 1942.
23. Ibid., 3 December 1942.
24. Goebbels, *Tagebücher*, 23 January 1942.
25. D.F. Morzik, *German Air Force Airlift Operations*, p. 191, quoted in Beevor, p. 360.
26. Domarus, vol. III, p. 1974.
27. Ibid., p. 1979.

XXXIII: 'Do you want total war?'

1. IMT, vol. 9, p. 440.
2. Paul, p. 233.
3. Overy, *Iron Man*, p. 212.
4. Irving, *Göring*, p. 377.
5. Goebbels, *Tagebücher*, 8 February 1943.
6. Below, p. 164.
7. BA-MA, MD 57, 3046; and shorthand notes taken by Koller, quoted in Irving, *Göring*, pp. 378–9.
8. Goebbels, *Tagebücher*, 2 February 1942.
9. Heiber *Goebbels Reden 1939–1945*, pp. 172ff.
10. Speer, p. 355.
11. Goebbels, *Tagebücher*, 2 March 1943.
12. Speer, p. 357.
13. Ibid., p. 358.
14. Speer, p. 360.
15. Speer, Nuremberg draft memoirs, quoted in Sereny, p. 373.
16. Goralski, p. 257.
17. Goebbels, *Tagebücher*, 1 March 1943.
18. Ibid., 2 March 1943.
19. Ibid.
20. Ibid.
21. Sereny, p. 374.
22. BA-MA, MD 62, 546ff., quoted in Irving, *Göring*, pp. 382–3.
23. Speer, pp. 364–5; Sereny, p. 375.
24. Speer, pp. 364–5.
25. Read and Fisher, *Fall of Berlin*, p. 114.

26. Peter Hoffmann, *Hitler's Personal Security*, p. 258.

27. Trevor-Roper, *The Bormann Letters*, p. 126.

28. Bracher, p. 519.

29. IMT, ND 2171-PS.

30. Norman Davies, *God's Playground: A History of Poland*, vol. II, p. 463, quoted in Bullock, *Hitler and Stalin*, p. 892.

31. IMT, ND 1919-PS.

32. Joanna Hanson, in Dear and Foot, p. 1260; Padfield, *Himmler*, p. 448; Martin Gibert, pp. 557ff.

33. NCA, vol. 3, pp. 719–75, ND 1061-PS.

34. *The Crime of Katyn*, pp. 101, 114ff., 214ff.

35. Irving, *Göring*, p. 384.

36. Goebbels, *Tagebücher*, 16 and 25 May 1943.

37. Semmler, p. 88.

38. Fitzsimons, pp. 92–3.

39. Dear and Foot, p. 523.

40. Galland, quoted in Fitzsimons, p. 93.

XXXIV: 'Call Me Meier!'

1. Felix Gilbert, pp. 40, 44.

2. Galland, quoted in Mosely, p. 303.

3. Ibid., p. 304.

4. Dear and Foot, p. 1001.

5. Goralski, p. 277.

6. Ibid.

7. Below, p. 179.

8. Martin Gilbert, p. 623.

9. Noble Frankland, *Bombing: the RAF Case*, in Fitzsimons, p. 145.

10. Semmler, p. 97.

11. PRO: WO208/4133.

12. Goebbels, *Tagebücher*, 30 November 1943.

13. Goebbels telegrams to Hitler, Christmas 1943 and New Year 1944, BAK, NL 118/100, quoted in Reuth, p. 324.

14. Below, p. 197.

15. IMT, vol. 9, pp. 355–7.

16. Ibid., pp. 357–60.

17. PRO WO208/685A; FO Report no. 794, H. Knatchbull Hugesson to Foreign Office.

18. Fleischhauer, pp. 183–4.

19. Dear and Foot, p. 853.

20. Bullock, *Hitler and Stalin*, p. 919; Irving, *Göring*, p. 427.

21. Goralski, pp. 319, 329, 335.

XXXV: Last Throw of the Dice

1. Schlabrendorff, pp. 103ff; Peter Hoffmann, *German Resistance*, pp. 317–24.

2. Kersten, p. 201.

3. Bloch, p. 403n.

4. Trevor-Roper, *Last Days of Hitler*, pp. 35–6.

5. Ibid.

6. J. von Lang, *Der Adjutant: Karl Wolff; Der Mann zwischen Hitler und Himmler* (Herbig, Munich, 1985), p. 251, quoted in Padfield, *Himmler*, p. 509.

7. Speer, p. 520.

8. Karl Thöt diary, quoted in Irving, *Göring*, p. 433.

9. Shirer, *Rise and Fall*, p. 1286.

10. Schlabrendorff, p. 113.

11. Trial details: Peter Hoffmann, *German Resistance*, pp. 525–7.

12. Execution details: Gedenkstätte Deutscher Widerstand.

13. Peter Hoffmann, *German Resistance*, p. 527.

14. Peter Longerich, *Joseph Goebbels und der Totale Krieg*, pp. 289ff., quoted in Reuth, pp. 329–30.

15. Semmler, pp. 146–7.

16. Goebbels, *Tagebücher*, 23 July 1944.

17. Reimann, p. 305.
18. Ibid., p. 306.
19. Veit Harlan, *Im Schatten meiner Filme: Selbstbiographie* (Gütersloh, 1966), pp. 184, 187–8, quoted in Kershaw, *Nemesis*, p. 713.
20. Fritz Hesse, *Das Spiel um Deutschland* (Munich 1953), *Hitler and the English* (London 1954), pp. 190–2, quoted in Martin Gilbert, p. 711, and Bloch, p. 416.
21. Erickson, *Road to Berlin*, note 84, Chapter 14; Padfield, *Himmler*, p. 524.
22. Hanson, pp. 85, 202; and in Dear and Foot, pp. 1261–2.
23. Guderian, p. 356.
24. Sereny, pp. 309–10.
25. Personal communication to author from the late F.W. Winterbotham.
26. Speer, p. 751, n 19.
27. Padfield, pp. 540–3; IfZ, MA 315, frames 2614201ff.
28. Willemer, pp. 40–2.
29. Dornberger, quoted in Paul, p. 243.
30. Goebbels, *Tagebücher*, 4 December 1944.
31. Semmler, pp. 174–5.
32. Callum Macdonald, *The Battle of the Bulge* (Macmillan 1984), quoted in Dear and Foot, p. 52.
33. Paul, p. 248.
34. HG order No 11, 16 January 1945, BA-MA, Lw 104/3, quoted in Irving, *Göring*, p. 451.

XXXVI: Götterdämmerung

1. Guderian, p. 315; the late Lt-Gen Bernd Freytag von Loringhoven, personal interview.
2. Hitler's condition: Freytag von Loringhoven, interview; Guderian, p. 443; Boldt,
   pp. 39–40, 82.
3. Guderian, p. 315.
4. Speer, pp. 566–7.
5. Guderian, p. 334; Read and Fisher, *Fall of Berlin*, p. 223.
6. Czech, p. 804; Erickson, *Road to Berlin*, 459; Read and Fisher, *Fall of Berlin*, p. 212.
7. Goebbels, *Tagebücher*, 28 January 1945.
8. Toland, *The Last 100 Days*, p. 17.
9. Speer, pp. 567–8.
10. Ibid.
11. Ibid., p. 577.
12. Domarus, vol. III, pp. 2195–8.
13. Trevor-Roper, *The Bormann Letters*, p. 164.
14. Speer, p. 571.
15. Chuikov, p. 120.
16. Guderian, 324–44; Freytag von Loringhoven, interview.
17. NA film T321/10/6800ff, quoted in Irving, *Göring*, p. 454 and note.
18. Semmler, pp. 180–1.
19. Goebbels, *Tagebücher*, 28 February 1945.
20. Semmler, p. 179.
21. R. Hewins, *Count Folke Bernadotte: His Life and Work* (Hutchinson, 1949), pp. 109, 118, quoted in Padfield, *Himmler*, p. 565.
22. Kersten, pp. 276–7.
23. Goebbels, *Tagebücher*, 16 March 1945.
24. Heinrici papers; Read and Fisher, *Fall of Berlin*, pp. 264–6; Ryan, pp. 82–5; Toland, *The Last 100 Days*, pp. 260–1.
25. Guderian, pp. 340–3.
26. Goebbels, *Tagebücher*, 11 March 1945.
27. Ibid., 14 March 1945.
28. Semmler, p. 185.
29. *Zeitschrift für Militärgeschichte*,

no. 2, 1965, GDR Military Publishing House, Potsdam.

30. Goebbels, *Tagebücher*, 11 March 1945.
31. Ibid., 26 March 1945.
32. Ibid., 31 March 1945.
33. Trevor-Roper, *The Bormann Letters*, pp. 177–8.
34. Speer, pp. 618–19; Ryan, pp. 142–4, 292–3, 302–3.
35. Speer, p. 619.
36. Semmler, pp. 192ff.
37. Speer, p. 619.
38. Erickson, *Road to Berlin*, p. 538; Chuikov, p. 140.

XXXVII: The End of the Road

1. Reimann, pp. 313–15.
2. Keitel, p. 198.
3. Speer, p. 633.
4. Irving, *Göring*, p. 460, quoting SAIC/X/5, 24 May 1945.
5. Koller, p. 21.
6. Ibid., pp. 45–50.
7. Keitel, pp. 200–3; Boldt, pp. 121–4; Koller, p. 54; Freytag von Loringhoven, interview.
8. Schellenberg, p. 448.
9. Speer, p. 644.
10. Keitel, p. 214.
11. Paul, p. 259.
12. Ibid., pp. 649–50.
13. IMT, ND 3569-PS.
14. NA Washington, NND 901065, Folder 2; Traudl Junge memoirs (unpublished).
15. Read and Fisher, *Fall of Berlin*, pp. 457–61; Chuikov, pp. 213–30; Dufving, personal interview.
16. Read and Fisher, *Fall of Berlin*, p. 463, Weidling diary.
17. Marian G. Streinert, *Die 23 Tage der Regierung Dönitz* (Düsseldorf 1967), p. 107, quoted in Bloch, p. 429.
18. Bloch, p. 433.
19. SAIC/13; Mosley, pp. 322–3; Paul, p. 265.
20. Andrus, p. 29.
21. Montgomery Hyde, *Lord Birkett* (Hamish Hamilton, 1964); Manvell and Fraenkel, *Göring*, p. 351.

SELECT BIBLIOGRAPHY

Unless indicated otherwise the place of publication is London.

ANDRUS, BURTON C. *The Infamous of Nuremberg* Leslie Frewin, 1969

ARONSON, SHLOMO *Reinhard Heydrich und die Frühgeschichte von Gestapo und SD* Stuttgart, Deutsche Verlagsanstalt, 1971

BARRACLOUGH, GEOFFREY *The Origins of Modern Germany*, Blackwell, 1979

BAYNES, N.H. (ed.) *The Speeches of Adolf Hitler, April 1922 – August 1939* (2 vols) Oxford, Oxford University Press, 1942

BEEVOR, ANTONY *Stalingrad* Penguin, 1999

BELOW, NICOLAUS VON *At Hitler's Side: The Memoirs of Hitler's Luftwaffe Adjutant 1937–1945* Greenhill Books, 2001

BENNECKE, HEINRICH *Hitler und die SA* Munich and Vienna, Günter Olzog, 1962

BEREZHKOV, VALENTIN *History in the Making* Moscow, Progress Publishers, 1982

Berlin Handbuch: Das Lexikon der Bundeshauptstadt Berlin, FAB, 1992

BEWLEY, CHARLES *Hermann Göring and the Third Reich: A Biography Based on Family and Official Records* New York, Devin-Adair, 1962

BLOCH, MICHAEL *Ribbentrop* Bantam, 1992

BLOOD-RYAN, A.W. *Göring, the Iron Man of Germany* Long, 1938

BODENSCHATZ, KARL *Jagd in Flanders Himmel* Munich, Knorr und Sirth, 1935

BOLDT, GERHARD *Die letzten Tage* Hamburg, Rowohlt, 1947

BOYD, CARL *The Extraordinary Envoy: General Hiroshi Oshima and*

Diplomacy in the Third Reich, 1934–1939 Washington, DC, University Press of America, 1980

BRACHER, KARL DIETRICH *The German Dictatorship: The Origins, Structure and Consequences of National Socialism* Penguin, 1991

BRENDON, PIERS *The Dark Valley: A Panorama of the Thirties* Cape, 2000

BROWDER, GEORGE C. *Foundations of the Nazi Police State: The Formation of Sipo and SD* Lexington, Kentucky, University of Kentucky Press, 1990
Hitler's Enforcers: The Gestapo and the SS Security Service in the Nazi Revolution New York, Oxford University Press, 1996

BUCHHEIM, HANS; BROSZAT, MARTIN; KRAUSNICK, HELMUT; JACOBSEN, HANS-ADOLF *The Anatomy of the SS State* Collins, 1968

BULLOCK, ALAN *Hitler: A Study in Tyranny* Penguin, 1983
Hitler and Stalin: Parallel Lives HarperCollins, 1991

BURCKHARDT, CARL J. *Meine Danziger Mission, 1937–1939* Munich, Verlag Georg D.W. Callwey, 1960

BURLEIGH, MICHAEL *The Third Reich: A New History* Macmillan, 2000

CECIL, ROBERT *The Myth of the Master Race: Rosenberg and the Nazi Ideology* Batsford, 1972

CHANNON, HENRY *The Ludwigs of Bavaria* Methuen, 1933

CHUIKOV, V.I. *The End of the Third Reich* Moscow, Progress Publishers, 1978

CHURCHILL, WINSTON S. *The Second World War, Vol 1: The Gathering Storm; Vol 2: Their Finest Hour* Penguin, 1985

CIANO, GALLEAZO (ed. Malcolm Muggeridge) *Ciano's Diary, 1937–1938*, Collins, 1952
(ed. Hugh Gibson) *The Ciano Diaries 1939–1943*, New York, Doubleday, 1946

COCKS, GEOFFREY *Psychotherapy in the Third Reich: The Göring Institute* New York, Oxford University Press, 1985

CORNISH, KIMBERLEY *The Jew of Linz: Wittgenstein, Hitler and their Secret Battle for the Mind* Century, 1998

The Crime of Katyn: Facts and Documents Polish Cultural Foundation, 1965

CZECH, DANUTA *Auschwitz Chronicles 1939–45* I.B. Tauris, 1990

DAHLERUS, BIRGER *The Last Attempt* Hutchinson, 1948

DEAR, I.C.B. and FOOT, M.R.D (eds) *The Oxford Companion to the*

Second World War Oxford and New York, Oxford University Press, 1995

Der Hitler-Prozess Munich, Deutscher Volksverlag, 1924

DELMER, SEFTON *Trail Sinister* Secker & Warburg, 1961

DEUERLEIN, ERNST *Der Aufstieg der NSDAP 1919–1933 in Augenzeugenberichten* Düsseldorf, Rauch, 1968

DIELS, RUDOLF *Lucifer ante Portas* Stuttgart, Deutsche Verlagsanstalt, 1950

DIMITROV, GEORGI, et al *The Reichstag Fire Trial* John Lane/The Bodley Head, 1934

DOMARUS, MAX (ed.) *Hitler: Reden und Proklamationen 1932-45* (4 vols) Munich, Süddeutscher Verlag, 1965

ERICKSON, JOHN *The Road to Stalingrad: Stalin's War with Germany, Vol. 1* Weidenfeld and Nicolson, 1983
The Road to Berlin: Stalin's War with Germany, Vol. 2 Weidenfeld and Nicolson, 1983

FEST, JOACHIM C. *The Face of the Third Reich* Weidenfeld and Nicolson, 1970
Hitler Weidenfeld and Nicolson, 1974

FITZSIMONS, BERNARD (ed.) *Warplanes and Air Battles of World War II* Phoebus, 1973

FLEISCHHAUER, INGEBORG *Die Chance des Sonderfriedens: Deutsch-sowjetische Geheimgespräche 1941–1945,* Berlin, Siedler, 1986

FOOT, M.R.D *SOE: An Outline History of the Special Operations Executive 1940–46* BBC, 1984

FRANÇOIS-PONCET, ANDRÉ *The Fateful Years* Gollancz, 1949

FRANK, HANS *Im Angesicht des Galgens* Munich, Gräfelfing, 1953

FRENCH YELLOW BOOK *Documents Diplomatiques Français, 1938–9* Paris, Ministère des Affaires Étrangères

FREI, NORBERT *National Socialist Rule in Germany: The Führer State 1933–1945* Blackwell, 1993

FRISCHAUER, WILLI *Goering* Odhams, 1951
Himmler: The Evil Genius of the Third Reich Odhams, 1953

FRITZSCHE, HANS *The Sword in the Scales – as told to Hildegard Springer* (trs. Diana Pike and Heinrich Fraeker) Alan Wingate, 1953

GALLAND, ADOLF *The First and the Last* Methuen, 1955

GILBERT, FELIX (ed.) *Hitler Directs His War* New York, Oxford University Press, 1951

GILBERT, G.M. *Nuremberg Diary* Eyre & Spottiswoode, 1948

GILBERT, MARTIN *The Holocaust: The Jewish Tragedy* Collins, 1986

GISEVIUS, HANS BERND *To the Bitter End* Westport, Connecticut, Greenwood Press, 1975

GOEBBELS, JOSEPH *Die Tagebücher von Joseph Goebbels: Sämtliche Fragmente*, edited by Elke Fröhlich for the Institut für Zeitgeschichte, Munich, in collaboration with the Bundesarchiv, Munich, K.G. Saur, 1987, 1995, 2000
Die Zweite Revolution: Briefe an Zeitgenossen Zwickau, 1926
Vom Kaiserhof zur Reichskanzlei Munich, Eher, 1934
Revolution der Deutschen: 14 Jahre Nationalsozialismus Oldenburg, 1933
Kampf um Berlin Munich, Eher, 1934
My Part in Germany's Fight Hurst & Blackett, 1935

GOLDHAGEN, DANIEL JONAH *Hitler's Willing Executioners: Ordinary Germans and the Holocaust* Abacus, 1997

GORDON, HAROLD J. *Hitler and the Beer Hall Putsch* Princeton, NJ, Princeton University Press, 1972

GRABER, G.S. *History of the SS* Robert Hale, 1978

GRITZBACH, ERICH *Hermann Göring: The Man and his Work* Hurst and Blackett, 1939

GRUNBERGER, RICHARD *A Social History of the Third Reich* Penguin, 1974

GUDERIAN, HEINZ *Panzer Leader* New York, Ballantine Books, 1952

HALDER, COLONEL-GENERAL FRANZ *Kriegstagebuch* Kohlhammer, Stuttgart, 1963
Hitler als Feldherr, Munich, Münchener-Dom Verlag, 1949

HALE, ORON J. *The Captive Press in the Third Reich* Princeton, NJ, Princeton University Press, 1964

HALIFAX, LORD *Fulness of Days* Collins, 1957

HANSER, RICHARD *Prelude to Terror: The Rise of Hitler 1919–1923* Rupert Hart-Davis, 1971

HANSON, JOANNA K.M. *The Civilian Population and the Warsaw Uprising of 1944*, Cambridge University Press, 1982

HASSELL, ULRICH VON *The Von Hassell Diaries, 1938–1944* Hamish Hamilton, 1948

HAUNER, MILAN *Hitler: A Chronology of his Life and Time* Macmillan, 1983

HEIBER, HELMUT (ed.) *Reichsführer: Briefe an und von Himmler* Stuttgart, Deutsche Verlagsanstalt, 1968
Goebbels Reden 1932–1939 Munich, 1971

Goebbels Reden 1939–1945 Munich, 1972

HEIDEN, KONRAD *Geschichte des Nationalsozialismus* Berlin, Rowohlt, 1932
Der Führer Gollancz, 1944

HENDERSON, SIR NEVILE *Failure of a Mission: Berlin 1938–1939* Hodder and Stoughton, 1940

HERWARTH, HANS VON with STARR, S. FREDERICK *Against Two Evils* New York, Rawson, Wade, 1981

HESSE, FRITZ *Hitler and the English* Wingate, 1954

HESTON, LEONARD and RENATA *The Medical Casebook of Adolf Hitler* Kimber, 1979

HEYDRICH, LINA *Leben mit einem Kriegsverbrecher* Pfaffenhofen, Verlag W. Ludwig, 1976

HILDEBRAND, KLAUS *The Third Reich* Routledge, 1991

HITLER, ADOLF *Mein Kampf* Hutchinson, 1969
Hitler's Secret Conversations New York, Signet, 1961
The Testament of Adolf Hitler: The Hitler–Bormann Documents, Cassell, 1961
Hitler. Reden, Schriften, Anordnungen: Februar 1925 bis Januar 1933 (5 vols) Munich, Institut für Zeitgeschichte, 1992–8

HOFFMANN, HEINRICH *Hitler Was My Friend* Burke, 1955

HOFFMANN, PETER *The History of the German Resistance* Macdonald and Jane's, 1977
Hitler's Personal Security Cambridge, Mass, MIT, 1979

HÖHNE, HEINZ *The Order of the Death's Head: The Story of Hitler's SS* Secker & Warburg, 1969

HÖSS, RUDOLF *Commandant of Auschwitz* Weidenfeld and Nicolson, 1959

HYDE, H. MONTGOMERY *Lord Birkett* Hamish Hamilton, 1964

IRVING, DAVID *The War Path: Hitler's Germany 1933–1939* Macmillan, 1983
Hitler's War Macmillan, 1983
Göring Macmillan, 1989

ISHERWOOD, CHRISTOPHER *Berlin Stories* New York, New Directions, 1963

JÄCKEL, EBERHARD and KUHN, EXEL (eds) *Hitler: Sämtliche Aufzeichnungen 1905–1924,* Stuttgart, 1980

JOCHMANN, WERNER (ed.) *Nationalsozialismus und Revolution: Ursprung und Geschichte der NSDAP in Hamburg 1922–1933. Dokumente* Frankfurt am Main, 1963

KEEGAN, JOHN *The First World War* Pimlico, 1999

KEITEL, FIELD MARSHAL WILHELM *Memoirs* Kimber, 1965

KELLEY, DOUGLAS M. *22 Cells in Nuremberg*, W.H. Allen, 1947

KERSHAW, IAN *Hitler 1889–1936: Hubris* Allen Lane, The Penguin Press, 1998

Hitler 1936–1945: Nemesis Allen Lane, The Penguin Press, 2000

KERSTEN, FELIX *The Kersten Memoirs 1940–1945* Hutchinson, 1956

KLOTZ, HELMUT *The Berlin Diaries* Jarrolds, 1934

KNOPP, GUIDO *Hitlers Helfer* Munich, Goldmann, 1996

KOCH, H.W. (ed.) *Aspects of the Third Reich* Macmillan, 1985

KOEHL, R.L. *The Black Corps: The Structure and Power Struggles of the Nazi SS* Madison, Wisconsin, University of Wisconsin Press, 1983

KOLLER, KARL *Der letzte Monat* Munich, Bechtle, 1985

KORDT, ERICH *Nicht aus den Akten: Die Wilhelmstrasse in Frieden und Krieg* Stuttgart, 1950

LARGE, DAVID CLAY *Between Two Fires: Europe's Path in the 1930s* New York, Norton, 1990

LEWIN, RONALD *Ultra Goes to War: The Secret Story* Hutchinson, 1978

LIFTON, ROBERT JAY *The Nazi Doctors: Medical Killing and the Psychology of Genocide* New York, Basic Books, 1986

LUDECKE, KURT *I Knew Hitler* Jarrolds, 1938

MacDONALD, CALLUM *The Lost Battle: Crete 1941* Macmillan, 1993

McGOVERN, JAMES *Martin Bormann* Arthur Barker, 1968

MANVELL, ROGER and FRAENKEL, HEINRICH
Doctor Goebbels: His Life and Death Heinemann, 1960
Hermann Göring Heinemann, 1962
Heinrich Himmler Heinemann, 1965
Adolf Hitler: The Man and the Myth Granada, 1978

MARLEY, LORD *The Brown Book of the Hitler Terror and the Burning of the Reichstag* John Lane/The Bodley Head, 1933

MASER, WERNER *Die Frühgeschichte der NSDAP: Hitlers Weg bis 1924* Frankfurt, Athenäum, 1965

MEISSNER, HANS-OTTO *Magda Goebbels: A Biography* Sidgwick & Jackson, 1980

MOSLEY, LEONARD *The Reich Marshal: A Biography of Hermann Goering* Weidenfeld and Nicolson, 1974

MÜLLER, Karl-Alexander von *Im Wandel einer Welt. Erinnerungen 1919–1932* Munich, 1966

Nazi–Soviet Relations, 1939–41. Documents from the Archives of the German Foreign Office Washington, D.C., US Department of State, 1948

NOAKES, J. and PRIDHAM, G. (eds) *Documents on Nazism* Jonathan Cape, 1974
(eds) *Nazism 1919–1945: A Documentary Reader* (4 vols) Exeter, 1983-98

OVEN, WILFRED VON *Mit Goebbels bis zum Ende* (2 vols) Buenos Aires, Dürer, 1949–50

OVERY, RICHARD *Goering: The 'Iron Man'* Routledge & Kegan Paul, 1984
Why the Allies Won Jonathan Cape, 1995
Interrogations: The Nazi Elite in Allied Hands, 1945 Allen Lane, The Penguin Press, 2001

PADFIELD, PETER *Himmler: Reichsführer-SS* Macmillan, 1990
Hess: Flight for the Führer Weidenfeld and Nicolson, 1991

PAPEN, FRANZ VON *Memoirs* Deutsch, 1952

PAUL, WOLFGANG *Hermann Göring: Hitler Paladin or Puppet?* Arms and Armour, 1998

PICK, F.W. *The Art of Dr Goebbels* Robert Hale, 1942

POLISH WHITE BOOK *Documents Diplomatiques, 1938–9: Offical Documents Concerning Polish–German and Polish–Soviet Relations* Polish Ministry for Foreign Affairs

PRICE, MORGAN PHILIPS *Dispatches from the Weimar Republic* Pluto Press, 1999

READ, ANTHONY and FISHER, DAVID *The Deadly Embrace: Hitler, Stalin and the Nazi–Soviet Pact, 1939–1941* Michael Joseph, 1988
Kristallnacht: Unleashing the Holocaust Michael Joseph, 1989
The Fall of Berlin Hutchinson, 1992

RECK-MALLECZEWEN, FRIEDRICH *Diary of a Man in Despair* Duck Editions, 2000

REIMANN, VIKTOR *The Man Who Created Hitler: Joseph Goebbels* Kimber, 1976

REUTH, RALF GEORG *Goebbels: The Life of Joseph Goebbels, the Mephistolean Genius of Nazi Propaganda* Constable, 1993

RHODES JAMES, ROBERT (ed.) *Chips: The Diaries of Sir Henry Channon* Weidenfeld and Nicolson, 1976

RIBBENTROP, JOACHIM VON *The Ribbentrop Memoirs* Weidenfeld and Nicolson, 1954

RICH, NORMAN *Hitler's War Aims* (2 vols) New York, W.W. Norton,

1973, 1974

RICHIE, ALEXANDRA *Faust's Metropolis: A History of Berlin* Harper Collins, 1998

RIESS, CURT *Joseph Goebbels* Hollis and Carter, 1949

RÖHM, ERNST *Die Geschichte eines Hochverräters* Munich, Eher, 1930

ROMMEL, FIELD MARSHAL ERWIN *The Rommel Papers* Collins, 1953

ROSENBAUM, RON *Explaining Hitler: The Search for the Origins of his Evil* Macmillan, 1998

RYAN, CORNELIUS *The Last Battle* Collins, 1966

SCHACHT, HJALMAR *Account Settled* Weidenfeld and Nicolson, 1948

My First Seventy-Six Years Weidenfeld and Nicolson, 1955

SCHELLENBERG, WALTER *The Schellenberg Memoirs* André Deutsch, 1956

SCHLABRENDORFF, FABIAN VON *Revolt Against Hitler* Eyre and Spottiswoode, 1948

SCHMIDT, PAUL *Hitler's Interpreter* Heinemann, 1951

SEMMLER, RUDOLF *Goebbels – The Man Next to Hitler* Westhouse, 1947

SERENY, GITTA *Albert Speer: His Battle with Truth* Picador, 1996

SHIRER, WILLIAM L. *The Rise and Fall of the Third Reich* Pan Books, 1981

The Nightmare Years 1930–1940 New York, Bantam, 1985

Berlin Diary New York, Bonanza Books, 1984

SOMMER, ERICH, F. *Das Memorandum: Wie der Sowjetunion der Krieg erklärt wurde* Munich, Herbig, 1981

Botschafter Graf Schulenburg: Der letzte Vertreter des Deutschen Reiches in Moskau Asendorf, MUT, 1987

SNYDER, LOUIS L. *Hitler's Elite: Biographical Sketches of Nazis who Shaped the Third Reich* David & Charles, 1990

SPEER, ALBERT *Inside the Third Reich* Sphere, 1983

STACHURA, PETER D. *Gregor Strasser and the Rise of Nazism* Allen & Unwin, 1983

STEIN, G.H. *The Waffen SS* Oxford, Oxford University Press, 1966

STONE, NORMAN *Hitler* Hodder & Stoughton, 1980

STRASSER, OTTO *Hitler and I* Jonathan Cape, 1940

Mein Kampf: Eine politische Autobiographie Frankfurt, Heinrich Heine, 1969

STUDNITZ, HANS-GEORG VON *While Berlin Burns* Weidenfeld and Nicolson, 1953

TAYLOR, A.J.P. *The Origins of the Second World War* Penguin, 1964

TOBIAS, FRITZ *Der Reichstagsbrand* Rastatt, G. Groete'sche Verlagsbuchhandlung, 1962

TOLAND, JOHN *Adolf Hitler* Doubleday, 1976
The Last 100 Days New York, Random House, 1966

TREVOR-ROPER, H.R. (ed.) *Hitler's Table Talk* Weidenfeld and Nicolson, 1953
The Bormann Letters Weidenfeld and Nicolson, 1954
The Last Days of Hitler Macmillan, 1987

TUSA, ANNE and JOHN *The Nuremberg Trial* Macmillan, 1983

VAT, DAN VAN DER *The Good Nazi: The Life and Lies of Albert Speer* New York, Houghton Mifflin, 1997

WARLIMONT, WALTER *Inside Hitler's Headquarters, 1939–45* Weidenfeld & Nicolson, 1964

WEIZSÄCKER, ERNST VON *Memoirs* Gollancz, 1951

WELLES, SUMNER *The Time for Decision* New York, Harper, 1944

WHALEY, BARTON *Codeword Barbarossa* Cambridge, Mass, MIT Press, 1973

WHEATLEY, RONALD *Operation Sea Lion* Oxford, Clarendon Press, 1958

WHITING, CHARLES *The Hunt for Martin Bormann: The Truth* Leo Cooper, 1996

WIGHTON, CHARLES *Heydrich: Hitler's Most Evil Henchman* Odhams, 1962

WILAMOWITZ-MOELLENDORFF, FANNY VON *Carin Göring* Berlin, Martin Warneck, 1934

WILLEMER, WILLIAM *The German Defence of Berlin* Berlin, HQ USAREUR, 1953

WINTERBOTHAM, F.W. *The Ultra Secret* Futura, 1975

YOUNG, DESMOND *Rommel* Collins, 1950

INDEX

Lutze, SA-Obengruppenführer Viktor 355, 363, 365, 368, 376
Lützow (battleship) 626
Lützow, Colonel Günther 858
Luxembourg 631
Luxemburg, Rosa 37, 43
LVZ *see* Air Defence Zone

Macdonald, Ramsay 398, 402
Mackensen, August von 496, 553
Magistrati, Counsellor 564
Maikowski, Hanne 277, 286
Majdanek death camp 756, 847
Malta 674, 768, 813
Manchester Guardian 43, 317
Mann, Golo 334
Mann, Heinrich 334
Mann, Thomas 334, 341
Manstein, General Erich von 570, 617, 784
Mantel, Police President 97
Markart, Hans 448
Mastnyyy Dr Vojtech 468–9, 505
Masur, Norbert 895
Matsuoka, Yosuke 680
Maurice, Emil 109, 151, 153
Mautendorf Castle 30, 477, 549
Mauthausen concentration camp 474, 814, 852
Maximilian of Baden, Prince 18, 19, 21, 45
Mayr, Captain Karl 53, 58, 73
Meissner, Dr Otto 225, 244–5, 266, 267, 271, 362
Memel (1939) 542–3, 544
Mers-el-Kebir: destruction of French fleet 643–4
Messerschmitt, Willi 177, 691, 818–19
Messerschmitt fighters 415, 818–19, 843, 853–4
Metaxas, General Ioannis 547
MI6 615
Michael, King of Romania 659
Miklas, Wilhelm 463, 464, 465, 469, 473
Milch, Field Marshal Erhard: relationship with Göring 177, 178, 205, 241, 300–1; and development of Luftwaffe 324–5; on 'vacation tour' with Göring 357; and defence of Air Ministry 366; at Hitler's oath of allegiance ceremony 377; and aircraft production 378, 415, 416; sends fighters to Franco 425; as Göring's deputy 494, 507, 534, 559; and Mussolini's demands 579, 580; cancels aircraft development work 621; organises air fleet in Oslo 627; proposes invasion of Britain 636–7; appointed Field Marshal 646; in temporary command 654; takes North Africa plans to Göring 674; takes over aircraft

production from Udet 718, 719, 720; relationship with Speer 743–4, 745; and Stalingrad airlift 773, 780; as member of Central Planning Committee 783; achieves miracles 795; and conspiracy 796, 797; sets up Fighter Aircraft Staff 822; and Me-262 fiasco 843; intervenes on Galland's behalf 859; on Göring and Hitler 634
Mölders, Werner 719, 720; widow 770
Molotov, Vyacheslav 565, 566–7, 568, 573, 599, 600, 659–63, 708
Monte Cassino (1944) 824
Montezemolo, Colonel Giuseppe 777
Montgomery, General Bernard 710, 768, 769, 775, 848, 852–3, 879, 914
Morell, Dr Theodor 495, 539–40, 833, 881, 894, 896, 897, 899
Morris, Leland 738
Moscow: 'Miracle of' 731–4; retreat from 739–41
Mosse family 333
Muchow, Reinhold 318
Muff, General Wolfgang 463, 465, 466
Müller, Heinrich ('Gestapo Müller') 348, 511, 512, 527, 563, 724–5, 798, 827
Müller, Hermann 193
Müller, Lt Josef 827
Müller, Professor Karl Alexander von 95, 96
Münchener Post 200
Munich: Räterepublik 45–7, 51, 58; 14th Alarm Company 49, 54; volatility and political meetings 50–1; Einwohnerwehr (home guard) 54, 58, 59, 65; political situation (1922) 65–8; *putsch* (1923) 92–102, 105, 106; 'House of German Art' 440–1, 485; 'Exhibition of Degenerate Art' (1937) 441
Munich Agreement (1938) 501–4, 542
Münster, Bishop of 729
Munthe, Axel 433
Mussolini, Benito: wants nothing to do with Göring or Hitler 113, 124; and Göring's visits (1931) 218, (1932) 255, (1933) 323; sidelines Balbo 324; captivated by Magda Goebbels 335; signs treaty with Austria 335; his villa an example to Göring 335; tit-for-tats with Göring 357, 378; complains at German rearmament 388; and invasion of Abyssinia 409; and Spanish Civil War 425, 426; and *Anschluss* 433–4; pays state visit to Germany 434; joins Anti-Comintern Pact 445, 446; and *Anschluss* 460, 467, 470; and Hitler's visit to Rome 483; opinion of Ribbentrop 484; wants German mobilisation postponed 501; and Munich conference 501–2, 503; unimpressed by Ribbentrop's efforts 506–7;